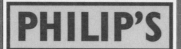

STREET ATLAS
Cheshire

First published in 1995 by

Philip's, a division of
Octopus Publishing Group Ltd
2–4 Heron Quays, London E14 4JP

Second colour edition 2002
Third impression with revisions 2004

ISBN 0-540-08113-2 (spiral)

© Philip's 2004

Ordnance Survey®

This product includes mapping data licensed
from Ordnance Survey® with the permission of
the Controller of Her Majesty's Stationery Office.
© Crown copyright 2004. All rights reserved.
Licence number 100011710.

Printed and bound in Spain
by Cayfosa-Quebecor

Contents

III   **Key to map symbols**

IV   **Key to map pages**

VI   **Route planning**

VIII   **Administrative and Postcode boundaries**

1   **Street maps** at 3½ inches to 1 mile

237   **Street map of Chester city centre** at 7 inches to 1 mile

238   **Town maps** of Altrincham, Cheadle and Gatley, Stockport, Hyde, Romiley, Sale and Stalybridge

243   **Index** of towns and villages

244   **Index** of streets, hospitals, industrial estates, railway stations, schools, shopping centres, universities and places of interest

Digital Data

The exceptionally high-quality mapping found in this atlas is available as digital data in TIFF format, which is easily convertible to other bitmapped (raster) image formats.

The index is also available in digital form as a standard database table. It contains all the details found in the printed index together with the National Grid reference for the map square in which each entry is named.

For further information and to discuss your requirements, please contact Philip's on 020 7644 6932 or james.mann@philips-maps.co.uk

Key to map symbols

Symbol	Description
(22a)	**Motorway** with junction number
	Primary route – dual/single carriageway
	A road – dual/single carriageway
	B road – dual/single carriageway
	Minor road – dual/single carriageway
	Other minor road – dual/single carriageway
– – –	**Road under construction**
	Pedestrianised area
DY7	**Postcode boundaries**
	County and unitary authority boundaries
	Railway
– – –	**Railway under construction**
	Tramway, miniature railway
	Rural track, private road or narrow road in urban area
	Gate or obstruction to traffic (restrictions may not apply at all times or to all vehicles)
– – –	**Path, bridleway, byway open to all traffic, road used as a public path**

The representation in this atlas of a road, track or path is no evidence of the existence of a right of way

58 / 230 / 237	**Adjoining page indicators**

The map area within the pink band is shown at a larger scale on the page indicated by the red block and arrow

Abbr	Full	Abbr	Full
Acad	**Academy**	Mkt	**Market**
Allot Gdns	**Allotments**	Meml	**Memorial**
Cemy	**Cemetery**	Mon	**Monument**
C Ctr	**Civic Centre**	Mus	**Museum**
CH	**Club House**	Obsy	**Observatory**
Coll	**College**	Pal	**Royal Palace**
Crem	**Crematorium**	PH	**Public House**
Ent	**Enterprise**	Recn Gd	**Recreation Ground**
Ex H	**Exhibition Hall**	Resr	**Reservoir**
Ind Est	**Industrial Estate**	Ret Pk	**Retail Park**
IRB Sta	**Inshore Rescue Boat Station**	Sch	**School**
	Boat Station	Sh Ctr	**Shopping Centre**
Inst	**Institute**	TH	**Town Hall/House**
Ct	**Law Court**	Trad Est	**Trading Estate**
L Ctr	**Leisure Centre**	Univ	**University**
LC	**Level Crossing**	Wks	**Works**
Liby	**Library**	YH	**Youth Hostel**

Symbol	Description
Walsall	**Railway station**
	Private railway station
	Bus, coach station
	Ambulance station
	Coastguard station
	Fire station
	Police station
✚	**Accident and Emergency entrance to hospital**
H	**Hospital**
✚	**Place of worship**
i	**Information Centre** (open all year)
P	**Parking**
P&R	**Park and Ride**
PO	**Post Office**
⚊	**Camping site**
	Caravan site
	Golf course
	Picnic site
Prim Sch	**Important buildings, schools, colleges, universities and hospitals**
River Medway	**Water name**
	River, stream
	Lock, weir
	Water
	Tidal water
	Woods
	Houses
Church	**Non-Roman antiquity**
ROMAN FORT	**Roman antiquity**

■ The small numbers around the edges of the maps identify the 1 kilometre National Grid lines ■ The dark grey border on the inside edge of some pages indicates that the mapping does not continue onto the adjacent page

The scale of the maps on the pages numbered in blue is 5.52 cm to 1 km • 3½ inches to 1 mile • 1: 18103

0	¼	½	¾	1 mile
0	250 m	500 m	750 m	1 kilometre

The scale of the maps on pages numbered in red is 11.04 cm to 1 km • 7 inches to 1 mile • 1: 9051.4

0	220 yards	440 yards	660 yards	½ mile
0	125 m	250 m	375 m	½ kilometre

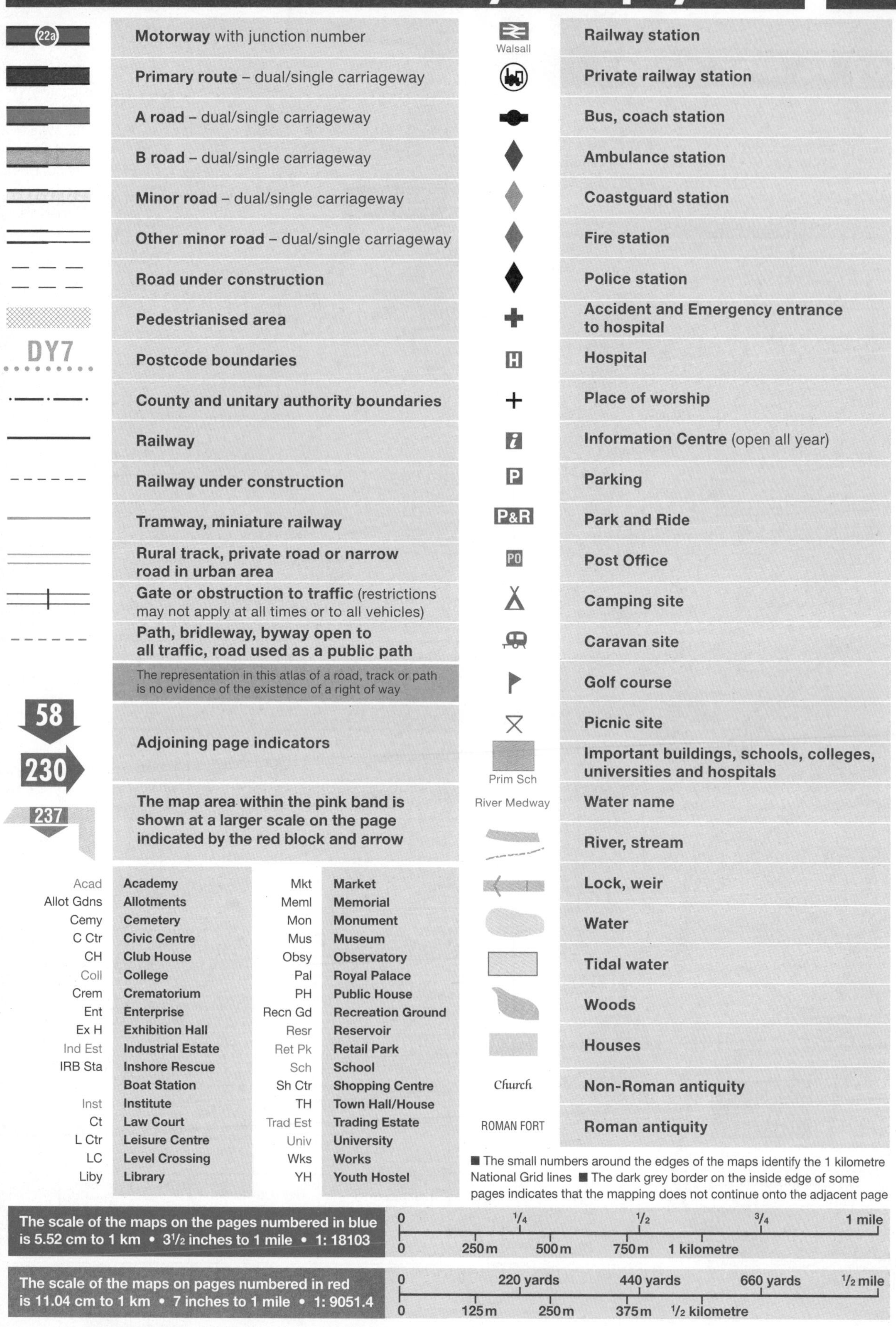

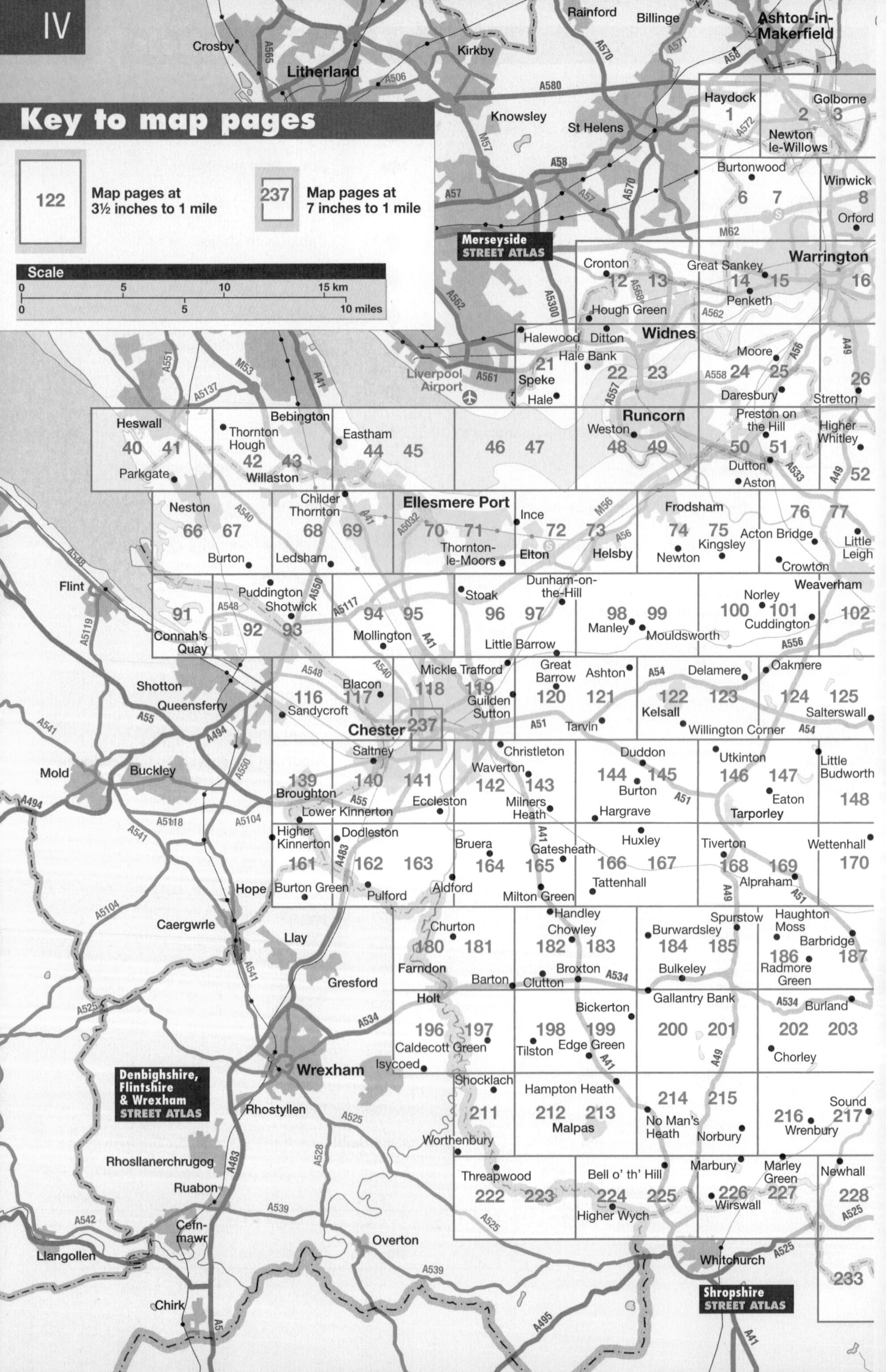

Key to map pages

| 122 | Map pages at 3½ inches to 1 mile | 237 | Map pages at 7 inches to 1 mile |

Scale

0   5   10   15 km

0   5   10 miles

Crosby

Litherland

Rainford   Billinge   Ashton-in-Makerfield

Kirkby

Knowsley

St Helens

Merseyside STREET ATLAS

Haydock **1**   Golborne **3**
2
Newton le-Willows

Burtonwood **6**   **7**   Winwick **8**
Orford

Cronton **12** **13**   Great Sankey **14** **15**   **Warrington** **16**
Penketh
Hough Green   A562

Widnes   Moore   **24** **25**   **26**
Halewood   Ditton   Daresbury   Stretton
Hale Bank   **22** **23**
Liverpool Airport   Speke **21**
Hale   Weston **48** **49**   **Runcorn**   Preston on the Hill **50** **51**   Higher Whitley
Dutton   **52**
Aston

Heswall **40** **41**   Bebington   Thornton Hough   Eastham **44** **45**   **46** **47**   Weston **48** **49**
Parkgate   **42** **43**   Willaston

Neston **66** **67**   Childer Thornton **68** **69**   **Ellesmere Port** **70** **71**   Ince **72** **73**   Frodsham **74** **75**   **76** **77**
Burton   Ledsham   Thornton-le-Moors   Elton   Helsby   Newton   Kingsley   Acton Bridge   Little Leigh
Crowton

Flint   Puddington   Shotwick **94** **95**   Stoak **96** **97**   Dunham-on-the-Hill   **98** **99**   Norley **100** **101**   Weaverham
91   **92** **93**   Mollington   Little Barrow   Manley   Mouldsworth   Cuddington **102**
Connah's Quay

Shotton   Blacon   Mickle Trafford **118** **119**   Great Barrow **120**   Ashton **121**   Delamere **122** **123**   Oakmere **124** **125**
Queensferry   Sandycroft **116** **117**   Guilden Sutton   Kelsall   Willington Corner   Salterswall
Chester **237**   Tarvin

Mold   Buckley   Saltney   Christleton   Duddon **144** **145**   Utkinton **146** **147**   Little Budworth
139 **140** **141**   Waverton **142** **143**   Burton   Eaton **148**
Broughton   Eccleston   Milners Heath   Hargrave   **Tarporley**
Lower Kinnerton

Higher Kinnerton   Dodleston   Bruera   Gatesheath   Huxley   Tiverton **168** **169**   Wettenhall **170**
Caergwrle   **161** **162** **163** **164** **165** **166** **167**   Alpraham
Hope   Burton Green   Pulford   Aldford   Milton Green   Tattenhall
Llay

Gresford   Churton   Handley   Chowley   Burwardsley **184** **185**   Spurstow   Haughton Moss   Barbridge
180 **181** **182** **183**   Radmore Green **186** **187**
Farndon   Broxton   Bulkeley
Holt   Barton   Clutton   Bickerton   Gallantry Bank   Burland
196 **197** **198** **199** **200** **201** **202** **203**
Caldecott Green   Tilston   Edge Green   Chorley
Isycoed

Denbighshire, Flintshire & Wrexham STREET ATLAS

Wrexham   Shocklach   Hampton Heath   No Man's Heath **214** **215**   Wrenbury **216** **217**
Rhostyllen   **211**   **212** **213**   Norbury   Sound
Worthenbury   **Malpas**

Rhosllanerchrugog   Threapwood   Bell o' th' Hill   Marbury **226** **227**   Marley Green   Newhall
Ruabon   **222** **223** **224** **225**   Wirswall **228**
Higher Wych

Cefn-mawr   Overton   Whitchurch   **233**
Llangollen

Shropshire STREET ATLAS

Chirk

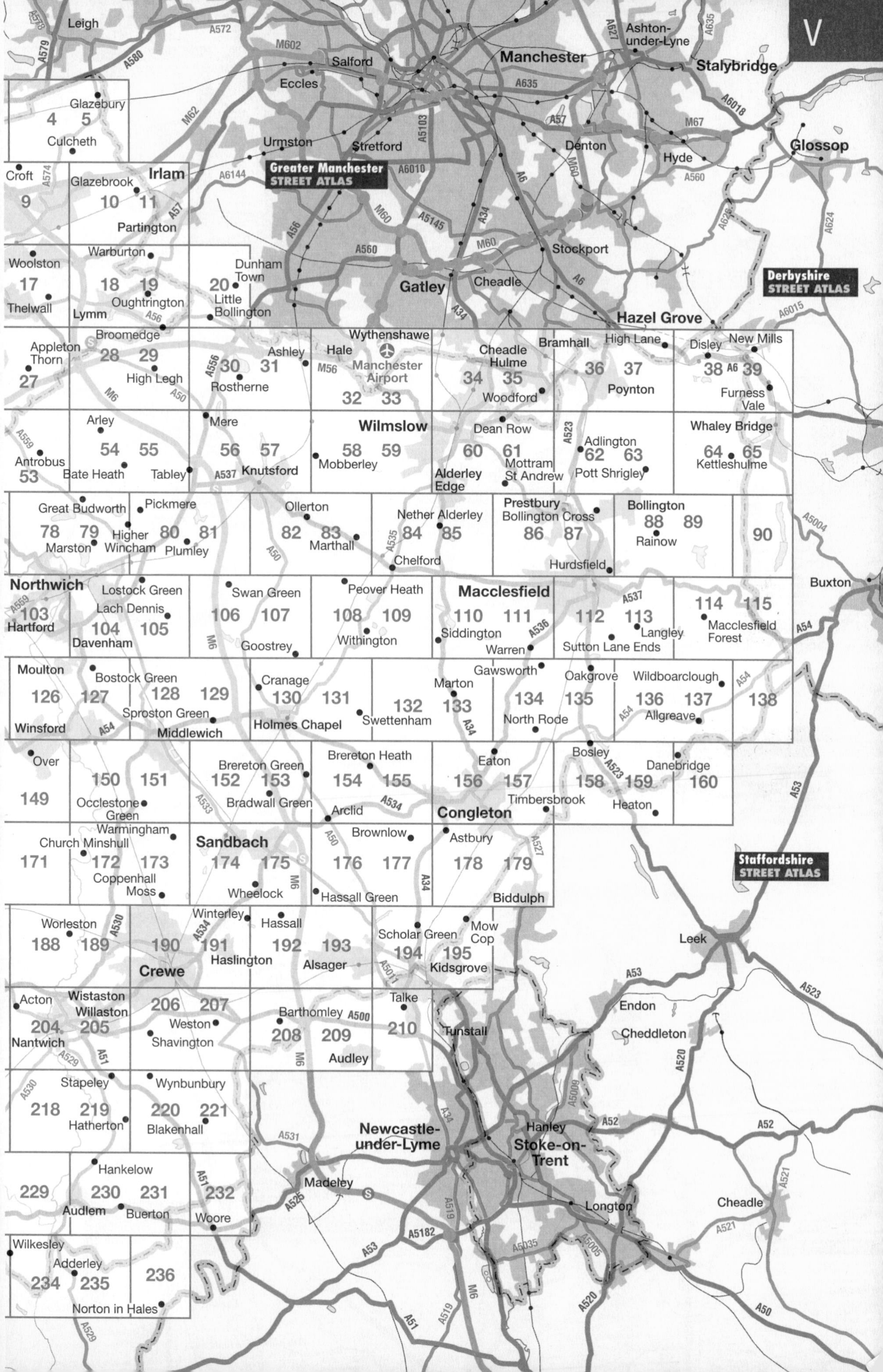

V
Leigh
A572
A579
A580
M602
Salford
Eccles
Manchester
Ashton-under-Lyne
A627
A635
Stalybridge
A635
A6018
M67
Glossop
Glazebury
4
5
Culcheth
M62
Urmston
Stretford
A5103
A57
Denton
Hyde
A560
Greater Manchester STREET ATLAS
A6010
A6144
Croft
A574
9
Glazebrook
Irlam
10
11
A57
Partington
A56
M60
A5145
A34
A6
M60
A626
A624
Woolston
Warburton
17
18
19
Thelwall
Lymm
Oughtrington
A56
Dunham Town
20
Little Bollington
A560
Gatley
Cheadle
Stockport
A6
A34
Hazel Grove
Derbyshire STREET ATLAS
A6015
Appleton Thorn
27
Broomedge
28
29
High Legh
M6
A50
A556
30
31
Rostherne
Ashley
Wythenshawe
Hale
M56
Manchester Airport
32
33
Cheadle Hulme
34
35
Woodford
Bramhall
High Lane
36
37
Poynton
Disley
New Mills
38
A6
39
Furness Vale
A559
Antrobus
53
Arley
54
55
Bate Heath
Tabley
Mere
56
57
A537
Knutsford
Wilmslow
58
59
Mobberley
Dean Row
60
61
Alderley Edge
Mottram St Andrew
A523
Adlington
62
63
Pott Shrigley
Whaley Bridge
64
65
Kettleshulme
Great Budworth
78
79
Marston
Pickmere
Higher Wincham
80
81
Plumley
Ollerton
82
83
Marthall
A50
Nether Alderley
A535
84
85
Chelford
Prestbury
Bollington Cross
86
87
Hurdsfield
Bollington
88
89
Rainow
90
A5004
Buxton
Northwich
A559
103
Hartford
Lostock Green
Lach Dennis
104
105
Davenham
Swan Green
106
107
M6
Goostrey
Peover Heath
108
109
Withington
Macclesfield
110
111
Siddington
A536
Warren
112
A537
113
Langley
Sutton Lane Ends
114
115
Macclesfield Forest
A54
Moulton
126
127
Winsford
Bostock Green
128
129
Sproston Green
A54
Middlewich
Cranage
130
131
Holmes Chapel
Swettenham
132
Marton
133
A34
Gawsworth
134
135
North Rode
Oakgrove
Wildboarclough
136
137
A54
Allgreave
A54
138
Over
149
150
151
Occlestone Green
Brereton Green
152
153
A533
Bradwall Green
Brereton Heath
154
155
Arclid
A534
Eaton
156
157
Congleton
Timbersbrook
Bosley
A523
158
159
Heaton
Danebridge
160
A53
Warmingham
Church Minshull
171
172
173
Coppenhall Moss
Sandbach
174
175
M6
Wheelock
A50
Brownlow
176
177
Hassall Green
A34
Astbury
178
179
A527
Biddulph
Staffordshire STREET ATLAS
Worleston
188
189
A530
Winterley
A534
190
191
Crewe
Haslington
Hassall
192
193
Alsager
Scholar Green
194
195
Mow Cop
Kidsgrove
A5011
Leek
A53
A523
Acton
Wistaston
Willaston
204
205
Nantwich
A529
A51
206
207
Weston
Shavington
Barthomley
A500
208
209
M6
Audley
Talke
210
Tunstall
Endon
Cheddleton
A520
A530
Stapeley
218
219
Hatherton
Wynbunbury
220
221
Blakenhall
A531
Newcastle-under-Lyme
A34
A5009
Hanley
Stoke-on-Trent
A52
A52
A521
229
Hankelow
230
231
Audlem
Buerton
A51
232
Woore
Madeley
A525
A519
Longton
Cheadle
A521
A5182
A53
A5035
A5005
Wilkesley
Adderley
234
235
236
Norton in Hales
A529
A51
A519
M6
A520
A50

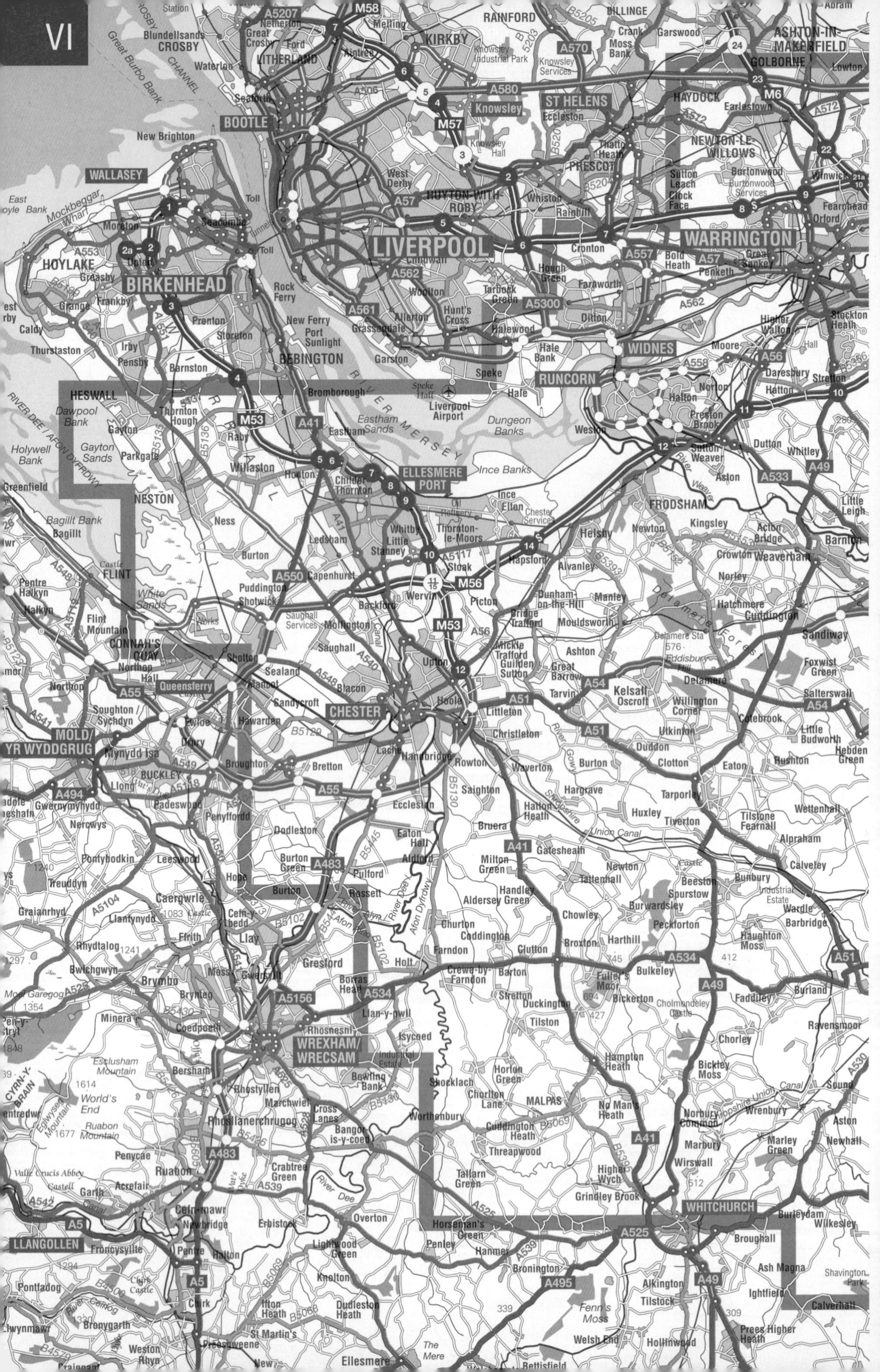

CROSBY
LITHERLAND
KIRKBY
RAINFORD
BILLINGE
ASHTON-IN-MAKERFIELD
GOLBORNE
BOOTLE
ST HELENS
HAYDOCK
NEWTON-LE-WILLOWS
WALLASEY
PRESCOT
HUYTON-WITH-ROBY
LIVERPOOL
WARRINGTON
HOYLAKE
BIRKENHEAD
WIDNES
RUNCORN
BEBINGTON
HESWALL
ELLESMERE PORT
NESTON
FRODSHAM
FLINT
CONNAH'S QUAY
Queensferry
CHESTER
MOLD/YR WYDDGRUG
BUCKLEY
WREXHAM/WRECSAM
MALPAS
WHITCHURCH
LLANGOLLEN
Liverpool Airport
RIVER MERSEY
Delamere Forest
Ellesmere
M58
M57
M6
M53
M56
A580
A57
A562
A561
A5300
A557
A41
A550
A55
A5117
A56
A51
A54
A494
A483
A534
A5156
A49
A525
A5
A495
A539
A533

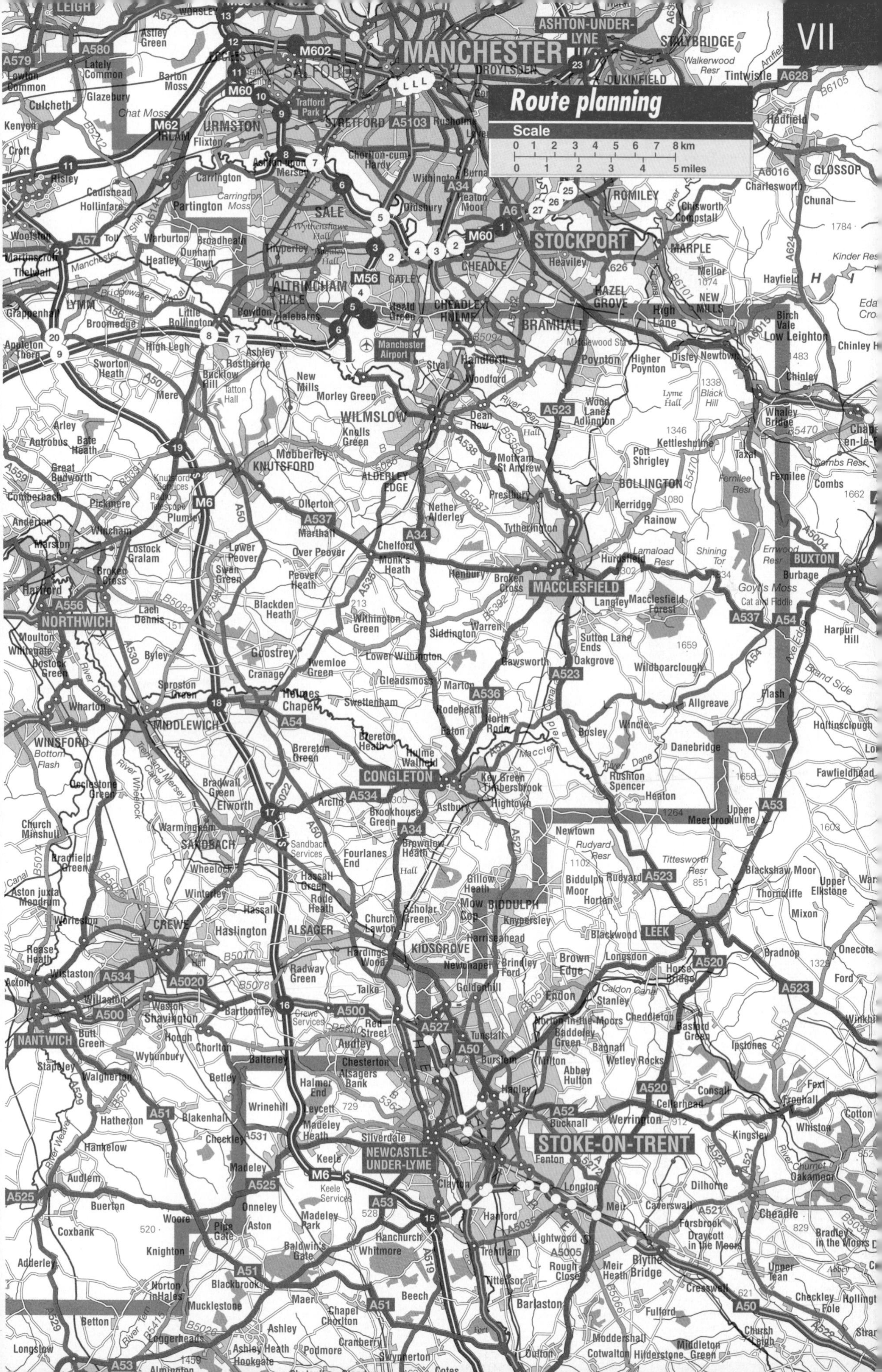
Route planning
Scale
0 1 2 3 4 5 6 7 8 km
0 1 2 3 4 5 miles
MANCHESTER
SALFORD
ASHTON-UNDER-LYNE
STALYBRIDGE
DROYLSDEN
DUKINFIELD
Tintwistle
Hadfield
GLOSSOP
Charlesworth
Chunal
ROMILEY
Chisworth
Compstall
STOCKPORT
MARPLE
Heaviley
Mellor
HAZEL GROVE
NEW MILLS
High Lane
Hayfield
Birch Vale
Low Leighton
Chinley
Whaley Bridge
Chapel-en-le-Frith
BUXTON
Burbage
Leigh
Worsley
Astley Green
Eccles
Lately Common
Lowton Common
Glazebury
Culcheth
Barton Moss
Trafford Park
Chat Moss
Kenyon
Croft
URMSTON
IRLAM
Flixton
Stretford
Rusholme
Chorlton-cum-Hardy
Withington
Ashton upon Mersey
Carrington
Risley
Cadishead
Hollinfare
Partington
Carrington Moss
SALE
Wythenshawe Hall
Didsbury
Heaton Moor
Woolston
Warburton
Broadheath
Dunham Town
Timperley
Manchester Ship Canal
Martinscroft
Thelwall
Heatley
CHEADLE
GATLEY
ALTRINCHAM
HALE
Halebarns
Bowdon
Heald Green
CHEADLE HULME
BRAMHALL
Grappenhall
LYMM
Bridgewater Canal
Broomedge
Little Bollington
Appleton Thorn
High Legh
Ashley
Rostherne
Bucklow Hill
Sworton Heath
Manchester Airport
Styal
Handforth
Woodford
Poynton
Higher Poynton
Disley
Newtown
Middlewood Sta
Mere
Tatton Hall
New Mills
Morley Green
WILMSLOW
Dean Row
Lyme Hall
Black Hill
Wood Lanes
Adlington
Arley
Antrobus
Bate Heath
Knolls Green
Mobberley
KNUTSFORD
Great Budworth
Comberbach
Pickmere
Knutsford Services
ALDERLEY EDGE
Mottram St Andrew
Pott Shrigley
Kettleshulme
Taxal
Fernilee
Combs
Combs Resr
BOLLINGTON
Kerridge
Rainow
Prestbury
Nether Alderley
Ollerton
Marthall
Plumley
Anderton
Wincham
Marston
Lostock Gralam
Lower Peover
Over Peover
Chelford
Monk's Heath
Tytherington
Hurdsfield
Lamaload Resr
Shining Tor
Errwood Resr
Harford
Broken Cross
Swan Green
Peover Heath
Henbury
MACCLESFIELD
Goyt's Moss
Cat and Fiddle
NORTHWICH
Lach Dennis
Blackden Heath
Withington Green
Langley
Macclesfield Forest
Siddington
Warren
Sutton Lane Ends
Oakgrove
Moulton
Whitegate
Bostock Green
Byley
Goostrey
Cranage
Twemloe Green
Lower Withington
Gawsworth
Wildboarclough
Harpur Hill
Gleadsmoss
Marton
Flash
Sproston Green
Holmes Chapel
Swettenham
Allgreave
Wharton
MIDDLEWICH
Rodeheath
North Rode
Bosley
Wincle
Hollinsclough
WINSFORD
Bottom Flash
Brereton Heath
Brereton Green
Hulme Walfield
Danebridge
Rushton Spencer
Heaton
Fawfieldhead
CONGLETON
Key Green
Timbersbrook
Hightown
Astbury
Occlestone Green
Bradwall Green
Elworth
Arclid
Brookhouse Green
Church Minshull
Warmingham
SANDBACH
Sandbach Services
Newtown
Rudyard Resr
Upper Hulme
Meerbrook
Fourlanes End
Brownlow Heath
Tittesworth Resr
Bradfield Green
Wheelock
Hassall Green
Gillow Heath
Biddulph Moor
Rudyard
Blackshaw Moor
Upper Elkstone
Thorncliffe
Aston juxta Mondrum
Winterley
Rode Heath
Mow Cop
BIDDULPH
Horton
Mixon
Worleston
CREWE
Hassall
Haslington
ALSAGER
Church Lawton
Scholar Green
Knypersley
Blackwood
LEEK
Reaseheath
Harriseahead
KIDSGROVE
Hardings Wood
Radway Green
Newchapel
Brindley Ford
Brown Edge
Longsdon
Horse Bridge
Bradnop
Onecote
Wistaston
Crewe Hall
Acton
Willaston
Talke
Goldenhill
Endon
Caldon Canal
Stanley
Ford
NANTWICH
Weston
Shavington
Barthomley
Crewe Services
Red Street
Audley
Tunstall
Norton-in-the-Moors
Baddeley Green
Cheddleton
Basford Green
Butt Green
Hough
Chorlton
Burslem
Milton
Bagnall
Wetley Rocks
Ipstones
Stapeley
Wybunbury
Balterley
Chesterton
Alsagers Bank
Abbey Hulton
Walgherton
Betley
Halmer End
Hanley
Consall
Foxt
Froghall
Wrinehill
Leycett
Cellarhead
Hatherton
Blakenhall
Madeley Heath
Bucknall
Werrington
Whiston
Cotton
Checkley
Silverdale
STOKE-ON-TRENT
Kingsley
Hankelow
NEWCASTLE-UNDER-LYME
Keele
Fenton
Audlem
Madeley
Clayton
Longton
Dilhorne
Oakamoor
Buerton
Onneley
Keele Services
Caverswall
Woore
Aston
Madeley Park
Hanford
Meir
Forsbrook
Cheadle
Coxbank
Pipe Gate
Hanchurch
Lightwood
Draycott in the Moors
Bradley in the Moors
Knighton
Baldwin's Gate
Whitmore
Trentham
Blythe Bridge
Adderley
Rough Close
Meir Heath
Upper Tean
Norton in Hales
Blackbrook
Tittensor
Cresswell
Mucklestone
Beech
Barlaston
Maer
Chapel Chorlton
Checkley
Fole
Hollington
Betton
Fulford
Church Leigh
Loggerheads
Ashley
Cranberry
Moddershall
Longslow
Ashley Heath
Podmore
Swynnerton
Middleton Green
Hookgate
Cotwalton
Hilderstone
Almington
Cotes
Dutton
River Dane
River Wheelock
River Weaver
River Tern
River Dean
River Churnet
Trent and Mersey Canal
Macclesfield Canal
Axe Edge
Brand Side
M6
M60
M62
M56
M602
A6
A34
A50
A51
A52
A53
A54
A57
A500
A520
A523
A527
A534
A537
A556
A580
A628
A5103
A5020

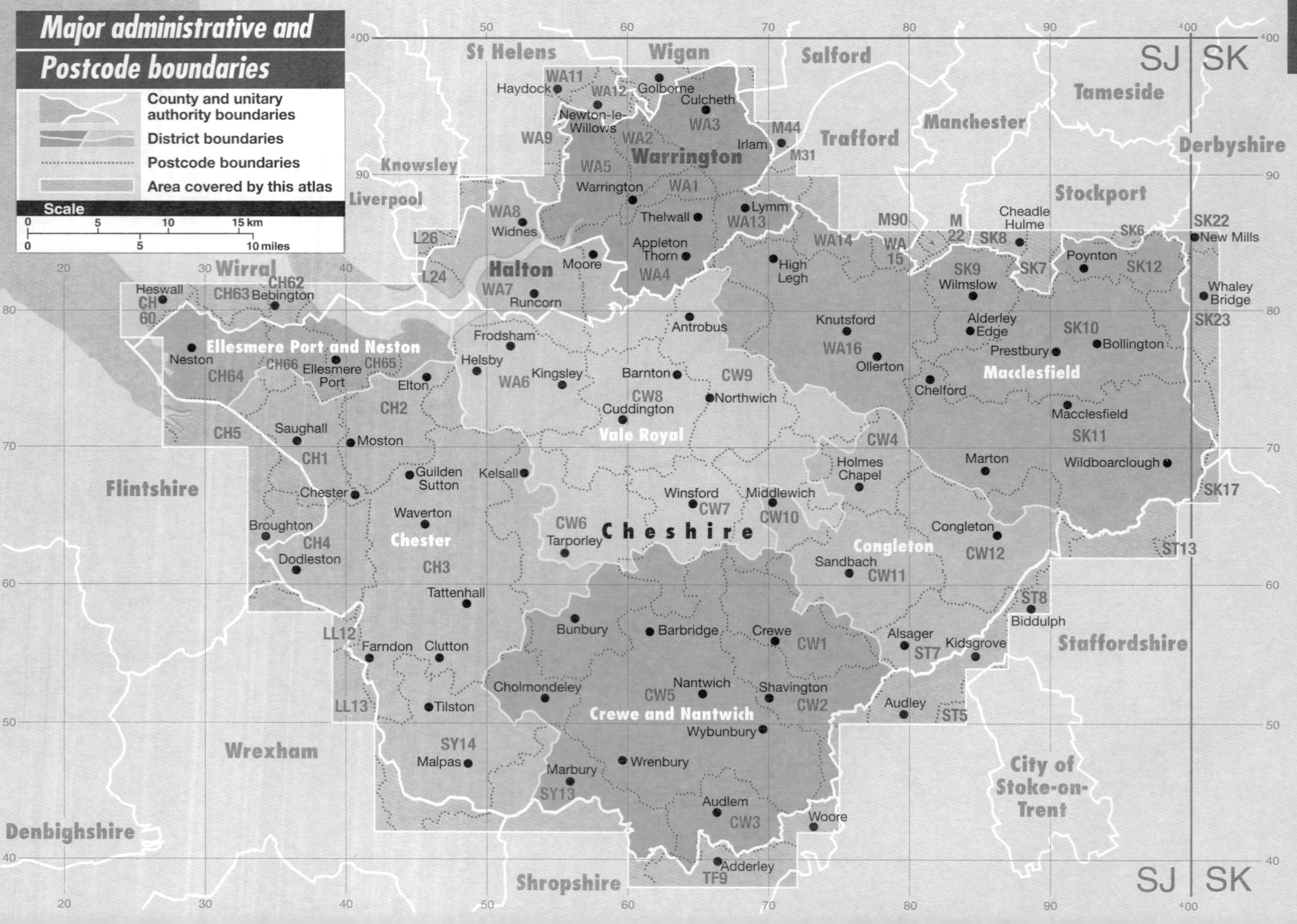

Major administrative and Postcode boundaries

— County and unitary authority boundaries
— District boundaries
······ Postcode boundaries
■ Area covered by this atlas

Scale
0   5   10   15 km
0   5   10 miles

2

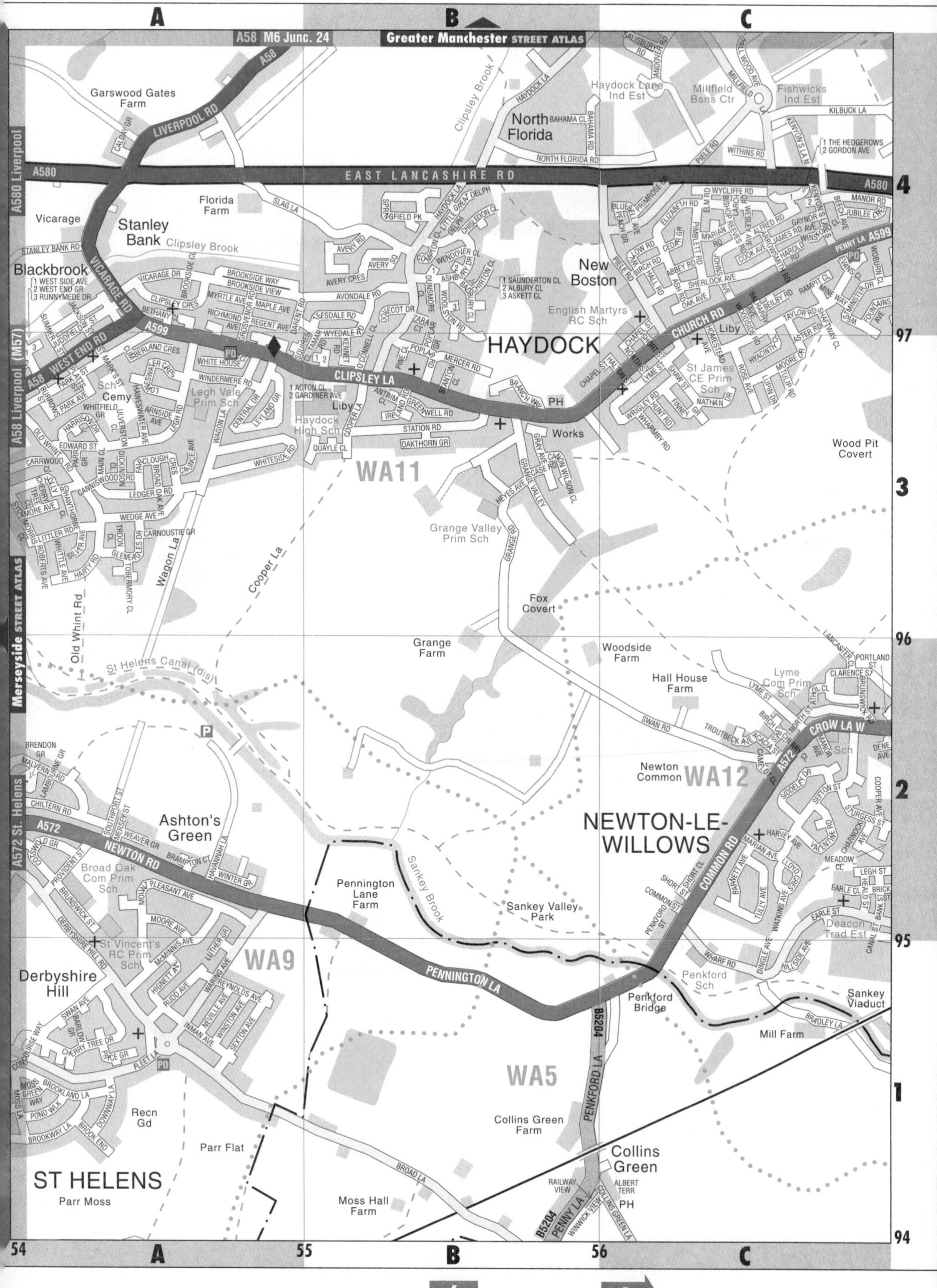
A
B
C
A58 M6 Junc. 24
Greater Manchester STREET ATLAS
A580 Liverpool
A58 Liverpool (M57)
Merseyside STREET ATLAS
A572 St. Helens
Garswood Gates Farm
LIVERPOOL RD
A58
CALDAY GR
A580
EAST LANCASHIRE RD
Florida Farm
SLAG LA
Vicarage
Stanley Bank
Clipsley Brook
STANLEY BANK RD
Blackbrook
1 WEST SIDE AVE
2 WEST END GR
3 RUNNYMEDE DR
VICARAGE RD
VICARAGE DR
BROOKSIDE WAY
BROOKSIDE VIEW
BROOKSIDE CL
CLIPSLEY CRES
MYRTLE AVE
MAPLE AVE
RICHMOND AVE
REGENT AVE
GROSVENOR RD
BETHANY CL
A599
A58 WEST END RD
WHITE HOUSE
WINDERMERE RD
Legh Vale Prim Sch
Cemy
Sch
PARK AVE
WHITFIELD GR
EDWARD ST
OLD WHINT RD
CARRWOOD RD
HAWESWATER AVE
ARNSIDE AVE
CENTRAL DR
LEYLAND GR
WAGON LA
ULVERSTON AVE
DICKINSON CL
CLOUGH CRES
BROAD OAK AVE
CANNISWOOD RD
LEDGER RD
WEDGE AVE
WHITESIDE RD
CARNOUSTIE GR
SILVER AVE
HARTY RD
WHITTLE AVE
LITTLER RD
ROBERTS AVE
SYCAMORE AVE
TROON CL
GLENEAGLES DR
TOBERMORY CL
Wagon La
Old Whint Rd
Cooper La
Clipsley Brook
HAYDOCK LA
North Florida
BAHAMA CL
BAHAMA RD
NORTH FLORIDA RD
Haydock Lane Ind Est
Millfield Bsns Ctr
Fishwicks Ind Est
SALISBURY RD
ANDOVER RD
MILLFIELD
KILBUCK LA
PIELE RD
WITHINS RD
KENYON'S LA
1 THE HEDGEROWS
2 GORDON AVE
AVERY RD
AVERY SQ
AVERY CRES
AVONDALE RD
SPRINGFIELD PK
LITTLE DELPH
GREAT DELPH
CHISLEDON CL
WENDOVER CL
ASHBURY DR
DUNSMORE CL
WOOLSTON RD
1 SAUNDERTON CL
2 ALBURY CL
3 ASKETT CL
ESKDALE RD
WYEDALE RD
DOVECOT DR
ZARA CT
POPLAR GR
PINE CL
MERCER RD
STANTON CL
O'CONNELL CL
KENNET CL
CLIPSLEY LA
1 ACTON CL
2 GARDINER AVE
Haydock High Sch
Liby
COOPER LA
STATION RD
OAKTHORN GR
QUAYLE CL
ANTRIM CL
GREENWELL RD
IRELAND RD
BRANCH WAY
PH
Works
HAYDOCK
WA11
HEYES AVE
GRANGE VALLEY
GRAY AVE
CASE RD
CANON WILSON CL
Grange Valley Prim Sch
GRANGE DR
New Boston
English Martyrs RC Sch
BLUEBELL AVE
PRIMROSE DR
PEACH GR
ELIZABETH RD
WYCLIFFE RD
ELM RD
BISHOP REEVES RD
MARIAN AVE
PIMBLETT RD
CEDAR GR
ABBEY RD
LOW RD
BIRCH RD
HALL RD
ASH RD
SHERLOCK AVE
OAK AVE
ALFRED RD
COOK AVE
JAMES RD
GAYNOR AVE
HAROLD AVE
WINSFORD CL
MANOR RD
JUBILEE CRES
PENNY LA
A599
CHURCH RD
BEILBY RD
RAMPIT CL
MINE WAY
TAYLOR RD
ASTER RD
HYACINTH
MOORE DR
LUPIN DR
TULIP RD
SHAFTWAY CL
FOUNTAINS AVE
Liby
St James CE Prim Sch
CHAPEL ST
NATHAN DR
WRIGLEY RD
HUNT RD
FINNEY GR
WHARMBY RD
ROSE AVE
HOMESTEAD AVE
WOODSIDE RD
Wood Pit Covert
Fox Covert
Grange Farm
Woodside Farm
Hall House Farm
Lyme Com Prim Sch
LYME ST
SWAN RD
TROUTBECK AVE
LANCASTER CL
PORTLAND ST
CLARENCE ST
BRUNSWICK RD
CROW LA W
A572
Newton Common
WA12
NEWTON-LE-WILLOWS
COMMON RD
SIDDELEY DR
SEFTON ST
STURGESS ST
HARVEY AVE
MARIAN AVE
LLOYD AVE
CHARNOCK AVE
MEADOW CL
LEIGH ST
EARLE CL
EARLE ST
BRICK ST
BANK ST
Deacon Trad Est
CANAL ST
BARNETT AVE
TULLY AVE
WATKINS AVE
DINGLE AVE
HAYSIDE AVE
WHARF RD
Penkford Sch
SHORT ST
COMMON ST
PENKFORD ST
Sankey Viaduct
BRADLEY LA
Mill Farm
St Helens Canal (dis)
P
BRENDON GR
MALVERN RD
CHILTERN RD
A572
NEWTON RD
SOUTHPORT ST
MERSEY ST
WEAVER GR
Ashton's Green
BRAMPTON CT
HAVANNAH LA
WINTER GR
Broad Oak Com Prim Sch
PROVIDENT ST
BRUNSWICK ST
DERBYSHIRE HILL RD
MOUNT PLEASANT AVE
MOORE AVE
St Vincent's RC Prim Sch
McMINNIS AVE
LUTHER GR
HIGNETT AVE
WARING AVE
REYNOLDS AVE
RUDD AVE
NEVILLE AVE
WINSTON AVE
SEXTON AVE
INMAN AVE
WA9
Derbyshire Hill
SWAN AVE
BARLOW GR
CHERRY TREE DR
PACE GR
FLEET LA
PO
BROOKLAND LA
MOSS GREEN WAY
POND WLK
BROOKWAY LA
BROOK END
DOWNWAY LA
Recn Gd
Parr Flat
ST HELENS
Parr Moss
Pennington Lane Farm
Sankey Brook
Sankey Valley Park
PENNINGTON LA
Penkford Bridge
B5204
PENKFORD LA
WA5
Collins Green Farm
Collins Green
RAILWAY VIEW
ALBERT TERR
PH
PENNY LA
WINWICK VIEW
COLLINS GREEN LA
BROAD LA
Moss Hall Farm
4
97
3
96
2
95
1
94
54
55
56

6

2

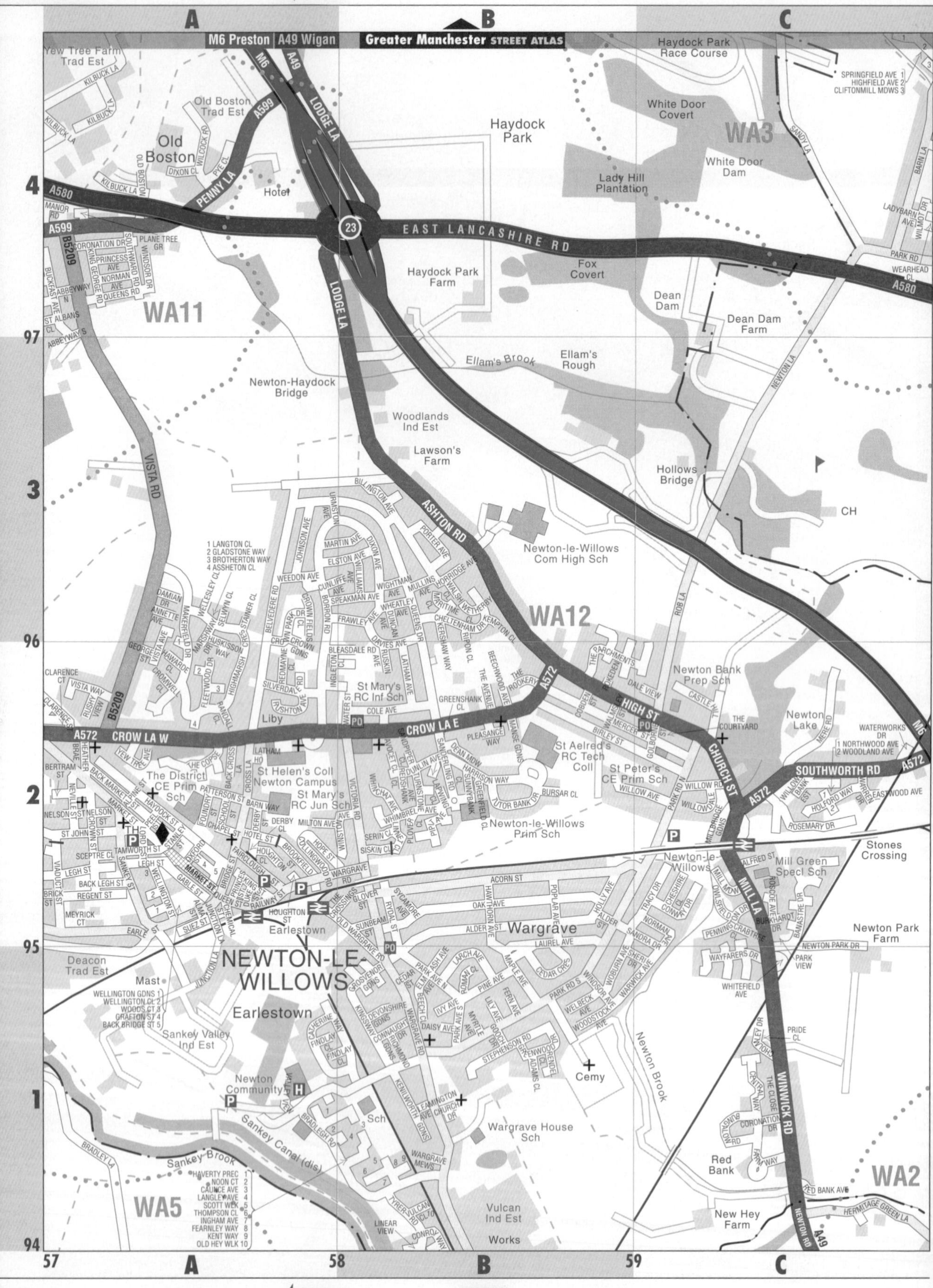

M6 Preston | A49 Wigan | Greater Manchester STREET ATLAS

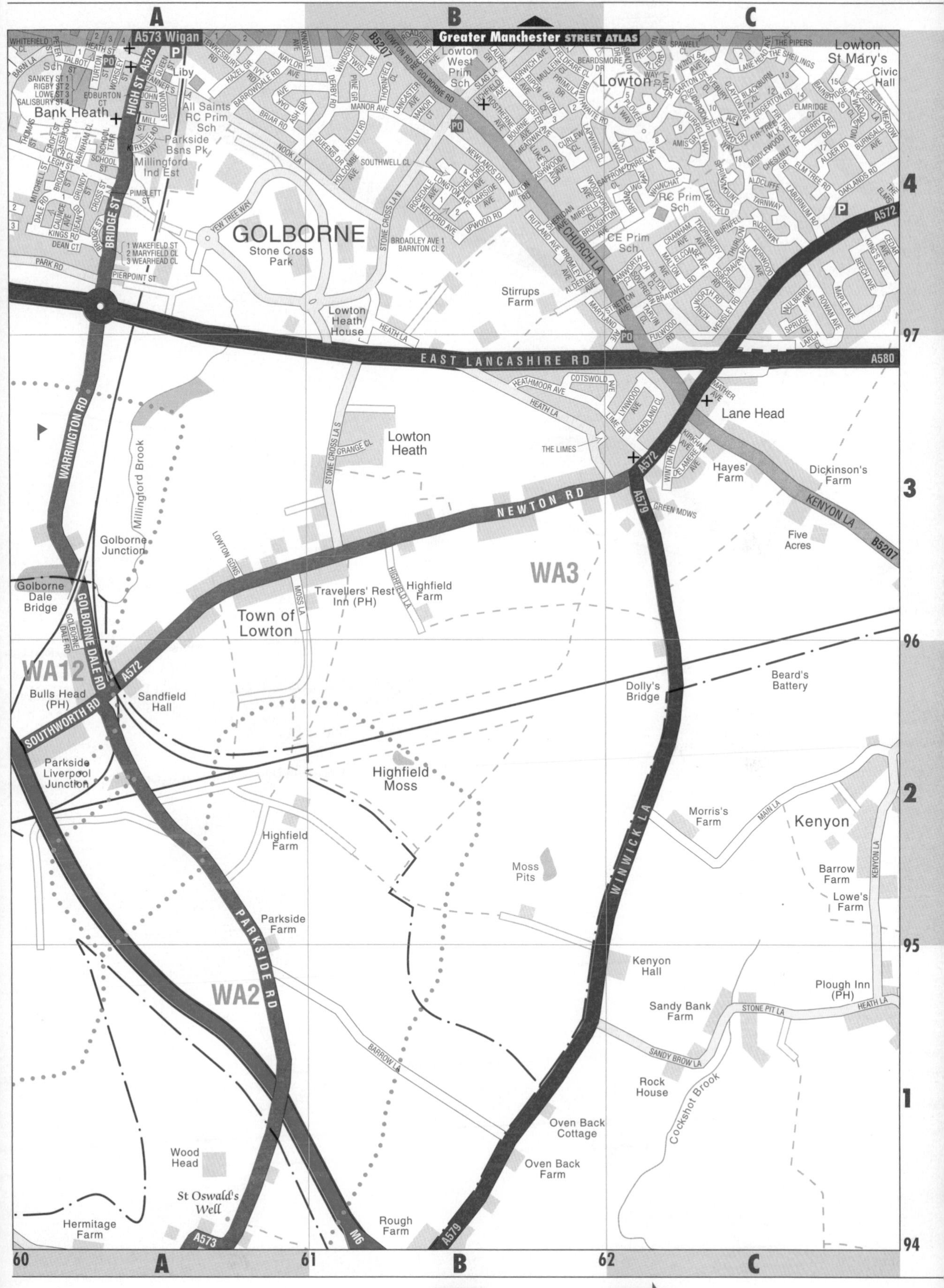

3

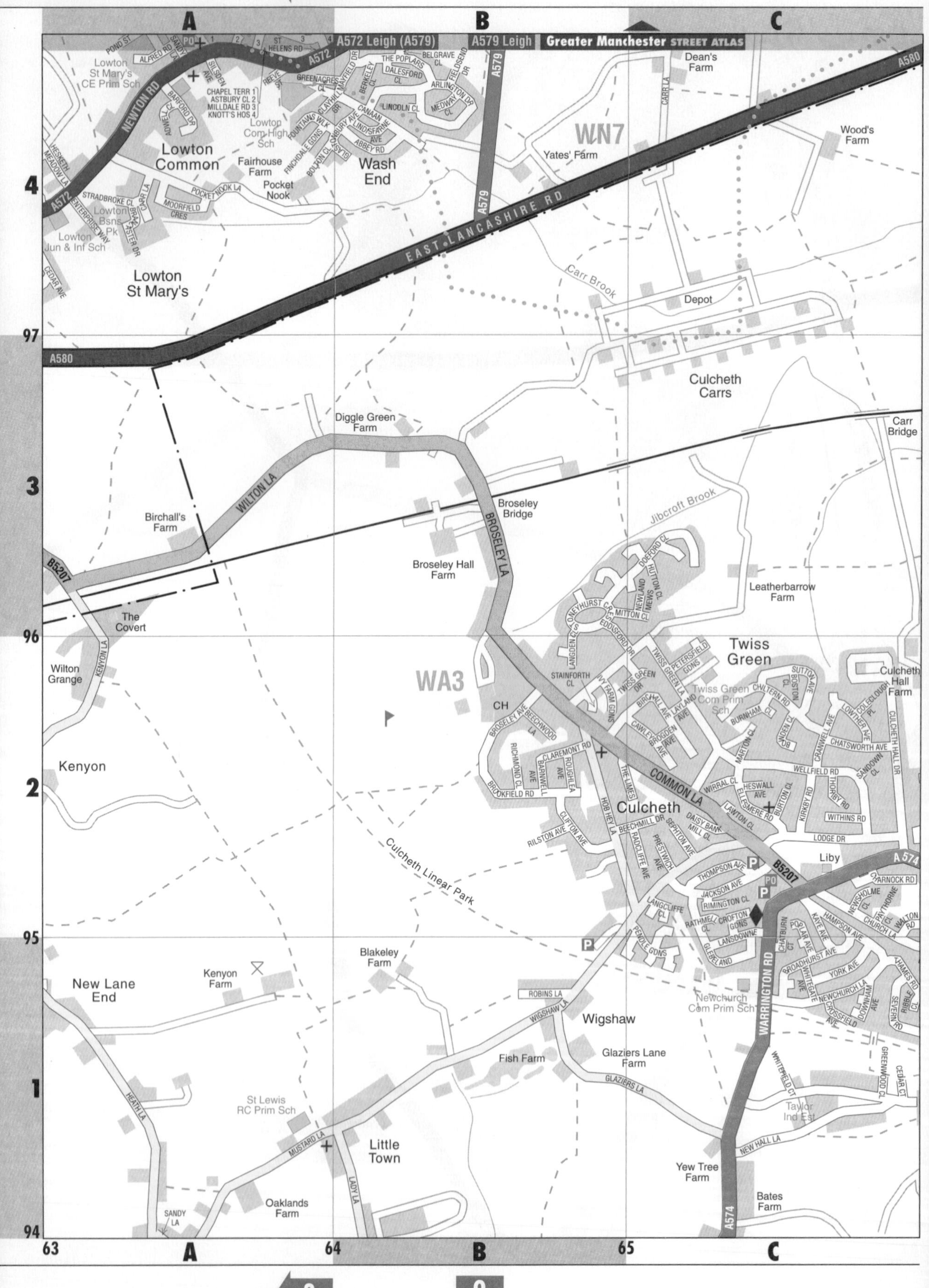
A
B
C
A572 Leigh (A579)
A579 Leigh
Greater Manchester STREET ATLAS
Lowton St Mary's CE Prim Sch
Lowton Common
Lowtop Com High Sch
Fairhouse Farm
Pocket Nook
Wash End
Lowton Bsns Pk
Lowton Jun & Inf Sch
Lowton St Mary's
Dean's Farm
WN7
Yates' Farm
Wood's Farm
EAST LANCASHIRE RD
A580
A579
A572
NEWTON RD
Carr Brook
Depot
Culcheth Carrs
Carr Bridge
Diggle Green Farm
WILTON LA
Birchall's Farm
Broseley Bridge
BROSELEY LA
Jibcroft Brook
Broseley Hall Farm
Leatherbarrow Farm
B5207
The Covert
Wilton Grange
KENYON LA
WA3
CH
Twiss Green
Twiss Green Com Prim Sch
Culcheth Hall Farm
Kenyon
COMMON LA
Culcheth
Liby
A 574
Culcheth Linear Park
Blakeley Farm
Kenyon Farm
New Lane End
ROBINS LA
WIGSHAW LA
Wigshaw
Newchurch Com Prim Sch
WARRINGTON RD
Fish Farm
Glaziers Lane Farm
GLAZIERS LA
Taylor Ind Est
HEATH LA
St Lewis RC Prim Sch
MUSTARD LA
Little Town
LADY LA
NEW HALL LA
Yew Tree Farm
Oaklands Farm
SANDY LA
Bates Farm
A574
4
97
3
96
2
95
1
94
63
64
65

3

9

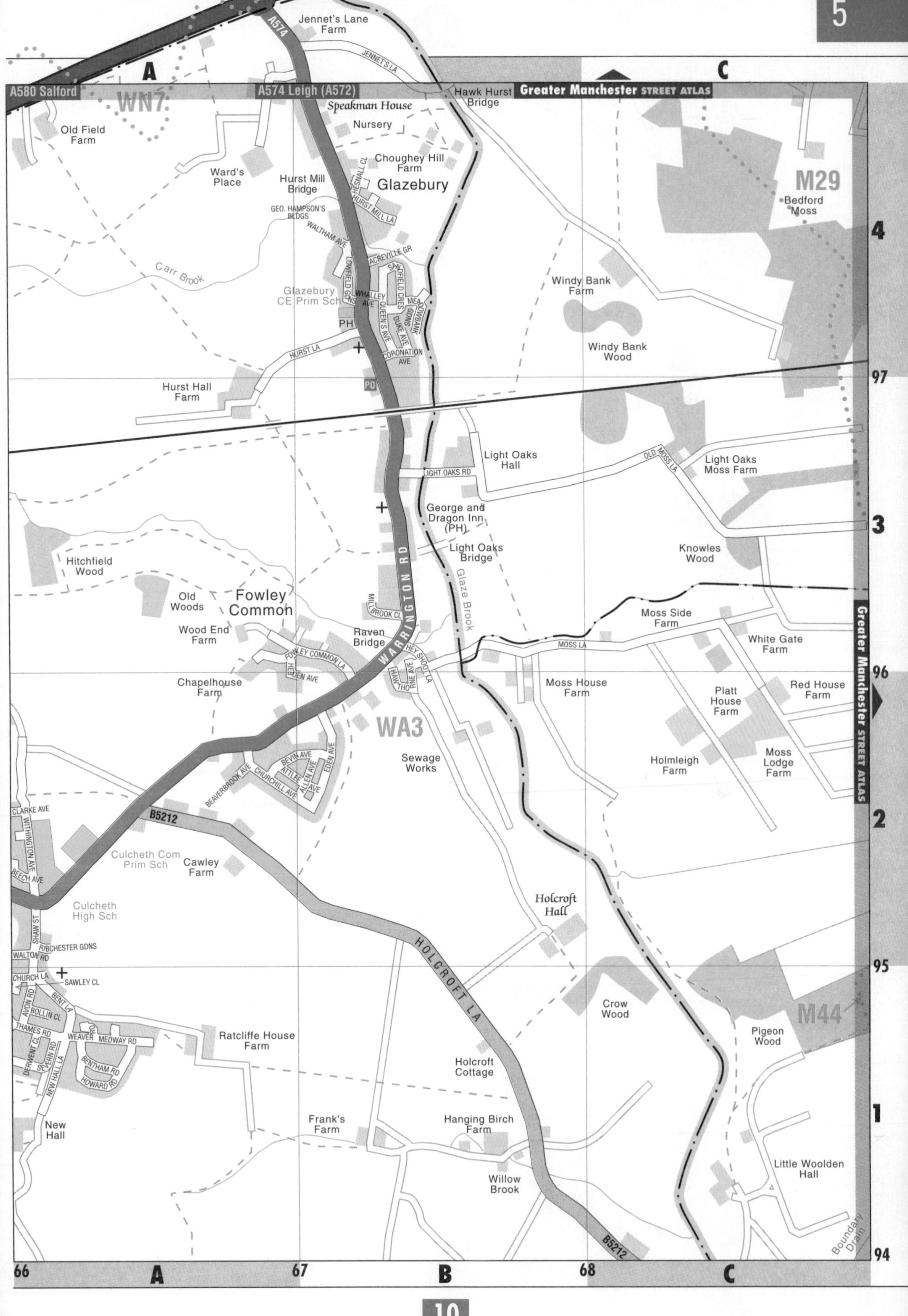

A580 Salford

A574 Leigh (A572)

WN7

M29

Jennet's Lane Farm

JENNET'S LA

Hawk Hurst Bridge

Speakman House

Nursery

Old Field Farm

Ward's Place

Choughey Hill Farm

Hurst Mill Bridge

Glazebury

GEO. HAMPSON'S BLDGS

Carr Brook

Bedford Moss

Windy Bank Farm

Glazebury CE Prim Sch

WALTHAM AVE

LOWFIELD GDNS

HESNALL CL

HURST MILL LA

WHALLEY AVE

SMALLFIELD CRES

ACREVILLE GR

GDNS

MEA

QUEEN'S AVE

DUKE AVE

CORONATION AVE

Windy Bank Wood

PH

HURST LA

PO

Hurst Hall Farm

97

Light Oaks Hall

LIGHT OAKS RD

Light Oaks Moss Farm

OLD MOSS LA

Hitchfield Wood

George and Dragon Inn (PH)

Light Oaks Bridge

Knowles Wood

3

WARRINGTON RD

Glaze Brook

Old Woods

Fowley Common

MILLBROOK CL

Wood End Farm

FOWLEY COMMON LA

HEYDEN AVE

Raven Bridge

HAW THORN AVE

SHOTT CL

Moss Side Farm

MOSS LA

White Gate Farm

96

Chapelhouse Farm

WA3

Moss House Farm

Red House Farm

Platt House Farm

BEVIN AVE

ATTLEE AVE

ALLEN AVE

EDEN AVE

CHURCHILL AVE

Sewage Works

Holmleigh Farm

Moss Lodge Farm

BEAVERBROOK AVE

CLARKE AVE

WITHINGTON AVE

B5212

2

BEECH AVE

Culcheth Com Prim Sch

Cawley Farm

Culcheth High Sch

SMITH LA

RIBCHESTER GDNS

WALTON RD

Holcroft Hall

HOLCROFT LA

95

CHURCH LA

SAWLEY CL

M44

AVON RD

BOLLIN CL

BENTLA

Crow Wood

Pigeon Wood

THAMES RD

WEAVER

MEDWAY RD

BERWENT CL

SEVERN RD

NEW HALL LA

BENTHAM RD

HOWARD RD

Ratcliffe House Farm

Holcroft Cottage

New Hall

Frank's Farm

Hanging Birch Farm

1

Little Woolden Hall

Willow Brook

B5212

Boundary Drain

94

66   A   67   B   68   C

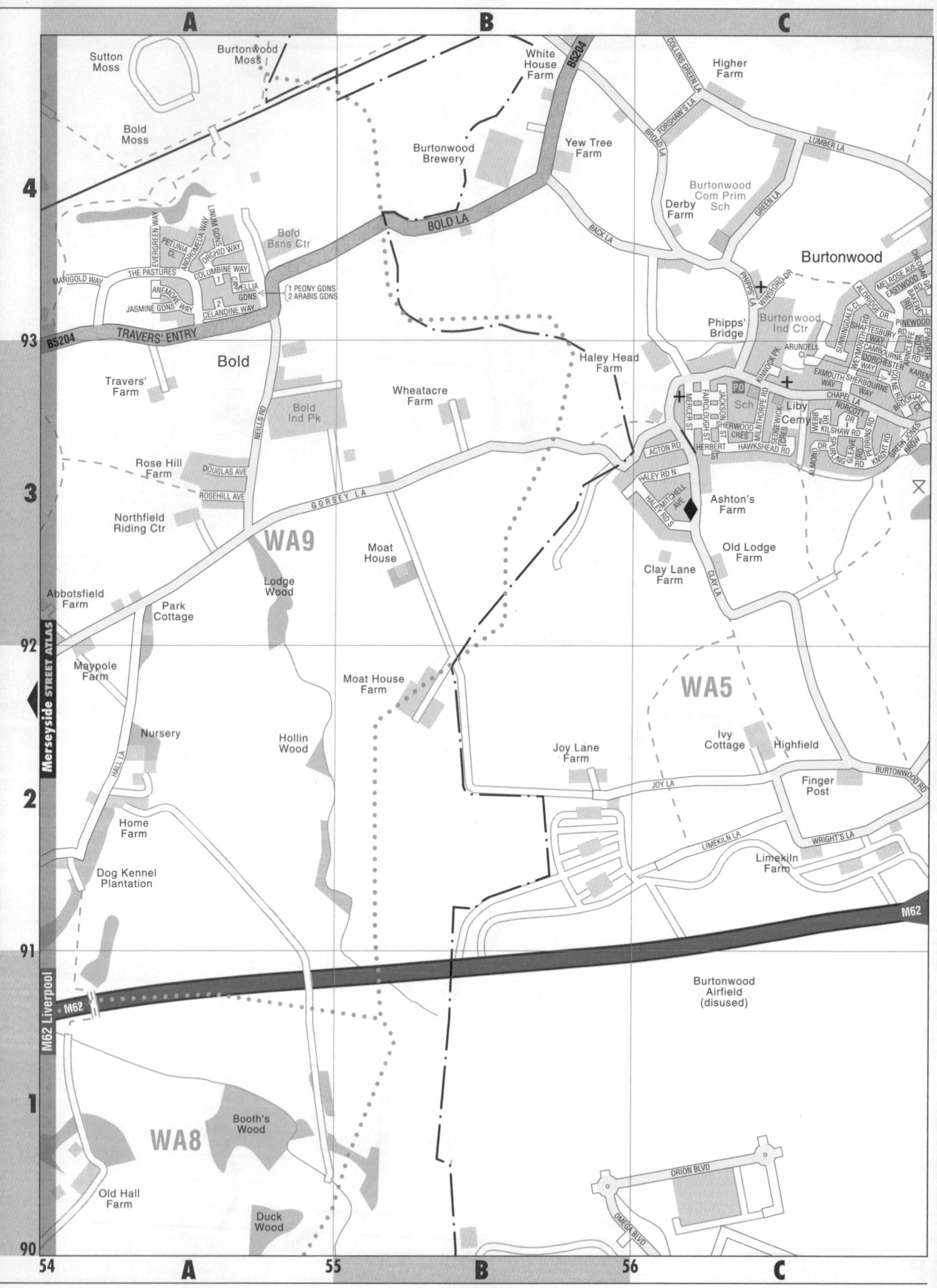

A   B   C

Sutton
Moss

Burtonwood
Moss

White
House
Farm

Higher
Farm

B5204

COLLINS GREEN LA

Bold
Moss

Burtonwood
Brewery

Yew Tree
Farm

FORSHAW'S LA

BROAD LA

LUMBER LA

GREEN LA

Burtonwood
Com Prim
Sch

Derby
Farm

4

BOLD LA

BACK LA

PHIPPS LA

WINDSOR DR

Burtonwood

Bold
Bsns Ctr

EVERGREEN WAY

PETUNIA CL

ANEMONE WAY

ANDROMEDA WAY

ORCHID WAY

LINUM GDNS

COLUMBINE WAY

CAMELLIA GDNS

THE PASTURES

MARIGOLD WAY

JASMINE GDNS

CELANDINE WAY

1 PEONY GDNS
2 ARABIS GDNS

MELROSE AVE

EASTWOOD

CHEDDAR

PINEWOOD

ALTHORPE DR

SHAFTESBURY

CAMBOURNE

DORCHESTER WAY

KAREN CL

Burtonwood
Ind Ctr

93

B5204

TRAVERS' ENTRY

Bold

Phipps'
Bridge

Haley Head
Farm

KINLOCK PK

ARUNDELL CL

WYMOUTH WAY

SHERBOURNE WAY

BROOKVALE

Travers'
Farm

Wheatacre
Farm

EXMOUTH WAY

CHAPEL LA

NORCOTT DR

PERRINS RD

KILSHAW RD

GREEN JONES RD

Bold
Ind Pk

NEILLS RD

MERCER ST

PO

FAIRCLOUGH ST

JACKSON ST

MILNTHORPE RD

Liby
Cemy

Rose Hill
Farm

Sch

SHERWOOD CRES

HERBERT ST

HAWKSHEAD RD

GLEW

KNYPERSLEY RD

ALMOND

DOUGLAS AVE

Acton Rd

ROSEHILL AVE

GORSEY LA

HALEY RD N

3

Northfield
Riding Ctr

WA9

Moat
House

HALEY RD S

MITCHELL AVE

Ashton's
Farm

Old Lodge
Farm

Lodge
Wood

Clay Lane
Farm

CLAY LA

Abbotsfield
Farm

Park
Cottage

92

Maypole
Farm

Moat House
Farm

WA5

Nursery

Hollin
Wood

Joy Lane
Farm

Ivy
Cottage

Highfield

Finger
Post

BURTONWOOD RD

HALL LA

JOY LA

Home
Farm

2

LIMEKILN LA

WRIGHT'S LA

Limekiln
Farm

Dog Kennel
Plantation

M62

91

M62 Liverpool

M62

Burtonwood
Airfield
(disused)

1

WA8

Booth's
Wood

ORION BLVD

Old Hall
Farm

Duck
Wood

OMEGA BLVD

90

54   A   55   B   56   C

Merseyside STREET ATLAS

2

8

A B C

Bradlegh Old Hall
New Bradlegh Hall Farm
BRADLEY LA
HALL LA
Vulcan Village
Sankey Canal (dis)
WA12
HEY WOOD CL
LONDON ROW
CHESTER ROW
SHEFFIELD ROW
LIVERPOOL ROW
MANCHESTER ROW
DERBY ROW
WARGRAVE RD
KIRKACRE AVE
HEY LOCK CL
TYRER RD
CONROY WAY
Newton Brook
Cop Holt Farm
NEWTON RD
A49
4
LUMBER LA
Boarded Barn Farm
MELROSE AVE
BAKEWELL RD
FIR TREE LA
Hall Lane Farm
CH
ALDER ROOT LA
Alder Root Farm
WA2
The Old Vicarage
Red House Farm
Stoneyard Cottage
Asps Wood
PINEWOOD RD
ALDER LA
93
ROXBOROUGH CL
CAMBOURNE RD
KAREN CL
CHAPEL LA
Clayton's House Farm
The Fiddle i'th Bag Inn
Lower Alder Root Farm
Primrose Hill Farm
HOLLINS LA
FARMER'S LA
Tan House Farm
Sankey Brook
WATERY LA
WA5
Sankey Valley Park
Hollins Park
3
BROWNING DR
Phipps' Brook
Brook Head Farm
ALDER LA
Causey Bridge
TAN HOUSE LA
Forest Farm
Causeway Bridges Farm
Works
92
DELPH LA
M62
MILL LA
CLARENDON CT
CRAVEN CT
CALVER RD
BISHOPS CT
Dial Post Farm
TAURUS PK
Gemini
WARRINGTON
2
Burtonwood Service Area
EUROPA BVD
Superstore
WEST QUAY RD
Superstores
Gemini Bsns Pk
8
CROMWELL AVE
CHARON WAY
HOLYHEAD CL
FAIRBOURNE CL
ST ASAPH DR
RUTHIN CL
CHEPSTOW CL
PETERSTONE CL
GOLDCLIFFE CL
WELSHPOOL CL
CRESSWELL CL
LAMPETER CL
BALA CL
91
FALCONERS GN
KINGSWOOD RD
EASTER CT
NEWBRIDGE CL
Little Moss Wood
HARLECH CL
BRECON CT
COLWYN CL
A574
TOURNEY GN
BURTONWOOD RD
CASTLE GN
DELTA CRES
PENMARK CL
STANNER CL
Callands Prim Sch
PO
GRANSTON CL
CARTMEL CL
TENBY CL
LYDSTEP CT
SUMMERFIELD AVE
HERALDS GN
WESTBROOK CRES
CARDIGAN CL
PENSARN GDNS
RIDGEBORNE CL
NEWBOROUGH CL
ROSSETT CL
TINTERN CL
SAUNDERSFOOT CL
LANGLAND CL
RUTTER AVE
PHOENIX AVE
LEWIS AVE
DAGNALL AVE
CONWAY AVE
MARSHALL AVE
Kingswood
PENDINE CL
CARMARTHEN CL
CALLANDS RD
LYDBURY CL
BARMOUTH CL
KILFORD CL
CALDWELL AVE
Dallam
1
DOVE CL
COPPICE GN
WESTBROOK WAY
Calland's Farmhouse
Callands
GRESFORD CL
WREXHAM CL
CORWEN CL
NORTH PARK BROOK RD
Dallam Com Prim Sch
BOULTING AVE
BARDSLEY AVE
MULLEN CL
PO
HARRISON SQ
St Philip (Westbrook) CE Prim Sch
Liby
Superstore
WILLOUGHBY CL
RALEIGH CL
GRANT CL
LADYWOOD RD
MARCROSS CL
CANDLESTON CL
BOVERTON CL
ABERDARE CL
HAYSCASTLE CL
HOOTON AVE
HINDLE AVE
GALE AVE
HIGHAM AVE
LONGSHAW ST
HAWLEY'S LA
HAWLEY'S CL
TAYLOR ST
1 MATLOCK CL
2 TENBURY CL
Westbrook Centre
BLACKSHAW DR
WARD CL
WESTBROOK CTR
BEECROFT CL
Big Wood
WHITTLE AVE
FIRMAN CL
P
BARFORD
GARWOOD CL
CARVER CL
MARES CL
CABOT CL
DRAKE CL
PURDY CL
A574
HARROGATE CL
BRISTOW CL
SHACKLETON CL
Gullivers World Theme Park
90

57 58 59
A B C

15
8

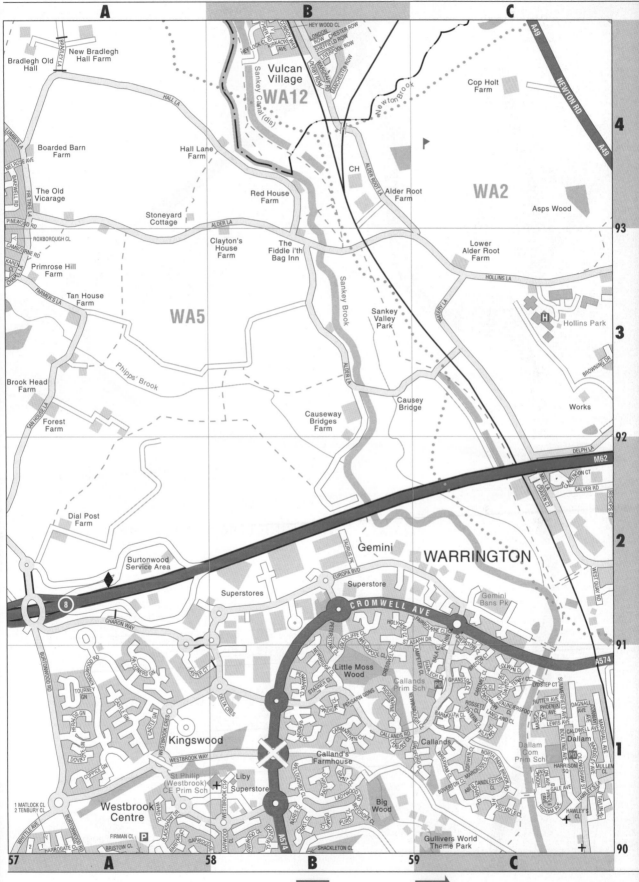

7
3

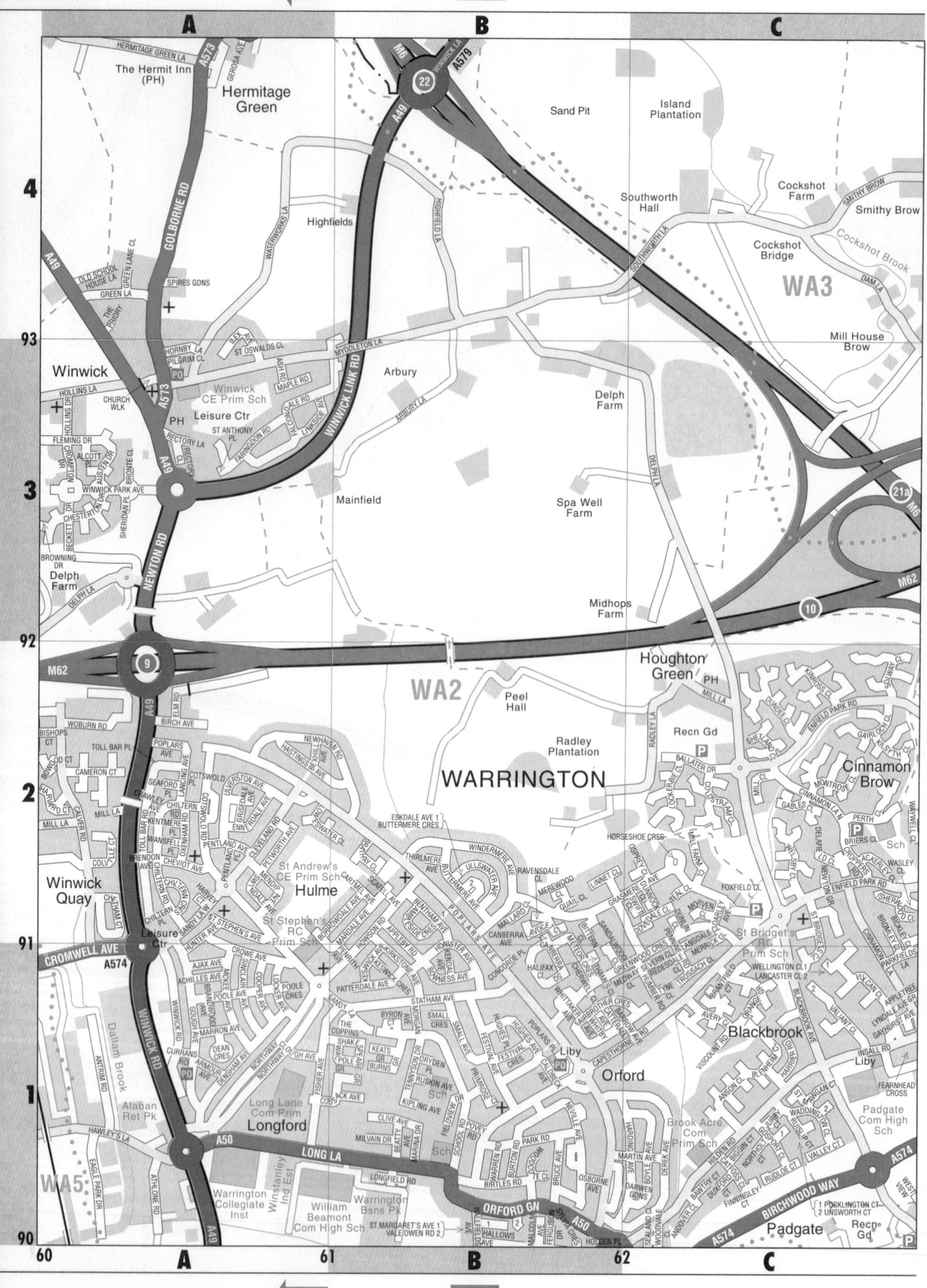

The Hermit Inn (PH)
Hermitage Green
Sand Pit
Island Plantation
Southworth Hall
Cockshot Farm
Smithy Brow
Cockshot Bridge
Cockshot Brook
WA3
Mill House Brow
Highfields
Winwick
Winwick CE Prim Sch
Leisure Ctr
Arbury
Delph Farm
Mainfield
Spa Well Farm
Midhops Farm
Houghton Green
WA2
Peel Hall
Radley Plantation
Recn Gd
WARRINGTON
Cinnamon Brow
Winwick Quay
St Andrew's CE Prim Sch
Hulme
St Stephen's RC Prim Sch
St Bridget's RC Prim Sch
Blackbrook
Orford
Liby
Dallam Brook
Alaban Ret Pk
Long Lane Com Prim
Longford
Brook Acre Com Prim Sch
Padgate Com High Sch
WA5
Warrington Collegiate Inst
Winstanley Ind Est
William Beamont Com High Sch
Warrington Bsns Pk
Padgate
M62
M6
A49
A573
A574
A50
A579
CROMWELL AVE
WINWICK RD
NEWTON RD
LONG LA
ORFORD GN
BIRCHWOOD WAY
WINWICK LINK RD
GOLBORNE RD

7
16

4

10

A B C

Sandy La
Wildings Old La
Heath La
Mustard Ave
Croft Heath Gdns
Croft Prim Sch
PH
Deacons Cl
Abbey Cl
Croft
Lord St
Kingsmead Ct
Smithy Brow
Oak St
Arkenshaw Rd
Round Thorn
Betsyfield Dr
Gerrard Rd
Birchall St
Maythorn Ave
Chadwick Ave
Churchfields
Eaves Brow Rd
Wadeson Way
Browmere Dr
Gosling Rd
Smithy La
New La
Lady La
Brook House Farm
Clares Farm
Hope Farm
A574
Laneside
HM Remand Centre
Warrington Rd
Eaves Farm
Stone Platt
Rowe Farm
Eaves Brow
Hey Farm
Cross La
Silver La
M62
Eaves Brow Farm
Springfield Farm
Mill Houses
Spring La
Hop Pole Farm
Millhouse La
Mast
M6
Cross Lane S
CH
Kelvin Cl
Risley
Trident Ind Est
Clayton Rd
Melbury Ct
Raglan Ct
Leacroft Rd
Daten Pk
Temple Ct
Daten Ave
Heaton Ct
Maxwell St
The Quadrant
Adlington Ct
WA3
Smithills Cl
Birchwood Science Pk
Birchwood Park Ave
Reynold Ave
Griffith Ave
Kelvin St
Stokes St
Gawsworth Ct
Risley Rd
Birchwood Tech Pk
Dalton St
The Beacons
1 Centurion Cl
2 Vanguard Ct
3 Renown Cl
4 Barham Ct
Chadwick Pl
Walton La
Dewar St
Faraday St
Cavendish Ave
Cavendish Pl
Ravenhurst Ct
Trinity Ct
Davy Ave
The Genesis Ctr
Sandycroft Cl
Marlow Cl
Montcliffe Cl
Turton Cl
Cadshaw Cl
Dunscar Cl
Havisham Cl
Copperfield Cl
Bracken Cl
Trefoil Cl
Heather Cl
Norden Cl
Eccleston Cl
Violet Ct
Campion Cl
Locking Stumps Com Prim Sch
Garrett Field
Newton Ave
Thompson St
Birchwood
Aston Ave
Keyes Gdn
Holmes Cl
Lords La
Redvales Ct
Hawkshaw Cl
Aspull Cl
Strawberry Cl
Fern Cl
Armstrong Cl
Glover Rd
Stonecrop Cl
Delenty Dr
Fernbank Cl
Powell Ave
Pheasant Cl
Keyes Cl
Admirals Rd
Sovereign Ct 1
Nuttall Ct 2
Windle Ct 3
Topping Ct
Locking Stumps La
Deanwater Cl
Picton Cl
Carden Cl
Beeston Cl
Carrington Cl
Elton Cl
Hapsford Cl
Kinnerton Dr
Ledham Cl
Kelsall Cl
Cutland La
Warrington Rd
Ordnance Ave
Redshank La
Redpoll La
Dunnock Gr
Goldfinch La
Kestrel La
Linnet Gr
Partridge Cl
Kingfisher Cl
Wren Cl
Woodpecker Cl
Swallow Cl
Fieldfare Cl
Dove Cl
Oakwood
Jay Cl
Chaffinch Cl
Sch
Oakwood Gate
Bickerton Cl
Birchwood Ave
Fox Wood Sch
Forbes Cl
Talbot Cl
Noble Cl
Nightingale Cl
Whinchat Dr
Mallard La
Teal Gr
Halliday Cl
Burrough Cl
Chatfield Dr
Ramsey Cl
Layton Cl
Harcourt Cl
Curlew Gr
Pipit La
Admirals Rd
Miles Cl
Lyster Cl
Liby
Birchwood Com High Sch
Latham Cl
Brock Rd
Sp Ctr
Hamnett Ct
Ainscough Rd
Patterson Cl
Woodhouse Cl
Rawlings Cl
Benson Rd
Birchwood Centre
Birchwood One Bsns Pk
Birchwood Blvd
Dewhurst Rd
Birchwood
St Andrews Cl
Mathers Cl
Enfield Park Rd
Tweed Cl
Muir Cl
Braemar Cl
Oban Gr
Stonehaven Dr
Nairn Cl
Strumness Cl
Blackledge Cl
Rowland Cl
Dig La
Birchwood Office Pk
Crab La
Jervis Cl
Aspinall Cl
Aviemore Dr
Stirrup Cl
1 Waywell Cl
2 Cottam Dr
3 Libson Cl
4 Timmis Cl
5 Wasley Cl
Warrington Univ Coll (Padgate Campus)
Cinnamon Pk
Bickley Cl
Parkfields La
WA2
College Cl
Long Barn La
Arran Cl
Canada Cl
Appletree Gr
Fearnhead La
Cross Farm
Kings Rd
Ronald Dr
Barnes Ave
Nook La
B5210
Blackburne Cl
Longbarn Blvd
Capenhurst Ave
Mere Rd
Chapel Cross Rd
Windscale Rd
Fearnhead
Dounrey Cl
Orchard St
Meadow La
Winfrith Rd
Anderson Cl
Station Rd
Edgars Dr
Harpers Rd
Fallowfield Gr
Freshfields Dr
Lovage Cl
Sorrel Cl
Burnet Cl
Sage Cl
Saffron Cl
Woolston Grange Ave
Woolston Moss
Moss Lane Farm
Station Road N
Carpenter Gr
Peasley Cl
Pasture La
Oxmead Cl
Longbarn Prim Sch
Longbarn
Padgate CE Prim Sch
WA1
Brookfield Farm
West View
Church Rd
Guildford Cl
Mullion Gr
Mayberry Gr
Duckworth Gr
Station Road S
1 Shawbury Gr
2 Colemere Cl
Grosvenor Grange
Aston Ct
Greys Ct
Kingsland Grange
Long Barn La
Woolston Park
Poulton Cres
Totton Ct
Hardwick Grange
Moss La
Nicol Ave
Padgate

4 93 3 92 2 91 1 90

63 A 64 B 65 C

17 10

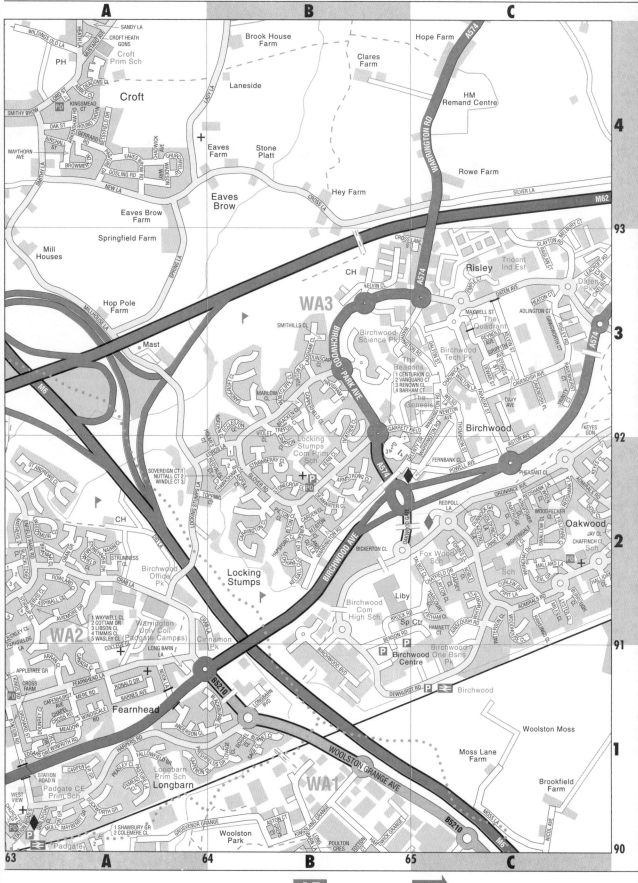

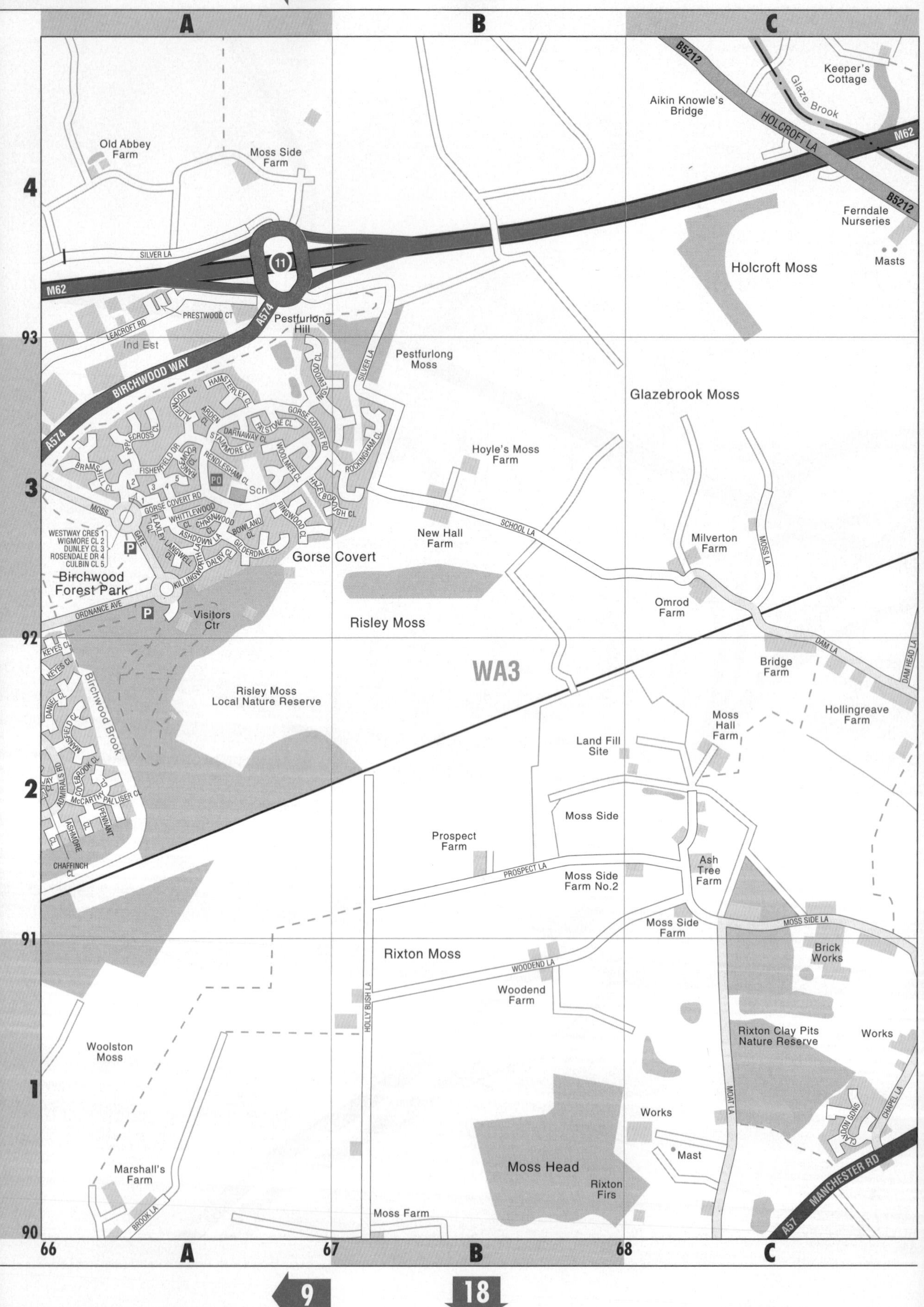
A   **B**   **C**

4

Old Abbey Farm

Moss Side Farm

B5212

Aikin Knowle's Bridge

Keeper's Cottage

Glaze Brook

HOLCROFT LA

M62

B5212

Ferndale Nurseries

Holcroft Moss

Masts

SILVER LA

M62

(11)

93

LEACROFT RD

PRESTWOOD CT

A574

Pestfurlong Hill

Pestfurlong Moss

Glazebrook Moss

Ind Est

BIRCHWOOD WAY

A574

HAMSTERLEY CL

GORSE COVERT RD

SILVER LA

Hoyle's Moss Farm

Milverton Farm

MOSS LA

3

BRAMSHILL DR

FISHERFIELD DR

ECROSS

WHITTLEWOOD CL

DARNAWAY CL

TALSTONE CL

WOOLMER CL

RENDLESHAM CL

HAZELBOROUGH CL

ROCKINGHAM CL

PO

Sch

New Hall Farm

SCHOOL LA

Omrod Farm

MOSS

GORSE COVERT RD

RALEY

LANGWELL

ASHDOWN

CHARNWOOD CL

BOWLAND

BIRCHWOOD CL

GILDERDALE CL

Gorse Covert

Risley Moss

Bridge Farm

DAM LA

WESTWAY CRES 1
WIGMORE CL 2
DUNLEY CL 3
ROSENDALE DR 4
CULBIN CL 5.

P

GATE

KILLINGWORTH

DALBY CL

Birchwood Forest Park

WA3

Moss Hall Farm

Hollingreave Farm

92

ORDNANCE AVE

P

Visitors Ctr

KEYES CL

KEYES CL

DANIEL CL

Birchwood Brook

Risley Moss Local Nature Reserve

Land Fill Site

Moss Side

DAM LA

2

MCKEAN ST

TRASK CL

MCCARTHY

PALLISER CL

PENNANT

ASHMORE CL

Prospect Farm

Moss Side

Ash Tree Farm

CHAFFINCH CL

PROSPECT LA

Moss Side Farm No.2

Moss Side Farm

MOSS SIDE LA

Brick Works

91

Rixton Moss

WOODEND LA

Woodend Farm

HOLLY BUSH LA

Rixton Clay Pits Nature Reserve

Works

1

Woolston Moss

MOAT LA

Works

Marshall's Farm

Moss Head

Rixton Firs

Mast

LYDIATE GDNS

CHAPEL LA

MANCHESTER RD

A57

90

BROOK LA

Moss Farm

66   67   68

A   **B**   **C**

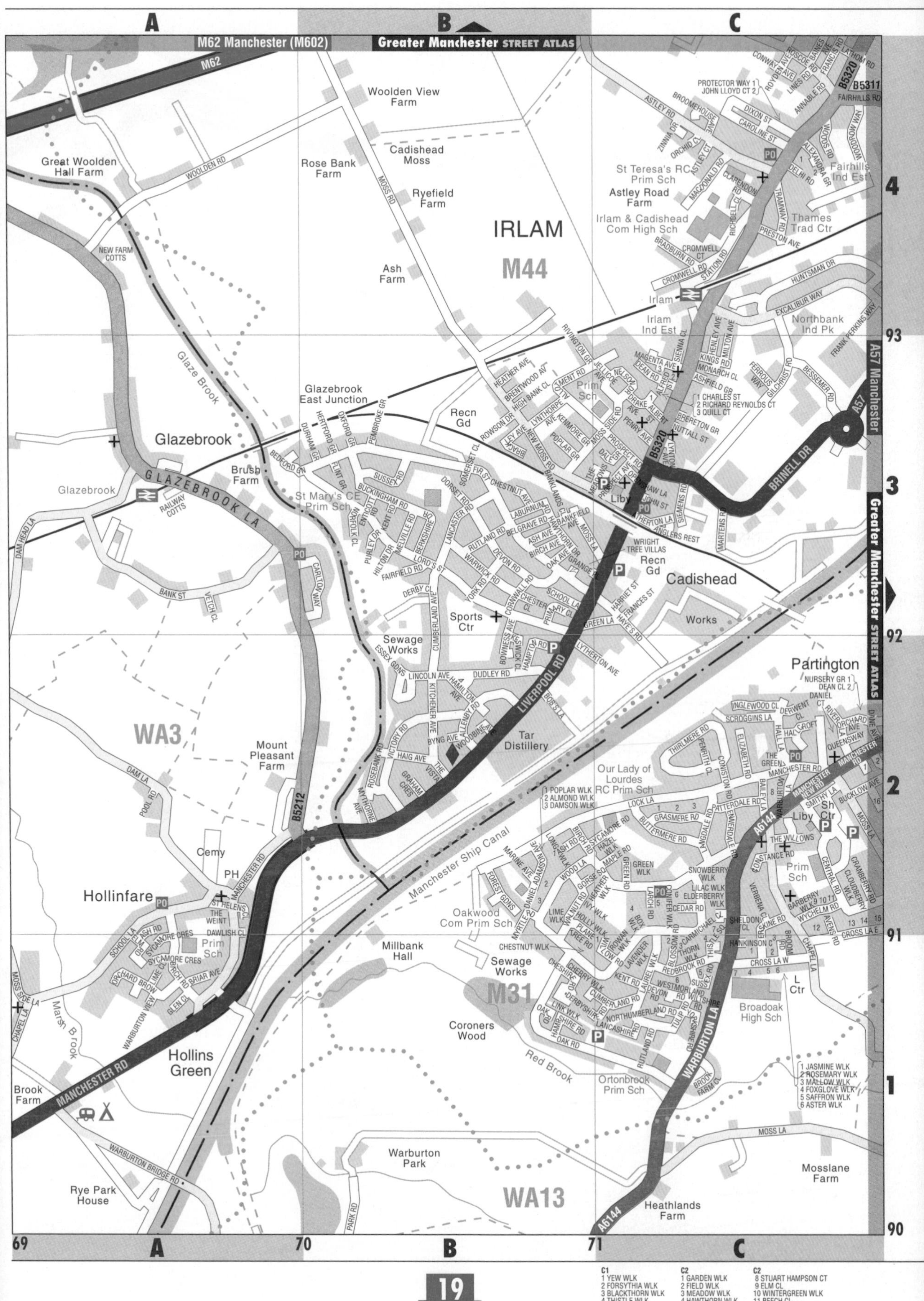

M62 Manchester (M602)

Greater Manchester STREET ATLAS

M62

Woolden View Farm

Great Woolden Hall Farm

Woolden Rd

Rose Bank Farm

Cadishead Moss

Moss Rd

Ryefield Farm

New Farm Cotts

Ash Farm

IRLAM

M44

CONWAY GR

ROSCOE RD

GAINES

FRANCIS RD

B5320

B5311

FAIRHILLS RD

PROTECTOR WAY 1
JOHN LLOYD CT 2

ASTLEY RD

BROOMEHOUSE

ROY GRAVE

LINES RD

ANNABLE RD

NOSS RD

WOOLS RD

St Teresa's RC Prim Sch

ORCHARD CL

ASTLEY RD

DIXON ST

CAROLINE ST

PO

FAIRHILLS IND EST

ZINNIA

CLARENDON

DELHI RD

Astley Road Farm

MACDONALD

RICHELIEU

CROMWELL

DOXEY RD

Irlam & Cadishead Com High Sch

CROMWELL

STATION RD

Irlam

CROMWELL

HUNTSMAN DR

PRESTON AVE

Thames Trad Ctr

Glaze Brook

Glazebrook

Glazebrook East Junction

Glazebrook

Glazebrook

GLAZEBROOK LA

Brush Farm

RAILWAY COTTS

Irlam Ind Est

EXCALIBUR WAY

Northbank Ind Pk

HEATHER AVE

BRENTWOOD AV

HIGH BANK CL

Recn Gd

RIVINGTON GR

MAGENTA AVE

KINGS RD

HENLEY AVE

MILTON AVE

ASHFIELD GR

FERROUS WAY

GILCHRIST RD

BESSEMER RD

FRANK PERKINS WAY

A57 Manchester

93

A57

Prim Sch

1 CHARLES ST
2 RICHARD REYNOLDS CT
3 QUILL CT

BRERETON GR

BRINELL DR

3

Greater Manchester STREET ATLAS

DAM HEAD LA

HERTFORD GR

OXFORD GR

DURHAM GR

FLINT GR

PEMBROKE GR

BEDFORD GR

St Mary's CE Prim Sch

SUSSEX

BUCKINGHAM RD

DORSET RD

SOMERSET CL

ROWSON DR

LYTHORPE

KENMORE GR

NEW MOSS RD

PARKLANDS

POPLAR GR

PROSPECT

ALDER AVE

B5320

ANGLERS REST

Liby

JOHN ST

SHAW LA

92

PURLEY AVE

HILTON GR

NORFOLK CL

MELVILLE RD

KENT RD

LANCASTER RD

DEVON RD

BELGRAVE RD

LABURNUM

ASH AVE

BIRCH AVE

ORANGE

MOSS LA

Cadishead

FAIRFIELD RD

LORD'S ST

WARWICK RD

RUTLAND RD

OAK AVE

DERBY CL

CRANWALL RD

CHESTER RD

SCHOOL RD

HARRIE ST

ST FRANCES ST

Recn Gd

Works

WRIGHT TREE VILLAS

WA3

Mount Pleasant Farm

Sports Ctr

BOWNESS AVE

HAMPTON

BYE ST A

Sewage Works

LINCOLN AVE

HAMILTON

DUDLEY RD

KITCHENER AVE

GREEN LA W

HAYES ST

LYTHERTON AVE

P

Partington

NURSERY GR 1
DEAN CL 2

DANIEL

Tar Distillery

Liverpool Rd

INGLEWOOD CL

SCROGGINS LA

DERWENT CL

HALL CROFT

RIVER

ORCHARD AVE

QUEENSWAY

PINE ST

MANCHESTER RD

2

B5212

DAM LA

POOL RD

VETCH CL

BANK ST

CARLOW WAY

VICTORY RD

ROSEBANK RD

HAIG AVE

GRAHAM CRES

ANYTHORNE

1 POPLAR WLK
2 ALMOND WLK
3 DAMSON WLK

Our Lady of Lourdes RC Prim Sch

LOCK LA

THIRLMERE RD

PENRITH

CONISTON RD

GRASMERE RD

BUTTERMERE RD

ELIZABETH RD

PATTERDALE RD

ENNERDALE

THE GREEN

BAILEY LA

MANCHESTER RD

SMITHY LA

BUCKLOW AVE

MOSS LA

Sh Ctr

Liby Ctr

P

P

Prim Sch

CRANBERRY

CLOUDBERRY

Cemy

PH

Hollinfare

MANCHESTER RD

PO

St Helens THE WEINT

DAWLISH CL

Prim Sch

SCHOOL LA

ASH RD

SYCAMORE CRES

SYCAMORE VIEW

LIME TREE

GLEN CL

BATAR AVE

Millbank Hall

Oakwood Com Prim Sch

CHESTNUT WLK

Sewage Works

MARINE AVE

FOREST GDNS

LIME WLK

MYRTLE

IVY WLK

HOLLY WLK

BROWN

GORSE WLK

MOOR HEATHER

SYCAMORE RD

HAZEL

MAPLE RD

WOOD LA

GREEN RD

LILAC WLK

ELDERBERRY

CEDAR RD

LARCH RD

SNOWBERRY WLK

VERBENA RD

SHELDON

BARBERRY WLK 9 10 11

WYCHELM RD

12

13 14 15

CROSS LA E

91

MOSS SIDE LA

CHAPEL LA

Marsh Brook

Hollins Green

ORCHARD BROW

SHORROCKS

CHERRY WLK

CHESHIRE

LAVENDER

KENT RD

SHRUBBERY

LINK WLK

OAK RD

SHIRE

WESTMOR RD

CUMBERLAND RD

LANCASHIRE

NORTHUMBERLAND RD

RUTLAND RD

WARBURTON LA

BROADOAK HIGH SCH

Broadoak High Sch

CROSS LA W

L Ctr

1 JASMINE WLK
2 ROSEMARY WLK
3 MALLOW WLK
4 FOXGLOVE WLK
5 SAFFRON WLK
6 ASTER WLK

Brook Farm

WARBURTON BRIDGE RD

M31

Coroners Wood

Red Brook

Ortonbrook Prim Sch

BROOK FARM RD

MOSS LA

1

Rye Park House

PARK RD

Warburton Park

Heathlands Farm

WA13

A6144

Mosslane Farm

90

69 A 70 B 71 C

C1
1 YEW WLK
2 FORSYTHIA WLK
3 BLACKTHORN WLK
4 THISTLE WLK
5 MAGNOLIA CL
6 LOBELIA WLK
7 IRIS WLK

C2
1 GARDEN WLK
2 FIELD WLK
3 MEADOW WLK
4 HAWTHORN WLK
5 MAY WLK
6 PINE WLK
7 ROSE WLK

C2
8 STUART HAMPSON CT
9 ELM CL
10 WINTERGREEN WLK
11 BEECH CL
12 CAMOMILE WLK
13 CHARLOCK WLK
14 WOODRUFF WLK
15 COLUMBINE WLK
16 WORTHINGTON AVE

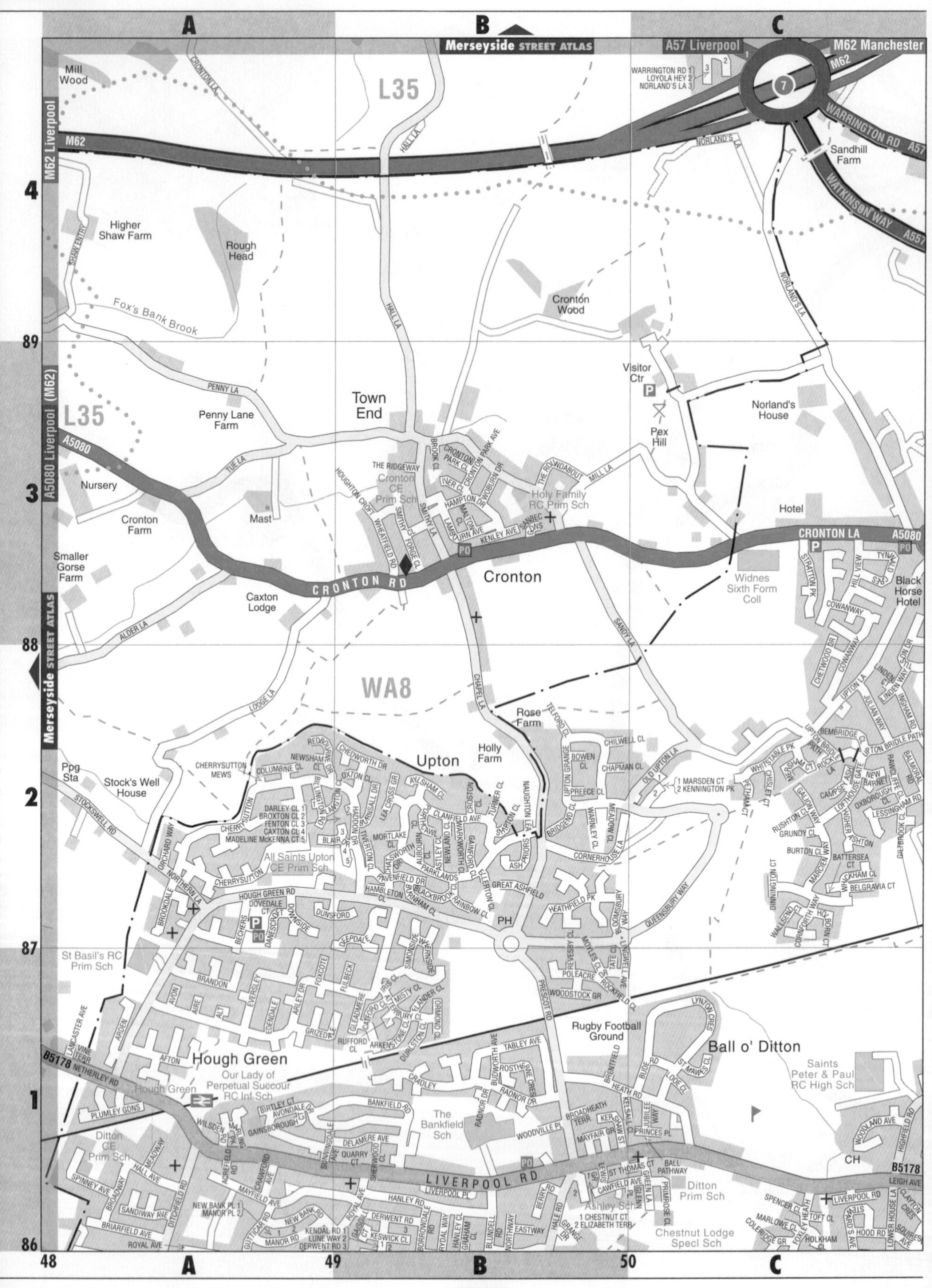
A
B
C
Merseyside STREET ATLAS
A57 Liverpool
M62 Manchester
WARRINGTON RD 1
LOYOLA HEY 2
NORLAND'S LA 3
M62
WARRINGTON RD A57
WATKINSON WAY A557
Sandhill Farm
Mill Wood
CRONTON LA
L35
HALL LA
M62 Liverpool
4
Higher Shaw Farm
SHAW ENTRY
Rough Head
Fox's Bank Brook
Cronton Wood
NORLAND'S LA
89
A5080 Liverpool (M62)
PENNY LA
Penny Lane Farm
L35
Town End
Visitor Ctr
Pex Hill
Norland's House
A5080
Nursery
TUE LA
Mast
THE RIDGEWAY
Cronton CE Prim Sch
HOUGHTON CROFT
BROOK CL
CRONTON PARK CL
CRONTON PARK AVE
WOBURN DR
THE ROUNDABOUT
MILL LA
Holy Family RC Prim Sch
3
Cronton Farm
Hotel
CRONTON LA
A5080
Smaller Gorse Farm
CRONTON RD
Cronton
Caxton Lodge
Widnes Sixth Form Coll
STRATTON PK
HILL VIEW
Black Horse Hotel
COWANWAY
ALDER LA
SANDY LA
88
Merseyside STREET ATLAS
LODGE LA
WA8
CHAPEL LA
Rose Farm
TELFORD CL
Holly Farm
Upton
CHILWELL CL
BOWEN CL
CHAPMAN CL
OLD UPTON LA
1 MARSDEN CT
2 KENNINGTON PK
Ppg Sta
Stock's Well House
CHERRYSUTTON MEWS
STOCKSWELL RD
2
DARLEY CL 1
BROXTON CL 2
FENTON CL 3
CAXTON CL 4
MADELINE McKENNA CT 5
All Saints Upton CE Prim Sch
CHERRYSUTTON
NORTHERN LA
ORCHARD WAY
HOUGH GREEN RD
DOVEDALE CT
GREAT ASHFIELD
CORNERHOUSE LA
HEATHFIELD PK
QUEENSBURY WAY
PH
BROOKDALE
87
St Basil's RC Prim Sch
BRANDON
PRESCOT RD
WOODSTOCK GR
Rugby Football Ground
LYNTON CRES
Ball o' Ditton
Saints Peter & Paul RC High Sch
LANCASTER AVE
VINE TERR
B5178 NETHERLEY RD
Hough Green
Our Lady of Perpetual Succour RC Inf Sch
Hough Green
TABLEY AVE
1
PLUMLEY GDNS
BANKFIELD RD
The Bankfield Sch
WOODVILLE PL
Ditton CE Prim Sch
LIVERPOOL RD
B5178
CH
Ditton Prim Sch
Ashley Sch
1 CHESTNUT CT
2 ELIZABETH TERR
Chestnut Lodge Specl Sch
NEW BANK PL 1
MANOR PL 2
KENDAL RD 1
LUNE WAY 2
DERWENT RD 3
ROYAL AVE
86
48
49
50
A
B
C

22

14

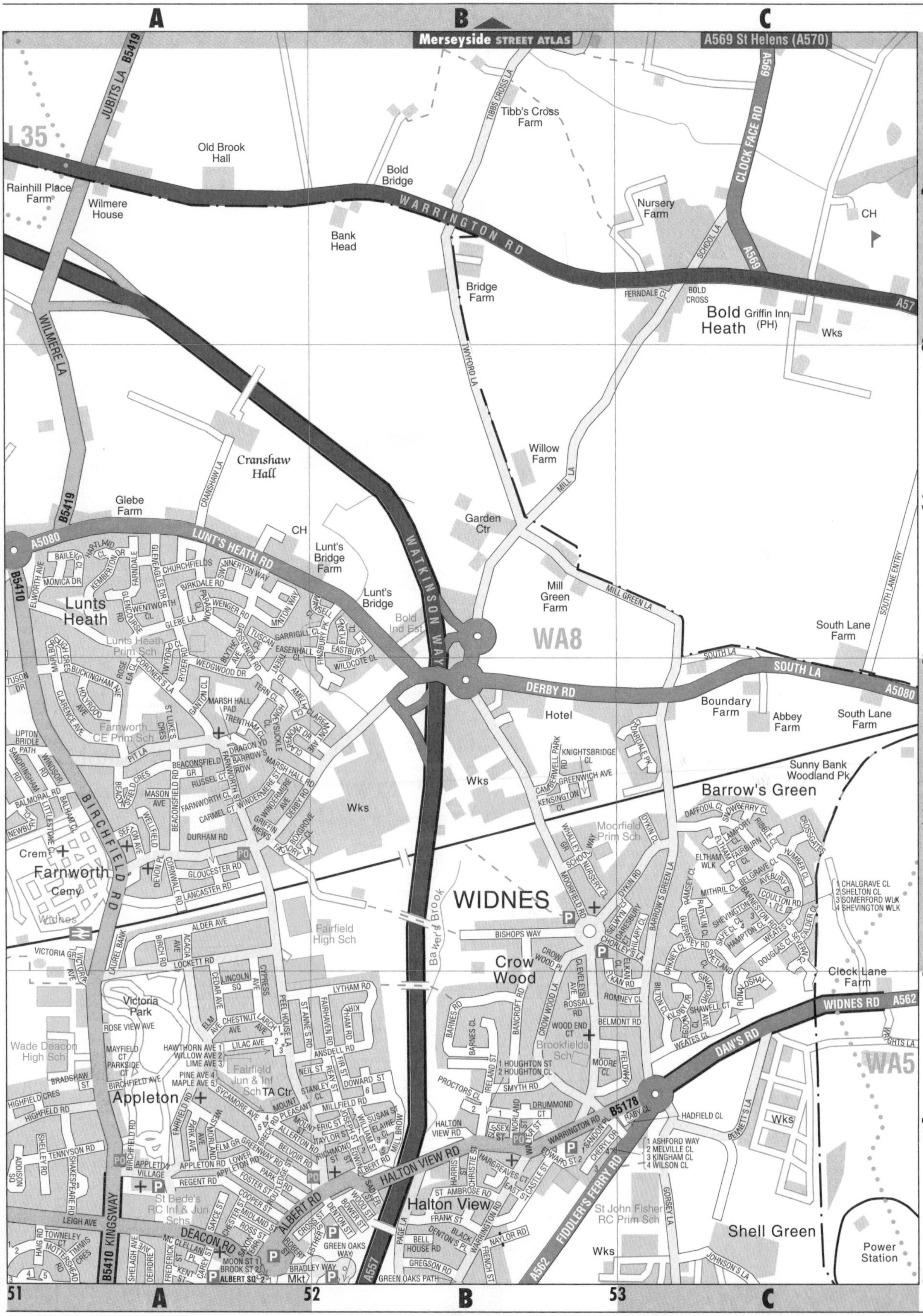
A
B
C
Merseyside STREET ATLAS
A569 St Helens (A570)
L35
JUBITS LA B5419
Old Brook Hall
Rainhill Place Farm
Wilmere House
Bold Bridge
Bank Head
WARRINGTON RD
Tibb's Cross Farm
TIBBS CROSS LA
CLOCK FACE RD
A569
Nursery Farm
SCHOOL LA
CH
Bridge Farm
FERNDALE CL
BOLD CROSS
Bold Heath
Griffin Inn (PH)
Wks
A57
89
4
WILMERE LA
TWYFORD LA
Cranshaw Hall
CRANSHAW LA
Willow Farm
MILL LA
Glebe Farm
B5419
Garden Ctr
3
A5080
LUNT'S HEATH RD
Lunt's Bridge Farm
Lunt's Bridge
Mill Green Farm
MILL GREEN LA
WATKINSON WAY
SOUTH LANE ENTRY
South Lane Farm
Lunts Heath
Lunts Heath Prim Sch
Bold Ind Est
WA8
88
SOUTH LA
A5080
DERBY RD
Hotel
Boundary Farm
Abbey Farm
South Lane Farm
Farnworth CE Prim Sch
KNIGHTSBRIDGE CL
GREENWICH AVE
KENSINGTON CL
Sunny Bank Woodland Pk
Barrow's Green
Wks
2
Moorfield Prim Sch
Crem
Farnworth
Cemy
Widnes
WIDNES
1 CHALGRAVE CL
2 SHELTON CL
3 SOMERFORD WLK
4 SHEVINGTON WLK
Fairfield High Sch
BISHOPS WAY
Bawers Brook
Crow Wood
87
Clock Lane Farm
Victoria Park
WIDNES RD
A562
DAN'S RD
WA5
Wade Deacon High Sch
Fairfield Jun & Inf Sch
TA Ctr
Brookfields Sch
Appleton
1 HOUGHTON ST
2 HOUGHTON CL
B5178
1 ASHFORD WAY
2 MELVILLE CL
3 KINGHAM CL
4 WILSON CL
HADFIELD CL
Wks
1
HALTON VIEW RD
Halton View
St Bede's RC Inf & Jun Schs
St John Fisher RC Prim Sch
FIDDLER'S FERRY RD
A562
Shell Green
Power Station
Wks
B5410 KINGSWAY
A557
ALBERT RD
DEACON RD
Mkt
GREEN OAKS PATH
86
51
52
53

A1
1 CLAYTON CRES
2 HENDERSON RD
3 SQUIRES AVE
4 BRUNNER RD
5 MOND RD

B1
1 PARR ST
2 RUNNYMEDE CT
3 CLIFFE ST
4 HENRY ST
5 RUNNYMEDE GDNS
6 KNOWLES ST
7 RUNNYMEDE WLK

23
14

13
6

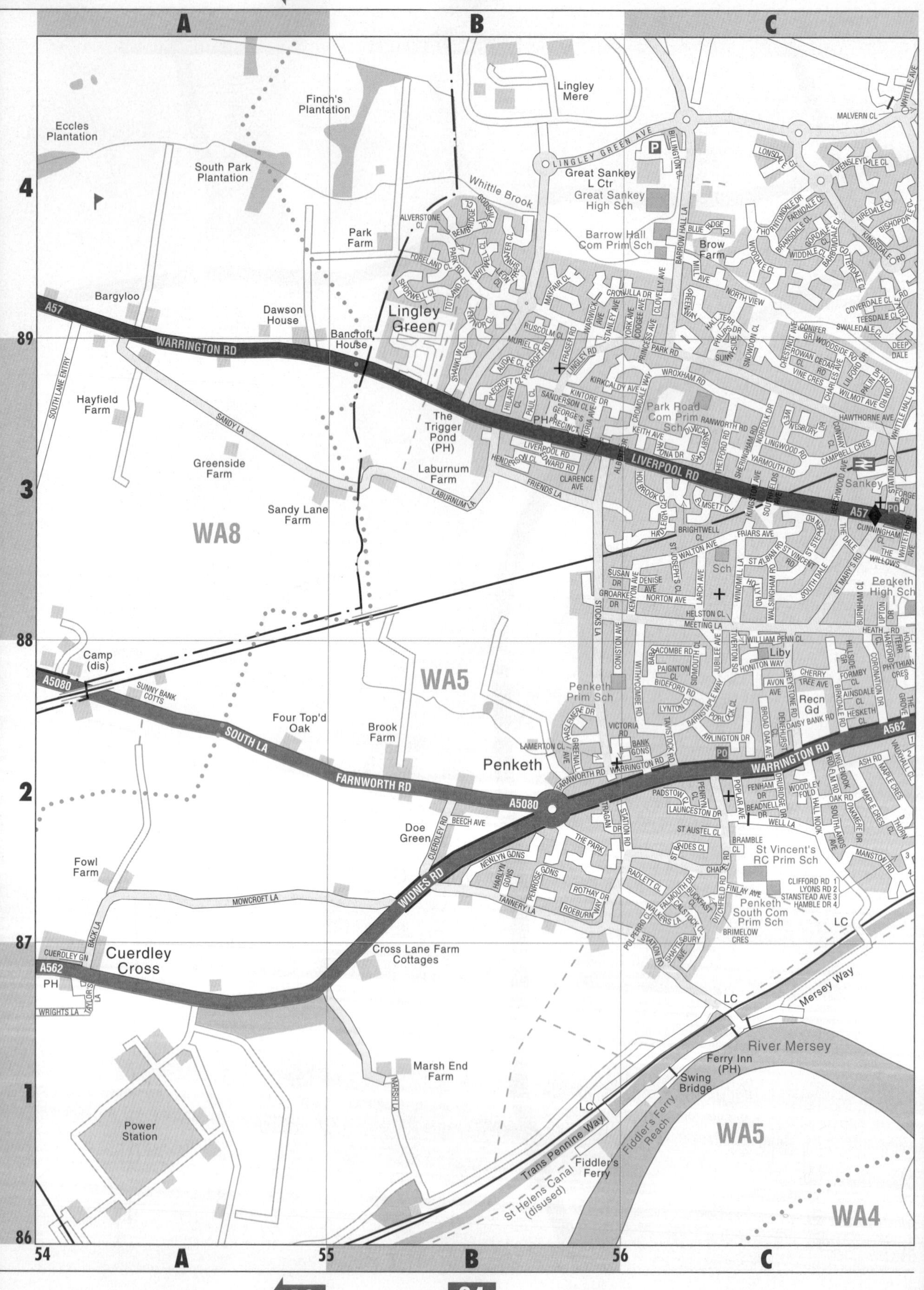
A
B
C
4
89
3
88
2
87
1
86
54
55
56
Eccles Plantation
Finch's Plantation
South Park Plantation
Lingley Mere
LINGLEY GREEN AVE
Great Sankey L Ctr
Great Sankey High Sch
Barrow Hall Com Prim Sch
Brow Farm
Whittle Brook
Park Farm
Bargyloo
Dawson House
Bancroft House
Lingley Green
A57
WARRINGTON RD
Hayfield Farm
SANDY LA
The Trigger Pond (PH)
Greenside Farm
Laburnum Farm
LABURNUM LA
Sandy Lane Farm
WA8
LIVERPOOL RD
Park Road Com Prim Sch
Sankey
Penketh High Sch
Camp (dis)
A5080
SUNNY BANK COTTS
WA5
SOUTH LA
Four Top'd Oak
Brook Farm
FARNWORTH RD
Penketh
Penketh Prim Sch
Liby
Recn Gd
A562
Doe Green
BEECH AVE
WIDNES RD
Fowl Farm
MOWCROFT LA
St Vincent's RC Prim Sch
Penketh South Com Prim Sch
CLIFFORD RD 1
LYONS RD 2
STANSTEAD AVE 3
HAMBLE DR 4
Cuerdley Cross
Cross Lane Farm Cottages
LC
Mersey Way
River Mersey
Ferry Inn (PH)
Swing Bridge
Marsh End Farm
Power Station
Trans Pennine Way
St Helens Canal (disused)
Fiddler's Ferry
Fiddler's Ferry Reach
WA4
A
B
C

13
24

7
16

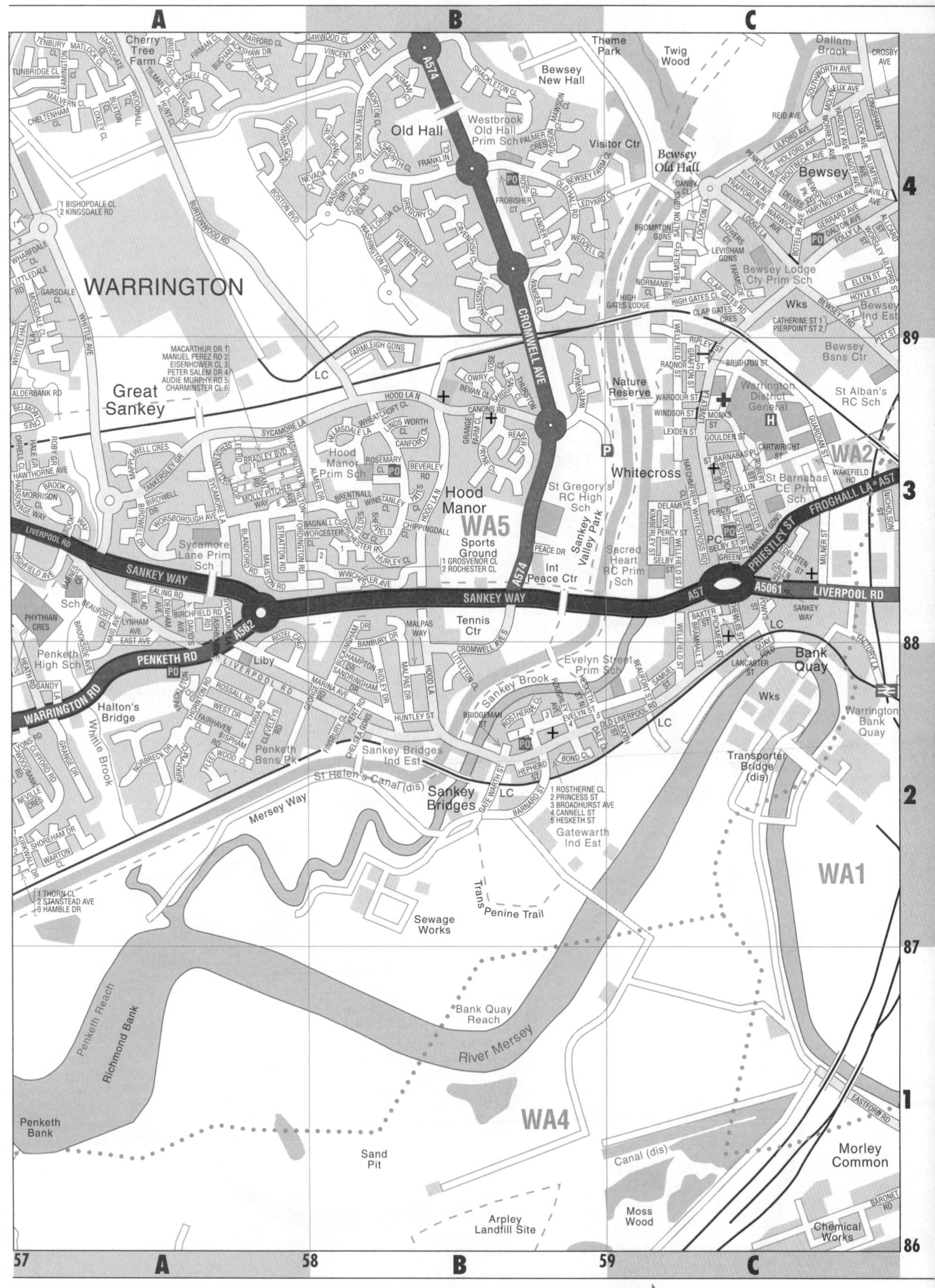
A
B
C
WARRINGTON
Great Sankey
Old Hall
Hood Manor
WA5
Whitecross
Bewsey
Bewsey Old Hall
Sankey Bridges
Bank Quay
WA1
WA2
WA4
River Mersey
Bank Quay Reach
Penketh Bank
Penketh Reach
Richmond Bank
Sand Pit
Arpley Landfill Site
Moss Wood
Morley Common
Chemical Works
Sewage Works
Trans Penine Trail
Mersey Way
St Helen's Canal (dis)
Canal (dis)
Sankey Way
Cromwell Ave
Liverpool Rd
Penketh Rd
Warrington Rd
Priestley St
Froghall La
Cherry Tree Farm
Theme Park
Twig Wood
Dallam Brook
Bewsey New Hall
Westbrook Old Hall Prim Sch
Visitor Ctr
Nature Reserve
Warrington District General
St Alban's RC Sch
St Gregory's RC High Sch
Sankey Valley Park
Sacred Heart RC Prim Sch
Int Peace Ctr
Sports Ground
Tennis Ctr
Hood Manor Prim Sch
Sycamore Lane Prim Sch
Penketh High Sch
Halton's Bridge
Whittle Brook
Penketh Bsns Pk
Sankey Bridges Ind Est
Gatewarth Ind Est
Evelyn Street Prim Sch
St Barnabas CE Prim Sch
Bewsey Lodge Cty Prim Sch
Bewsey Bsns Ctr
Bewsey Ind Est
Transporter Bridge (dis)
Warrington Bank Quay
Sankey Brook
57
58
59
86
87
88
89
1
2
3
4

25
16

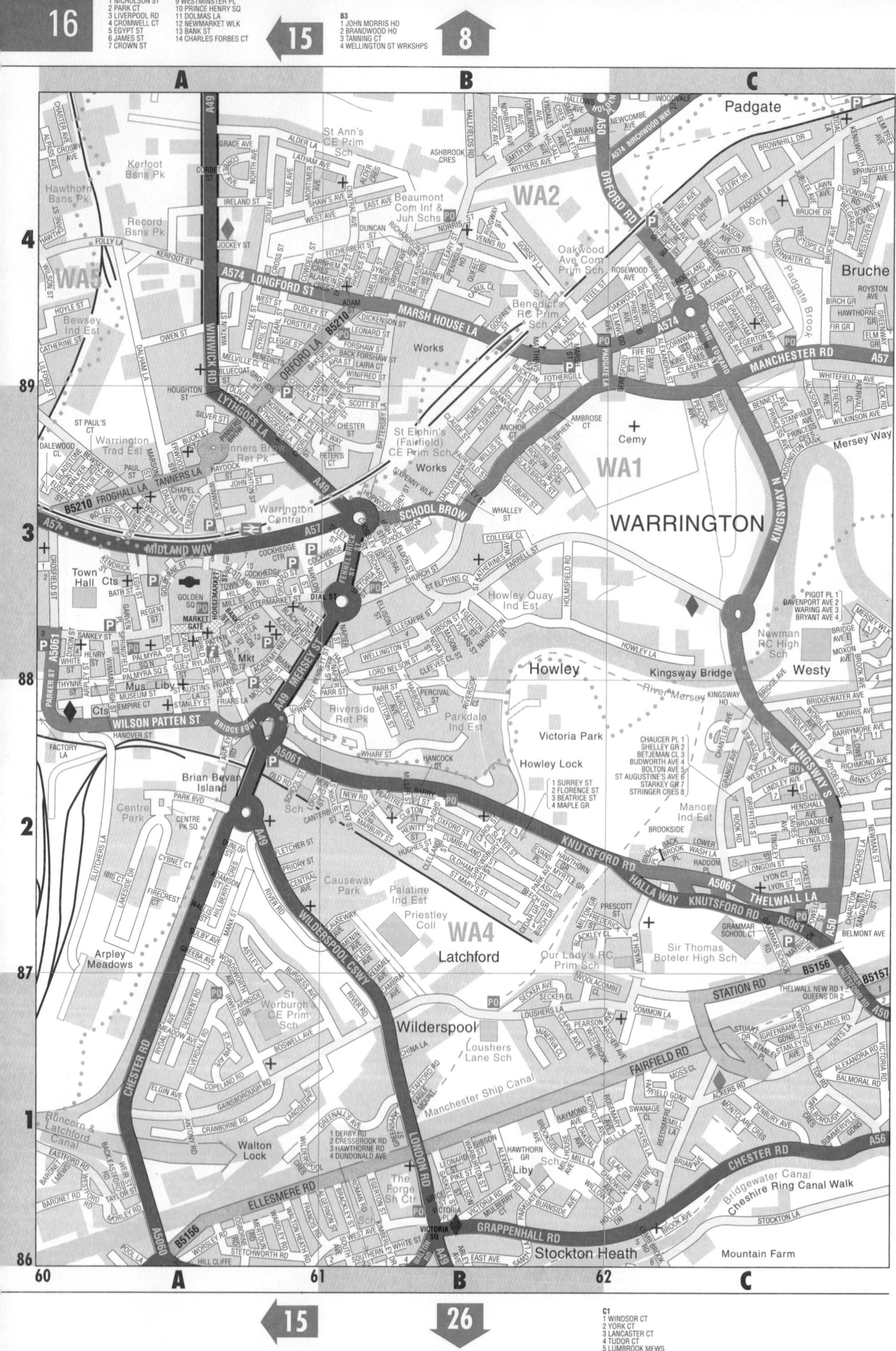

9
18

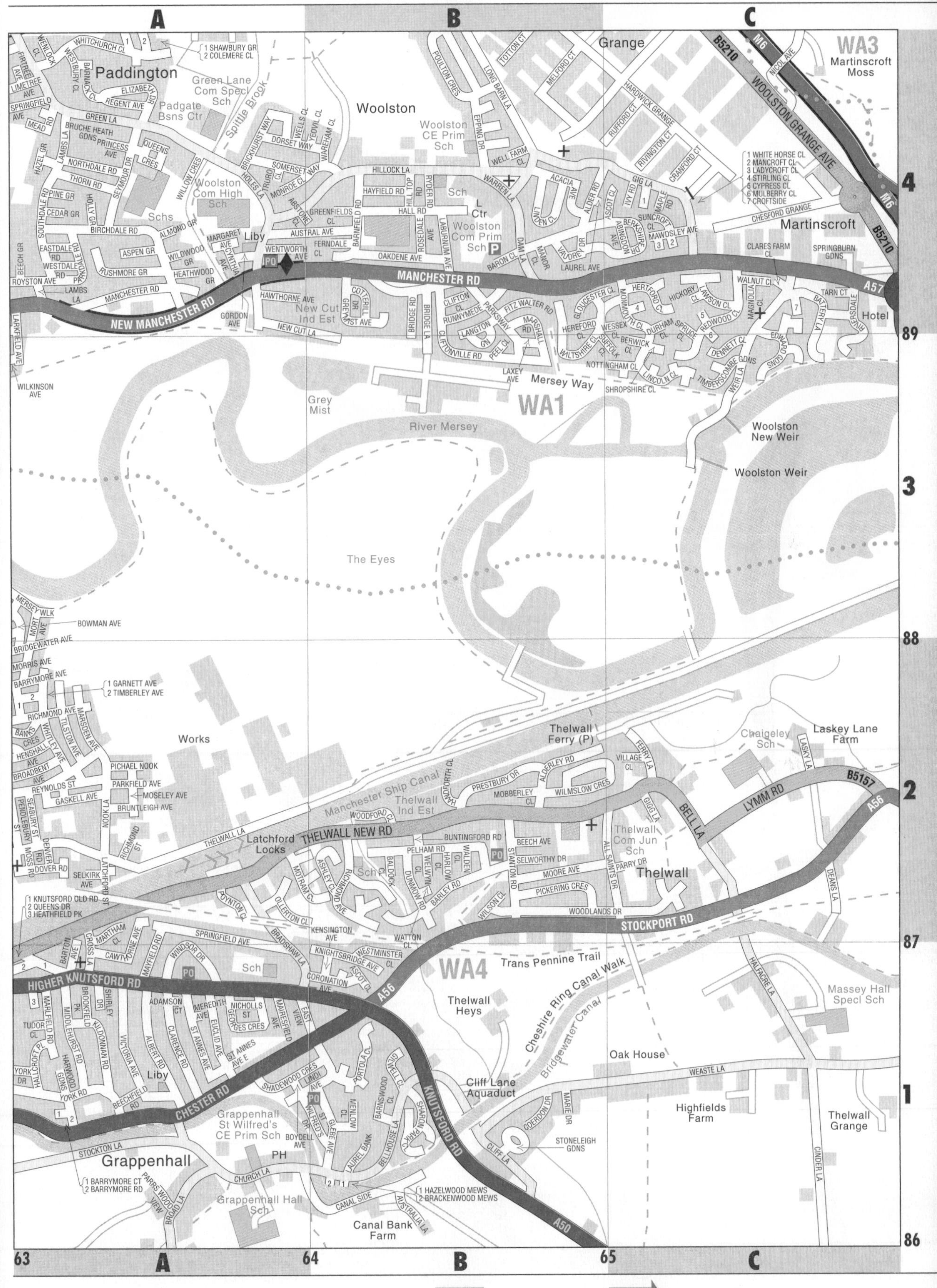
A
B
C
Paddington
Woolston
Grange
WA3
Martinscroft Moss
Green Lane Com Specl Sch
Padgate Bsns Ctr
Spittle Brook
Woolston CE Prim Sch
Woolston Com High Sch
Schs
Liby
L Ctr
Woolston Com Prim Sch
Martinscroft
Hotel
1 SHAWBURY GR
2 COLEMERE CL
1 WHITE HORSE CL
2 MANCROFT CL
3 LADYCROFT CL
4 STIRLING CL
5 CYPRESS CL
6 MULBERRY CL
7 CROFTSIDE
WOOLSTON GRANGE AVE
B5210
M6
CHESFORD GRANGE
CLARES FARM CL
SPRINGBURN GDNS
MANCHESTER RD
NEW MANCHESTER RD
A57
New Cut Ind Est
NEW CUT LA
HAWTHORNE AVE
Mersey Way
WA1
Grey Mist
River Mersey
Woolston New Weir
Woolston Weir
The Eyes
4
3
2
1
89
88
87
86
BOWMAN AVE
BRIDGEWATER AVE
1 GARNETT AVE
2 TIMBERLEY AVE
Works
PICHAEL NOOK
PARKFIELD AVE
MOSELEY AVE
BRUNTLEIGH AVE
Manchester Ship Canal
Thelwall Ind Est
Thelwall Ferry (P)
Chaigeley Sch
Laskey Lane Farm
B5157
LYMM RD
BELL LA
A56
Latchford Locks
THELWALL NEW RD
THELWALL LA
Thelwall Com Jun Sch
Thelwall
STOCKPORT RD
1 KNUTSFORD OLD RD
2 QUEENS DR
3 HEATHFIELD PK
HIGHER KNUTSFORD RD
WA4
Trans Pennine Trail
Cheshire Ring Canal Walk
Bridgewater Canal
Thelwall Heys
Massey Hall Specl Sch
Oak House
Cliff Lane Aquaduct
Highfields Farm
Thelwall Grange
WEASTE LA
CHESTER RD
KNUTSFORD RD
A50
Grappenhall St Wilfred's CE Prim Sch
Grappenhall
PH
Grappenhall Hall Sch
Canal Bank Farm
STOCKTON LA
CHURCH LA
CANAL SIDE
1 BARRYMORE CT
2 BARRYMORE RD
1 HAZELWOOD MEWS
2 BRACKENWOOD MEWS
STONELEIGH GDNS
CINDER LA
HALFACRE LA
63
64
65

27
18

17
10

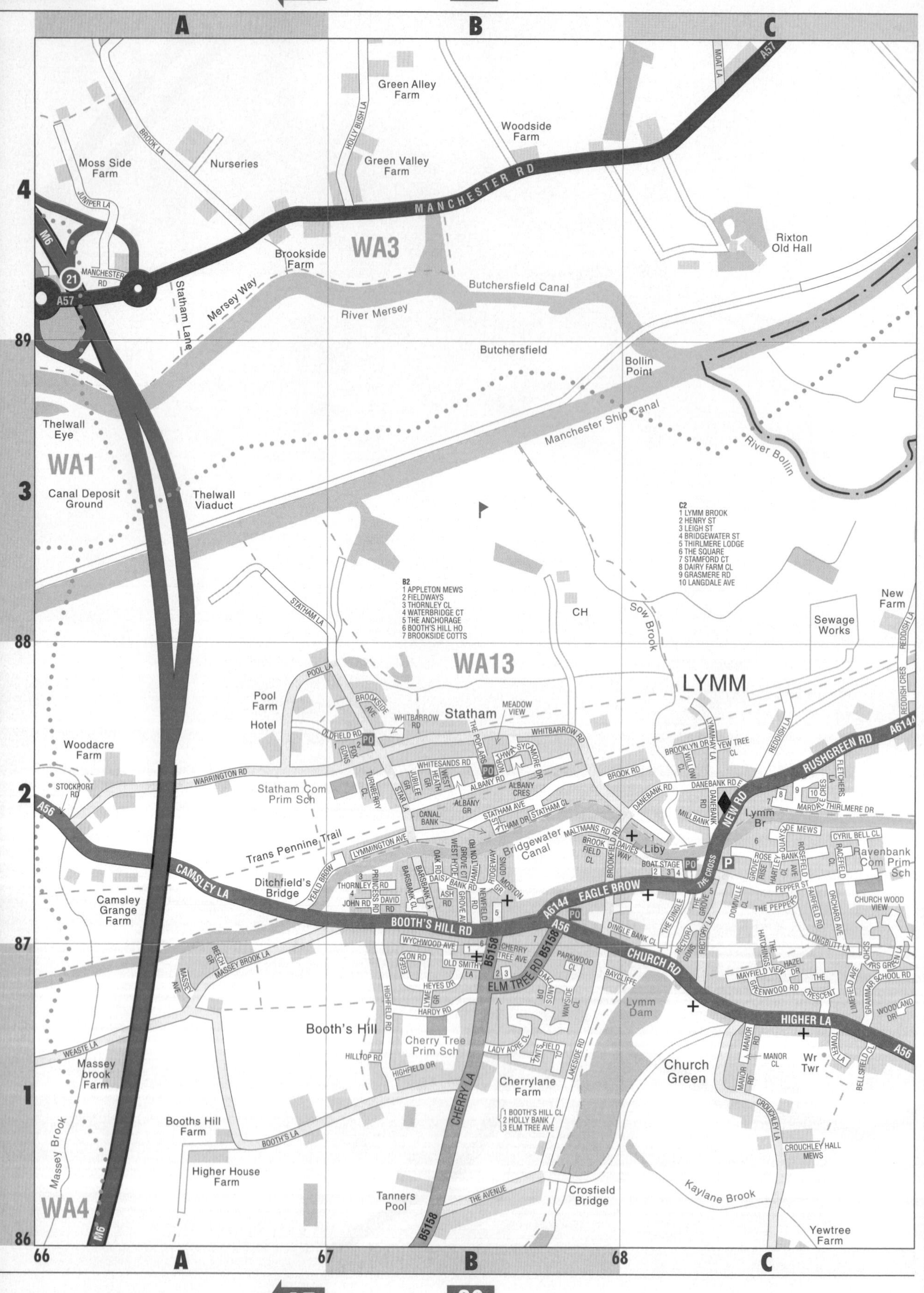
A
B
C
4
89
3
88
2
87
1
86
66
67
68
Green Alley Farm
Woodside Farm
Moss Side Farm
Nurseries
Green Valley Farm
MANCHESTER RD
A57
MOAT LA
BROOK LA
HOLLY BUSH LA
JUNIPER LA
M6
21
MANCHESTER RD
Brookside Farm
WA3
Rixton Old Hall
Statham Lane
Mersey Way
Butchersfield Canal
River Mersey
Butchersfield
Bollin Point
Thelwall Eye
WA1
Manchester Ship Canal
River Bollin
Canal Deposit Ground
Thelwall Viaduct
C2
1 LYMM BROOK
2 HENRY ST
3 LEIGH ST
4 BRIDGEWATER ST
5 THIRLMERE LODGE
6 THE SQUARE
7 STAMFORD CT
8 DAIRY FARM CL
9 GRASMERE RD
10 LANGDALE AVE
B2
1 APPLETON MEWS
2 FIELDWAYS
3 THORNLEY CL
4 WATERBRIDGE CT
5 THE ANCHORAGE
6 BOOTH'S HILL HO
7 BROOKSIDE COTTS
STATHAM LA
CH
Sow Brook
New Farm
Sewage Works
REDDISH LA
REDDISH CRES
WA13
LYMM
POOL LA
Pool Farm
Hotel
BROOKSIDE AVE
WHITBARROW RD
Statham
MEADOW VIEW
OLDFIELD RD
WHITBARROW RD
Woodacre Farm
FOX GDNS
THE POPLARS
SYCAMORE DR
WHITESANDS RD
BROOKLYN DR
YEW TREE CL
RUSHGREEN RD
A6144
WARRINGTON RD
STOCKPORT RD
Statham Com Prim Sch
TURNBERRY CL
JUBILEE GR
HEATH GR
WEST AVE
ALBANY RD
ALBANY CRES
BROOK RD
DANEBANK RD
LYMMHAY LA
WILLOW CL
FLETCHERS LA
A56
STAR LA
ALBANY GR
CANAL BANK
STATHAM AVE
STATHAM DR
STATHAM CL
MILLBANK
DANEBANK RD
NEW RD
MARDALE CRES
THIRLMERE DR
Lymm Br
DE MEWS
CYRIL BELL CL
Trans Pennine Trail
LYMMINGTON AVE
MALTMANS RD
Bridgewater Canal
BROOKFIELD CL
BROOKFIELD RD
DAVIES WAY
Liby
BOAT STAGE
THE CROSS
ROSE BANK
ROSEFIELD
Ravenbank Com Prim Sch
CAMSLEY LA
Ditchfield's Bridge
YEALD BROW
THORNLEY
PRINCESS RD
JOHN RD
DAVID RD
BARSBANK CL
BARSBANK LA
OAK RD
DAISY BANK RD
WEST HYDE
ASH RD
GROVE CT
GROVE AVE
HAMILTON RD
NEWFIELD
RIDGEWAY GR
MOSTON GDNS
EAGLE BROW
THE DINGLE
GROVE RISE
HARTLEY AVE
QUAY CL
PEPPER ST
THE PEPPERS
FAIRFIELD RD
ORCHARD AVE
CHURCH WOOD VIEW
Camsley Grange Farm
BOOTH'S HILL RD
B5158
DINGLE BANK CL
RECTORY GDNS
RECTORY LA
THE GROVE
DOMVILLE
THE HATCHINGS
LONGBUTT LA
WYCHWOOD AVE
CHERRY TREE AVE
PARKWOOD CL
CHURCH RD
BEECH GR
MASSEY BROOK LA
EGERTON RD
OLD SMITHY LA
BAYCLIFFE
MAYFIELD VIEW
HAZEL
GREENWOOD RD
THE CRESCENT
GRAMMAR SCHOOL RD
MASSEY AVE
HEYES DR
ELM TREE RD
LYME GR
OAKLANDS DR
WAYSIDE CL
Lymm Dam
LIMEFIELD AVE
WOODLAND DR
HARDY RD
Booth's Hill
HIGHER LA
WEASTE LA
HIGHFIELD RD
Cherry Tree Prim Sch
LADY ACRE CL
HUNTSFIELD CL
LAKESIDE RD
MANOR AVE
MANOR CL
Wr Twr
TOWER LA
BELLSFIELD CL
HILLTOP RD
Church Green
Massey brook Farm
HIGHFIELD DR
Cherrylane Farm
MANOR RD
CHERRY LA
1 BOOTH'S HILL CL
2 HOLLY BANK
3 ELM TREE AVE
CROUCHLEY LA
Booths Hill Farm
BOOTH'S LA
CROUCHLEY HALL MEWS
Massey Brook
Higher House Farm
Tanners Pool
THE AVENUE
Crosfield Bridge
Kaylane Brook
WA4
Yewtree Farm

17
28

11
20

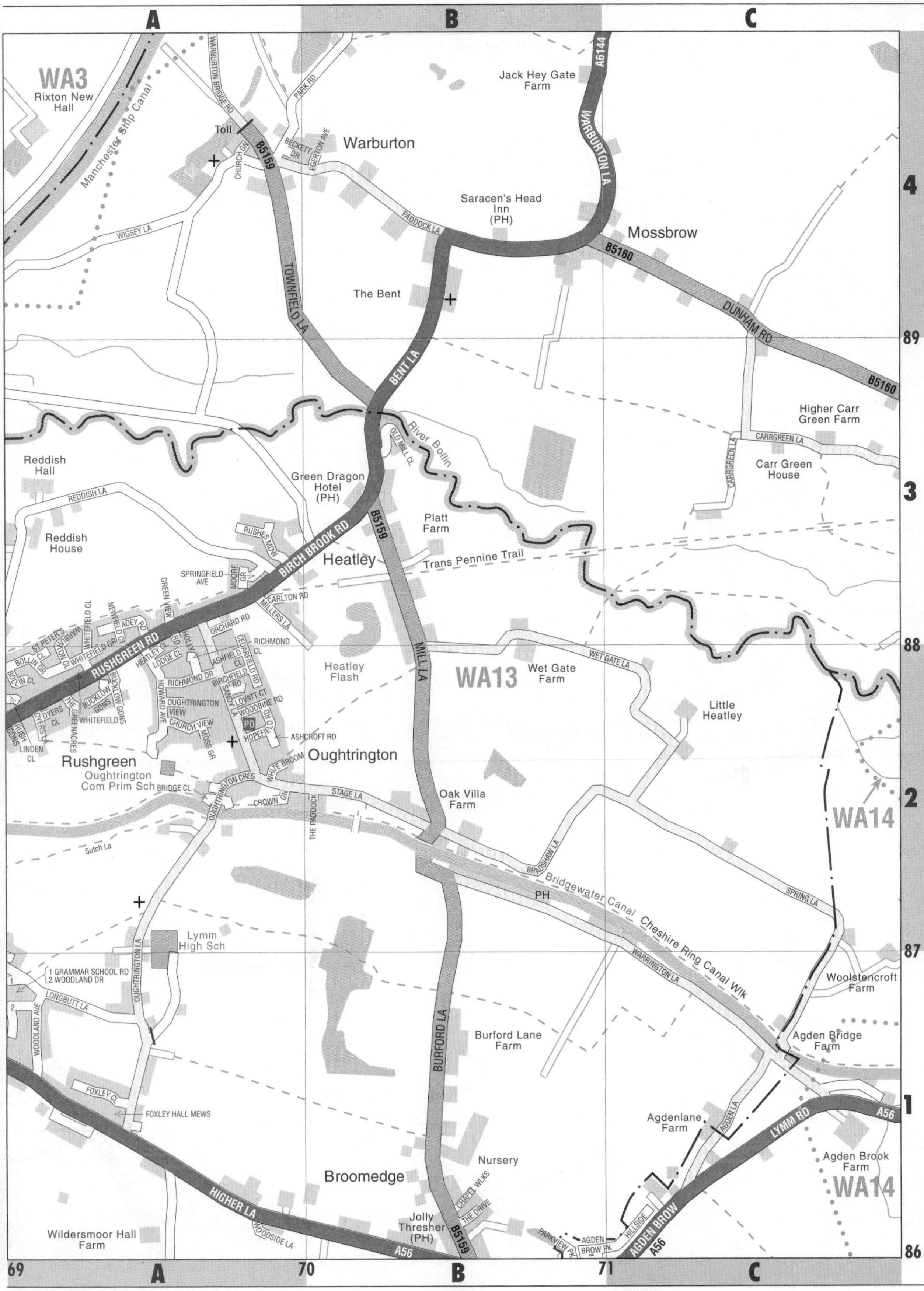
A
B
C
WA3
Rixton New Hall
Manchester Ship Canal
Warburton Bridge Rd
Toll
Church Gn
B5159
Park Rd
Beckett Dr
Egerton Ave
Warburton
Jack Hey Gate Farm
A6144
Warburton La
Saracen's Head Inn (PH)
Paddock La
Wigsey La
Mossbrow
B5160
Townfield La
The Bent
Dunham Rd
Bent La
B5160
Higher Carr Green Farm
Carrgreen La
River Bollin
Old Mill Cl
Reddish Hall
Green Dragon Hotel (PH)
Carr Green House
Reddish La
Platt Farm
Reddish House
Rushes Mdw
Birch Brook Rd
B5159
Heatley
Trans Pennine Trail
Springfield Ave
Moore Gr
Carlton Rd
Millers La
Green View
Newfield Cl
Adey Rd
Orchard Rd
Richmond Cl
St Peter's
Whitefield Gr
Rushgreen Rd
Holly
Cedarfield Rd
Ashfield Cl
Heatley Cl
Lodge Cl
Birchfield Rd
Richmond Dr
Heatley Flash
Mill La
WA13
Wet Gate Farm
Wet Gate La
Bollin Dr
Bollin Cl
Bucklow Gdns
The Greenacres
Howard Ave
Oughtrington View
Sandy La
Lovatt Ct
Woodbine Rd
Little Heatley
Dyers Cl
Whitefield
Church View
PO
Hopefield Rd
Ashcroft Rd
Rush Gdns
Linden Cl
Moss Gr
Rushgreen
White Broom
Oughtrington
Oughtrington Com Prim Sch
Bridge Cl
Oughtrington Cres
Crown Gn
The Paddock
Stage La
Oak Villa Farm
WA14
Sutch La
Bradshaw La
Bridgewater Canal
PH
Spring La
Cheshire Ring Canal Wlk
Lymm High Sch
Oughtrington La
1 Grammar School Rd
2 Woodland Dr
Warrington La
Woolstencroft Farm
Longbutt La
Woodland Ave
Burford Lane Farm
Burford La
Agden Bridge Farm
Foxley Cl
Foxley Hall Mews
Agdenlane Farm
Agden La
Lymm Rd
A56
Nursery
Agden Brook Farm
Broomedge
Chapel Wlks
WA14
Higher La
The Drive
Jolly Thresher (PH)
Hillside
Agden Brow
Wildersmoor Hall Farm
Woodside La
A56
B5159
Parkview Pk
Agden Brow Pk
A56
4
89
3
88
2
87
1
86
69
70
71

29
20

19

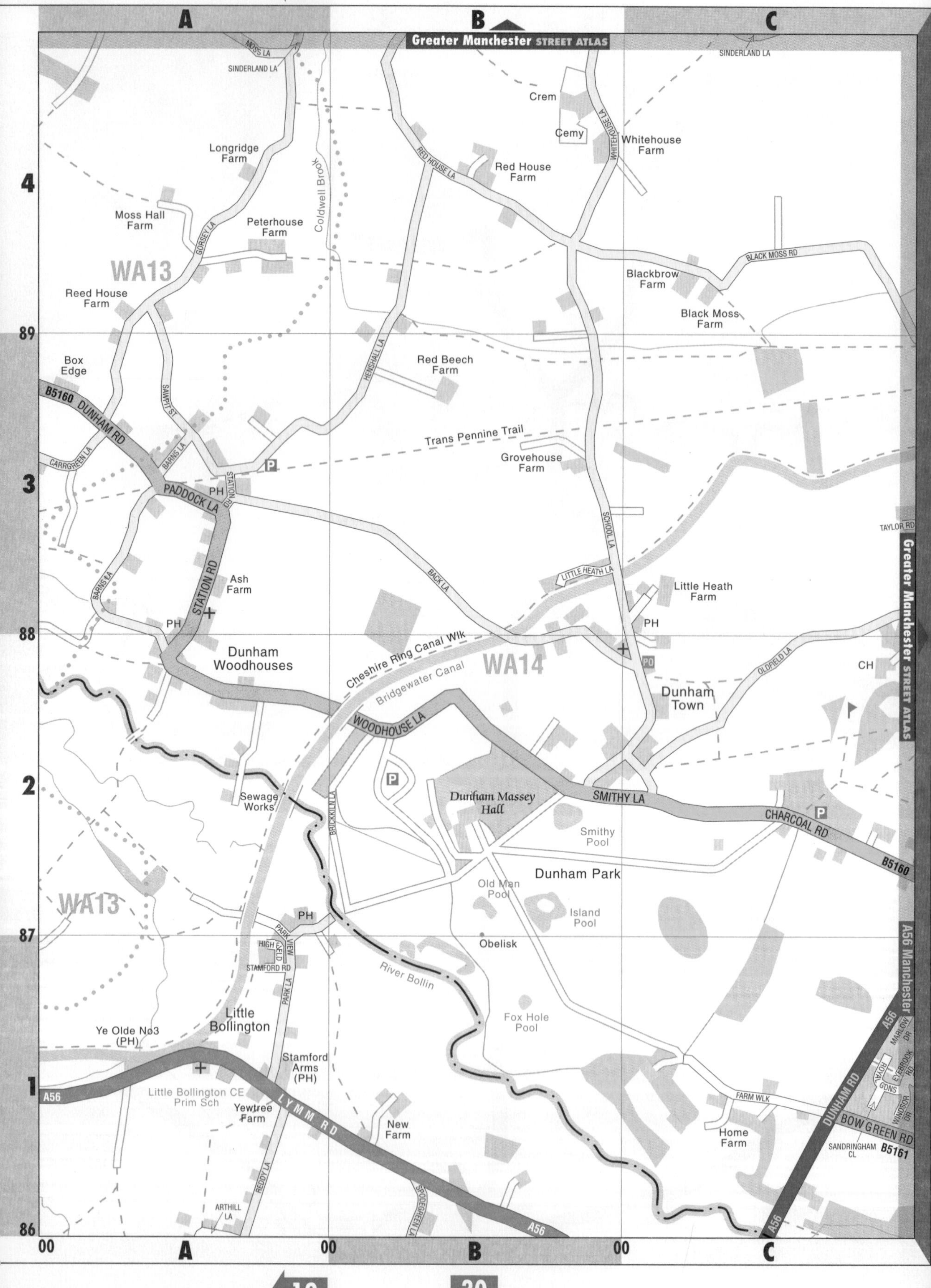
A
B
C
Greater Manchester STREET ATLAS
MOSS LA
SINDERLAND LA
Crem
Cemy
Whitehouse Farm
WHITEHOUSE LA
Longridge Farm
RED HOUSE LA
Red House Farm
Coldwell Brook
Moss Hall Farm
Peterhouse Farm
GORSEY LA
WA13
BLACK MOSS RD
Blackbrow Farm
Reed House Farm
Black Moss Farm
Box Edge
HENSHALL LA
Red Beech Farm
B5160
DUNHAM RD
SAWPIT ST
Trans Pennine Trail
CARRGREEN LA
BARNS LA
Grovehouse Farm
P
PADDOCK LA
PH
STATION RD
SCHOOL LA
TAYLOR RD
BACK LA
LITTLE HEATH LA
Ash Farm
Little Heath Farm
BARNS LA
PH
PH
Cheshire Ring Canal Wlk
Dunham Woodhouses
WA14
PO
Bridgewater Canal
OLDFIELD LA
CH
Dunham Town
WOODHOUSE LA
Dunham Massey Hall
SMITHY LA
Sewage Works
BRICKKILN LA
Smithy Pool
CHARCOAL RD
B5160
Dunham Park
Old Man Pool
WA13
Island Pool
PH
PARK VIEW
HIGH FIELD
Obelisk
STAMFORD RD
River Bollin
PARK LA
Little Bollington
Fox Hole Pool
Ye Olde No3 (PH)
Stamford Arms (PH)
A56
Little Bollington CE Prim Sch
LYMM RD
Yewtree Farm
New Farm
FARM WLK
Home Farm
DUNHAM RD
BOW GREEN RD
SANDRINGHAM CL
B5161
ROYAL GDNS
MARLOW DR
EYEBROOK RD
WINDSOR DR
REDDY LA
ARTHILL LA
SPODEGREEN LA
A56
A56 Manchester
Greater Manchester STREET ATLAS
4
89
3
88
2
87
1
86
00
00
00

19
30

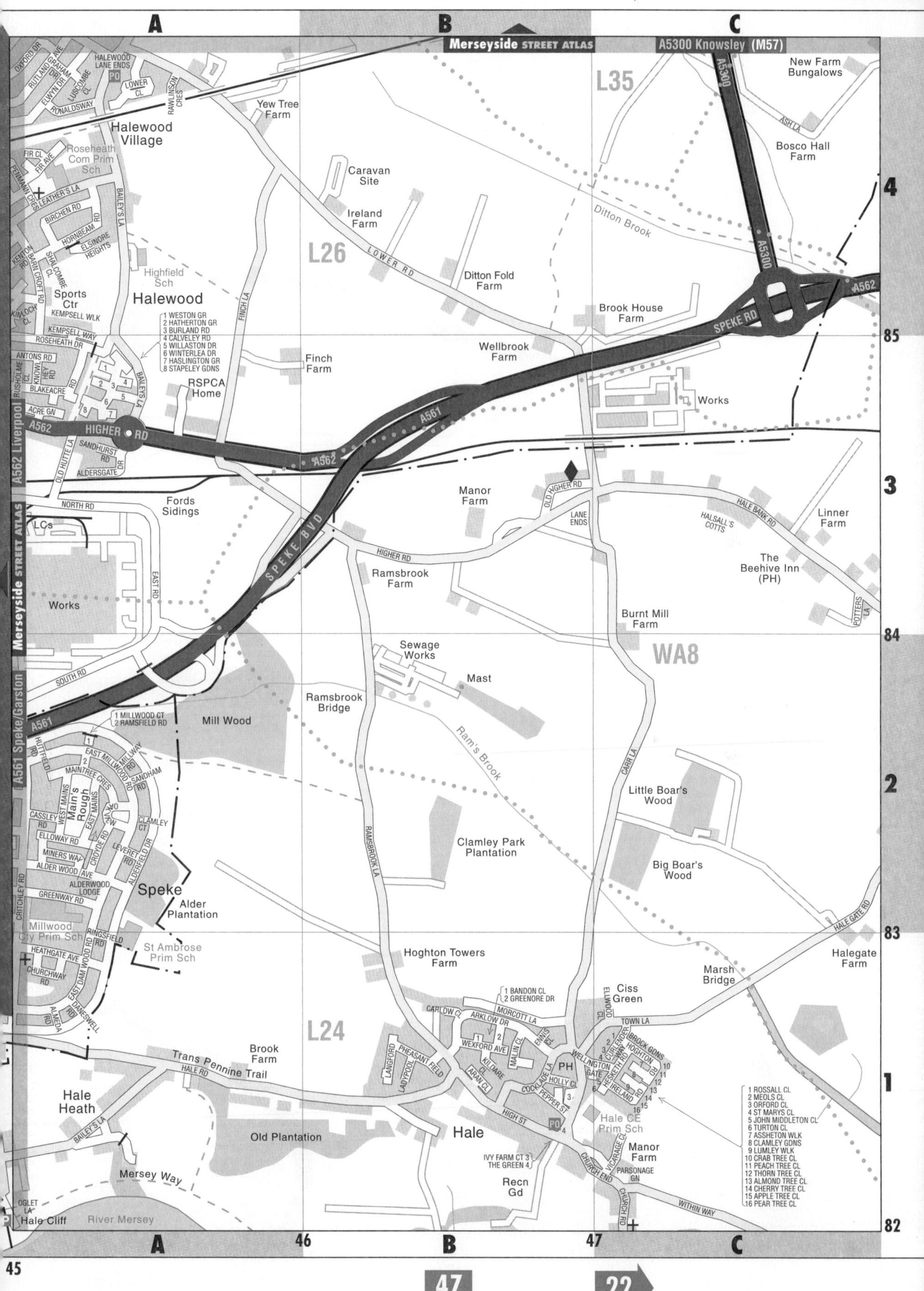

Merseyside STREET ATLAS

A5300 Knowsley (M57)

New Farm
Bungalows

L35

Halewood
Lane Ends

PO

Halewood
Village

Yew Tree
Farm

Bosco Hall
Farm

ASH LA

A5300

Roseheath
Com Prim
Sch

LEATHER'S LA

Caravan
Site

4

Ireland
Farm

L26

LOWER RD

Ditton Brook

A562

Highfield
Sch

Ditton Fold
Farm

Brook House
Farm

SPEKE RD

85

Sports
Ctr

Halewood

1 WESTON GR
2 HATHERTON GR
3 BURLAND RD
4 CALVELEY RD
5 WILLASTON DR
6 WINTERLEA DR
7 HASLINGTON GR
8 STAPELEY GDNS

Finch
Farm

Wellbrook
Farm

Works

KEMPSELL WLK
KEMPSELL WAY
ROSEHEATH DR

A561

RSPCA
Home

ANTONS RD

ACRE GN

HIGHER RD

A562

A562

Manor
Farm

OLD HIGHER RD

3

Fords
Sidings

LANE
ENDS

HALE BANK RD

Linner
Farm

NORTH RD

LCs

HIGHER RD

HALSALL'S
COTTS

SPEKE BLVD

EAST RD

Ramsbrook
Farm

The
Beehive Inn
(PH)

Works

SOUTH RD

Burnt Mill
Farm

POTTERS LA

84

Sewage
Works

WA8

A561

1 MILLWOOD CT
2 RAMSFIELD RD

Ramsbrook
Bridge

Mast

Mill Wood

EAST MILLWAY

Ram's Brook

CARR LA

Little Boar's
Wood

2

Main's
Rough

Speke

Clamley Park
Plantation

Big Boar's
Wood

HALE GATE RD

Alder
Plantation

83

Millwood
Cty Prim Sch

St Ambrose
Prim Sch

Hoghton Towers
Farm

Marsh
Bridge

Halegate
Farm

Ciss
Green

CHURCHWAY
RD

L24

1 BANDON CL
2 GREENORE DR

CARLOW CL

ARKLOW DR

MORCOTT LA

TOWN LA

Brook
Farm

Trans Pennine Trail

HALE RD

PHEASANT FIELD

WEXFORD AVE

KILDARE

PH

WELLINGTON GATE

BROCK GDNS

HOGHTON CL

1 ROSSALL CL
2 MEOLS CL
3 ORFORD CL
4 ST MARYS CL
5 JOHN MIDDLETON CL
6 TURTON CL
7 ASSHETON WLK
8 CLAMLEY GDNS
9 LUMLEY WLK
10 CRAB TREE CL
11 PEACH TREE CL
12 THORN TREE CL
13 ALMOND TREE CL
14 CHERRY TREE CL
15 APPLE TREE CL
16 PEAR TREE CL

1

Hale
Heath

BAILEY'S LA

Old Plantation

Hale

HIGH ST

PEPPER ST

HOLLY CL

Hale CE
Prim Sch

Manor
Farm

PARSONAGE
GN

Mersey Way

IVY FARM CT 3
THE GREEN 4

Recn
Gd

CHURCH RD

WITHIN WAY

Hale Cliff

River Mersey

82

← 21

12

B4
1 LEVENS WAY
2 RIDSDALE
3 LONSDALE CL
4 LEIGH GREEN CL
5 APPLEBY WLK
6 AYCLIFFE WLK

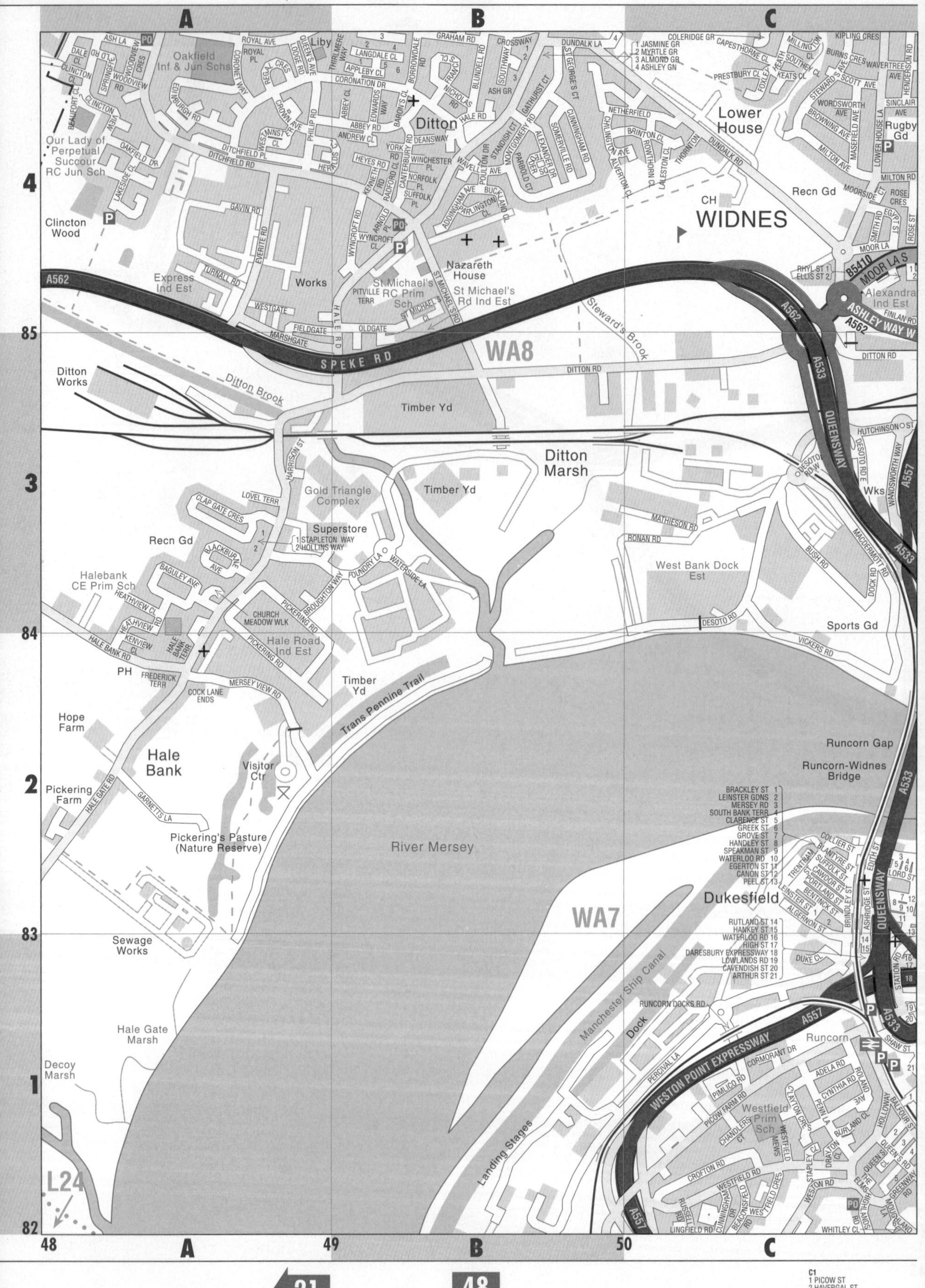

C1
1 PICOW ST
2 HAVERGAL ST
3 CURZON ST
4 LIGHTBURN ST
5 STANLEY VILLAS
6 SOUTHLANDS MEWS

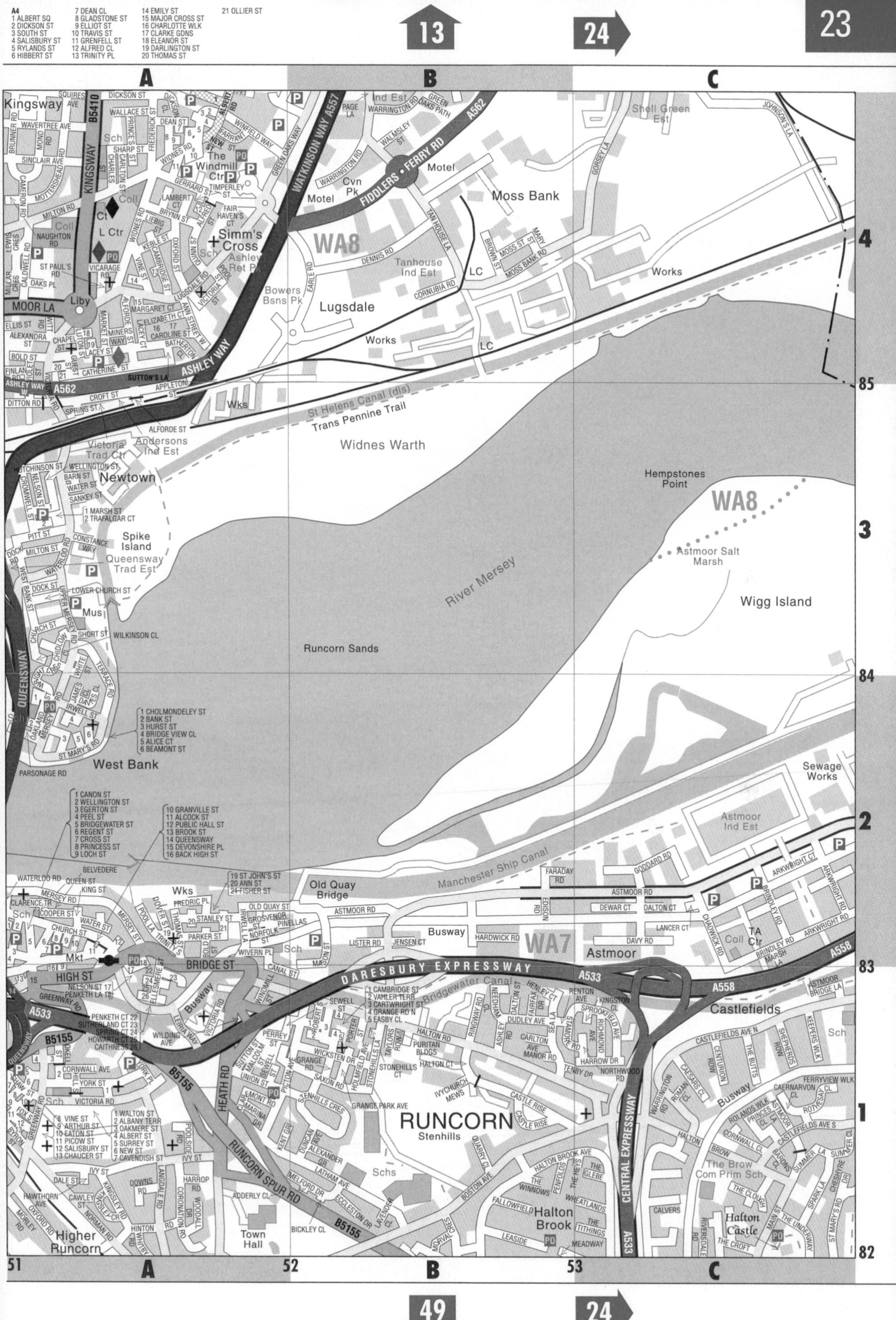

A4
1 ALBERT SQ
2 DICKSON ST
3 SOUTH ST
4 SALISBURY ST
5 RYLANDS ST
6 HIBBERT ST
7 DEAN CL
8 GLADSTONE ST
9 ELLIOT ST
10 TRAVIS ST
11 GRENFELL ST
12 ALFRED CL
13 TRINITY PL
14 EMILY ST
15 MAJOR CROSS ST
16 CHARLOTTE WLK
17 CLARKE GDNS
18 ELEANOR ST
19 DARLINGTON ST
20 THOMAS ST
21 OLLIER ST

23
14

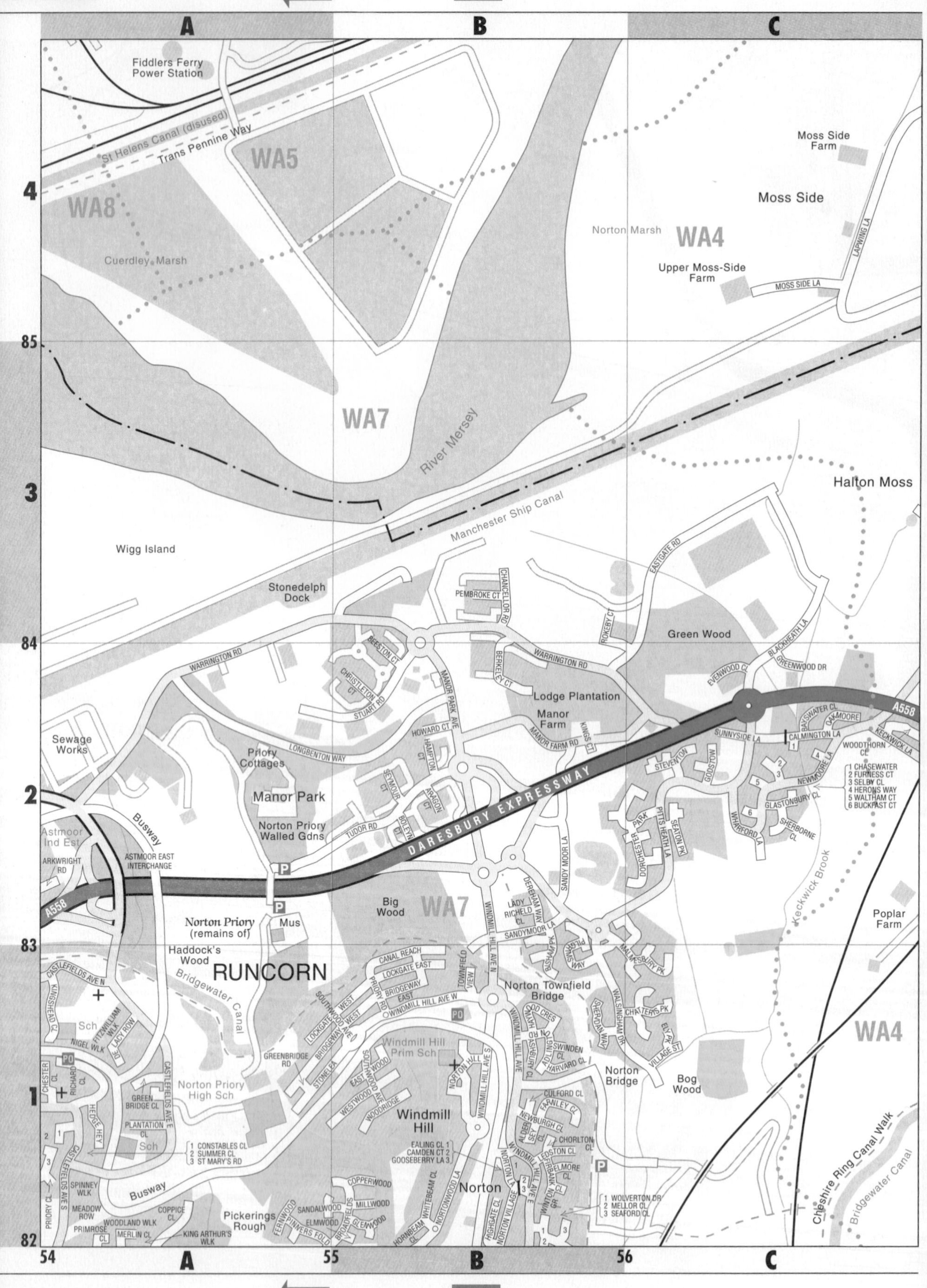
A
B
C
4
85
3
84
2
83
1
82
54
55
56
Fiddlers Ferry
Power Station
St Helens Canal (disused)
Trans Pennine Way
WA5
WA8
Cuerdley Marsh
Norton Marsh
WA4
Moss Side
Farm
Moss Side
Upper Moss-Side
Farm
MOSS SIDE LA
LAPWING LA
WA7
River Mersey
Halton Moss
Manchester Ship Canal
Wigg Island
Stonedelph
Dock
PEMBROKE CT
CHANCELLOR RD
EASTGATE RD
ROKEBY CT
Green Wood
BLACKHEATH LA
EVENWOOD CL
GREENWOOD DR
WARRINGTON RD
BEESTON CT
CHRISTLETON CT
STUART RD
MANOR PARK AVE
BERKELEY CT
Lodge Plantation
Manor
Farm
MANOR FARM RD
KINGS CT
HOWARD CT
HAMPTON CT
Sewage
Works
LONGBENTON WAY
Priory
Cottages
Manor Park
SEYMOUR CT
ARAGON CT
BOLEYN CT
TUDOR RD
Norton Priory
Walled Gdns
DARESBURY EXPRESSWAY
A558
SUNNYSIDE LA
CALMINGTON LA
BAKSWATER CL
OAKMOORE
KECKWICK LA
WOODTHORN CL
1 CHASEWATER
2 FURNESS CT
3 SELBY CL
4 HERONS WAY
5 WALTHAM CT
6 BUCKFAST CT
NEWMOORE LA
GLASTONBURY CL
SHERBORNE CL
WHARFORD LA
STEVENTON
GODSTOW
DORCHESTER PARK
PITTS HEATH LA
SEATON PK
SANDY MOOR LA
Keckwick Brook
Poplar
Farm
Astmoor
Ind Est
ARKWRIGHT RD
Busway
ASTMOOR EAST
INTERCHANGE
P
Norton Priory
(remains of)
Mus
Big
Wood
WA7
DEREHAM WAY
LADY RICHELD CL
SANDYMOOR LA
WINDMILL HILL AVE N
BASHAM PK
PILGRIMS WAY
MALMESBURY PK
Haddock's
Wood
RUNCORN
Bridgewater Canal
CASTLEFIELDS AVE N
KINGSHEAD CL
FITZWILLIAM WLK
DE LACY ROW
NIGEL WLK
Sch
PO
CANAL REACH
LOCKGATE EAST
BRIDGEWAY EAST
TOWNFIELD VIEW
WINDMILL HILL AVE W
PRIORY RD
SOUTHWOOD AVE
LOCKGATE WEST
BRIDGEWAY WEST
Norton Townfield
Bridge
WALSINGHAM DR
CHATTERIS PK
ELY PK
VILLAGE ST
SWINDEN CL
HARVARD CL
Windmill Hill
Prim Sch
GREENBRIDGE RD
STONELEA
EASTWOOD
WESTWOOD
WOODRIDGE
NORTON HILL
WINDMILL HILL AVE S
Norton
Bridge
Bog
Wood
WA4
CHESTER CL
RICHARD CL
HEDGE HEY
GREEN BRIDGE CL
CASTLEFIELDS AVE E
PLANTATION CL
Norton Priory
High Sch
1 CONSTABLES CL
2 SUMMER CL
3 ST MARY'S RD
Windmill
Hill
EALING CL 1
CAMDEN CT 2
GOOSEBERRY LA 3
CULFORD CL
FARNLEY CL
NEWBURGH CL
CHORLTON CL
LEDSTON CL
ELMORE CL
CASTLEFIELDS AVE S
SPINNEY WLK
MEADOW ROW
PRIMROSE CL
PRIORY CL
WOODLAND WLK
MERLIN CL
COPPICE CL
KING ARTHUR'S WLK
Busway
Pickerings
Rough
FERNWOOD
SANDALWOOD
PINNERS FOLD
ELMWOOD
BROADFIELDS
GREENWOOD
MILLWOOD
COPPERWOOD
HORNBEAM
WHITEBEAM CL
NORTONWOOD LA
Norton
HIGHGATE CL
NORTON VILLAGE
NORTON LA
WINDMILL HILL AVE E
1 WOLVERTON DR
2 MELLOR CL
3 SEAFORD CL
Cheshire Ring Canal Walk
Bridgewater Canal

23
50

A B C

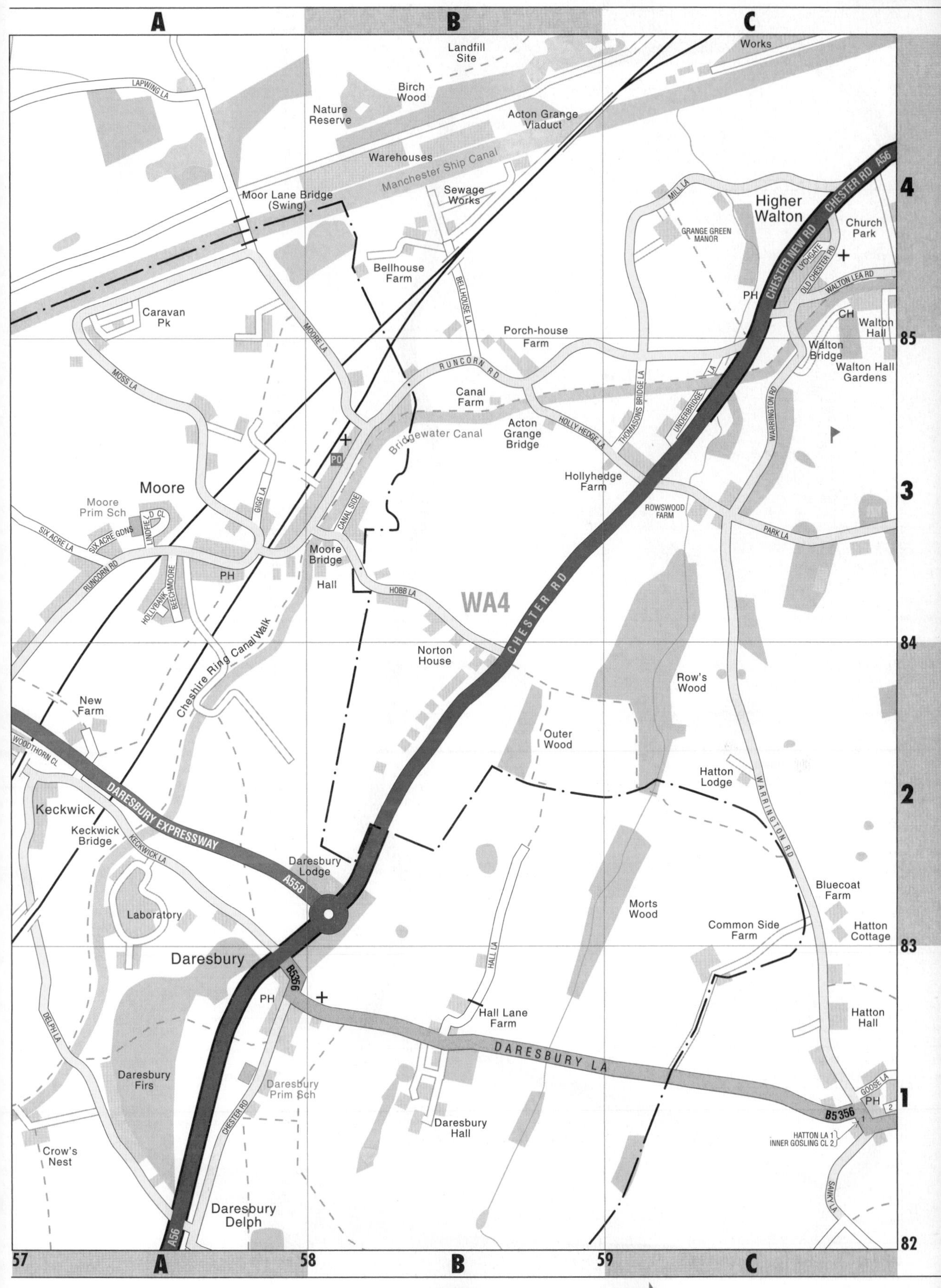
Landfill Site
Works
Birch Wood
Nature Reserve
Acton Grange Viaduct
Warehouses
Manchester Ship Canal
Moor Lane Bridge (Swing)
Sewage Works
Higher Walton
Church Park
GRANGE GREEN MANOR
CHESTER NEW RD
CHESTER RD
A56
Bellhouse Farm
Caravan Pk
PH
CH
Walton Hall
Walton Bridge
Walton Hall Gardens
Porch-house Farm
Canal Farm
Acton Grange Bridge
Bridgewater Canal
Hollyhedge Farm
ROWSWOOD FARM
Moore
Moore Prim Sch
Moore Bridge
Hall
WA4
Norton House
Row's Wood
Outer Wood
Hatton Lodge
New Farm
Keckwick
Keckwick Bridge
DARESBURY EXPRESSWAY
A558
Daresbury Lodge
Laboratory
Bluecoat Farm
Morts Wood
Common Side Farm
Hatton Cottage
Daresbury
B5356
Hall Lane Farm
Hatton Hall
DARESBURY LA
Daresbury Firs
Daresbury Prim Sch
Daresbury Hall
HATTON LA 1
INNER GOSLING CL 2
Crow's Nest
Daresbury Delph
LAPWING LA
MOORE LA
MOSS LA
BELLHOUSE LA
RUNCORN RD
HOLLY HEDGE LA
THOMASONS BRIDGE LA
UNDERBRIDGE LA
MILL LA
LYCHGATE
OLD CHESTER RD
WALTON LEA RD
WARRINGTON RD
PARK LA
CANAL SIDE
GIGG LA
SIX ACRE LA
SIX ACRE GDNS
LINDFIELD CL
HOLLYBANK
BEECHMOORE
HOBB LA
CHESTER RD
Cheshire Ring Canal Walk
WOODTHORN CL
KECKWICK LA
HALL LA
DELPH LA
GOOSE LA
SANKY LA
PO
4
85
3
84
2
83
1
82
57
58
59

A B C

25
16

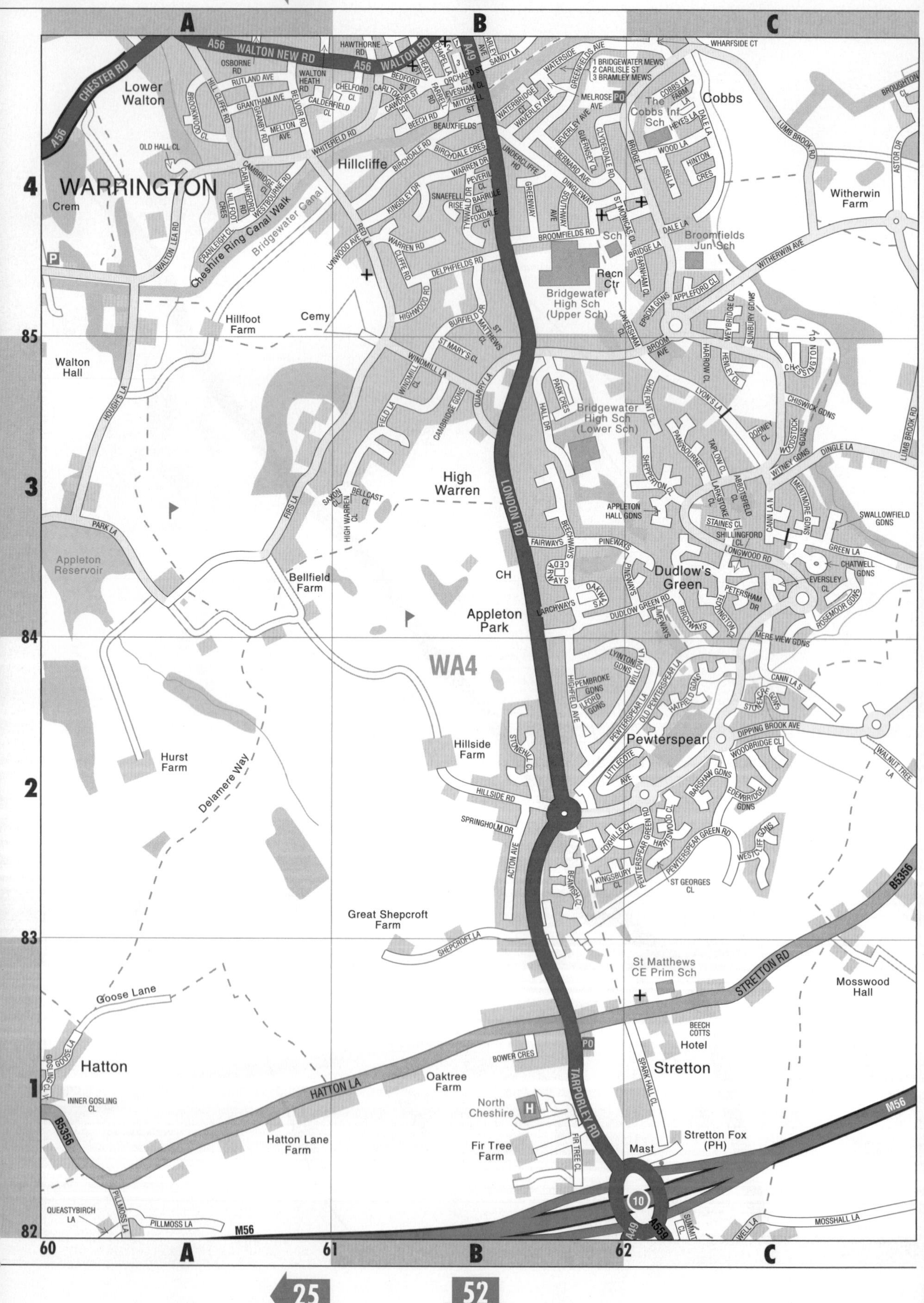
A
B
C
WARRINGTON
Lower Walton
Hillcliffe
Cobbs
Witherwin Farm
Walton Hall
Hillfoot Farm
Cemy
High Warren
Appleton Reservoir
Bellfield Farm
Appleton Park
WA4
Dudlow's Green
Pewterspear
Hurst Farm
Hillside Farm
Delamere Way
Great Shepcroft Farm
St Matthews CE Prim Sch
Mosswood Hall
Goose Lane
Hatton
Stretton
Oaktree Farm
North Cheshire
Hatton Lane Farm
Fir Tree Farm
Stretton Fox (PH)
Mast
Hotel
Bridgewater High Sch (Upper Sch)
Bridgewater High Sch (Lower Sch)
Broomfields Jun Sch
The Cobbs Inf Sch
Recn Ctr
Crem
LONDON RD
TARPORLEY RD
STRETTON RD
HATTON LA
A56 WALTON NEW RD
CHESTER RD
Cheshire Ring Canal Walk
Bridgewater Canal
M56
B5356
60
61
62
85
84
83
82
4
3
2
1

25
52

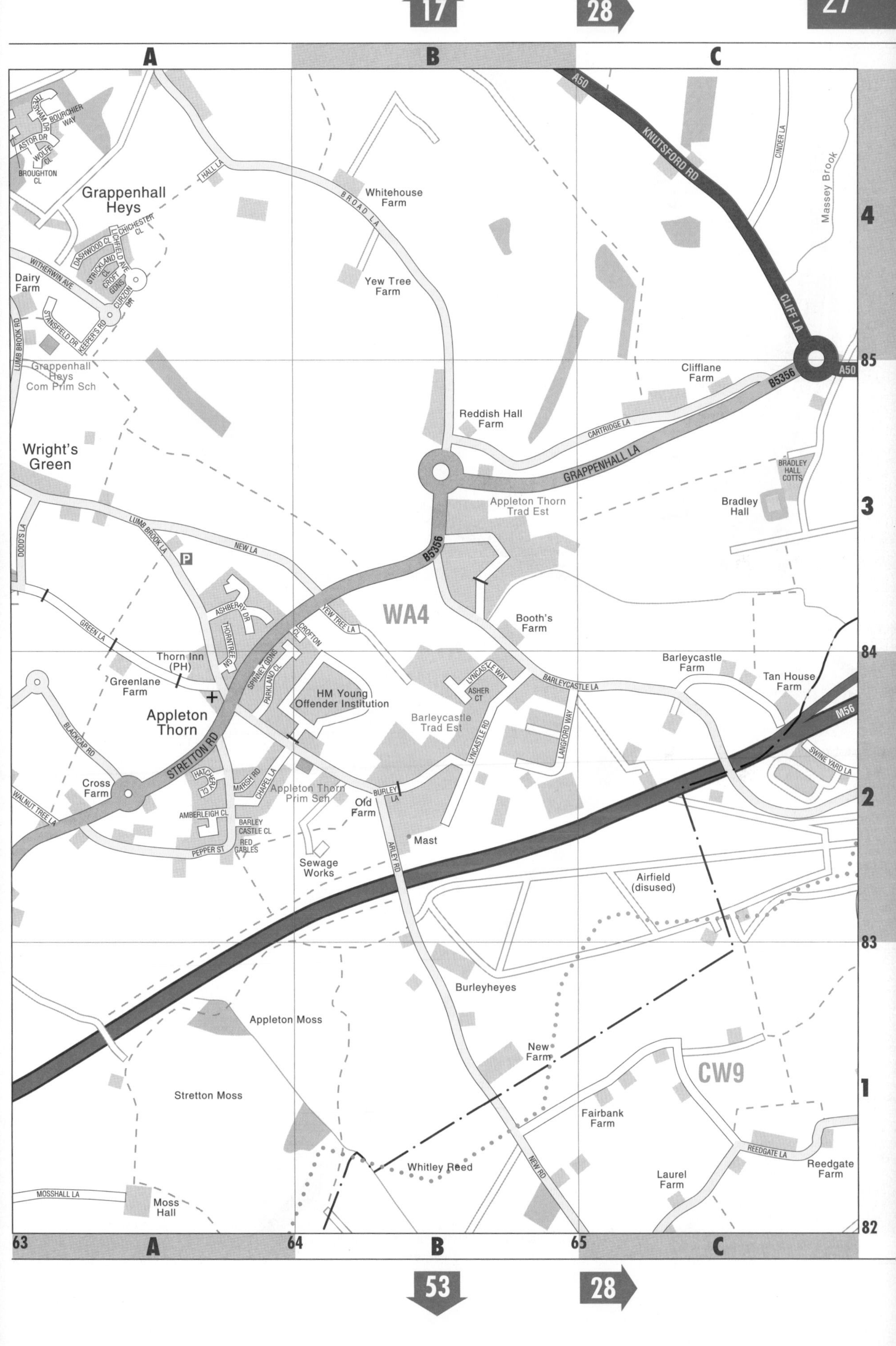

A
B
C

Grappenhall Heys

A50
KNUTSFORD RD

CINDER LA

Massey Brook

4

ASTOR DR
WOLFE CL
BROUGHTON CL
BOURCHIER WAY
JESSAMINE

HALL LA

BROAD LA

Whitehouse Farm

CHICHESTER CL
DASHWOOD CL
LOCHFIELD AVE
STRICKLAND AVE
CROFT GDNS
CLIFTON

Yew Tree Farm

WITHERWIN AVE

Dairy Farm

LUMB BROOK RD

STANSFIELD DR
ICKEEPER'S RD

Grappenhall Heys Com Prim Sch

Reddish Hall Farm

CARTRIDGE LA

Clifflane Farm

CLIFF LA

B5356

85

A50

Wright's Green

GRAPPENHALL LA

BRADLEY HALL COTTS

DODD'S LA

LUMB BROOK LA

NEW LA

P

Appleton Thorn Trad Est

Bradley Hall

3

GREEN LA

ASHBERRY DR

THORNTREE LN

NEW TREE LA

B5356

WA4

Booth's Farm

Barleycastle Farm

Tan House Farm

84

Thorn Inn (PH)

Greenlane Farm

SPINNEY GDNS
PARKLAND CT
CROFTON

HM Young Offender Institution

LYNCASTLE WAY
ASHER CT

BARLEYCASTLE LA

M56

Appleton Thorn

STRETTON RD

MATSCH RD
CHAPELLA

Barleycastle Trad Est

LYNCASTLE RD

LANGFORD WAY

SWINE YARD LA

BLACKCAP RD

HATCH

Cross Farm

Appleton Thorn Prim Sch

Old Farm

BURLEY LA

2

WALNUT TREE LA

AMBERLEIGH CL

BARLEY CASTLE CL
RED GABLES

PEPPER ST

Mast

ARLEY RD

Airfield (disused)

Sewage Works

83

Burleyheyes

New Farm

CW9

Appleton Moss

1

Stretton Moss

Fairbank Farm

REEDGATE LA

Reedgate Farm

MOSSHALL LA

Whitley Reed

NEW RD

Laurel Farm

82

Moss Hall

63
A
64
B
65
C

27
18

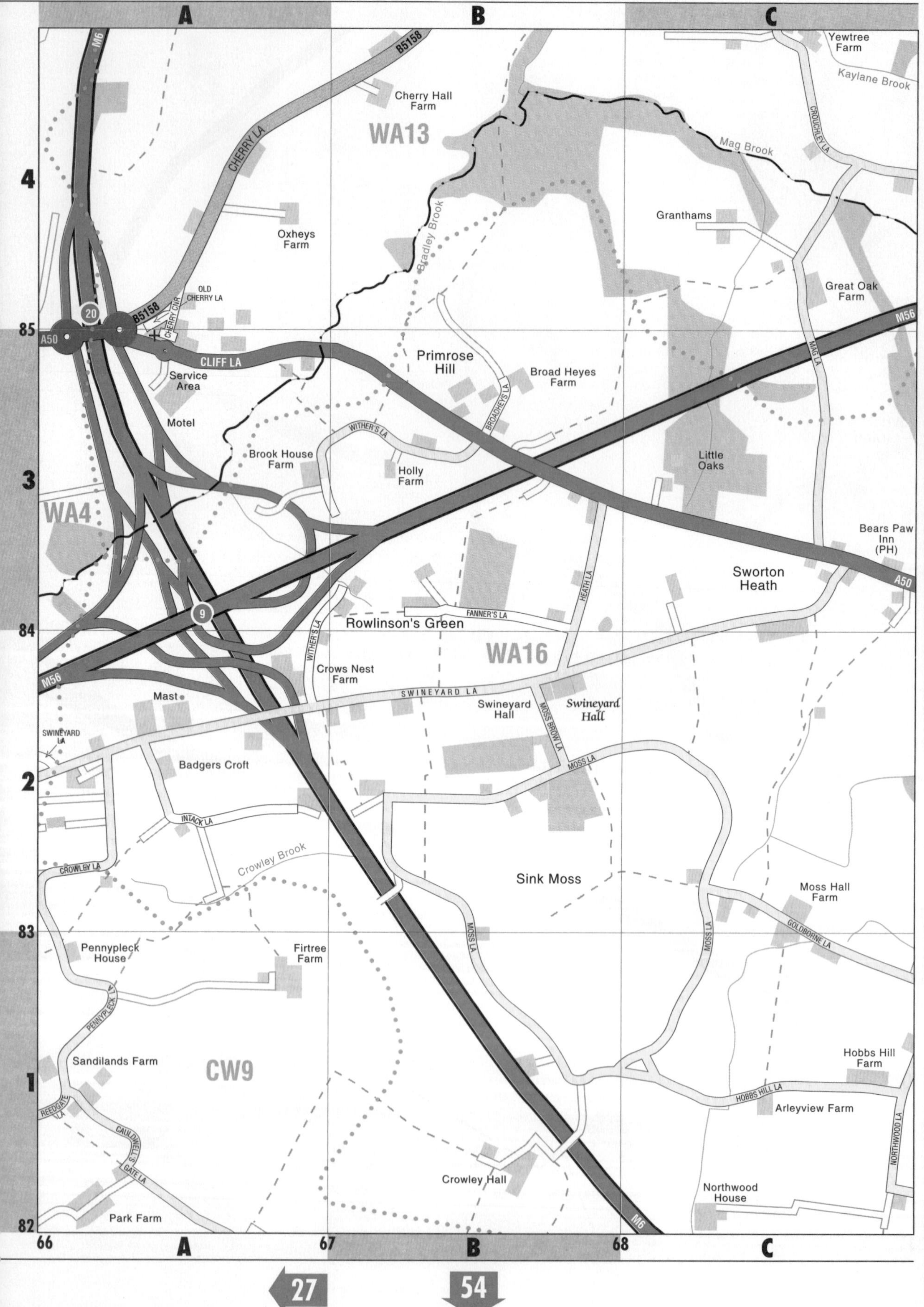
A
B
C
M6
B5158
Cherry Hall
Farm
Yewtree
Farm
Kaylane Brook
WA13
CHERRY LA
Mag Brook
CROUCHLEY LA
4
Oxheys
Farm
Granthams
Bradley Brook
OLD
CHERRY LA
CHERRY CNR
B5158
20
Great Oak
Farm
M56
85
A50
CLIFF LA
Primrose
Hill
MAG LA
Service
Area
Broad Heyes
Farm
BROADHEYS LA
Motel
WITHER'S LA
Brook House
Farm
Holly
Farm
Little
Oaks
3
WA4
Bears Paw
Inn
(PH)
HEATH LA
Sworton
Heath
A50
9
FANNER'S LA
Rowlinson's Green
84
WITHER'S LA
WA16
M56
Crows Nest
Farm
SWINEYARD LA
Mast
Swineyard
Hall
MOSS BROW LA
Swineyard
Hall
SWINEYARD
LA
Badgers Croft
MOSS LA
2
INTACK LA
Crowley Brook
CROWLEY LA
Sink Moss
Moss Hall
Farm
GOLDBORNE LA
83
MOSS LA
MOSS LA
Pennypleck
House
Firtree
Farm
PENNYPLECK LA
Sandilands Farm
CW9
Hobbs Hill
Farm
1
HOBBS HILL LA
REEDGATE LA
Arleyview Farm
CAULDWELL'S GATE LA
NORTHWOOD LA
Crowley Hall
Northwood
House
Park Farm
M6
82
66
67
68

27
54

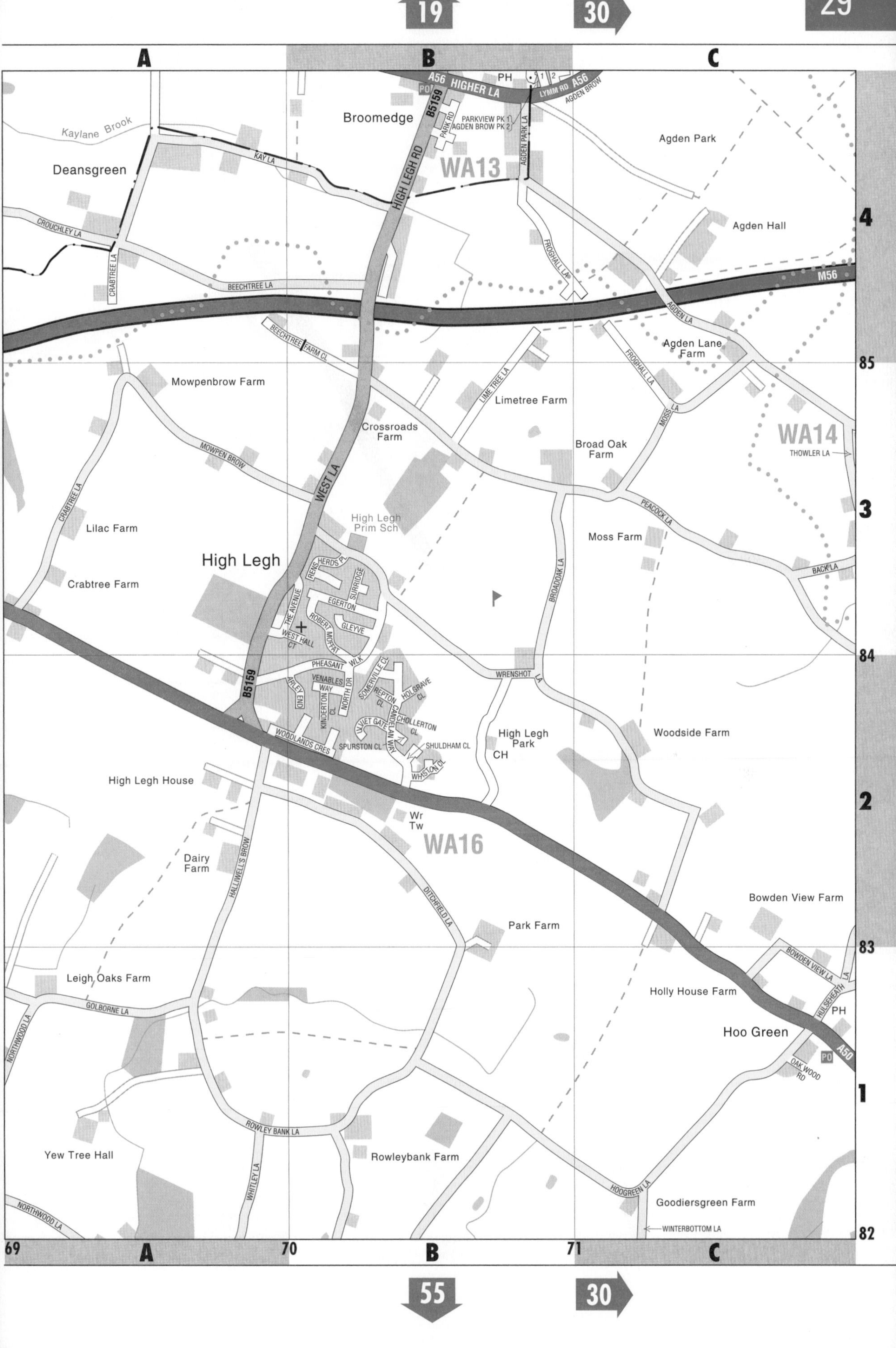
19
30
A
B
C
HIGHER LA
A56
PH
LYMM RD
AGDEN BROW
B5159
Broomedge
PARKVIEW PK 1
AGDEN BROW PK 2
PARK RD
Agden Park
Kaylane Brook
Deansgreen
KAY LA
HIGH LEGH RD
WA13
AGDEN PARK LA
CROUCHLEY LA
Agden Hall
FROGHALL LA
CRABTREE LA
BEECHTREE LA
M56
AGDEN LA
BEECHTREE FARM CL
Agden Lane Farm
Mowpenbrow Farm
LIME TREE LA
Limetree Farm
FROGHALL LA
MOSS LA
WA14
Crossroads Farm
THOWLER LA
Broad Oak Farm
MOWPEN BROW
WEST LA
CRABTREE LA
PEACOCK LA
Lilac Farm
High Legh Prim Sch
Moss Farm
High Legh
HERDS PL
RENS
SURRIDGE
BROADOAK LA
BACK LA
Crabtree Farm
EGERTON
THE AVENUE
ROBERT
GLEYVE
MOFFAT
WEST HALL CT
PHEASANT WLK
WRENSHOT LA
B5159
VENABLES WAY
SOMERVILLE CL
HOLGRAVE CL
ARLEY END
KINDERTON CL
NORTH DR
REPTON CL
CANDELAN WAY
CHOLLERTON CL
LYVIET GATE
High Legh Park
CH
WOODLANDS CRES
SPURSTON CL
SHULDHAM CL
WHISTON CL
Woodside Farm
High Legh House
Wr Tw
WA16
Dairy Farm
HALLIWELL'S BROW
DITCHFIELD LA
Bowden View Farm
Park Farm
BOWDEN VIEW LA
Leigh Oaks Farm
HULSEHEATH LA
Holly House Farm
PH
GOLBORNE LA
Hoo Green
NORTHWOOD LA
PO
A50
OAK WOOD RD
ROWLEY BANK LA
Yew Tree Hall
Rowleybank Farm
WHITLEY LA
HOOGREEN LA
Goodiersgreen Farm
NORTHWOOD LA
WINTERBOTTOM LA
4
85
3
84
2
83
1
82
69
70
71
55
30

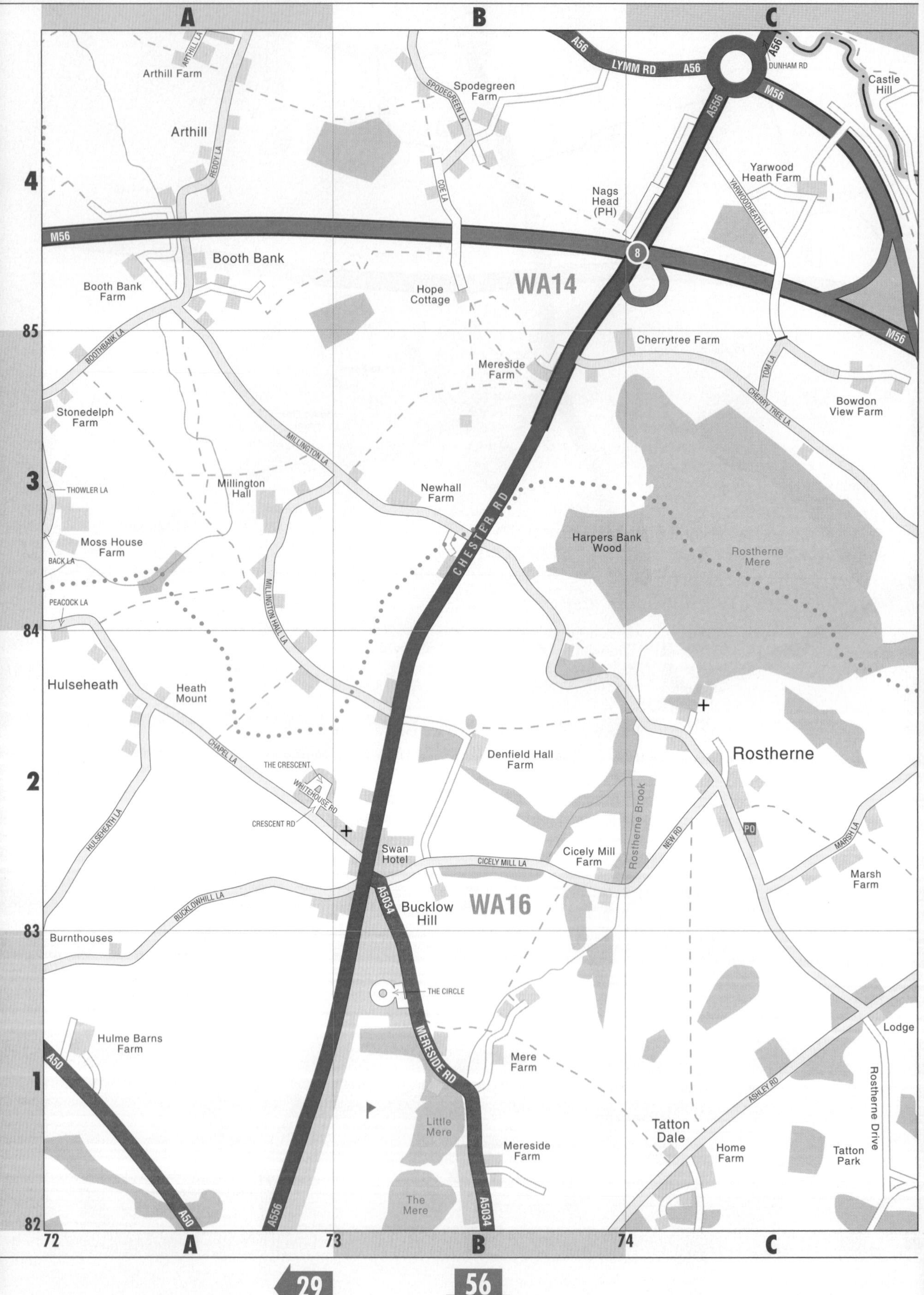

A
B
C

4

Arthill Farm

ARTHILL LA

Spodegreen Farm

SPODEGREEN LA

A56
LYMM RD
A56

A556

DUNHAM RD

Castle Hill

Arthill

REDDY LA

COE LA

M56

Yarwood Heath Farm

YARWOODHEATH LA

Nags Head (PH)

M56

Booth Bank

WA14

85

Booth Bank Farm

BOOTHBANK LA

Hope Cottage

8

Cherrytree Farm

TOM LA

CHERRY TREE LA

Bowdon View Farm

Mereside Farm

Stonedelph Farm

MILLINGTON LA

3

THOWLER LA

Millington Hall

Newhall Farm

CHESTER RD

Harpers Bank Wood

Rostherne Mere

Moss House Farm

BACK LA

MILLINGTON HALL LA

PEACOCK LA

84

Hulseheath

Heath Mount

+

Rostherne

2

HULSEHEATH LA

CHAPEL LA

THE CRESCENT

WHITEHOUSE RD

CRESCENT RD

+

Denfield Hall Farm

ROSTHERNE BROOK

NEW RD

MARSH LA

Marsh Farm

PO

Swan Hotel

CICELY MILL LA

Cicely Mill Farm

BUCKLOWHILL LA

A5034

Bucklow Hill

WA16

83

Burnthouses

A50

Hulme Barns Farm

A556

MERESIDE RD

THE CIRCLE

Mere Farm

ASHLEY RD

Lodge

ROSTHERNE DRIVE

1

Tatton Dale

Home Farm

Tatton Park

Little Mere

Mereside Farm

A5034

The Mere

82

72
A
73
B
74
C

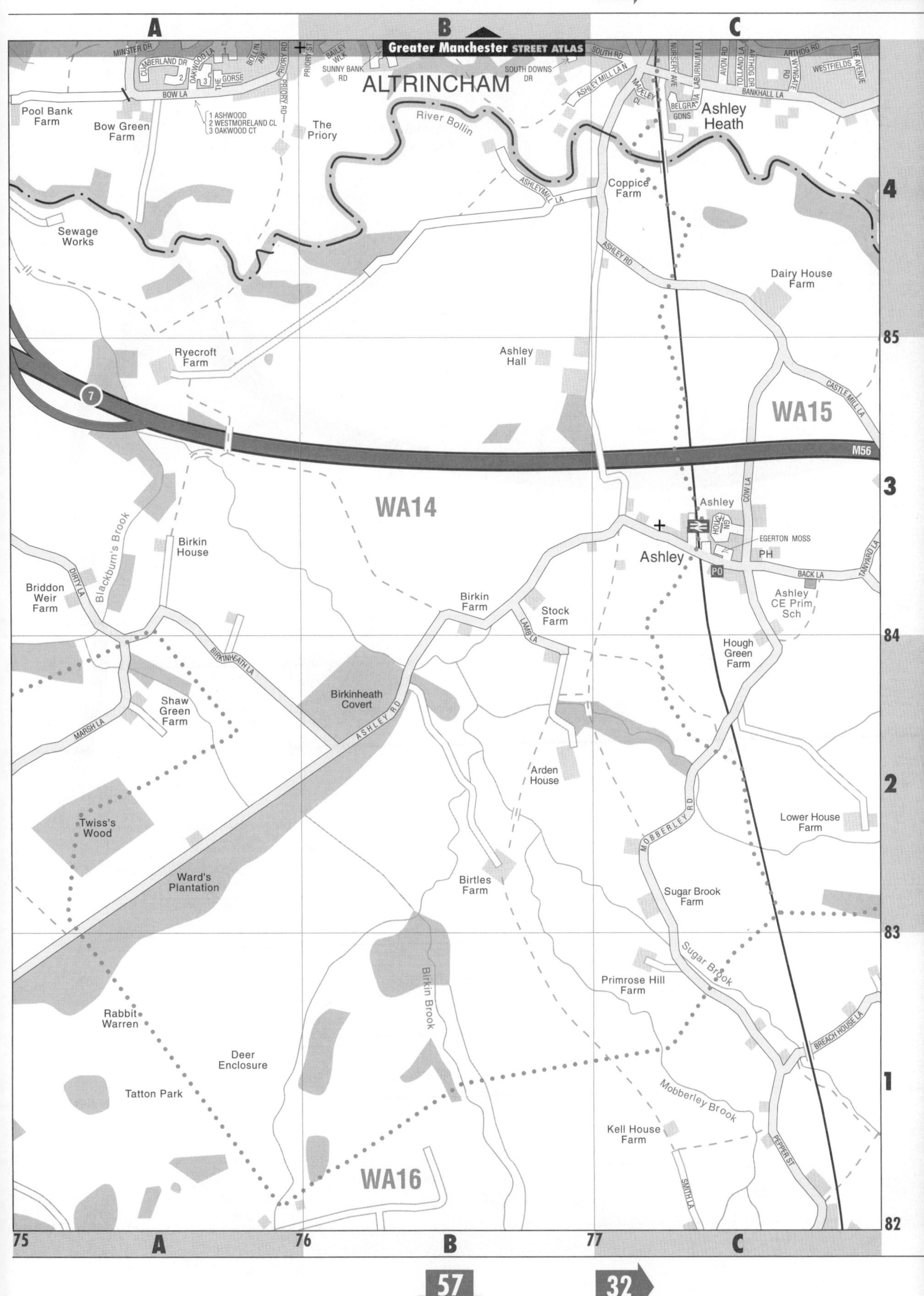
Greater Manchester STREET ATLAS
A
B
C
ALTRINCHAM
Ashley Heath
Pool Bank Farm
Bow Green Farm
The Priory
River Bollin
Sewage Works
Coppice Farm
Dairy House Farm
Ryecroft Farm
Ashley Hall
WA15
M56
WA14
Ashley
Birkin House
Briddon Weir Farm
Blackburn's Brook
Birkin Farm
Stock Farm
Ashley CE Prim Sch
Hough Green Farm
Shaw Green Farm
Birkinheath Covert
Arden House
Lower House Farm
Twiss's Wood
Ward's Plantation
Birtles Farm
Sugar Brook Farm
Sugar Brook
Primrose Hill Farm
Birkin Brook
Rabbit Warren
Deer Enclosure
Tatton Park
Mobberley Brook
Kell House Farm
WA16
MINSTER DR
CUMBERLAND DR
OAKWOOD LA
THE GORSE
BOLLIN AVE
PRIORY RD
PRIORY ST
BAILEY WLK
SUNNY BANK RD
SOUTH DOWNS DR
SOUTH RD
ASHLEY MILL LA N
MADELEY CL
NURSERY AVE
LABURNUM LA
AVON RD
TOLLAND LA
ARTHOG DR
ARTHOG RD
WYNGATE RD
WESTFIELDS
THE AVENUE
BANKHALL LA
BELGRAVIA GDNS
BOW LA
1 ASHWOOD
2 WESTMORELAND CL
3 OAKWOOD CT
ASHLEYMILL LA
ASHLEY RD
CASTLE MILL LA
COW LA
EGERTON MOSS
PH
PO
BACK LA
TANYARD LA
DIRTY LA
LAMB LA
BIRKINHEATH LA
MARSH LA
MOBBERLEY RD
BREACH HOUSE LA
PEPPER ST
SMITH LA
7
4
85
3
84
2
83
1
82
75
76
77

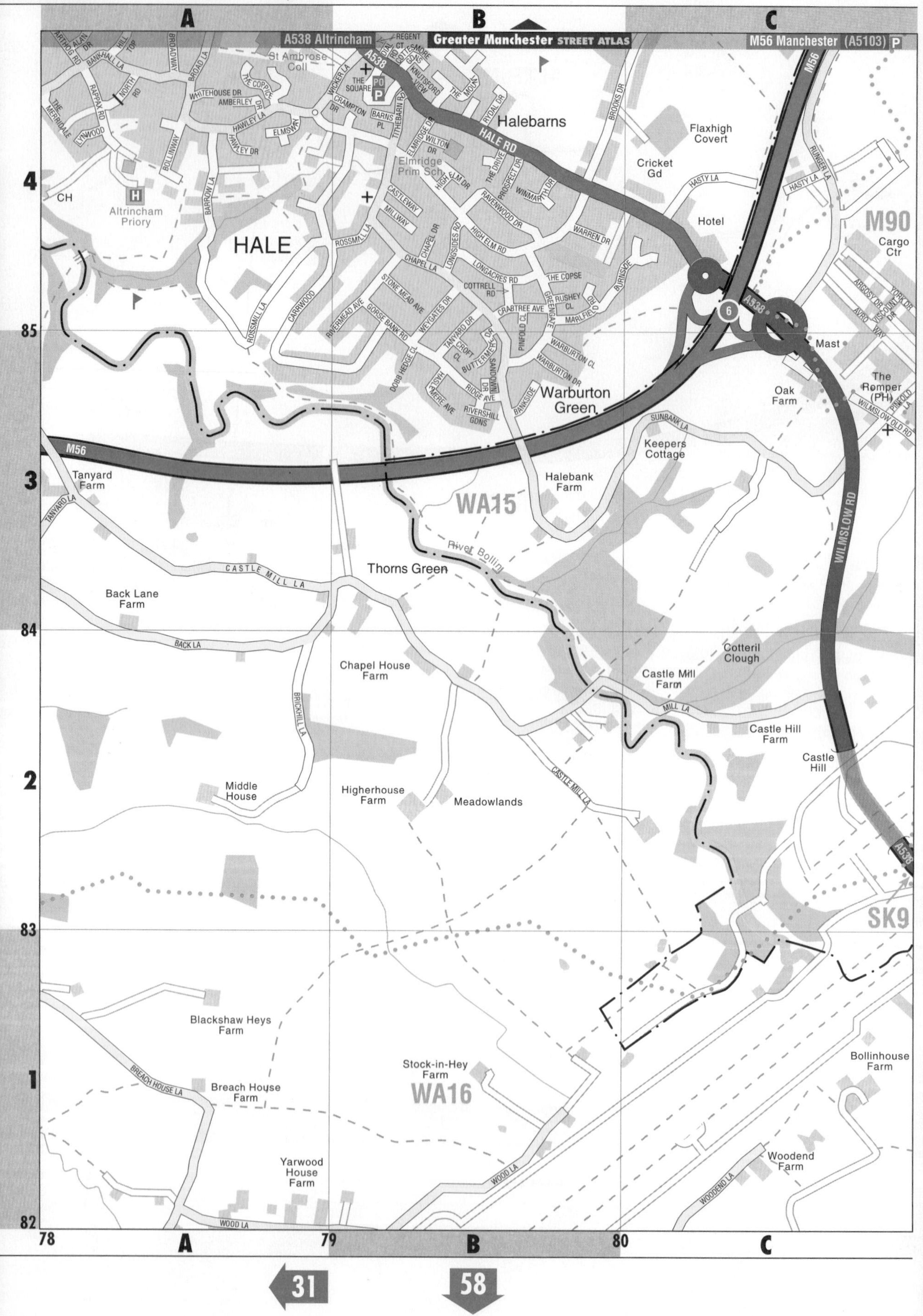

A   B   C

A538 Altrincham   **Greater Manchester** STREET ATLAS   M56 Manchester (A5103) P

St Ambrose Coll

Halebarns

HALE RD

Flaxhigh Covert

Cricket Gd

M90

Cargo Ctr

4

CH

Altrincham Priory

HALE

Hotel

Warren Dr

85

Warburton Green

Mast

6

A538

Oak Farm

The Romper (PH)

Keepers Cottage

3

Tanyard Farm

M56

WA15

Halebank Farm

River Bollin

Thorns Green

CASTLE MILL LA

Sunbank La

WILMSLOW RD

84

Back Lane Farm

BACK LA

Chapel House Farm

Castle Mill Farm

Cotteril Clough

MILL LA

Castle Hill Farm

Castle Hill

2

Middle House

Higherhouse Farm

Meadowlands

CASTLE MILL LA

83

SK9

Blackshaw Heys Farm

Bollinhouse Farm

1

Breach House Farm

BREACH HOUSE LA

Stock-in-Hey Farm

WA16

WOOD LA

Yarwood House Farm

Woodend Farm

WOODEND LA

82

78   A   79   B   80   C

WOOD LA

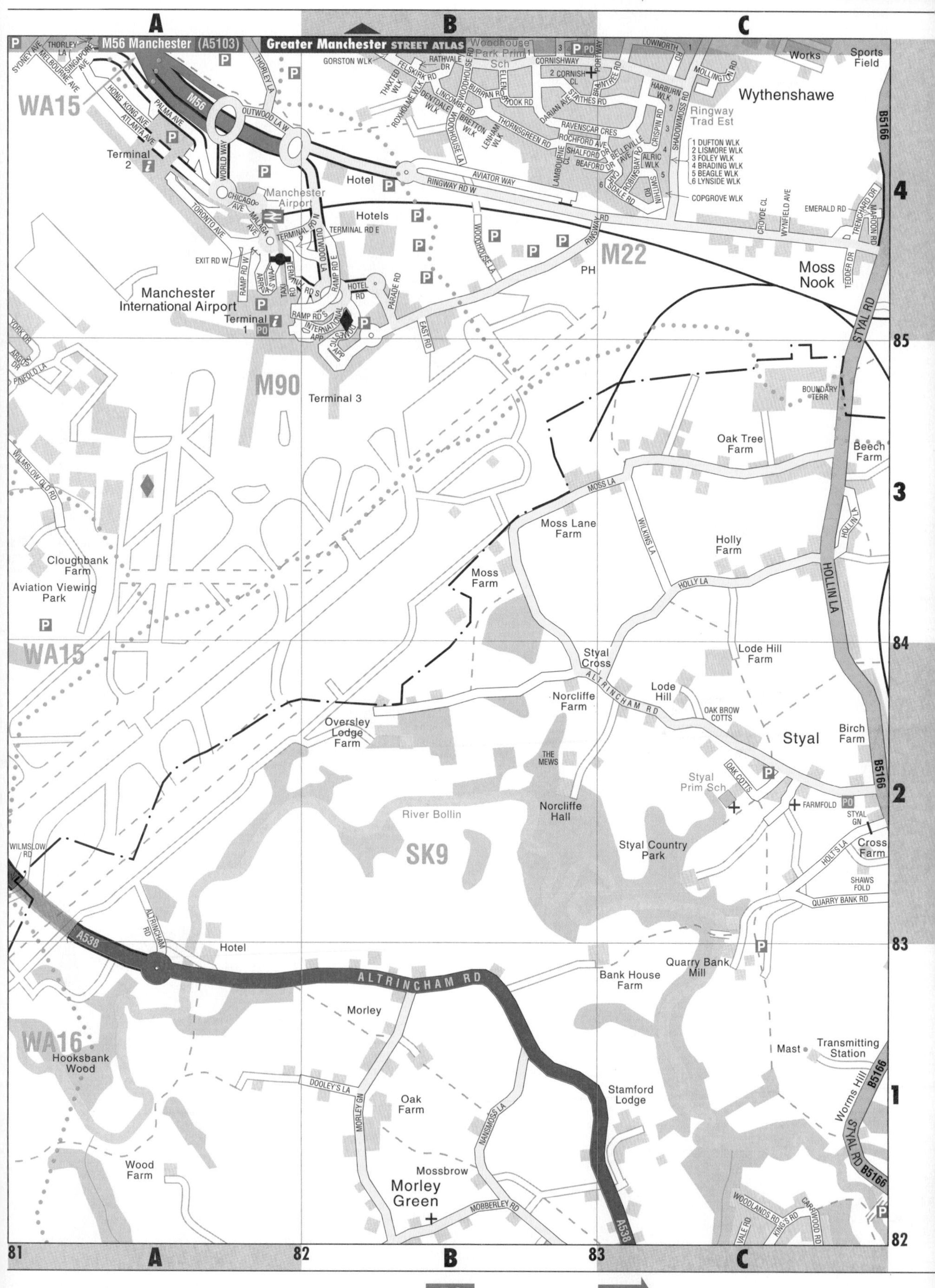
A
B
C
M56 Manchester (A5103)
Greater Manchester STREET ATLAS
WA15
Terminal 2
Manchester Airport
Hotel
Hotels
RINGWAY RD W
AVIATOR WAY
Manchester International Airport
Terminal 1
Terminal 3
M90
M22
PH
Woodhouse Park Prim Sch
Wythenshawe
Ringway Trad Est
Works
Sports Field
1 DUFTON WLK
2 LISMORE WLK
3 FOLEY WLK
4 BRADING WLK
5 BEAGLE WLK
6 LYNSIDE WLK
COPGROVE WLK
EMERALD RD
Moss Nook
STYAL RD
B5166
BOUNDARY TERR
Oak Tree Farm
Beech Farm
MOSS LA
Moss Lane Farm
WILKINS LA
Holly Farm
HOLLY LA
HOLLIN LA
Moss Farm
Cloughbank Farm
Aviation Viewing Park
WILMSLOW OLD RD
Styal Cross
Lode Hill Farm
Lode Hill
OAK BROW COTTS
ALTRINCHAM RD
Norcliffe Farm
Oversley Lodge Farm
Styal
Birch Farm
THE MEWS
Styal Prim Sch
OAK COTTS
FARMFOLD
STYAL GN
Norcliffe Hall
River Bollin
SK9
Styal Country Park
Cross Farm
HOLT'S LA
SHAWS FOLD
QUARRY BANK RD
WILMSLOW RD
A538
Hotel
Quarry Bank Mill
Bank House Farm
Morley
WA16
Hooksbank Wood
Mast
Transmitting Station
DOOLEY'S LA
Oak Farm
Stamford Lodge
Worms Hill
MORLEY GN
NANSMOSS LA
Wood Farm
Mossbrow
Morley Green
MOBBERLEY RD
WOODLANDS RD
KING'S RD
CARRWOOD RD
VALE RD
85
84
83
82
4
3
2
1
81
82
83

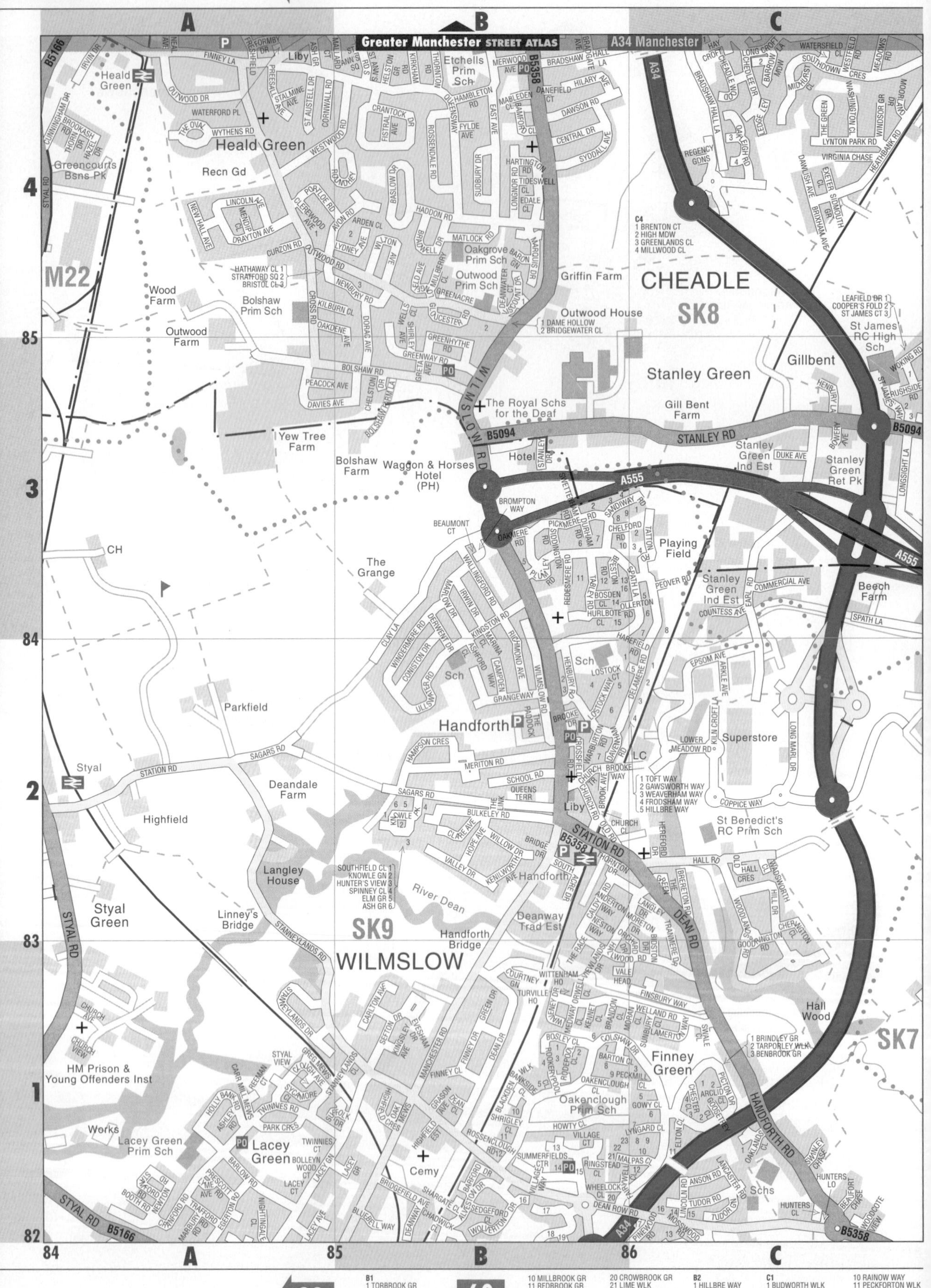

B3
1 TARVIN WAY
2 OVERTON WAY
3 STRETTON WAY
4 BIRTLES WAY
5 PEACOCK WAY
6 KELSALL WAY

7 CUDDINGTON WAY
8 WILLASTON WAY
9 NORBURY WAY
10 PICKMERE CT
11 EASTHAM WAY
12 UPTON WAY
13 ASTON WAY

14 HOOTON WAY
15 CHRISTLETON WAY
16 CRANAGE WAY

C3
1 SUTTON WAY
2 CHELFORD CT
3 SOMERFORD WAY
4 TATTON CT
5 MARTON WAY
6 NANTWICH WAY

7 HASSALL WAY
8 MARTHALL WAY

B1
1 TORBROOK GR
2 CLIFFBROOK GR
3 BENSON WLK
4 CARDENBROOK GR
5 TIMBERSBROOK GR
6 DE TRAFFORD MEWS
7 LADYBROOK GR
8 FODEN WLK
9 TAME WLK

10 MILLBROOK GR
11 REDBROOK GR
12 SHELLBROOK GR
13 TIVERTON DR
14 DEAN ROW CT
15 RINGSTEAD DR
16 DRAYTON CL
17 KNIGHTSBRIDGE CL
18 KINGSBURY DR
19 QUEENSBURY CL

20 CROWBROOK GR
21 LIME WLK
22 DINGLEBROOK GR
23 WADEBROOK GR

B2
1 HILLBRE WAY
2 SEALAND WAY
3 ECCLESTON WAY
4 HELSBY WAY
5 HEATLEY WAY
6 ELWORTH WAY
7 PARKGATE WAY

C1
1 BUDWORTH WLK
2 EDLESTONE GR
3 WOODCOTT GR
4 KETTLESHULME WLK
5 TILSTON WLK
6 SNAPEBROOK GR
7 DAIRYBROOK GR
8 APPLETON WLK
9 MOORSBROOK GR

10 RAINOW WAY
11 PECKFORTON WLK
12 SALTERSBROOK GR
13 PINWOOD CT
14 KINGSTON CT
15 MELROSE CT
16 SEYMOUR HO
17 HAZELDEAN CT

36

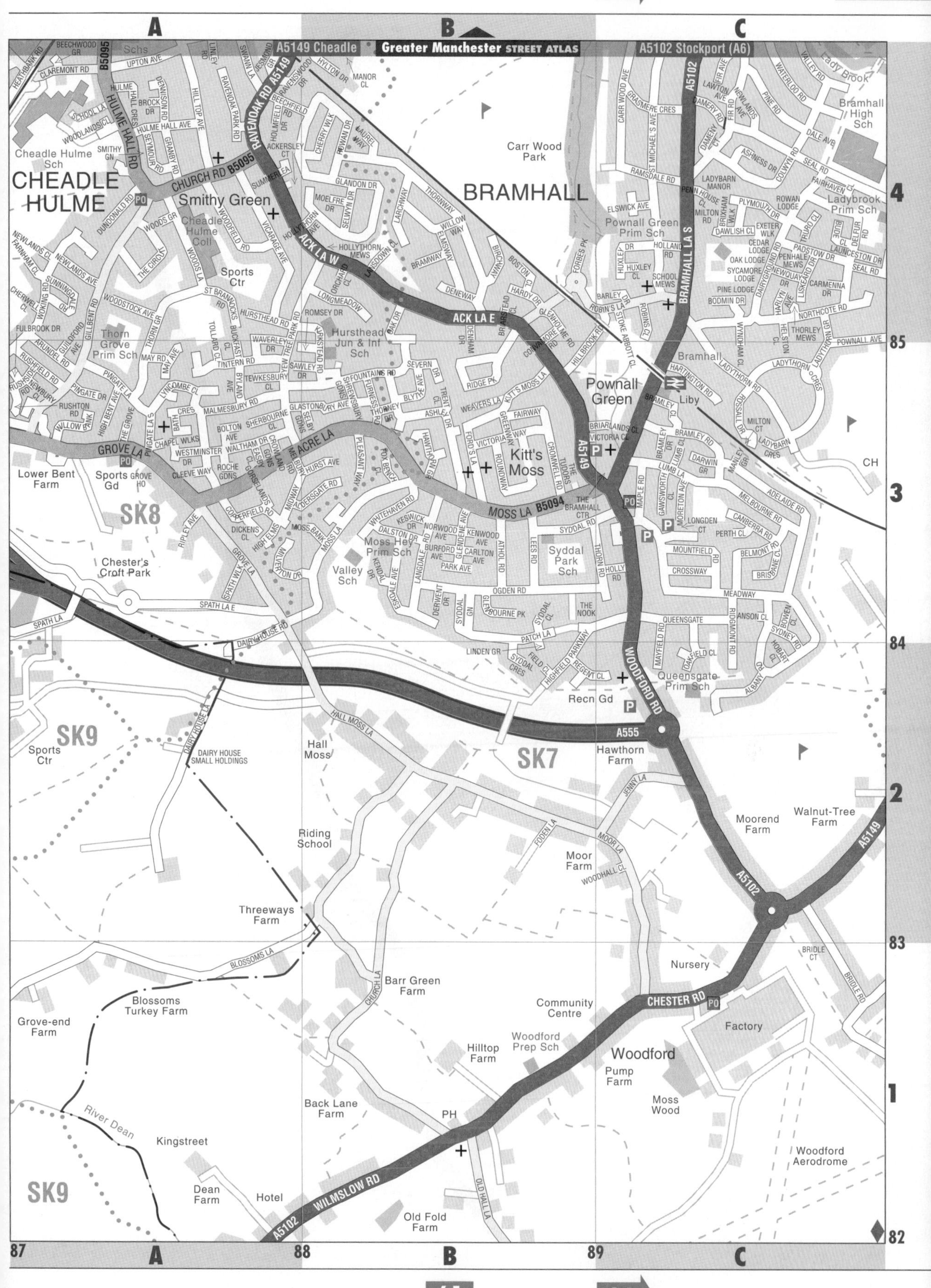

A
B
C
A5149 Cheadle
Greater Manchester STREET ATLAS
A5102 Stockport (A6)
CHEADLE HULME
Cheadle Hulme Sch
Smithy Green
Cheadle Hulme Coll
Sports Ctr
Thorn Grove Prim Sch
Hursthead Jun & Inf Sch
BRAMHALL
Carr Wood Park
Bramhall High Sch
Ladybrook Prim Sch
Pownall Green Prim Sch
Pownall Green
Bramhall
Liby
Kitt's Moss
Lower Bent Farm
Sports Gd
SK8
Chester's Croft Park
Moss Hey Prim Sch
Valley Sch
Syddal Park Sch
THE BRAMHALL CTR
Queensgate Prim Sch
Recn Gd
CH
SK9
Sports Ctr
DAIRY HOUSE SMALL HOLDINGS
Hall Moss
SK7
Hawthorn Farm
Moorend Farm
Walnut-Tree Farm
Riding School
Moor Farm
Threeways Farm
Nursery
Barr Green Farm
Blossoms Turkey Farm
Grove-end Farm
Community Centre
Factory
Woodford Prep Sch
Hilltop Farm
Woodford
Pump Farm
Moss Wood
Back Lane Farm
PH
River Dean
Kingstreet
Woodford Aerodrome
SK9
Dean Farm
Hotel
Old Fold Farm
CHURCH RD B5095
HULME HALL RD
RAVENOAK RD A5149
ACK LA W
ACK LA E
BRAMHALL LA S
A5102
A5149
GROVE LA
ACRE LA
MOSS LA B5094
WOODFORD RD
A555
CHESTER RD
WILMSLOW RD
A5102
HALL MOSS LA
DAIRY HOUSE LA
BLOSSOMS LA
CHURCH LA
OLD HALL LA
MOOR LA
FODEN LA
JENNY LA
WOODHALL CL
BRIDLE RD
SPATH LA E
GROVE LA
4
85
3
84
2
83
1
82
87
88
89

61

36

35

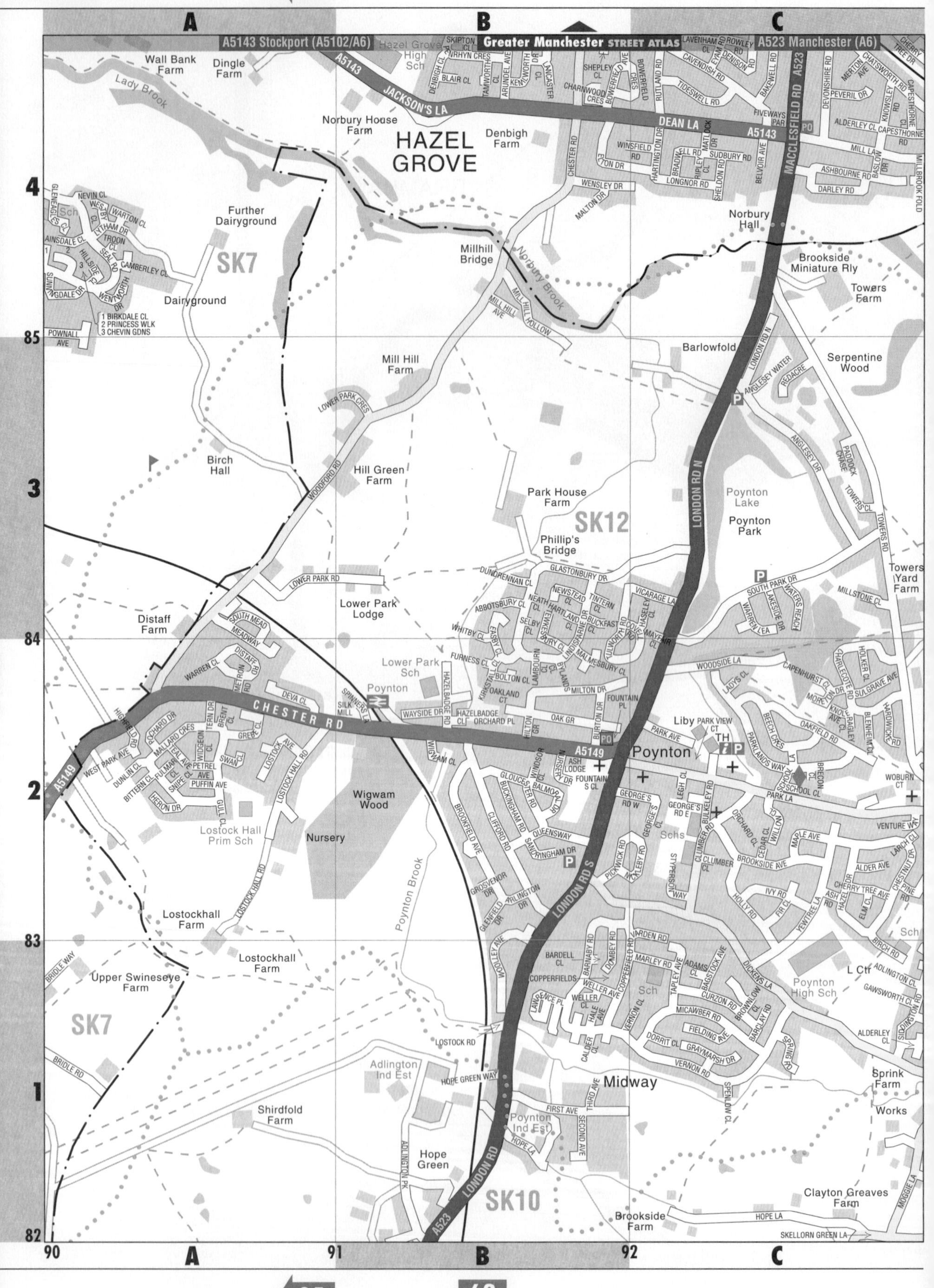
A
B
C
A5143 Stockport (A5102/A6)
Greater Manchester STREET ATLAS
A523 Manchester (A6)
Wall Bank Farm
Dingle Farm
Lady Brook
Hazel Grove High Sch
JACKSON'S LA
DEAN LA
A5143
Norbury House Farm
HAZEL GROVE
Denbigh Farm
Further Dairyground
SK7
Dairyground
Millhill Bridge
Norbury Brook
Norbury Hall
Brookside Miniature Rly
Towers Farm
MACCLESFIELD RD
A523
Barlowfold
Serpentine Wood
Mill Hill Farm
LOWER PARK CRES
WOODFORD RD
Birch Hall
Hill Green Farm
Park House Farm
SK12
Phillip's Bridge
LONDON RD N
Poynton Lake
Poynton Park
Towers Yard Farm
LOWER PARK RD
Lower Park Lodge
Distaff Farm
Lower Park Sch
Poynton
CHESTER RD
A5149
Liby
TH
Poynton
Wigwam Wood
Nursery
Lostock Hall Prim Sch
LONDON RD S
Schs
Poynton Brook
Lostockhall Farm
Lostockhall Farm
Upper Swineseye Farm
SK7
L Ctr
Poynton High Sch
Adlington Ind Est
Midway
Poynton Ind Est
Shirdfold Farm
Hope Green
LONDON RD
A523
SK10
Brookside Farm
HOPE LA
SKELLORN GREEN LA
Clayton Graves Farm
Sprink Farm
Works
4
85
3
84
2
83
1
82
90
91
92

35

62

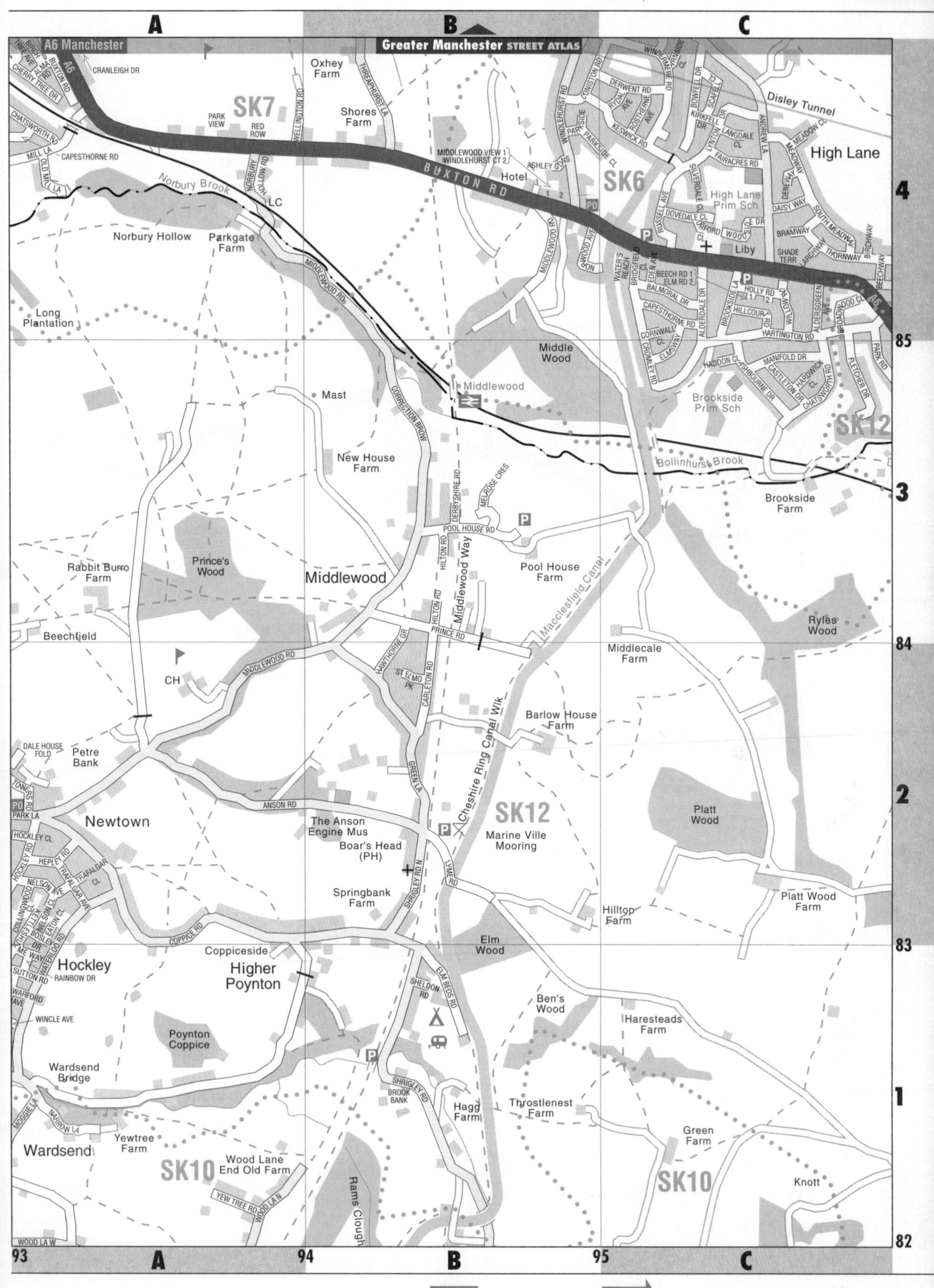

38

Greater Manchester STREET ATLAS

A6 Manchester

CRANLEIGH DR

SK7

Oxhey Farm

Shores Farm

PARK VIEW

RED ROW

Norbury Brook

Capesthorne Rd

Norbury Hollow

Parkgate Farm

Long Plantation

Mast

New House Farm

Middlewood

Rabbit Burro Farm

Prince's Wood

Middlewood

Beechfield

CH

Newtown

Petre Bank

Dale House Fold

Coppiceside

Higher Poynton

Hockley

RAINBOW DR

Poynton Coppice

Wardsend Bridge

Wincle Ave

Wardsend

Yewtree Farm

SK10

Wood Lane End Old Farm

Rams Clough

Middlewood View 1
Windlehurst Ct 2

Buxton Rd

Hotel

Ashley Dvns

PO

Middle Wood

Middlewood

Pool House Rd

Pool House Farm

Middlewood Way

Derbyshire Rd

Hilton Rd

Prince Rd

Cheshire Ring Canal Wlk

St Elmo Pk

Carleton Rd

Hawthorne Gr

Green La

Anson Rd

The Anson Engine Mus

Boar's Head (PH)

Springbank Farm

Sheldon Rd

Elm Beds Rd

Brook Bank

Shrigley Rd

Hagg Farm

Macclesfield Canal

SK12

Marine Ville Mooring

Elm Wood

Lyme Rd

Shrigley Rd N

SK6

High Lane

Disley Tunnel

High Lane Prim Sch

Liby

SK12

Middle cale Farm

Barlow House Farm

Platt Wood

Platt Wood Farm

Hilltop Farm

Ben's Wood

Haresteads Farm

Throstlenest Farm

Green Farm

Knott

SK10

Ryles Wood

Brookside Prim Sch

Brookside Farm

Bollinhurst Brook

37

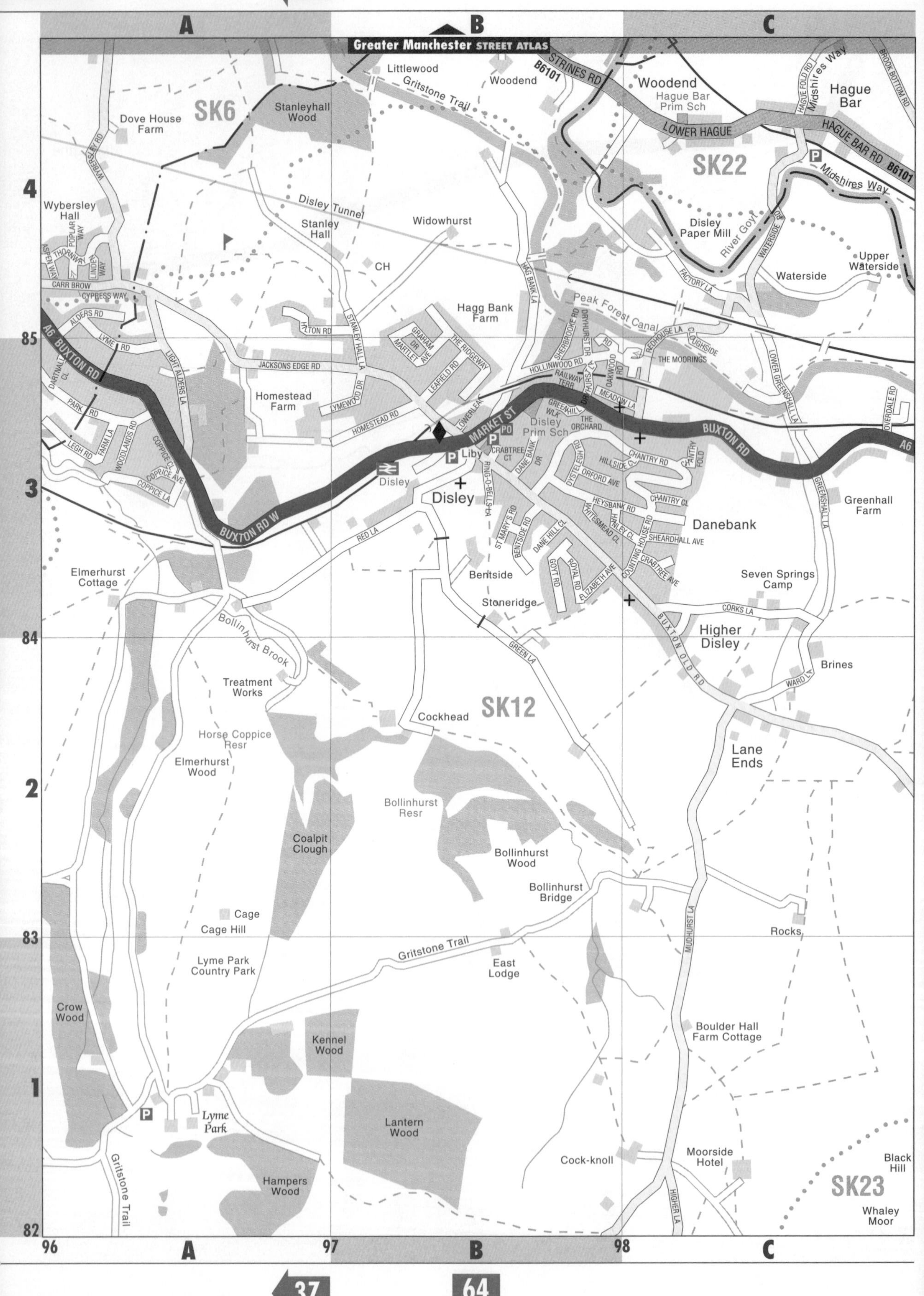
A
B
C
Greater Manchester STREET ATLAS
SK6
SK22
SK12
SK23
Littlewood
Woodend
Gritstone Trail
Stanleyhall Wood
Dove House Farm
Woodend
Hague Bar Prim Sch
Hague Bar
LOWER HAGUE
HAGUE BAR RD
B6101
STRINES RD
Midshires Way
Wybersley Hall
Disley Tunnel
Stanley Hall
Widowhurst
Disley Paper Mill
River Goyt
Upper Waterside
Waterside
CH
Hagg Bank Farm
Peak Forest Canal
THE MOORINGS
Homestead Farm
JACKSONS EDGE RD
HOMESTEAD RD
A6 BUXTON RD
MARKET ST
Disley Prim Sch
Liby
Disley
BUXTON RD
BUXTON RD W
A6
Greenhall Farm
Danebank
Elmerhurst Cottage
RED LA
Bentside
Stoneridge
Seven Springs Camp
CORKS LA
Higher Disley
Brines
Bollinhurst Brook
Treatment Works
Cockhead
GREEN LA
BUXTON OLD RD
Lane Ends
Horse Coppice Resr
Elmerhurst Wood
Bollinhurst Resr
Coalpit Clough
Bollinhurst Wood
Bollinhurst Bridge
Cage
Cage Hill
Rocks
Lyme Park Country Park
Gritstone Trail
East Lodge
Crow Wood
Kennel Wood
Boulder Hall Farm Cottage
Lyme Park
Lantern Wood
Cock-knoll
Moorside Hotel
Black Hill
Whaley Moor
Hampers Wood
MUDHURST LA
HIGHER LA
4
85
3
84
2
83
1
82
96
97
98

37

64

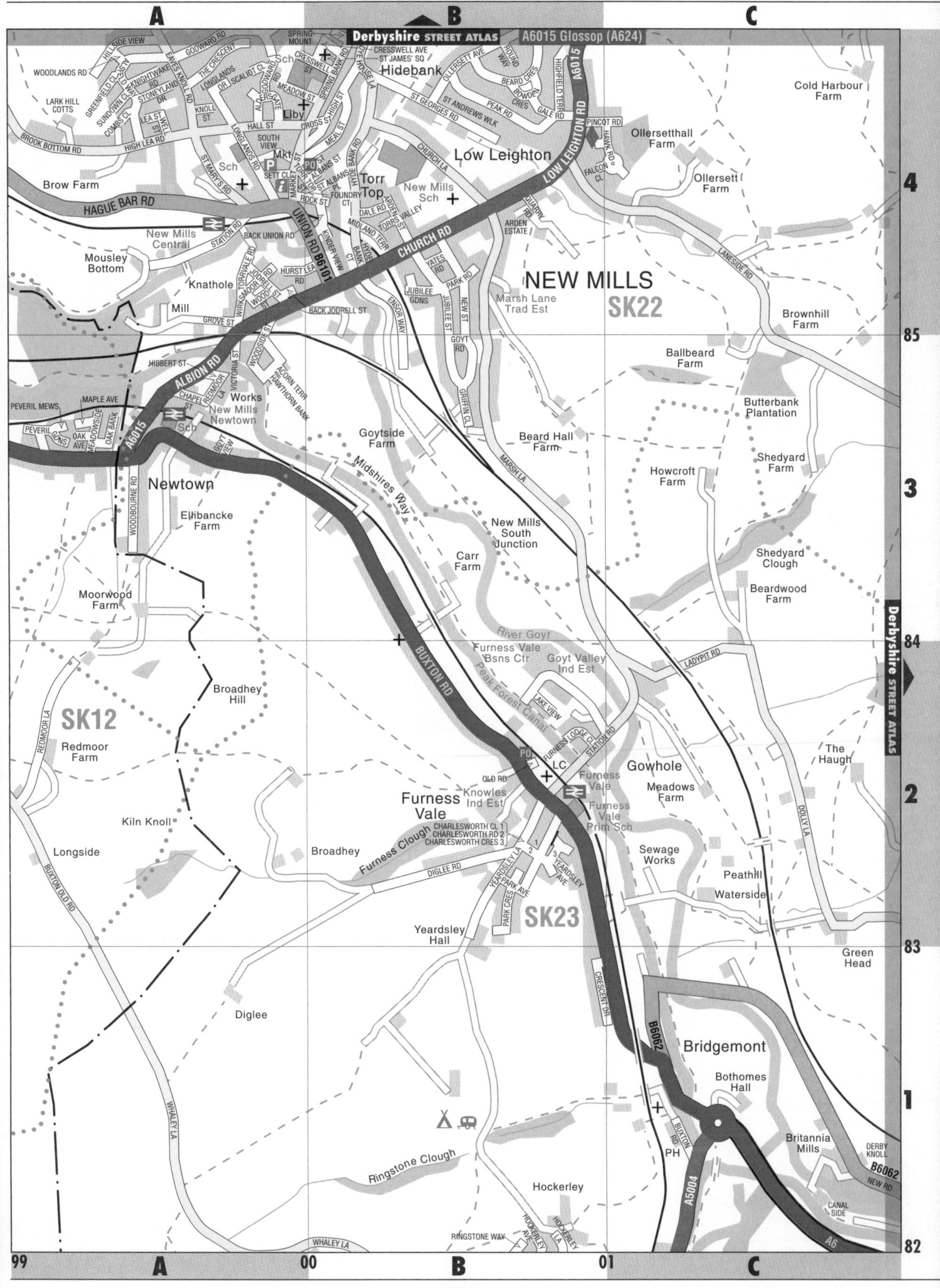

A6015 Glossop (A624)

HILLSIDE VIEW
GOWARD RD
SPRING
MOUNT
CRESSWELL AVE
ST JAMES' SQ

WOODLANDS RD
GREENFOLD CL
KNIGHTWAKE RD
FAVERS ANHAL RD
STONELAND DR
GODWARD RD
THE CRESCENT
CRESSWELL AVE
CRESSWELL BANK
LYTE HOUSE LA
MEADOW ST
SCALLOT CL
CH
Hidebank
ST ANDREWS WLK
ST GEORGES RD
OLLERSETT AVE
ROUND WAY
BEARD CRES
BEARD CRES
BLANOE
GALE RD
PEAK CRES
HIGHFIELD TERR
A6015

Cold Harbour
Farm

LARK HILL
COTTS
GREENFOLD CL
SUMOVIN CL
COMBS ST
KNOLL ST
LEA ST
HALL ST
Lib
CROSS HIGH ST
MEAL ST
CHURCH RD
Ollersetthall
Farm

BROOK BOTTOM RD
HIGH LEA RD
SOUTH VIEW
Sch
Mkt
PO
Torr
Top
New Mills
Sch
Low Leighton
DUFFY
PINCOT RD
HAWK RD
FALCON
CL
Ollersett
Farm

Brow Farm
HAGUE BAR RD
ST MARY'S RD
ST ALBANS RD
ST ALBANS PL
FOUNDRY ST
Rock St
DALE RD
TORR VALLEY
ARDEN
ESTATE
LANESIDE RD

New Mills
Central
STATION RD
BACK UNION RD
KINDER VIEW
UNION RD B6101
YATES
PARK RD
NEW MILLS
SK22
Brownhill
Farm

Mousley
Bottom
Knathole
HURST LEA RD
BACK JODRELL ST
ENSOR WAY
JUBILEE
GDNS
JUBILEE ST
NEW ST
GOYT RD
Marsh Lane
Trad Est
Ballbeard
Farm

Mill
GROVE ST
HIBBERT ST
CHURCH RD
WOODSIDE ST
VICTORIA ST
ACORN TERR
HAWTHORN BANK
GRIFFIN CL
MARSH LA
Butterbank
Plantation

PEVERIL MEWS
MAPLE AVE
ALBION RD
CHAPEL ST
A6015
Works
New Mills
Newtown
Sch
Goytside
Farm
Beard Hall
Farm
Shedyard
Farm

PEVERIL RONS
OAK AVE
OAK BANK
MEADOWSIDE
WOODBOURNE RD
GOYT VIEW
Midshires Way
Howcroft
Farm

Newtown
Ellibancke
Farm
New Mills
South
Junction
Shedyard
Clough

SK12
Moorwood
Farm
Broadhey
Hill
Carr
Farm
BUXTON RD
River Goyt
Furness Vale
Bsns Ctr
Peak Forest Canal
Goyt Valley
Ind Est
LADYPIT RD
Beardwood
Farm

REDMOOR LA
Redmoor
Farm
LAKE VIEW
FURNESS LODGE CL
STATION RD
The
Haugh

Kiln Knoll
Furness Clough
Knowles
Ind Est
OLD RD
PO
LC
Furness
Vale
Furness
Vale
Prim Sch
Gowhole
Meadows
Farm
DOLLY LA

Longside
BUXTON OLD RD
WHALEY LA
Broadhey
Furness
Vale
CHARLESWORTH CL 1
CHARLESWORTH RD 2
CHARLESWORTH CRES 3
DIGLEE RD
PARK CRES
PARK AVE
YEARDSLEY LA
YEARDSLEY AVE
Sewage
Works
Peathill
Waterside

SK23
Yeardsley
Hall
Green
Head

Diglee
CRESSETT DR
B6062
Bridgemont
Bothomes
Hall

Ringstone Clough
Hockerley
RINGSTONE WAY
HOCKERLEY AVE
HOCKERLEY LA
BUXTON RD
PH
A5004
Britannia
Mills
DERBY
KNOLL
B6062
NEW RD

WHALEY LA
CANAL
SIDE
A6

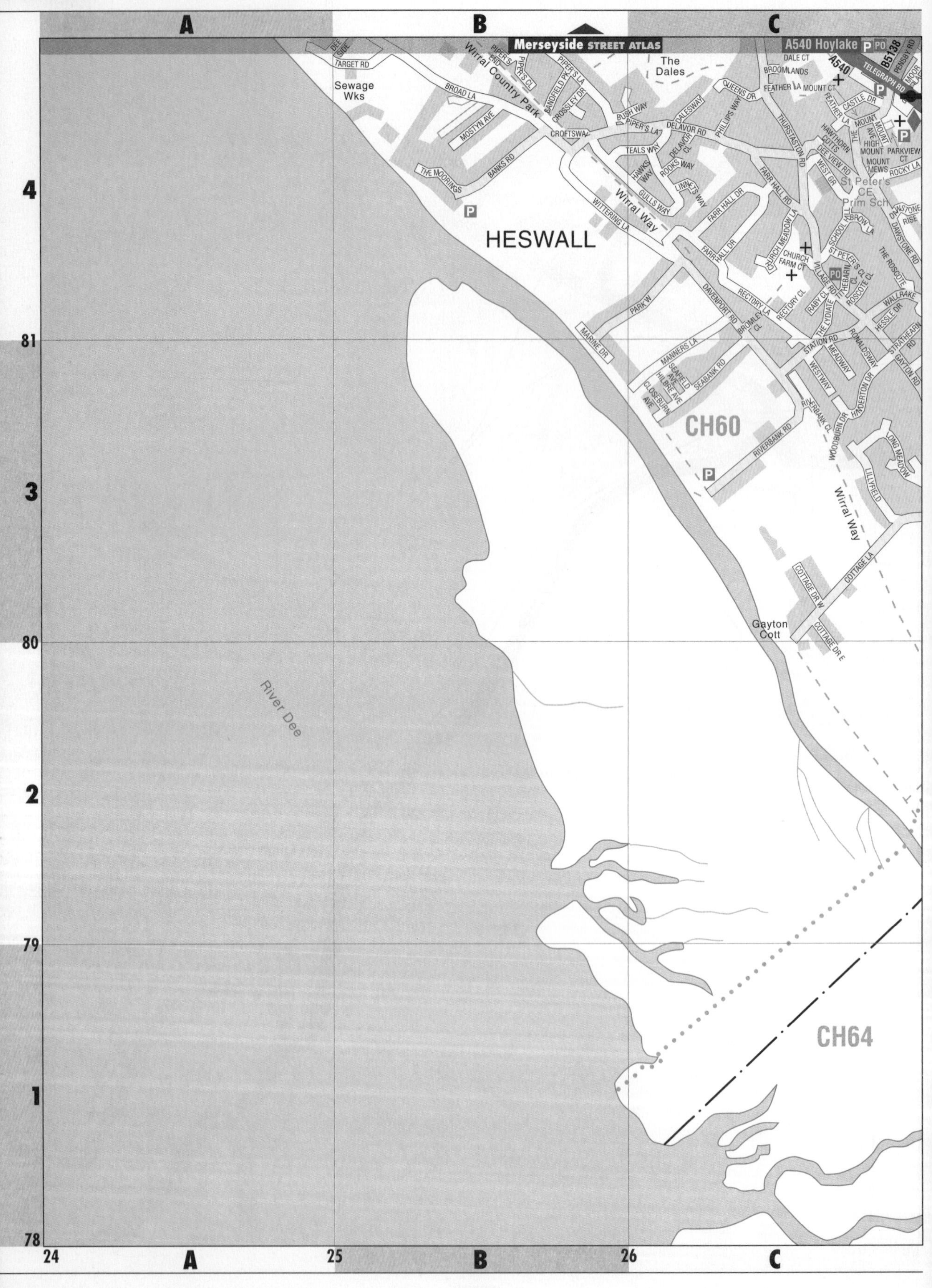

A   B   C

A540 Hoylake

The Dales

Sewage Wks

Wirral Country Park

HESWALL

St Peter's CE Prim Sch

CH60

Wirral Way

River Dee

Gayton Cott

CH64

4

81

3

80

2

79

1

78

24   A   25   B   26   C

42

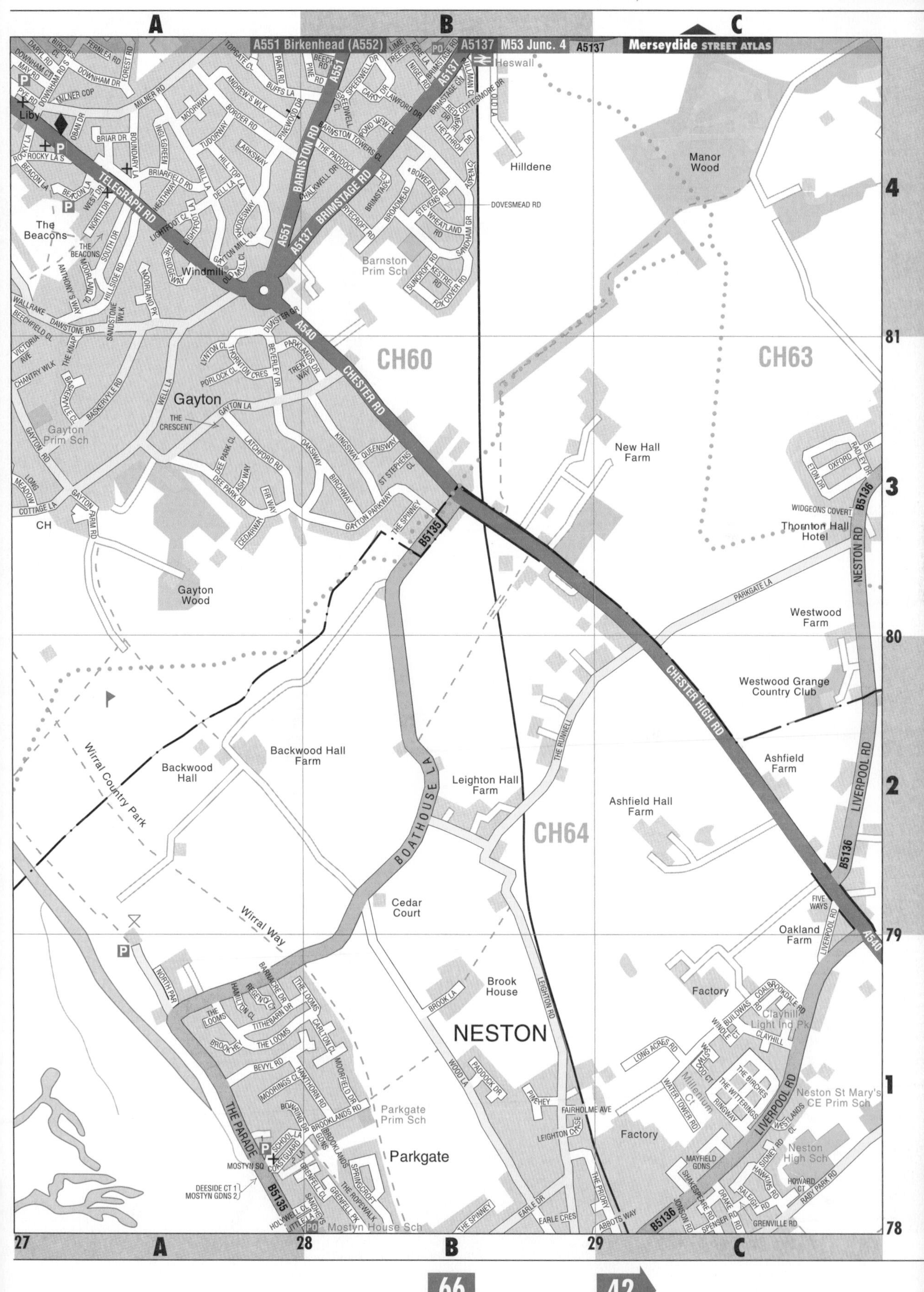

A
B
C
A551 Birkenhead (A552)
A5137 M53 Junc. 4
A5137
Merseydide STREET ATLAS
Heswall
Hilldene
Manor Wood
DOVESMEAD RD
The Beacons
Windmill
Barnston Prim Sch
TELEGRAPH RD
BARNSTON RD
BRIMSTAGE RD
A551
A5137
A540
CHESTER RD
CH60
CH63
Gayton
Gayton Prim Sch
THE CRESCENT
New Hall Farm
CH
Gayton Wood
B5135
WIDGEONS COVERT
Thornton Hall Hotel
NESTON RD
B5136
PARKGATE LA
Westwood Farm
Westwood Grange Country Club
CHESTER HIGH RD
Backwood Hall Farm
Backwood Hall
Wirral Country Park
Leighton Hall Farm
THE RUNNELL
Ashfield Farm
LIVERPOOL RD
Ashfield Hall Farm
CH64
BOATHOUSE LA
Cedar Court
Wirral Way
FIVE WAYS
Oakland Farm
Brook House
NORTH PAR
Factory
Clayhill Light Ind Pk
NESTON
LEIGHTON RD
Millenium Ct
Neston St Mary's CE Prim Sch
THE PARADE
Parkgate Prim Sch
Factory
Parkgate
Neston High Sch
MOSTYN SQ
DEESIDE CT 1
MOSTYN GDNS 2
Mostyn House Sch
27
28
29
78
79
80
81
1
2
3
4

66

42

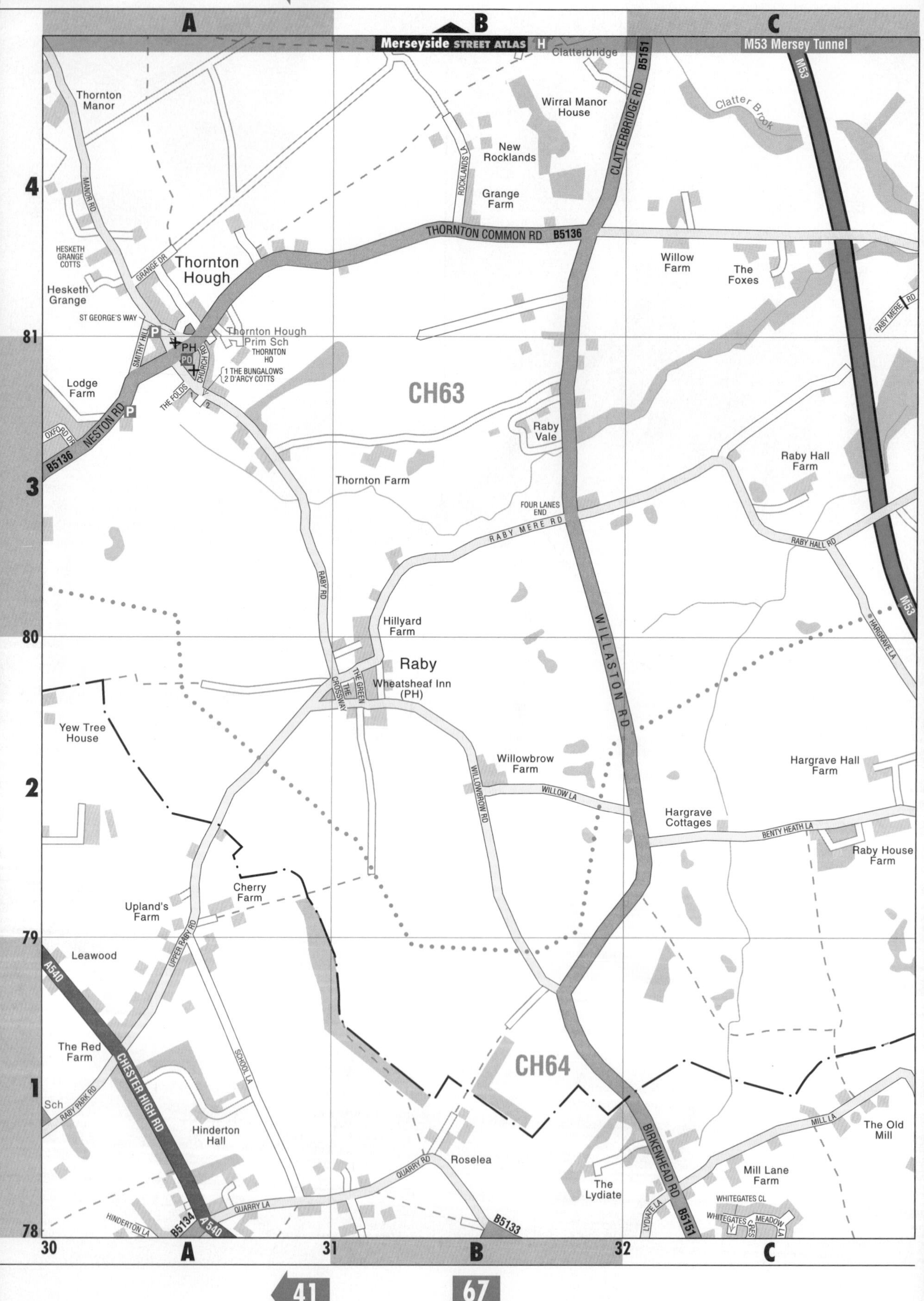

A   **B**   H   **C**

Merseyside STREET ATLAS

Clatterbridge

M53 Mersey Tunnel

Thornton Manor

Wirral Manor House

New Rocklands

Grange Farm

4

Willow Farm

The Foxes

RABY MERE RD

HESKETH GRANGE COTTS

Thornton Hough

ROCKLANDS LA

MANOR RD

GRANGE DR

THORNTON COMMON RD   B5136

CLATTERBRIDGE RD

B5151

M53

Clatter Brook

Hesketh Grange

St George's Way

SMITHY HILL

P

PH

PO

CH63

Raby Vale

Raby Hall Farm

81

Thornton Hough Prim Sch

THORNTON HO

1 THE BUNGALOWS

2 D'ARCY COTTS

CHURCH RD

Lodge Farm

THE FOLDS

P

NESTON RD

OXFORD DR

B5136

Thornton Farm

RABY RD

FOUR LANES END

RABY MERE RD

WILLASTON RD

Raby Hall Farm

RABY HALL RD

M53

HARGRAVE LA

3

Hillyard Farm

80

Raby

THE GREEN

THE CROSSWAY

Wheatsheaf Inn (PH)

Yew Tree House

Willowbrow Farm

WILLOWBROW RD

WILLOW LA

Hargrave Hall Farm

Hargrave Cottages

BENTY HEATH LA

Raby House Farm

2

Upland's Farm

Cherry Farm

UPPER RABY RD

79

Leewood

A540

The Red Farm

CHESTER HIGH RD

SCHOOL LA

Raby Park Rd

Sch

CH64

Hinderton Hall

MILL LA

The Old Mill

1

Roselea

QUARRY RD

BIRKENHEAD RD

Mill Lane Farm

LYDIATE LA

B5151

The Lydiate

WHITEGATES CL

WHITEGATES CS

MEADOW LA

HINDERTON LA

B5134

A540

QUARRY LA

B5133

78

30   **A**   31   **B**   32   **C**

44

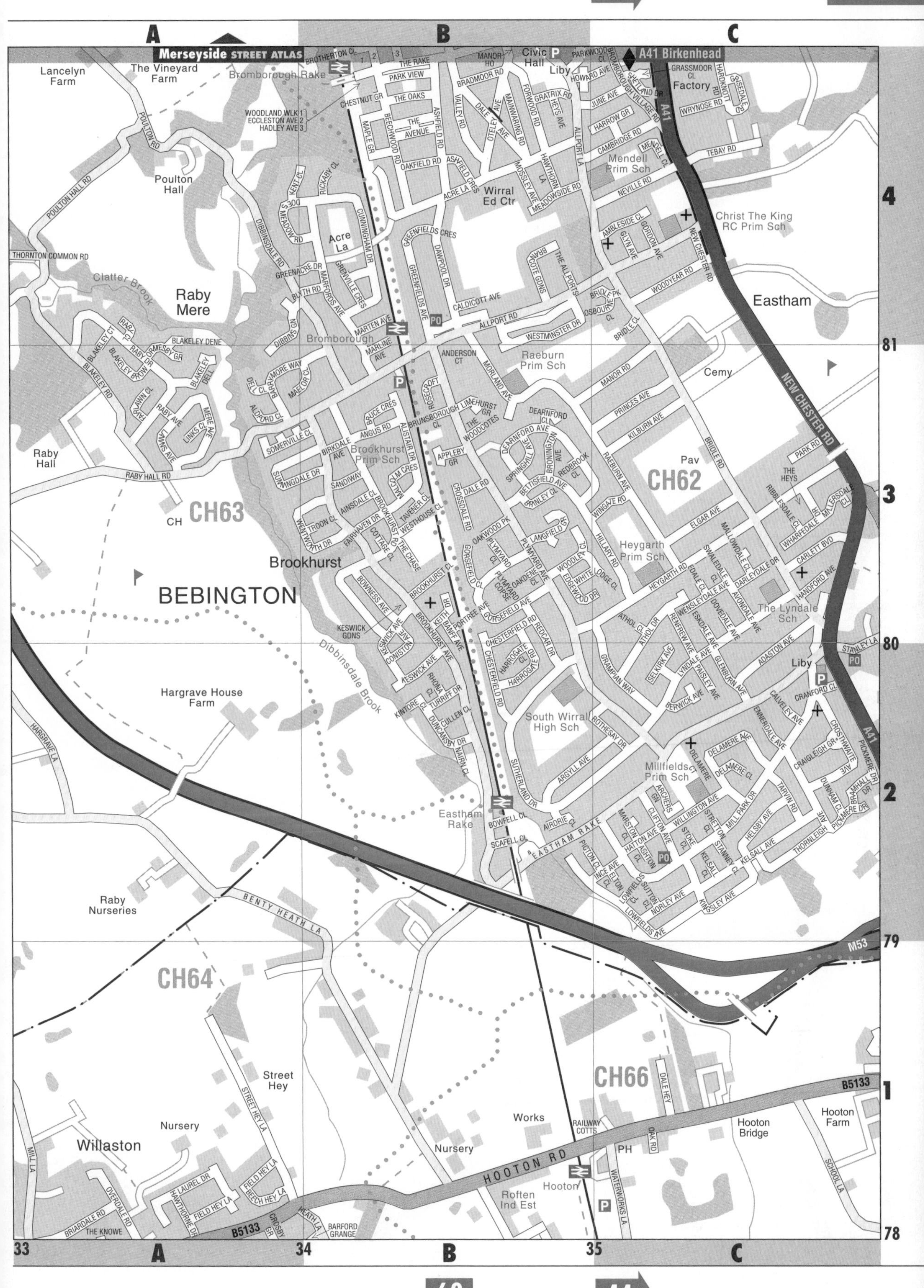
A
B
C
Merseyside STREET ATLAS
A41 Birkenhead
Lancelyn Farm
The Vineyard Farm
Bromborough Rake
Civic Hall
Liby
Factory
Poulton Hall
Mendell Prim Sch
Wirral Ed Ctr
Christ The King RC Prim Sch
Acre La
Raby Mere
Clatter Brook
Eastham
Bromborough
Raeburn Prim Sch
Cemy
NEW CHESTER RD
Raby Hall
Brookhurst Prim Sch
Pav
CH62
CH63
CH
Heygarth Prim Sch
Brookhurst
BEBINGTON
The Lyndale Sch
Dibbinsdale Brook
Hargrave House Farm
South Wirral High Sch
Millfields Prim Sch
Eastham Rake
Raby Nurseries
BENTY HEATH LA
M53
CH64
CH66
Street Hey
Nursery
Willaston
Works
Hooton Bridge
Hooton Farm
HOOTON RD
Hooton
Rofton Ind Est
B5133
4
3
2
1
81
80
79
78
33
34
35

68

44

43

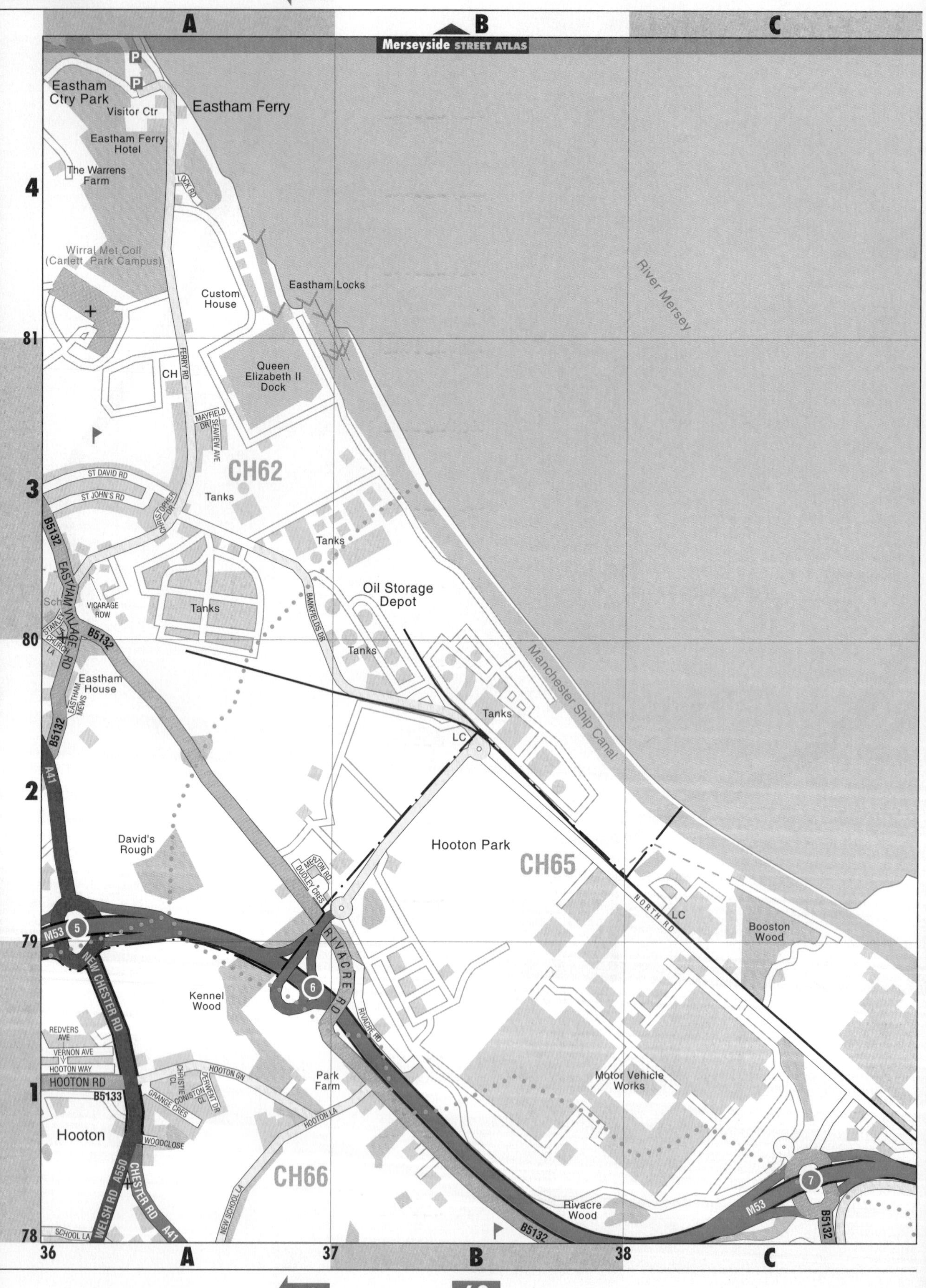
Merseyside STREET ATLAS
A
B
C
Eastham Ctry Park
Visitor Ctr
Eastham Ferry
Eastham Ferry Hotel
The Warrens Farm
LOCK RD
Wirral Met Coll (Carlett Park Campus)
Custom House
Eastham Locks
River Mersey
Queen Elizabeth II Dock
CH
FERRY RD
MAYFIELD DR
SEAVIEW AVE
CH62
ST DAVID RD
ST JOHN'S RD
CHRISTOPHER DR
Tanks
B5132
EASTHAM VILLAGE RD
VICARAGE ROW
Oil Storage Depot
BANKFIELDS DR
STANLEY LA
CHURCH LA
Eastham House
EASTHAM MEWS
Manchester Ship Canal
LC
A41
Hooton Park
CH65
David's Rough
MERTON RD
DUDLEY CRES
NORTH RD
Booston Wood
M53
RIVACRE RD
Kennel Wood
NEW CHESTER RD
REDVERS AVE
VERNON AVE
HOOTON WAY
HOOTON RD
B5133
HOOTON GN
CHRISTIE CL
CONISTON CL
DERWENT DR
GRANGE CRES
Park Farm
Motor Vehicle Works
HOOTON LA
Hooton
WOODCLOSE
CH66
NEW SCHOOL LA
A550
WELSH RD
CHESTER RD
SCHOOL LA
Rivacre Wood
4
81
3
80
2
79
1
78
36
37
38

43

69

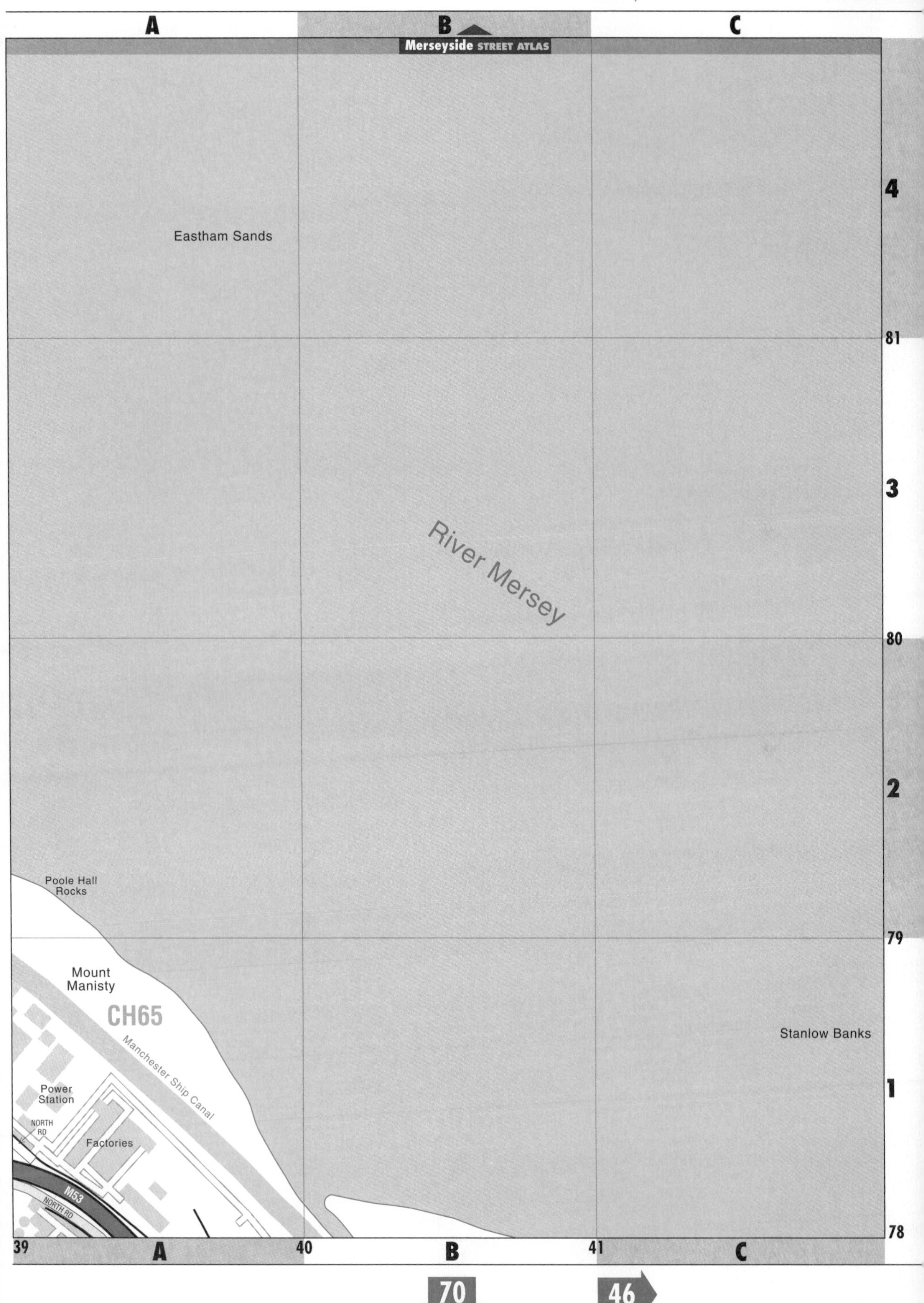

46

A   **B**   **C**

Merseyside STREET ATLAS

Eastham Sands

River Mersey

Poole Hall
Rocks

Mount
Manisty

CH65

Manchester Ship Canal

Stanlow Banks

Power
Station

NORTH
RD

Factories

M53

NORTH RD

4

81

3

80

2

79

1

78

39   **A**   40   **B**   41   **C**

70

46

45

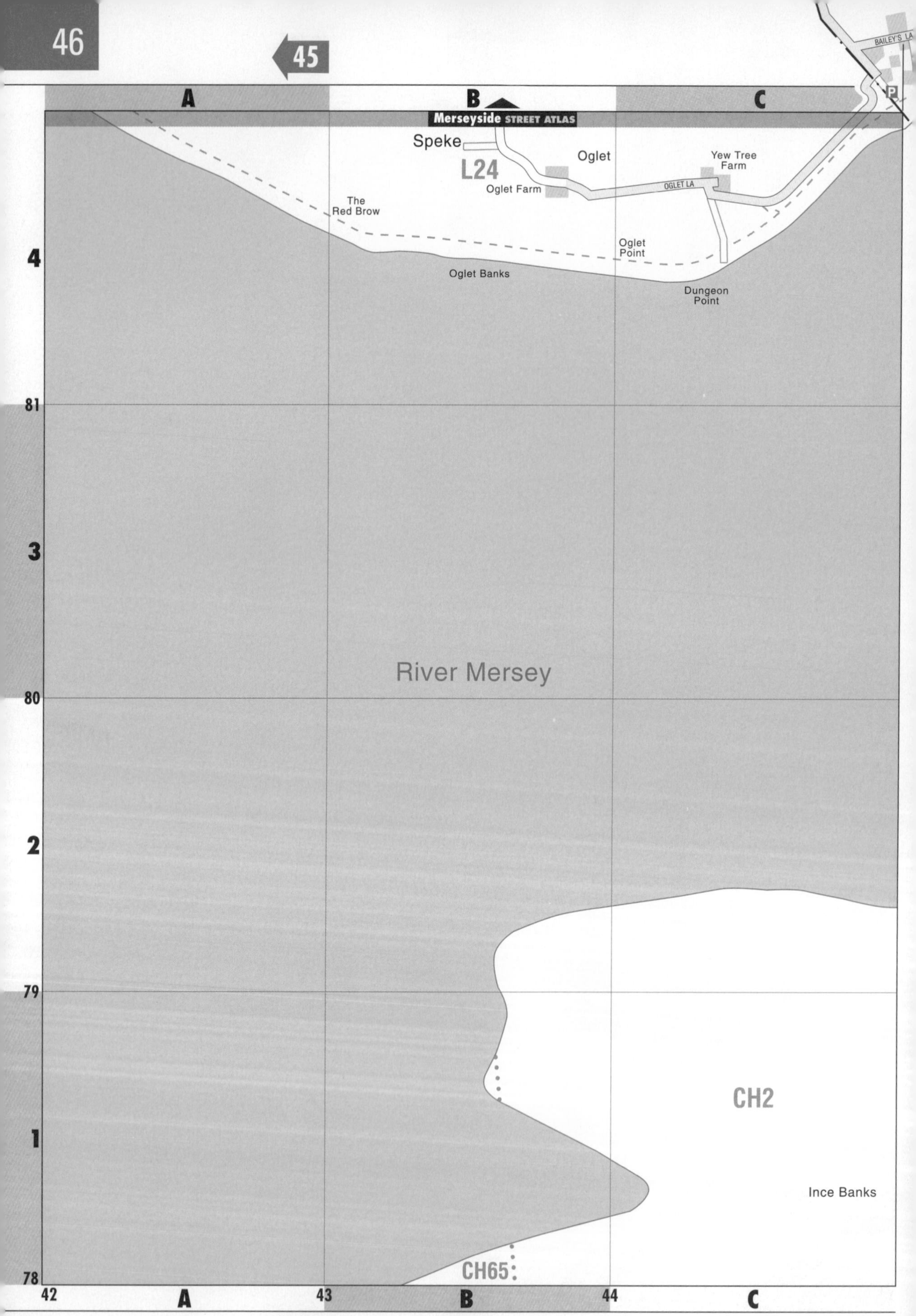

A

C

P

BAILEY'S LA

Speke

L24

Oglet

Yew Tree
Farm

The
Red Brow

Oglet Farm

OGLET LA

Oglet
Point

4

Oglet Banks

Dungeon
Point

81

3

River Mersey

80

2

79

CH2

1

Ince Banks

CH65

78

42   A   43   B   44   C

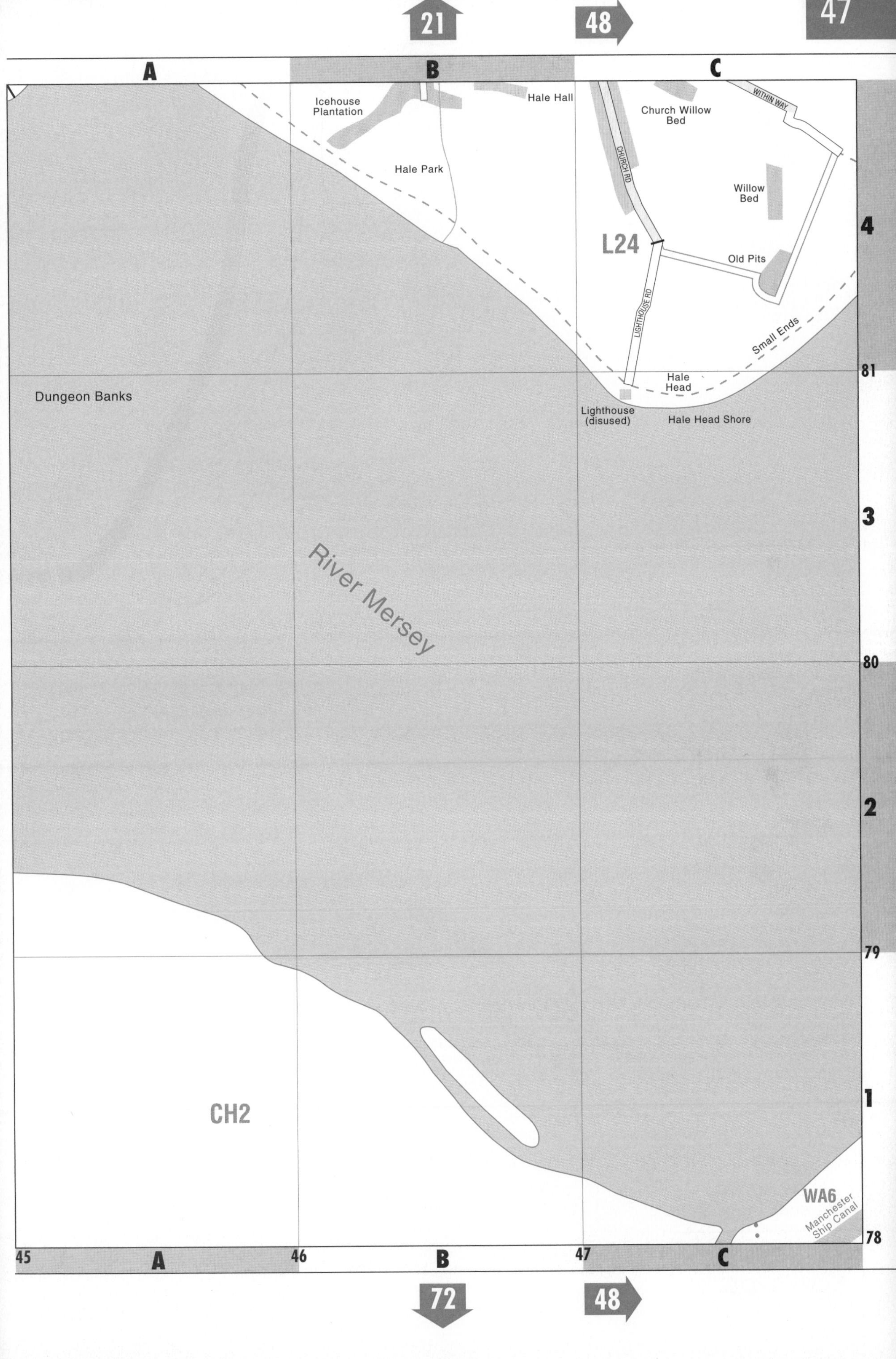

A

Icehouse
Plantation

Hale Hall

B

Church Willow
Bed

WITHIN WAY

C

Hale Park

CHURCH RD

Willow
Bed

L24

4

Old Pits

LIGHTHOUSE RD

Small Ends

81

Dungeon Banks

Hale
Head

Lighthouse
(disused)

Hale Head Shore

River Mersey

3

80

2

79

CH2

1

WA6
*Manchester
Ship Canal*

78

47
22

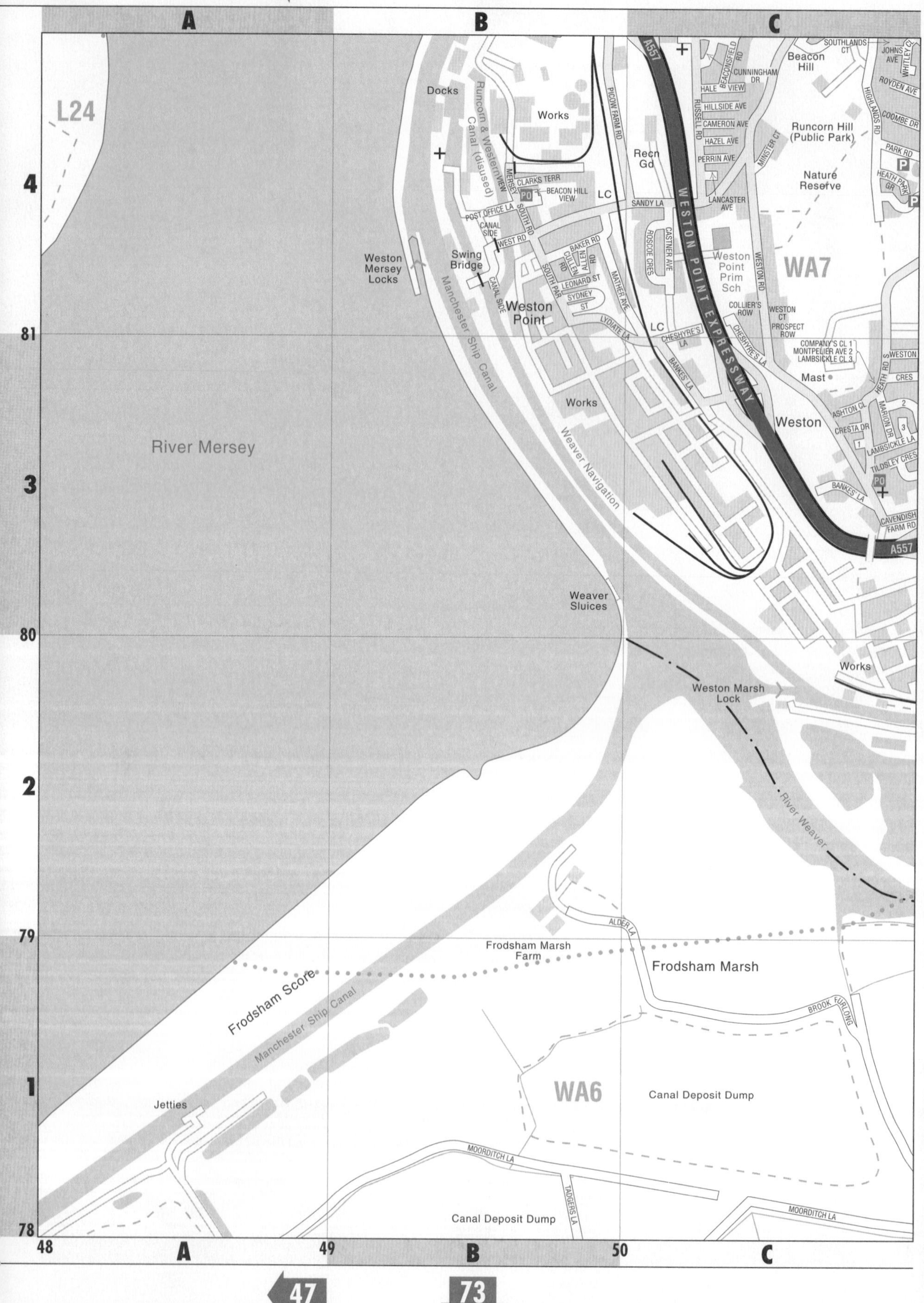
A
B
C
L24
River Mersey
Docks
Runcorn & Western Canal (disused)
Works
Weston Mersey Locks
Swing Bridge
Weston Point
Manchester Ship Canal
Weaver Navigation
Weaver Sluices
Recn Gd
WESTON POINT EXPRESSWAY
A557
Beacon Hill
Runcorn Hill (Public Park)
Nature Reserve
WA7
Weston Point Prim Sch
Mast
Weston
Works
Weston Marsh Lock
River Weaver
Frodsham Marsh Farm
Frodsham Marsh
Frodsham Score
Manchester Ship Canal
Jetties
WA6
Canal Deposit Dump
Canal Deposit Dump
ALDER LA
BROOK FURLONG
MOORDITCH LA
TADGERS LA
MOORDITCH LA
SANDY LA
PICOW FARM RD
CLARKS TERR
BEACON HILL VIEW
POST OFFICE LA
CANAL SIDE
WEST RD
SOUTH RD
BAKER RD
LEONARD ST
SYDNEY ST
SOUTH PAR
MATHER AVE
LYDIATE LA
CHESHYRE'S LA
BANKES' LA
ROSCOE CRES
CASTNER AVE
WESTON RD
COLLIER'S ROW
WESTON CT
PROSPECT ROW
LANCASTER AVE
PERRIN AVE
HAZEL AVE
CAMERON AVE
HILLSIDE AVE
HALE VIEW
CUNNINGHAM DR
BEACONSFIELD RD
RUSSELL RD
MINSTER CT
SOUTHLANDS CT
JOHNS AVE
WHITLEY CL
ROYDEN AVE
COOMBE DR
HIGHLANDS RD
PARK RD
HEATH PARK GR
COMPANY'S CL 1
MONTPELIER AVE 2
LAMBSICKLE CL 3
HEATH RD S
WESTON CRES
ASHTON CL
CRESTA DR
MARION DR
LAMBSICKLE LA
TILDSLEY CRES
BANKES' LA
CAVENDISH FARM RD
LC
LC
4
81
3
80
2
79
1
78
48
49
50

47
73

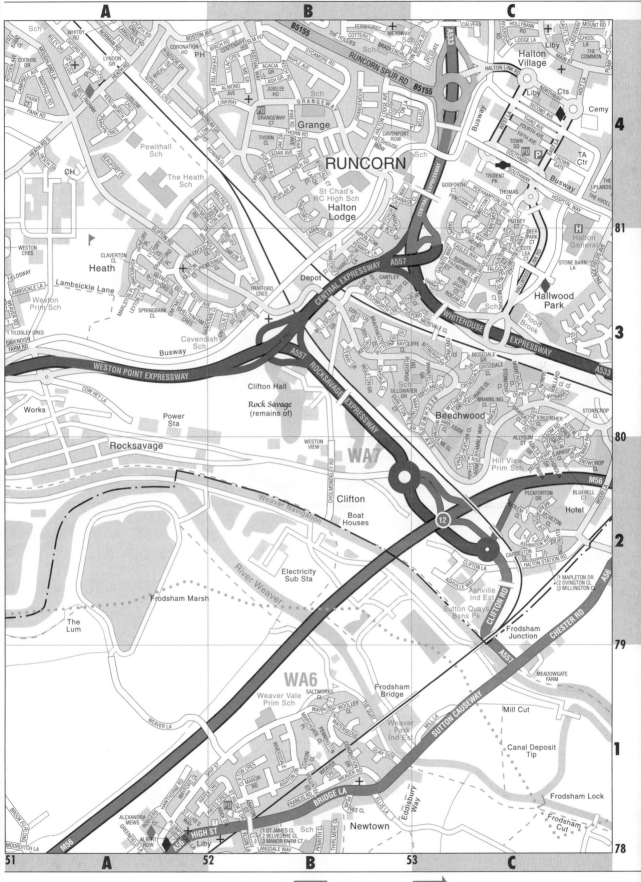
23
50

A B C

RUNCORN
Halton Village
Grange
Halton Lodge
Heath
Beechwood
Clifton
Rocksavage
Newtown
Hallwood Park
WA7
WA6

B5155
RUNCORN SPUR RD
A533
CENTRAL EXPRESSWAY
A557
WHITEHOUSE EXPRESSWAY
WESTON POINT EXPRESSWAY
ROCKSAVAGE EXPRESSWAY
M56
A56
CHESTER RD
SUTTON CAUSEWAY
BRIDGE LA
HIGH ST
CLIFTON RD
HALTON STATION RD
HALTON LINK RD
HALLWOOD LINK RD
HOSPITAL WAY
SOUTHWAY
NORTHWAY
Busway
Lambsickle Lane
Eddisbury Way

St Chad's RC High Sch
Pewithall Sch
The Heath Sch
Cavendish Sch
Weston Prim Sch
Hill View Prim Sch
Weaver Vale Prim Sch
Halton General
TA Ctr
Cemy
Depot
Clifton Hall
Rock Savage (remains of)
Power Sta
Works
Boat Houses
Electricity Sub Sta
Ashville Ind Est
Sutton Quays Bsns Pk
Frodsham Junction
Frodsham Marsh
Frodsham Bridge
Weaver Park Ind Est
The Lum
Mill Cut
Canal Deposit Tip
Frodsham Lock
Frodsham Cut
Weaver Navigation
River Weaver
Flood Brook
Meadowgate Farm

1 TILDSLEY CRES
1 MAPLETON DR
2 OVINGTON CL
3 MILLINGTON CL
1 ST JAMES CL
2 BELVEDERE CL
3 MANOR FARM CT

4
81
3
80
2
79
1
78

51 A 52 B 53 C

49
24

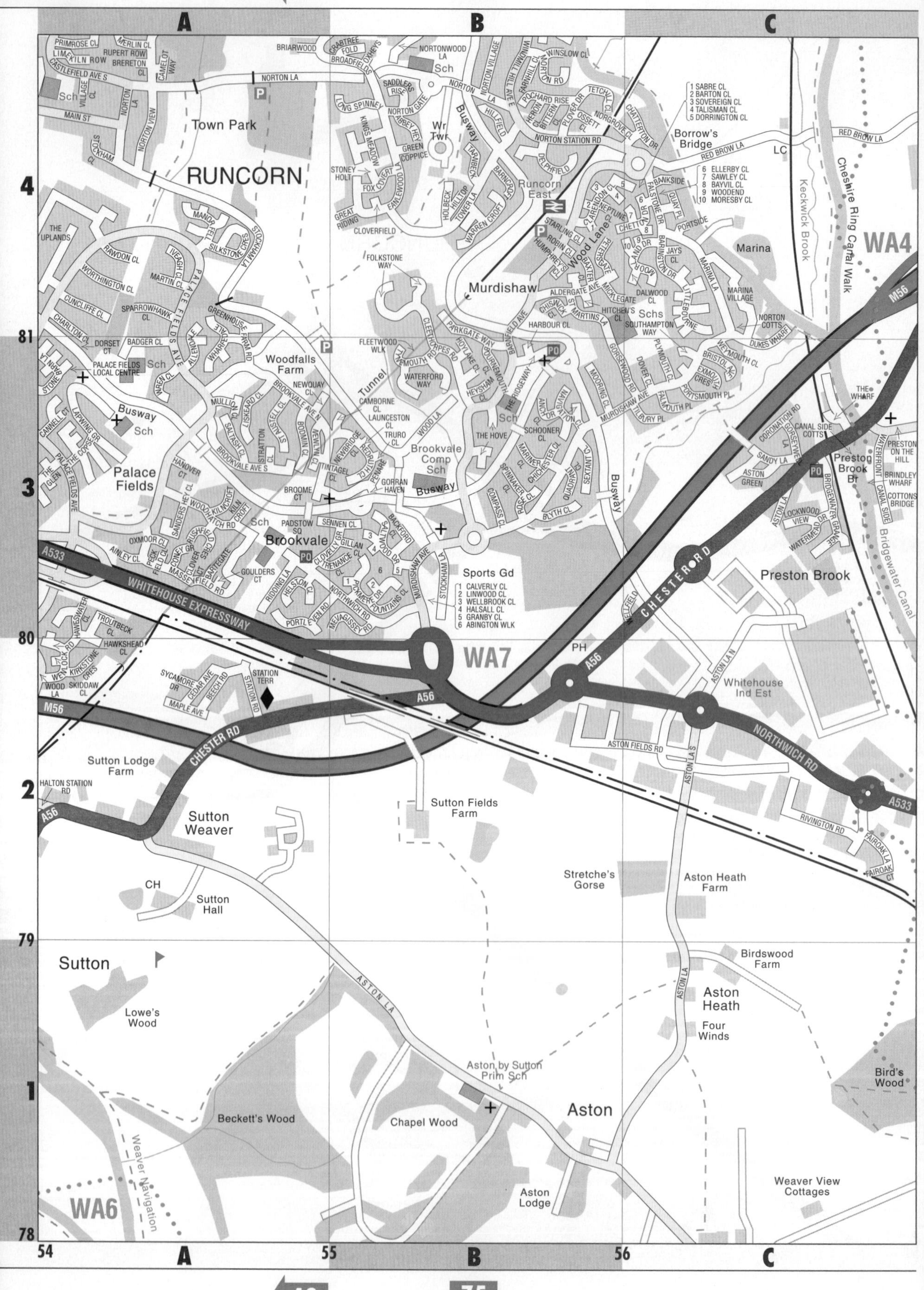
A
B
C
4
81
3
80
2
79
1
78
54
55
56
RUNCORN
Town Park
Runcorn East
Murdishaw
Borrow's Bridge
Marina
Marina Village
WA4
M56
Cheshire Ring Canal Walk
Keckwick Brook
Red Brow La
LC
1 SABRE CL
2 BARTON CL
3 SOVEREIGN CL
4 TALISMAN CL
5 DORRINGTON CL
6 ELLERBY CL
7 SAWLEY CL
8 BAYVIL CL
9 WOODEND
10 MORESBY CL
Norton La
Norton Station Rd
Norton Village
Wood Lane
Busway
Tunnel
Wr Twr
Sch
Schs
Palace Fields
Woodfalls Farm
Brookvale
Brookvale Comp Sch
Sports Gd
1 CALVERLY CL
2 LINWOOD CL
3 WELLBROOK CL
4 HALSALL CL
5 GRANBY CL
6 ABINGTON WLK
A533
Whitehouse Expressway
WA7
A56
Chester Rd
PH
Preston Brook
Whitehouse Ind Est
Northwich Rd
Aston Fields Rd
Bridgewater Canal
Sutton Lodge Farm
Halton Station Rd
Sutton Weaver
Sutton Fields Farm
Stretche's Gorse
Aston Heath Farm
CH
Sutton Hall
Sutton
Lowe's Wood
Aston La
Birdswood Farm
Aston Heath
Four Winds
Aston by Sutton Prim Sch
Aston
Beckett's Wood
Chapel Wood
Weaver Navigation
Bird's Wood
Weaver View Cottages
Aston Lodge
WA6

25
52

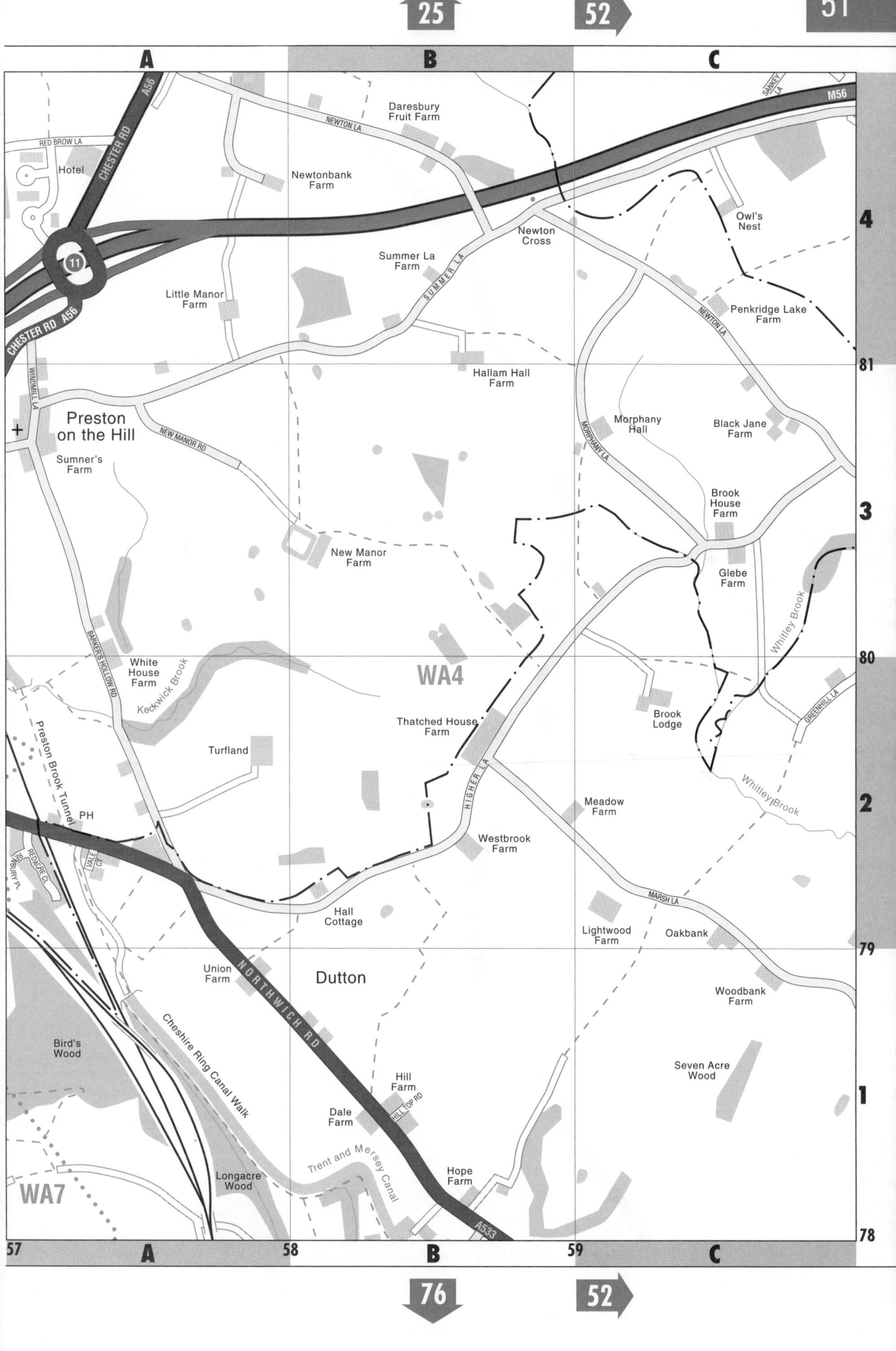
A
B
C
Daresbury Fruit Farm
NEWTON LA
SANKEY LA
M56
RED BROW LA
Hotel
CHESTER RD
A56
Newtonbank Farm
Owl's Nest
4
Newton Cross
11
Summer La Farm
SUMMER LA
Little Manor Farm
CHESTER RD A56
Penkridge Lake Farm
NEWTON LA
81
WINDMILL LA
Hallam Hall Farm
Preston on the Hill
NEW MANOR RD
Morphany Hall
MORPHANY LA
Black Jane Farm
Sumner's Farm
Brook House Farm
3
New Manor Farm
Glebe Farm
Whitley Brook
BARKER'S HOLLOW RD
80
White House Farm
Keckwick Brook
WA4
GREENHILL LA
Brook Lodge
Thatched House Farm
Preston Brook Tunnel
Turfland
HIGHER LA
Whitley Brook
2
Meadow Farm
PH
Westbrook Farm
REDACRE CL
VALE CT
MARSH LA
Hall Cottage
Lightwood Farm
Oakbank
79
Union Farm
NORTHWICH RD
Dutton
Woodbank Farm
Bird's Wood
Cheshire Ring Canal Walk
Seven Acre Wood
Hill Farm
1
Dale Farm
HILL TOP RD
Trent and Mersey Canal
Longacre Wood
Hope Farm
WA7
A533
78
57
58
59

76
52

51
26

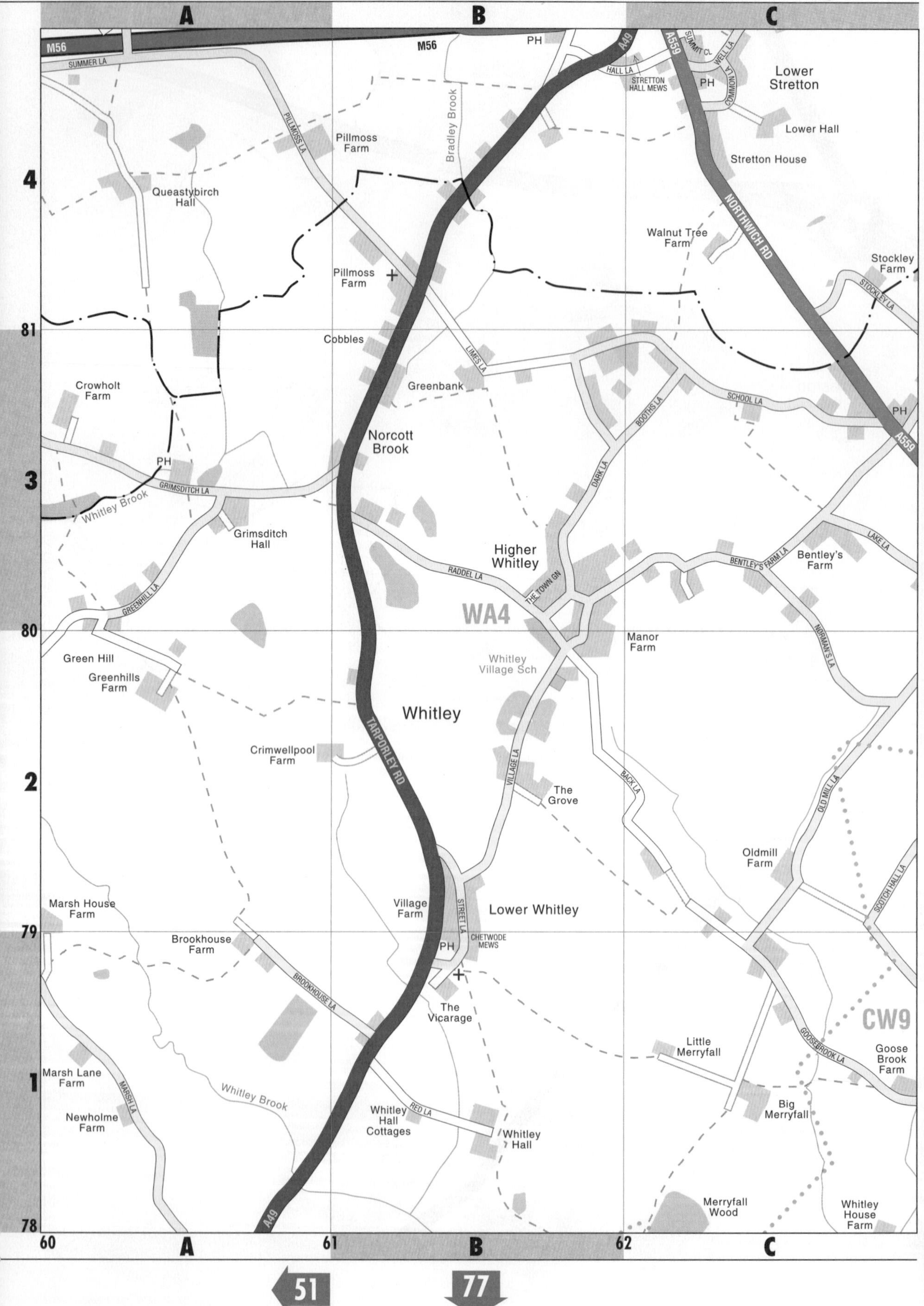
A
B
C
4
81
3
80
2
79
1
78
60
61
62
M56
SUMMER LA
PH
HALL LA
STRETTON HALL MEWS
A559
Lower Stretton
Lower Hall
Stretton House
PILLMOSS LA
Pillmoss Farm
Bradley Brook
A49
Queastybirch Hall
Walnut Tree Farm
NORTHWICH RD
Stockley Farm
STOCKLEY LA
Pillmoss Farm
Cobbles
LIMES LA
Greenbank
Crowholt Farm
SCHOOL LA
BOOTHS LA
Norcott Brook
DARK LA
GRIMSDITCH LA
Whitley Brook
Grimsditch Hall
Higher Whitley
RADDEL LA
THE TOWN GN
BENTLEY'S FARM LA
Bentley's Farm
LAKE LA
GREENHILL LA
WA4
Manor Farm
NORMAN'S LA
Green Hill
Greenhills Farm
Whitley Village Sch
Whitley
TARPORLEY RD
Crimwellpool Farm
VILLAGE LA
The Grove
BACK LA
OLD MILL LA
Oldmill Farm
SCOTCH HALL LA
Marsh House Farm
Village Farm
STREET LA
Lower Whitley
Brookhouse Farm
CHETWODE MEWS
BROOKHOUSE LA
The Vicarage
CW9
Little Merryfall
GOOSEBROOK LA
Goose Brook Farm
Marsh Lane Farm
MARSH LA
Whitley Brook
Newholme Farm
Whitley Hall Cottages
RED LA
Whitley Hall
Big Merryfall
Merryfall Wood
Whitley House Farm

51
77

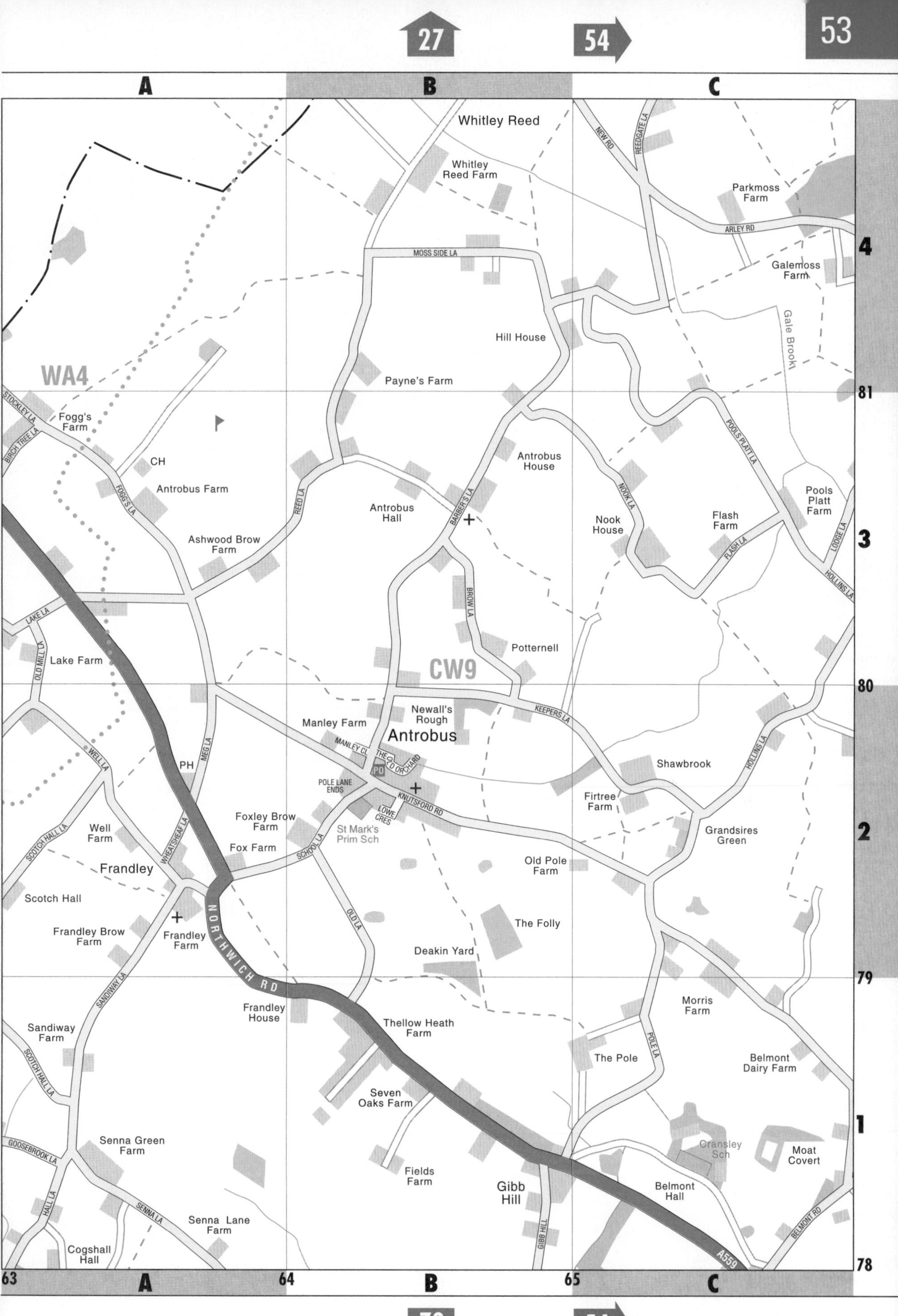

A **B** **C**

4

Whitley Reed

NEW RD

REEDGATE LA

Parkmoss
Farm

ARLEY RD

Whitley
Reed Farm

Galemoss
Farm

MOSS SIDE LA

Gale Brook

81

Hill House

WA4

Payne's Farm

Antrobus
House

Pools Platt LA

STOCKLEY LA

Fogg's
Farm

BIRCH TREE LA

CH

Antrobus Farm

FOGG'S LA

REED LA

BARBER'S LA

Antrobus
Hall

Nook
House

NOOK LA

Flash
Farm

FLASH LA

Pools
Platt
Farm

HOLLINS LA

LOOSE LA

3

Ashwood Brow
Farm

LAKE LA

OLD MILL LA

Lake Farm

BROW LA

Potternell

CW9

Newall's
Rough

KEEPERS LA

80

MEG LA

Manley Farm

Antrobus

HOLLINS LA

PH

WELL LA

MANLEY CL

THE OLD ORCHARD
PO

Shawbrook

SCOTCH HALL LA

Well
Farm

WHEATSHEAF LA

Foxley Brow
Farm

Fox Farm

SCHOOL LA

POLE LANE
ENDS

St Mark's
Prim Sch

LOWE
CRES

KNUTSFORD RD

Firtree
Farm

Grandsires
Green

2

Frandley

Scotch Hall

NORTHWICH RD

OLD LA

Old Pole
Farm

Frandley Brow
Farm

Frandley
Farm

The Folly

POLE LA

Morris
Farm

Deakin Yard

79

SANDIWAY LA

Frandley
House

Thellow Heath
Farm

The Pole

Belmont
Dairy Farm

SCOTCH HALL LA

Sandiway
Farm

Seven
Oaks Farm

1

GOOSEBROOK LA

Senna Green
Farm

Fields
Farm

GIBB HILL

Gibb
Hill

Cransley
Sch

Moat
Covert

Belmont
Hall

BELMONT RD

HALL LA

SENNA LA

Senna Lane
Farm

A559

Cogshall
Hall

78

53
28

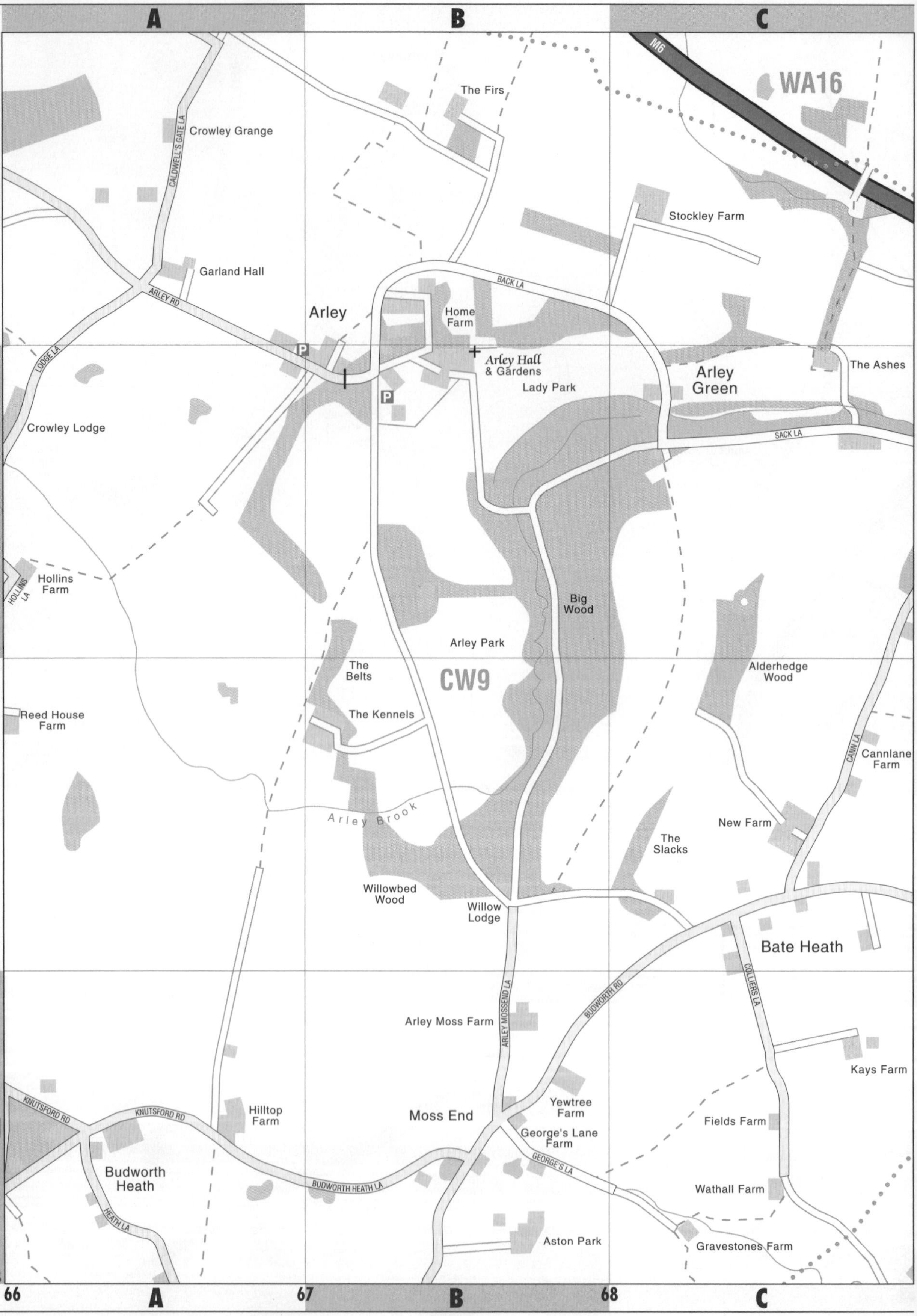

A **B** **C**

WA16

M6

The Firs

Crowley Grange

4

Stockley Farm

Garland Hall

ARLEY RD

CALDWELL'S GATE LA

BACK LA

Arley

Home Farm

P

Arley Hall & Gardens

The Ashes

81

Arley Green

LODGE LA

Crowley Lodge

P

Lady Park

SACK LA

3

HOLLINS LA

Hollins Farm

Big Wood

Arley Park

Alderhedge Wood

80

The Belts

CW9

Reed House Farm

The Kennels

CANAL LA

Cannlane Farm

2

Arley Brook

New Farm

The Slacks

Willowbed Wood

Willow Lodge

Bate Heath

COLLIERS LA

79

Arley Moss Farm

ARLEY MOSSEND LA

BUDWORTH RD

Kays Farm

1

KNUTSFORD RD

KNUTSFORD RD

Hilltop Farm

Moss End

Yewtree Farm

George's Lane Farm

Fields Farm

Budworth Heath

HEATH LA

BUDWORTH HEATH LA

GEORGE'S LA

Wathall Farm

Aston Park

Gravestones Farm

78

66 **A** 67 **B** 68 **C**

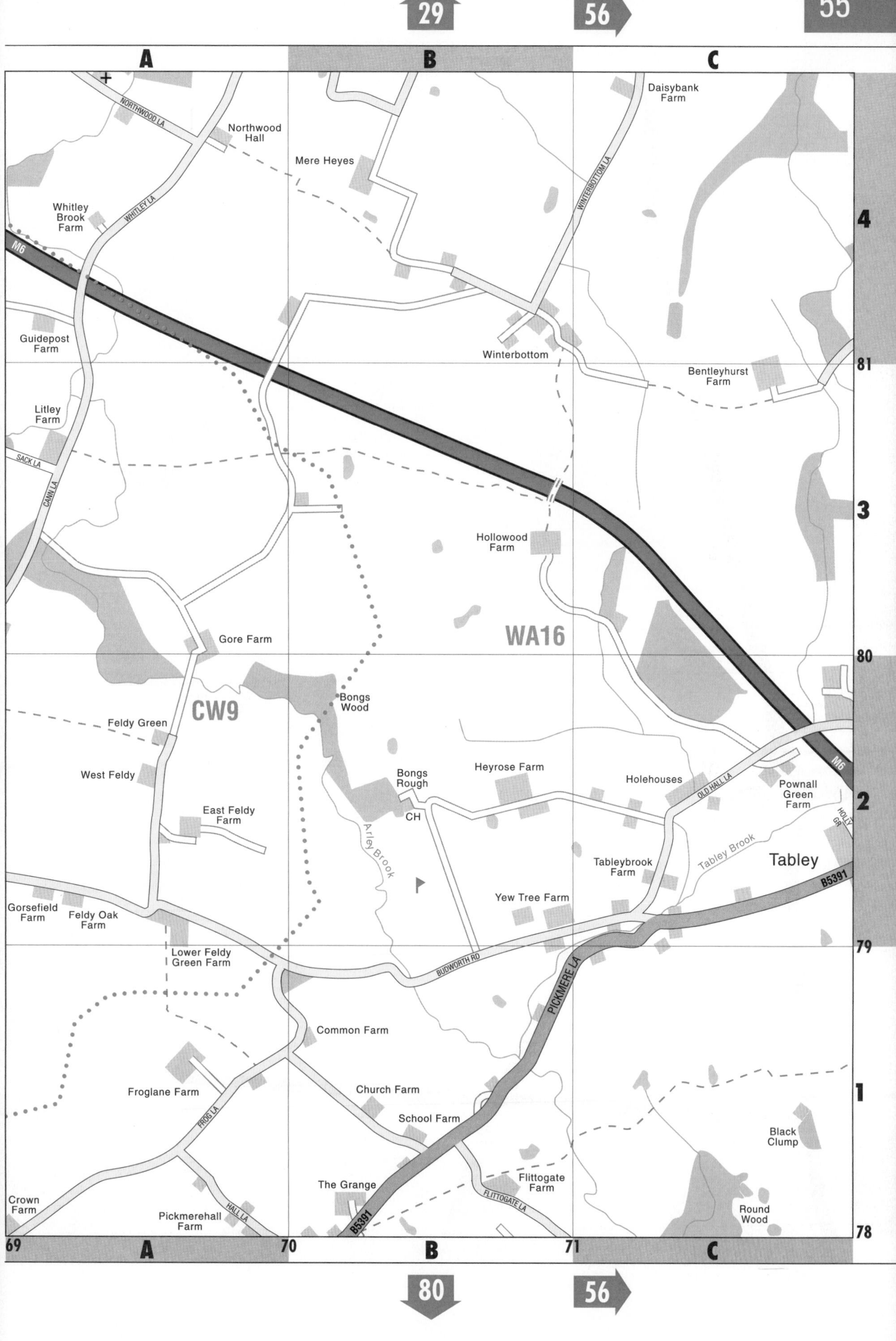

A
B
C

Northwood Hall
Mere Heyes
Daisybank Farm
NORTHWOOD LA
Whitley Brook Farm
WHITLEY LA
M6
Guidepost Farm
Winterbottom
WINTERBOTTOM LA
Bentleyhurst Farm
81
Litley Farm
SACK LA
CANAL LA
4
3
Hollowood Farm
Gore Farm
WA16
80
Bongs Wood
CW9
Feldy Green
West Feldy
Bongs Rough
Heyrose Farm
Holehouses
OLD HALL LA
Pownall Green Farm
M6
East Feldy Farm
CH
Arley Brook
Tabley Brook
Tabley
HOLLY GR
2
Gorsefield Farm
Feldy Oak Farm
Tableybrook Farm
B5391
Lower Feldy Green Farm
BUDWORTH RD
Yew Tree Farm
79
Common Farm
PICKMERE LA
Froglane Farm
Church Farm
Black Clump
1
FROG LA
School Farm
Crown Farm
The Grange
Flittogate Farm
FLITTOGATE LA
Round Wood
78
Pickmerehall Farm
HALL LA
B5391

69
A
70
B
71
C

55
30

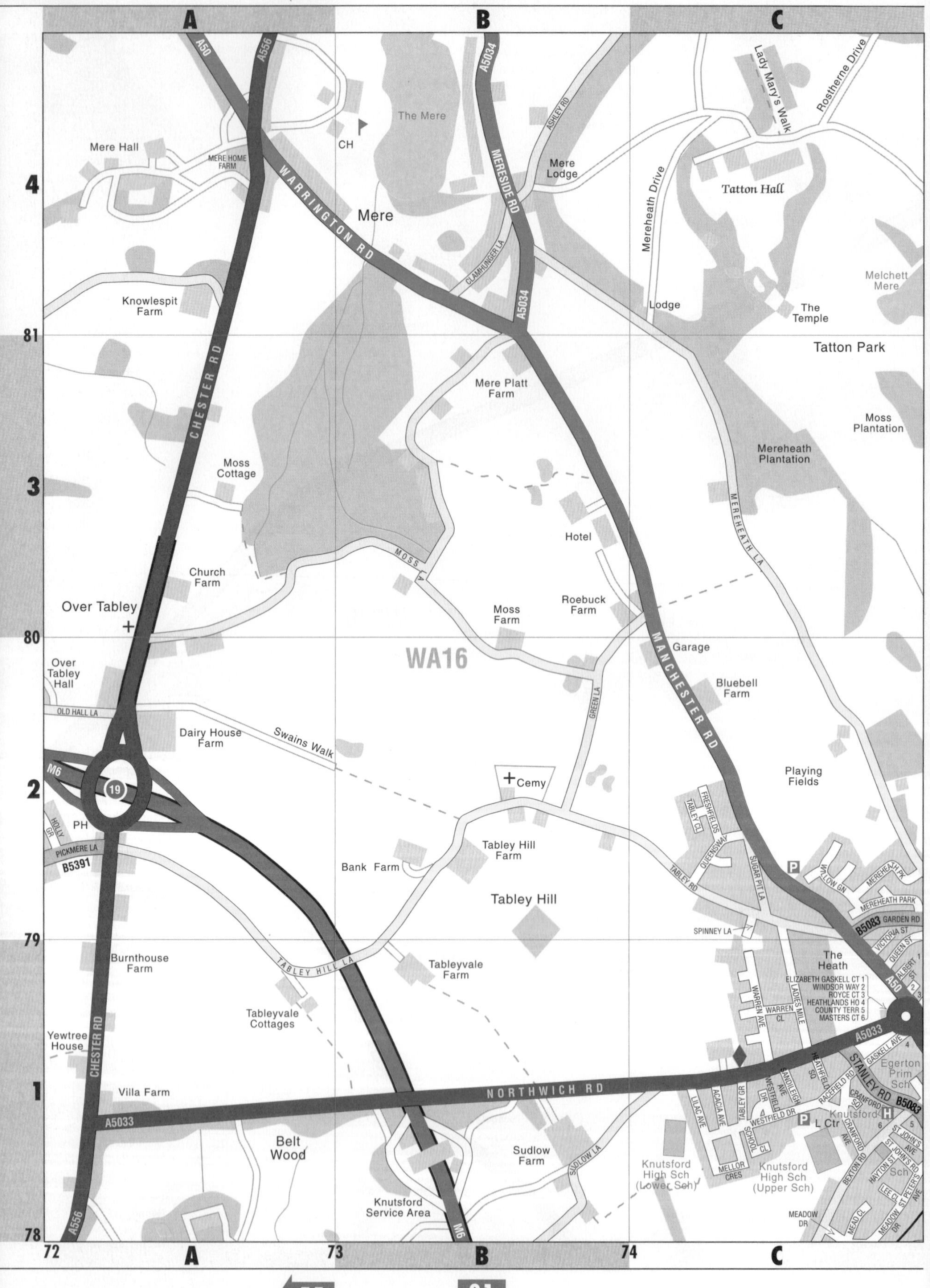
A
B
C
4
81
3
80
2
79
1
78
72
73
74
Mere Hall
MERE HOME FARM
CH
The Mere
WARRINGTON RD
Mere
MERESIDE RD
ASHLEY RD
Mere Lodge
Lady Mary's Walk
Rostherne Drive
Tatton Hall
Mereheath Drive
Knowlespit Farm
CLAMHUNGER LA
A5034
Lodge
The Temple
Melchett Mere
Tatton Park
CHESTER RD
Mere Platt Farm
Moss Plantation
Mereheath Plantation
Moss Cottage
MEREHEATH LA
Hotel
MOSS LA
Church Farm
Over Tabley
Roebuck Farm
Moss Farm
WA16
MANCHESTER RD
Garage
Over Tabley Hall
Bluebell Farm
OLD HALL LA
GREEN LA
Dairy House Farm
Swains Walk
M6
19
Cemy
Playing Fields
PH
HOLLY GR
PICKMERE LA
B5391
FRESHFIELDS
TABLEY CL
QUEENSWAY
SUGAR PIT LA
TABLEY RD
Tabley Hill Farm
Bank Farm
Tabley Hill
WILLOW GN
MEREHEATH PK
MEREHEATH PARK
B5083
GARDEN RD
VICTORIA ST
QUEEN ST
SPINNEY LA
The Heath
Burnthouse Farm
TABLEY HILL LA
Tableyvale Farm
ELIZABETH GASKELL CT 1
WINDSOR WAY 2
ROYCE CT 3
HEATHLANDS HO 4
COUNTY TERR 5
MASTERS CT 6
WARREN AVE
WARREN CL
LADIES MILE
Tableyvale Cottages
Yewtree House
A5033
GASKELL AVE
Egerton Prim Sch
STANLEY RD
NORTHWICH RD
Villa Farm
LILAC AVE
ACACIA AVE
TABLEY GR
WESTFIELD DR
SANDILEIGH AVE
HEATHFIELD SQ
RACEFIELD RD
CRANFORD SQ
Knutsford
L Ctr
SCHOOL CL
CRANFORD AVE
ST JOHN'S AVE
ST JOHN'S RD
Belt Wood
Sudlow Farm
SUDLOW LA
Knutsford High Sch (Lower Sch)
MELLOR CRES
Knutsford High Sch (Upper Sch)
BEXTON RD
HAYTON ST
LEE CL
ST PETER'S AVE
MEADOW DR
MEAD CL
Knutsford Service Area
A556
A50

55
81

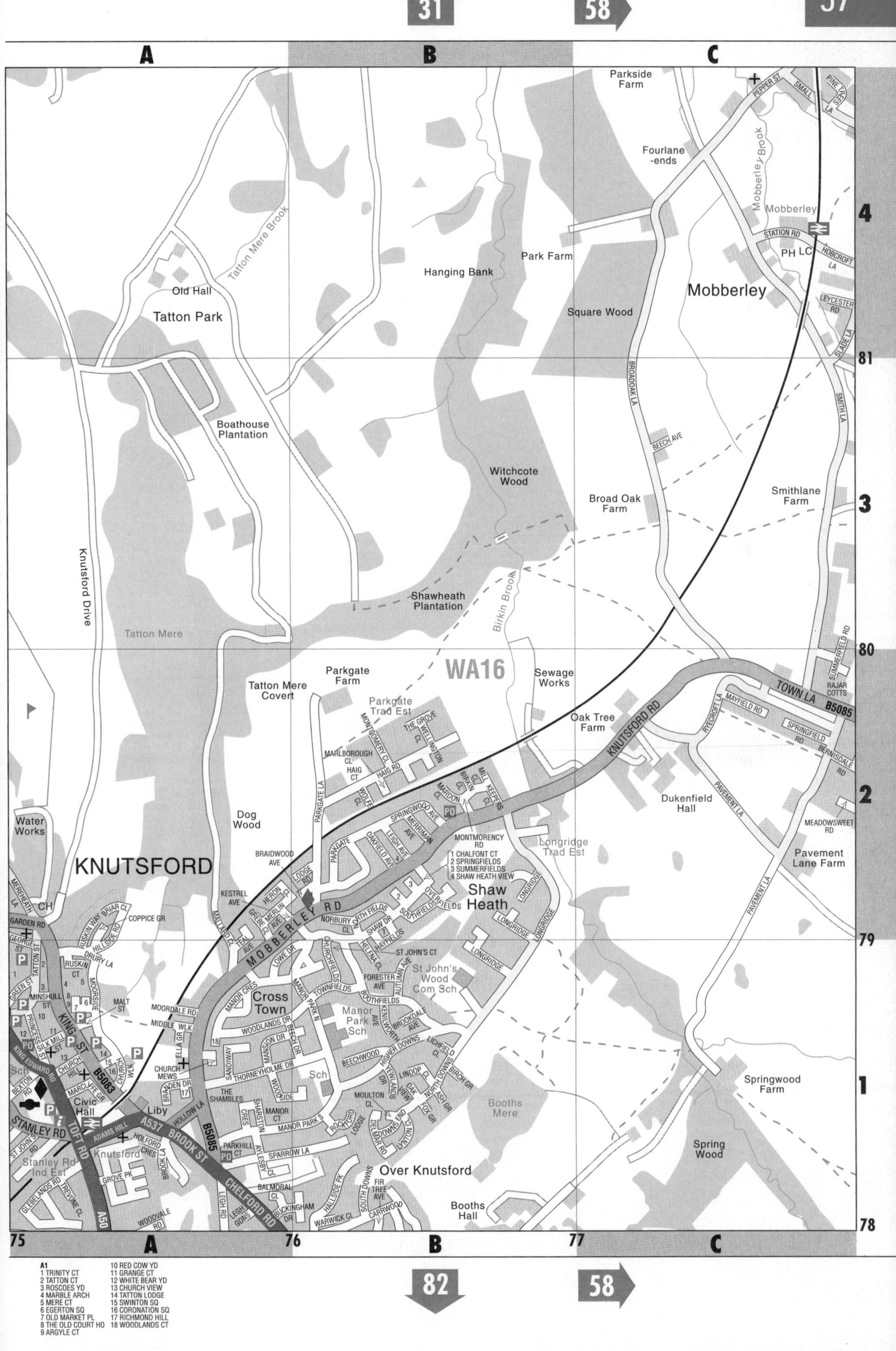
31
58
A
B
C
Parkside Farm
Fourlane -ends
Mobberley Brook
Mobberley
STATION RD
PH
LC
HOBCROFT LA
PEPPER ST
SMALL LA
PINE TREE CL
LEYCESTER RD
SLADE LA
SMITH LA
Mobberley
Park Farm
Hanging Bank
Square Wood
Tatton Mere Brook
Old Hall
Tatton Park
Boathouse Plantation
BROADOAK LA
BEECH AVE
Witchcote Wood
Broad Oak Farm
Smithlane Farm
Knutsford Drive
Shawheath Plantation
Birkin Brook
Tatton Mere
WA16
Parkgate Farm
Tatton Mere Covert
Sewage Works
Parkgate Trad Est
TOWN LA
B5085
SUMMERFIELD RD
RAJAR COTTS
Oak Tree Farm
KNUTSFORD RD
MAYFIELD RD
RYECROFT LA
SPRINGFIELD RD
BERNISDALE RD
MONTGOMERY CL
THE GROVE
WELLINGTON CL
MARLBOROUGH CL
HAIG CT
HAIG RD
WOLFE CL
PARKGATE LA
MILL CT
KEEPERS CL
BIRKIN CL
MARDON CL
PO
Dukenfield Hall
PAVEMENT LA
MEADOWSWEET RD
Water Works
Dog Wood
SPRINGWOOD AVE
MERRIMAN AVE
LEIGH AVE
OAKFIELD AVE
PARKGATE
MONTMORENCY RD
1 CHALFONT CT
2 SPRINGFIELDS
3 SUMMERFIELDS
4 SHAW HEATH VIEW
Longridge Trad Est
Pavement Lane Farm
BRAIDWOOD AVE
KNUTSFORD
LODGE RD
KESTREL AVE
HERON CL
MERLIN CL
GREBE CL
TEAL AVE
MALLARD CL
MOBBERLEY RD
NORBURY CL
NORTH FIELDS
SHAW DR
HAYFIELDS
OVERFIELDS
SOUTHFIELDS
Shaw Heath
LONGRIDGE
MEREHEATH LA
CH
GARDEN RD
RUSKIN WAY
BRIAR CL
COPPICE GR
HILLSIDE RD
DRURY LA
GEORGE ST
TATTON ST
RUSKIN CT
GREEN ST
MINSHULL ST
MOORSIDE
MALT ST
ST JOHN'S CT
LOWE DR
CHURCHFIELDS
HELENA CL
AUTUMN AVE
FORESTER AVE
St John's Wood Com Sch
MANOR CRES
Cross Town
TOWNFIELDS
MANOR PARK N
BOOTHFIELDS
Manor Park Sch
KENILWORTH AVE
BROOKDALE AVE
MOORDALE RD
MIDDLE WLK
WOODLANDS DR
BEECH DR
PRINCESS ST
SILK MILL ST
KING ST
CHURCH WLK
ELLA GR
CHURCH MEWS
SANDIWAY
MANSION DR
THORNEYHOLME DR
WOODSIDE
BEECHWOOD
HIGHER DOWNS
LICHFIELD CL
Sch
LINDOP CL
OAK VIEW
NORTH DOWNS
BIRCH GR
KING EDWARD RD
BEXTON RD
CHURCH HILL
MARCLIFFE GR
B5083
Civic Hall
BRADDEN DR
THE SHAMBLES
SHARSTON CRES
MANOR CT
MOULTON CL
Booths Mere
Springwood Farm
STANLEY RD
TOFT RD
ADAMS HILL
Liby
HOLLOW LA
A537
BROOK ST
B5085
MANOR PARK S
ROCKFORD LODGE
DELMAR RD
DOWNS END
FOX GR
ASH GR
ST JOHN'S RD
HOLFORD CRES
Knutsford
PARKHILL CT
AYLESBY CL
SPARROW LA
Spring Wood
Stanley Rd Ind Est
GROVE PK
BROOK LA
CHELFORD RD
Over Knutsford
GLEBELANDS RD
TREVONE CL
A50
WOODVALE RD
LEGH RD
LEGH GDNS
BALMORAL CL
BUCKINGHAM DR
HALLSIDE PK
SOUTH DOWNS
FIR TREE AVE
CARRWOOD
WARWICK CL
Booths Hall
4
81
3
80
2
79
1
78
75
76
77
82
58
A1
1 TRINITY CT
2 TATTON CT
3 ROSCOES YD
4 MARBLE ARCH
5 MERE CT
6 EGERTON SQ
7 OLD MARKET PL
8 THE OLD COURT HO
9 ARGYLE CT
10 RED COW YD
11 GRANGE CT
12 WHITE BEAR YD
13 CHURCH VIEW
14 TATTON LODGE
15 SWINTON SQ
16 CORONATION SQ
17 RICHMOND HILL
18 WOODLANDS CT

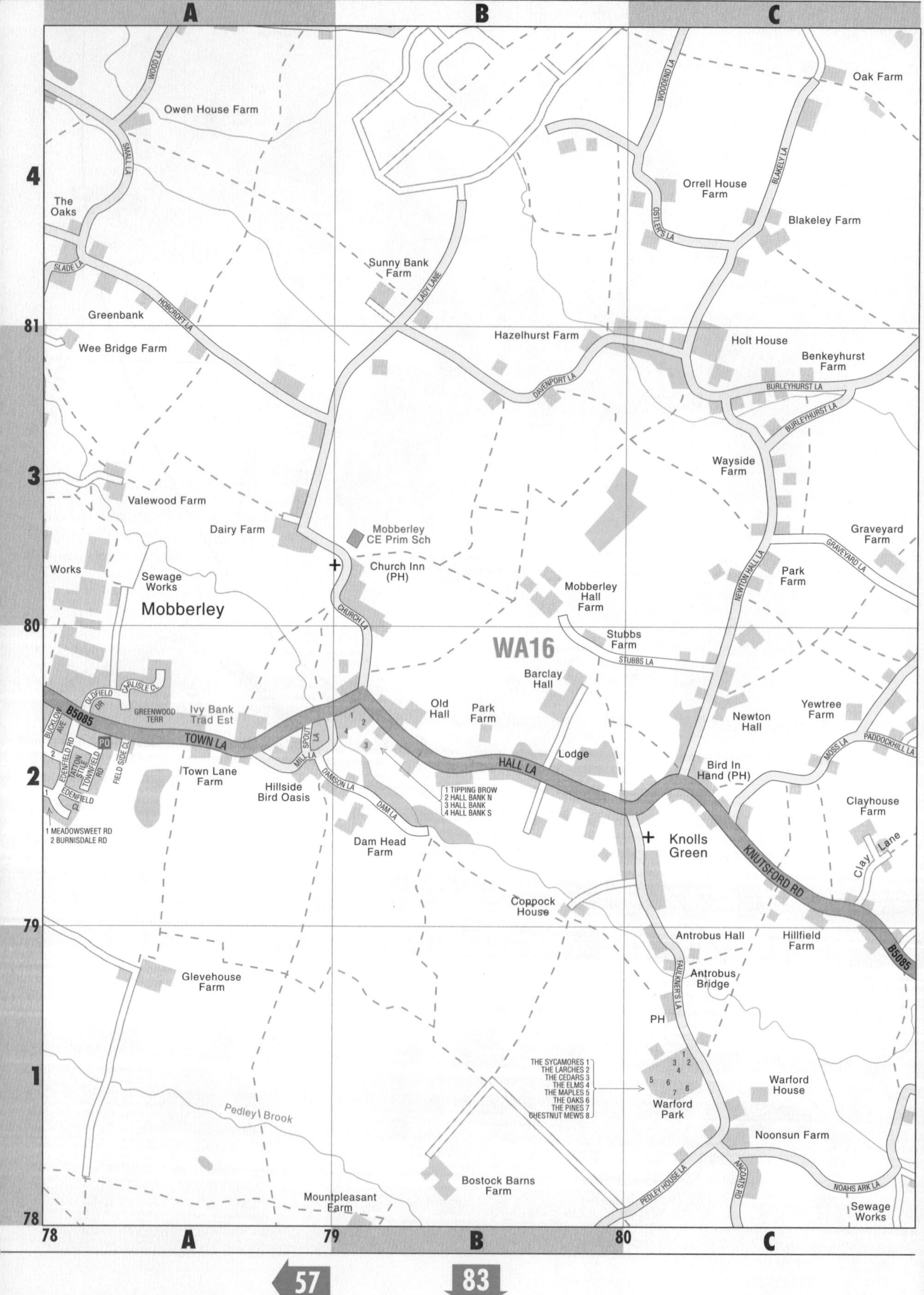
57
32
A
B
C
4
3
2
1
81
80
79
78
Owen House Farm
The Oaks
Greenbank
Wee Bridge Farm
Valewood Farm
Dairy Farm
Works
Sewage Works
Mobberley
Sunny Bank Farm
Mobberley CE Prim Sch
Church Inn (PH)
Hazelhurst Farm
Orrell House Farm
Oak Farm
Blakeley Farm
Holt House
Benkeyhurst Farm
Wayside Farm
Graveyard Farm
Park Farm
Mobberley Hall Farm
Stubbs Farm
WA16
Barclay Hall
Old Hall
Park Farm
Ivy Bank Trad Est
Town Lane Farm
Hillside Bird Oasis
Dam Head Farm
Lodge
Newton Hall
Yewtree Farm
Bird In Hand (PH)
Clayhouse Farm
Knolls Green
Coppock House
Antrobus Hall
Hillfield Farm
Antrobus Bridge
PH
Glevehouse Farm
Warford Park
Warford House
Noonsun Farm
Bostock Barns Farm
Mountpleasant Farm
Sewage Works
Pedley Brook
WOOD LA
SMALL LA
SLADE LA
HOBCROFT LA
LADY LANE
DAVENPORT LA
WOODEND LA
OSTLER'S LA
BLAKELY LA
BURLEYHURST LA
GRAVEYARD LA
NEWTON HALL LA
STUBBS LA
CHURCH LA
B5085
TOWN LA
HALL LA
KNUTSFORD RD
MOSS LA
PADDOCKHILL LA
Clay Lane
FAULKNER'S LA
PEDLEY HOUSE LA
ANCOATS RD
NOAHS ARK LA
OLDFIELD DR
CARLISLE CL
GREENWOOD TERR
BUCKLOW AVE
EDENFIELD RD
TATTON STILE
TOWNFIELD RD
FIELD SIDE CL
EDENFIELD CL
SPOUT LA
MILL LA
DAMSON LA
DAM LA
PO
1 MEADOWSWEET RD
2 BURNISDALE RD
1 TIPPING BROW
2 HALL BANK N
3 HALL BANK
4 HALL BANK S
THE SYCAMORES 1
THE LARCHES 2
THE CEDARS 3
THE ELMS 4
THE MAPLES 5
THE OAKS 6
THE PINES 7
CHESTNUT MEWS 8
78
79
80
57
83

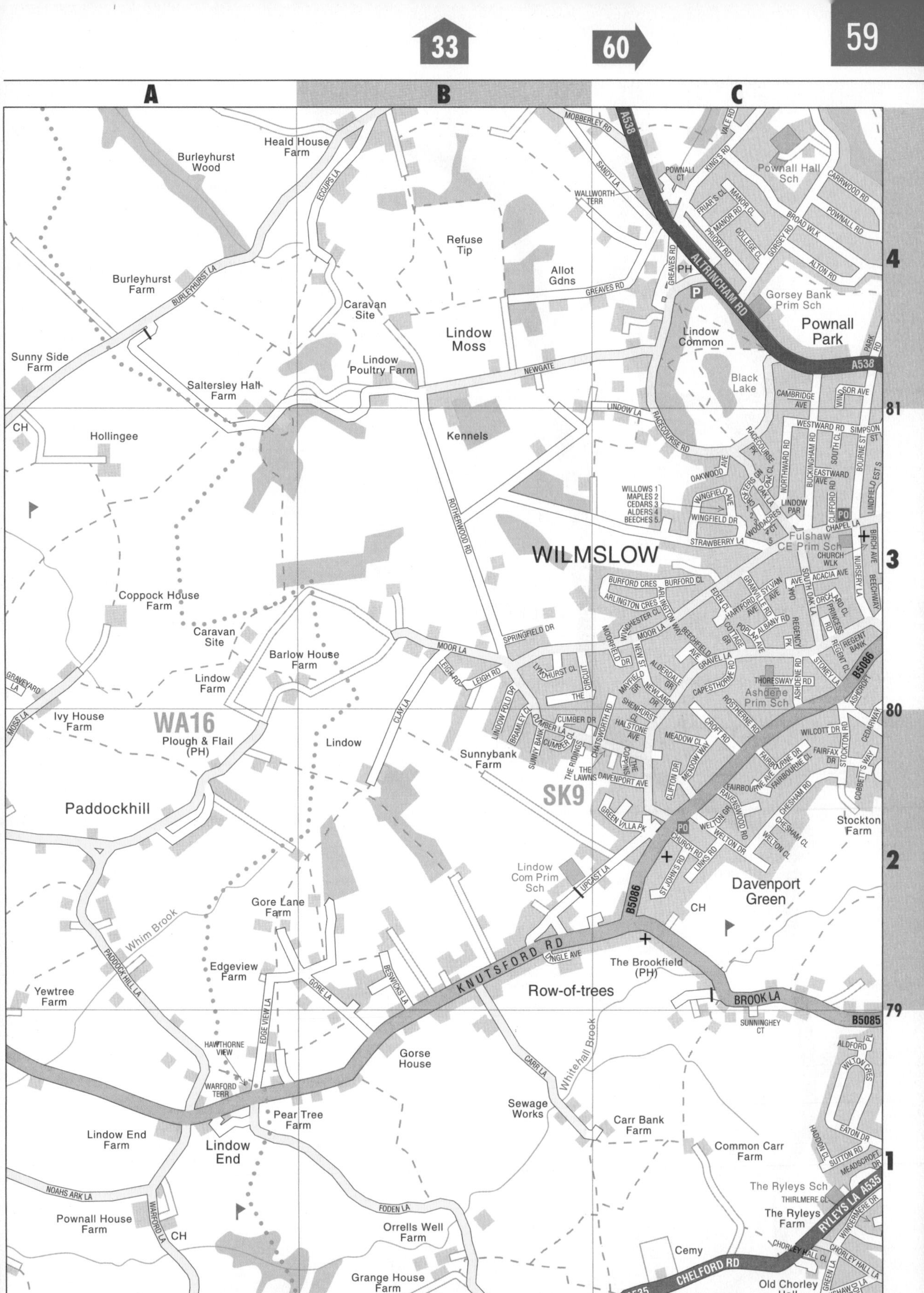
A
B
C
4
81
3
80
2
79
1
78
81
82
83
Heald House Farm
Burleyhurst Wood
Burleyhurst Farm
BURLEYHURST LA
ECCUPS LA
Refuse Tip
Allot Gdns
Caravan Site
Lindow Moss
Lindow Poultry Farm
Sunny Side Farm
Saltersley Hall Farm
NEWGATE
GREAVES RD
MOBBERLEY RD
SANDY LA
WALLWORTH TERR
A538
POWNALL CT
VALE RD
KING'S RD
Pownall Hall Sch
CARRWOOD RD
FRIAR'S CL
MANOR CL
MANOR RD
PRIORY RD
COLLEGE CL
GORSEY RD
BROAD WLK
POWNALL RD
ALTON RD
ALTRINCHAM RD
PH
P
Gorsey Bank Prim Sch
Pownall Park
Lindow Common
Black Lake
CAMBRIDGE AVE
WINDSOR AVE
PARK RD
CH
Hollingee
Kennels
LINDOW LA
RACECOURSE RD
RACECOURSE PK
WESTWARD RD
SIMPSON ST
OAKWOOD AVE
NORTHWARD RD
BUCKINGHAM RD
SOUTH CL
BOURNE ST
LINDFIELD EST S
EASTWARD AVE
CLIFFORD RD
LINDOW PAR
WILLOWS 1
MAPLES 2
CEDARS 3
ALDERS 4
BEECHES 5
WINGFIELD AVE
WINGFIELD DR
WOODACRES CT
PO
CHAPEL LA
STRAWBERRY LA
Fulshaw CE Prim Sch
CHURCH WLK
BIRCH AVE
ROTHERWOOD RD
WILMSLOW
BURFORD CRES
BURFORD CL
ARLINGTON CRES
ARLINGTON WAY
WINCHESTER CL
EDEN CL
HARTFORD AVE
SYLVAN AVE
OAK AVE
SOUTH OAK LA
ACACIA AVE
NURSERY LA
BEECHWAY
Coppock House Farm
Caravan Site
Barlow House Farm
Lindow Farm
MOOR LA
SPRINGFIELD DR
MOORFIELD DR
NEW ST
BEECHFIELD AVE
COTTAGE GR
POPLAR AVE
ALBANY RD
REGENCY PK
PRINCESS RD
REGENT CL
REGENT BANK
STONEY LA
B5086
GRAVEYARD LA
LEIGH RD
LYNDHURST CL
THE CIRCUIT
ALDERDALE GR
GRAVEL LA
MAYFIELD GR
NEWLANDS DR
CAPESTHORNE RD
THORESWAY RD
ASHDENE RD
Ashdene Prim Sch
ASHCROFT
CEDARWAY
MOSS LA
Ivy House Farm
WA16
Plough & Flail (PH)
Lindow
CLAY LA
LINDOW FOLD DR
BRAMLEY CL
CUMBER DR
CUMBER LA
CUMBER CL
SUNNY BANK
THE RIDINGS
THE LAWNS
CHATSWORTH RD
SHENHURST CL
HALSTONE AVE
THE COPPINS
MEADOW CL
MEADOW WAY
CROFT RD
ROSTHERNE RD
WILCOTT DR
FAIRFAX DR
STOCKTON RD
COBBETT'S WAY
Sunnybank Farm
DAVENPORT AVE
CLIFTON DR
FAIRBOURNE AVE
FAIRBOURNE DR
FAIRBOURNE CL
RAVENSWOOD RD
CHESHAM RD
SK9
Paddockhill
GREEN VILLA PK
WELTON GR
WELTON DR
CHESHAM CL
WELTON CL
CHURCH RD
LINKS RD
ST JOHN'S RD
Stockton Farm
Lindow Com Prim Sch
UPCAST LA
Davenport Green
Gore Lane Farm
Whim Brook
PADDOCK HILL LA
Edgeview Farm
KNUTSFORD RD
DINGLE AVE
The Brookfield (PH)
BESWICKS LA
GORE LA
Row-of-trees
BROOK LA
B5085
SUNNINGHEY CT
Yewtree Farm
EDGE VIEW LA
HAWTHORNE VIEW
WARFORD TERR
Gorse House
Whitehall Brook
CARR LA
Sewage Works
ALDFORD PL
WILTON CRES
Pear Tree Farm
Lindow End Farm
Lindow End
Carr Bank Farm
Common Carr Farm
EATON DR
HADDON CL
SUTTON RD
MEADSCROFT DR
NOAHS ARK LA
WARFORD LA
The Ryleys Sch
THIRLMERE CL
The Ryleys Farm
RYLEYS LA
A535
WINDERMERE DR
Pownall House Farm
FODEN LA
Orrells Well Farm
Cemy
CHORLEY HALL CL
CHORLEY HALL LA
CHELFORD RD
GREEN LA
Grange House Farm
Old Chorley Hall
BLACKSHAW LA
DOWNSWAY

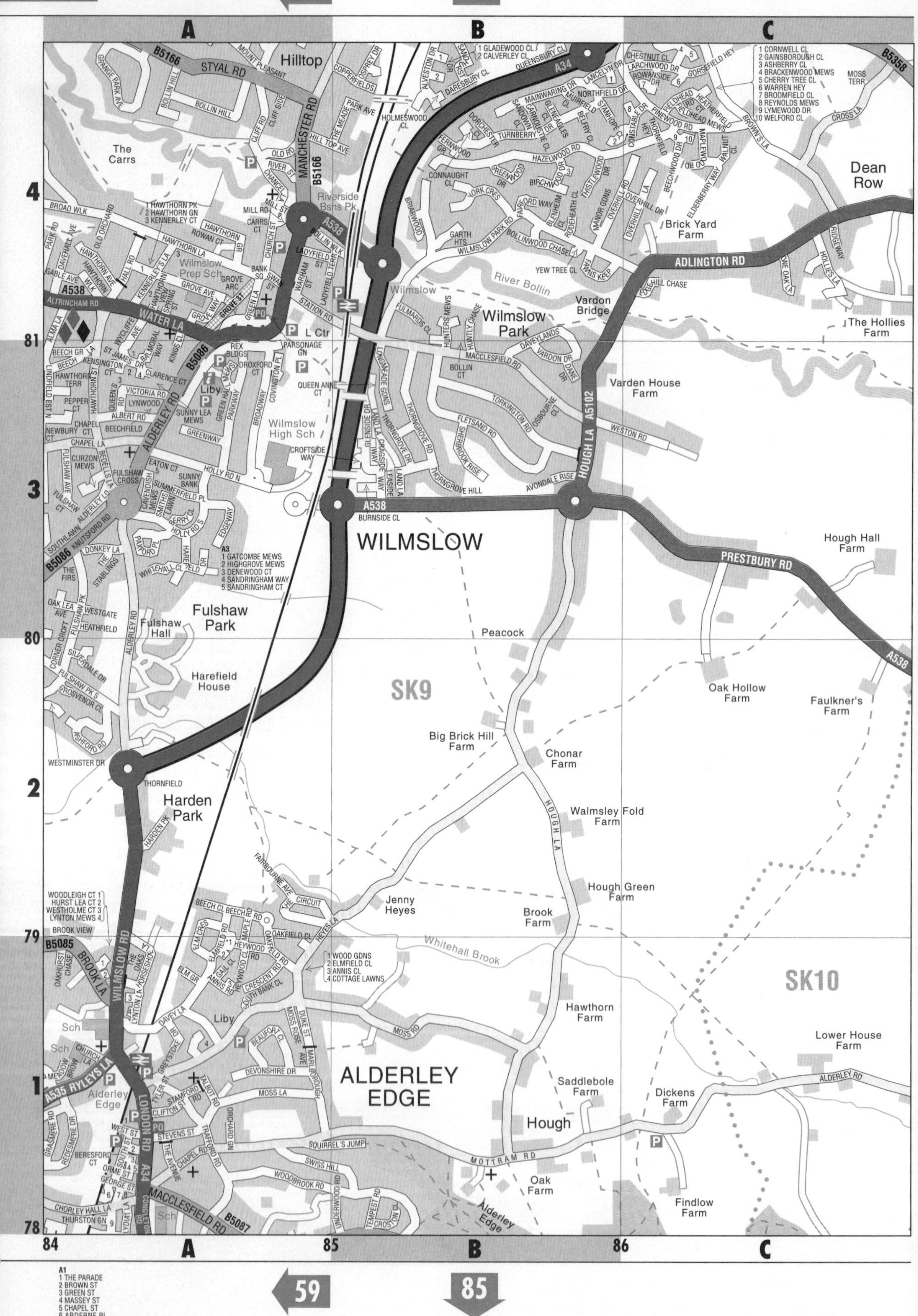

A B C

Hotel
WILMSLOW RD
A5102
DEAN ROW RD B5358
Upton House
WOODFORD RD
+
A5102
Unicorn (PH)
B5358
OLD HALL LA
Old Hall Farm
Woodford Aerodrome
SK7
River Dean
New Hall Farm
Works
Dairyhouse Wood
4
Nurseries
Hollies Farm
Vicar Farm
SK9
LEES LA
Pitlane Farm
Lumb Farm
WOODFORD LA
Florence Farm
Bent Farm
81
Newton Hall Farm
WILMSLOW RD
Garage
Dandy Farm
MILL LA
Parkwood House
Carr House
3
Boundary Farm
Mottram Bridge
Willot Hall
Woodside Farm
Mill Lane Farm
MILL LA
Collins Wood
Dean Farm
80
Ivy Cottage
SK10
River Bollin
Brook House Farm
Top o' th' Hill
BONIS HALL LA
CH
2
Mottram Hall Hotel
WILMSLOW RD
Brook Cottage
Mottram Park House
Parkside Farm
Mottram Wood
Mottram Old Hall
79
B5358
Mottram St Andrew Stud Farm
WILMSLOW OLD RD
BLACKHURST BROW
Higher Yewards Farm
SMITHY LA
Woodside Farm
Mottram St Andrew
RUSHTON FOLD
Kirkleyditch Farm
MOSS LA
THE CRESCENT
PO
Mottram Cross (restored)
1
BUTLEY LANES
ALDERLEY RD
+
PRIEST LA
Mottram St Andrew Prim Sch
PH
Sewage Works
Brook House Farm
OAK RD
WILMSLOW RD
Legh Hall
A538
78

87 A 88 B 89 C

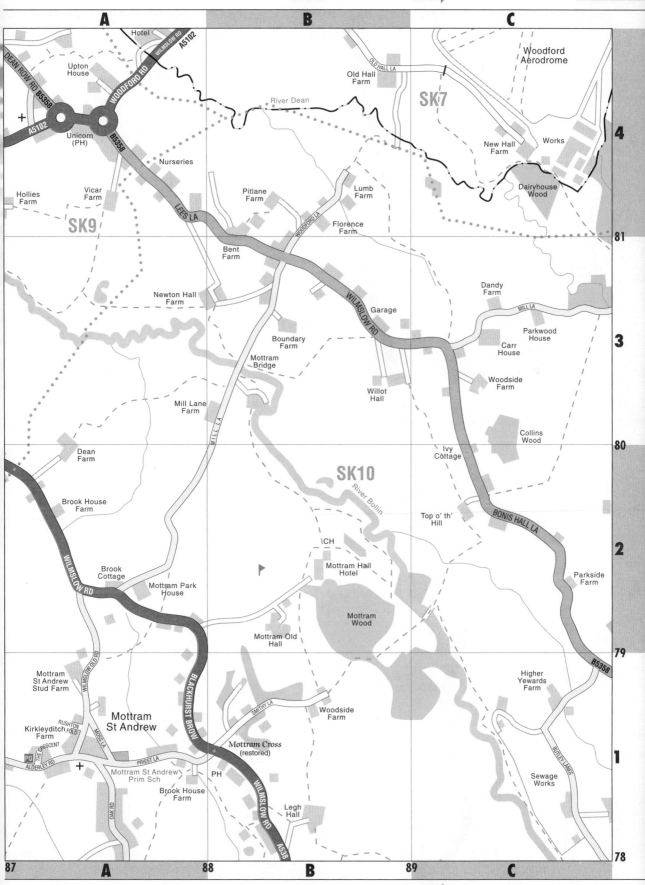

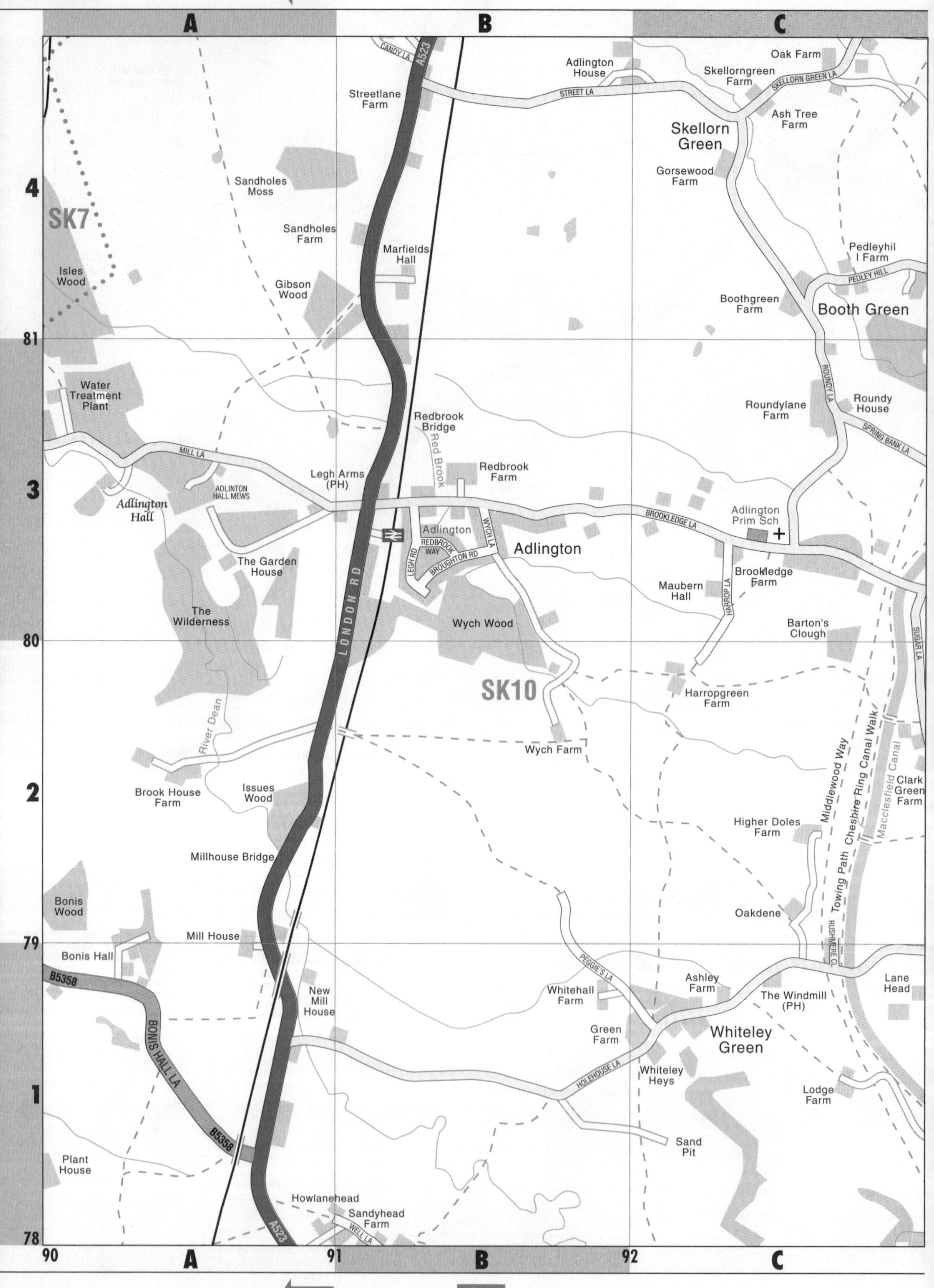

A   **B**   **C**

CANDY LA

A523

Adlington
House

Streetlane
Farm

STREET LA

Oak Farm

Skellorngreen
Farm

SKELLORN GREEN LA

Ash Tree
Farm

**Skellorn
Green**

Sandholes
Moss

4

SK7

Isles
Wood

Sandholes
Farm

Gibson
Wood

Marfields
Hall

Gorsewood
Farm

Pedleyhil
l Farm

PEDLEY HILL

Boothgreen
Farm

Booth Green

81

Water
Treatment
Plant

MILL LA

Redbrook
Bridge

Red Brook

Roundylane
Farm

ROUNDY LA

Roundy
House

SPRING BANK LA

Legh Arms
(PH)

Redbrook
Farm

BROOKLEDGE LA

Adlington
Prim Sch

3

*Adlington
Hall*

ADLINTON
HALL MEWS

LONDON RD

LEGH RD

REDBROOK
WAY

BROUGHTON RD

WYCH LA

Adlington

Maubern
Hall

HARROP LA

Brookledge
Farm

SUGAR LA

The Garden
House

*The
Wilderness*

Wych Wood

Barton's
Clough

80

River Dean

SK10

Wych Farm

Harropgreen
Farm

Middlewood Way

Cheshire Ring Canal Walk

Macclesfield Canal

Clark
Green
Farm

2

Brook House
Farm

Issues
Wood

Higher Doles
Farm

Towing Path

Bonis
Wood

Mill House

Oakdene

RUSHMERE CL

79

Bonis Hall

B5358

BONIS HALL LA

New Mill
House

PEGGIE'S LA

Whitehall
Farm

Ashley
Farm

The Windmill
(PH)

Lane
Head

B5358

Green
Farm

HOLEHOUSE LA

Whiteley
Heys

**Whiteley
Green**

Lodge
Farm

1

Plant
House

Sand
Pit

A523

Howlanehead

Sandyhead
Farm

WELL LA

78

90   **A**   **91**   **B**   **92**   **C**

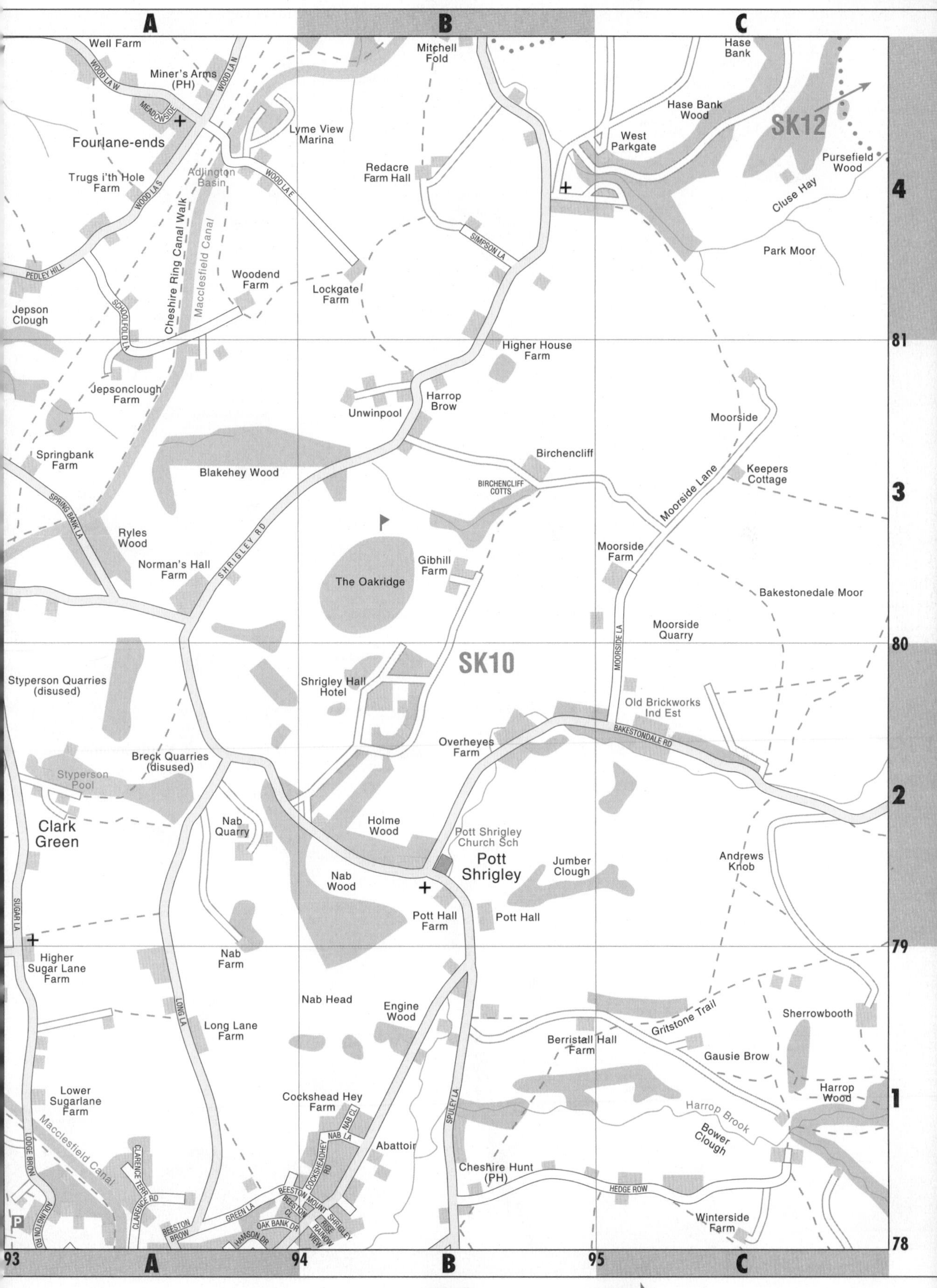
A
B
C
Well Farm
Miner's Arms (PH)
Fourlane-ends
Trugs i'th Hole Farm
Adlington Basin
Lyme View Marina
Mitchell Fold
Redacre Farm Hall
Hase Bank
Hase Bank Wood
West Parkgate
SK12
Pursefield Wood
Cluse Hay
Park Moor
Cheshire Ring Canal Walk
Macclesfield Canal
Woodend Farm
Lockgate Farm
Jepson Clough
Higher House Farm
Jepsonclough Farm
Harrop Brow
Unwinpool
Moorside
Springbank Farm
Blakehey Wood
Birchencliff
BIRCHENCLIFF COTTS
Keepers Cottage
Moorside Lane
Ryles Wood
Norman's Hall Farm
Gibhill Farm
The Oakridge
Moorside Farm
Bakestonedale Moor
Moorside Quarry
SK10
Styperson Quarries (disused)
Shrigley Hall Hotel
Old Brickworks Ind Est
Overheyes Farm
Breck Quarries (disused)
Styperson Pool
Clark Green
Nab Quarry
Holme Wood
Pott Shrigley Church Sch
Pott Shrigley
Jumber Clough
Andrews Knob
Nab Wood
Pott Hall Farm
Pott Hall
Higher Sugar Lane Farm
Nab Farm
Nab Head
Engine Wood
Long Lane Farm
Berristall Hall Farm
Gritstone Trail
Sherrowbooth
Gausie Brow
Harrop Wood
Lower Sugarlane Farm
Cockshead Hey Farm
Harrop Brook
Bower Clough
Abattoir
Cheshire Hunt (PH)
Winterside Farm
WOOD LA W
MEADOWSIDE
WOOD LA N
WOOD LA E
WOOD LA S
PEDLEY HILL
SCHOOLFOLD LA
SIMPSON LA
SPRING BANK LA
SHRIGLEY RD
MOORSIDE LA
BAKESTONDALE RD
SUGAR LA
LONG LA
SPULEY LA
HEDGE ROW
LODGE BROW
ADLINGTON RD
CLARENCE TERR
CLARENCE RD
BEESTON BROW
GREEN LA
HAMSON DR
OAK BANK DR
BEESTON CL
BEESTON MOUNT
COCKSHEADHEY RD
NAB CL
NAB LA
SHRIGLEY RISE
RAINOW VIEW
4
81
3
80
2
79
1
78
93
94
95

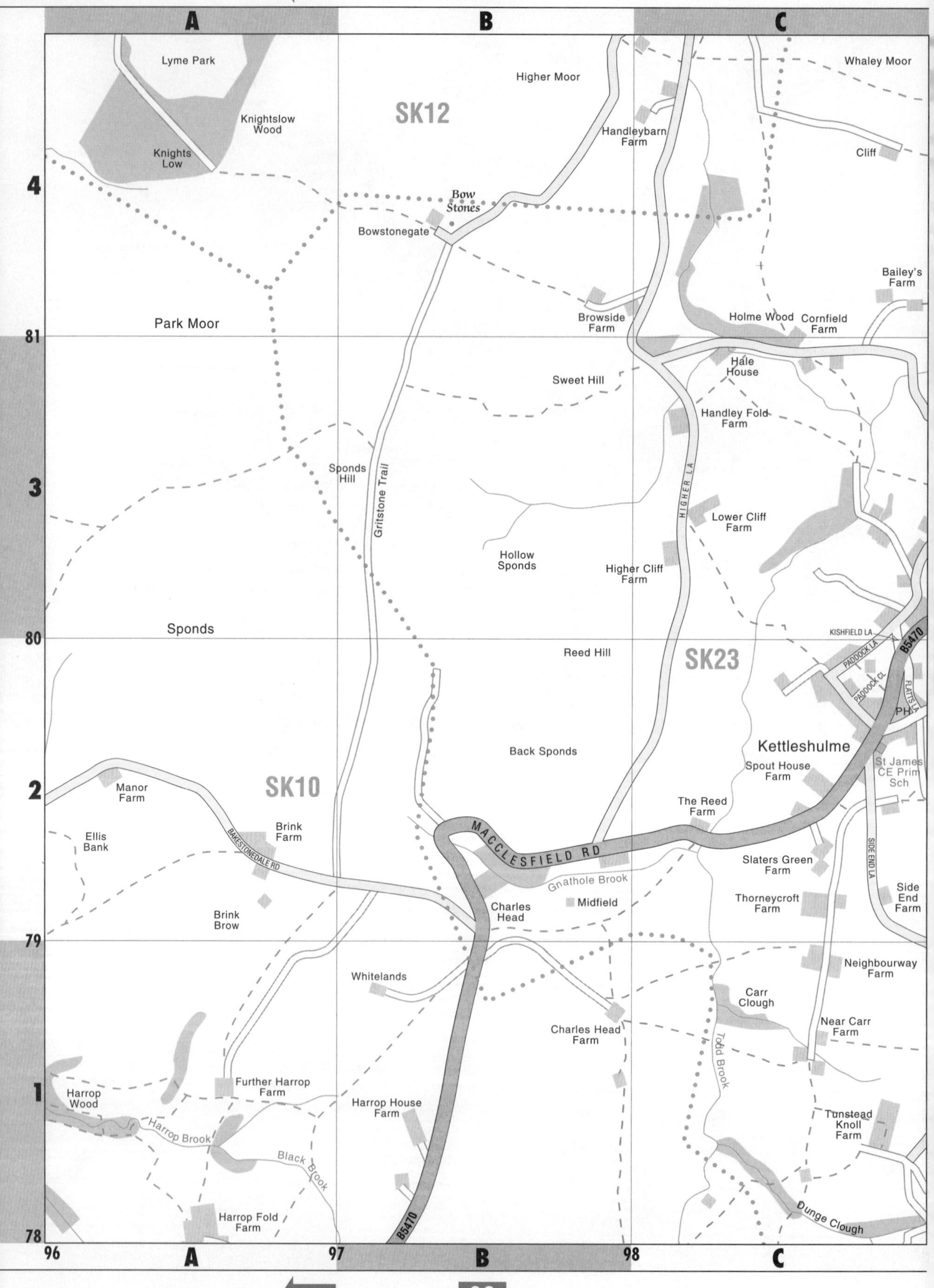

A   B   C

Lyme Park

Knightslow
Wood

Knights
Low

SK12

Higher Moor

Whaley Moor

Handleybarn
Farm

Cliff

Bow
Stones

4

Bowstonegate

Bailey's
Farm

Park Moor

Browside
Farm

Holme Wood

Cornfield
Farm

81

Sweet Hill

Hale
House

Handley Fold
Farm

Sponds
Hill

Gritstone Trail

HIGHER LA

Lower Cliff
Farm

3

Hollow
Sponds

Higher Cliff
Farm

80

Sponds

Reed Hill

SK23

KISHFIELD LA

B5470

PADDOCK LA

PADDOCK CL

FLATS LA

Back Sponds

Kettleshulme

PH

St James
CE Prim
Sch

Spout House
Farm

2

Manor
Farm

SK10

Brink
Farm

The Reed
Farm

Slaters Green
Farm

Ellis
Bank

BAKESTONEDALE RD

MACCLESFIELD RD

Thorneycroft
Farm

Side
End
Farm

SIDE END LA

Gnathole Brook

Brink
Brow

Charles
Head

Midfield

79

Whitelands

Neighbourway
Farm

Charles Head
Farm

Carr
Clough

Near Carr
Farm

Todd Brook

Harrop
Wood

Further Harrop
Farm

Harrop House
Farm

1

Harrop Brook

Tunstead
Knoll
Farm

Black Brook

B5470

Harrop Fold
Farm

Dunge Clough

78

96   A   97   B   98   C

39

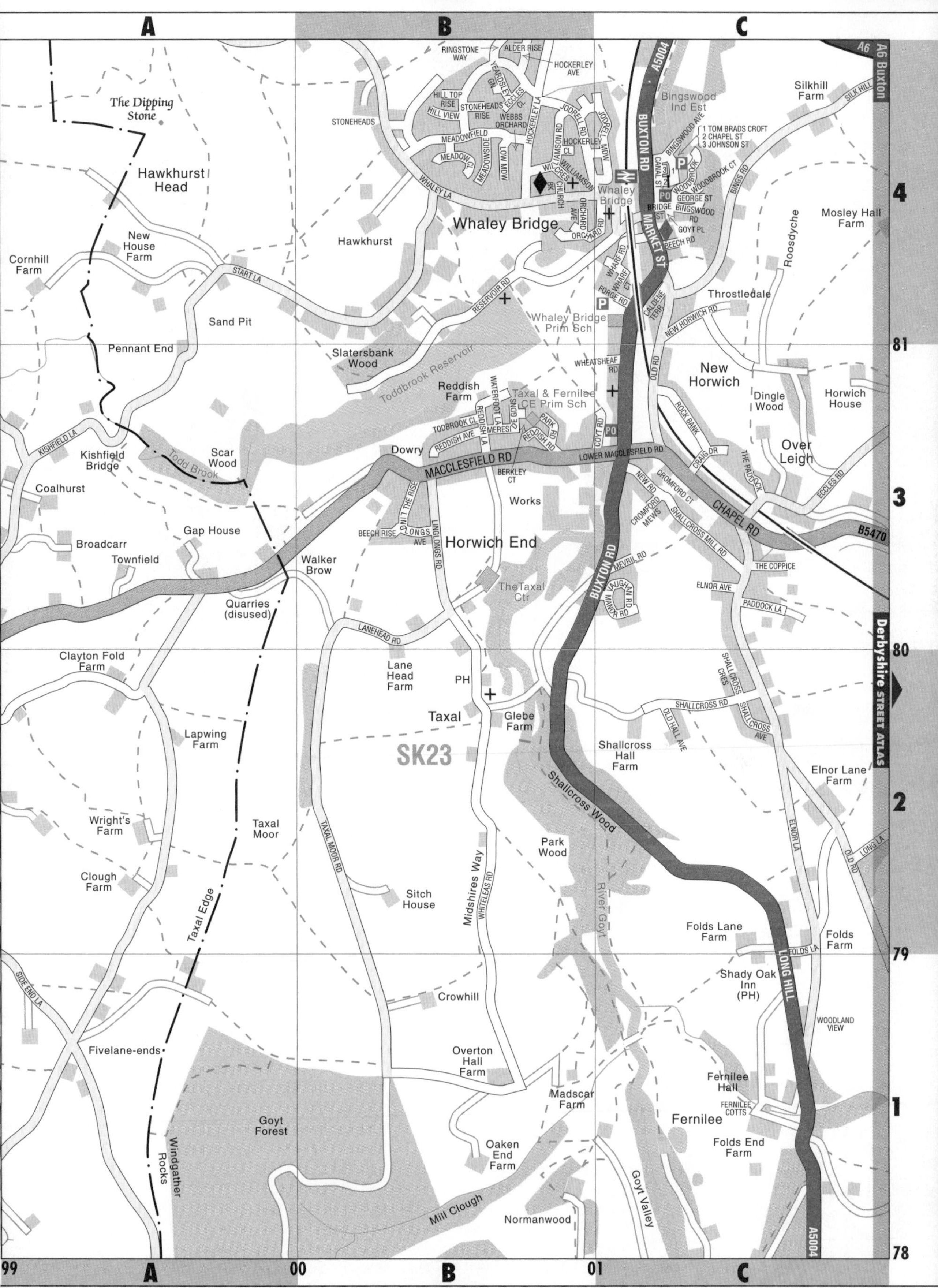
A
B
C
The Dipping Stone
Hawkhurst Head
New House Farm
Cornhill Farm
Hawkhurst
Sand Pit
Pennant End
Slatersbank Wood
Toddbrook Reservoir
Reddish Farm
Kishfield Bridge
Scar Wood
Todd Brook
Coalhurst
Broadcarr
Townfield
Gap House
Walker Brow
Quarries (disused)
Dowry
Works
Horwich End
The Taxal Ctr
Clayton Fold Farm
Lane Head Farm
PH
Taxal
Glebe Farm
SK23
Lapwing Farm
Wright's Farm
Taxal Moor
Clough Farm
Taxal Edge
Sitch House
Midshires Way
Park Wood
Shallcross Wood
River Goyt
Crowhill
Fivelane-ends
Overton Hall Farm
Madscar Farm
Goyt Forest
Oaken End Farm
Windgather Rocks
Mill Clough
Normanwood
Goyt Valley
Whaley Bridge
Whaley Bridge Prim Sch
Taxal & Fernilee CE Prim Sch
Bingswood Ind Est
Silkhill Farm
Mosley Hall Farm
Roosdyche
Throstledale
New Horwich
Dingle Wood
Horwich House
Over Leigh
Shallcross Hall Farm
Elnor Lane Farm
Folds Lane Farm
Folds Farm
Shady Oak Inn (PH)
Fernilee Hall
Fernilee
Folds End Farm
A6 Buxton
A5004
B5470
BUXTON RD
MARKET ST
MACCLESFIELD RD
LOWER MACCLESFIELD RD
CHAPEL RD
LONG HILL
RINGSTONE WAY
ALDER RISE
HOCKERLEY AVE
HILL TOP RISE
HILL VIEW
YEARDSLEY GN
STONEHEADS RISE
ECCLES CL
WEBBS ORCHARD
HOCKERLEY LA
JODRELL RD
JODRELL MDW
STONEHEADS
MEADOWFIELD
MEADOW CL
MEADOWSIDE
LOW MDW
WILLIAMSON RD
HOCKERLEY CL
WILLIAMSON
CHURCH
WHALEY LA
ORCHARD AVE
ORCHARD RD
START LA
RESERVOIR RD
WHARF RD
WHARF CT
FORGE RD
CALDENE TERR
1 TOM BRADS CROFT
2 CHAPEL ST
3 JOHNSON ST
BINGSWOOD AVE
WOODBROOK
WOODBROOK CT
BINGS RD
CANAL ST
GEORGE ST
BRIDGE ST
BINGSWOOD RD
GOYT PL
BEECH RD
SILK HILL
NEW HORWICH RD
OLD RD
WHEATSHEAF RD
WATERFOOT LA
BONGS CL
TODBROOK CL
REDDISH LA
REDDISH AVE
MERESIDE
PARK RD
REDDISH RD
GOYT RD
BERKLEY CT
ROCK BANK
CRAIG DR
THE PADDOCK
ECCLES RD
NEW RD
CROMFORD CT
CROMFORD MEWS
SHALLCROSS MILL RD
IN THE RISE
BEECH RISE
LONGS AVE
LINGLONGS RD
MEVRIL RD
VAUGHAN RD
MANOR RD
THE COPPICE
ELNOR AVE
PADDOCK LA
LANEHEAD RD
SHALLCROSS CRES
SHALLCROSS RD
OLD HALL AVE
SHALLCROSS AVE
ELNOR LA
OLD RD
LONG LA
TAXAL MOOR RD
WHITELEAS RD
FOLDS LA
WOODLAND VIEW
FERNILEE COTTS
SIDE END LA
KISHFIELD LA
PO
P
Derbyshire STREET ATLAS
4
81
3
80
2
79
1
78
99
00
01

90

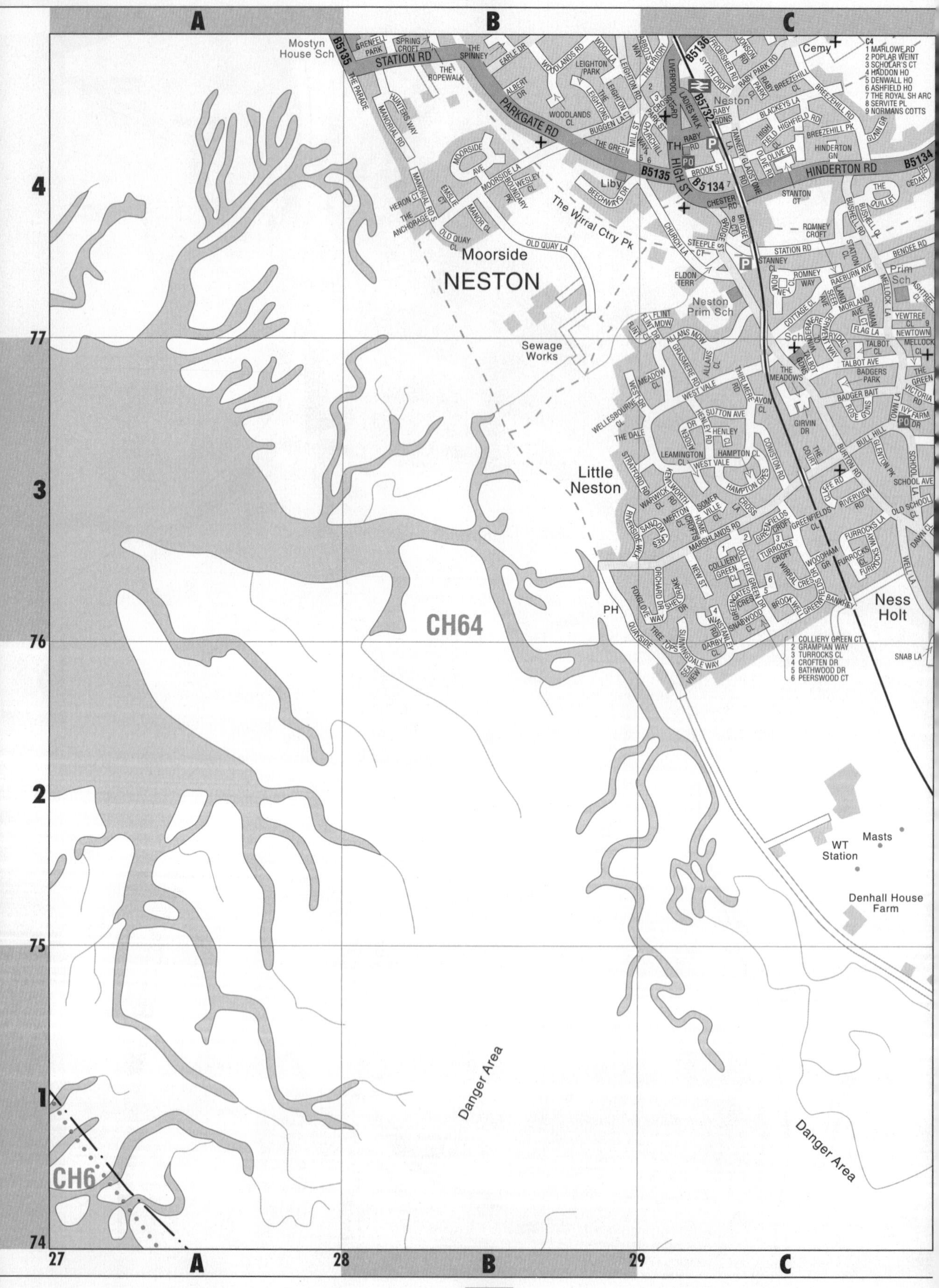

Mostyn
House Sch

B5135
STATION RD
GRENFELL
PARK
SPRING
CROFT
THE SPINNEY
EARLE DR
WOODLANDS RD
WOOD LA
LEIGHTON RD
THE PRIORY
RABY PARK RD
BREEZEHILL
Cemy

C4
1 MARLOWE RD
2 POPLAR WEINT
3 SCHOCAR'S CT
4 HADDON HO
5 DENWALL HO
6 ASHFIELD HO
7 THE ROYAL SH ARC
8 SERVITE PL
9 NORMANS COTTS

THE PARADE
HUNTERS WAY
MANORIAL RD
PARKGATE RD
THE ROPEWALK
LEIGHTON
PARK
WOODLANDS
CL
BUGGEN LA
THE GREEN
MILL ST
LIVERPOOL RD
LADIES WALK
B5136
RABY
GDNS
BLACKEYS LA
BREEZEHILL RD
HINTERTON
GN
GLAN CR
THE
QUILLE
CEDARS

4

HERON CT
MANOR CL
MOORSIDE
AVE
MOORSIDE LA
WESLEY
PK
LibV
BECHWRYS
HIGH ST
CHURCH LA
CHESTER RD
HINDERTON RD
B5134
STANTON
CT
BUSHELL CL
BUSHELL RD
STATION CL
THE ANCHORAGE
EGRETTE
CROFT
OLD QUAY
CL
OLD QUAY LA
The Wirral Ctry Pk
STEEPLE
CT
BRIDGE ST
ROMNEY
CROFT
STATION RD
BENDEE RD

Moorside
NESTON

ELDON
TERR
Neston
Prim Sch
STANNEY
ROMNEY
WAY
RAEBURN RD
MORLAND
RYDLE CL
COTTAGE CL
FLAG LA
PRIM
SCH
YEWTREE
CL
NEWTOWN
MELLOCK LA

77

Sewage
Works
FLINT
MDW
ALLANS MDW
SWIFT CL
Sch
TALBOT AVE
TALBOT CT
THE
MEADOWS
BADGERS
PARK
VICTORIA
RD
THE
GREEN
IVY FARM
PO
DR

3

WELLESBOURNE
CL
THE DALE
MEADOW
CL
GRASMERE RD
WEST VALE
SUTTON AVE
AVON
CONISTON RD
HENLEY
GIRVIN DR
BADGER BAIT
BULL HILL
CLAYTON PK
SCHOOL AVE

Little
Neston
STRATFORD RD
WARWICK CL
LEAMINGTON
CL
HAMPTON
CL
HAMPTON CRES
WEST VALE
RIVERVIEW
RD
LYFE RD
GREENFIELDS
FURROCKS LA
OLD SCHOOL LA
DAWN CL

CH64

RIVERSIDE WAY
PADWORTH
MERTON
CROFT
SOMER
VILLE
CL
MARSHLANDS RD
COLLIERY
GREEN
CL
GREENFIELDS
CROFT
GREENFIELDS
TURROCKS
CROFT
WIRRAL MEWS
WOODHAM
GR
FURROCKS LA
WELL LA

PH
ORCHARD DR
NEW ST
COLLIERY
GREEN
CRES
SHELL
CL
GATES
CRES
SNOWBOOD
TURROCKS CL
BROOK AVE
BANKHEY
Ness
Holt

QUAYSIDE
FLING OUT
WAY
TREE
TOPS
WANSTANLEY
CL
DARBY
CL
GREEN LA

76

SUNNINGDALE WAY
1 COLLIERY GREEN CT
2 GRAMPIAN WAY
3 TURROCKS CL
4 CROFTEN DR
5 BATHWOOD DR
6 PEERSWOOD CT
SNAB LA

2

WT
Station
Masts

Denhall House
Farm

75

Danger Area

1

Danger Area

CH6

74

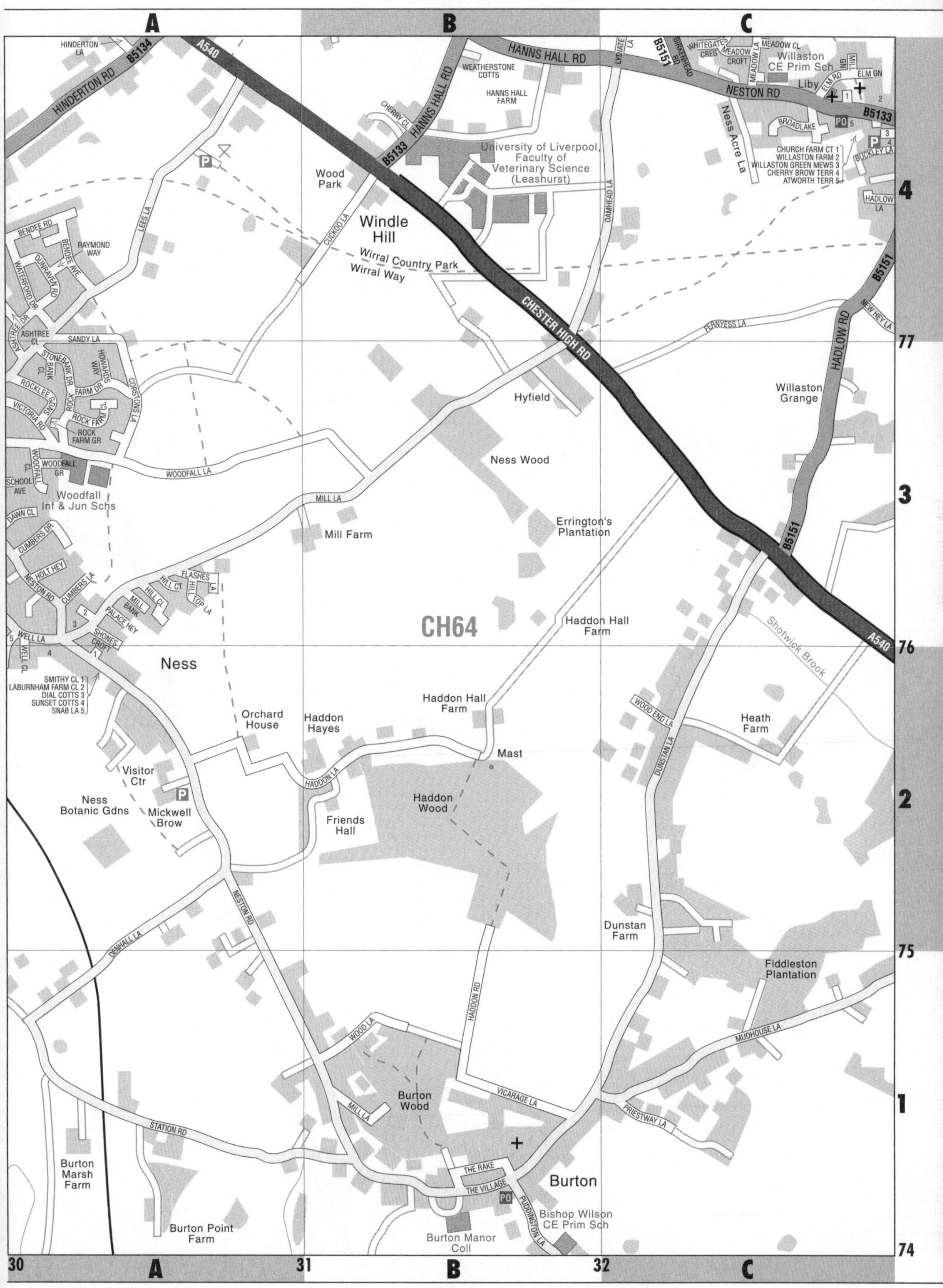
A
B
C
HINDERTON LA
HINDERTON RD
B5134
A540
HANNS HALL RD
B5151
WHITEGATES CRES
MEADOW CROFT
MEADOW LA
MEADOW CL
Willaston CE Prim Sch
NESTON RD
Liby
ELM RD
ELM GN
MILL
B5133
WEATHERSTONE COTTS
HANNS HALL FARM
CHERRY CL
HANNS HALL RD
University of Liverpool, Faculty of Veterinary Science (Leashurst)
Wood Park
Ness Acre La
BROADLAKE
PO
CHURCH FARM CT 1
WILLASTON FARM 2
WILLASTON GREEN MEWS 3
CHERRY BROW TERR 4
ATWORTH TERR 5
BUCKLEY LA
HADLOW LA
LYDIATE LA
DAMHEAD LA
Windle Hill
CUCKOO LA
LEES LA
Wirral Country Park
Wirral Way
BENDEE RD
RAYMOND WAY
BENDEE AVE
DUNRAVEN RD
WATERFORD DR
ASHTREE DR
ASHTREE CL
SANDY LA
STONEBANK DR
HOWARDS WAY
CORSTONS LA
ROCKLEE GDNS
ROCK FARM DR
ROCK FARM CL
ROCK FARM GR
VICTORIA RD
CHESTER HIGH RD
FERNYESS LA
NEW HEY LA
B5151
HADLOW RD
Willaston Grange
Hyfield
Ness Wood
WOODFALL LA
WOODFALL CL
WOODFALL GR
SCHOOL AVE
Woodfall Inf & Jun Schs
DAWN CL
CUMBERS DR
HOLT HEY
NESTON RD
CUMBERS LA
MILL LA
Mill Farm
Errington's Plantation
FLASHES LA
HILL CT
HILL CL
HILL TOP LA
MILL BANK
PALACE HEY
SHONES CROFT
WELL LA
WELL CL
CH64
Haddon Hall Farm
Shotwick Brook
A540
Ness
SMITHY CL 1
LABURNHAM FARM CL 2
DIAL COTTS 3
SUNSET COTTS 4
SNAB LA 5
Orchard House
Haddon Hayes
Haddon Hall Farm
WOOD END LA
DUNSTAN LA
Heath Farm
Mast
HADDON LA
Visitor Ctr
Ness Botanic Gdns
Mickwell Brow
Haddon Wood
Friends Hall
NESTON RD
DENHALL LA
Dunstan Farm
Fiddleston Plantation
HADDON RD
WOOD LA
MUDHOUSE LA
Burton Wood
MILL LA
VICARAGE LA
PRIESTWAY LA
STATION RD
THE RAKE
THE VILLAGE
Burton
Burton Marsh Farm
PUDDINGTON LA
Bishop Wilson CE Prim Sch
Burton Point Farm
Burton Manor Coll
4
77
3
76
2
75
1
74
30
31
32

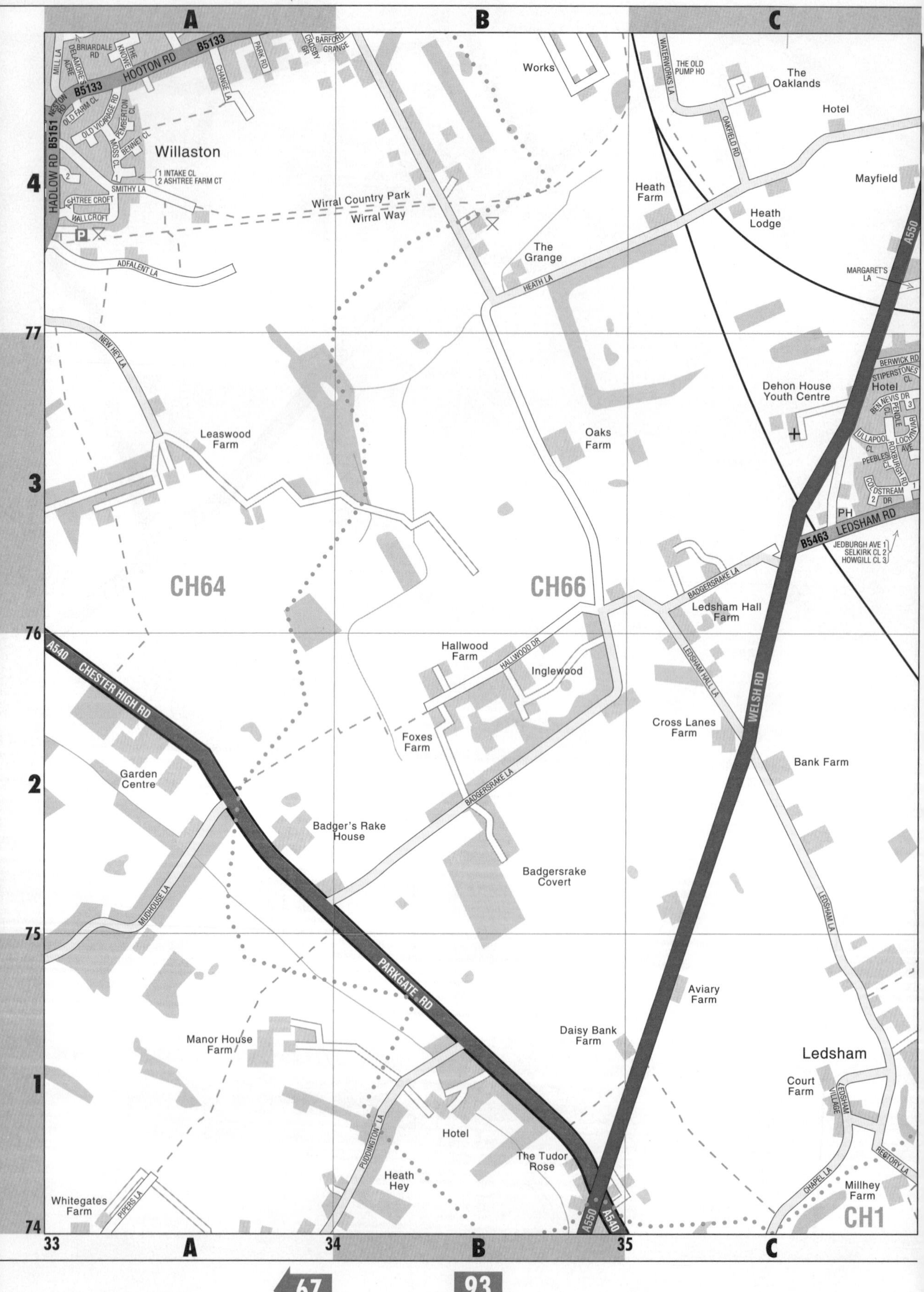

A
B
C

MILL LA
DELAMORE PL
BRIARDALE RD
DELAMORE RD
THE KNOWE
HOOTON RD
B5133
PARK RD
BARFORD GRANGE
CHAISY CROSSY
Works

HESTON RD
B5133
OLD FARM CL
OLD VICARAGE RD
PEMBERTON CL
CHANGE LA
B5151
BENNET CL
TQ SISSON CL
Willaston
1 INTAKE CL
2 ASHTREE FARM CT
ASHTREE CROFT
SMITHY LA
HADLOW RD
B5151
HALLCROFT
P
ADFALENT LA

The Oaklands
WATERWORKS LA
THE OLD PUMP HO
OAKFIELD RD
Hotel
Mayfield
Heath Farm
Heath Lodge
A550
MARGARET'S LA

4

Wirral Country Park
Wirral Way
The Grange
HEATH LA

77

NEW HEY LA
Leaswood Farm
Oaks Farm
Dehon House Youth Centre
Hotel
BERWICK RD
STIPERSTONES CL
BEN NEVIS DR
PENDLE
ULLAPOOL CL
LOCHINVAR
PEEBLES
ROXBURGH AVE
COQUSTREAM DR

3

CH64
CH66
PH
LEDSHAM RD
B5463
JEDBURGH AVE 1
SELKIRK CL 2
HOWGILL CL 3

Ledsham Hall Farm
BADGERSRAKE LA

76

A540
CHESTER HIGH RD
Hallwood Farm
HALLWOOD DR
Inglewood
HALLWOOD LA
Cross Lanes Farm
LEDSHAM HALL LA
WELSH RD
Bank Farm

Foxes Farm
BADGERSRAKE LA

2

Garden Centre
Badger's Rake House
Badgersrake Covert
Aviary Farm
LEDSHAM LA

MUDHOUSE LA

75

PARKGATE RD

Manor House Farm
Daisy Bank Farm
Ledsham
Court Farm
LEDSHAM VILLAGE

1

PUDDINGTON LA
Hotel
The Tudor Rose
CHAPEL LA
A510
A540
REGORY LA
Millhey Farm

Whitegates Farm
PIPERS LA
Heath Hey
CH1

74

33
A
34
B
35
C

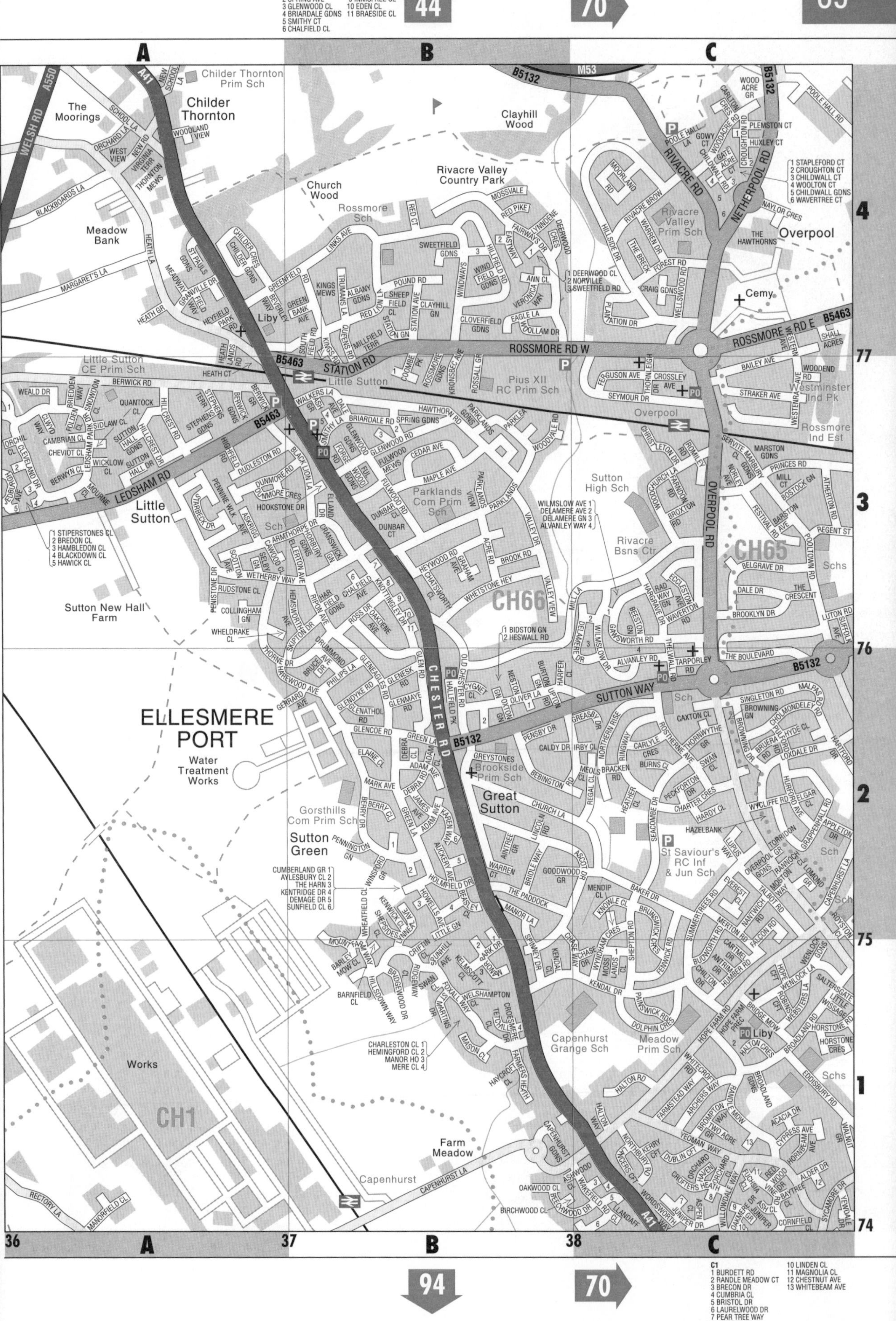

← 69

B3
1 CHURCH WLK
2 CHURCH PAR
3 WORCESTER WLK
4 CRESSINGTON GDNS
5 CHARLES PRICE GDNS
6 THE COURT HO

▲ 45

B3
7 HIGHFIELD RD N
8 ASHFIELD RD N
9 WOODFIELD RD N
10 WELLINGTON CL
11 SHREWSBURY RD
12 WATERLOO CL

13 WELLESLEY WLK

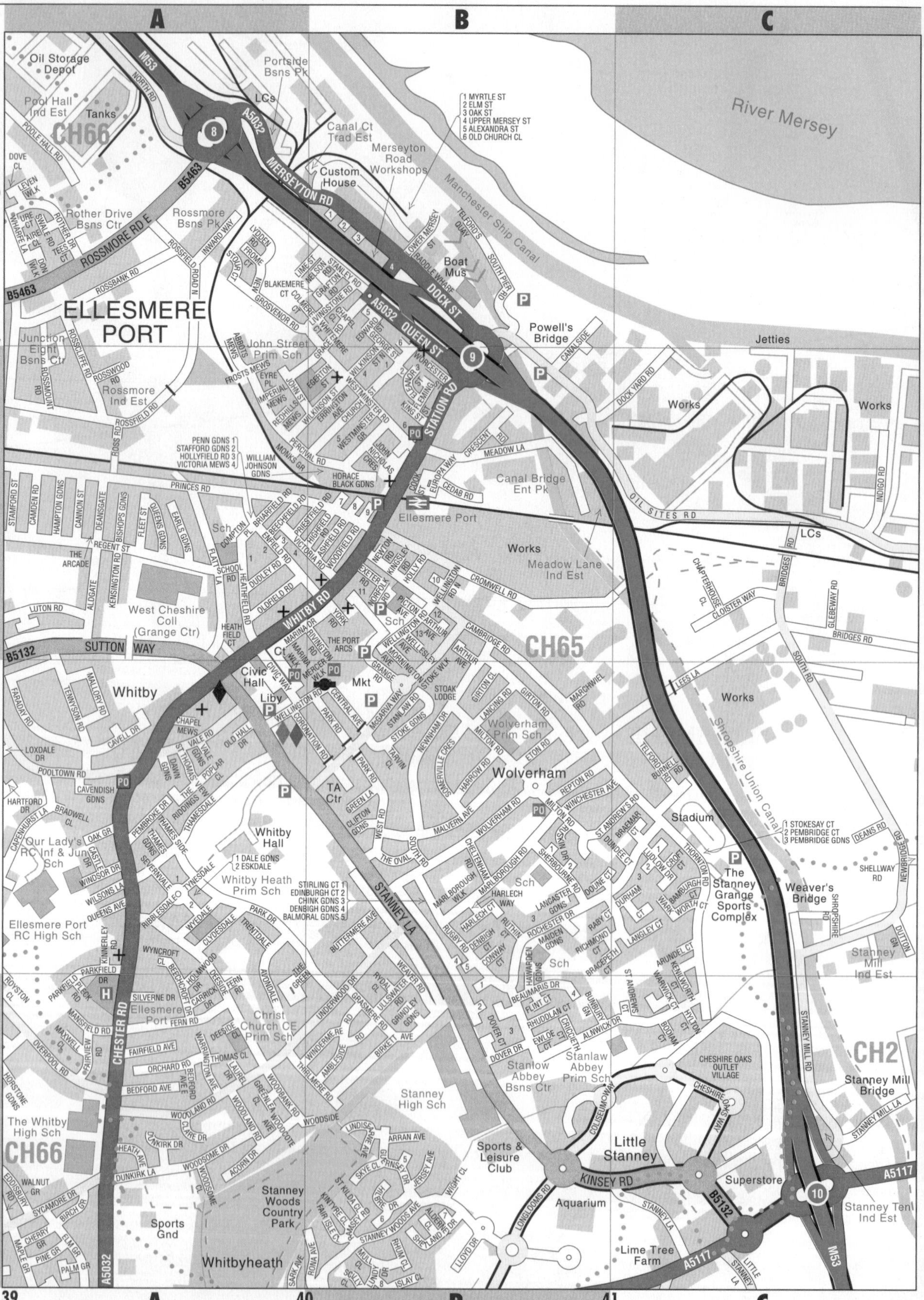

A **B** **C**

River Mersey

Oil Storage Depot

Pool Hall Ind Est

Tanks

CH66

Portside Bsns Pk

LCs

Canal Ct Trad Est

Custom House

Merseyton Road Workshops

Manchester Ship Canal

1 MYRTLE ST
2 ELM ST
3 OAK ST
4 UPPER MERSEY ST
5 ALEXANDRA ST
6 OLD CHURCH CL

4

ROSSMORE RD E

Rossmore Bsns Pk

MERSEYTON RD

A5032 QUEEN ST

DOCK ST

Boat Mus

Powell's Bridge

Jetties

B5463

ELLESMERE PORT

77

Junction Eight Bsns Ctr

Rossmore Ind Est

John Street Prim Sch

STATION RD

Canal Side

Dock Yard Rd

Works

Works

P

P

3

Penn Gdns 1
Stafford Gdns 2
Hollyfield Rd 3
Victoria Mews 4

William Johnson Gdns

Horace Black Gdns

Princes Rd

Ellesmere Port

Canal Bridge Ent Pk

Meadow La

Works

Meadow Lane Ind Est

Oil Sites Rd

LCs

Cloister Way

Bridges Rd

CH65

WHITBY RD

West Cheshire Coll (Grange Ctr)

76 B5132 SUTTON WAY

Civic Hall

Liby

Mkt

The Port Arcs

Wolverham Prim Sch

Works

South Rd

Whitby

Chapel Mews

Wolverham

Tees La

2

Our Lady's RC Inf & Jun Sch

Whitby Hall

Whitby Heath Prim Sch

TA Ctr

STANNEY LA

Stadium

The Stanney Grange Sports Complex

Weaver's Bridge

Shropshire Union Canal

Stanney Mill Ind Est

1 STOKESAY CT
2 PEMBRIDGE CT
3 PEMBRIDGE GDNS

1 DALE GDNS
2 ESKDALE

STIRLING CT 1
EDINBURGH CT 2
CHINK GDNS 3
DENBIGH GDNS 4
BALMORAL GDNS 5

Ellesmere Port RC High Sch

75

CHESTER RD

Ellesmere Port Fern Rd

Christ Church CE Prim Sch

Stanney High Sch

Stanlow Abbey Bsns Ctr

Stanlaw Abbey Prim Sch

Cheshire Oaks Outlet Village

Stanney Mill Bridge

CH2

The Whitby High Sch

CH66

1

KINSEY RD

Sports & Leisure Club

Aquarium

Little Stanney

Superstore

Stanney Ten Ind Est

Sports Gnd

Stanney Woods Country Park

B5132

A5117

Lime Tree Farm

A5117

M53

10

A5117

74 **39** **A** **40** **B** **41** **C**

Whitbyheath

A5032

← 69

B1
1 BUCKINGHAM RD
2 SANDRINGHAM GDNS
3 FOTHERINGAY CT
4 CAERNARVON CT
5 BARDSEY CL
6 ANGLESEY CL
7 ORKNEY CL
8 CUMBRAE DR

▲ 95

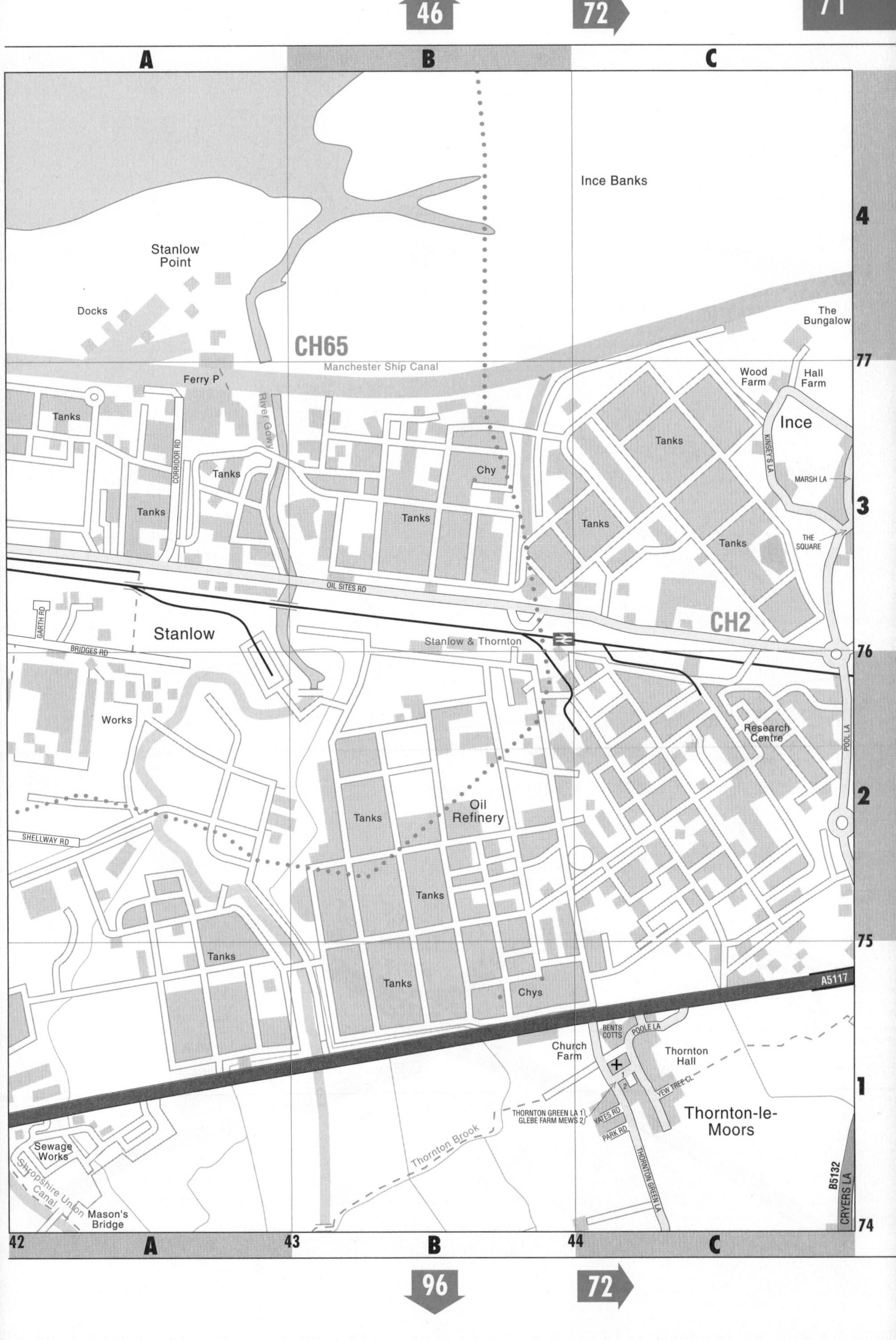

A B C

4

Ince Banks

Stanlow
Point

Docks

CH65

Ferry P

Manchester Ship Canal

The
Bungalow

77

Wood
Farm

Hall
Farm

Tanks

Tanks

Chy

Tanks

Ince

KINSEY'S LA

MARSH LA

THE
SQUARE

3

Tanks

Tanks

Tanks

CORRIDOR RD

River Gowy

OIL SITES RD

CH2

76

GARTH RD

Stanlow

BRIDGES RD

Stanlow & Thornton

Research
Centre

POOL LA

Works

Oil
Refinery

Tanks

2

SHELLWAY RD

Tanks

75

Tanks

Tanks

A5117

Tanks

Chys

BENTS
COTTS

POOLE LA

Church
Farm

Thornton
Hall

YEW TREE CL

1

Thornton-le-
Moors

YATES RD

THORNTON GREEN LA

PARK RD

THORNTON GREEN LA 1
GLEBE FARM MEWS 2

Sewage
Works

Shropshire Union Canal

Mason's
Bridge

Thornton Brook

B5132

CRYERS LA

74

← 71
↑ 47

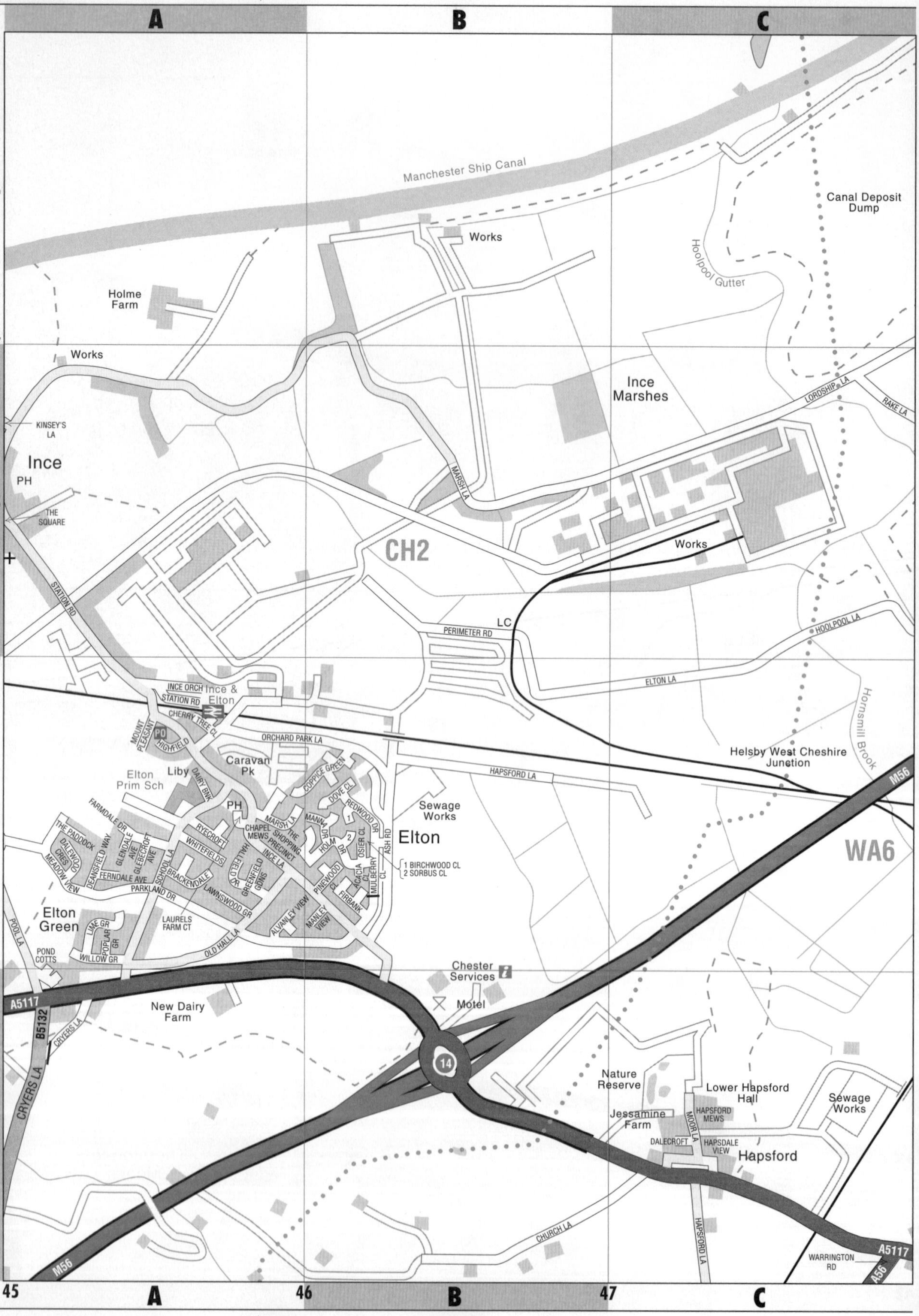

A **B** **C**

4

Manchester Ship Canal

Canal Deposit Dump

Works

Holme Farm

77

Works

Ince Marshes

Hoolpool Gutter

LORDSHIP LA
RAKE LA

KINSEY'S LA

Ince

PH

3

THE SQUARE

CH2

Works

STATION RD

MARSH LA

HOOLPOOL LA

76

PERIMETER RD

LC

ELTON LA

Hornsmill Brook

INCE ORCH
Ince & Elton
STATION RD

CHERRY TREE CL

ORCHARD PARK LA

Helsby West Cheshire Junction

MOUNT PLEASANT
HIGHFIELD
PO

Caravan Pk

HAPSFORD LA

M56

Liby
Dairy Pbk

Elton Prim Sch

COPPICE GREEN

DOVE CL

REDWOOD CL

Sewage Works

WA6

PH

2

FARMDALE DR

MARSH THE

MANLEY RD

RYECROFT

CHAPEL MEWS SHOPPING PRECINCT

HOLM DR

OSIER CL

1 BIRCHWOOD CL
2 SORBUS CL

Elton

THE PADDOCK
DALEHEAD GRES RD
MEADOW VIEW

DEANSFIELD WAY
GLENDALE AVE
GLEBCROFT AVE

SCHOOL LA
BRACKENDALE

WHITEFIELDS

INCE LA
HALLFIELD CL
GREENFIELD GDNS

PINEWOOD

ACACIA

MULBERRY CL

ASH RD

FERNDALE AVE

PARKLAND DR

LAWNSWOOD GR

ALVANLEY VIEW

FIRBANK

Elton Green

LIME GR
POPLAR GR

LAURELS FARM CT

OLD HALL LA

MANLEY VIEW

POOL LA

Pond Cotts

WILLOW GR

75

A5117

B5132

CRYERS LA

New Dairy Farm

Chester Services 𝑖

Motel

Nature Reserve

Lower Hapsford Hall

Sewage Works

CRYERS LA

14

Jessamine Farm

HAPSFORD MEWS

DALECROFT

HAPSDALE VIEW

Hapsford

MOOR LA

1

CHURCH LA

HAPSFORD LA

WARRINGTON RD

A5117

A56

74

45

A 46 **B** 47 **C**

M56

48
74

A B C

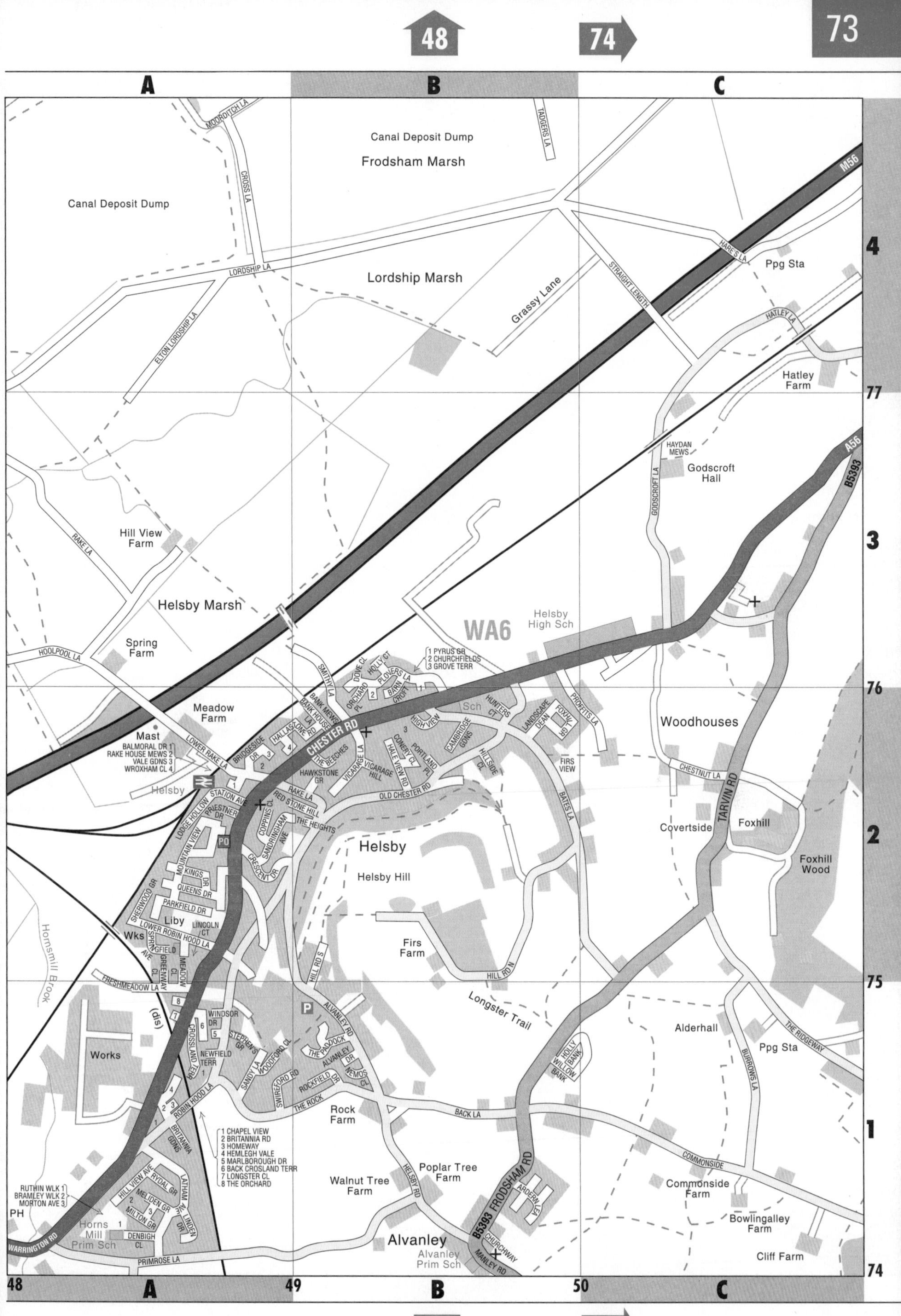
Canal Deposit Dump
Frodsham Marsh
Canal Deposit Dump
Lordship Marsh
Grassy Lane
Hill View Farm
Helsby Marsh
Spring Farm
Meadow Farm
Mast
BALMORAL DR 1
RAKE HOUSE MEWS 2
VALE GDNS 3
WROXHAM CL 4
Helsby
WA6
Helsby High Sch
1 PYRUS GR
2 CHURCHFIELDS
3 GROVE TERR
CHESTER RD
Sch
Woodhouses
Godscroft Hall
HAYDAN MEWS
Hatley Farm
Ppg Sta
Helsby
Helsby Hill
Liby
Wks
Works
Hornsmill Brook
Firs Farm
Longster Trail
Covertside
Foxhill
Foxhill Wood
Alderhall
Ppg Sta
Rock Farm
1 CHAPEL VIEW
2 BRITANNIA RD
3 HOMEWAY
4 HEMLEGH VALE
5 MARLBOROUGH DR
6 BACK CROSLAND TERR
7 LONGSTER CL
8 THE ORCHARD
Poplar Tree Farm
Walnut Tree Farm
RUTHIN WLK 1
BRAMLEY WLK 2
MORTON AVE 3
PH
Horns Mill Prim Sch
Alvanley
Alvanley Prim Sch
Commonside Farm
Bowlingalley Farm
Cliff Farm
TARVIN RD
FRODSHAM RD
WARRINGTON RD
M56
A56
B5393
77
76
75
74
4
3
2
1
48
49
50

A B C

98
74

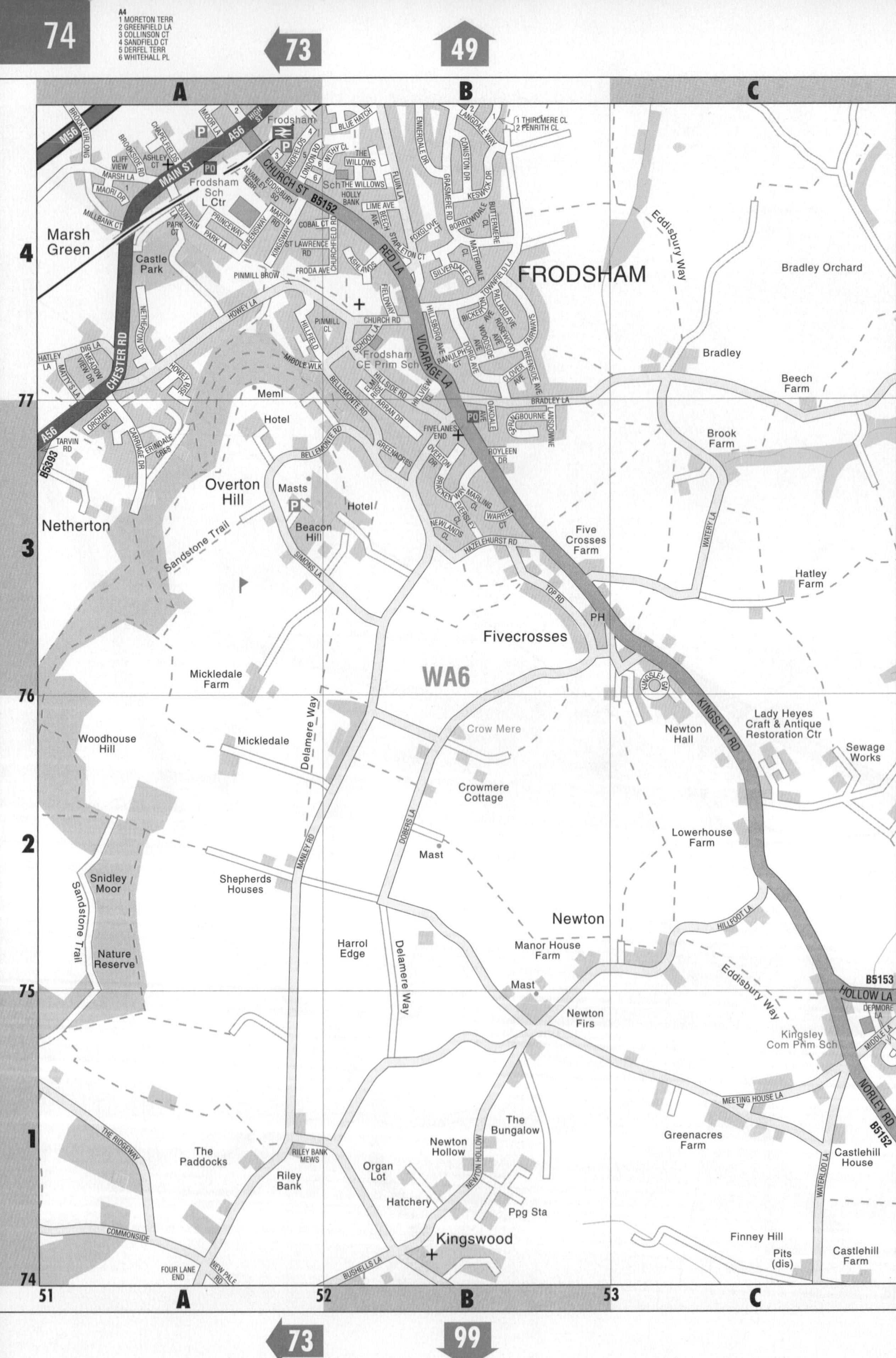

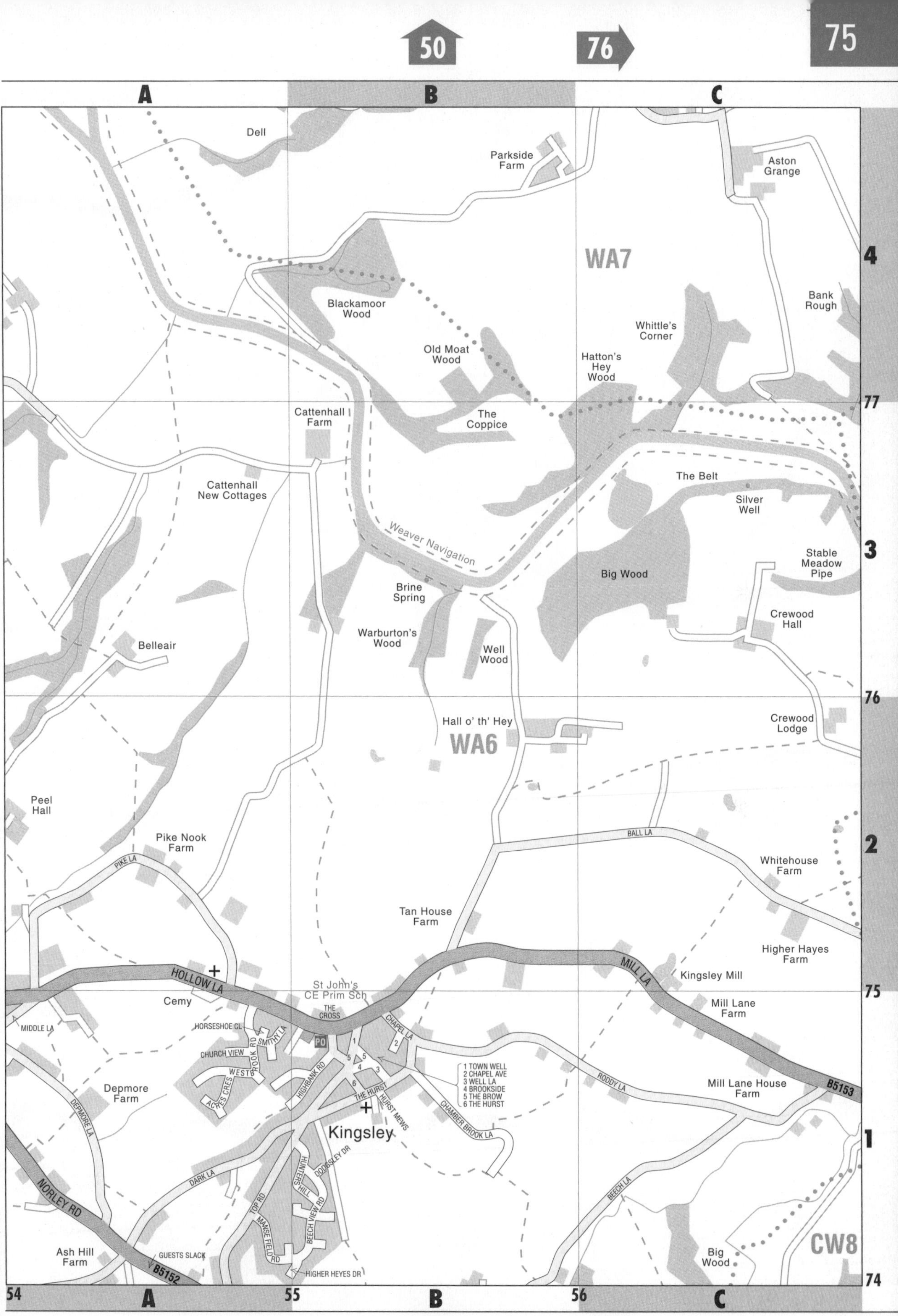
A
B
C
Dell
Parkside Farm
Aston Grange
WA7
4
Blackamoor Wood
Bank Rough
Whittle's Corner
Old Moat Wood
Hatton's Hey Wood
77
Cattenhall Farm
The Coppice
The Belt
Cattenhall New Cottages
Silver Well
Weaver Navigation
3
Stable Meadow Pipe
Big Wood
Brine Spring
Crewood Hall
Warburton's Wood
Belleair
Well Wood
76
Hall o' th' Hey
Crewood Lodge
WA6
Peel Hall
Pike Nook Farm
BALL LA
2
PIKE LA
Whitehouse Farm
Tan House Farm
Higher Hayes Farm
HOLLOW LA
MILL LA
Kingsley Mill
St John's CE Prim Sch
75
Cemy
Mill Lane Farm
THE CROSS
MIDDLE LA
HORSESHOE CL
SMITHY LA
CHAPEL LA
PO
CHURCH VIEW
BROOK RD
WEST B
ACRES CRES
1 TOWN WELL
2 CHAPEL AVE
3 WELL LA
4 BROOKSIDE
5 THE BROW
6 THE HURST
RODDY LA
Mill Lane House Farm
B5153
Depmore Farm
DEPMORE LA
HIGHBANK RD
THE HURST
HURST MEWS
CHAMBER BROOK LA
Kingsley
1
DARK LA
HUNTERS HILL
DODSLEY DR
NORLEY RD
TOP RD
BEECH VIEW RD
MANSE FIELD RD
BEECH LA
Ash Hill Farm
GUESTS SLACK
B5152
HIGHER HEYES DR
Big Wood
CW8
74
54
55
56

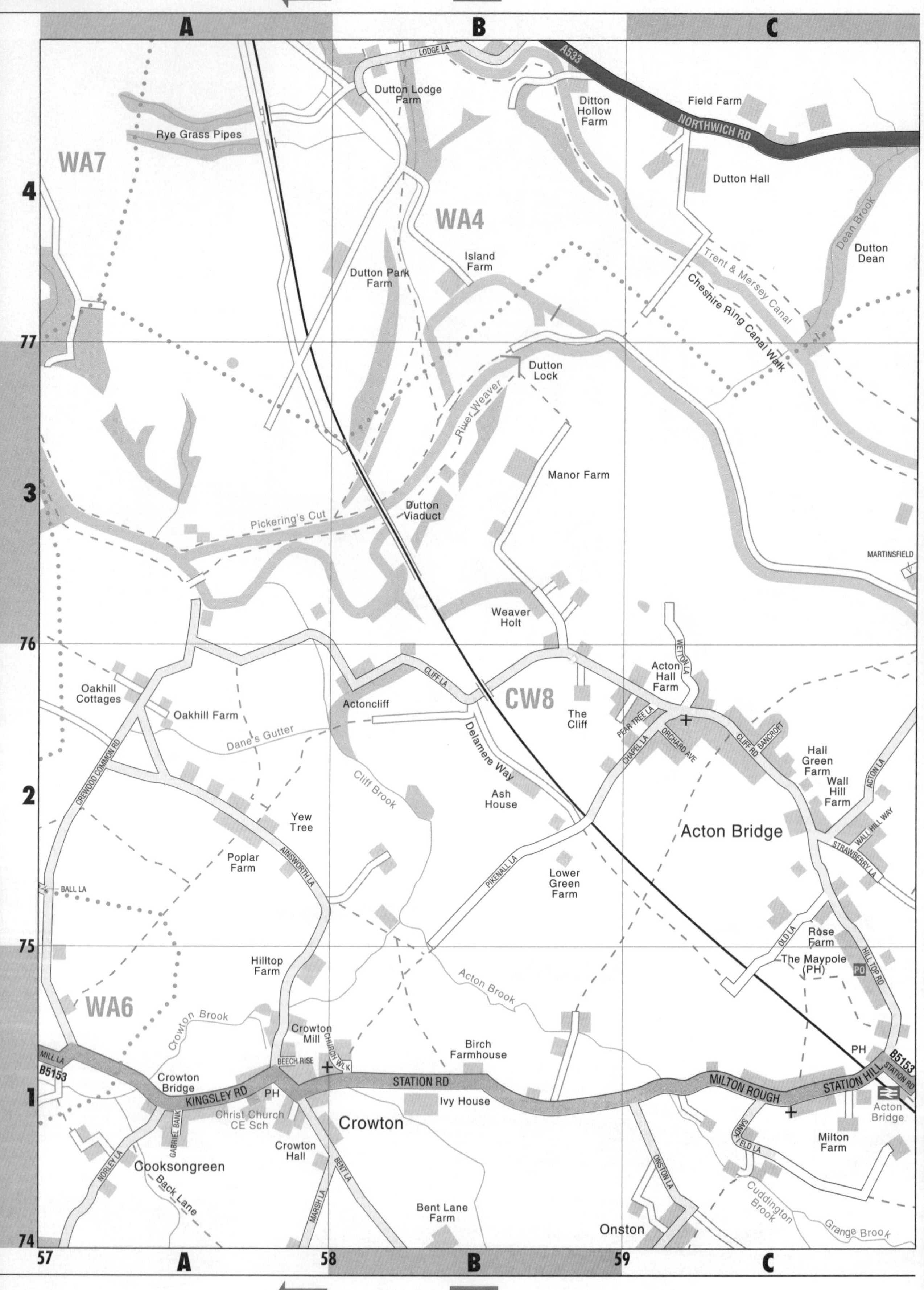

A   B   C

WA7

Rye Grass Pipes

Dutton Lodge Farm

Ditton Hollow Farm

A533

NORTHWICH RD

Field Farm

4

WA4

Island Farm

Dutton Park Farm

Dutton Hall

Cheshire Ring Canal Walk

Trent & Mersey Canal

Dutton Dean

Dean Brook

77

River Weaver

Dutton Lock

Manor Farm

MARTINSFIELD

3

Pickering's Cut

Dutton Viaduct

Weaver Holt

Acton Hall Farm

WELTON LA

76

Oakhill Cottages

Oakhill Farm

Dane's Gutter

CREWOOD COMMON RD

Actoncliff

CLIFF LA

CW8

The Cliff

PEAR TREE LA

CHAPEL LA

ORCHARD AVE

CLIFF RD

BANCROFT

Hall Green Farm

Wall Hill Farm

ACTON LA

Delamere Way

Cliff Brook

Ash House

2

Yew Tree

AINSWORTH LA

Poplar Farm

PIKENALL LA

Lower Green Farm

Acton Bridge

STRAWBERRY LA

Wall Hill Way

BALL LA

Rose Farm

OLD LA

75

Hilltop Farm

Acton Brook

The Maypole (PH)

PO

HILL TOP RD

WA6

Crowton Brook

Crowton Mill

BEECH RISE

CHURCH WLK

Birch Farmhouse

PH

STATION HILL RD

STATION RD

Acton Bridge

MILL LA

B5153

Crowton Bridge

KINGSLEY RD

PH

GABRIEL BANK

Christ Church CE Sch

Ivy House

Crowton

MILTON ROUGH

B5153

1

NORLEY LA

Crowton Hall

MARSH LA

BENT LA

Milton Farm

KINGS BD LA

ONSTON LA

Cuddington Brook

Grange Brook

Cooksongreen

Back Lane

Bent Lane Farm

Onston

74

57   A   58   B   59   C

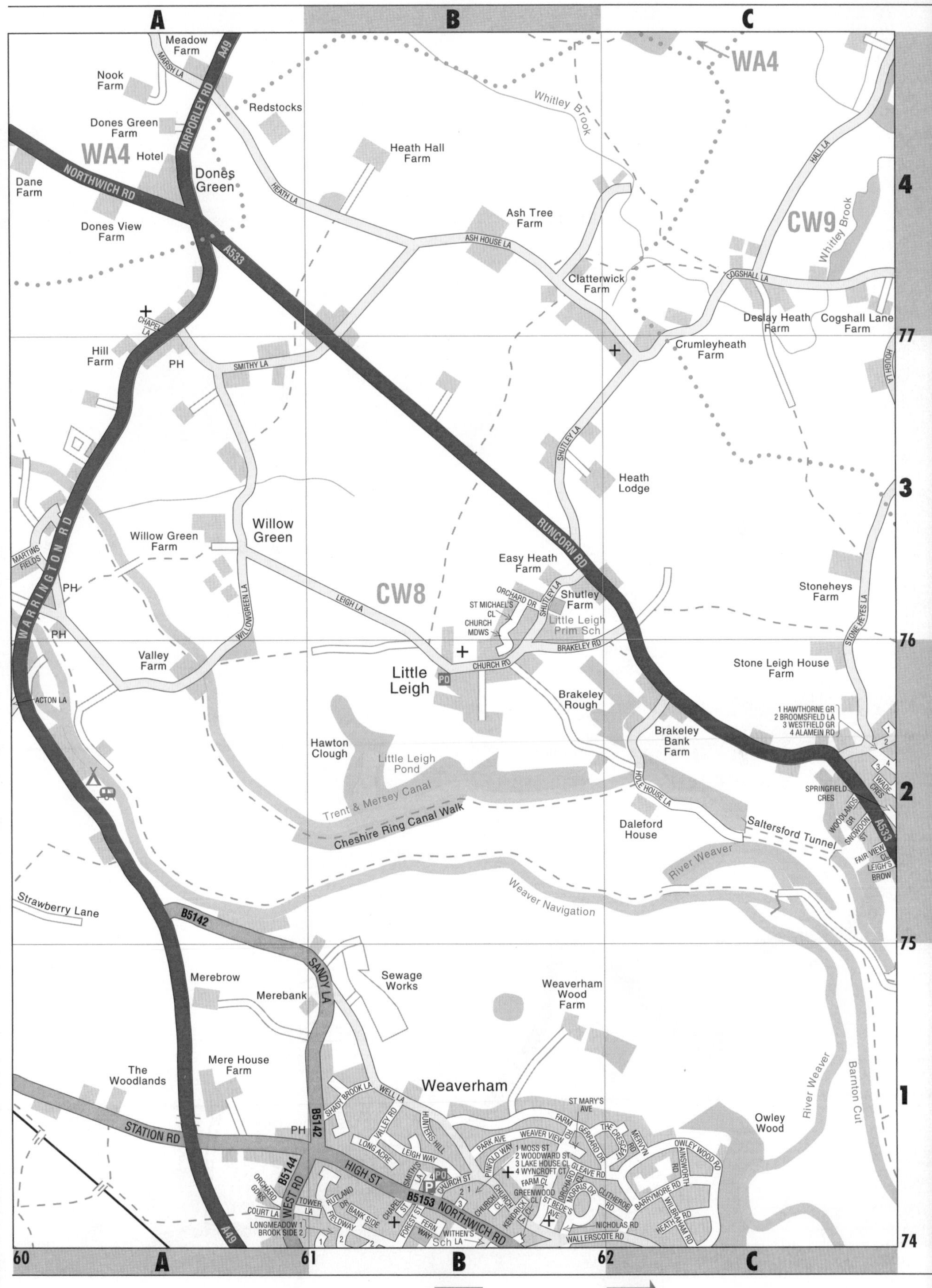
A
B
C
Meadow Farm
Nook Farm
Redstocks
Dones Green Farm
WA4
Hotel
Dane Farm
Dones Green
Heath Hall Farm
Whitley Brook
WA4
NORTHWICH RD
TARPORLEY RD
A49
MARSH LA
HEATH LA
Dones View Farm
A533
Ash Tree Farm
ASH HOUSE LA
HALL LA
CW9
Whitley Brook
Clatterwick Farm
COGSHALL LA
Deslay Heath Farm
Cogshall Lane Farm
CHAPEL LA
Hill Farm
PH
SMITHY LA
Crumleyheath Farm
HOUGH LA
SHUTLEY LA
Heath Lodge
Willow Green
Willow Green Farm
RUNCORN RD
MARTINS FIELDS
WARRINGTON RD
PH
Easy Heath Farm
CW8
Stoneheys Farm
ORCHARD DR
SHUTLEY LA
Shutley Farm
ST MICHAEL'S CL
CHURCH MDWS
Little Leigh Prim Sch
LEIGH LA
WILLOWGREEN LA
PH
STONE HEYS LA
Valley Farm
BRAKELEY RD
CHURCH RD
Little Leigh
PO
Stone Leigh House Farm
ACTON LA
Brakeley Rough
1 HAWTHORNE GR
2 BROOMSFIELD LA
3 WESTFIELD GR
4 ALAMEIN RD
Hawton Clough
Little Leigh Pond
Brakeley Bank Farm
Trent & Mersey Canal
HOLE HOUSE LA
SPRINGFIELD CRES
WADE CRES
Cheshire Ring Canal Walk
Daleford House
Saltersford Tunnel
WOODLANDS GR
SNOWDON ST
A533
River Weaver
FAIR VIEW CL
LEIGH'S BROW
Strawberry Lane
Weaver Navigation
B5142
Merebrow
SANDY LA
Sewage Works
Merebank
Weaverham Wood Farm
The Woodlands
Mere House Farm
Weaverham
Owley Wood
River Weaver
Barnton Cut
SHADY BROOK LA
WELL LA
ST MARY'S AVE
STATION RD
B5142
PH
VALLEY RD
HUNTERS HILL
PARK AVE
WEAVER VIEW
FARM CL
GERRARD DR
THE CRESCENT
MERVYN RD
OWLEY WOOD RD
AINSWORTH RD
LONG ACRE
LEIGH WAY
PINFOLD WAY
1 MOSS ST
2 WOODWARD ST
3 LAKE HOUSE CL
4 WYNCROFT CT
GLEAVE RD
B5144
HIGH ST
SMITHS LA
PO
CHURCH ST
FARM CL
GREENWOOD CL
CHURCH CL
ORCHARD
CLITHEROE RD
BARRYMORE RD
WILBRAHAM RD
ORCHARD GDNS
WEST RD
RUTLAND DR
TOWER LA
CHAPEL ST
B5153
NORTHWICH RD
MORRIS DR
KENDRICK CL
ST BEDE'S AVE
HEATH RD
COURT LA
BANK SIDE
FIELDWAY
FOREST ST
FERN WAY
WITHEN'S LA
Sch
NICHOLAS RD
WALLERSCOTE RD
LONGMEADOW 1
BROOK SIDE 2
A49
77
76
75
74
4
3
2
1
60
61
62
A
B
C

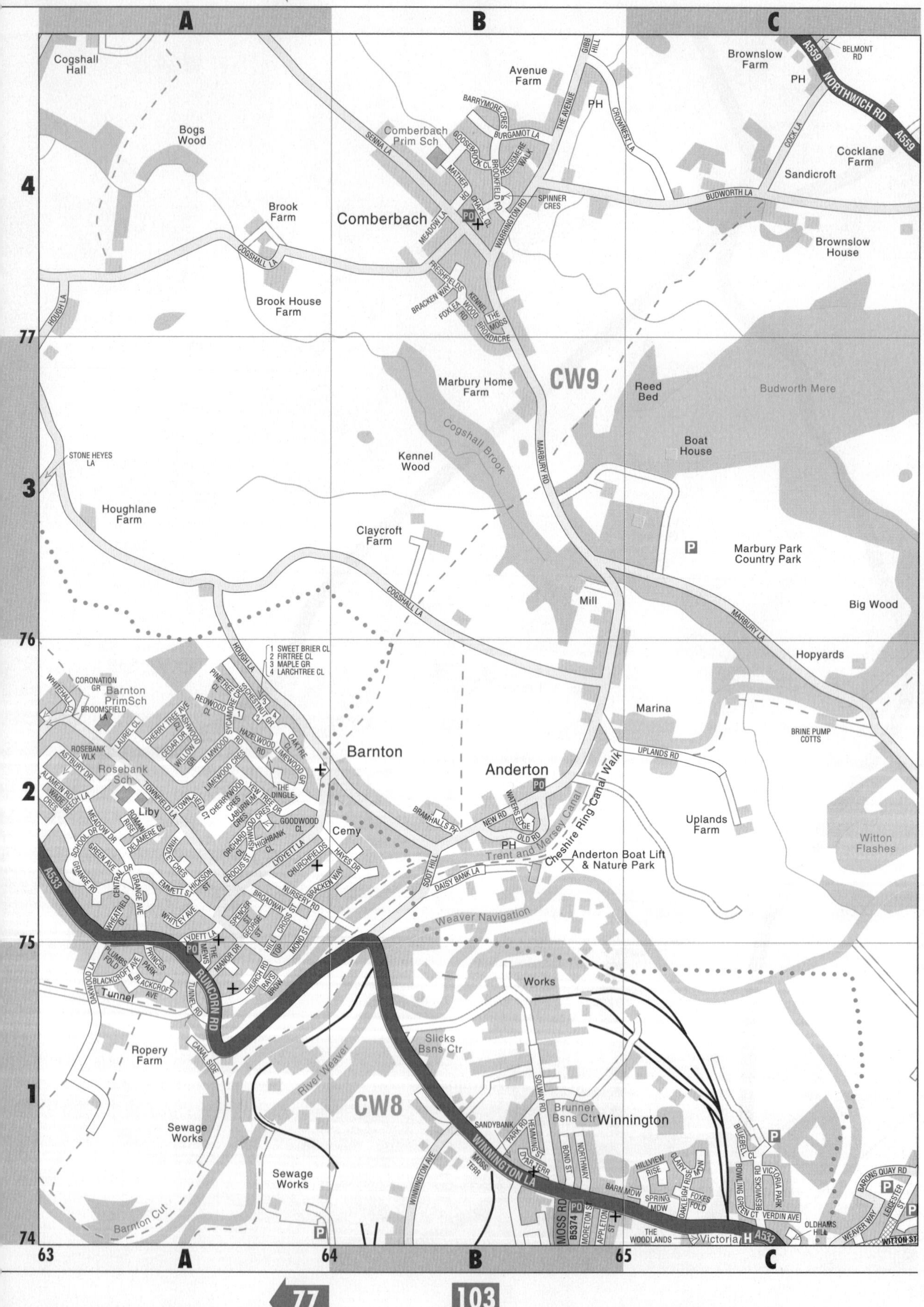

A   B   C

Cogshall
Hall

Bogs
Wood

Brownslow
Farm

PH

BELMONT
RD

A559

NORTHWICH RD

A559

COCK LA

Cocklane
Farm

Sandicroft

Brownslow
House

Avenue
Farm

BARRYMORE CRES

GIBB HILL

PH

CROWNEST LA

THE AVENUE

4

Comberbach
Prim Sch

BURGAMOT LA

SENNA LA

GOOSEBANK CL

BROOKFIELD

REEDSMERE WALK

WARRINGTON RD

SPINNER
CRES

BUDWORTH LA

Brook
Farm

MATHER DR

MEADOW LA

CHAPEL LA

PO

Comberbach

COGSHALL LA

FRESHFIELDS

BRACKEN WAY

FOXLEY
WOOD
RD

KENNEL LA

THE
MOSS

BROADACRE

Brook House
Farm

HOUGH LA

77

Marbury Home
Farm

Cogshall Brook

CW9

MARBURY RD

Reed
Bed

Budworth Mere

Boat
House

Kennel
Wood

Stone Heyes
LA

3

Houghlane
Farm

Claycroft
Farm

COGSHALL LA

P

Marbury Park
Country Park

Big Wood

MARBURY LA

76

1 SWEET BRIER CL
2 FIRTREE CL
3 MAPLE GR
4 LARCHTREE CL

Mill

Hopyards

BRINE PUMP
COTTS

CORONATION
GR

WHITEHALL

Barnton
Prim Sch

BROOMSFIELD
LA

HOUGH LA

PINETREE CL

CHESTNUT GR

REDWOOD CL

CHERRY TREE AVE

CEDAR AVE

ASHWOOD

WILLOW GR

ELMWOOD CL

SYCAMORE GR

HAZELWOOD RD

LIMEWOOD CRES

OAK TREE RD

LIMEWOOD CL

Barnton

Marina

UPLANDS RD

Rosebank
Sch

ROSEBANK
WLK

ASTBURY DR

LAUREL CL

LABURNUM CRES

THE
DINGLE

YEW TREE GR

Anderton

PO

Uplands
Farm

Witton
Flashes

2

ALAMEIN RD

WHEATFIELD

BEECH LA

WADE CRES

MEADOW DR

ELLAMERE CL

ROMAN WAY

TOWNFIELD LA

TOWN FIELD

CHERRYWOOD CRES

CROCUS ST

ORCHARD RD

HIGHBANK
CL

GOODWOOD
CL

LYDYETT LA

HAYES DR

BRAMHALLS PK

NEW RD

WATERS EDGE

OLD RD

PH

Cheshire Ring Canal Walk

BRINE
PUMP

Liby

SCHOOL DR

GREEN AVE

CENTRAL DR

GRANGE AVE

EMMETT ST

HICKSON ST

ASHWOOD GR

CHURCHFIELDS

NURSERY RD

BRACKEN WAY

SCOTT HILL

DAISY BANK LA

Trent and Mersey Canal

Anderton Boat Lift
& Nature Park

Cerny

A533

GRANGE RD

WHITLEY AVE

SPENCER ST

BROADWAY

GEORGE ST

HILL CROSS

MANOR RD

POND ST

Weaver Navigation

75

PLUMBS
FOLD

THE
MEWS

LYDYETT LA

PRINCES AVE

PARK

BLACKCROFT AVE

RUNCORN RD

CHURCH RD

BROOK

PO

Works

Tunnel

TUNNEL RD

CANAL SIDE

TOWNFIELD

Ropery
Farm

River Weaver

CW8

Slicks
Bsns Ctr

1

Sewage
Works

WINNINGTON AVE

SANDYBANK

Brunner
Bsns Ctr

Winnington

SOLWAY RD

BOND ST

NORTHWICH RD

BUXFIELD CL

P

VICTORIA PARK

BOWLING GREEN CT

VERDIN AVE

BARONS QUAY RD

LEICESTER

Sewage
Works

WINNINGTON LA

MOSS RD

B5374

PO

PARK RD

HEMMING ST

DYAR TERR

APPLETON ST

HILLVIEW
RISE

BARN MDW

SPRING
MDW

OAKLEIGH RISE

CLAY LA

FOXES
FOLD

OLD SCHOOL RD

OAKDALE
CH

OLDHAMS
HILL

WEAVER WAY

P

74

Barnton Cut

P

THE
WOODLANDS

Victoria
H

A533

WITTON ST

63   A   64   B   65   C

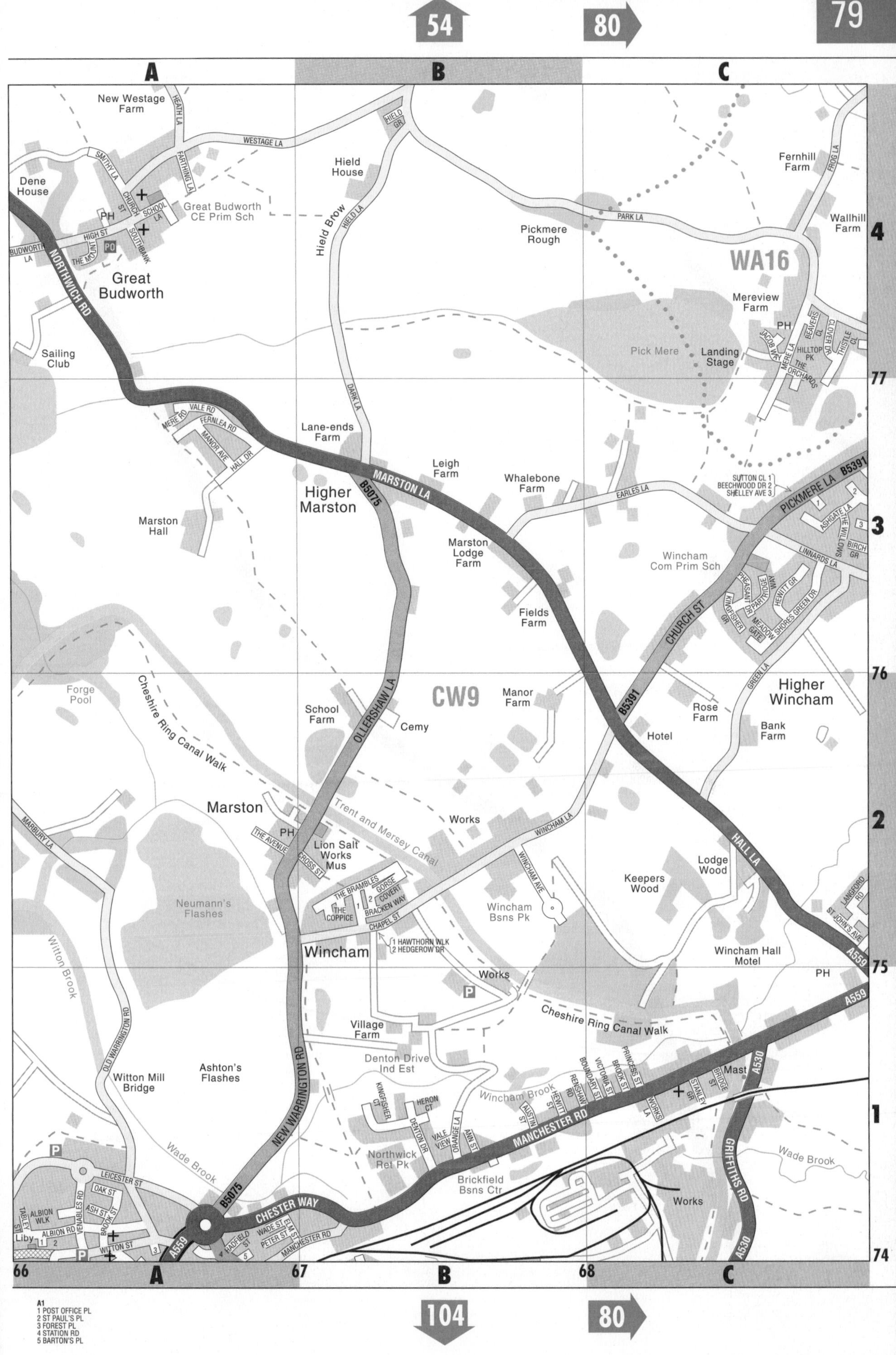

79
55

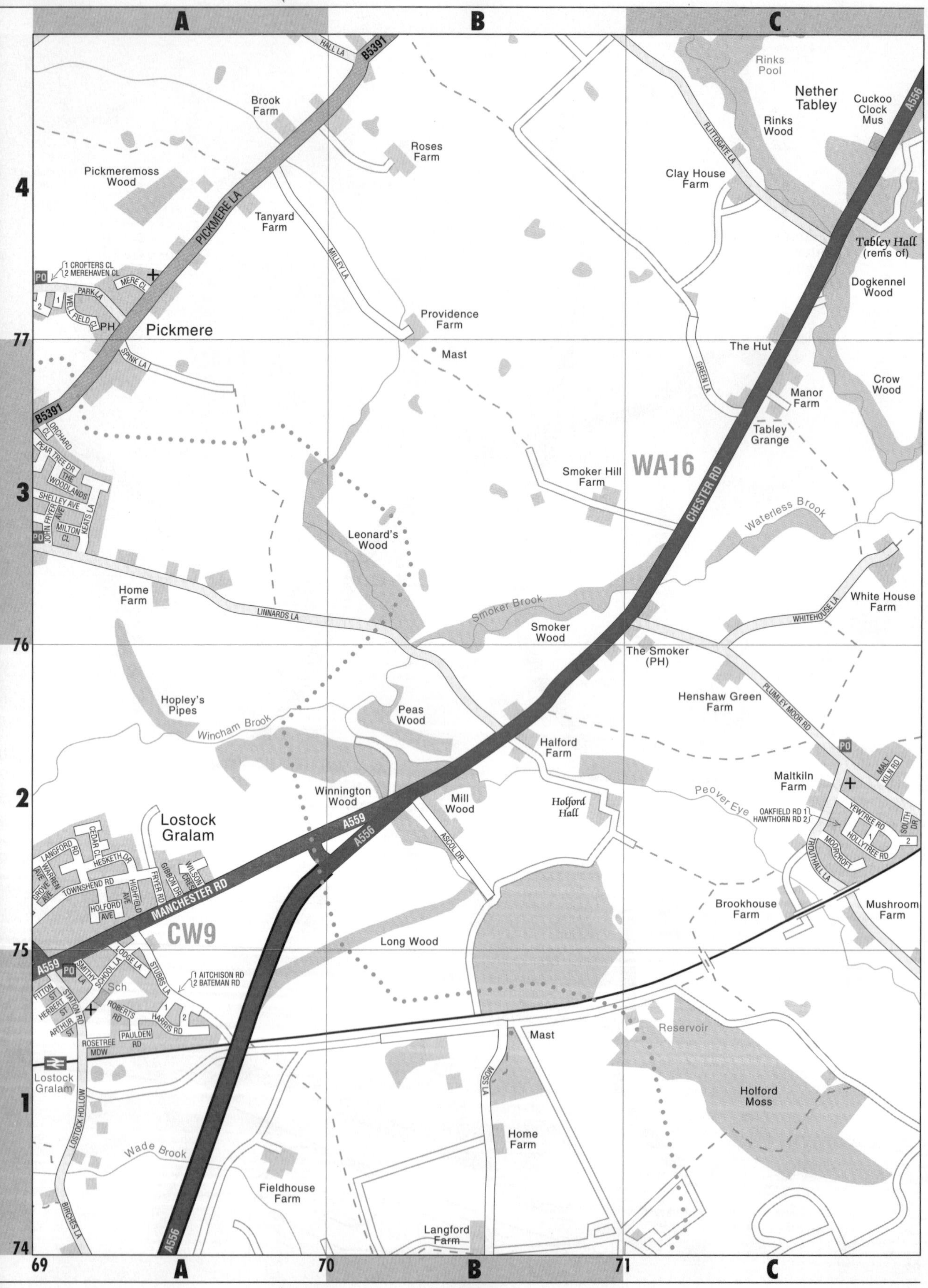
A
B
C
4
3
2
1
77
76
75
74
69
70
71
B5391
HALL LA
Brook Farm
Roses Farm
Pickmeremoss Wood
PICKMERE LA
Tanyard Farm
MILLEY LA
1 CROFTERS CL
2 MEREHAVEN CL
PO
MERE CL
PARK LA
WELL FIELD CL
PH
Pickmere
Providence Farm
Mast
SPINK LA
ORCHARD CL
PEAR TREE DR
THE WOODLANDS
SHELLEY AVE
JOHN FRYER AVE
MILTON CL
KEATS LA
Home Farm
LINNARDS LA
Leonard's Wood
Hopley's Pipes
Wincham Brook
Peas Wood
Winnington Wood
Lostock Gralam
LANGFORD RD
CEDAR CL
HESKETH DR
WARREN AVE
GROVE AVE
TOWNSHEND RD
HIGHFIELD AVE
HOLFORD AVE
GIBBON DR
FRYER RD
WILSON CRES
MANCHESTER RD
A559
A556
CW9
SMITHY LA
SCHOOL LA
LODGE LA
STUBBS LA
1 AITCHISON RD
2 BATEMAN RD
Sch
FITTON ST
HERBERT ST
STATION RD
ARTHUR ST
ROBERTS RD
HARRIS RD
PAULDEN RD
ROSETREE MDW
Lostock Gralam
LOSTOCK HOLLOW
Wade Brook
BIRCHES LA
Mill Wood
ASCOL DR
Long Wood
Mast
MOSS LA
Home Farm
Fieldhouse Farm
Langford Farm
Rinks Pool
Nether Tabley
Cuckoo Clock Mus
Rinks Wood
FLITTOGATE LA
Clay House Farm
Tabley Hall (rems of)
Dogkennel Wood
The Hut
GREEN LA
Manor Farm
Crow Wood
Tabley Grange
Smoker Hill Farm
WA16
CHESTER RD
Waterless Brook
White House Farm
WHITEHOUSE LA
Smoker Brook
Smoker Wood
The Smoker (PH)
Henshaw Green Farm
PLUMLEY MOOR RD
Halford Farm
Maltkiln Farm
MALT KILN RD
Peover Eye
Holford Hall
OAKFIELD RD 1
HAWTHORN RD 2
YEWTREE RD
HOLLYTREE RD
MOORCROFT
TROUTHALL LA
SOUTH DR
Brookhouse Farm
Mushroom Farm
Reservoir
Holford Moss

79
105

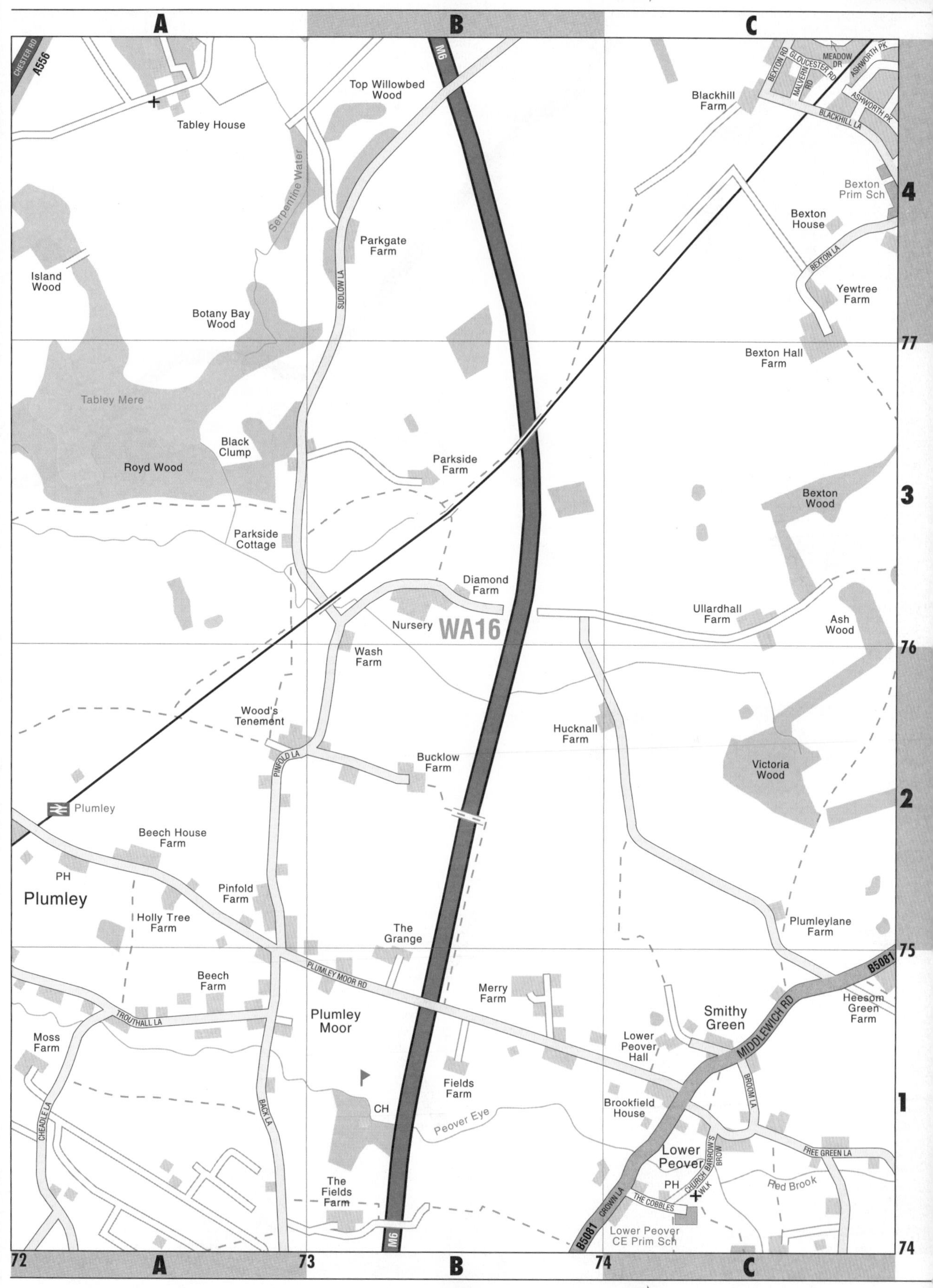

CHESTER RD
A556

Top Willowbed Wood

Blackhill Farm

MEADOW DR
BEXTON RD
GLOUCESTER RD
MALVERN RD
ASHWORTH PK
BLACKHILL LA

Tabley House

Bexton Prim Sch

4

Parkgate Farm

Bexton House

Island Wood

SUDLOW LA

Botany Bay Wood

Serpentine Water

Yewtree Farm

BEXTON LA

77

Bexton Hall Farm

Tabley Mere

Black Clump

Parkside Farm

Bexton Wood

3

Royd Wood

Parkside Cottage

Diamond Farm

Ullardhall Farm

Ash Wood

Nursery WA16

76

Wash Farm

Wood's Tenement

Hucknall Farm

Victoria Wood

PINFOLD LA

Bucklow Farm

2

Plumley

Beech House Farm

Plumleylane Farm

PH

Pinfold Farm

75
B5081

Plumley

Holly Tree Farm

The Grange

PLUMLEY MOOR RD

Smithy Green

Heesom Green Farm

MIDDLEWICH RD

Beech Farm

TROUTHALL LA

Merry Farm

Lower Peover Hall

BROOM LA

Moss Farm

Plumley Moor

Fields Farm

Brookfield House

1

CHEADLE LA

BACK LA

CH

Peover Eye

Lower Peover

BARROW'S BROW

FREE GREEN LA

Red Brook

The Fields Farm

CROWN LA

PH

WLK

THE COBBLES

CHURCH

B5081

Lower Peover CE Prim Sch

M6

74

81
57

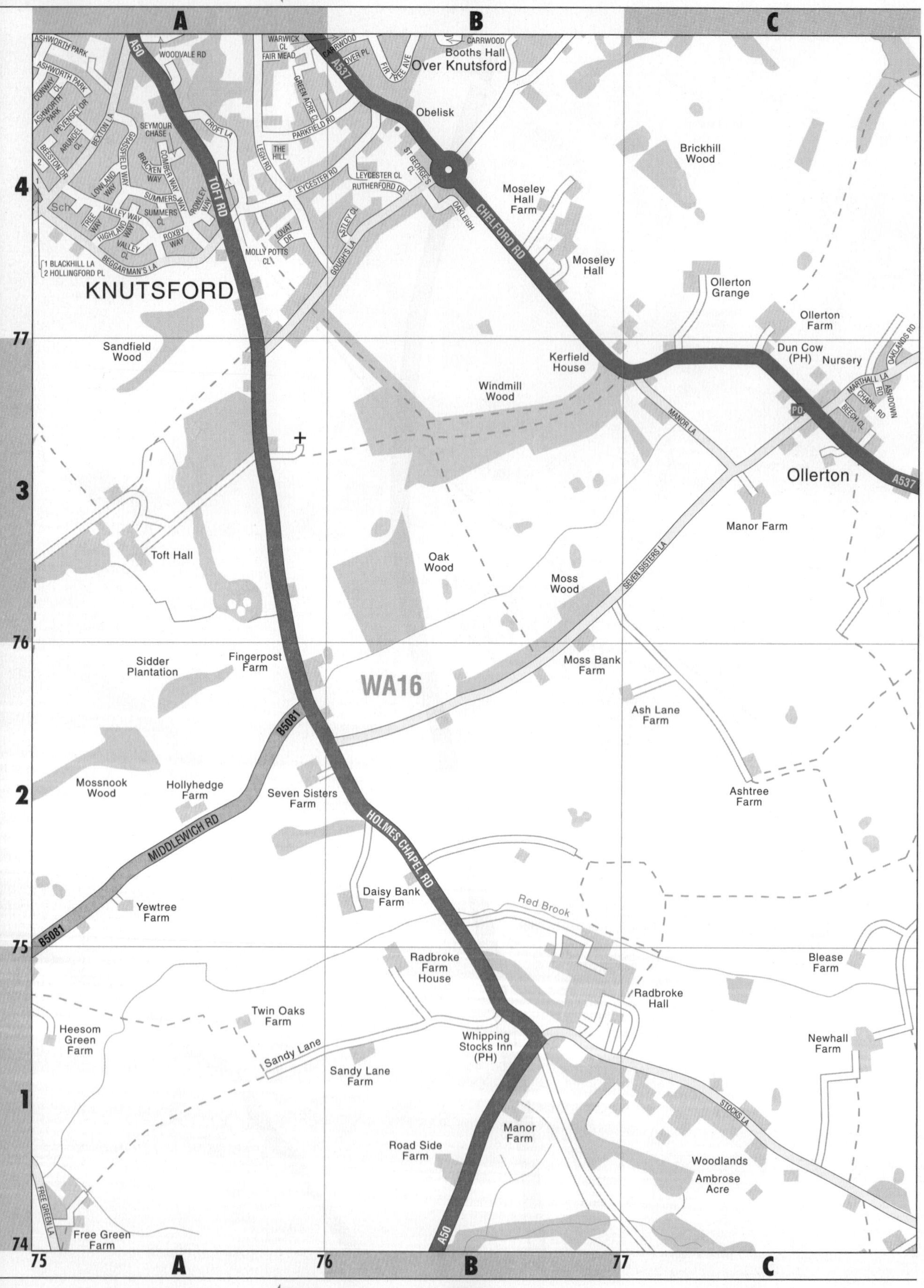
A
B
C
KNUTSFORD
Over Knutsford
Booths Hall
Obelisk
Brickhill Wood
Moseley Hall Farm
Moseley Hall
Ollerton Grange
Ollerton Farm
Dun Cow (PH)
Nursery
Kerfield House
Windmill Wood
Sandfield Wood
Ollerton
Manor Farm
Toft Hall
Oak Wood
Moss Wood
Sidder Plantation
Fingerpost Farm
WA16
Moss Bank Farm
Ash Lane Farm
Mossnook Wood
Hollyhedge Farm
Seven Sisters Farm
Ashtree Farm
Daisy Bank Farm
Yewtree Farm
Red Brook
Radbroke Farm House
Radbroke Hall
Blease Farm
Twin Oaks Farm
Heesom Green Farm
Whipping Stocks Inn (PH)
Newhall Farm
Sandy Lane
Sandy Lane Farm
Manor Farm
Road Side Farm
Woodlands
Ambrose Acre
Free Green Farm
A50
A537
B5081
TOFT RD
CHELFORD RD
MANOR LA
SEVEN SISTERS LA
MIDDLEWICH RD
HOLMES CHAPEL RD
STOCKS LA
FREE GREEN LA
1 BLACKHILL LA
2 HOLLINGFORD PL
4
3
2
1
77
76
75
74

81
107

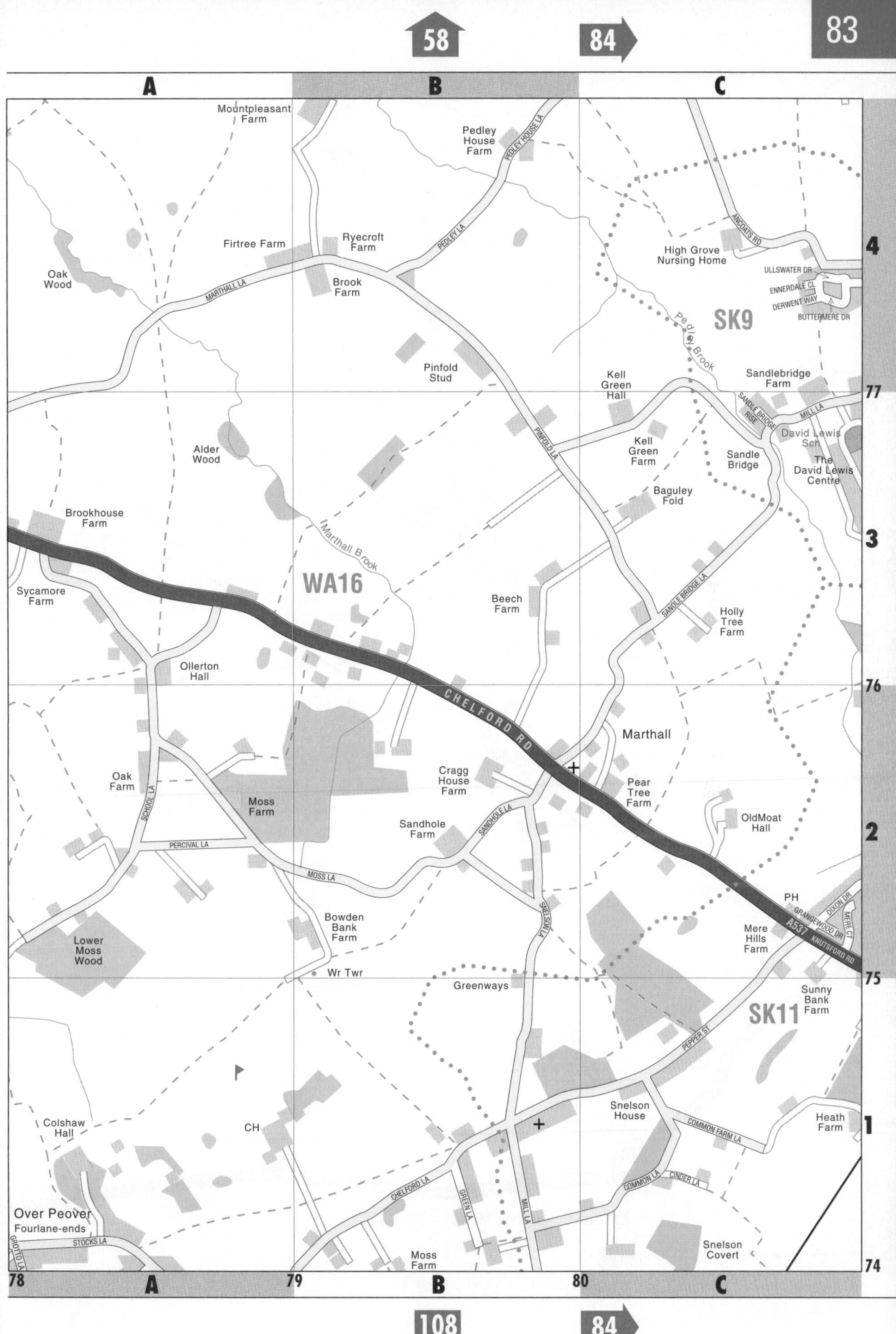
A
B
C
Mountpleasant Farm
Pedley House Farm
PEDLEY HOUSE LA
Firtree Farm
Ryecroft Farm
PEDLEY LA
ANCOATS RD
High Grove Nursing Home
ULLSWATER DR
ENNERDALE CL
DERWENT WAY
BUTTERMERE DR
Oak Wood
MARTHALL LA
Brook Farm
Pedley Brook
SK9
Pinfold Stud
Kell Green Hall
Sandlebridge Farm
SANDLE BRIDGE RISE
MILL LA
David Lewis Sch
The David Lewis Centre
Alder Wood
PINFOLD LA
Kell Green Farm
Sandle Bridge
Baguley Fold
Brookhouse Farm
Marthall Brook
WA16
Sycamore Farm
Beech Farm
SANDLE BRIDGE LA
Holly Tree Farm
Ollerton Hall
CHELFORD RD
Marthall
Oak Farm
Cragg House Farm
Pear Tree Farm
SCHOOL LA
Moss Farm
Sandhole Farm
SANDHOLE LA
OldMoat Hall
PERCIVAL LA
MOSS LA
PH
DIXON DR
MERE CT
GRANGEWOOD DR
A537
KNUTSFORD RD
Bowden Bank Farm
SNELSON LA
Mere Hills Farm
Lower Moss Wood
Wr Twr
Greenways
Sunny Bank Farm
SK11
PEPPER ST
Colshaw Hall
CH
Snelson House
COMMON FARM LA
Heath Farm
CHELFORD LA
GREEN LA
COMMON LA
CINDER LA
Over Peover
Fourlane-ends
MILL LA
GROTTO LA
STOCKS LA
Moss Farm
Snelson Covert
4
77
3
76
2
75
1
74
78
79
80
A
B
C

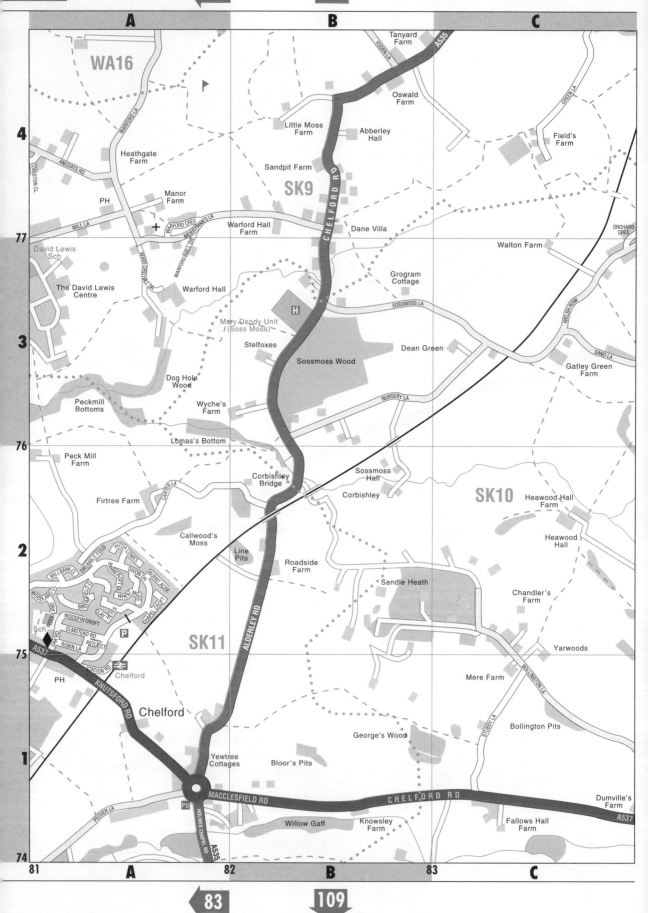

A   B   C

4

WA16

Tanyard
Farm

A535

Oswald
Farm

Little Moss
Farm

Abberley
Hall

Field's
Farm

GREEN LA

Heathgate
Farm

Sandpit Farm

ANGOATS RD

CONISTON CL

WARFORD LA

SK9

CHELFORD RD

77

Manor
Farm

PH

MILL LA

WARFORD CRES

MERRYMAN'S LA

Warford Hall
Farm

Dane Villa

Walton Farm

ORCHARD
CRES

David Lewis
Sch

WARFORD HALL DR

Warford Hall

Grogram
Cottage

WELSH ROW

The David Lewis
Centre

WARFORD DR

H

SOSSMOSS LA

Mary Dendy Unit
/ (Soss Moss)

Walton Farm

3

Stelfoxes

Dean Green

SAND LA

Dog Hole
Wood

Sossmoss Wood

Gatley Green
Farm

Peckmill
Bottoms

Wyche's
Farm

NURSERY LA

76

Lomas's Bottom

Peck Mill
Farm

CARTER LA

Corbishley
Bridge

Sossmoss
Hall

SK10

Heawood Hall
Farm

Firtree Farm

Corbishley

Callwood's
Moss

Line
Pits

Heawood
Hall

2

MILLBANK

DRUMBLE FIELD

HITCHLOWES

BURNT ACRE

ALDERLEY RD

Roadside
Farm

Sandle Heath

Chandler's
Farm

WOODLAND CL

BROMFIELD

BIRCHCROFT DR

DIXON DR

WYCH MOSS

Yarwoods

WOODLAND

CLAY ACRES

CURZON CROFT

WOODFIN CROFT

ROLLINGTON LA

ELMSTEAD RD

ASTLE CT

Mere Farm

Sch

DALE RD

ROBIN LA

P

SK11

75

A537

STATION RD

Chelford

PH

KNUTSFORD RD

Chelford

George's Wood

STUBBY LA

Bollington Pits

1

Yewtree
Cottages

Bloor's Pits

Dumville's
Farm

PO

MACCLESFIELD RD

CHELFORD RD

Fallows Hall
Farm

A537

PEOVER LA

HOLMES CHAPEL RD

A535

Willow Gaff

Knowsley
Farm

74

81   A   82   B   83   C

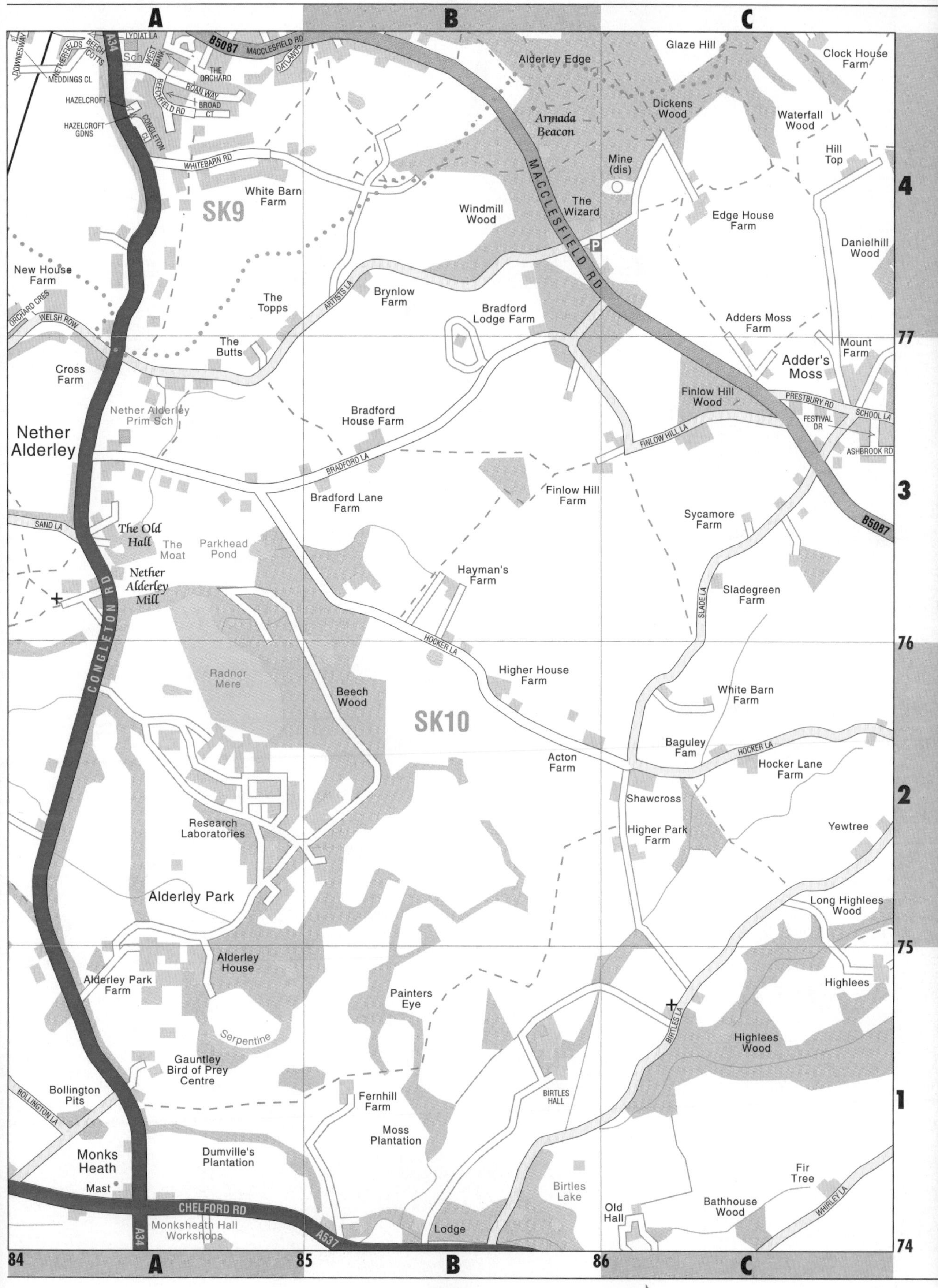
A
B
C
Alderley Edge
Glaze Hill
Clock House Farm
Dickens Wood
Armada Beacon
Waterfall Wood
Hill Top
Mine (dis)
White Barn Farm
SK9
Windmill Wood
The Wizard
Edge House Farm
Danielhill Wood
New House Farm
The Topps
Brynlow Farm
Bradford Lodge Farm
Adders Moss Farm
The Butts
Mount Farm
Adder's Moss
Cross Farm
Finlow Hill Wood
Nether Alderley Prim Sch
Bradford House Farm
Nether Alderley
Bradford Lane Farm
Finlow Hill Farm
Sycamore Farm
The Old Hall
The Moat
Parkhead Pond
Nether Alderley Mill
Hayman's Farm
Sladegreen Farm
Radnor Mere
Beech Wood
Higher House Farm
White Barn Farm
SK10
Baguley Fam
Acton Farm
Hocker Lane Farm
Shawcross
Research Laboratories
Higher Park Farm
Yewtree
Alderley Park
Long Highlees Wood
Alderley House
Alderley Park Farm
Painters Eye
Highlees
Serpentine
Highlees Wood
Gauntley Bird of Prey Centre
Bollington Pits
Fernhill Farm
Moss Plantation
Monks Heath
Dumville's Plantation
Fir Tree
Mast
Birtles Lake
Old Hall
Bathhouse Wood
Monksheath Hall Workshops
Lodge
MACCLESFIELD RD
B5087
CONGLETON RD
A34
CHELFORD RD
A537
WHITEBARN RD
ARTISTS LA
WELSH ROW
ORCHARD CRES
BRADFORD LA
FINLOW HILL LA
PRESTBURY RD
SCHOOL LA
FESTIVAL DR
ASHBROOK RD
SAND LA
SLADE LA
HOCKER LA
BIRTLES LA
BIRTLES HALL
BOLLINGTON LA
WHIRLEY LA
LYDIAT LA
DOWNESWAY
NETHERFIELDS
BEECH COTTS
MEDDINGS CL
HAZELCROFT
HAZELCROFT GDNS
CONGLETON CL
WEST BANK
THE ORCHARD
ROAN WAY
BEECHFIELD RD
BROAD CT
OATLANDS
Sch
4
77
3
76
2
75
1
74
84
85
86

85
61

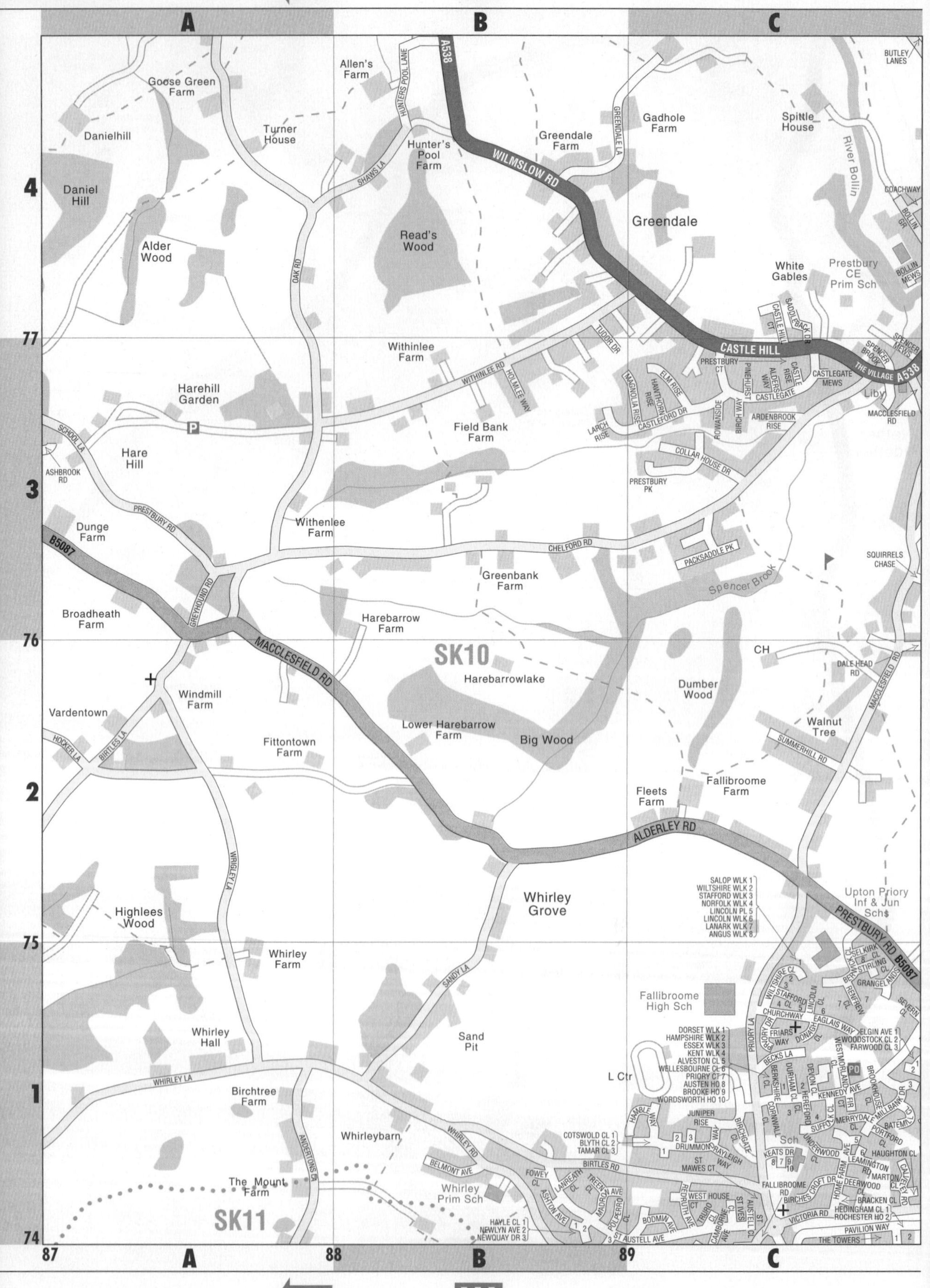
A
B
C
Goose Green Farm
Allen's Farm
Danielhill
Turner House
Hunter's Pool Farm
Greendale Farm
Gadhole Farm
Spittle House
River Bollin
Daniel Hill
Alder Wood
Read's Wood
WILMSLOW RD
Greendale
White Gables
Prestbury CE Prim Sch
CASTLE HILL
THE VILLAGE
A538
Withinlee Farm
WITHINLEE RD
Harehill Garden
Field Bank Farm
Hare Hill
Dunge Farm
Withenlee Farm
CHELFORD RD
PACKSADDLE PK
Greenbank Farm
Spencer Brook
Broadheath Farm
Harebarrow Farm
SK10
MACCLESFIELD RD
Harebarrowlake
CH
Dumber Wood
Windmill Farm
Vardentown
Lower Harebarrow Farm
Big Wood
Walnut Tree
Fittontown Farm
Fallibroome Farm
Fleets Farm
ALDERLEY RD
Whirley Grove
Upton Priory Inf & Jun Schs
PRESTBURY RD B5087
Highlees Wood
Whirley Farm
Fallibroome High Sch
Sand Pit
Whirley Hall
L Ctr
WHIRLEY LA
Birchtree Farm
Whirleybarn
The Mount Farm
Whirley Prim Sch
SK11
B5087
87
88
89
74
75
1
2
76
3
77
4

85
111

62
88
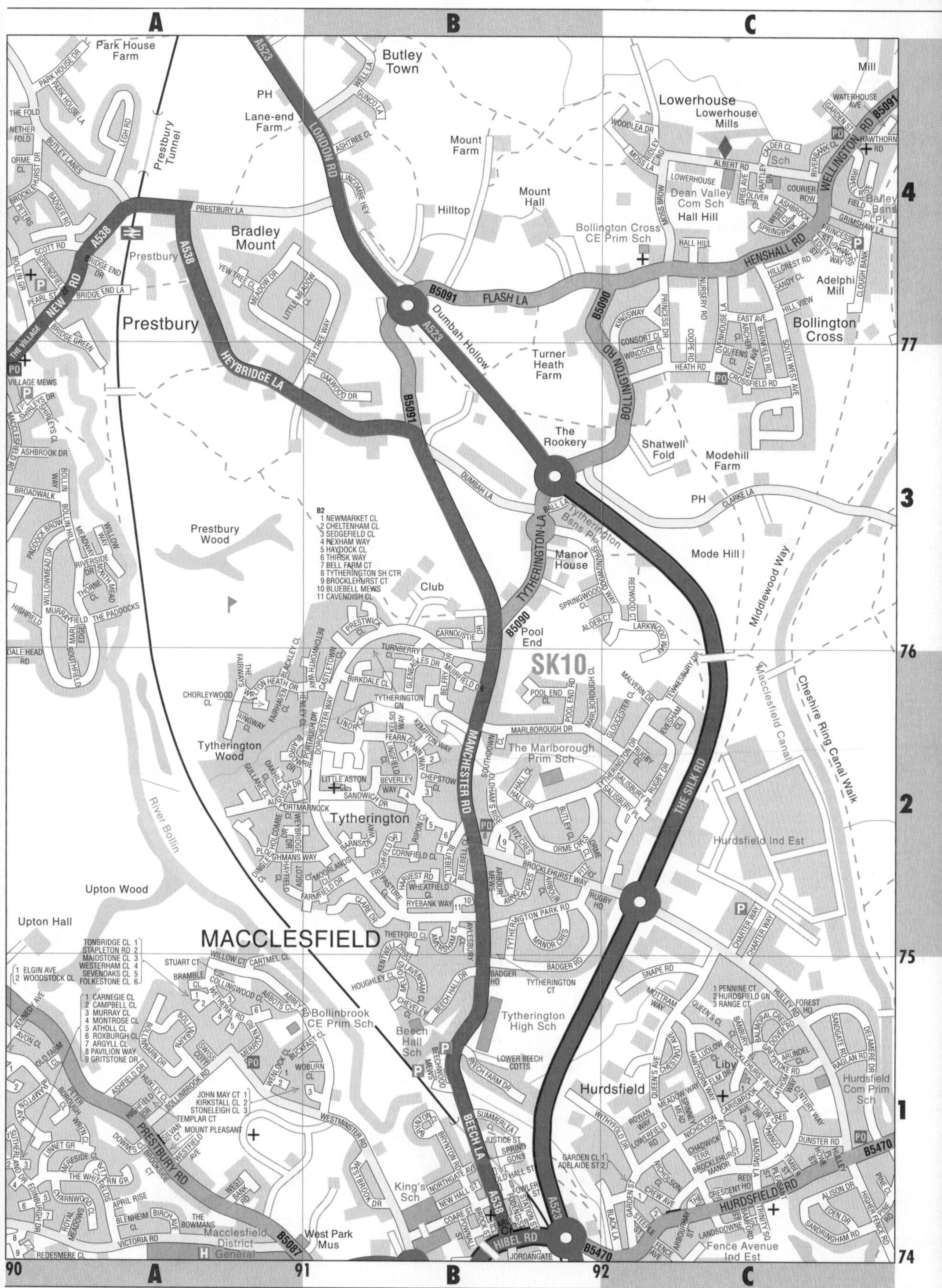
A
B
C
4
3
2
1
77
76
75
74
90
91
92
Park House Farm
Butley Town
PH
Lane-end Farm
Prestbury Tunnel
Mount Farm
Mount Hall
Hilltop
Lowerhouse
Lowerhouse Mills
Dean Valley Com Sch
Hall Hill
Bollington Cross CE Prim Sch
Mill
Bradley Mount
Prestbury
LONDON RD
PRESTBURY LA
A538
A523
B5091
FLASH LA
Dumbah Hollow
HEYBRIDGE LA
B5090
BOLLINGTON RD
HENSHALL RD
WELLINGTON RD
Adelphi Mill
Bollington Cross
Turner Heath Farm
The Rookery
Shatwell Fold
Modehill Farm
PH
CLARKE LA
DUMBAH LA
Prestbury Wood
Tytherington Bsns Pk
Manor House
Mode Hill
Middlewood Way
TYTHERINGTON LA
Club
Pool End
SK10
Macclesfield Canal
Cheshire Ring Canal Walk
THE SILK RD
MANCHESTER RD
Tytherington Wood
The Marlborough Prim Sch
Tytherington
River Bollin
Hurdsfield Ind Est
Upton Wood
Upton Hall
MACCLESFIELD
Bollinbrook CE Prim Sch
Beech Hall Sch
Tytherington High Sch
Hurdsfield
Hurdsfield Com Prim Sch
Liby
PRESTBURY RD
BEECH LA
HURDSFIELD RD
B5470
King's Sch
West Park Mus
Macclesfield District General
B5087
HIBEL RD
JORDANGATE
Fence Avenue Ind Est
B2
1 NEWMARKET CL
2 CHELTENHAM CL
3 SEDGEFIELD CL
4 HEXHAM WAY
5 HAYDOCK CL
6 THIRSK WAY
7 BELL FARM CT
8 TYTHERINGTON SH CTR
9 BROCKLEHURST CT
10 BLUEBELL MEWS
11 CAVENDISH CL
TONBRIDGE CL 1
STAPLETON RD 2
MAIDSTONE CL 3
WESTERHAM CL 4
SEVENOAKS CL 5
FOLKESTONE CL 6
1 ELGIN AVE
2 WOODSTOCK CL
1 CARNEGIE CL
2 CAMPBELL CL
3 MURRAY CL
4 MONTROSE CL
5 ATHOLL CL
6 ROXBURGH CL
7 ARGYLL CL
8 PAVILION WAY
9 GRITSTONE DR
JOHN MAY CT 1
KIRKSTALL CL 2
STONELEIGH CL 3
TEMPLAR CT
MOUNT PLEASANT
1 PENNINE CT
2 HURDSFIELD GN
3 RANGE CT
GARDEN CL 1
ADELAIDE ST 2
112
88

87
63

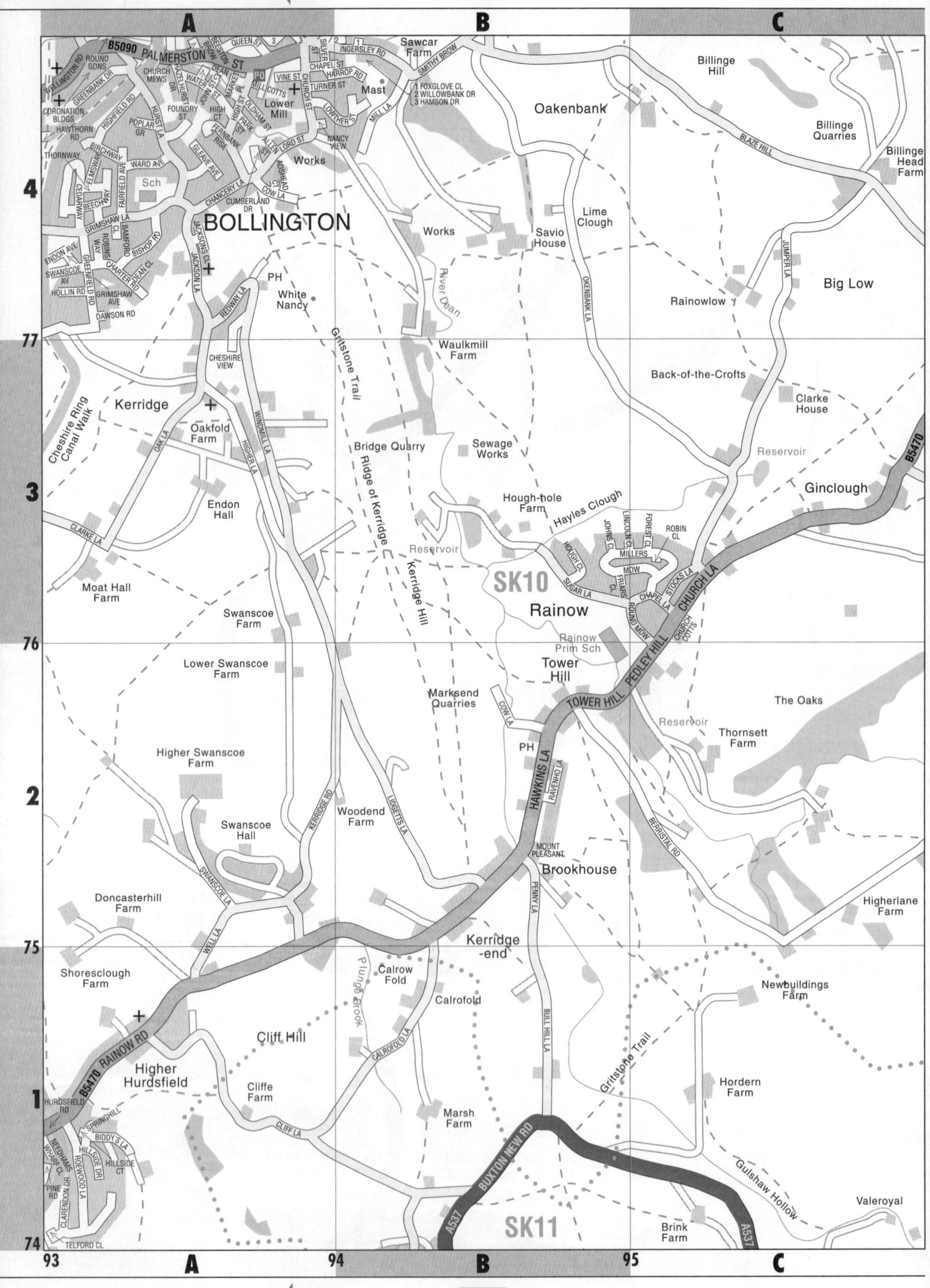
A
B
C
4
77
3
76
2
75
1
74
93
94
95
BOLLINGTON
B5090 PALMERSTON ST
Sawcar Farm
Billinge Hill
Oakenbank
Billinge Quarries
Billinge Head Farm
BLAZE HILL
Lower Mill
Mast
Works
Sch
Lime Clough
Savio House
Works
PH
White Nancy
River Dean
Big Low
Rainowlow
Waulkmill Farm
Back-of-the-Crofts
Clarke House
Kerridge
Cheshire Ring Canal Walk
Oakfold Farm
Gritstone Trail
Bridge Quarry
Sewage Works
Reservoir
B5470
Ginclough
Endon Hall
Ridge of Kerridge
Hough-hole Farm
Hayles Clough
Kerridge Hill
Reservoir
SK10
Rainow
Moat Hall Farm
Swanscoe Farm
Rainow Prim Sch
Tower Hill
Lower Swanscoe Farm
Marksend Quarries
TOWER HILL
PEDLEY HILL
CHURCH LA
The Oaks
Reservoir
Thornsett Farm
PH
Higher Swanscoe Farm
HAWKINS LA
Woodend Farm
Swanscoe Hall
MOUNT PLEASANT
Brookhouse
Doncasterhill Farm
Higherlane Farm
Kerridge -end
Shoresclough Farm
Calrow Fold
Plunge Brook
Calrofold
Newbuildings Farm
Cliff Hill
B5470 RAINOW RD
Higher Hurdsfield
Cliffe Farm
Gritstone Trail
Hordern Farm
Marsh Farm
BUXTON NEW RD
A537
Gulshaw Hollow
Valeroyal
SK11
Brink Farm
A537

87
113

64
90

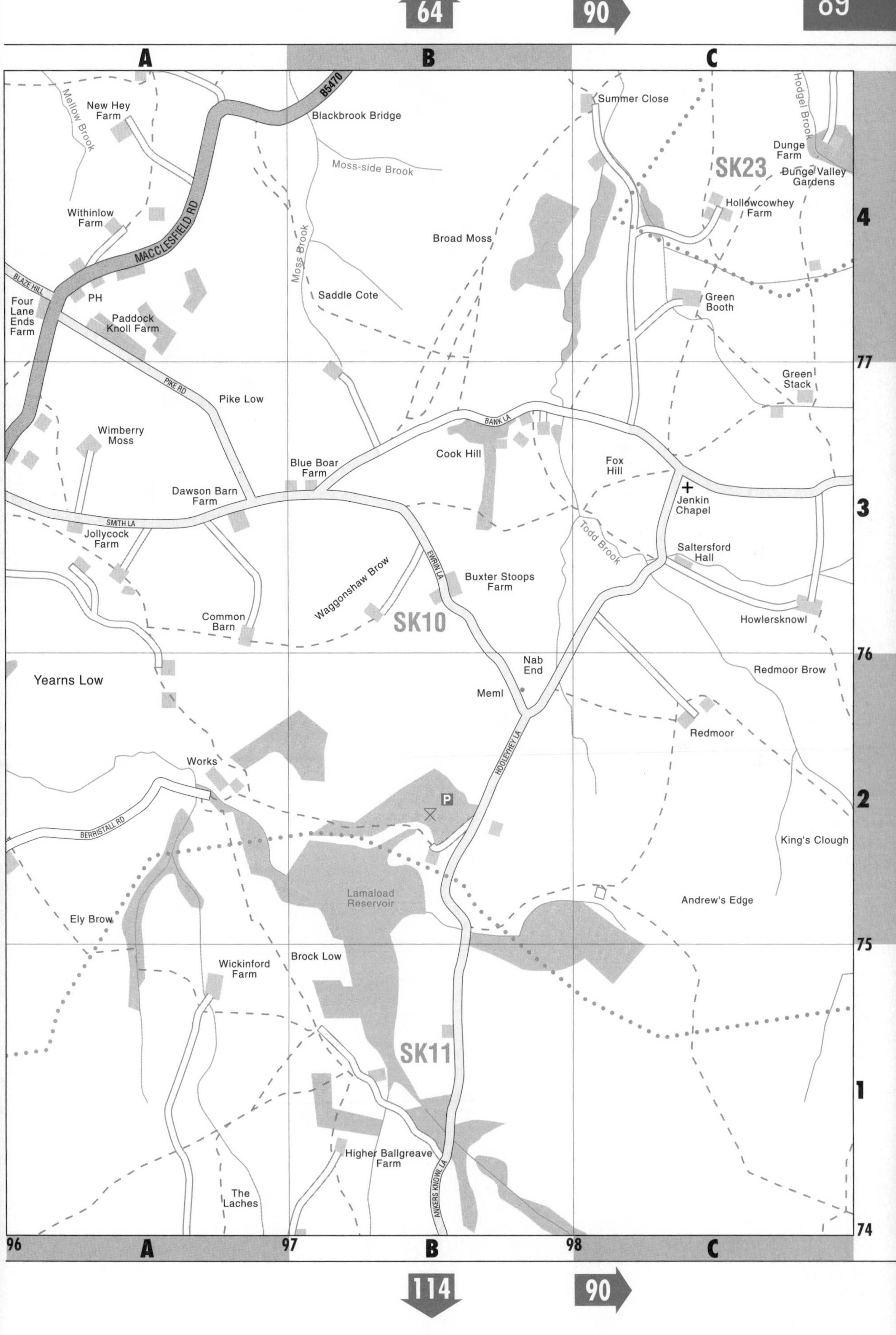
A
B
C
New Hey Farm
Mellow Brook
B5470
Blackbrook Bridge
Moss-side Brook
Summer Close
Hodgel Brook
Dunge Farm
SK23
Dunge Valley Gardens
Hollowcowhey Farm
Withinlow Farm
MACCLESFIELD RD
Moss Brook
Broad Moss
BLAZE HILL
Four Lane Ends Farm
PH
Paddock Knoll Farm
Saddle Cote
Green Booth
Green Stack
PIKE RD
Pike Low
Wimberry Moss
BANK LA
Cook Hill
Fox Hill
Blue Boar Farm
Dawson Barn Farm
Jenkin Chapel
SMITH LA
Jollycock Farm
Todd Brook
Saltersford Hall
Waggonshaw Brow
EWRIN LA
Buxter Stoops Farm
Common Barn
SK10
Howlersknowl
Yearns Low
Nab End
Redmoor Brow
Meml
Redmoor
Works
HOOLEYHEY LA
P
BERRISTALL RD
King's Clough
Lamaload Reservoir
Andrew's Edge
Ely Brow
Wickinford Farm
Brock Low
SK11
Higher Ballgreave Farm
ANKERS KNOWL LA
The Laches
4
77
3
76
2
75
1
74
96
97
98

114
90

89
65

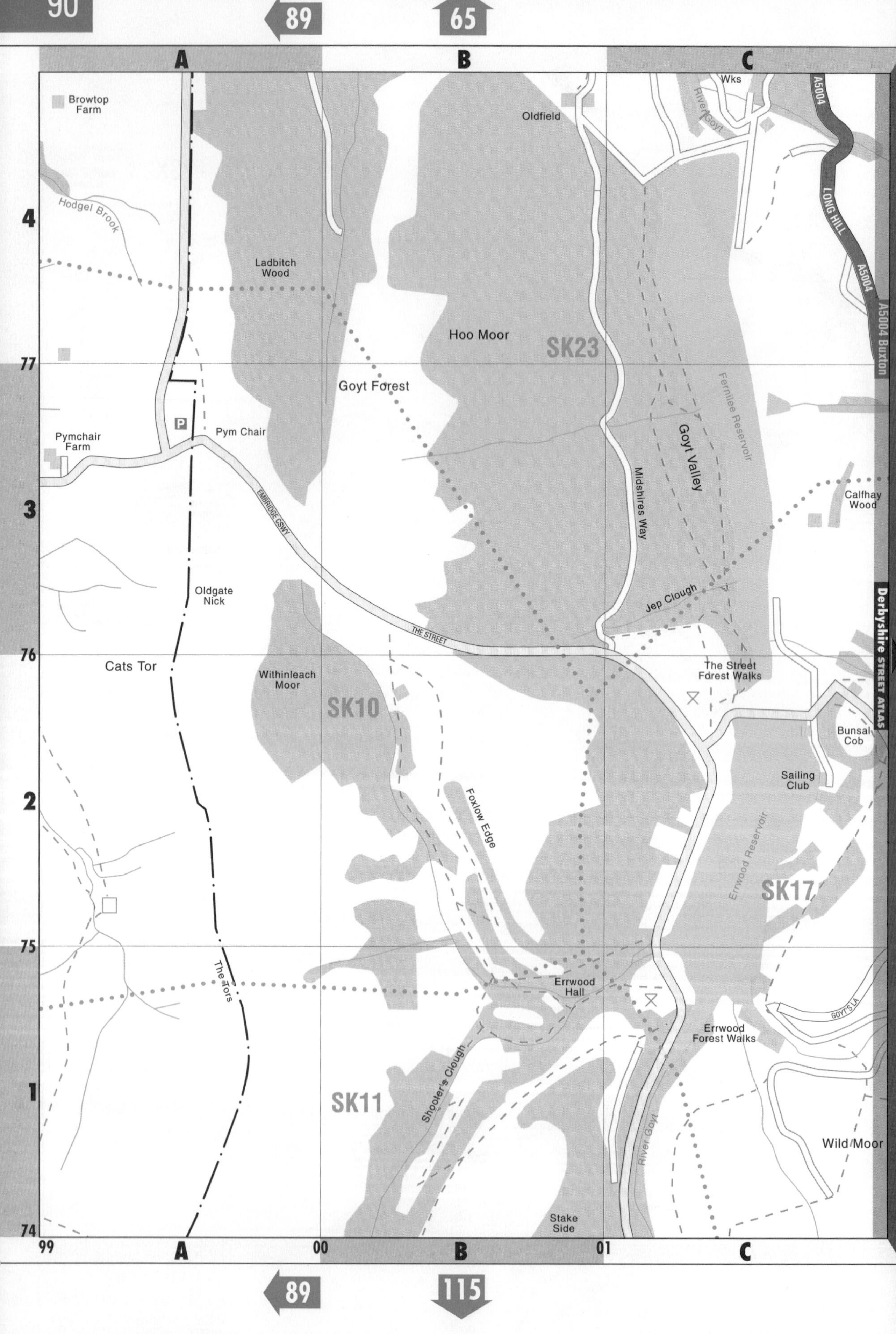
A
B
C
Browtop Farm
Oldfield
Wks
River Goyt
A5004
LONG HILL
A5004
A5004 Buxton
Hodgel Brook
4
Ladbitch Wood
Hoo Moor
SK23
77
Goyt Forest
Fernilee Reservoir
Pymchair Farm
Pym Chair
Goyt Valley
Midshires Way
3
EMBRIDGE CSWY
Calfhay Wood
Oldgate Nick
Jep Clough
THE STREET
76
Cats Tor
Withinleach Moor
SK10
The Street Forest Walks
Derbyshire STREET ATLAS
Bunsal Cob
Sailing Club
2
Foxlow Edge
Errwood Reservoir
SK17
75
The Tors
Errwood Hall
GOYT'S LA
Errwood Forest Walks
Shooter's Clough
1
SK11
River Goyt
Wild Moor
Stake Side
74
99
00
01

89
115

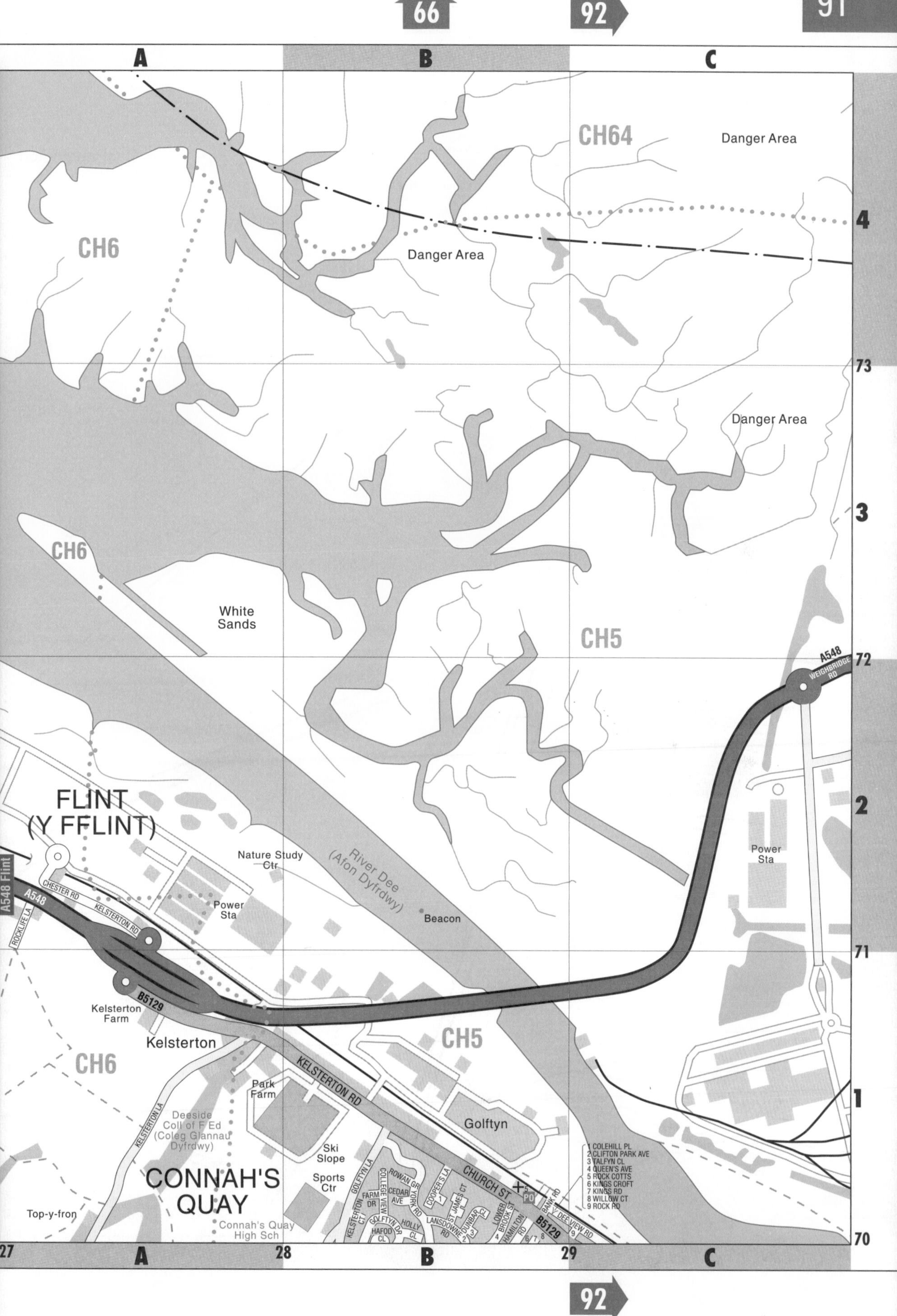

A **B** **C**

CH64

Danger Area

CH6

Danger Area

4

73

CH6

3

White
Sands

CH5

A548
WEIGHBRIDGE RD

72

FLINT
(Y FFLINT)

Nature Study
Ctr

River Dee
(Afon Dyfrdwy)

Power
Sta

2

A548 Flint

CHESTER RD

A548

Power
Sta

Beacon

KELSTERTON RD

ROCKLIFE LA

71

B5129

Kelsterton
Farm

Kelsterton

CH5

1

CH6

KELSTERTON LA

Park
Farm

KELSTERTON RD

Golftyn

Deeside
Coll of F Ed
(Coleg Glannau
Dyfrdwy)

Ski
Slope

1 COLEHILL PL
2 CLIFTON PARK AVE
3 TALFYN CL
4 QUEEN'S AVE
5 ROCK COTTS
6 KINGS CROFT
7 KING'S RD
8 WILLOW CT
9 ROCK RD

CONNAH'S
QUAY

Sports
Ctr

CHURCH ST
PO

Top-y-fron

Connah's Quay
High Sch

GOLFTYN LA
COLLEGE VIEW
FARM DR
CEDAR AVE
KELSTERTON CT
GOLFTYN CL
HAFOD CL
HOLLY CL
ROWAN GR
YORK RD
LANSDOWNE RD
COOPER'S LA
ST JAMES CT
DUBAO CT
BROOKE ST
HAMILTON RD
BANK RD
DEE VIEW RD

B5129

A **B** **C**

27 28 29

70

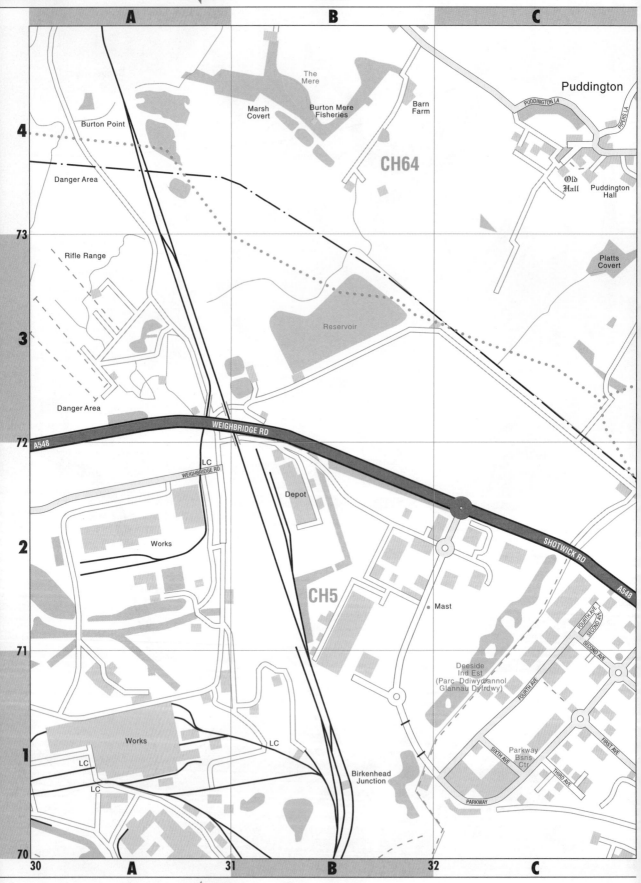

A B C

The Mere

Marsh Covert

Burton Mere Fisheries

Barn Farm

Puddington

PUDDINGTON LA

PIPERS LA

Burton Point

4

CH64

Old Hall

Puddington Hall

Danger Area

73

Rifle Range

Platts Covert

3

Reservoir

Danger Area

WEIGHBRIDGE RD

72

A548

LC

WEIGHBRIDGE RD

Depot

SHOTWICK RD

2

Works

CH5

Mast

A548

FOURTH AVE

SECOND AVE

SECOND AVE

71

Deeside Ind Est (Parc Ddiwydiannol Glannau Dyfrdwy)

FOURTH AVE

Works

LC

LC

1

LC

Birkenhead Junction

Parkway Bsns Ctr

SIXTH AVE

FIRST AVE

THIRD AVE

LC

PARKWAY

70

30 A 31 B 32 C

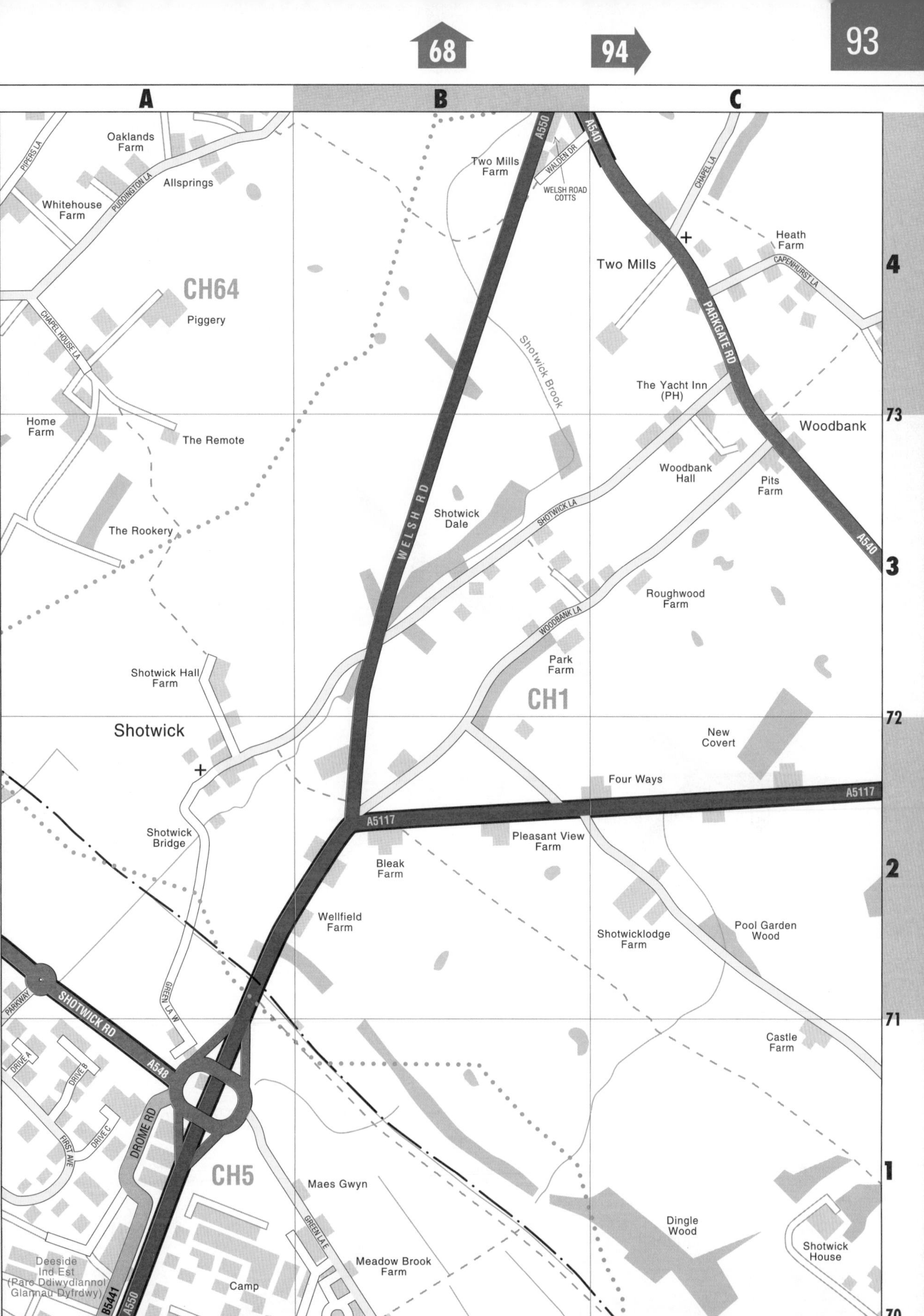
68
94
A
B
C
Oaklands Farm
Allsprings
Whitehouse Farm
PIPERS LA
PUDDINGTON LA
CH64
Piggery
CHAPEL HOUSE LA
Home Farm
The Remote
The Rookery
Shotwick Hall Farm
Shotwick
Shotwick Bridge
Two Mills Farm
WALDEN DR
WELSH ROAD COTTS
A550
A540
Two Mills
CHAPEL LA
Heath Farm
CAPENHURST LA
PARKGATE RD
Shotwick Brook
The Yacht Inn (PH)
Woodbank
Woodbank Hall
Pits Farm
WELSH RD
Shotwick Dale
SHOTWICK LA
Roughwood Farm
WOODBANK LA
Park Farm
CH1
New Covert
Four Ways
A5117
Pleasant View Farm
Bleak Farm
Wellfield Farm
Shotwicklodge Farm
Pool Garden Wood
Castle Farm
PARKWAY
SHOTWICK RD
A548
GREEN LA W
DRIVE A
DRIVE B
DRIVE C
FIRST AVE
DROME RD
CH5
Maes Gwyn
GREEN LA E
Meadow Brook Farm
Dingle Wood
Shotwick House
Deeside Ind Est (Parc Ddiwydiannol Glannau Dyfrdwy)
Camp
B5441
4
73
3
72
2
71
1
70
33
34
35
116

93
69

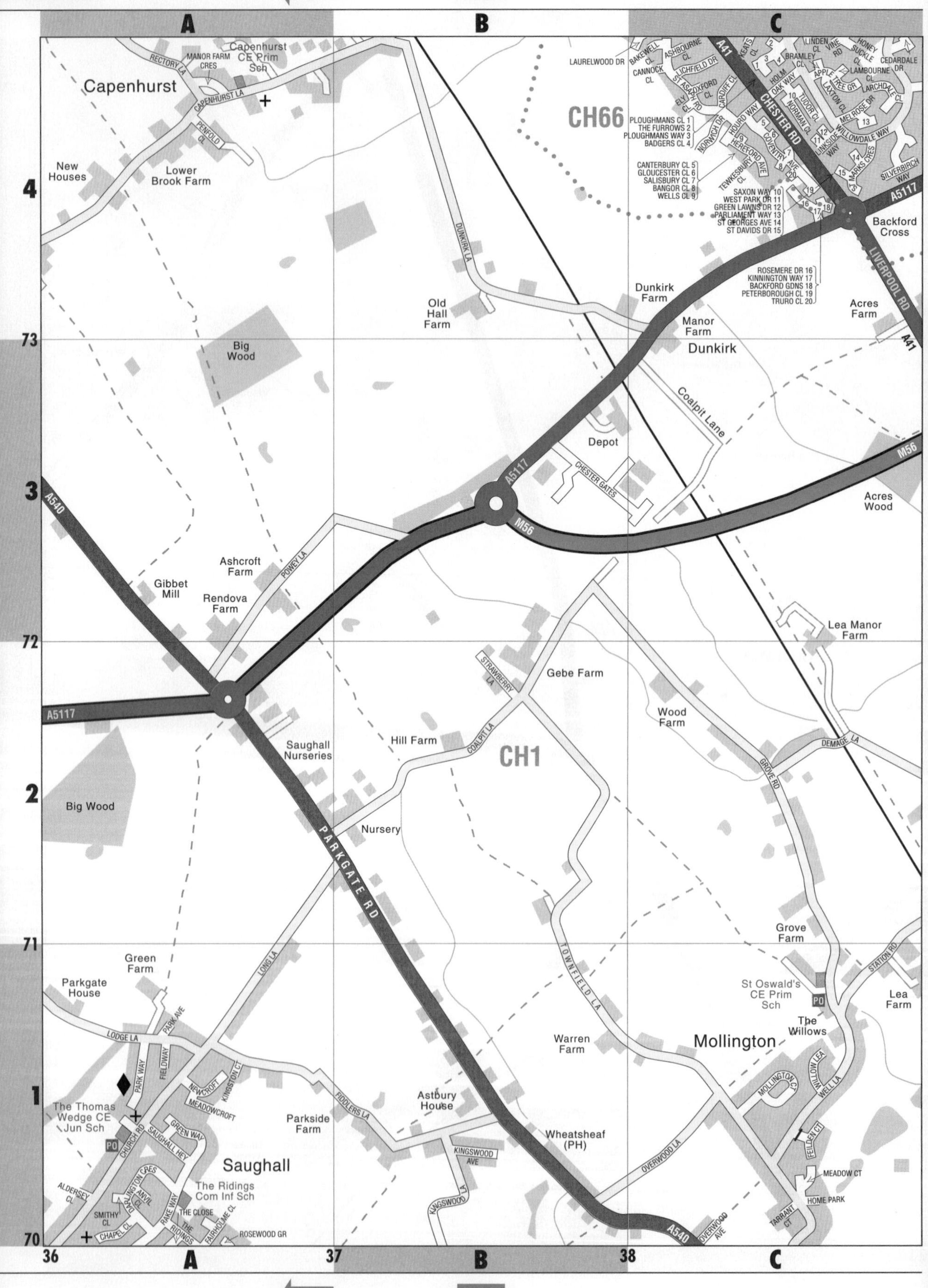
Capenhurst
Capenhurst CE Prim Sch
MANOR FARM CRES
RECTORY LA
CAPENHURST LA
PENFOLD CL
New Houses
Lower Brook Farm
CH66
LAURELWOOD DR
BAKEWELL CL
ASHBOURNE CL
CANNOCK CL
LICHFIELD DR
OXFORD CL
CHESTER RD
PLOUGHMANS CL 1
THE FURROWS 2
PLOUGHMANS WAY 3
BADGERS CL 4
CANTERBURY CL 5
GLOUCESTER CL 6
SALISBURY CL 7
BANGOR CL 8
WELLS CL 9
SAXON WAY 10
WEST PARK DR 11
GREEN LAWNS DR 12
PARLIAMENT WAY 13
ST GEORGES AVE 14
ST DAVIDS DR 15
ROSEMERE DR 16
KINNINGTON WAY 17
BACKFORD GDNS 18
PETERBOROUGH CL 19
TRURO CL 20
Backford Cross
A5117
LIVERPOOL RD
A41
Big Wood
DUNKIRK LA
Old Hall Farm
Dunkirk Farm
Manor Farm
Dunkirk
Acres Farm
Coalpit Lane
Depot
CHESTER GATES
M56
Acres Wood
A540
Ashcroft Farm
Gibbet Mill
Rendova Farm
POWEY LA
Lea Manor Farm
Gebe Farm
STRAWBERRY LA
Wood Farm
Hill Farm
COALPIT LA
Saughall Nurseries
CH1
DEMAGE LA
GROVE RD
Big Wood
Nursery
PARKGATE RD
Grove Farm
Green Farm
Parkgate House
LONG LA
TOWNFIELD LA
St Oswald's CE Prim Sch
STATION RD
Lea Farm
PO
The Willows
LODGE LA
PARK AVE
Warren Farm
Mollington
PARK WAY
FIELDWAY
KINGSTON CT
NEWCROFT
MEADOWCROFT
MOLLINGTON CT
WILLOW LEA
WELL LA
The Thomas Wedge CE Jun Sch
Astbury House
FIDDLERS LA
Parkside Farm
Wheatsheaf (PH)
FEILDEN CT
CHURCH RD
SAUGHALL HEY
GREEN WAY
KINGSWOOD AVE
OVERWOOD LA
MEADOW CT
Saughall
HOME PARK
The Ridings Com Inf Sch
KINGSWOOD LA
ALDERSEY CL
DARLINGTON CRES
ANVIL CL
SMITHY CL
RAKE WAY
THE CLOSE
THE RIDINGS
CHAPEL CL
FAIRHOLME CL
ROSEWOOD GR
OVERWOOD AVE
TARRANT CT
A B C
4 73 3 72 2 71 1 70
36 37 38

93
117

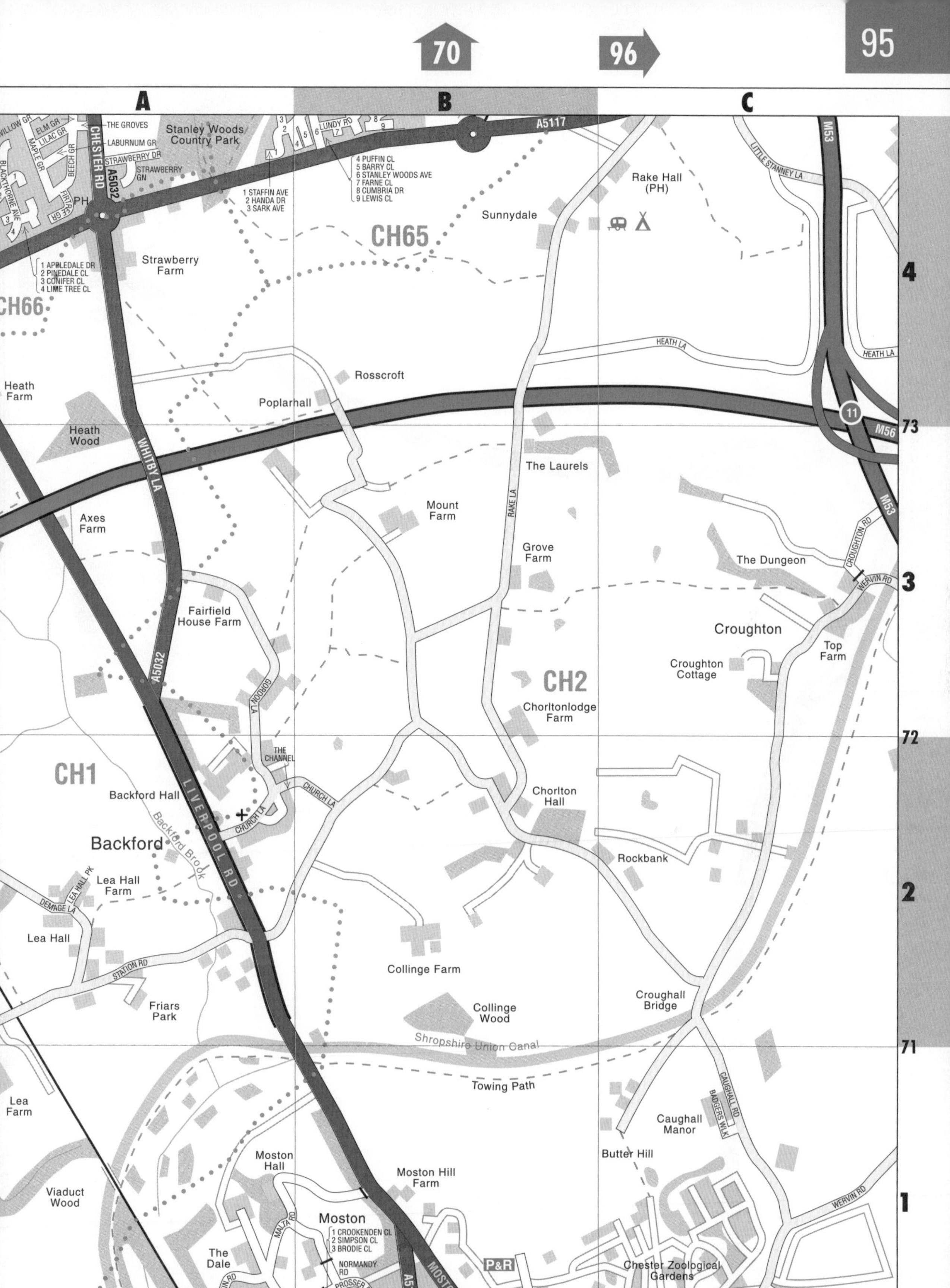
A
B
C
Stanley Woods Country Park
THE GROVES
LABURNUM GR
STRAWBERRY DR
STRAWBERRY GN
CHESTER RD
A5032
A5117
LUNDY RD
1 STAFFIN AVE
2 HANDA DR
3 SARK AVE
4 PUFFIN CL
5 BARRY CL
6 STANLEY WOODS AVE
7 FARNE CL
8 CUMBRIA DR
9 LEWIS CL
1 APPLEDALE DR
2 PINEDALE CL
3 CONIFER CL
4 LIME TREE CL
Strawberry Farm
CH65
CH66
Sunnydale
Rake Hall (PH)
LITTLE STANNEY LA
M53
HEATH LA
Heath Farm
Heath Wood
Rosscroft
Poplarhall
M56
11
The Laurels
WHITBY LA
Axes Farm
Mount Farm
RAKE LA
Grove Farm
The Dungeon
CROUGHTON RD
WERVIN RD
Croughton
Top Farm
Croughton Cottage
Fairfield House Farm
A5032
GORDON LA
CH2
Chorltonlodge Farm
CH1
THE CHANNEL
CHURCH LA
Backford Hall
LIVERPOOL RD
Chorlton Hall
Backford
Backford Brook
Rockbank
Lea Hall Farm
LEA HALL PK
DEMAGE LA
Lea Hall
STATION RD
Friars Park
Collinge Farm
Collinge Wood
Croughall Bridge
Shropshire Union Canal
Towing Path
Lea Farm
Caughall Manor
CAUGHALL RD
BADGERS WLK
Butter Hill
Viaduct Wood
Moston Hall
Moston Hill Farm
Moston
1 CROOKENDEN CL
2 SIMPSON CL
3 BRODIE CL
MALTA RD
NORMANDY RD
The Dale
ALAMEIN RD
PROSSER RD
SIMPSON RD
CROOKENDEN RD
CHARLES RD
SALERNO RD
A5116
MOSTON RD
A41
4 DAUNCEY CL
5 HARINGTON CL
6 HARINGTON RD
P&R
Chester Zoological Gardens
FLAG LA N
GREENACRES
ACRES LA
4
73
3
72
2
71
1
70
39
40
41

95
71

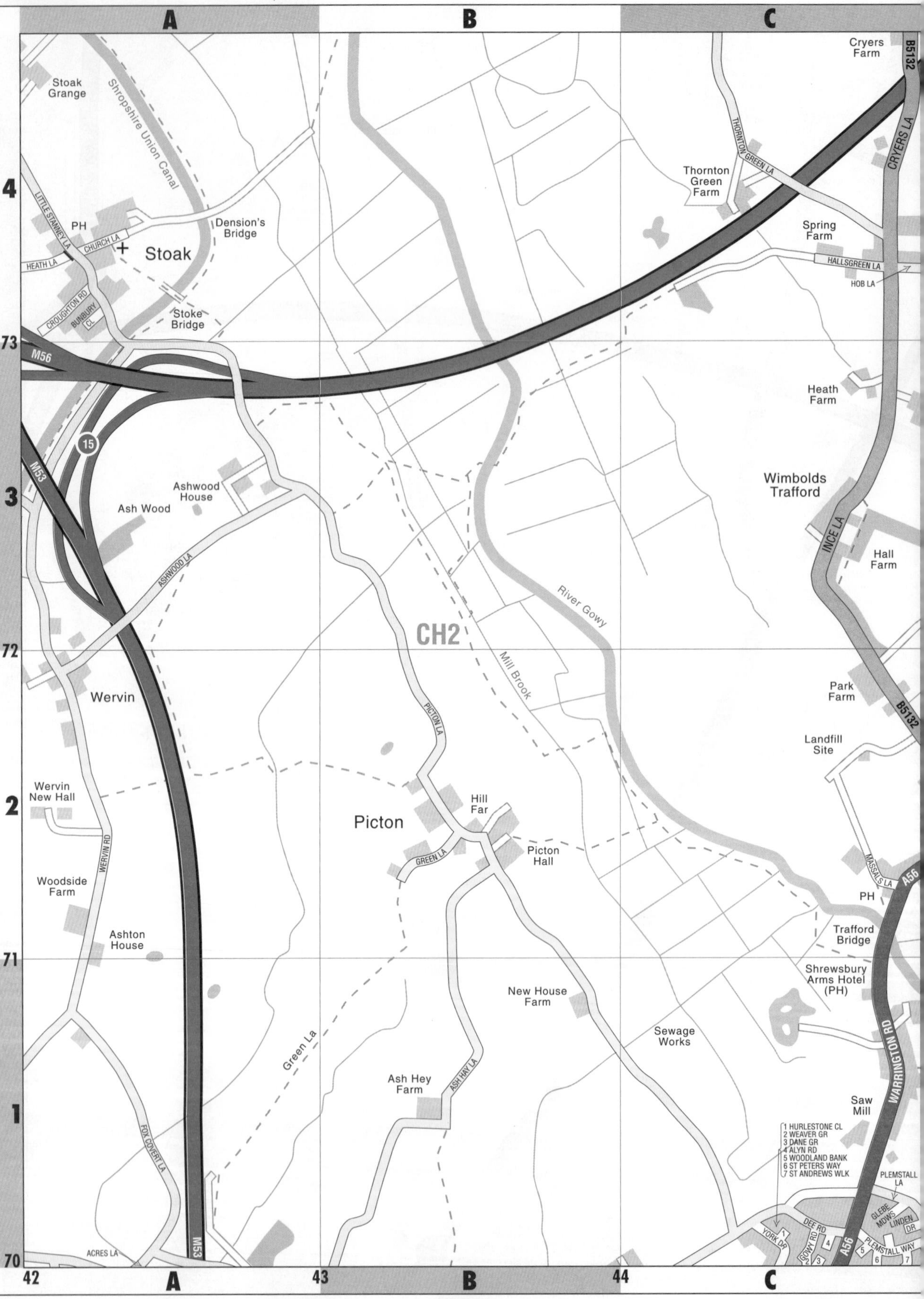

A   B   C

Cryers
Farm

B5132

Stoak
Grange

Shropshire Union Canal

Thornton
Green
Farm

THORNTON GREEN LA

CRYERS LA

4

LITTLE STANNEY LA

PH

Dension's
Bridge

CHURCH LA

Stoak

Spring
Farm

HALLSGREEN LA

HEATH LA

HOB LA

CROUGHTON RD

BUNBURY CL

Stoke
Bridge

73

M56

Heath
Farm

15

Ashwood
House

Wimbolds
Trafford

INCE LA

3

M53

Ash Wood

Hall
Farm

River Gowy

ASHWOOD LA

72

CH2

Mill Brook

Park
Farm

B5132

Wervin

PICTON LA

Landfill
Site

Wervin
New Hall

Hill
Far

2

GREEN LA

Picton

Picton
Hall

MASSIES LA

PH

A56

Woodside
Farm

WERVIN RD

Trafford
Bridge

Ashton
House

Shrewsbury
Arms Hotel
(PH)

71

New House
Farm

WARRINGTON RD

Green La

Sewage
Works

FOX COVERT LA

Ash Hey
Farm

ASH HAY LA

Saw
Mill

1 HURLESTONE CL
2 WEAVER GR
3 DANE GR
4 ALYN RD
5 WOODLAND BANK
6 ST PETERS WAY
7 ST ANDREWS WLK

1

M53

PLEMSTALL
LA

ACRES LA

PLEMSTALL WAY

GLEBE
MDWS

LINDEN
DR

DEE RD

SWAY RD

A56

70

YORK DR

42   43   44

A   B   C

95
119

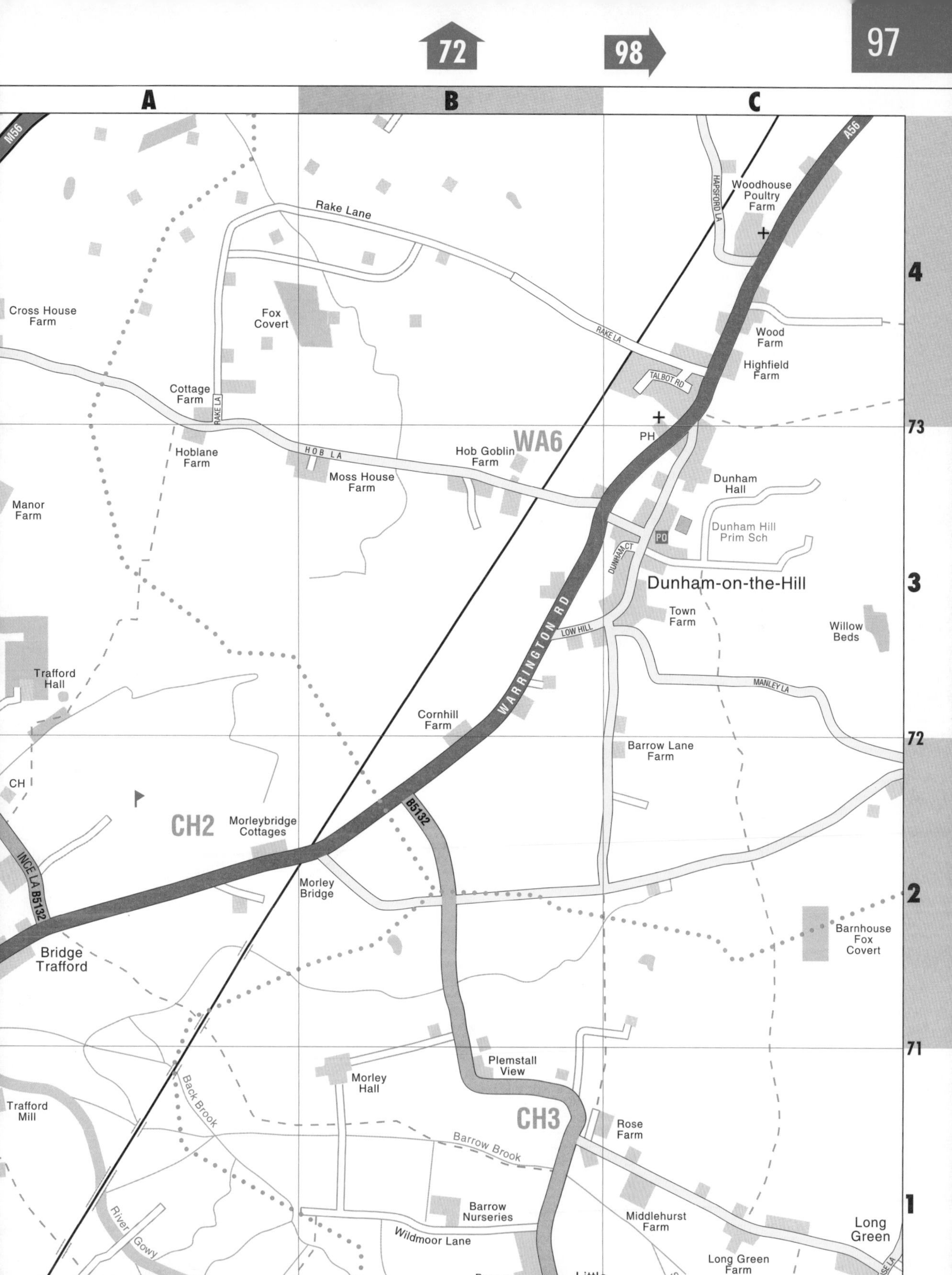

A B C

M56

Rake Lane

Woodhouse
Poultry
Farm

HAPSFORD LA

A56

Cross House
Farm

Fox
Covert

RAKE LA

Wood
Farm

Highfield
Farm

TALBOT RD

4

Cottage
Farm

RAKE LA

HOB LA

Hob Goblin
Farm

WA6

PH

73

Hoblane
Farm

Moss House
Farm

Dunham
Hall

Manor
Farm

DUNHAM CT

PO

Dunham Hill
Prim Sch

Town
Farm

Dunham-on-the-Hill

Willow
Beds

3

Trafford
Hall

LOW HILL

WARRINGTON RD

MANLEY LA

CH

Cornhill
Farm

Barrow Lane
Farm

72

CH2

Morleybridge
Cottages

B5132

INCE LA B5132

Morley
Bridge

Barnhouse
Fox
Covert

2

Bridge
Trafford

71

Back Brook

Plemstall
View

Trafford
Mill

Morley
Hall

CH3

Rose
Farm

Barrow Brook

Middlehurst
Farm

Long
Green

1

River Gowy

Barrow
Nurseries

Long Green
Farm

BARNHOUSE LA

BRIDGEND

Wildmoor Lane

Barrow
Lodge

Little
Barrow

Salters Brook

PLEMSTALL LA

Plemstall

Hough
Farm

B5132

70

45 A 46 B 47 C

97
73

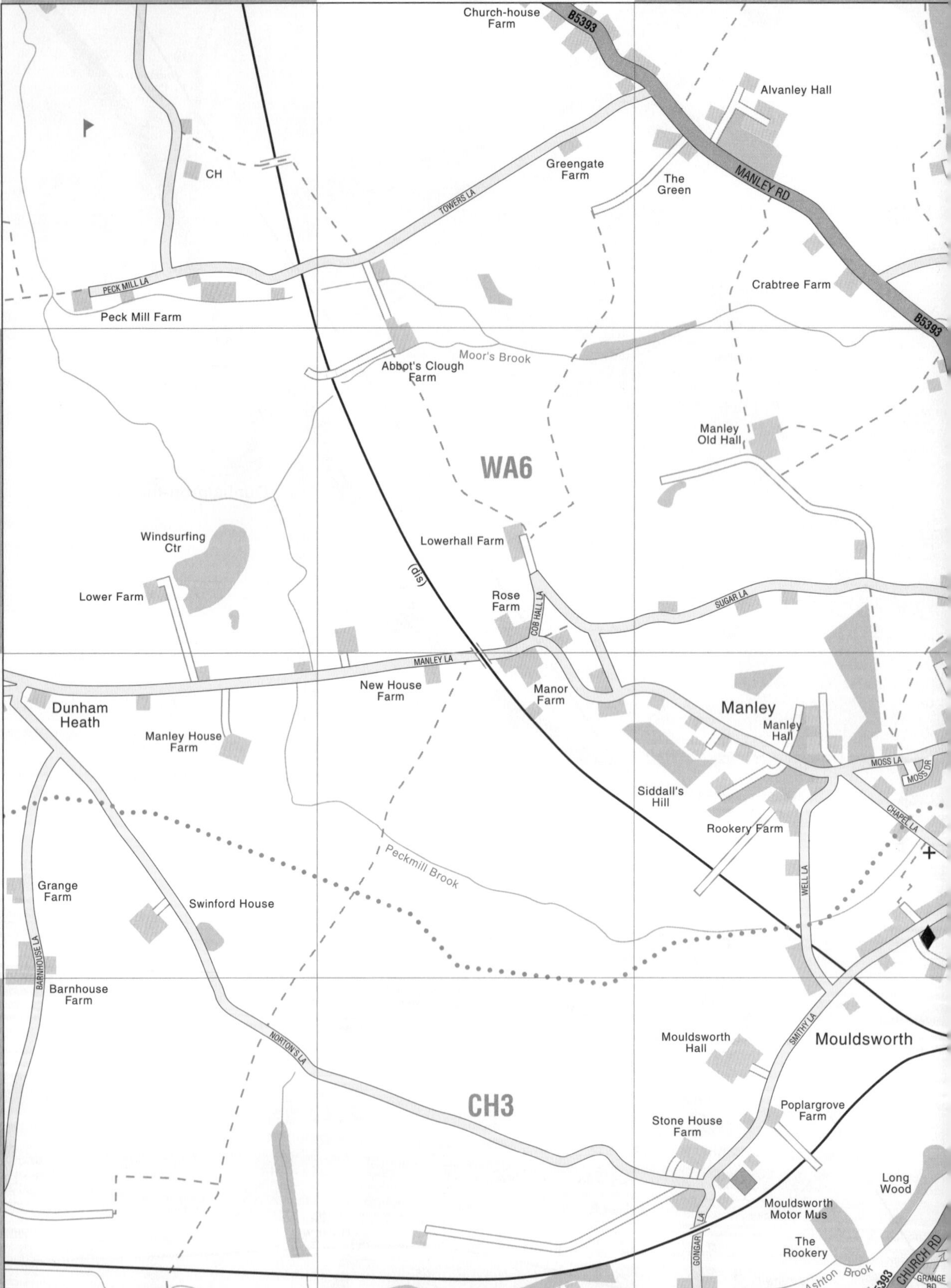

A   B   C

4

Church-house Farm

B5393

Alvanley Hall

Greengate Farm

CH

The Green

MANLEY RD

TOWERS LA

Crabtree Farm

PECK MILL LA

B5393

Peck Mill Farm

73

Abbot's Clough Farm

Moor's Brook

Manley Old Hall

WA6

3

Windsurfing Ctr

Lowerhall Farm

Lower Farm

Rose Farm

SUGAR LA

COB HALL LA

A49(T)

72

MANLEY LA

Manor Farm

Manley

New House Farm

Manley Hall

Dunham Heath

Manley House Farm

MOSS LA

MOSS DR

Siddall's Hill

CHAPEL LA

2

Peckmill Brook

Rookery Farm

WELL LA

Grange Farm

Swinford House

BARNHOUSE LA

71

Barnhouse Farm

SMITHY LA

Mouldsworth Hall

Mouldsworth

NORTON'S LA

Poplargrove Farm

CH3

1

Stone House Farm

Long Wood

Mouldsworth Motor Mus

GONGAR LA

The Rookery

Ashton Brook

B5393

CHURCH RD

GRANGE RD

70

48   A   49   B   50   C

74
100

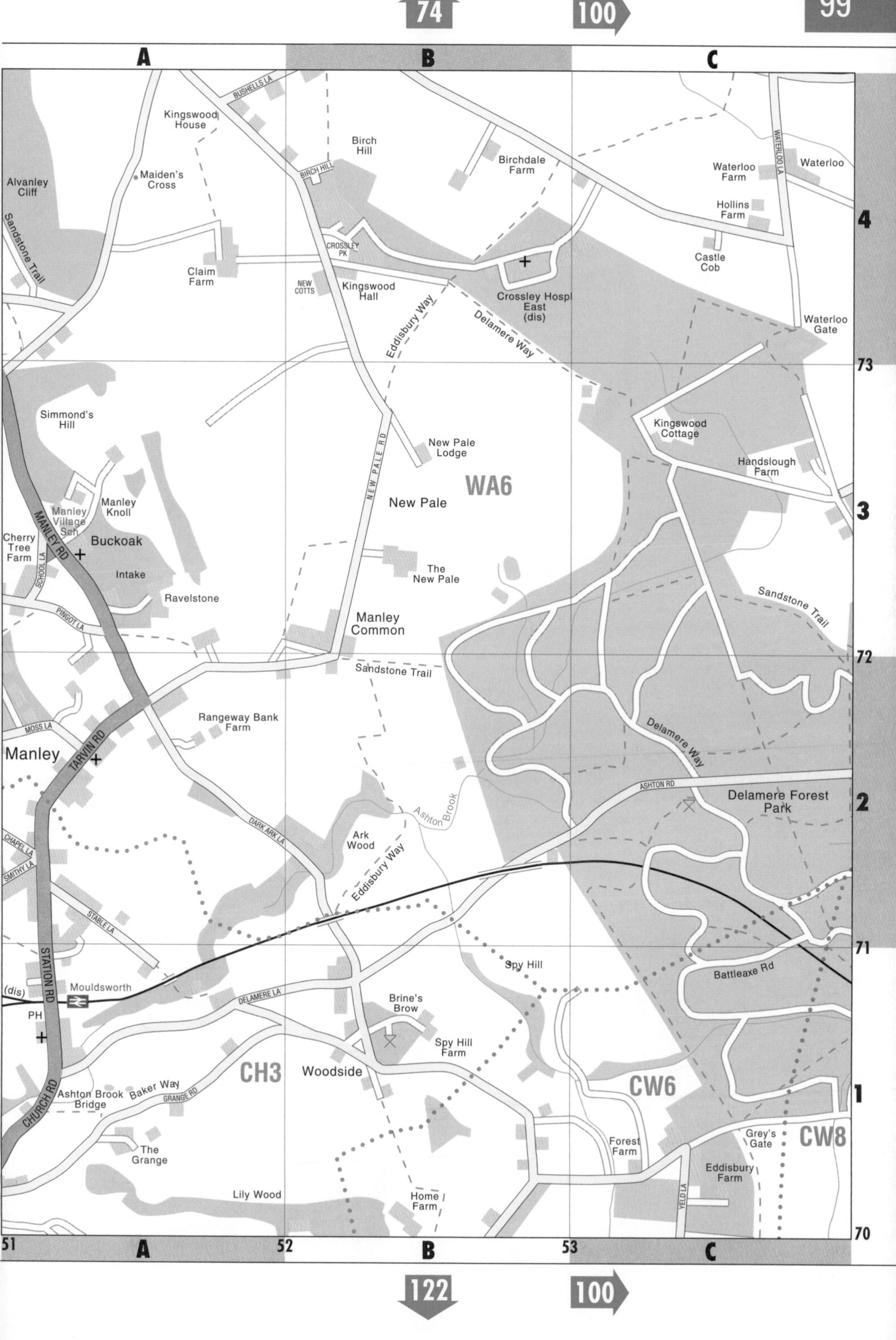
A
B
C
BUSHELLS LA
Kingswood House
Birch Hill
Birchdale Farm
Waterloo Farm
WATERLOO LA
Waterloo
Alvanley Cliff
Maiden's Cross
BIRCH HILL
Hollins Farm
Sandstone Trail
CROSSLEY PK
Castle Cob
Claim Farm
NEW COTTS
Kingswood Hall
Crossley Hospl East (dis)
Eddisbury Way
Delamere Way
Waterloo Gate
Simmond's Hill
Kingswood Cottage
New Pale Lodge
Handslough Farm
WA6
NEW PALE RD
Manley Knoll
Manley Village Sch
New Pale
MANLEY RD
Cherry Tree Farm
Buckoak
SCHOOL LA
The New Pale
Intake
Sandstone Trail
Ravelstone
Manley Common
PINGOT LA
Sandstone Trail
Rangeway Bank Farm
MOSS LA
Delamere Way
Manley
TARVIN RD
ASHTON RD
Delamere Forest Park
Ashton Brook
DARK ARK LA
Ark Wood
CHAPEL LA
SMITHY LA
Eddisbury Way
STABLE LA
STATION RD
Spy Hill
Mouldsworth
(dis)
Battleaxe Rd
DELAMERE LA
Brine's Brow
PH
Spy Hill Farm
CH3
Woodside
CW6
Ashton Brook Bridge
Baker Way
GRANGE RD
CHURCH RD
Forest Farm
Grey's Gate
CW8
The Grange
Eddisbury Farm
Lily Wood
Home Farm
YELD LA
51
52
53
4
73
3
72
2
71
1
70

122
100

99
75

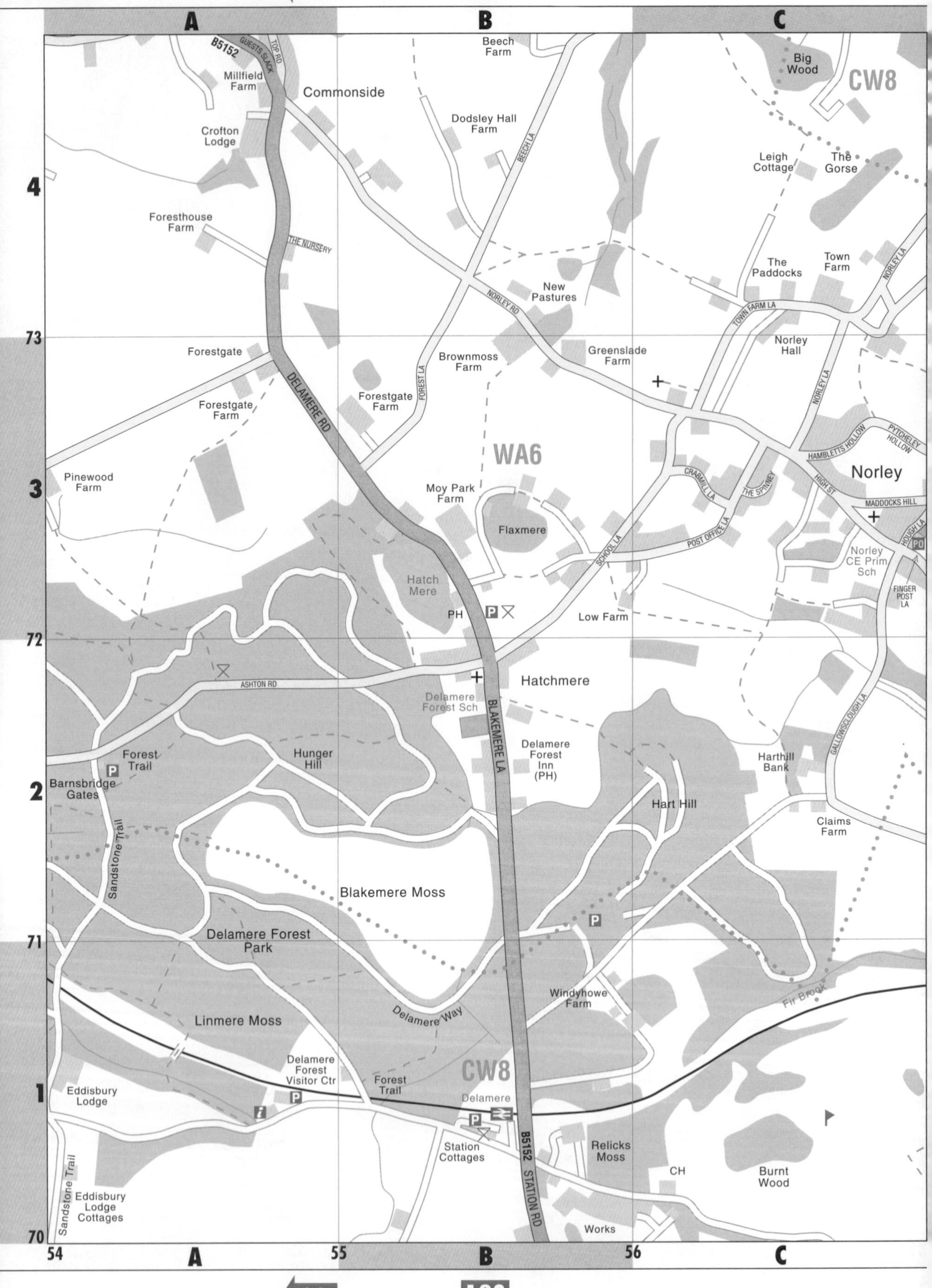
A
B
C
4
73
3
72
2
71
1
70
54
55
56
Beech Farm
Big Wood
CW8
B5152
GUESTS SLACK
TOP RD
Millfield Farm
Commonside
Dodsley Hall Farm
BEECH LA
Crofton Lodge
Leigh Cottage
The Gorse
Foresthouse Farm
THE NURSERY
The Paddocks
Town Farm
NORLEY LA
New Pastures
NORLEY RD
TOWN FARM LA
Forestgate
Brownmoss Farm
Greenslade Farm
Norley Hall
DELAMERE RD
FOREST LA
Forestgate Farm
NORLEY LA
Forestgate Farm
WA6
HAMBLETTS HOLLOW
PYTCHELEY HOLLOW
Pinewood Farm
CRABMILL LA
THE SPINNEY
HIGH ST
Norley
Moy Park Farm
MADDOCKS HILL
Flaxmere
POST OFFICE LA
SCHOOL LA
HOUGH LA
PO
Hatch Mere
Norley CE Prim Sch
FINGER POST LA
PH
Low Farm
ASHTON RD
Hatchmere
Delamere Forest Sch
BLAKEMERE LA
GALLOWSCLOUGH LA
Forest Trail
Hunger Hill
Delamere Forest Inn (PH)
Harthill Bank
Barnsbridge Gates
Hart Hill
Claims Farm
Sandstone Trail
Blakemere Moss
Delamere Forest Park
Windyhowe Farm
Fir Brook
Linmere Moss
Delamere Way
Delamere Forest Visitor Ctr
CW8
Forest Trail
Eddisbury Lodge
Delamere
B5152 STATION RD
Station Cottages
Relicks Moss
CH
Burnt Wood
Sandstone Trail
Eddisbury Lodge Cottages
Works

99
123

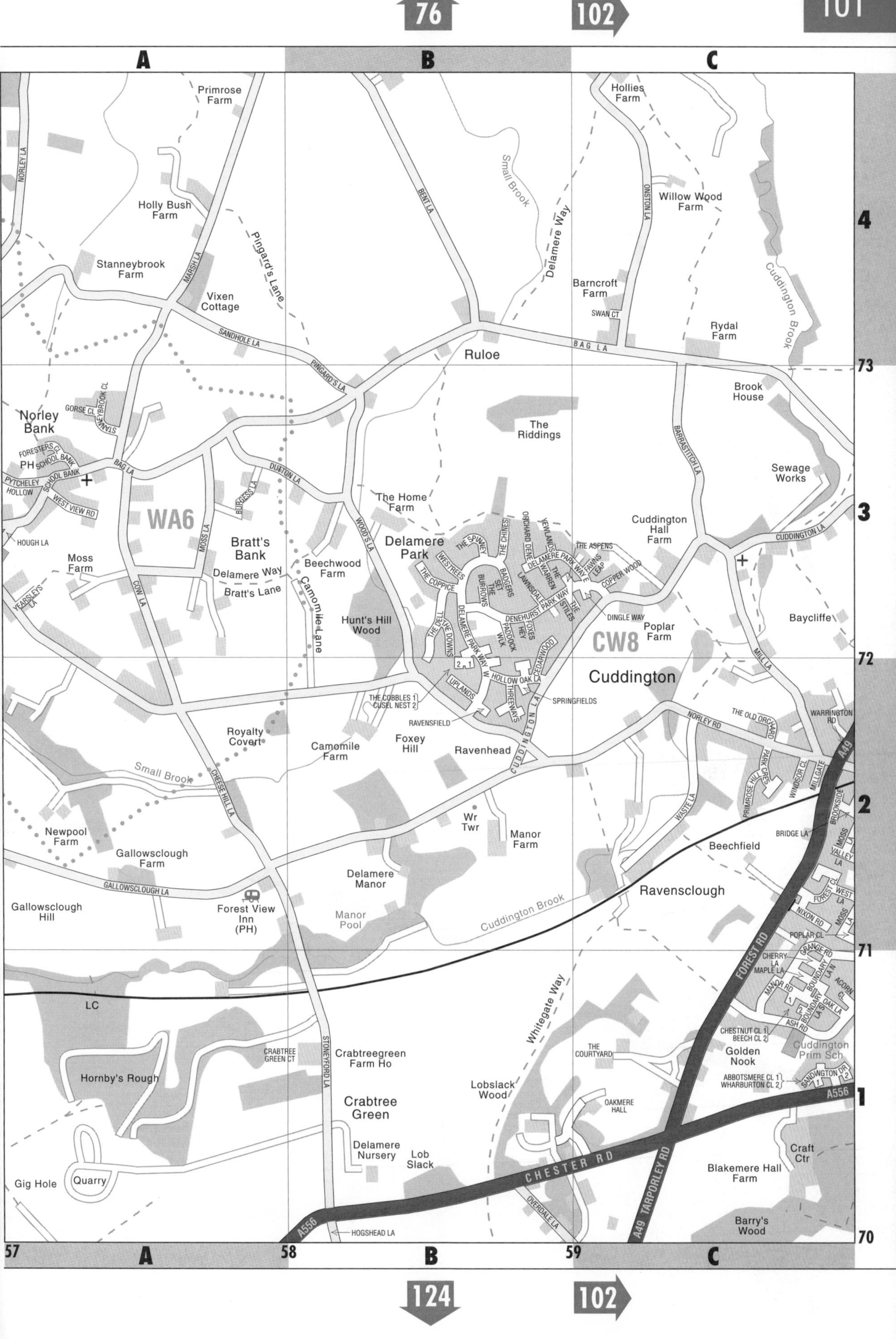

NORLEY LA
Primrose Farm
Holly Bush Farm
Stanneybrook Farm
MARSH LA
Pingard's Lane
SANDHOLE LA
Vixen Cottage
Small Brook
Delamere Way
Hollies Farm
ONSTON LA
Willow Wood Farm
Barncroft Farm
SWAN CT
BAG LA
Ruloe
Rydal Farm
Cuddington Brook

4

73

Norley Bank
GORSE CL
STANNEYBROOK CL
FORESTERS CL
PH
SCHOOL BANK
PYTCHELEY HOLLOW
WEST VIEW RD
HOUGH LA
BAG LA
BURGESS CL
DURTON LA
The Home Farm
The Riddings
Brook House
BARRASTITCH LA
Sewage Works
Cuddington Hall Farm

3

Moss Farm
YEASLEYS LA
COW LA
MOSS LA
WA6
Bratt's Bank
Delamere Way
Bratt's Lane
Beechwood Farm
Camomile Lane
WOOD'S LA
Hunt's Hill Wood
Delamere Park
THE SPINNEY
THE CHINES
ORCHARD DENE
THE WARREN
YEWLANDS
DELAMERE PARK WAY E
DELAMERE PARK WAY W
THE CHIVES
(WESTREYS)
THE COPPICE
THE BURROWS
BADGERS SET
LAWNSHALL HEY
FOXES
DENEHURST WLK
CEDARWOOD
THE ASPENS
DAWNS LEAP
COPPER WOOD
Dingle Way
Poplar Farm
CUDDINGTON LA
Baycliffe
MILL LA

72

Royalty Covert
CHEESE HILL LA
Small Brook
Camomile Farm
THE FELL DOWNS
DELAMERE PARK WAY W
HOLLOW OAK LA
Foxey Hill
THE CUBBLES 1
CUSEL NEST 2
RAVENSFIELD
UPLANDS
2 n 1
SPRINGFIELDS
Ravenhead
CUDDINGTON LA
CW8
Cuddington
NORLEY RD
THE OLD ORCHARD
WARRINGTON RD
WINDSOR CL
MILLGATE
PARK CRES
PRIMROSE HILL
A49
BROOKSIDE
MOSS LA
VALLEY LA
WEST LA

2

Newpool Farm
Gallowsclough Farm
GALLOWSCLOUGH LA
Gallowsclough Hill
Forest View Inn (PH)
Delamere Manor
Manor Pool
Wr Twr
Manor Farm
Cuddington Brook
Ravensclough
Beechfield
BRIDGE LA
NIXON RD
POPLAR CL
FOREST RD

71

LC
Crabtreegreen Farm Ho
CRABTREE GREEN CT
STONYFORD LA
Crabtreegreen Farm Ho
Whitegate Way
ORANGE RD
CHERRY LA
MAPLE LA
MANOR RD
ASH RD
BOUNDARY LA
OAK LA
ACORN
Cuddington Prim Sch

Hornby's Rough
Crabtree Green
THE COURTYARD
Lobslack Wood
CHESTNUT CL 1
BEECH CL 2
Golden Nook
ABBOTSMERE CL 1
WHARBURTON CL 2
SANDWTON DR?
1 2
A556

1

Gig Hole
Quarry
Delamere Nursery
Lob Slack
OAKMERE HALL
Craft Ctr
Blakemere Hall Farm
Barry's Wood
A49 TARPORLEY RD
CHESTER RD
A556
HOGSHEAD LA
OVERDALE LA

70

101
77

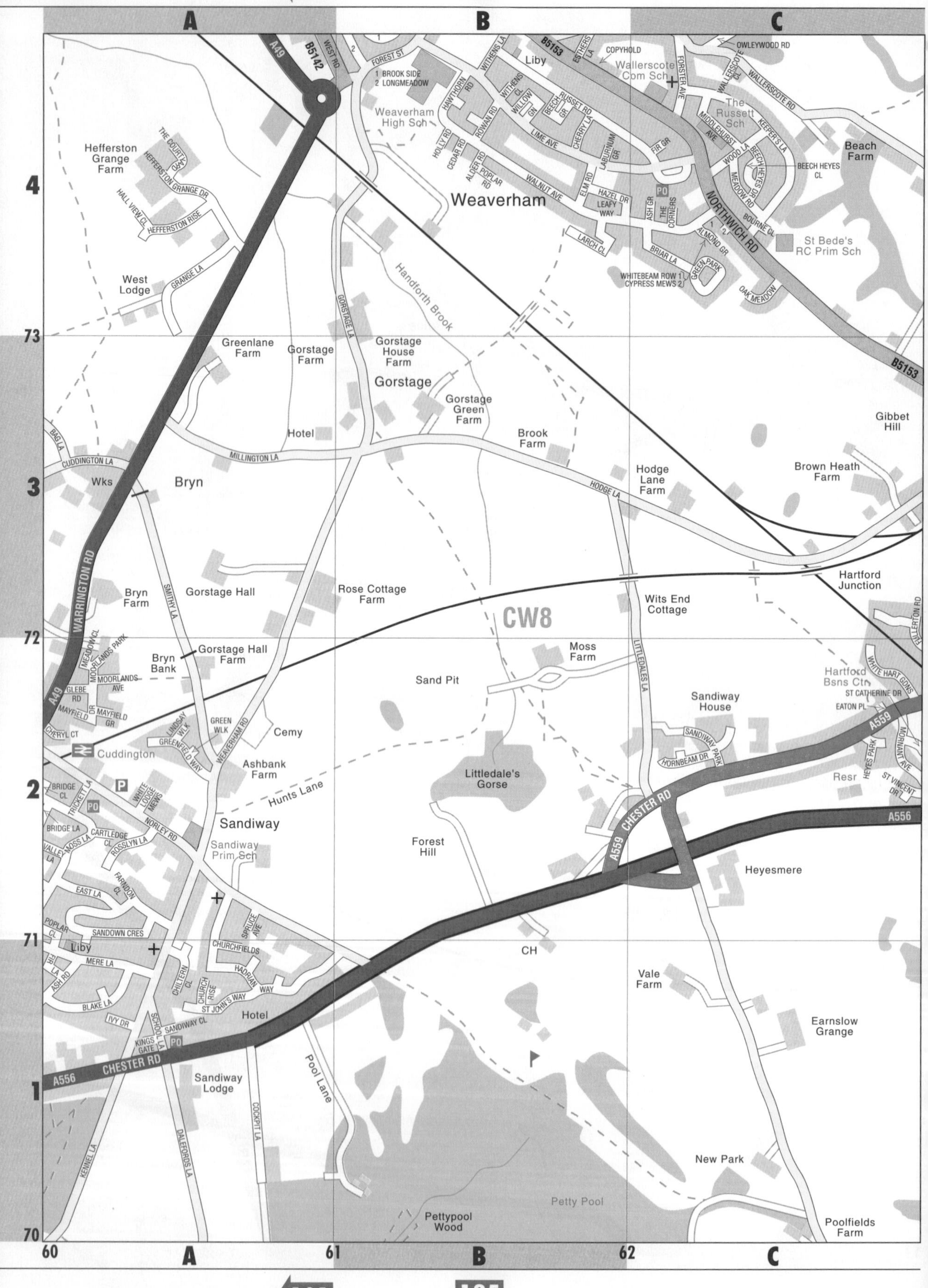
A
B
C
Weaverham
Gorstage
Bryn
Sandiway
Cuddington
Hefferston Grange Farm
West Lodge
Greenlane Farm
Gorstage Farm
Gorstage House Farm
Gorstage Green Farm
Brook Farm
Hodge Lane Farm
Hotel
Wks
Bryn Farm
Gorstage Hall
Rose Cottage Farm
Wits End Cottage
Hartford Junction
CW8
Gorstage Hall Farm
Bryn Bank
Moss Farm
Sand Pit
Cemy
Ashbank Farm
Hunts Lane
Littledale's Gorse
Forest Hill
Sandiway Prim Sch
Sandiway House
Hartford Bsns Ctr
Resr
Heyesmere
CH
Vale Farm
Earnslow Grange
Sandiway Lodge
Pool Lane
New Park
Petty Pool
Pettypool Wood
Poolfields Farm
Beach Farm
Gibbet Hill
Brown Heath Farm
St Bede's RC Prim Sch
The Russett Sch
Wallerscote Com Sch
Weaverham High Sch
Handforth Brook
Liby
WARRINGTON RD
CHESTER RD
NORTHWICH RD
MILLINGTON LA
HODGE LA
SMITHY LA
GORSTAGE LA
LITTLEDALES LA
WEAVERHAM RD
NORLEY RD
A49
B5142
B5153
A559
A556
1 BROOK SIDE
2 LONGMEADOW
WHITEBEAM ROW 1
CYPRESS MEWS 2
4
3
2
1
73
72
71
70
60
61
62

101
125

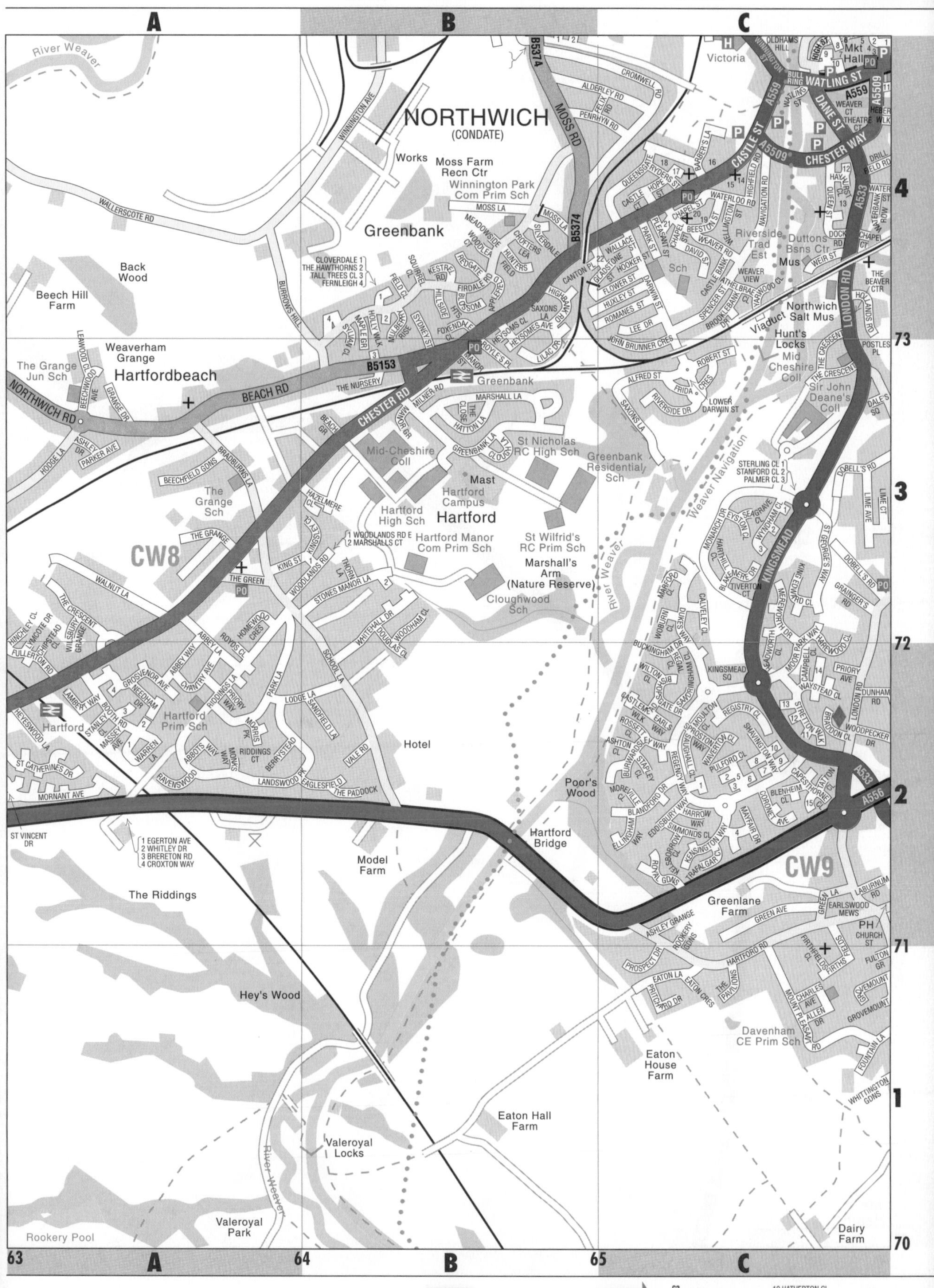

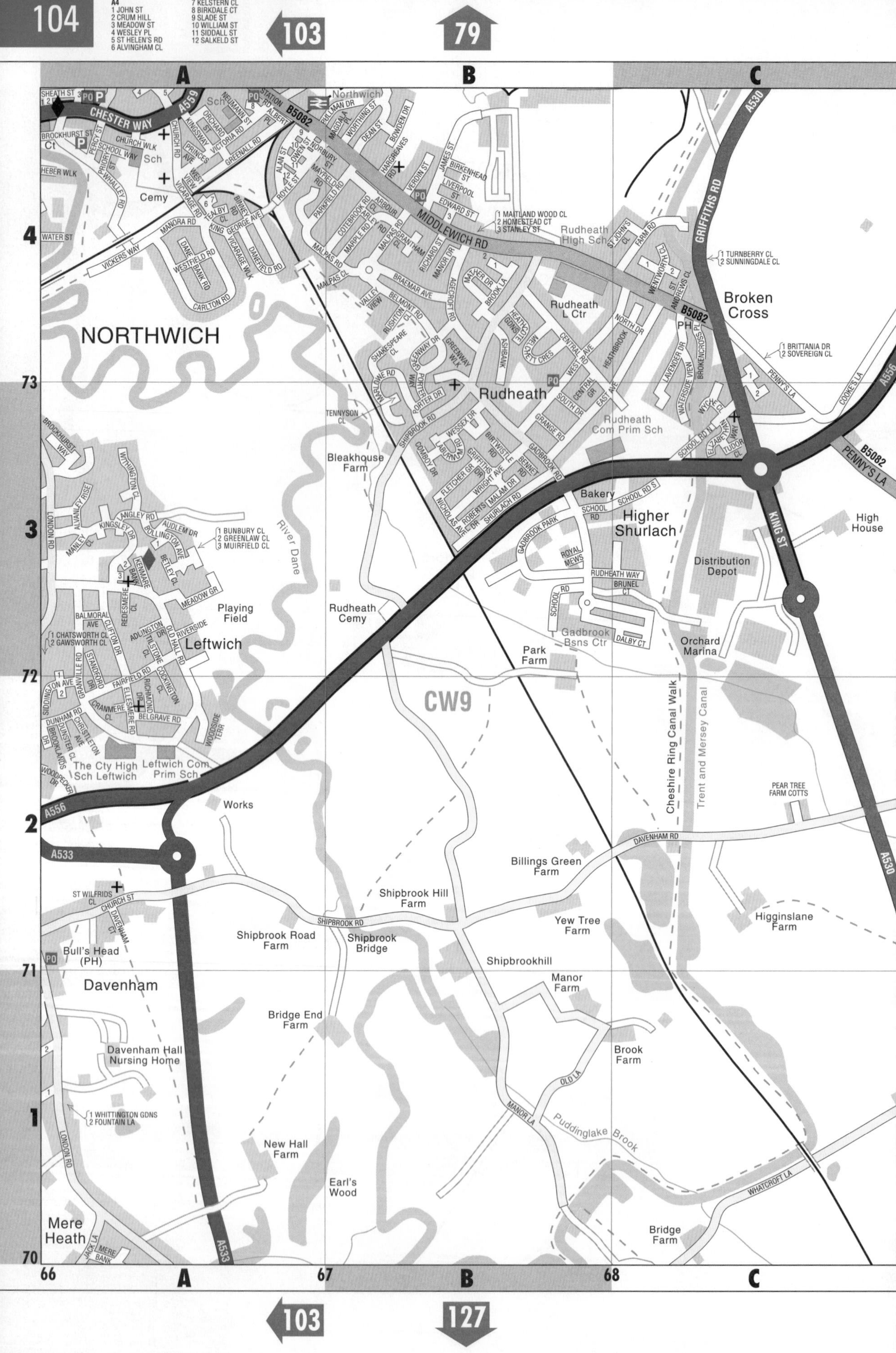

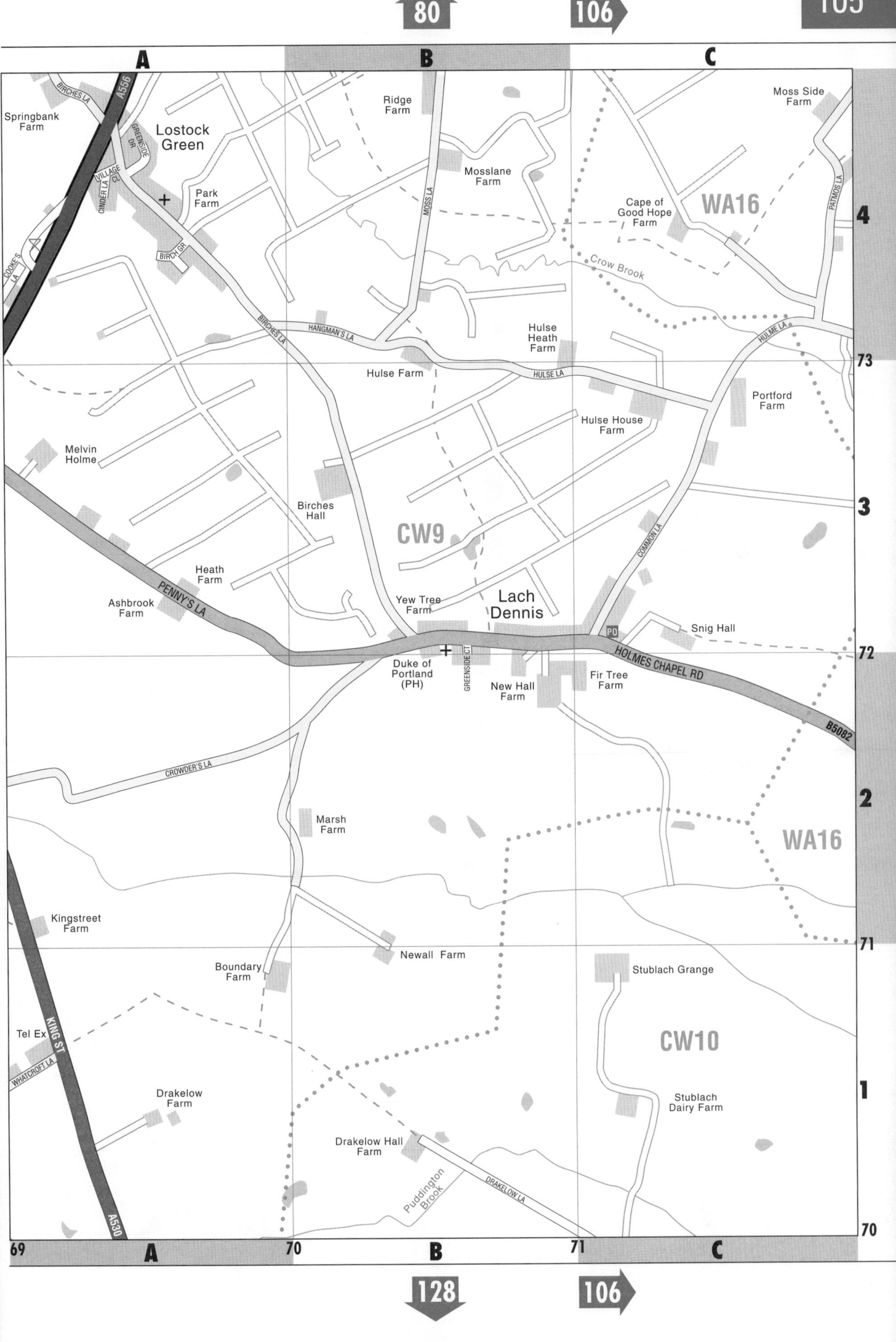
80
106
A
B
C
Springbank Farm
Lostock Green
Park Farm
Ridge Farm
Mosslane Farm
Moss Side Farm
Cape of Good Hope Farm
WA16
Crow Brook
Hulse Heath Farm
Hulse Farm
HANGMAN'S LA
HULSE LA
HULME LA
PATMOS LA
Portford Farm
Hulse House Farm
Melvin Holme
Birches Hall
CW9
Heath Farm
Ashbrook Farm
PENNY'S LA
Yew Tree Farm
Lach Dennis
PO
Snig Hall
Duke of Portland (PH)
GREENSIDE CT
New Hall Farm
Fir Tree Farm
HOLMES CHAPEL RD
B5082
COMMON LA
CROWDER'S LA
Marsh Farm
WA16
Kingstreet Farm
Newall Farm
Boundary Farm
Stublach Grange
Tel Ex
KING ST
WHATCROFT LA
CW10
Drakelow Farm
Stublach Dairy Farm
Drakelow Hall Farm
Puddington Brook
DRAKELOW LA
A530
A556
BIRCHES LA
GREENSIDE DR
VILLAGE CL
CINDER LA
BIRCH GR
COOKE'S LA
MOSS LA
4
73
3
72
2
71
1
70
69
70
71
128
106

105
81

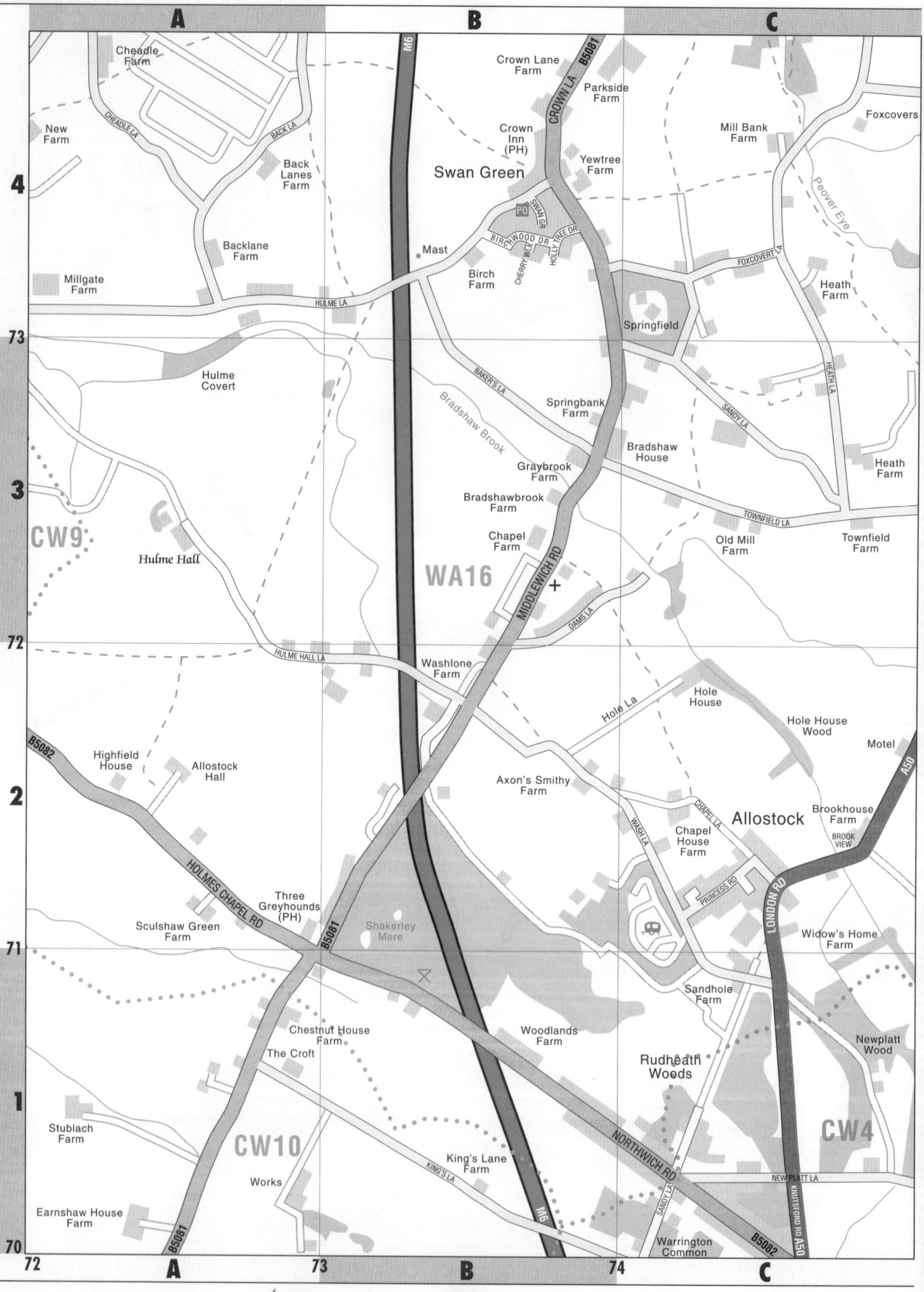

A　**B**　**C**

Cheadle Farm

New Farm

CREADLE LA

BACK LA

Back Lanes Farm

4

Backlane Farm

Millgate Farm

HULME LA

Crown Lane Farm

CROWN LA

B5081

Parkside Farm

Crown Inn (PH)

Yewtree Farm

Swan Green

Mill Bank Farm

Foxcovers

PO

SWAN GR

BIRCHWOOD DR

CHERRY WLK

HOLLY TREE DR

Mast

Birch Farm

Peover Eye

FOXCOVERT LA

Heath Farm

Springfield

73

Hulme Covert

Bradshaw Brook

BAKER'S LA

Springbank Farm

Bradshaw House

SANDY LA

TOWNFIELD LA

Heath Farm

CW9

Hulme Hall

Graybrook Farm

Bradshawbrook Farm

Chapel Farm

MIDDLEWICH RD

WA16

+

Old Mill Farm

Townfield Farm

3

HULME HALL LA

Washlone Farm

DAMS LA

Hole La

Hole House

Hole House Wood

Motel

72

B5082

Highfield House

Allostock Hall

Axon's Smithy Farm

CHAPEL LA

Chapel House Farm

Allostock

Brookhouse Farm

BROOK VIEW

A50

2

HOLMES CHAPEL RD

Sculshaw Green Farm

Three Greyhounds (PH)

B5081

Shakerley Mere

WASH LA

PRINCESS RD

LONDON RD

Widow's Home Farm

Chestnut House Farm

The Croft

Woodlands Farm

Sandhole Farm

Newplatt Wood

71

Stublach Farm

CW10

Works

Earnshaw House Farm

King's Lane Farm

KING'S LA

NORTHWICH RD

SANDY LA

Rudheath Woods

CW4

NEW PLATT LA

B5082 A50

KNUTSFORD RD

1

B5081

M6

Warrington Common

70

72　**A**　**73**　**B**　**74**　**C**

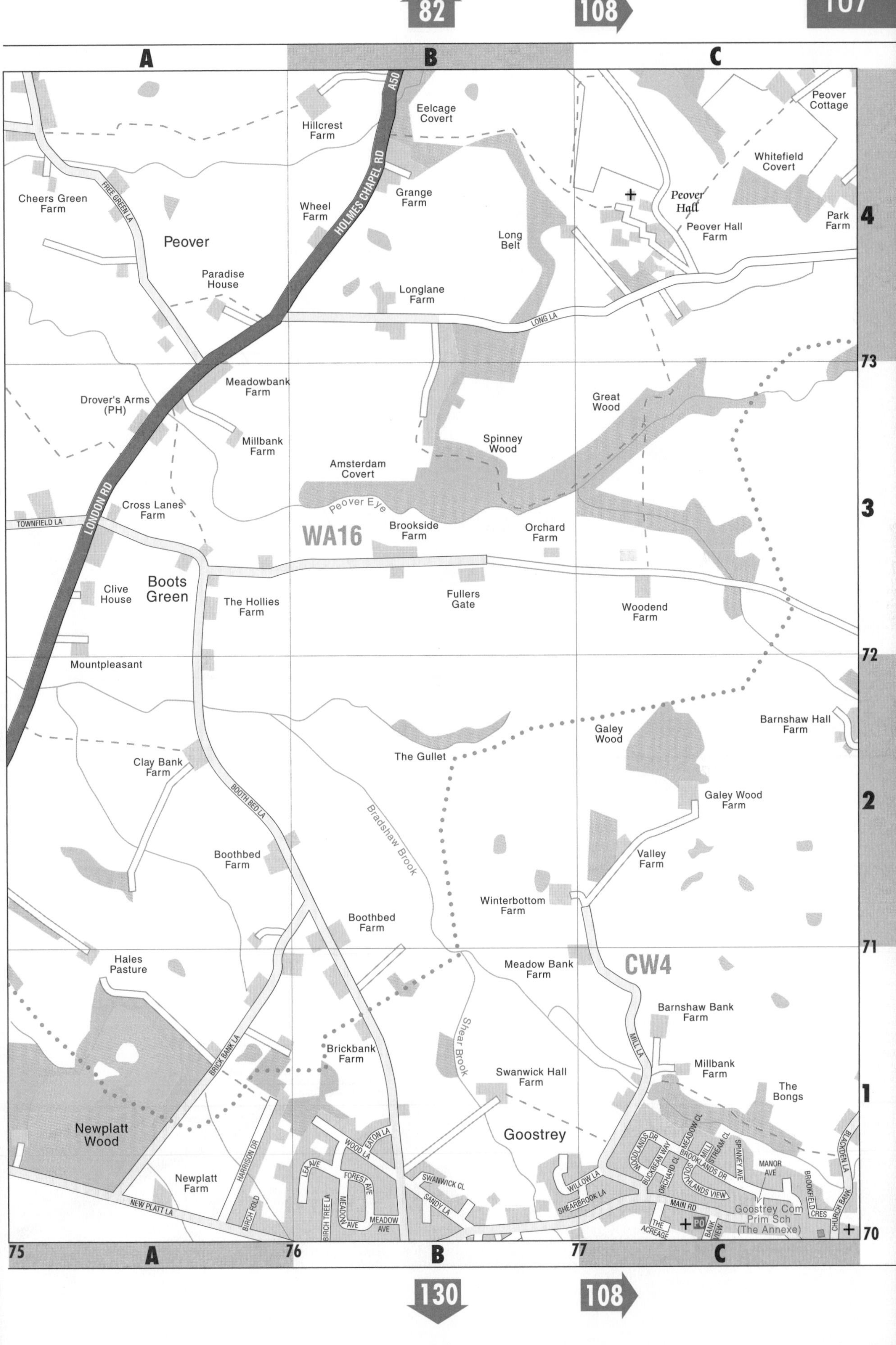

A
B
C

A50

Peover Cottage

Hillcrest Farm

Eelcage Covert

Whitefield Covert

Cheers Green Farm

Peover

Wheel Farm

Grange Farm

HOLMES CHAPEL RD

Peover Hall

Park Farm

4

Peover Hall Farm

Long Belt

FREE GREEN LA

Paradise House

Longlane Farm

LONG LA

73

Meadowbank Farm

Drover's Arms (PH)

Great Wood

Millbank Farm

Spinney Wood

Amsterdam Covert

LONDON RD

Cross Lanes Farm

TOWNFIELD LA

Peover Eye

WA16

Brookside Farm

Orchard Farm

3

Boots Green

Clive House

The Hollies Farm

Fullers Gate

Woodend Farm

72

Mountpleasant

Clay Bank Farm

The Gullet

Galey Wood

Barnshaw Hall Farm

BOOTH BED LA

Bradshaw Brook

Galey Wood Farm

2

Boothbed Farm

Valley Farm

Boothbed Farm

Winterbottom Farm

71

Hales Pasture

Meadow Bank Farm

CW4

BRICK BANK LA

Shear Brook

MILL LA

Barnshaw Bank Farm

Millbank Farm

The Bongs

1

Brickbank Farm

Swanwick Hall Farm

BLACKDEN LA

Newplatt Wood

HARRISON DR

Goostrey

WOADLANDS DR

BUCKBEAN WAY

MEADOW CL

ORCHARD CL

BROOKLANDS DR

SPINNEY AVE

MANOR AVE

BROOKFIELDS CRES

CHURCH BANK

Newplatt Farm

LEA AVE

WOOD LA

EATON LA

FOREST AVE

SWANWICK CL

SANDY LA

WILLOW LA

SHEARBROOK LA

MAIN RD

BANK VIEW

THE ACREAGE

PO

Goostrey Com Prim Sch (The Annexe)

NEW PLATT LA

BIRCH FOLD

BIRCH TREE LA

MEADOW AVE

MEADOW AVE

70

107
83

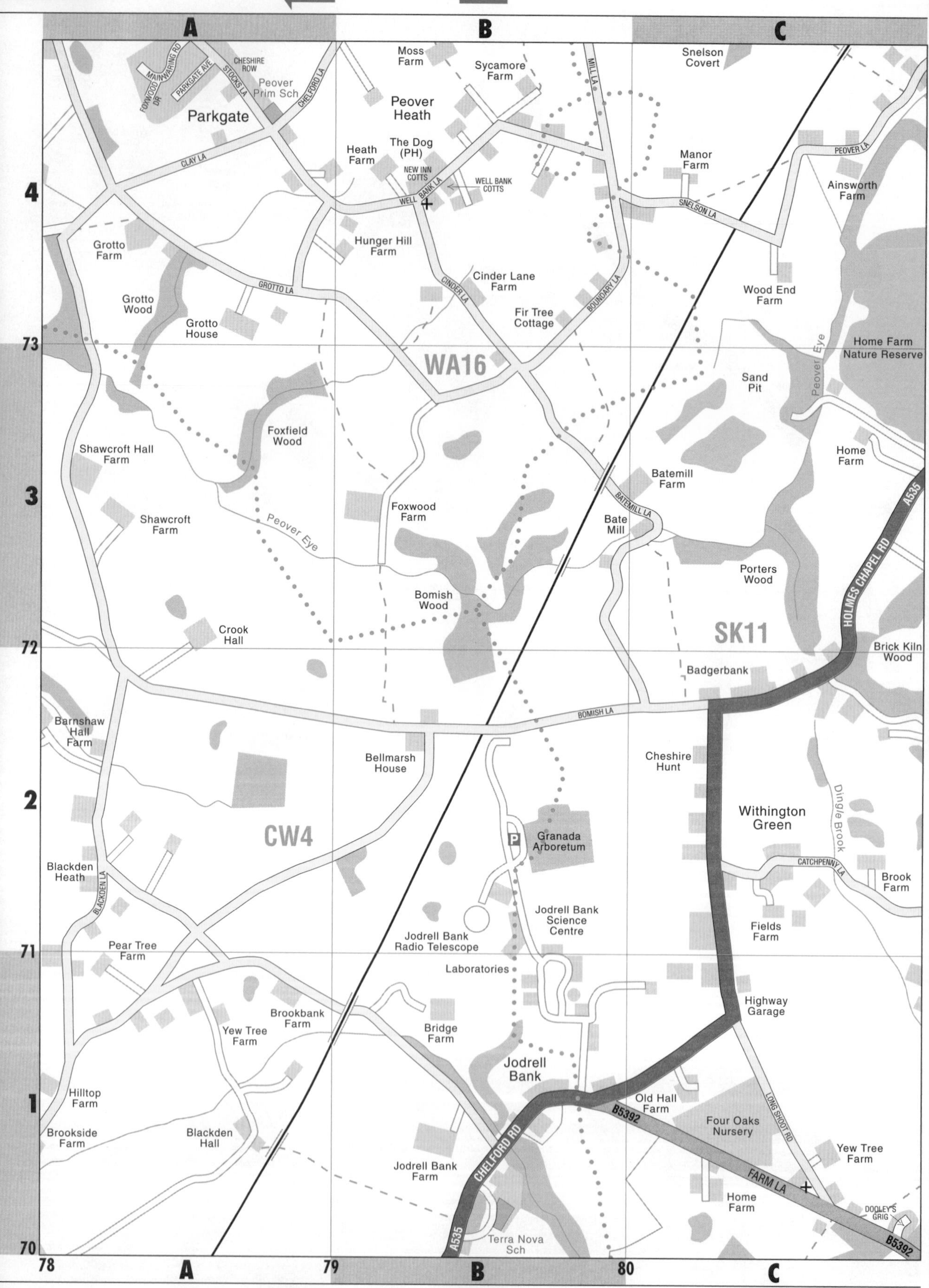
A
B
C
Parkgate
Peover Prim Sch
CHESHIRE ROW
STOCKS LA
CHELFORD LA
PARKGATE AVE
MAINWARING RD
FOXWOOD DR
CLAY LA
Moss Farm
Sycamore Farm
Peover Heath
Heath Farm
The Dog (PH)
NEW INN COTTS
WELL BANK COTTS
WELL BANK LA
MILL LA
Snelson Covert
Manor Farm
SNELSON LA
PEOVER LA
Ainsworth Farm
Grotto Farm
Hunger Hill Farm
Grotto Wood
GROTTO LA
Grotto House
CINDER LA
Cinder Lane Farm
Fir Tree Cottage
BOUNDARY LA
Wood End Farm
Home Farm Nature Reserve
Peover Eye
WA16
Sand Pit
Foxfield Wood
Shawcroft Hall Farm
Home Farm
Batemill Farm
BATEMILL LA
Bate Mill
Shawcroft Farm
Foxwood Farm
Porters Wood
A535
HOLMES CHAPEL RD
Bomish Wood
Crook Hall
SK11
Brick Kiln Wood
Badgerbank
BOMISH LA
Barnshaw Hall Farm
Bellmarsh House
Cheshire Hunt
Withington Green
Dingle Brook
CW4
P
Granada Arboretum
CATCHPENNY LA
Blackden Heath
BLACKDEN LA
Brook Farm
Jodrell Bank Science Centre
Fields Farm
Jodrell Bank Radio Telescope
Pear Tree Farm
Laboratories
Highway Garage
Brookbank Farm
Yew Tree Farm
Bridge Farm
Jodrell Bank
Hilltop Farm
Old Hall Farm
B5392
LONG SHOOT RD
Four Oaks Nursery
Brookside Farm
Blackden Hall
CHELFORD RD
Yew Tree Farm
Jodrell Bank Farm
FARM LA
Home Farm
DOOLEY'S GRIG
Terra Nova Sch
73
72
71
70
4
3
2
1
78
79
80

107
131

84
110

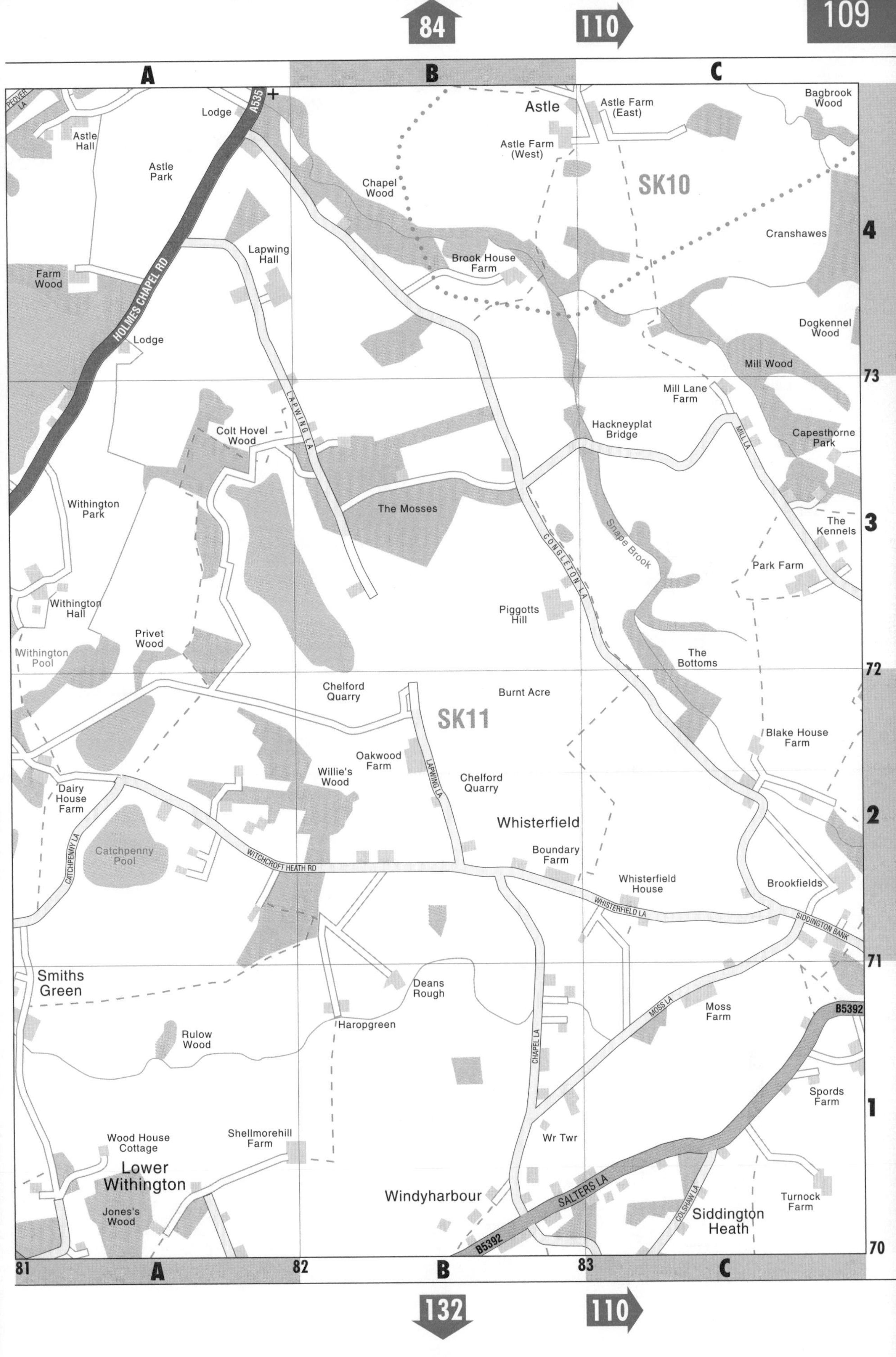
A
B
C
PEOVER LA
Lodge
A535
Astle
Astle Farm (East)
Bagbrook Wood
Astle Hall
Astle Farm (West)
Astle Park
Chapel Wood
SK10
4
Cranshawes
Lapwing Hall
Brook House Farm
Farm Wood
HOLMES CHAPEL RD
Lodge
Dogkennel Wood
Mill Wood
73
Mill Lane Farm
LAPWING LA
Hackneyplat Bridge
Colt Hovel Wood
MILL LA
Capesthorne Park
Withington Park
The Mosses
3
The Kennels
CONGLETON LA
Snape Brook
Park Farm
Withington Hall
Piggotts Hill
Privet Wood
Withington Pool
The Bottoms
72
Chelford Quarry
Burnt Acre
SK11
Blake House Farm
Oakwood Farm
Willie's Wood
LAPWING LA
Chelford Quarry
Dairy House Farm
2
Whisterfield
Catchpenny Pool
CATCHPENNY LA
WITCHCROFT HEATH RD
Boundary Farm
Whisterfield House
Brookfields
WHISTERFIELD LA
SIDDINGTON BANK
71
Smiths Green
Deans Rough
B5392
MOSS LA
Moss Farm
Haropgreen
Rulow Wood
CHAPEL LA
Spords Farm
1
Wood House Cottage
Shellmorehill Farm
Wr Twr
Lower Withington
SALTERS LA
Turnock Farm
Jones's Wood
Windyharbour
COLSHAW LA
Siddington Heath
B5392
70
81
A
82
B
83
C

132
110

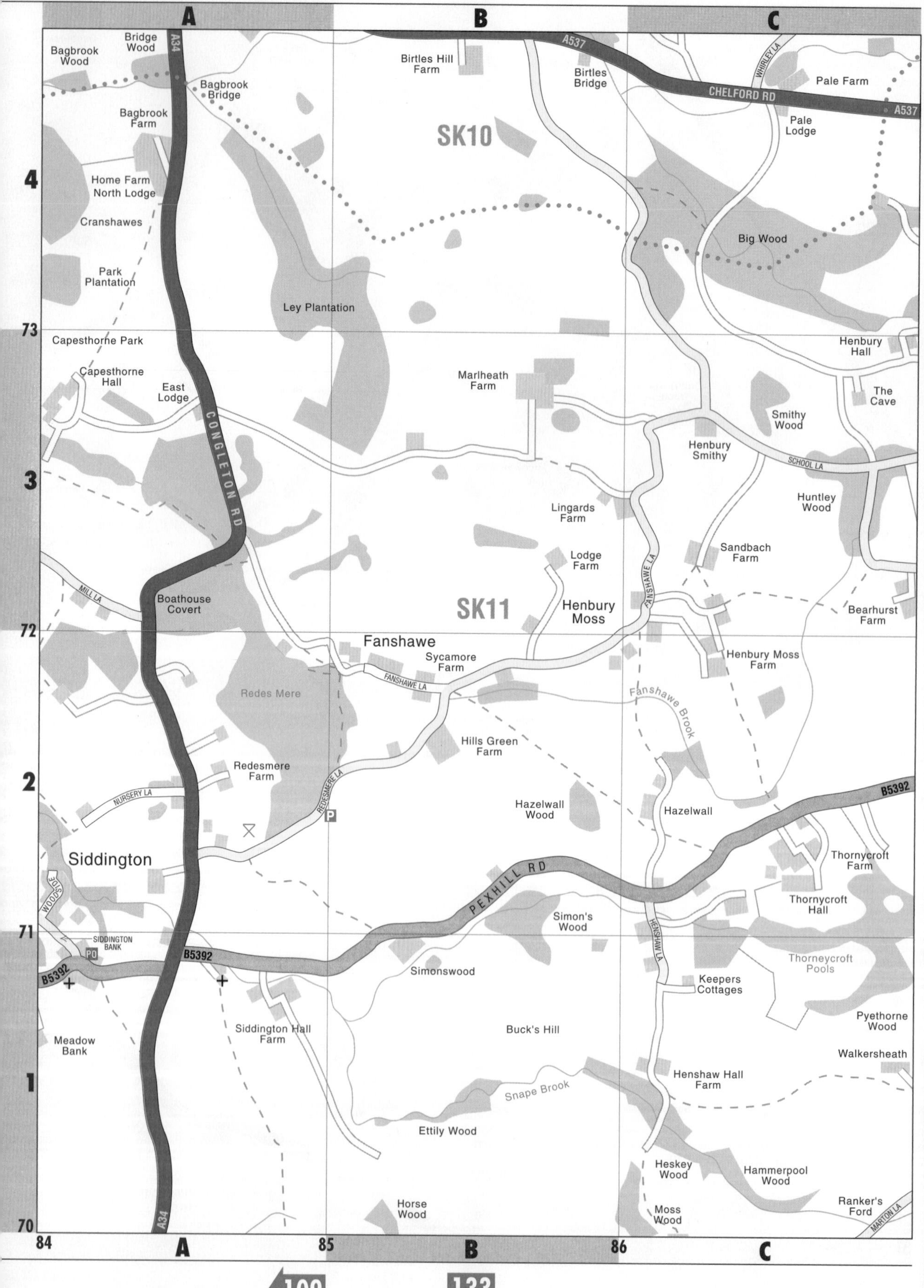
A
B
C
Bagbrook Wood
Bridge Wood
A34
Bagbrook Bridge
Bagbrook Farm
Birtles Hill Farm
A537
Birtles Bridge
WHIRLEY LA
Pale Farm
CHELFORD RD
Pale Lodge
SK10
Home Farm North Lodge
Cranshawes
Big Wood
Park Plantation
Ley Plantation
Capesthorne Park
Capesthorne Hall
East Lodge
Marlheath Farm
Henbury Hall
The Cave
Smithy Wood
Henbury Smithy
SCHOOL LA
CONGLETON RD
Huntley Wood
Lingards Farm
Lodge Farm
Sandbach Farm
FANSHAWE LA
MILL LA
Boathouse Covert
SK11
Henbury Moss
Bearhurst Farm
Fanshawe
Sycamore Farm
Henbury Moss Farm
Redes Mere
Fanshawe Brook
Hills Green Farm
Redesmere Farm
NURSERY LA
REDESMERE LA
Hazelwall Wood
Hazelwall
B5392
Siddington
PEXHILL RD
Thornycroft Farm
WOODSIDE
Thornycroft Hall
Simon's Wood
HENSHAW LA
SIDDINGTON BANK
PO
Simonswood
Thorneycroft Pools
Keepers Cottages
Siddington Hall Farm
Buck's Hill
Pyethorne Wood
Meadow Bank
Walkersheath
Henshaw Hall Farm
Snape Brook
Ettily Wood
Heskey Wood
Hammerpool Wood
Horse Wood
Moss Wood
Ranker's Ford
MARTON LA
4
73
3
72
2
71
1
70
84
85
86

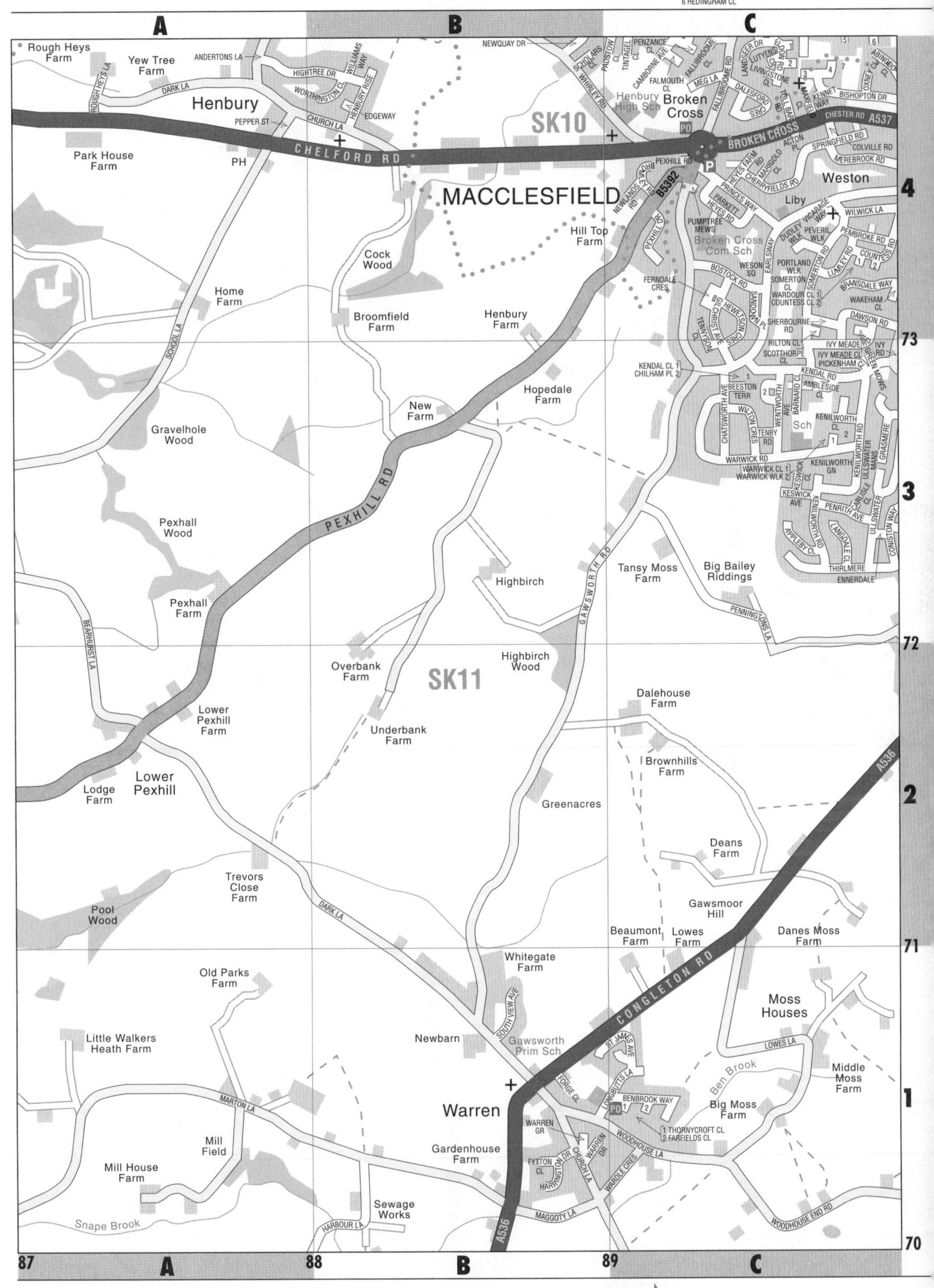

C4
1 ASHBOURNE MEWS
2 SHELBOURNE MEWS
3 ALDERNEY CL
4 BLANFORD DR
5 THE TOWERS
6 HEDINGHAM CL

7 MARLBOROUGH HO

A

B

C

Rough Heys Farm
Yew Tree Farm
ANDERTONS LA
Henbury
Park House Farm
PH
Home Farm
SCHOOL LA
Gravelhole Wood
Pexhall Wood
BEARHURST LA
Pexhall Farm
Lower Pexhill Farm
Lower Pexhill
Lodge Farm
Pool Wood
Trevors Close Farm
DARK LA
MARTON LA
Old Parks Farm
Little Walkers Heath Farm
Mill Field
Mill House Farm
Snape Brook

HIGHTREE DR
WILLIAMS WAY
WORTHINGTON CL
HENBURY RISE
EDGEWAY
DARK LA
PEPPER ST
CHURCH LA
CHELFORD RD
Cock Wood
Broomfield Farm
Henbury Farm
New Farm
PEXHILL RD
Hopedale Farm
Highbirch
Overbank Farm
SK11
Underbank Farm
GAWSWORTH RD
Highbirch Wood
Whitegate Farm
SOUTH VIEW AVE
Gawsworth Prim Sch
Newbarn
FORGE CL
Warren
Gardenhouse Farm
WARREN GR
FYTTON CL
HARRINGTON DR
CHURCH LA
MAGGOTY LA
HARBOUR LA
Sewage Works
A536

NEWQUAY DR
SCHOLARS
PADSTOW
WHIRLEY RD
WHIRLEY RD
SK10
MACCLESSFIELD
Hill Top Farm
Henbury High Sch
B5392
PEXHILL RD
NEWLANDS RD
PENZANCE CL
TINTAGEL CL
CAMBORNE AVE
FALMOUTH CL
MEG LA
HEYES FARM
PRINCES WAY
HEYES RD
Pumptree Mews
WESON RD
BOSTOCK RD
FERNDALE CRES
HEWE SON PL
SANDON PL
CHRIST ME
TENNYSON CL
HILTON CL
SCOTTHORPE CL
KENDAL CL 1
CHILHAM PL 2
CHATSWORTH AVE
WENTWORTH
Tansy Moss Farm
PENNINGTON LA
Big Bailey Riddings
Dalehouse Farm
Brownhills Farm
Greenacres
Deans Farm
Gawsmoor Hill
CONGLETON RD
A536
Beaumont Farm
Lowes Farm
Danes Moss Farm
Moss Houses
LOWES LA
Ben Brook
Middle Moss Farm
Big Moss Farm
ST JAMES AVE
LONGBUTTS LA
BENBROOK WAY
WOODHOUSE LA
1 THORNYCROFT CL
2 FARFIELDS CL
WARDLE CRES
WOODHOUSE END RD

Broken Cross
Broken Cross PO
SK10
CHESTER RD
A537
Weston
Liby
Broken Cross Com Sch
Broken Cross Com Sch
SHERBOURNE RD
Sch
WARWICK RD
WARWICK CL 1
WARWICK WLK 2
KESWICK AVE
PENRITH CL

111
87

SK10

MACCLESFIELD

Moss Lane

SK11

Byrons Wood

Gurnett

Moss Rose Football Gnd
(Macclesfield Town FC)

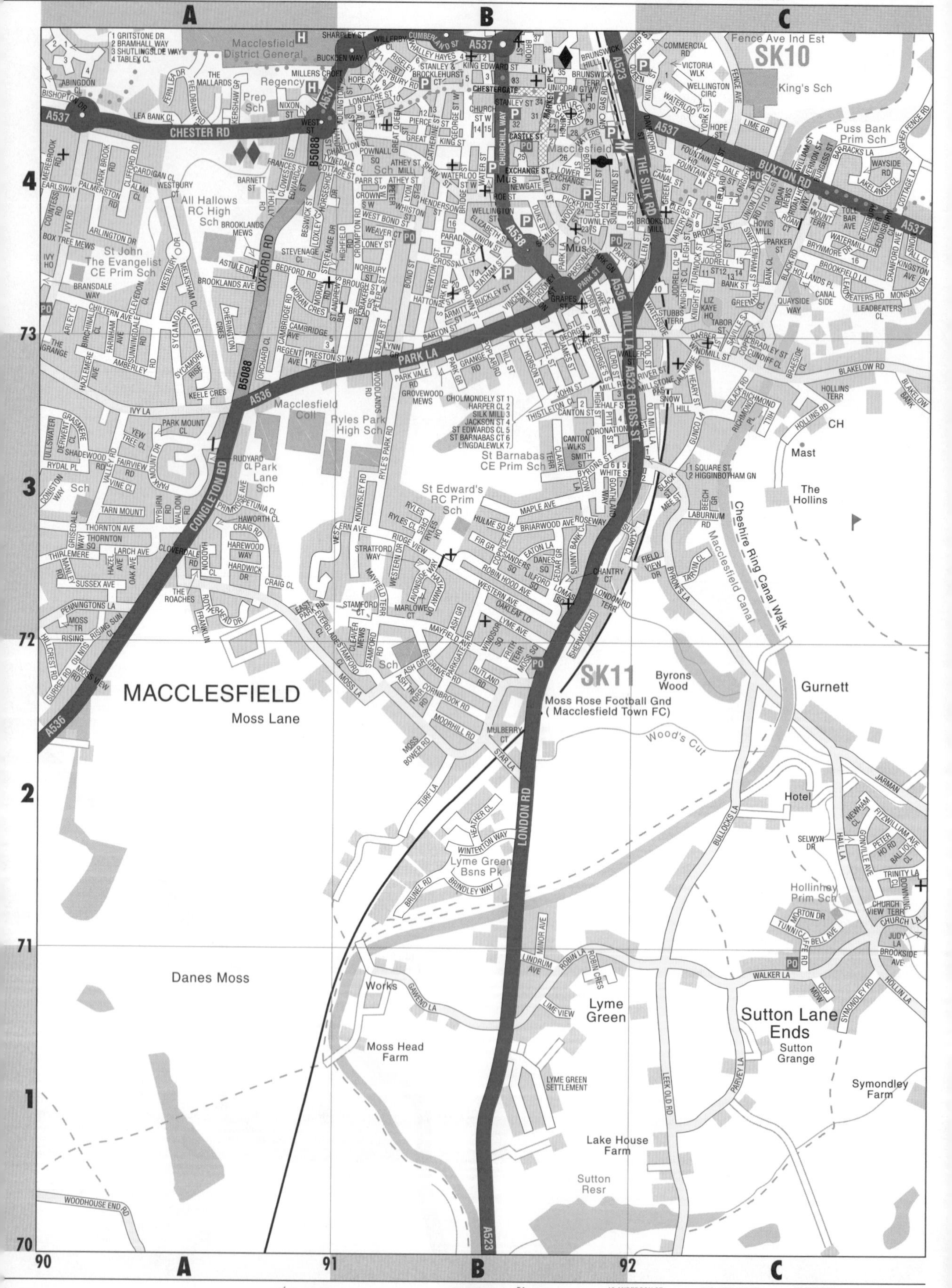

Danes Moss

Wood's Cut

Lyme Green

Sutton Lane Ends

Sutton Grange

Moss Head Farm

Lyme Green Settlement

Lake House Farm

Sutton Resr

Symondley Farm

111
135

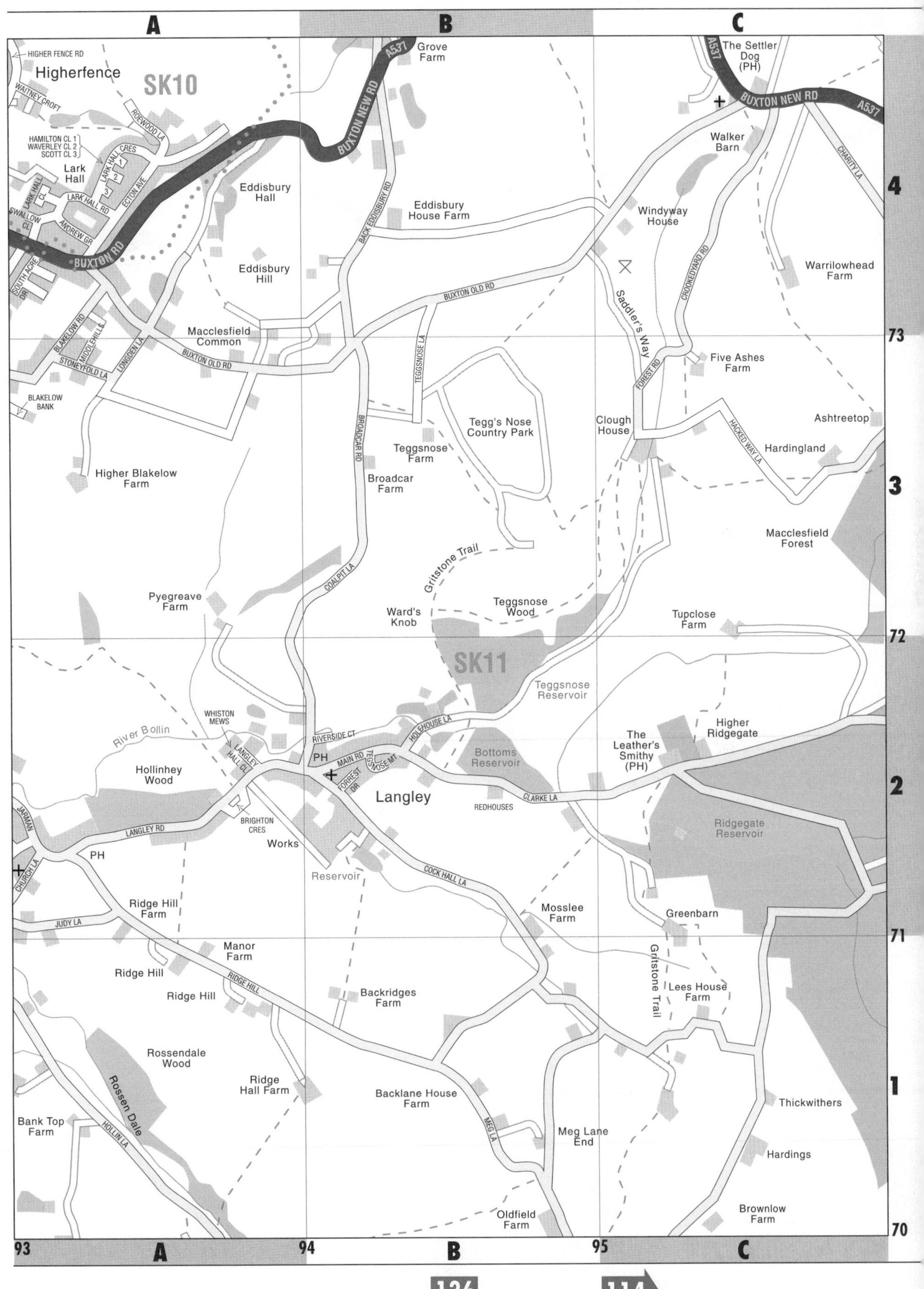

A
B
C

SK10

Higherfence

HIGHER FENCE RD

WAITNEY CROFT

ROE WOOD LA

HAMILTON CL 1
WAVERLEY CL 2
SCOTT CL 3

Lark Hall

LARK HALL CRES

ECTON LANE

LARK HALL RD

ANDREW GR

LARK HALL

SWALLOW CL

SOUTH ACRE DR

Buxton Rd
BUXTON RD

BLAKELOW RD

MIDDLE HILLS

STONEYFOLD LA

LONGDEN LA

BUXTON OLD RD

Macclesfield Common

BLAKELOW BANK

Higher Blakelow Farm

BROADCAR RD

COALPIT LA

Eddisbury Hall

Eddisbury Hill

Grove Farm

A537

BUXTON NEW RD

BACK EDDISBURY RD

Eddisbury House Farm

Buxton Old Rd
BUXTON OLD RD

TEGGSNOSE LA

Teggsnose Farm

Broadcar Farm

Tegg's Nose Country Park

Gritstone Trail

Pyegreave Farm

Ward's Knob

Teggsnose Wood

Teggsnose Wood

The Settler Dog (PH)

BUXTON NEW RD
A537

Walker Barn

Windyway House

CHARITY LA

CROOKEDYARD RD

FOREST RD

Saddler's Way

Five Ashes Farm

Clough House

Warrilowhead Farm

HACKED WAY LA

Ashtreetop

Hardingland

Macclesfield Forest

Tupclose Farm

73

4

3

72

SK11

River Bollin

WHISTON MEWS

LANGLEY HALL CL

RIVERSIDE CT

MAIN RD

PH

FORREST DR

Langley

Hollinhey Wood

JARMAN

CHURCH LA

PH

Ridge Hill Farm

JUDY LA

Ridge Hill

Ridge Hill

Ridge Hill
RIDGE HILL

Rossendale Wood

Rossen Dale

HOLLIN LA

Bank Top Farm

LANGLEY RD

BRIGHTON CRES

Works

Reservoir

COCK HALL LA

Manor Farm

Backridges Farm

Ridge Hall Farm

Backlane House Farm

MEG LA

Oldfield Farm

Teggsnose Reservoir

Bottoms Reservoir

The Leather's Smithy (PH)

CLARKE LA

REDHOUSES

Mosslee Farm

Higher Ridgegate

Ridgegate Reservoir

Greenbarn

Gritstone Trail

Lees House Farm

Meg Lane End

Thickwithers

Hardings

Brownlow Farm

71

2

1

70

93
A
94
B
95
C

A　　　　　B　　　　　C

4

The Laches

Ankers Knowl
Farm

Turnshawflat

A537

Fox Stake

Longclough
Farm

A537

BUXTON NEW RD

Hindsclough
Farm

Fieldhead
Farm

73

Greenways
Farm

Brookhouse

HACKED WAY LA

Whitehills

Long
Clough

Tor Brook

ANKERS LA

CHARITY LA

3

The Stanley Arms
(PH)

Torgate
Farm

Chapel House
Farm

Chambers
Farm

Macclesfield
Forest

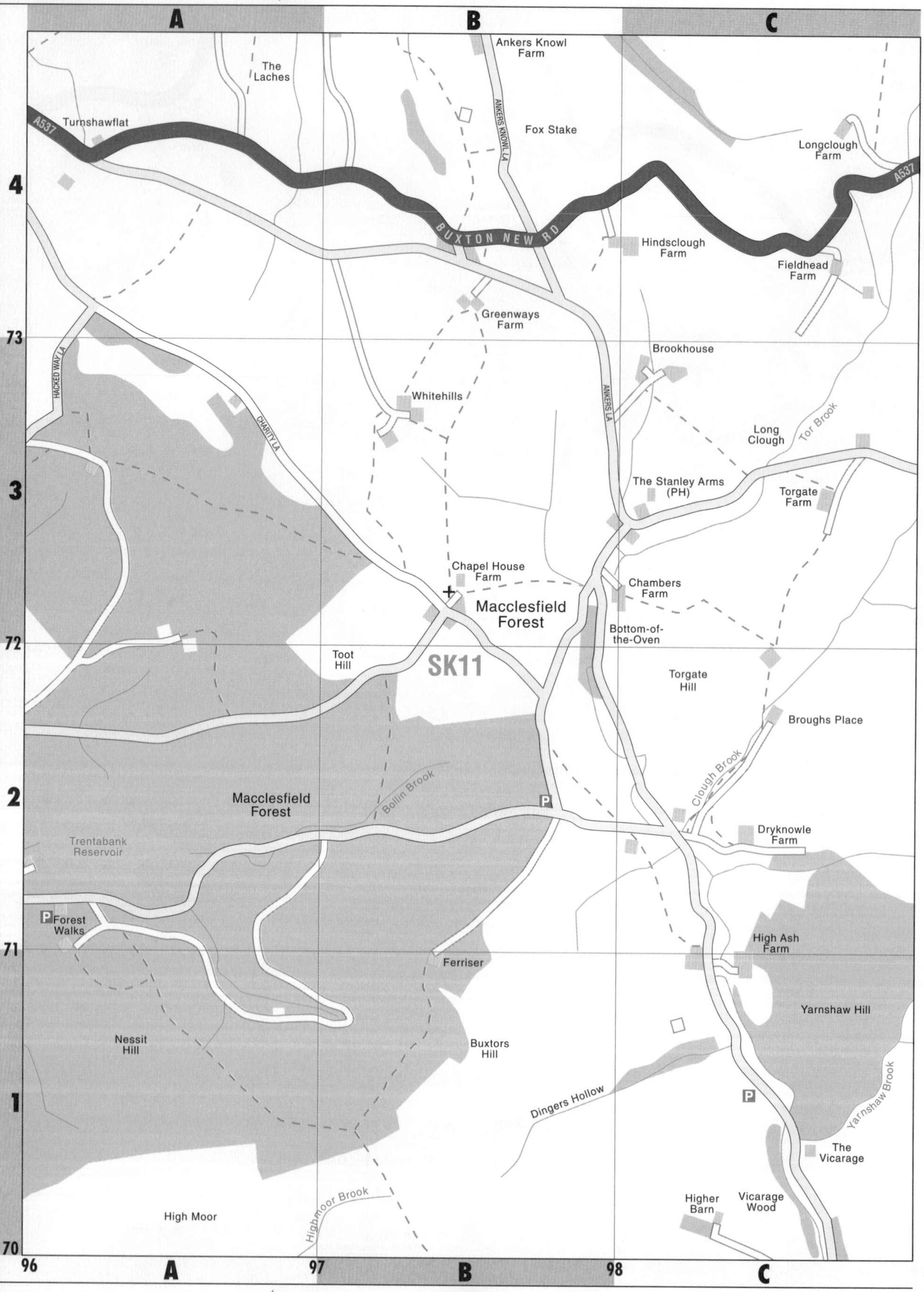

Toot
Hill

SK11

Bottom-of-
the-Oven

72

Torgate
Hill

Broughs Place

Bollin Brook

Clough Brook

2

Macclesfield
Forest

P

Dryknowle
Farm

Trentabank
Reservoir

71

P Forest
Walks

Ferriser

High Ash
Farm

Yarnshaw Hill

Nessit
Hill

Buxtors
Hill

P

Yarnshaw Brook

1

Dingers Hollow

The
Vicarage

High Moor

Highmoor Brook

Higher
Barn

Vicarage
Wood

70

96　　　　　97　　　　　98

A　　　　　B　　　　　C

90

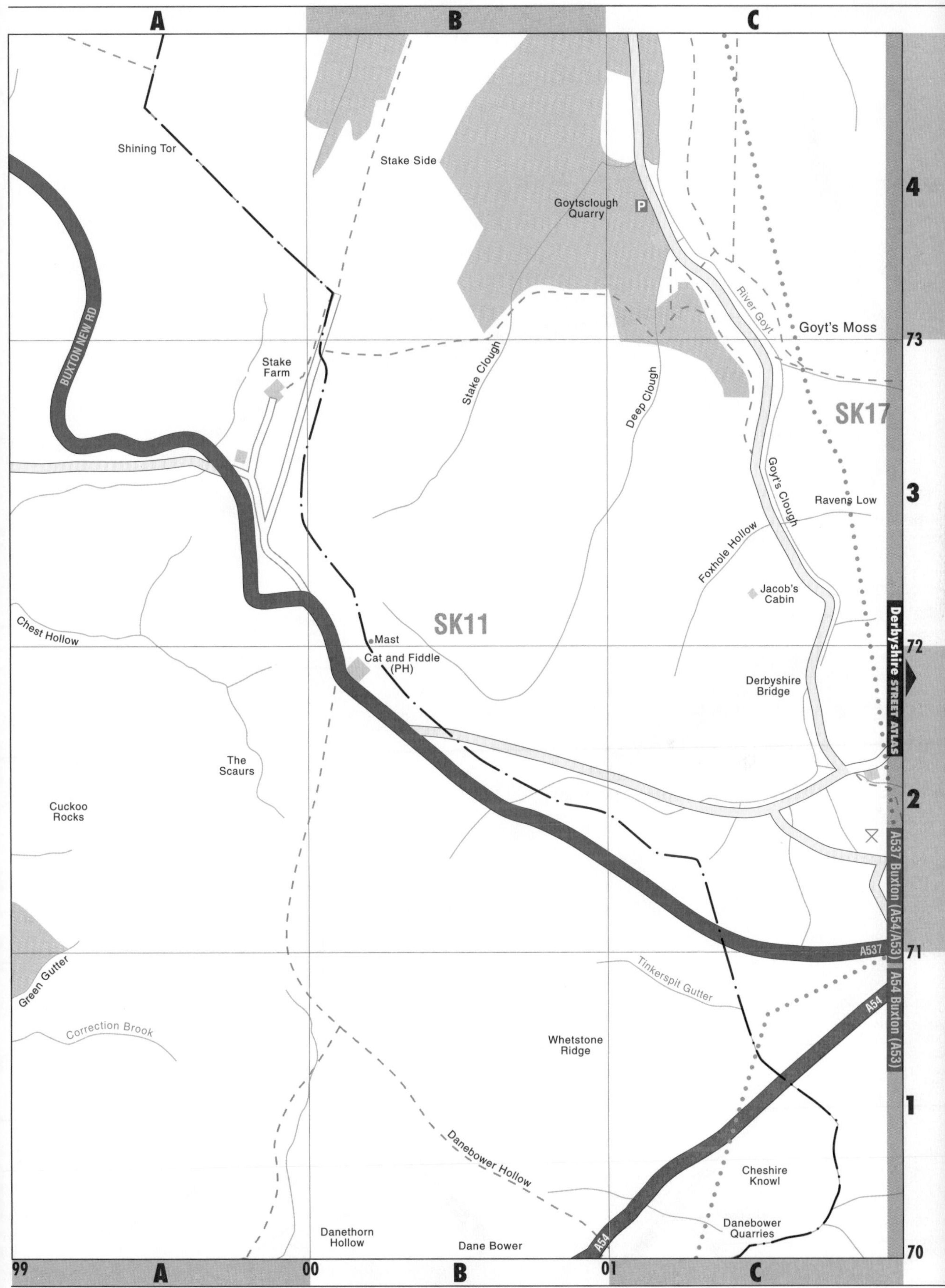

A
B
C
Shining Tor
Stake Side
Goytsclough Quarry
P
River Goyt
Goyt's Moss
BUXTON NEW RD
Stake Farm
Stake Clough
Deep Clough
SK17
Goyt's Clough
Ravens Low
Foxhole Hollow
Jacob's Cabin
Chest Hollow
SK11
Mast
Cat and Fiddle (PH)
Derbyshire Bridge
Derbyshire STREET ATLAS
The Scaurs
Cuckoo Rocks
A537 Buxton (A54/A53)
A537
Tinkerspit Gutter
A54 Buxton (A53)
A54
Green Gutter
Correction Brook
Whetstone Ridge
Danebower Hollow
Cheshire Knowl
Danebower Quarries
Danethorn Hollow
Dane Bower
A54
4
73
3
72
2
71
1
70
99
00
01

138

93

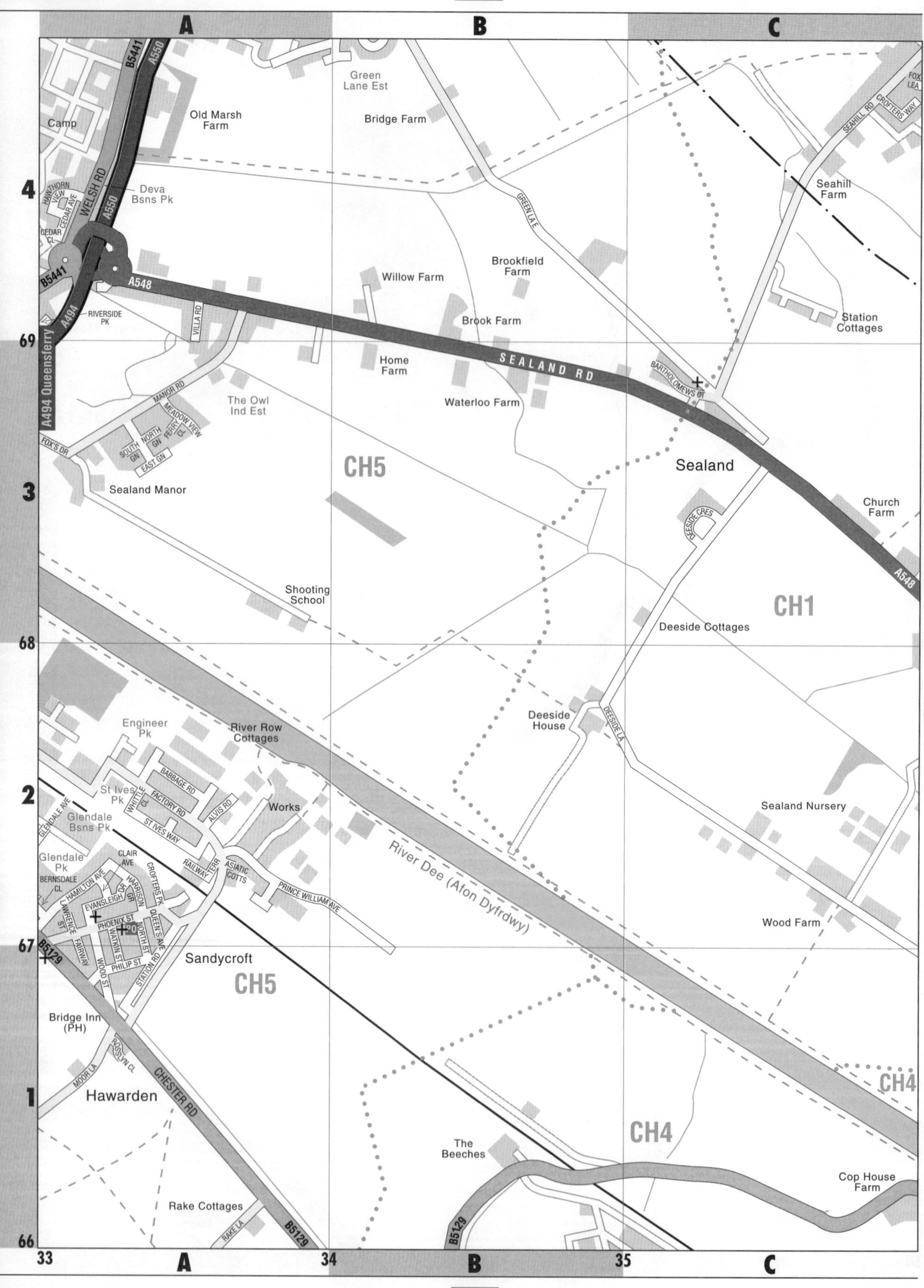
A
B
C
4
69
3
68
2
67
1
66
33
34
35
Green Lane Est
Old Marsh Farm
Bridge Farm
Camp
Deva Bsns Pk
WELSH RD
B5441
A550
A494
A548
A494 Queensferry
RIVERSIDE PK
VILLA RD
Willow Farm
Brookfield Farm
Brook Farm
Home Farm
SEALAND RD
Waterloo Farm
GREEN LA E
The Owl Ind Est
MANOR RD
MEADOW VIEW
FOX'S DR
Sealand Manor
CH5
Sealand
BARTHOLOMEWS CT
DEESIDE CRES
Church Farm
Seahill Farm
SEAHILL RD
CROFTERS WAY
FOX LEA
Station Cottages
CH1
Deeside Cottages
Shooting School
Deeside House
DEESIDE LA
Engineer Pk
River Row Cottages
St Ives Pk
Glendale Bsns Pk
Glendale Pk
Works
BABBAGE RD
FACTORY RD
ST IVES WAY
ALVIS RD
WHITTLE CL
GLENDALE AVE
RAILWAY TERR
ASIATIC COTTS
PRINCE WILLIAM AVE
CLAIR AVE
HAMILTON AVE
BERNSDALE CL
EVANSLEIGH DR
HARRISON GR
CROFTERS PK
PHOENIX ST
NORTH ST
QUEEN'S AVE
WATKIN ST
LAWRENCE ST
FAIRWAY
WOOD ST
PHILIP ST
STATION RD
River Dee (Afon Dyfrdwy)
Sealand Nursery
Wood Farm
Sandycroft
CH5
B5129
Bridge Inn (PH)
ROSLYN CL
MOOR LA
Hawarden
CHESTER RD
Rake Cottages
RAKE LA
The Beeches
CH4
CH4
Cop House Farm

139

94
118

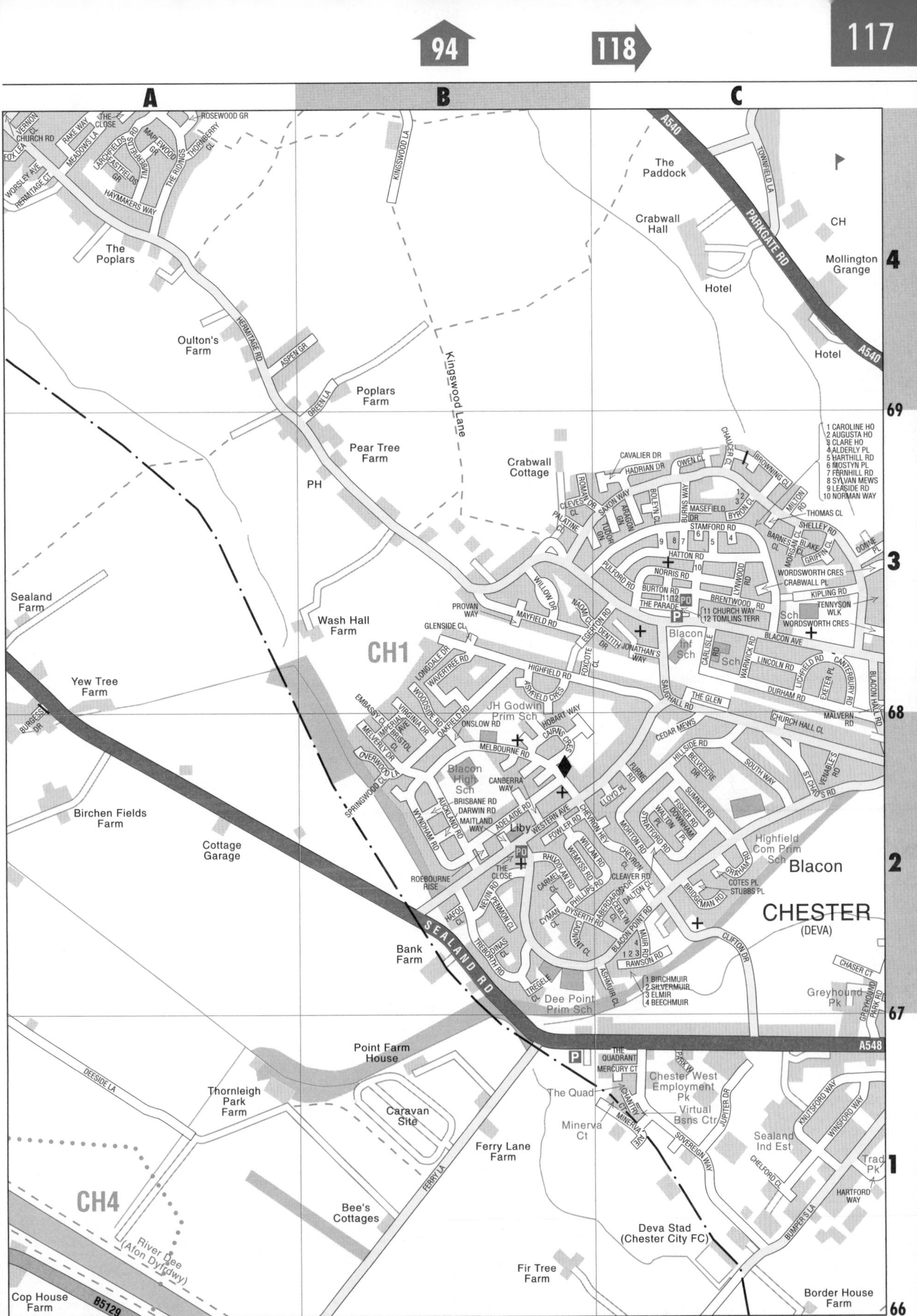
A
B
C
The Paddock
Crabwall Hall
Hotel
CH
Mollington Grange
The Poplars
Oulton's Farm
Poplars Farm
Pear Tree Farm
PH
Kingswood Lane
Crabwall Cottage
Sealand Farm
Wash Hall Farm
CH1
Yew Tree Farm
JH Godwin Prim Sch
Blacon High Sch
Blacon Inf Sch
Birchen Fields Farm
Cottage Garage
Bank Farm
SEALAND RD
Dee Point Prim Sch
Highfield Com Prim Sch
Blacon
CHESTER
(DEVA)
Greyhound Pk
Point Farm House
Thornleigh Park Farm
Caravan Site
The Quad
Minerva Ct
Chester West Employment Pk
Virtual Bsns Ctr
Sealand Ind Est
Trad Pk
Ferry Lane Farm
CH4
Bee's Cottages
River Dee (Afon Dyfrdwy)
Deva Stad (Chester City FC)
Fir Tree Farm
Border House Farm
Cop House Farm
B5129
A540
A548
PARKGATE RD
1 CAROLINE HO
2 AUGUSTA HO
3 CLARE HO
4 ALDERLY PL
5 HARTHILL RD
6 MOSTYN PL
7 FERNHILL RD
8 SYLVAN MEWS
9 LEASIDE RD
10 NORMAN WAY
11 CHURCH WAY
12 TOMLINS TERR
1 BIRCHMUIR
2 SILVERMUIR
3 ELMIR
4 BEECHMUIR
4
3
2
1
69
68
67
66
36
37
38

140
118

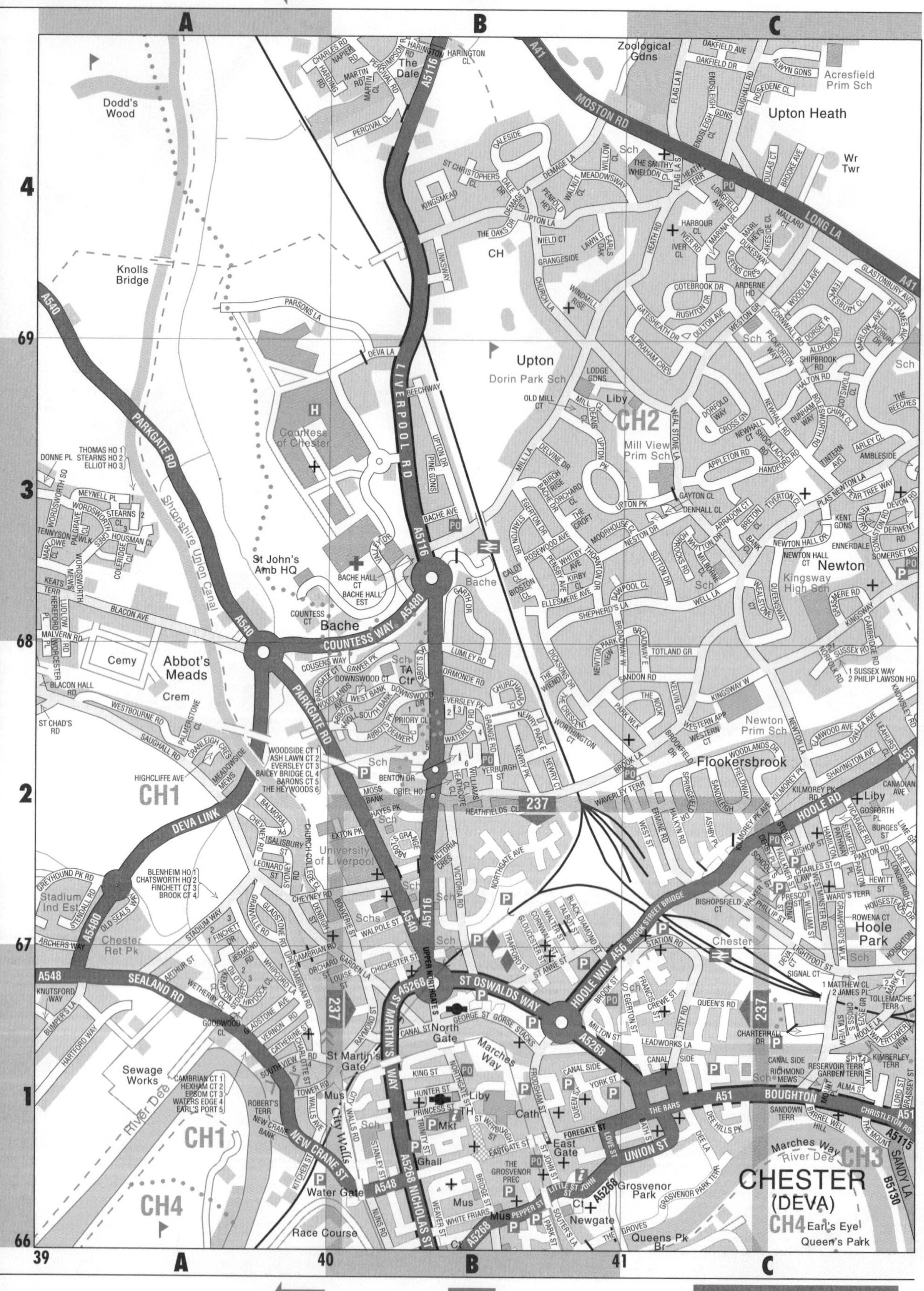

For full street detail of the highlighted area see page 237.

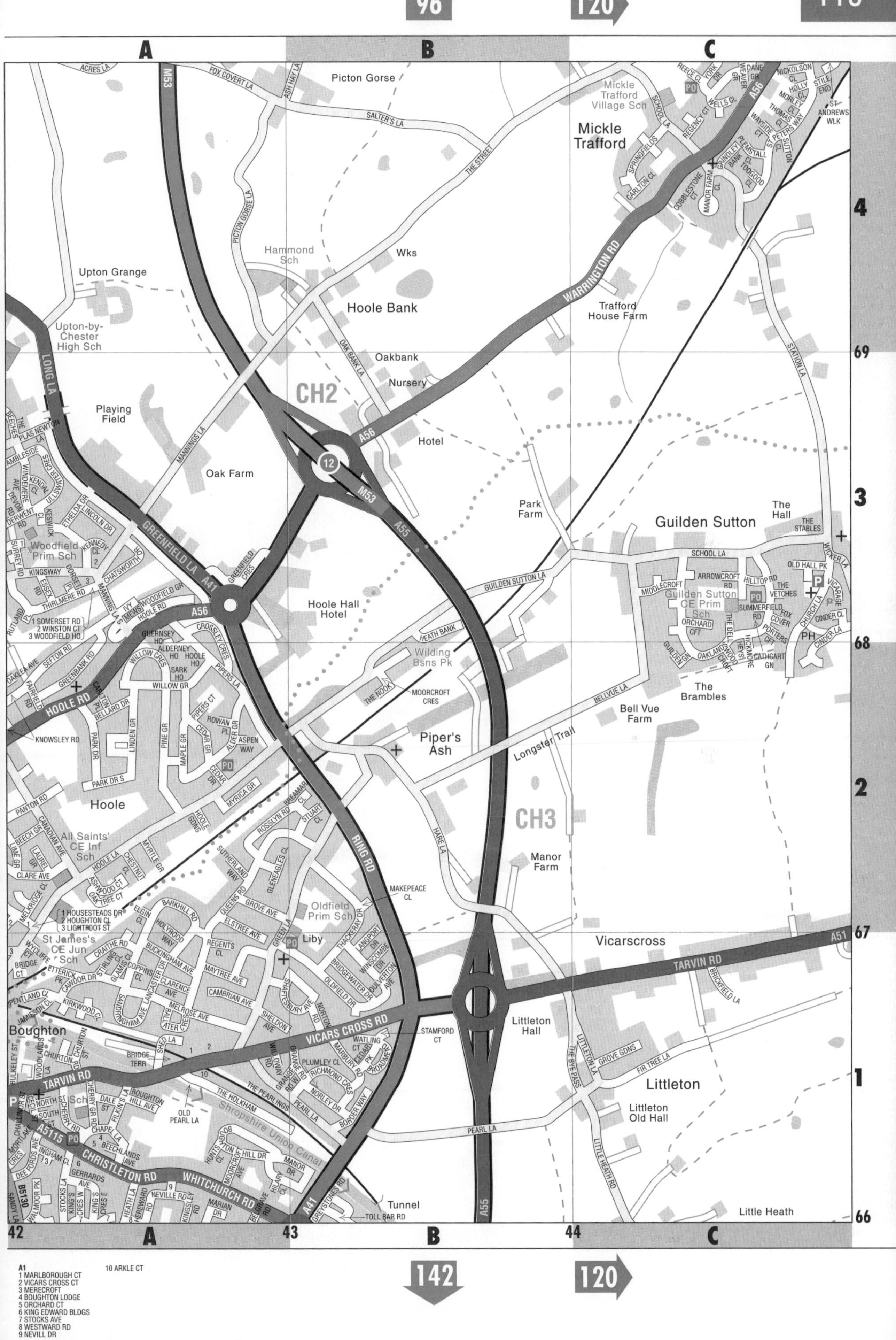
96
120
A
B
C
Picton Gorse
Mickle Trafford Village Sch
Mickle Trafford
Hammond Sch
Wks
Upton Grange
Hoole Bank
Trafford House Farm
Upton-by-Chester High Sch
Oakbank
Nursery
CH2
Playing Field
Hotel
Oak Farm
Park Farm
The Hall
Guilden Sutton
THE STABLES
Woodfield Prim Sch
Hoole Hall Hotel
Guilden Sutton CE Prim Sch
Wilding Bsns Pk
The Brambles
Bell Vue Farm
Piper's Ash
Longster Trail
Hoole
CH3
All Saints' CE Inf Sch
Manor Farm
Oldfield Prim Sch
Liby
St James's CE Jun Sch
Vicarscross
Boughton
Littleton Hall
Littleton
Littleton Old Hall
Shropshire Union Canal
Tunnel
Little Heath
M53
A56
A41
A55
A51
A5115
B5130
WARRINGTON RD
GREENFIELD LA
HOOLE RD
RING RD
TARVIN RD
VICARS CROSS RD
CHRISTLETON RD
WHITCHURCH RD
LONG LA
PEARL LA
BELLVUE LA
GUILDEN SUTTON LA
SCHOOL LA
HARE LA
STATION LA
4
3
2
1
69
68
67
66
42
43
44
142
120
A1
1 MARLBOROUGH CT
2 VICARS CROSS CT
3 MERECROFT
4 BOUGHTON LODGE
5 ORCHARD CT
6 KING EDWARD BLDGS
7 STOCKS AVE
8 WESTWARD RD
9 NEVILL DR
10 ARKLE CT

119
97

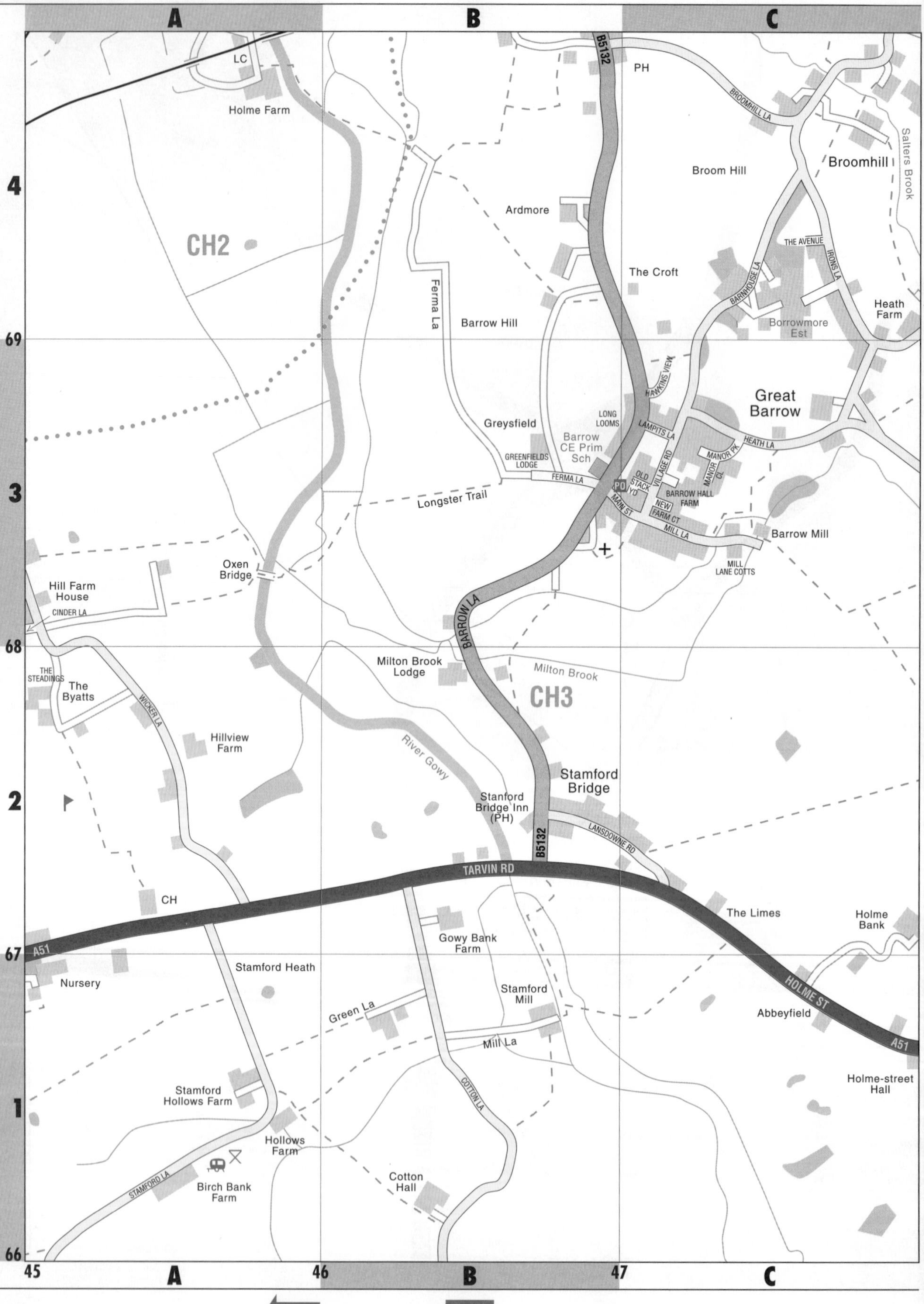

A **B** **C**

4

LC

Holme Farm

CH2

Ardmore

Ferma La

Barrow Hill

The Croft

B5132

PH

Broom Hill

BROOMHILL LA

Broomhill

THE AVENUE

BARNHOUSE LA

IRONS LA

Salters Brook

Heath Farm

Borrowmore Est

69

Greysfield

Longster Trail

FERMA LA

GREENFIELDS LODGE

LONG LOOMS

Barrow CE Prim Sch

HAWKINS VIEW

LAMPITS LA

VILLAGE RD

Great Barrow

MANOR PK

HEATH LA

MANOR CL

OLD STACK YD

PO

NEW FARM CT

BARROW HALL FARM

MAIN ST

MILL LA

Barrow Mill

MILL LANE COTTS

+

3

Hill Farm House

CINDER LA

Oxen Bridge

68

THE STEADINGS

The Byatts

WICKER LA

Hillview Farm

River Gowy

Milton Brook Lodge

BARROW LA

Milton Brook

CH3

Stamford Bridge

Stanford Bridge Inn (PH)

B5132

LANSDOWNE RD

2

CH

Gowy Bank Farm

The Limes

Holme Bank

A51

TARVIN RD

67

Nursery

Stamford Heath

Green La

Stamford Mill

Mill La

COTTON LA

Abbeyfield

HOLME ST

A51

Holme-street Hall

1

Stamford Hollows Farm

Hollows Farm

STAMFORD LA

Birch Bank Farm

Cotton Hall

66

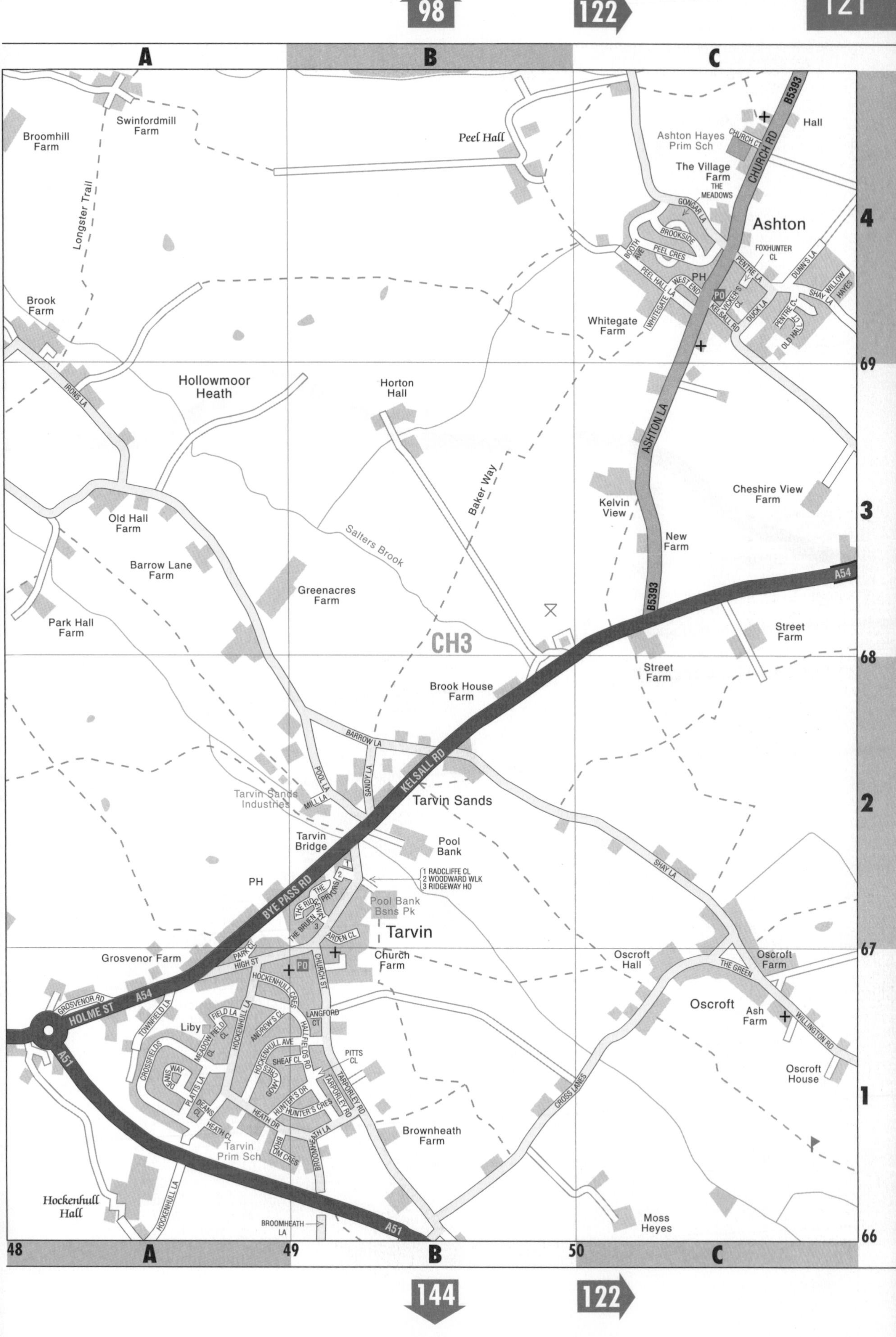

A B C

4

69

3

68

2

67

1

66

Broomhill Farm
Swinfordmill Farm
Longster Trail
Brook Farm
Hollowmoor Heath

Peel Hall

Ashton Hayes Prim Sch
Hall
CHURCH RD
B5393
The Village Farm
THE MEADOWS
CHURCH CL
GONGAR LA
BROOKSIDE
Ashton
PEEL CRES
BOOTH AVE
WEST END
PH
PO
WHITEGATE LA
FOXHUNTER CL
PENTRE LA
VICKERS CL
KELSALL RD
DUCK LA
DUNN'S LA
PENTRE CT
SHAY LA
WILLOW HAYES
OLD HALL

Whitegate Farm

Irons La
Old Hall Farm
Barrow Lane Farm
Park Hall Farm
Greenacres Farm

Horton Hall
Baker Way
Salters Brook

Ashton La
Kelvin View
B5393
New Farm
Cheshire View Farm

CH3

Brook House Farm
Street Farm
Street Farm
A54

BARROW LA
KELSALL RD
SANDY LA
POOL LA
MILL LA
Tarvin Sands Industries
Tarvin Sands
Pool Bank
SHAY LA

Tarvin Bridge
BYE PASS RD
PARK CL
HIGH ST
THE RIDGEWAY
THE BRIARS
PRIORS 3
PH
2
1 RADCLIFFE CL
2 WOODWARD WLK
3 RIDGEWAY HO
Pool Bank Bsns Pk
ARDEN CL
Tarvin
Church Farm
Oscroft Hall
THE GREEN
Oscroft Farm
Oscroft

Grosvenor Farm
GROSVENOR RD
HOLME ST
A54
A51
TOWNFIELD LA
HOCKENHULL CRES
CHURCH ST
PO
ANDREW'S CL
MEADOW FIELD CL
HOCKENHULL LA AVE
FIELD LA CL
HALL FIELDS RD
LANGFORD CT
FAIRDILEY RD
PITTS CL
Ash Farm
WILLINGTON RD
Oscroft House
Liby
CROSSFIELDS
PLATTS LA
LANE WAY
DEANS CL
HEATH CL
HUNTER'S DR
HUNTER'S CRES
SHEAF CL
HEATH DR
ELM CRES
Tarvin Prim Sch
CROSS LANES

Brownheath Farm

Hockenhull Hall
HOCKENHULL LA
BROOMHEATH LA
A51
Moss Heyes

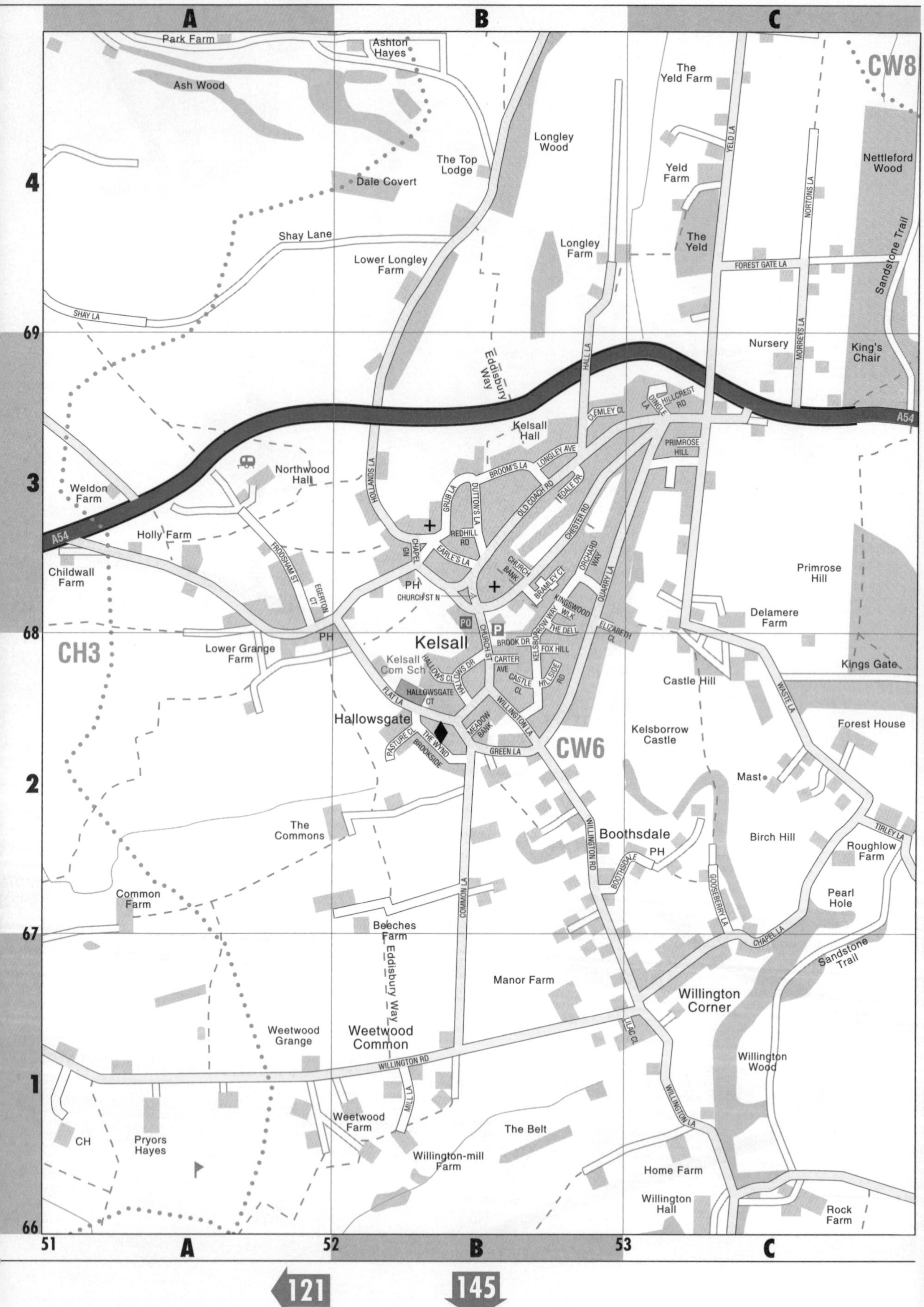

A B C

CW8

Park Farm

Ash Wood

Ashton Hayes

Longley Wood

The Top Lodge

The Yeld Farm

Nettleford Wood

4

Dale Covert

Yeld Farm

Shay Lane

Lower Longley Farm

Longley Farm

The Yeld

FOREST GATE LA

SHAY LA

Nursery

King's Chair

69

Weldon Farm

Northwood Hall

Eddisbury Way

Kelsall Hall

CEMLEY CL

HILLCREST RD

PRIMROSE HILL

A54

A54

3

Holly Farm

BROOM'S LA

LONGLEY AVE

Primrose Hill

Childwall Farm

HOLLANDS LA

GRUB LA

DUTTONS LA

OLD COACH RD

EDALE DR

CHESTER RD

CHAPEL GN

REDHILL RD

EARLE'S LA

CHURCH BANK

BRAMLEY CT

ORCHARD WAY

QUARRY LA

Delamere Farm

PH

CHURCH ST N

KINGSWOOD WAY

KELSBORROW WAY

THE DELL

ELIZABETH CL

Kings Gate

68

EGERTON CT

PH

PO

P

BROOK DR

FOX HILL

CH3

Lower Grange Farm

Kelsall Com Sch

HALLON'S CLO DR

CARTER AVE

CASTLE CL

HILLSIDE

WILLINGTON LA

Castle Hill

Forest House

Kelsall

FLAT LA

HALLOWSGATE CT

MEADOW BANK

Kelsborrow Castle

Hallowsgate

PASTURE CT

THE WYND

BROOMSIDE

GREEN LA

CW6

Mast

Birch Hill

Roughlow Farm

2

The Commons

Boothsdale

TIRLEY LA

WILLINGTON RD

PH

Pearl Hole

Common Farm

COMMON LA

BOOTHSDALE

GOOSEBERRY LA

CHAPEL LA

Sandstone Trail

67

Beeches Farm

Eddisbury Way

Manor Farm

Willington Corner

Weetwood Grange

Weetwood Common

WILLINGTON RD

LILAC CL

Willington Wood

1

CH

Pryors Hayes

Weetwood Farm

MILL LA

The Belt

Willington-mill Farm

Home Farm

Willington Hall

Rock Farm

66

51 A 52 B 53 C

100
124

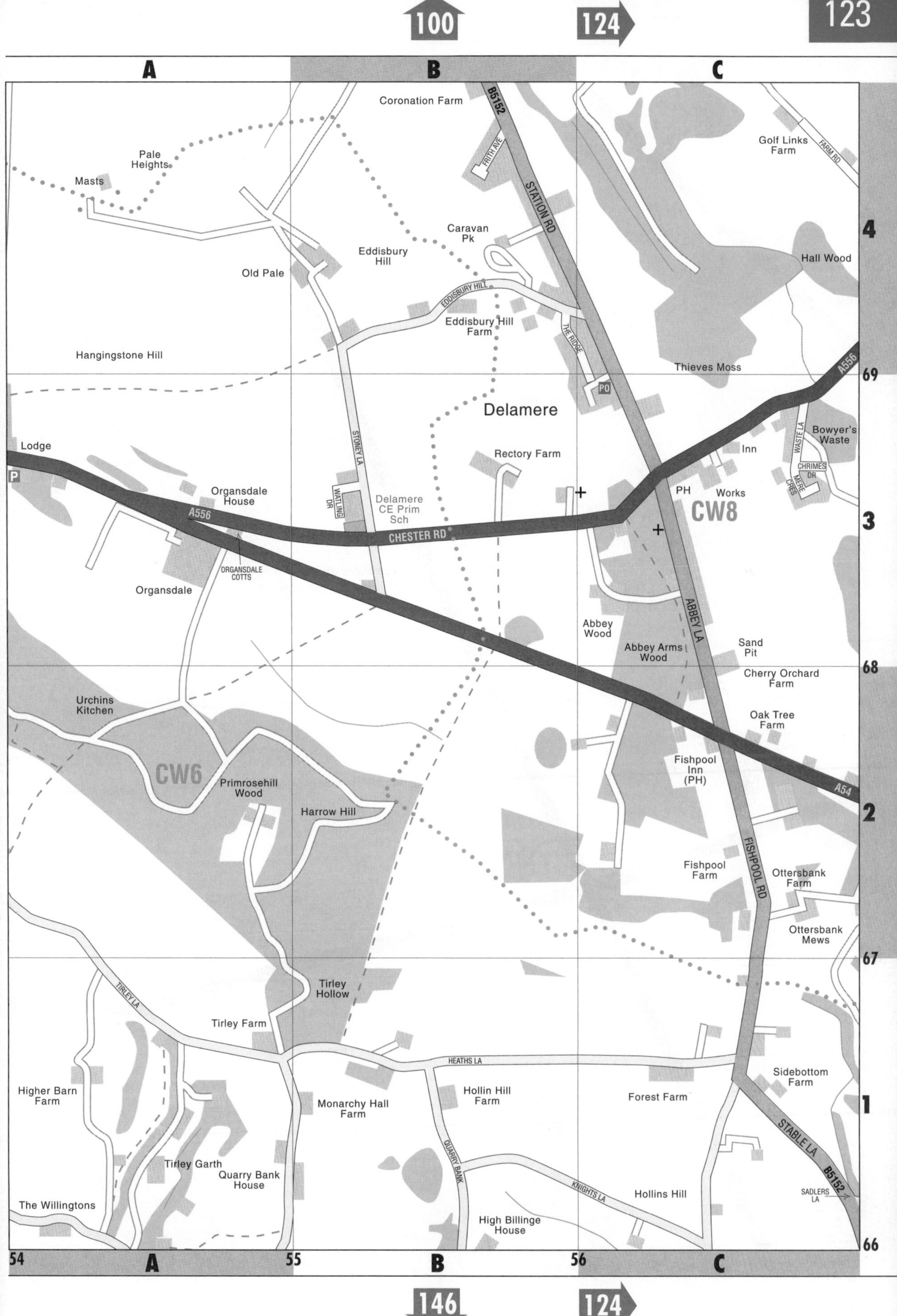
A
B
C
Coronation Farm
B5152
FRITH AVE
STATION RD
Golf Links Farm
FARM RD
Pale Heights
Masts
Caravan Pk
4
Hall Wood
Eddisbury Hill
Old Pale
EDDISBURY HILL
Eddisbury Hill Farm
THE RIDGE
Hangingstone Hill
Thieves Moss
A556
69
PO
Delamere
Lodge
Rectory Farm
STONEY LA
Inn
WASTE LA
Bowyer's Waste
P
Organsdale House
WATLING DR
Delamere CE Prim Sch
PH
Works
CHRIMES DR
MERE CRES
A556
CHESTER RD
CW8
3
ORGANSDALE COTTS
Organsdale
ABBEY LA
Abbey Wood
Abbey Arms Wood
Sand Pit
Cherry Orchard Farm
68
Urchins Kitchen
Oak Tree Farm
CW6
Primrosehill Wood
Fishpool Inn (PH)
A54
2
Harrow Hill
Fishpool Farm
FISHPOOL RD
Ottersbank Farm
Ottersbank Mews
67
TIRLEY LA
Tirley Hollow
Tirley Farm
HEATHS LA
Higher Barn Farm
Hollin Hill Farm
Sidebottom Farm
Monarchy Hall Farm
Forest Farm
1
STABLE LA
QUARRY BANK
Tirley Garth
Quarry Bank House
KNIGHTS LA
B5152
Hollins Hill
SADLERS LA
The Willingtons
High Billinge House
66
54
55
56

146
124

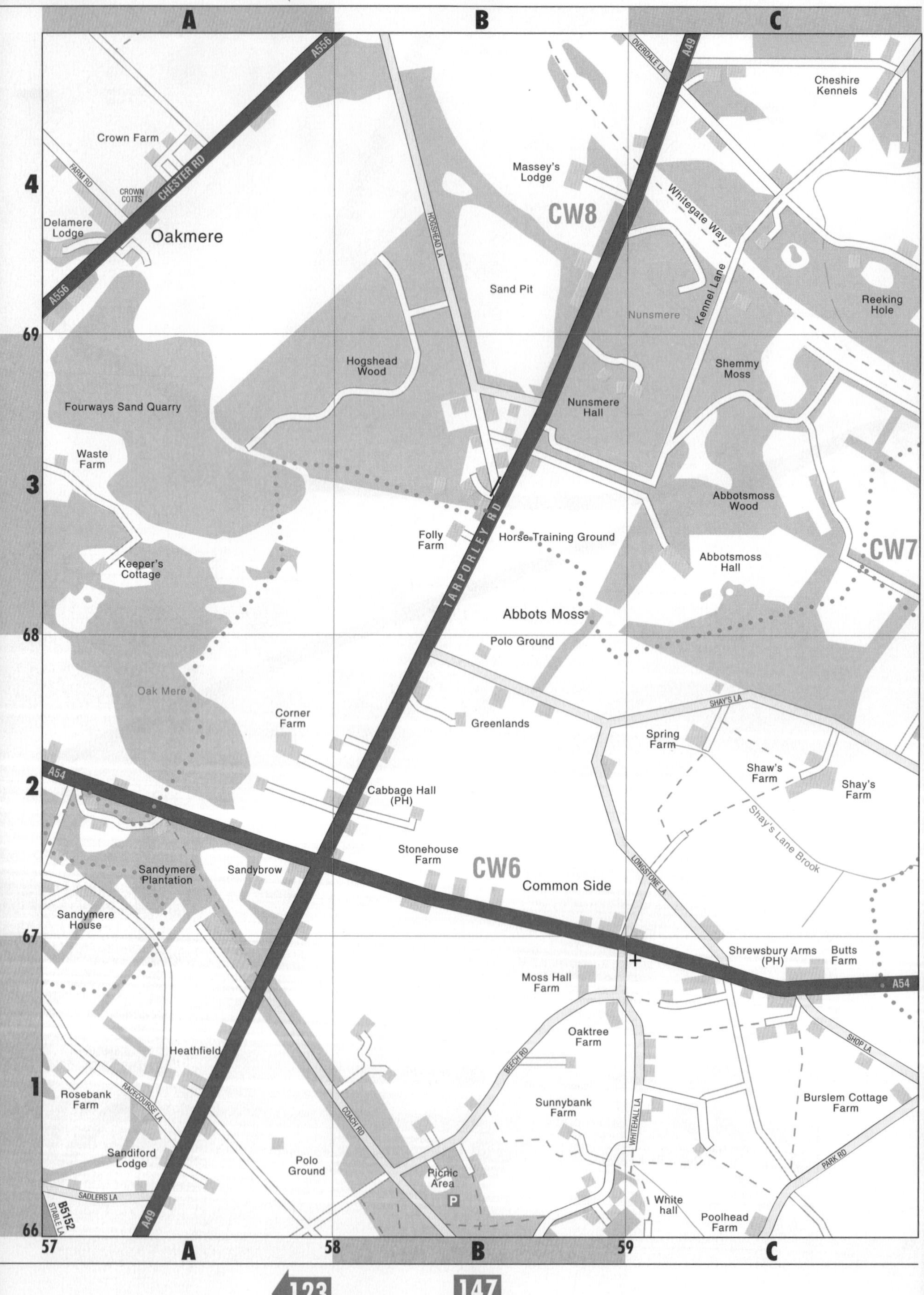

A **B** **C**

A556

Crown Farm

FARM RD

CROWN COTTS

CHESTER RD

Delamere Lodge

4

Oakmere

A556

Massey's Lodge

CW8

HORSEHEAD LA

Sand Pit

Nunsmere

OVERDALE LA

A49

Whitegate Way

Kennel Lane

Cheshire Kennels

Reeking Hole

69

Hogshead Wood

Nunsmere Hall

Shemmy Moss

Fourways Sand Quarry

Waste Farm

3

Keeper's Cottage

Folly Farm

TARPORLEY RD

Horse Training Ground

Abbotsmoss Wood

Abbotsmoss Hall

CW7

Abbots Moss

68

Oak Mere

Polo Ground

SHAY'S LA

Corner Farm

Greenlands

Spring Farm

Shaw's Farm

Shay's Farm

Shay's Lane Brook

A54

2

Sandymere Plantation

Sandybrow

Cabbage Hall (PH)

Stonehouse Farm

CW6

Common Side

LONGSTONE LA

Shrewsbury Arms (PH)

Butts Farm

Sandymere House

67

A54

SHOP LA

Heathfield

RACECOURSE LA

Moss Hall Farm

Oaktree Farm

BEECH RD

WHITEHALL LA

Burslem Cottage Farm

PARK RD

1

Rosebank Farm

Sandiford Lodge

SADLERS LA

B5152

STABLE LA

A49

COACH RD

Polo Ground

Picnic Area

P

Sunnybank Farm

White hall

Poolhead Farm

66

57 **A** **58** **B** **59** **C**

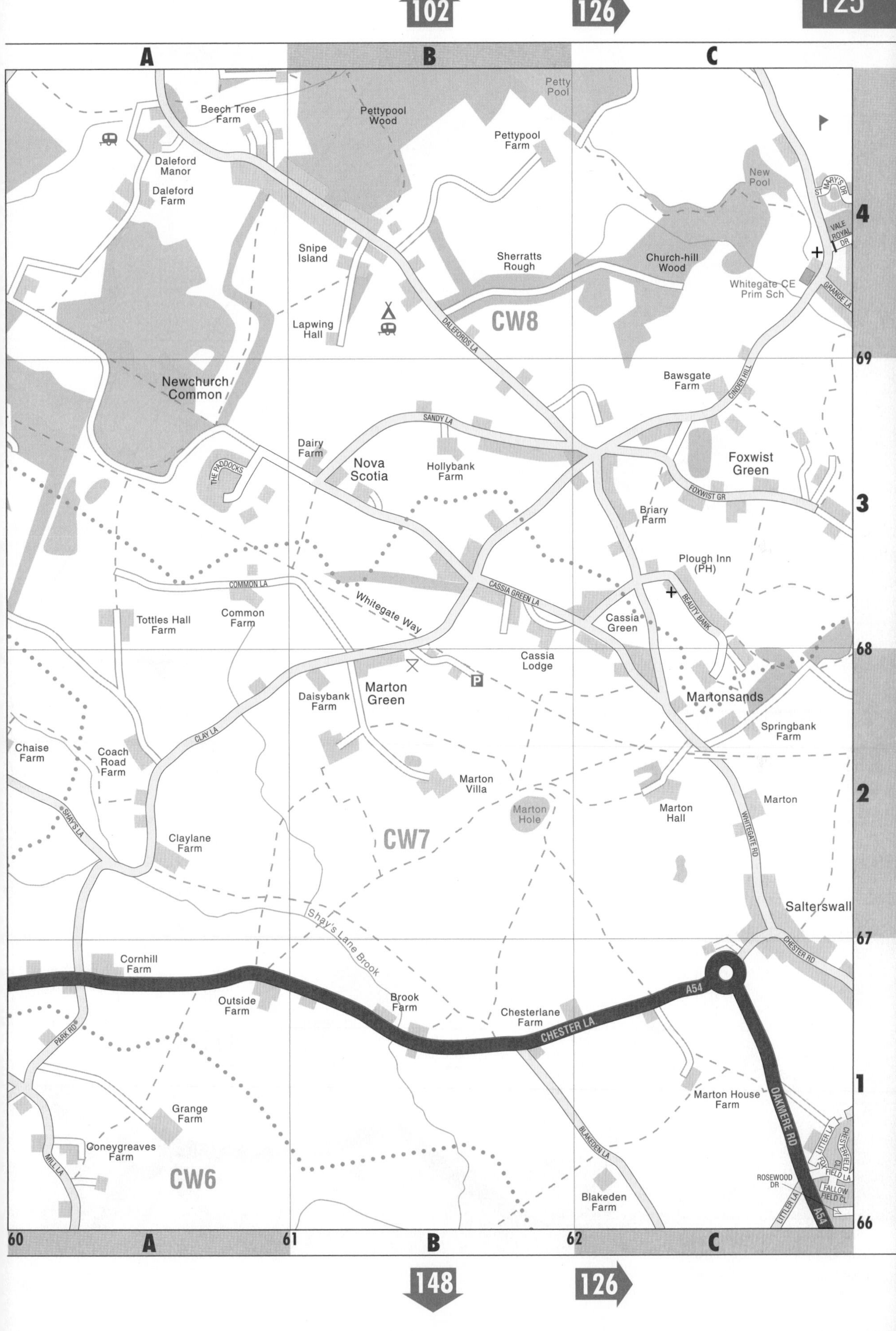
A
B
C
Petty Pool
Beech Tree Farm
Pettypool Wood
Pettypool Farm
Daleford Manor
Daleford Farm
New Pool
ST MARY'S DR
VALE ROYAL DR
Snipe Island
Sherratts Rough
Church-hill Wood
Whitegate CE Prim Sch
GRANGE LA
Lapwing Hall
CW8
DALEFORDS LA
Newchurch Common
Bawsgate Farm
CINDER HILL
SANDY LA
Dairy Farm
THE PADDOCKS
Nova Scotia
Hollybank Farm
Foxwist Green
FOXWIST GR
Briary Farm
Plough Inn (PH)
COMMON LA
CASSIA GREEN LA
Tottles Hall Farm
Common Farm
Whitegate Way
Cassia Green
BEAUTY BANK
Cassia Lodge
Marton Green
Daisybank Farm
Martonsands
CLAY LA
Springbank Farm
Chaise Farm
Coach Road Farm
Marton Villa
Marton
Marton Hole
Marton Hall
SHAY'S LA
CW7
Claylane Farm
WHITEGATE RD
Salterswall
Shay's Lane Brook
CHESTER RD
Cornhill Farm
A54
Outside Farm
Brook Farm
Chesterlane Farm
CHESTER LA.
PARK RD
OAKMERE RD
Marton House Farm
Grange Farm
BLAKEDEN LA
LITTLER LA
CHESTERFIELD CL
FOX FIELD LA
FALLOW FIELD CL
Coneygreaves Farm
MILL LA
CW6
ROSEWOOD DR
Blakeden Farm
LITTLER LA
A54
4
69
3
68
2
67
1
66
60
61
62

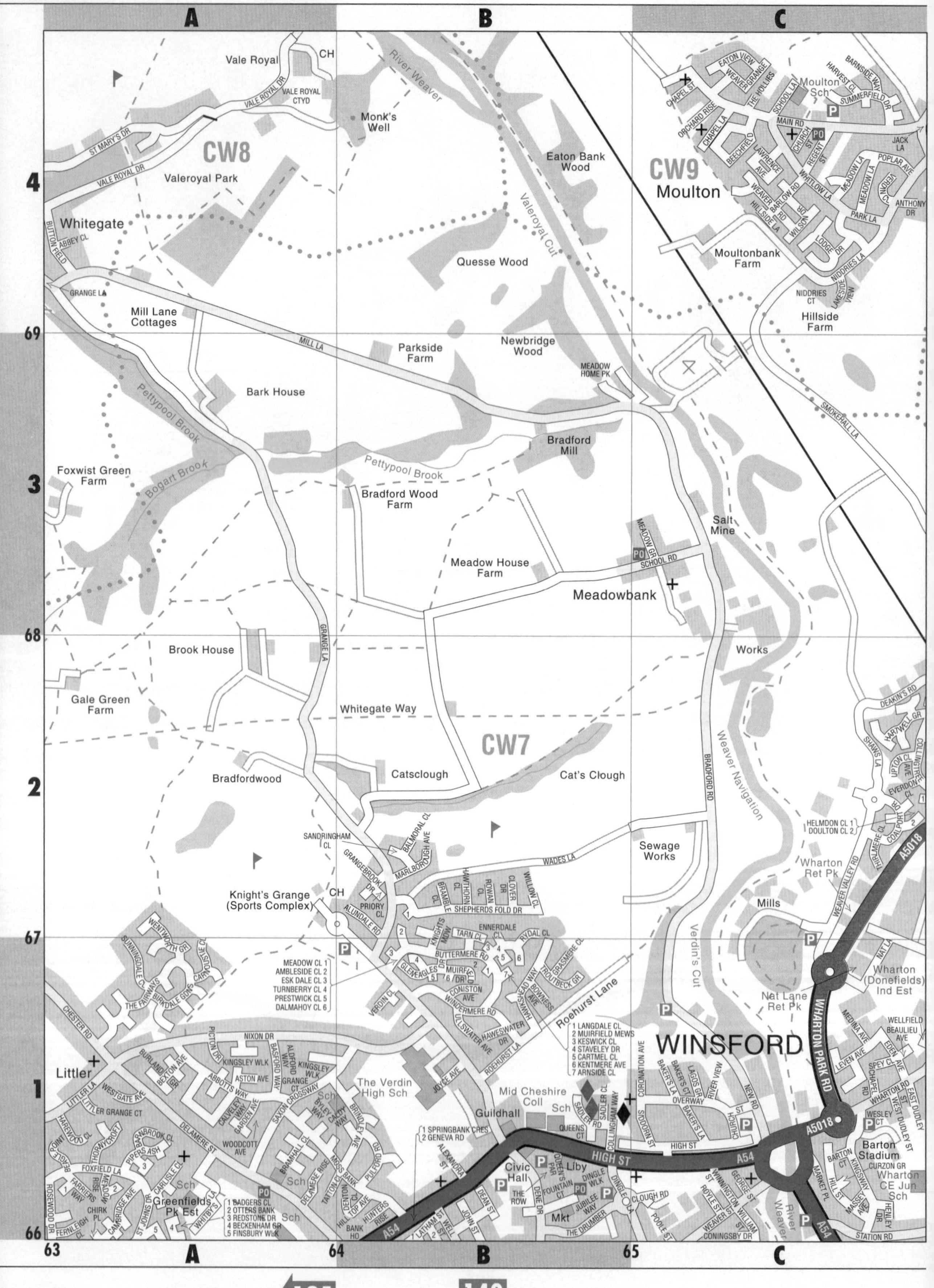

125
103

A

B

C

CH

Vale Royal

VALE ROYAL DR

VALE ROYAL CTYD

River Weaver

Monk's Well

Eaton Bank Wood

ST MARY'S DR

CW8

Valeroyal Park

Valeroyal Cut

Quesse Wood

EATON VIEW

WEAVER GRANGE

THE HOLLIES

Moulton Sch

CHAPEL ST

ORCHARD RISE

CHAPEL LA

MAIN RD

PO

HARVEST CL

BARNSIDE WAY

SUMMERFIELD DR

SCHOOL LA

REGENT ST

WHITLOW LA

WILSON BK

LODGE RD

CW9
Moulton

JACK LA

POPLAR AVE

MEADOW LA

ANTHONY DR

PARK LA

4

Whitegate

BUTTON FIELD

ABBEY CL

GRANGE LA

Mill Lane Cottages

MILL LA

Parkside Farm

Newbridge Wood

MEADOW HOME PK

Moultonbank Farm

HILLSIDE LA

NIDDRIES LA

NIDDRIES CT

LANES IDE

LAKE VIEW

Hillside Farm

SMOKEHALL LA

69

Pettypool Brook

Bark House

Bradford Mill

Bogart Brook

Pettypool Brook

Bradford Wood Farm

Salt Mine

3

Foxwist Green Farm

Meadow House Farm

MEADOW RD

SCHOOL RD

PO

Meadowbank

68

Brook House

GRANGE LA

Whitegate Way

Works

Gale Green Farm

CW7

Weaver Navigation

DEAKIN'S RD

HARTWELL GR

SHAW'S LA

UPTON CL

EVERDON CL

COALPORT

2

Bradfordwood

Catsclough

Cat's Clough

Sewage Works

BALMORAL CL

MARLBOROUGH AVE

SANDRINGHAM CL

GRANGEBROOK

BRADFORD RD

HELMDON CL 1

DOULTON CL 2

Wharton Ret Pk

A5018

HAWTHORN CL

BRAMBLE CL

ROWAN CL

CLOVER CL

WILLOW CL

WADES LA

Verdin's Cut

Mills

P

KNIGHT'S GRANGE

CH

Knight's Grange
(Sports Complex)

PRIORY CL

ALUNDALE RD

KNIGHTS MDW

TARN CL

SHEPHERDS FOLD DR

ENNERDALE

RYDAL CL

GRASMERE GR

Nat Lane Ret Pk

Wharton
(Donefields)
Ind Est

67

P

MEADOW CL 1
AMBLESIDE CL 2
ESK DALE CL 3
TURNBERRY CL 4
PRESTWICK CL 5
DALMAHOY CL 6

WENTWORTH

THE FAIRWAYS

SUNNINGDALE

BURLAND

GLENEAGLES

MUIRFIELD DR

BUTTERMERE RD

CONISTON AVE

WINDERMERE RD

ULLSWATER AVE

HAWESWATER DR

GRASMERE GR

WAY BUSINESS

PROCTERS GR

Roehurst Lane

ROEHURST LA

1 LANGDALE CL
2 MUIRFIELD MEWS
3 KESWICK CL
4 STAVELEY DR
5 CARTMEL CL
6 KENTMERE AVE
7 ARNSIDE CL

P

CORONATION AVE

VERDIN'S CUT

WINSFORD

WELLFIELD

BEAULIEU AVE

LEVEN DR

WHARTON RD

EAST DUDLEY

WEST DUDLEY

WESLEY CT

P

1

CHESTER RD

Littler

WENTWORTH

PICTON DR

NIXON DR

KINGSLEY WLK

ABBOTS WAY

ASTON AVE

KINGSLEY WAY

GRANGE

CROSSWAY

SAXON WAY

The Verdin High Sch

JOYCE AVE

Sch

BRINDLEY AVE

1 SPRINGBANK CRES
2 GENEVA RD

Mid Cheshire Coll

Guildhall

SADLER RD

Sch

QUEENS CT

SADLER RD

CHURCH ST

OVERWAY

BAKERS LA

NEW RD

River View

Barton Stadium

CURZON GR

Wharton
CE Jun Sch

LITTLER LA

LITTLER GRANGE CT

WESTGATE AVE

DELAMERE AVE

BROMHALL CT

WOODCOTT AVE

DELAMERE ST

TATTON CL

The Verdin High Sch

HUNTERS

WELL

LATHAM ST

JOHN ST

ALEXANDRA ST

DENE DR

High St

QUEENS DR

Civic Hall

THE ROW

Liby

FOUNTAIN

PO

JUBILEE WAY

DINGLE WLK

CLOUGH RD

HIGH ST

WEAVER ST

WILLIAM ST

GEORGE ST

MARKET PL

HILL ST

HENLEY DR

Greenfields Pk Est

ROSEWOOD DR

FERN LEIGH

FINSBURY WLK

1 BADGERS CL
2 OTTERS BANK
3 REDSTONE DR
4 BECKENHAM GR
5 FINSBURY WLK

Sch

PO

Mkt

THE DRUMBER

A54

River Weaver

CONINGSBY DR

STATION RD

WHARTON PARK RD

A5018

66

63

A

64

B

65

C

104
128

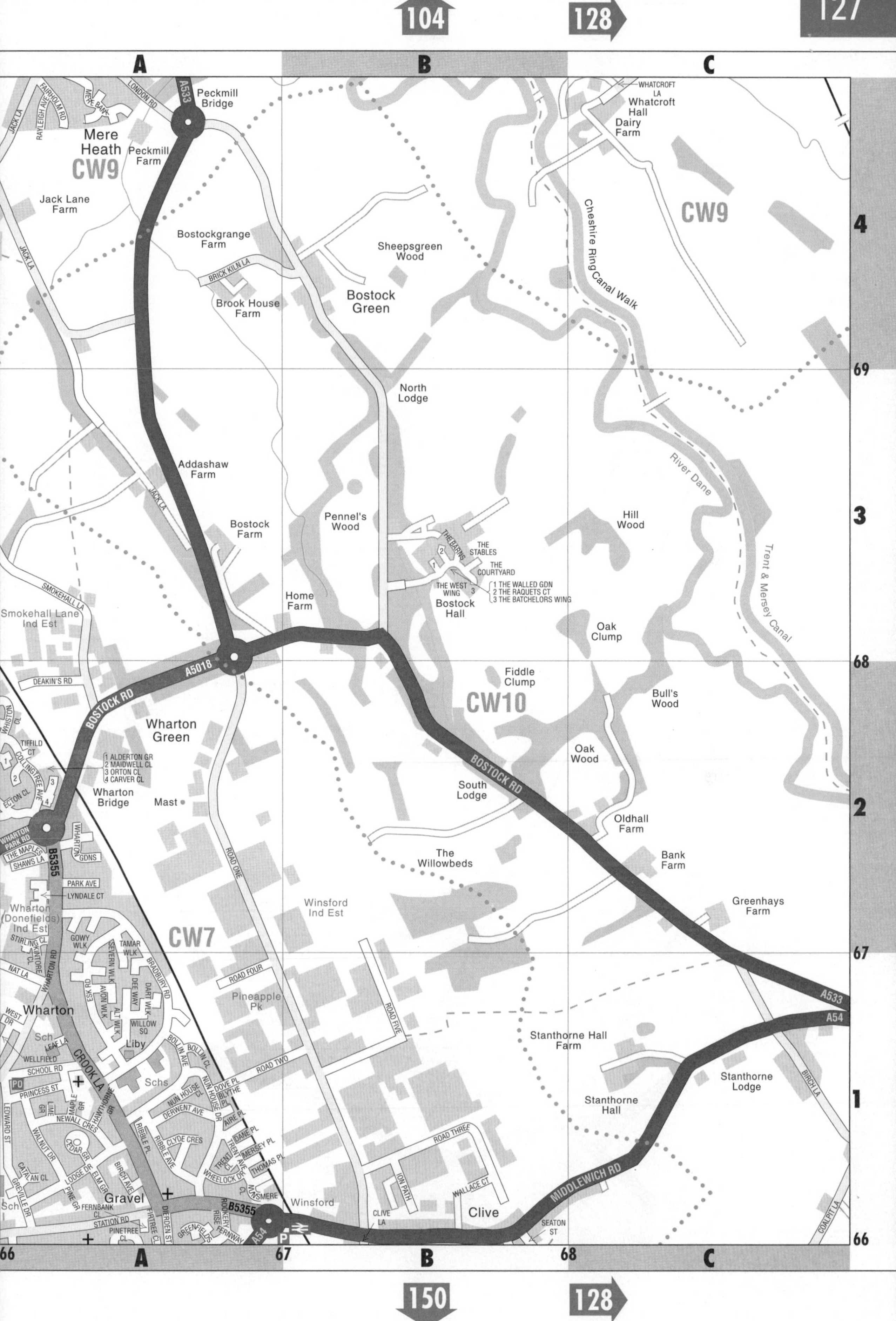
A
B
C
Peckmill Bridge
Mere Heath
Peckmill Farm
CW9
Jack Lane Farm
Bostockgrange Farm
Brook House Farm
Sheepsgreen Wood
Bostock Green
Whatcroft Hall
Dairy Farm
Cheshire Ring Canal Walk
North Lodge
Addashaw Farm
Bostock Farm
Pennel's Wood
Home Farm
Bostock Hall
River Dane
Hill Wood
Trent & Mersey Canal
Oak Clump
Fiddle Clump
CW10
Bull's Wood
Oak Wood
Smokehall Lane Ind Est
Wharton Green
Wharton Bridge
Mast
South Lodge
Oldhall Farm
Bank Farm
The Willowbeds
Winsford Ind Est
Greenhays Farm
Wharton (Donefields) Ind Est
CW7
Pineapple Pk
Wharton
Stanthorne Hall Farm
Stanthorne Lodge
Stanthorne Hall
Gravel
Winsford
Clive
BOSTOCK RD
A5018
A533
A54
B5355
MIDDLEWICH RD
CROOK LA
ROAD ONE
1 ALDERTON GR
2 MAIDWELL CL
3 ORTON CL
4 CARVER CL
1 THE WALLED GDN
2 THE RAQUETS CT
3 THE BATCHELORS WING
4
3
2
1
69
68
67
66

150
128

127
105

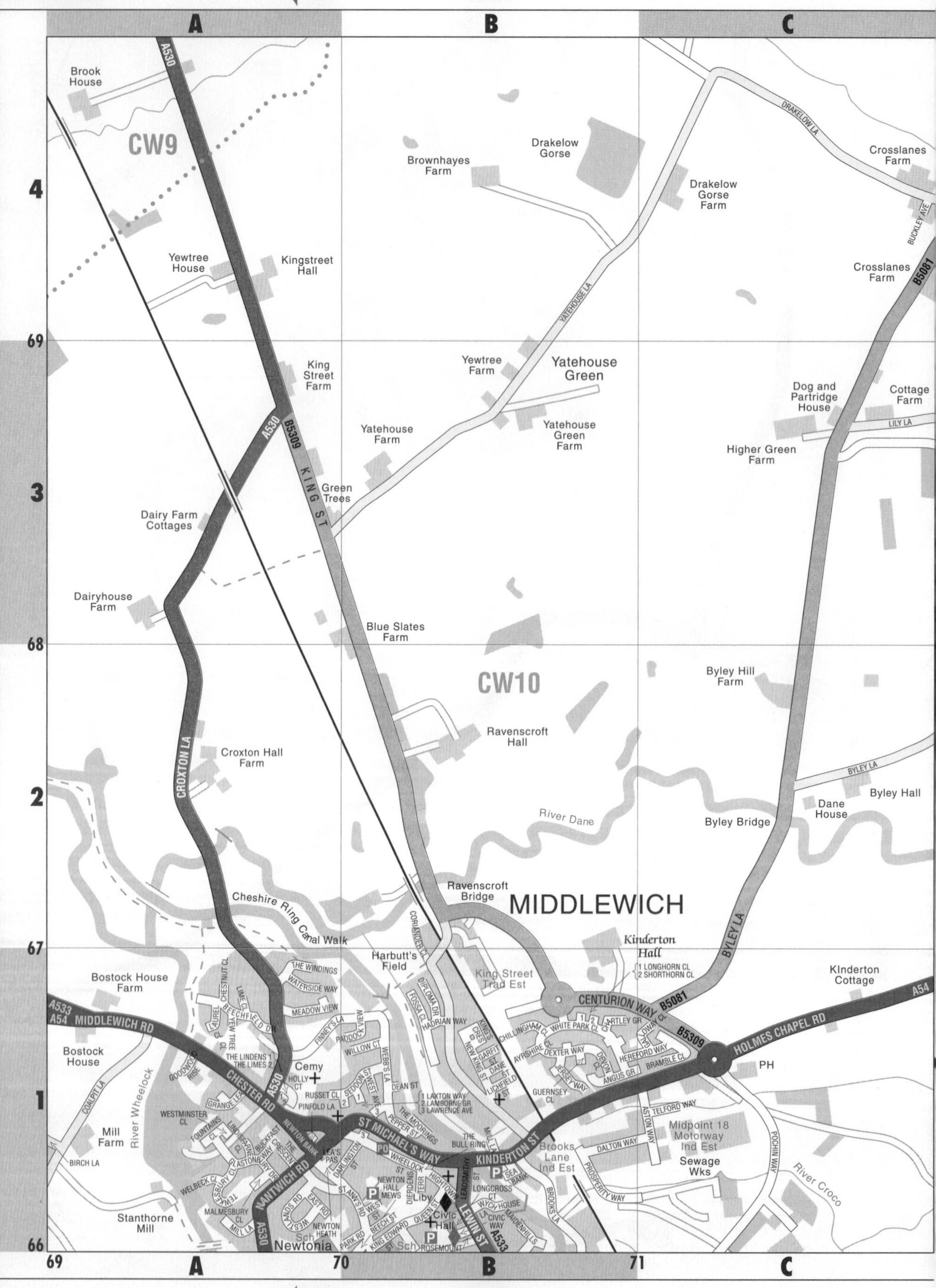
A
B
C
4
69
3
68
2
67
1
66
69
70
71
CW9
CW10
MIDDLEWICH
Brook House
Drakelow Gorse
Brownhayes Farm
Drakelow Gorse Farm
Crosslanes Farm
DRAKELOW LA
BUCKLEY AVE
Yewtree House
Kingstreet Hall
Crosslanes Farm
YATEHOUSE LA
B5081
King Street Farm
Yewtree Farm
Yatehouse Green
Dog and Partridge House
Cottage Farm
LILY LA
Yatehouse Farm
Yatehouse Green Farm
Higher Green Farm
A530
B5309
KING ST
Green Trees
Dairy Farm Cottages
Dairyhouse Farm
Blue Slates Farm
Byley Hill Farm
Ravenscroft Hall
CROXTON LA
Croxton Hall Farm
BYLEY LA
Byley Hall
Dane House
River Dane
Byley Bridge
Ravenscroft Bridge
Cheshire Ring Canal Walk
Kinderton Hall
1 LONGHORN CL
2 SHORTHORN CL
Harbutt's Field
King Street Trad Est
Bostock House Farm
Kinderton Cottage
A533
A54
MIDDLEWICH RD
CENTURION WAY
HOLMES CHAPEL RD
Bostock House
CHESTER RD
Cemy
PH
River Wheelock
COALPIT LA
Mill Farm
BIRCH LA
ST MICHAEL'S WAY
KINDERTON ST
Brooks Lane Ind Est
Midpoint 18 Motorway Ind Est
Sewage Wks
River Croco
POCHIN WAY
TELFORD WAY
DALTON WAY
PROSPERITY WAY
ASTON WAY
NANTWICH RD
Stanthorne Mill
Newtonia
Civic Hall
Liby
LEADSMITHY
LEWIN ST
BROOKS LA
WESTMINSTER CL
GRANGE LA
GOODWOOD RISE
THE LINDENS
THE LIMES
WELBECK CL
MALMESBURY CL
MILL LA
WATERSIDE WAY
MEADOW VIEW
THE WINDINGS
WILLOW CT
PADDOCK VIEW
FINNEY'S LA
RUSSET CL
PINFOLD LA
DEAN ST
1 LAXTON WAY
2 LAMBORNE GR
3 LAWRENCE AVE
PEPPER ST
THE MOORINGS
THE BULL RING
WHEELOCK ST
NEWTON HALL MEWS
QUEEN ST
KING EDWARD ST
ROSEMOUNT
PARK RD
NEWTON HEATH
EAST RD
DARLINGTON ST
HADRIAN WAY
DIPLOMA DR
FOSSA CL
CORIANDER CL
CHILLINGHAM CL
WHITE PARK CL
CHARTLEY GR
AYRSHIRE CL
DEXTER WAY
HEREFORD WAY
BRAMBLE CL
ANGUS GR
JERSEY WAY
GUERNSEY CL
LICHFIELD ST
DANE ST
GARFIT ST
NEW KING ST
LONGCROSS CT
WYCH HOUSE LA
CIVIC WAY
MAIDENHILLS
SEA BANK
LEA'S PAS
SEDDON ST
WEBB'S LA
HOLLY CT
NEWTON BANK

127
151

106
130

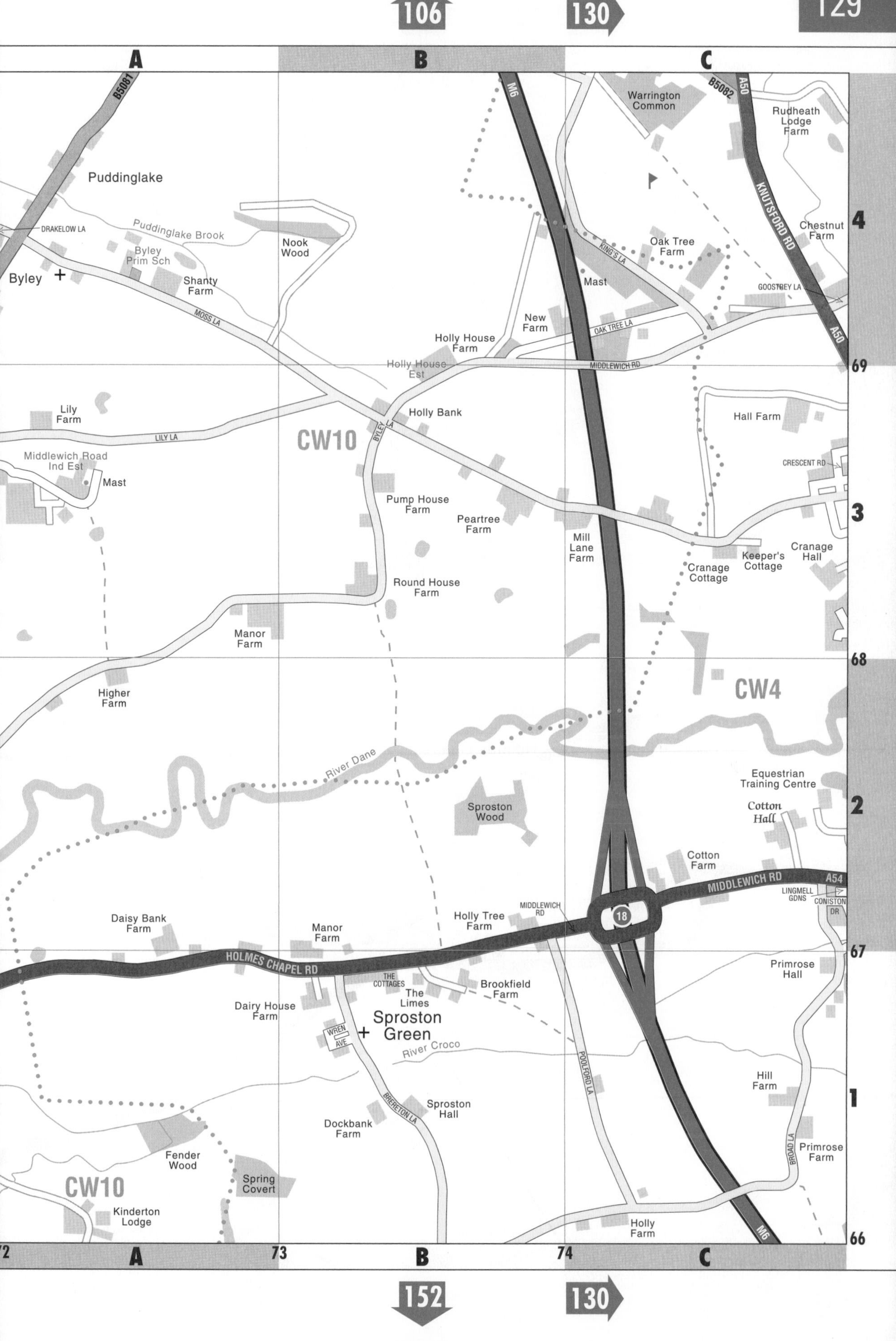
A
B
C
B5081
Puddinglake
DRAKELOW LA
Puddinglake Brook
Byley Prim Sch
Byley
Shanty Farm
Nook Wood
MOSS LA
M6
Warrington Common
B5082
A50
Rudheath Lodge Farm
KNUTSFORD RD
Chestnut Farm
Oak Tree Farm
KING'S LA
Mast
GOOSTREY LA
New Farm
OAK TREE LA
Holly House Farm
Holly House Est
MIDDLEWICH RD
Lily Farm
LILY LA
CW10
BYLEY LA
Holly Bank
Hall Farm
Middlewich Road Ind Est
Mast
CRESCENT RD
Pump House Farm
Peartree Farm
Mill Lane Farm
Cranage Cottage
Keeper's Cottage
Cranage Hall
Round House Farm
Manor Farm
Higher Farm
CW4
River Dane
Equestrian Training Centre
Sproston Wood
Cotton Hall
Cotton Farm
MIDDLEWICH RD
A54
LINGMELL GDNS
CONISTON DR
Daisy Bank Farm
Manor Farm
Holly Tree Farm
MIDDLEWICH RD
18
HOLMES CHAPEL RD
THE COTTAGES
The Limes
Brookfield Farm
Primrose Hall
Dairy House Farm
WREN AVE
Sproston Green
River Croco
POOLFORD LA
Hill Farm
BRERETON LA
Sproston Hall
Dockbank Farm
BROAD LA
Primrose Farm
Fender Wood
Spring Covert
CW10
Kinderton Lodge
Holly Farm
4
69
3
68
2
67
1
66
72
73
74

152
130

129
107

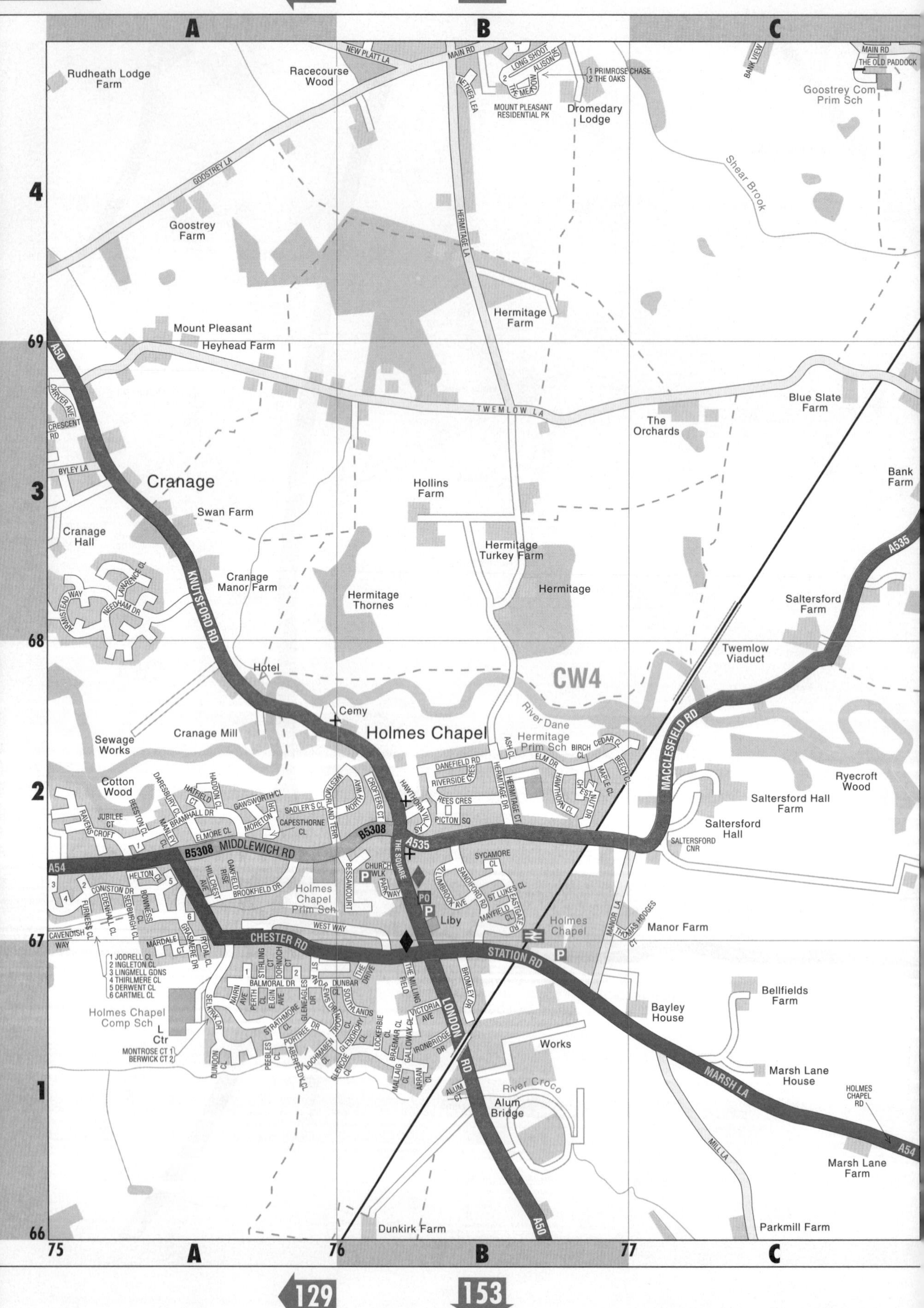
A
B
C
4
3
2
1
69
68
67
66
75
76
77
Rudheath Lodge Farm
Racecourse Wood
Goostrey Farm
Mount Pleasant
Heyhead Farm
Dromedary Lodge
MOUNT PLEASANT RESIDENTIAL PK
1 PRIMROSE CHASE
2 THE OAKS
Goostrey Com Prim Sch
THE OLD PADDOCK
Shear Brook
Hermitage Farm
The Orchards
Blue Slate Farm
TWEMLOW LA
Cranage
Swan Farm
Cranage Hall
Cranage Manor Farm
Hollins Farm
Hermitage Turkey Farm
Hermitage Thornes
Hermitage
Bank Farm
Saltersford Farm
Twemlow Viaduct
CW4
Hotel
River Dane
Cemy
Holmes Chapel
Hermitage Prim Sch
Cranage Mill
Sewage Works
Cotton Wood
KNUTSFORD RD
MACCLESFIELD RD
Ryecroft Wood
Saltersford Hall Farm
Saltersford Hall
SALTERSFORD CNR
B5308 MIDDLEWICH RD
A535
A54
A50
Holmes Chapel Prim Sch
PO
Liby
CHESTER RD
STATION RD
Holmes Chapel
Manor Farm
1 JODRELL CL
2 INGLETON CL
3 LINGMELL GDNS
4 THIRLMERE CL
5 DERWENT CL
6 CARTMEL CL
Holmes Chapel Comp Sch
L Ctr
MONTROSE CT 1
BERWICK CT 2
LONDON RD
Bayley House
Bellfields Farm
Works
Marsh Lane House
MARSH LA
HOLMES CHAPEL RD
River Croco
Alum Bridge
MILL LA
Marsh Lane Farm
Dunkirk Farm
Parkmill Farm

129
153

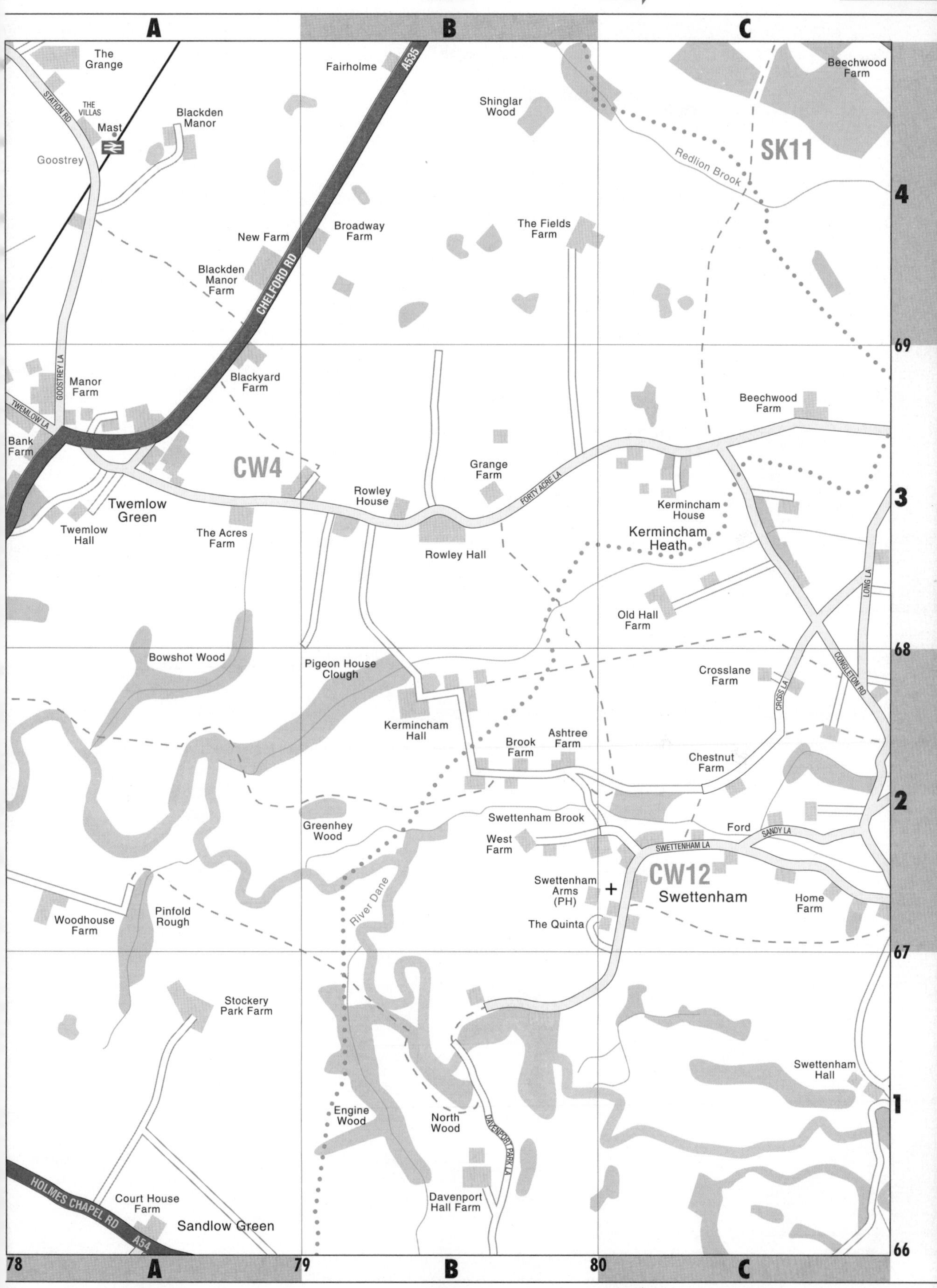
108
132
132

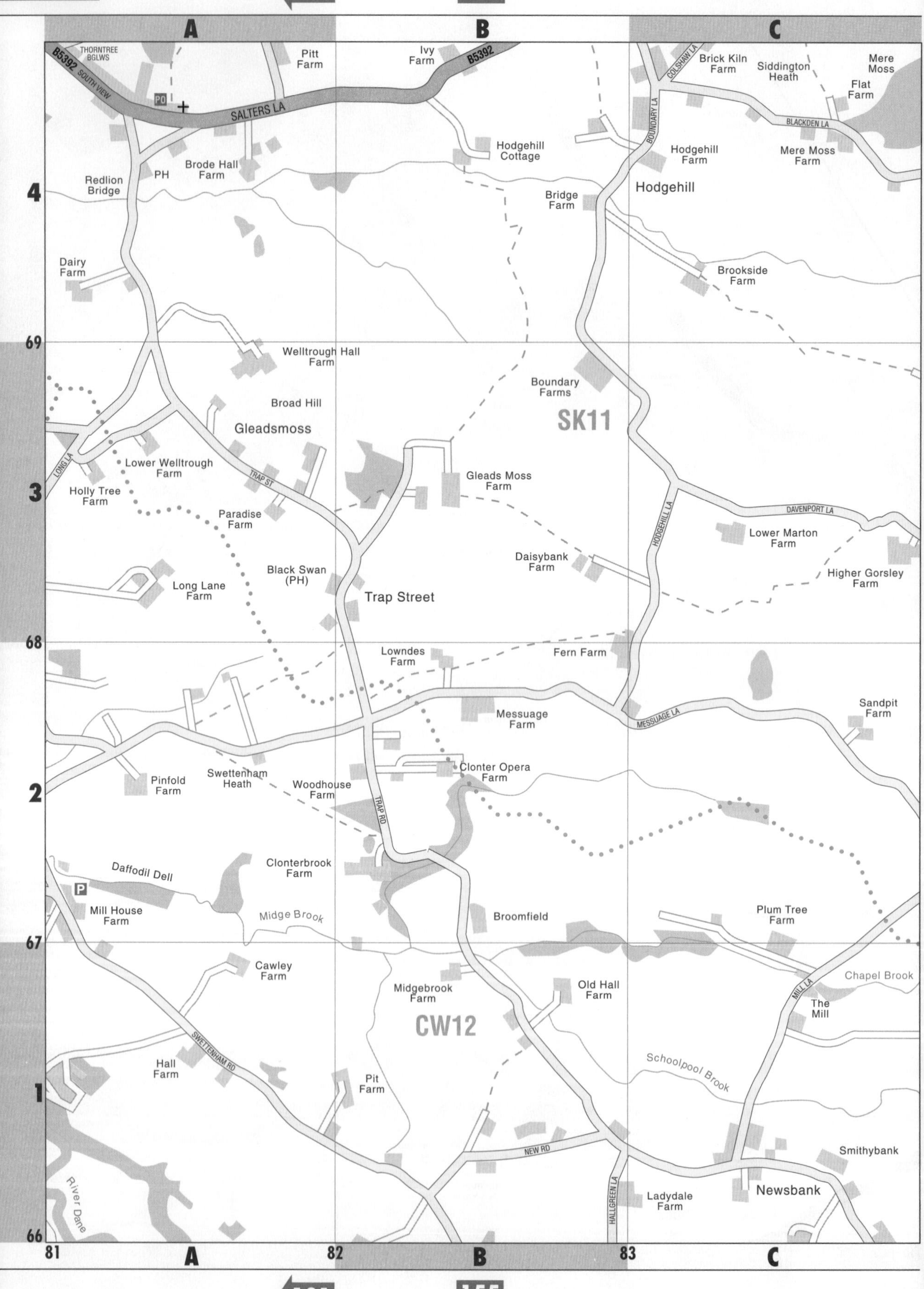

THORNTREE BGLWS
B5392 SOUTH VIEW
PO
Pitt Farm
Ivy Farm
B5392
Brick Kiln Farm
COLSHAW LA
Siddington Heath
Mere Moss
Flat Farm
SALTERS LA
Hodgehill Cottage
BOUNDARY LA
Hodgehill Farm
BLACKDEN LA
Mere Moss Farm
Redlion Bridge
PH
Brode Hall Farm
Bridge Farm
Hodgehill
4
Dairy Farm
Brookside Farm
Welltrough Hall Farm
69
Broad Hill
Boundary Farms
SK11
Gleadsmoss
LONG LA
TRAP ST
Lower Welltrough Farm
Gleads Moss Farm
DAVENPORT LA
HODGEHILL LA
3
Holly Tree Farm
Paradise Farm
Lower Marton Farm
Black Swan (PH)
Daisybank Farm
Higher Gorsley Farm
Long Lane Farm
Trap Street
68
Lowndes Farm
Fern Farm
Sandpit Farm
Messuage Farm
MESSUAGE LA
Pinfold Farm
Swettenham Heath
Woodhouse Farm
Clonter Opera Farm
2
TRAP RD
Daffodil Dell
Clonterbrook Farm
Plum Tree Farm
P
Mill House Farm
Midge Brook
Broomfield
MILL LA
Chapel Brook
67
Cawley Farm
Midgebrook Farm
Old Hall Farm
The Mill
CW12
Schoolpool Brook
SWETTENHAM RD
Hall Farm
Pit Farm
Smithybank
1
HALLGREEN LA
NEW RD
Ladydale Farm
Newsbank
River Dane
66

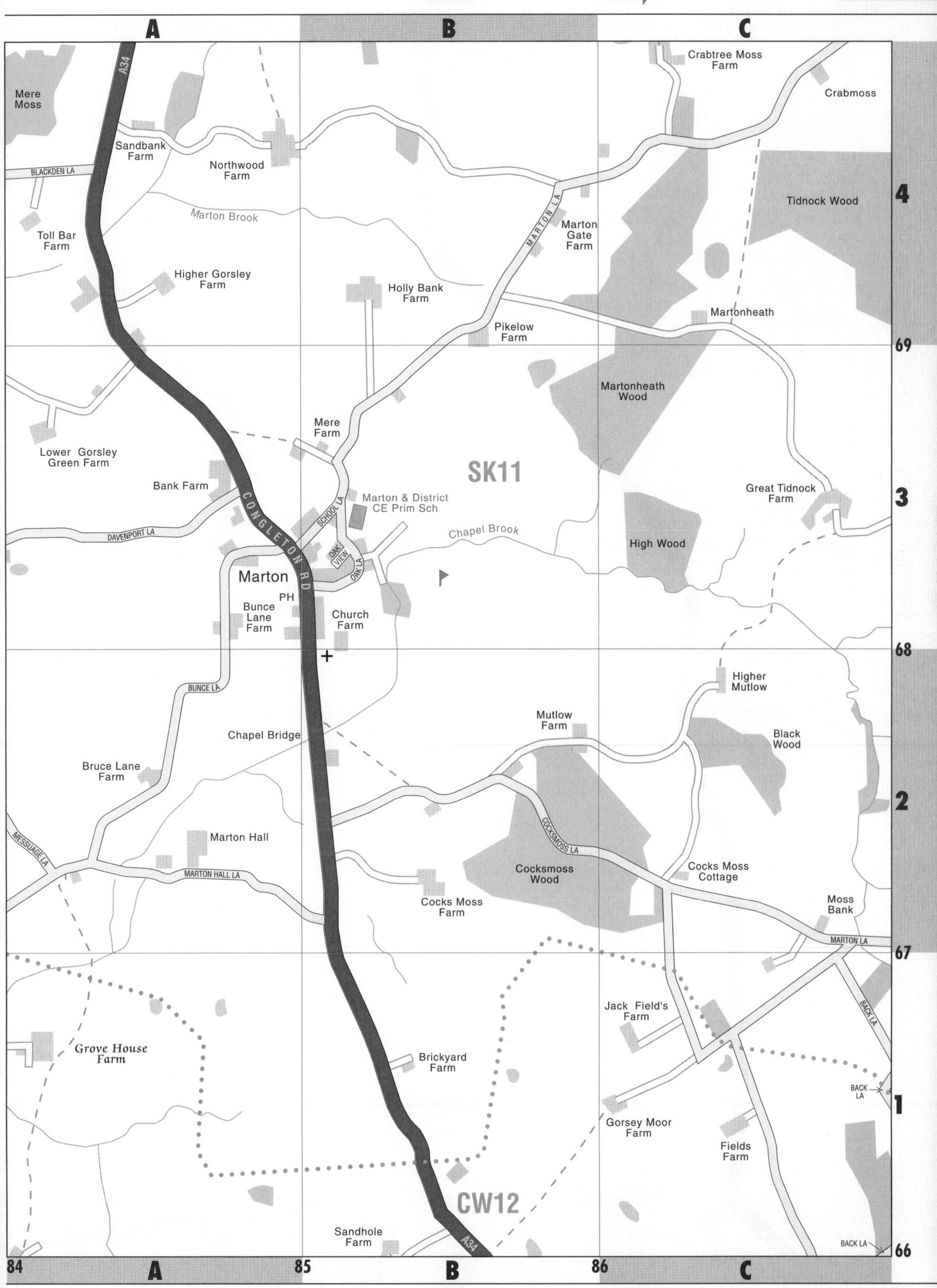

A
B
C

Mere Moss

Sandbank Farm

Northwood Farm

BLACKDEN LA

Marton Brook

Toll Bar Farm

Higher Gorsley Farm

Holly Bank Farm

Crabtree Moss Farm

Crabmoss

Tidnock Wood

4

MARTON LA

Marton Gate Farm

Pikelow Farm

Martonheath

69

Lower Gorsley Green Farm

Bank Farm

DAVENPORT LA

CONGLETON RD

SCHOOL LA

Mere Farm

Marton & District CE Prim Sch

OAK VIEW

OAK LA

SK11

Chapel Brook

Martonheath Wood

High Wood

Great Tidnock Farm

3

Marton

PH

Bunce Lane Farm

Church Farm

+

68

BUNCE LA

Bruce Lane Farm

MESSUAGE LA

Chapel Bridge

Marton Hall

MARTON HALL LA

Higher Mutlow

Mutlow Farm

Black Wood

Cocksmoss Wood

COCKSMOSS LA

Cocks Moss Farm

Cocks Moss Cottage

Moss Bank

MARTON LA

67

2

Grove House Farm

Brickyard Farm

Jack Field's Farm

BACK LA

Gorsey Moor Farm

Fields Farm

BACK LA

1

Sandhole Farm

CW12

A34

BACK LA

66

84
A
85
B
86
C

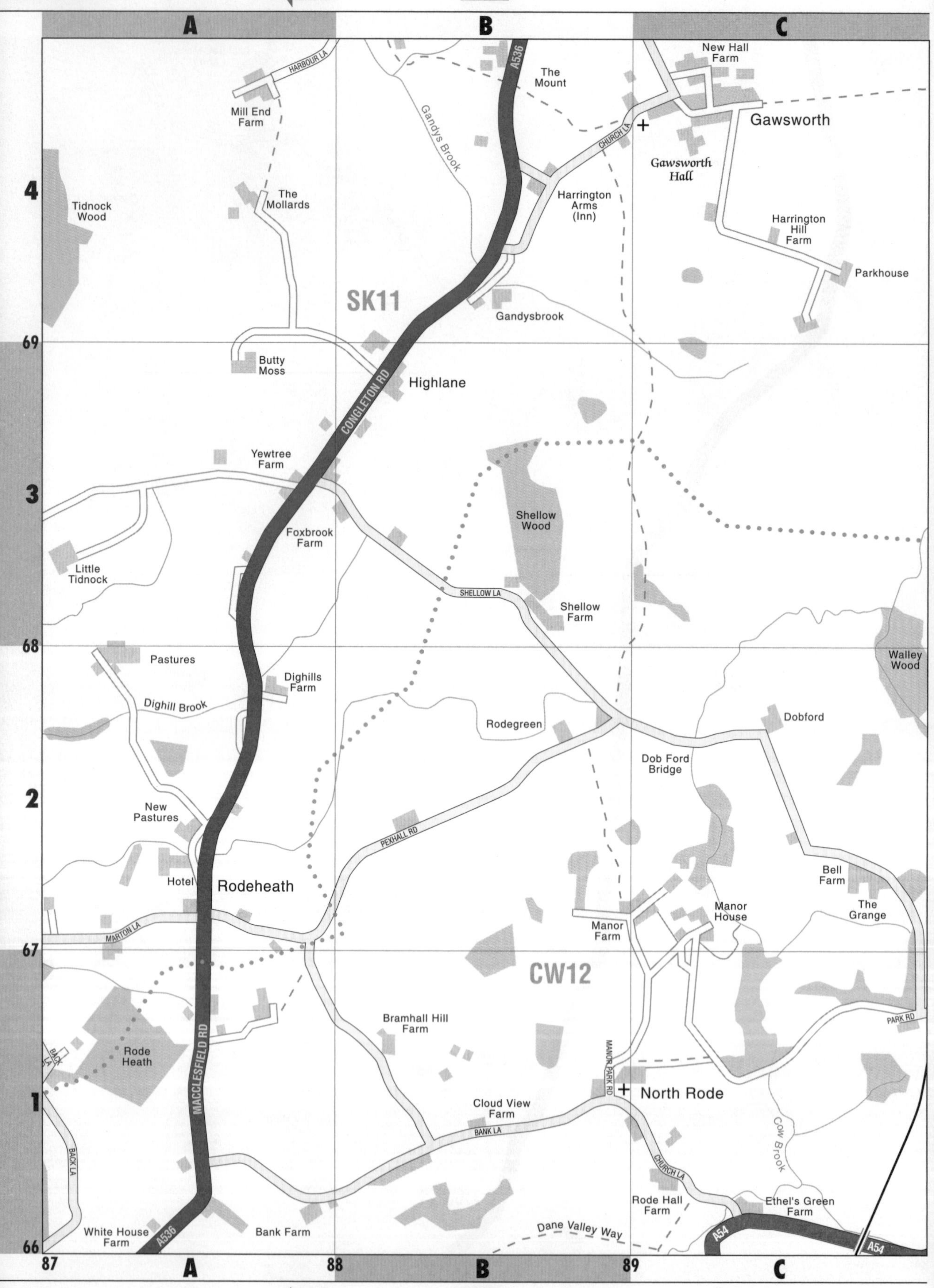
A
B
C
4
3
2
1
69
68
67
66
87
88
89
SK11
CW12
A536
HARBOUR LA
Mill End Farm
The Mount
New Hall Farm
Gawsworth
Gandys Brook
CHURCH LA
Gawsworth Hall
Tidnock Wood
The Mollards
Harrington Arms (Inn)
Harrington Hill Farm
Parkhouse
Gandysbrook
Butty Moss
Highlane
CONGLETON RD
Yewtree Farm
Shellow Wood
Foxbrook Farm
Little Tidnock
SHELLOW LA
Shellow Farm
Pastures
Dighills Farm
Walley Wood
Dighill Brook
Rodegreen
Dobford
Dob Ford Bridge
New Pastures
PEXHALL RD
Bell Farm
Hotel
Rodeheath
The Grange
Manor House
Manor Farm
MARTON LA
PARK RD
Bramhall Hill Farm
MACCLESFIELD RD
BACK LA
Rode Heath
MANOR PARK RD
North Rode
Cloud View Farm
BANK LA
Cow Brook
CHURCH LA
Rode Hall Farm
Ethel's Green Farm
Dane Valley Way
White House Farm
Bank Farm
A54

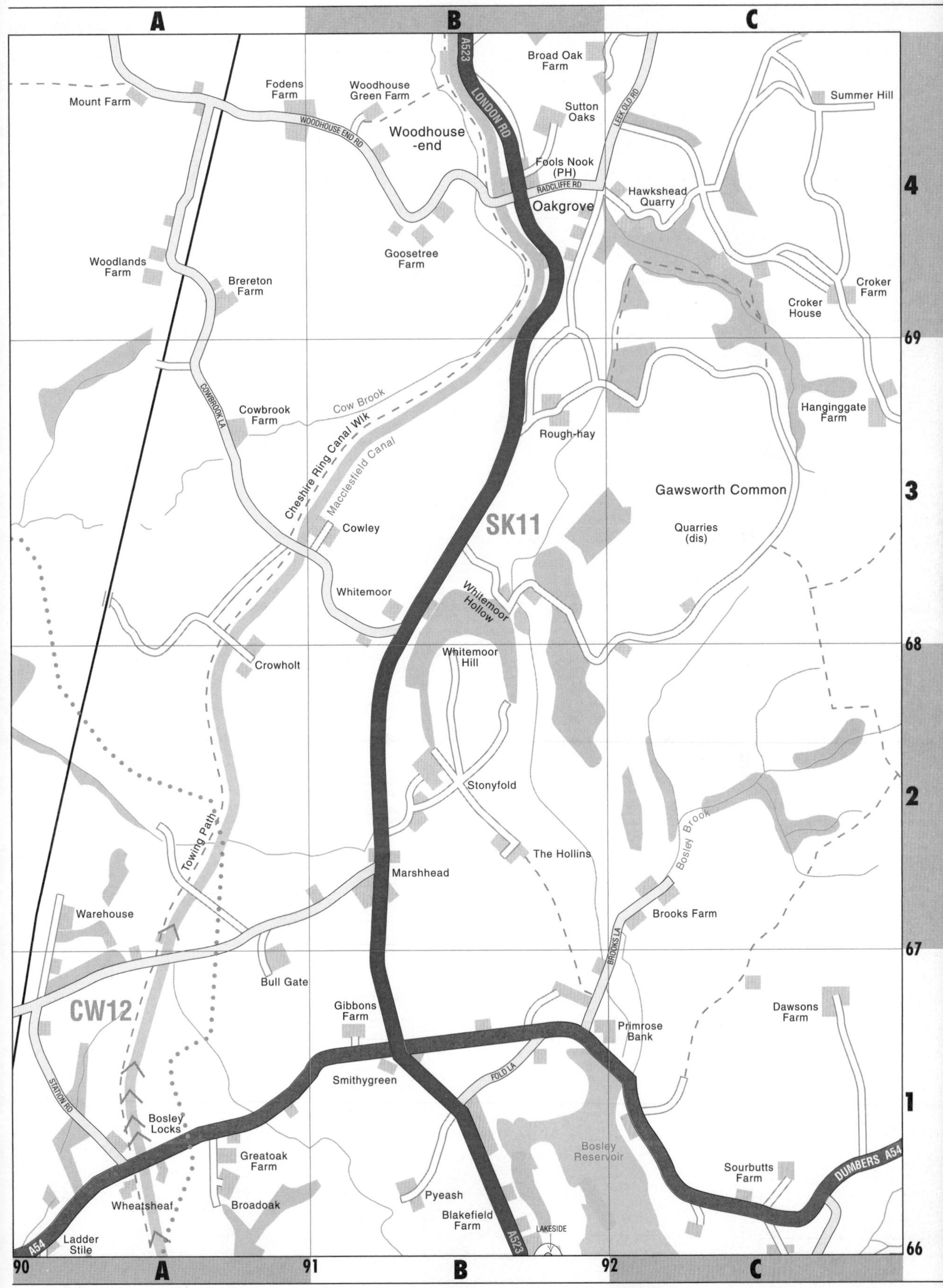

Mount Farm

Fodens Farm

Woodhouse Green Farm

Broad Oak Farm

Summer Hill

Sutton Oaks

WOODHOUSE END RD

Woodhouse -end

Fools Nook (PH)

RADCLIFFE RD

Oakgrove

Hawkshead Quarry

LONDON RD

A523

LEEK OLD RD

Woodlands Farm

Brereton Farm

Goosetree Farm

Croker House

Croker Farm

COWBROOK LA

Cowbrook Farm

Cow Brook

Cheshire Ring Canal WIK

Macclesfield Canal

Rough-hay

Hanginggate Farm

69

Gawsworth Common

SK11

Quarries (dis)

3

Cowley

Whitemoor

Whitemoor Hollow

Crowholt

Whitemoor Hill

68

Stonyfold

Bosley Brook

2

Towing Path

The Hollins

Marshhead

Brooks Farm

Warehouse

BROOKS LA

67

CW12

Bull Gate

Gibbons Farm

Primrose Bank

Dawsons Farm

STATION RD

Smithygreen

FOLD LA

1

Bosley Locks

Greatoak Farm

Bosley Reservoir

Sourbutts Farm

DUMBERS A54

Wheatsheaf

Broadoak

Pyeash

Blakefield Farm

A523

LAKESIDE

A54

Ladder Stile

66

90

91

92

135
113

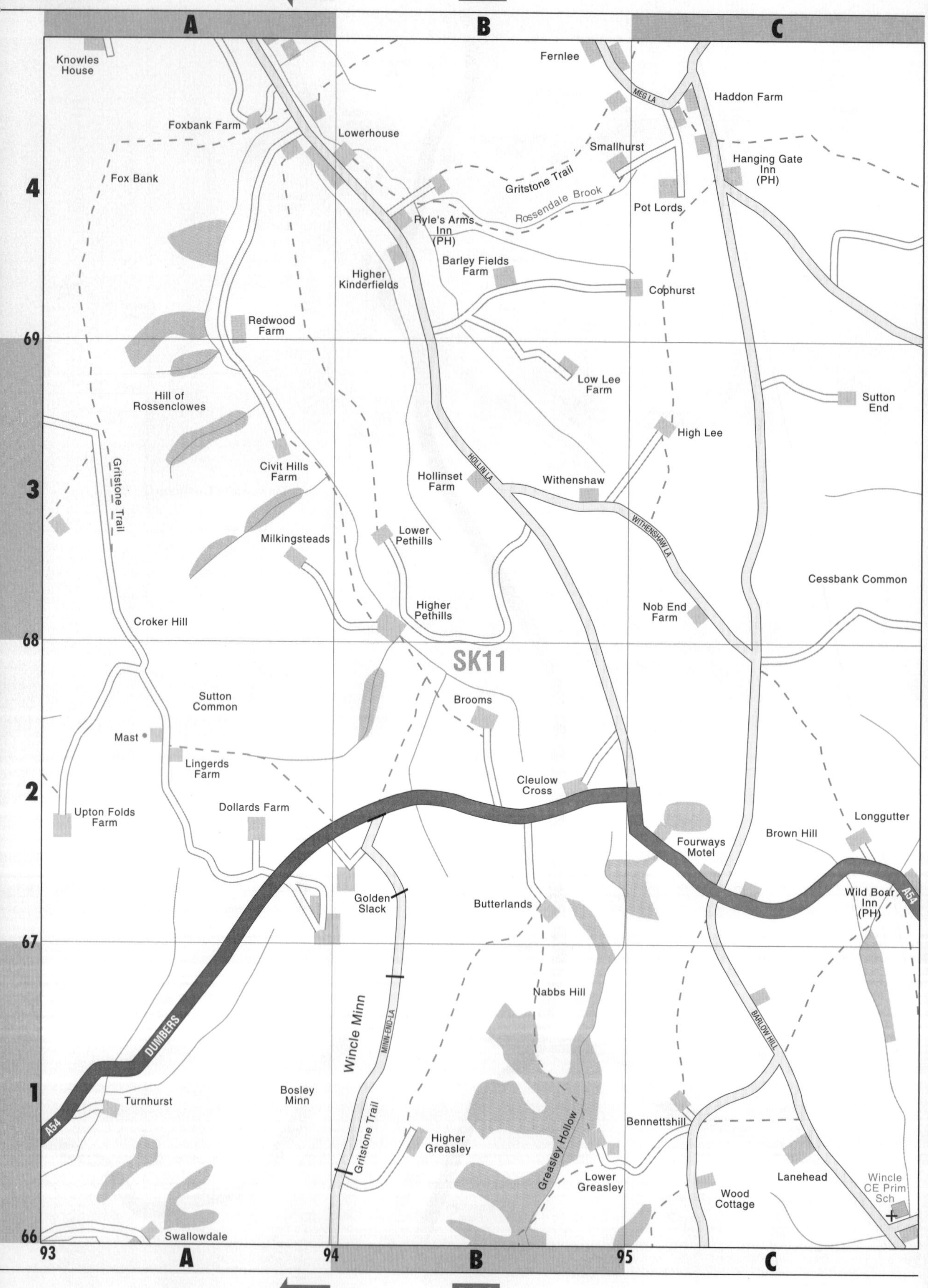
A
B
C
Knowles House
Fernlee
Haddon Farm
MEG LA
Foxbank Farm
Lowerhouse
Smallhurst
Hanging Gate Inn (PH)
Fox Bank
Gritstone Trail
Rossendale Brook
Pot Lords
Ryle's Arms Inn (PH)
Barley Fields Farm
Higher Kinderfields
Cophurst
Redwood Farm
Low Lee Farm
Hill of Rossenclowes
Sutton End
High Lee
Civit Hills Farm
HOLLIN LA
Hollinset Farm
Withenshaw
Gritstone Trail
WITHENSHAW LA
Lower Pethills
Milkingsteads
Cessbank Common
Nob End Farm
Higher Pethills
Croker Hill
SK11
Sutton Common
Brooms
Mast
Lingerds Farm
Cleulow Cross
Upton Folds Farm
Dollards Farm
Longgutter
Brown Hill
Fourways Motel
Wild Boar Inn (PH)
A54
Golden Slack
Butterlands
Nabbs Hill
DUMBERS
Wincle Minn
MINN-END-LA
BARLOW HILL
Bosley Minn
Turnhurst
A54
Bennettshill
Gritstone Trail
Higher Greasley
Greasley Hollow
Lower Greasley
Lanehead
Wincle CE Prim Sch
Wood Cottage
Swallowdale
4
69
3
68
2
67
1
66
93
94
95
A
B
C

135
159

114
138

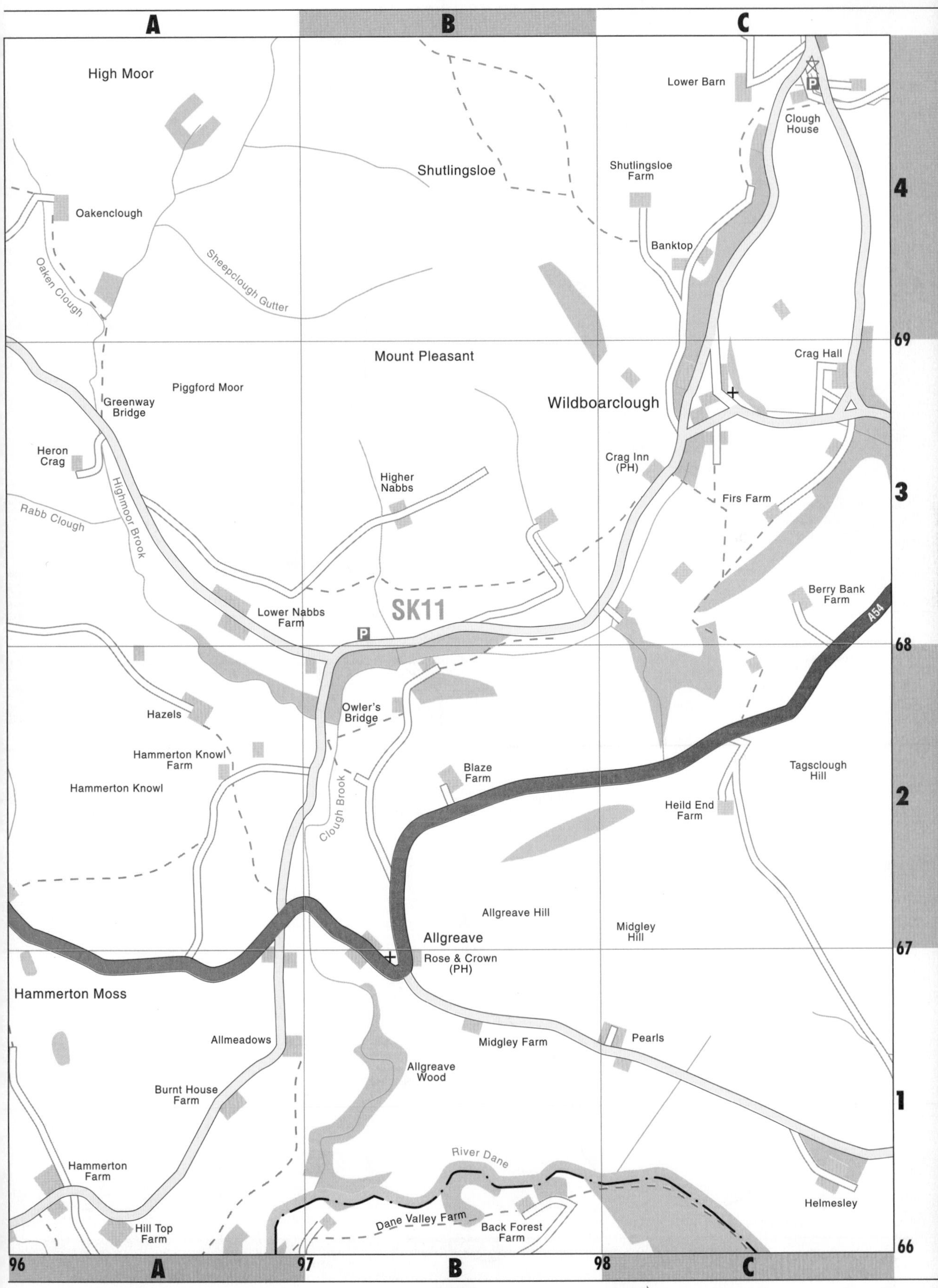

High Moor

Oakenclough

Oaken Clough

Sheepclough Gutter

Shutlingsloe

Lower Barn

Shutlingsloe
Farm

Clough
House

Banktop

4

69

Mount Pleasant

Wildboarclough

Crag Hall

Greenway
Bridge

Piggford Moor

Highmoor Brook

Heron
Crag

Rabb Clough

Higher
Nabbs

Crag Inn
(PH)

Firs Farm

3

Lower Nabbs
Farm

SK11

Berry Bank
Farm

A54

68

Hazels

Owler's
Bridge

Clough Brook

Blaze
Farm

Heild End
Farm

Tagsclough
Hill

2

Hammerton Knowl
Farm

Hammerton Knowl

Allgreave Hill

Midgley
Hill

67

Allgreave

Rose & Crown
(PH)

Hammerton Moss

Allmeadows

Midgley Farm

Pearls

Burnt House
Farm

Allgreave
Wood

1

Hammerton
Farm

River Dane

Helmesley

Hill Top
Farm

Dane Valley Farm

Back Forest
Farm

66

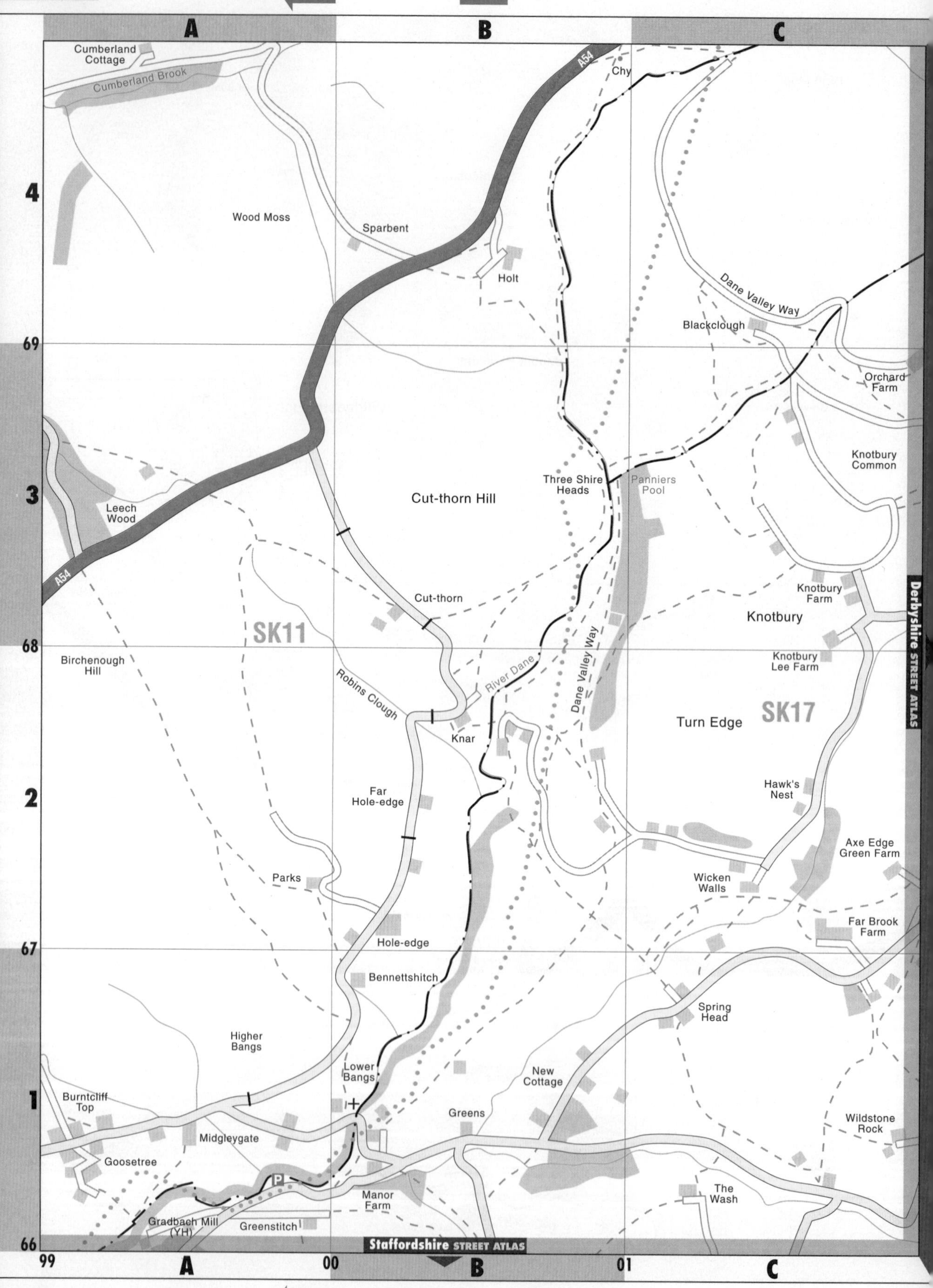

A   B   C

Cumberland
Cottage
Cumberland Brook

Wood Moss

Sparbent

A54

Chy

4

Holt

Dane Valley Way

Blackclough

69

Orchard
Farm

Leech
Wood

3

Cut-thorn Hill

Three Shire
Heads

Panniers
Pool

Knotbury
Common

A54

Cut-thorn

Knotbury
Farm

Knotbury

SK11

Robins Clough

River Dane

Dane Valley Way

Knotbury
Lee Farm

68

Birchenough
Hill

Knar

Turn Edge   SK17

Far
Hole-edge

Hawk's
Nest

2

Parks

Axe Edge
Green Farm

Wicken
Walls

67

Hole-edge

Far Brook
Farm

Bennettshitch

Spring
Head

Higher
Bangs

Lower
Bangs

New
Cottage

1

Burntcliff
Top

Greens

Wildstone
Rock

Midgleygate

Goosetree

P

Manor
Farm

The
Wash

Gradbach Mill
(YH)

Greenstitch

66

99   A   00   B   01   C

Derbyshire STREET ATLAS

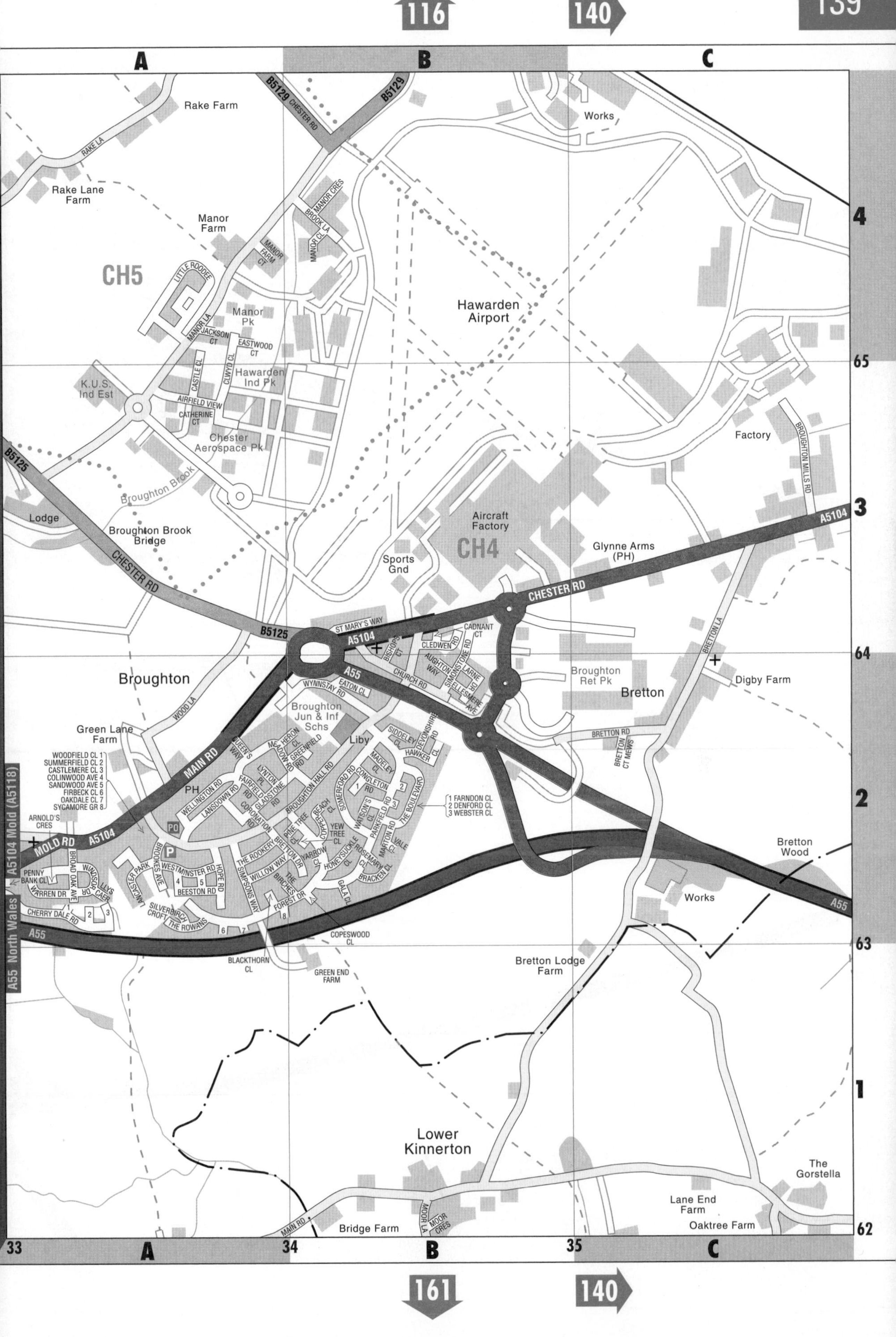

Rake Farm

B5129 CHESTER RD
B5129

Works

Rake Lane
Farm

RAKE LA

MANOR CRES

4

Manor
Farm

BROOK LA

CH5

LITTLE RODDEE

MANOR
FARM
CT

Hawarden
Airport

Factory

MANOR CL

BROUGHTON MILLS RD

65

Manor
Pk

EASTWOOD
CT

MANOR LA

JACKSON
CT

CLWYD CL

Hawarden
Ind Pk

B5125

CASTLE CL

CASTLE VIEW

AIRFIELD VIEW

K.U.S.
Ind Est

CATHERINE
CT

Chester
Aerospace Pk

Broughton Brook

Aircraft
Factory

Glynne Arms
(PH)

A5104

3

Lodge

Broughton Brook
Bridge

CHESTER RD

CH4

Sports
Gnd

CHESTER RD

B5125

A5104

ST MARY'S WAY

CADNANT
CT

Broughton
Ret Pk

BRETTON LA

Bretton

64

BISHOPS CL

CLEDWEN

AUGHTON WAY

MANASTONE RD

LARNE

GILLESMERE

Digby Farm

Broughton

WOOD LA

CHURCH RD

Broughton
Jun & Inf
Schs

EATON CL

A55

WYNNSTAY RD

Liby

SIDDELEY
CL

DEVONSHIRE RD

HAWKER

BECTON RD

Bretton
Ret Pk

BRETTON RD

BRETTON
CT MEWS

Green Lane
Farm

MAIN RD

MC HEGON
CL

QUEENS WAY

GREENFIELD
RD

MADELEY
CL

CONGLETON
RD

1 FARNDON CL
2 DENFORD CL
3 WEBSTER CL

Bretton
Wood

WOODFIELD CL 1
SUMMERFIELD CL 2
CASTLEMERE CL 3
COLINWOOD AVE 4
SANDWOOD AVE 5
FIRBECK CL 6
OAKDALE CL 7
SYCAMORE GR 8

PH

WELLINGTON RD

LANSDOWN RD

LINTON RD

FAIRFIELD RD

GLADSTONE RD

CONGLETON RD

SOMERFORD RD

WATSON'S CL

MARTIN RD

PARKFIELD RD

ROSEMARY CL

BRACKETT CL

2

Arnold's
Cres

MOLD RD

A5104

PO

BROOKES AVE

THE ROOKERY

BRETTON CL

PINE TREE

BEACH

YEW
TREE
CL

HONEYSUCKLE

THE VALE

GALT CL

Bretton
Wood

A55

PENNY
BANK CL

BROAD OAK AVE

LEA PARK

WESTMINSTER RD

HOPE RD

WILLOW WAY

THE BINCHES

FOREST DR

Works

WARREN DR

WINDSOR CL

SALLY'S
CROFT

4 5

BEESTON RD

SIMPSONS WAY

YARROW

CHERRY DALE RD

LINCOLN DR

1 2 3

SILVERBIRCH
CROFT THE ROWANS

6 7

8

A55

63

A55 North Wales / A5104 Mold (A5118)

BLACKTHORN
CL

GREEN END
FARM

COPESWOOD
CL

Bretton Lodge
Farm

1

Lower
Kinnerton

The
Gorstella

Lane End
Farm

MAIN RD

MOOR LA

MOOR
CRES

Oaktree Farm

62

139
117

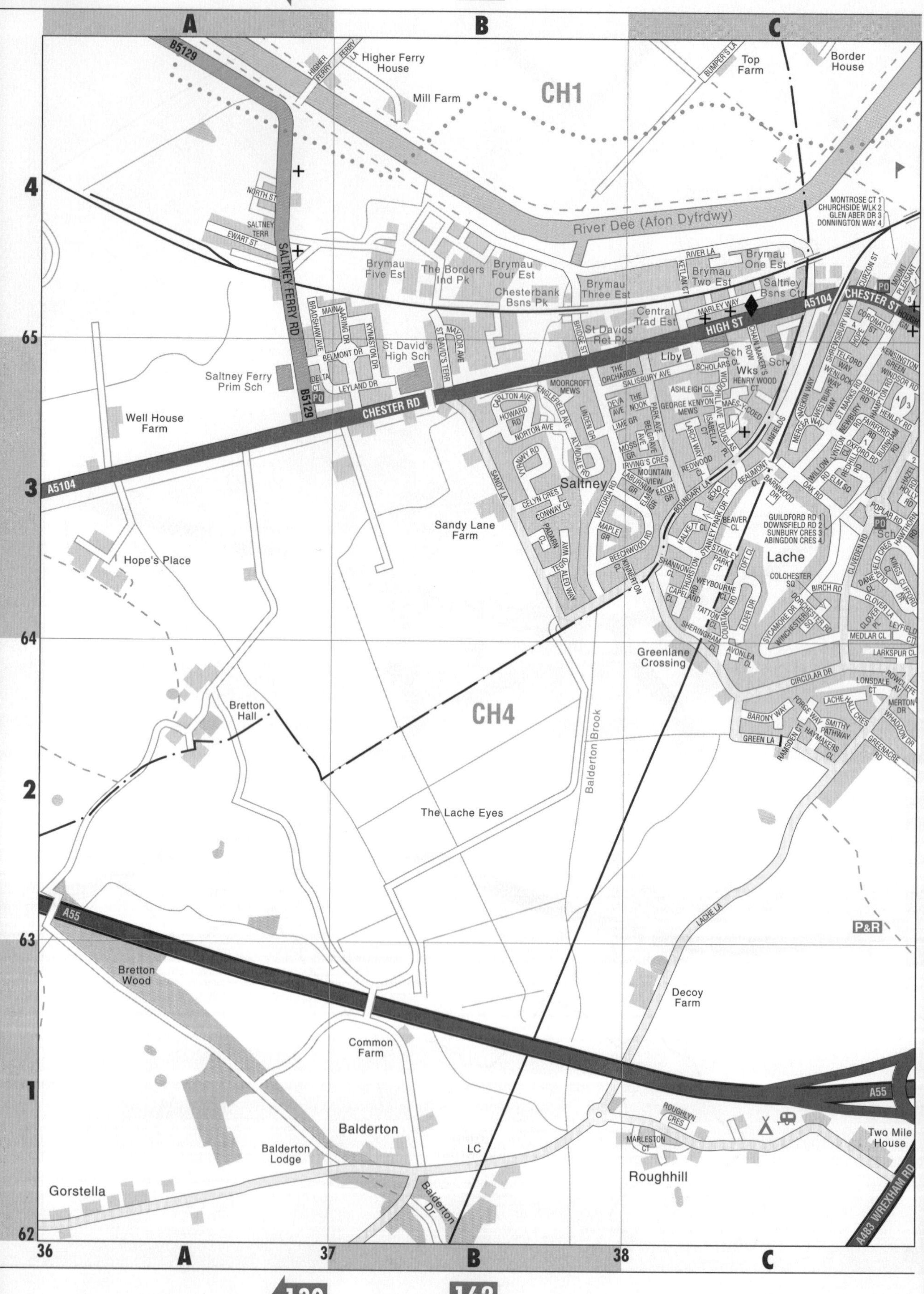
A
B
C
CH1
CH4
River Dee (Afon Dyfrdwy)
Higher Ferry House
Mill Farm
Top Farm
Border House
Brymau Five Est
The Borders Ind Pk
Brymau Four Est
Chesterbank Bsns Pk
Brymau Three Est
Brymau Two Est
Brymau One Est
Saltney Bsns Ctr
Central Trad Est
St Davids' Ret Pk
St David's High Sch
Saltney Ferry Prim Sch
Well House Farm
Saltney
Sandy Lane Farm
Hope's Place
Lache
Greenlane Crossing
Bretton Hall
The Lache Eyes
Bretton Wood
Common Farm
Decoy Farm
Balderton
Balderton Lodge
Gorstella
Roughhill
Two Mile House
Balderton Brook
A5104
B5129
A55
A483 WREXHAM RD
CHESTER RD
HIGH ST
CHESTER ST
SALTNEY FERRY RD
LACHE LA
CIRCULAR DR
MONTROSE CT 1
CHURCHSIDE WLK 2
GLEN ABER DR 3
DONNINGTON WAY 4
GUILDFORD RD 1
DOWNSFIELD RD 2
SUNBURY CRES 3
ABINGDON CRES 4
P&R
LC
36
37
38
62
63
64
65
1
2
3
4

139
162

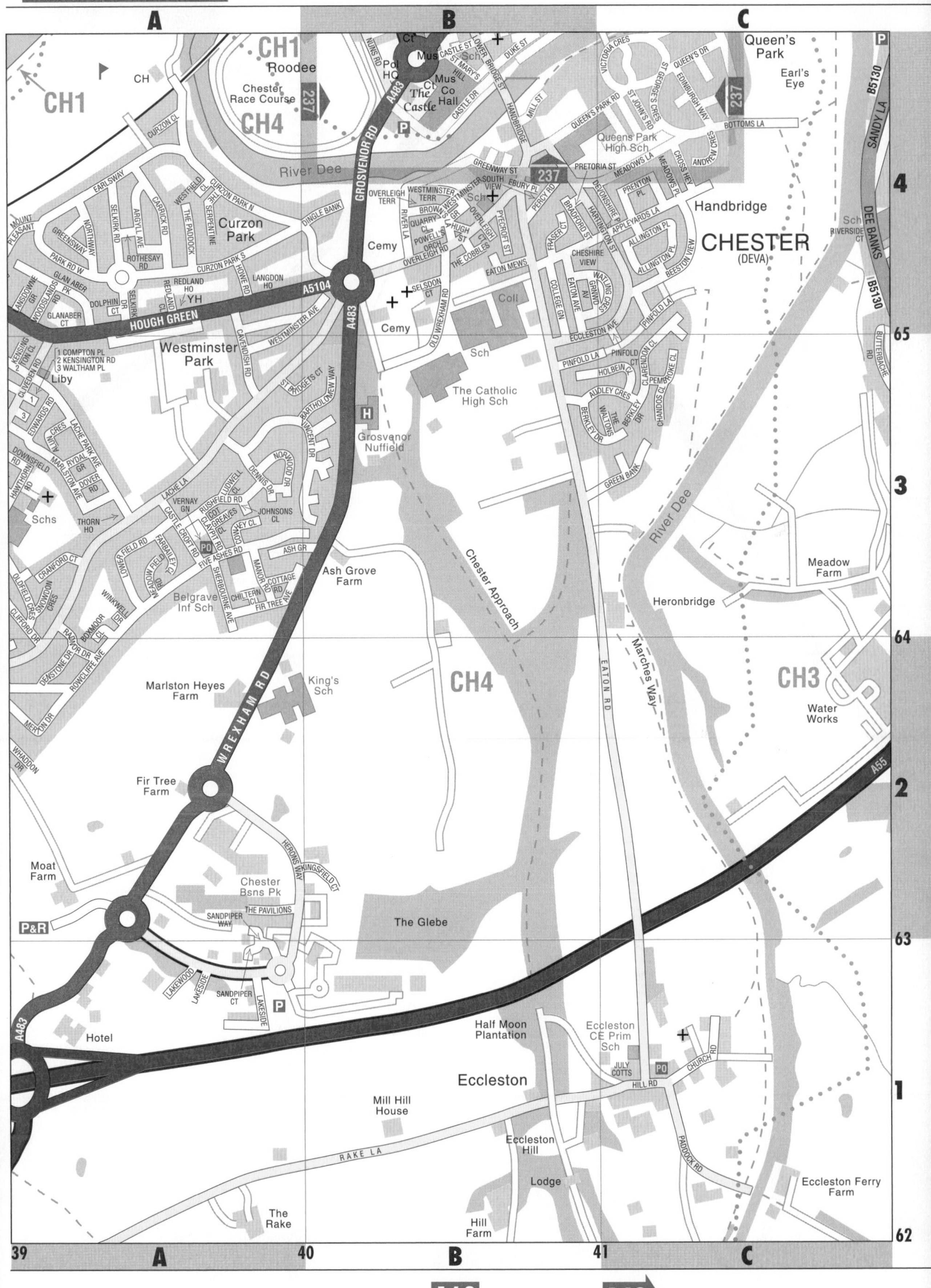

141
119

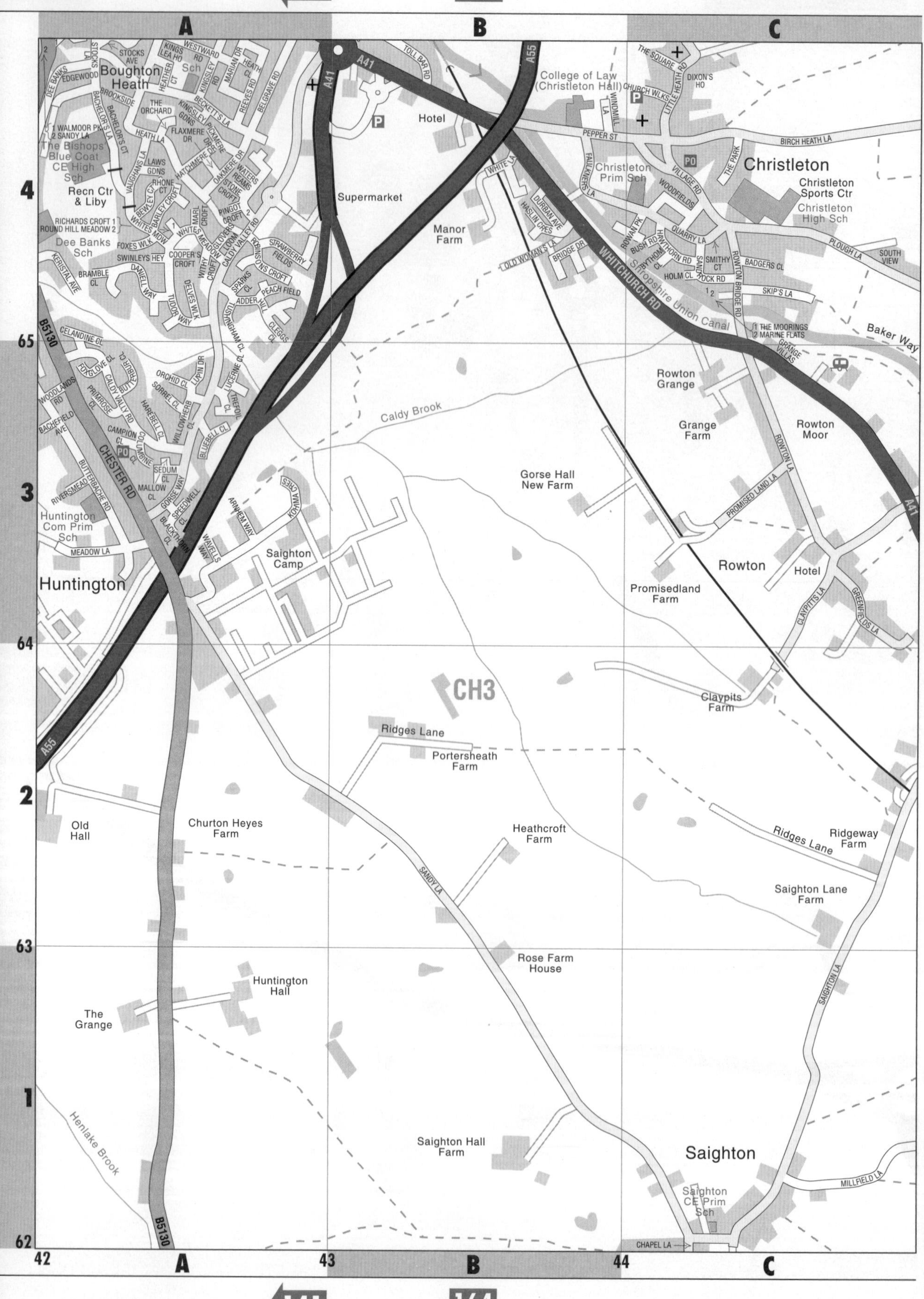
A
B
C
4
65
3
64
2
63
1
62
42
43
44
Boughton Heath
Sch
The Bishops' Blue Coat CE High Sch
Recn Ctr & Liby
Dee Banks Sch
STOCKS AVE
EDGEWOOD
DEE BANKS
BROOKSIDE
THE ORCHARD
KINGSLEY GDNS
FLAXMERE DR
HEATH LA
VAUGHANS LA
LAWS GDNS
RHONE CT
BEWLEY CT
BARLEY CROFT
WHITES MDW
FOXES WLK
SWINLEYS HEY
COOPER'S CROFT
DANIELL WAY
TUDOR WAY
DELVES WLK
BRAMBLE CL
KERISTAL AVE
1 WALMOOR PK
2 SANDY LA
RICHARDS CROFT 1
ROUND HILL MEADOW 2
WESTWARD RD
KINGS LEA HO
HEATHER CT
KINGSLEY RD
MARIAN DR
BECKETT'S LA
REEVES RD
BELGRAVE RD
HATCHMERE DR
PICKMERE DR
OAKMERE DR
STONE CROFT
PINGOT CROFT
WATERS REACH
MARL CROFT
WITHY CROFT
GLOVERS LOOM
CALDY VALLEY RD
ROBINSONS CROFT
STRAWBERRY FIELDS
SPARKS CL
ADDER HILL
PEACH FIELD
CLEGGS CL
TUSHINGHAM CL
LUCERNE CL
TREFOIL CL
BLUEBELL CL
WILLOWHERB CL
HAREBELL CL
LUPIN DR
ORCHID CL
SORREL CL
CELANDINE CL
FOXGLOVE CL
CALDY VALLY RD
BUTTERBUR CL
PRIMROSE CL
CAMPION CL
COLUMBINE CL
SEDUM CL
MALLOW CL
GORSE WAY
SPEEDWELL
BLACKTHORN CL
WOODLANDS RD
BACHEFIELD AVE
BUTTERBACHE RD
RIVERSMEAD
CHESTER RD
B5130
Huntington Com Prim Sch
MEADOW LA
Huntington
ARNHEM WAY
KOHIMA CRES
WAVELLS WAY
Saighton Camp
A41
A55
TOLL BAR RD
Hotel
Supermarket
Manor Farm
WHITE LA
OLD WOMAN'S LA
College of Law (Christleton Hall)
THE SQUARE
DIXON'S HO
LITTLE HEATH RD
CHURCH WLKS
WINDMILL LA
PEPPER ST
BIRCH HEATH LA
Christleton Prim Sch
FAULKNERS LA
DURBAN AVE
HASLIN CRES
BRIDGE DR
VILLAGE RD
WOODFIELDS
THE PARK
Christleton
Christleton Sports Ctr
Christleton High Sch
ROWAN PK
BUSH RD
RYTHOM CL
HAWTHORN RD
QUARRY LA
SMITHY CT
SANDROCK RD
HOLM CL
ROWTON BRIDGE RD
BADGERS CL
SKIP'S LA
PLOUGH LA
SOUTH VIEW
WHITCHURCH RD
Shropshire Union Canal
1 THE MOORINGS
2 MARINE FLATS
GRANGE VILLAS
Baker Way
Rowton Grange
Grange Farm
Rowton Moor
Caldy Brook
Gorse Hall New Farm
ROWTON LA
PROMISED LAND LA
Rowton
Hotel
Promisedland Farm
CLAYPITS LA
GREENFIELDS LA
CH3
Claypits Farm
Ridges Lane
Portersheath Farm
Old Hall
Churton Heyes Farm
Heathcroft Farm
Ridges Lane
Ridgeway Farm
Saighton Lane Farm
SANDY LA
SAIGHTON LA
Rose Farm House
Huntington Hall
The Grange
Henlake Brook
Saighton Hall Farm
Saighton
MILLFIELD LA
Saighton CE Prim Sch
CHAPEL LA
PO
P

141
164

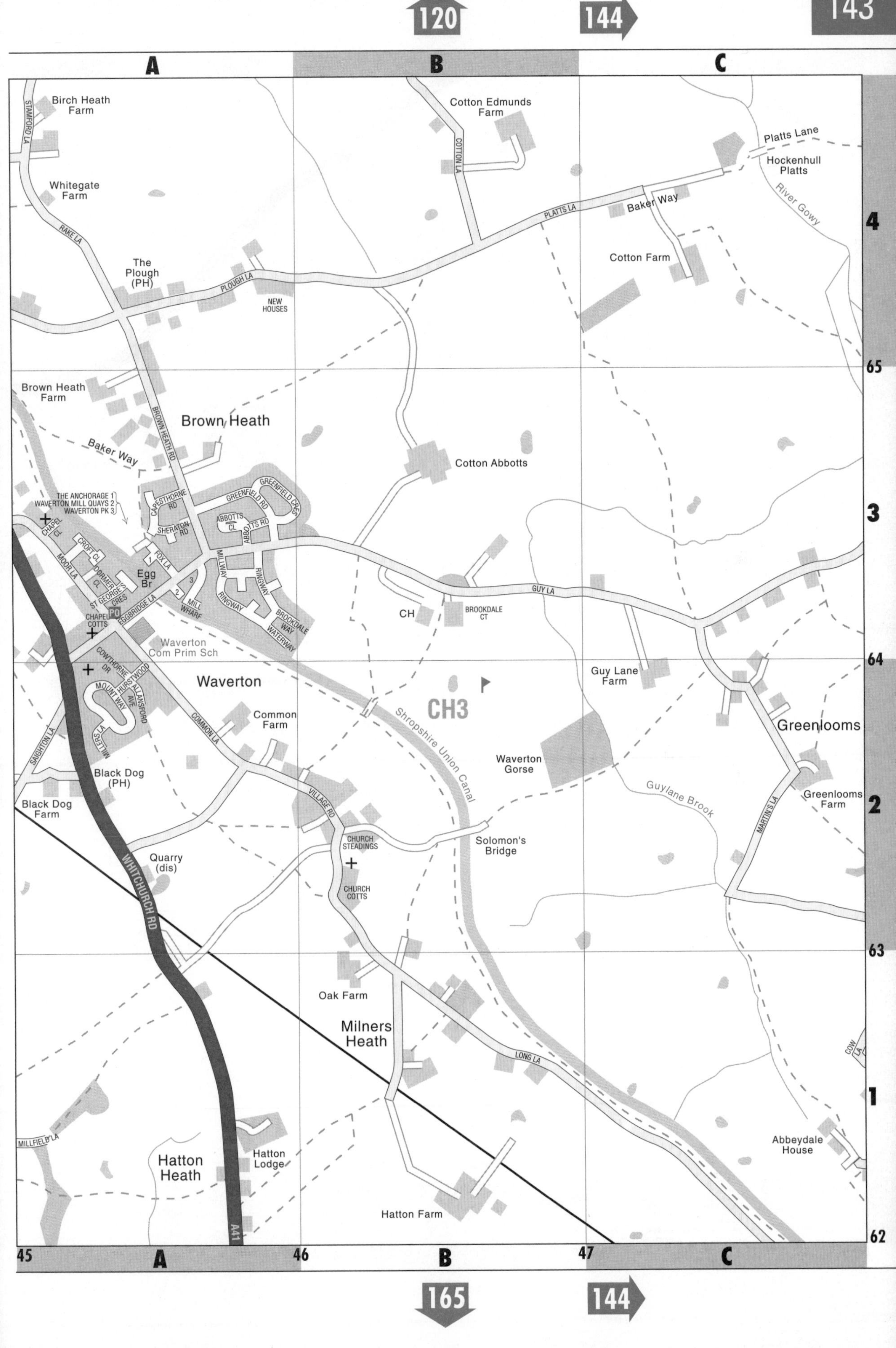

A B C

Birch Heath Farm

Cotton Edmunds Farm

STAMFORD LA

Platts Lane

Hockenhull Platts

Whitegate Farm

River Gowy

PLATTS LA

Baker Way

RAKE LA

4

The Plough (PH)

Cotton Farm

PLOUGH LA

NEW HOUSES

65

Brown Heath Farm

BROWN HEATH RD

Brown Heath

Baker Way

Cotton Abbotts

THE ANCHORAGE 1
WAVERTON MILL QUAYS 2
WAVERTON PK 3

3

GREENFIELD RD

GREENFIELD CRES

CAPESTHORNE RD

ABBOTTS CL

SHERATON RD

CHAPEL CL

ABBOTTS RD

MOOR LA

FOX LA

CROFT CL

MORTIMERS CL

Egg Br

MILLWAY

RINGWAY

St GEORGE'S CRES

ST GEORGE'S

MILL WHARF

RINGWAY

GUY LA

CH

BROOKDALE CT

CHAPEL COTTS

PO

BROOKDALE WAY

Waverton Com Prim Sch

64

COWTHORNE DR

HURSTWOOD

ALLINSFORD

EGGBRIDGE LA

Waverton

Guy Lane Farm

MOUNT WAY

MILLERS CT

Common Farm

Shropshire Union Canal

CH3

Waverton Gorse

Greenlooms

COMMON LA

Black Dog (PH)

VILLAGE RD

Guylane Brook

MARTINS LA

Greenlooms Farm

2

Black Dog Farm

SAIGHTON LA

CHURCH STEADINGS

Solomon's Bridge

Quarry (dis)

CHURCH COTTS

63

WHITCHURCH RD

Oak Farm

Milners Heath

LONG LA

1

MILLFIELD LA

COW LA

Hatton Lodge

Abbeydale House

Hatton Heath

A41

Hatton Farm

62

45 A 46 B 47 C

A
B
C

Baker Way
HOCKENHILL LA
Broom Bank
AUSTINE HILL
A51
TARPORLEY RD
Platts Lane
Platts La
Sheaf Farm
CROSS LANES
BROOMHEATH LA
Duddon Hall

4

Old Moss
Duddon Heath
TARPORLEY RD

PLATTS LA

Cross Lanes Farm
Old Moss Farm
OLD MOSS LA
Moss Lane Farm
The Moss
Warren House Farm
BURTON LA
MILL LA

65

RYECROFT LA

Smithy Farm
SIDE LA

GUY LA

DUDDON HOOK LA

Stapleford Hall
BROOKHOUSE LA

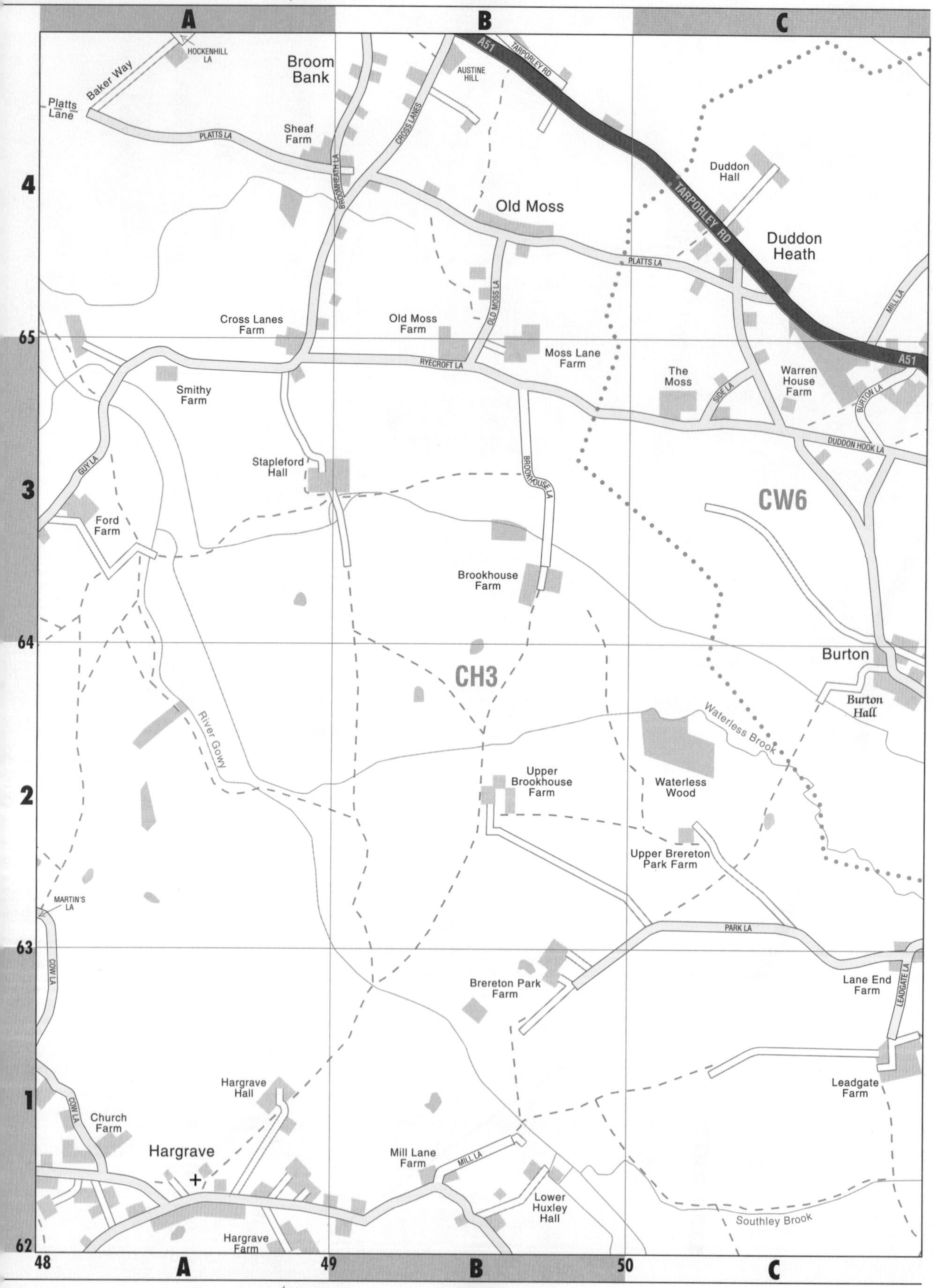

CW6

3

Ford Farm

Brookhouse Farm

64

Burton

CH3
Burton Hall

River Gowy

Waterless Brook

Upper Brookhouse Farm
Waterless Wood

2

Upper Brereton Park Farm

MARTIN'S LA

PARK LA

63

COW LA
Brereton Park Farm
Lane End Farm
LEADGATE LA

1

Hargrave Hall
Leadgate Farm

COW LA
Church Farm

Hargrave
Mill Lane Farm
MILL LA

Lower Huxley Hall

Southley Brook

Hargrave Farm

62

48
A
49
B
50
C

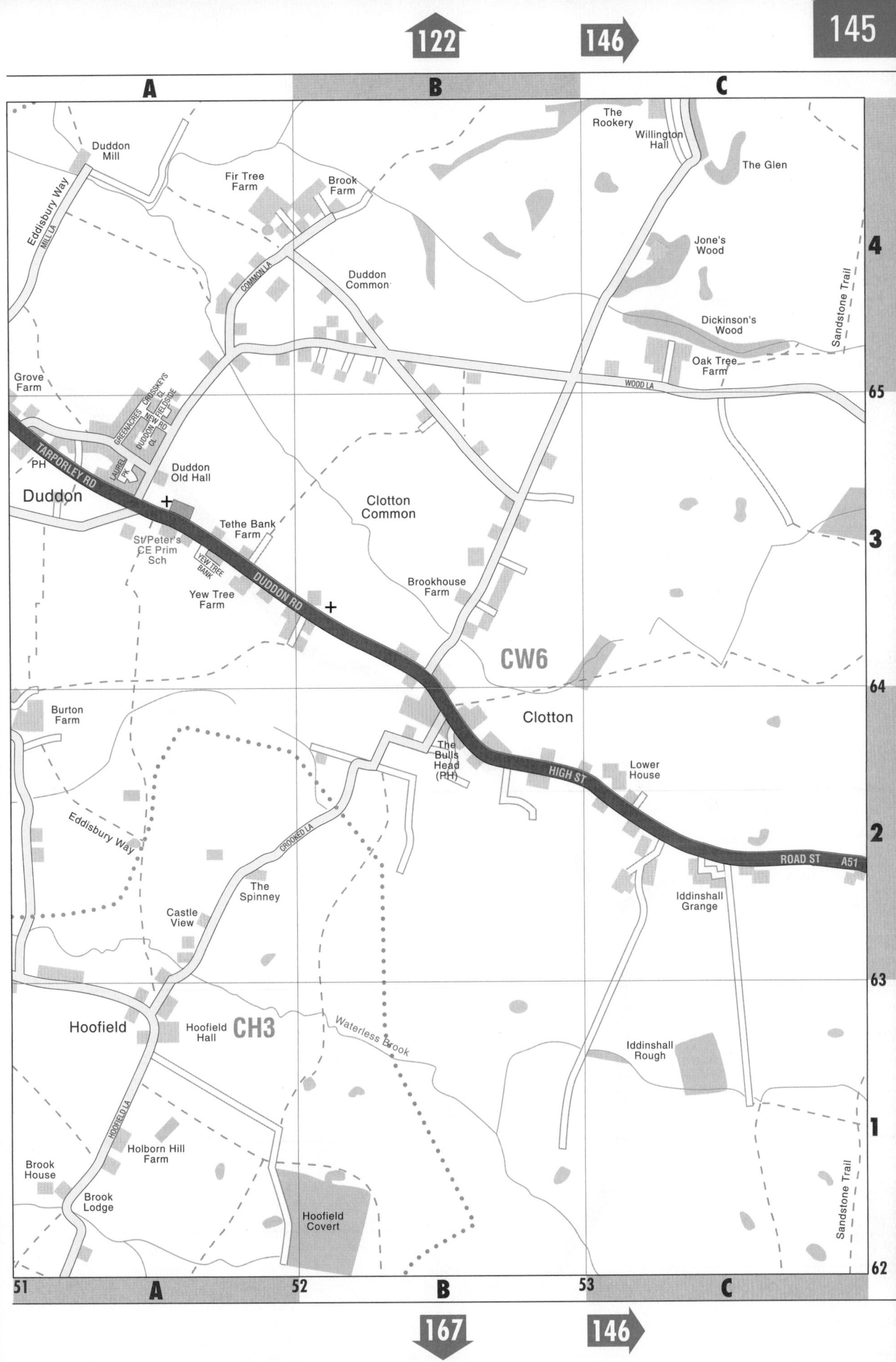
A
B
C
Duddon Mill
Eddisbury Way
MILL LA
Fir Tree Farm
Brook Farm
The Rookery
Willington Hall
The Glen
Jone's Wood
Duddon Common
COMMON LA
Sandstone Trail
Dickinson's Wood
Oak Tree Farm
WOOD LA
Grove Farm
CROSSKEYS CL
FIELDSIDE
NEW RD
GREENACRES
DUDDON CL
TARPORLEY RD
PH
LAUREL PK
Duddon Old Hall
Duddon
Clotton Common
Tethe Bank Farm
St Peter's CE Prim Sch
YEW TREE BANK
DUDDON RD
Yew Tree Farm
Brookhouse Farm
CW6
Burton Farm
Clotton
The Bulls Head (PH)
HIGH ST
Lower House
Eddisbury Way
CROOKED LA
The Spinney
Castle View
ROAD ST
A51
Iddinshall Grange
Hoofield
Hoofield Hall
CH3
Waterless Brook
Iddinshall Rough
HOOFIELD LA
Holborn Hill Farm
Brook House
Brook Lodge
Hoofield Covert
Sandstone Trail
4
65
3
64
2
63
1
62
51
52
53
A
B
C

145
123

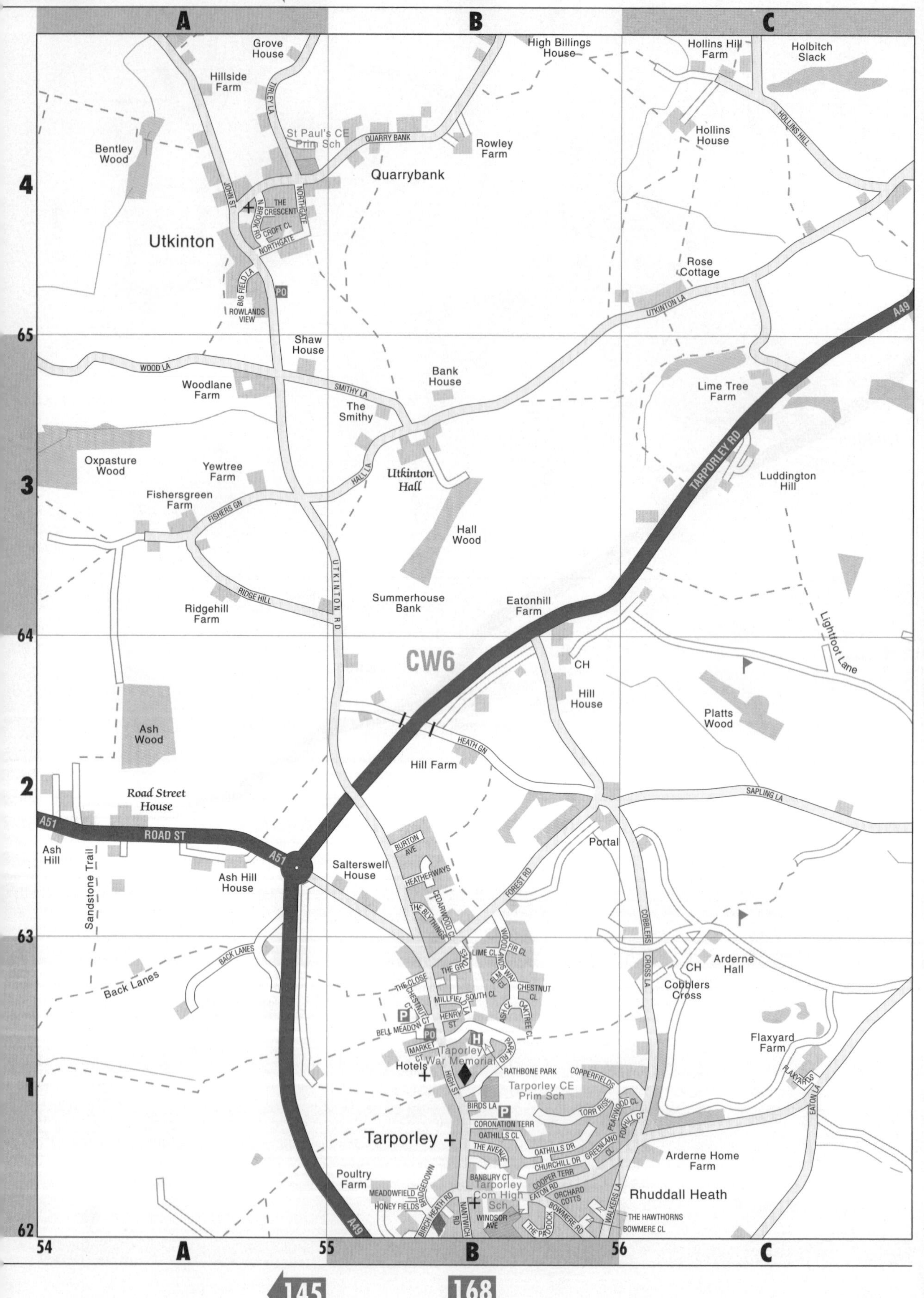
A
B
C
4
3
2
1
65
64
63
62
54
55
56
Grove House
Hillside Farm
Bentley Wood
St Paul's CE Prim Sch
Quarrybank
Rowley Farm
High Billings House
Hollins Hill Farm
Holbitch Slack
Hollins House
Utkinton
Rose Cottage
Shaw House
Bank House
Woodlane Farm
The Smithy
Lime Tree Farm
Oxpasture Wood
Yewtree Farm
Fishersgreen Farm
Utkinton Hall
Luddington Hill
Hall Wood
Ridgehill Farm
Summerhouse Bank
Eatonhill Farm
CW6
CH
Hill House
Platts Wood
Lightfoot Lane
Ash Wood
Hill Farm
Road Street House
Ash Hill
Ash Hill House
Sandstone Trail
Salterswell House
Portal
Back Lanes
Arderne Hall
Cobblers Cross
Flaxyard Farm
Tarporley War Memorial
Hotels
Tarporley CE Prim Sch
Tarporley
Arderne Home Farm
Poultry Farm
Tarporley Com High Sch
Rhuddall Heath
THE HAWTHORNS
BOWMERE CL
A49
A51
ROAD ST
TARPORLEY RD
UTKINTON RD
UTKINTON LA
WOOD LA
SMITHY LA
HALL LA
FISHERS GN
RIDGE HILL
HEATH GN
SAPLING LA
QUARRY BANK
TIRLEY LA
JOHN ST
NORTHGATE
THE CRESCENT
CROFT CL
BIG FIELD LA
ROWLANDS VIEW
HOLLINS HILL
FOREST RD
BURTON AVE
HEATHERWAYS
CEDARWOOD CL
COBBLERS CROSS LA
LIME CL
FIR CL
CHESTNUT CL
OAKTREE CL
THE CLOSE
THE GROVES
HENRY ST
HIGH ST
PARK RD
RATHBONE PARK
COPPERFIELDS
BIRDS LA
CORONATION TERR
OATHILLS CL
OATHILLS DR
THE AVENUE
CHURCHILL DR
COOPER TERR
EATON RD
ORCHARD COTTS
BOWMERE RD
THE PADDOCK
WINDSOR AVE
BANBURY CT
MEADOWFIELD
HONEY FIELDS
BRIDGEDOWN
BIRCH HEATH RD
NANTWICH RD
WALKERS LA
GREENLAND
FOXHILL CT
EATON LA
FLAXYARDS
BELL MEADOW CT
MARKET CT
BACK LANES
PO
H
P

145
168

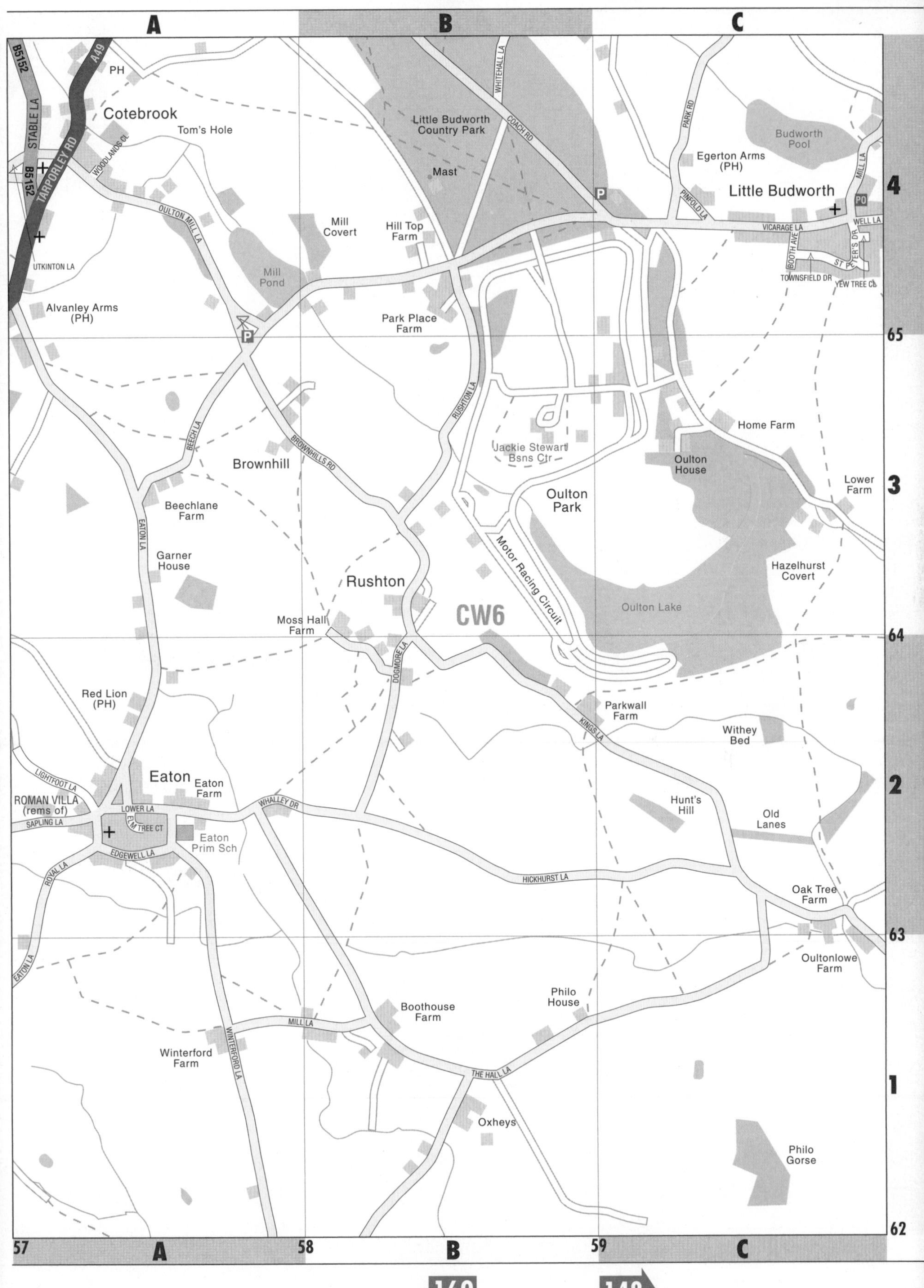

124
148
169
148

A B C

Cotebrook

PH

Tom's Hole

Little Budworth
Country Park

Mast

Egerton Arms
(PH)

Budworth
Pool

Little Budworth

PO

VICARAGE LA

TOWNSFIELD DR   YEW TREE CL

Mill Covert

Hill Top
Farm

P

Mill
Pond

Park Place
Farm

65

Alvanley Arms
(PH)

UTKINTON LA

P

Home Farm

Oulton
House

Lower
Farm

3

Brownhill

Beechlane
Farm

Jackie Stewart
Bsns Ctr

Oulton
Park

Garner
House

Rushton

Hazelhurst
Covert

Moss Hall
Farm

CW6

Oulton Lake

64

Red Lion
(PH)

Parkwall
Farm

Withey
Bed

Eaton

Eaton
Farm

Hunt's
Hill

Old
Lanes

ROMAN VILLA
(rems of)

LOWER LA   ELM TREE CT

WHALLEY DR

Eaton
Prim Sch

2

SAPLING LA

EDGEWELL LA

HICKHURST LA

Oak Tree
Farm

63

EATON LA

Oultonlowe
Farm

Boothouse
Farm

Philo
House

MILL LA

Winterford
Farm

THE HALL LA

1

Oxheys

Philo
Gorse

62

57   58   B   59   C

57 A 58 B 59 C

147 125

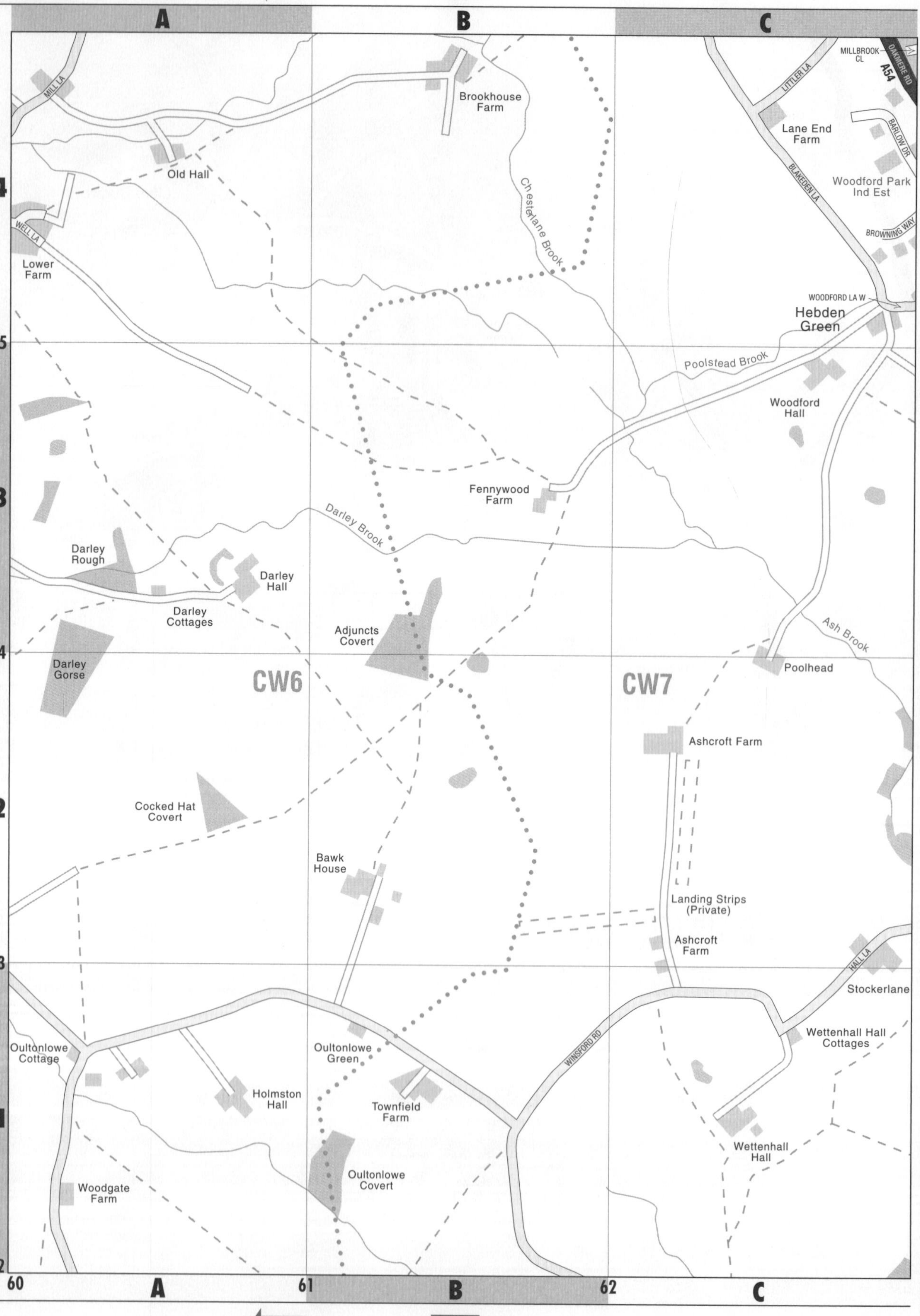

A B C

MILL LA

Old Hall

Brookhouse
Farm

Chesterlane Brook

MILLBROOK
CL

OAKMERE RD

LITTLER LA

A54

Lane End
Farm

BARLOW DR

Woodford Park
Ind Est

BLAKEMERE LA

BROWNING WAY

4

WELL LA

Lower
Farm

WOODFORD LA W

Hebden
Green

65

Poolstead Brook

Woodford
Hall

Fennywood
Farm

3

Darley Brook

Darley
Rough

Darley
Hall

Darley
Cottages

Ash Brook

Adjuncts
Covert

64

Darley
Gorse

CW6

CW7

Poolhead

Ashcroft Farm

2

Cocked Hat
Covert

Bawk
House

Landing Strips
(Private)

Ashcroft
Farm

63

HALL LA

Stockerlane

Oultonlowe
Cottage

Oultonlowe
Green

WINSFORD RD

Wettenhall Hall
Cottages

Holmston
Hall

Townfield
Farm

1

Wettenhall
Hall

Woodgate
Farm

Oultonlowe
Covert

62

60

A

61

B

62

C

147 170

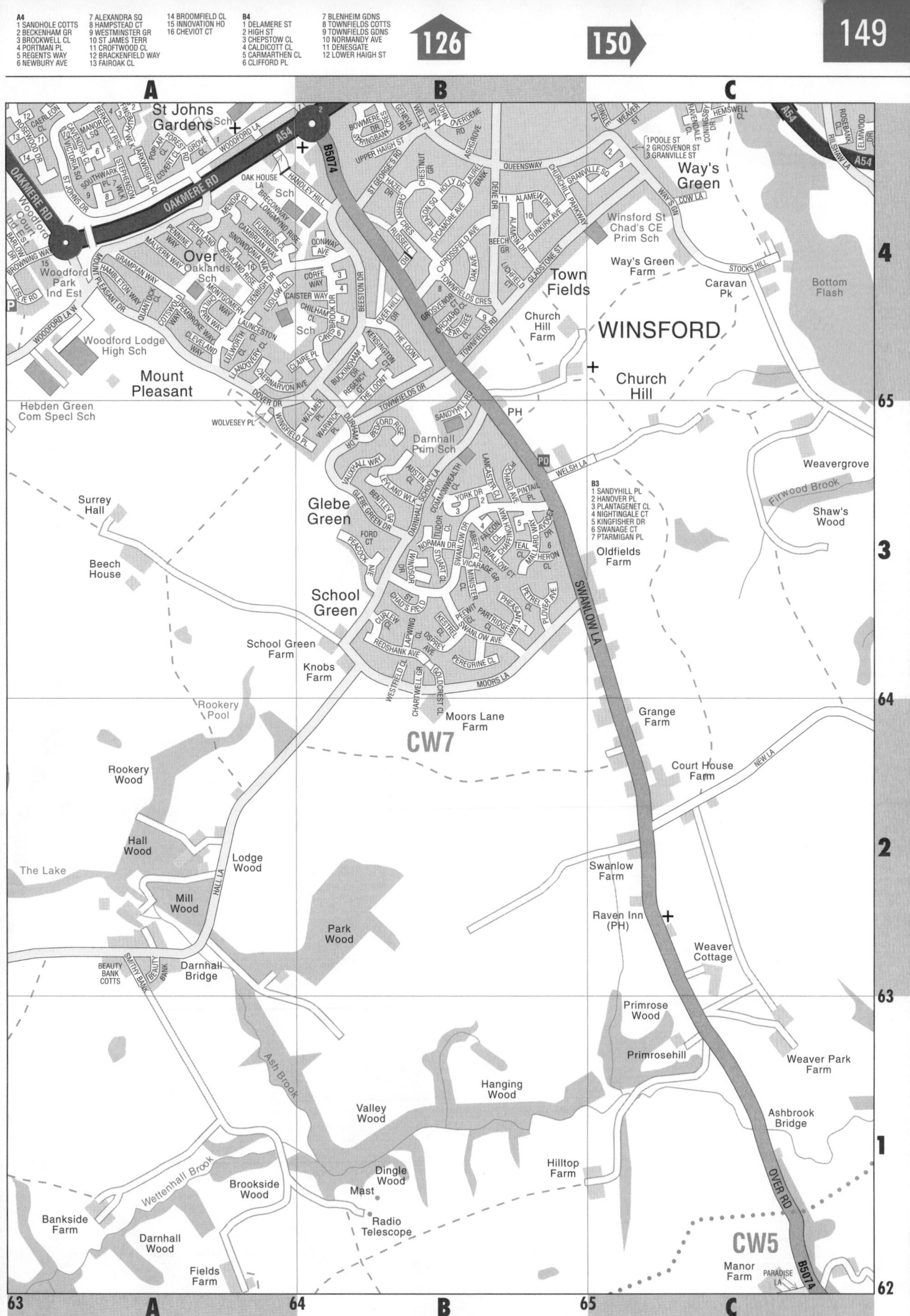
A4
1 SANDHOLE COTTS
2 BECKENHAM GR
3 BROCKWELL CL
4 PORTMAN PL
5 REGENTS WAY
6 NEWBURY AVE
7 ALEXANDRA SQ
8 HAMPSTEAD CT
9 WESTMINSTER GR
10 ST JAMES TERR
11 CROFTWOOD CL
12 BRACKENFIELD WAY
13 FAIROAK CL
14 BROOMFIELD CL
15 INNOVATION HO
16 CHEVIOT CT
B4
1 DELAMERE ST
2 HIGH ST
3 CHEPSTOW CL
4 CALDICOTT CL
5 CARMARTHEN CL
6 CLIFFORD PL
7 BLENHEIM GDNS
8 TOWNFIELDS COTTS
9 TOWNFIELDS GDNS
10 NORMANDY AVE
11 DENESGATE
12 LOWER HAIGH ST
126
150
A
B
C
St Johns Gardens
Sch
A54
B5074
OAKMERE RD
Woodford Court Ind Est
Woodford Park Ind Est
Over
Oaklands Sch
Woodford Lodge High Sch
Mount Pleasant
Hebden Green Com Specl Sch
Way's Green
1 POOLE ST
2 GROSVENOR ST
3 GRANVILLE ST
Winsford St Chad's CE Prim Sch
Way's Green Farm
Caravan Pk
Bottom Flash
Town Fields
Church Hill Farm
WINSFORD
Church Hill
PH
Darnhall Prim Sch
PO
WELSH LA
B3
1 SANDYHILL PL
2 HANOVER PL
3 PLANTAGENET CL
4 NIGHTINGALE CT
5 KINGFISHER DR
6 SWANAGE CT
7 PTARMIGAN PL
Oldfields Farm
Weavergrove
Firwood Brook
Shaw's Wood
Surrey Hall
Glebe Green
Beech House
School Green
School Green Farm
Knobs Farm
SWANLOW LA
MOORS LA
Rookery Pool
Moors Lane Farm
CW7
Grange Farm
Court House Farm
NEW LA
Rookery Wood
Hall Wood
The Lake
Lodge Wood
Mill Wood
HALL LA
Swanlow Farm
Raven Inn (PH)
Park Wood
Weaver Cottage
BEAUTY BANK COTTS
SMITHY BANK
BEAUTY BANK
Darnhall Bridge
Primrose Wood
Primrosehill
Weaver Park Farm
Ash Brook
Hanging Wood
Valley Wood
Ashbrook Bridge
Hilltop Farm
Dingle Wood
Mast
Wettenhall Brook
Brookside Wood
Radio Telescope
Bankside Farm
Darnhall Wood
Fields Farm
OVER RD
CW5
Manor Farm
PARADISE LA
B5074
4
3
2
1
65
64
63
62
63
64
65

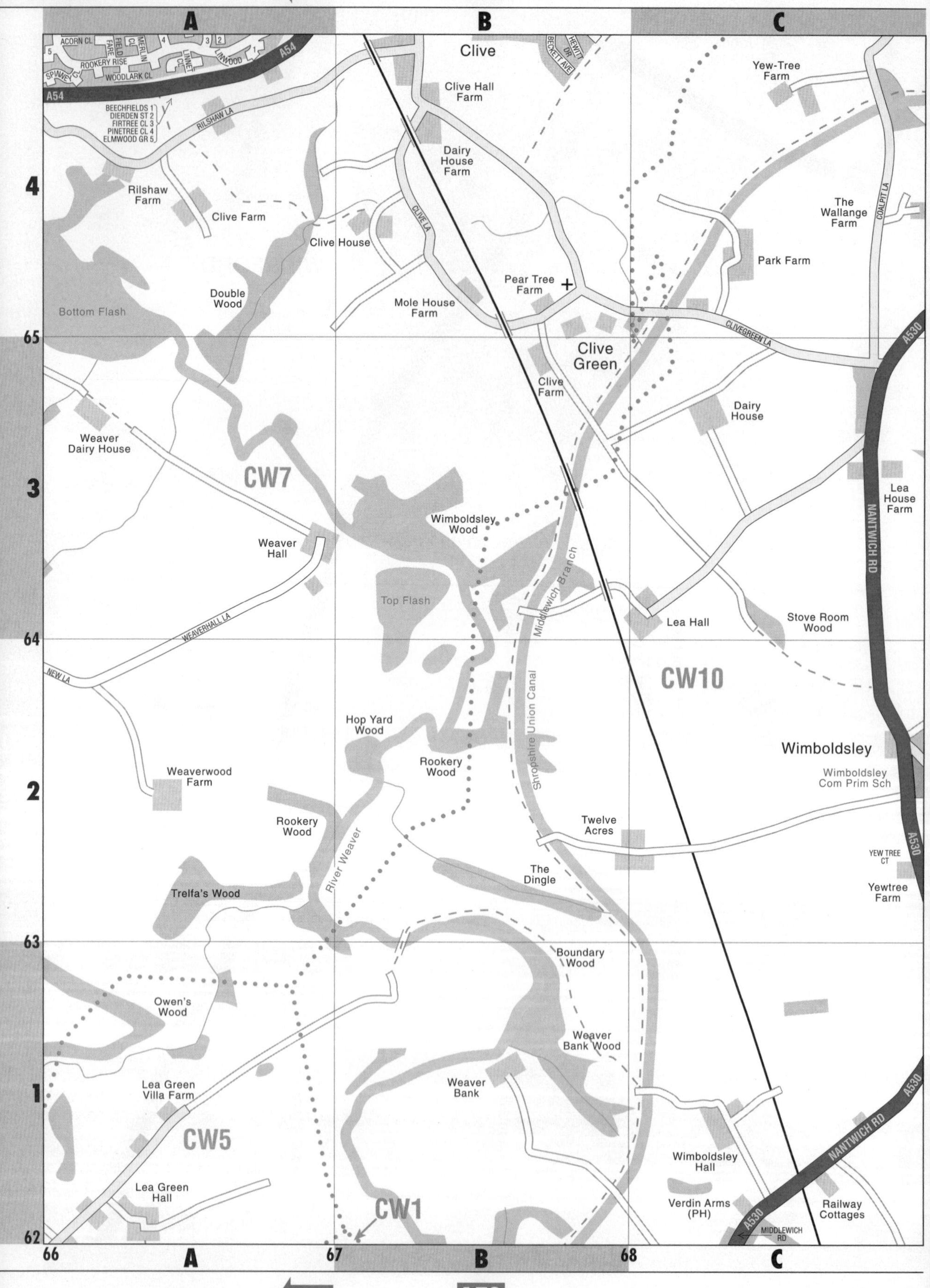

A   B   C

4

Clive

Clive Hall
Farm

Dairy
House
Farm

Rilshaw
Farm

Clive Farm

Clive House

Double
Wood

Mole House
Farm

Pear Tree
Farm

Yew-Tree
Farm

The
Wallange
Farm

Park Farm

Bottom Flash

BEECHFIELDS 1
DIERDEN ST 2
FIRTREE CL 3
PINETREE CL 4
ELMWOOD GR 5

RILSHAW LA

CLIVE LA

A54

A530

COALPIT LA

NANTWICH RD

CLIVEGREEN LA

65

Clive Green

Clive
Farm

Dairy
House

Lea
House
Farm

Weaver
Dairy House

CW7

Weaver
Hall

Wimboldsley
Wood

3

WEAVERHALL LA

Top Flash

Middlewich Branch

Lea Hall

Stove Room
Wood

CW10

64

NEW LA

Shropshire Union Canal

Hop Yard
Wood

Rookery
Wood

Twelve
Acres

Wimboldsley

Wimboldsley
Com Prim Sch

Weaverwood
Farm

2

Rookery
Wood

River Weaver

The
Dingle

YEW TREE
CT

Yewtree
Farm

Trelfa's Wood

63

Boundary
Wood

Owen's
Wood

Weaver
Bank Wood

Lea Green
Villa Farm

Weaver
Bank

1

CW5

Wimboldsley
Hall

Lea Green
Hall

CW1

Verdin Arms
(PH)

Railway
Cottages

A530

MIDDLEWICH
RD

NANTWICH RD

62

66   A   67   B   68   C

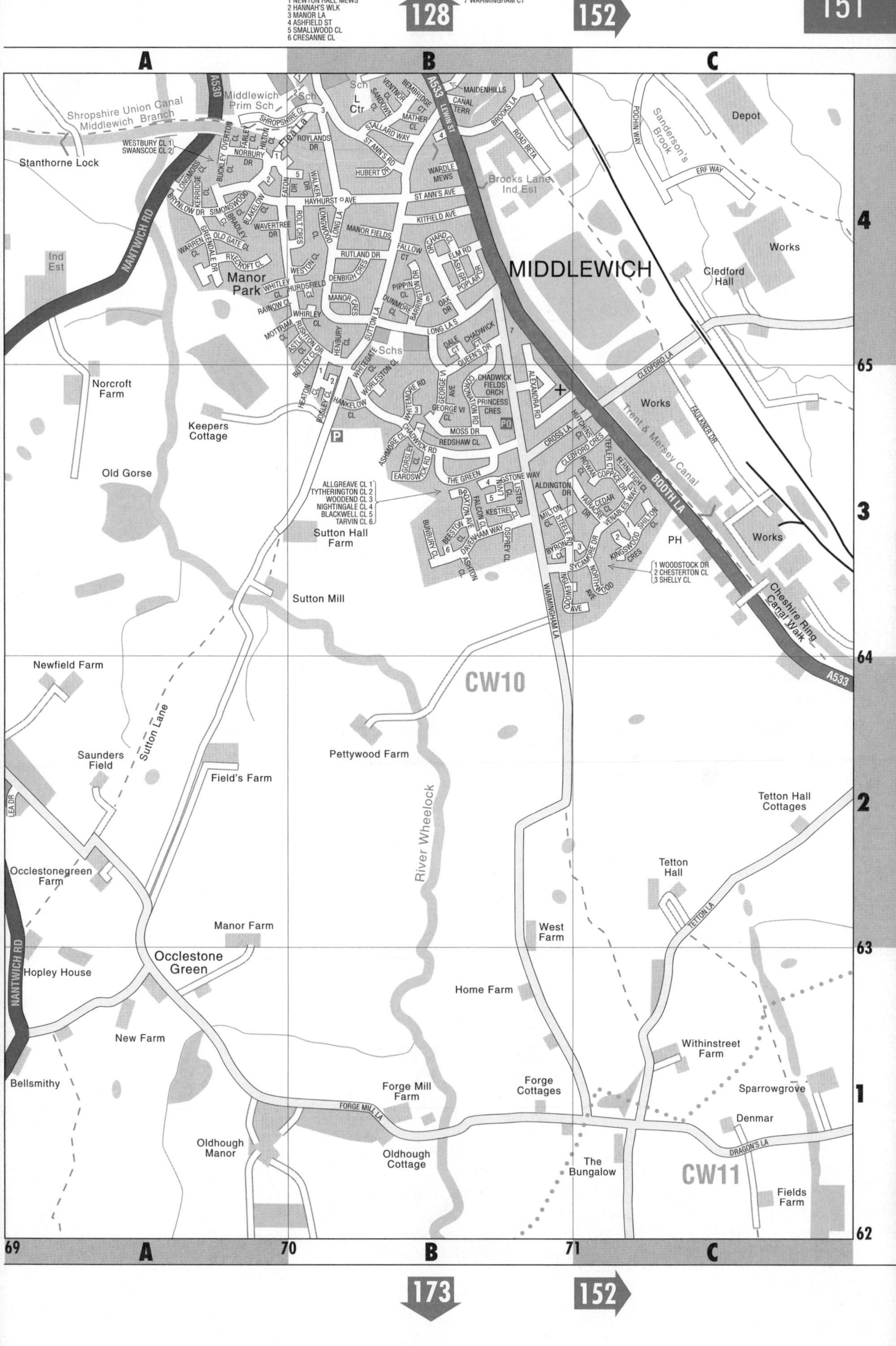

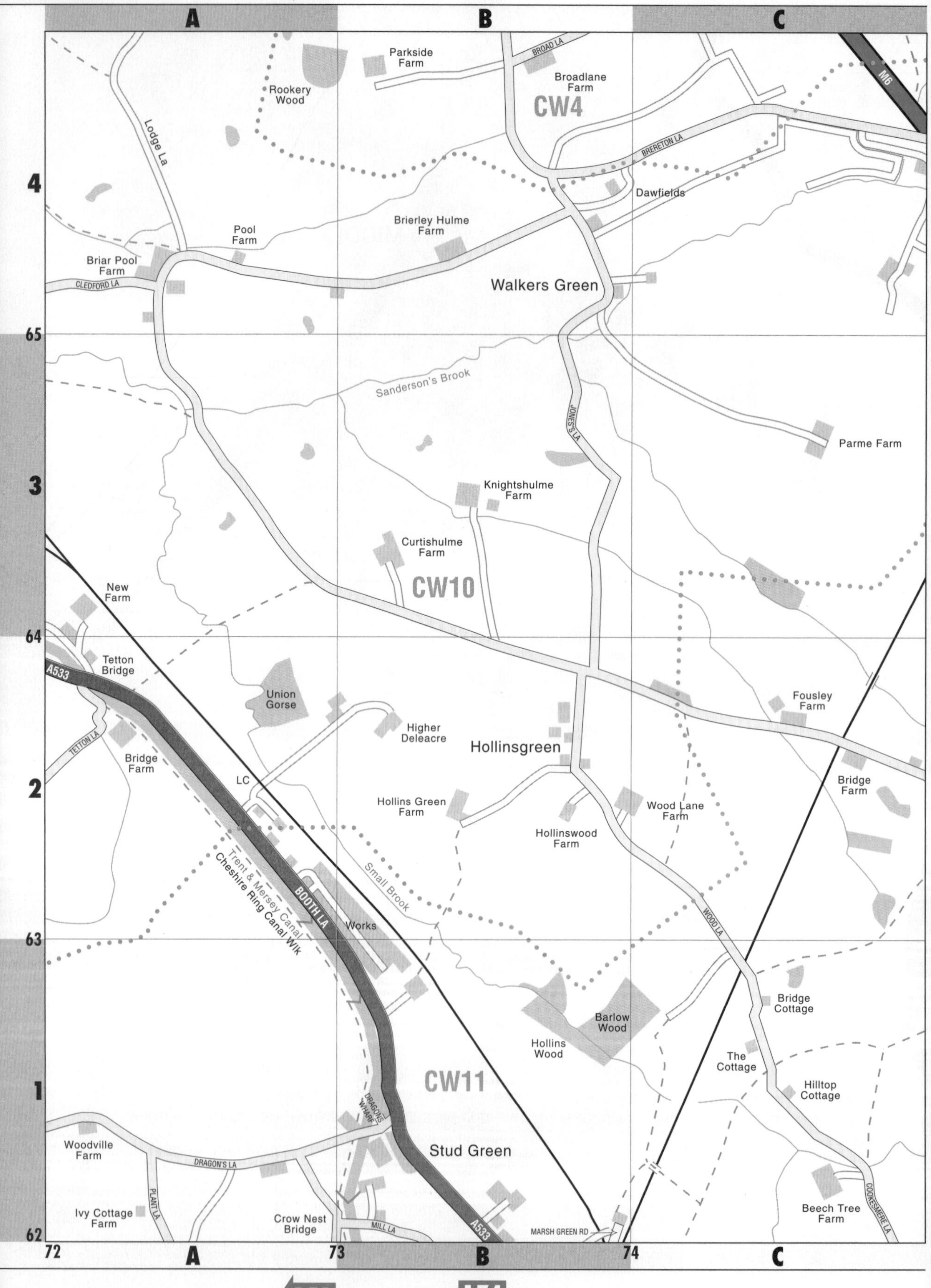
151
129
A
B
C
Parkside Farm
BROAD LA
Broadlane Farm
CW4
M6
Rookery Wood
Lodge La
BRERETON LA
4
Dawfields
Pool Farm
Brierley Hulme Farm
Briar Pool Farm
CLEDFORD LA
Walkers Green
65
Sanderson's Brook
JONES'S LA
Parme Farm
3
Knightshulme Farm
Curtishulme Farm
CW10
New Farm
64
Tetton Bridge
A533
Union Gorse
Fousley Farm
Higher Deleacre
TETTON LA
Bridge Farm
Hollinsgreen
Bridge Farm
2
LC
Hollins Green Farm
Wood Lane Farm
Hollinswood Farm
Trent & Mersey Canal
Cheshire Ring Canal Wlk
BOOTH LA
Small Brook
WOOD LA
Works
63
Barlow Wood
Bridge Cottage
Hollins Wood
The Cottage
1
CW11
Hilltop Cottage
DRAGONS WHARF
Woodville Farm
DRAGON'S LA
Stud Green
PLANT LA
Ivy Cottage Farm
Crow Nest Bridge
MILL LA
A533
MARSH GREEN RD
Beech Tree Farm
COOKESMERE LA
62
72
A
73
B
74
C
151
174

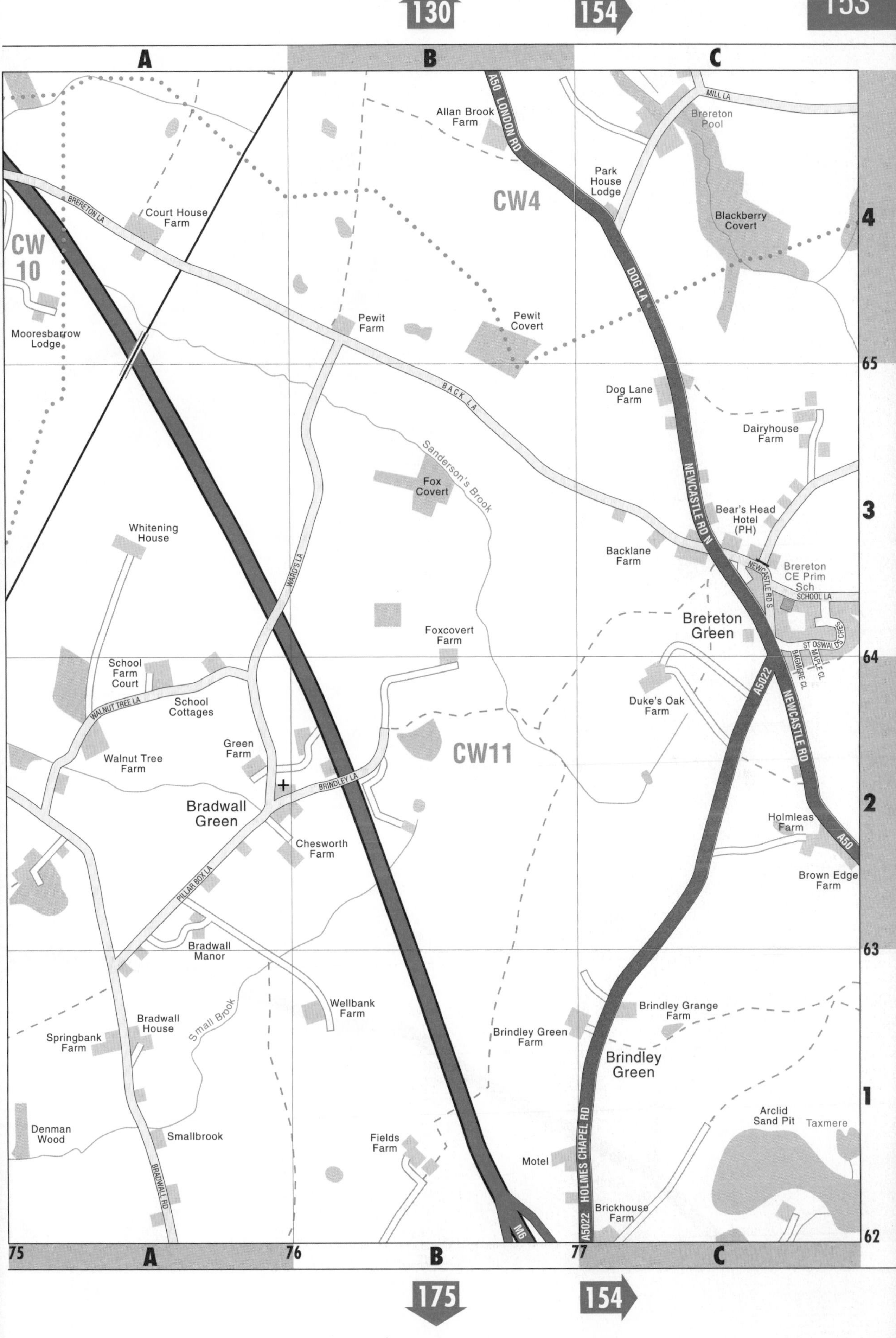
A
B
C
Allan Brook Farm
A50 LONDON RD
MILL LA
Brereton Pool
Park House Lodge
CW4
Blackberry Covert
4
BRERETON LA
Court House Farm
CW 10
DOG LA
Mooresbarrow Lodge
Pewit Farm
Pewit Covert
65
BACK LA
Dog Lane Farm
Dairyhouse Farm
Sanderson's Brook
Fox Covert
NEWCASTLE RD N
3
Whitening House
Bear's Head Hotel (PH)
Backlane Farm
Brereton CE Prim Sch
NEWCASTLE RD S
SCHOOL LA
WARD'S LA
Brereton Green
Foxcovert Farm
ST OSWALDS CRES
BAGMERE CL
MAPLE CL
64
School Farm Court
WALNUT TREE LA
School Cottages
A5022
NEWCASTLE RD
Duke's Oak Farm
Green Farm
CW11
Walnut Tree Farm
BRINDLEY LA
2
Bradwall Green
Holmleas Farm
A50
Chesworth Farm
PILLAR BOX LA
Brown Edge Farm
Bradwall Manor
63
Wellbank Farm
Brindley Grange Farm
Bradwall House
Small Brook
Springbank Farm
Brindley Green Farm
Brindley Green
A5022 HOLMES CHAPEL RD
1
Arclid Sand Pit
Taxmere
Denman Wood
Smallbrook
Fields Farm
Motel
BRADWALL RD
Brickhouse Farm
M6
62
75
76
77

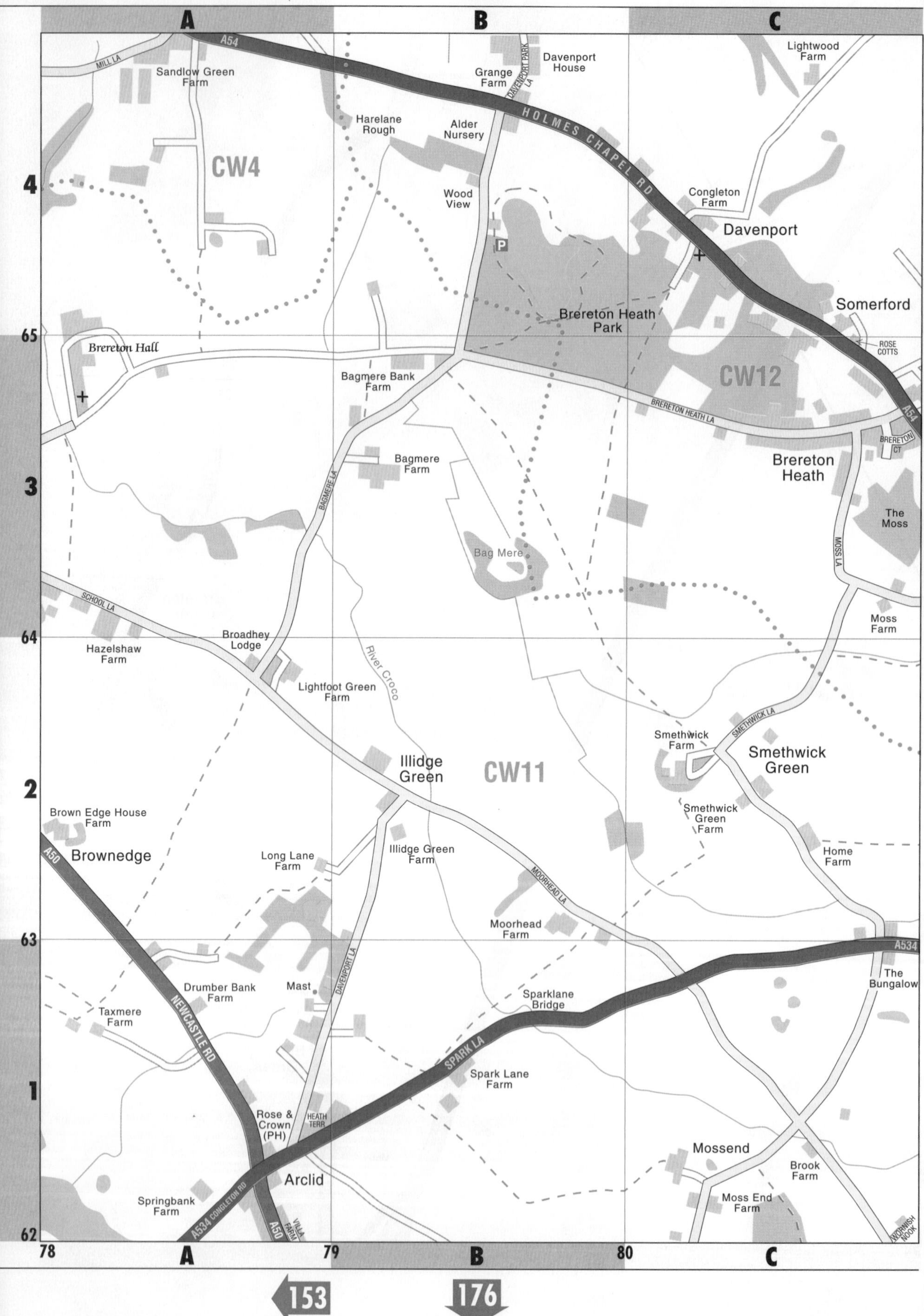

A   B   C

A54

MILL LA

Sandlow Green
Farm

Grange
Farm

DAVENPORT PARK LA

Davenport
House

Lightwood
Farm

CW4

Harelane
Rough

Alder
Nursery

HOLMES CHAPEL RD

Congleton
Farm

Wood
View

Davenport

4

P

Brereton Heath
Park

Somerford

65

Brereton Hall

CW12

ROSE
COTTS

Bagmere Bank
Farm

BRERETON HEATH LA

BRERETON
CT

Bagmere
Farm

Brereton
Heath

BAGMERE LA

The
Moss

3

Bag Mere

MOSS LA

Moss
Farm

SCHOOL LA

Broadhey
Lodge

64

Hazelshaw
Farm

River Croco

Lightfoot Green
Farm

SMETHWICK LA

Smethwick
Farm

Smethwick
Green

Illidge
Green

CW11

2

Brown Edge House
Farm

Long Lane
Farm

Illidge Green
Farm

Smethwick
Green
Farm

Home
Farm

A50

Brownedge

MOORHEAD LA

63

A534

Moorhead
Farm

The
Bungalow

NEWCASTLE RD

Drumber Bank
Farm

Mast

DAVENPORT LA

Sparklane
Bridge

Taxmere
Farm

SPARK LA

Spark Lane
Farm

1

Rose &
Crown
(PH)

HEATH
TERR

Mossend

Brook
Farm

A534 CONGLETON RD

Arclid

A50

VILLA
FRONT

Moss End
Farm

IVY NOOK

Springbank
Farm

62

78   A   79   B   80   C

132
156

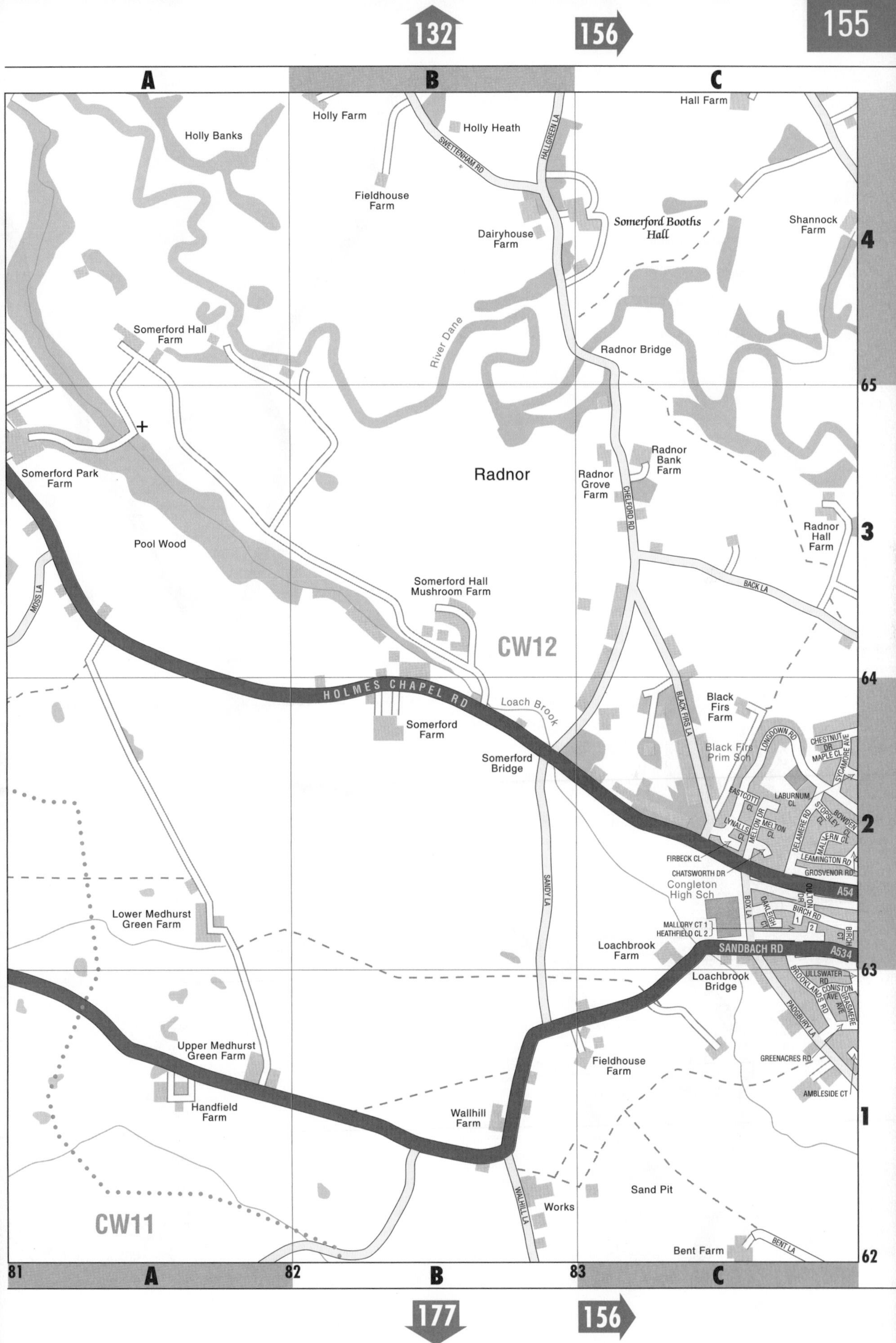
A
B
C
Holly Farm
Holly Heath
Hall Farm
Holly Banks
SWETTENHAM RD
HALLGREEN LA
Fieldhouse Farm
Somerford Booths Hall
Shannock Farm
Dairyhouse Farm
4
River Dane
Somerford Hall Farm
Radnor Bridge
65
Radnor
Radnor Bank Farm
Radnor Grove Farm
Somerford Park Farm
CHELFORD RD
Radnor Hall Farm
3
Pool Wood
BACK LA
MOSS LA
Somerford Hall Mushroom Farm
CW12
64
HOLMES CHAPEL RD
Loach Brook
Black Firs Farm
BLACK FIRS LA
Somerford Farm
Somerford Bridge
Black Firs Prim Sch
LONGDOWN RD
CHESTNUT DR
MAPLE CL
SYCAMORE AVE
EASTCOTT CL
LABURNUM CL
2
LYNALLS CL
MELTON DR
MELTON CL
DELAMERE RD
STOPSLEY CL
BOWDEN CL
MALVERN CL
FIRBECK CL
LEAMINGTON RD
CHATSWORTH DR
GROSVENOR RD
SANDY LA
Congleton High Sch
A54
BOX LA
OAKLEIGH CT
OULTON DR
BIRCH RD
Lower Medhurst Green Farm
MALLORY CT 1
HEATHFIELD CL 2
BIRCH CT
Loachbrook Farm
SANDBACH RD
A534
63
Loachbrook Bridge
ULLSWATER RD
BROOKLANDS RD
CONISTON AVE
GRASMERE AVE
PADGBURY LA
Upper Medhurst Green Farm
Fieldhouse Farm
GREENACRES RD
AMBLESIDE CT
Handfield Farm
1
Wallhill Farm
Sand Pit
Works
WALHILL LA
CW11
BENT LA
Bent Farm
62
81
A
82
B
83
C

177
156

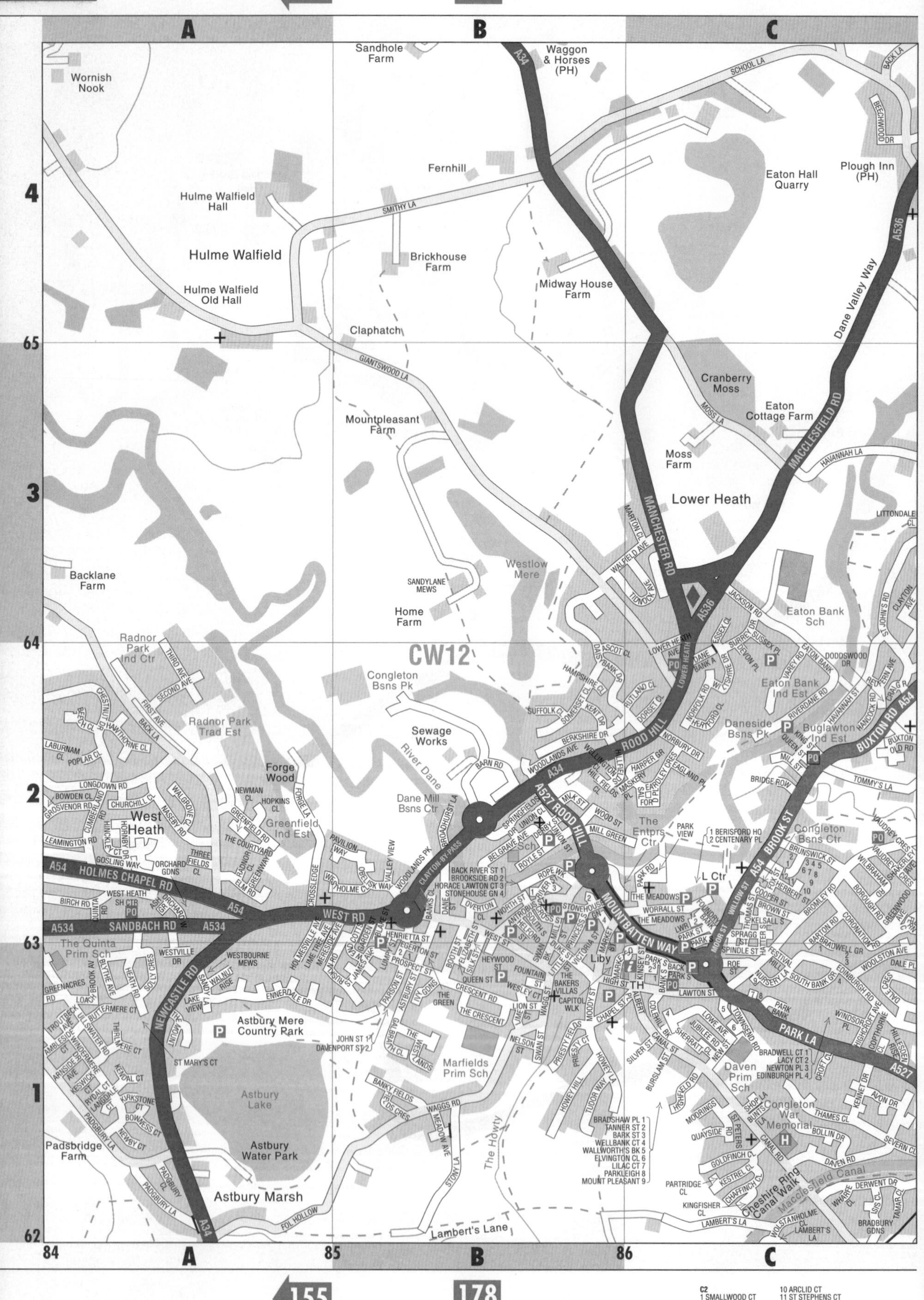

C2
1 SMALLWOOD CT
2 SOMERFORD CT
3 CRANAGE CT
4 GOOSTREY CT
5 MOSTON CT
6 BETCHTON CT
7 RODE CT
8 TETTON CT
9 NEWBOLD CT
10 ARCLID CT
11 ST STEPHENS CT
12 ELWORTH CT

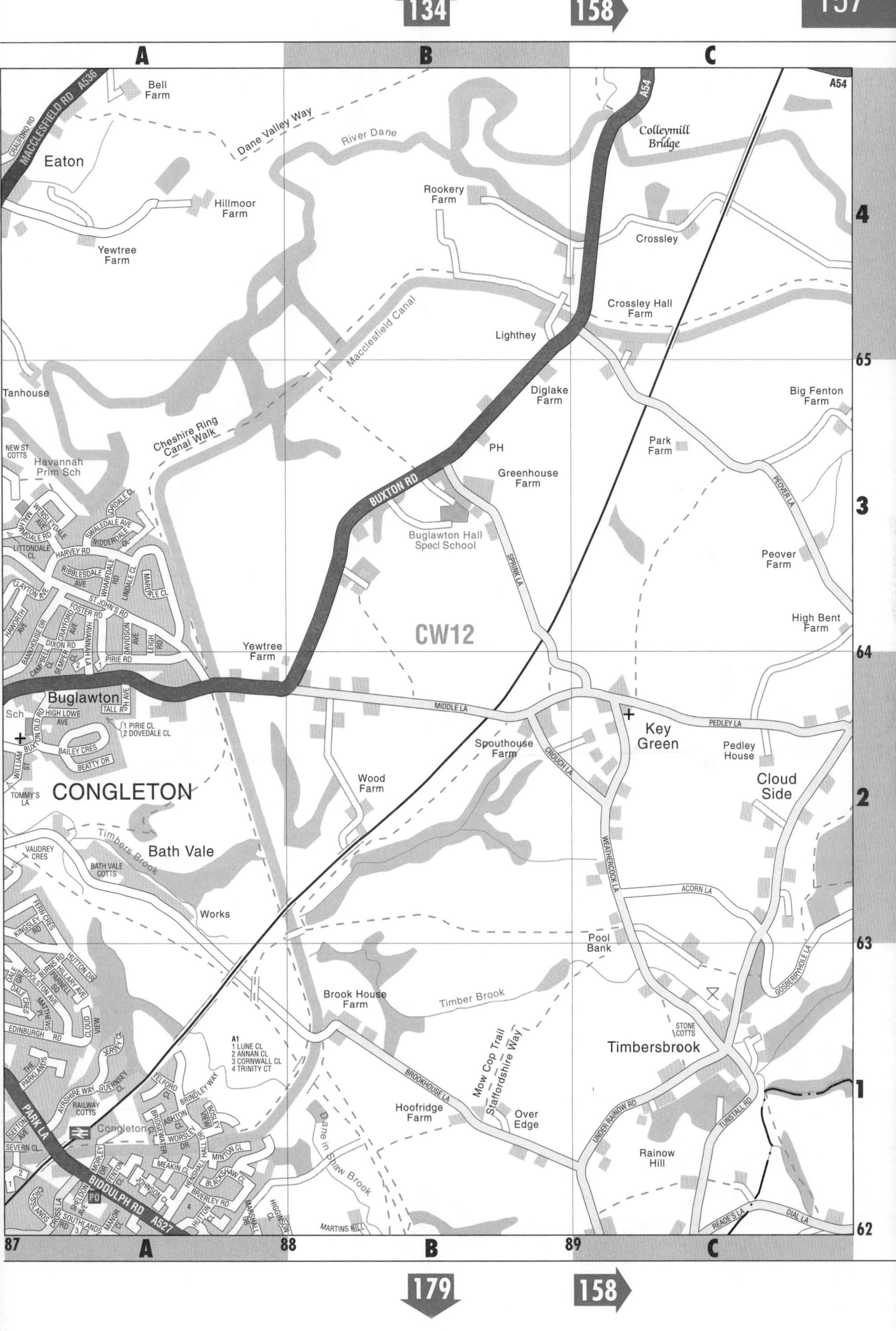
A
B
C
Bell Farm
Eaton
MACCLESFIELD RD A536
Dane Valley Way
River Dane
Colleymill Bridge
A54
Hillmoor Farm
Rookery Farm
Yewtree Farm
Crossley
Crossley Hall Farm
Macclesfield Canal
Lighthey
Tanhouse
Diglake Farm
Big Fenton Farm
Cheshire Ring Canal Walk
PH
Park Farm
Havannah Prim Sch
Greenhouse Farm
BUXTON RD
PEOVER LA
Buglawton Hall Specl School
Peover Farm
SPRINK LA
CW12
High Bent Farm
Yewtree Farm
Buglawton
MIDDLE LA
PEDLEY LA
Key Green
Spouthouse Farm
CROUCH LA
Pedley House
Cloud Side
Wood Farm
CONGLETON
Bath Vale
Timbers Brook
WEATHERCOCK LA
ACORN LA
Works
Pool Bank
GOSBERRYHOLE LA
Brook House Farm
Timber Brook
A1
1 LUNE CL
2 ANNAN CL
3 CORNWALL CL
4 TRINITY CT
Mow Cop Trail
Staffordshire Way
STONE COTTS
Timbersbrook
BROOKHOUSE LA
Hoofridge Farm
Over Edge
UNDER RAINOW RD
TUNSTALL RD
Congleton
Dane in Shaw Brook
Rainow Hill
PARK LA
BIDDULPH RD A527
READE'S LA
DIAL LA
MARTINS HILL
4
65
3
64
2
63
1
62
87
88
89

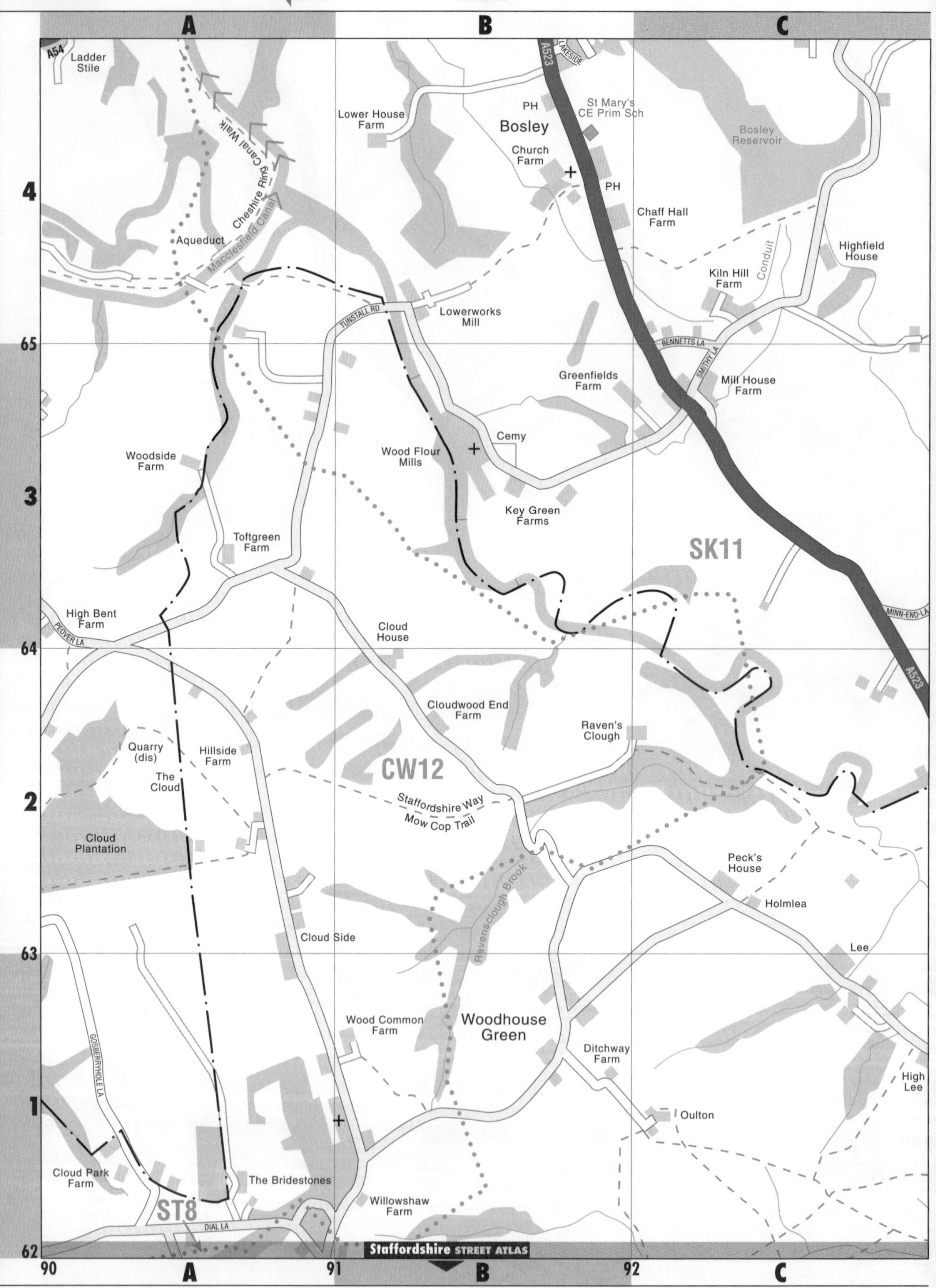

Staffordshire STREET ATLAS

B
C
A54
Ladder Stile
Lower House Farm
PH
Bosley
St Mary's CE Prim Sch
Bosley Reservoir
Church Farm
PH
Chaff Hall Farm
Cheshire Ring Canal Walk
Macclesfield Canal
Aqueduct
Highfield House
Kiln Hill Farm
Conduit
A523
LAKESIDE
TUNSTALL RD
Lowerworks Mill
BENNETTS LA
SMITHY LA
Greenfields Farm
Mill House Farm
Cemy
Wood Flour Mills
Woodside Farm
Key Green Farms
Toftgreen Farm
SK11
High Bent Farm
PEOVER LA
Cloud House
MINN-END-LA
Cloudwood End Farm
Raven's Clough
Quarry (dis)
Hillside Farm
The Cloud
CW12
Staffordshire Way
Mow Cop Trail
Cloud Plantation
Peck's House
Ravensclough Brook
Holmlea
Cloud Side
Lee
Wood Common Farm
Woodhouse Green
GOSBERRYHOLE LA
Ditchway Farm
High Lee
Oulton
Cloud Park Farm
The Bridestones
Willowshaw Farm
ST8
DIAL LA
4
65
3
64
2
63
1
62
90
91
92

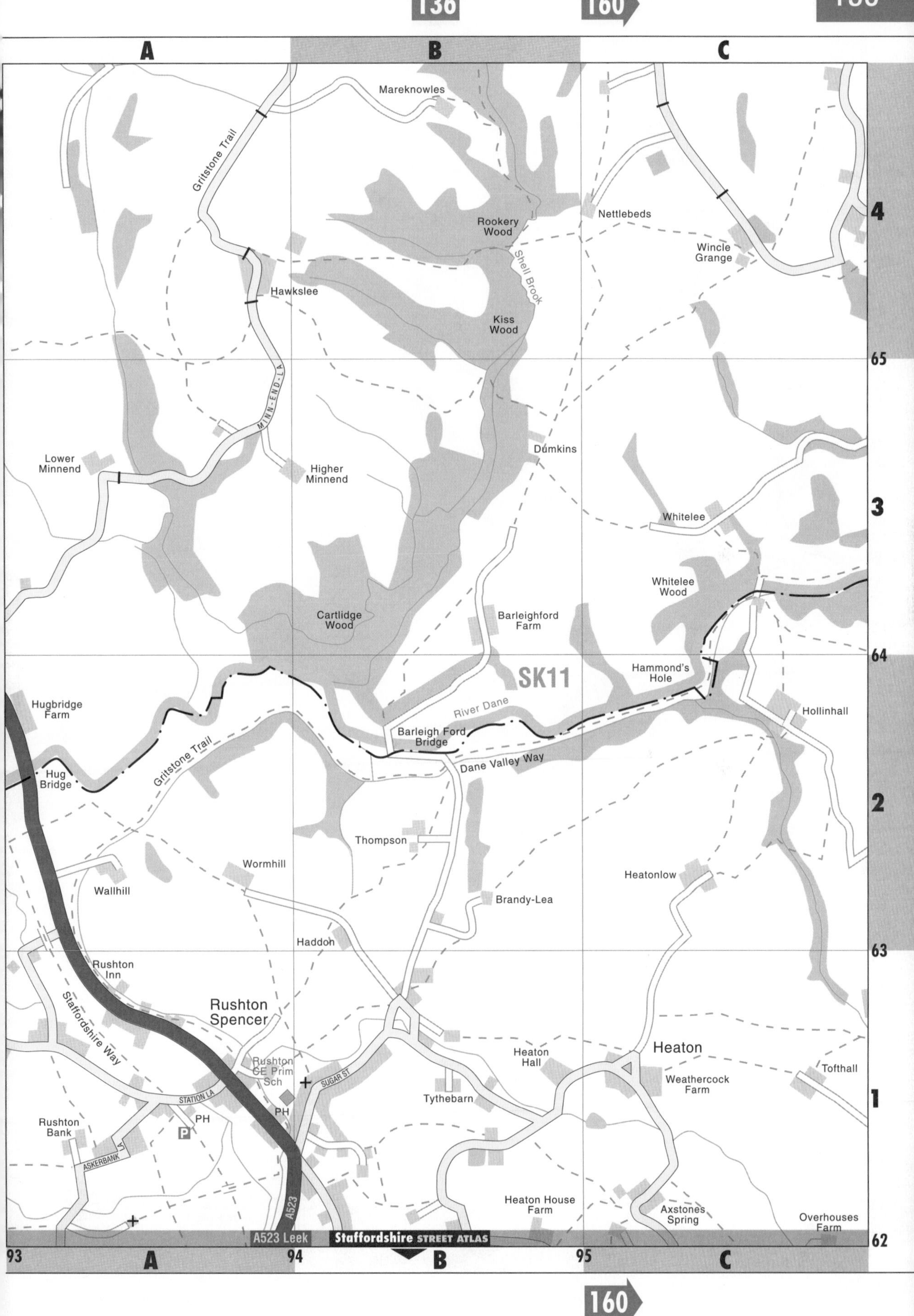

A
B
C

Mareknowles

Gritstone Trail

Rookery
Wood

Nettlebeds

Shell Brook

Wincle
Grange

4

Hawkslee

Kiss
Wood

MINN-END-LA

65

Lower
Minnend

Dumkins

Higher
Minnend

Whitelee

3

Whitelee
Wood

Cartlidge
Wood

Barleighford
Farm

SK11

Hammond's
Hole

64

Hugbridge
Farm

River Dane

Gritstone Trail

Barleigh Ford
Bridge

Hollinhall

Hug
Bridge

Dane Valley Way

2

Thompson

Wormhill

Heatonlow

Wallhill

Brandy-Lea

Haddon

63

Staffordshire Way

Rushton
Inn

Rushton
Spencer

Heaton

Tofthall

Rushton
CE Prim
Sch

SUGAR ST

Heaton
Hall

Weathercock
Farm

1

STATION LA

PH

Tythebarn

Rushton
Bank

PH

P

ASKERBANK

A523

Heaton House
Farm

Axstones
Spring

Overhouses
Farm

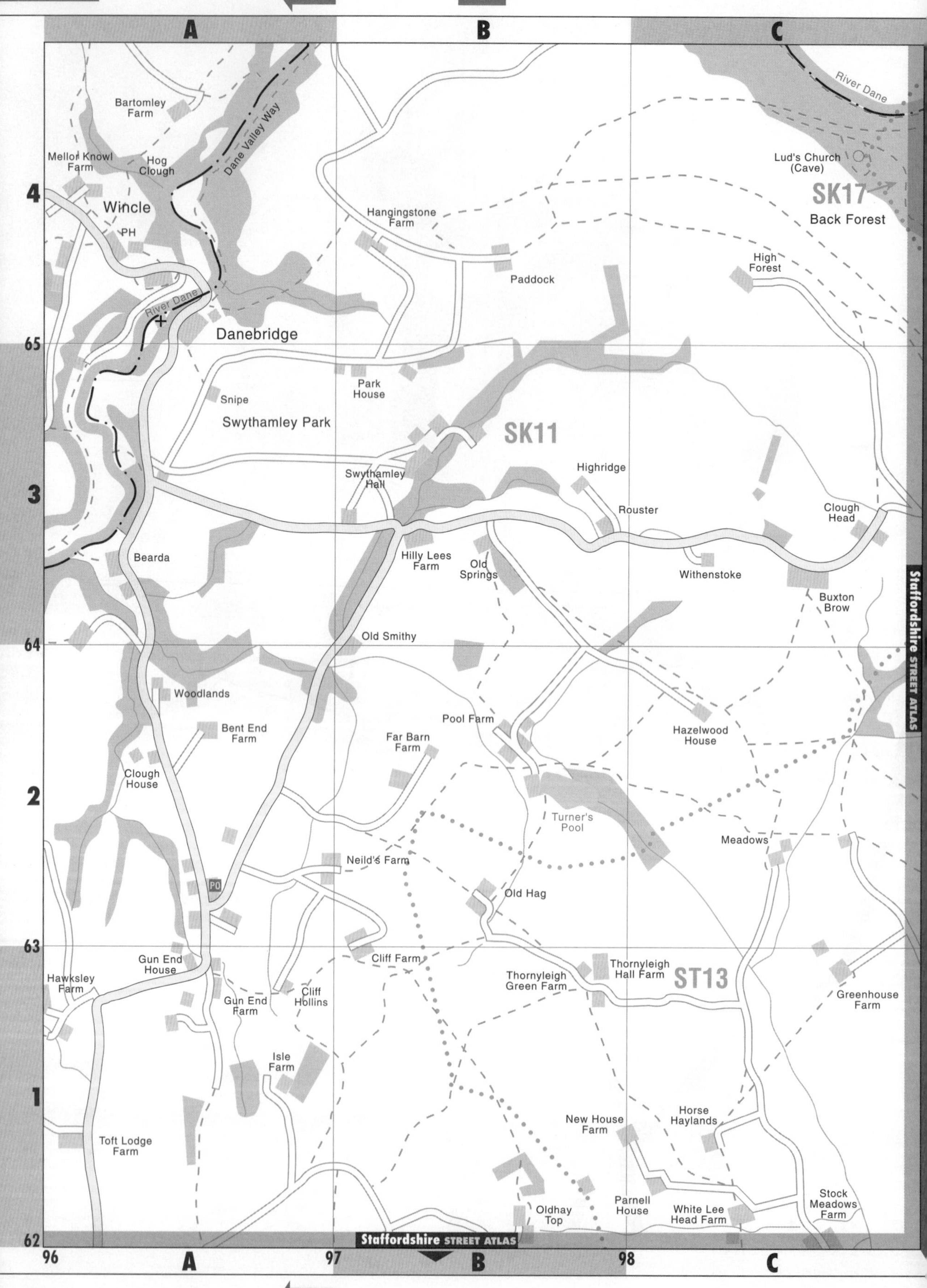

A   B   C

159

River Dane

Bartomley
Farm

Mellor Knowl
Farm

Hog
Clough

Dane Valley Way

Wincle

PH

River Dane

Danebridge

Hangingstone
Farm

Paddock

Lud's Church
(Cave)

SK17

Back Forest

High
Forest

Snipe

Park
House

Swythamley Park

SK11

Highridge

Swythamley
Hall

Rouster

Clough
Head

Bearda

Hilly Lees
Farm

Old
Springs

Withenstoke

Buxton
Brow

Old Smithy

Woodlands

Pool Farm

Hazelwood
House

Bent End
Farm

Far Barn
Farm

Clough
House

Turner's
Pool

Meadows

Neild's Farm

Old Hag

PO

Cliff Farm

Gun End
House

Thornyleigh
Green Farm

Thornyleigh
Hall Farm

ST13

Greenhouse
Farm

Hawksley
Farm

Gun End
Farm

Cliff
Hollins

Isle
Farm

New House
Farm

Horse
Haylands

Toft Lodge
Farm

Oldhay
Top

Parnell
House

White Lee
Head Farm

Stock
Meadows
Farm

Staffordshire STREET ATLAS

65

64

63

62

96   97   98

4

3

2

1

Staffordshire STREET ATLAS

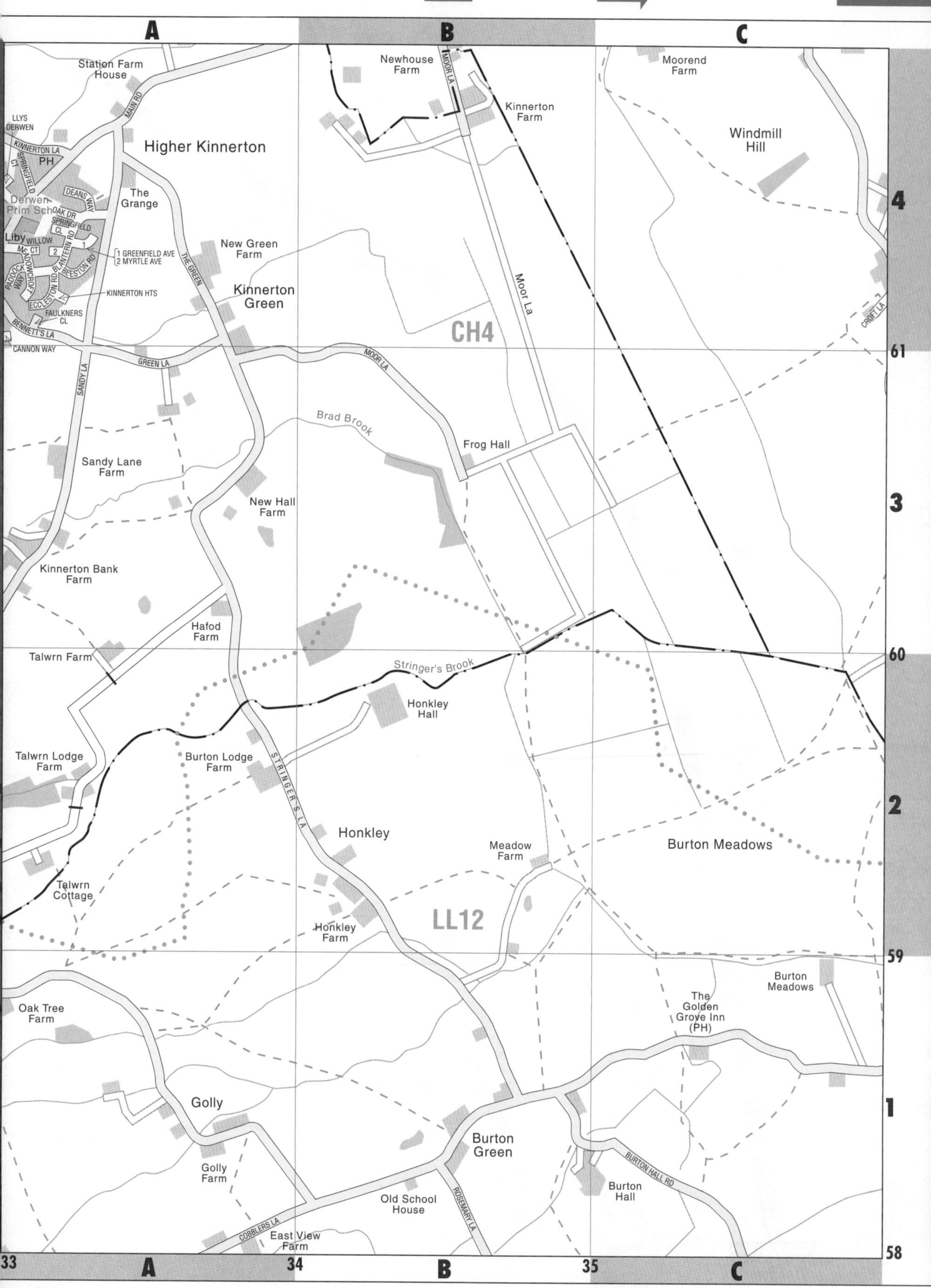

A

Station Farm
House

LLYS
DERWEN

KINNERTON LA
PH

SPRINGFIELD

DEANS WAY

Derwen
Prim Sch

OAK DR

SPRINGFIELD
CL

WILLOW

Liby

McC CT

PADDOCK
WAY

MEADOWCROFT

FAULKNERS
CL

BENNETT'S LA

CANNON WAY

SANDY LA

ECCLESTON RD

BEESTON RD

ANTERN RD

The Grange

Higher Kinnerton

New Green
Farm

1 GREENFIELD AVE
2 MYRTLE AVE

THE GREEN

Kinnerton
Green

KINNERTON HTS

GREEN LA

MOOR LA

Sandy Lane
Farm

Brad Brook

New Hall
Farm

Kinnerton Bank
Farm

Hafod
Farm

Talwrn Farm

Talwrn Lodge
Farm

Burton Lodge
Farm

STRINGER'S LA

Honkley

Honkley
Farm

Talwrn
Cottage

LL12

Oak Tree
Farm

Golly

Golly
Farm

COBBLERS LA

East View
Farm

B

Newhouse
Farm

MOOR LA

Kinnerton
Farm

Moor La

CH4

Frog Hall

Stringer's Brook

Honkley
Hall

Meadow
Farm

Honkley
Hall

Old School
House

ROSEMARY LA

Burton
Green

C

Moorend
Farm

Windmill
Hill

CROFT LA

4

61

3

60

Burton Meadows

2

59

Burton
Meadows

The
Golden
Grove Inn
(PH)

1

Burton
Hall

BURTON HALL RD

58

161

140

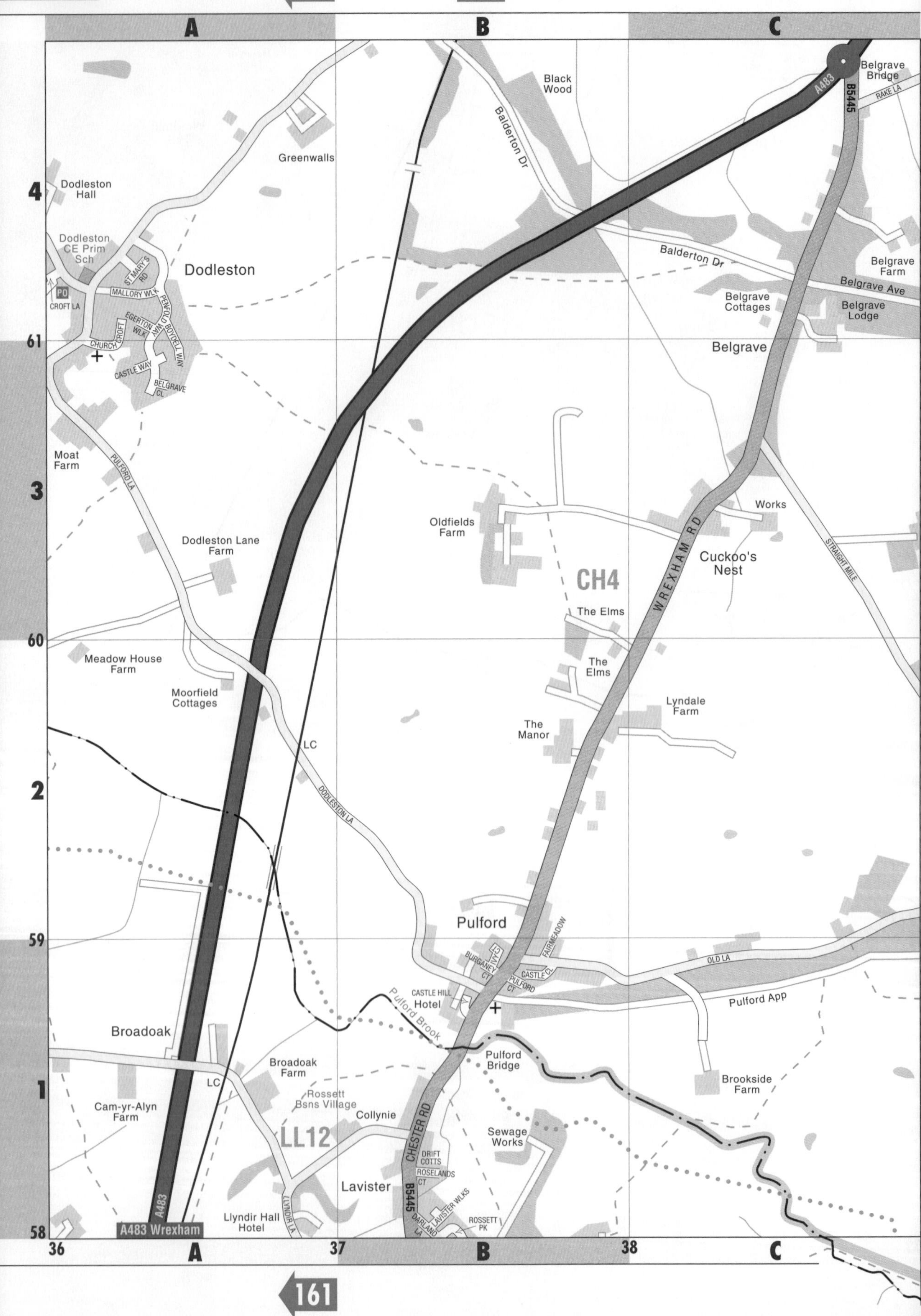

A
B
C
4
3
2
1
61
60
59
58
36
37
38
Dodleston Hall
Dodleston CE Prim Sch
Dodleston
PO
CROFT LA
ST MARY'S RD
MALLORY WLK
PENFOLD WAY
BOYDELL WAY
EGERTON WLK
CROFT
CHURCH
CASTLE WAY
BELGRAVE CL
Greenwalls
Black Wood
Balderton Dr
Belgrave Bridge
A483
B5445
RAKE LA
Belgrave Farm
Belgrave Ave
Belgrave Cottages
Belgrave Lodge
Belgrave
Moat Farm
PULFORD LA
Dodleston Lane Farm
Oldfields Farm
Works
Cuckoo's Nest
STRAIGHT MILE
WREXHAM RD
CH4
The Elms
Meadow House Farm
Moorfield Cottages
Lyndale Farm
The Manor
LC
DODLESTON LA
Pulford
FAIRMEADOW
BURGANEY CT
CASTLE CL
PULFORD CT
OLD LA
CASTLE HILL Hotel
Pulford App
Pulford Brook
Broadoak
Pulford Bridge
Broadoak Farm
Brookside Farm
Cam-yr-Alyn Farm
Rossett Bsns Village
Collynie
Sewage Works
LL12
CHESTER RD
DRIFT COTTS
ROSELANDS CT
Lavister
LAVISTER WLKS
Llyndir Hall Hotel
LLYNDIR LA
DARLAND LA
ROSSETT PK
A483 Wrexham

161

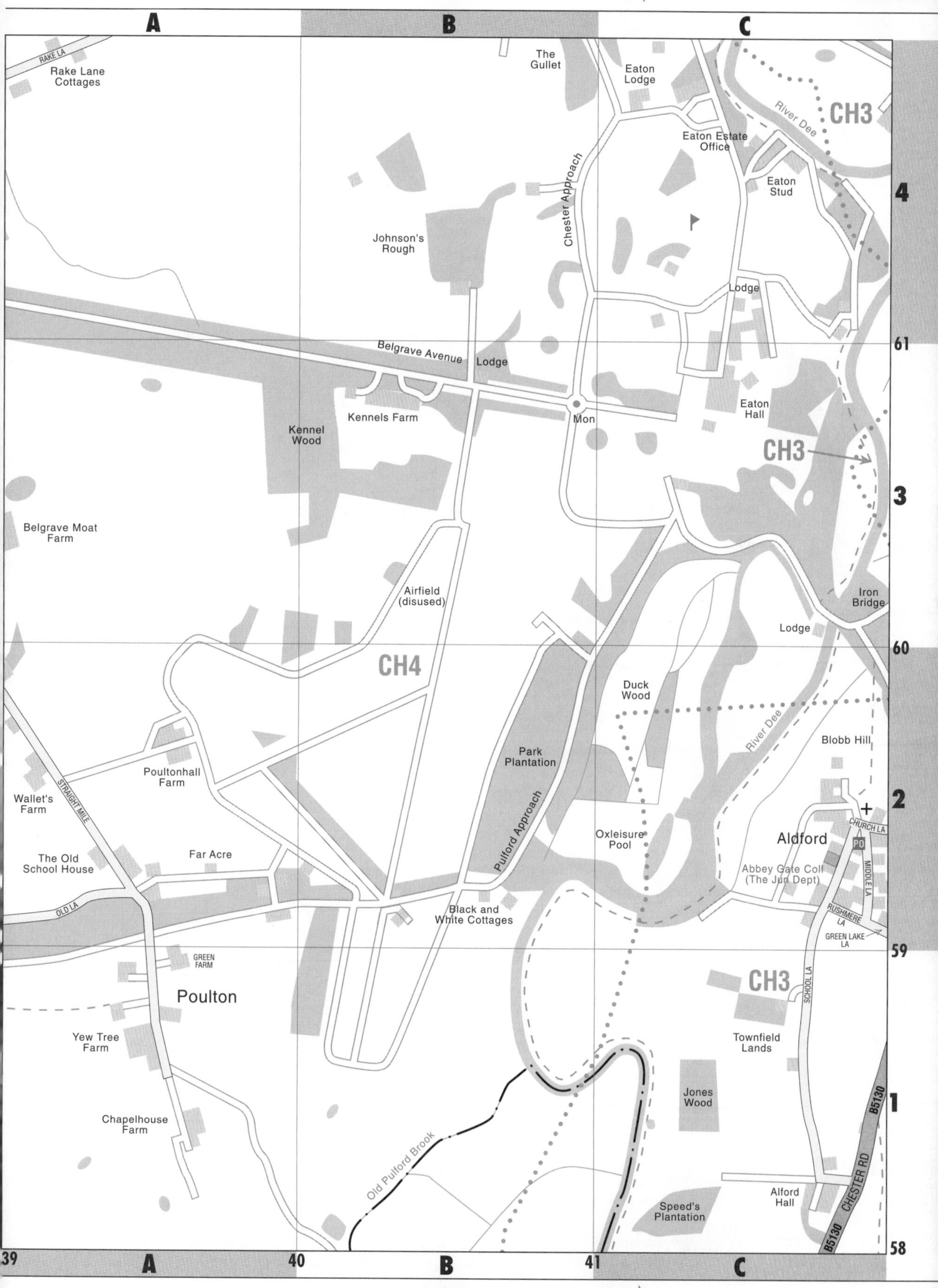

A B C

Rake Lane
Cottages

RAKE LA

The Gullet

Eaton
Lodge

River Dee

CH3

4

Chester Approach

Eaton Estate
Office

Eaton
Stud

Johnson's
Rough

Lodge

Belgrave Avenue

Lodge

61

Mon

Kennels Farm

Eaton
Hall

Kennel
Wood

CH3

3

Belgrave Moat
Farm

Iron
Bridge

Airfield
(disused)

Lodge

60

CH4

Duck
Wood

Park
Plantation

Blobb Hill

Poultonhall
Farm

Pulford Approach

Aldford

2

STRAIGHT MILE

Wallet's
Farm

CHURCH LA

Oxleisure
Pool

The Old
School House

Far Acre

Abbey Gate Coll
(The Jun Dept)

MIDDLE LA

OLD LA

RUSHMERE LA

Black and
White Cottages

GREEN LAKE LA

GREEN
FARM

59

Poulton

CH3

SCHOOL LA

Yew Tree
Farm

Townfield
Lands

Jones
Wood

B5130

1

Chapelhouse
Farm

CHESTER RD

Alford
Hall

Old Pulford Brook

Speed's
Plantation

B5130

39 A 40 B 41 C 58

163
142

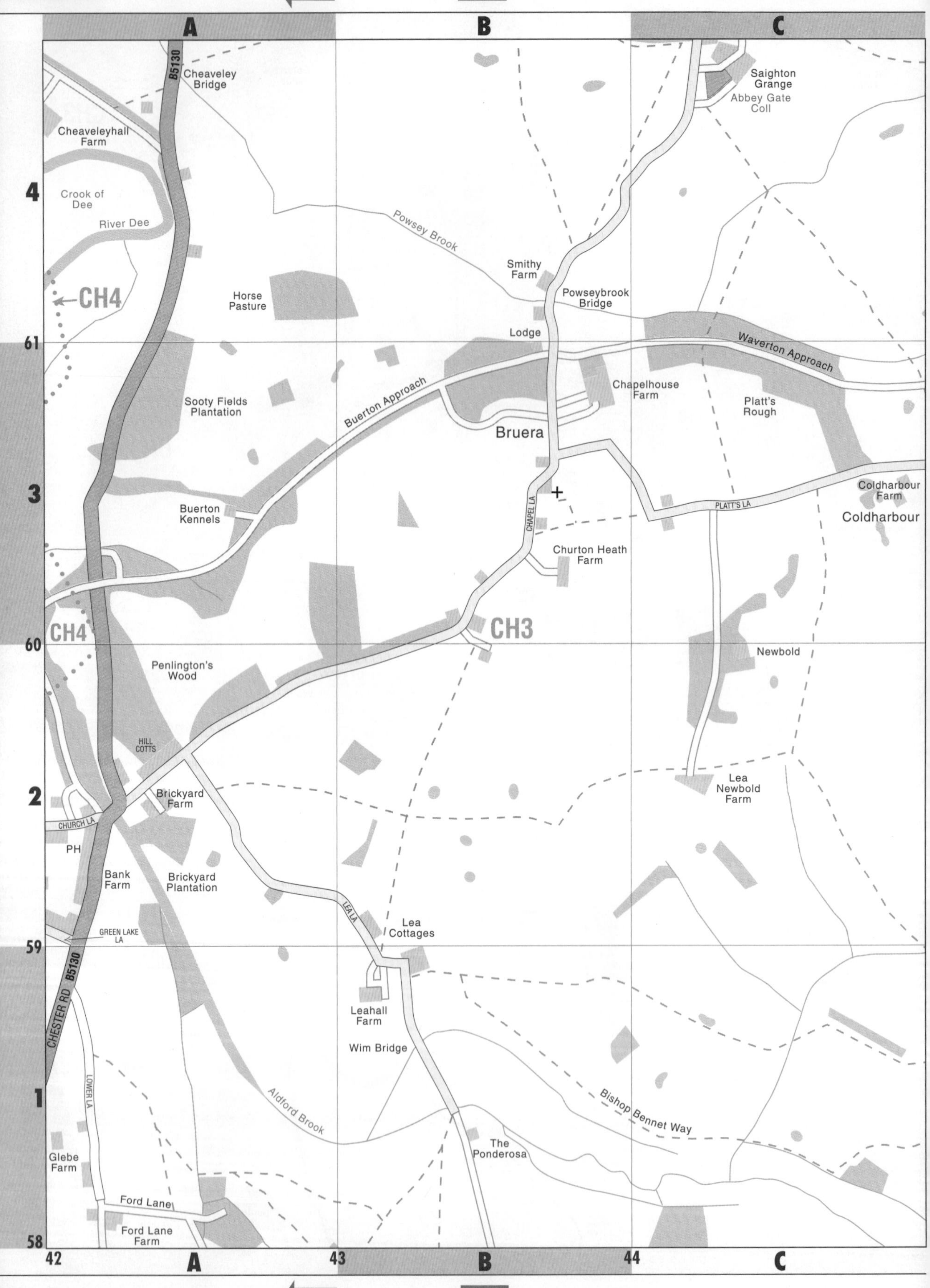
A
B
C
B5130
Cheaveley Bridge
Saighton Grange
Abbey Gate Coll
Cheaveleyhall Farm
4
Crook of Dee
River Dee
Powsey Brook
Smithy Farm
CH4
Horse Pasture
Powseybrook Bridge
Lodge
61
Waverton Approach
Sooty Fields Plantation
Buerton Approach
Chapelhouse Farm
Platt's Rough
Bruera
3
Buerton Kennels
CHAPEL LA
PLATT'S LA
Coldharbour Farm
Coldharbour
Churton Heath Farm
CH4
CH3
60
Newbold
Penlington's Wood
HILL COTTS
2
Brickyard Farm
Lea Newbold Farm
CHURCH LA
PH
Bank Farm
Brickyard Plantation
LEA LA
GREEN LAKE LA
Lea Cottages
59
B5130
CHESTER RD
Leahall Farm
Wim Bridge
1
LOWER LA
Aldford Brook
Bishop Bennet Way
The Ponderosa
Glebe Farm
Ford Lane
Ford Lane Farm
58
42
43
44
A
B
C

163
181

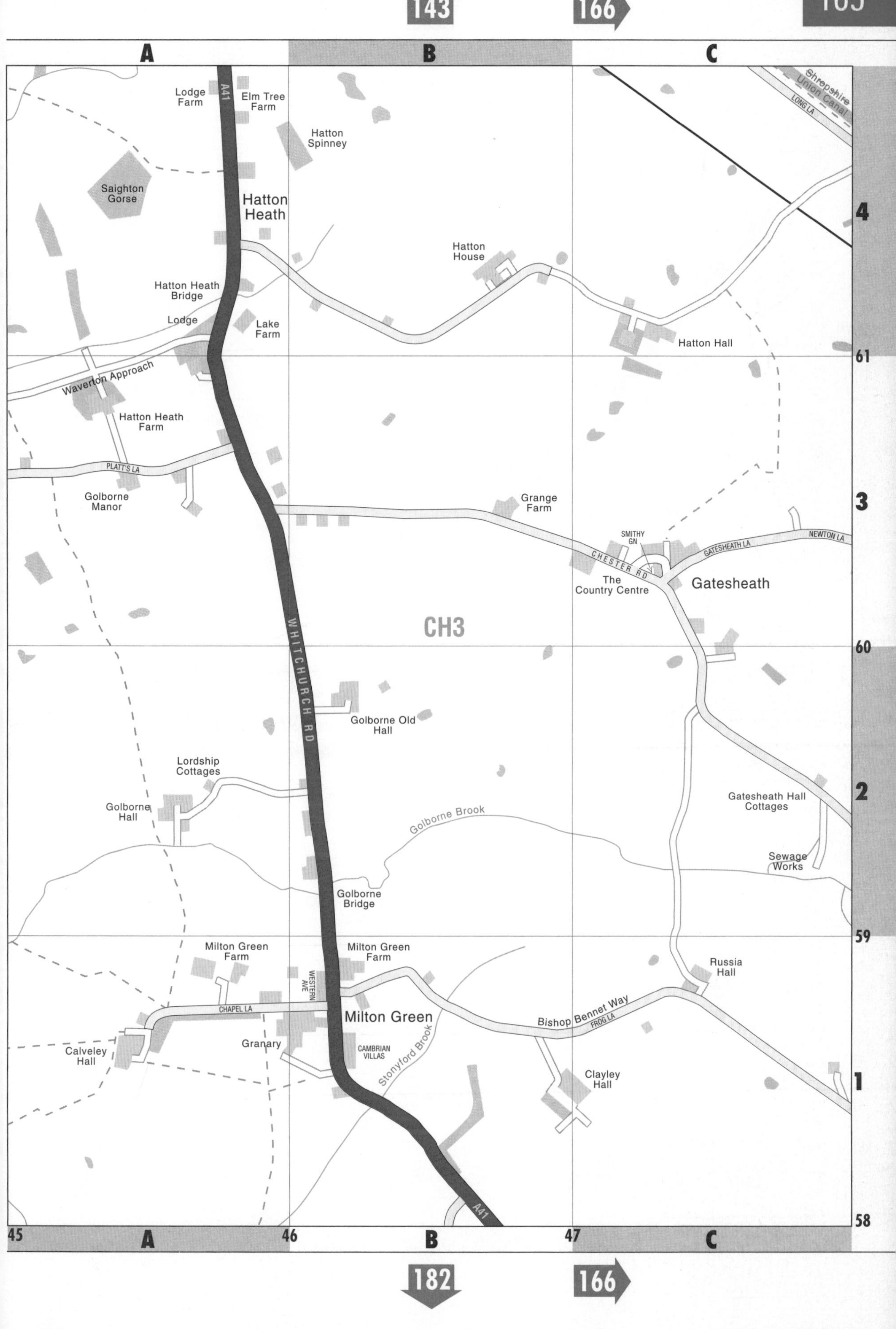
A
B
C
Lodge Farm
Elm Tree Farm
A41
Hatton Spinney
Shropshire Union Canal
LONG LA
Saighton Gorse
Hatton Heath
4
Hatton House
Hatton Heath Bridge
Lodge
Lake Farm
Hatton Hall
61
Waverton Approach
Hatton Heath Farm
PLATT'S LA
Golborne Manor
Grange Farm
3
SMITHY GN
CHESTER RD
GATESHEATH LA
NEWTON LA
The Country Centre
Gatesheath
CH3
WHITCHURCH RD
60
Golborne Old Hall
Lordship Cottages
2
Golborne Hall
Gatesheath Hall Cottages
Golborne Brook
Sewage Works
Golborne Bridge
59
Milton Green Farm
Milton Green Farm
WESTERN AVE
Russia Hall
CHAPEL LA
Milton Green
Bishop Bennet Way
FROG LA
Calveley Hall
Granary
CAMBRIAN VILLAS
Stonyford Brook
Clayley Hall
1
A41
58
45
46
47

165 144

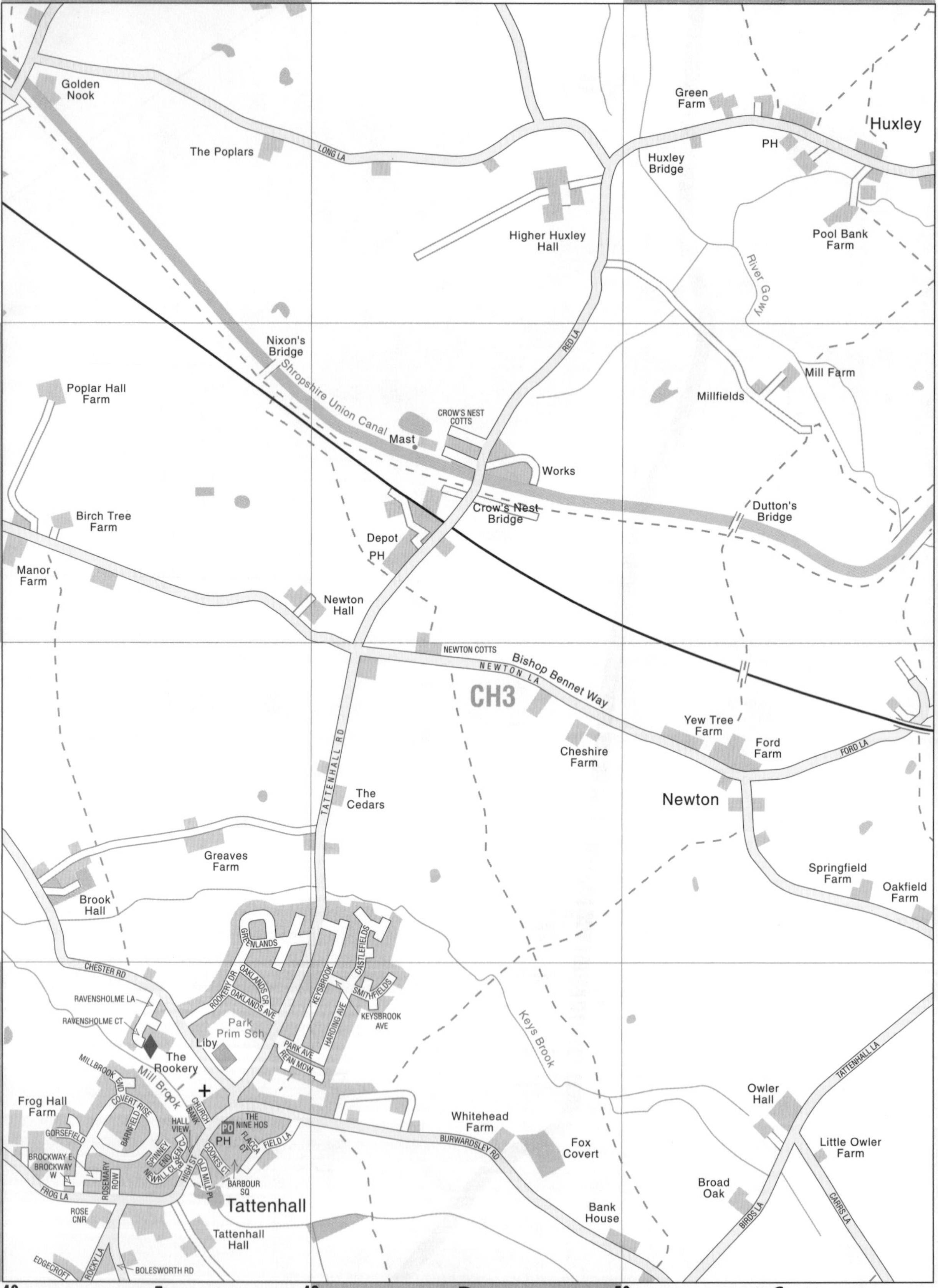

A   **B**   **C**

Golden Nook

The Poplars

LONG LA

Green Farm

Huxley

PH

Huxley Bridge

Higher Huxley Hall

Pool Bank Farm

River Gowy

4

Nixon's Bridge

RED LA

Shropshire Union Canal

CROW'S NEST COTTS

Mast

Works

Mill Farm

Millfields

61

Poplar Hall Farm

Birch Tree Farm

Crow's Nest Bridge

Dutton's Bridge

3

Manor Farm

Depot PH

Newton Hall

NEWTON COTTS

Bishop Bennet Way

NEWTON LA

CH3

Yew Tree Farm

Ford Farm

FORD LA

60

The Cedars

TATTENHALL RD

Cheshire Farm

Newton

2

Greaves Farm

Springfield Farm

Oakfield Farm

Brook Hall

CHESTER RD

GREENLANDS

KEYSBROOK

CASTLEFIELDS

SMITHFIELDS

Keys Brook

59

RAVENSHOLME LA

RAVENSHOLME CT

OAKLANDS CR

OAKLANDS AVE

ROOKERY DR

Park Prim Sch

Liby

HARDING AVE

PARK AVE

BEAN MDW

KEYSBROOK AVE

Owler Hall

TATTENHALL LA

The Rookery

MILLBROOK END

Mill Brook

CHURCH BANK

Frog Hall Farm

GORSEFIELD

COVERT RISE

BARNFIELD

ROSEMARY ROW

SPINNEY

NEWALL CR

HALL VIEW

HIGH ST

OLD MILL PL

PO PH

THE NINE HOS

FIELD LA

Whitehead Farm

BURWARDSLEY RD

Fox Covert

Little Owler Farm

1

BROCKWAY E

BROCKWAY W

FROG LA

ROSE CNR

ROCKY LA

CROSS ST

BARBOUR SQ

Tattenhall

Bank House

Broad Oak

BIRDS LA

CARRS LA

EDGECROFT

BOLESWORTH RD

Tattenhall Hall

58

48   **A**   **49**   **B**   **50**   **C**

165 183

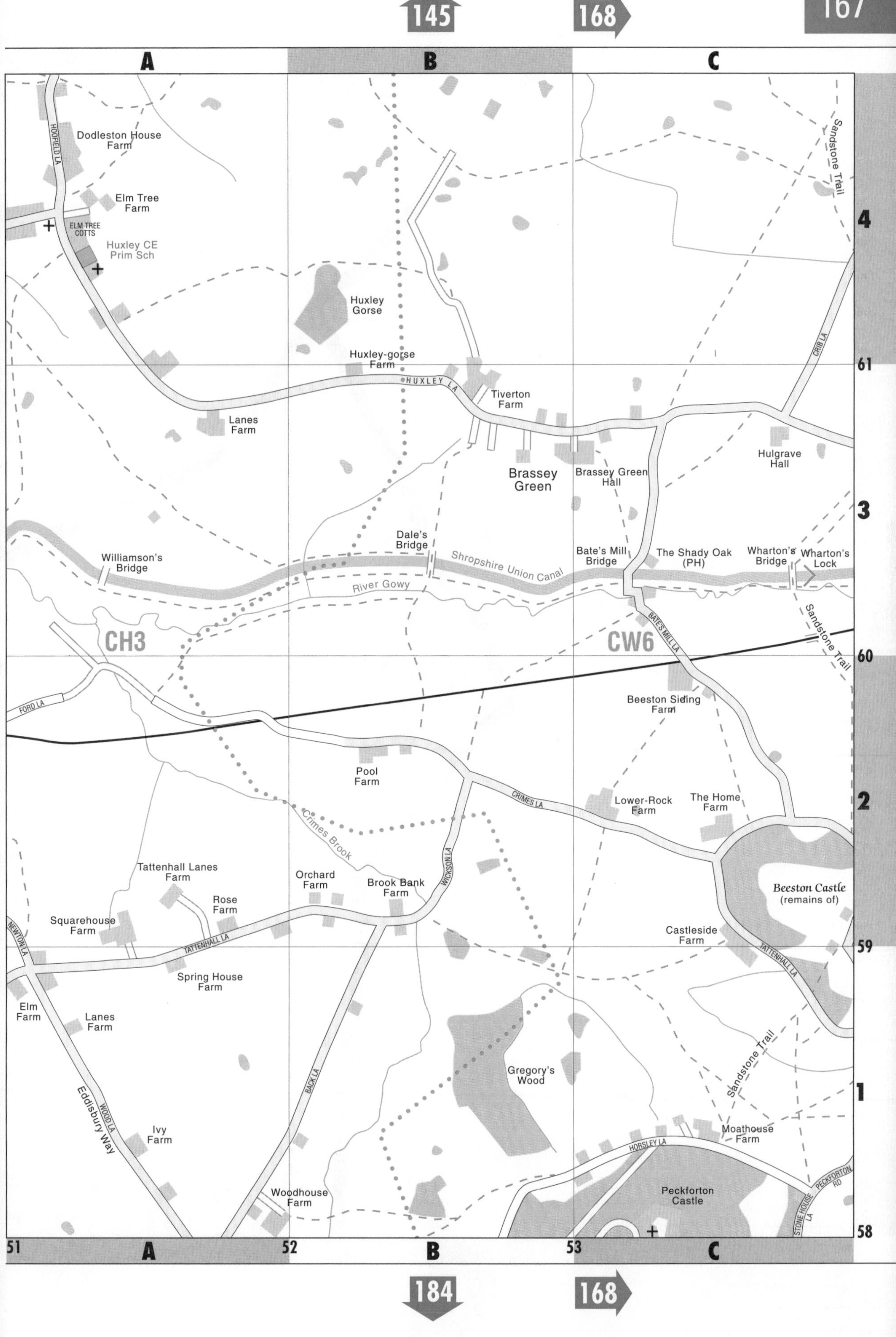
A
B
C
Dodleston House Farm
HOOFIELD LA
Elm Tree Farm
ELM TREE COTTS
Huxley CE Prim Sch
Huxley Gorse
Huxley-gorse Farm
HUXLEY LA
Tiverton Farm
Lanes Farm
Brassey Green
Brassey Green Hall
Hulgrave Hall
CRIB LA
Sandstone Trail
Dale's Bridge
Williamson's Bridge
Shropshire Union Canal
River Gowy
Bate's Mill Bridge
The Shady Oak (PH)
Wharton's Bridge
Wharton's Lock
CH3
CW6
BATE'S MILL LA
FORD LA
Beeston Siding Farm
Pool Farm
CRIMES LA
Lower-Rock Farm
The Home Farm
Crimes Brook
Beeston Castle
(remains of)
Tattenhall Lanes Farm
Orchard Farm
Brook Bank Farm
WICKSON LA
Rose Farm
Squarehouse Farm
NEWTON LA
TATTENHALL LA
Castleside Farm
Spring House Farm
Elm Farm
Lanes Farm
Gregory's Wood
BACK LA
Eddisbury Way
WOOD LA
Ivy Farm
Moathouse Farm
HORSLEY LA
Woodhouse Farm
Peckforton Castle
PECKFORTON RD
STONE HOUSE LA
4
61
3
60
2
59
1
58
51
52
53

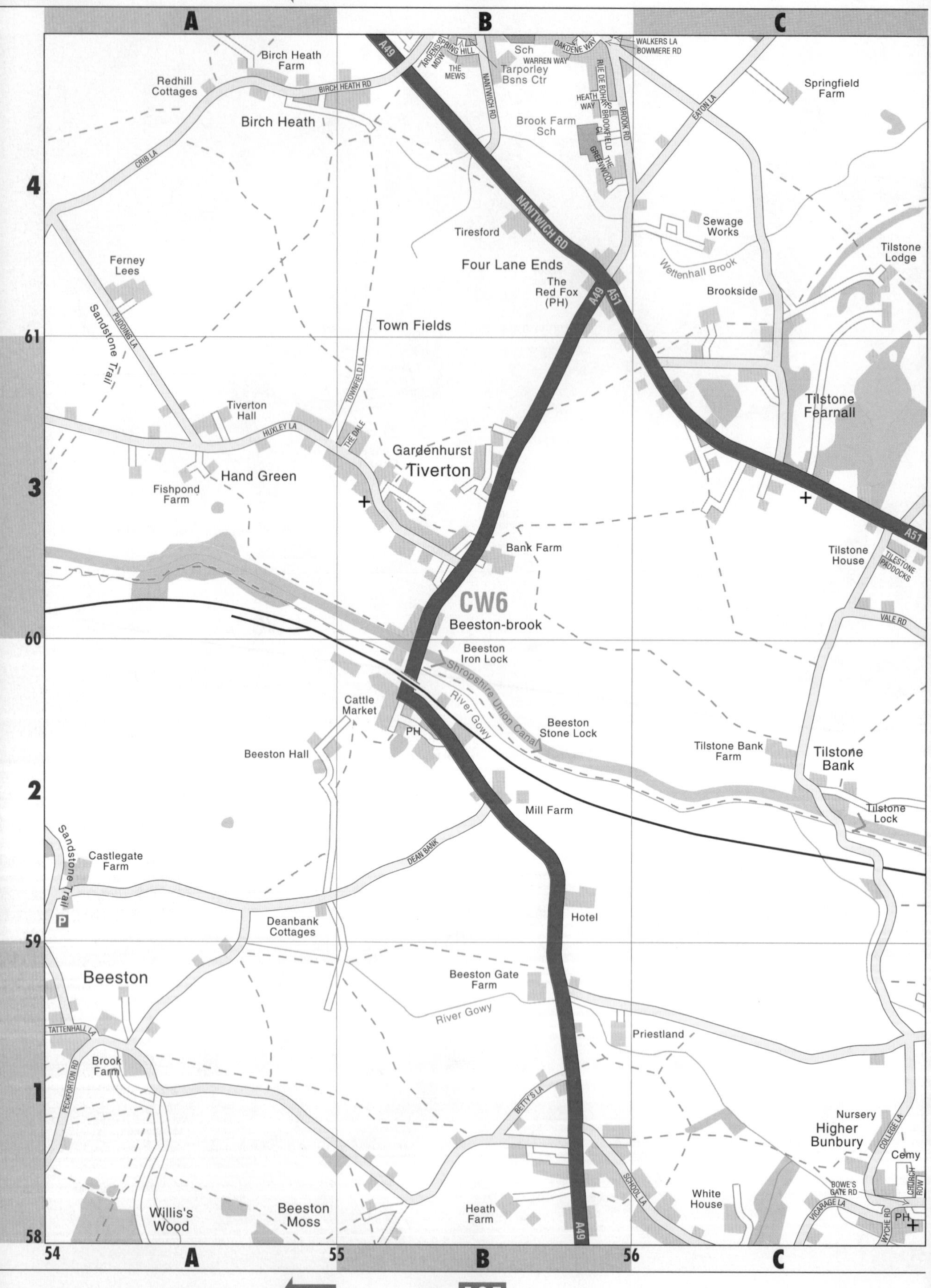
A
B
C
Birch Heath Farm
Redhill Cottages
BIRCH HEATH RD
Birch Heath
CRIB LA
Sch
Tarporley Bsns Ctr
WARREN WAY
OAKDENE WAY
WALKERS LA
BOWMERE RD
SPRING HILL
THE MEWS
NANTWICH RD
Brook Farm Sch
HEATH WAY
BROOK RD
EATON LA
Springfield Farm
A49
NANTWICH RD
Tiresford
Four Lane Ends
The Red Fox (PH)
A51
Sewage Works
Wettenhall Brook
Brookside
Tilstone Lodge
Ferney Lees
PUDDING LA
Sandstone Trail
Town Fields
TOWNFIELD LA
Tiverton Hall
HUXLEY LA
THE DALE
Gardenhurst
Tiverton
Hand Green
Fishpond Farm
Tilstone Fearnall
Bank Farm
Tilstone House
TILESTONE PADDOCKS
CW6
Beeston-brook
VALE RD
Beeston Iron Lock
Shropshire Union Canal
River Gowy
Cattle Market
PH
Beeston Stone Lock
Beeston Hall
Tilstone Bank Farm
Tilstone Bank
Mill Farm
Tilstone Lock
Castlegate Farm
DEAN BANK
Hotel
Deanbank Cottages
P
Beeston
Beeston Gate Farm
River Gowy
Priestland
TATTENHALL LA
Brook Farm
PECKFORTON RD
BETTY'S LA
Nursery
Higher Bunbury
COLLEGE LA
Cemy
SCHOOL LA
White House
BOWE'S GATE RD
CHURCH ROW
VICARAGE LA
WYCHE RD
PH
Willis's Wood
Beeston Moss
Heath Farm
4
61
3
60
2
59
1
58
54
55
56

147
170

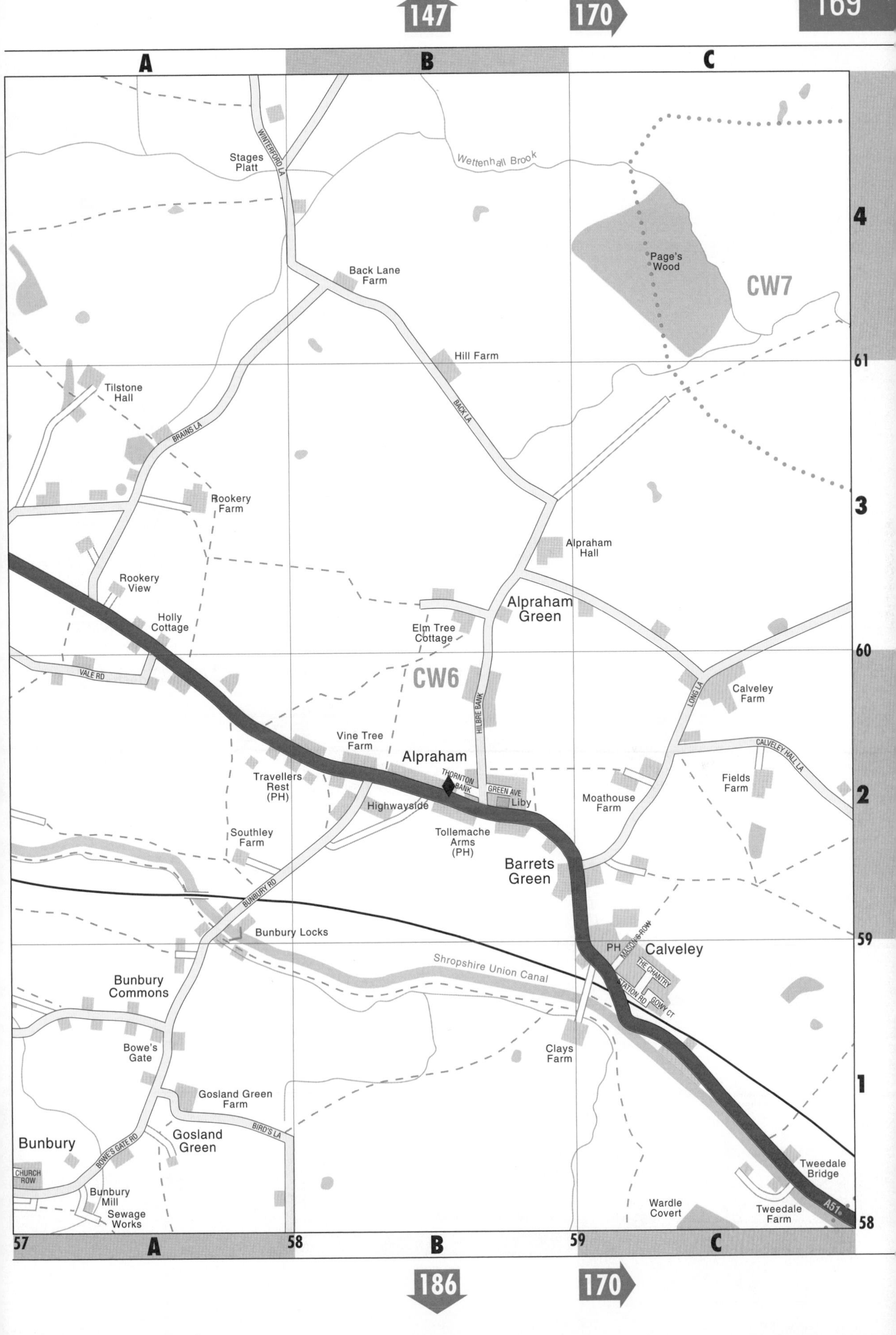
A
B
C
Stages Platt
WINTERFORD LA
Wettenhall Brook
Page's Wood
CW7
Back Lane Farm
Hill Farm
Tilstone Hall
BRAINS LA
BACK LA
Rookery Farm
Alpraham Hall
Rookery View
Holly Cottage
Alpraham Green
Elm Tree Cottage
VALE RD
CW6
HILBRE BANK
LONG LA
Calveley Farm
CALVELEY HALL LA
Vine Tree Farm
Alpraham
Travellers Rest (PH)
THORNTON BANK
GREEN AVE
Liby
Highwayside
Moathouse Farm
Fields Farm
Tollemache Arms (PH)
Southley Farm
Barrets Green
BUNBURY RD
Bunbury Locks
PH
MASONS ROW
Calveley
THE CHANTRY
Shropshire Union Canal
STATION RD
GOWY CT
Bunbury Commons
Bowe's Gate
Clays Farm
Gosland Green Farm
BIRD'S LA
Gosland Green
Bunbury
BOWE'S GATE RD
CHURCH ROW
Bunbury Mill
Sewage Works
Wardle Covert
Tweedale Bridge
Tweedale Farm
A51
4
61
3
60
2
59
1
58
57
58
59

186
170

A **B** **C**

CW6

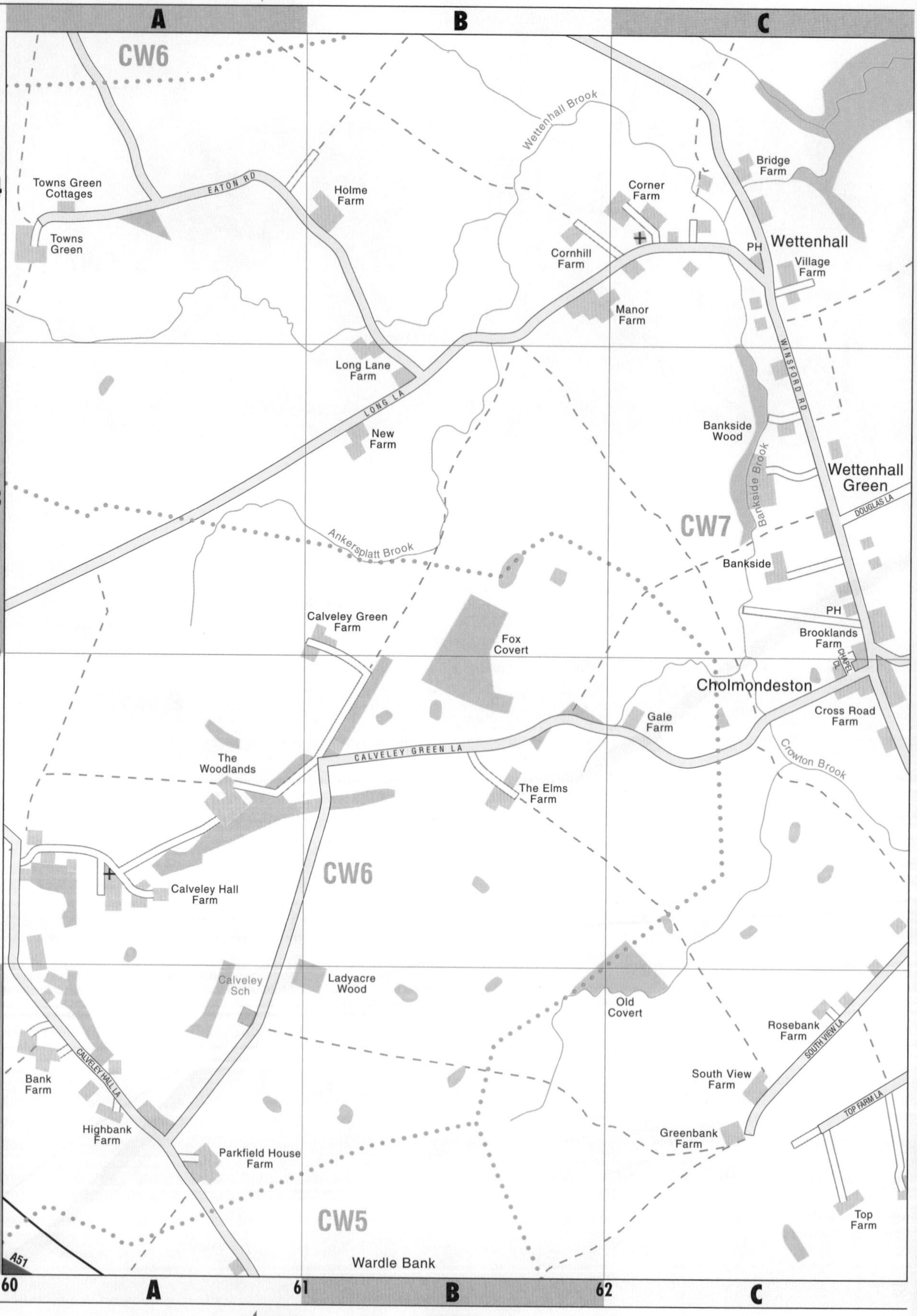

Towns Green Cottages

Towns Green

EATON RD

Holme Farm

Wettenhall Brook

Corner Farm

Bridge Farm

PH Wettenhall

Cornhill Farm

Village Farm

Manor Farm

4

61

Long Lane Farm

LONG LA

New Farm

Bankside Wood

WINSFORD RD

Bankside Brook

Wettenhall Green

DOUGLAS LA

3

Ankersplatt Brook

CW7

Bankside

Calveley Green Farm

Fox Covert

PH

Brooklands Farm

CHAPEL

60

Cholmondeston

Gale Farm

Cross Road Farm

The Woodlands

CALVELEY GREEN LA

The Elms Farm

Crowton Brook

2

CW6

Calveley Hall Farm

59

Calveley Sch

Ladyacre Wood

Old Covert

Rosebank Farm

SOUTH VIEW LA

Bank Farm

CALVELEY HALL LA

South View Farm

1

Highbank Farm

Parkfield House Farm

Greenbank Farm

TOP FARM LA

Top Farm

A51

CW5

Wardle Bank

58

60 **A** **61** **B** **62** **C**

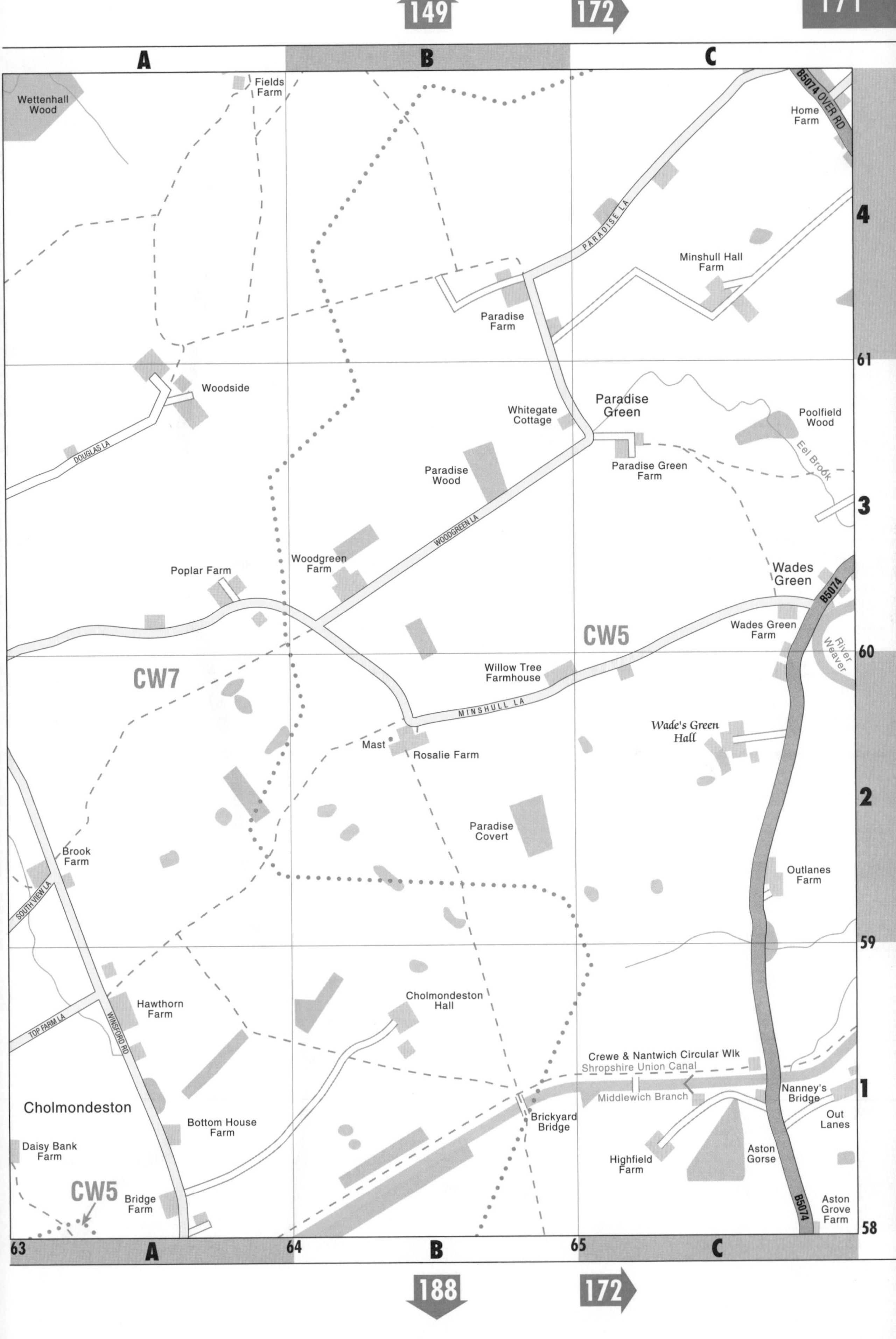

A   B   C

Wettenhall Wood

Fields Farm

B5074 OVER RD

Home Farm

PARADISE LA

4

Minshull Hall Farm

Paradise Farm

61

Woodside

DOUGLAS LA

Whitegate Cottage

Paradise Green

Poolfield Wood

Eel Brook

Paradise Wood

Paradise Green Farm

3

Poplar Farm

Woodgreen Farm

WOODGREEN LA

Wades Green

B5074

River Weaver

CW5

Wades Green Farm

60

Willow Tree Farmhouse

MINSHULL LA

CW7

Mast   Rosalie Farm

Wade's Green Hall

2

Paradise Covert

Outlanes Farm

Brook Farm

SOUTH VIEW LA

59

Cholmondeston Hall

Hawthorn Farm

TOP FARM LA   WINSFORD RD

Crewe & Nantwich Circular Wlk
Shropshire Union Canal

Nanney's Bridge

1

Middlewich Branch

Out Lanes

Cholmondeston

Bottom House Farm

Brickyard Bridge

Highfield Farm

Aston Gorse

Daisy Bank Farm

CW5

Bridge Farm

B5074

Aston Grove Farm

58

63   A   64   B   65   C

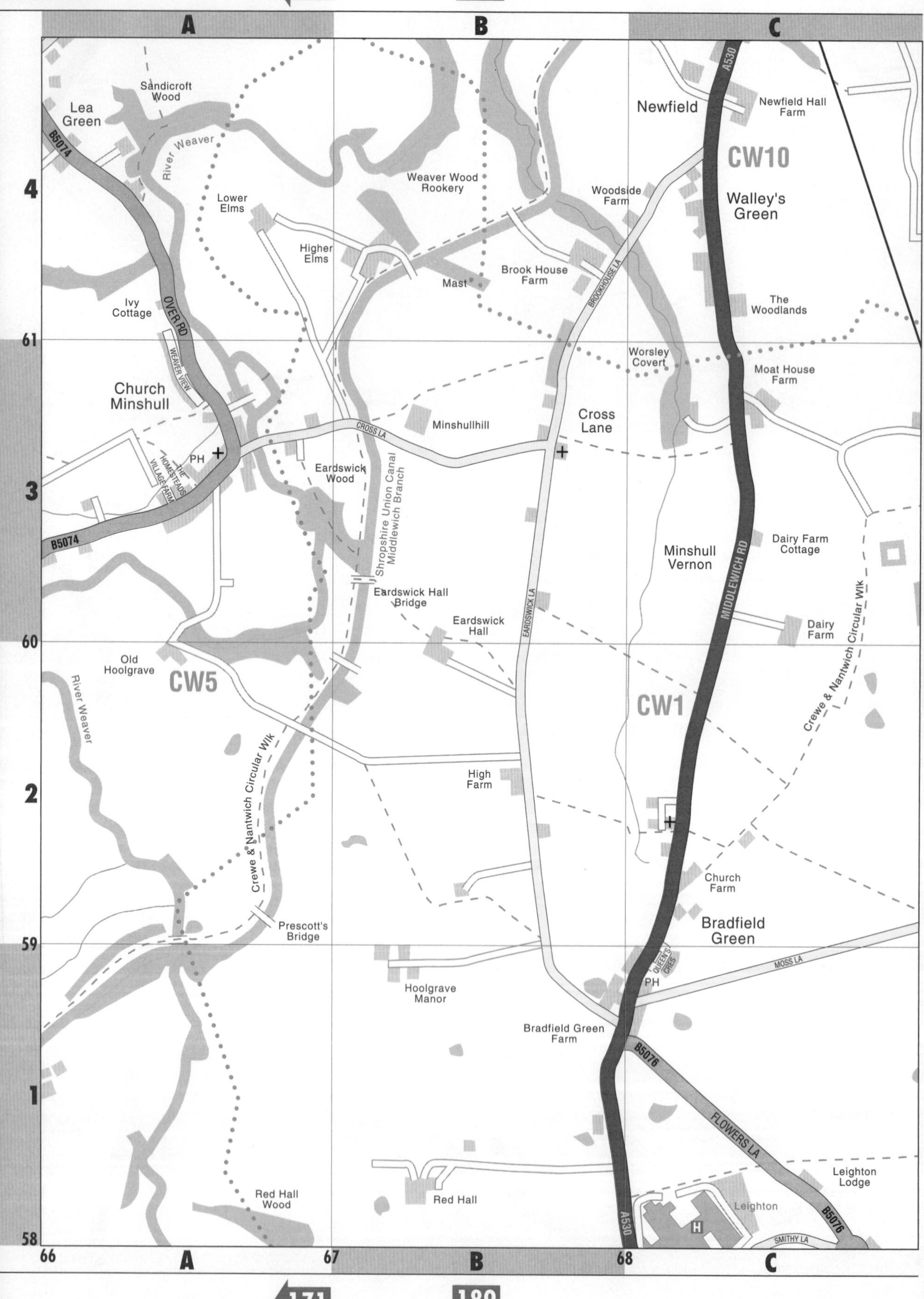

A B C

Lea
Green
Sandicroft
Wood
River Weaver
Lower
Elms
Higher
Elms
Mast
Weaver Wood
Rookery
Brook House
Farm
Woodside
Farm
Newfield
Newfield Hall
Farm
CW10
Walley's
Green
The
Woodlands
Ivy
Cottage
OVER RD
WEAVER VIEW
B5074
61
Church
Minshull
THE HOMESTEAD
VILLAGE FARM
PH
CROSS LA
Eardswick
Wood
Minshullhill
Cross
Lane
Worsley
Covert
Moat House
Farm
BROADHOUSE LA
3
B5074
Shropshire Union Canal
Middlewich Branch
Eardswick Hall
Bridge
Eardswick
Hall
EARDSWICK LA
Minshull
Vernon
MIDDLEWICH RD
Dairy Farm
Cottage
Dairy
Farm
Crewe & Nantwich Circular Wlk
60
Old
Hoolgrave
CW5
River Weaver
Crewe & Nantwich Circular Wlk
High
Farm
CW1
2
Church
Farm
59
Prescott's
Bridge
Hoolgrave
Manor
Bradfield
Green
QUEEN'S CRES
PH
MOSS LA
1
Bradfield Green
Farm
B5076
FLOWERS LA
Leighton
Lodge
Red Hall
Wood
Red Hall
A530
Leighton
H
B5076
58
SMITHY LA
66 A 67 B 68 C

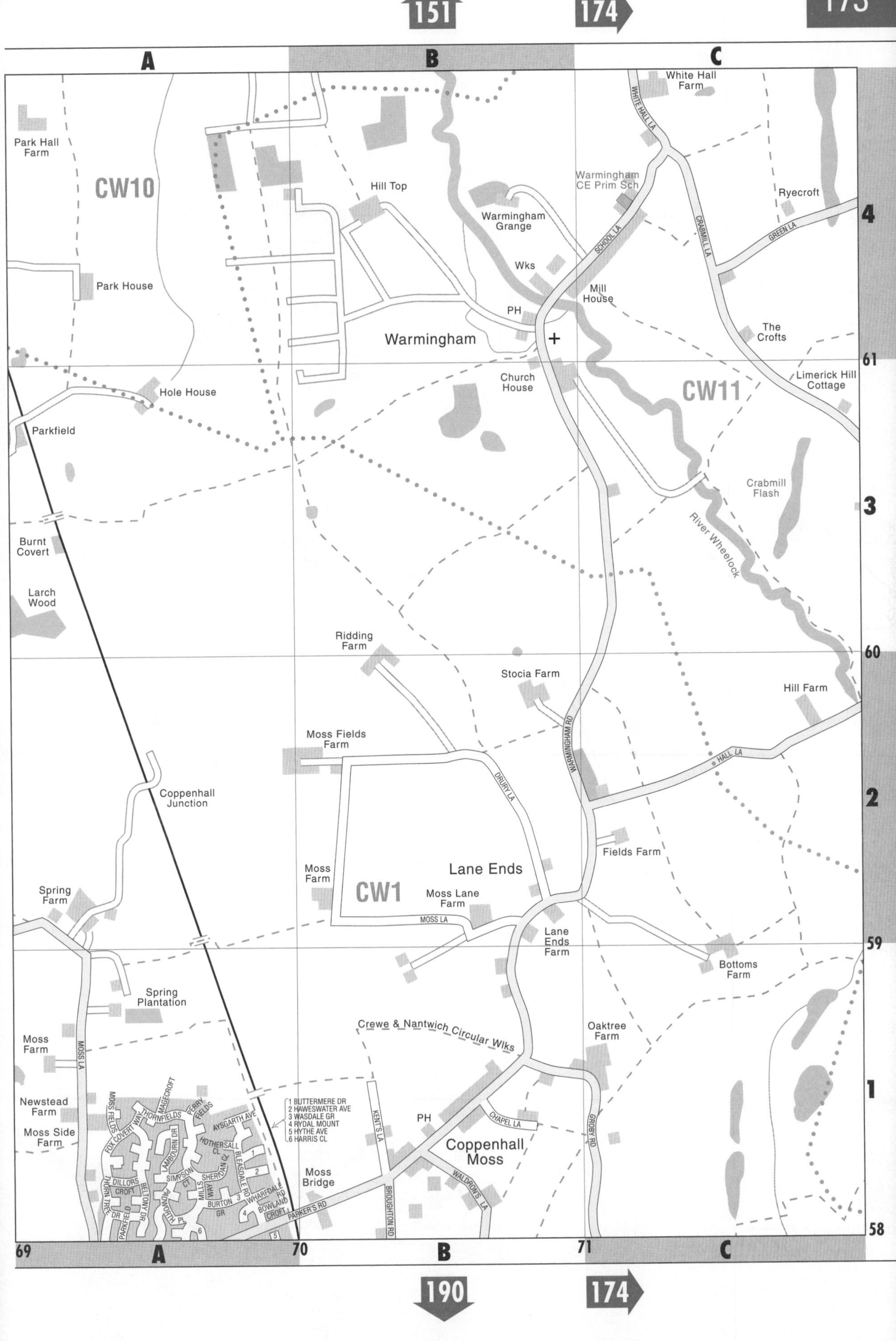

A   B   C

Park Hall Farm

CW10

Park House

Hole House

Parkfield

Burnt Covert

Larch Wood

Hill Top

Warmingham Grange

Wks

PH

Warmingham

Church House

Ridding Farm

Moss Fields Farm

Coppenhall Junction

Moss Farm

CW1

Moss Lane Farm

MOSS LA

Lane Ends

Spring Farm

Spring Plantation

Moss Farm

Newstead Farm

Moss Side Farm

Crewe & Nantwich Circular Wlks

1 BUTTERMERE DR
2 HAWESWATER AVE
3 WASDALE GR
4 RYDAL MOUNT
5 HYTHE AVE
6 HARRIS CL

Moss Bridge

PH

Coppenhall Moss

White Hall Farm

Warmingham CE Prim Sch

Mill House

Ryecroft

The Crofts

Limerick Hill Cottage

CW11

Crabmill Flash

River Wheelock

Hill Farm

Stocia Farm

HALL LA

Fields Farm

Lane Ends Farm

Bottoms Farm

Oaktree Farm

WARMINGHAM RD

DRURY LA

WHITE HALL LA

SCHOOL LA

CRABMILL LA

GREEN LA

4

61

3

60

2

59

1

58

KENT'S LA

CHAPEL LA

GRIBY RD

BROUGHTON RD

WALDRONS LA

PARKER'S RD

MOSS LA

FOX COVERT WALK
HORNFIELDS
MAGSCROFT
FERRY FIELDS
AYSGARTH AVE
HOTHERSALL CL
LAMBOURN DR
SIMYSON ST
SHERIDAN CL
BURTON GR
BLEASDALE RD
WHARFDALE
BOWLAND CROFT
PARKFIELD
DILLORS CROFT
THORN TREE DR
BELMONT WAY
FITHDALE RD
RINDONDT

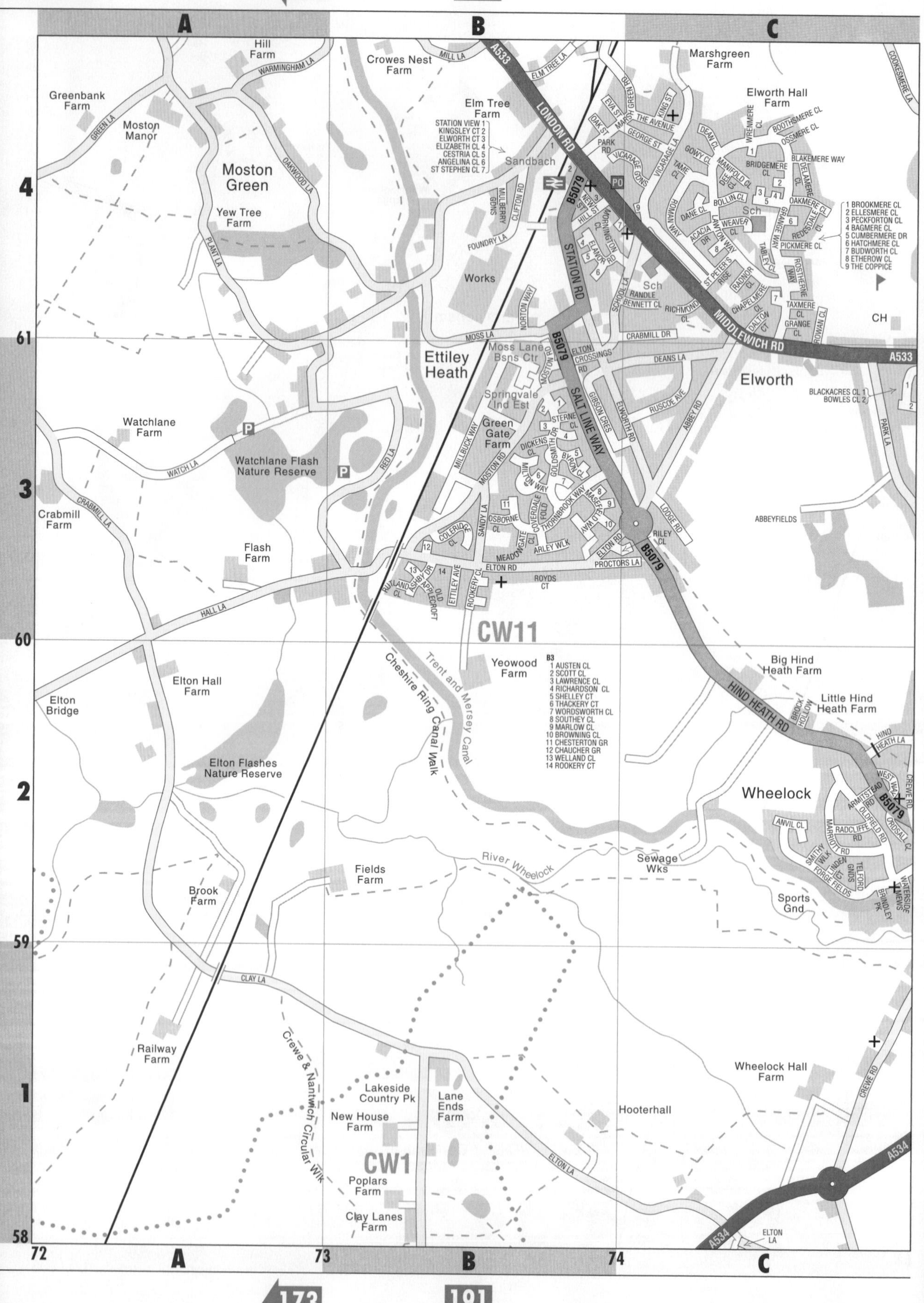

A B C

4

Greenbank Farm

Hill Farm

Moston Manor

Moston Green

Yew Tree Farm

Crowes Nest Farm

Elm Tree Farm

STATION VIEW 1
KINGSLEY CT 2
ELWORTH CT 3
ELIZABETH CL 4
CESTRIA CL 5
ANGELINA CL 6
ST STEPHEN CL 7

Sandbach

Works

Marshgreen Farm

Elworth Hall Farm

1 BROOKMERE CL
2 ELLESMERE CL
3 PECKFORTON CL
4 BAGMERE CL
5 CUMBERMERE DR
6 HATCHMERE CL
7 BUDWORTH CL
8 ETHEROW CL
9 THE COPPICE

Sch

CH

61

Ettiley Heath

Moss Lane Bsns Ctr

Springvale Ind Est

Green Gate Farm

Elworth

BLACKACRES CL 1
BOWLES CL 2

3

Watchlane Farm

Watchlane Flash Nature Reserve

Crabmill Farm

Flash Farm

ABBEYFIELDS

CW11

60

Elton Hall Farm

Elton Bridge

Elton Flashes Nature Reserve

Yeowood Farm

B3
1 AUSTEN CL
2 SCOTT CL
3 LAWRENCE CL
4 RICHARDSON CL
5 SHELLEY CT
6 THACKERY CT
7 WORDSWORTH CL
8 SOUTHEY CL
9 MARLOW CL
10 BROWNING CL
11 CHESTERTON GR
12 CHAUCER GR
13 WELLAND CL
14 ROOKERY CT

Big Hind Heath Farm

Little Hind Heath Farm

HIND HEATH RD

Wheelock

2

Brook Farm

Fields Farm

River Wheelock

Sewage Wks

Sports Gnd

Wheelock Hall Farm

59

Clay La

Railway Farm

1

Lakeside Country Pk

New House Farm

Lane Ends Farm

Hooterhall

CW1

Poplars Farm

Clay Lanes Farm

58

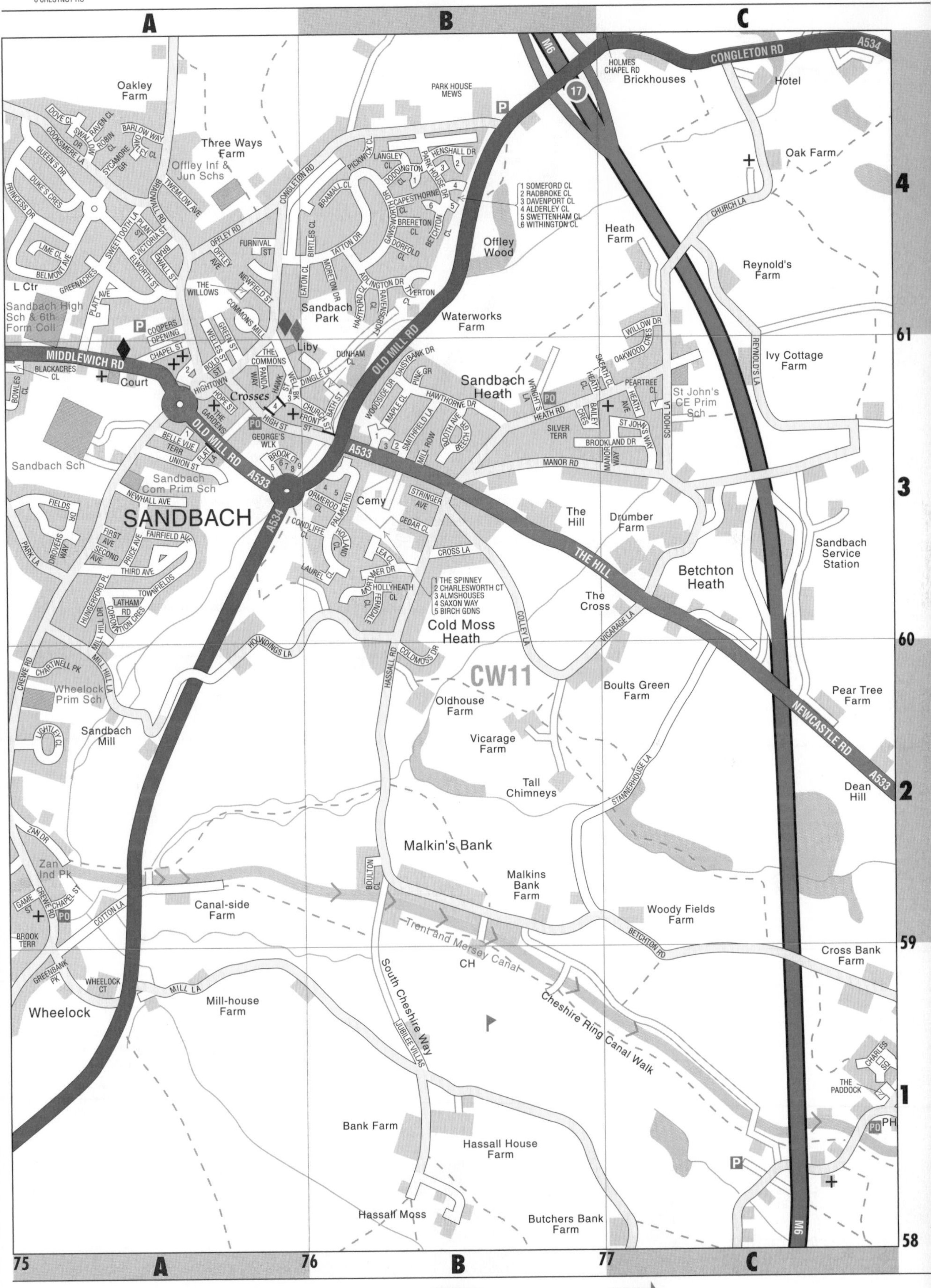

A3
1 CECIL RIGBY CL
2 WESLEY AVE
3 CROWN BANK
4 MARKET SQ
5 BROOKHOUSE RD
6 CHESTNUT HO
7 OAK HO
8 ASH HO
9 ELM HO

153
176
192
176

A B C

4 61 3 60 2 59 1 58

1 SOMEFORD CL
2 RADBROKE CL
3 DAVENPORT CL
4 ALDERLEY CL
5 SWETTENHAM CL
6 WITHINGTON CL

1 THE SPINNEY
2 CHARLESWORTH CT
3 ALMSHOUSES
4 SAXON WAY
5 BIRCH GDNS

Oakley Farm
Three Ways Farm
Offley Inf & Jun Schs
Park House Mews
Holmes Chapel Rd
Brickhouses
Hotel
Oak Farm
Heath Farm
Reynold's Farm
Offley Wood
Ivy Cottage Farm
Waterworks Farm
St John's CE Prim Sch
Sandbach Heath
Liby
Sandbach Park
Sandbach Mill
L Ctr
Sandbach High Sch & 6th Form Coll
Court
Crosses
The Gardens
SANDBACH
Sandbach Sch
Sandbach Com Prim Sch
Cemy
The Hill
Drumber Farm
The Cross
Betchton Heath
Sandbach Service Station
Cold Moss Heath
Pear Tree Farm
Dean Hill
CW11
Oldhouse Farm
Boults Green Farm
Vicarage Farm
Tall Chimneys
Wheelock Prim Sch
Malkin's Bank
Malkins Bank Farm
Woody Fields Farm
Cross Bank Farm
Zan Ind Pk
Canal-side Farm
Trent and Mersey Canal
CH
Cheshire Ring Canal Walk
THE PADDOCK
Wheelock
Mill-house Farm
South Cheshire Way
Bank Farm
Hassall House Farm
Hassall Moss
Butchers Bank Farm

MIDDLEWICH RD
OLD MILL RD
CONGLETON RD
A534
CHURCH LA
NEWCASTLE RD
A533
THE HILL
M6

75 76 77

175
154

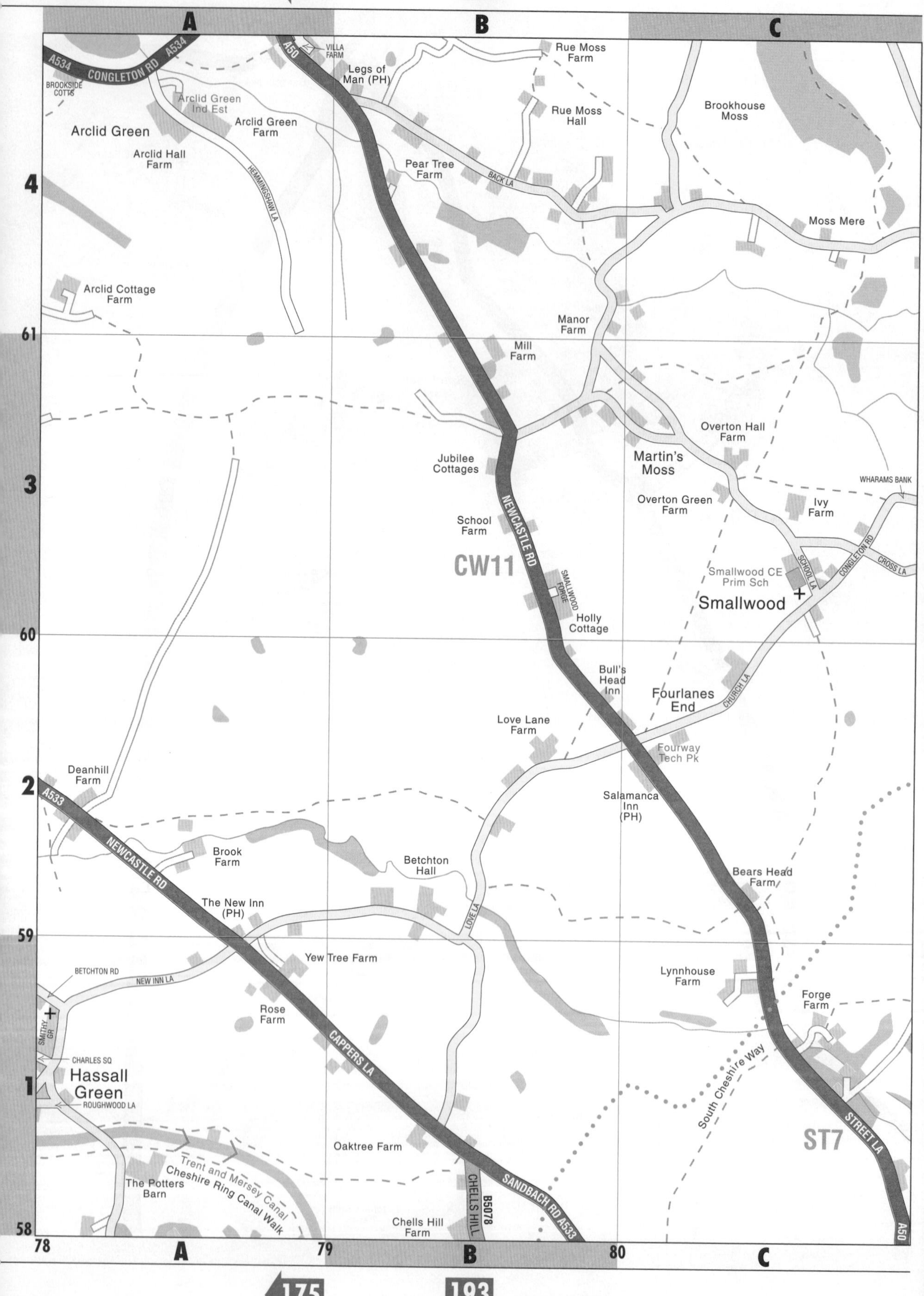
A
B
C
A534 CONGLETON RD A534
BROOKSIDE COTTS
A50
VILLA FARM
Legs of Man (PH)
Rue Moss Farm
Arclid Green Ind Est
Arclid Green
Arclid Green Farm
Rue Moss Hall
Brookhouse Moss
Arclid Hall Farm
HEMMINGSHAW LA
Pear Tree Farm
BACK LA
Moss Mere
Arclid Cottage Farm
Manor Farm
Mill Farm
Overton Hall Farm
Jubilee Cottages
Martin's Moss
WHARAMS BANK
Overton Green Farm
Ivy Farm
NEWCASTLE RD
School Farm
CW11
SMALLWOOD FORGE
Smallwood CE Prim Sch
SCHOOL LA
CONGLETON RD
CROSS LA
Smallwood
Holly Cottage
Bull's Head Inn
Fourlanes End
CHURCH LA
Love Lane Farm
Fourway Tech Pk
Deanhill Farm
A533
Salamanca Inn (PH)
NEWCASTLE RD
Brook Farm
Betchton Hall
Bears Head Farm
The New Inn (PH)
LOVE LA
Yew Tree Farm
BETCHTON RD
NEW INN LA
Lynnhouse Farm
Forge Farm
Rose Farm
SMITHY GR
CAPPERS LA
CHARLES SQ
Hassall Green
ROUGHWOOD LA
South Cheshire Way
STREET LA
ST7
Oaktree Farm
Trent and Mersey Canal
Cheshire Ring Canal Walk
The Potters Barn
CHELLS HILL
B5078
SANDBACH RD A533
Chells Hill Farm
A50
4
61
3
60
2
59
1
58
78
79
80

175
193

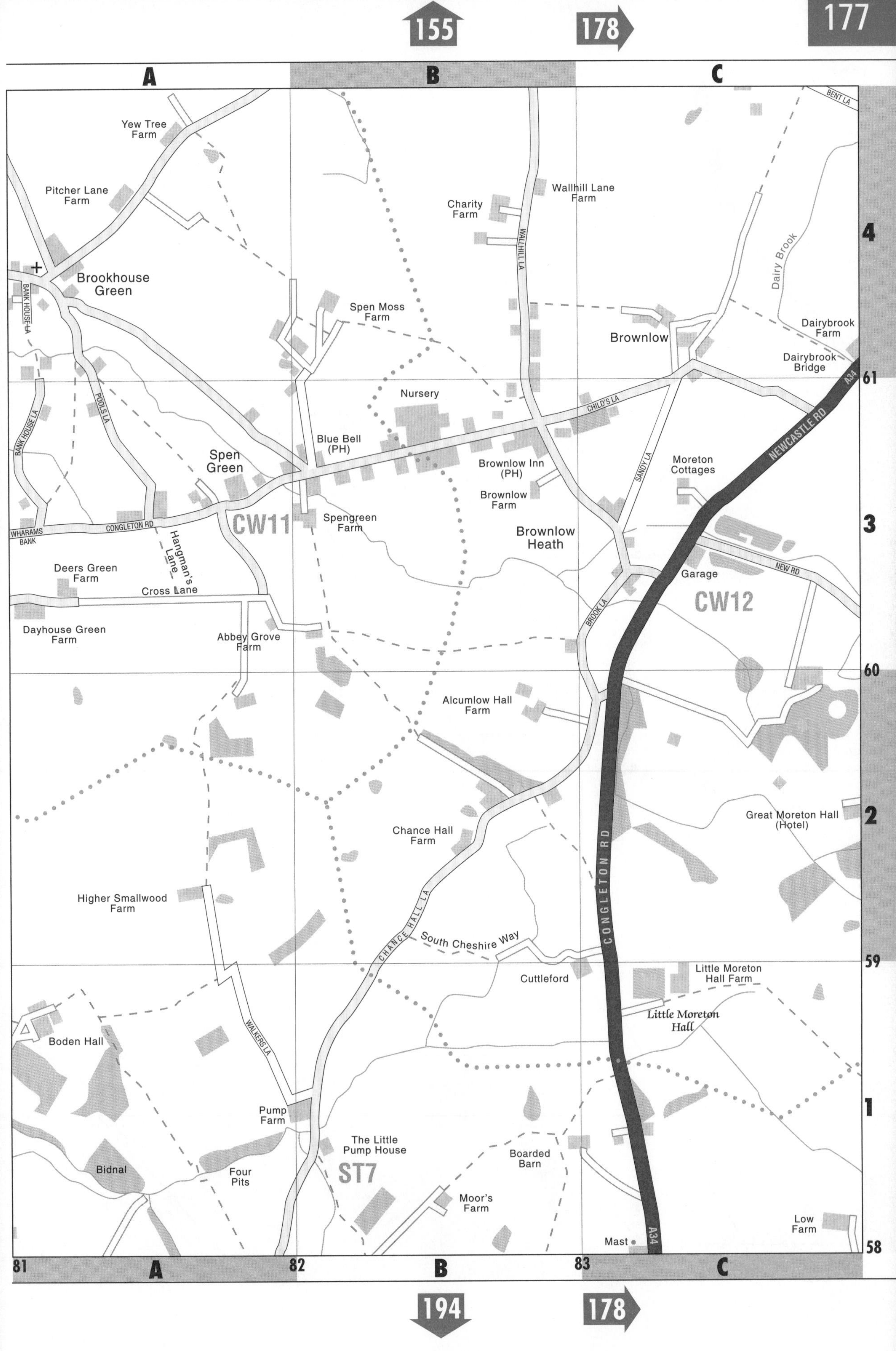

A
B
C

4

Yew Tree Farm

Pitcher Lane Farm

Wallhill Lane Farm

Charity Farm

WALLHILL LA

BENT LA

Brookhouse Green

Spen Moss Farm

Brownlow

Dairybrook Farm

Dairy Brook

BANK HOUSE LA

Dairybrook Bridge

61

A34

POOL'S LA

Nursery

CHILD'S LA

NEWCASTLE RD

Blue Bell (PH)

Spen Green

Brownlow Inn (PH)

Moreton Cottages

SANDY LA

3

BANK HOUSE LA

CW11

Spengreen Farm

Brownlow Farm

Brownlow Heath

NEW RD

CONGLETON RD

WHARAMS BANK

Hangman's Lane

Garage

CW12

Deers Green Farm

Cross Lane

BROOK LA

Dayhouse Green Farm

Abbey Grove Farm

60

Alcumlow Hall Farm

Great Moreton Hall (Hotel)

2

Higher Smallwood Farm

Chance Hall Farm

CONGLETON RD

CHANCE HALL LA

South Cheshire Way

Little Moreton Hall Farm

59

Cuttleford

Little Moreton Hall

Boden Hall

WALKERS LA

Pump Farm

1

Bidnal

Four Pits

The Little Pump House

ST7

Boarded Barn

Moor's Farm

Low Farm

Mast

A34

58

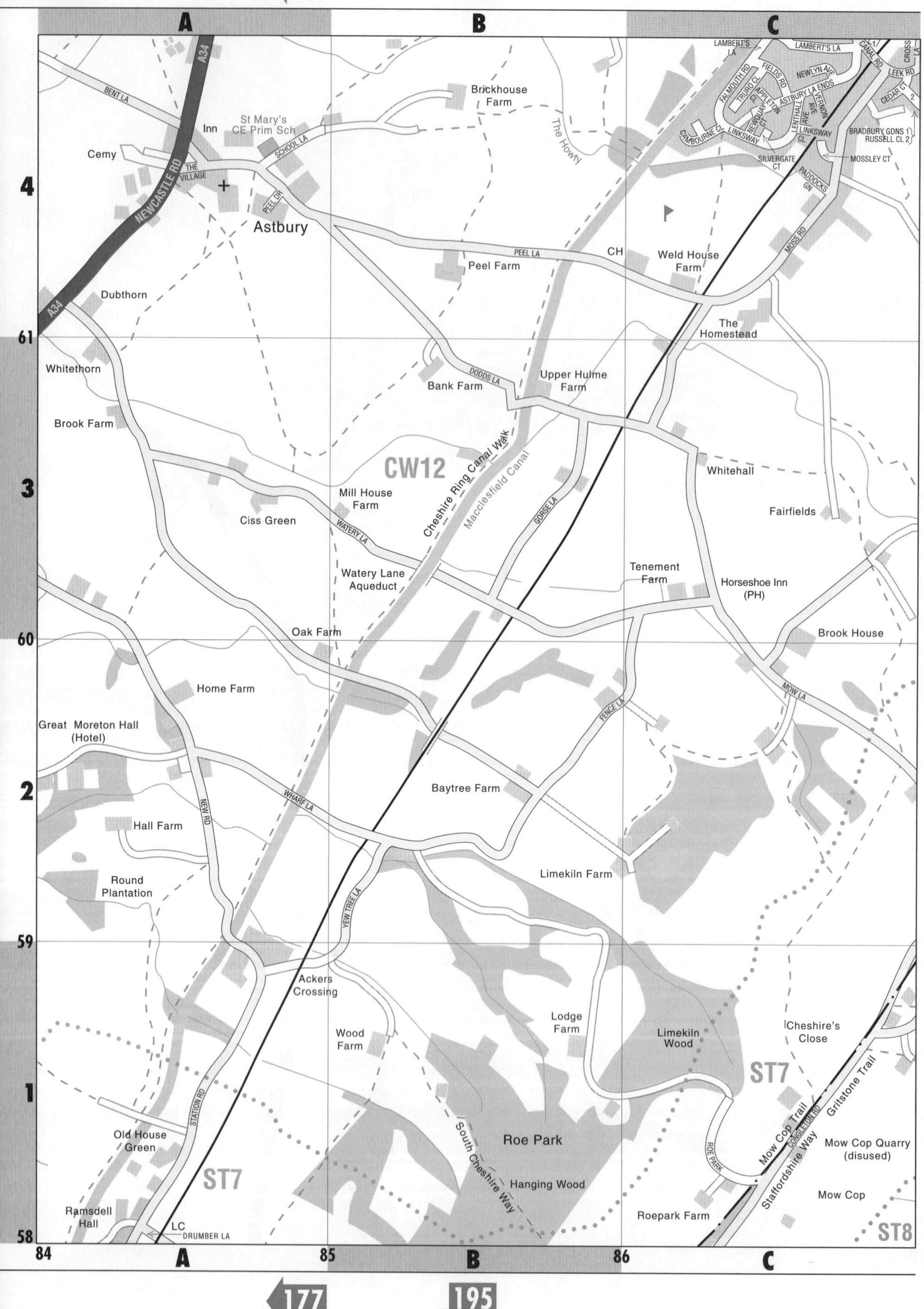

A   B   C

A   B   C

4

61

3

60

2

59

1

58

84   85   86

A34

BENT LA

St Mary's
CE Prim Sch

Inn

SCHOOL LA

Cemy

THE VILLAGE

NEWCASTLE RD

PEEL DR

Astbury

Dubthorn

Whitethorn

Brook Farm

Home Farm

Great Moreton Hall
(Hotel)

Hall Farm

Round
Plantation

NEW RD

STATION RD

WHARF LA

YEW TREE LA

Old House
Green

ST7

Ramsdell
Hall

LC
DRUMBER LA

Ackers
Crossing

Wood
Farm

Oak Farm

WATERY LA

Ciss Green

Mill House
Farm

Watery Lane
Aqueduct

CW12

Cheshire Ring Canal Walk

Macclesfield Canal

Bank Farm

Brickhouse
Farm

The Howty

Peel Farm

PEEL LA

DODDS LA

Upper Hulme
Farm

Baytree Farm

FENCE LA

Limekiln Farm

Lodge
Farm

Roe Park

South Cheshire Way

Hanging Wood

CH

Weld House
Farm

MOSS RD

The Homestead

Whitehall

Fairfields

Tenement
Farm

Horseshoe Inn
(PH)

Brook House

MOW LA

Limekiln
Wood

Cheshire's
Close

ST7

Roepark Farm

ROE PARK

Mow Cop Trail

CONGLETON RD

Staffordshire Way

Gritstone Trail

Mow Cop Quarry
(disused)

Mow Cop

ST8

LAMBERT'S
LA

LAMBERT'S LA

CANAL RD

LEEK RD

CROSS LA

FALMOUTH RD

TRURO CL

FIELDS RD

NEWLYN AVE

ASTBURY LANE ENDS

CAMBOURNE CL

LINKSWAY

NEWQUAY CT

APPLETON CL

LENTHALL AVE

VERNON AVE

CEDAR CT

BRADBURY GDNS 1
RUSSELL CL 2

MOSSLEY CT

SILVERGATE
CT

PADDOCKS
GN

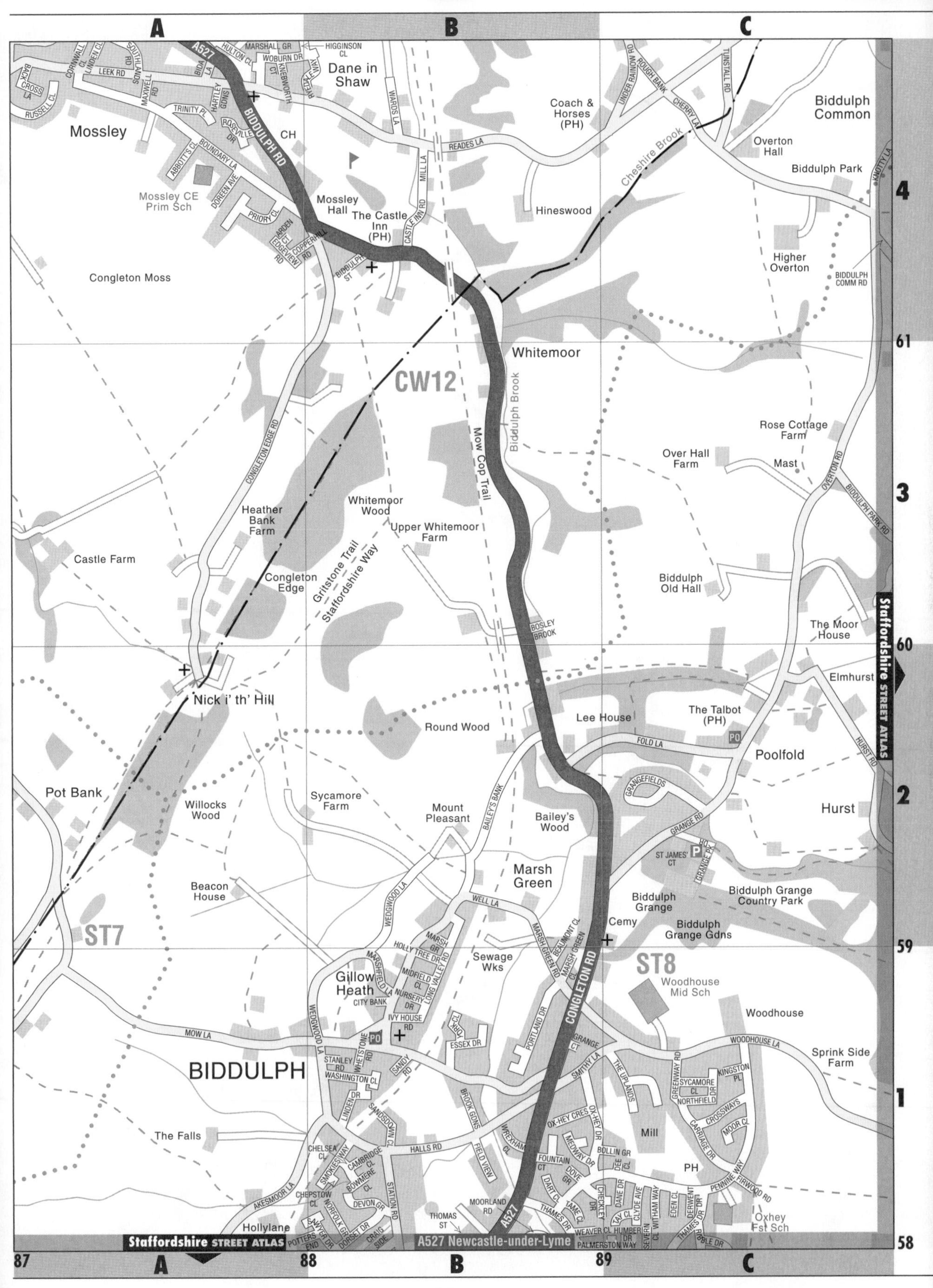
A
B
C
Mossley
Dane in Shaw
Coach & Horses (PH)
Biddulph Common
Overton Hall
Biddulph Park
Mossley CE Prim Sch
Mossley Hall
The Castle Inn (PH)
Hineswood
Cheshire Brook
Higher Overton
Congleton Moss
Whitemoor
CW12
Biddulph Brook
Mow Cop Trail
Rose Cottage Farm
Over Hall Farm
Mast
Heather Bank Farm
Whitemoor Wood
Upper Whitemoor Farm
Castle Farm
Congleton Edge
Gritstone Trail
Staffordshire Way
Biddulph Old Hall
The Moor House
Nick i' th' Hill
Elmhurst
Lee House
The Talbot (PH)
Round Wood
Poolfold
Pot Bank
Willocks Wood
Sycamore Farm
Mount Pleasant
Bailey's Wood
Hurst
Marsh Green
Biddulph Grange
Biddulph Grange Country Park
Beacon House
Cemy
Biddulph Grange Gdns
ST7
Sewage Wks
ST8
Gillow Heath
Woodhouse Mid Sch
Woodhouse
BIDDULPH
Sprink Side Farm
The Falls
Mill
PH
Hollylane
Oxhey Fst Sch
A527
BIDDULPH RD
CONGLETON RD
CONGLETON EDGE RD
MOW LA
WEDGWOOD LA
HALLS RD
WOODHOUSE LA
GRANGE RD
FOLD LA
OVERTON RD
READES LA
Staffordshire STREET ATLAS
A527 Newcastle-under-Lyme
87
88
89
4
61
3
60
2
59
1
58

163

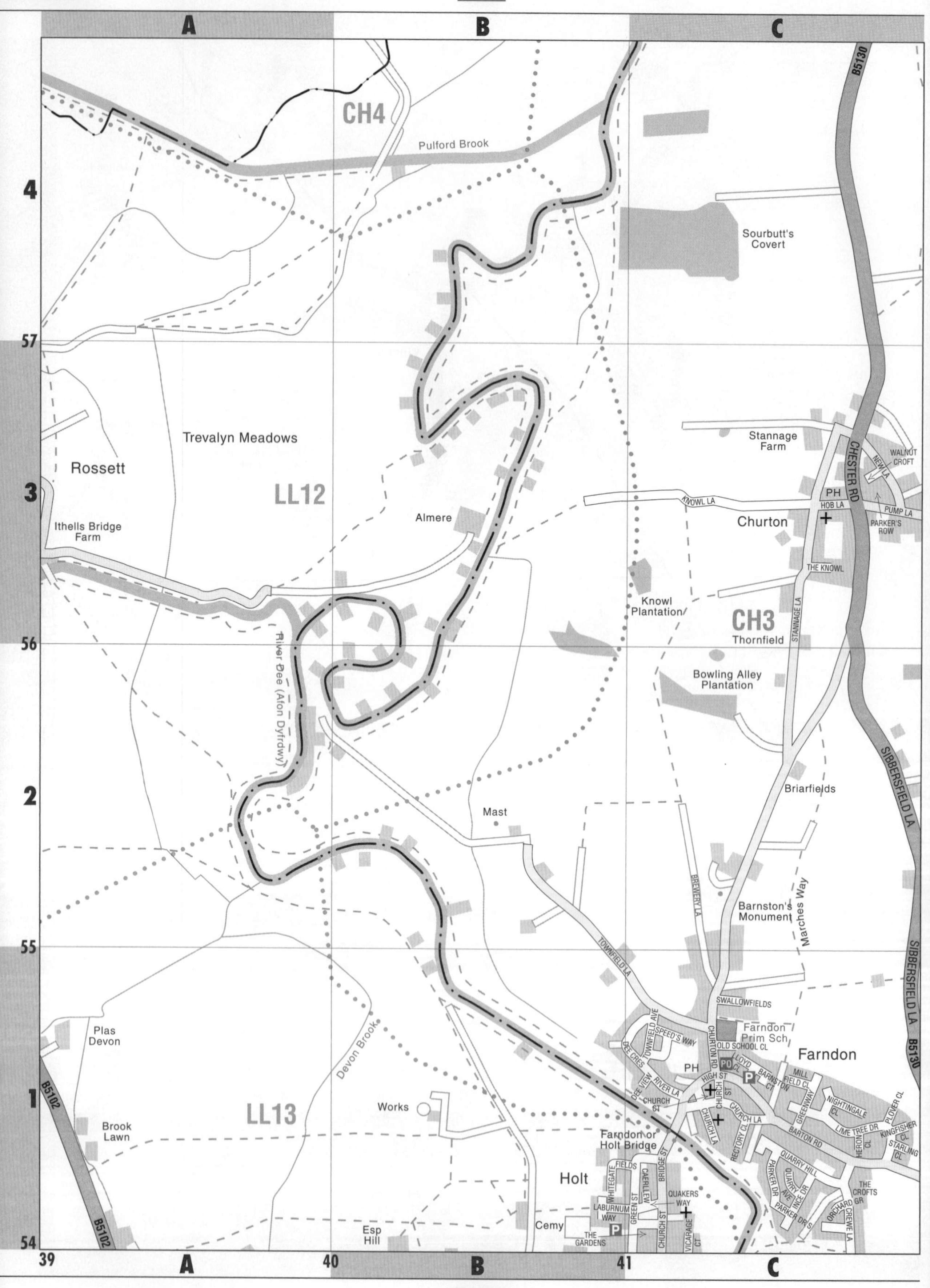

A
B
C
CH4
Pulford Brook
Sourbutt's Covert
B5130
Trevalyn Meadows
Rossett
LL12
Almere
Ithells Bridge Farm
Stannage Farm
CHESTER RD
NEW LA
WALNUT CROFT
KNOWL LA
PH
HOB LA
PUMP LA
Churton
PARKER'S ROW
THE KNOWL
Knowl Plantation
CH3
Thornfield
STANNAGE LA
Bowling Alley Plantation
River Dee (Afon Dyfrdwy)
SIBBERSFIELD LA
Briarfields
Mast
BREWERY LA
Barnston's Monument
Marches Way
TOWNFIELD LA
SWALLOWFIELDS
Farndon Prim Sch
Farndon
Plas Devon
Devon Brook
DOWNFIELD AVE
SPEED'S WAY
DEE CRES
CHURTON RD
OLD SCHOOL CL
PH
PO
LLOYD CL
BARNSTON CT
MILL FIELD CL
HIGH ST
DEE VIEW
RIVER LA
CHURCH CT
CHURCH ST
CHURCH LA
GREENWAY
NIGHTINGALE CL
PLOVER CL
B5102
Works
LL13
Brook Lawn
RECTORY CL
BARTON RD
LIME TREE DR
KINGFISHER CL
HERON CL
STARLING CL
Farndon or Holt Bridge
QUARRY HILL
Holt
WHITEGATE FIELDS
CAERLLEW
BRIDGE ST
PARKER DR
QUARRY AVE
QUINCE DR
PARKER DR S
THE CROFTS
QUAKERS WAY
LABURNUM WAY
GREEN ST
ORCHARD GR
CREWE LA
Esp Hill
Cemy
THE GARDENS
CHURCH ST
VICARAGE CT
4
57
56
3
2
55
1
54
39
40
41

196

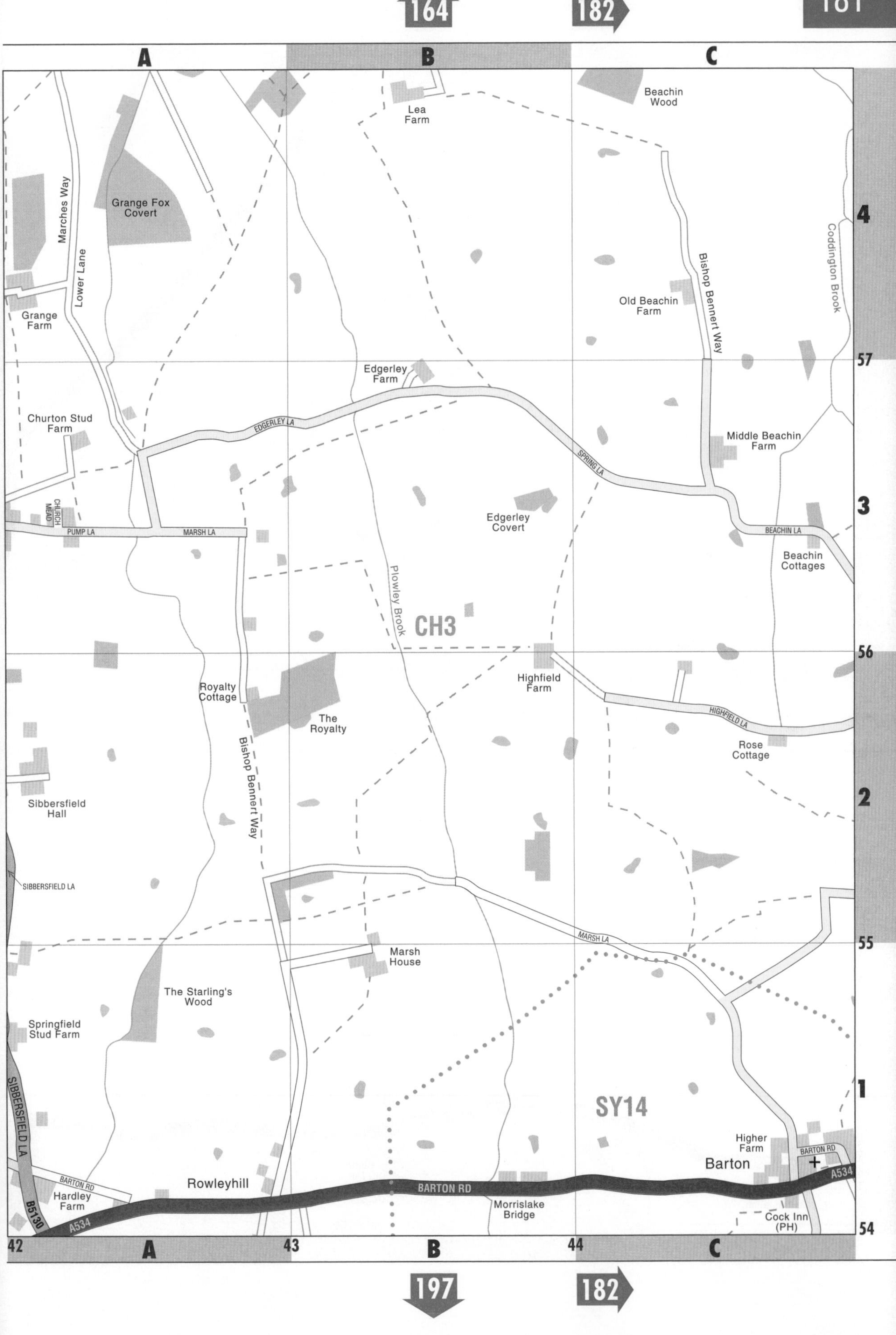

A
B
C

Marches Way

Grange Fox Covert

Lower Lane

Grange Farm

Beachin Wood

4

Bishop Bennert Way

Old Beachin Farm

Coddington Brook

57

Churton Stud Farm

Edgerley Farm

EDGERLEY LA

SPRING LA

Middle Beachin Farm

CHURCH MEAD

PUMP LA

MARSH LA

Edgerley Covert

BEACHIN LA

Beachin Cottages

3

Plowley Brook

CH3

Highfield Farm

56

Royalty Cottage

The Royalty

Bishop Bennert Way

HIGHFIELD LA

Rose Cottage

Sibbersfield Hall

2

SIBBERSFIELD LA

Marsh House

MARSH LA

55

The Starling's Wood

Springfield Stud Farm

SIBBERSFIELD LA

SY14

1

Higher Farm

Barton

BARTON RD

A534

Hardley Farm

Rowleyhill

BARTON RD

B5130

A534

Morrislake Bridge

BARTON RD

Cock Inn (PH)

54

181
165

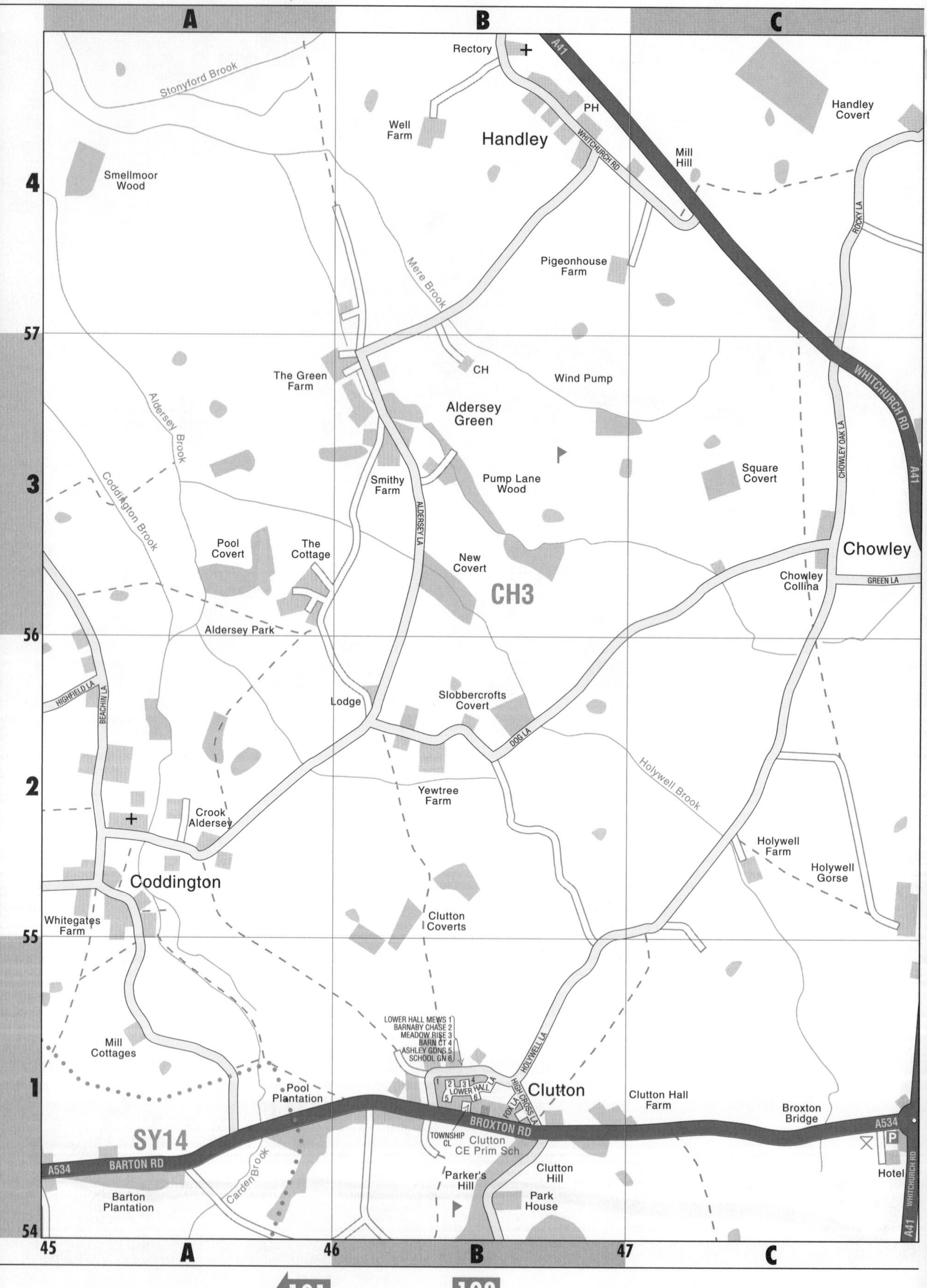
A
B
C
Rectory
A41
Stonyford Brook
Well
Farm
Handley
PH
WHITCHURCH RD
Handley
Covert
Mill
Hill
Smellmoor
Wood
ROCKY LA
Mere Brook
Pigeonhouse
Farm
The Green
Farm
CH
Wind Pump
WHITCHURCH RD
Aldersey Brook
Aldersey
Green
Coddington Brook
Smithy
Farm
Pump Lane
Wood
Square
Covert
CHOWLEY OAK LA
A41
ALDERSEY LA
Pool
Covert
The
Cottage
New
Covert
Chowley
CH3
Chowley
Collina
GREEN LA
Aldersey Park
HIGHFIELD LA
BEACHIN LA
Lodge
Slobbercrofts
Covert
DOG LA
Holywell Brook
Yewtree
Farm
Crook
Aldersey
Holywell
Farm
Holywell
Gorse
Coddington
Whitegates
Farm
Clutton
Coverts
LOWER HALL MEWS 1
BARNABY CHASE 2
MEADOW RISE 3
BARN CT 4
ASHLEY GDNS 5
SCHOOL GN 6
Mill
Cottages
HOLYWELL LA
LOWER HALL
Clutton
HIGH CROSS LA
FOX LA
Clutton Hall
Farm
Pool
Plantation
Broxton
Bridge
BROXTON RD
A534
SY14
TOWNSHIP
CL
Clutton
CE Prim Sch
A534
BARTON RD
Carden Brook
Parker's
Hill
Clutton
Hill
Hotel
WHITCHURCH RD
Barton
Plantation
Park
House
A41
4
57
3
56
2
55
1
54
45
46
47

181
198

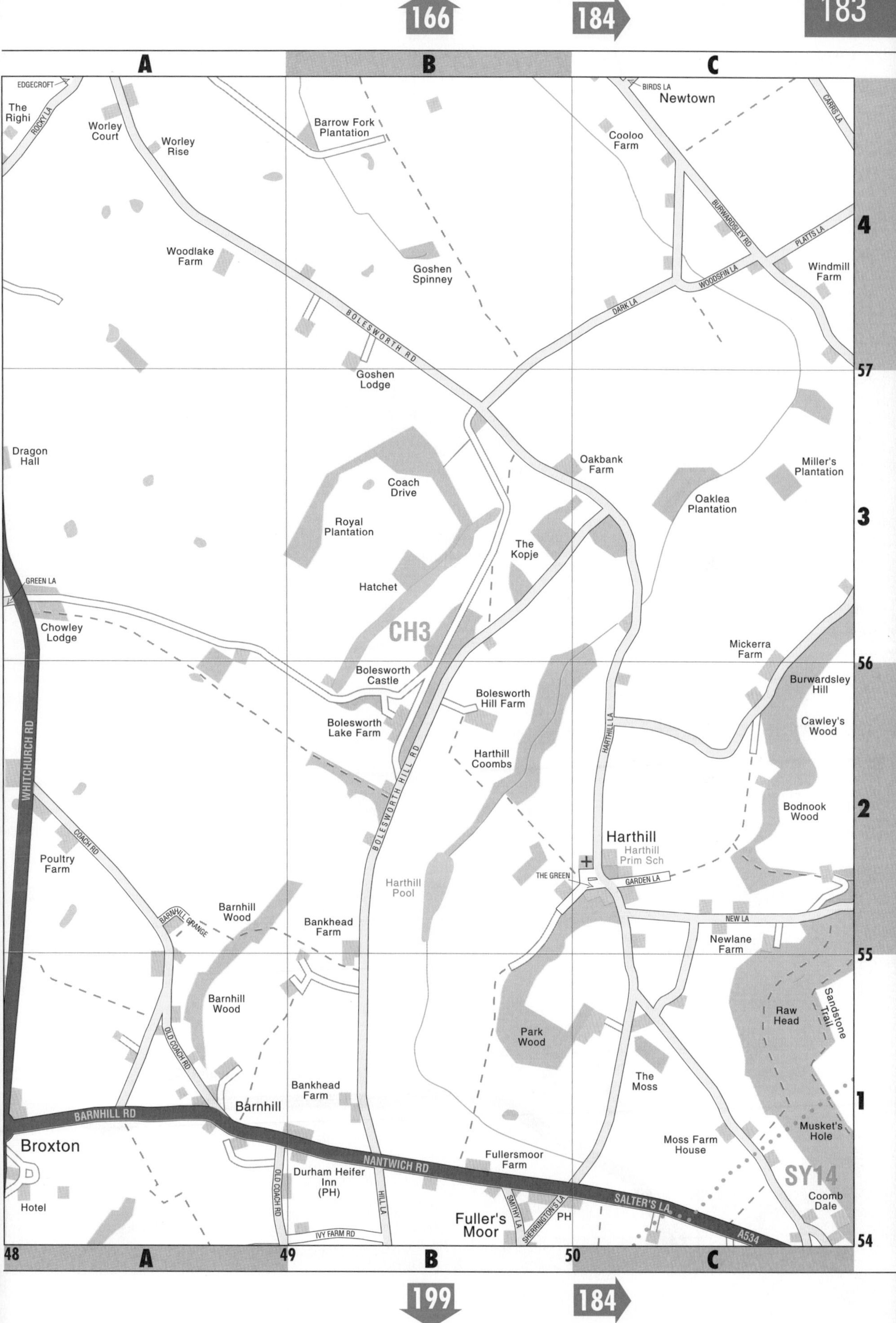

A B C

EDGECROFT
The Righi
ROCK LA
Worley Court
Worley Rise
Woodlake Farm

Barrow Fork Plantation
Goshen Spinney

Newtown
BIRDS LA
CARRS LA
Cooloo Farm
BURWARDSLEY RD
PLATTS LA
Windmill Farm
WOODSFIN LA
DARK LA

4

BOLESWORTH RD
Goshen Lodge

57

Dragon Hall
Coach Drive
Royal Plantation
Hatchet

Oakbank Farm
The Kopje

Oaklea Plantation

Miller's Plantation

3

GREEN LA
Chowley Lodge

CH3

Mickerra Farm

56

Bolesworth Castle
Bolesworth Lake Farm

Bolesworth Hill Farm
Harthill Coombs

Burwardsley Hill
Cawley's Wood

WHITCHURCH RD
COACH RD
Poultry Farm

BOLESWORTH HILL RD
Harthill Pool

HARTHILL LA
Harthill
Harthill Prim Sch
THE GREEN
GARDEN LA

Bodnook Wood

2

BARNHILL GRANGE
Barnhill Wood
Bankhead Farm

NEW LA
Newlane Farm

55

OLD COACH RD
Barnhill Wood

Park Wood

Raw Head
Sandstone Trail

The Moss

1

BARNHILL RD
Barnhill
Bankhead Farm

Musket's Hole

Broxton
Hotel

NANTWICH RD
OLD COACH RD
HILL LA
Durham Heifer Inn (PH)
IVY FARM RD

Fullersmoor Farm

SMITH LA
SHERRINGTON'S LA
Fuller's Moor
PH
SALTER'S LA

Moss Farm House

SY14

A534
Coomb Dale

183
167

A
B
C
The Table Rock
Wood Farm
WOOD BACK LA
Honeyend Farm
CARRS LA
PLATTS LA
Fly Fishery
Eddisbury Way
Pennsylvania Wood
Stanner Nab
Lodge
4
Outlanes Farm
Spring House Farm
57
BURWARDSLEY RD
Hall
Burwardsley Hall
CH3
OUT LA
River Gowy
PO
HARTHILL RD
Broad Rough
ROCK LA
Waste Hill
HILL LA
QUARRYBANK COTTS
QUARRYBANK
SCHOOL LA
Cheshire Workshops
PH
3
Curdlands House
CHURCH RD
Willow Hill
Burwardsley
BARRACKS LA
Higher Burwardsley
Peckforton Hills
Peckforton
PECKFORTON HALL LA
Sandstone Trail
SARRA LA
CW6
STONE HOUSE LA
FOWLERS BENCH LA
56
Cawley Lodge Farm
Willow Hill
Stonehouse Farm
Grig Hill Farm
Peckforton Gap
Hillside Farm
2
Droppingstone Farm
Bulkeley Hill
NEW LA
Sycamore Farm
Common Farm
Rawhead Farm
55
Bulkeley Mill
SY14
COPPERMINE LA
MILL GR
MILL VIEW CL
YEW TREE CL
Bulkeley
Bridge Farm
1
Bickerton Hill
WREXHAM RD
A534
The Bickerton Poacher (PH)
SANDY LA
HITCHENS LA
White House Farm
CHOLMONDELEY LA
Tower Wood
Chiflik Farm
The Grange
A534
WREXHAM RD
54
51
52
53
A
B
C

183
200

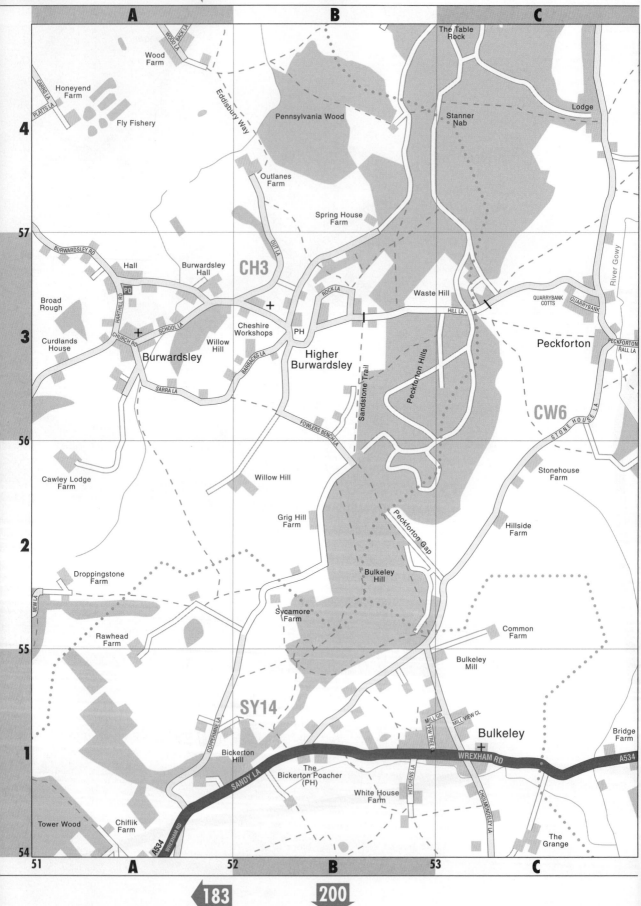

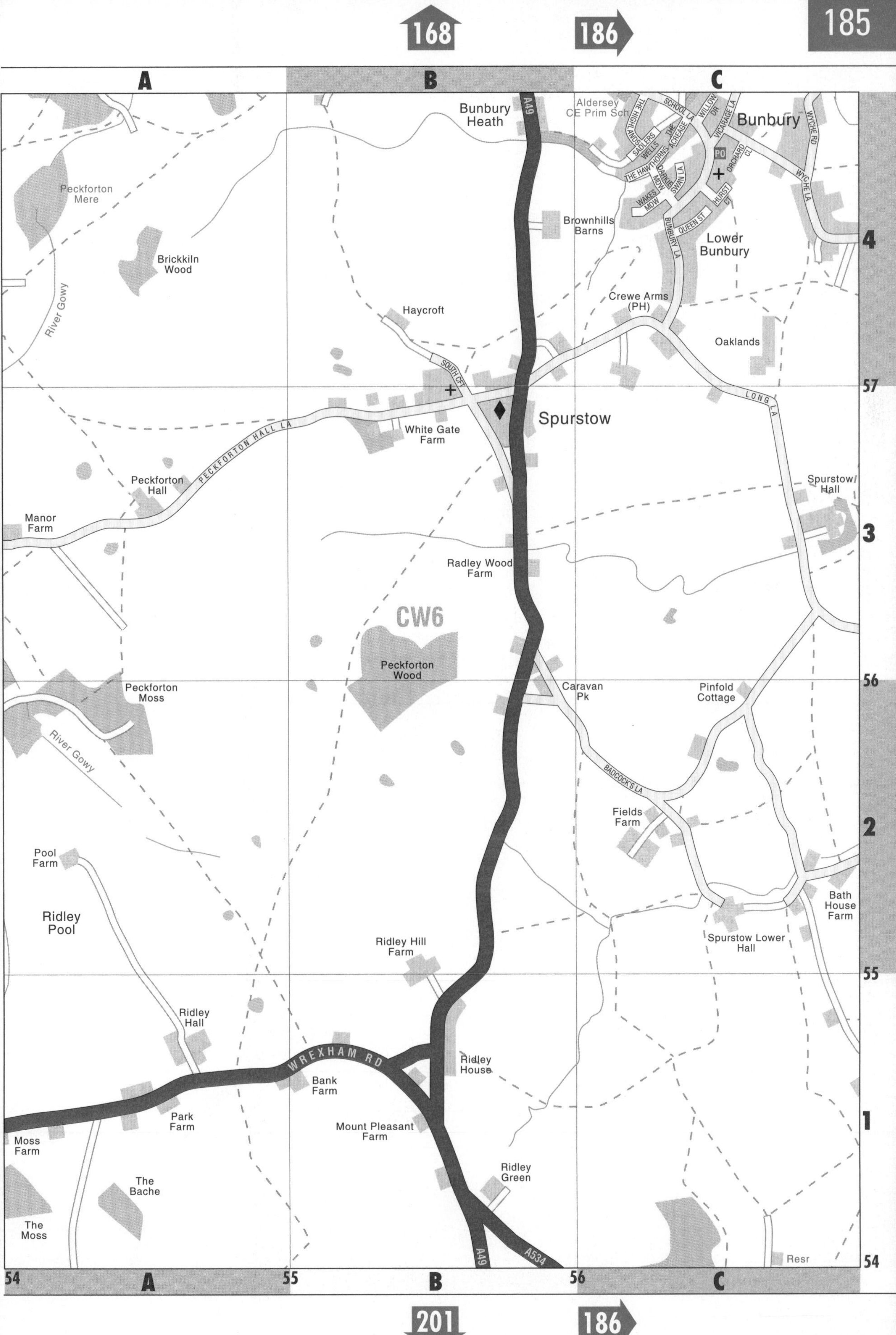

A B C

Peckforton
Mere

Brickkiln
Wood

River Gowy

Bunbury
Heath

Aldersey
CE Prim Sch

Bunbury

THE HAWTHORNS
SCHOOL LA
WILLOW DR
VICARAGE LA
WYCHE LA

THE SADLERS
WELLS

Brownhills
Barns

WAKES
MDW
DARBISHIRE
LYTH AV
BUNBURY LA
QUEEN ST
HURST CT
ORCHARD CL

PO

Lower
Bunbury

Haycroft

Crewe Arms
(PH)

Oaklands

LONG LA

57

SOUTH CFT

White Gate
Farm

Spurstow

Spurstow
Hall

PECKFORTON HALL LA

Peckforton
Hall

Manor
Farm

Radley Wood
Farm

3

CW6

Peckforton
Wood

Peckforton
Moss

Caravan
Pk

Pinfold
Cottage

56

River Gowy

BADCOCK'S LA

Fields
Farm

2

Pool
Farm

Bath
House
Farm

Ridley
Pool

Spurstow Lower
Hall

55

Ridley
Hall

Ridley Hill
Farm

WREXHAM RD

Bank
Farm

Ridley
House

1

Park
Farm

Mount Pleasant
Farm

Moss
Farm

The Bache

Ridley
Green

The
Moss

A49
A534

Resr

54
54 55 56

A B C

185
169

A **B** **C**

4

WYCHE LA
BIRD'S LA
Woodworth
Green

Woodworth Green
Farm

CW5

GREEN LA

57

Wardle
Hall

Church
Farm

Haughton Hall
Farm

Haughton

Long
Wood

3

HALL LA

Moss
Farm

Haughton
Hall

Firs
Farm

Pool
Covert

Nag's Head
(PH)

Oak Farm

56

CW6

Yewtree
House

LONG LA

Garners
Farm

Peartree
Farm

Laurel
Farm

THE
COURTYARD

Rookery
Farm

Yew Tree
Farm

2

Capper's Lane
Farm

Radmore
Green

CAPPER'S LA

55

Spa
Plantation

Longfields

Spurstow Spa
(Saline)

Brindley Hall
Farm

BRINDLEY HALL RD

CW5

Old
House

1

High Ash
Farm

Brook
Farm

Clay Fields
Farm

54

A 58 **B** 59 **C**

Ash
House

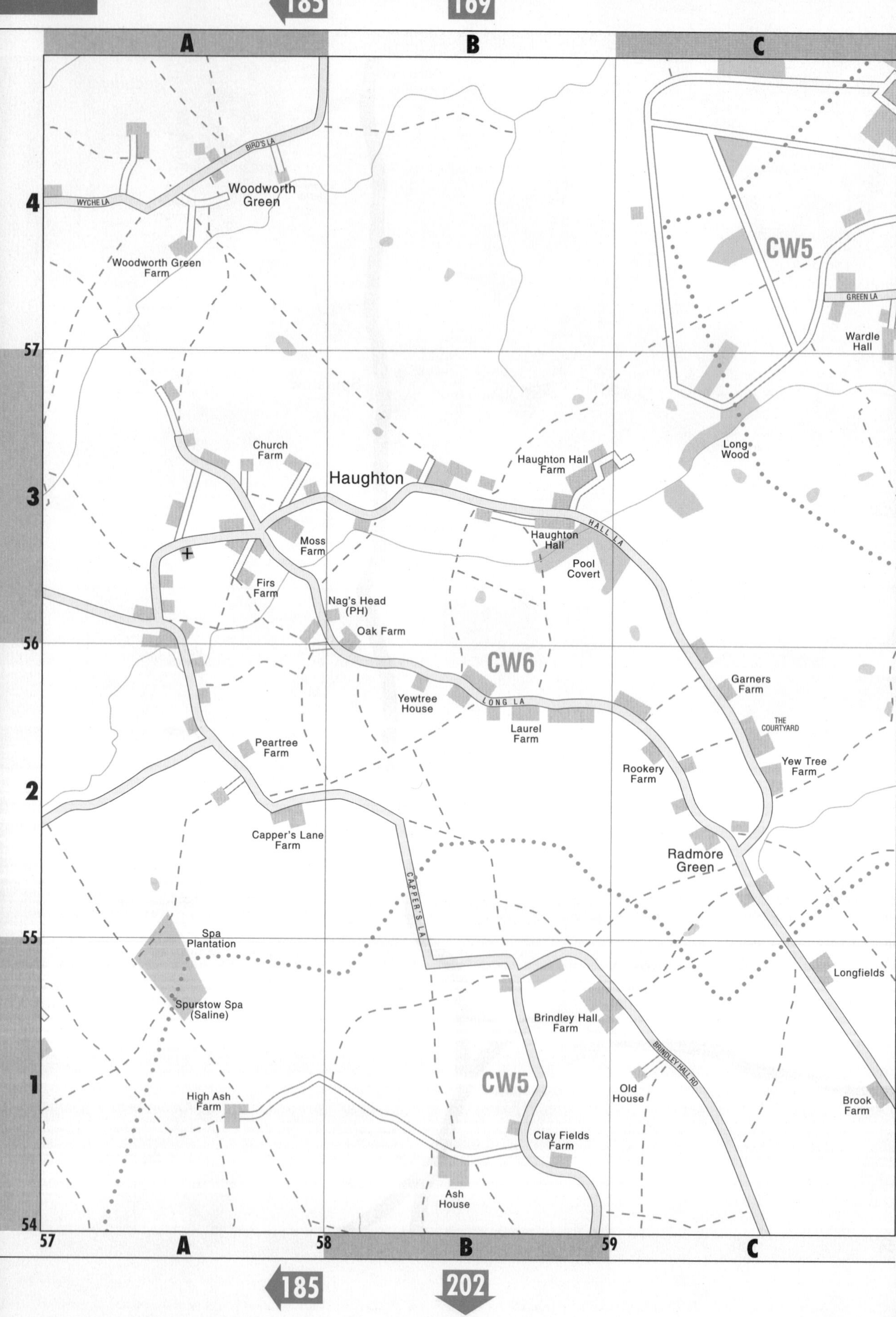

170
188

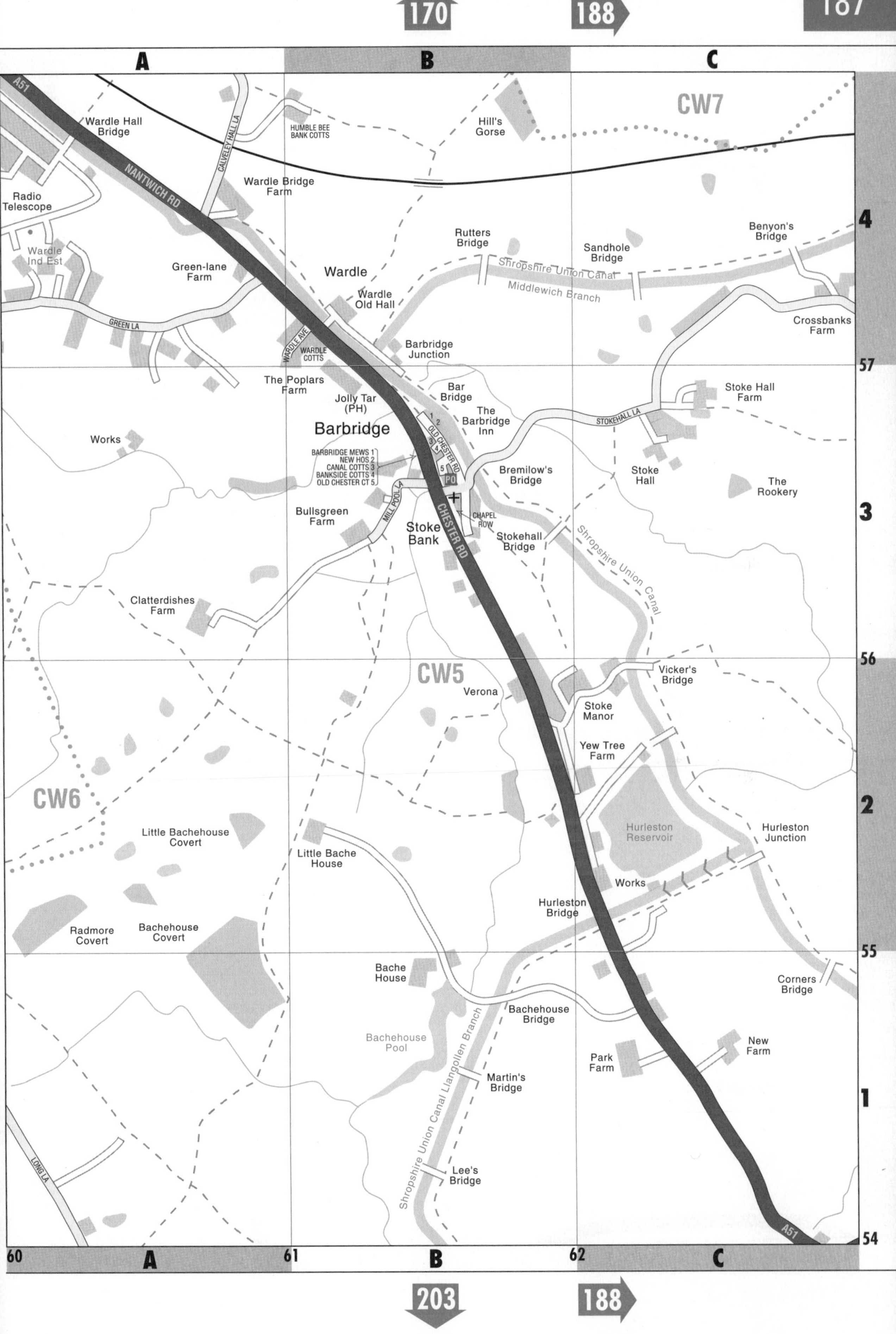
A
B
C
CW7
A51
Wardle Hall Bridge
HUMBLE BEE BANK COTTS
Hill's Gorse
CALVELEY HALL LA
NANTWICH RD
Wardle Bridge Farm
Radio Telescope
Rutters Bridge
Sandhole Bridge
Benyon's Bridge
Wardle Ind Est
Green-lane Farm
Wardle
Shropshire Union Canal
Middlewich Branch
Wardle Old Hall
GREEN LA
WARDLE AVE
WARDLE COTTS
Barbridge Junction
Crossbanks Farm
The Poplars Farm
Bar Bridge
Stoke Hall Farm
Jolly Tar (PH)
The Barbridge Inn
STOKEHALL LA
Barbridge
OLD CHESTER RD
Works
BARBRIDGE MEWS 1
NEW HOS 2
CANAL COTTS 3
BANKSIDE COTTS 4
OLD CHESTER CT 5
PO
Bremilow's Bridge
Stoke Hall
The Rookery
MILL POOL LA
CHAPEL ROW
Bullsgreen Farm
Stoke Bank
CHESTER RD
Stokehall Bridge
Shropshire Union Canal
Clatterdishes Farm
CW5
Verona
Vicker's Bridge
Stoke Manor
Yew Tree Farm
CW6
Little Bachehouse Covert
Hurleston Reservoir
Hurleston Junction
Little Bache House
Works
Hurleston Bridge
Radmore Covert
Bachehouse Covert
Bache House
Corners Bridge
Bachehouse Bridge
Bachehouse Pool
Shropshire Union Canal Llangollen Branch
Park Farm
New Farm
Martin's Bridge
Lee's Bridge
LONG LA
A51
4
57
3
56
2
55
1
54
60
61
62

203
188

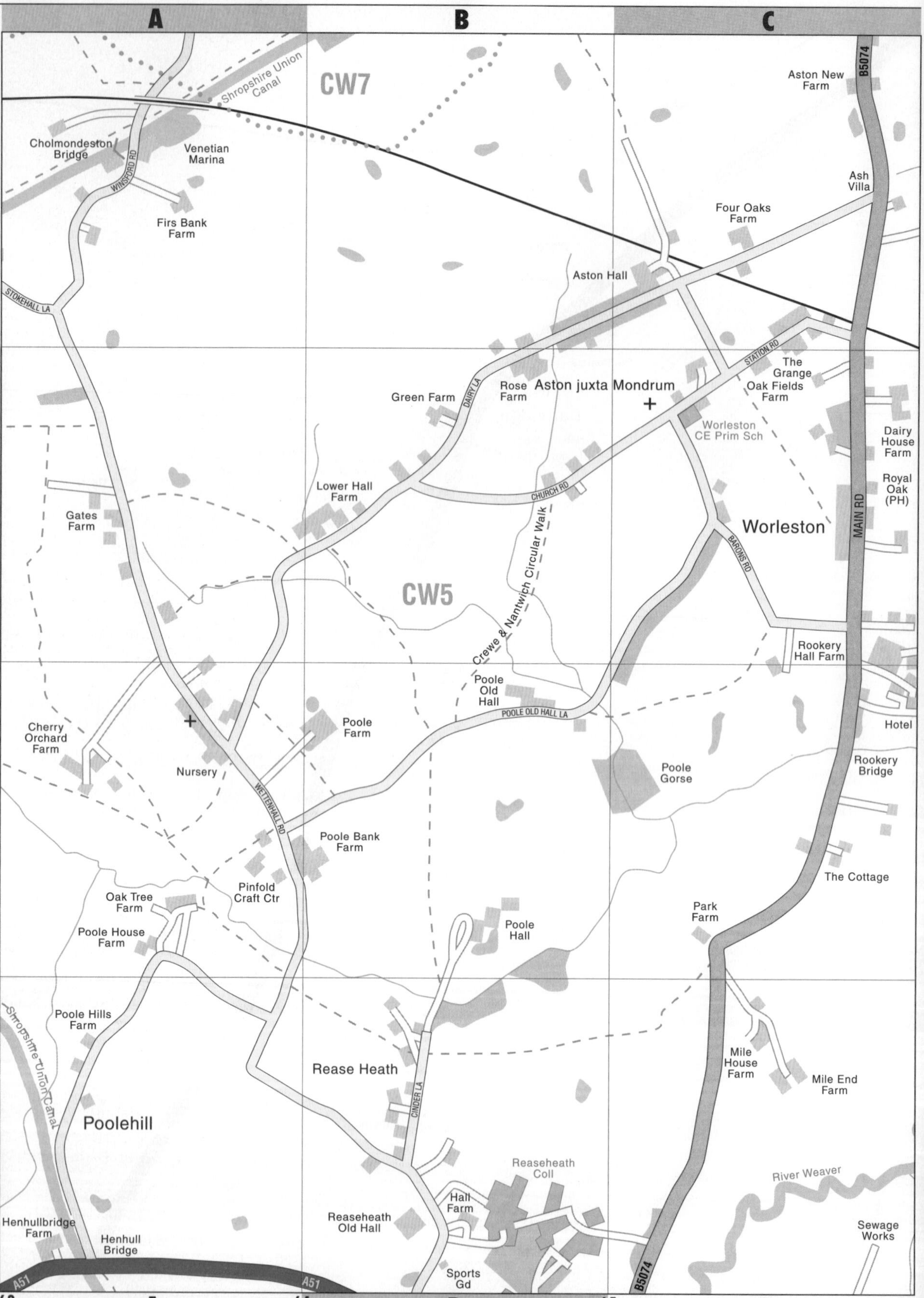

187
171

A

B

C

Shropshire Union Canal

CW7

Cholmondeston Bridge

WINSFORD RD

Venetian Marina

Aston New Farm

B5074

Ash Villa

4

Firs Bank Farm

Four Oaks Farm

Aston Hall

STOKEHALL LA

57

Green Farm

DAIRY LA

Rose Farm

Aston juxta Mondrum

+

STATION RD

The Grange

Oak Fields Farm

Worleston CE Prim Sch

Dairy House Farm

Lower Hall Farm

CHURCH RD

MAIN RD

Royal Oak (PH)

3

Gates Farm

Crewe & Nantwich Circular Walk

CW5

Worleston

BARONS RD

Cherry Orchard Farm

+

Nursery

Poole Farm

Poole Old Hall

POOLE OLD HALL LA

Rookery Hall Farm

56

Hotel

Poole Gorse

Rookery Bridge

WETTENHALL RD

Poole Bank Farm

2

The Cottage

Oak Tree Farm

Pinfold Craft Ctr

Poole House Farm

Poole Hall

Park Farm

55

Poole Hills Farm

Mile House Farm

Mile End Farm

Shropshire Union Canal

Rease Heath

CINDER LA

1

Poolehill

Reaseheath Coll

River Weaver

Hall Farm

Henhullbridge Farm

Reaseheath Old Hall

Sewage Works

Henhull Bridge

B5074

Sports Gd

54

A51

A51

63

A

64

B

65

C

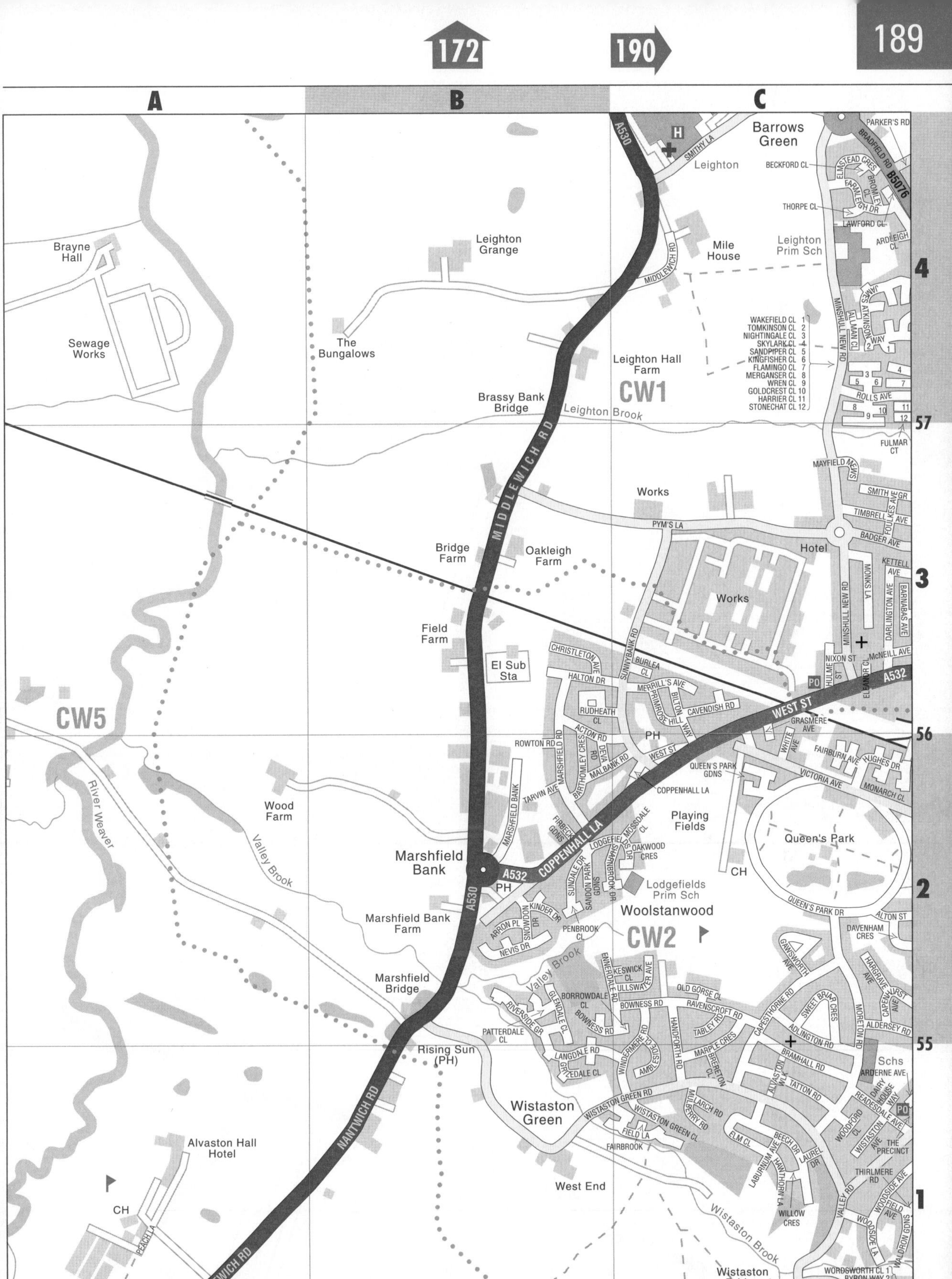
A
B
C
Barrows Green
Leighton
Brayne Hall
Leighton Grange
Mile House
Leighton Prim Sch
Sewage Works
The Bungalows
Leighton Hall Farm
CW1
Brassy Bank Bridge
Leighton Brook
MIDDLEWICH RD
Works
PYM'S LA
Hotel
Bridge Farm
Oakleigh Farm
Works
Field Farm
El Sub Sta
CW5
WEST ST
A532
River Weaver
Wood Farm
Valley Brook
Playing Fields
Queen's Park
Marshfield Bank
COPPENHALL LA
Lodgefields Prim Sch
Woolstanwood
Marshfield Bank Farm
CW2
Marshfield Bridge
Rising Sun (PH)
Wistaston Green
Alvaston Hall Hotel
West End
NANTWICH RD
Wistaston Brook
Wistaston Bridge
Robinson's Corner
MIDDLEWICH RD
A530
4
3
2
1
57
56
55
54
66
67
68

189
173

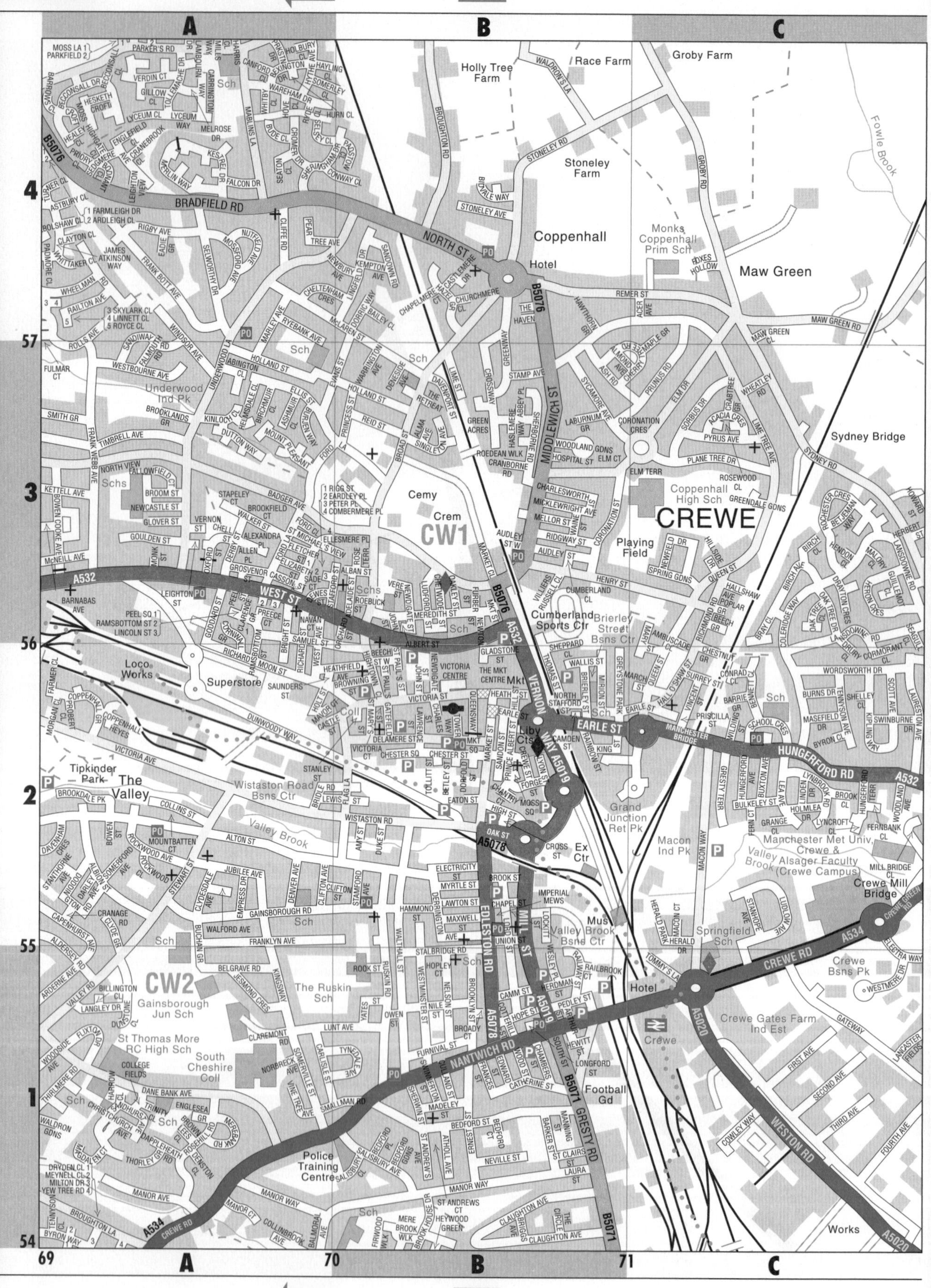
A
B
C
4
57
3
56
2
55
1
54
69
70
71
CREWE
CW1
CW2
Coppenhall
Maw Green
Holly Tree Farm
Race Farm
Groby Farm
Stoneley Farm
Monks Coppenhall Prim Sch
Sydney Bridge
Coppenhall High Sch
Playing Field
Cemy
Crem
Cumberland Sports Ctr
Brierley Street Bsns Ctr
Underwood Ind Pk
Loco Works
Superstore
Tipkinder Park
The Valley
Wistaston Road Bsns Ctr
Valley Brook
Victoria Centre
The Mkt Centre
Mkt
Liby
Cts
Coll
Grand Junction Ret Pk
Macon Ind Pk
Ex Ctr
Mus
Valley Brook Bsns Ctr
Manchester Met Univ, Crewe & Alsager Faculty (Crewe Campus)
Crewe Mill Bridge
Springfield Sch
Crewe Bsns Pk
Crewe Gates Farm Ind Est
Crewe
Hotel
Football Gd
The Ruskin Sch
Gainsborough Jun Sch
St Thomas More RC High Sch
South Cheshire Coll
Police Training Centre
Works
Fowle Brook
BRADFIELD RD
NORTH ST
WEST ST
NANTWICH RD
CREWE RD
HUNGERFORD RD
EARLE ST
VERNON WAY
MIDDLEWICH ST
EDLESTON RD
MILL ST
GRESTY RD
WESTON RD
MANCHESTER BRIDGE
DUNWOODY WAY
MAW GREEN RD
REMER ST
GROBY RD
BROUGHTON RD
A532
A534
A5019
A5020
A5078
B5071
B5076

189
206

174
192

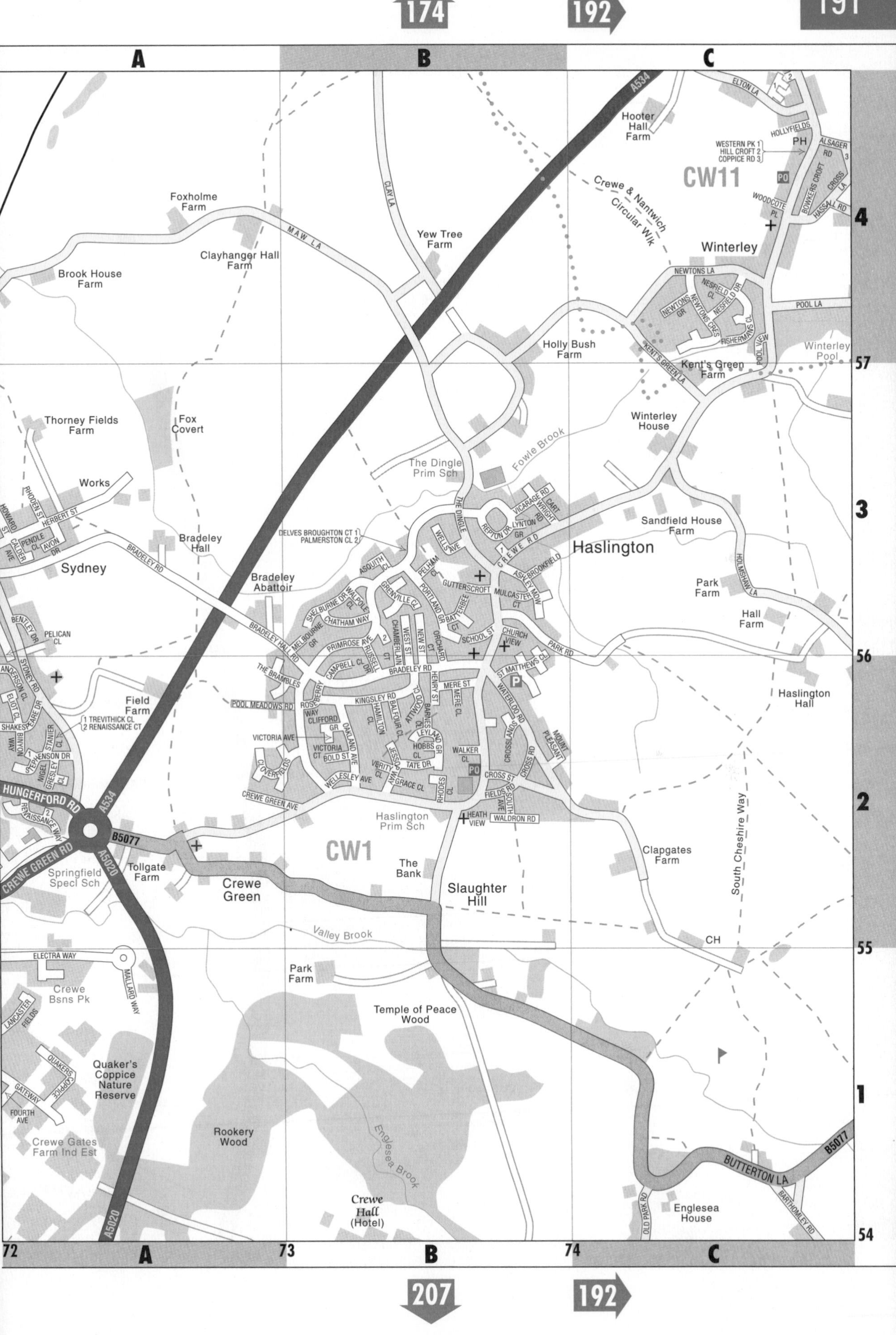
A
B
C
Foxholme Farm
Brook House Farm
Clayhanger Hall Farm
Yew Tree Farm
Hooter Hall Farm
CW11
Crewe & Nantwich Circular Wlk
Winterley
Holly Bush Farm
Kent's Green Farm
Winterley Pool
Winterley House
Thorney Fields Farm
Fox Covert
Works
Bradeley Hall
Sydney
Bradeley Abattoir
The Dingle Prim Sch
Fowle Brook
Haslington
Sandfield House Farm
Park Farm
Hall Farm
Haslington Hall
Field Farm
Haslington Prim Sch
CW1
The Bank
Slaughter Hill
Clapgates Farm
South Cheshire Way
Crewe Green
Tollgate Farm
Springfield Specl Sch
Valley Brook
CH
Park Farm
Temple of Peace Wood
Crewe Bsns Pk
Quaker's Coppice Nature Reserve
Rookery Wood
Englesea Brook
Crewe Gates Farm Ind Est
Crewe Hall (Hotel)
Englesea House
BUTTERTON LA
B5077
A534
A5020
HUNGERFORD RD
CREWE GREEN RD
CREWE GREEN AVE
BRADELEY RD
BRADELEY HALL RD
MAW LA
CLAY LA
ELTON LA
HOLLYFIELDS
ALSAGER RD
WESTERN PK 1
HILL CROFT 2
COPPICE RD 3
NEWTONS LA
POOL LA
KENT'S GREEN LA
CREWE RD
PARK RD
HOLMSHAW LA
DELVES BROUGHTON CT 1
PALMERSTON CL 2
1 TREVITHICK CL
2 RENAISSANCE CT
POOL MEADOWS RD
VICTORIA AVE
ELECTRA WAY
MALLARD WAY
OLD PARK RD
BARTHOMLEY RD
57
56
55
54
4
3
2
1
72
73
74

207
192

191
175

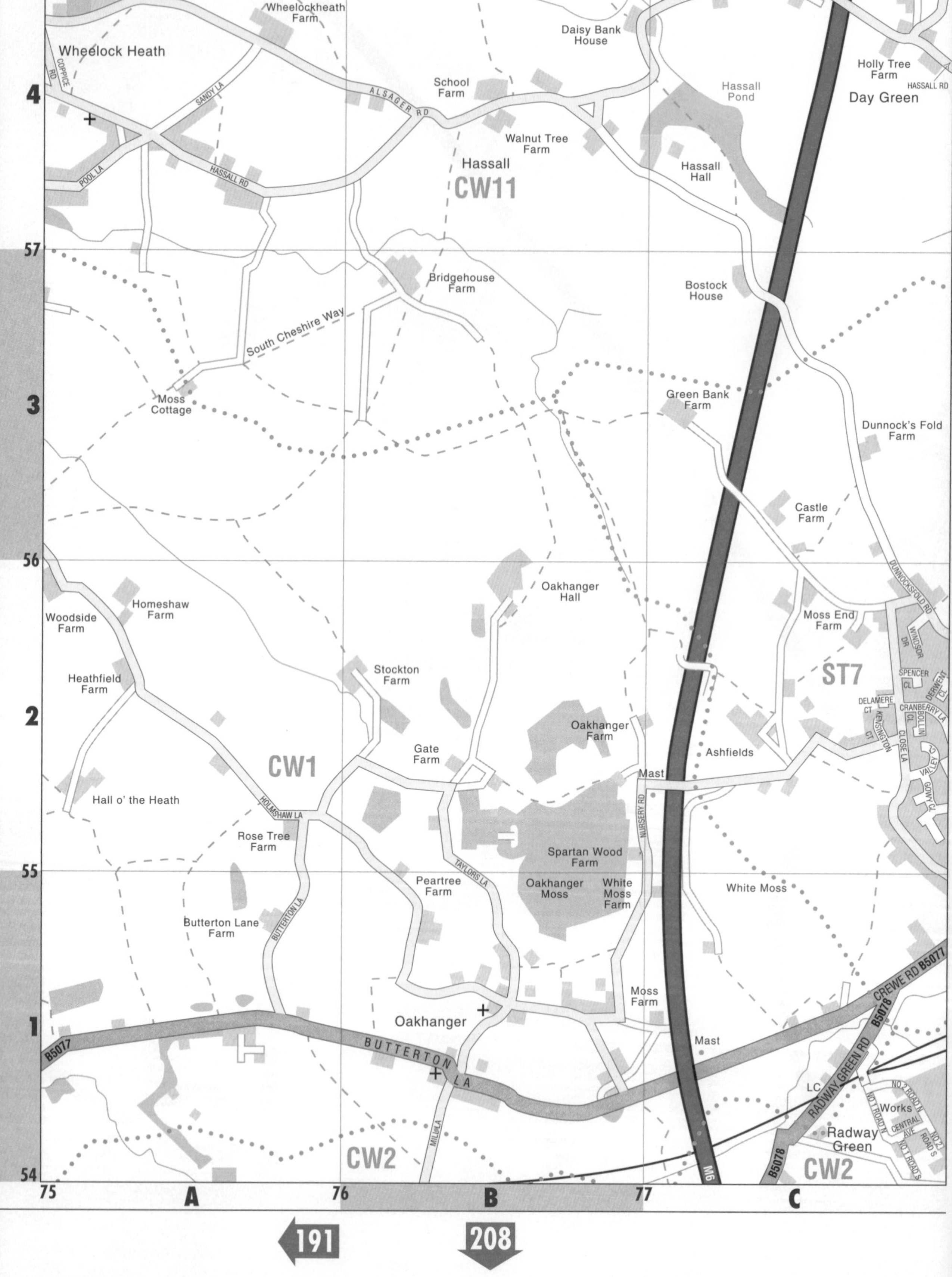
A
B
C
Whitehall Farm
Wheelockheath Farm
Wheelock Heath
Fingerpost Farm
Daisy Bank House
School Farm
Hassall Pond
Holly Tree Farm
Day Green
HASSALL RD
ALSAGER RD
SANDY LA
POOL LA
HASSALL RD
Walnut Tree Farm
Hassall
CW11
Hassall Hall
Bridgehouse Farm
Bostock House
South Cheshire Way
Moss Cottage
Green Bank Farm
Dunnock's Fold Farm
Castle Farm
Oakhanger Hall
Homeshaw Farm
Woodside Farm
Moss End Farm
ST7
Heathfield Farm
Stockton Farm
Oakhanger Farm
Gate Farm
Ashfields
CW1
Mast
Hall o' the Heath
HOLMSHAW LA
NURSERY RD
Rose Tree Farm
Spartan Wood Farm
Peartree Farm
TAYLORS LA
Oakhanger Moss
White Moss Farm
White Moss
Butterton Lane Farm
BUTTERTON LA
Moss Farm
Oakhanger
CREWE RD B5077
B5078
B5077
Mast
RADWAY GREEN RD
LC
Works
Radway Green
MILL LA
CW2
CW2
M6
4
3
2
1
57
56
55
54
75
76
77

191
208

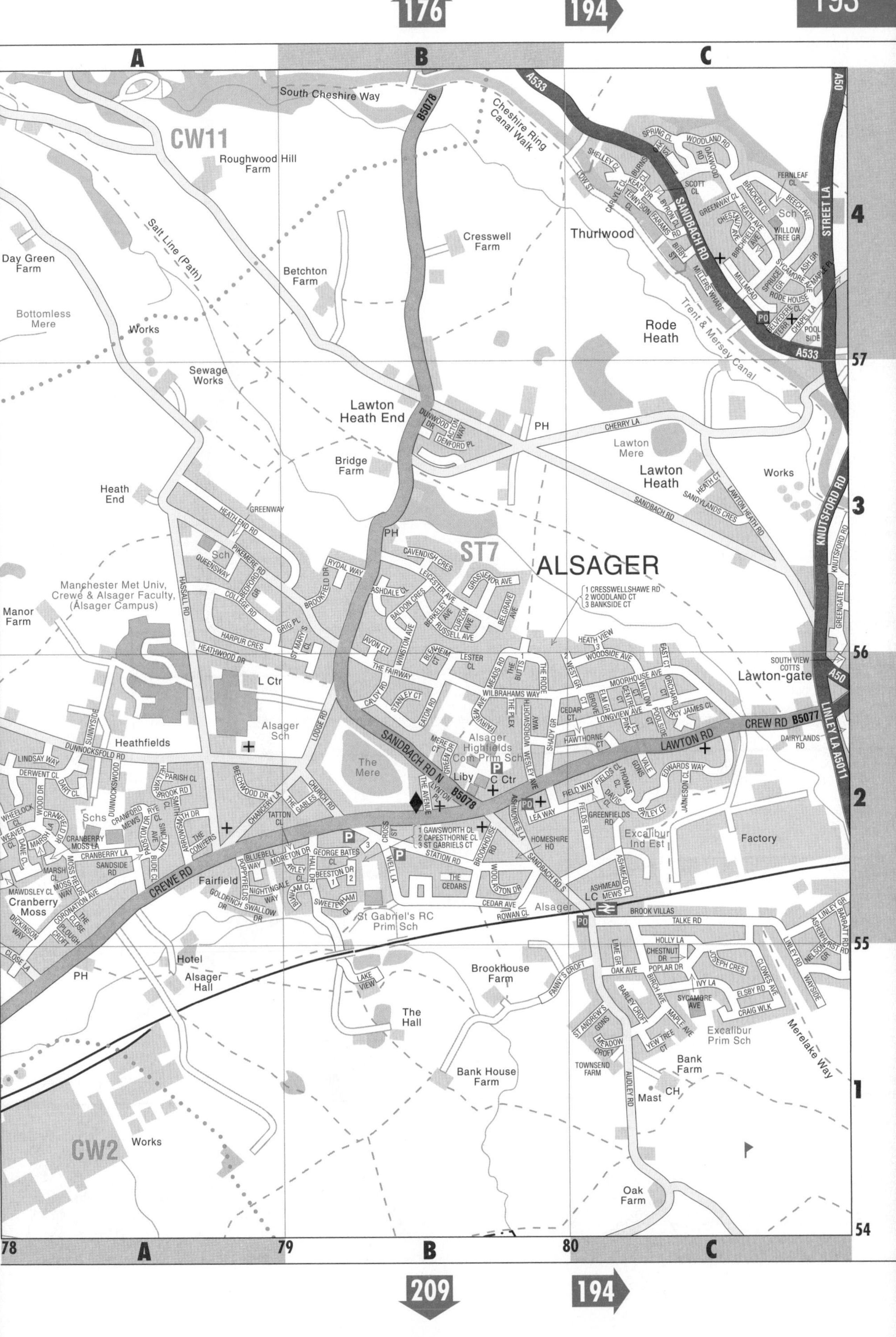
A
B
C
CW11
South Cheshire Way
Cheshire Ring Canal Walk
Roughwood Hill Farm
Salt Line (Path)
Day Green Farm
Bottomless Mere
Works
Sewage Works
Betchton Farm
Cresswell Farm
Thurlwood
Rode Heath
Trent & Mersey Canal
Lawton Heath End
Bridge Farm
PH
Lawton Mere
Lawton Heath
Works
Heath End
ST7
ALSAGER
Manchester Met Univ, Crewe & Alsager Faculty, (Alsager Campus)
Manor Farm
1 CRESSWELLSHAWE RD
2 WOODLAND CT
3 BANKSIDE CT
Lawton-gate
L Ctr
Alsager Sch
Heathfields
The Mere
Alsager Highfields Com Prim Sch
Liby
C Ctr
Schs
1 GAWSWORTH CL
2 CAPESTHORNE CL
3 ST GABRIELS CT
Excalibur Ind Est
Factory
Fairfield
Cranberry Moss
St Gabriel's RC Prim Sch
Alsager
Hotel
Alsager Hall
Brookhouse Farm
The Hall
Excalibur Prim Sch
Bank House Farm
Bank Farm
Mast
Merelake Way
Works
CW2
Oak Farm
CREWE RD
SANDBACH RD N
LAWTON RD
CREW RD B5077
KNUTSFORD RD
LINLEY LA A5011
STREET LA
A533
A50
B5078
4
3
2
1
57
56
55
54
78
79
80

193
177

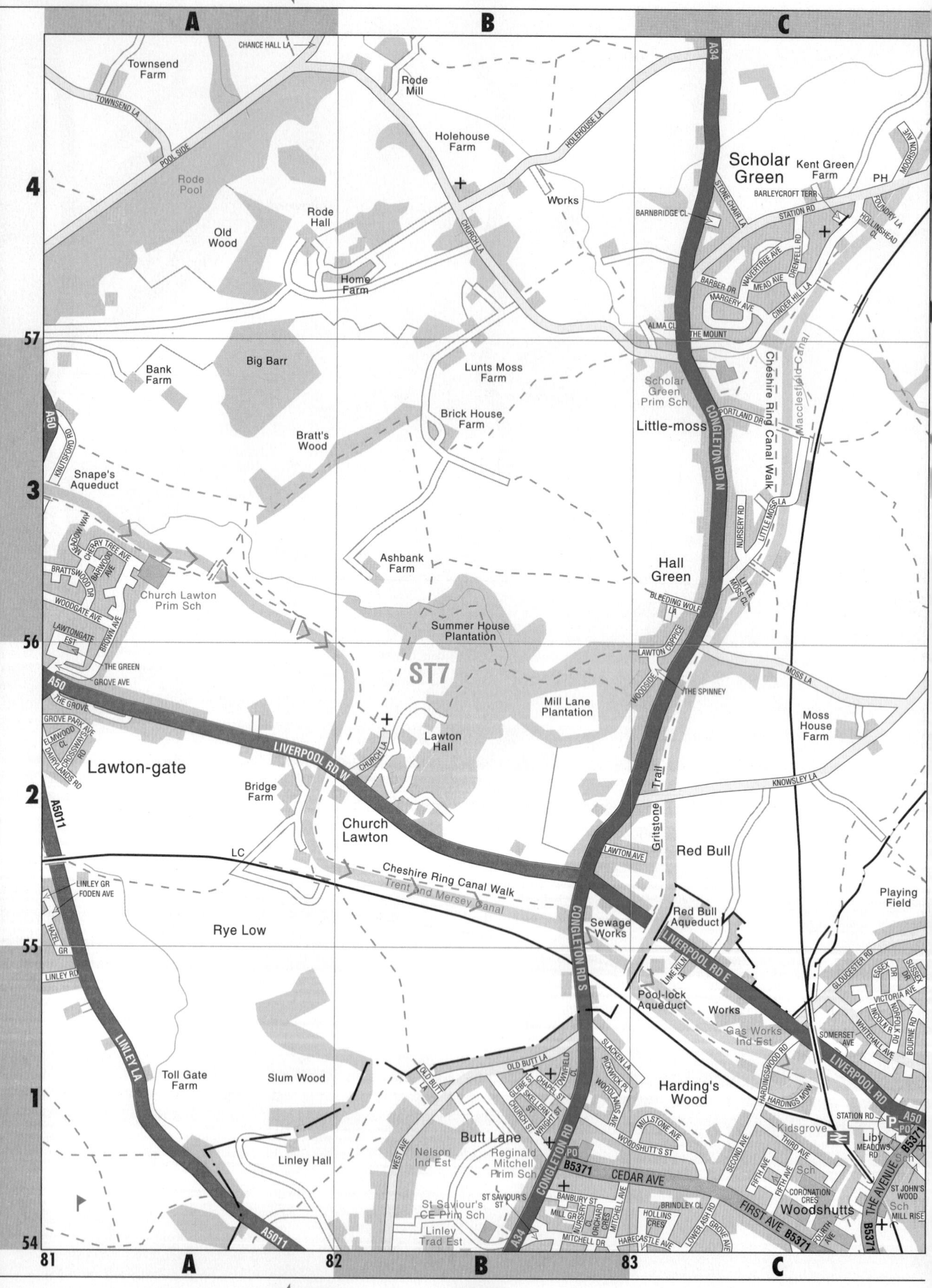
A
B
C
Townsend Farm
TOWNSEND LA
CHANCE HALL LA
POOL SIDE
Rode Pool
Old Wood
Rode Mill
Holehouse Farm
HOLEHOUSE LA
Rode Hall
Home Farm
CHURCH LA
Works
Scholar Green
Kent Green Farm
PH
BARLEYCROFT TERR
STATION RD
BARNBRIDGE CL
STONE CHAIR LA
FOUNDRY LA
HOLLINSHEAD CL
MOORSON AVE
WAVERTREE AVE
DRENFELL RD
MEAD AVE
BARBER DR
MARGERY AVE
CINDER HILL LA
ALMA CL
THE MOUNT
A34
4
57
Bank Farm
Big Barr
Lunts Moss Farm
Scholar Green Prim Sch
Brick House Farm
Bratt's Wood
Little-moss
PORTLAND DR
Cheshire Ring Canal Walk
Macclesfield Canal
CONGLETON RD N
A50
KNUTSFORD RD
Snape's Aqueduct
3
MEADOW WAY
CHERRY TREE AVE
BRATTSWOOD DR
BARWOOD AVE
Church Lawton Prim Sch
WOODGATE AVE
BROWN AVE
LAWTONGATE EST
THE GREEN
GROVE AVE
Ashbank Farm
NURSERY RD
LITTLE MOSS LA
LITTLE MOSS CL
Hall Green
BLEEDING WOLF LA
Summer House Plantation
56
ST7
LAWTON COPPICE
WOODSIDE
THE SPINNEY
MOSS LA
Mill Lane Plantation
Moss House Farm
THE GROVE
GROVE PARK AVE
ELMWOOD CL
CROSSWAYS RD
DAIRYLANDS RD
Lawton-gate
LIVERPOOL RD W
CHURCH LA
Lawton Hall
Bridge Farm
2
A5011
Church Lawton
Gritstone Trail
KNOWSLEY LA
LAWTON AVE
Red Bull
LC
Cheshire Ring Canal Walk
Trent and Mersey Canal
LINLEY GR
FODEN AVE
HAZEL GR
Rye Low
Sewage Works
CONGLETON RD S
Red Bull Aqueduct
Playing Field
55
LINLEY RD
LIVERPOOL RD E
LIME KILN LA
Pool-lock Aqueduct
Works
Gas Works Ind Est
GLOUCESTER RD
ESSEX DR
SUSSEX DR
VICTORIA AVE
LINCOLN RD
NORFOLK RD
WHITEHALL AVE
BOURNE RD
SOMERSET AVE
LINLEY LA
Toll Gate Farm
Slum Wood
OLD BUTT LA
GLEBE ST
CHAPEL ST
TOWNFIELD CL
SKELLERN ST
CHURCH ST
WRIGHT ST
SLACKEN LA
PICKWICK PL
WOODLANDS AVE
Harding's Wood
HARDINGSWOOD RD
HARDINGS MDW
LIVERPOOL RD
1
Butt Lane
MILLSTONE AVE
WOODSHUTT'S ST
STATION RD
Kidsgrove
Liby
MEADOWS RD
THIRD AVE
SECOND AVE
FIFTH AVE
Sch
Linley Hall
WEST AVE
Nelson Ind Est
Reginald Mitchell Prim Sch
PO
B5371
CEDAR AVE
CONGLETON RD
ST SAVIOUR'S ST
St Saviour's CE Prim Sch
BANBURY ST
MILL GR
NURSERY CL
ORCHARD CRES
MITCHELL AVE
BRINDLEY CL
HOLLINS CRES
LOWER ASH RD
GROVE AVE
FIRST AVE
CORONATION CRES
Woodshutts
FOURTH AVE
THE AVENUE
ST JOHN'S WOOD
Sch
MILL RISE
Linley Trad Est
MITCHELL DR
HARECASTLE AVE
54
81
82
83

193
210

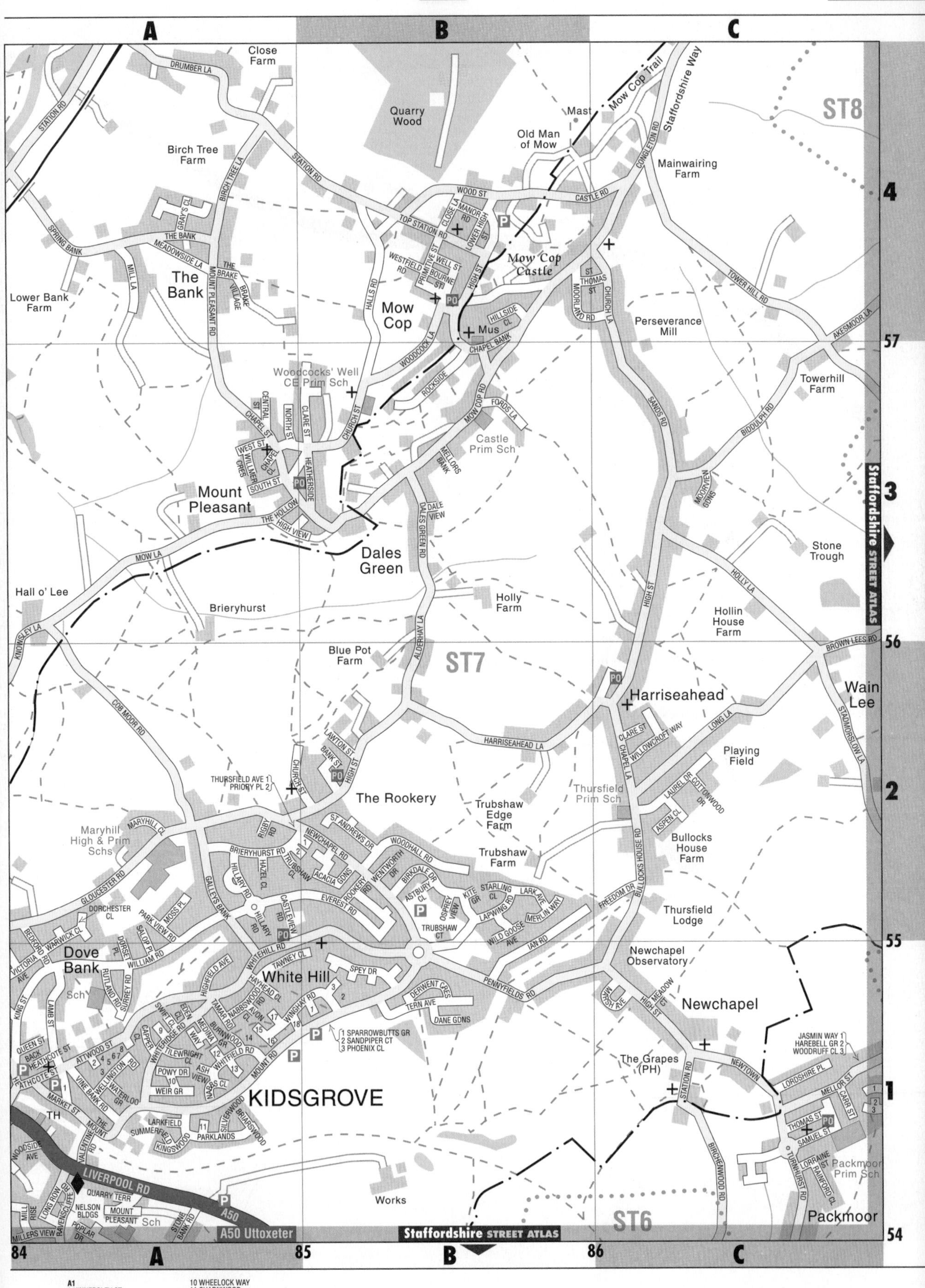

A1
1 KINNERSLEY ST
2 GILBERT CL
3 NAPIER GDNS
4 PEEL CT
5 BANK CT
6 HIGHERLAND CT
7 WESLEY GDNS
8 VICTORIA CT
9 SWALLOW CL
10 WHEELOCK WAY
11 CHARNWOOD
12 DIAMOND AVE
13 MOSSFIELD CRES
14 LITTLE ROW
15 BRIGHTS AVE
16 BIRCHES WAY
17 SILVERMINE CL
18 MAGPIE CRES

180

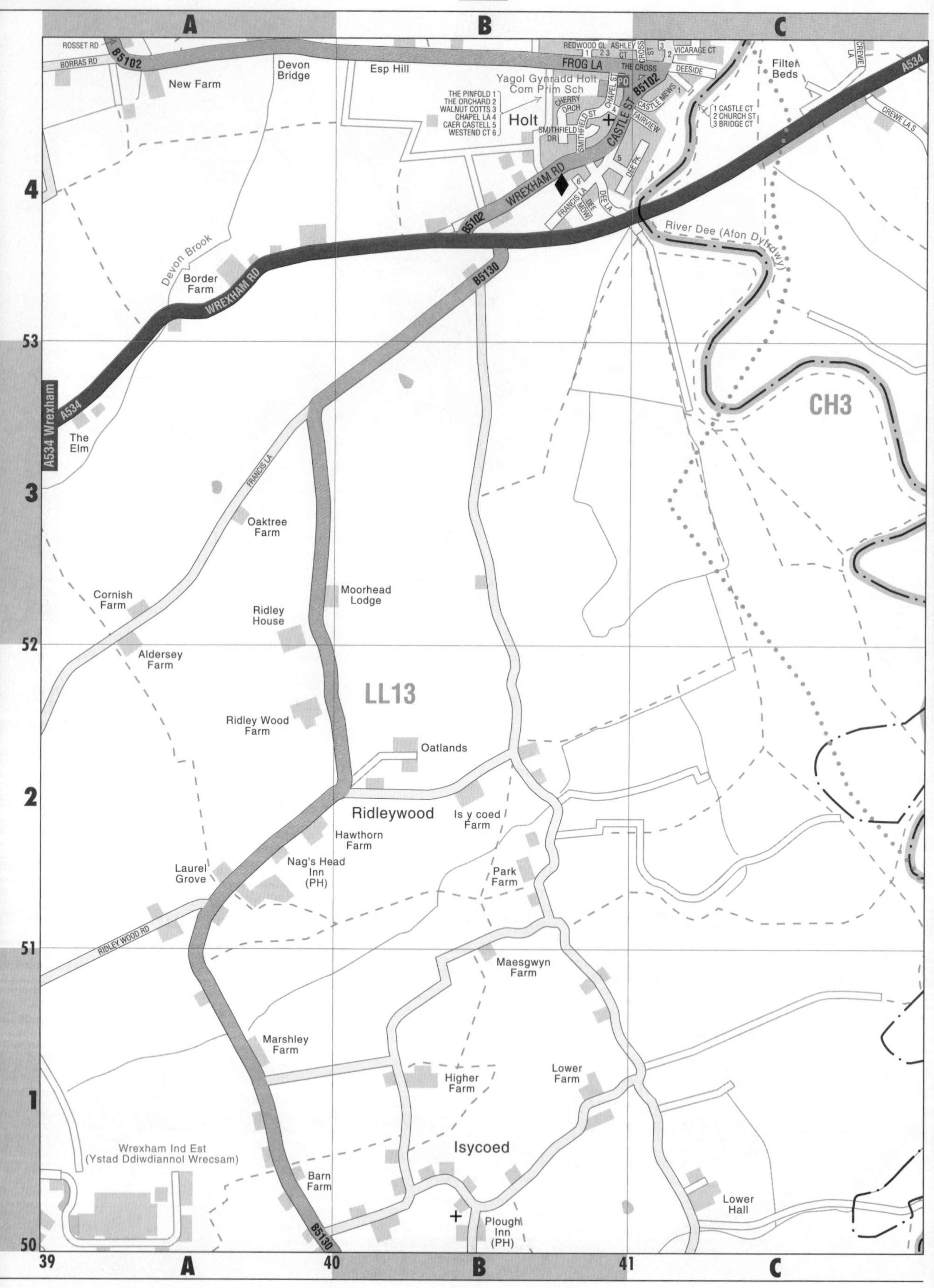

A
B
C
ROSSET RD
BORRAS RD
B5102
New Farm
Devon Bridge
Esp Hill
REDWOOD CL
ASHLEY CT
CROSS ST
VICARAGE CT
FROG LA
THE CROSS
DEESIDE
Filter Beds
CREWE LA
A534
Yagol Gynradd Holt Com Prim Sch
THE PINFOLD 1
THE ORCHARD 2
WALNUT COTTS 3
CHAPEL LA 4
CAER CASTELL 5
WESTEND CT 6
CHERRY ORCH
Holt
SMITHFIELD DR
SMITHFIELD ST
CHAPEL ST
CASTLE ST
CASTLE MEWS
FAIRVIEW
1 CASTLE CT
2 CHURCH ST
3 BRIDGE CT
CREWE LA S
WREXHAM RD
DEE PK
FRANCIS LA
DEE MDW
DEE LA
River Dee (Afon Dyfrdwy)
Devon Brook
Border Farm
WREXHAM RD
B5130
CH3
A534 Wrexham
The Elm
FRANCIS LA
Oaktree Farm
Cornish Farm
Moorhead Lodge
Ridley House
Aldersey Farm
LL13
Ridley Wood Farm
Oatlands
Ridleywood
Is y coed Farm
Hawthorn Farm
Laurel Grove
Nag's Head Inn (PH)
Park Farm
RIDLEY WOOD RD
Maesgwyn Farm
Marshley Farm
Higher Farm
Lower Farm
Isycoed
Wrexham Ind Est (Ystad Ddiwdiannol Wrecsam)
Barn Farm
Lower Hall
Plough Inn (PH)
B5130
53
52
51
50
4
3
2
1
39
40
41

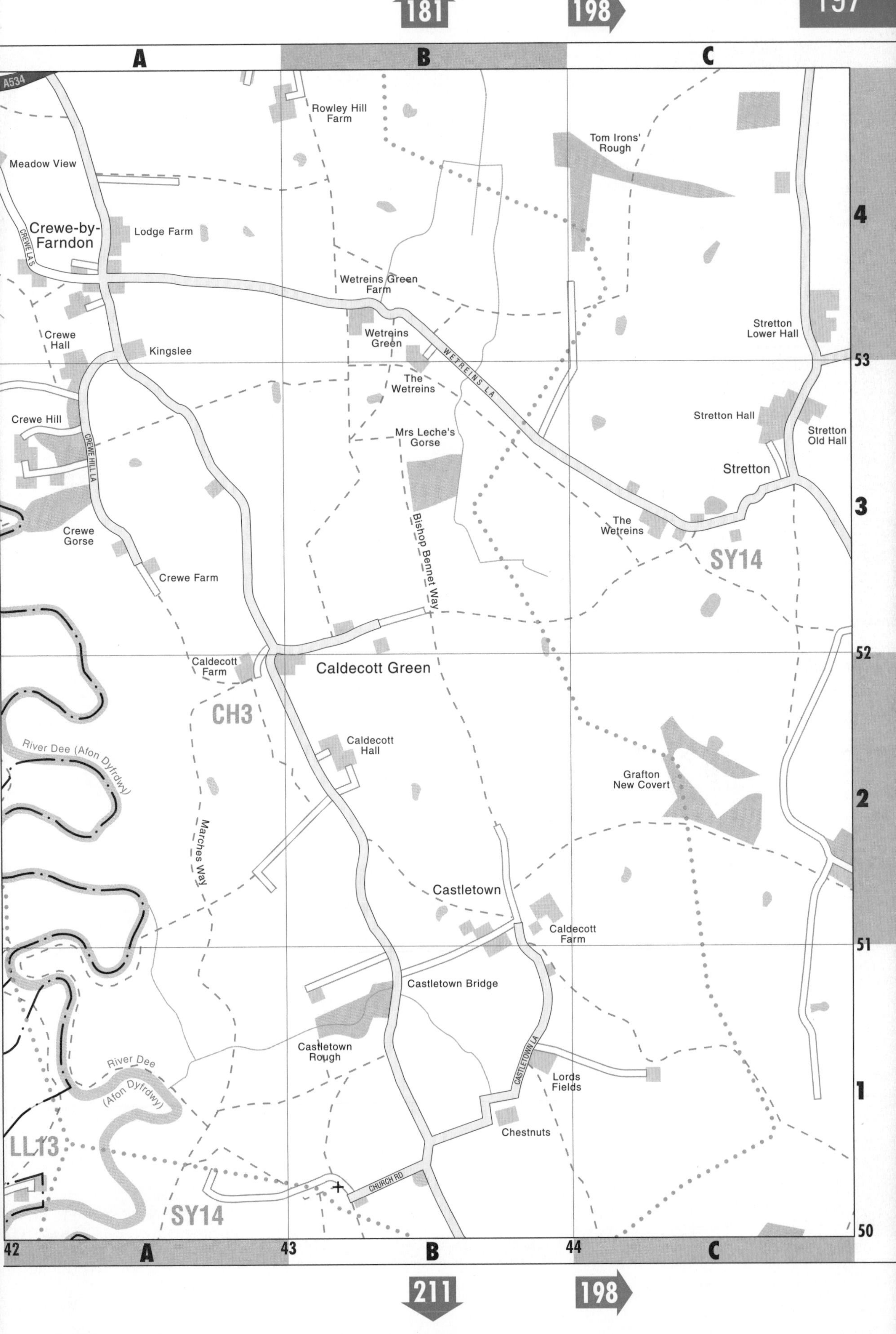
A
B
C
A534
Rowley Hill Farm
Tom Irons' Rough
Meadow View
Crewe-by-Farndon
CREWE LA S
Lodge Farm
4
Wetreins Green Farm
Crewe Hall
Wetreins Green
Kingslee
Stretton Lower Hall
WETREINS LA
53
The Wetreins
Crewe Hill
Mrs Leche's Gorse
Stretton Hall
Stretton Old Hall
CREWE HILL LA
Stretton
3
Crewe Gorse
Bishop Bennet Way
The Wetreins
SY14
Crewe Farm
52
Caldecott Farm
Caldecott Green
CH3
River Dee (Afon Dyfrdwy)
Caldecott Hall
Grafton New Covert
2
Marches Way
Castletown
Caldecott Farm
51
Castletown Bridge
Castletown Rough
River Dee
(Afon Dyfrdwy)
CASTLETOWN LA
Lords Fields
1
Chestnuts
LL13
CHURCH RD
SY14
50
42
43
44

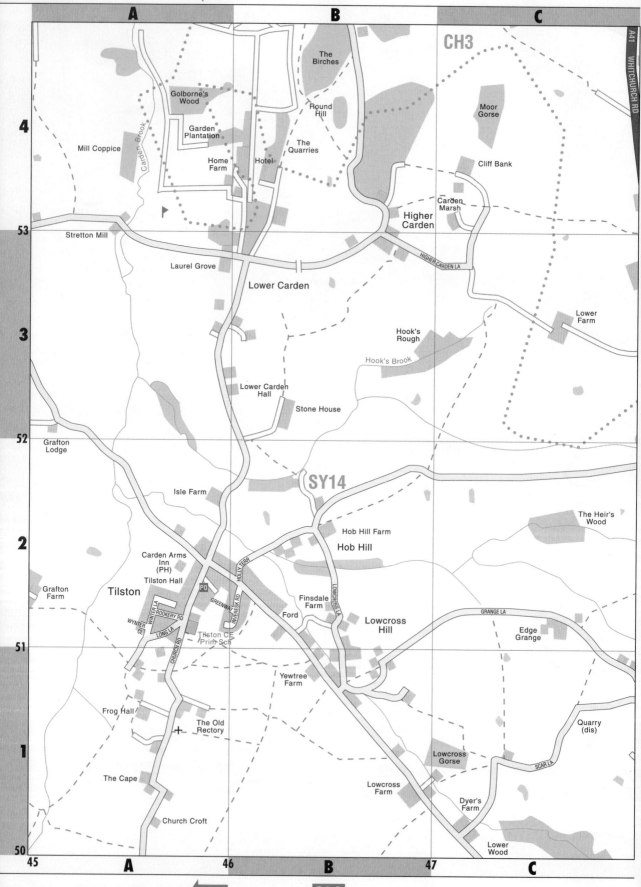

A   B   C

CH3

Moor Gorse

The Birches

Golborne's Wood

Round Hill

Garden Plantation

The Quarries

Cliff Bank

Mill Coppice

Home Farm

Hotel

Carden Marsh

Higher Carden

4

Stretton Mill

Laurel Grove

HIGHER CARDEN LA

53

Lower Carden

Lower Farm

Hook's Rough

Hook's Brook

3

Lower Carden Hall

Stone House

Grafton Lodge

52

SY14

The Heir's Wood

Isle Farm

Hob Hill Farm

Hob Hill

2

Carden Arms Inn (PH)

Tilston Hall

Grafton Farm

Tilston

PO

GREENWAY

HOLLY TERR

INVERESK RD

Finsdale Farm

Ford

LOWCROSS LA

Lowcross Hill

GRANGE LA

Edge Grange

WINTER LA

ROOKERY RD

WYNTER CL

LONG LA

CHURCH RD

Tilston CE Prim Sch

51

Yewtree Farm

Quarry (dis)

Frog Hall

The Old Rectory

Lowcross Gorse

SCAR LA

1

The Cape

Lowcross Farm

Dyer's Farm

Church Croft

Lower Wood

50

45   A   46   B   47   C

A41 WHITCHURCH RD

Carden Brook

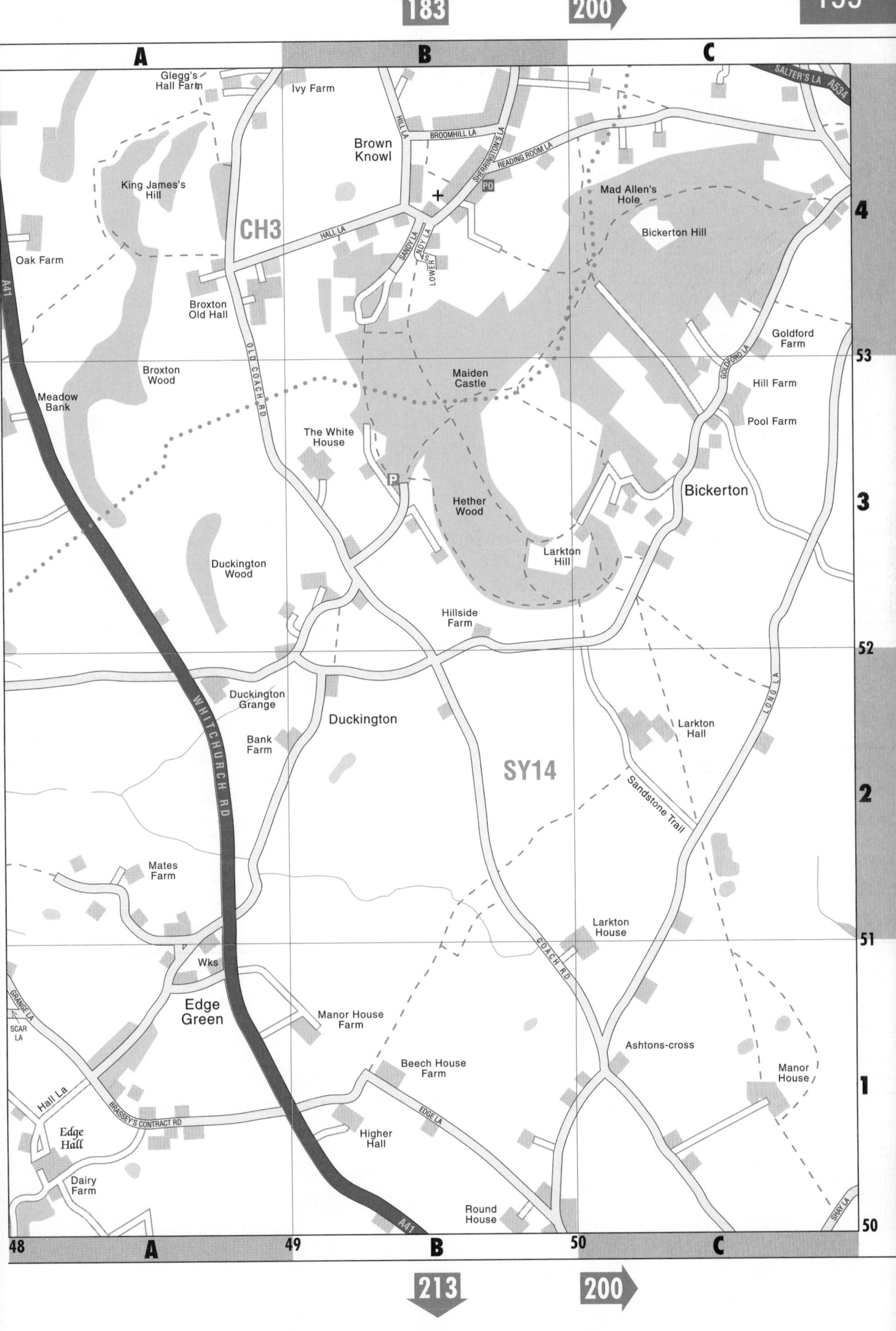

A
B
C

Glegg's Hall Farm
Ivy Farm
BROOMHILL LA
SHERRINGTON'S LA
SALTER'S LA
A534
Brown Knowl
HILL LA
READING ROOM LA
Mad Allen's Hole
PO
King James's Hill
CH3
HALL LA
LADY LA
LS LOWER
SANDY LA
Bickerton Hill
4
Oak Farm
A41
Broxton Old Hall
OLD COACH RD
Goldford Farm
GOLDFORD LA
53
Broxton Wood
Maiden Castle
Hill Farm
Pool Farm
Meadow Bank
The White House
P
Bickerton
Duckington Wood
Hether Wood
Larkton Hill
3
Hillside Farm
52
Duckington Grange
Larkton Hall
Duckington
Bank Farm
SY14
Sandstone Trail
2
WHITCHURCH RD
LONG LA
Mates Farm
Larkton House
51
Wks
Edge Green
GRANGE LA
SCAR LA
Manor House Farm
Ashtons-cross
Manor House
Beech House Farm
1
Hall La
BRASSEY'S CONTRACT RD
EDGE LA
Edge Hall
Higher Hall
Dairy Farm
A41
Round House
SHAY LA
50

48
A
49
B
50
C

A B C

4

A534

WREXHAM RD

Standstone Trail

Gallantry Bank

Bickerton Farm

Gallantry-bank Farm

Bulkeley Hall

Walnut Tree Farm

Manor Farm

BULKELEY HALL LA

CHOLMONDELEY LA

Bulkeleyhay

CW6

Yewtree Farm

Townsend Farm

LONG LA

Bickerton Holy Trinity CE Prim Sch

53

Bickerton Hall

Fields Farm

Gate House Farm

Manor Farm

3

Egerton Green

Green Farm

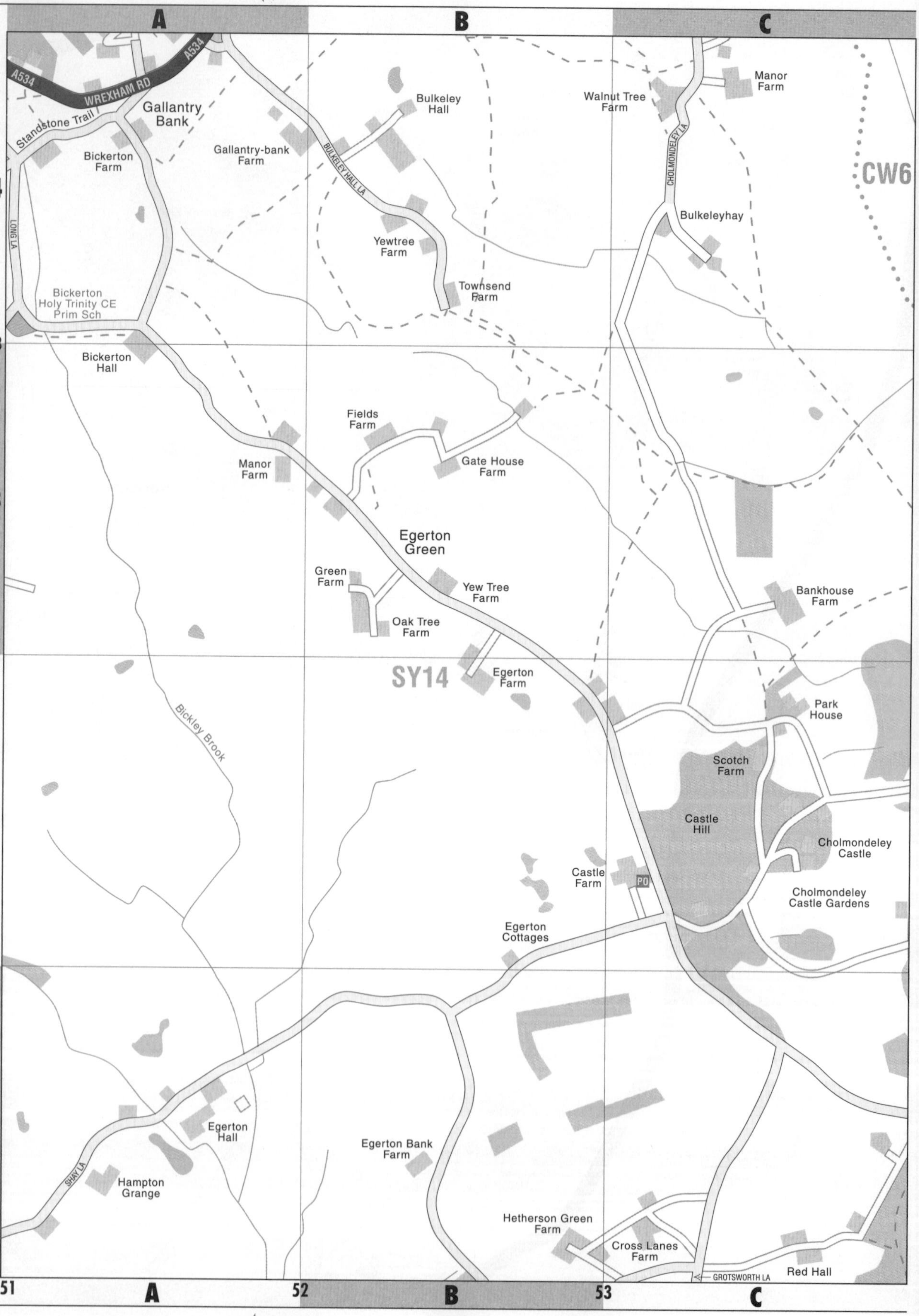

Yew Tree Farm

Bankhouse Farm

Oak Tree Farm

52

SY14

Egerton Farm

Park House

Bickley Brook

Scotch Farm

Castle Hill

Cholmondeley Castle

2

Castle Farm

Cholmondeley Castle Gardens

PO

Egerton Cottages

51

Egerton Hall

SHAY LA

1

Egerton Bank Farm

Hampton Grange

Hetherson Green Farm

Cross Lanes Farm

GROTSWORTH LA

Red Hall

50

51 A 52 B 53 C

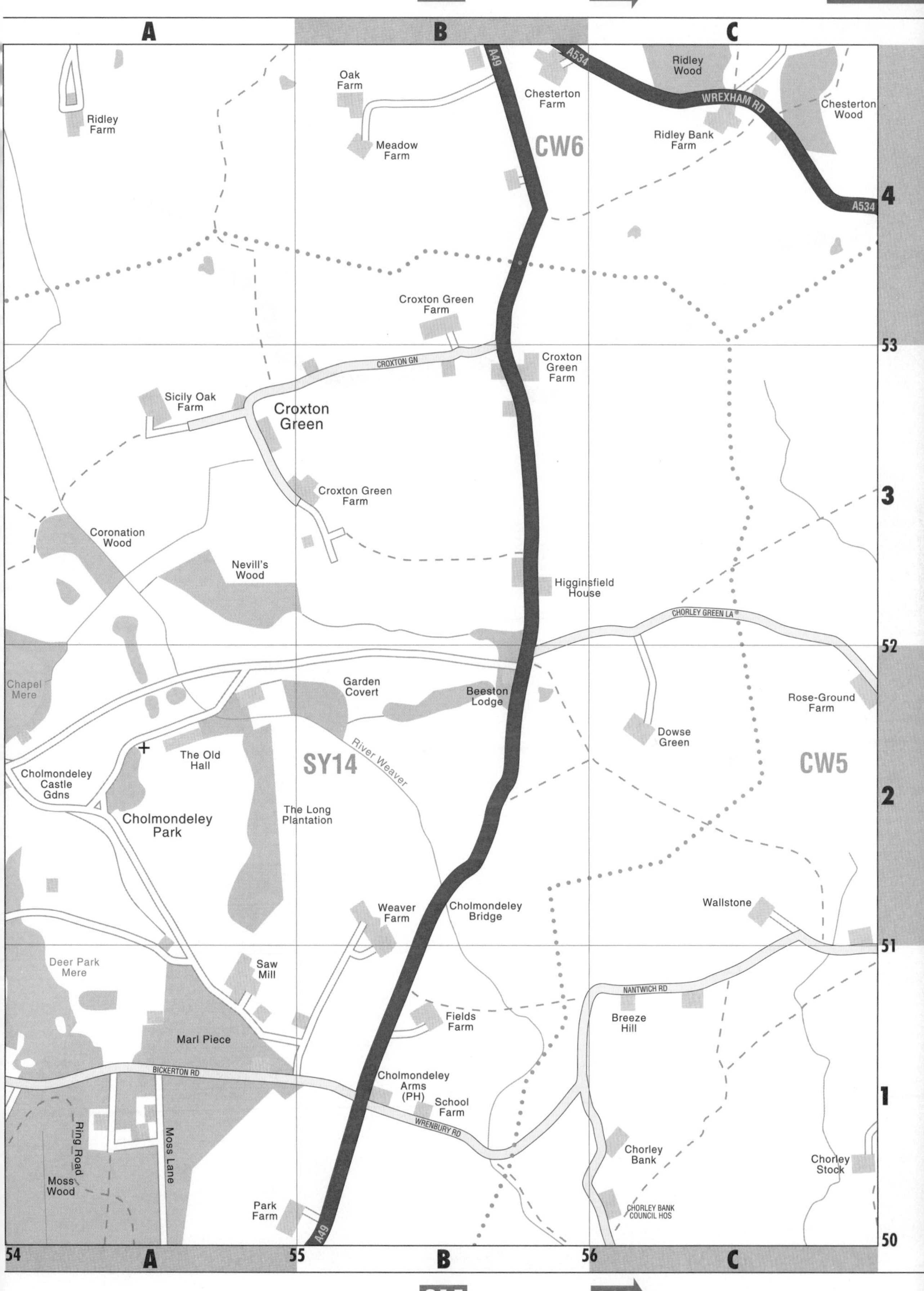

A   B   C

Ridley
Farm

Oak
Farm

A49

A534

Ridley
Wood

WREXHAM RD

Chesterton
Farm

Chesterton
Wood

Meadow
Farm

CW6

Ridley Bank
Farm

4

A534

Croxton Green
Farm

53

CROXTON GN

Croxton
Green
Farm

Sicily Oak
Farm

Croxton
Green

Croxton Green
Farm

3

Coronation
Wood

Nevill's
Wood

Higginsfield
House

CHORLEY GREEN LA

52

Chapel
Mere

Garden
Covert

Beeston
Lodge

Rose-Ground
Farm

River Weaver

SY14

The Old
Hall

Dowse
Green

CW5

2

Cholmondeley
Castle
Gdns

The Long
Plantation

Cholmondeley
Park

Deer Park
Mere

Saw
Mill

Weaver
Farm

Cholmondeley
Bridge

Wallstone

51

NANTWICH RD

Marl Piece

Fields
Farm

Breeze
Hill

BICKERTON RD

Cholmondeley
Arms
(PH)

School
Farm

Chorley
Bank

Chorley
Stock

1

Ring Road

Moss Lane

WRENBURY RD

Moss
Wood

Park
Farm

A49

CHORLEY BANK
COUNCIL HOS

50

54   A   55   B   56   C

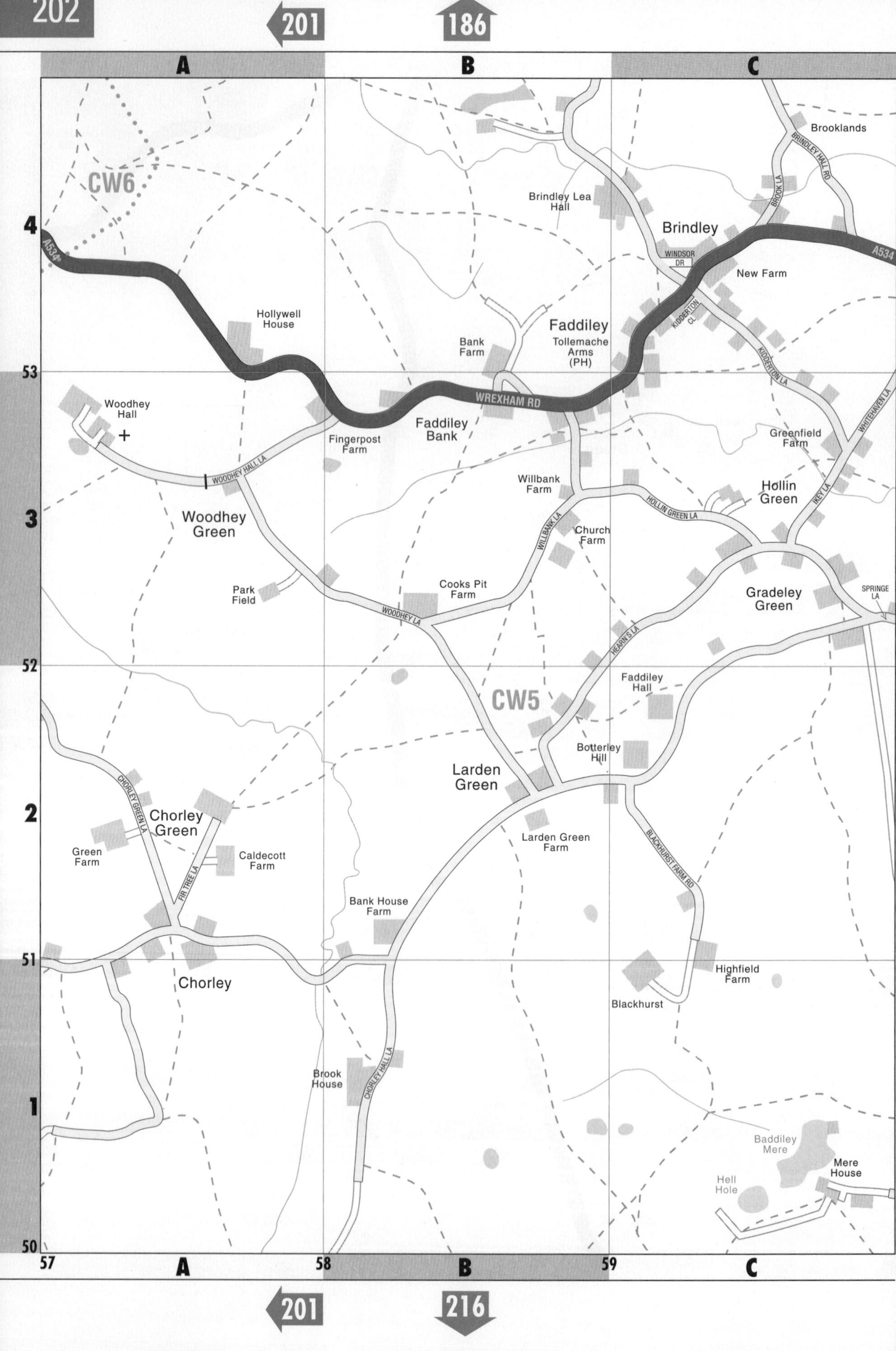

A534

CW6

Hollywell House

Woodhey Hall

Woodhey Green

Fingerpost Farm

Park Field

Chorley Green La

Green Farm

Chorley Green

Caldecott Farm

Fir Tree La

Chorley

Brook House

Chorley Hall La

WOODHEY HALL LA

Faddiley Bank

WREXHAM RD

Bank Farm

Faddiley

Tollemache Arms (PH)

Brindley Lea Hall

Brindley

Windsor Dr

New Farm

Brooklands

Brindley Hall Rd

Brook La

Kidderton Cl

Kidderton La

A534

Greenfield Farm

Hollin Green

Whitehaven La

Irey La

Willbank Farm

Church Farm

Willbank La

Hollin Green La

Cooks Pit Farm

WOODHEY LA

Hearn's La

Gradeley Green

Springe La

Faddiley Hall

CW5

Larden Green

Botterley Hill

Larden Green Farm

Blackhurst Farm Rd

Bank House Farm

Highfield Farm

Blackhurst

Baddiley Mere

Hell Hole

Mere House

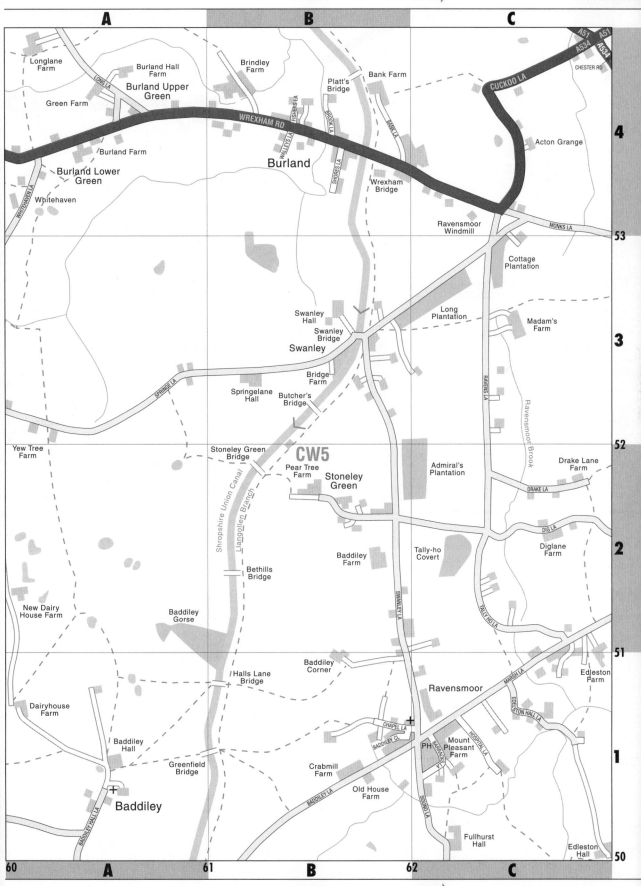
187

204

A B C

Longlane Farm
Burland Hall Farm
Burland Upper Green
Green Farm
LONG LA
Brindley Farm
Platt's Bridge
Bank Farm
CUCKOO LA
A51
A534
CHESTER RD
WREXHAM RD
FISHERS LA
BROOK LA
BANK LA
WALLEYS LA
Burland Farm
Burland
Acton Grange
Burland Lower Green
SHORES LA
Wrexham Bridge
WHITEHAVEN LA
Whitehaven
Ravensmoor Windmill
MONKS LA
Cottage Plantation
Long Plantation
Swanley Hall
Madam's Farm
Swanley Bridge
Swanley
SPRINGE LA
Bridge Farm
Springelane Hall
Butcher's Bridge
RAVENS LA
Ravensmoor Brook
Yew Tree Farm
Stoneley Green Bridge
CW5
Pear Tree Farm
Stoneley Green
Admiral's Plantation
Drake Lane Farm
DRAKE LA
Shropshire Union Canal
Llangollen Branch
DIG LA
Baddiley Farm
Tally-ho Covert
Diglane Farm
Bethills Bridge
SWANLEY LA
New Dairy House Farm
Baddiley Gorse
TALLY HO LA
Baddiley Corner
Halls Lane Bridge
Ravensmoor
MARSH LA
Edleston Farm
EDLESTON HALL LA
Dairyhouse Farm
CHAPEL LA
BADDILEY CL
Baddiley Hall
PH
BARRACKS LA
Mount Pleasant Farm
HOSPITAL LA
Greenfield Bridge
Crabmill Farm
Old House Farm
Baddiley
BADDILEY LA
SOUND LA
BADDILEY HALL LA
Fullhurst Hall
Edleston Hall
4
53
3
52
2
51
1
50
60
61
62

A B C

217

204

203
188

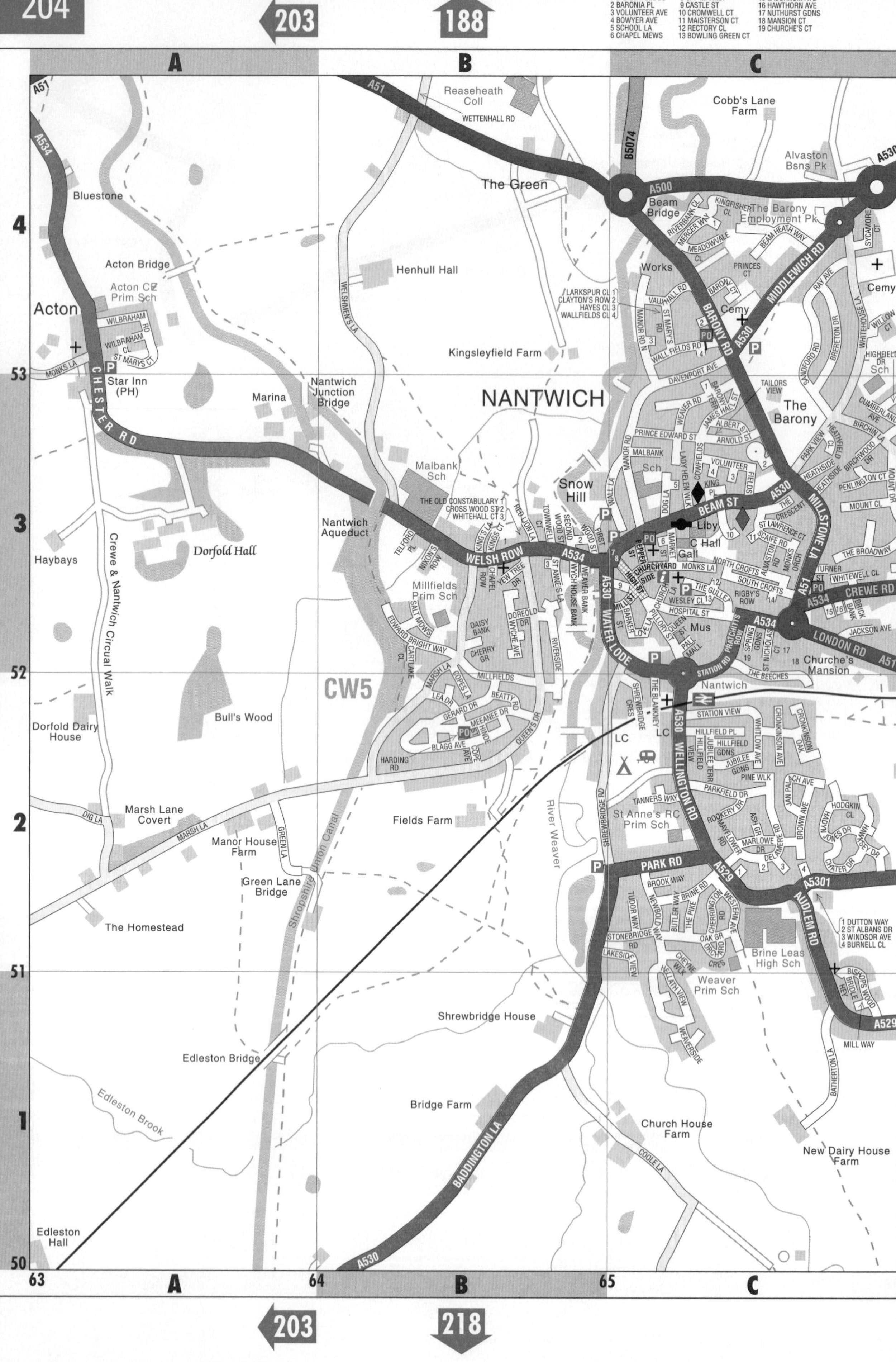
C3
1 BARONY BLDGS
2 BARONIA PL
3 VOLUNTEER AVE
4 BOWYER AVE
5 SCHOOL LA
6 CHAPEL MEWS
7 SWINE MARKET
8 OAT MARKET
9 CASTLE ST
10 CROMWELL CT
11 MAISTERSON CT
12 RECTORY CL
13 BOWLING GREEN CT
14 ROOKERY CL
15 LABURNUM AVE
16 HAWTHORN AVE
17 NUTHURST GDNS
18 MANSION CT
19 CHURCHE'S CT
A
B
C
4
3
2
1
53
52
51
50
63
64
65
Reaseheath Coll
WETTENHALL RD
Cobb's Lane Farm
Alvaston Bsns Pk
The Green
Beam Bridge
The Barony Employment Pk
Bluestone
Acton Bridge
Henhull Hall
Acton CE Prim Sch
Acton
Works
Cemy
Kingsleyfield Farm
LARKSPUR CL 1
CLAYTON'S ROW 2
HAYES CL 3
WALLFIELDS CL 4
Star Inn (PH)
Marina
Nantwich Junction Bridge
NANTWICH
The Barony
Malbank Sch
Snow Hill
THE OLD CONSTABULARY 1
CROSS WOOD ST 2
WHITEHALL CT 3
Haybays
Dorfold Hall
Nantwich Aqueduct
Liby
C Hall
Gall
Mus
Millfields Prim Sch
Crewe & Nantwich Circual Walk
CW5
Churche's Mansion
Nantwich
Dorfold Dairy House
Bull's Wood
LC
Marsh Lane Covert
Manor House Farm
Fields Farm
St Anne's RC Prim Sch
River Weaver
Green Lane Bridge
Shropshire Union Canal
The Homestead
1 DUTTON WAY
2 ST ALBANS DR
3 WINDSOR AVE
4 BURNELL CL
Brine Leas High Sch
Weaver Prim Sch
Shrewbridge House
Edleston Bridge
Edleston Brook
Bridge Farm
Church House Farm
New Dairy House Farm
Edleston Hall
A51
A534
A530
A500
B5074
A529
A5301
CHESTER RD
WELSH ROW
BEAM ST
WATER LODE
WELLINGTON RD
PARK RD
LONDON RD
CREWE RD
MILLSTONE LA
BARONY RD
MIDDLEWICH RD
AUDLEM RD
BADDINGTON LA
COOLE LA
MARSH LA
DIG LA
GREEN LA
WELSHMEN'S LA
SHREWBRIDGE RD
MILL WAY
BATHERTON LA

203
218

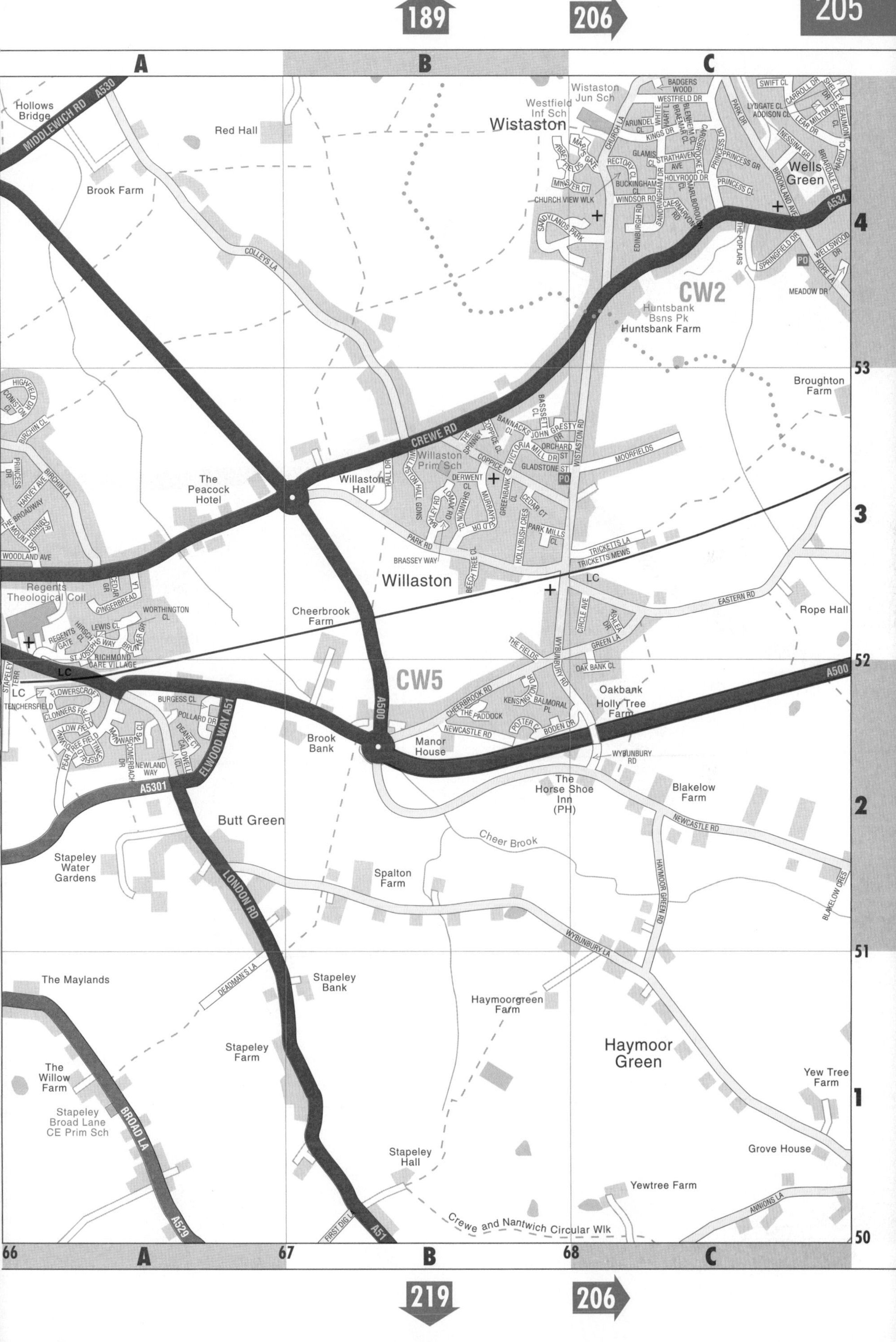
189
206
A
B
C
Hollows Bridge
MIDDLEWICH RD A530
Red Hall
Brook Farm
COLLEYS LA
Westfield Inf Sch
Wistaston Jun Sch
Wistaston
BADGERS WOOD
WESTFIELD DR
SWIFT CL
LYDGATE CL
ADDISON CL
CARROLL DR
SHELLEY DR
BEAUMONT
MILTON DR
LEAR DR
NESSINA GR
BRIARDALE CL
HARDY CL
CHURCH LA
ARUNDEL CL
KINGS DR
WHITE HART L
BRAEMAR CL
BLENHEIM CL
CARISBROOKE CL
PARK DR
ABBEYFIELDS
MARS GATE
RECTORY CL
GLAMIS CL
STRATHAVEN AVE
PRINCESS DR
PRINCESS GR
PRINCESS CL
HOLYROOD DR
BUCKINGHAM CL
SANDRINGHAM DR
MARLBOROUGH
MINSTER CT
CHURCH VIEW WLK
WINDSOR RD
CAERNARVON RD
EDINBURGH RD
Wells Green
BROOKLAND AVE
A534
SANDYLANDS PARK
THE POPLARS
SPRINGFIELD DR
WELLSWOOD DR
ROPE LA
MEADOW DR
CW2
Huntsbank Bsns Pk
Huntsbank Farm
53
4
Broughton Farm
HIGHFIELD DR
CONISTON CL
BIRCHIN CL
PRINCESS DR
HARVEY AVE
BIRCHIN LA
THE BROADWAY
MOUNT DR
HORNBY DR
WOODLAND AVE
The Peacock Hotel
CREWE RD
THE SPINNEY
COPPICE CL
BANNACKS CL
BASSETT CL
JOHN GRESTY DR
ORCHARD ST
VICTORIA MILL DR
WISTASTON RD
MOORFIELDS
Willaston Prim Sch
COPPICE RD
GLADSTONE ST
DERWENT CL
Willaston Hall
HALL DR
WILLASTON HALL GDNS
SHANNON CL
MURRAYFIELD DR
GREENBANK CL
CEDAR CT
LOMAX RD
BARLEY RD
HOLLYBUSH CRES
PARK MILLS CL
PARK RD
BRASSEY WAY
BEECH TREE CL
TRICKETTS LA
TRICKETTS MEWS
3
Willaston
LC
Regents Theological Coll
CEDAR GR
GINGERBREAD LA
WORTHINGTON CL
LEWIS CL
REGENTS GATE
HIRSCH CL
ST JOSEPHS WAY
BRUNNER GR
RICHMOND CARE VILLAGE
Cheerbrook Farm
EASTERN RD
Rope Hall
CIRCLE AVE
ASHLEA DR
GREEN LA
THE FIELDS
WYBUNBURY RD
OAK BANK CL
52
STAPELEY TERR
LC
TENCHERSFIELD
FLOWERSCROFT
CLONNERS FIELD
LOW FIELD
PEAR TREE FIELD
MAINWARING DR
COMBERBACH DR
BURGESS CL
POLLARD DR
DEANE CT
CALDWELL CL
NEWLAND WAY
ELWOOD WAY A51
A5301
CW5
A500
Brook Bank
CHEERBROOK RD
THE PADDOCK
KENSINGTON DR
BALMORAL PL
POTTER CL
BODEN DR
NEWCASTLE RD
Manor House
Oakbank
Holly Tree Farm
A500
WYBUNBURY RD
The Horse Shoe Inn (PH)
Blakelow Farm
2
Butt Green
Stapeley Water Gardens
Cheer Brook
NEWCASTLE RD
LONDON RD
Spalton Farm
HAYMOOR GREEN RD
BLAKELOW CRES
WYBUNBURY LA
51
The Maylands
DEADMAN'S LA
Stapeley Bank
Haymoorgreen Farm
Stapeley Farm
Haymoor Green
The Willow Farm
Stapeley Broad Lane CE Prim Sch
BROAD LA
Yew Tree Farm
1
Grove House
Stapeley Hall
Yewtree Farm
ANNIONS LA
A529
FIRST DIG LA
A51
Crewe and Nantwich Circular Wlk
50
66
A
67
B
68
C
219
206

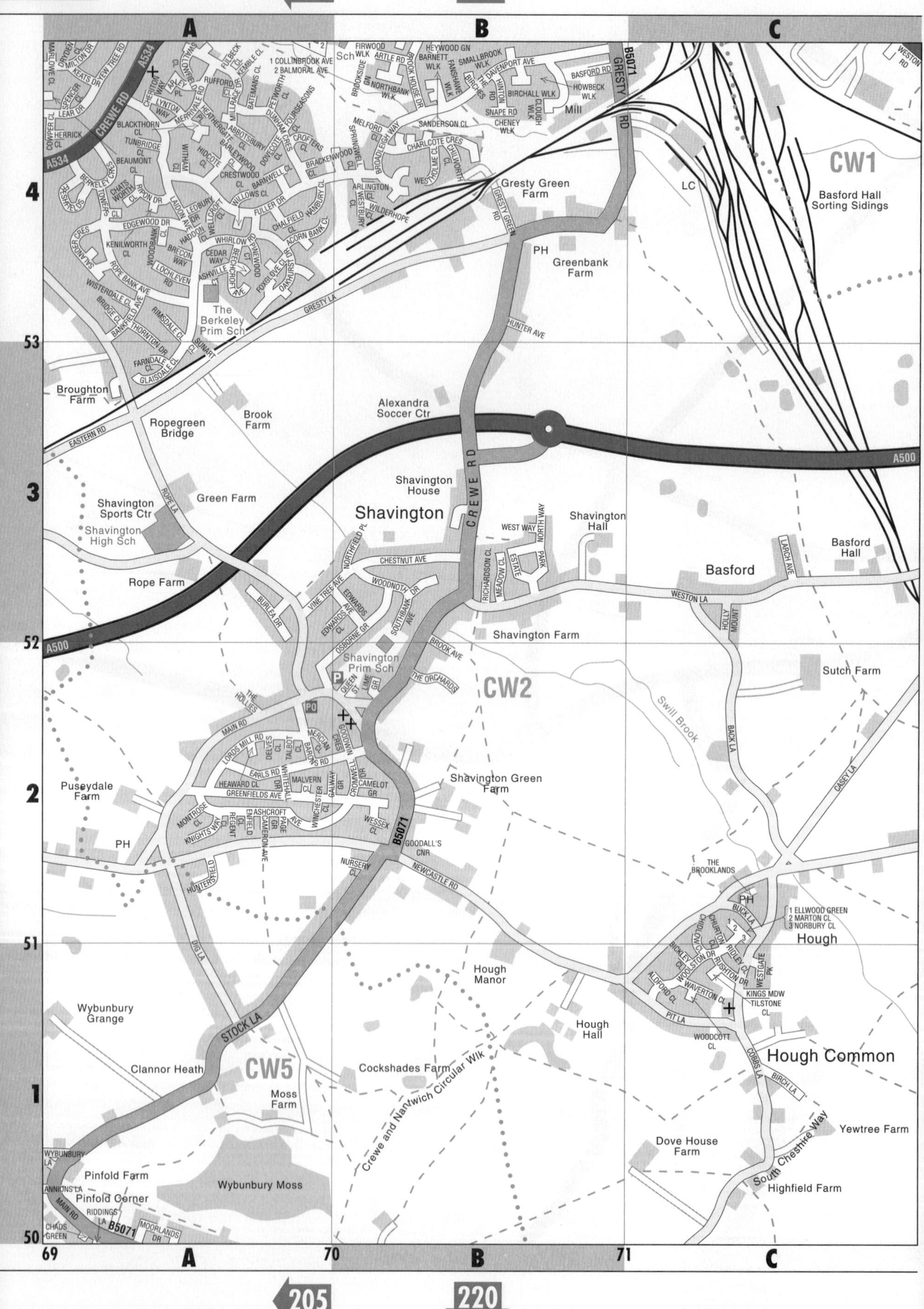
205
190
A
B
C
4
3
2
1
53
52
51
50
69
70
71
CW1
CW2
CW5
Basford Hall Sorting Sidings
LC
Gresty Green Farm
Greenbank Farm
PH
Mill
Sch
The Berkeley Prim Sch
Broughton Farm
Ropegreen Bridge
Brook Farm
Alexandra Soccer Ctr
Shavington House
Shavington
Shavington Hall
Basford Hall
Basford
Shavington Sports Ctr
Shavington High Sch
Green Farm
Rope Farm
Shavington Farm
Shavington Prim Sch
Sutch Farm
Swill Brook
Puseydale Farm
Shavington Green Farm
GOODALL'S CNR
THE BROOKLANDS
Hough
Hough Manor
Hough Hall
Hough Common
Wybunbury Grange
Clannor Heath
Cockshades Farm
Moss Farm
Crewe and Nantwich Circular Wlk
Yewtree Farm
Dove House Farm
South Cheshire Way
Highfield Farm
Pinfold Farm
Pinfold Corner
Wybunbury Moss
CHADS GREEN
A534
CREWE RD
A500
B5071
GRESTY RD
GRESTY LA
EASTERN RD
ROPE LA
WESTON LA
WESTON RD
BACK LA
CASEY LA
NEWCASTLE RD
STOCK LA
DIG LA
MAIN RD
PIT LA
COBBS LA
BIRCH LA
WYBUNBURY LA
ANNIONS LA
RIDDINGS LA
MOORLANDS DR
1 COLLINBROOK AVE
2 BALMORAL AVE
1 ELLWOOD GREEN
2 MARTON CL
3 NORBURY CL

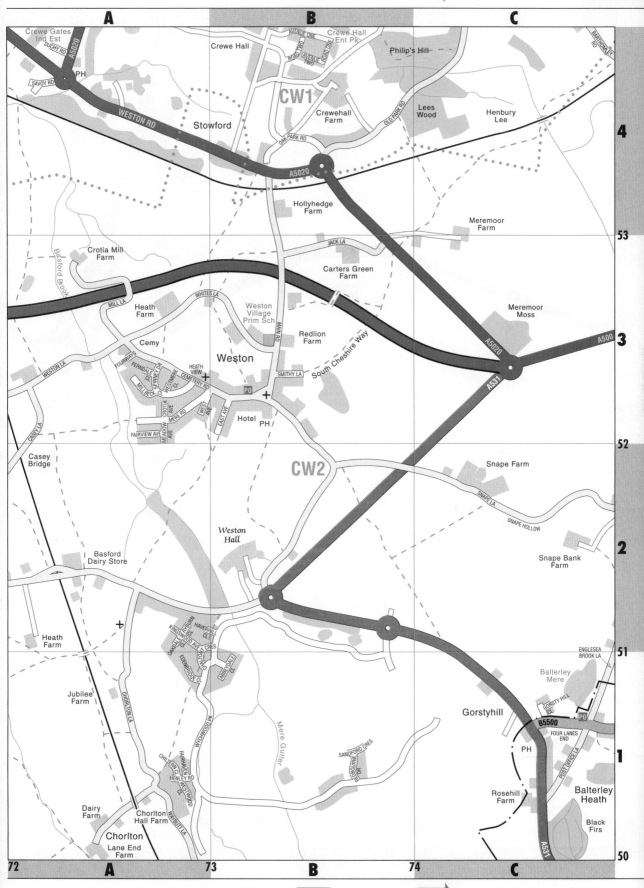

Crewe Gates Ind Est
A5020
DUCHY RD
PH
SAVOY RD
WESTON RD
Stowford
Crewe Hall
AVENUE ONE
ROAD TWO
AVENUE TWO
Crewe Hall Ent Pk
ROAD ONE
Philip's Hill
BARTHOMLEY RD
CW1
Crewehall Farm
Oak Park Rd
OAK PARK RD
Old Park Rd
Lees Wood
Henbury Lee
4
A5020
Hollyhedge Farm
Meremoor Farm
53
JACK LA
Carters Green Farm
Badford Brook
Crotia Mill Farm
MILL LA
Heath Farm
WHITES LA
Weston Village Prim Sch
MAIN RD
Redlion Farm
South Cheshire Way
Meremoor Moss
A5020
A531
A500
3
WESTON LA
CASEY LA
Cemy
FOURWAYS
PERNDALE CL
SPINNEY DR
WESTMERE CL
MILL BECK
CROTIA AVE
MEADOW
MERE RD
FAIRVIEW AVE
HEATH VIEW
CEMETERY RD
WEST AVE
EAST AVE
PO
Weston
SMITHY LA
Hotel
PH
52
Casey Bridge
CW2
Snape Farm
Weston Hall
SNAPE LA
SNAPE HOLLOW
Snape Bank Farm
2
Basford Dairy Store
Heath Farm
KINGSWOOD AVE
RYBURN CL
HAVERHILL CRES
OAKDALE CL
CHALTON CL
EDENBRIDGE CL
ABBEYDALE CL
WYCHWOOD PK
Mere Gutter
ENGLESEA BROOK LA
Balterley Mere
51
Jubilee Farm
CHORLTON LA
Gorstyhill
GORSTY HILL CL
PO
Dairy Farm
Chorlton Hall Farm
Chorlton
Lane End Farm
CHILTERN CL
FAIRHAVEN RD
HENLEY RD
WESTWOOD CL
WALBUTT LA
SANDFORD CRES
REDBOURNE DR
B5500
FOUR LANES END
PH
POST OFFICE LA
Balterley Heath
Rosehill Farm
Black Firs
A531
1
50

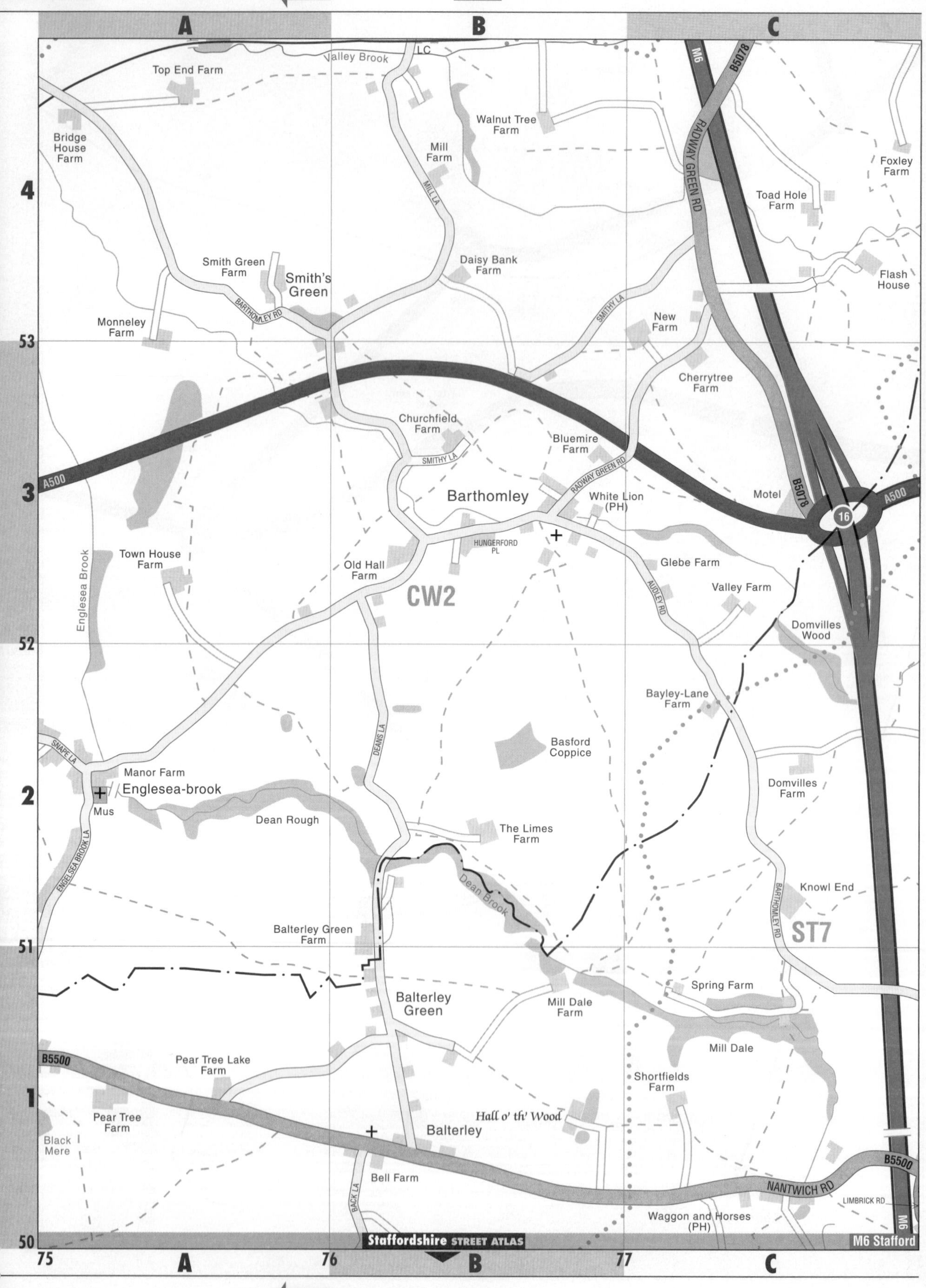
A
B
C
Valley Brook
LC
Top End Farm
Bridge House Farm
Walnut Tree Farm
Mill Farm
MILL LA
M6
B5078
RADWAY GREEN RD
Foxley Farm
Toad Hole Farm
4
Smith Green Farm
Smith's Green
Daisy Bank Farm
BARTHOMLEY RD
Monneley Farm
SMITHY LA
New Farm
Flash House
53
Cherrytree Farm
Churchfield Farm
SMITHY LA
Bluemire Farm
A500
RADWAY GREEN RD
3
Barthomley
White Lion (PH)
Motel
B5078
16
A500
HUNGERFORD PL
Town House Farm
Old Hall Farm
Glebe Farm
Englesea Brook
CW2
AUDLEY RD
Valley Farm
Domvilles Wood
52
Bayley-Lane Farm
DEANS LA
Basford Coppice
SNAPE LA
Manor Farm
Englesea-brook
2
Mus
Domvilles Farm
Dean Rough
The Limes Farm
ENGLESEA BROOK LA
Dean Brook
Knowl End
BARTHOMLEY RD
Balterley Green Farm
ST7
51
Spring Farm
Balterley Green
Mill Dale Farm
Mill Dale
B5500
Pear Tree Lake Farm
Shortfields Farm
1
Pear Tree Farm
Hall o' th' Wood
Balterley
Black Mere
B5500
Bell Farm
NANTWICH RD
LIMBRICK RD
BACK LA
Waggon and Horses (PH)
M6
50
Staffordshire STREET ATLAS
M6 Stafford
75
76
77

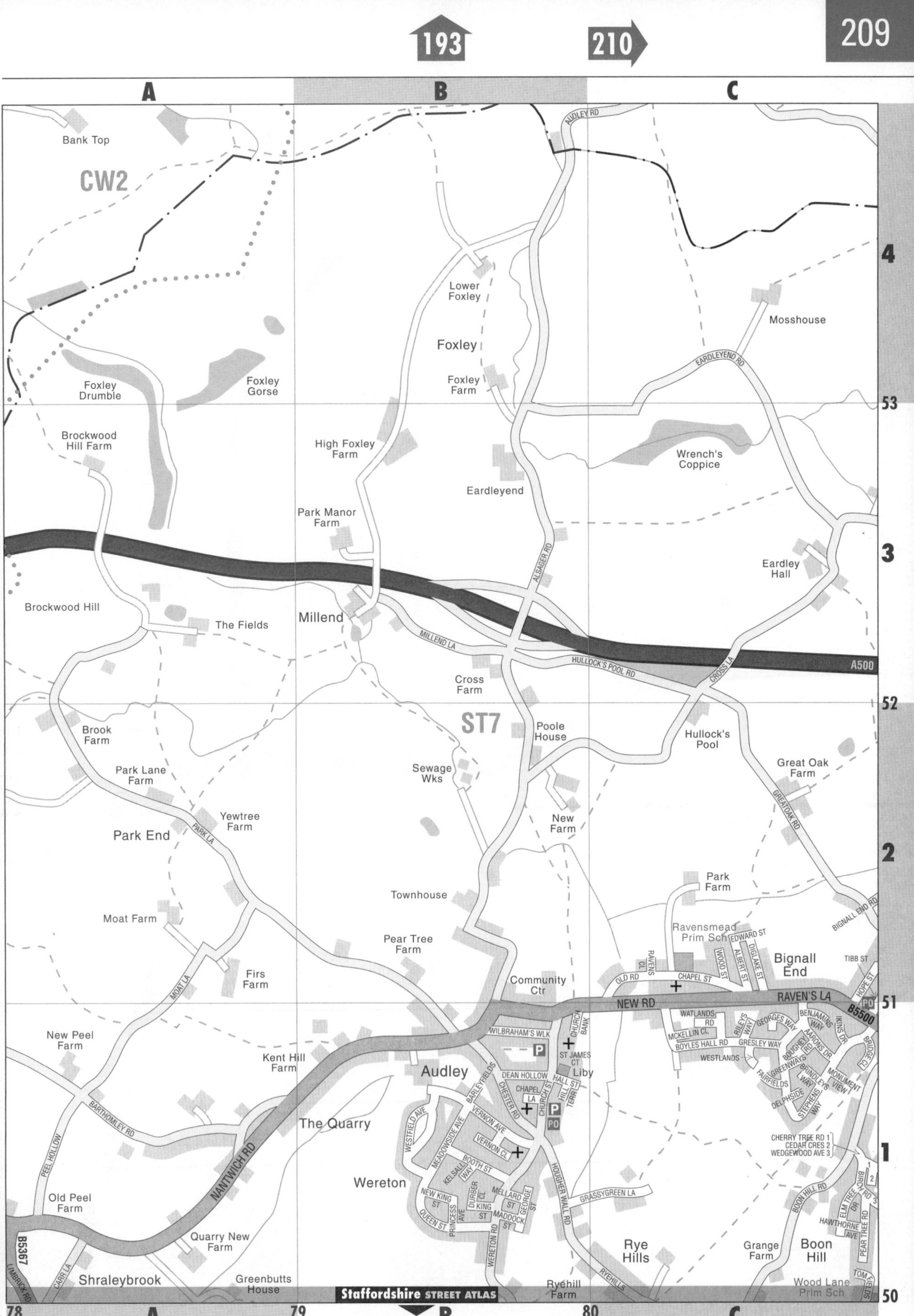

A B C

4

53

3

52

2

51

1

50

CW2

Bank Top

Lower
Foxley

Foxley

Mosshouse

EARDLEYEND RD

Foxley
Farm

Foxley
Drumble

Foxley
Gorse

High Foxley
Farm

Wrench's
Coppice

Brockwood
Hill Farm

Eardleyend

ALSAGER RD

AUDLEY RD

Park Manor
Farm

Eardley
Hall

Brockwood Hill

The Fields

Millend

MILLEND LA

HULLOCK'S POOL RD

CROSS LA

A500

Cross
Farm

ST7

Poole
House

Hullock's
Pool

Brook
Farm

Great Oak
Farm

Park Lane
Farm

Sewage
Wks

New
Farm

GREAT OAK RD

Park End

Yewtree
Farm

PARK LA

Park
Farm

BIGNALL END RD

Moat Farm

Townhouse

Ravensmead
Prim Sch

EDWARD ST

Bignall
End

TIBB ST

MOAT LA

Pear Tree
Farm

WOOD ST

ALBERT ST

Firs
Farm

Community
Ctr

RAVENS CL

OLD RD

CHAPEL ST

RAVEN'S LA

NEW RD

B5500

New Peel
Farm

Wilbraham's Wlk

WATLANDS
RD

GEORGES WAY

BENJAMINS
WAY

HOPE ST

IKINS DR

BARONS DR

BARTHOMLEY RD

Kent Hill
Farm

BAGLEYFIELDS

CHURCH
BANK

St James
Ct

MCKELLIN CL.

BILL'S
WAY

GRESLEY WAY

BANGUY

GREENWAYS

MONUMENT
VIEW

Audley

DEAN HOLLOW

Liby

BOYLES HALL RD

WESTLANDS

FAIRFIELDS

STEPHENS
WAY

NANTWICH RD

CHESTER RD

VERNON AVE

CHAPEL
LA

HALL ST

ST JAMES
TERR

DELPHSIDE

WESTFIELD AVE

MEADOWSIDE AVE

VERNON CT.

CHURCH ST

CHERRY TREE RD 1
CEDAR CRES 2
WEDGEWOOD AVE 3

The Quarry

BOOTH ST

PO

Wereton

KEL SALL
WAY

DURBER
CL

MELLARD ST

GEORGE ST

GRASSYGREEN LA

Grange
Farm

Boon
Hill

BOON HILL RD

ELM TREE AVE

HAWTHORNE
AVE

PEAR TREE RD

Old Peel
Farm

NEW KING
ST

PRINCESS
AVE

QUEEN ST

KING
ST

MADDOCK
ST

WERETON RD

HOUGHER WALL RD

Rye
Hills

RYEHILLS

Wood Lane
Prim Sch

B5367

TIMBRICK RD

Quarry New
Farm

Shraleybrook

Greenbutts
House

Ryehill
Farm

78 A 79 B 80 C

209
194

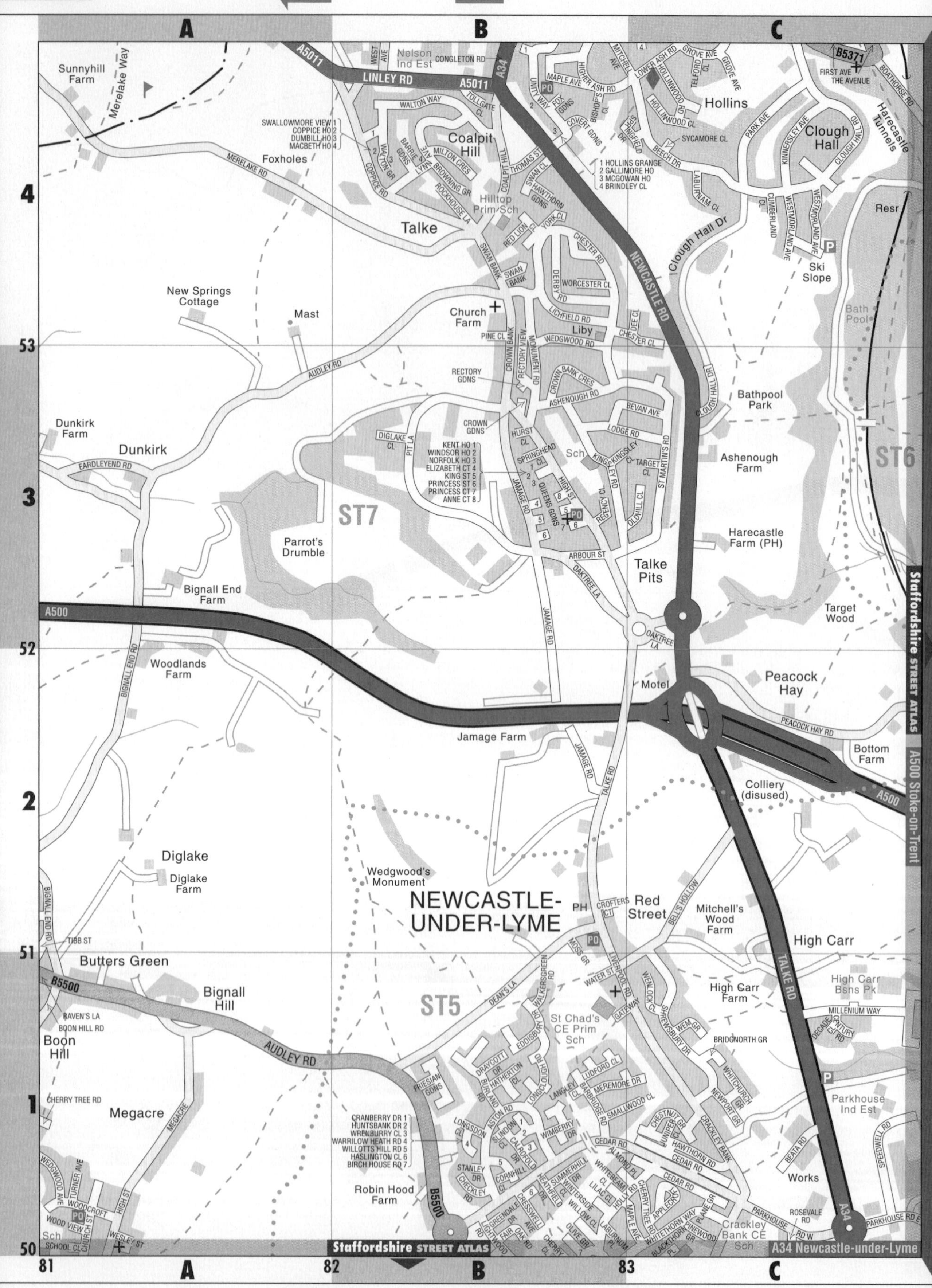
A
B
C
A5011
LINLEY RD
A5011
A34
WEST AVE
Nelson Ind Est
CONGLETON RD
Sunnyhill Farm
Merelake Way
WALTON WAY
TOLLGATE CL
SWALLOWMORE VIEW 1
COPPICE HO 2
DUMBILL HO 3
MACBETH HO 4
Coalpit Hill
MILTON CRES
BROWNING GR
ROCKHOUSE LA
WALTON GR
COPPICE RD
COALPIT HILL
THOMAS ST
SWAN CL
HAWTHORN GDNS
Hilltop Prim Sch
Foxholes
MERELAKE RD
Talke
RED LION CL
YORK CL
SWAN BANK
MAPLE AVE
UNITY WAY
FOX GDNS
HIGHER ASH RD
BISHOP'S CL
COVERT GDNS
MITCHELL AVE
SPRINGFIELD DR
1 HOLLINS GRANGE
2 GALLIMORE HO
3 MCGOWAN HO
4 BRINDLEY CL
LOWER ASH RD
GROVE AVE
HOLLINWOOD RD
HOLLINWOOD CL
TELFORD CL
Hollins
SYCAMORE CL
BEECH DR
LABURNAM CL
PARK AVE
KINNERSLEY AVE
Clough Hall
CLOUGH HALL RD
B5371
FIRST AVE
THE AVENUE
BOATHORSE RD
Harecastle Tunnels
CUMBERLAND CL
WESTMORLAND AVE
WESTMORLAND AVE
Resr
Ski Slope
Clough Hall Dr
NEWCASTLE RD
CHESTER RD
DERBY RD
WORCESTER CL
LICHFIELD RD
DEE CL
CHESTER CL
Liby
WEDGWOOD RD
New Springs Cottage
Mast
Church Farm
PINE CL
CROWN BANK
RECTORY VIEW
MONUMENT RD
53
AUDLEY RD
RECTORY GDNS
CROWN BANK CRES
ASHENOUGH RD
BEVAN AVE
LODGE RD
CLOUGH HALL DR
Bathpool Park
Bath Pool
CROWN GDNS
DIGLAKE CL
PIT LA
KENT HO 1
WINDSOR HO 2
NORFOLK HO 3
ELIZABETH CT 4
KING ST 5
PRINCESS ST 6
PRINCESS CT 7
ANNE CT 8
HURST CL
SPRINGHEAD CL
KINGSLEY RD
KINGSLEY CL
TARGET CL
ST MARTIN'S RD
Sch
Ashenough Farm
ST6
Dunkirk Farm
Dunkirk
EARDLEYEND RD
ST7
JAMAGE RD
QUEENS GDNS
HIGH ST
REGENCY CL
OLDHILL CL
PO
Parrot's Drumble
Harecastle Farm (PH)
ARBOUR ST
OAKTREE LA
Talke Pits
Bignall End Farm
A500
Target Wood
JAMAGE RD
OAKTREE LA
52
BIGNALL END RD
Woodlands Farm
Motel
Peacock Hay
PEACOCK HAY RD
Jamage Farm
JAMAGE RD
TALKE RD
Bottom Farm
Colliery (disused)
A500
2
Diglake
Diglake Farm
Wedgwood's Monument
NEWCASTLE-UNDER-LYME
PH
CROFTERS CT
Red Street
BELL'S HOLLOW
Mitchell's Wood Farm
High Carr
BIGNALL END RD
TIBB ST
51
Butters Green
B5500
Bignall Hill
DEAN'S LA
WALKERSGREEN RD
MOSS GR
WATER ST
LIVERPOOL RD
ST5
GATEWAY
St Chad's CE Prim Sch
WENLOCK CL
SHREWSBURY DR
WEM GR
High Carr Farm
TALKE RD
High Carr Bsns Pk
MILLENIUM WAY
DECADE CL
CENTURY RD
BRIDGNORTH GR
RAVEN'S LA
BOON HILL RD
Boon Hill
AUDLEY RD
FRIESIAN GDNS
DRAYCOTT DR
EDDISBURY DR
HATHERTON CL
BURLAND RD
LONGLOUGH RD
LUDFORD CL
MEREMORE DR
SMALLWOOD CL
LANGLEY CL
BARBRIDGE RD
WHITCHURCH GR
NEWPORT GR
1
CHERRY TREE RD
Megacre
MEGACRE
CRANBERRY DR 1
HUNTSBANK DR 2
WRENBURY CL 3
WARRILOW HEATH RD 4
WILLOTTS HILL RD 5
HASLINGTON CL 6
BIRCH HOUSE RD 7
LONGSDON CL
ASTON RD
WIMBERRY DR
CHESTNUT GR
JUNIPER CL
CRACKLEY BANK
HAWTHORN RD
CEDAR RD
ALMOND PL
Parkhouse Ind Est
BEATA RD
SPEEDWELL RD
Works
STANLEY DR
CHECKLEY RD
CORNHILL
HEATHFIELD DR
SUMMERHILL DR
WINTERSIDE CL
WHITEBEAM CL
LILAC CL
HOLLY RD
CHERRY TREE RD
APPLECROFT
PLANE GR
PARKHOUSE RD W
ROSEVALE RD
A34
PARKHOUSE RD E
Robin Hood Farm
B5500
TURNER AVE
WEDGWOOD AVE
WOODCROFT
WOOD VIEW
CHURCH ST
HIGH ST
WESLEY ST
GREENDALE DR
CRESSWELL AVE
FAIR OAK RD
LIGHTWOOD RD
CHERRY CL
OLIVE GR
WILLOW CL
LABURNUM PL
MAPLE AVE
WHITETHORN WAY
BLACKTHORN PL
PINEWOOD GR
Crackley Bank CE Sch
Sch
SCHOOL CL
50
81
82
83
Staffordshire STREET ATLAS
A34 Newcastle-under-Lyme
A500 Stoke-on-Trent
4
3

209

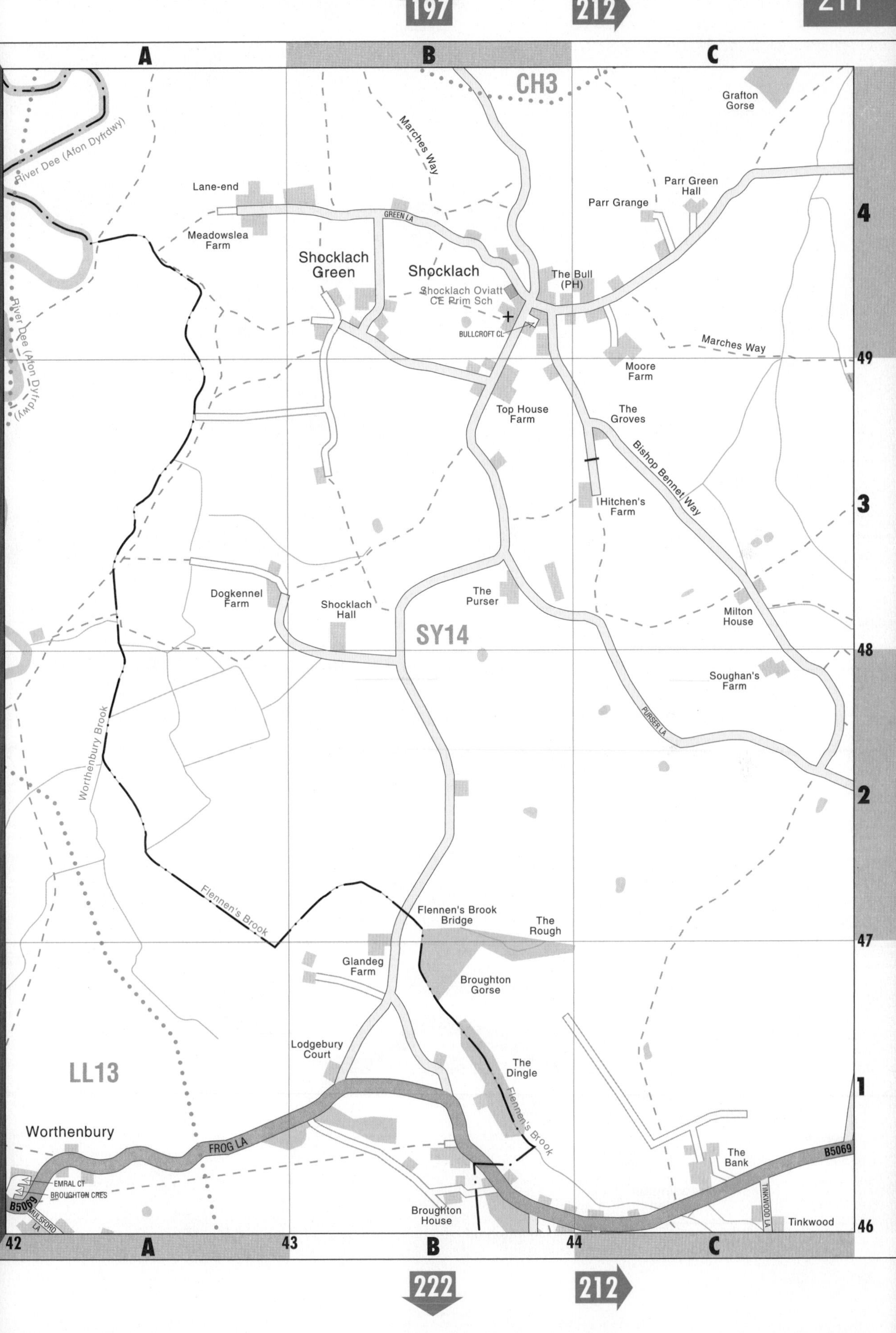

A B C

CH3

Grafton
Gorse

River Dee (Afon Dyfrdwy)

Lane-end

Parr Green
Hall

4

Meadowslea
Farm

Green La

Parr Grange

Shocklach
Green

Shocklach

The Bull
(PH)

Shocklach Oviatt
CE Prim Sch

River Dee (Afon Dyfrdwy)

Bullcroft Cl.

Marches Way

49

Moore
Farm

Top House
Farm

The Groves

Bishop Bennet Way

3

Hitchen's
Farm

Dogkennel
Farm

Shocklach
Hall

The Purser

Milton
House

SY14

48

Soughan's
Farm

Worthenbury Brook

Purser La

2

Flennen's Brook

Flennen's Brook
Bridge

The
Rough

47

Glandeg
Farm

Broughton
Gorse

Lodgebury
Court

LL13

The
Dingle

Flennen's Brook

1

Worthenbury

Frog La

The
Bank

B5069

Emral Ct
Broughton Cres

B5069

Bulsford La

Broughton
House

Tinkwood La

Tinkwood

46

42 A 43 B 44 C

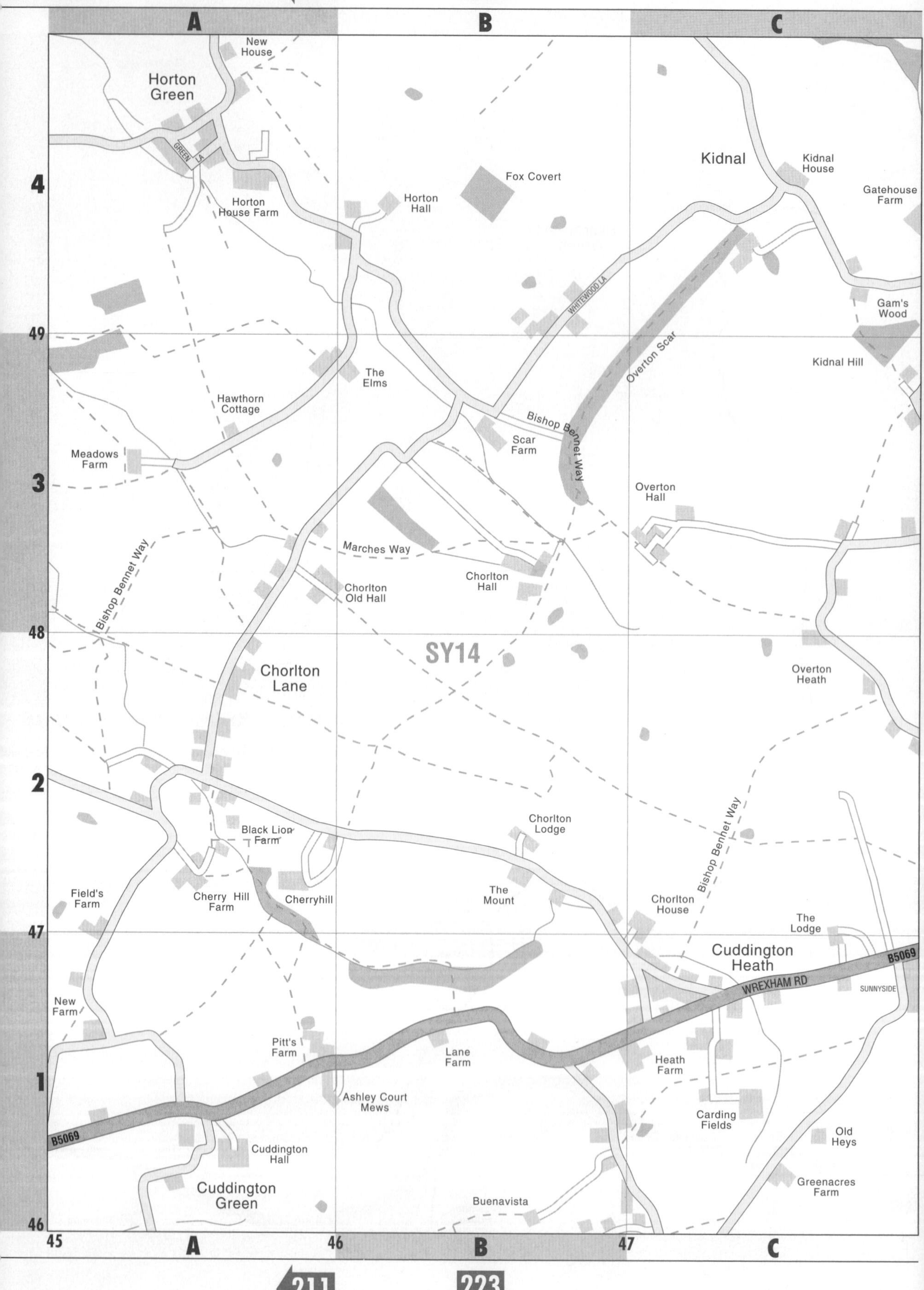

A   B   C

New House

Horton Green

Fox Covert

Kidnal

Kidnal House

Gatehouse Farm

Horton House Farm

Horton Hall

4

GREEN LA

WHITEWOOD LA

Gam's Wood

49

The Elms

Hawthorn Cottage

Bishop Bennet Way

Overton Scar

Kidnal Hill

Scar Farm

Meadows Farm

3

Overton Hall

Bishop Bennet Way

Marches Way

Chorlton Hall

SY14

Chorlton Old Hall

48

Chorlton Lane

Overton Heath

2

Black Lion Farm

Chorlton Lodge

Bishop Bennet Way

Field's Farm

Cherry Hill Farm

Cherryhill

The Mount

Chorlton House

The Lodge

47

Cuddington Heath

B5069

New Farm

WREXHAM RD

SUNNYSIDE

Pitt's Farm

Lane Farm

Heath Farm

1

Ashley Court Mews

Carding Fields

Old Heys

B5069

Cuddington Hall

Greenacres Farm

Cuddington Green

Buenavista

46

45   A   46   B   47   C

199
214

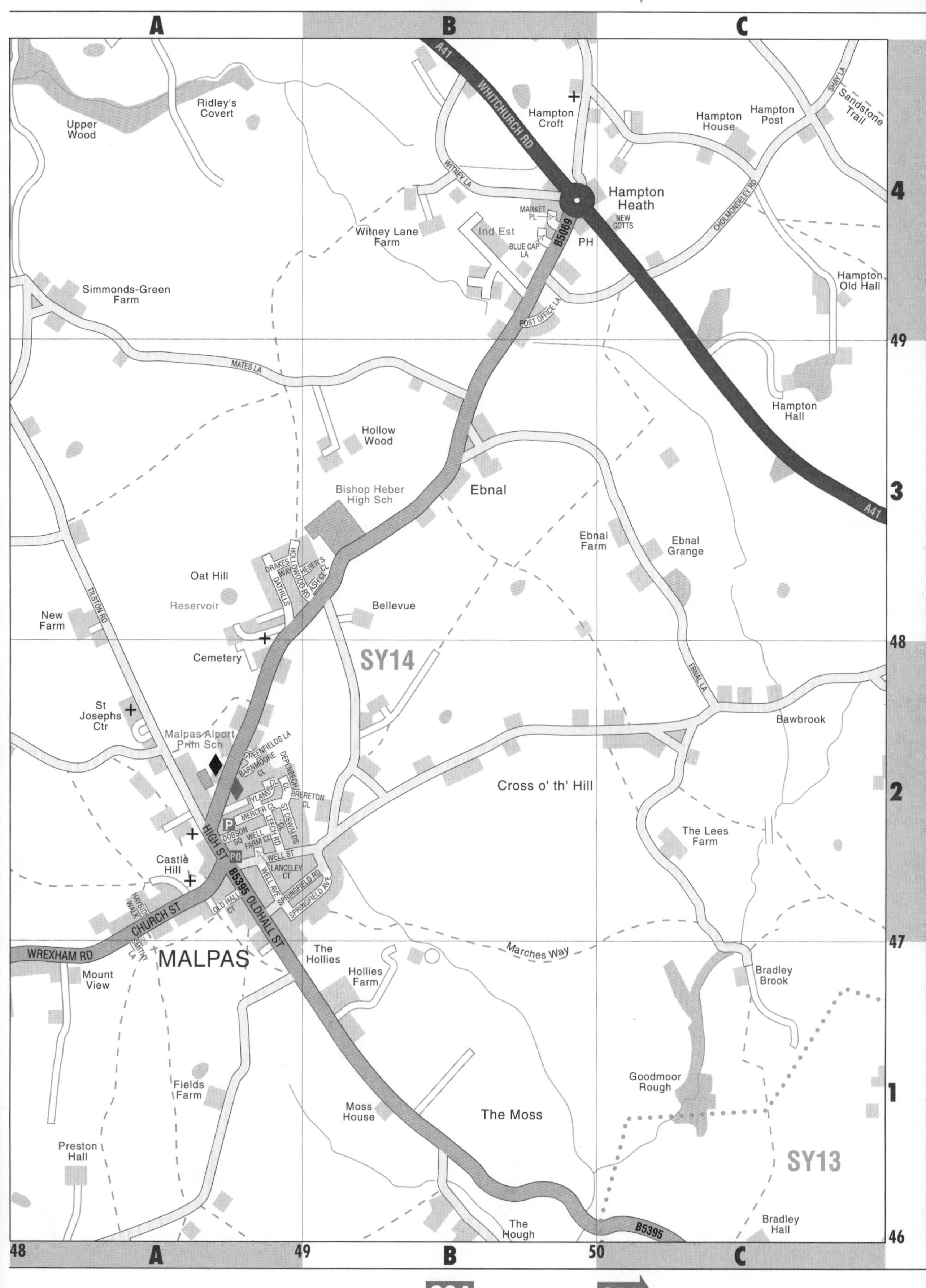
A
B
C
Upper Wood
Ridley's Covert
Hampton Croft
Hampton House
Hampton Post
Sandstone Trail
SHAY LA
WHITCHURCH RD
A41
WITNEY LA
Hampton Heath
MARKET PL
NEW COTTS
CHOLMONDELEY RD
Witney Lane Farm
Ind Est
BLUE CAP LA
B5069
PH
Hampton Old Hall
Simmonds-Green Farm
POST OFFICE LA
MATES LA
Hampton Hall
Hollow Wood
Bishop Heber High Sch
Ebnal
Ebnal Farm
Ebnal Grange
Oat Hill
Reservoir
Bellevue
New Farm
TILSTON RD
Cemetery
SY14
EBNAL LA
St Josephs Ctr
Malpas Alport Prim Sch
GREENFIELDS LA
BARNMOORE CL
DEPENBECH CL
BRETON CL
Bawbrook
Cross o' th' Hill
HIGH ST
MERCER CL
DOBSON SQ
WELL FARM CL
LEECH RD
ST OSWALDS
WELL ST
Castle Hill
LANCELEY CT
WELL AVE
SPRINGFIELD RD
SPRINGFIELD AVE
B5395
OLDHALL ST
OLD HALL CT
HAYSIDE WALK
CHURCH ST
The Lees Farm
WREXHAM RD
SMITHY LA
MALPAS
The Hollies
Hollies Farm
Marches Way
Bradley Brook
Mount View
Fields Farm
Goodmoor Rough
Moss House
The Moss
Preston Hall
SY13
The Hough
B5395
Bradley Hall
4
49
3
48
2
47
1
46
48
49
50

224
214

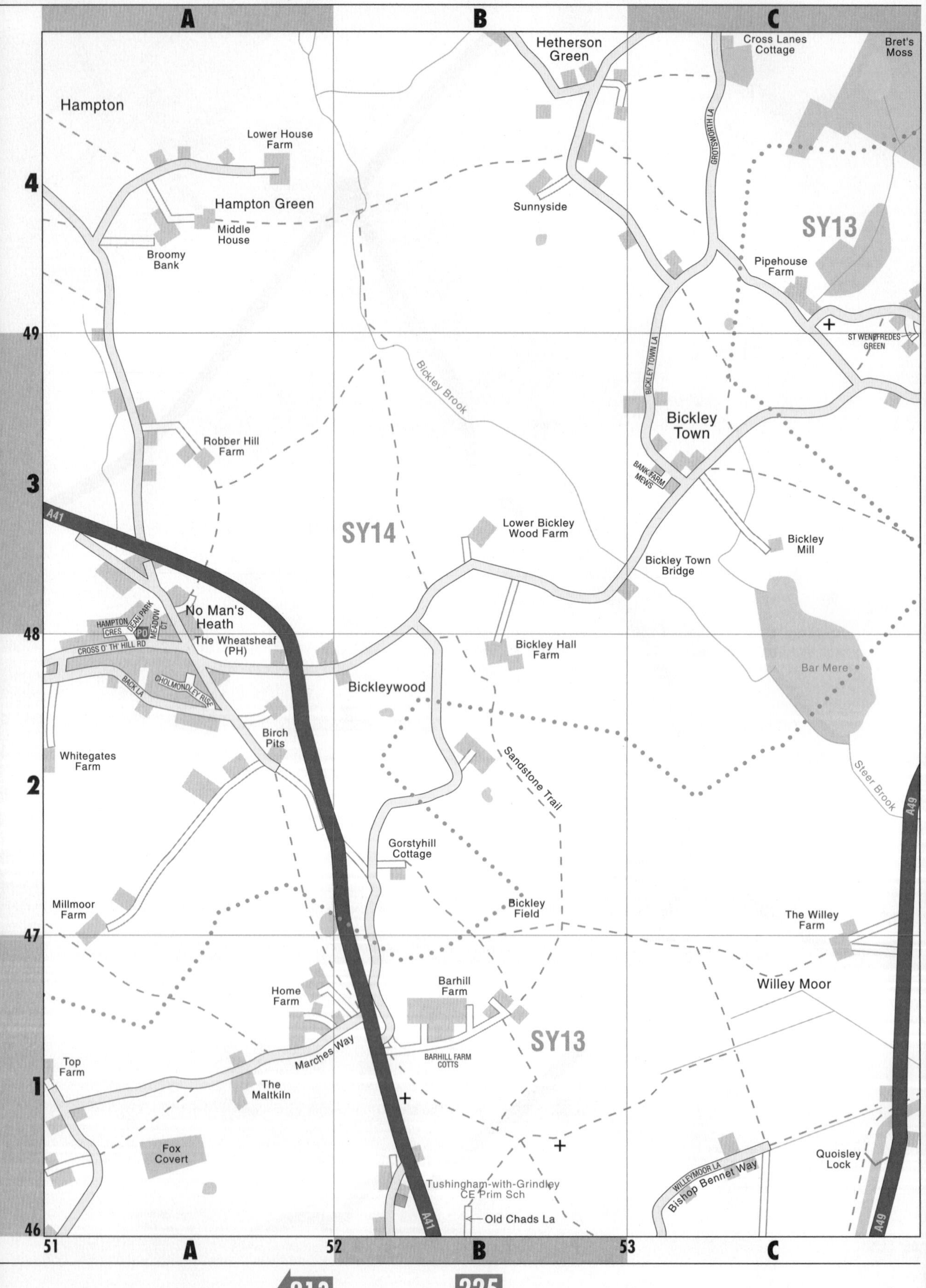

A   **B**   **C**

Hetherson Green

Cross Lanes Cottage

Bret's Moss

Hampton

Lower House Farm

Sunnyside

SY13

Pipehouse Farm

4

Hampton Green

Middle House

Broomy Bank

St WENEFREDES GREEN

49

Bickley Brook

Bickley Town

Robber Hill Farm

BANK FARM MEWS

3

A41

SY14

Lower Bickley Wood Farm

Bickley Mill

Bickley Town Bridge

No Man's Heath

HAMPTON CRES

DEAN PARK CT

MEADOW CT

PO

The Wheatsheaf (PH)

Bickley Hall Farm

Bar Mere

48

CROSS O' TH' HILL RD

Bickleywood

BACK LA

CHOLMONDELEY RISE

Birch Pits

Whitegates Farm

Sandstone Trail

Steer Brook

A49

2

Gorstyhill Cottage

Millmoor Farm

Bickley Field

The Willey Farm

47

Home Farm

Barhill Farm

Willey Moor

Marches Way

SY13

1

Top Farm

The Maltkiln

BARHILL FARM COTTS

Fox Covert

Quoisley Lock

WILLEYMOOR LA

Bishop Bennet Way

Tushingham-with-Grindley CE Prim Sch

A41

Old Chads La

A49

46

51   **A**   52   **B**   53   **C**

201
216

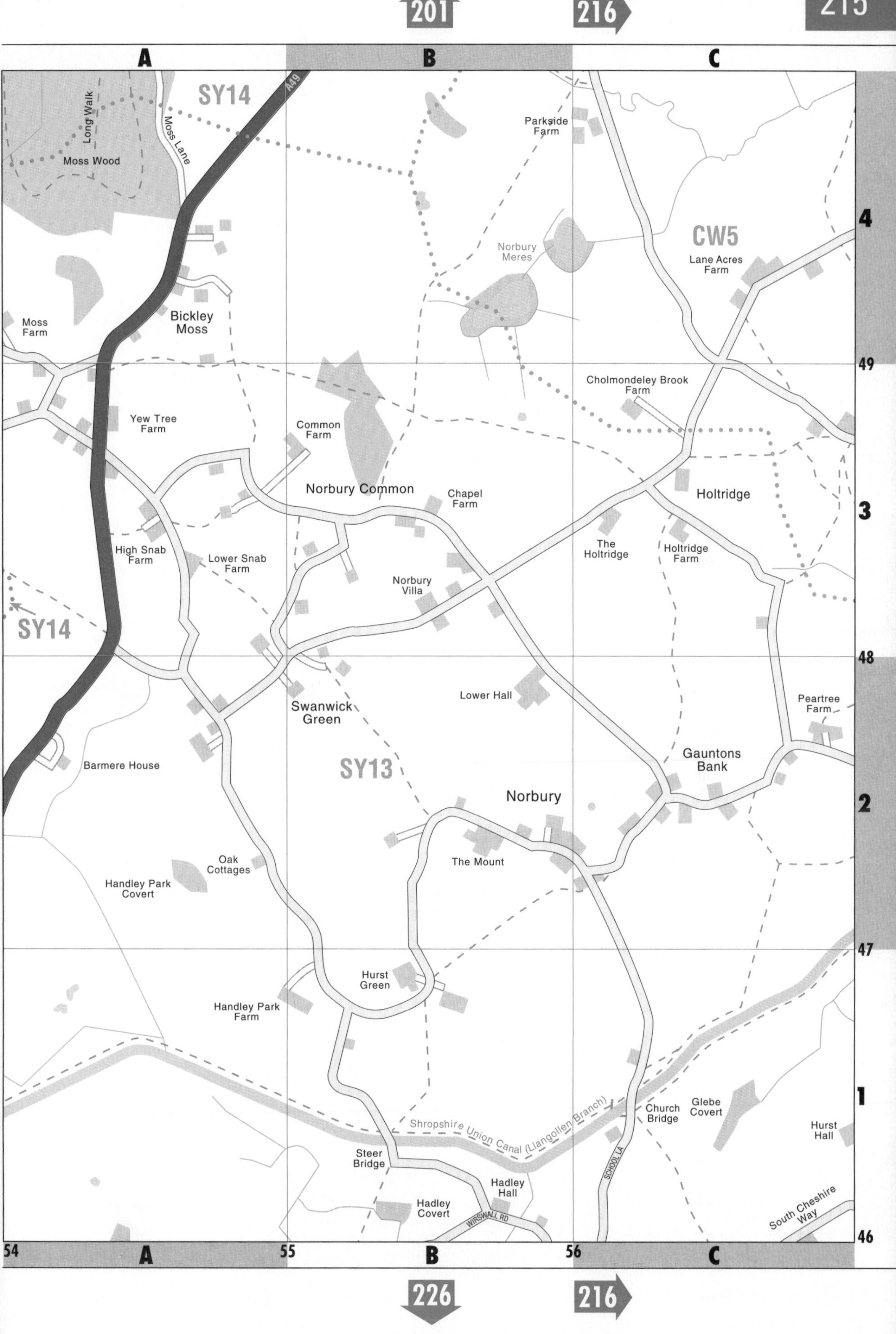
A
B
C
SY14
A49
Long Walk
Moss Lane
Moss Wood
Parkside Farm
4
CW5
Norbury Meres
Lane Acres Farm
Moss Farm
Bickley Moss
49
Cholmondeley Brook Farm
Yew Tree Farm
Common Farm
Norbury Common
Chapel Farm
Holtridge
3
High Snab Farm
Lower Snab Farm
The Holtridge
Holtridge Farm
Norbury Villa
SY14
48
Lower Hall
Peartree Farm
Swanwick Green
Gauntons Bank
Barmere House
SY13
Norbury
2
The Mount
Oak Cottages
Handley Park Covert
47
Hurst Green
Handley Park Farm
1
Glebe Covert
Church Bridge
Shropshire Union Canal (Llangollen Branch)
Hurst Hall
Steer Bridge
School La
Hadley Hall
Hadley Covert
Wirswall Rd
South Cheshire Way
46
54
55
56

226
216

215
202

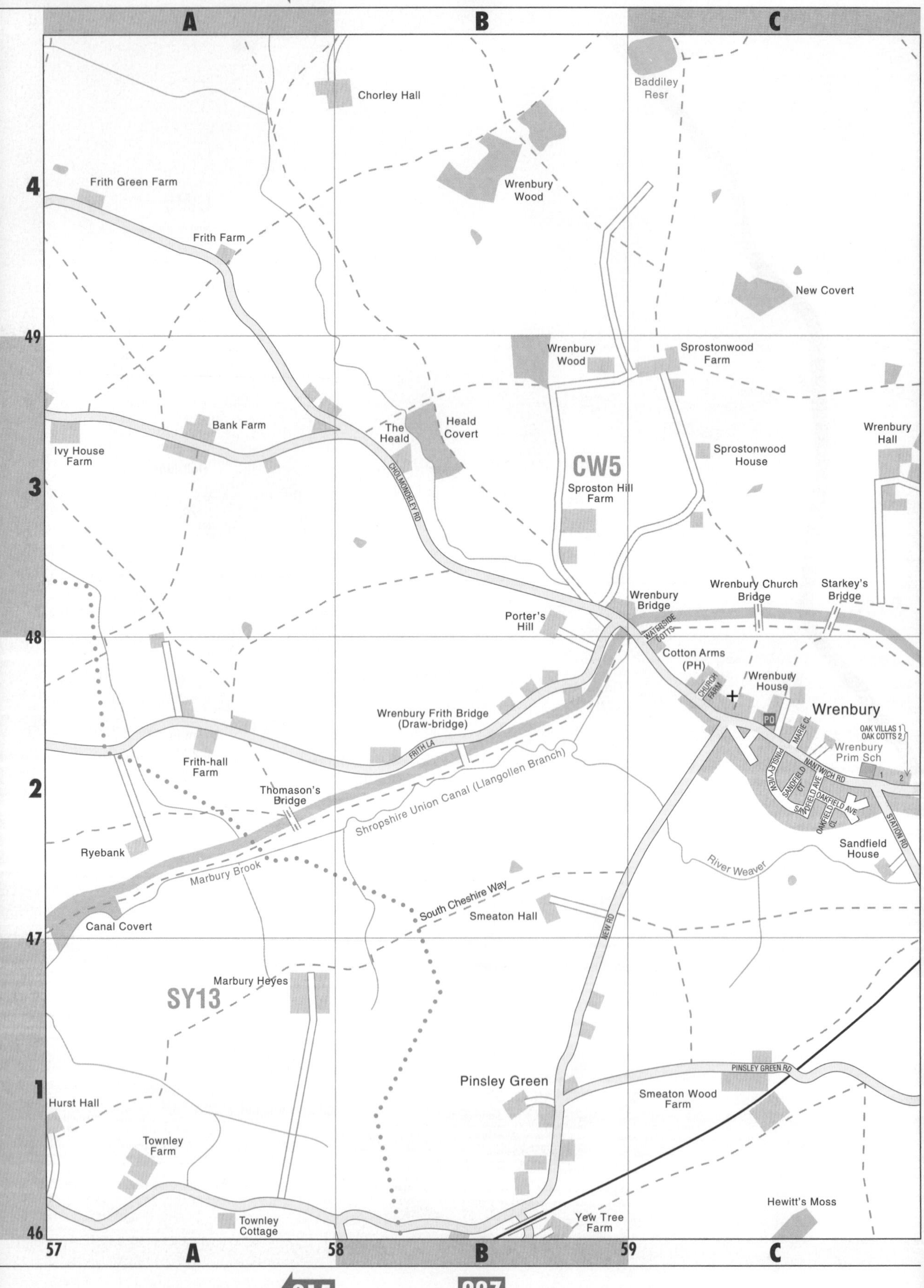
A
B
C
4
49
3
48
2
47
1
46
57
58
59
Chorley Hall
Baddiley Resr
Frith Green Farm
Wrenbury Wood
Frith Farm
New Covert
Wrenbury Wood
Sprostonwood Farm
Bank Farm
The Heald
Heald Covert
Wrenbury Hall
Ivy House Farm
CW5
Sprostonwood House
CHOLMONDELEY RD
Sproston Hill Farm
Wrenbury Bridge
Wrenbury Church Bridge
Starkey's Bridge
Porter's Hill
WATERSIDE COTTS
Cotton Arms (PH)
CHURCH FARM
Wrenbury House
Wrenbury
PO
Wrenbury Frith Bridge (Draw-bridge)
MARIE CL
OAK VILLAS 1
OAK COTTS 2
Wrenbury Prim Sch
FRITH LA
NANTWICH RD
Frith-hall Farm
Shropshire Union Canal (Llangollen Branch)
PINSLEY VIEW
SANDFIELD CT
SANDFIELD AVE
OAKFIELD AVE
OAKFIELD CL
Thomason's Bridge
STATION RD
Ryebank
Sandfield House
River Weaver
Marbury Brook
South Cheshire Way
Smeaton Hall
Canal Covert
NEW RD
Marbury Heyes
SY13
PINSLEY GREEN RD
Pinsley Green
Smeaton Wood Farm
Hurst Hall
Townley Farm
Hewitt's Moss
Townley Cottage
Yew Tree Farm

215
227

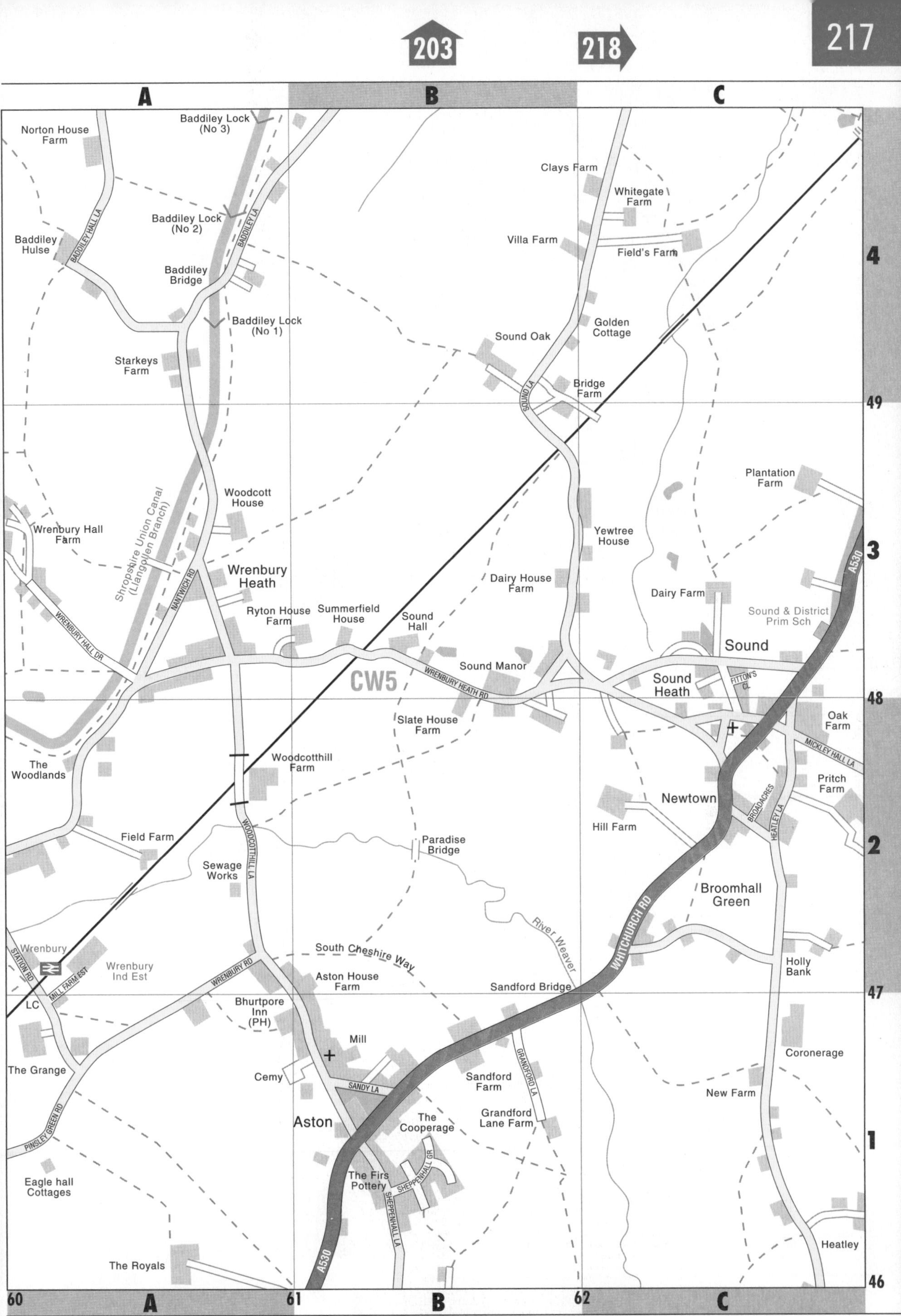

203
218

A   **B**   **C**

Norton House Farm

Baddiley Lock (No 3)

Baddiley Hulse

Baddiley Lock (No 2)

BADDILEY HALL

BADDILEY LA

Baddiley Bridge

Baddiley Lock (No 1)

Starkeys Farm

Clays Farm

Whitegate Farm

Villa Farm

Field's Farm

Sound Oak

Golden Cottage

SOUND LA

Bridge Farm

4

49

Shropshire Union Canal (Llangollen Branch)

NANTWICH RD

Woodcott House

Wrenbury Hall Farm

WRENBURY HALL DR

Wrenbury Heath

Ryton House Farm

Summerfield House

Sound Hall

Plantation Farm

Yewtree House

Dairy House Farm

Dairy Farm

Sound & District Prim Sch

Sound

3

A530

CW5

WRENBURY HEATH RD

Sound Manor

Sound Heath

FITTON'S CL

48

The Woodlands

Woodcotthill Farm

Slate House Farm

Oak Farm

MICKLEY HALL LA

Pritch Farm

Newtown

BROADACRES

HEATLEY LA

Field Farm

WOODCOTTHILL LA

Sewage Works

Paradise Bridge

Hill Farm

Broomhall Green

2

River Weaver

WHITCHURCH RD

Holly Bank

Wrenbury

STATION RD

MILL FARM EST

Wrenbury Ind Est

South Cheshire Way

WRENBURY RD

Aston House Farm

Sandford Bridge

Coronerage

47

LC

Bhurtpore Inn (PH)

Mill

Cemy

SANDY LA

Sandford Farm

GRANDFORD LA

New Farm

The Grange

Aston

The Cooperage

Grandford Lane Farm

PINSLEY GREEN RD

Eagle hall Cottages

The Firs Pottery

SHEPPENHALL GR

SHEPPENHALL LA

1

The Royals

A530

Heatley

46

60   **A**   61   **B**   62   **C**

228
218

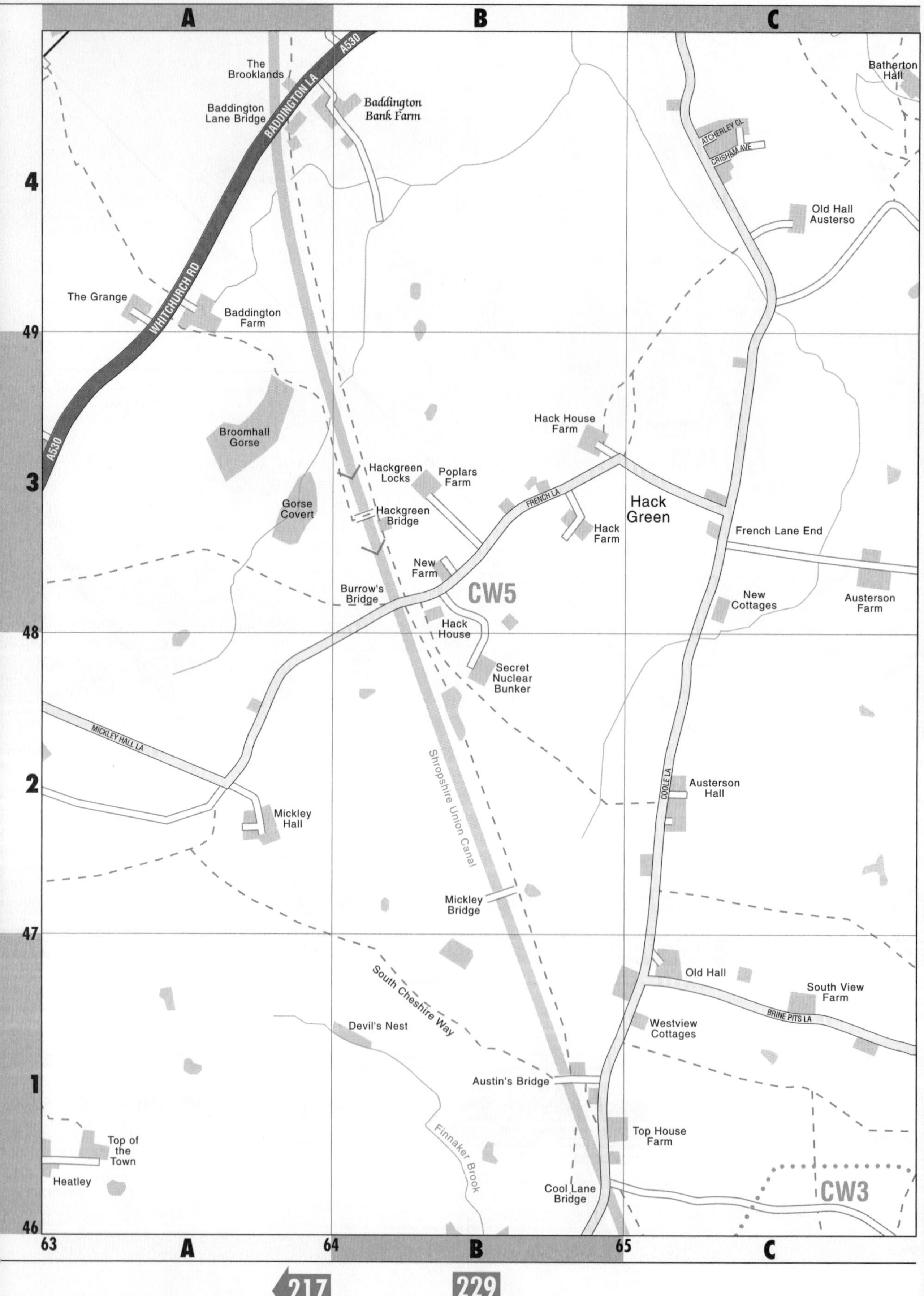

A   **B**   **C**

4

49

3

48

2

47

1

46

Batherton Hall

ATCHERLEY CL
CRISHAM AVE

Old Hall Austerso

The Brooklands

BADDINGTON LA
A530

Baddington Lane Bridge

Baddington Bank Farm

Baddington Lane Bridge

The Grange

WHITCHURCH RD

Baddington Farm

A530

Broomhall Gorse

Gorse Covert

Hackgreen Locks

Hackgreen Bridge

Poplars Farm

New Farm

Burrow's Bridge

Hack House Farm

FRENCH LA

Hack Farm

Hack Green

French Lane End

New Cottages

Austerson Farm

CW5

Hack House

Secret Nuclear Bunker

MICKLEY HALL LA

Mickley Hall

Shropshire Union Canal

Mickley Bridge

COOLE LA

Austerson Hall

Old Hall

South View Farm

BRINE PITS LA

South Cheshire Way

Devil's Nest

Westview Cottages

Austin's Bridge

Finnaker Brook

Top House Farm

Top of the Town

Heatley

Cool Lane Bridge

CW3

63   **A**   64   **B**   65   **C**

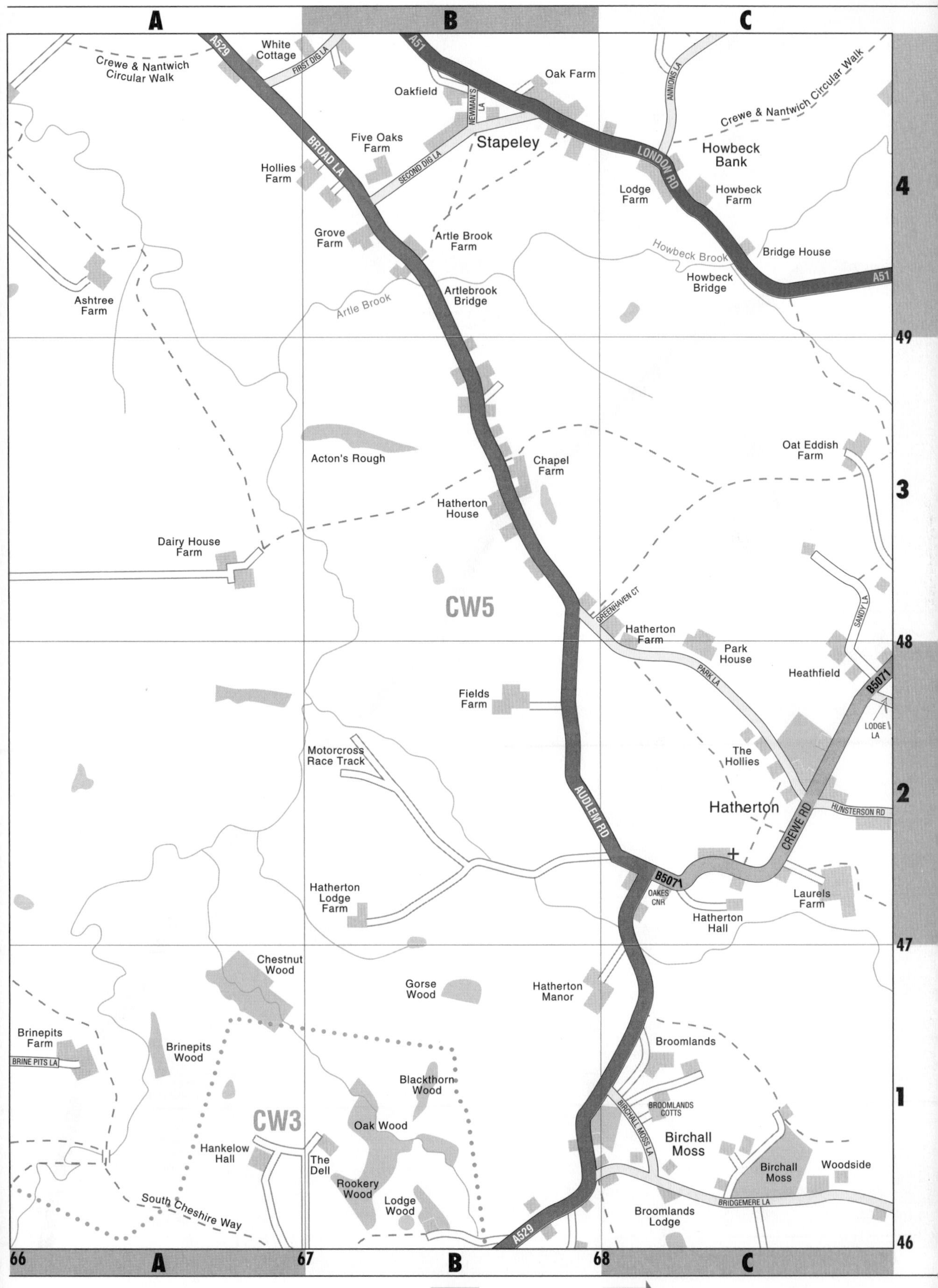

A • B • C

Crewe & Nantwich Circular Walk

White Cottage

A529 BROAD LA

FIRST DIG LA

NEWMAN'S LA

Oakfield

Oak Farm

Five Oaks Farm

A51

Stapeley

SECOND DIG LA

Hollies Farm

ANNIONS LA

Crewe & Nantwich Circular Walk

Howbeck Bank

LONDON RD

Lodge Farm

Howbeck Farm

Grove Farm

Artle Brook Farm

Bridge House

Artlebrook Bridge

Howbeck Brook

A51

Artle Brook

Howbeck Bridge

4

49

Acton's Rough

Chapel Farm

Oat Eddish Farm

Hatherton House

3

SANDY LA

CW5

GREENHAVEN CT

Hatherton Farm

Park House

Heathfield

48

B5071

Dairy House Farm

Fields Farm

PARK LA

LODGE LA

Motorcross Race Track

The Hollies

2

Hatherton

CREWE RD

HUNSTERSON RD

AUDLEM RD

B507

OAKES CNR

Laurels Farm

Hatherton Lodge Farm

Hatherton Hall

47

Chestnut Wood

Gorse Wood

Hatherton Manor

Brinepits Farm

BRINE PITS LA

Brinepits Wood

Blackthorn Wood

Broomlands

BIRCHALL MOSS LA

BROOMLANDS COTTS

1

CW3

Oak Wood

Birchall Moss

Birchall Moss

Woodside

Hankelow Hall

The Dell

Rookery Wood

Lodge Wood

Broomlands Lodge

BRIDGEMERE LA

South Cheshire Way

A529

46

219
206

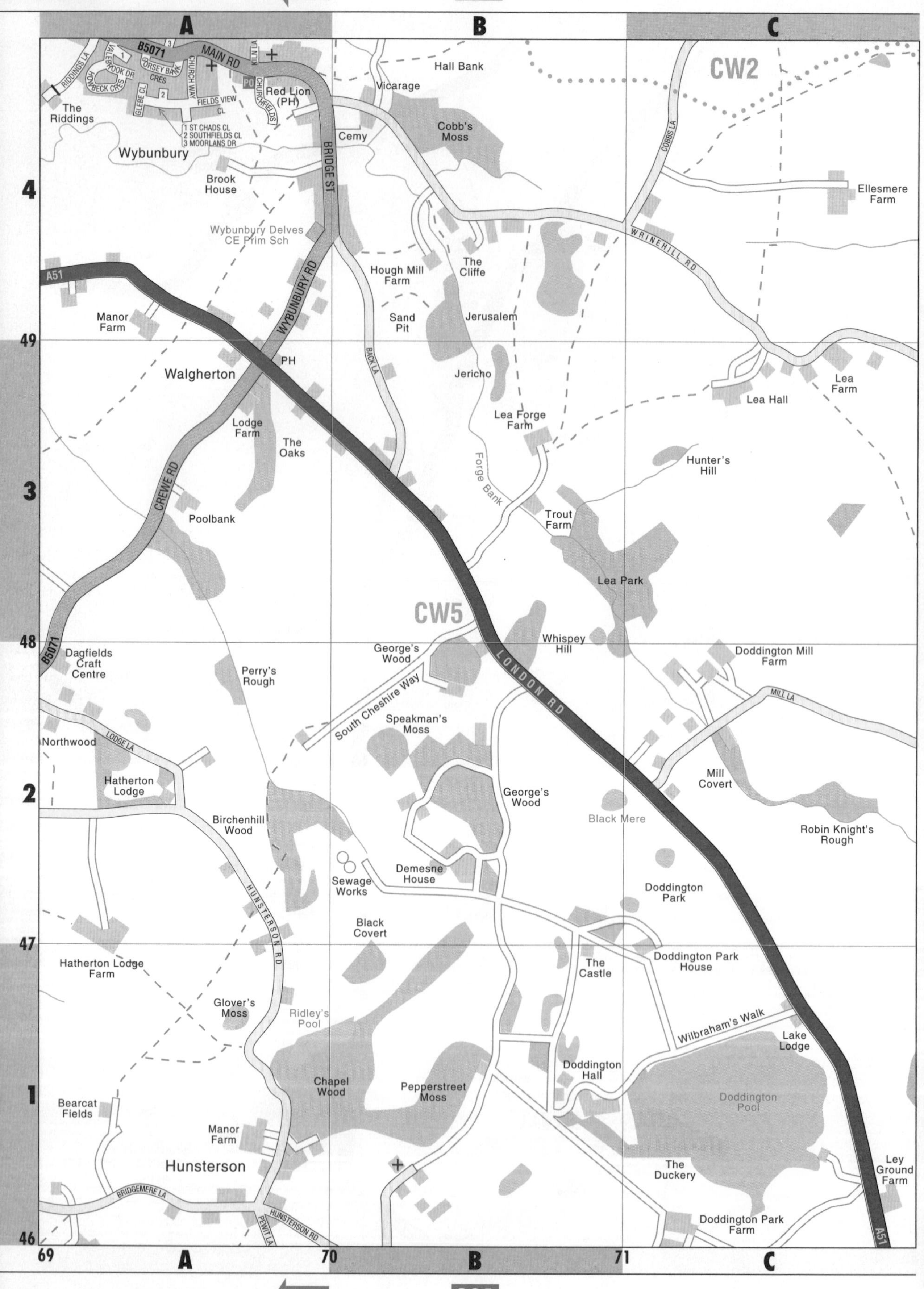
A
B
C
CW2
CW5
B5071
MAIN RD
KILN LA
RIDDINGS LA
VALEBROOK DR
GORSEY BANK CRES
CHURCH WAY
HOWBECK CRES
GLEBE CL
FIELDS VIEW CL
CHURCHFIELDS
1 ST CHADS CL
2 SOUTHFIELDS CL
3 MOORLANS DR
The Riddings
Wybunbury
Red Lion (PH)
Vicarage
Hall Bank
Cemy
Cobb's Moss
COBBS LA
Ellesmere Farm
Brook House
BRIDGE ST
Wybunbury Delves CE Prim Sch
WRINEHILL RD
A51
Hough Mill Farm
The Cliffe
WYBUNBURY RD
Sand Pit
Jerusalem
Manor Farm
Walgherton
PH
BACK LA
Jericho
Lea Hall
Lea Farm
Lodge Farm
The Oaks
Lea Forge Farm
Hunter's Hill
CREWE RD
Forge Bank
Poolbank
Trout Farm
Lea Park
Whispey Hill
Dagfields Craft Centre
George's Wood
LONDON RD
Doddington Mill Farm
Perry's Rough
South Cheshire Way
Speakman's Moss
MILL LA
Northwood
LODGE LA
Hatherton Lodge
George's Wood
Mill Covert
Birchenhill Wood
Black Mere
Robin Knight's Rough
Sewage Works
Demesne House
Doddington Park
HUNSTERSON RD
Black Covert
Hatherton Lodge Farm
The Castle
Doddington Park House
Glover's Moss
Ridley's Pool
Wilbraham's Walk
Lake Lodge
Chapel Wood
Pepperstreet Moss
Doddington Hall
Bearcat Fields
Doddington Pool
Manor Farm
Hunsterson
The Duckery
Ley Ground Farm
BRIDGEMERE LA
PEWIT LA
Doddington Park Farm
4
49
3
48
2
47
1
46
69
70
71

219
231

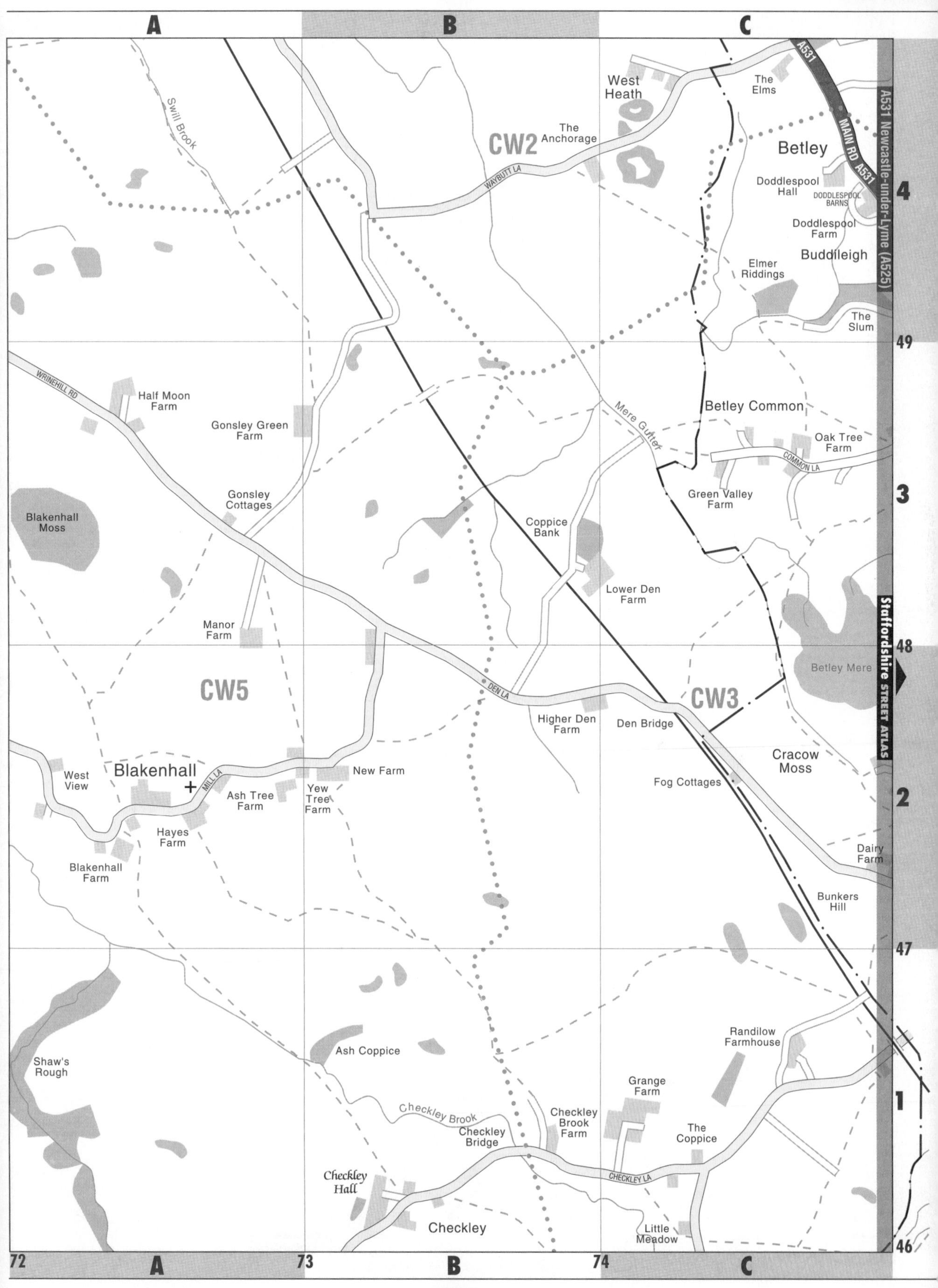

A B C

West Heath
CW2
The Anchorage
WAYBUTT LA
MAIN RD A531
A531
The Elms
Betley
Doddlespool Hall
DODDLESPOOL BARNS
Doddlespool Farm
Buddileigh
Elmer Riddings
The Slum
A531 Newcastle-under-Lyme (A525)

Swill Brook

Half Moon Farm
WRINEHILL RD
Gonsley Green Farm
Gonsley Cottages
Blakenhall Moss
Manor Farm

Betley Common
Oak Tree Farm
COMMON LA
Green Valley Farm
Mere Gutter
Coppice Bank
Lower Den Farm

CW5
DEN LA
Higher Den Farm
Den Bridge
CW3
Betley Mere
Cracow Moss
Fog Cottages

West View
Blakenhall
Ash Tree Farm
Yew Tree Farm
New Farm
MILL LA
Hayes Farm
Blakenhall Farm

Dairy Farm
Bunkers Hill

Shaw's Rough

Ash Coppice
Checkley Brook
Checkley Bridge
Checkley Brook Farm
Checkley Hall
Checkley
CHECKLEY LA
Grange Farm
Randilow Farmhouse
The Coppice
Little Meadow

Staffordshire STREET ATLAS

4
49
3
48
2
47
1
46

72 A 73 B 74 C

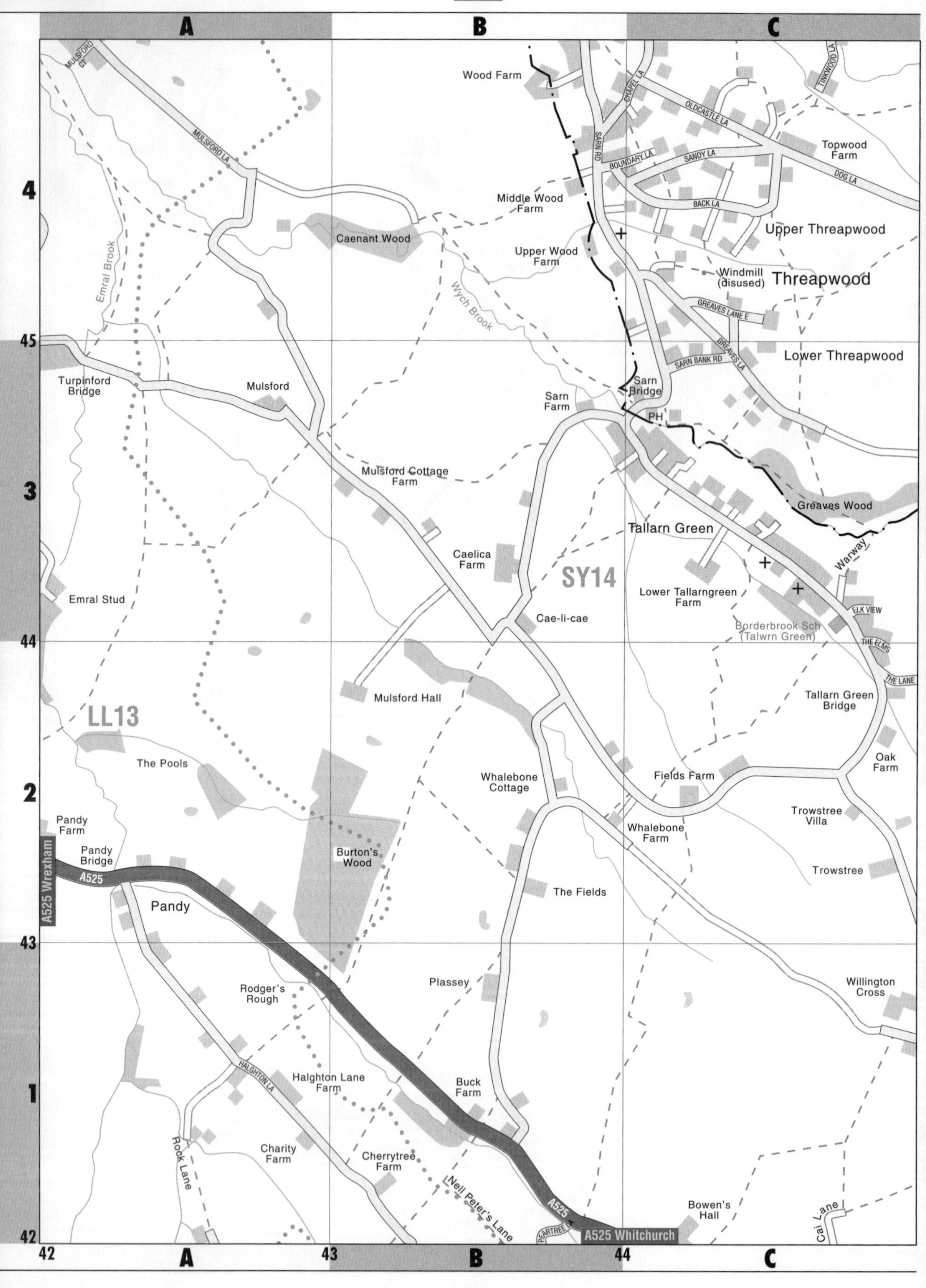

Wood Farm

Middle Wood Farm

Upper Wood Farm

Caenant Wood

CHAPEL LA

SARN RD

OLDCASTLE LA

TINKWOOD LA

BOUNDARY LA

SANDY LA

Topwood Farm

DOG LA

BACK LA

Upper Threapwood

Windmill (disused)

Threapwood

GREAVES LANE E

Lower Threapwood

GREAVES LA

SARN BANK RD

Sarn Bridge

Sarn Farm

PH

Wych Brook

Turpinford Bridge

Mulsford

Greaves Wood

Mulsford Cottage Farm

Tallarn Green

Caelica Farm

SY14

Warway

Emral Stud

Lower Tallarngreen Farm

ELK VIEW

Cae-li-cae

Borderbrook Sch (Talwrn Green)

THE ELMS

THE LANE

LL13

Mulsford Hall

Tallarn Green Bridge

The Pools

Oak Farm

Whalebone Cottage

Fields Farm

Pandy Farm

Burton's Wood

Whalebone Farm

Trowstree Villa

Pandy Bridge

A525

Trowstree

The Fields

Pandy

A525 Wrexham

Rodger's Rough

Plassey

Willington Cross

HALGHTON LA

Halghton Lane Farm

Buck Farm

Rock Lane

Charity Farm

Cherrytree Farm

Nell Peter's Lane

Bowen's Hall

Cae Lane

PEARTREE LA

A525

A525 Whitchurch

Emral Brook

MULSFORD LA

MULSFORD CT

4

45

3

44

2

43

1

42

A

B

C

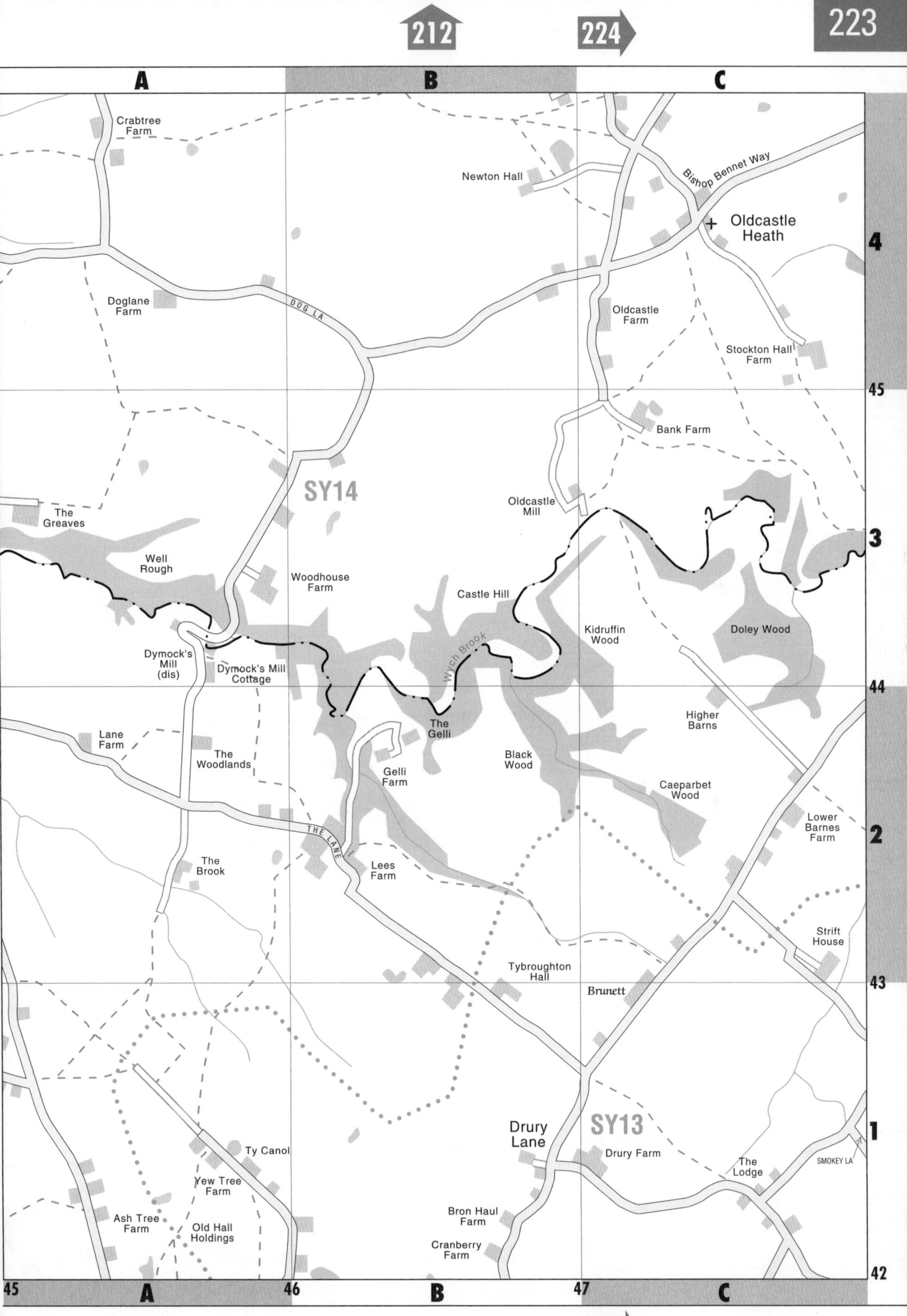

A

B

C

Crabtree
Farm

Newton Hall

Bishop Bennet Way

Oldcastle
Heath

Doglane
Farm

DOG LA

Oldcastle
Farm

Stockton Hall
Farm

4

45

SY14

Bank Farm

The
Greaves

Oldcastle
Mill

3

Well
Rough

Woodhouse
Farm

Castle Hill

Kidruffin
Wood

Doley Wood

Wych Brook

Dymock's
Mill
(dis)

Dymock's Mill
Cottage

The Gelli

Higher
Barns

44

Lane
Farm

The
Woodlands

Gelli
Farm

Black
Wood

Caeparbet
Wood

Lower
Barnes
Farm

2

THE LANE

The
Brook

Lees
Farm

Strift
House

Tybroughton
Hall

43

Brunett

Drury
Lane

SY13

Drury Farm

1

Ty Canol

The
Lodge

SMOKEY LA

Yew Tree
Farm

Ash Tree
Farm

Old Hall
Holdings

Bron Haul
Farm

Cranberry
Farm

42

A

B

C

223
213

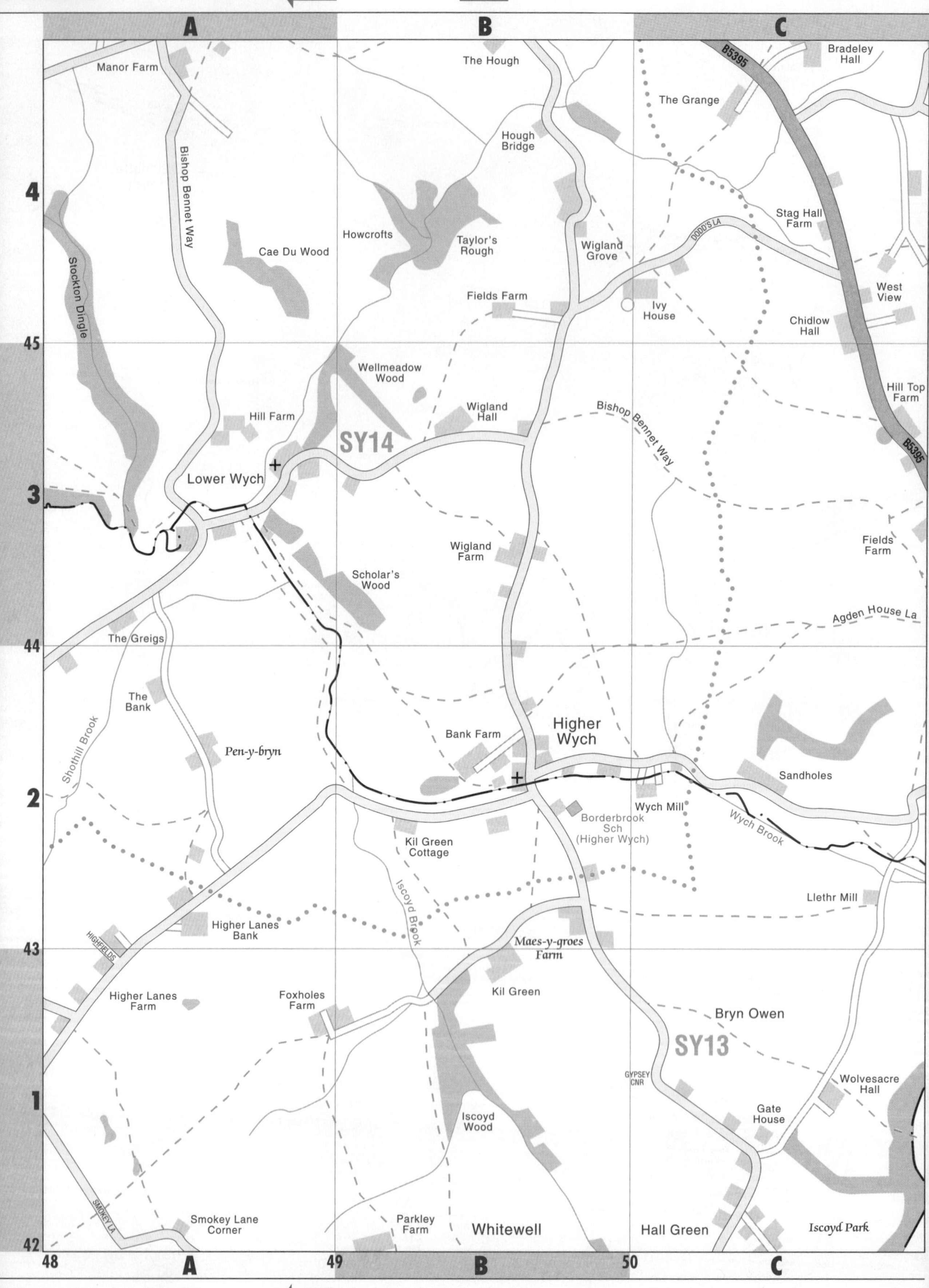
A
B
C
Manor Farm
The Hough
Bradeley Hall
B5395
The Grange
Hough Bridge
Bishop Bennet Way
4
Stag Hall Farm
Howcrofts
Taylor's Rough
Cae Du Wood
Wigland Grove
DODD'S LA
Stockton Dingle
West View
Fields Farm
Ivy House
Chidlow Hall
45
Wellmeadow Wood
Hill Top Farm
Wigland Hall
Bishop Bennet Way
Hill Farm
SY14
B5395
Lower Wych
3
Fields Farm
Wigland Farm
Scholar's Wood
Agden House La
The Greigs
44
The Bank
Higher Wych
Bank Farm
Shothill Brook
Pen-y-bryn
Sandholes
2
Wych Mill
Borderbrook Sch (Higher Wych)
Wych Brook
Kil Green Cottage
Llethr Mill
Iscoyd Brook
Higher Lanes Bank
HIGHFIELDS
Maes-y-groes Farm
43
Kil Green
Higher Lanes Farm
Foxholes Farm
Bryn Owen
SY13
GYPSEY CNR
1
Wolvesacre Hall
Iscoyd Wood
Gate House
SMOKEY LA
Smokey Lane Corner
Parkley Farm
Whitewell
Hall Green
Iscoyd Park
42
48
A
49
B
50
C

223

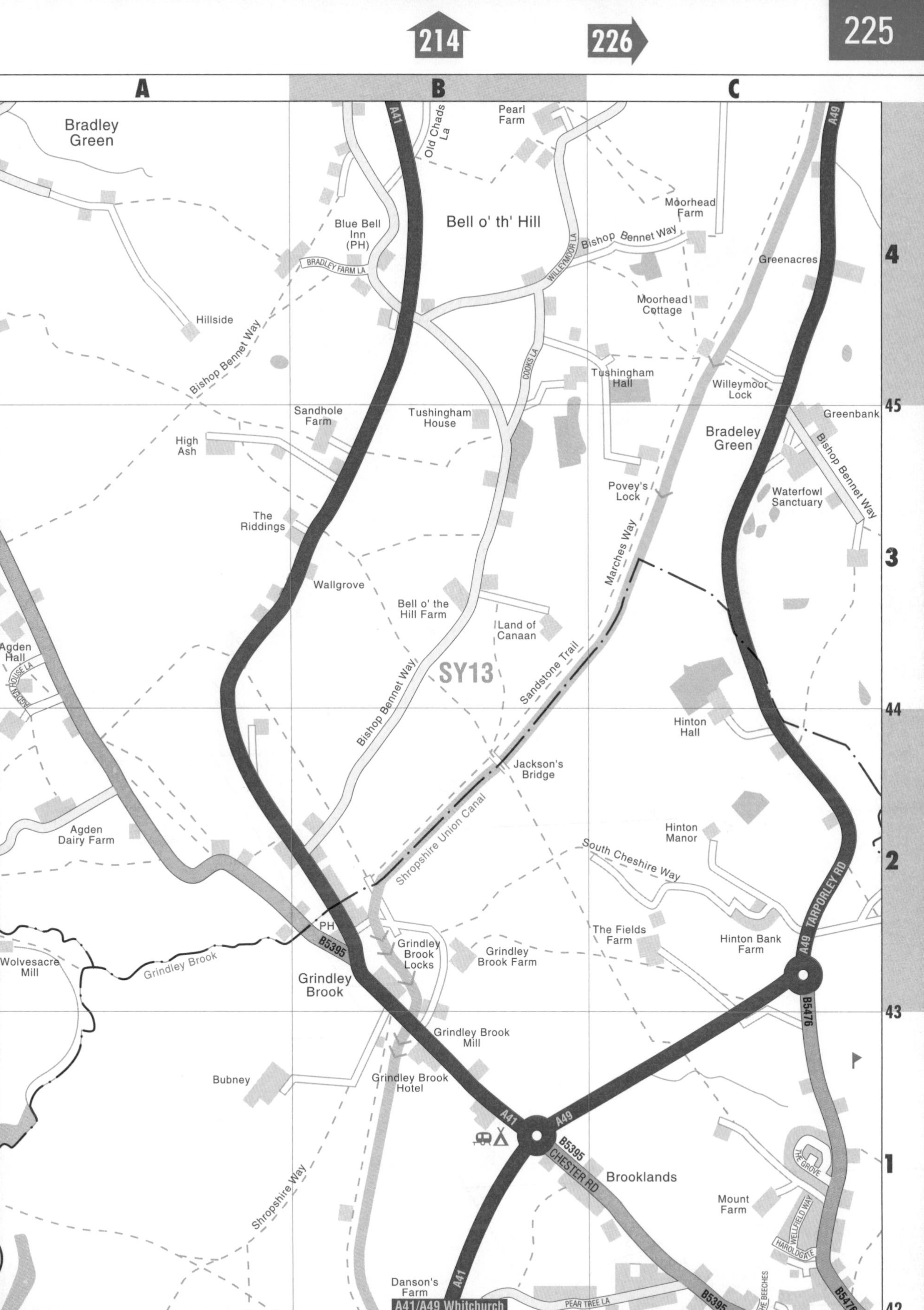
A
B
C
Bradley Green
Pearl Farm
Old Chads La
A41
A49
Bell o' th' Hill
Blue Bell Inn (PH)
Bradley Farm La
Moorhead Farm
Bishop Bennet Way
Willeymoor La
Greenacres
Moorhead Cottage
Hillside
Bishop Bennet Way
Cooks La
Tushingham Hall
Willeymoor Lock
Sandhole Farm
Tushingham House
High Ash
Bradeley Green
Greenbank
Bishop Bennet Way
Povey's Lock
Waterfowl Sanctuary
The Riddings
Marches Way
Wallgrove
Bell o' the Hill Farm
Land of Canaan
Agden Hall
Agden House La
SY13
Sandstone Trail
Bishop Bennet Way
Hinton Hall
Jackson's Bridge
Shropshire Union Canal
Agden Dairy Farm
Hinton Manor
South Cheshire Way
Tarporley Rd
PH
The Fields Farm
Hinton Bank Farm
Wolvesacre Mill
Grindley Brook
B5395
Grindley Brook Locks
Grindley Brook Farm
Grindley Brook
B5476
Grindley Brook Mill
Bubney
Grindley Brook Hotel
Brooklands
Chester Rd
The Grove
Mount Farm
Shropshire Way
Wellfield Way
Harrogate
Danson's Farm
A41/A49 Whitchurch
Pear Tree La
The Beeches
4
45
3
44
2
43
1
42
51
52
53

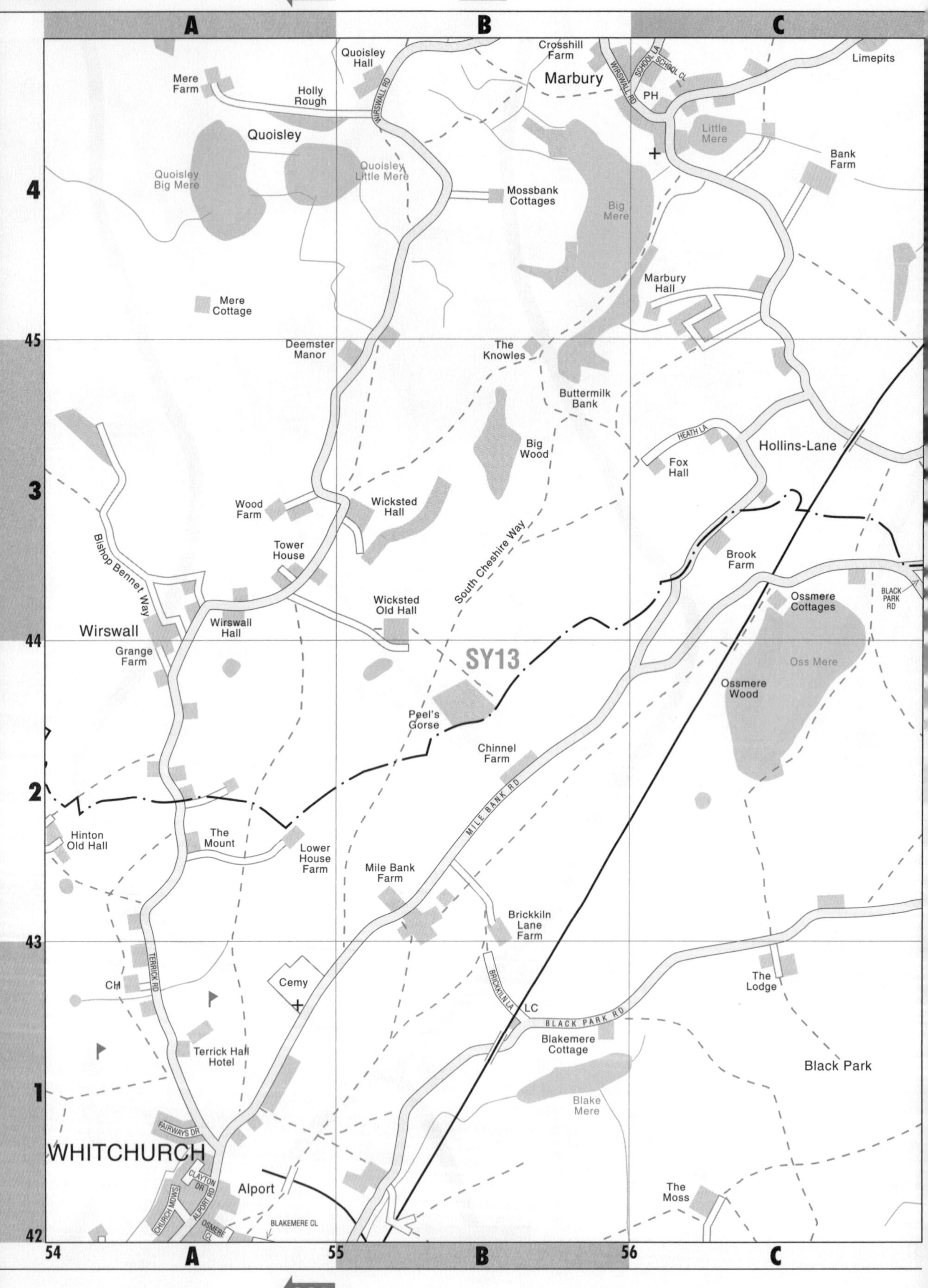

A | B | C

Limepits

Mere Farm

Holly Rough

Quoisley Hall

Crosshill Farm

Marbury

PH

Little Mere

Bank Farm

Quoisley

Quoisley Big Mere

Quoisley Little Mere

Mossbank Cottages

Big Mere

4

Marbury Hall

Mere Cottage

45

Deemster Manor

The Knowles

Buttermilk Bank

Heath La

Hollins-Lane

Big Wood

Fox Hall

Wood Farm

Wicksted Hall

South Cheshire Way

Brook Farm

3

Bishop Bennet Way

Tower House

Wicksted Old Hall

Ossmere Cottages

BLACK PARK RD

Wirswall

Wirswall Hall

44

SY13

Oss Mere

Ossmere Wood

Grange Farm

Peel's Gorse

Chinnel Farm

Hinton Old Hall

The Mount

Lower House Farm

Mile Bank Farm

Mile Bank Rd

2

Terrick Rd

Ch

Cemy

Brickkiln Lane Farm

The Lodge

43

Brickkiln La

LC

BLACK PARK RD

Terrick Hall Hotel

Blakemere Cottage

Black Park

1

Fairways Dr

Blake Mere

WHITCHURCH

Clayton Dr Rd

Alport Rd

Alport

Church Mews

Osmere Cl

BLAKEMERE CL

The Moss

42

54 | A | 55 | B | 56 | C

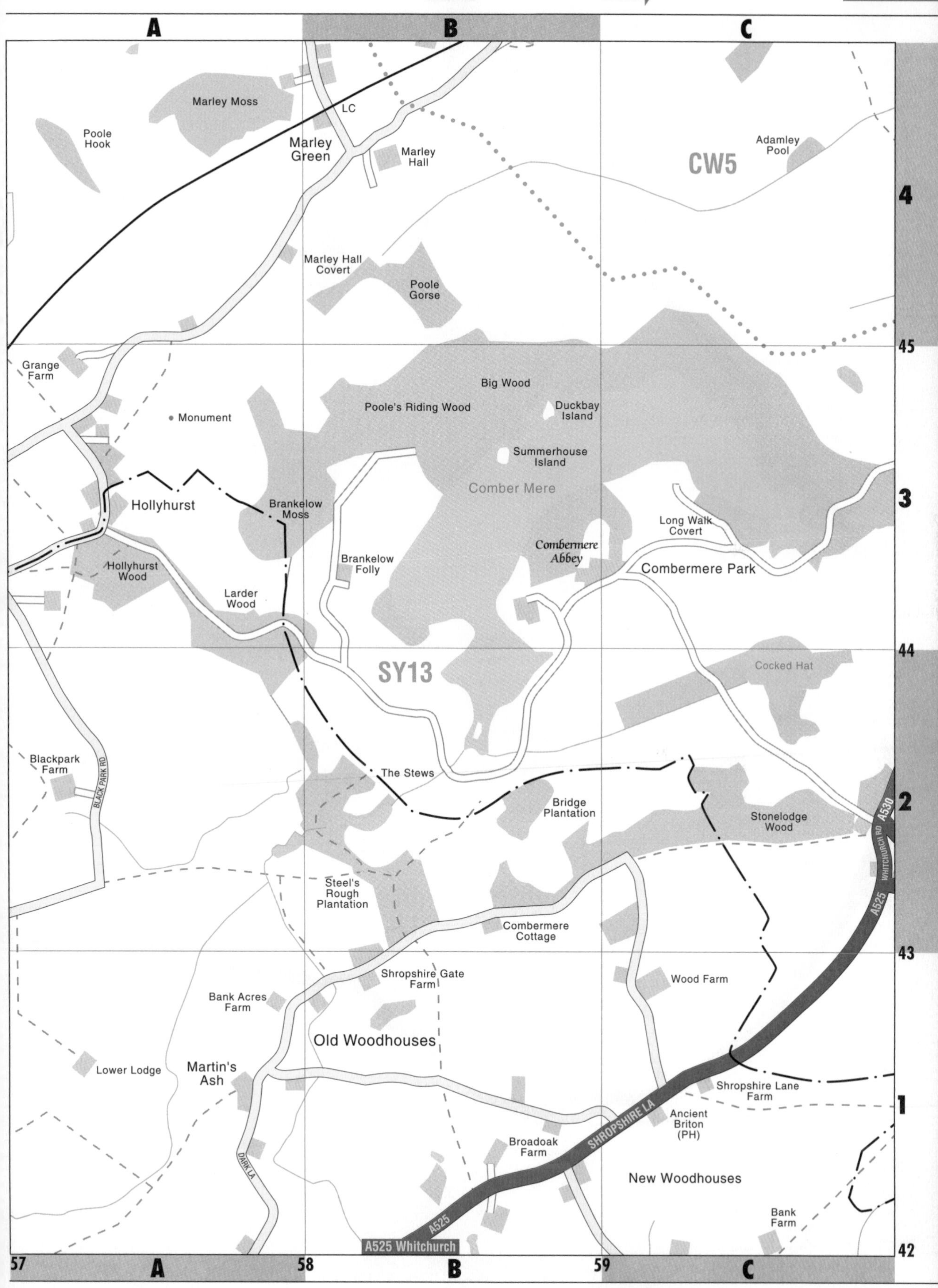

Marley Moss

Poole Hook

LC

Marley Green

Marley Hall

CW5

Adamley Pool

4

Marley Hall Covert

Poole Gorse

45

Grange Farm

Monument

Big Wood

Poole's Riding Wood

Duckbay Island

Summerhouse Island

Comber Mere

3

Hollyhurst

Brankelow Moss

Long Walk Covert

Combermere Abbey

Combermere Park

Hollyhurst Wood

Larder Wood

Brankelow Folly

SY13

Cocked Hat

44

Blackpark Farm

BLACK PARK RD

The Stews

Bridge Plantation

Stonelodge Wood

A530

WHITCHURCH RD

2

Steel's Rough Plantation

Combermere Cottage

A525

43

Shropshire Gate Farm

Wood Farm

Bank Acres Farm

Old Woodhouses

Lower Lodge

Martin's Ash

Shropshire Lane Farm

1

Broadoak Farm

SHROPSHIRE LA

Ancient Briton (PH)

DARL LA

New Woodhouses

Bank Farm

A525

A525 Whitchurch

42

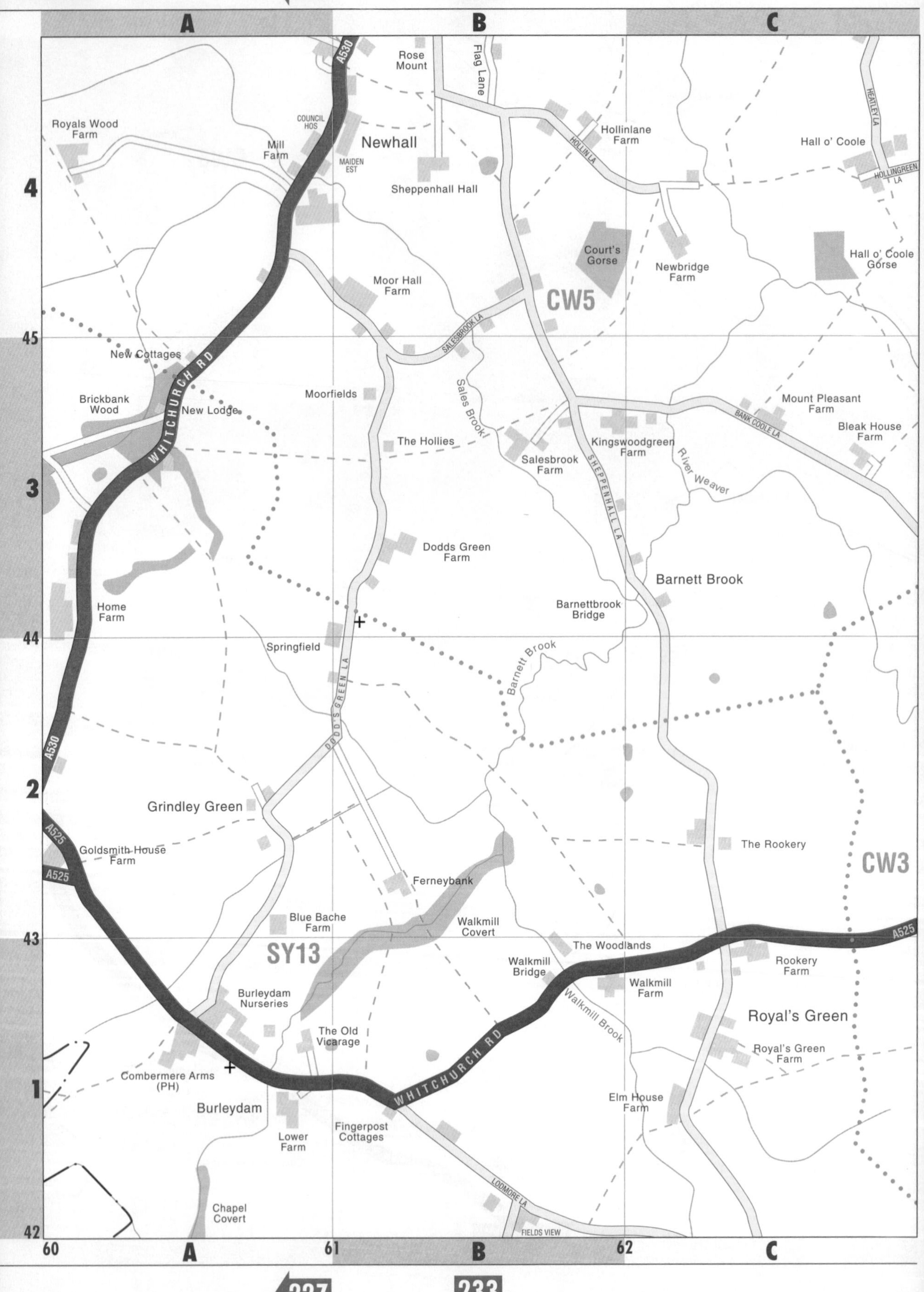

A B C

4

Royals Wood Farm

Mill Farm

COUNCIL HOS

Rose Mount

Newhall

Flag Lane

Hollinlane Farm

Hall o' Coole

HEATLEY LA

MAIDEN EST

Sheppenhall Hall

Court's Gorse

HOLLIN LA

Newbridge Farm

Hall o' Coole Gorse

HOLLINGREEN LA

CW5

45

New Cottages

Moor Hall Farm

SALESBROOK LA

Moorfields

Mount Pleasant Farm

BANK COOLE LA

Bleak House Farm

Brickbank Wood

New Lodge

WHITCHURCH RD

The Hollies

Sales Brook

Salesbrook Farm

Kingswoodgreen Farm

River Weaver

3

Home Farm

Dodds Green Farm

SHEPPENHALL LA

Barnett Brook

44

A530

Springfield

DODDS GREEN LA

Barnett Brook

Barnettbrook Bridge

2

A525

Grindley Green

Goldsmith House Farm

A525

Ferneybank

The Rookery

CW3

A525

43

Blue Bache Farm

SY13

Walkmill Covert

The Woodlands

Rookery Farm

Burleydam Nurseries

Walkmill Bridge

Walkmill Farm

Royal's Green

The Old Vicarage

Walkmill Brook

WHITCHURCH RD

Royal's Green Farm

1

Combermere Arms (PH)

Burleydam

Lower Farm

Fingerpost Cottages

Elm House Farm

Chapel Covert

LOOMORE LA

FIELDS VIEW

42

60 A 61 B 62 C

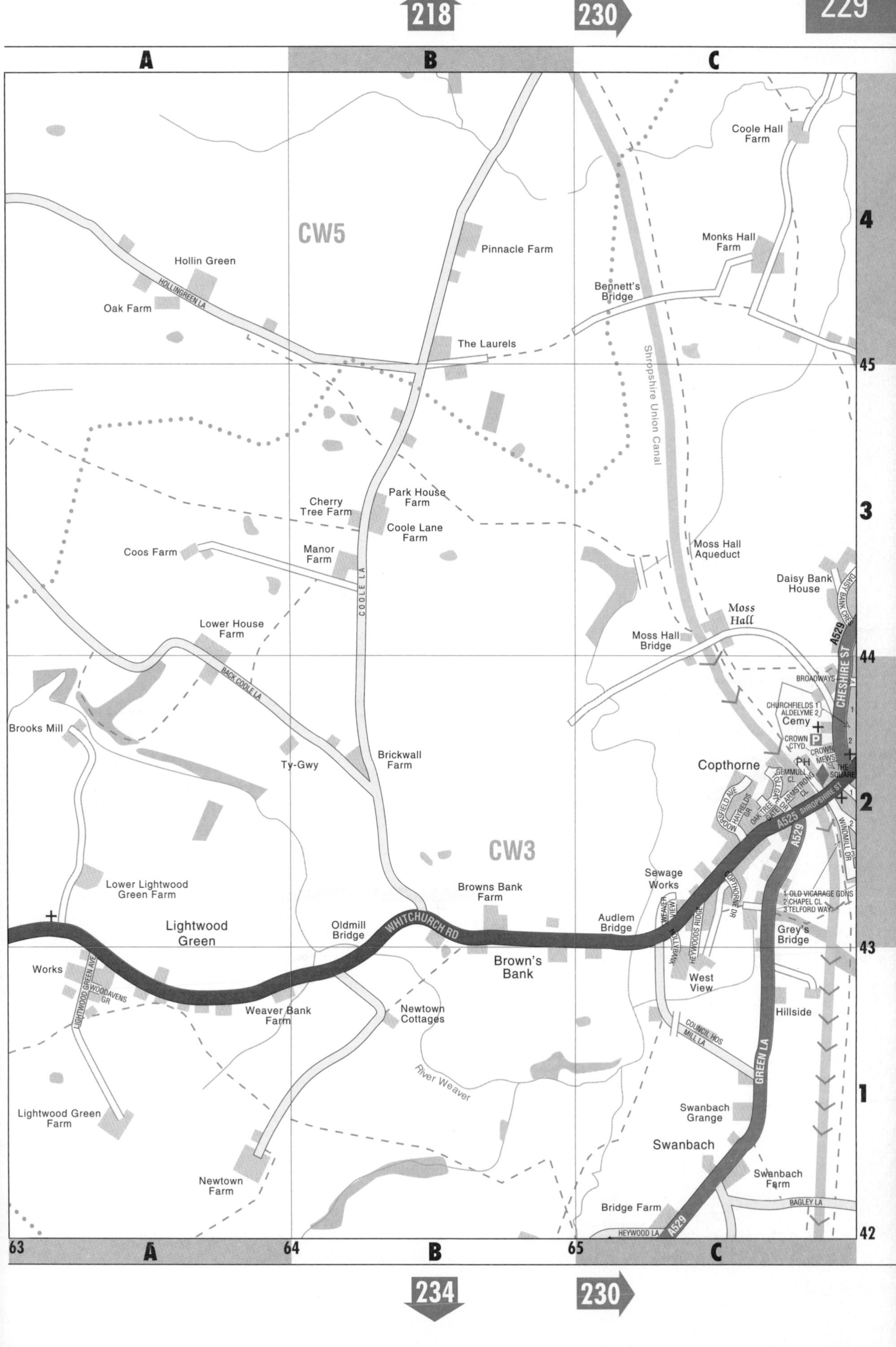

4

45

3

44

2

43

1

42

CW5

Coole Hall Farm

Monks Hall Farm

Pinnacle Farm

Bennett's Bridge

Hollin Green

HOLLINGREEN LA

Oak Farm

The Laurels

Shropshire Union Canal

Cherry Tree Farm

Park House Farm

Coole Lane Farm

Moss Hall Aqueduct

Coos Farm

Manor Farm

COOLE LA

Daisy Bank House

Moss Hall

Lower House Farm

Moss Hall Bridge

CHESHIRE ST

A529

BROADWAYS

BACK COOLE LA

CHURCHFIELDS 1
ALDELYME 2

Brooks Mill

Cemy

CROWN
CTYD

CROWN
MEWS

Ty-Gwy

Brickwall Farm

PH

Copthorne

GEMMULL
CL

OAK TREE CT

GATE ARMSTRONG CL

THE SQUARE

MOORESFIELD AVE

HATFIELDS GR

A525 SHRAWBY ST

A529

WINDMILL DR

CW3

Browns Bank Farm

Sewage Works

A525

A529

COPTHORNE DR

1 OLD VICARAGE GDNS
2 CHAPEL CL
3 TELFORD WAY

Lower Lightwood Green Farm

Oldmill Bridge

WHITCHURCH RD

Audlem Bridge

WEAVER WAY

HEYWOODS RIDGE

Grey's Bridge

Lightwood Green

Brown's Bank

West View

Hillside

Works

LIGHTWOOD GREEN AVE

WOODAVENS GR

Weaver Bank Farm

Newtown Cottages

COUNCIL HOS
MILL LA

GREEN LA

Swanbach Grange

Lightwood Green Farm

River Weaver

Swanbach

Swanbach Farm

Newtown Farm

Bridge Farm

HEYWOOD LA

A529

BAGLEY LA

229
219

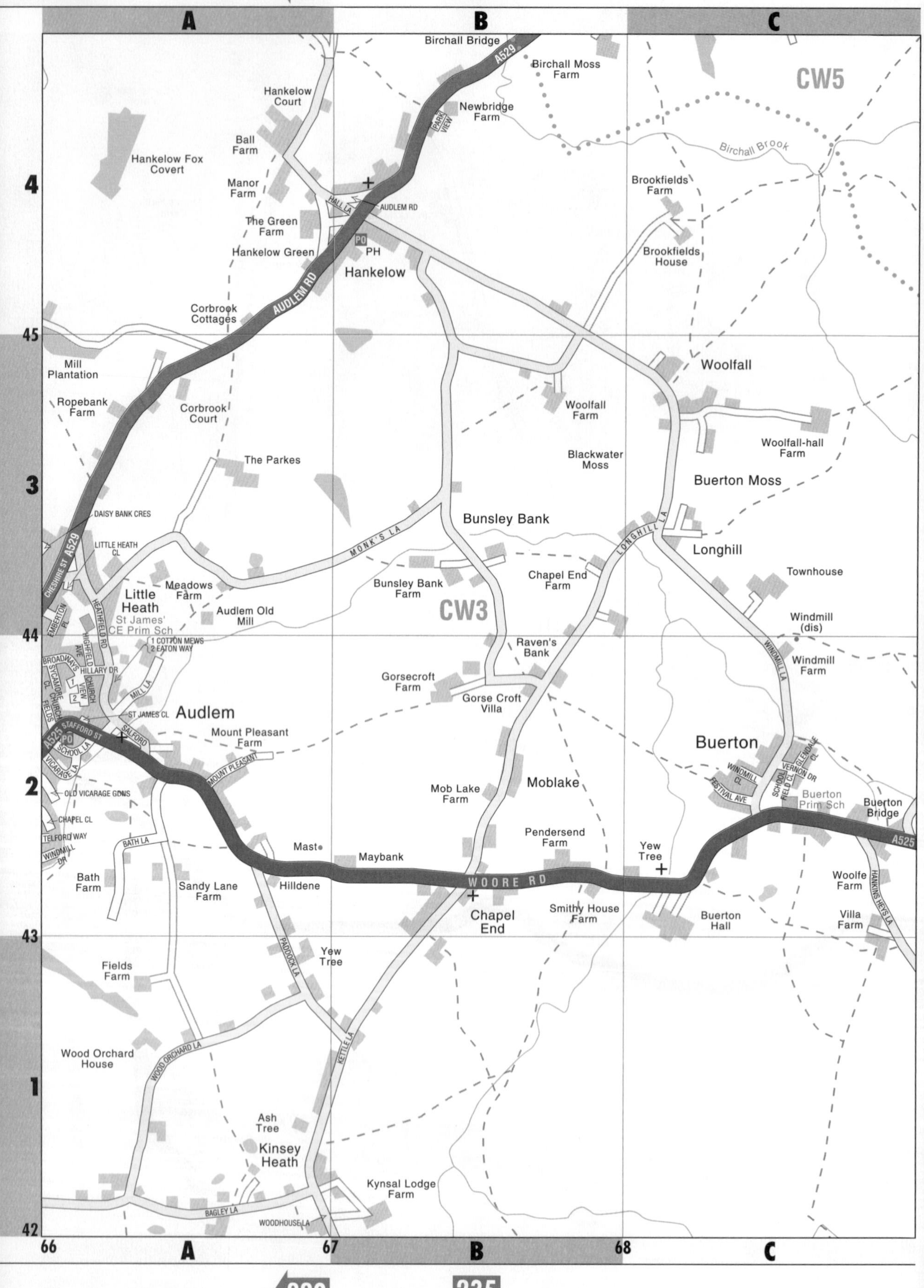
A
B
C
Birchall Bridge
A529
Birchall Moss Farm
CW5
Hankelow Court
Newbridge Farm
PARK VIEW
Ball Farm
Birchall Brook
Hankelow Fox Covert
Manor Farm
4
HALL LA
AUDLEM RD
Brookfields Farm
The Green Farm
PO
PH
Hankelow Green
Brookfields House
Hankelow
AUDLEM RD
Corbrook Cottages
45
Mill Plantation
Woolfall
Ropebank Farm
Corbrook Court
Woolfall Farm
Woolfall-hall Farm
The Parkes
Blackwater Moss
3
Buerton Moss
DAISY BANK CRES
Bunsley Bank
LONGHILL LA
LITTLE HEATH CL
MONK'S LA
Longhill
A529
CHESHIRE ST
Townhouse
Meadows Farm
Chapel End Farm
Little Heath
Bunsley Bank Farm
EMBERTON PL
HEATHFIELD RD
Audlem Old Mill
CW3
Windmill (dis)
St James' CE Prim Sch
44
1 COTTON MEWS
2 EATON WAY
Raven's Bank
BROADWAYS
HIGHFIELD AVE
Windmill Farm
SYCAMORE CL
HILLARY DR
Gorsecroft Farm
WINDMILL LA
CHURCH FIELDS
CHURCH VIEW
MILL LA
Gorse Croft Villa
ST JAMES CL
Audlem
STAFFORD ST
A525
SALFORD
Mount Pleasant Farm
Buerton
PO
SCHOOL LA
GLENDALE CL
MOUNT PLEASANT
VERNON DR
VICARAGE LA
WINDMILL CL
2
Moblake
OLD VICARAGE GDNS
Mob Lake Farm
SCHOOL FIELD CL
FESTIVAL AVE
Buerton Prim Sch
Buerton Bridge
CHAPEL CL
TELFORD WAY
Pendersend Farm
A525
BATH LA
WINDMILL DR
Mast
Yew Tree
Maybank
Bath Farm
Sandy Lane Farm
WOORE RD
Hilldene
Woolfe Farm
Smithy House Farm
Chapel End
HANKINS HEYS LA
Buerton Hall
Villa Farm
43
Yew Tree
PADDOCK LA
Fields Farm
KETTLE LA
Wood Orchard House
WOOD ORCHARD LA
1
Ash Tree
Kinsey Heath
Kynsal Lodge Farm
BAGLEY LA
WOODHOUSE LA
42
66
A
67
B
68
C

229
235

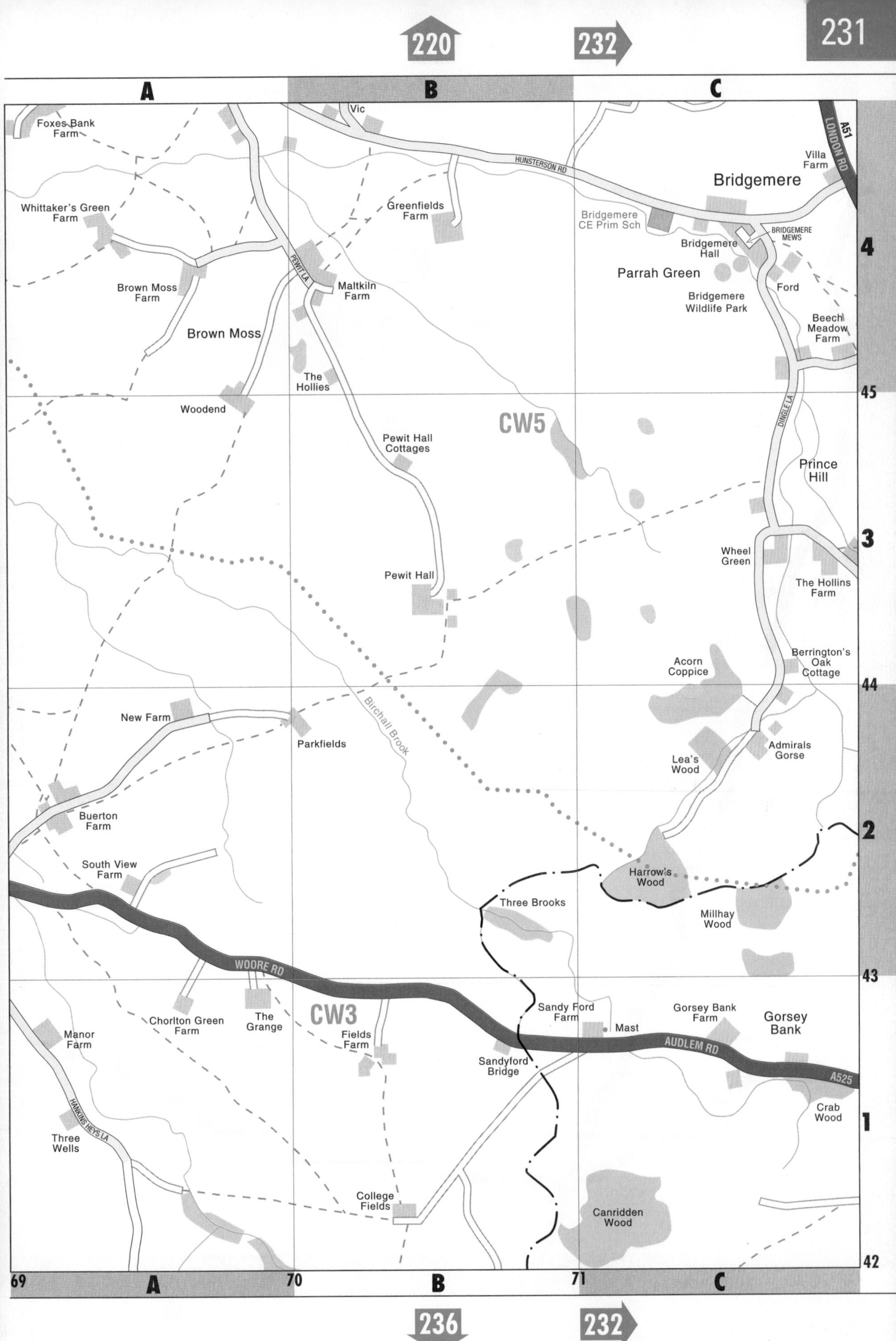
A
B
C
Vic
Foxes Bank Farm
HUNSTERSON RD
A51
LONDON RD
Villa Farm
Bridgemere
Whittaker's Green Farm
Greenfields Farm
Bridgemere CE Prim Sch
BRIDGEMERE MEWS
Bridgemere Hall
4
PEWIT LA
Parrah Green
Brown Moss Farm
Maltkiln Farm
Ford
Bridgemere Wildlife Park
Brown Moss
Beech Meadow Farm
The Hollies
45
Woodend
DINGLE LA
CW5
Pewit Hall Cottages
Prince Hill
3
Wheel Green
Pewit Hall
The Hollins Farm
Acorn Coppice
Berrington's Oak Cottage
44
New Farm
Birchall Brook
Parkfields
Admirals Gorse
Lea's Wood
Buerton Farm
2
South View Farm
Harrow's Wood
Three Brooks
Millhay Wood
WOORE RD
43
Chorlton Green Farm
The Grange
CW3
Sandy Ford Farm
Gorsey Bank Farm
Gorsey Bank
Manor Farm
Fields Farm
Mast
AUDLEM RD
Sandyford Bridge
A525
Crab Wood
1
HAWKINS HEYS LA
Three Wells
College Fields
Canridden Wood
42
69
70
71

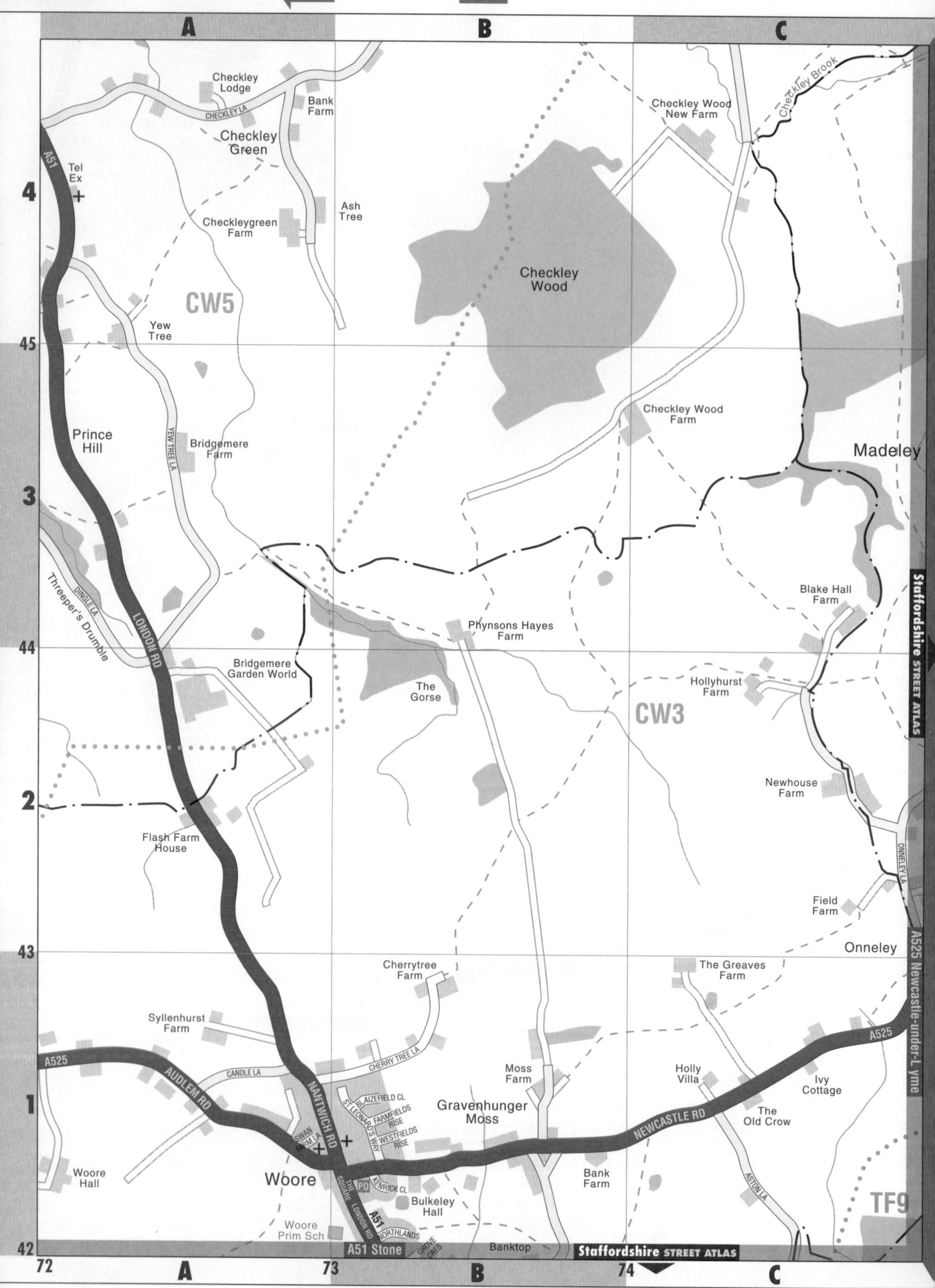

A · B · C

4

45

3

44

2

43

1

42

72 · A · 73 · B · 74 · C

CW5

Checkley Lodge
Bank Farm
CHECKLEY LA
Checkley Green
Tel Ex
Checkleygreen Farm
Ash Tree
Yew Tree
YEW TREE LA
Prince Hill
Bridgemere Farm
Threeper's Drumble
DINGLE LA
LONDON RD
Bridgemere Garden World
The Gorse
Flash Farm House
A51

Checkley Wood New Farm
Checkley Wood
Checkley Wood Farm
Madeley
Checkley Brook
Blake Hall Farm
Phynsons Hayes Farm
Hollyhurst Farm
CW3
Newhouse Farm
Onneley
ONNELEY LA
Field Farm
The Greaves Farm
Staffordshire STREET ATLAS
A525 Newcastle-under-Lyme

Cherrytree Farm
Syllenhurst Farm
A525
AUDLEM RD
CANDLE LA
CHERRY TREE LA
NANTWICH RD
BLAIZEFIELD CL
ST LEONARDS WAY
FARMFIELDS RISE
WESTFIELDS RISE
SWAN BANK LA
THE SQUARE
LONDON RD
PO
KENRICK CL
Woore
Woore Hall
Bulkeley Hall
Woore Prim Sch
NORTHLANDS
A51 Stone
GROVE CRES
Banktop
Gravenhunger Moss
Moss Farm
Bank Farm
Newcastle RD
Holly Villa
The Old Crow
Ivy Cottage
ASTON LA
TF9

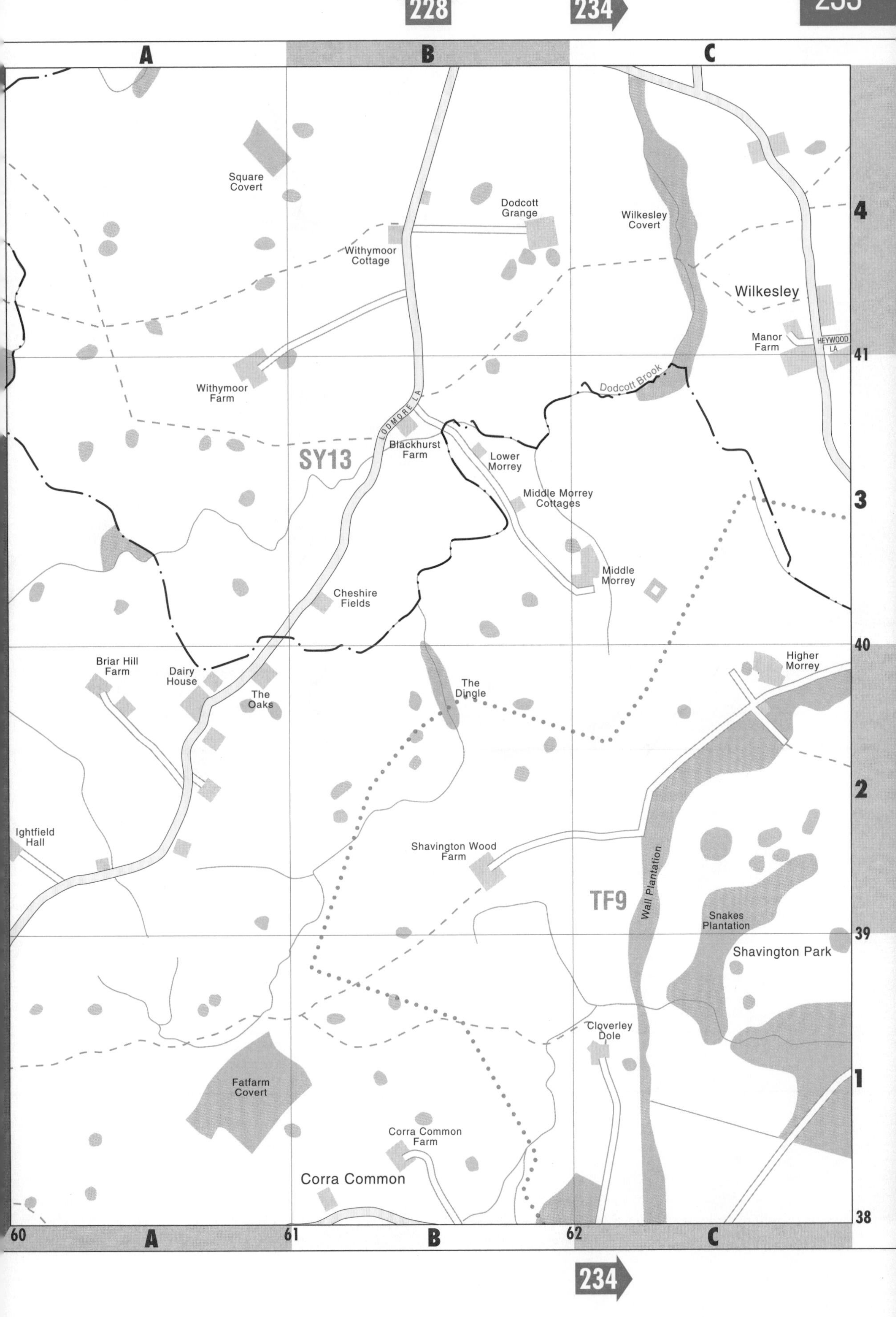

A
B
C

4

Square Covert

Dodcott Grange

Wilkesley Covert

Withymoor Cottage

Wilkesley

Manor Farm

HEYWOOD LA

41

Withymoor Farm

Dodcott Brook

SY13

Blackhurst Farm

Lower Morrey

3

Middle Morrey Cottages

Middle Morrey

Cheshire Fields

Briar Hill Farm

40

Higher Morrey

Dairy House

The Oaks

The Dingle

2

Ightfield Hall

Shavington Wood Farm

TF9

Wall Plantation

Snakes Plantation

39

Shavington Park

Cloverley Dole

1

Fatfarm Covert

Corra Common Farm

Corra Common

38

233
229

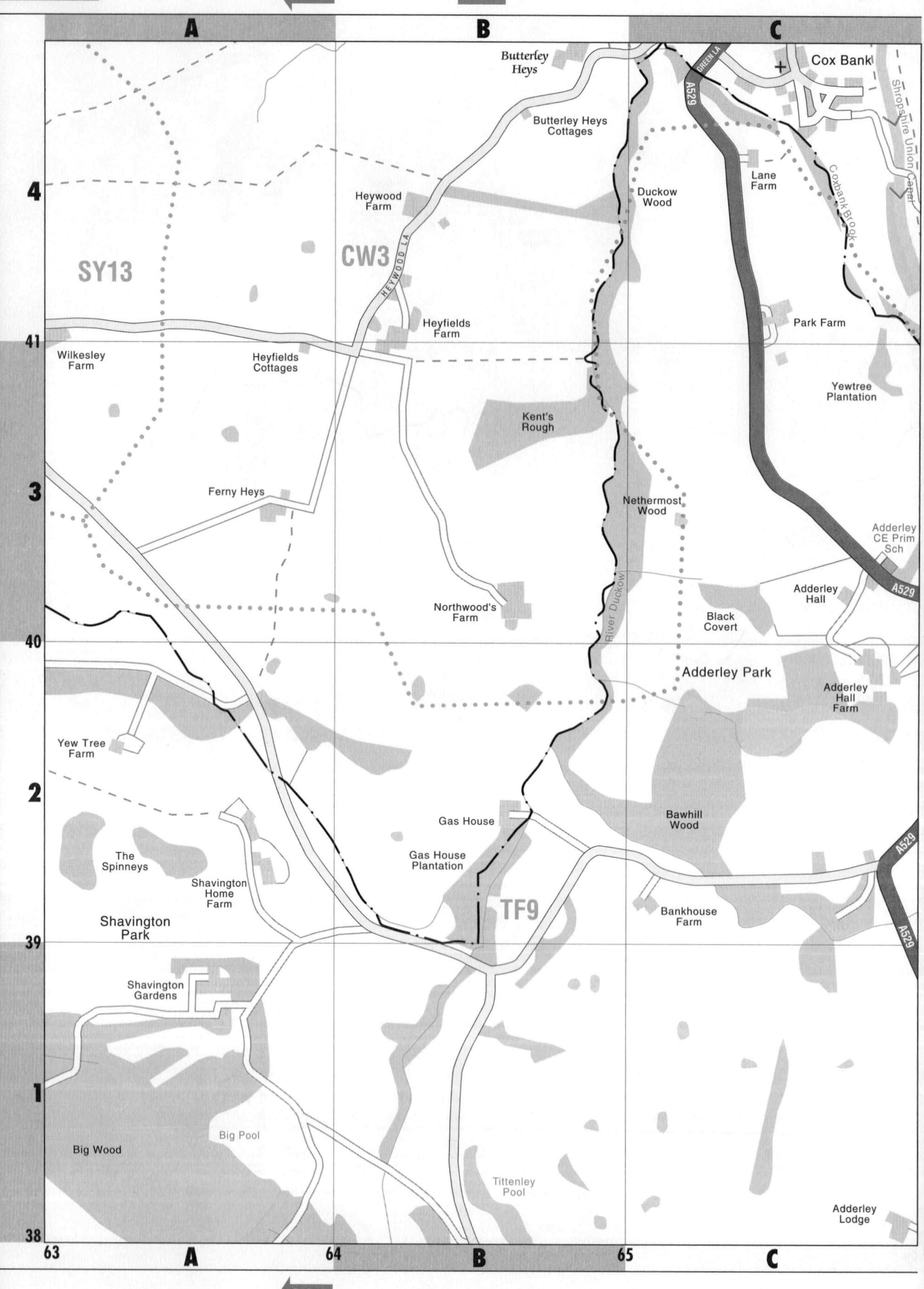
A
B
C
Butterley Heys
Cox Bank
GREEN LA
A529
Shropshire Union Canal
Butterley Heys Cottages
Lane Farm
Coxbank Brook
Heywood Farm
Duckow Wood
4
SY13
CW3
HEYWOOD LA
Heyfields Farm
Park Farm
41
Wilkesley Farm
Heyfields Cottages
Yewtree Plantation
Kent's Rough
3
Ferny Heys
Nethermost Wood
Adderley CE Prim Sch
Adderley Hall
Northwood's Farm
River Duckow
Black Covert
40
Adderley Park
Adderley Hall Farm
Yew Tree Farm
2
Gas House
Bawhill Wood
The Spinneys
Gas House Plantation
Shavington Home Farm
Bankhouse Farm
Shavington Park
TF9
39
Shavington Gardens
1
Big Pool
Big Wood
Tittenley Pool
Adderley Lodge
38
63
64
65

233

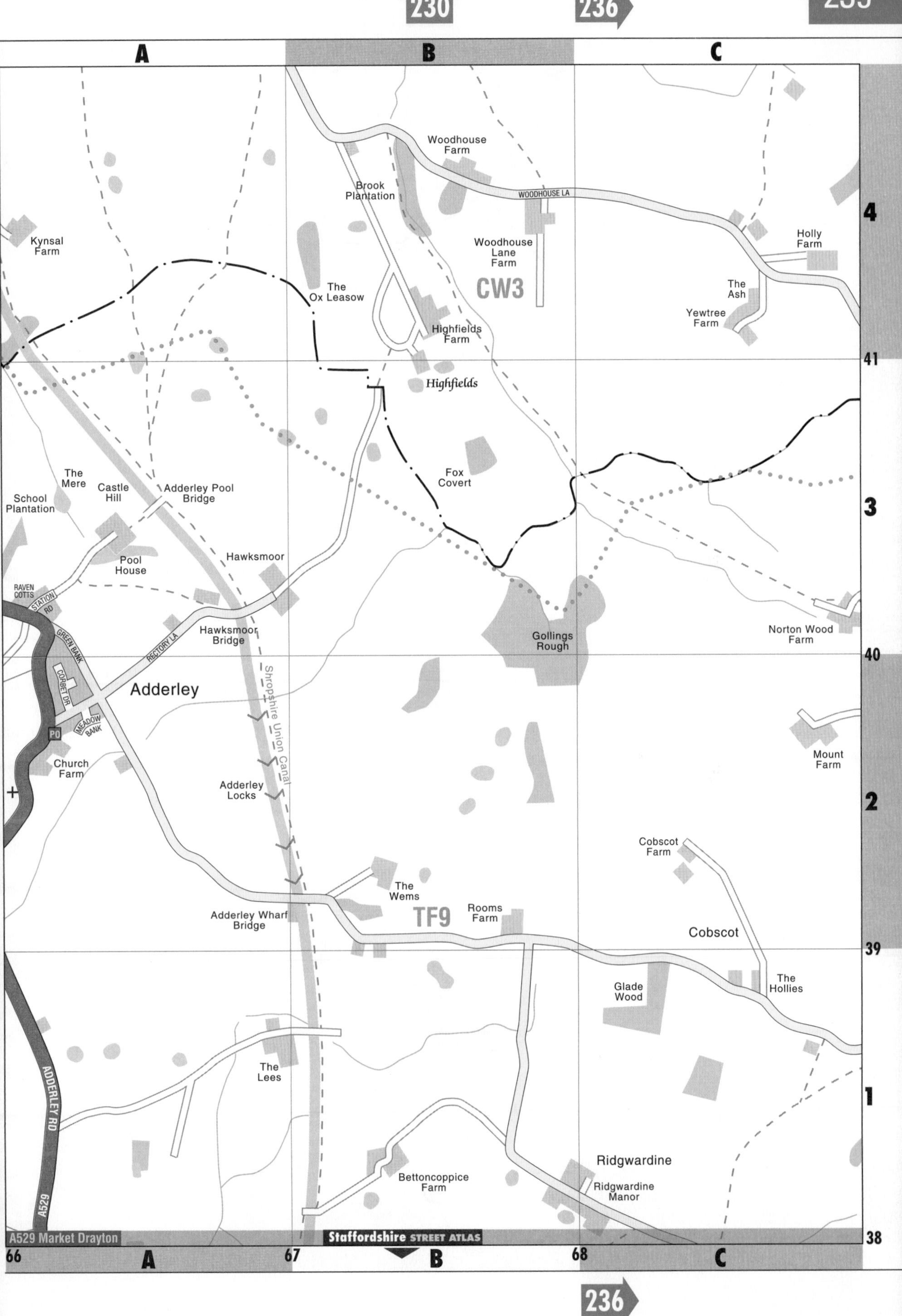

A

B

C

4

Kynsal
Farm

Woodhouse
Farm

Brook
Plantation

WOODHOUSE LA

Holly
Farm

The
Ox Leasow

Woodhouse
Lane
Farm

CW3

The
Ash

Yewtree
Farm

Highfields
Farm

41

Highfields

The
Mere

School
Plantation

Castle
Hill

Adderley Pool
Bridge

Fox
Covert

3

Hawksmoor

RAVEN
COTTS

STATION RD

Pool
House

Norton Wood
Farm

GREEN BANK

RECTORY LA

Hawksmoor
Bridge

Gollings
Rough

40

PO

CORBET DR

Adderley

Shropshire Union Canal

MEADOW BANK

Church
Farm

Mount
Farm

Adderley
Locks

2

Cobscot
Farm

Adderley Wharf
Bridge

The
Wems

TF9

Rooms
Farm

Cobscot

39

ADDERLEY RD

A529

The
Lees

Glade
Wood

The
Hollies

1

Bettoncoppice
Farm

Ridgwardine

Ridgwardine
Manor

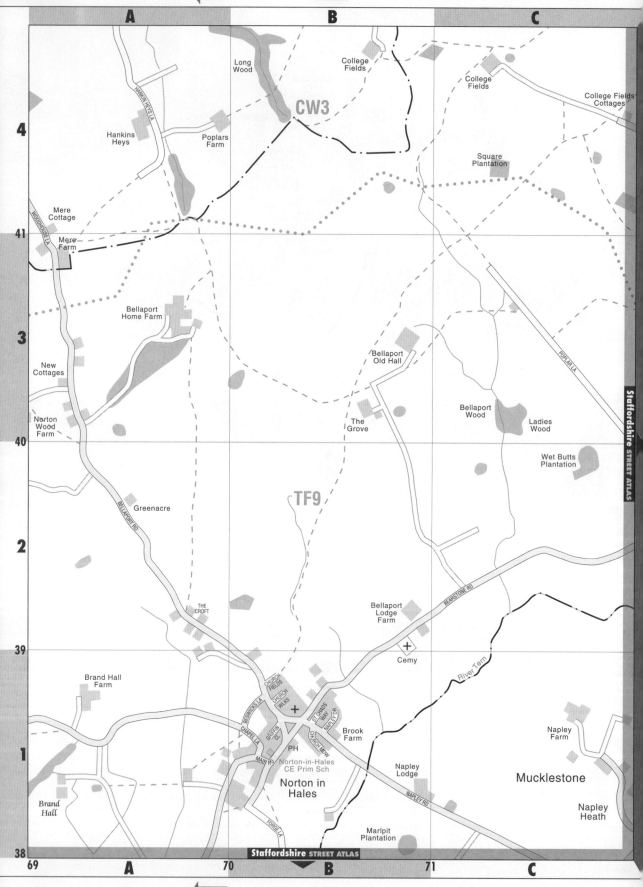

A   B   C

Long Wood

College Fields

CW3

College Fields

College Fields Cottages

Hankins Heys

Poplars Farm

Square Plantation

Mere Cottage

41

Mere Farm

Bellaport Home Farm

3

New Cottages

Bellaport Old Hall

Bellaport Wood

Ladies Wood

POPLAR LA

Norton Wood Farm

The Grove

40

Wet Butts Plantation

Greenacre

TF9

BELLAPORT RD

2

Bellaport Lodge Farm

BEARSTONE RD

THE CROFT

39

Cemy

River Tern

Brand Hall Farm

CHURCH FIELDS

CHURCH WLKS

BESWICKS LA

ST CHADS WAY

NAPLEY DR

Brook Farm

Napley Farm

CHAPEL LA

GRIFFIN CL

CHURCH MDW

1

PH

Napley Lodge

Mucklestone

MAIN RD

Norton-in-Hales CE Prim Sch

Brand Hall

Norton in Hales

Napley Heath

FORGE LA

NAPLEY RD

Marlpit Plantation

Staffordshire STREET ATLAS

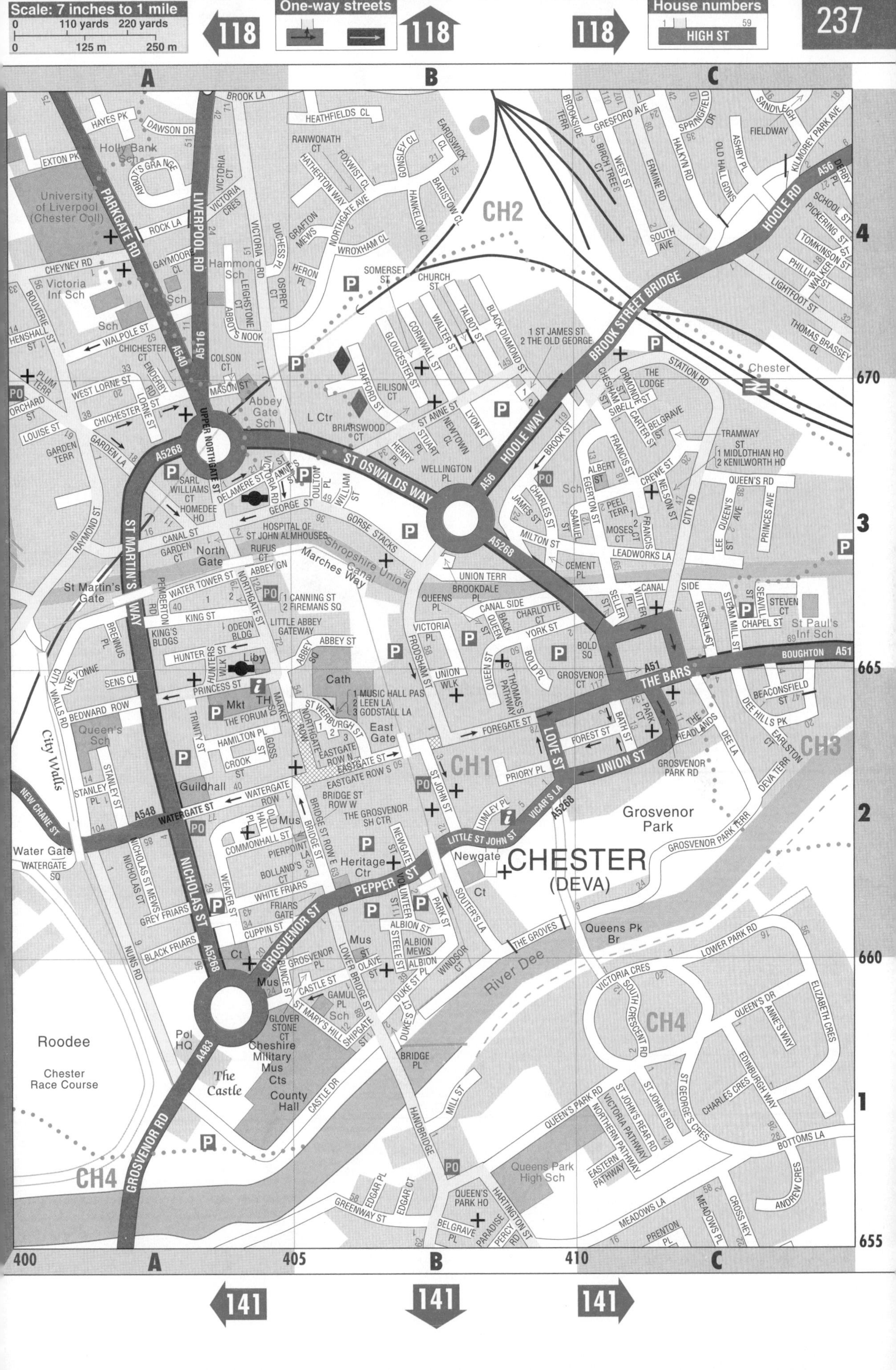
Scale: 7 inches to 1 mile
0 110 yards 220 yards
0 125 m 250 m
118
One-way streets
118
118
House numbers
1 59
HIGH ST
237
A
B
C
4
3
2
1
670
665
660
655
400
405
410
CH2
CH1
CH3
CH4
CH4
CHESTER
(DEVA)
BROOK LA
HEATHFIELDS CL
HAYES PK
DAWSON DR
Holly Bank Sch
EXTON PK
ABBOT'S GRANGE
University of Liverpool (Chester Coll)
PARKGATE RD
LIVERPOOL RD
VICTORIA CT
VICTORIA CRES
ROCK LA
CHEYNEY RD
GAYMOORE CL
Victoria Inf Sch
Hammond Sch
Sch
BOUVERIE ST
HENSHALL ST
WALPOLE ST
CHICHESTER CT
ENDERBY RD
A5116
A540
COLSON CT
MASON ST
ABBOT'S NOOK
LEIGHSTONE CT
VICTORIA RD
DUCHESS PL
OSPREY CT
HERON PL
GRAFTON MEWS
RANWONATH CT
HATHERTON WAY
FOXWIST CL
GONSLEY CL
EARDSWICK CL
NORTHGATE AVE
HANKELOW CL
BARISTOW CL
WROXHAM CL
SOMERSET ST
CHURCH ST
WALTER ST
TALBOT ST
BLACK DIAMOND ST
GLOUCESTER ST
CORNWALL ST
TRAFFORD ST
EILISON CT
BRIARSWOOD CT
L Ctr
ST ANNE ST
NEWTOWN CL
LYON ST
HENRY PL
STUART PL
1 ST JAMES ST
2 THE OLD GEORGE
PLUM TERR
ORCHARD ST
WEST LORNE ST
LORNE ST
CHICHESTER ST
LOUISE ST
GARDEN TERR
GARDEN LA
Abbey Gate Sch
UPPER NORTHGATE ST
A5268
SARL WILLIAMS CT
HOMEDEE HO
DELAMERE ST
ST ANNE'S ST
OULTON PL
WILLIAM ST
GEORGE ST
ST OSWALDS WAY
WELLINGTON PL
HOSPITAL OF ST JOHN ALMHOUSES
GORSE STACKS
CANAL ST
GARDEN CT
North Gate
RUFUS CT
RAYMOND ST
ST MARTIN'S WAY
Shropshire Union Canal
Marches Way
St Martin's Gate
WATER TOWER ST
ABBEY GN
PEMBERTON RD
NORTHGATE ST
1 CANNING ST
2 FIREMANS SQ
KING ST
KING'S BLDGS
ODEON BLDG
LITTLE ABBEY GATEWAY
ABBEY ST
ABBEY SQ
BRENNUS PL
HUNTER ST
HUNTERS WLK
Liby
CITY WALLS RD
THE YONNE
SENS CL
PRINCESS ST
Mkt
TH
MARKET SQ
Cath
1 MUSIC HALL PAS
2 LEEN LA
3 GODSTALL LA
BEDWARD ROW
TRINITY ST
THE FORUM
ST WERBURGH ST
NORTHGATE ROW
East Gate
Queen's Sch
City Walls
HAMILTON PL
CROOK ST
GOSS ST
EASTGATE ROW N
EASTGATE ST
EASTGATE ROW S
Guildhall
STANLEY PL
STANLEY ST
WATERGATE ROW
WATERGATE ST
A548
NEW CRANE ST
BRIDGE ST ROW W
THE GROSVENOR SH CTR
BRIDGE ST ROW E
Water Gate
WATERGATE SQ
NICHOLAS ST MEWS
NICHOLAS ST
OLD HALL PL
COMMONHALL ST
Mus
PIERPOINT LA
BOLLAND'S CT
WHITE FRIARS
Heritage Ctr
NEWGATE ST
PEPPER ST
VOLUNTEER ST
GREY FRIARS
WEAVER ST
FRIARS GATE
CUPPIN ST
BLACK FRIARS
NUNS RD
GROSVENOR ST
Ct
GROSVENOR PL
BUNCE ST
CASTLE ST
GAMUL PL
LOWER BRIDGE ST
ST OLAVE ST
ALBION ST
ALBION MEWS
STEELE ST
DUKE ST
ALBION PL
PARK ST
WINDSOR CT
Mus
Sch
GLOVER STONE CT
ST MARY'S HILL
SHIPGATE ST
DUKE'S CT
Pol HQ
A483
Cheshire Military Mus
Cts
County Hall
Roodee
Chester Race Course
The Castle
CASTLE DR
GROSVENOR RD
BRIDGE PL
MILL ST
HANDBRIDGE
GREENWAY ST
EDGAR PL
EDGAR CT
QUEEN'S PARK HO
BELGRAVE PL
PARADISE
PERCY RD
HARRINGTON ST
Queens Park High Sch
QUEEN'S PARK RD
VICTORIA PATHWAY
NORTHERN PATHWAY
EASTERN PATHWAY
ST JOHN'S REAR RD
ST JOHN'S RD
ST GEORGE'S CRES
MEADOWS LA
MEADOWS PL
PRENTON PL
CROSS HEY
ANDREW CRES
BOTTOMS LA
CHARLES CRES
EDINBURGH WAY
QUEEN'S DR
ANNE'S WAY
ELIZABETH CRES
SOUTH CRESCENT RD
VICTORIA CRES
LOWER PARK RD
River Dee
Queens Pk Br
THE GROVES
SOUTER'S LA
Newgate
LITTLE ST JOHN ST
LUMLEY PL
VICAR'S LA
ST JOHN ST
Grosvenor Park
GROSVENOR PARK TERR
GROSVENOR PARK RD
PRIORY PL
UNION ST
LOVE ST
FOREST ST
BATH ST
PARK CT
THE HEADLANDS
DEE LA
DEVA TERR
EARLSTON CT
DEE HILLS PK
BEACONSFIELD ST
BOUGHTON A51
THE BARS
A51
GROSVENOR CT
FOREGATE ST
FRODSHAM ST
VICTORIA PL
UNION WLK
QUEEN ST
ST THOMAS'S PATHWAY
BOLD PL
BOLD SQ
YORK ST
BACK QUEEN ST
CHARLOTTE CT
CANAL SIDE
QUEENS PL
BROOKDALE PL
UNION TERR
A5268
MILTON ST
CEMENT PL
LEADWORKS LA
SELLER ST
WITTER PL
CANAL SIDE
RUSSELL ST
STEAM MILL ST
SEAVILL ST
CHAPEL ST
STEVEN CT
St Paul's Inf Sch
JAMES ST
CHARLES ST
SAMUEL ST
EGERTON ST
PEEL TERR
MOSES CT
FRANCIS ST
CREWE ST
NELSON ST
CITY RD
QUEEN'S RD
QUEEN'S AVE
LEE ST
PRINCES AVE
TRAMWAY ST
1 MIDLOTHIAN HO
2 KENILWORTH HO
ALBERT ST
Sch
BROOK ST
HOOLE WAY
A56
BROOK STREET BRIDGE
CHESHAM ST
ORMONDE ST
SIBELL ST
CARTER ST
BELGRAVE ST
FRANCIS ST
THE LODGE
STATION RD
Chester
HOOLE RD
A56 DERBY PL
KILMOREY PARK AVE
SCHOOL ST
PICKERING ST
TOMKINSON ST
PHILLIP ST
WALKER ST
LIGHTFOOT ST
THOMAS BRASSEY CL
BROOKSIDE TERR
BIRCH TREE CT
GRESFORD AVE
WEST ST
ERMINE RD
HALKYN RD
SPRINGFIELD DR
OLD HALL GDNS
ASHBY PL
FIELDWAY
SANDILEIGH
SOUTH AVE
141
141
141

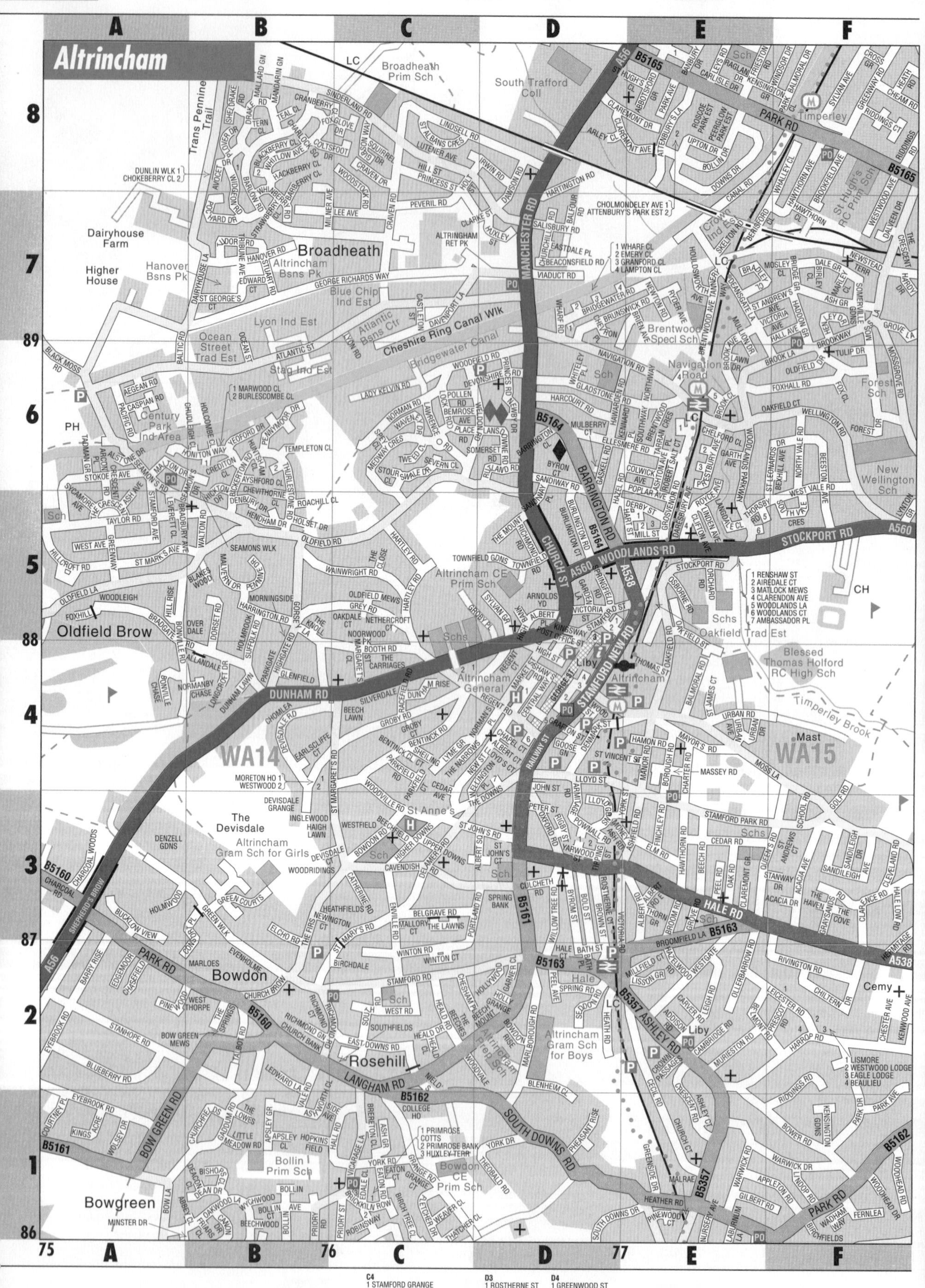

D5
1 POLICE ST
2 STAMFORD WAY
3 STAMFORD SQ
4 OLD MARKET PL

E6
1 LYNGARTH HO
2 ASTBURY CL
3 THELWALL CL
4 THE WOODS
5 SELWORTH CL

Altrincham

C4
1 STAMFORD GRANGE
2 EASINGWOLD

D3
1 ROSTHERNE ST
2 WILLIAM WLK

D4
1 GREENWOOD ST
2 THE CAUSEWAY
3 CROSS ST
4 BREWERY ST
5 GRAFTON MALL
6 LLOYD SQ
7 OSBOURNE PL

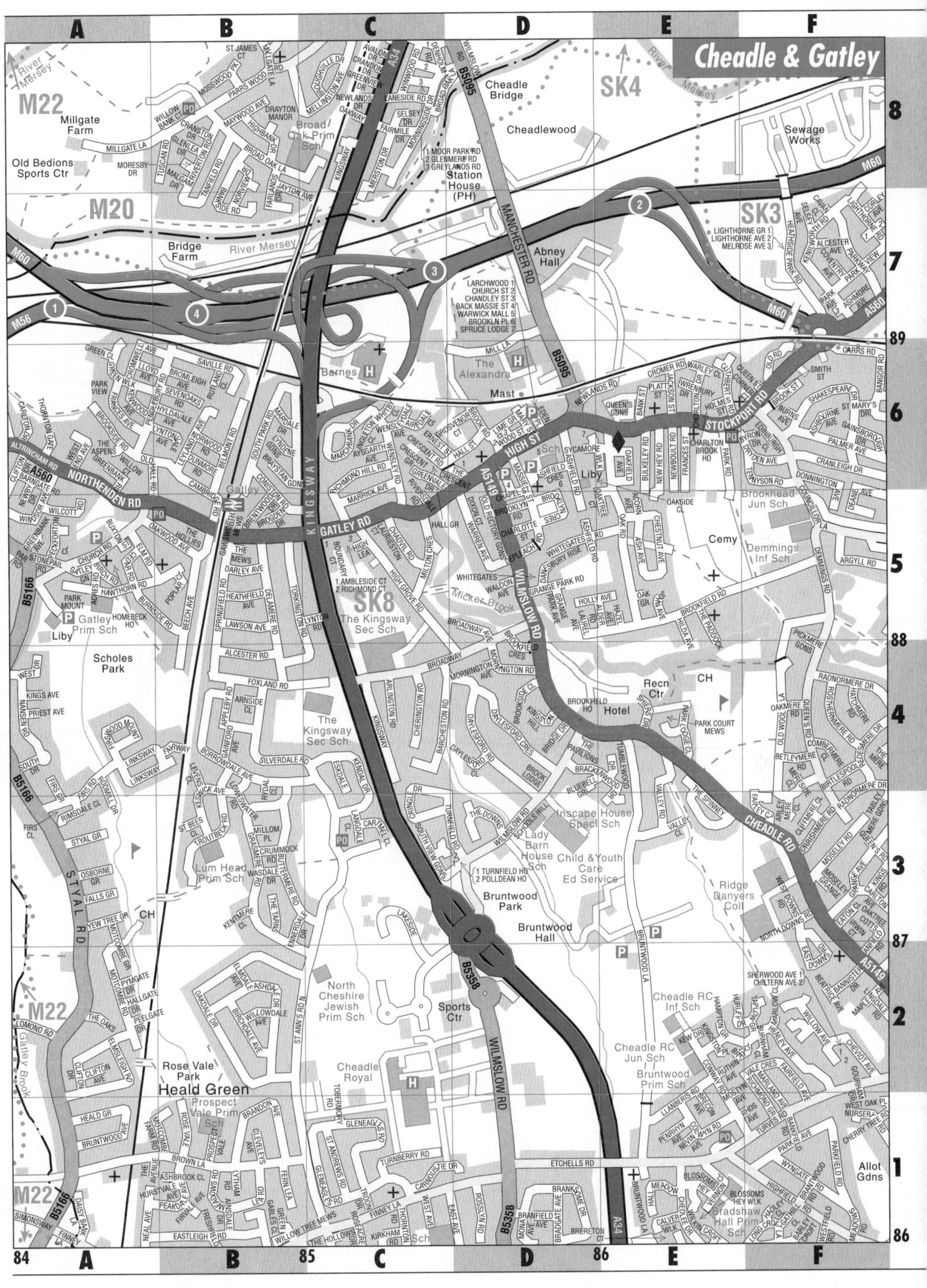
Cheadle & Gatley
A
B
C
D
E
F
8
7
6
5
4
3
2
1
89
88
87
86
84
85
86
M22
M20
SK4
SK3
SK8
Millgate Farm
Old Bedions Sports Ctr
Bridge Farm
River Mersey
Cheadle Bridge
Cheadlewood
Sewage Works
Station House (PH)
Abney Hall
Barnes
The Alexandra
Mast
KINGSWAY
MANCHESTER RD
HIGH ST
STOCKPORT RD
GATLEY RD
NORTHENDEN RD
WILMSLOW RD
CHEADLE RD
STYAL RD
Gatley
Scholes Park
Liby
Gatley Prim Sch
The Kingsway Sec Sch
Micker Brook
Brookhead Jun Sch
Cemy
Demmings Inf Sch
Recn Ctr
Hotel
CH
Inscape House Specl Sch
Lady Barn House Sch
Child & Youth Care Ed Service
Ridge Danyers Coll
Bruntwood Park
Bruntwood Hall
Lum Head Prim Sch
North Cheshire Jewish Prim Sch
Sports Ctr
Cheadle Royal
Cheadle RC Inf Sch
Cheadle RC Jun Sch
Bruntwood Prim Sch
Rose Vale Park
Heald Green
Prospect Vale Prim Sch
Bradshaw Hall Prim Sch
Allot Gdns
Gatley Brook
A560
A5149
A34
B5095
B5166
B5358
M56
M60
ETCHELLS RD

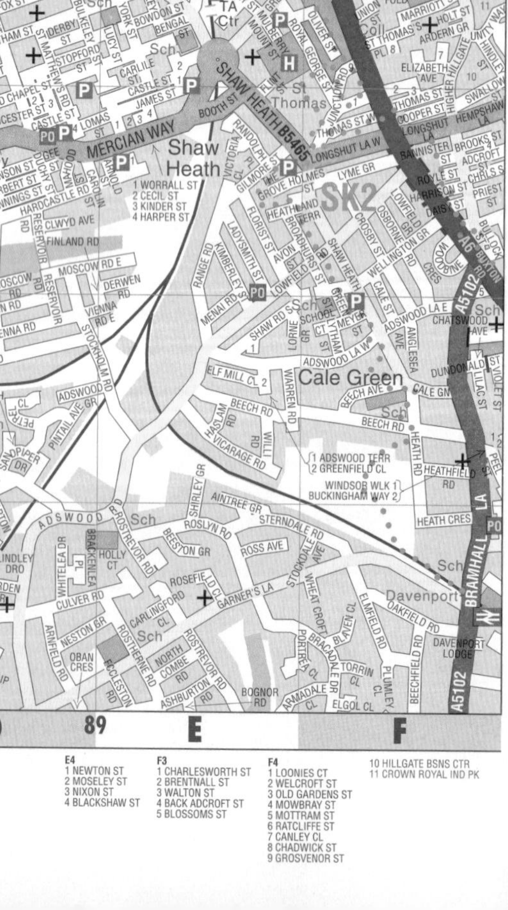

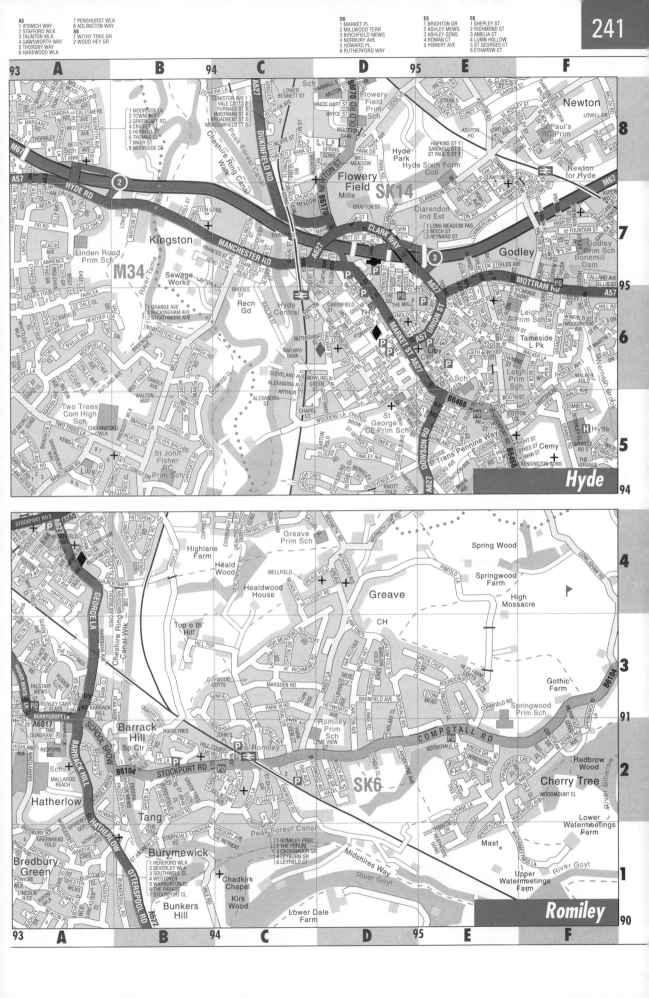

A5
1 IPSWICH WAY
2 STAFFORD WLK
3 TAUNTON WLK
4 GAWSWORTH WAY
5 THORSBY WAY
6 HAREWOOD WLK

7 PENSHURST WLK
8 ADLINGTON WAY
A6
1 WITHY TREE GR
2 WOOD HEY GR

D6
1 MARKET PL
2 MILLWOOD TERR
3 BIRCHFIELD MEWS
4 NORBURY AVE
5 HOWARD PL
6 RUTHERFORD WAY

E5
1 BRIGHTON GR
2 ASHLEY MEWS
3 ASHLEY GDNS
4 ROWAN CT
5 HIBBERT AVE

E6
1 SHEPLEY ST
2 RICHMOND ST
3 AMELIA ST
4 LUMN HOLLOW
5 ST GEORGES CT
6 ETHAROW CT

Hyde

Romiley

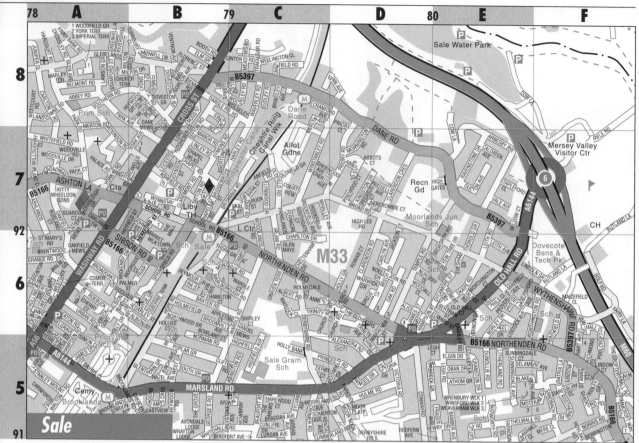

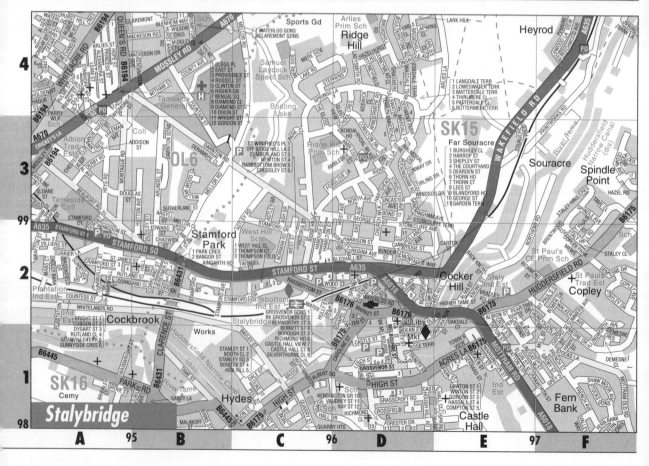

Church Rd 6 Beckenham BR2..........**53** C6

Place name	**Location number**	**Locality, town or village**	**Postcode district**	**Page and grid square**
May be abbreviated on the map	Present when a number indicates the place's position in a crowded area of mapping	Shown when more than one place has the same name	District for the indexed place	Page number and grid reference for the standard mapping

Public and commercial buildings are highlighted in magenta   **Places of interest** are highlighted in blue with a star★

Abbreviations used in the index

Acad	**Academy**	Comm	**Common**	Gd	**Ground**	L	**Leisure**	Prom	**Prom**
App	**Approach**	Cott	**Cottage**	Gdn	**Garden**	La	**Lane**	Rd	**Road**
Arc	**Arcade**	Cres	**Crescent**	Gn	**Green**	Liby	**Library**	Recn	**Recreation**
Ave	**Avenue**	Cswy	**Causeway**	Gr	**Grove**	Mdw	**Meadow**	Ret	**Retail**
Bglw	**Bungalow**	Ct	**Court**	H	**Hall**	Meml	**Memorial**	Sh	**Shopping**
Bldg	**Building**	Ctr	**Centre**	Ho	**House**	Mkt	**Market**	Sq	**Square**
Bsns, Bus	**Business**	Ctry	**Country**	Hospl	**Hospital**	Mus	**Museum**	St	**Street**
Bvd	**Boulevard**	Cty	**County**	HQ	**Headquarters**	Orch	**Orchard**	Sta	**Station**
Cath	**Cathedral**	Dr	**Drive**	Hts	**Heights**	Pal	**Palace**	Terr	**Terrace**
Cir	**Circus**	Dro	**Drove**	Ind	**Industrial**	Par	**Parade**	TH	**Town Hall**
Cl	**Close**	Ed	**Education**	Inst	**Institute**	Pas	**Passage**	Univ	**University**
Cnr	**Corner**	Emb	**Embankment**	Int	**International**	Pk	**Park**	Wk, Wlk	**Walk**
Coll	**College**	Est	**Estate**	Intc	**Interchange**	Pl	**Place**	Wr	**Water**
Com	**Community**	Ex	**Exhibition**	Junc	**Junction**	Prec	**Precinct**	Yd	**Yard**

Index of localities, towns and villages

Acton 204 A4	Cheadle 239	Haslington 191 C3	Mere 56 B4	Sound 217 C3
Acton Bridge 76 C2	Chelford 84 A1	Hassall Green 176 A1	Mickle Trafford 119 C4	Speke 21 A2
Adderley 235 A2	Chester 118 C1	Hatherton 219 C2	Middlewich 128 B2	Sproston Green 129 B1
Adlington 62 B3	Cholmondeston 170 C2	Hatton 26 A1	Milton Green 165 B1	Spurstow 185 B3
Alderley Edge 60 B1	Chorlton 207 A1	Haughton 186 B3	Mobberley 57 C4	St Helens 1 A1
Aldford 163 C2	Christleton 142 C4	Hawarden 116 A1	Mollington 94 C1	Stalybridge 242
Allostock 106 C2	Church Minshull 172 A3	Haydock 1 B3	Moore 25 A3	Stanlow 71 A3
Alpraham 169 B2	Churton 180 C3	Haymoor Green 205 C1	Mottram St Andrew ...61 A1	Stapeley 219 B4
Alsager 193 C3	Clutton 182 B1	Hazel Grove 36 B4	Mouldsworth 98 C1	Stoak 96 A4
Altrincham 31 B4	Coddington 182 A2	Helsby 73 B2	Moulton 126 C4	Stockport 240
Altrincham 238	Collins Green 1 C1	Henbury 111 A4	Mount Pleasant 195 A3	Stretton 26 C1
Alvanley 73 B1	Comberbach 78 B4	Heswall 40 B4	Mow Cop 195 B4	Styal 33 C2
Anderton 78 B2	Congleton 157 A2	High Lane 37 C4	Nantwich 204 B3	Sutton 50 A1
Antrobus 53 B2	Connah's Quay 91 A1	High Legh 29 A3	Neston 66 B4	Sutton Lane Ends 112 C1
Appleton Thorn 27 A2	Cranage 130 A3	Higher Kinnerton 161 A4	Nether Alderley 85 A3	Swettenham 131 C2
Ashley 31 C3	Crewe 190 C3	Higher Walton 25 C4	New Mills 39 B4	Tabley 55 C2
Ashton 121 C4	Crewe-by-Farndon 197 A4	Higher Wincham 79 C2	Newcastle-under-Lyme 210 B2	Talke 210 B4
Astbury 178 A4	Croft 9 A4	Hollinfare 11 A2	Newhall 228 B4	Tarporley 146 B1
Aston 217 B1	Cronton 12 B3	Hollins Green 11 A1	Newton-le-Willows ...2 A1	Tarvin 121 B2
Audlem 230 A2	Crowton 76 B1	Holmes Chapel 130 B2	No Man's Heath 214 A3	Tattenhall 166 A1
Audley 209 B1	Cuddington 101 C2	Holt 196 B4	Norley 100 C3	The Bank 195 A4
Backford 95 A2	Culcheth 4 C2	Hooton 44 A1	Northwich 103 B4	Thornton Hough 42 A4
Barbridge 187 B3	Daresbury 25 A1	Hough Common 206 C1	Norton in Hales 236 B1	Thornton-le-Moors ...71 C1
Barnton 78 B2	Davenham 104 A1	Huntington 142 A3	Oakmere 124 A4	Threapwood 222 C4
Barthomley 208 B3	Delamere 123 B3	Huxley 166 C4	Ollerton 82 C3	Tilston 198 A2
Barton 181 C1	Disley 38 B3	Hyde 241	Packmoor 195 C1	Tiverton 168 B3
Bate Heath 54 C2	Dodleston 162 A4	Irlam 11 B4	Partington 11 C2	Utkinton 146 A4
Bebington 43 A3	Duddon 145 A3	Isycoed 196 B1	Peckforton 184 C3	Warmingham 173 B4
Beeston 168 A1	Dunham-on-the-Hill ...97 C3	Kelsall 122 B2	Peover 107 A4	Warren 111 B1
Bell o' th' Hill 225 B4	Dutton 51 B1	Kettleshulme 64 C2	Pickmere 80 A4	Warrington 16 C3
Betley 221 C4	Eaton 147 A2	Kidsgrove 195 A1	Picton 96 B2	Waverton 143 A2
Bickerton 199 C2	Eaton (nr Congleton) ..157 A4	Kingsley 75 C2	Plumley 81 A2	Weaverham 77 B1
Bickley Town 214 C3	Eccleston 141 B1	Knutsford 57 A2	Pott Shrigley 63 B2	Weston 207 B3
Biddulph 179 A1	Edge Green 199 A1	Lach Dennis 105 B3	Poynton 36 C2	Wettenhall 170 C4
Blacon 117 C2	Ellesmere Port 70 A4	Langley 113 B2	Prestbury 87 A4	Whaley Bridge 65 B4
Blakenhall 221 A2	Elton 72 B2	Lavister 162 B1	Preston on the Hill ...51 A3	Whitchurch 226 A1
Bold Heath 13 C4	Faddiley 202 B4	Lawton Heath 193 C3	Puddington 92 C4	Whitegate 126 A4
Bollington 88 A4	Farndon 180 C1	Lawton Heath End 193 B3	Pulford 162 B2	Whitewell 224 B1
Bosley 158 B4	Fowley Common 5 A3	Lawton-gate 194 A2	Rainow 88 B3	Whitley 52 B2
Bradwall Green 153 A2	Frodsham 74 B4	Ledsham 68 C1	Ravensmoor 203 C1	Widnes 22 C4
Bramhall 35 B4	Gatesheath 165 C3	Lindow End 59 A1	Rode Heath 193 C4	Willaston 68 A4
Brereton Green 153 C3	Gatley 239	Little Bollington 20 A1	Romiley 241	Willaston (nr Nantwich) 205 B3
Bridgemere 231 C4	Glazebury 5 B4	Little Budworth 147 C4	Rostherne 30 C2	Wilmslow 60 B3
Broomedge 19 B1	Golborne 3 A4	Little Leigh 77 B2	Royal's Green 228 C1	Wimbolds Trafford ...96 C3
Broughton 139 A2	Goostrey 107 B1	Lostock Gralam 80 A2	Runcorn 23 B1	Wimboldsley 150 C2
Brown Knowl 199 B4	Gorstyhill 207 C1	Lostock Green 105 A4	Rushton Spencer 159 A1	Wincle 160 A4
Broxton 183 A1	Grappenhall Heys 27 A4	Lower Kinnerton 139 B1	Saighton 142 C1	Winsford 126 C1
Buerton 230 C2	Great Barrow 120 C3	Lower Peover 81 C1	Sale 242	Winwick 8 A3
Bulkeley 184 C1	Great Budworth 79 A4	Lymm 18 C2	Sandbach 175 A3	Wistaston 205 B4
Bunbury 185 C4	Guilden Sutton 119 C3	Macclesfield 112 A2	Saughall 94 A1	Withington Green 108 C2
Burland 203 B4	Hale 21 B1	Macclesfield Forest ...114 B3	Scholar Green 194 C4	Woodford 35 C1
Burton 67 B1	Halewood 21 A4	Madeley 232 C3	Sealand 116 C3	Woore 232 A1
Burton Green 161 B1	Hampton 214 A4	Malpas 213 A1	Shavington 206 B3	Worleston 188 C3
Burtonwood 6 C4	Handforth 34 B2	Manley 99 A2	Shocklach 211 B4	Worthenbury 211 A1
Burwardsley 184 A3	Hargrave 144 A1	Marbury 226 B4	Shotwick 93 A2	Wrenbury 216 C2
Capenhurst 94 A4	Hartford 103 B3	Marston 79 A2	Siddington 110 A2	Wybunbury 220 A4
Cheadle 34 C4	Harthill 183 C2	Marton 133 A3	Smallwood 176 C3	Wythenshawe 33 C4

1

108 Steps 29 SK11 ... 112 B4

A

Aarons Dr ST7 ... 209 C1
Abbey Cl
Altrincham WA14 ... 238 B1
Croft WA3 ... 9 A4
Whitegate CW8 ... 126 A4
Widnes WA8 ... 22 B4
Abbey Fields CW2 ... 205 B4
Abbey Gate Coll CH3 ... 164 C4
Abbey Gate Coll (The Jun Dept) CH3 ... 163 C2
Abbey Gate Sch CH2 ... 237 A4
Abbey Gn CH1 ... 237 A3
Abbey Hey WA7 ... 50 B4
Abbey La Delamere CW8 ... 123 C3
Hartford CW8 ... 103 A2
Abbey Pl CW1 ... 190 B3
Abbey Rd Golborne WA3 ... 4 B4
Haydock WA11 ... 1 C4
Macclesfield SK10 ... 87 A1
Sale M33 ... 242 A8
Sandbach CW11 ... 174 C3
Stockport SK8 ... 240 A1
Widnes WA8 ... 22 B4
Abbey Sq CH1 ... 237 B3
Abbey St CH1 ... 237 B3
Abbey Way CW8 ... 103 A2
Abbeydale Cl CW2 ... 207 B1
Abbeyfields CW11 ... 174 C3
Abbeyway N WA11 ... 2 A4
Abbeyway S WA11 ... 2 A4
Abbot's Dr CH2 ... 118 B2
Abbot's Grange CH2 ... 237 A4
Abbot's Nook CH2 ... 237 A4
Abbots Cl
Macclesfield SK10 ... 87 A1
Sale M33 ... 242 D7
Abbots Ct M33 ... 242 D7
Abbots Knoll CH2 ... 118 B2
Abbots Mews CH65 ... 70 A3
Abbots Pk CH2 ... 118 B2
Abbots Way
Hartford CW8 ... 103 A2
Neston CH64 ... 41 C1
Abbotsbury Cl
Poynton SK12 ... 36 B3
Wistaston CW2 ... 206 A4
Abbotsfield Cl WA4 ... 26 C3
Abbotsford Gr WA14 ... 238 E8
Abbotsmere Cl CW8 ... 101 C1
Abbott's Cl CW12 ... 179 A4
Abbotts Cl Runcorn WA7 ... 49 A4
Waverton CH3 ... 143 A3
Abbotts Rd CH3 ... 143 A3
Abbotts Way CW7 ... 126 A1
Aber Rd SK8 ... 240 A2
Abercrombie Ct M33 ... 242 D7
Aberdare Cl WA5 ... 7 C1
Aberdaron Dr CH1 ... 117 C2
Aberdeen Cres SK3 ... 240 D4
Aberdeen Gr SK3 ... 240 D4
Aberfeldy Cl CW4 ... 130 A1
Abingdon Ave WA1 ... 17 C4
Abingdon Cl SK11 ... 111 C4
Abingdon Cres CH4 ... 140 C3
Abingdon St OL6 ... 242 A2
Abington Cl CW1 ... 190 A3
Abington Rd M33 ... 242 C5
Abington Wlk WA7 ... 50 B3
Abstone Cl WA1 ... 17 A4
Acacia Ave
Altrincham WA15 ... 238 F3
Denton M34 ... 241 A7
Knutsford WA16 ... 56 C1
Warrington WA1 ... 17 B4
Widnes WA8 ... 13 A2
Wilmslow SK9 ... 59 C3
Acacia Cl CH2 ... 72 B2
Acacia Cres CW1 ... 190 C3
Acacia Dr
Altrincham WA15 ... 238 F3
Ellesmere Port CH66 ... 69 C1
Sandbach CW11 ... 174 C4
Acacia Gdns ST7 ... 195 B2
Acacia Gr Runcorn WA7 ... 49 B4
4 Stockport SK5 ... 240 F8
Acacia St WA12 ... 1 C2
Academy St WA1 ... 16 A3
Academy Way WA1 ... 16 A3
Acer Ave CW1 ... 190 C4
Achilles Ave WA2 ... 8 A1
Ack La E SK7 ... 35 B4
Ack La W SK7,SK8 ... 35 B4
Ackerley Cl WA2 ... 8 C2
Ackers La WA4 ... 16 C1
Ackers Rd WA4 ... 16 C1
Ackersley Ct SK8 ... 35 A4
Acorn Ave SK8 ... 239 E5
Acorn Bank Cl CW2 ... 206 A4
Acorn Bsns Ctr SK4 ... 240 D5
Acorn Cl Cuddington CW8 ... 101 C1
Winsford CW7 ... 150 A4
Acorn Dr CH65 ... 70 A1
Acorn La CW12 ... 157 C2
Acorn St WA12 ... 2 B2
Acorn Terr SK22 ... 39 A3
Acre Gn L26 ... 21 A3
Acre La Bebington CH62 ... 43 B4
Bramhall SK7,SK8 ... 35 B3
Heswall CH60 ... 41 B4
Acre Rd CH66 ... 69 B3
Acre St SK6 ... 241 B2
Acreage The
Bunbury CW6 ... 185 C4
Goostrey CW4 ... 107 C1
Acrefield Ave SK4 ... 240 B8
Acrefield Rd WA8 ... 12 A1
Acres Cres WA6 ... 75 A1
Acres La Chester CH2 ... 118 B4
Stalybridge SK15 ... 242 E1
Acres Rd SK8 ... 239 A5
Acresfield Prim Sch CH2 ... 118 C4
Acreville Gr WA3 ... 5 B4
Acton Ave WA4 ... 26 B2
Acton Bridge Sta CW8 ... 76 C1
Acton CE Prim Sch CW5 ... 204 A4
Acton Cl WA11 ... 1 B3
Acton La CW8 ... 76 C2
Acton Pl SK11 ... 111 C4
Acton Rd Burtonwood WA5 ... 6 C3
Crewe CW2 ... 189 B3
Acton Way ST7 ... 193 B3
Adam Ave CH66 ... 69 B2
Adam Cl CH66 ... 69 B2
Adam St WA2 ... 16 B4
Adams Cl
Newton-le-W WA12 ... 2 B1
Poynton SK12 ... 36 C1
Adams Hill WA16 ... 57 A1
Adamson Ct WA4 ... 17 A1
Adamson St WA4 ... 16 A2
Adaston Ave CH62 ... 43 C2
Adcroft St SK1 ... 240 F3
Adder Hill CH3 ... 142 A4
Adderley CE Prim Sch TF9 ... 234 C3
Adderly Cl WA7 ... 23 B1
Addingham Ave WA8 ... 22 B4
Addison Ave OL6 ... 242 A3
Addison Cl CW2 ... 205 C4
Addison Rd WA15 ... 238 E2
Addison Sq WA8 ... 13 A1
Adela Rd WA7 ... 22 C1
Adelaide Rd Blacon CH1 ... 117 B2
Bramhall SK7 ... 35 C3
Stockport SK3 ... 240 D4
Adelaide Sch CW1 ... 190 B3
Adelaide St Crewe CW1 ... 190 B3
Macclesfield SK10 ... 87 C1
Adey Rd WA13 ... 19 A3
Adfalent La CH64 ... 68 A4
Adlington Cl SK12 ... 36 C1
Adlington Ct WA3 ... 9 C3
Adlington Dr
Northwich CW9 ... 104 A3
Sandbach CW11 ... 175 B4
Adlington Ind Est SK10 ... 36 B1
Adlington Pk SK10 ... 36 B1
Adlington Prim Sch SK10 ... 62 C3
Adlington Rd
Bollington SK10 ... 63 A1
Crewe CW2 ... 189 C2
Runcorn WA7 ... 24 B1
Wilmslow SK9 ... 60 C4
Adlington St SK11 ... 112 B4
Adlington Sta SK10 ... 62 B3
Adlington Way 8 M34 ... 241 A5
Adlinton Hall Mews SK10 ... 62 A3
Admirals Rd WA3 ... 9 C2
Adshall Rd SK8 ... 240 A1
Adshead Ct SK10 ... 88 A4
Adswood Gr SK3 ... 240 D2
Adswood La E SK2 ... 240 F2
Adswood La W SK3 ... 240 F2
Adswood Prim Sch SK3 ... 240 E1
Adswood Rd SK3 ... 240 D1
Adswood Terr SK3 ... 240 E2
Adwell Cl WA3 ... 4 A4
Aegean Rd WA14 ... 238 A6
Afton WA8 ... 12 A1
Agden Brow WA13 ... 19 C1
Agden Brow Pk WA13 ... 29 B4
Agden House La SY13 ... 225 A3
Agden La
Broomedge WA13 ... 19 C1
Little Bollington WA13 ... 29 C4
Agden Park La WA13 ... 29 B4
Agecroft Rd
Northwich CW9 ... 104 B4
Romiley SK6 ... 241 A1
Aingarth Ho SK15 ... 242 C2
Ainley Cl WA7 ... 50 A3
Ainscough Rd WA3 ... 9 C2
Ainsdale Cl
Bebington CH63 ... 43 B3
Bramhall SK7 ... 36 A4
Warrington WA5 ... 14 C2
Ainsdale Dr SK8 ... 239 B1
Ainsworth La CW8 ... 76 A2
Ainsworth Rd CW8 ... 77 C1
Aintree Gr
Ellesmere Port CH66 ... 69 B2
Stockport SK3 ... 240 E1
Airdrie Cl CH62 ... 43 B2
Aire WA8 ... 12 A1
Aire Cl CH65 ... 70 A4
Aire Pl CW7 ... 127 A1
Airedale Cl Gatley SK8 ... 239 C6
Warrington WA5 ... 14 C4
Airedale Ct WA14 ... 238 E5
Airfield View CH4 ... 139 A3
Aitchison Rd CW9 ... 80 A1
Ajax Ave WA2 ... 8 A1
Akesmoor La
Biddulph ST8 ... 179 A1
Kidsgrove ST7 ... 195 C4
Alamein Cres WA2 ... 16 B4
Alamein Dr Romiley SK6 ... 241 F2
Winsford CW7 ... 149 B4
Alamein Rd Barnton CW8 ... 78 A2
Chester CH2 ... 95 A1
Alan Dr WA15 ... 32 A4
Alan Rd SK4 ... 240 B8
Alan St CW9 ... 104 A4
Alandale Rd SK3 ... 240 C3
Alban Ret Pk WA2 ... 8 A1
Alban St CW1 ... 190 B3
Albany Cres WA13 ... 18 B2
Albany Gdns CH66 ... 69 B4
Albany Gr WA13 ... 18 B2
Albany Rd Bramhall SK7 ... 35 C2
Lymm WA13 ... 18 B2
Wilmslow SK9 ... 59 C3
Albany Terr WA7 ... 23 A1
Albert Ct WA14 ... 238 D4
Albert Dr Neston CH64 ... 66 B4
Warrington WA5 ... 14 B3
Albert Pl
Altrincham WA14 ... 238 D5
Congleton CW12 ... 156 C1
Northwich CW9 ... 104 A4
Albert Rd
Altrincham WA15 ... 238 E3
Bollington SK10 ... 87 C4
Hyde SK14 ... 241 D6
Sale M33 ... 242 C6
Stockport SK4 ... 240 A7
Warrington WA4 ... 17 A1
Widnes WA8 ... 13 A1
Wilmslow SK9 ... 60 A3
Albert Rd E WA15 ... 238 E3
Albert Row WA6 ... 49 A1
Albert Sq
Altrincham WA14 ... 238 D3
Stalybridge SK15 ... 242 C1
1 Widnes WA8 ... 23 A4
Albert St Audley ST7 ... 209 C2
Chester CH2 ... 237 C3
Crewe CW1 ... 190 B3
Hyde SK14 ... 241 F7
Irlam M44 ... 11 C3
Knutsford WA16 ... 56 C1
Macclesfield SK11 ... 112 B4
Nantwich CW5 ... 204 C3
Runcorn WA7 ... 23 A1
Stockport SK3 ... 240 D5
Albert Terr WA5 ... 1 C1
Alberta St SK1 ... 240 F4
Albion Cl SK4 ... 240 E7
Albion Gdns SK15 ... 242 E1
Albion Gr M33 ... 242 A6
Albion Ho SK15 ... 242 F2
Albion Mews CH1 ... 237 B2
Albion Pl CH4 ... 237 B1
Albion Rd New Mills SK22 ... 39 A3
Northwich CW9 ... 79 A1
Albion St Chester CH1 ... 237 B2
Crewe CW2 ... 190 A2
Sale M33 ... 242 B6
Stalybridge SK15 ... 242 E2
Albion Trad Est OL6 ... 242 A3
Albion Wlk CW9 ... 79 A1
Albury Cl WA11 ... 1 B4
Alcester Ave SK3 ... 239 F7
Alcester Rd SK8 ... 239 B4
Alcock St WA7 ... 23 A2
Alcott Pl WA2 ... 8 A3
Aldcliffe WA3 ... 3 C4
Aldelyme CW3 ... 229 C2
Alder Ave Poynton SK12 ... 36 C2
Widnes WA8 ... 13 A2
Alder Cres WA2 ... 16 B4
Alder Ct SK10 ... 87 B3
Alder Dr
Ellesmere Port CH66 ... 69 C1
Stalybridge SK15 ... 242 F3
Alder Gr Chester CH2 ... 119 A2
Denton M34 ... 241 A7
Stockport SK3 ... 240 C4
Alder La
Burtonwood WA2,WA5 ... 7 B4
Cronton WA8 ... 12 A3
Frodsham WA6,WA7 ... 48 B2
Warrington WA2 ... 16 A4
Alder Rd Cheadle SK8 ... 239 E5
Golborne WA3 ... 3 C4
Warrington WA1 ... 17 B4
Weaverham CW8 ... 102 B4
Alder Rise SK23 ... 65 B4
Alder Root La WA2 ... 7 B4
Alder St WA12 ... 2 B2
Alder Wood Ave L24 ... 21 A2
Alderbank Rd WA5 ... 15 A3
Alderdale Dr SK6 ... 37 C4
Alderdale Gr SK9 ... 59 C3
Alderfield Dr L24 ... 21 A2
Aldergate Ave WA7 ... 50 B4
Alderhay La ST7 ... 195 B3
Alderley Ave WA3 ... 3 B4
Alderley Cl
Hazel Grove SK7 ... 36 C4
Poynton SK12 ... 36 C1
Sandbach CW11 ... 175 B4
Alderley Edge★ SK9 ... 60 B1
Alderley Edge Com Prim Sch SK9 ... 60 A1
Alderley Edge Sch for Girls SK9 ... 60 A1
Alderley Edge Sta SK9 ... 60 A1
Alderley Lodge SK9 ... 60 A3
Alderley Rd
Alderley Edge SK10,SK9 ... 60 C1
Chelford SK10 ... 84 B2
Northwich CW8 ... 103 C4
Prestbury SK10 ... 86 C2
Warrington WA4 ... 17 B2
Wilmslow SK9 ... 60 A3
Alderley Wlk 14 SK11 ... 112 C4
Alderly Pl CH1 ... 117 C3
Alderman Bolton Inf & Jun Sch WA4 ... 16 C2
Alderney Cl
Ellesmere Port CH65 ... 70 B1
3 Macclesfield SK11 ... 111 C4
Alderney Ho CH2 ... 119 A2
Alders SK9 ... 59 C3
Alders Rd SK12 ... 38 A4
Alders Way SK10 ... 86 C3
Aldersey CE Prim Sch CW6 ... 185 C4
Aldersey Cl Runcorn WA7 ... 24 B1
Saughall CH1 ... 94 A1
Aldersey La CH3 ... 182 B3
Aldersey Rd CW2 ... 190 A1
Aldersgate SK22 ... 39 A4
Aldersgate Dr L26 ... 21 A3
Aldersgate Rd SK7,SK8 ... 35 B3
Aldersgreen Ave SK6 ... 37 C4
Alderton Gr CW7 ... 127 A2
Alderwood Ave SK4 ... 240 A5
Alderwood Lo L24 ... 21 A2
Aldewood Cl WA3 ... 10 A3
Aldford Cl Bebington CH63 ... 43 A3
Hough Common CW2 ... 206 C1
Aldford Pl SK9 ... 59 C1
Aldford Rd CH2 ... 118 C3
Aldford Way CW7 ... 126 A1
Aldgate CH65 ... 70 A3
Aldington Dr CW10 ... 151 B3
Aldridge Dr WA5 ... 6 C4
Aled Way CH4 ... 140 B3
Alexander Dr WA8 ... 22 B4
Alexander Gr WA7 ... 23 B1
Alexandra Ave SK14 ... 241 C6
Alexandra Cl SK3 ... 240 C2
Alexandra Gr M44 ... 11 C4
Alexandra Hospl The SK8 ... 239 D6
Alexandra Ind Est WA8 ... 22 C4
Alexandra Mews WA6 ... 49 A1
Alexandra Park Inf Sch SK3 ... 240 C3
Alexandra Park Jun Sch SK3 ... 240 C3
Alexandra Pl CW1 ... 190 A3
Alexandra Rd
Dukinfield M34 ... 241 A8
Middlewich CW10 ... 151 B3
Sale M33 ... 242 D5
Stockport SK4 ... 240 C7
Warrington WA4 ... 16 C1
Warrington, Stockton Heath WA4 ... 16 B1
Alexandra Sq 7 CW7 ... 149 A4
Alexandra St
Ashton-u-Lyne OL6 ... 242 A4
Ellesmere Port CH65 ... 70 B4
Hyde SK14 ... 241 C5
Warrington WA1 ... 16 C4
Widnes WA8 ... 23 A4
Winsford CW7 ... 126 B1
Alforde St WA8 ... 23 A4
Alfred Cl 12 WA8 ... 23 A4
Alfred Rd Golborne WA3 ... 4 A4
Haydock WA11 ... 1 C4
Alfred St
Ashton-u-Lyne OL6 ... 242 A4
Dukinfield SK14 ... 241 C7
Irlam M44 ... 11 C3
Newton-le-W WA12 ... 2 C2
Northwich CW8 ... 103 C3
Widnes WA8 ... 23 A4
Alger Mews OL6 ... 242 A4
Alger St OL6 ... 242 A4
Algernon St Runcorn WA7 ... 22 C2
Warrington WA1 ... 16 B3
Warrington, Stockton Heath WA4 ... 16 B1
Algreave Rd SK3 ... 240 A4
Alice Ct WA8 ... 23 A2
Alice St M33 ... 242 D6
Alison Ct 4 SK4 ... 240 B7
Alison Dr Goostrey CW4 ... 130 B4
Macclesfield SK10 ... 87 C1
Alistair Dr CH63 ... 43 B3
All Hallows RC High Sch SK11 ... 112 A4
All Saints CE Prim Sch
Runcorn WA7 ... 23 A2
Stockport SK4 ... 240 D7
All Saints Dr WA4 ... 17 C2
All Saints RC Prim Sch WA3 ... 3 A4
All Saints Upton CE Prim Sch WA8 ... 12 A2
All Saints' CE Inf Sch CH2 ... 119 A2
All Saints' Rd SK4 ... 240 E8
Allandale WA14 ... 238 B4
Allans Cl CH64 ... 66 C3
Allans Mdw CH64 ... 66 C4
Allansford Ave CH3 ... 143 A2
Allcard St WA5 ... 15 C4
Allen Ave WA3 ... 5 B2
Allen Dr CW9 ... 103 C1
Allen Pl CW1 ... 190 A3
Allen Rd WA7 ... 48 B4
Allen St Bollington SK10 ... 88 A4
Allen St *continued*
Macclesfield SK11 ... 112 C4
Warrington WA2 ... 16 A3
Allenby Rd M44 ... 11 B2
Allendale WA7 ... 50 A3
Allerby Way WA3 ... 3 C4
Allerton Rd WA8 ... 13 A1
Allgreave Cl CW10 ... 151 B3
Allington Pl CH4 ... 141 C4
Allman Cl CW1 ... 189 C4
Allotment Rd M44 ... 11 B3
Allport La CH62 ... 43 B4
Allport Rd CH62,CH63 ... 43 B4
Allports The CH62 ... 43 B4
Allumbrook Ave CW4 ... 130 B2
Allysum Ct WA7 ... 49 C2
Alma Ave CW1 ... 190 B3
Alma Cl
Macclesfield SK11 ... 112 A4
Scholar Green ST7 ... 194 C4
Alma La SK9 ... 60 A4
Alma Rd SK7 ... 37 A4
Alma St Chester CH2 ... 118 C1
Newton-le-W WA12 ... 2 A2
Stalybridge SK15 ... 242 E2
Almeda Rd L24 ... 21 A1
Almer Dr WA5 ... 15 B3
Almond Ave Crewe CW1 ... 190 C3
Runcorn WA7 ... 49 B4
Almond Cl SK3 ... 240 C4
Almond Dr WA5 ... 6 C3
Almond Gr
Warrington WA1 ... 17 A4
Weaverham CW8 ... 102 C4
Widnes WA8 ... 22 B4
Almond Pl ST5 ... 210 C1
Almond Tree Cl L24 ... 21 C1
Almond Wlk M31 ... 11 B2
Almshouses CW11 ... 175 B3
Alnwick Dr CH65 ... 70 B1
Alpass Ave WA5 ... 16 A4
Alpine St WA12 ... 2 A2
Alport Rd SY13 ... 226 A1
Alpraham Cres CH2 ... 118 C3
Alric Wlk M22 ... 33 C4
Alsager Highfields Com Prim Sch ST7 ... 193 B2
Alsager Rd Audley ST7 ... 209 B3
Haslington CW11 ... 192 B4
Alsager Sch ST7 ... 193 A2
Alsager Sta ST7 ... 193 C2
Alsfeld Way SK22 ... 39 A4
Alstone Dr WA14 ... 238 A6
Alt WA8 ... 12 A1
Alt Wlk CW7 ... 127 A1
Alton Dr SK10 ... 87 C1
Alton Rd SK9 ... 59 C4
Alton St CW2 ... 190 A2
Altrincham Bsns Pk WA14 ... 238 B7
Altrincham CE Prim Sch WA14 ... 238 D5
Altrincham General Hospl WA14 ... 238 D4
Altrincham Gram Sch for Boys WA14 ... 238 D2
Altrincham Gram Sch for Girls
Altrincham WA14 ... 238 B3
Altrincham WA14 ... 238 C3
Altrincham Prep Sch WA14 ... 238 D1
Altrincham Priory Hospl WA15 ... 32 A4
Altrincham Rd Styal SK9 ... 33 C2
Wilmslow SK9 ... 33 B1
Altrincham Sta WA15 ... 238 E4
Altringham Ret Pk WA14 ... 238 C7
Alum Ct CW4 ... 130 B1
Alun Cres CH4 ... 141 A3
Alundale Rd CW7 ... 126 B2
Alvanley Cres SK3 ... 240 C2
Alvanley Dr WA6 ... 73 B1
Alvanley Prim Sch WA6 ... 73 B1
Alvanley Rd
Ellesmere Port CH66 ... 69 C2
Helsby WA6 ... 73 B1
Alvanley Rise CW9 ... 104 A3
Alvanley Terr WA6 ... 74 A4
Alvanley View CH2 ... 72 A2
Alvanley Way CH66 ... 69 C2
Alvaston Ave SK4 ... 240 B6
Alvaston Bsns Pk CW5 ... 204 C4
Alvaston Rd CW5 ... 204 C3
Alvaston Wlk CW2 ... 189 C1
Alverstone Cl WA5 ... 14 B4
Alverton Cl WA8 ... 22 B4
Alveston Cl SK10 ... 86 C1
Alveston Dr SK9 ... 60 B4
Alvingham Cl 6 CW9 ... 104 A4
Alvis Rd CH5 ... 116 A2
Alwyn Gdns CH2 ... 118 C4
Alyn Rd CH2 ... 96 C1
Alyndale Rd CH4 ... 140 B3
Ambassador Pl WA15 ... 238 E5
Amberleigh Cl WA4 ... 27 A2
Amberley Dr WA15 ... 32 A4
Amberley Rd SK11 ... 112 A3
Ambleside Chester CH2 ... 119 A3
Stalybridge SK15 ... 242 D3
Ambleside Cl
Bebington CH62 ... 43 C4
Macclesfield SK11 ... 111 C3
Runcorn WA7 ... 49 C3
Winsford CW7 ... 126 B2
Wistaston CW2 ... 189 C1
Ambleside Cres WA2 ... 8 B2

Ambleside Ct
Congleton CW12 ....155 C1
Gatley SK8 ....239 C5
Stalybridge SK15 ......242 D3
Ambleside Rd CH65 ....70 B1
Ambrose Ct WA1 ....16 B3
Ambuscade Cl CW1 ....190 C3
Amelia Cl WA8 ....13 A2
Amelia St 3 Hyde SK14 .241 E6
Warrington WA2 ....16 B4
Amersham Cl SK10 ......87 B2
Amis Gr WA3 ....3 C4
Amy St CW2 ....190 B2
Anchor Cl WA7 ....50 B3
Anchor Ct WA1 ....16 B3
Anchorage The
5 Lymm WA13 ....18 B2
Neston CH64 ....66 B4
Waverton CH3 ....143 A3
Ancoats Rd WA16,SK9 ...83 C4
Anderson Cl Crewe CW1 191 A2
Warrington WA2 ....9 A1
Anderson Ct CH62 ......43 B3
Anderson St 10 SK11 ...112 B4
Andersons Ind Est WA8 .23 A3
Anderton Boat Lift & Nature Park★ CW9 ....78 B2
Anderton Way SK9 ......34 B2
Andertons La SK10,SK11 .86 A1
Andover Cl WA2 ....8 C1
Andover Rd WA11 ....1 C4
Andrew Cl WA8 ....22 B4
Andrew Cres CH4 ......237 C1
Andrew Gr SK10 ....113 A4
Andrew La SK6 ....37 C4
Andrew St Hyde SK14 ...241 F7
Stockport SK4 ....240 D6
Andrew's Cl CH3 ......121 A1
Andrew's Wlk CH60 .....41 A4
Andromeda Way WA9 ....6 A4
Anemone Way WA9 ......6 A4
Anfield Rd Cheadle SK8 ..239 F3
Sale M33 ....242 C7
Angel St M34 ....241 A8
Angelina Cl CW11 ......174 B4
Anglers Rest M44 ....11 C3
Anglesea Ave SK2 ......240 F2
Anglesey Cl 6 CH65 .....70 B1
Anglesey Dr SK12 ....36 C3
Anglesey Gr SK8 ....240 A2
Anglesey Water SK12 ....36 C3
Angus Gr CW10 ....128 B1
Angus Rd CH63 ....43 B3
Angus Wlk SK10 ....86 C1
Ankers Knowl La SK11 .114 B4
Ankers La SK11 ....114 B3
Ann Cl CH66 ....69 B4
Ann St Dukinfield SK14 ..241 C7
Northwich CW9 ....79 B1
Runcorn WA7 ....23 A2
Stockport SK5 ....240 E8
Ann St W WA8 ....23 A4
Annable Rd M44 ....11 C4
Annan Cl 2 CW12 ......157 A1
Anne Ct ST7 ....210 B3
Anne's Way CH4 ....237 C1
Annette Ave WA12 ....2 A3
Annie St WA2 ....16 B3
Annions La CW5 ....205 C1
Annis Cl SK9 ....60 A1
Annis Rd SK9 ....60 A1
Ansdell Rd WA8 ....13 B1
Ansley Gr SK4 ....240 B7
Anson Cl Bramhall SK7 ...35 C3
Warrington WA2 ....8 C1
Anson Engine Mus The★ SK12 ....37 B2
Anson Rd Handforth SK9 ..34 C1
Poynton SK12 ....37 A2
Anthony Dr CW9 ....126 C4
Anthony's Way CH60 ....41 A4
Antons Rd L26 ....21 A3
Antony Rd WA4 ....16 A1
Antrim Cl WA11 ....1 B3
Antrim Dr CH66 ....69 C1
Antrim Rd WA2 ....8 A1
Antrobus St CW12 .....156 B2
Anvil Cl Haslington CW11 174 C2
Saughall CH1 ....94 A1
Apple Market St 10 CW9 ....103 C4
Apple Tree Cl L24 ....21 C1
Apple Tree Gr CH66 .....94 C4
Appleby Cl
Macclesfield SK11 ......111 C3
Stockport SK3 ....240 D1
Widnes WA8 ....22 B4
Appleby Gr CH62 ....43 B4
Appleby Rd Gatley SK8 ..239 B4
Warrington WA2 ....8 B2
Appleby Wlk 2 WA8 .....22 B4
Applecroft ST5 ....210 C1
Applecross Cl WA3 ......10 A3
Appledale Dr CH1 ....95 A4
Applefield CW8 ....103 B4
Appleford Cl WA4 ....26 C4
Appleton Cl CW12 ......178 C4
Appleton Ct M33 ....242 B6
Appleton Dr CH65 ....69 C2
Appleton Hall Gdns WA4 26 C3
Appleton Mews 1 WA13 .18 B2
Appleton Rd
Altrincham WA15 ....238 F1
Chester CH2 ....118 C3
Widnes WA8 ....13 A1
Appleton St
Northwich CW8 ....78 B1
Widnes WA8 ....23 A4
Appleton Thorn Prim Sch WA4 ....27 B2
Appleton Thorn Trad Est WA4 ....27 B3
Appleton Village WA8 ...13 A1
Appleton Wlk 8 SK9 ....34 C1
Appletree Gr WA2 ....8 C1
Appleyards La CH4 .....141 C4
April Rise SK10 ....87 A1
Apsley Cl WA14 ....238 B1
Apsley Gr WA14 ....238 B1
Apsley St SK1 ....240 F5
Arabis Gdns WA9 ....6 A4
Aragon Ct WA7 ....24 B2
Aragon Gn CH1 ....117 C3
Aran Cl L24 ....21 B1
Arbour Cl
Macclesfield SK10 ....87 B2
Northwich CW9 ....104 B4
Arbour Cres SK10 ....87 B2
Arbour Mews SK10 ......87 B2
Arbour St ST7 ....210 B3
Arbourhay St SK10 ......87 C1
Arbury Ave SK3 ....240 A3
Arbury La WA2 ....8 B3
Arcade The
Ellesmere Port CH65 .....70 A3
3 Northwich CW9 ......103 C4
Archer Ave WA4 ....16 C1
Archer Cl SK10 ....87 C4
Archers Gn CH62 ....43 C2
Archers Way Blacon CH1 118 A2
Ellesmere Port CH66 .....69 C1
Arclid Cl SK9 ....34 C1
Arclid Ct 10 CW12 .....156 C2
Arclid Green Ind Est CW11 ....176 A4
Arcon Pl WA14 ....238 A6
Arden WA8 ....12 A1
Arden Cl Gatley SK8 .....34 B4
Tarvin CH3 ....121 B2
Warrington WA3 ....10 A3
Arden Ct CW12 ....179 A4
Arden Dr CH64 ....66 C3
Arden Est SK22 ....39 B4
Arden St SK22 ....39 B4
Ardenbrook Rise SK10 ...86 C3
Ardens Mdw CW6 ....168 B4
Ardern Gr SK1 ....240 F4
Ardern Lea WA6 ....73 B1
Arderne Ave CW2 ....190 A1
Arderne Ho CH2 ....118 C4
Arderne Pl 6 SK9 ....60 A1
Ardleigh Cl CW1 ....189 C4
Argosy Dr M90 ....32 C4
Argyle Ct 9 WA16 ....57 A1
Argyll Ave Bebington CH62 43 B2
Chester CH4 ....141 A4
Argyll Cl SK10 ....87 A1
Argyll Rd SK8 ....239 F5
Argyll St OL6 ....242 B3
Ariel Wlk 11 WA3 ....3 C4
Arkenshaw Rd WA3 ....9 A4
Arkenstone Cl WA8 ......12 B1
Arkle Ave SK8,SK9 ....34 C2
Arkle Ct 10 CH3 ....119 A1
Arklow Dr L24 ....21 B1
Arkwright Cl CW7 ......149 A4
Arkwright Ct WA7 ....23 C2
Arkwright Rd WA7 ....23 C2
Arley Ave WA4 ....26 B4
Arley Cl Alsager ST7 ....193 B2
Altrincham WA14 ....238 D8
Chester CH2 ....118 C3
Macclesfield SK11 ......112 A4
Arley Dr WA8 ....12 A1
Arley End WA16 ....29 B2
Arley Hall & Gdns★ CW9 54 B3
Arley Mere Cl SK8 .....239 F3
Arley Mossend La CW9 ..54 B1
Arley Pl CW2 ....206 A4
Arley Rd Antrobus CW9 ...54 A4
Appleton Thorn WA4 .....27 B2
Northwich CW9 ....104 B4
Arley Wlk CW11 ....174 B3
Arlies Cl SK15 ....242 D4
Arlies La SK15 ....242 E4
Arlies Prim Sch SK15 ..242 D4
Arlies St OL6 ....242 A4
Arlington Ave M34 .....241 A6
Arlington Cl CW2 ......206 B4
Arlington Cres SK9 ......59 C3
Arlington Dr
Golborne WA3,WN7 ....4 B4
Macclesfield SK11 ......112 A4
Poynton SK12 ....36 B2
Warrington WA5 ....14 C2
Arlington Rd SK8 ......239 C4
Arlington Way SK9 ......59 C3
Armadale Cl SK3 ....240 F1
Armentieres Way SK15 .242 D1
Armistead Way CW4 ...130 A3
Armitage Rd WA14 .....238 D3
Armitstead Rd CW11 ...174 C2
Armitt St SK11 ....112 B4
Armour Ave WA2 ....8 A1
Armoury Court Mews 4 SK11 ....112 A3
Armoury St SK3 ....240 E4
Armoury Twrs 5 SK11 ..112 A3
Armstrong Cl
Audlem CW3 ....229 C2
Warrington WA3 ....9 B2
Armthorpe Dr CH66 .....69 B3
Arncliffe Dr WA5 ....6 C3
Arndale WA7 ....49 C3
Arnesby Ave M33 ......242 E7
Arnfield Rd SK3 ....240 D1
Arnhem Cres WA2 ....16 B4
Arnhem Way CH3 ......142 A3
Arnold Pl WA8 ....22 B4
Arnold St Nantwich CW5 .204 C3
Stockport SK3 ....240 E3
Arnold's Cres CH4 .....139 A2
Arnolds Yd WA14 ....238 D5
Arnside Ave
Congleton CW12 ....156 A1
Haydock WA11 ....1 A3
Arnside Cl Gatley SK8 ...239 B4
High Lane SK6 ....37 C4
Winsford CW7 ....126 B1
Arnside Dr SK14 ....241 C8
Arnside Gr Sale M33 ....242 B8
Warrington WA4 ....16 A1
Arpley Rd WA1 ....16 A2
Arpley St WA1 ....16 A2
Arradon Ct CH2 ....118 C3
Arran Ave
Ellesmere Port CH65 .....70 B1
Sale M33 ....242 C5
Arran Cl
Holmes Chapel CW4 .....130 B1
Warrington WA2 ....9 A1
Arran Dr WA6 ....74 B3
Arrivals Way M90 ....33 A4
Arron Pl CW2 ....189 B2
Arrowcroft Rd CH3 .....119 C3
Arrowsmith Dr ST7 .....193 A2
Arrowsmith Rd WA11 .....1 C4
Arthill La WA14 ....30 A4
Arthog Dr WA15 ....31 C4
Arthog Rd WA15 ....31 C4
Arthur Ave CH65 ....70 B3
Arthur St Blacon CH1 ...118 A1
Crewe CW2 ....190 B1
Hyde SK14 ....241 C5
Lostock Gralam CW9 .....80 A1
Runcorn WA7 ....23 A1
Warrington WA2 ....16 A3
Artists La SK10 ....85 B4
Artle Rd CW2 ....206 B4
Arundel Ave SK7 ....36 B4
Arundel Cl
Knutsford WA16 ....82 A4
Macclesfield SK10 ....87 C1
Wistaston CW2 ....205 C4
Arundel Ct CH65 ....70 C2
Arundel Rd SK8 ....35 A3
Arundel St OL6 ....242 B3
Arundell Cl WA5 ....6 C3
Ascol Dr WA16 ....80 B2
Ascot Ave WA7 ....49 A3
Ascot Cl Congleton CW12 156 B2
Macclesfield SK10 ....87 B2
Warrington WA4 ....17 B1
Warrington, Martinscroft WA1 ....17 C4
Ascot Dr CH66 ....69 C2
Ash Ave Altrincham WA14 238 A5
Cheadle SK8 ....239 E5
Irlam M44 ....11 B3
Newton-le-W WA12 ....2 B1
Ash Cl Ellesmere Port CH66 69 C1
Holmes Chapel CW4 .....130 B2
Malpas SY14 ....213 B3
Tarporley CW6 ....146 B1
Ash Ct SK4 ....240 B7
Ash Gr
Altrincham, Bowdon WA14 238 C1
Altrincham, Timperley WA15 ....238 F7
Chester CH4 ....141 A3
Congleton CW12 ....156 A2
Ellesmere Port CH66 .....69 B3
Gatley SK8 ....34 A4
Golborne WA3 ....3 A4
Handforth SK9 ....34 B2
Knutsford WA16 ....57 B1
Macclesfield SK11 ......112 B2
Middlewich CW10 ....151 B4
Nantwich CW5 ....204 C2
Rode Heath ST7 ....193 C4
Runcorn WA7 ....49 B4
Stalybridge SK15 ....242 C3
Warrington WA4 ....16 B2
Weaverham CW8 ....102 C4
Widnes WA8 ....22 B4
Ash Grove Sch SK11 ...112 B2
Ash Hay La CH2 ....96 B1
Ash Ho 8 CW11 ....175 A3
Ash House La CW8 ......77 B4
Ash La Warrington WA4 ..26 C4
Widnes WA8 ....22 A4
Ash Lawn Ct CH2 ....118 B2
Ash Lo SK12 ....36 B2
Ash Priors WA8 ....12 B2
Ash Rd Crewe CW1 .....190 B3
Cuddington CW8 ....101 C1
Elton CH2 ....72 B2
Haydock WA11 ....1 C4
Hollinfare WA3 ....11 A1
Lymm WA13 ....18 B2
Partington M31 ....11 B2
Poynton SK12 ....36 C2
Warrington WA5 ....14 C2
Winwick WA2 ....8 A3
Ash St Northwich CW9 ....79 A1
Stockport SK3 ....240 B4
Ash Terr SK11 ....112 B2
Ash View ST7 ....195 A1
Ash Way CH60 ....41 A3
Ashbank CW9 ....104 B4
Ashberry Cl SK9 ....60 B4
Ashberry Dr WA4 ....27 A3
Ashbourne Ave
Cheadle SK8 ....239 F6
Ashbourne Ave *continued*
Runcorn WA7 ....49 A3
Ashbourne Cl CH66 .....94 C4
Ashbourne Dr SK6 ....37 C3
Ashbourne Mews 1 SK11 ....111 C4
Ashbourne Rd
Hazel Grove SK7 ....36 C4
Warrington WA5 ....15 A3
Ashbrook Ave WA7 ......49 C2
Ashbrook Cl SK8 ....239 B1
Ashbrook Cres WA2 .....16 B4
Ashbrook Dr SK10 ....87 A3
Ashbrook Rd
Bollington SK10 ....87 C4
Nether Alderley SK10 .....85 C3
Ashburn Gr SK4 ....240 D7
Ashburn Rd SK4 ....240 D7
Ashburton Rd SK3 ......240 E1
Ashbury Cl WA7 ....24 B1
Ashbury Dr WA11 ....1 B4
Ashby Dr CW11 ....174 B3
Ashby Pl CH2 ....237 C4
Ashcroft SK9 ....59 C3
Ashcroft Ave CW2 ......206 A2
Ashcroft Rd WA13 ....19 A2
Ashdale Cl ST7 ....193 B3
Ashdale Dr SK8 ....239 B2
Ashdene Prim Sch SK9 ..59 C3
Ashdene Rd SK9 ....59 C3
Ashdown La WA3 ....10 A3
Ashdown Rd
Ollerton WA16 ....82 C3
Stockport SK4 ....240 C7
Ashenhurst Rd ST7 .....193 C2
Ashenough Rd ST7 .....210 B3
Asher Ct WA4 ....27 B2
Ashfield Cl WA13 ....19 A2
Ashfield Cres
Bebington CH62 ....43 B4
Blacon CH1 ....117 B3
Cheadle SK8 ....239 D6
Ashfield Dr SK10 ....87 A1
Ashfield Gr M44 ....11 C3
Ashfield Ho 6 CH64 .....66 C4
Ashfield Rd
Altrincham WA15 ....238 E3
Bebington CH62 ....43 B4
Cheadle SK8 ....239 D6
Ellesmere Port CH65 .....70 B3
Sale M33 ....242 B7
Ashfield Rd N 8 CH65 ...70 B3
Ashfield St 4 CW10 .....151 B4
Ashford Cl SK9 ....34 B2
Ashford Rd SK9 ....60 A2
Ashford Way WA8 ....13 B1
Ashgate La CW9 ....79 C3
Ashgrove CW7 ....149 B4
Ashlands Frodsham WA6 ..74 B4
Sale M33 ....242 A7
Ashlea Dr CW5 ....205 C3
Ashleigh Cl CH4 ....140 C3
Ashley CE Prim Sch WA15 ....31 C3
Ashley Cl WA4 ....17 B2
Ashley Ct
Altrincham WA15 ....238 E1
Frodsham WA6 ....74 A4
Holt LL13 ....196 B4
Ashley Dr Bramhall SK7 ...35 B3
Hartford CW8 ....103 A3
Ashley Gdns Clutton CH3 182 B1
High Lane SK6 ....37 B4
3 Hyde SK14 ....241 E5
Ashley Gn WA8 ....22 B4
Ashley Grange CW9 .....103 C2
Ashley Mdw CW1 ....191 B3
Ashley Mews 2 SK14 ....241 E5
Ashley Mill La N WA14 ...31 C4
Ashley Rd
Altrincham WA15 ....238 E2
Ashley WA14,WA15 ....31 C4
Handforth SK9 ....34 A1
Mere WA16 ....56 B4
Runcorn WA7 ....23 B1
Ashley Ret Pk WA8 ......23 A4
Ashley Sch WA8 ....12 B1
Ashley St SK14 ....241 E8
Ashley Sta WA15 ....31 C3
Ashley Way WA8 ....23 A4
Ashley Way W WA8 ......22 C4
Ashleymill La WA14 .....31 B4
Ashleys The 6 SK4 .....240 B7
Ashmead Cl ST7 ....193 C2
Ashmead Mews ST7 .....193 C2
Ashmore Ave SK3 ....239 F7
Ashmore Cl
Middlewich CW10 ....151 B3
Warrington WA3 ....10 A2
Ashmore's La ST7 ......193 B2
Ashmuir Cl Blacon CH1 ..117 C2
Crewe CW1 ....190 A3
Ashness Dr SK7 ....35 C4
Ashridge St WA7 ....22 C2
Ashton Ave
Altrincham WA14 ....238 E6
Macclesfield SK10 ....86 B1
Ashton Cl Bebington CH62 .43 C2
Congleton CW12 ....157 A1
Frodsham WA6 ....49 B1
Middlewich CW10 ....151 B3
Northwich CW9 ....103 C2
Runcorn WA7 ....48 C3
Ashton Ct WA6 ....49 B1
Ashton Dr WA6 ....49 B1
Ashton Hayes Prim Sch CH3 ....121 C4
Ashton Ho SK14 ....241 E8
Ashton House SK14 ....241 E8
Ashton La CH3 ....121 C3
Ashton Rd Manley WA6 ...99 C2
Newton-le-W WA12 ....2 B3
Norley WA6 ....100 A2
Ashton Sixth Form Coll OL6 ....242 B3
Ashton St WA2 ....16 A3
Ashtree Cl Neston CH64 ..67 A4
Prestbury SK10 ....87 B4
Ashtree Croft CH64 ......68 A4
Ashtree Dr CH64 ....67 A4
Ashtree Farm Ct CH64 ...68 A4
Ashurst Dr SK3 ....240 B1
Ashville Ct CW2 ....206 A4
Ashville Ind Est WA7 ....49 C2
Ashville Way WA7 ....49 C2
Ashwood WA14 ....31 A4
Ashwood Ave
Golborne WA3 ....3 B4
Warrington WA1 ....16 C4
Ashwood Cl Barnton CW8 .78 A2
Ellesmere Port CH66 .....69 B1
Ashwood Cres CW8 .....78 A2
Ashwood Ct CH2 ....119 A2
Ashwood La CH2 ....96 A3
Ashwood Rd SK12 ....38 B3
Ashworth Cl WA14 .....238 B1
Ashworth Pk WA16 ....81 C4
Asiatic Cotts CH5 ......116 A2
Askerbank La SK11 .....159 A1
Askett Cl WA11 ....1 B4
Askrigg Ave CH66 ....69 A3
Aspen Cl
Ellesmere Port CH66 .....69 C1
Heswall CH60 ....41 B4
Kidsgrove ST7 ....195 C2
Stockport SK4 ....240 A5
Aspen Gn M34 ....241 A6
Aspen Gr Saughall CH1 ..117 A4
Warrington WA1 ....17 A4
Aspen Way Chester CH2 .119 A2
High Lane SK6 ....38 A4
Aspen Wood SK14 ......241 F7
Aspens The
Cuddington CW8 ....101 B3
Gatley SK8 ....239 A6
Aspinall Cl WA2 ....9 A2
Aspull Cl WA3 ....9 B2
Asquith Cl CW1 ....191 B3
Assheton Cl WA12 ....2 A2
Assheton Wlk L24 ....21 C1
Astbury Cl
2 Altrincham WA15 .....238 E6
Crewe CW1 ....190 A4
Golborne WA3 ....4 A4
Kidsgrove ST7 ....195 B2
Astbury Cres SK3 ......240 D2
Astbury Dr CW8 ....78 A2
Astbury Lane Ends CW12 ....178 C4
Astbury Mere Ctry Pk★ CW12 ....156 A1
Astbury St CW12 ....156 B1
Aster Cres WA7 ....49 C3
Aster Rd WA11 ....1 C4
Aster Wlk M31 ....11 C1
Astle Cl CW10 ....151 B4
Astle Ct SK11 ....84 A2
Astley Cl Knutsford WA16 .82 B4
Warrington WA4 ....16 A2
Widnes WA8 ....12 B2
Astley Ct M44 ....11 C4
Astley Gr SK15 ....242 C3
Astley Rd Irlam M44 .....11 C4
Stalybridge SK15 ....242 C2
Astley St SK4 ....240 E5
Astmoor Bridge La WA7 .23 C1
Astmoor East Intc WA7 ..24 A2
Astmoor Ind Est WA7 ...23 C2
Astmoor La WA7 ....23 C1
Astmoor Prim Sch WA7 .23 C1
Aston Ave CW7 ....126 A1
Aston by Sutton Prim Sch WA7 ....50 B1
Aston Cl SK3 ....240 C2
Aston Ct WA1 ....9 B1
Aston Fields Rd WA7 ....50 C2
Aston Gn WA7 ....50 C3
Aston La Runcorn WA7 ...50 C3
Sutton WA7 ....50 B1
Woore CW3 ....232 C1
Aston La N WA7 ....50 C2
Aston La S WA7 ....50 C2
Aston Rd ST5 ....210 B1
Aston Way
Middlewich CW10 ....128 C1
13 Wilmslow SK9 ....34 B3
Astor Dr WA4 ....26 C4
Astule Dr SK11 ....112 A4
Atcherley Cl CW5 ......218 C4
Athelbrae Cl CW8 ......103 C4
Atherton Inf Sch CH65 ..69 C3
Atherton La M44 ....11 C3
Atherton Rd CH65 ....69 C3
Atherton St SK3 ....240 D4
Athey St SK11 ....112 B4
Athey St Mill SK11 .....112 B4
Athlone Ave SK8 ....240 C1
Athlone Rd WA2 ....8 A1
Athol Cl Bebington CH62 ..43 C3
Newton-le-W WA12 ....1 C2
Athol Dr CH62 ....43 C3
Athol Rd SK7 ....35 B3
Athol St SK4 ....240 D7

Atholl Ave CW2 ... 190 B1
Atholl Cl SK10 ... 87 A1
Atkinson Ho 2 M33 ... 242 B7
Atkinson Rd M33 ... 242 A7
Atlanta Ave M90 ... 33 A4
Atlantic Bsns Ctr WA14 ... 238 C7
Atlantic St WA14 ... 238 B6
Attenbury's La WA14 ... 238 E8
Attenbury's Park Est
WA14 ... 238 E8
Atterbury Cl WA8 ... 12 B1
Attlee Ave WA3 ... 5 B2
Attwood Cl CW1 ... 191 B2
Attwood St ST7 ... 195 A1
Atworth Terr CH64 ... 67 C4
Aubourn Cl WA8 ... 12 B2
Auburn Ave SK14 ... 241 E5
Auckery Ave CH66 ... 69 B2
Auckland Rd CH1 ... 117 B2
Audie Murphy Rd WA5 ... 15 A3
Audlem Cl WA7 ... 49 C2
Audlem Dr CW9 ... 104 A3
Audlem Rd Audlem CW3 ... 230 A4
Hatherton CW5 ... 219 B2
Nantwich CW5 ... 204 C2
Woore CW3 ... 232 A1
Audley Cres CH4 ... 141 C3
Audley Rd Alsager ST7 ... 193 C1
Barthomley CW2,ST7 ... 208 C3
Newcastle-u-L ST7,ST5 ... 210 A1
Talke ST7 ... 210 A3
Audley St
Ashton-u-Lyne OL6 ... 242 B2
Crewe CW1 ... 190 B3
Audley St W CW1 ... 190 B3
Audre Cl WA5 ... 14 B3
Aughton Way CH4 ... 139 B2
Augusta Dr SK10 ... 87 A2
Austell Rd 3 M22 ... 33 B4
Austen Cl 1 CW11 ... 174 B3
Austen Dr WA2 ... 8 A3
Austen Ho SK10 ... 86 C1
Austin Cl CW7 ... 149 B3
Austin St CW9 ... 79 B1
Austine Hill CH3 ... 144 B4
Austral Ave WA1 ... 17 B4
Australia La WA4 ... 17 B1
Autumn Ave WA16 ... 57 B1
Avalon Dr M20 ... 239 C8
Avebury Cl Golborne WA3 ... 3 C4
Widnes WA8 ... 13 C2
Avens Rd M31 ... 11 C2
Avenue One CW1 ... 207 B4
Avenue St 3 SK1 ... 240 F6
Avenue The
Alderley Edge SK9 ... 60 A1
Alsager ST7 ... 193 B2
Altrincham WA15 ... 31 C4
Bebington CH62 ... 43 B4
Comberbach CW9 ... 78 B4
Gatley SK8 ... 239 A1
Great Barrow CH3 ... 120 C4
High Legh WA16 ... 29 B3
Kidsgrove ST7 ... 194 C1
Lymm WA13 ... 18 B1
Marston CW9 ... 79 A2
Newton-le-W WA12 ... 2 B2
Sandbach CW11 ... 174 C4
Tarporley CW6 ... 146 B1
Avenue Two CW1 ... 207 B4
Avery Cl WA2 ... 8 C1
Avery Cres WA11 ... 1 B4
Avery Rd WA11 ... 1 B4
Avery Sq WA11 ... 1 B4
Aviator Way SK9 ... 33 B4
Aviemore Dr WA2 ... 9 A2
Avocet Cl
Newton-le-W WA12 ... 2 B2
Warrington WA2 ... 8 B2
Avocet Dr
Altrincham WA14 ... 238 B8
Winsford CW7 ... 149 B3
Avon WA8 ... 12 A1
Avon Ave WA5 ... 14 C2
Avon Cl Kidsgrove ST7 ... 195 A1
Macclesfield SK10 ... 87 A1
Neston CH64 ... 66 C3
Avon Ct ST7 ... 193 B3
Avon Dr Congleton CW12 ... 156 C1
Crewe CW1 ... 191 A3
Avon Rd Altrincham WA15 ... 31 C4
Culcheth WA3 ... 5 A1
Gatley SK8 ... 34 B4
Avon St SK3 ... 240 E3
Avon Wlk CW7 ... 127 A1
Avondale CH65 ... 70 A1
Avondale Ave CH62 ... 43 C3
Avondale Dr WA8 ... 12 A1
Avondale High Sch SK3 ... 240 B3
Avondale Ind Est SK3 ... 240 B3
Avondale Lodge M33 ... 242 B5
Avondale Rd Haydock WA11 ... 1 B4
Stockport SK3 ... 240 C4
Avondale Rise SK9 ... 60 B3
Avonlea Cl CH4 ... 140 C3
Avonside Way SK11 ... 112 B3
Avro Way M90 ... 32 C4
Aycliffe Wlk 6 WA8 ... 22 B4
Aylesbury Cl
Ellesmere Port CH66 ... 69 B2
Macclesfield SK10 ... 87 B2
Aylesby Cl WA16 ... 57 A1
Aylsham Cl WA8 ... 12 B2
Aylwin Dr M33 ... 242 C5
Ayrshire Cl CW10 ... 128 B1
Ayrshire Way CW12 ... 157 A1
Aysgarth Ave
Cheadle SK8 ... 239 C6
Crewe CW1 ... 173 A1
Romiley SK6 ... 241 D4
Ayshford Cl WA14 ... 238 B6
Azalea Gr WA7 ... 49 C2

B

Babbacombe Rd WA5 ... 14 C2
Babbage Rd CH5 ... 116 A2
Bache Ave CH2 ... 118 B3
Bache Dr CH2 ... 118 B3
Bache Hall Ct CH2 ... 118 B3
Bache Hall Est CH2 ... 118 B3
Bache Sta CH2 ... 118 B3
Bachefield Ave CH3 ... 142 A3
Bachelor's Ct CH3 ... 142 A4
Bachelor's La CH3 ... 142 A4
Back Bridge St WA12 ... 2 A2
Back Brook Pl WA4 ... 16 C2
Back Crosland Terr WA6 ... 73 A1
Back Cross La
Congleton CW12 ... 179 A4
Newton-le-W WA12 ... 2 A2
Back Eastford Rd WA4 ... 16 A1
Back Eddisbury Rd
SK11 ... 113 B4
Back Forshaw St WA2 ... 16 B4
Back Heathcote St ST7 ... 195 A1
Back High St WA7 ... 23 A1
Back Jodrell St SK22 ... 39 A4
Back Knowl St SK15 ... 242 E2
Back La Alpraham CW6 ... 169 B3
Altrincham WA15 ... 32 A2
Alvanley WA6 ... 73 B1
Bate Heath CW9 ... 54 B4
Beeston CH3 ... 167 B1
Betley CW2 ... 208 B1
Brereton Green CW11 ... 153 B3
Burtonwood WA5 ... 6 B4
Congleton CW12 ... 156 A2
Duddon CW6 ... 145 A3
Eaton (nr Congleton)
CW12 ... 156 C4
High Legh WA14 ... 29 C3
Lower Peover WA16 ... 106 A4
Marton CW12,SK11 ... 133 C1
No Man's Heath SY14 ... 214 A2
Partington WA14 ... 20 B3
Plumley WA16 ... 81 A1
Shavington CW2 ... 206 C2
Smallwood CW11 ... 176 B4
Threapwood SY14 ... 222 C4
Warrington WA5 ... 14 A2
Whitley WA4 ... 52 C2
Wybunbury CW5 ... 220 B3
Back Lanes CW6 ... 146 A1
Back Legh St WA12 ... 2 A2
Back Market St WA12 ... 2 A2
Back Massie St SK8 ... 239 D6
Back Paradise St 17
SK11 ... 112 B4
Back Park St CW12 ... 156 C1
Back Queen St CH1 ... 237 B3
Back River St CW12 ... 156 B2
Back Union Rd SK22 ... 39 B4
Back Wallgate 27 SK11 ... 112 B4
Back Water St 2 SK1 ... 240 F6
Backford Cl WA7 ... 50 B3
Backford Gdns CH1 ... 94 C4
Badbury Cl WA11 ... 1 B4
Badcock's La CW6 ... 185 C2
Baddeley Cl SK3 ... 240 D1
Baddiley Cl CW5 ... 203 B1
Baddiley Hall La CW5 ... 217 A4
Baddiley La CW5 ... 203 B1
Baddington La CW5 ... 204 B1
Badger Ave CW1 ... 190 A3
Badger Bait CH64 ... 66 C3
Badger Cl WA7 ... 50 A3
Badger Ho SK10 ... 87 B1
Badger Rd
Macclesfield SK10 ... 87 B1
Prestbury SK10 ... 87 A4
Badgers Cl
Christleton CH3 ... 142 C4
Ellesmere Port CH66 ... 94 C4
Winsford CW7 ... 126 A1
Badgers Pk CH64 ... 66 C3
Badgers Set CW8 ... 101 B3
Badgers Wlk CH2 ... 95 C1
Badgers Wood CW2 ... 205 C4
Badgersrake La
Ellesmere Port CH66 ... 68 C3
Ledsham CH66 ... 68 B2
Bag La
Cuddington CW8,WA6 ... 101 C4
Norley WA6 ... 101 A3
Bagley La CW3 ... 230 A1
Bagmere Cl
Brereton Green CW11 ... 153 C2
Sandbach CW11 ... 174 C4
Bagmere La CW11 ... 154 A3
Bagnall Cl WA5 ... 15 B3
Bagot Ave WA5 ... 15 C4
Bagstock Ave SK12 ... 36 C1
Baguley Ave WA8 ... 22 A3
Baguley Cres SK3 ... 240 D2
Baguley La M33 ... 242 E5
Baguley Rd M33 ... 242 E6
Bahama Cl WA11 ... 1 B4
Bahama Rd WA11 ... 1 B4
Bailey Ave CH65 ... 69 C3
Bailey Bridge Cl CH2 ... 118 B2
Bailey Bsns Pk SK10 ... 87 C4
Bailey Cl CW1 ... 190 B4
Bailey Cres
Congleton CW12 ... 157 A2
Sandbach CW11 ... 175 B3
Bailey Ct ST7 ... 193 C2
Bailey La M31 ... 11 C2
Bailey Wlk WA14 ... 31 B4
Bailey's Bank ST8 ... 179 B2
Bailey's La Hale L24 ... 21 A1
Halewood L26 ... 21 A4
Baileys Cl WA8 ... 13 A3
Bainbridge Ave WA3 ... 3 C4
Baines Ave M44 ... 11 C4
Baker Dr CH66 ... 69 C2
Baker Rd WA7 ... 48 B4
Baker St
Macclesfield SK11 ... 112 B4
Stalybridge SK15 ... 242 E1
Stockport SK4 ... 240 E7
Baker's Ct CW7 ... 126 C1
Baker's La CW7 ... 126 C1
Bakers Pl WA2 ... 16 A4
Bakers Villas The CW12 ... 156 B1
Bakestondale Rd SK10 ... 63 C2
Bakewell Cl CH66 ... 94 C4
Bakewell Rd
Burtonwood WA5 ... 7 A4
Hazel Grove SK7 ... 36 C4
Bakewell St SK3 ... 240 D3
Bala Cl WA5 ... 7 C1
Baldock Cl WA4 ... 17 B2
Baldon Cres ST7 ... 193 B3
Balfour Cl CW1 ... 191 B2
Balfour Rd WA14 ... 238 D7
Balfour St WA7 ... 22 C1
Balham Cl WA8 ... 13 A2
Balharry Ave WA11 ... 1 C4
Ball La Bollington SK10 ... 87 B3
Kingsley WA6 ... 75 C2
Ball Pathway WA8 ... 12 C1
Ballantyne Way 10 WA3 ... 3 C4
Ballater Cres CH3 ... 119 A1
Ballater Dr WA2 ... 8 C2
Balliol Cl Romiley SK6 ... 241 C4
Sutton Lane Ends SK11 ... 112 C2
Balmoral Ave
Crewe CW2 ... 190 A1
Northwich CW9 ... 104 A3
Balmoral Cl
Knutsford WA16 ... 57 A1
Willaston (nr Nantwich)
CW5 ... 205 B2
Winsford CW7 ... 126 B2
Balmoral Cres SK10 ... 87 C1
Balmoral Ct 3 SK4 ... 240 A7
Balmoral Dr Helsby WA6 ... 73 A2
High Lane SK6 ... 37 C4
Holmes Chapel CW4 ... 130 A1
Poynton SK12 ... 36 B2
Sale WA14 ... 238 F8
Stalybridge SK15 ... 242 D3
Balmoral Gdns CH65 ... 70 B2
Balmoral Pk CH1 ... 118 A2
Balmoral Rd
Altrincham WA15 ... 238 E4
Stockport SK4 ... 240 A7
Warrington WA4 ... 16 C1
Widnes WA8 ... 13 A2
Balmoral Way SK9 ... 60 A3
Baltic Rd WA14 ... 238 A6
Bamber Ave M33 ... 242 E5
Bamburgh Ct CH65 ... 70 C2
Bamford Cl Gatley SK8 ... 34 B4
Runcorn WA7 ... 49 B4
Bamford St
Macclesfield SK10 ... 87 C1
Stockport SK1 ... 240 F4
Banastre Dr WA12 ... 2 C2
Banbury Cl SK10 ... 87 C1
Banbury Ct CW6 ... 146 B1
Banbury Dr
Altrincham WA14 ... 238 E8
Warrington WA5 ... 15 B3
Banbury St
Kidsgrove ST7 ... 194 B1
11 Stockport SK1 ... 240 F5
Bancroft CW8 ... 76 C2
Bancroft Rd WA8 ... 13 B1
Bandon Cl L24 ... 21 B1
Banff Ave CH63 ... 43 B3
Bangor Cl CH66 ... 94 C4
Bangor Rd SK8 ... 239 F6
Bangor St
Ashton-u-Lyne OL6,SK15 ... 242 B2
Stockport SK5 ... 240 F8
Bank Cl Chester CH2 ... 118 C3
Macclesfield SK11 ... 112 C4
Neston CH64 ... 67 A3
Bank Coole La CW5 ... 228 C3
Bank Ct 5 ST7 ... 195 A1
Bank Farm Mews SY14 ... 214 C3
Bank Gdns WA5 ... 14 C2
Bank Ho CW7 ... 126 B1
Bank House La
Helsby WA6 ... 73 B2
Smallwood CW11 ... 177 A3
Bank La Burland CW5 ... 203 B4
Congleton CW12 ... 134 B1
Rainow SK10 ... 89 B3
Bank Mews WA6 ... 73 B2
Bank Rd
Connah's Quay CH5 ... 91 B1
Romiley SK6 ... 241 A3
Bank Side CW8 ... 77 B1
Bank Sq SK9 ... 60 A4
Bank St Cheadle SK8 ... 239 E6
Congleton CW12 ... 156 C1
Hollinfare WA3 ... 11 A3
Bank St *continued*
Hyde SK14 ... 241 D7
Kidsgrove ST7 ... 195 B2
Newton-le-W WA12 ... 1 C2
Sale M33 ... 242 C7
13 Warrington WA1 ... 16 A3
Widnes WA8 ... 23 A2
Bank The ST7 ... 195 A4
Bank View CW4 ... 107 C1
Bankes' La WA7 ... 48 C3
Bankfield Ave Irlam M44 ... 11 B3
Stockport SK4 ... 240 C5
Wistaston CW2 ... 206 A4
Bankfield Rd
Cheadle SK8 ... 239 F1
Widnes WA8 ... 12 B1
Bankfield Sch The WA8 ... 12 B1
Bankfield St SK5 ... 240 E7
Bankfield Trad Est SK5 ... 240 E8
Bankfields Dr CH65,CH62 ... 44 A3
Bankhall La WA14,WA15 ... 31 C4
Bankhall Rd SK4 ... 240 A6
Bankhey CH64 ... 66 C3
Bankhouse Dr CW12 ... 157 A3
Banklands Cl M44 ... 11 B3
Banks Cl CW12 ... 156 B2
Banks Cres WA4 ... 16 C2
Banks Rd CH60 ... 40 B4
Bankside Altrincham WA15 ... 32 B3
Runcorn WA7 ... 50 C4
Bankside Cl
Barbridge CW5 ... 187 B3
Handforth SK9 ... 34 B1
Bankside Ct ST7 ... 193 C3
Bankside Rd M20 ... 239 B7
Banky Fields CW12 ... 156 B1
Bann St SK3 ... 240 E4
Bannacks Cl CW5 ... 205 B3
Bannister Dr SK8 ... 239 F2
Bannister St SK1 ... 240 F3
Barbauld St WA1 ... 16 A3
Barber Dr ST7 ... 194 C4
Barber St SK11 ... 112 C3
Barber's La Antrobus CW9 ... 53 B3
Northwich CW8 ... 103 C4
Barberry Cl WA14 ... 238 B7
Barberry Wlk M31 ... 11 C2
Barbondale Cl WA5 ... 14 C4
Barbour Sq CH3 ... 166 A1
Barbridge Mews CW5 ... 187 B3
Barbridge Rd ST5 ... 210 B1
Barcheston Rd SK8 ... 239 C4
Barclay Rd SK12 ... 36 C1
Bardell Cl SK12 ... 36 B1
Bardsey Cl 5 CH65 ... 70 B1
Bardsley Ave WA5 ... 7 C1
Bardsley St SK4 ... 240 D7
Barford Cl WA5 ... 7 A1
Barford Dr Golborne WA3 ... 4 A4
Handforth SK9 ... 34 B1
Barford Grange CH66 ... 68 B4
Barham Ct WA3 ... 9 B2
Barhill Farm Cotts SY13 ... 214 B1
Barington Dr WA7 ... 50 C4
Baristow Cl CH2 ... 237 B4
Bark St CW12 ... 156 C1
Barker St Crewe CW2 ... 190 B1
Nantwich CW5 ... 204 C3
Barker's Hollow Rd WA4 ... 51 A3
Barkhill Rd CH2 ... 119 A4
Barley Castle Cl WA4 ... 27 A2
Barley Croft Alsager ST7 ... 193 C1
Cheadle SK8 ... 239 F1
Chester CH3 ... 142 A4
Barley Dr SK7 ... 35 C4
Barley Mow Cl CH66 ... 69 B1
Barley Rd WA4 ... 17 B2
Barleycastle La WA4,CW9 ... 27 B2
Barleycastle Trad Est
WA4 ... 27 B2
Barleycroft Terr ST7 ... 194 C4
Barleyfields ST7 ... 209 B1
Barleywood Cl CW2 ... 206 A4
Barlow Dr CW7 ... 148 C4
Barlow Fold SK6 ... 241 D3
Barlow Fold Rd SK6 ... 241 D3
Barlow Gr WA9 ... 1 A1
Barlow Hill SK11 ... 136 C1
Barlow Rd
Altrincham WA14 ... 238 B7
Handforth SK9 ... 34 A1
Moulton CW9 ... 126 C4
Barlow Way CW11 ... 175 A4
Barmouth Cl WA5 ... 7 C1
Barn Croft WA6 ... 73 B2
Barn Croft Rd L26 ... 21 A4
Barn Ct CH3 ... 182 B1
Barn La WA3 ... 2 C4
Barn Mdw CW8 ... 78 C1
Barn Rd CW12 ... 156 B2
Barn St WA8 ... 23 A3
Barn Way WA12 ... 2 A2
Barnabas Ave CW1 ... 189 C3
Barnaby Chase CH3 ... 182 B1
Barnaby Rd SK12 ... 36 B1
Barnack Cl WA1 ... 17 A4
Barnacre Dr CH64 ... 41 A1
Barnard Ave SK4 ... 240 B6
Barnard Cl SK11 ... 111 C3
Barnard St WA5 ... 15 B2
Barnbridge Cl ST7 ... 194 C4
Barnbrook Cl CW7 ... 126 A1
Barncroft WA7 ... 50 B4
Barncroft Cl SK11 ... 84 A2
Barnes Ave
Stockport SK4 ... 240 A6
Warrington WA2 ... 9 A1
Barnes Cl Blacon CH1 ... 117 C3
Barnes Cl *continued*
Haslington CW1 ... 191 B2
Warrington WA5 ... 15 A3
Widnes WA8 ... 13 B1
Barnes Hospl SK8 ... 239 C6
Barnes Rd WA8 ... 13 B1
Barneston Rd WA8 ... 13 C2
Barnett Ave WA12 ... 1 C2
Barnett St SK11 ... 112 A4
Barnett Wlk CW2 ... 206 B4
Barnfield CH3 ... 166 A1
Barnfield Ave
Romiley SK6 ... 241 D3
Runcorn WA7 ... 50 B3
Barnfield Cl CH66 ... 69 B1
Barnfield Rd
Bollington SK10 ... 87 C3
Warrington WA1 ... 17 B4
Barngate Rd SK8 ... 239 A6
Barnham Cl WA3 ... 3 A4
Barnhill Grange CH3 ... 183 A2
Barnhill Rd CH3 ... 183 A1
Barnhouse La
Great Barrow CH3 ... 120 C4
Mouldsworth CH3 ... 98 A2
Barnmoore Cl SY14 ... 213 A2
Barns La WA14 ... 20 A3
Barns Pl WA15 ... 32 B4
Barns The CW10 ... 127 B3
Barnside Way
Macclesfield SK10 ... 87 B2
Moulton CW9 ... 126 C4
Barnstaple Way WA5 ... 14 C2
Barnston Ct CH3 ... 180 C1
Barnston Prim Sch CH60 ... 41 B4
Barnston Rd CH60 ... 41 B4
Barnston Towers Cl
CH60 ... 41 B4
Barnswood Cl WA4 ... 17 B1
Barnton Cl WA3 ... 3 B4
Barnton Prim Sch CW8 ... 78 A2
Barnwell Ave WA3 ... 4 B2
Barnwell Cl CW2 ... 206 A4
Barnwood Dr CH4 ... 140 C3
Baron Cl WA1 ... 17 B4
Baron Gn SK8 ... 34 B4
Baron's Cl WA8 ... 22 B4
Baronet Mews WA4 ... 16 A1
Baronet Rd WA4 ... 16 A1
Baronia Pl 2 CW5 ... 204 C3
Barons Cl WA7 ... 23 C1
Barons Ct CH2 ... 118 B2
Barons Quay Rd CW9 ... 78 C1
Barons Rd
Shavington CW2 ... 206 A2
Worleston CW5 ... 188 C3
Barony Bldgs 1 CW5 ... 204 C3
Barony Ct CW5 ... 204 C4
Barony Employment Pk The
CW5 ... 204 C4
Barony Rd CW5 ... 204 C4
Barony Terr CW5 ... 204 C3
Barony Way CH4 ... 140 C3
Barrack Hill SK6 ... 241 A2
Barrack Hill Cl SK6 ... 241 A3
Barrack Hill Prim Sch
SK6 ... 241 A2
Barracks La
Burwardsley CH3 ... 184 B3
Macclesfield SK10 ... 112 C4
Ravensmoor CW5 ... 203 C1
Barracks Sq 3 SK11 ... 112 A3
Barrastitch La CW8 ... 101 C3
Barratt Rd ST7 ... 193 C2
Barrel Well Hill CH2 ... 118 C1
Barrie Gdns ST7 ... 210 B4
Barrie Gr CW1 ... 190 C2
Barrington Cl WA14 ... 238 D6
Barrington Dr CW10 ... 151 B4
Barrington Rd WA14 ... 238 D5
Barrow Ave WA2 ... 8 C1
Barrow CE Prim Sch
CH3 ... 120 B3
Barrow Hall Com Prim Sch
WA5 ... 14 C4
Barrow Hall Farm CH3 ... 120 C3
Barrow Hall La WA5 ... 14 C4
Barrow La
Altrincham WA15 ... 32 A4
Culcheth WA2,WA3 ... 3 B1
Great Barrow CH3 ... 120 B3
Tarvin CH3 ... 121 B2
Barrow Mdw SK8 ... 34 C4
Barrow's Brow WA16 ... 81 C1
Barrow's Green La WA8 ... 13 C2
Barrow's Row WA8 ... 13 A2
Barrowdale Rd WA3 ... 3 A4
Barrows Cl CW1 ... 190 A4
Barrule Cl WA4 ... 26 B4
Barry Cl CH65 ... 95 B4
Barry Rise WA14 ... 238 A2
Barry St WA4 ... 16 B2
Barrymore Ave WA4 ... 16 C2
Barrymore Cres CW9 ... 78 B4
Barrymore Ct WA4 ... 17 A1
Barrymore Rd
Runcorn WA7 ... 49 A4
Warrington WA4 ... 17 A1
Weaverham CW8 ... 77 C1
Barrymore Way CH63 ... 43 A3
Bars The CH2 ... 237 C2
Barsbank Cl WA13 ... 18 B2
Barsbank La WA13 ... 18 B2
Barshaw Gdns WA4 ... 26 C2
Barston Ave CH65 ... 69 C3
Bartegate WA7 ... 50 A3
Bartholomew Way CH4 ... 141 B3
Bartholomews Ct CH5 ... 116 C3

Barthomley Cres CW2 ...189 B2
Barthomley Rd
Audley ST7 ...209 A1
Barthomley CW2 ...208 A4
Betley ST7 ...208 C2
Barton Ave WA4 ...17 A1
Barton Cl Runcorn WA7 ...50 B4
Wilmslow SK9 ...34 B1
Barton Ct CW7 ...126 C1
Barton Fold SK14 ...241 D5
Barton Rd
Barton CH3,SY14 ...181 B1
Congleton CW12 ...156 C2
Farndon CH3 ...180 C1
Barton St SK11 ...112 B3
Barton Stad CW7 ...126 C1
Bartons Pl 5 CW9 ...79 A1
Barwick Pl M33 ...242 A6
Barwood Ave ST7 ...194 A3
Basford Rd CW2 ...206 B4
Basford Way CW7 ...126 A1
Basil St SK4 ...240 E7
Baskervyle Cl CH60 ...41 A3
Baskervyle Rd CH60 ...41 A3
Baslow Dr Gatley SK8 ...34 B4
Hazel Grove SK7 ...36 C4
Basssett Cl CW5 ...205 B3
Batchelors Wing The CW10 ...127 B3
Bate's Mill La CW6 ...167 C3
Bateman Rd CW9 ...80 A1
Batemans Cl CW2 ...206 A4
Batemill Cl SK10 ...86 C1
Batemill La WA16,SK11 ...108 B3
Bates La WA6 ...73 B2
Bath Cres SK8 ...35 A3
Bath La CW3 ...230 A2
Bath Pl WA4 ...238 D2
Bath St Altrincham WA14 ...238 D2
Chester CH1 ...237 C2
Sandbach CW11 ...175 B3
Warrington WA1 ...16 A3
Bath Vale Cotts CW12 ...157 A2
Batherton Cl WA8 ...23 A4
Batherton La CW5 ...204 C1
Bathwood Dr CH64 ...66 C3
Batterbee Ct CW1 ...191 B3
Battersby La WA2 ...16 B3
Battersea Ct WA8 ...12 C2
Battery La WA1 ...17 C4
Bawtry Ct WA2 ...8 C1
Baxter Cl WA7 ...50 B4
Baxter Rd M33 ...242 B6
Baxter St WA5 ...15 C3
Baycliffe WA13 ...18 B1
Baycliffe Cl WA7 ...49 B3
Bayley Rd CW5 ...205 B3
Bayley St SK15 ...242 C1
Bayswater Cl WA7 ...24 C2
Baytree Ave M34 ...241 A8
Baytree Cl CH66 ...69 C1
Bayvil Cl WA7 ...50 C4
Beach Gr CW8 ...103 B3
Beach Rd CW8 ...103 A3
Beachin La CH3 ...182 A2
Beacon Hill View WA7 ...48 B4
Beacon La CH60 ...41 A4
Beacon Rd SK6 ...241 A1
Beacons The
Heswall CH60 ...41 A4
Warrington WA3 ...9 C3
Beaconsfield Cres WA8 ...13 A2
Beaconsfield Gr WA8 ...13 A2
Beaconsfield Rd
Altrincham WA14 ...238 D7
Runcorn WA7 ...22 C1
Widnes WA8 ...13 A2
Beaconsfield St CH2 ...237 C2
Beadnell Dr WA5 ...14 C2
Beaford Dr M22 ...33 C4
Beagle Point CW7 ...126 A1
Beagle Wlk M22 ...33 C4
Beam Heath Way CW5 ...204 C4
Beam St CW5 ...204 C3
Beamish Cl WA4 ...26 B2
Beamont Com Inf & Jun Schs WA2 ...16 B4
Beamont St WA8 ...23 A2
Beard Cres SK22 ...39 B4
Beardsmore Dr WA3 ...3 C4
Bearhurst La SK11 ...111 A2
Bearstone Rd TF9 ...236 C2
Beasley Cl CH66 ...69 B2
Beata Rd ST5 ...210 C1
Beatrice Ave SK8 ...239 F2
Beatrice St WA4 ...16 B2
Beatty Ave WA2 ...8 B1
Beatty Dr CW12 ...157 A2
Beatty Rd CW5 ...204 B2
Beaufort Ave M33 ...242 C5
Beaufort Chase SK9 ...34 C1
Beaufort Cl
Alderley Edge SK9 ...60 A1
Runcorn WA7 ...49 A4
Warrington WA5 ...15 A3
Widnes WA8 ...22 A4
Beaufort Rd
Ashton-u-Lyne OL6 ...242 A3
Sale M33 ...242 C5
Beaufort St WA5 ...15 C2
Beaulieu WA15 ...238 F2
Beaulieu Ave CW7 ...126 C1
Beaumaris Dr CH65 ...70 B1
Beaumont Cl
Biddulph ST8 ...179 B2
Chester CH4 ...140 C3
Wistaston CW2 ...205 C4
Beaumont Ct SK9 ...34 B3
Beauty Bank
Whitegate CW7 ...125 C3
Winsford CW7 ...149 A2
Beauty Bank Cotts CW7 149 A2
Beauxfields WA4 ...26 B4
Beaver Cl CH4 ...140 C3
Beaver Ctr The CW9 ...103 C4
Beaverbrook Ave WA3 ...5 A2
Beavers Cl WA16 ...79 C4
Bebbington Cl M33 ...242 F5
Bebington Rd CH66 ...69 B2
Becconsall Cl CW1 ...190 A4
Becconsall Dr CW1 ...190 A4
Bechers WA8 ...12 A2
Beckenham Gr CW7 ...126 A1
Beckett Ave CW7 ...150 B4
Beckett Dr Lymm WA13 ...19 A4
Winwick WA2 ...8 A3
Beckett's La CH3 ...142 A4
Beckford Cl CW1 ...189 C4
Becks La SK10 ...86 C1
Becontree Ave M34 ...241 A8
Bedells La SK9 ...60 A3
Bedford Ave
Ellesmere Port CH65 ...70 A1
Hyde SK14 ...241 E7
Bedford Ave E CH65 ...70 A1
Bedford Ct CW2 ...190 B1
Bedford Gdns CW2 ...190 B1
Bedford Gn M44 ...11 A3
Bedford Gr ST7 ...193 A3
Bedford Pl CW2 ...190 B1
Bedford Rd
Kidsgrove ST7 ...195 A2
Macclesfield SK11 ...112 A4
Bedford Rise CW7 ...149 B3
Bedford St Crewe CW2 ...190 B1
Warrington WA4 ...26 B4
Bedward Row CH1 ...237 A2
Beech Ave Culcheth WA3 ...5 A2
Frodsham WA6 ...74 B4
Gatley SK8 ...239 B5
Golborne WA3 ...3 C4
Haydock WA11 ...1 C4
Mobberley WA16 ...57 C3
Rode Heath ST7 ...193 C4
Stockport SK3 ...240 F2
Warrington, Penketh WA5 ...14 B2
Warrington, Thelwall WA4 ...17 B2
Beech Cl
Alderley Edge SK9 ...60 A2
Congleton CW12 ...156 A2
Cuddington CW8 ...101 C1
Holmes Chapel CW4 ...130 B2
Newton-le-W WA12 ...2 B1
Ollerton WA16 ...82 C3
11 Partington M31 ...11 C2
Beech Cotts
Alderley Edge SK9 ...85 A4
Stretton WA4 ...26 C1
Beech Cres SK12 ...36 C2
Beech Dr Knutsford WA16 ...57 B1
Talke ST7 ...210 C4
Wistaston CW2 ...189 C1
Beech Farm Dr SK10 ...87 B1
Beech Gr Chester CH2 ...119 A2
Crewe CW1 ...190 C3
Ellesmere Port CH1 ...95 A4
Lymm WA13 ...18 A1
Macclesfield SK11 ...112 C3
Sandbach CW11 ...175 B3
Warrington WA1 ...17 A4
Warrington, Latchford WA4 ...16 B2
Weaverham CW8 ...102 B4
Wilmslow SK9 ...60 A3
Winsford CW7 ...149 B4
Beech Hall Dr SK10 ...87 B1
Beech Hall Sch SK10 ...87 B1
Beech Hey La CH64 ...43 A1
Beech Heyes Cl CW8 ...102 C4
Beech Heyes Dr CW8 ...102 C4
Beech La Barnton CW8 ...78 A2
Eaton CW6 ...147 A3
Macclesfield SK10 ...87 B1
Norley WA6 ...75 C1
Romiley SK6 ...241 C2
Wilmslow SK9 ...60 A3
Beech Lawn WA14 ...238 C4
Beech Mount WA14 ...238 D2
Beech Rd
Alderley Edge SK9 ...60 A2
Altrincham WA15 ...238 E3
Heswall CH60 ...41 B4
High Lane SK6 ...37 C4
Little Budworth CW6 ...124 B1
Runcorn WA7 ...49 B4
Sale M33 ...242 D6
Stockport SK2,SK3 ...240 F2
Sutton WA7 ...50 A2
Warrington WA4 ...26 B4
Whaley Bridge SK23 ...65 C4
Beech Rise Crowton CW8 ...76 A1
Whaley Bridge SK23 ...65 B3
Beech St Hyde SK14 ...241 D7
Middlewich CW10 ...128 B1
Beech St W CW1 ...190 B2
Beech Tree Cl CW5 ...205 B3
Beech View Rd WA6 ...75 B1
Beechcroft Ave CW2 ...206 A4
Beechcroft Dr CH65 ...70 A1
Beeches SK9 ...59 C3
Beeches The
Altrincham WA14 ...238 C2
Chester CH2 ...119 A3
Helsby WA6 ...73 B2
Nantwich CW5 ...204 C3
Whitchurch SY13 ...225 C1
Beechfield
Altrincham WA14 ...238 C3
Moulton CW9 ...126 C4
Wilmslow SK9 ...60 A3
Beechfield Ave SK9 ...59 C3
Beechfield Cl CH60 ...41 A4
Beechfield Dr CW10 ...128 A1
Beechfield Gdns CW8 ...103 A3
Beechfield Rd
Alderley Edge SK9 ...85 A4
Cheadle SK8 ...35 A4
Ellesmere Port CH65 ...70 A3
Stockport SK3 ...240 F1
Warrington WA4 ...17 A1
Beechfields CW7 ...150 A4
Beechlands Ave CH3 ...119 A1
Beechmill Dr WA3 ...4 C2
Beechmoore WA4 ...25 A3
Beechmuir CH1 ...117 C2
Beechtree Farm Cl WA16 29 B4
Beechtree La WA13 ...29 A4
Beechurst Rd SK8 ...240 B1
Beechway Bollington SK10 ...88 A4
Chester CH2 ...118 B3
High Lane SK6 ...37 C4
Wilmslow SK9 ...59 C3
Beechways WA4 ...26 B3
Beechways Dr CH64 ...66 B4
Beechwood
Altrincham WA14 ...238 B1
Knutsford WA16 ...57 B1
Beechwood Ave
Hartford CW8 ...103 A3
Newton-le-W WA12 ...2 B2
Romiley SK6 ...241 D2
Runcorn WA7 ...49 C3
Stalybridge SK15 ...242 F4
3 Stockport SK5 ...240 F8
Warrington, Great Sankey WA5 ...14 C3
Warrington, Padgate WA1 ...16 C4
Beechwood Dr
Alsager ST7 ...193 A2
Eaton (nr Congleton) CW12 ...156 C4
Ellesmere Port CH66 ...69 B1
Higher Wincham CW9 ...79 C3
Wilmslow SK9 ...60 C4
Beechwood Gr SK8 ...35 A4
Beechwood La
Culcheth WA3 ...4 B2
Stalybridge SK15 ...242 F4
Beechwood Mews SK10 ...87 B1
Beechwood Prim Sch WA7 ...49 C3
Beechwood Rd
Bebington CH62 ...43 B4
Broughton CH4 ...140 C3
Beechwood Sch CW1 ...190 B3
Beecroft Cl WA5 ...7 B1
Beeley St SK14 ...241 E6
Beeston Ave WA15 ...238 F6
Beeston Brow SK10 ...88 A4
Beeston Castle* CW6 ...167 C2
Beeston Cl Bollington SK10 63 B1
Holmes Chapel CW4 ...130 A2
Middlewich CW10 ...151 B3
Warrington WA3 ...9 B2
Beeston Ct WA7 ...24 B2
Beeston Dr Alsager ST7 ...193 B2
Knutsford WA16 ...82 A4
Winsford CW7 ...149 B4
Beeston Gn CH66 ...69 C3
Beeston Gr SK3 ...240 E1
Beeston Mount SK10 ...63 B1
Beeston Rd
Broughton CH4 ...139 A2
Handforth SK9 ...34 B3
Higher Kinnerton CH4 ...161 A4
Beeston St CW8 ...103 C4
Beeston Terr SK11 ...111 C3
Beeston View CH4 ...141 C4
Beggarman's La WA16 ...82 A4
Beilby Rd WA11 ...1 C4
Belfry Cl SK9 ...60 B4
Belfry Dr SK10 ...87 B2
Belgrave Ave
Alsager ST7 ...193 B3
Broughton CH4 ...140 C3
Congleton CW12 ...156 B2
Warrington WA1 ...16 C4
Belgrave Cl
Dodleston CH4 ...162 A3
Golborne WN7 ...4 B4
Widnes WA8 ...13 C2
Belgrave Dr CH65 ...69 C3
Belgrave Inf Sch CH4 ...141 A3
Belgrave Pl CH4 ...237 B1
Belgrave Rd
Altrincham WA14 ...238 C3
Chester CH3 ...142 A4
Crewe CW2 ...190 A1
Irlam M44 ...11 B3
Macclesfield SK11 ...112 B2
Northwich CW9 ...104 A2
Sale M33 ...242 A6
Belgrave St CH2 ...237 C3
Belgravia Ct WA8 ...12 C2
Belgravia Gdns WA15 ...31 C4
Bell Ave SK11 ...112 C2
Bell Farm Ct 7 SK10 ...87 B2
Bell House Rd WA8 ...13 B1
Bell La WA4 ...17 C2
Bell Meadow Ct CW6 ...146 B1
Bell's Hollow ST5 ...210 C2
Bellaport Rd TF9 ...236 A2
Bellard Dr CH2 ...119 A2
Bellcast Cl WA4 ...26 B3
Belldale Cl SK4 ...240 A6
Belle Vue Terr CW11 ...175 A3
Bellemonte Rd WA6 ...74 B4
Belleville Ave M22 ...33 C4
Bellhouse La
Higher Walton WA4 ...25 B4
Warrington WA4 ...17 B1
Bellingham Dr WA7 ...49 A4
Bellsfield Cl WA13 ...18 C1
Bellvue La CH3 ...119 C2
Belmont Ave
Macclesfield SK10 ...86 B1
Sandbach CW11 ...175 A4
Warrington WA4 ...16 C2
Belmont Cl SK4 ...240 E7
Belmont Cres WA5 ...15 A3
Belmont Rd
Altrincham WA15 ...238 E2
Bramhall SK7 ...35 C3
Gatley SK8 ...239 B6
Great Budworth CW9 ...53 C1
Northwich CW9 ...104 B4
Sale M33 ...242 A8
Widnes WA8 ...13 C1
Belmont St SK4 ...240 E7
Belmont Way SK4 ...240 E7
Beltony Dr CW1 ...173 A1
Belvedere WA7 ...23 A2
Belvedere Cl WA6 ...49 B1
Belvedere Dr CH1 ...117 C2
Belvedere Rd WA12 ...2 A3
Belvedere Terr ST7 ...193 C4
Belvoir Ave SK7 ...36 C4
Belvoir Rd
Warrington WA4 ...26 A4
Widnes WA8 ...13 A1
Bembridge Cl
Widnes WA8 ...12 C2
Warrington WA5 ...14 B4
Bembridge Ct CW10 ...151 B4
Bemrose Ave WA14 ...238 C6
Ben Nevis Dr CH66 ...68 C3
Benbow St 7 M33 ...242 B7
Benbrook Gr SK9 ...34 C1
Benbrook Way SK11 ...111 C1
Bendee Ave CH64 ...67 A4
Bendee Rd CH64 ...67 A4
Bengal Sq OL6 ...242 A4
Bengal St SK3 ...240 E4
Benjamins Way ST7 ...209 C1
Bennet Cl CH64 ...68 A4
Bennet Rd CW9 ...104 B3
Bennett Ave WA1 ...16 C3
Bennett Cl Crewe CW1 ...190 C2
4 Stockport SK3 ...240 C4
Bennett St
Stalybridge SK15 ...242 D1
3 Stockport SK3 ...240 C4
Warrington WA1 ...16 A3
Bennett's La
Higher Kinnerton CH4 ...161 A4
Widnes WA8 ...13 C1
Bennetts La SK11 ...158 C3
Benson Rd WA3 ...9 B2
Benson Wlk 3 SK9 ...34 B1
Bent La Astbury CW12 ...178 A4
Crowton CW8 ...101 B4
Culcheth WA3 ...5 A1
Lymm WA13 ...19 B3
Bentham Ave WA2 ...8 B2
Bentham Rd WA3 ...5 A1
Bentinck Cl WA14 ...238 C4
Bentinck Rd WA14 ...238 C4
Bentinck St WA7 ...22 C2
Bentley Dr CW1 ...191 A3
Bentley Gr CW7 ...149 B3
Bentley's Farm La WA4 ...52 C3
Bentleys The SK5 ...240 F7
Benton Dr CH2 ...118 B2
Bents Cotts CH2 ...71 C1
Bentside Rd SK12 ...38 B3
Benty Heath La CH64, CH66 ...43 A2
Beresford Ct SK9 ...60 A1
Beresford St WA1 ...16 C4
Berisford Cl WA15 ...238 E7
Berisford Ho CW12 ...156 C2
Berkeley Ave ST7 ...193 B3
Berkeley Cl Golborne WN7 ...4 B4
Hyde SK14 ...241 D5
Berkeley Cres
Hyde SK14 ...241 D5
Wistaston CW2 ...206 A4
Berkeley Ct WA7 ...24 B2
Berkeley Prim Sch The CW2 ...206 A4
Berkeley Rise CW7 ...149 A4
Berkley Ct SK23 ...65 B3
Berkley Dr CH4 ...141 B3
Berkshire Cl SK10 ...86 C1
Berkshire Dr
Congleton CW12 ...156 B2
Irlam M44 ...11 B3
Warrington WA1 ...17 C4
Berlin Rd SK3 ...240 D2
Bernard Ave WA4 ...26 B4
Bernisdale Rd WA16 ...57 C2
Bernsdale Cl CH5 ...116 A2
Berristal Rd SK10 ...88 C2
Berry Cl
Ellesmere Port CH66 ...69 B2
Wilmslow SK9 ...60 A3
Berry Dr CH66 ...69 B2
Berry Rd WA8 ...12 B1
Berrycroft La SK6 ...241 A3
Berrystead CW8 ...103 A2
Bertram St
Newton-le-W WA12 ...2 A2
Bertram St *continued*
Sale M33 ...242 E6
Berwick Ave CH62 ...43 C2
Berwick Cl
Macclesfield SK10 ...86 C1
Warrington WA1 ...17 C3
Berwick Ct CW4 ...130 A1
Berwick Gdns CH66 ...69 A3
Berwick Gr CH66 ...69 A3
Berwick Rd CH66 ...69 A3
Berwyn Ave SK8 ...240 B1
Berwyn Cl CH66 ...69 A3
Bessancourt CW4 ...130 B2
Bessemer Rd M44 ...11 C3
Beswick St SK11 ...112 A4
Beswicks La
Lindow End SK9 ...59 B2
Norton in Hales TF9 ...236 B1
Beswicks Rd CW8 ...78 C1
Betchton Cl CW11 ...175 B4
Betchton Ct 6 CW12 ...156 C2
Betchton Rd CW11 ...175 C1
Betchworth Cres WA7 ...49 B3
Betchworth Way SK10 ...87 B2
Bethany Cl WA11 ...1 A4
Betjeman Cl WA4 ...16 C2
Betjeman Way CW1 ...190 C3
Betley Cl CW9 ...104 A3
Betley St CW1 ...190 B2
Betleymere Rd SK8 ...239 F4
Betsyfield Dr WA3 ...9 A4
Bettisfield Ave CH62 ...43 B3
Betty's La CW6 ...168 B1
Bevan Ave ST7 ...210 C3
Bevan Cl WA5 ...15 B3
Beverley Ave
Denton M34 ...241 A6
Warrington WA4 ...26 B4
Beverley Dr CH60 ...41 A3
Beverley Rd WA5 ...15 B3
Beverley Way
Ellesmere Port CH66 ...69 A4
Macclesfield SK10 ...87 B2
Beverley Wlk SK6 ...241 A1
Bevin Ave WA3 ...5 A2
Bevyl Rd CH64 ...41 A1
Bewley Ct CH3 ...142 A4
Bewsey Bsns Ctr WA5 ...15 C3
Bewsey Farm Cl WA5 ...15 B4
Bewsey Ind Est WA5 ...16 A4
Bewsey Lodge Cty Prim Sch WA5 ...15 C4
Bewsey Pk Cl WA5 ...15 C4
Bewsey Rd WA2,WA5 ...16 A3
Bewsey St 8 WA2 ...16 A3
Bexhill Ave
Altrincham WA15 ...238 F6
Warrington WA2 ...8 A2
Bexington Dr CW1 ...190 A4
Bexton Ave CW7 ...126 A1
Bexton La WA16 ...82 A4
Bexton Prim Sch WA16 ...81 C4
Bexton Rd WA16 ...56 C1
Bibby Ave WA1 ...16 C3
Bibby St ST7 ...193 C4
Bickerton Ave WA6 ...74 B4
Bickerton Cl WA3 ...9 B2
Bickerton Holy Trinity CE Prim Sch SY14 ...200 A4
Bickerton Rd
Altrincham WA14 ...238 B6
Bickley Town SY14 ...201 A1
Bickerton Way 1 CW9 ...103 C2
Bickley Cl
Hough Common CW2 ...206 C1
Runcorn WA7 ...23 B1
Warrington WA2 ...8 C2
Bickley Town La SY14 ...214 C3
Bicknell Cl WA5 ...15 A4
Bida La CW12 ...179 A4
Biddulph Common Rd ST8 ...179 C4
Biddulph Grange Ctry Pk* ST8 ...179 C2
Biddulph Grange Gdn* ST8 ...179 C2
Biddulph Park Rd ST8 ...179 C3
Biddulph Rd
Biddulph ST7 ...195 C3
Congleton CW12 ...179 A4
Biddulph St CW12 ...179 B4
Biddy's La SK10 ...88 A1
Bideford Rd WA5 ...14 C2
Bidston Cl CH2 ...118 B3
Bidston Dr SK9 ...34 C1
Bidston Gn CH66 ...69 B2
Bidvale Way CW1 ...190 B4
Big Field La CW6 ...146 A4
Biggin Ct WA2 ...8 C1
Bignall End Rd
Audley ST7 ...210 A2
Newcastle-u-L ST7 ...210 A2
Billington Ave WA12 ...2 B3
Billington Cl Crewe CW2 190 A1
Warrington WA5 ...14 C4
Billington Rd WA8 ...12 A2
Bilson Dr SK3 ...240 B3
Bilton Cl WA8 ...13 C1
Bilton Way CW2 ...189 C3
Bings Rd SK23 ...65 C4
Bingswood Ave SK23 ...65 C4
Bingswood Ind Est SK23 ...65 C4
Bingswood Rd SK23 ...65 C4
Binney Rd CW9 ...104 A4
Binns St SK15 ...242 B1

Binyon Way CW1 .....191 A2
Birbeck St SK15 .....242 C1
Birch Ave Alsager ST7 ..193 C1
  Crewe CW1 ....190 C3
  Irlam M44 ....11 B3
  Macclesfield SK10 .....87 A1
  Romiley SK6 ....241 D2
  Sale M33 ....242 B5
  3 Stockport SK4 .....240 B8
  Wilmslow SK9 ....59 C3
  Winsford CW7 ......127 A1
Birch Brook Rd WA13 ...19 B3
Birch Cl Crewe CW1 ....190 C3
  Holmes Chapel CW4 ...130 B2
Birch Cres WA12 ....1 C1
Birch Ct CW12 ....155 C2
Birch Fold CW11 ......107 A1
Birch Gdns CW11 ......175 B3
Birch Gr
  Ellesmere Port CH66 ....70 A1
  Higher Wincham CW9 ...79 C3
  Knutsford WA16 ......57 B1
  Lostock Green CW9 ...105 A4
  Warrington, Bruche WA1 ..16 C4
  Warrington, Latchford WA4 .16 B2
Birch Heath La CH3 ...142 C4
Birch Heath Rd CW6 ...168 B4
Birch Hill WA6 ....99 B4
Birch House Rd ST5 ...210 B1
Birch La
  Hough Common CW2 ...206 C1
  Winsford CW10 ......127 C1
Birch Rd Audley ST7 ...209 C1
  Chester CH4 ....140 C3
  Congleton CW12 .....155 C2
  Gatley SK8 ....239 A5
  Haydock WA11 ....1 C4
  Hollinfare WA3 ......11 A1
  Partington M31 ......11 B2
  Poynton SK12 ....36 C1
  Runcorn WA7 ....49 B4
  Widnes WA8 ....13 A2
Birch Rise CH2 ....118 B3
Birch Tree Ave SK7 ....37 A4
Birch Tree Cl WA14 ...238 C1
Birch Tree Ct CH2 ....237 C4
Birch Tree La
  Antrobus WA4 ....53 A3
  Goostrey CW4 ....107 B1
  The Bank ST7 ....195 A4
Birch Tree Rd **17** WA3 ...3 C4
Birch Way SK10 ....86 C3
Birchall Ave WA3 ......4 C2
Birchall Moss La CW5 ..219 C1
Birchall Wlk CW2 .....206 B4
Birchdale WA14 ......238 C2
Birchdale Ave SK8 ....239 B2
Birchdale Cres WA4 ....26 B4
Birchdale Rd
  Warrington, Appleton WA4 ..26 B4
  Warrington, Paddington
    WA1 ....17 A4
Birchen Rd L26 ....21 A4
Birchencliff Cotts SK10 ..63 B3
Birchenwood Rd ST6,
  ST7 ....195 C1
Birches Cl CH60 ....41 A4
Birches Croft Dr SK10 ..86 C1
Birches La CW9 ......105 A4
Birches The
  Broughton CH4 ......139 A2
  Crewe CW2 ....206 B4
  Neston CH64 ....41 C1
Birches Way **16** ST7 ...195 A1
Birchfield Ave
  Rode Heath ST7 .....193 C4
  Widnes WA8 ....13 A1
Birchfield Mews **3**
  SK14 ....241 D6
Birchfield Rd Lymm WA13 ..19 A2
  Stockport SK3 ....240 A3
  Warrington WA5 .....15 A3
  Widnes, Appleton WA8 ...13 A1
  Widnes, Farnworth WA8 ...13 A4
Birchfields WA15 .....238 F1
Birchgate Cl SK10 .....86 C1
Birchin Cl CW5 ......205 A3
Birchin La CW5 ......205 A3
Birchinall Cl SK11 ....112 A4
Birchmuir CH1 ....117 C2
Birchmuir Cl CW1 ....190 A4
Birchvale Ave SK6 ....241 D3
Birchway Bollington SK10 ..88 A4
  Bramhall SK7 ....35 B4
  Heswall CH60 ....41 B3
  High Lane SK6 ....37 C4
Birchways WA4 ....26 C3
Birchwood Ave WA2,WA3 ..9 B2
Birchwood Bvd WA3 .....9 B1
Birchwood CE Prim Sch
  WA3 ....9 C2
Birchwood Cl
  Ellesmere Port CH66 ....69 B1
  Elton CH2 ....72 B2
  Stockport SK4 ....240 A5
Birchwood Com High Sch
  WA3 ....9 B2
Birchwood Dr
  Lower Peover WA16 ...106 B4
  Nantwich CW5 ......204 C3
  Wilmslow SK9 ....60 B4
Birchwood Office Pk WA2 ..9 A2

Birchwood One Bsns Pk
  WA3 ....9 C1
Birchwood Park Ave WA3 ..9 B3
Birchwood Science Pk
  WA3 ....9 B3
Birchwood Sta WA3 .....9 C1
Birchwood Tech Pk WA3 ..9 C3
Birchwood Way WA2 .....8 C1
Bird Hall La SK3 ....240 B2
Bird Hall Rd SK8 ......240 C1
Birdwell Dr WA5 ....15 A3
Bird's La CW6 ....186 A4
Birds La Tarporley CW6 ..146 B1
  Tattenhall CH3 ......166 C1
Birkdale Ave CH63 .....43 A3
Birkdale Cl Bramhall SK7 ..36 A4
  Macclesfield SK10 .....87 B3
Birkdale Ct **8** CW9 ...104 A4
Birkdale Dr ST7 ......195 B2
Birkdale Gdns CW7 ....126 A1
Birkdale Rd
  Warrington WA5 .....14 C2
  Widnes WA8 ....13 A3
Birkenhead Rd CH64 ....42 C1
Birkenhead St CW9 ....104 B4
Birkett Ave CH65 ......70 B1
Birkin Cl WA16 ....57 B2
Birkinheath La WA14 ...31 A2
Birley Ave WA15 .....238 F7
Birley St WA12 ....2 B2
Birstall Ct WA7 ....49 B4
Birtles Cl
  Sandbach CW11 .....175 B4
  Stockport SK8 ......240 A1
Birtles Hall SK10 ......85 B1
Birtles La SK10 ....85 C1
Birtles Rd
  Macclesfield SK10 .....86 B1
  Warrington WA2 ......8 B1
Birtles Way **4** SK9 ...34 B3
Birtlespool Rd SK8 ....239 F4
Birtley Ct WA8 ....12 A1
Birtwistle Rd CW9 ....104 B3
Bisham Pk WA7 ....24 B1
Bishop Heber High Sch
  SY14 ....213 B3
Bishop Rd SK10 ......111 C4
Bishop Reeves Rd WA11 ..1 C4
Bishop St CH2 ....118 C2
Bishop Wilson CE Prim Sch
  CH64 ....67 B1
Bishop's Cl
  Stockport SK8 ......240 A1
  Talke ST7 ....210 B4
Bishopdale Cl WA5 .....14 C2
Bishopgates Dr CW9 ...103 C2
Bishops Cl WA14 .....238 B1
Bishops Ct
  Broughton CH4 ......139 A2
  Warrington WA2 ......8 A2
Bishops Gdns CH65 ....70 A3
Bishops Way WA8 ......13 B2
Bishops Wood CW5 ....204 C1
**Bishops' Blue Coat CE High
  Sch** CH3 ....142 A4
Bishopsfield Ct CH2 ...118 C2
Bishopton Dr SK11 ....111 C4
Bispham Rd WA5 ......15 A2
Bittern Cl Poynton SK12 ..36 A2
  Runcorn WA7 ....50 B4
  Warrington WA2 ......8 B1
Bittern Gr SK10 ......87 A1
Bk Adcroft St **4** SK1 ..240 F3
Bk Grosvenor St SK15 ..242 D1
Bk Melbourne St SK15 ..242 D1
Black Denton's Pl WA8 ...13 B1
Black Diamond St CH2 ..237 B4
Black Firs La CW12 ....155 C2
Black Firs Prim Sch
  CW12 ....155 C2
Black Friars CH1 ......237 A2
Black La SK10 ....87 C1
Black Lion La CH66 ....69 B3
Black Moss Rd WA14 ...20 C4
Black Park Rd SY13 ....226 B1
Black Rd SK11 ....112 C4
Blackacres Cl CW11 ...174 C3
Blackberry La WA14 ...238 B1
Blackboards La CH66 ...69 A4
Blackbrook Ave WA2 .....8 C1
Blackbrook Cl WA8 .....12 B2
Blackburn Cl WA3 ......3 C4
Blackburne Ave WA8 ...22 A3
Blackburne Cl WA2 ......9 B1
Blackcap Rd WA4 ......27 A4
Blackcroft Ave CW8 ....78 A1
Blackden La
  Goostrey CW4 ......108 A2
  Siddington SK11 .....132 C4
Blackdown Cl CH66 ....69 A3
Blackeys La CH64 ......66 C4
Blackheath La WA7 ....24 C3
Blackhill La WA16 .....81 C4
Blackhurst Brow SK10 ..61 B1
Blackhurst Farm Rd
  CW5 ....202 C2
Blackhurst St WA1 .....16 A3
Blackledge Cl WA2 ......9 A2
Blackley Cl
  Macclesfield SK10 .....87 A2
  Warrington WA4 .....16 B2
Blackshaw Cl CW12 ...157 A1
Blackshaw Dr WA5 ......7 A1
Blackshaw La SK9 .....59 C1
Blackshaw St
  20 Macclesfield SK11 ..112 B4
  4 Stockport SK3 ....240 E4

Blackthorn Cl
  Broughton CH4 ......139 A2
  Huntington CH3 .....142 A3
  Wistaston CW2 .....206 A4
Blackthorn Pl ST5 .....210 C1
Blackthorne Ave CH1 ...95 A4
Blackwell Cl CW10 ....151 B3
Blacon Ave CH1 ......118 A3
Blacon Hall Jun Sch
  CH1 ....117 C3
Blacon Hall Rd CH1 ....117 C3
Blacon High Sch CH1 ...117 C3
Blacon Inf Sch CH1 ....117 C3
Blacon Point Rd CH1 ...117 C3
Blagg Ave CW5 ......204 B2
Blair Cl SK7 ....36 B4
Blair Dr WA8 ....12 B4
Blairgowrie Dr SK10 ....87 A2
Blaizefield Cl CW3 .....232 B1
Blake Cl Blacon CH1 ...117 C3
  Wistaston CW2 .....189 C1
Blake La SK8 ....102 A1
Blake St CW12 ....156 B2
Blakeacre Rd L26 ......21 A3
Blakeden La CW7 .....148 C4
Blakeley Ct CH63 ......43 A4
Blakeley Dell CH63 .....43 A4
Blakeley Dene CH63 ....43 A4
Blakeley Rd CH63 ......43 A4
Blakelow Bank SK11 ...112 C3
Blakelow Cl CW10 ....151 A4
Blakelow Cres CW5 ....205 C2
Blakelow Rd SK11 .....112 C3
Blakely La WA16 ......58 C4
Blakemere Ave M33 ...242 E5
Blakemere Cl SY13 ....226 A1
Blakemere Ct CH65 ....70 B4
Blakemere Dr CW9 ....103 C3
Blakemere La WA6 ....100 B2
Blakemere Way CW11 ..174 C4
Blakeswood WA14 ....238 B5
Blandford Ct SK15 ....242 D2
Blandford Dr
  4 Macclesfield SK11 ..111 C4
  Northwich CW9 .....103 C2
Blandford Ho SK15 ....242 D2
Blandford Rd
  Stockport SK4 ......240 C6
  Warrington WA5 .....15 A4
Blandford St SK15 ....242 D2
Blankney The CW5 ....204 C2
Blantern Rd CH4 .....161 A4
Blantyre St WA7 ......22 C2
Blaven Cl SK3 ....240 F1
Blaze Hill SK10 ....88 C3
Bleasdale Rd
  Crewe CW1 ....173 A1
  Newton-le-W WA12 ....2 B2
Bleeding Wolf La ST7 ..194 C3
Blenheim Cl
  Altrincham WA14 ....238 D2
  Davenham CW9 .....103 C2
  Macclesfield SK10 .....87 A1
  Poynton SK12 ....36 C2
  Warrington WA2 ......8 C1
  Wilmslow SK9 ....60 B4
  Wistaston CW2 .....205 C2
Blenheim Ct ST7 .....193 B3
Blenheim Gdns **7** CW7 ..149 B4
Blenheim Ho CH1 .....118 A2
Blenheim Way OL6 ....242 A4
**Blessed Thomas Holford RC
  High Sch** WA15 ....238 E4
Bloom St SK3 ....240 E4
Bloomsbury Way WA8 ...12 B2
Blossom Hts CW8 .....103 B4
Blossom Rd M31 ......11 C1
Blossoms Hey SK8 ....239 E1
Blossoms Hey Wlk SK8 ..239 E1
Blossoms La SK7 ......35 A1
Blossoms St **5** SK2 ...240 F3
Blue Cap La SY14 .....213 B4
Blue Chip Bsns Pk
  WA14 ....238 C2
Blue Hatch WA6 ......74 B1
Blue Planet Aquarium The ★
  CH65 ....70 B1
Blue Ridge Cl WA5 .....14 C4
Bluebell Ave WA11 ......1 C4
Bluebell Cl
  Huntington CH3 .....142 A3
  Macclesfield SK10 .....87 B2
  Northwich CW8 ......78 C1
Bluebell Ct WA7 ......49 C2
Bluebell Gr SK8 ......239 D4
Bluebell La SK10 ......87 B2
Bluebell Mews **10** SK10 ..87 B2
Bluebell Way
  Alsager ST7 ....193 A2
  Handforth SK9 ......34 B1
Blueberry Rd WA14 ....238 A2
Bluecoat St WA2 ......16 A4
Blundell Rd WA8 ......22 B4
Blyth Cl Macclesfield SK10 ..86 C1
  Runcorn WA7 ....50 B3
Blyth Rd CH63 ....43 B4
Blythe Ave Bramhall SK7 ..35 B3
  Congleton CW12 .....156 A1
  Widnes WA8 ....13 A3
Blythe Pl CW7 ....127 A1
Blythings The CW6 ....146 B2
Board St OL6 ....242 A4
Boardman Cl SK5 .....240 F8
Boat Mus ★ CH65 .....70 B4
Boat Stage WA11 ......18 C2
Boathorse Rd ST7 ....210 C4

Boathouse La CH64 ....41 B2
Bob's La M44 ....11 B2
Boddens Hill Rd SK4 ...240 A6
Boden Dr CW5 ....205 B2
Boden St SK11 ....112 B4
Bodiam Ct CH65 ......70 C1
Bodmin Ave SK10 ......86 C1
Bodmin Cl WA7 ......50 C3
Bodmin Dr SK7 ....35 C4
Bodnant Cl CW1 .....190 A4
Bold Bsns Ctr WA9 ......6 A4
Bold Cross WA8 ....13 C4
Bold Ind Est WA8 ......13 B3
Bold Ind Park WA9 ......6 A3
Bold La WA5,WA9 ......6 B4
Bold Pl CH1 ....237 B3
Bold Sq CH2 ....237 B3
Bold St Altrincham WA14 ..238 D3
  Haslington CW1 .....191 B2
  Runcorn WA7 ....23 A2
  Sandbach CW11 .....175 A3
  Warrington WA1 .....16 A3
  Widnes WA8 ....23 A4
Bolesworth Hill Rd CH3 ..183 B2
Bolesworth Rd
  Chester CH2 ....118 C3
  Tattenhall CH3 .....183 B4
Boleyn Cl CH1 ....117 C3
Boleyn Ct WA7 ....24 B2
Bolland's Ct CH1 .....237 A2
Bolleyn Wood Ct SK9 ...34 A1
Bollin Ave
  Altrincham WA14 ....238 B1
  Winsford CW7 ......127 A1
Bollin Cl Alsager ST7 ...192 C2
  Culcheth WA3 ....5 A1
  Lymm WA13 ....19 A2
  Sandbach CW11 .....174 C4
  Winsford CW7 ......127 A1
Bollin Ct
  Altrincham WA14 ....238 B1
  Wilmslow SK9 ....60 B3
Bollin Dr
  Altrincham WA14 ....238 E8
  Congleton CW12 .....156 C1
  Lymm WA13 ....19 A2
Bollin Gr ST8 ....179 C1
Bollin Hill Prestbury SK10 ..87 A3
  Wilmslow SK9 ....60 A4
Bollin Mews SK10 .....86 C4
Bollin Prim Sch WA14 ..238 B1
Bollin Sq WA14 ......238 B1
Bollin Way SK10 ......87 A3
Bollin Wlk SK9 ....60 B4
Bollinbarn SK10 ......87 A1
Bollinbrook CE Prim Sch
  SK10 ....87 A1
Bollinbrook Rd SK10 ....87 A1
Bollington Ave CW9 ...104 A3
Bollington Cross CE Prim Sch
  SK10 ....87 C3
Bollington La SK10 .....84 C1
Bollington Rd SK10 ....87 C3
Bollinway WA15 ......32 A4
Bollinwood Chase SK9 ..60 B4
Bolshaw Cl CW1 .....190 A4
Bolshaw Farm La SK8 ...34 B3
Bolshaw Prim Sch SK8 ...34 B4
Bolshaw Rd SK8 ......34 B3
Bolton Ave Bramhall SK8 ..35 A3
  Warrington WA4 .....16 C2
Bolton Cl Golborne WA3 ....4 A4
  Poynton SK12 ....36 B2
Bombay Rd SK3 ......240 C3
Bombay St OL6 ......242 A4
Bomish La CW4,SK11 ..108 B2
Bonar Cl SK3 ....240 C4
Bonar Rd **5** SK3 .....240 C4
Bond Cl WA5 ....15 B2
Bond St
  Macclesfield SK11 ....112 B4
  Northwich CW8 ......78 B1
  Stalybridge SK15 ....242 D3
Bonis Hall La SK10 .....61 C3
Bonnyfield SK6 ......241 B2
Bonville Chase WA14 ..238 A4
Bonville Rd WA14 ....238 A4
Boon Hill Rd ST7 .....209 C1
Booth Ave Ashton CH3 ..121 C4
  Little Budworth CW6 ...147 C4
  Sandbach CW11 .....175 B3
Booth Bed La WA16,
  CW4 ....107 A2
Booth Cl SK15 ....242 C1
Booth La CW10 ......151 C2
Booth Rd
  Altrincham WA14 ....238 C4
  Handforth SK9 ......34 A1
  Hartford CW8 ......103 A2
  Sale M33 ....242 B8
Booth St Audley ST7 ...209 B1
  Congleton CW12 .....156 B1
  Hyde SK14 ....241 E5
  Stockport SK3 ......240 E3
  Warrington WA5 .....15 C2
Booth's Rd Cl WA13 ....18 B1
Booth's Hill Ho **6** WA13 ..18 B2
Booth's Hill Rd WA13 ...18 B2
Booth's La WA13 ......18 A1
Boothbank La WA14 ....30 A3
Boothby St **8** SK11 ...112 B4
Boothfields WA16 ......57 B1
Booths La WA4 ....52 C3
Boothsdale CW6 ......122 B2
Border Rd CH60 ......41 A4
Border Way CH3 ......119 B1

**Borderbrook Sch (Higher
  Wych)** SY14 ....224 B2
**Borderbrook Sch (Talwrn
  Green)** SY14 ......222 C3
Borders Ind Pk The
  CH4 ....140 B4
Bordon St SK3 ......240 B3
Borough Arc SK14 ....241 D6
Borough Rd
  Altrincham WA15 ....238 E4
  Congleton CW12 .....156 C2
Borough St SK15 .....242 D1
Borras Rd LL13 ......196 A4
Borron Rd WA12 ....2 A3
Borrowdale Ave
  Gatley SK8 ....239 B4
  Warrington WA2 ......8 B2
Borrowdale Cl
  Crewe CW2 ....189 C2
  Frodsham WA6 ......74 B4
Borrowdale Rd WA8 ....22 B4
Borrowdale Terr SK15 ..242 D4
Borrowmore Est CH3 ...120 C4
Bosden Cl SK9 ....34 B3
Bosden Fold SK1 .....240 F4
Bosley Brook CW12 ...179 B3
Bosley Cl
  Middlewich CW10 ....151 B3
  Wilmslow SK9 ....34 B3
Bosley Dr SK12 ....37 A2
Bosley Rd SK3 ....240 A4
Bosley View CW12 ....157 A1
Bostock Gn CH65 ......69 C3
Bostock Hall CW10 ...127 B3
Bostock Rd
  Macclesfield SK11 ....111 C4
  Moulton CW7,CW10 ...127 B2
Bostock St WA5 ......15 C3
Boston Ave WA7 ......23 B1
Boston Bvd WA5 ......15 A4
Boston Cl Bramhall SK7 ..35 B4
  Culcheth WA3 ....4 C2
Boston St SK14 ....241 E6
Boswell Ave WA4 .....16 A1
Boteler Ave WA5 ......15 C4
Bottom St SK14 ......241 F7
Bottoms La CH4 ......237 C1
Boughey Rd ST7 .....209 C1
Boughton CH2 ....118 C3
Boughton Heath Prim Sch
  CH3 ....142 A1
Boughton Hill Ave CH3 ..119 A1
Boughton Hill Dr CH3 ...119 A1
Boughton Lodge **4**
  CH3 ....119 A1
Boulderstone Rd SK15 ..242 D4
Boulevard The
  Broughton CH4 ......139 A2
  Ellesmere Port CH65 ...69 C2
Boulting Ave WA5 ......7 C1
Boulton Cl CW11 .....175 B2
Boundary Ct SK8 .....239 C5
Boundary La
  Chester CH4 ....140 C3
  Congleton CW12 .....179 C1
  Heswall CH60 ....41 A4
  Peover WA16,SK11 ...108 C3
  Siddington SK11 .....132 C4
  Threapwood SY14 ...222 C4
Boundary La N CW8 ...101 C1
Boundary La S CW8 ...101 C1
Boundary Pk CH64 ....66 C4
Boundary Rd SK8 .....240 C4
Boundary St
  Northwich CW9 ......79 C1
  Warrington WA1 .....16 C4
Boundary Terr SK9 ....33 C3
Bourchier Way WA4 .....27 A4
Bourne Ave WA3 ....3 B4
Bourne Cl CW8 ......102 C4
Bourne Rd ST7 ......194 C3
Bourne St Mow Cop ST7 ..195 B4
  Stockport SK4 ......240 E8
  Wilmslow SK9 ....59 C3
Bournemouth Cl WA7 ...50 B3
Bournville Ave SK4 ....240 E6
Bouverie St CH2 .....237 A4
Boverton Cl WA5 ......7 C1
Bow Green Mews WA14 ..238 B2
Bow Green Rd WA14 ...238 A1
Bowla WA14 ....31 A4
Bow St SK3 ....240 C4
Bowden Cl
  Congleton CW12 .....156 C2
  Culcheth WA3 ....4 C2
  Warrington WA1 .....16 C4
Bowden Cres SK22 .....39 C4
Bowden Dr CW9 ......104 B4
Bowden View La WA16 ..29 C1
Bowdon CE Prim Sch
  WA14 ....238 C1
Bowdon Prep Sch
  WA14 ....238 C2
Bowdon Rd WA14 ....238 C1
Bowdon Rise WA14 ...238 D2
Bowdon St SK3 ......240 E4
Bowe's Gate Rd CW6 ...169 A1
Bowen Cl Bramhall SK7 ..35 C4
  Widnes WA8 ....12 B1
Bowen Cooke Ave CW1 ..190 A3
Bowen St CW2 ......190 A2
Bower Ave SK4 ......240 C6
Bower Cres WA4 ......26 C4
Bower Gr SK15 ......242 F2
Bower Rd
  Altrincham WA15 ....238 F1
  Heswall CH60 ....41 B4
Bower St WA8 ....13 B1

Bowerfield Ave SK7 36 B4
Bowerfield Cres SK7 36 C4
Bowerfold La SK4 240 D6
Bowers Bsns Pk WA8 23 A4
Bowery Ave SK8 34 C3
Bowfell Cl CH62 43 B2
Bowfell Dr SK6 37 C4
Bowker St SK14 241 E7
Bowkers Croft CW11 191 C4
Bowland Cl Runcorn WA7 49 C3
Warrington WA3 10 A3
Bowland Croft CW1 173 A1
Bowland Ct M33 242 B6
Bowland Rise CW7 149 A4
Bowles Cl CW11 175 A3
Bowling Green Ct
13 Nantwich CW5 204 C3
Northwich CW8 78 C1
Bowling Green St SK14 241 D6
Bowman Ave WA4 17 A3
Bowman Cres OL6 242 A3
Bowmans The SK10 87 A1
Bowmere Cl
Biddulph ST8 179 B1
Tarporley CW6 146 B1
Bowmere Dr CW7 149 B4
Bowmere Rd CW6 146 B1
Bowness Ave
Bebington CH63 43 B3
Irlam M44 11 B2
Warrington WA2 8 B1
Winsford CW7 126 B1
Bowness Cl CW4 130 A2
Bowness Ct CW12 156 A1
Bowness Rd CW2 189 B2
Bowood Ct WA2 8 A2
Bowring Dr CH64 41 A1
Bowyer Ave 4 CW5 204 C3
Box La CW12 155 C2
Box Tree Mews SK11 112 A4
Box Wlk M31 11 C2
Boxgrove Cl WA8 13 A2
Boxmoor Cl CH4 141 A3
Boydell Ave
Warrington WA4 17 A1
Warrington, Westy WA4 16 C2
Boydell Way CH4 162 A3
Boyle Ave WA2 8 C1
Boyles Hall Rd ST7 209 C1
Brabyns Ave SK6 241 D3
Bracadale Dr SK3 240 F1
Bracepeth Ct CH65 70 B2
Bracken Cl
Broughton CH4 139 B2
Macclesfield SK10 86 C1
Rode Heath ST7 193 C4
Warrington WA3 9 B3
Bracken Rd CH66 69 C2
Bracken Way
Barnton CW8 78 A2
Comberbach CW9 78 B4
Frodsham WA6 74 B3
Higher Wincham CW9 79 B2
Knutsford WA16 82 A4
Brackendale Elton CH2 72 A2
Runcorn WA7 49 B4
Brackenfield Way 12
CW7 149 A4
Brackenlea Pl SK3 240 D1
Brackenwood Cl CW2 206 A4
Brackenwood Dr SK8 239 E4
Brackenwood Mews
Warrington WA4 17 B1
Wilmslow SK9 60 C4
Brackley Ave M44 11 B3
Brackley St Runcorn WA7 22 C2
Warrington WA4 16 B1
Bradburn Rd M44 11 C4
Bradburns La CW8 103 A3
Bradbury Ave WA14 238 A5
Bradbury Gdns CW12 156 C1
Bradbury Rd CW7 127 A1
Bradbury St SK14 241 E5
Braddan Ave M33 242 C5
Braddon Cl CW9 103 C2
Bradeley Hall Rd CW1 191 A3
Bradeley Rd CW1 191 B2
Bradfield Rd CW1 190 A4
Bradford La SK10 85 B3
Bradford Rd CW7 126 C2
Bradford St CH4 141 B4
Bradgate Ave SK8 239 D1
Bradgate Rd WA14 238 A5
Brading Wlk M22 33 C4
Bradlegh Rd WA12 2 A1
Bradley Bvd WA5 15 A3
Bradley Cl
Altrincham WA15 238 E7
Middlewich CW10 151 A4
Bradley Farm La SY13 225 B4
Bradley Fold SK15 242 E2
Bradley Hall Cotts WA4 27 A3
Bradley La Frodsham WA6 74 B3
Newton-le-W WA5,WA12 2 A1
Bradley St SK11 112 C3
Bradley Way WA8 13 A1
Bradmoor Rd CH62 43 B4
Bradshaw Ave CH4 140 A4
Bradshaw Com Prim Sch
WA4 17 A1
Bradshaw Hall La
Cheadle SK8 34 C4
Gatley SK8 34 B4
Bradshaw Hall Prim Sch
SK8 239 E1
Bradshaw La Lymm WA13 19 B2
Warrington WA4 17 A2
Bradshaw Pl CW12 156 C1
Bradshaw St WA8 13 A1
Bradwall Rd CW11 175 A4
Bradwall St CW11 175 A4
Bradwell Cl CH65 70 A2
Bradwell Ct CW12 156 C1
Bradwell Dr SK8 34 B4
Bradwell Gr CW12 156 C2
Bradwell Rd Golborne WA3 3 C4
Hazel Grove SK7 36 C4
Bradwen Cl M34 241 A5
Braemar Ave CW9 104 B4
Braemar Cl
Holmes Chapel CW4 130 B1
Warrington WA2 9 A2
Wistaston CW2 205 C4
Braemar Ct CH65 70 C2
Braeside Cl
11 Ellesmere Port CH66 69 B3
Macclesfield SK11 112 C3
Braidwood Ave WA16 57 B2
Brains La CW6 169 A3
Braintree Rd M22 33 C4
Braithwaite Cl WA7 49 B3
Braithwaite Rd WA3 3 B4
Brake The ST7 195 A4
Brake Village ST7 195 A4
Brakeley Rd CW8 77 B2
Bramall Cl CW11 175 B4
Bramall St SK14 241 D8
Bramble Cl Chester CH3 142 A4
Macclesfield SK10 87 A1
Warrington WA5 14 C2
Winsford CW7 126 B2
Bramble Way WA7 49 C2
Brambles The
Haslington CW1 191 A2
Higher Wincham CW9 79 B2
Brambling Cl WA7 49 C3
Brambling Way WA3 3 C4
Bramhall Cl Sale M33 242 E5
Winsford CW7 126 A1
Bramhall Ctr The SK7 35 C3
Bramhall Dr
Bebington CH62 43 C2
Holmes Chapel CW4 130 A2
Bramhall High Sch SK7 35 C4
Bramhall La SK2,SK3 240 F1
Bramhall La S SK7 35 C4
Bramhall Rd CW2 189 C1
Bramhall St WA5 15 C3
Bramhall Sta SK7 35 C3
Bramhall Way SK11 112 A4
Bramhalls Pk CW9 104 B4
Bramley Cl Bramhall SK7 35 C3
Ellesmere Port CH66 94 C4
Wilmslow SK9 59 B2
Bramley Cres SK4 240 B5
Bramley Ct CW6 122 B3
Bramley Dr SK7 35 C3
Bramley Mews WA4 26 B4
Bramley Rd SK7 35 C3
Bramley Wlk WA6 73 A1
Brampton Ave SK10 87 A1
Brampton Ct WA9 1 A2
Bramshill Ct WA3 10 A3
Bramway Bramhall SK7 35 B4
High Lane SK6 37 C4
Brancaster Dr WA3 4 A4
Branch Way WA11 1 B3
Brancote Gdns CH62 43 B4
Branden Dr WA16 57 A1
Brandon WA8 12 A1
Brandon Ave SK8 239 B1
Brandon Cl SK9 34 B1
Brandwood Ave WA2 8 A1
Brandwood Ho 2 WA1 16 B3
Branfield Ave SK8 239 D1
Branksome Dr SK8 239 D1
Branksome Rd SK4 240 B5
Bransdale Cl WA5 14 C4
Bransdale Way SK11 111 C4
Brantfield Ct WA2 8 C1
Brantwood Rd
Cheadle SK8 239 F1
Stockport SK4 240 C8
Brassey St CH3 118 C1
Brassey Way CW5 205 B3
Brassey's Contract Rd
SY14 199 A1
Brathay Cl WA2 8 B2
Brattswood Dr ST7 194 A3
Bray Cl Cheadle SK8 239 E2
Crewe CW1 190 C3
Runcorn WA7 49 B3
Bray Rd CH4 140 C3
Braystan Gdns SK8 239 B6
Breach House La WA16 32 A1
Bread St SK11 112 B4
Breamar Cl CH3 119 B2
Breck Rd WA8 13 A1
Breck The CH66 69 C4
Brecon Ave SK8 239 E1
Brecon Cl SK12 36 C2
Brecon Ct WA5 7 C1
Brecon Dr 3 CH66 69 C1
Brecon Way CW2 206 A4
Breconway CW7 149 A4
Bredbury Gn SK6 241 A1
Bredon Cl CH66 69 A3
Breen Cl CH3 166 A1
Breezehill Cl CH64 66 C4
Breezehill Pk CH64 66 C4
Breezehill Rd CH64 66 C4
Brendon Ave WA2 8 A2
Brendon Gr WA9 1 A2
Brennus Pl CH1 237 A3
Brent Cl SK12 36 A2
Brent Rd SK4 240 C5
Brentfield WA8 12 B1
Brentnall Cl WA5 15 B3
Brentnall St 2 SK1 240 F3
Brenton Ave M33 242 A6
Brenton Ct 1 SK8 34 C4
Brentwood M33 242 A6
Brentwood Ave
Altrincham WA14 238 E7
Irlam M44 11 B3
Brentwood Cl SK15 242 F2
Brentwood Cres WA14 238 E6
Brentwood Dr SK8 239 B5
Brentwood Rd CH1 117 C3
Brentwood Specl Sch
WA14 238 E7
Brereton CE Prim Sch
CW11 153 C3
Brereton Cl
Altrincham WA14 238 C1
Crewe CW2 189 C1
Malpas SY14 213 A2
Runcorn WA7 50 A4
Sandbach CW11 175 B4
Brereton Ct
Brereton Green CW12 154 C3
Cheadle SK8 239 E1
Brereton Dr CW5 204 C4
Brereton Gr M44 11 C3
Brereton Heath La
CW11,CW12 154 C3
Brereton Heath Pk★
CW12 154 B4
Brereton La
Brereton Green CW10,
CW11 153 A4
Sproston Green CW4 152 C4
Brereton Rd
Handforth SK9 34 C2
Hartford CW8 103 A2
Breton Cl CH2 118 C3
Bretton Ct Mews CH4 139 C2
Bretton Dr CH4 139 A2
Bretton La CH4 139 C3
Bretton Rd CH4 139 C2
Bretton Wlk M22 33 B4
Brewery La CH3 180 C2
Brewery St
4 Altrincham WA14 238 D4
Stockport SK1 240 F7
Brian Ave Warrington WA2 16 B4
Warrington, Stockton Heath
WA4 16 C1
Briar Ave WA3 11 A1
Briar Cl WA16 57 A2
Briar Dr CH60 41 A4
Briar La CW8 102 C4
Briar Rd WA3 3 A4
Briardale Cl CW2 205 C4
Briardale Gdns 4 CH66 69 B3
Briardale Rd
Ellesmere Port CH66 69 B3
Willaston CH64 43 A1
Briardene M34 241 A8
Briarfield Ave WA8 12 A1
Briarfield Rd
Ellesmere Port CH65 70 A3
Heswall CH60 41 A4
Briarlands Cl SK7 35 B3
Briars Mount SK4 240 A6
Briarstead Cl SK7 35 B4
Briarswood ST7 195 A1
Briarswood Ct CH2 237 B3
Briarwood Runcorn WA7 50 A4
Wilmslow SK9 60 B4
Briarwood Ave
Macclesfield SK11 112 B3
Warrington WA1 16 C4
Brick Bank CW5 204 C3
Brick Bank La WA16,
CW4 107 A1
Brick Kiln La CW10 127 A4
Brick St Newton-le-W WA12 1 C2
Newton-le-W WA12 2 A2
Warrington WA1 16 B3
Brickfield Bsns Ctr CW9 79 B1
Brickfield La CH3 119 C1
Brickhill La WA15 32 A2
Brickhurst Way WA1 17 A4
Brickkiln La
Little Bollington WA14 20 B2
Whitchurch SY13 226 B1
Brickkiln Row WA14 238 C1
Bridge Ave WA4 16 C2
Bridge Ave E WA4 16 C3
Bridge Cl Audley ST7 209 C1
Cuddington CW8 102 A2
Lymm WA13 19 A2
Wistaston CW2 206 A4
Bridge Ct Chester CH2 119 A1
Holt LL13 196 C4
Neston CH64 66 C4
Bridge Dr Cheadle SK8 239 D4
Christleton CH3 142 B4
Handforth SK9 34 B2
Bridge End Dr SK10 87 A4
Bridge End La SK10 87 A4
Bridge Foot WA1 16 A2
Bridge Gn SK10 87 A4
Bridge Gr WA15 238 F7
Bridge Hall Prim Sch
SK3 240 D2
Bridge La
Cuddington CW8 101 C2
Frodsham WA6 49 B1
Warrington, Appleton WA4 26 C4
Warrington, Woolston WA1 17 B4
Bridge Mdw CH66 69 C1
Bridge Pl CH4 237 B1
Bridge Rd WA1 17 B4
Bridge Row CW12 156 C2
Bridge St Broughton CH4 140 B4
Chester CH1 237 B2
Golborne WA3 3 A4
Holt LL13 180 C1
Macclesfield SK11 112 B4
Neston CH64 66 C4
Newton-le-W WA12 2 A2
Northwich CW9 79 C1
Runcorn WA7 23 A2
Stalybridge SK15 242 C1
Stockport SK1 240 F6
Warrington WA1 16 A3
Whaley Bridge SK23 65 C4
Wybunbury CW5 220 A4
Bridge St Row E CH1 237 B2
Bridge St Row W CH1 237 B2
Bridge Terr CH3 119 A1
Bridge View Cl WA8 23 A2
Bridgedown CW6 146 B1
Bridgefield Ave SK9 34 B1
Bridgefield St SK1 240 E6
Bridgeman Rd CH1 117 C2
Bridgeman St WA5 15 B2
Bridgemere CE Prim Sch
CW5 231 C4
Bridgemere Cl CW11 174 C4
Bridgemere Garden World★
CW5 232 A2
Bridgemere La CW5 220 A1
Bridgemere Mews CW5 231 C4
Bridgemere Way 5
CW9 103 C2
Bridgend CH2 97 A1
Bridgend Cl WA8 12 B2
Bridges Rd CH65 70 C3
Bridgeside Dr WA6 73 A2
Bridgewater Ave WA4 16 C2
Bridgewater Cl
Cheadle SK8 34 B4
Congleton CW12 157 A1
Bridgewater Dr CH3 119 B1
Bridgewater Grange
WA7 50 C3
Bridgewater High Sch (Lower
Sch) WA4 26 B3
Bridgewater High Sch (Upper
Sch) WA4 26 B4
Bridgewater Mews WA4 26 B4
Bridgewater Rd WA14 238 D7
Bridgewater St
4 Lymm WA13 18 C2
Runcorn WA7 23 A1
Sale M33 242 B7
Bridgeway E WA7 24 B1
Bridgeway W WA7 24 B1
Bridgewood Dr CH66 69 B1
Bridgfield Cl SK6 37 C4
Bridgnorth Gr ST5 210 C1
Bridle Cl CH62 43 C4
Bridle Ct SK7 35 C1
Bridle Hey CW5 204 C1
Bridle Pk CH62 43 C4
Bridle Rd Bebington CH62 43 C3
Crewe CW2 190 A2
Woodford SK7,SK10 35 C1
Bridle Way
Ellesmere Port CH66 69 B2
Woodford SK7 36 A1
Bridlemere Ct WA1 16 C4
Briedden Way CH66 69 A3
Brien Ave WA14 238 E7
Brierley Prim Sch CW1 190 B2
Brierley Rd CW12 157 A1
Brierley St Crewe CW1 190 B2
Stalybridge SK16 242 A1
Briers Cl WA2 8 C2
Brieryhurst Rd ST7 195 A2
Briggs Ave CW2 190 B1
Bright St
Ashton-u-Lyne OL6 242 A2
Crewe CW1 190 A3
Brighton Cres SK11 113 A2
Brighton Gr
1 Hyde SK14 241 E5
Sale M33 242 B7
Brighton Rd SK4 240 C5
Brighton Road Ind Est
SK4 240 B5
Brighton St WA5 15 C3
Brights Ave 15 ST7 195 A1
Brightwell Cl WA5 14 C3
Brimelow Cres WA5 14 C2
Brimstage Cl CH60 41 B4
Brimstage Gn CH60 41 B4
Brimstage Rd CH60 41 B4
Brindley Ave Sale M33 242 C8
Warrington WA4 16 C2
Winsford CW7 126 B1
Brindley Cl
Kidsgrove ST7 194 C1
Talke ST7 210 B4
Brindley Gr SK9 34 C1
Brindley Hall Rd
Burland CW5 186 C1
Faddiley CW5 202 C4
Brindley La CW11 153 B2
Brindley Pk CW11 174 C2
Brindley Rd WA7 23 C2
Brindley St WA7 22 C2
Brindley Way
Congleton CW12 157 A1
Macclesfield SK11 112 B2
Brindley Wharf WA7 50 C3
Brindleys Way ST7 209 C1
Brine Leas High Sch
CW5 204 C2
Brine Pits La CW5 218 C1
Brine Pump Cotts CW9 78 C2
Brine Rd CW5 204 C2
Brinell Dr M44 11 C3
Brinksway SK3 240 C4
Brinksway Trad Est 1
SK3 240 C4
Brinley Cl CH62 43 B3
Brinton Cl WA8 22 C4
Brisbane Cl SK7 35 C3
Brisbane Rd CH1 117 B2
Bristol Ave WA7 50 C3
Bristol Cl Blacon CH1 117 C3
Cheadle SK8 34 B4
Bristol Dr 5 CH66 69 C1
Bristow Cl WA5 15 A4
Britannia Gdns WA6 73 A1
Britannia Rd Helsby WA6 73 A1
Sale M33 242 C7
Brittania Dr CW9 104 C4
Brixham Ave SK8 34 C4
Brixham Wlk SK7 35 C4
Broad Ct SK9 85 A4
Broad Hey SK6 241 D3
Broad La Altrincham WA15 32 A4
Appleton Thorn WA4 27 B4
Burtonwood WA5 6 C4
Haydock WA5,WA9 1 B1
Heswall CH60 40 B4
Sproston Green CW4 129 C1
Stapeley CW5 205 A1
Broad Oak Ave
Broughton CH4 139 A2
Haydock WA11 1 A3
Warrington WA5 14 C2
Broad Oak Com Prim Sch
WA9 1 A2
Broad Oak La M20 239 B8
Broad Oak Prim Sch
M20 239 C8
Broad Rd M33 242 D7
Broad St CW1 190 B3
Broad Street Inf Sch
CW1 190 B3
Broad Wlk SK9 59 C4
Broadacre CW9 78 B3
Broadacres CW5 217 C2
Broadbent Ave WA4 16 C2
Broadbent St SK14 241 D8
Broadcar Rd SK11 113 B3
Broadfield Cl M34 241 A6
Broadfields WA7 50 B4
Broadheath Prim Sch
WA14 238 C8
Broadheath Terr WA8 12 B1
Broadheys La WA16 28 B3
Broadhurst Ave
Culcheth WA3 4 C1
Warrington WA5 15 B2
Broadhurst La CW12 156 B2
Broadhurst St SK3 240 F3
Broadlake CH64 67 C4
Broadland Gdns CH66 69 C1
Broadland Rd CH66 69 C1
Broadleigh Way CW2 206 B4
Broadley Ave WA3 3 B4
Broadmead Chester CH3 119 B1
Heswall CH60 41 B4
Broadoak High Sch M31 11 C1
Broadoak La
High Legh WA16 29 B3
Mobberley WA16 57 C3
Broadoaks Rd M33 242 A6
Broadwalk SK10 87 A3
Broadway
Altrincham WA15 32 A4
Barnton CW8 78 A2
Cheadle SK8 239 C4
Sale M33 242 A7
Widnes WA8 12 A1
Wilmslow SK9 60 A3
Broadway Ave SK8 239 D5
Broadway E CH2 118 C3
Broadway The CW5 204 C3
Broadway W CH2 118 B3
Broadways CW3 230 A2
Broadwood Cl SK6 37 C4
Broady Ct CW2 190 B1
Brock Dr SK8 35 A4
Brock Gdns L24 21 C1
Brock Hollow CW11 174 C2
Brock Rd WA3 9 B2
Brock St SK10 87 B1
Brockhurst St CW9 104 A4
Brockhurst Way CW9 104 A3
Brocklebank Dr CW8 103 C4
Brocklehurst Ave SK10 87 C1
Brocklehurst Ct 9 SK10 87 B2
Brocklehurst Dr SK10 87 A4
Brocklehurst Manor
SK10 87 C1
Brocklehurst Way SK10 87 B2
Brockway E CH3 166 A1
Brockway W CH3 166 A1
Brockwell Cl 3 CW7 149 A4
Brodie Cl CH2 95 B1
Brogden Ave WA3 4 C2
Brogden Dr SK8 239 B5
Brogden Gr M33 242 A5
Brogden Terr M33 242 A5
Broken Banks 21 SK11 112 B4
Broken Cross CW9 111 C4
Broken Cross Com Sch
SK11 111 C4
Brokencross Pl CW9 104 C4

Bromborough Rake Sta
CH62 43 B4
Bromborough Sta CH63 43 B4
Bromborough Village Rd
CH62 43 C4
Bromleigh Ave SK8 239 B6
Bromley Ave WA3 3 B4
Bromley Cl Crewe CW1 189 C4
Heswall CH60 40 C4
Warrington WA2 8 C2
Bromley Dr CW4 130 B1
Bromley Rd
Congleton CW12 156 C2
Macclesfield SK10 111 C4
Brompton Gdns WA5 15 C4
Brompton Rd SK4 240 A6
Brompton Way
Ellesmere Port CH66 69 C1
Handforth SK9 34 B3
Bronington Ave CH62 43 B3
Bronte Cl WA2 8 A3
Brook Acre Com Prim Sch
WA2 8 C1
Brook Ave
Altrincham WA15 238 E6
Handforth SK9 34 B2
Shavington CW2 206 B3
Warrington, Stockton Heath
WA4 16 C1
Warrington, Westy WA4 16 C3
Brook Bank SK12 37 B1
Brook Bottom Rd SK22 39 A4
Brook Cl
Altrincham WA15 238 E6
Crewe CW1 190 C2
Cronton WA8 12 B3
Brook Ct Chester CH1 118 A2
Sandbach CW11 175 A3
Brook Dr Kelsall CW6 122 B2
Warrington WA5 15 A3
Brook End WA9 1 A1
Brook Farm Sch CW6 168 B4
Brook Fm Cl M31 11 C1
Brook Furlong WA6 48 C1
Brook Gdns ST8 179 B1
Brook Hey CH64 41 A1
Brook House Dr CW2 206 B4
Brook La
Alderley Edge SK9 59 C2
Altrincham WA15 238 F6
Astbury CW12 177 C3
Broughton CH5 139 B4
Burland CW5 203 B4
Chester CH2 118 C2
Faddiley CW5 202 C4
Knutsford WA16 57 A1
Neston CH64 41 B1
Northwich CW9 104 B4
Warrington WA3 18 A4
Brook Lodge SK8 239 D4
Brook Pl WA4 16 C2
Brook Rd Cheadle SK8 239 D6
Ellesmere Port CH66 69 B3
Lymm WA13 18 B2
Tarporley CW6 168 B4
Brook Side CW8 102 B4
Brook St Cheadle SK8 239 F6
Chester CH2 237 B3
Congleton CW12 156 C2
Crewe CW2 190 B2
Golborne WA3 3 A4
Hyde SK14 241 E7
Knutsford WA16 57 A1
Macclesfield SK11 112 C4
Neston CH64 66 C4
Northwich CW9 79 A1
Northwich, Lostock Gralam
CW9 79 C1
Runcorn WA7 23 A1
Sale M33 242 C7
Widnes WA8 13 A1
Brook Street Bridge
CH2 237 C4
Brook Terr CW11 175 A2
Brook View
Alderley Edge SK9 60 A2
Allostock WA16 106 C2
Brook Villas ST7 193 C2
Brook Way
Nantwich CW5 204 C2
Warrington WA5 15 A3
Brook Well CH64 66 C3
Brookash Rd M22 34 A4
Brookdale WA8 12 A2
Brookdale Ave
Denton M34 241 B6
Knutsford WA16 57 B1
Brookdale Ct CH3 143 B3
Brookdale Pk CW2 190 A2
Brookdale Pl CH1 237 B3
Brookdale Way CH3 143 A3
Brooke Ave CH2 118 C4
Brooke Dean Com Sch
SK9 34 B2
Brooke Dr SK9 34 B2
Brooke Ho SK10 86 C1
Brooke Way SK9 34 B2
Brookes Ave CH4 139 A2
Brookfield CW1 191 B3
Brookfield Ave
Altrincham WA15 238 F8
Poynton SK12 36 B2
Romiley SK6 241 A4
Runcorn WA7 23 C1
Brookfield Cl Lymm WA13 18 B2
Brookfield Cl *continued*
Tarporley CW6 168 B4
Brookfield Cres
Cheadle SK8 239 D4
Goostrey CW4 107 C1
Brookfield Ct CW1 190 A3
Brookfield Dr
Alsager ST7 193 B3
Chester CH2 118 C2
Holmes Chapel CW4 130 A2
Brookfield Gr OL6 242 A2
Brookfield Ho SK8 239 D4
Brookfield La SK11 112 C4
Brookfield Pk WA4 17 A1
Brookfield Rd
Cheadle SK8 239 E5
Comberbach CW9 78 B4
Culcheth WA3 4 B2
Lymm WA13 18 B2
Brookfield St WA12 2 A2
Brookfields Sch WA8 13 B1
Brookhead Dr SK8 240 A2
Brookhead Jun Sch
SK8 239 F5
Brookhouse Cl SK10 86 C1
Brookhouse La
Church Minshull CW1,
CW10 172 B4
Congleton CW12 157 B1
Duddon CH3 144 B3
Whitley WA4 52 A1
Brookhouse Rd
Alsager ST7 193 B2
5 Sandbach CW11 175 A3
Brookhurst Ave CH63 43 B3
Brookhurst Cl CH63 43 B3
Brookhurst Prim Sch
CH63 43 B3
Brookhurst Rd CH63 43 B3
Brookland Ave CW2 205 C4
Brookland Dr CW11 175 C3
Brookland La WA9 1 A1
Brookland St WA1 16 C4
Brooklands Ave SK11 112 A4
Brooklands Cres M33 242 B5
Brooklands Ct M33 242 B5
Brooklands Dr
Goostrey CW4 107 C1
Northwich CW9 104 A2
Brooklands Gdns CH64 41 B1
Brooklands Gr CW1 190 A3
Brooklands Mews SK11 112 A4
Brooklands Pl M33 242 A5
Brooklands Rd
Congleton CW12 155 C1
Neston CH64 41 B1
Brooklands Sta M33 242 A5
Brooklands Station App
M33 242 A5
Brookledge La SK10 62 C3
Brookln Pl SK8 239 D6
Brooklyn Cres SK8 239 D5
Brooklyn Dr
Ellesmere Port CH65 69 C3
Lymm WA13 18 C2
Brooklyn Rd SK8 239 D5
Brooklyn St CW2 190 B1
Brookmere Cl CW11 174 C4
Brooks Ave SK14 241 E5
Brooks Dr WA15 32 B4
Brooks La Bosley SK11 135 C1
Middlewich CW10 128 B1
Brooks Lane Ind Est
CW10 151 B4
Brooks St SK1 240 F3
Brookside Ashton CH3 121 C4
Chester CH3 142 A4
Cuddington CW8 101 C2
Kelsall CW6 122 B2
Kingsley WA6 75 B1
Warrington WA4 16 C2
Brookside Ave
Lymm WA13 18 B2
Poynton SK12 36 C2
Sutton Lane Ends SK11 112 C1
Warrington, Great Sankey
WA5 15 A2
Warrington, Stockton Heath
WA4 16 B1
Brookside Cl
Cheadle SK8 239 D4
Haydock WA11 1 A4
Brookside Cotts
7 Lymm WA13 18 B2
Sandbach CW11 176 A4
Brookside Ct SK10 87 A1
Brookside Gn CW2 206 B4
Brookside La SK6 37 C4
Brookside Mill SK11 112 C4
Brookside Miniature Rly*
SK12 36 C4
Brookside Prim Sch
Ellesmere Port CH66 69 B2
Ellesmere Port CH66 69 C2
High Lane SK6 37 C3
Brookside Rd
Congleton CW12 156 B2
Frodsham WA6 74 A4
Gatley SK8 239 A6
Brookside Terr CH2 237 C4
Brookside View WA11 1 A4
Brookside Way WA11 1 A3
Brookvale Ave N WA7 50 A3
Brookvale Ave S WA7 50 A3
Brookvale Cl WA5 6 C3
Brookvale Comp Sch
WA7 50 B3
Brookvale Prim Sch WA7 50 A3
Brookway WA15 238 F7
Brookway La WA9 1 A1
Brookwood Cl WA4 26 A4
Broom Ave WA4 26 C3
Broom Cres CH3 121 A1
Broom La WA16 81 C1
Broom Rd
Altrincham WA15 238 E3
Partington M31 11 C1
Broom St CW1 190 A3
Broom's La CW6 122 B3
Broome Ct WA7 50 A3
Broomehouse Ave M44 11 C4
Broomfield Cl
Chelford SK11 84 A2
Wilmslow SK9 60 C4
14 Winsford CW7 149 A4
Broomfield La WA15 238 E3
Broomfield Rd SK4 240 C8
Broomfields Jun Sch
WA4 26 C4
Broomfields Rd WA4 26 B4
Broomgrove La M34 241 A8
Broomheath La CH3 144 B4
Broomhill La
Brown Knowl CH3 199 B4
Great Barrow CH3 120 C4
Broomlands CH60 40 C4
Broomlands Cotts CW5 219 C1
Broomsfield La CW8 78 A2
Broomville Ave M33 242 B6
Broseley Ave WA3 4 B2
Broseley La WA3 4 B3
Brotherton Cl CH62 43 B4
Brotherton Way WA12 2 A2
Brough St W SK11 112 B4
Broughton Ave WA3 3 B4
Broughton Cl WA4 26 C4
Broughton Cres SY14 211 A1
Broughton Hall Rd CH4 139 B2
Broughton Inf Sch CH4 139 B2
Broughton Jun Sch
CH4 139 B2
Broughton La CW2 189 C1
Broughton Mills Rd
CH4 139 C3
Broughton Rd
Adlington SK10 62 B3
Crewe CW1 190 B4
Stockport SK5 240 F8
Broughton Ret Pk CH4 139 C2
Broughton Way WA8 22 A3
Broughville Dr M20 239 C8
Brow Com Prim Sch The
WA7 23 C1
Brow La Antrobus CW9 53 B3
Heswall CH60 40 C4
Brow The WA6 75 B1
Browmere Dr WA3 9 A4
Brown Ave
Lawton-gate ST7 194 A3
Nantwich CW5 204 C2
Brown Heath Rd CH3 143 A3
Brown La SK8 239 B1
Brown Lees Cl CW2 190 A1
Brown Lees Rd ST7 195 C2
Brown St
2 Alderley Edge SK9 60 A1
Altrincham WA14 238 D3
Congleton CW12 156 C2
Macclesfield SK11 112 B4
1 Stockport SK1 240 E6
Widnes WA8 23 B4
Brown's La Chester CH4 141 B4
Wilmslow SK9 60 C4
Brownhill Dr WA1 16 C4
Brownhills Rd CW6 147 B3
Browning Ave WA8 22 C4
Browning Cl Blacon CH1 117 C3
10 Sandbach CW11 174 B3
Browning Dr
Ellesmere Port CH65 69 C2
Winwick WA2 8 A3
Browning Gn CH65 69 C2
Browning Gr ST7 210 B4
Browning St CW1 190 B2
Browning Way CW7 149 A4
Brownlow Cl SK12 36 C1
Broxton Ave CW10 151 B3
Broxton Cl WA8 12 B2
Broxton Rd Clutton CH3 182 B1
Ellesmere Port CH66 69 C3
Bruce Ave WA2 8 B1
Bruce Cres CH63 43 B3
Bruce Dr CH66 69 B2
Bruche Ave WA1 16 C4
Bruche Com Inf Sch
WA1 17 A4
Bruche Com Jun Sch
WA1 17 A4
Bruche Dr WA1 16 C4
Bruche Heath Gdns WA1 17 A4
Bruen The CH3 121 B2
Bruera Rd CH65 69 C2
Brunel Ct CW9 104 C3
Brunel Rd SK11 112 B2
Brunner Bsns Ctr CW8 78 B1
Brunner Gr CW5 205 A3
Brunner Rd WA8 23 A4
Brunsborough Cl CH62 43 B3
Brunswick Cres CH66 69 C2
Brunswick Ct 3 SK11 112 B4
Brunswick Hill SK11 112 B4
Brunswick Rd
Altrincham WA14 238 D7
Newton-le-W WA12 1 C2
Brunswick St
Congleton CW12 156 C2
Brunswick St *continued*
35 Macclesfield SK11 112 B4
St Helens WA9 1 A2
Brunswick Terr SK11 112 B4
Bruntleigh Ave WA4 17 A2
Bruntwood Ave SK8 239 A1
Bruntwood La SK8 239 E2
Bruntwood Prim Sch
SK8 239 E2
Brussels Rd SK3 240 D2
Bryant Ave WA4 16 C3
Bryce St SK14 241 D8
Brymau Five Est CH4 140 B4
Brymau Four Est CH4 140 B4
Brymau One Est CH4 140 C4
Brymau Three Est CH4 140 B4
Brymau Two Est CH4 140 C4
Brynlow Dr CW10 151 A4
Brynmore Dr SK11 112 C4
Brynn St WA8 23 A4
Brynton Cl SK10 87 B1
Brynton Rd SK10 87 B1
Buchan Cl WA5 15 A4
Buchan Gr CW2 190 A2
Buck La CW2 206 C2
Buckbean Way CW4 107 C1
Buckden Way SK11 112 B4
Buckfast Ave WA11 2 A4
Buckfast Cl Bramhall SK8 35 A3
Macclesfield SK10 87 B1
Poynton SK12 36 B3
Warrington WA5 14 C2
Buckfast Ct WA7 24 C2
Buckfast Way CW10 128 A1
Buckingham Ave
Chester CH3 119 A1
Denton M34 241 B6
Widnes WA8 13 A2
Buckingham Cl CW2 205 C4
Buckingham Dr
Davenham CW9 103 C2
Knutsford WA16 57 A1
Warrington WA5 15 B2
Winsford CW7 149 B4
Buckingham Rd
1 Ellesmere Port CH65 70 B1
Irlam M44 11 B3
Poynton SK12 36 B2
Stalybridge SK15 242 D3
Wilmslow SK9 59 C3
Buckingham Rd W SK4 240 A8
Buckingham Way SK2 240 F2
Buckland Cl WA8 22 B4
Buckley Ave CW10 128 C4
Buckley Cl CW10 151 A4
Buckley Dr SK6 241 A1
Buckley St
Macclesfield SK11 112 B4
Warrington WA2 16 A3
Bucklow Ave
Mobberley WA16 58 A2
Partington M31 11 C2
Bucklow Gdns WA13 19 A2
Bucklow View WA14 238 A3
Bucklow Wlk 11 SK11 112 C4
Bucklowhill La WA16 30 A2
Buckton St WA1 16 B4
Bude Cl Alsager ST7 193 A2
Bramhall SK7 35 C4
Crewe CW1 190 A4
Bude Rd WA8 12 C1
Budworth Ave
Warrington WA4 16 C2
Widnes WA8 12 B1
Budworth Cl Runcorn WA7 49 B4
Sandbach CW11 174 C4
Budworth Heath La CW9 54 B1
Budworth La CW9 78 C4
Budworth Rd
Bate Heath CW9 54 C1
Ellesmere Port CH66 69 C1
Sale M33 242 E5
Tabley WA16 55 B1
Budworth Wlk 1 SK9 34 C1
Buerton Prim Sch CW3 230 C2
Buffs La CH60 41 A4
Buggen La CH64 66 B4
Buglawton Hall Specl Sch
CW12 157 B3
Buglawton Ind Est
CW12 156 C2
Buglawton Prim Sch
CW12 157 A2
Buildwas Rd CH64 41 C1
Bulkeley Hall La SY14 200 B4
Bulkeley Rd Cheadle SK8 239 E6
Handforth SK9 34 B2
Poynton SK12 36 C2
Bulkeley St Chester CH3 119 A1
Stockport SK3 240 D4
Bull Hill CH64 66 C3
Bull Hill La SK10 88 B1
Bull Ring CW9 103 C4
Bull Ring The CW10 128 B1
Bullcroft Cl SY14 211 B4
Bullock St SK2 240 F3
Bullocks House Rd ST7 195 C2
Bullocks La SK11 112 C2
Bumper's La CH1 117 C1
Bunbury Cl
Middlewich CW10 151 B3
Northwich CW9 104 A3
Stoak CH2 96 A4
Bunbury Dr WA7 49 B3
Bunbury Gn CH65 70 B1
Bunbury La CW6 185 C4
Bunbury Rd CW6 169 B2
Bunce La SK11 133 A2
Bunce St CH4 237 A1
Bungalow Rd WA12 2 C1
Bungalows The CH63 42 A3
Bunham Cl ST7 193 B2
Bunkershill Rd SK6 241 B1
Bunting Cl 5 WA3 3 C4
Buntingford Rd WA4 17 B2
Bunts La CW12 156 C1
Burdett Rd 1 CH66 69 C1
Burfield Dr WA4 26 B4
Burford Ave SK7 35 B3
Burford Cl SK9 59 C3
Burford Cres SK9 59 C3
Burford La WA13 19 B1
Burgamot La CW9 78 B4
Burganey Ct CH4 162 B1
Burges St CH2 118 C2
Burgess Ave WA4 16 A1
Burgess Cl CW5 205 A2
Burgess Dr CH1 117 A3
Burgess La WA6 101 A3
Burgess Pl 18 CW8 103 C4
Burgess St SK10 112 C4
Burghley Cl SK15 242 D2
Burjen Way CW1 190 A3
Burkhardt Dr WA12 2 C2
Burkitt St SK14 241 E6
Burland Cl WA7 22 C1
Burland Gr CW7 126 A1
Burland Rd Halewood L26 21 A3
Newcastle-u-L ST5 210 B1
Burlea Cl CW2 189 C3
Burlea Dr CW2 206 A3
Burlescombe Cl WA14 238 B6
Burley Ct SK4 240 C6
Burley La WA4 27 B2
Burleyhurst La SK9,WA16 59 A4
Burlington Ct WA14 238 D5
Burlington Rd WA14 238 D5
Burnell Cl CW5 204 C2
Burnell Rd CH65 70 C2
Burnet Cl WA2 9 B1
Burnfell WA3 3 C4
Burnham Cl Cheadle SK8 239 F2
Culcheth WA3 4 C2
Warrington WA5 14 C3
Widnes WA8 12 B2
Burnham Rd CH4 140 C3
Burns Ave SK8 239 F6
Burns Cl
Ellesmere Port CH66 69 C2
Rode Heath ST7 193 C4
Burns Cres WA8 22 C4
Burns Dr CW1 190 C2
Burns Gr WA2 8 B1
Burns Rd CW12 157 A1
Burns Way CH1 117 C3
Burnsall Ave WA3 3 C4
Burnsall Dr WA8 12 B2
Burnside WA15 32 B4
Burnside Ave WA4 16 B1
Burnside Cl SK9 60 B3
Burnside Rd SK8 239 B5
Burnt Acre SK11 84 A2
Burnwood Gr ST7 195 A1
Burran Rd M22 33 B4
Burrough Cl WA3 9 C2
Burrows Hill CW8 103 A4
Burrows La WA6 73 C1
Burrows St WA11 1 A3
Burrows The CW8 101 B3
Bursar Cl WA12 2 B2
Burslam St CW12 156 C1
Burton Ave CW6 146 B2
Burton Cl Culcheth WA3 4 C2
Widnes WA8 12 C2
Burton Dr SK12 36 B2
Burton Gn CH66 69 B2
Burton Gr CW1 173 A1
Burton Hall Rd LL12 161 C1
Burton La CW6 144 C3
Burton Manor Coll CH64 67 B1
Burton Rd Blacon CH1 117 C3
Neston CH64 66 C3
Warrington WA2 8 B1
Burton St SK4 240 E7
Burtonwood Com Prim Sch
WA5 6 C4
Burtonwood Ind Ctr WA5 6 C4
Burtonwood Rd WA5 7 A1
Burtonwood Service Area
WA5 7 A2
Burwardsley Rd CH3 166 B1
Burwardsley Way CW9 103 C2
Bury St SK5 240 F7
Bush Rd Christleton CH3 142 C4
Widnes WA8 22 C3
Bush Way CH60 40 B4
Bushell Cl CH64 66 C4
Bushell Rd CH64 66 C4
Bushells La WA6 99 A4
Butler Way CW5 204 C2
Butley Cl
Macclesfield SK10 87 B2
Middlewich CW10 151 B4
Butley Lanes SK10 61 C1
Butterbache Rd CH3 142 A3
Butterbur Cl CH3 142 A3
Buttercup Dr SK3 240 D1
Buttermarket St WA1 16 A3
Buttermere Ave
Ellesmere Port CH65 70 B2
Warrington WA2 8 B2
Buttermere Cl WA6 74 B4
Buttermere Cres WA2 8 B2
Buttermere Ct CW12 156 A1
Buttermere Dr
Alderley Edge SK9 83 C4

But – Ced 251

Buttermere Dr *continued*
Altrincham WA15 .32 B3
Crewe CW1 .173 A1
Buttermere Gr WA7 .49 B3
Buttermere Rd
Gatley SK8 .239 B3
Partington M31 .11 C2
Winsford CW7 .126 B1
Buttermere Terr SK15 .242 D3
Butterton La CW1 .192 B1
Button Field CW8 .126 A4
Butts The Alsager ST7 .193 B2
Runcorn WA7 .23 C1
Buxton Ave CW1 .190 C2
Buxton Cl WA5 .15 A4
Buxton New Rd
Macclesfield Forest SK11 .114 B4
Rainow SK10 .88 B1
Buxton Old Rd
Congleton CW12 .157 A2
Disley SK12 .38 C2
Macclesfield SK11 .113 B4
Buxton Rd
Congleton CW12 .157 B3
Disley SK12 .38 C3
Hazel Grove SK7 .37 A4
High Lane SK12,SK6,SK7 .37 B4
Macclesfield SK10,SK11 .112 C4
New Mills SK22,SK23 .39 B2
Whaley Bridge SK23 .39 C1
Whaley Bridge, New Horwich SK23 .65 C3
Buxton Rd W SK12 .38 A3
Buxton St SK8 .239 A5
Bye Pass Rd CH3 .121 A2
Bye Pass The CH3 .119 C1
Byland Ave SK8 .35 A3
Byland Cl WA8 .13 B3
Bylands Cl SK12 .36 B2
Byley La Cranage CW10 .129 B3
Middlewich CW10 .128 C2
Byley Prim Sch CW10 .129 A4
Byley Way CW7 .126 A1
Byng Ave M44 .11 B2
Byrom St WA14 .238 D3
Byron Cl Blacon CH1 .117 C3
Crewe CW1 .190 C2
Middlewich CW10 .151 B3
Rode Heath ST7 .193 C4
Sandbach CW11 .174 B3
Byron Ct
Altrincham WA14 .238 D6
Warrington WA2 .8 B1
Byron Dr SK8 .239 F6
Byron St WA7 .23 A1
Byron Way CW2 .190 A1
Byron's La SK11 .112 C3
Byrons St SK11 .112 B3
Bythom Cl CH3 .142 C4

C

Cabot Cl WA5 .7 B1
Cabot Pl SK5 .240 F8
Cabul Cl WA2 .16 B4
Cadishead Prim Sch M44 11 C3
Cadnant Cl CH1 .117 B2
Cadnant Ct CH4 .139 B3
Cadshaw Cl WA3 .9 B3
Caer Castell LL13 .196 B4
Caerleon Cl CW7 .149 A4
Caerllew LL13 .180 C1
Caernarvon Ave CW7 .149 A4
Caernarvon Cl WA7 .23 C1
Caernarvon Ct 4 CH65 .70 B1
Caernarvon Rd CW2 .205 C4
Caesars Cl WA7 .23 C1
Cairns Cres CH1 .117 B2
Cairo St WA1 .16 A3
Caister Way CW7 .149 B4
Caithness Ct WA7 .23 A1
Calamine St SK11 .112 C3
Calcutta Rd SK3 .240 C3
Calday Gr WA11 .1 A4
Caldbeck Ave Sale M33 .242 E7
Warrington WA2 .8 B1
Caldene Terr SK23 .65 C4
Calder Ave CW1 .191 A3
Calder Cl Bollington SK10 .87 C4
Poynton SK12 .36 B1
Widnes WA8 .13 C2
Calder Way 7 CH66 .69 B3
Calderfield Cl WA4 .26 A4
Caldicott Ave CH62 .43 B4
Caldicott Cl 4 CW7 .149 B4
Caldwell Ave WA5 .7 C1
Caldwell Cl CW5 .205 A2
Caldwell Rd WA8 .23 A4
Caldwell's Gate La CW9 .54 A4
Caldy Cl CH2 .118 B3
Caldy Dr CH66 .69 B2
Caldy Rd Alsager ST7 .193 B2
Handforth SK9 .34 B2
Caldy Valley Rd CH3 .142 A4
Caldy Way CW7 .126 A1
Cale Gn SK2 .240 F2
Cale Green Prim Sch SK3 .240 F2
Cale St SK2 .240 F2
California Cl WA5 .15 B4
Calland Ave SK14 .241 F7
Callands Prim Sch WA5 .7 C1
Callands Rd WA5 .7 B1
Calmington La WA7 .24 C2
Calrofold Dr ST5 .210 B1
Calrofold La SK10 .88 B1
Calstock Cl WA5 .14 C2
Calveley Ave CH62 .43 C2
Calveley Cl CW9 .103 C3
Calveley Green La CW6, CW7 .170 B2
Calveley Hall La CW5, CW6 .170 A1
Calveley Rd Halewood L26 21 A3
Macclesfield SK10 .86 C1
Calveley Sch CW6 .170 A1
Calveley Way CW7 .126 A1
Calver Rd WA2 .8 A2
Calver Wlk SK8 .239 E1
Calverley Cl SK9 .60 B4
Calverly Cl WA7 .50 B3
Calverly Rd SK8 .240 A1
Calvers WA7 .23 C1
Camberley Cl SK7 .36 A4
Camberwell Park Rd WA8 .13 B2
Camborne Ave SK10 .111 C4
Camborne Cl WA7 .50 B3
Cambourne Cl CW12 .178 C4
Cambourne Rd WA5 .6 C3
Cambrai Ave WA4 .16 B1
Cambrian Ave CH3 .119 A1
Cambrian Cl CH66 .69 A3
Cambrian Rd SK3 .240 C4
Cambrian Villas CH3 .165 B1
Cambrian Way CW7 .149 A4
Cambridge Ave
Macclesfield SK11 .112 A4
Wilmslow SK9 .59 C4
Winsford CW7 .126 A1
Cambridge Cl
Biddulph ST8 .179 B1
Warrington WA4 .26 A4
Cambridge Gdns
Helsby WA6 .73 B2
Warrington WA4 .26 B3
Cambridge Rd
Altrincham WA15 .238 E2
Bebington CH62 .43 C4
Chester CH2 .118 C3
Ellesmere Port CH65 .70 B3
Gatley SK8 .239 B5
Macclesfield SK11 .112 A4
Cambridge Road Com Prim Sch CH65 .70 B3
Cambridge St
Runcorn WA7 .23 B1
Stalybridge SK15 .242 D2
Widnes WA8 .23 A4
Camden Ct WA7 .24 B1
Camden Rd CH65 .70 A3
Camden St CW1 .190 B2
Camellia Gdns WA9 .6 A4
Camelot Cl WA12 .1 C2
Camelot Gr CW2 .206 B2
Camelot Way WA7 .50 A4
Cameron Ave
Runcorn WA7 .48 C4
Shavington CW2 .206 A2
Cameron Ct WA2 .8 A2
Cameron Rd WA8 .23 A4
Camm St CW2 .190 B1
Camomile Wlk 12 M31 .11 C2
Campbell Ave WA7 .49 A4
Campbell Cl
Congleton CW12 .157 A2
Haslington CW1 .191 B2
Macclesfield SK10 .87 A1
Northwich CW9 .103 C2
Campbell Cres WA5 .14 C3
Campden Way SK9 .34 B2
Campion Cl
Huntington CH3 .142 A3
Warrington WA3 .9 B3
Campsey Ash WA8 .12 C2
Camrose Cl WA7 .49 B3
Camsley La WA13 .18 A2
Canaan WA3 .4 B4
Canada Cl WA2 .9 A1
Canadian Ave CH2 .119 A2
Canal Bank WA13 .18 B2
Canal Bridge Ent Pk CH65 .70 B3
Canal Cotts CW5 .187 B3
Canal Ct Trad Est CH65 .70 B4
Canal Rd
Altrincham WA14 .238 E8
Congleton CW12 .156 C1
Canal Reach WA7 .24 B1
Canal Side Barnton CW8 .78 A1
Chester CH2 .237 C3
Macclesfield SK11 .112 C4
Moore WA4 .25 B3
Preston on the Hill WA4 .50 C3
Runcorn WA7 .48 B4
Warrington WA4 .17 B1
Whaley Bridge SK23 .39 C1
Canal Side Cotts WA7 .50 C3
Canal St Chester CH1 .237 A3
Congleton CW12 .156 C1
Dukinfield SK14 .241 C7
Macclesfield SK11 .112 C4
Newton-le-W WA12 .1 C2
Runcorn WA7 .23 A1
Stalybridge SK15 .242 D1
Stockport SK1 .240 F4
Whaley Bridge SK23 .65 C4
Canal Terr CW10 .151 B4
Canalside CH65 .70 B3
Canberra Ave WA2 .8 B2
Canberra Rd SK7 .35 C3
Canberra Sq WA2 .8 B1
Canberra Way CH1 .117 B2
Candelan Way WA16 .29 B2
Candle La CW3 .232 A1
Candleston Cl WA5 .7 C1
Candy La SK10 .62 B4
Canford Cl Crewe CW1 .190 A4
Warrington WA5 .15 B3
Canley Cl 7 SK1 .240 F4
Cann La CW9 .55 A3
Cann La N WA4 .26 C3
Cann La S WA4 .26 C2
Cannell Ct WA7 .50 A3
Cannell St WA5 .15 B2
Canning St Chester CH1 .237 A3
7 Stockport SK4 .240 E6
Canniswood Rd WA11 .1 A3
Cannock Cl CH66 .94 C4
Cannock Dr SK4 .240 A6
Cannon St CH65 .70 A3
Cannon Way CH4 .161 A4
Canon Dr WA14 .238 B1
Canon St WA7 .22 C2
Canon Wilson Cl WA11 .1 B3
Canons Rd WA5 .15 B3
Canterbury Cl CH66 .94 C4
Canterbury Ct 2 SK10 .112 C4
Canterbury Rd
Blacon CH1 .117 C3
Widnes WA8 .22 B4
Canterbury St WA4 .16 B2
Cantley Cl WA7 .49 B3
Canton Pl CW8 .103 B4
Canton St SK11 .112 B3
Canton Wlks SK11 .112 B3
Canute Pl WA16 .57 A1
Capeland Cl CH4 .140 C3
Capenhurst Ave
Crewe CW2 .190 A2
Warrington WA2 .9 A1
Capenhurst CE Prim Sch CH1 .94 A4
Capenhurst Cl SK12 .36 C2
Capenhurst Gdns CH66 .69 B1
Capenhurst Grange Sch CH66 .69 C1
Capenhurst La
Capenhurst CH1 .94 A4
Ellesmere Port CH65 .70 A2
Capenhurst Sta CH1 .69 B1
Capesthorne Cl
Alsager ST7 .193 B2
Davenham CW9 .103 C2
Hazel Grove SK7 .36 C4
Holmes Chapel CW4 .130 A2
Sandbach CW11 .175 B4
Widnes WA8 .22 C4
Capesthorne Hall* SK11 .110 A3
Capesthorne Rd
Crewe CW2 .189 C2
Hazel Grove SK7 .36 C4
High Lane SK6 .37 C4
Warrington WA2 .8 B1
Waverton CH3 .143 A3
Wilmslow SK9 .59 C3
Capesthorne Way 16 SK11 .112 C4
Capitol Wlk CW12 .156 B1
Capper Cl ST7 .195 A1
Capper's La CW5,CW6 .186 B2
Cappers La CW11 .176 B1
Carden Cl WA3 .9 B2
Cardenbrook Gr 4 SK9 .34 B1
Cardeston Cl WA7 .49 C2
Cardiff Cl CH66 .94 C4
Cardigan Cl
Macclesfield SK11 .112 A4
Warrington WA5 .7 B1
Carey St WA8 .13 A1
Carisbrook Ave SK10 .87 C1
Carisbrook Dr CW7 .149 B4
Carisbrooke Cl CW2 .205 C4
Carleton Rd SK12 .37 B2
Carlett Bvd CH62 .43 C3
Carlile St SK3 .240 E4
Carlingford Cl SK3 .240 E1
Carlingford Rd WA4 .26 A4
Carlisle Cl
Macclesfield SK11 .111 C3
Mobberley WA16 .58 A2
Romiley SK6 .241 A1
Winsford CW7 .126 A1
Carlisle Dr WA14 .238 E8
Carlisle Rd CH1 .117 C3
Carlisle St
9 Alderley Edge SK9 .60 A1
Crewe CW2 .190 A1
Warrington WA4 .26 B4
Carlow Cl L24 .21 B1
Carlton Ave Bramhall SK7 .35 B3
Broughton CH4 .140 B3
Cheadle SK8 .239 F3
Handforth SK9 .34 B1
Romiley SK6 .241 D2
Runcorn WA7 .23 B1
Carlton Cl
Mickle Trafford CH2 .119 C4
Neston CH64 .41 B1
Carlton Cres CH66 .69 C4
Carlton Dr SK8 .239 A6
Carlton Pl CH2 .119 A2
Carlton Rd Lymm WA13 .19 A3
Northwich CW9 .104 A4
Sale M33 .242 A8
Stockport SK4 .240 A6
Carlton St
Warrington WA4 .26 B4
Widnes WA8 .23 A4
Carlton Way M44 .11 B3
Carlyle Cl ST7 .193 C4
Carlyle Cres CH66 .69 C2
Carlyn Ave M33 .242 D6
Carmarthen Cl
Warrington WA5 .7 B1
5 Winsford CW7 .149 B4
Carmel Cl CH1 .117 B2
Carmel Ct WA8 .13 A2
Carmenna Dr SK7 .35 C4
Carmichael Cl M31 .11 C2
Carmichael St SK3 .240 D4
Carnegie Cl SK10 .87 A1
Carnforth Dr M33 .242 A5
Carnoustie Cl
Wilmslow SK9 .60 B4
Winsford CW7 .126 A1
Carnoustie Dr
Gatley SK8 .239 C1
Macclesfield SK10 .87 B3
Carnoustie Gr WA11 .1 A3
Carol Dr CH60 .41 B4
Carol St WA4 .16 B2
Caroline St Irlam M44 .11 C4
Stalybridge SK15 .242 D1
Stockport SK3 .240 D3
Widnes WA8 .23 A4
Carpenter Gr WA2 .9 A1
Carr Brow SK6 .38 A4
Carr La Alderley Edge SK9 .59 B1
Audley ST7 .209 A1
Golborne WN7 .4 C4
Hale L24,WA8 .21 C2
Carr Mill Mews SK9 .34 A1
Carr St ST7 .195 C1
Carr Wood Ave SK7 .35 C4
Carrgate Rd M34 .241 B5
Carrgreen La WA13 .19 C3
Carriage Dr Biddulph ST8 179 C1
Frodsham WA6 .74 A3
Carriages The WA14 .238 C4
Carrick Dr CH65 .70 A1
Carrick Rd CH4 .141 A4
Carrington Cl WA3 .9 B2
Carrington Way CW1 .190 A4
Carroll Dr CW2 .205 C4
Carrs Ave SK8 .240 A2
Carrs Ct SK9 .60 A4
Carrs La CH3 .166 C1
Carrs Rd SK8 .239 F6
Carrwood
Altrincham WA15 .32 A4
Knutsford WA16 .57 B1
Carrwood Cl WA11 .1 A3
Carrwood Rd SK9 .59 C4
Carsdale Rd M22 .33 C4
Carter Ave CW6 .122 B2
Carter La SK11 .84 A2
Carter St Chester CH2 .237 C3
Stalybridge SK15 .242 E2
Cartier Cl WA5 .15 B4
Cartlake Cl CW5 .204 B3
Cartledge Cl CW8 .102 A2
Cartmel Ave WA2 .8 B2
Cartmel Cl Gatley SK8 .239 C3
Holmes Chapel CW4 .130 A2
Macclesfield SK10 .87 A1
Warrington WA5 .7 C1
Winsford CW7 .126 B1
Cartmel Dr CH66 .69 C1
Cartmell Cl WA7 .49 A3
Cartridge La WA4 .27 C3
Cartwright Rd CW1 .191 B3
Cartwright St
Runcorn WA7 .23 B1
Warrington WA5 .15 C3
Carver Ave CW4 .130 A3
Carver Cl CW7 .127 A2
Carver Rd WA15 .238 E2
Case Rd WA11 .1 B3
Casey La CW2 .206 C2
Cashmere Rd SK3 .240 C3
Caspian Rd WA14 .238 A6
Cassia Green La CW7 .125 B3
Cassley Rd L24 .21 A2
Casson St CW1 .190 A3
Castle Bank CW8 .103 C4
Castle Cl Broughton CH4 .139 A3
Kelsall CW6 .122 B2
Pulford CH4 .162 B1
Castle Croft Rd CH4 .141 A3
Castle Ct Holt LL13 .196 C4
Northwich CW8 .103 C4
Castle Dr Chester CH4 .237 B1
Ellesmere Port CH65 .70 A2
Heswall CH60 .40 C4
Castle Gn WA5 .7 A1
Castle Hall Cl SK15 .242 E1
Castle Hall Ct SK15 .242 D1
Castle Hall View SK15 .242 D1
Castle Hill
Newton-le-W WA12 .2 C2
Prestbury SK10 .86 C3
Pulford CH4 .162 B1
Castle Hill Ct SK10 .86 C4
Castle Hill Farm 16 CW8 .103 C4
Castle Inn Rd CW12 .179 B4
Castle Mews LL13 .196 C4
Castle Mill La WA15 .32 A3
Castle Prim Sch ST7 .195 B3
Castle Rd Kidsgrove ST7 .195 B4
Runcorn WA7 .49 C4
Castle Rise
Prestbury SK10 .86 C3
Runcorn WA7 .23 B1
Castle St Chester CH4 .237 B1
Crewe CW1 .190 B2
Holt LL13 .196 B4
Hyde SK14 .241 F7
Macclesfield SK11 .112 B4
Castle St *continued*
9 Nantwich CW5 .204 C3
Northwich CW8 .103 C4
Stalybridge SK15 .242 D1
Stockport SK3 .240 D3
Widnes WA8 .13 B1
Castle St Mall 32 SK11 .112 B4
Castle View Prim Sch WA7 .49 B4
Castle Way CH4 .162 A3
Castle Yd SK1 .240 F6
Castlefields CH3 .166 B2
Castlefields Ave E WA7 .24 A1
Castlefields Ave N WA7 .23 C1
Castlefields Ave S WA7 .24 A1
Castleford Dr SK10 .86 C3
Castlegate SK10 .86 C3
Castlegate Mews SK10 .86 C3
Castlemead Wlk CW9 .103 C2
Castlemere Cl CH4 .139 A2
Castlemere Dr CW1 .190 B4
Castleton Dr SK6 .37 C3
Castleton St WA14 .238 C7
Castletown Cl SK10 .87 B2
Castletown La CH3 .197 B1
Castleview Rd ST7 .195 A2
Castleway WA15 .32 B4
Catalan Cl CW7 .127 A1
Catalyst Mus* WA8 .23 A3
Catchpenny La SK11 .108 C2
Catford Cl WA8 .12 B1
Catfoss Cl WA2 .8 C1
Cathcart Gn CH3 .119 C3
Cathedral Church of Christ & the Blessed Virgin Mary CH1 .237 B2
Catherine Ct CH5 .139 A3
Catherine Rd WA14 .238 C3
Catherine St
Chester CH1 .118 A1
Crewe CW2 .190 B1
Hyde SK14 .241 D7
Macclesfield SK11 .112 B4
Warrington WA5 .15 C4
Warrington WA5 .16 A4
Widnes WA8 .23 A4
Catherine Way WA12 .2 A1
Catterall Ave WA2 .8 B1
Caughall Rd CH2 .95 C1
Caunce Ave Golborne WA3 .3 A4
Haydock WA11 .1 A3
Newton-le-W WA12 .2 B1
Causeway Ave WA4 .16 B2
Causeway Pk WA4 .16 B2
Causeway The 2 WA14 .238 D4
Cavalier Dr CH1 .117 C3
Cavan Cl SK3 .239 F7
Cavell Dr CH65 .70 A2
Cavendish Ave WA3 .9 C3
Cavendish Cl
11 Macclesfield SK10 .87 B2
Warrington WA5 .15 B4
Winsford CW7 .149 A4
Cavendish Cres ST7 .193 B3
Cavendish Farm Rd WA7 49 A3
Cavendish Gdns CH65 .70 A2
Cavendish Mews SK9 .60 A3
Cavendish Pl WA3 .9 C3
Cavendish Rd
Altrincham WA14 .238 C3
Chester CH4 .141 A3
Crewe CW2 .189 C3
Hazel Grove SK7 .36 C4
Cavendish Sch WA7 .49 B3
Cavendish St WA7 .22 C1
Cavendish Way CW4 .130 A2
Caversham Cl WA4 .26 C3
Cawdor Dr CH3 .119 A1
Cawdor St Runcorn WA7 .22 C2
Warrington WA4 .26 B4
Cawfield Ave WA8 .12 B1
Cawley Ave WA3 .4 C2
Cawley St
9 Macclesfield SK11 .112 C4
Runcorn WA7 .23 A1
Cawood Cl CH66 .69 A3
Cawthorne Ave WA4 .17 A1
Caxton Cl
Ellesmere Port CH66 .69 C2
Widnes WA8 .12 B2
Cecil Rd WA15 .238 E2
Cecil Rigby Cl 1 CW11 .175 A3
Cecil St Chester CH3 .119 A1
Stalybridge SK15 .242 E1
Stockport SK3 .240 E3
Cedab Rd CH65 .70 B3
Cedar Ave Alsager ST7 .193 B2
Altrincham WA14 .238 C4
Connah's Quay CH5 .116 A4
Connah's Quay CH5 .91 B1
Ellesmere Port CH66 .69 B3
Golborne WA3 .4 A4
Kidsgrove ST7 .194 B1
Runcorn WA7 .49 B4
Stalybridge SK15 .242 F3
Sutton WA7 .50 A2
Widnes WA8 .13 A1
Cedar Cl
Connah's Quay CH5 .116 A4
Holmes Chapel CW4 .130 B2
Lostock Gralam CW9 .80 A2
Middlewich CW10 .151 C3
Poynton SK12 .36 C2
Sandbach CW11 .175 B3
Cedar Cres Audley ST7 .209 C1

Cedar Cres *continued*
Newton-le-W WA12 2 B1
Cedar Ct Alsager ST7 193 C2
Congleton CW12 178 C4
Culcheth WA3 4 C1
Willaston (nr Nantwich)
CW5 205 B3
Cedar Dr Barnton CW8 78 A2
Chester CH2 119 A2
Cedar Gr Chester CH2 119 A2
Haydock WA11 1 C4
Macclesfield SK11 112 B3
Nantwich CW5 205 A3
Neston CH64 66 C4
Warrington WA1 17 A4
Warrington, Latchford WA4 16 B2
Winsford CW7 127 A1
Cedar Lo SK7 35 C4
Cedar Mews CH1 117 C2
Cedar Pk CH3 119 B1
Cedar Rd
Altrincham WA15 238 E3
Gatley SK8 239 A5
Newcastle-u-L ST5 210 B1
Partington M31 11 C2
Warrington WA5 14 C3
Weaverham CW8 102 B4
Cedar St
Ashton-u-Lyne OL6 242 A4
Newton-le-W WA12 2 B1
Cedar Way CW2 206 A4
Cedardale Dr CH66 94 C4
Cedardale Pk WA8 13 C2
Cedarfield Rd WA13 19 A2
Cedars SK9 59 C3
Cedars The Alsager ST7 193 B2
Mobberley WA16 58 C1
Cedarway Heswall CH60 41 A3
Wilmslow SK9 59 C3
Cedarways WA4 26 B3
Cedarwood CW8 101 B3
Cedarwood Ave SK4 240 A5
Cedarwood Cl CW6 146 B2
Celandine Cl CH3 142 A4
Celandine Way WA9 6 A4
Celyn Cres CH4 140 B3
Cement Pl CH2 237 B3
Cemetery Rd CW2 207 A3
Cemlyn Cl CH1 117 C2
Centenary Ho WA7 49 B4
Centenary Pl CW12 156 C2
Central Ave Alsager CW2 192 C1
Ellesmere Port CH65 70 B2
Warrington WA2 16 B4
Warrington, Latchford WA4 16 A2
Central Dr Barnton CW8 78 A2
Gatley SK8 34 B4
Haydock WA11 1 A3
Romiley SK6 241 C3
Central Expressway WA7 49 C4
Central Gr CW9 104 B4
Central Rd
Northwich CW9 104 B4
Partington M31 11 C2
Central St ST7 195 A3
Central Trad Est CH4 140 C4
Central Way
Altrincham WA14 238 D4
Newton-le-W WA12 2 C1
Centre Ct ST7 193 C2
Centre Park Sq WA1 16 A2
Centre Pk WA2 16 A2
Centurion Cl WA3 9 B2
Centurion Row WA7 23 C1
Centurion Way CW10 128 B1
Century Park Ind Area
WA14 238 A6
Century Rd ST5 210 C1
Century Way SK10 87 C1
Cestria Cl CW11 174 B4
Chadkirk Chapel★ SK6 241 C1
Chadkirk Rd SK6 241 B1
Chads Gn CW5 206 A1
Chadvil Rd SK8 239 C5
Chadwick Ave Croft WA3 9 A4
Warrington WA4 16 C1
Chadwick Cl SK9 34 B1
Chadwick Ct CW10 151 B4
Chadwick Fields Orch
CW10 151 B3
Chadwick Pl WA3 9 C3
Chadwick Rd
Middlewich CW10 151 B3
Runcorn WA7 23 C2
Chadwick St
Ashton-u-Lyne OL6 242 B2
8 Stockport SK1 240 F4
Chadwick Terr SK10 87 C1
Chaffinch Cl
Congleton CW12 156 C1
Warrington WA3 9 C2
Chaffinch Way CW7 149 B3
Chaigeley Sch WA4 17 C2
Chain Maker's Row CH4 140 C4
Chalfield Ave CH66 69 B3
Chalfield Cl
6 Ellesmere Port CH66 69 B3
Wistaston CW2 206 A4
Chalfont Cl WA4 26 C3
Chalfont Cres CW2 207 A1
Chalfont Ct WA16 57 B2
Chalgrave Cl WA8 13 C2
Chalkwell Dr CH60 41 B4
Challinor St CH3 119 A1
Chamber Brook La WA6 75 B1
Chamberlain Ct CW1 191 B3
Chambers St CW2 190 B1
Chance Hall La CW12,
ST7 177 B2
Chancel La SK9 60 A4
Chancellor Rd WA7 24 B3
Chancery La Alsager ST7 193 A2
Bollington SK10 88 A4
Chandler Way WA3 3 C4
Chandlers Ct WA7 22 C1
Chandley St SK8 239 D6
Chandos Cl CH4 141 C3
Change La CH64 68 A4
Channel The CH1 95 A2
Chantler Ave WA4 16 C2
Chantry Ave CW8 103 A2
Chantry Cl SK12 38 C3
Chantry Ct Blacon CH1 117 C1
Crewe CW1 190 B2
Macclesfield SK11 112 B3
Chantry Fold SK12 38 C3
Chantry Rd SK12 38 C3
Chantry The CW6 169 C1
Chantry Wlk CH60 41 A3
Chapel Ave WA6 75 B1
Chapel Bank ST7 195 B3
Chapel Cl Audlem CW3 229 C2
Cholmondeston CW7 170 C2
Comberbach CW9 78 B4
Ellesmere Port CH65 70 B4
Mount Pleasant ST7 195 A3
Saughall CH1 94 A1
Waverton CH3 143 A3
Chapel Cotts CH3 143 A3
Chapel Croft SK11 84 A2
Chapel Cross Rd WA2 9 A1
Chapel Ct
Altrincham WA14 238 D4
Hyde SK14 241 C5
Northwich CW9 103 C4
Wilmslow SK9 60 A3
Chapel Dr WA15 32 B4
Chapel Gn CW6 122 B3
Chapel House La CH64 93 A4
Chapel La
Acton Bridge CW8 76 C2
Alford CH3 164 B3
Allostock WA16 106 C2
Altrincham WA15 32 B4
Appleton Thorn WA4 27 A2
Audley ST7 209 B1
Burtonwood WA5 6 C3
Chester CH3 119 A1
Crewe CW1 173 B1
Dutton WA4 77 A4
Ellesmere Port CH66 68 C1
Hollins Green WA3 10 C1
Holt LL13 196 B4
Kelsall CW6 122 C1
Kidsgrove ST7 195 C2
Kingsley WA6 75 B1
Manley WA6,CH3 98 C2
Mere WA16 30 A2
Milton Green CH3 165 A1
Moulton CW9 126 C4
Norton in Hales TF9 236 B1
Partington M31 11 C1
Rainow SK10 88 C3
Ravensmoor CW5 203 B1
Rode Heath ST7 193 C4
Threapwood SY14 222 C4
Warrington WA4 26 B4
Widnes WA8 12 B2
Wilmslow SK9 60 A3
Withington Green SK11 109 B1
Chapel Mews
Ellesmere Port CH65 70 A2
Elton CH2 72 A2
6 Nantwich CW5 204 C3
Chapel Mus Mow Cop★
ST7 195 B4
Chapel Rd
Alderley Edge SK9 60 A1
Ollerton WA16 82 C3
Sale M33 242 B7
Warrington WA5 14 C2
Whaley Bridge SK23 65 C3
Winsford CW7 126 C1
Chapel Row
Barbridge CW5 187 B3
Nantwich CW5 204 B3
Chapel St
5 Alderley Edge SK9 60 A1
Audley ST7 209 C2
Bollington SK10 88 A4
Cheadle SK8 239 D5
Chester CH2 237 C3
Congleton CW12 156 B1
Crewe CW2 190 B2
Haydock WA11 1 C3
Higher Wincham CW9 79 B2
Holt LL13 196 B4
Hyde SK14 241 D6
Kidsgrove ST7 194 B1
Macclesfield SK11 112 B3
Moulton CW9 126 C4
Mount Pleasant ST7 195 A3
New Mills SK22 39 A3
Newton-le-W WA12 2 A2
Northwich CW8 103 C4
Sandbach CW11 175 A3
Sandbach, Wheelock
CW11 175 A2
Stalybridge SK15 242 D2
Weaverham CW8 77 B1
Whaley Bridge SK23 65 C4
Widnes WA8 23 A4
Chapel Terr WA3 4 A4
Chapel View WA6 73 A1
Chapel Wlks Bramhall SK8 35 A3
Broomedge WA13 19 B1
Sale M33 242 B7
Chapel Yd WA2 16 A3
Chapelfields WA6 74 A4
Chapelmere Cl CW11 174 C4
Chapelmere Ct CW1 190 B4
Chapman Cl WA8 12 B2
Chapterhouse Cl CH65 70 C3
Charcoal Rd WA14 20 C2
Charcoal Woods WA14 238 A3
Charity La SK11 114 A3
Charlcote Cres CW2 206 B4
Charlecote Rd SK12 36 C2
Charles Ave
Davenham CW9 103 C1
Warrington WA5 14 C3
Charles Cres CH4 237 C1
Charles Darwin Prim Sch
CW8 103 C4
Charles Forbes Ct 14
WA1 16 A3
Charles Price Gdns 5
CH65 70 B3
Charles Rd CH2 95 B1
Charles Sq CW11 175 C1
Charles St Chester CH2 237 B3
Chester, Hoole Pk CH2 118 C2
Crewe CW1 190 B2
Irlam M44 11 C3
Widnes WA8 23 A4
Charleston Cl CH66 69 B1
Charlesworth Cl SK23 39 B2
Charlesworth Cres SK23 39 B2
Charlesworth Ct CW11 175 B3
Charlesworth Rd SK23 39 B2
Charlesworth St
Crewe CW1 190 B3
1 Stockport SK1 240 F3
Charlock Sq WA14 238 B8
Charlock Wlk 13 M31 11 C2
Charlotte Ct CH1 237 B3
Charlotte St Cheadle SK8 239 D5
Chester CH1 118 A1
Macclesfield SK11 112 B4
Charlotte St W 14 SK11 112 B4
Charlotte Wlk 16 WA8 23 A4
Charlton Brook Ho SK8 239 E6
Charlton Cl WA7 50 A4
Charlton Dr M33 242 C6
Charlton St
Macclesfield SK11 112 B4
Warrington WA4 16 C2
Charminster Cl WA5 15 A3
Charnock Ave WA12 1 C2
Charnock Rd WA3 4 C2
Charnwood 11 ST7 195 A1
Charnwood Cl
Macclesfield SK10 87 A1
Warrington WA3 10 A3
Charnwood Cres SK7 36 B4
Charter Ave WA5 16 A4
Charter Cres CH66 69 C2
Charter Rd
Altrincham WA15 238 E4
Bollington SK10 88 A4
Charter Way SK10 87 C2
Charterhall Dr CH2 118 C1
Chartist Ho SK14 241 E6
Chartley Gr CW10 128 B1
Chartwell Gr CW7 149 B3
Chartwell Pk CW11 175 A2
Chase Dr CH66 69 C1
Chase The CH63 43 B3
Chase Way CH66 69 C1
Chasefield WA14 238 A2
Chaser Ct CH1 117 C2
Chasewater WA7 24 C2
Chatburn Ct WA3 4 C1
Chater Dr CW5 204 C2
Chatfield Dr WA3 9 C2
Chatham St
15 Macclesfield SK11 112 B4
Stockport SK3 240 D4
Chatham Way CW1 191 B3
Chatswood Ave SK2 240 F2
Chatsworth Ave
Culcheth WA3 4 C2
Macclesfield SK11 111 C3
Chatsworth Cl
Ellesmere Port CH66 69 B3
Northwich CW9 104 A3
Wistaston CW2 206 A4
Chatsworth Dr
Chester CH2 119 A3
Congleton CW12 155 C2
Widnes WA8 12 B2
Chatsworth Ho CH1 118 A2
Chatsworth Rd
Hazel Grove SK7 36 C4
High Lane SK6 37 C3
Wilmslow SK9 59 C2
Chatteris Pk WA7 24 C1
Chatterton Dr WA7 50 C4
Chatwell Gdns WA4 26 C3
Chaucer Cl CH1 117 C3
Chaucer Pl WA4 16 C2
Chaucer St WA7 23 A1
Chaucher Gr 12 CW11 174 B3
Cheadle Heath Prim Sch
SK3 240 A3
Cheadle Hulme Coll SK8 35 A4
Cheadle Hulme Sch SK8 35 A4
Cheadle La
Lower Peover WA16 106 A4
Plumley WA16 81 A1
Cheadle Old Rd SK3 240 C3
Cheadle Prim Sch SK8 239 D6
Cheadle RC Inf Sch SK8 239 E2
Cheadle RC Jun Sch
SK8 239 E2
Cheadle Rd SK8 239 F3
Cheadle Royal Hospl
SK8 239 C2
Cheadle Wood SK8 34 C4
Cheam Rd WA15 238 F8
Cheapside SK14 241 E7
Checkley Dr ST8 179 B1
Checkley La CW3 221 C1
Checkley Rd ST5 210 B1
Cheddar Gr WA5 6 C4
Chedlee Dr SK8 34 C4
Chedworth Dr WA8 12 B2
Cheerbrook Rd CW5 205 B2
Cheese Hill La WA6,
CW8 101 A2
Cheetham Gdns SK15 242 E1
Chelford Ave WA3 3 B4
Chelford CE Prim Sch
SK11 84 A2
Chelford Cl
Altrincham WA15 238 E6
Blacon CH1 117 C1
Warrington WA4 26 B4
Chelford Ct 2 SK9 34 C3
Chelford Gr SK3 240 D1
Chelford La WA16 83 B1
Chelford Rd
Chelford SK10,SK11 84 B1
Chelford, Marthall WA16,
SK11 83 B2
Congleton CW12 155 C3
Goostrey CW4 131 A4
Handforth SK9 34 B3
Henbury SK10 110 C4
Knutsford WA16 82 B4
Macclesfield SK10,SK11 111 B4
Nether Alderley SK9 84 B4
Nether Alderley, Monks Heath
SK10 85 A1
Prestbury SK10 86 B3
Chelford Sta SK11 84 A1
Chell St CW1 190 A3
Chells Hill CW11 176 B1
Chelmsford Rd SK3 240 C4
Chelsea Cl ST8 179 B1
Chelsea Gdns WA5 15 B2
Chelston Dr SK8 34 B3
Cheltenham Cl
2 Macclesfield SK10 87 B2
Warrington WA5 15 A4
Cheltenham Cres
Crewe CW1 190 A4
Runcorn WA7 49 A3
Cheltenham Dr
Newton-le-W WA12 2 B3
Sale M33 242 C6
Cheltenham Rd
Ellesmere Port CH65 70 B2
Stockport SK3 240 A3
Chemical St WA12 2 A2
Cheney Wlk CW2 206 B4
Chepstow Cl
Biddulph ST8 179 B1
Macclesfield SK10 87 B2
Warrington WA5 7 C1
3 Winsford CW7 149 B4
Cherington Cl SK9 34 C2
Cherington Cres SK11 112 A4
Cherington Rd SK8 239 C4
Cheriton Ave M33 242 C7
Cheriton Way CW2 206 A4
Cherrington Rd CW5 204 C2
Cherry Blossom Rd WA7 49 C2
Cherry Brow Terr CH64 67 C4
Cherry Cl
Newcastle-u-L ST5 210 B1
Newton-le-W WA12 1 C2
Willaston CH64 67 B4
Cherry Cnr WA13 28 A4
Cherry Cres CW7 149 B4
Cherry Ct M33 242 A6
Cherry Dale Rd CH4 139 A2
Cherry Gr
Ellesmere Port CH66 70 A1
Nantwich CW5 204 B3
Cherry Grove Prim Sch
CH3 119 A1
Cherry Grove Rd CH3 119 A1
Cherry La
Congleton CW12 179 C4
Cuddington CW8 101 C1
Lawton Heath ST7 193 C3
Lymm WA13 28 A4
Weaverham CW8 102 B4
Cherry Orch LL13 196 B4
Cherry Rd CH3 119 A1
Cherry Tree Ave
Barnton CW8 78 A2
Lawton-gate ST7 194 A3
Lymm WA13 18 B1
Poynton SK12 36 C2
Runcorn WA7 49 B4
Warrington WA5 14 C2
Cherry Tree Cl Elton CH2 72 A2
Hale L24 21 C1
Haydock WA11 1 A3
Romiley SK6 241 E2
Wilmslow SK9 60 C4
Cherry Tree Dr
Hazel Grove SK7 37 A4
St Helens WA9 1 A1
Cherry Tree La
Romiley SK6 241 E2
Rostherne WA16 30 C3
Cherry Tree La *continued*
Woore CW3 232 B1
Cherry Tree Prim Sch
WA13 18 B1
Cherry Tree Rd
Audley ST7 209 C1
Crewe CW1 190 C3
Golborne WA3 3 C4
Newcastle-u-L ST5 210 C1
Cherry Wlk Cheadle SK8 35 B4
Lower Peover WA16 106 B4
Partington M31 11 B1
Cherrycroft SK6 241 E1
Cherryfields Rd SK11 111 C4
Cherrysutton WA8 12 A2
Cherrysutton Mews WA8 12 A2
Cherrywood Cres CW8 78 A2
Cherwell Cl Cheadle SK8 35 A4
Warrington WA2 8 B1
Cheryl Ct CW8 102 A2
Cheryl Dr WA8 13 B1
Chesford Grange WA1 17 C4
Chesham Cl SK9 59 C2
Chesham Pl WA14 238 C2
Chesham Rd SK9 59 C2
Chesham St CH2 237 C3
Cheshire Cl WA12 2 C2
Cheshire Farm★ CH3 166 B2
Cheshire Military Mus★
CH4 237 A1
Cheshire Oaks Outlet Village
CH65 70 C1
Cheshire Oaks Way CH65 70 C1
Cheshire Rd M31 11 B1
Cheshire Row WA16 108 A4
Cheshire St CW3 229 C2
Cheshire View
Bollington SK10 88 A3
Chester CH4 141 C4
Cheshire Workshops★
CH3 184 B3
Cheshyre Dr WA7 23 C1
Cheshyre's La WA7 48 C4
Chessington Cl WA4 26 C3
Chester Aerospace Pk
CH4 139 A3
Chester Ave
Altrincham WA15 238 F2
Golborne WA3 3 B4
Chester Bsns Pk CH4 141 A2
Chester Cl Handforth SK9 34 C1
Irlam M44 11 B3
Runcorn WA7 24 A1
Talke ST7 210 C4
Chester Gates CH1 94 B3
Chester High Rd
Neston CH64 41 C2
Willaston CH64 67 B4
Chester La CW7 125 B1
Chester New Rd WA4 25 C4
Chester Rd Acton CW5 204 A3
Audley ST7 209 B1
Barbridge CW5 187 B3
Broughton CH4 139 B3
Churton CH3 180 C3
Connah's Quay CH6 91 A2
Daresbury WA4 25 A1
Delamere CW6,CW8 123 B3
Ellesmere Port, Great Sutton
CH66 69 B2
Ellesmere Port, Whitby
CH65,CH66 70 A1
Frodsham WA6 74 A4
Gatesheath CH3 165 C3
Hartford CW8 102 C2
Hartford, Greenbank CW8 103 B3
Hawarden CH5 116 A1
Hazel Grove SK7 36 B4
Helsby WA6 73 B2
Heswall CH60,CH64 41 B3
Higher Walton WA4 25 B3
Holmes Chapel CW4 130 A1
Huntington CH3 142 A3
Kelsall CW6 122 B3
Knutsford WA16 56 A3
Lavister LL12,CH4 162 B1
Macclesfield SK11 112 A4
Middlewich CW10 128 A1
Neston CH64 66 C4
Oakmere CW8 124 A4
Plumley WA16 80 C3
Poynton SK12 36 A2
Rostherne WA14 30 B3
Runcorn WA7 50 C3
Sutton WA7 50 A2
Tabley WA16 56 A1
Talke ST7 210 B4
Tattenhall CH3 166 A1
Warrington WA4 17 A1
Whitchurch SY13 225 B1
Winsford CW7 125 C1
Woodford SK7 35 C1
Chester Ret Pk CH1 118 A2
Chester Row WA12 7 B4
Chester Sq CW1 190 B2
Chester St Chester CH4 140 C4
Stockport SK3 240 D5
Warrington WA1 16 A3
Widnes WA8 13 A1
Chester Sta CH2 237 C3
Chester Toy & Doll Mus★
CH1 237 B2
Chester Way CW9 104 A4
Chester West Employment Pk
CH1 117 C1
Chester Wlks SK6 241 A1
Chester Zoological Gdns★
CH2 95 C1

Chesterbank Bsns Pk
CH4 140 B4
Chesterfield Cl CW7 125 C1
Chesterfield Gr OL6 242 A3
Chesterfield Rd CH62 43 B2
Chestergate
Macclesfield SK11 112 B4
Stockport SK3 240 E5
Chestergate Mall 34
SK11 112 B4
Chesterton Cl CW10 151 C3
Chesterton Dr
Winwick WA2 8 A3
Wistaston CW2 189 C1
Chesterton Gr 11 CW11 174 B3
Chestnut Ave
Cheadle SK8 239 E5
12 Ellesmere Port CH66 69 C1
Irlam M44 11 B3
Macclesfield SK10 87 C1
Rode Heath ST7 193 C4
Shavington CW2 206 B3
Warrington WA5 14 C3
Widnes WA8 13 A1
Chestnut Cl Chester CH2 119 A2
Cuddington CW8 101 C1
Middlewich CW10 128 A1
Tarporley CW6 146 B1
Wilmslow SK9 60 C4
Chestnut Ct
Tarporley CW6 146 B1
Widnes WA8 12 B1
Chestnut Dr Alsager ST7 193 C1
Congleton CW12 156 A2
Holmes Chapel CW4 130 B2
Poynton SK12 36 C2
Chestnut Gr Barnton CW8 78 A2
Bebington CH62 43 B4
Crewe CW1 190 C3
Golborne WA3 3 C4
Newcastle-u-L ST5 210 C1
Winsford CW7 149 B4
Chestnut Ho 6 CW11 175 A3
Chestnut La WA6 73 C2
Chestnut Lodge Specl Sch
WA8 12 C1
Chestnut Mews WA16 58 C1
Chestnut Villas SK4 240 B5
Chestnut Wlk M31 11 B1
Chesworth Cl SK1 240 F4
Chesworth Fold SK1 240 F4
Chetham Ct WA2 8 A2
Chetton Dr WA7 50 C4
Chetwode Mews WA4 52 B1
Chetwode St CW1 190 B3
Chetwood Dr WA8 12 C2
Cheveley Cl SK10 87 C1
Chevin Gdns SK7 36 A4
Cheviot Ave Cheadle SK8 239 F2
Warrington WA2 8 A2
Cheviot Cl
Ellesmere Port CH66 69 A3
Stockport SK4 240 D7
Cheviot Ct 16 CW7 149 A4
Chevithorne Cl WA14 238 B5
Chevron Cl CH1 117 C2
Chevron Hey CH1 117 C2
Chevron Pl WA14 238 D7
Cheyne Wlk CW5 204 C2
Cheyney Rd Blacon CH1 118 A2
Chester CH1 118 A2
Chicago Ave M90 33 A4
Chichester Cl
Grappenhall Heys WA4 27 A4
Runcorn WA7 50 B3
Chichester Ct CH1 237 A3
Chichester Rd SK6 241 C2
Chichester St CH1 237 A3
Chidlow Cl
Hough Common CW2 206 C2
Widnes WA8 23 A3
Child's La CW12 177 C3
Childer Cres CH66 69 A4
Childer Gdns CH66 69 A4
Childer Thornton Prim Sch
CH66 69 A4
Childwall Ct CH66 69 C4
Childwall Gdns CH66 69 C4
Childwall Rd CH66 69 C4
Chilham Cl CW7 149 B4
Chilham Pl SK11 111 C3
Chilington Ave WA8 22 B4
Chillingham Cl CW10 128 B1
Chiltern Ave Cheadle SK8 239 F2
Macclesfield SK11 112 A4
Chiltern Cl Chester CH4 141 A3
Cuddington CW8 102 A1
Hough Common CW2 207 A1
Chiltern Cres WA2 8 A2
Chiltern Dr WA15 238 F2
Chiltern Pl WA2 8 A2
Chiltern Rd Culcheth WA3 4 C2
St Helens WA9 1 A2
Warrington WA2 8 A2
Chiltern Way CW7 149 A4
Chilton Dr CH66 69 C1
Chilwell Cl WA8 12 B2
Chilworth Cl CW2 206 B4
China La WA4 16 B1
Chines The CW8 101 B3
Chink Gdns CH65 70 B2
Chinley Cl Sale M33 242 D5
Stockport SK4 240 B7
Chippingdall Cl WA5 15 B3
Chipstead Cl CW8 103 A2
Chirk Cl CH2 118 C3
Chirk Pl CW7 126 A1
Chirton Cl WA11 1 B4
Chisledon Cl WA11 1 B4
Chislet Ct WA8 12 C2
Chiswick Cl WA7 50 B4
Chiswick Gdns WA4 26 C3
Chokeberry Cl WA14 238 B8
Chollerton Cl WA16 29 B2
Cholmley Dr WA12 2 C1
Cholmondeley Ave
WA14 238 E8
Cholmondeley Castle Gdns*
SY14 201 A2
Cholmondeley La SY14 200 C4
Cholmondeley Rd
Ellesmere Port CH65 69 C2
Hampton SY14 213 C4
Runcorn WA7 49 B2
Wrenbury CW5 216 B3
Cholmondeley St WA8 23 A2
Cholmondely St SK11 112 B3
Cholmondley Rise SY14 214 A2
Chomlea WA14 238 B4
Chorley Bank Council Hos
CW5 201 C1
Chorley Green La CW5,
SY14 201 C3
Chorley Hall Cl SK9 59 C1
Chorley Hall La
Alderley Edge SK9 60 A1
Faddiley CW5 202 B1
Chorley St WA2 16 A3
Chorley's La WA8 13 C2
Chorleywood Cl SK10 87 A2
Chorlton Cl WA7 24 B1
Chorlton Dr SK8 239 E6
Chorlton La CW2 207 A1
Chowley Oak La CH3 182 C3
Chrimes Dr CW8 123 C3
Christ Church CE Prim Sch
CH65 70 A1
Christ Church CE Sch
CW8 76 A1
Christ The King RC Prim Sch
CH62 43 C4
Christchurch Ave CW2 190 A1
Christie Cl CH66 44 A1
Christie St WA8 13 A1
Christleton Ave
Crewe CW2 189 B3
Northwich CW9 104 A2
Christleton Ct WA7 24 B2
Christleton Dr CH66 69 C3
Christleton High Sch
CH3 142 C4
Christleton Prim Sch
CH3 142 C4
Christleton Rd CH3 119 A1
Christleton Sports Ctr
CH3 142 C4
Christleton Way 15 SK9 34 B3
Christopher Dr CH62 44 A3
Chudleigh Cl WA14 238 B6
Church Ave SK9 34 A1
Church Bank
Altrincham WA14 238 B2
Audley ST7 209 B1
Goostrey CW4 107 C1
Kelsall CW6 122 B3
Tattenhall CH3 166 A1
Church Bk SK23 65 B4
Church Brow
Altrincham WA14 238 B2
Hyde SK14 241 D5
Church Cl Handforth SK9 34 B2
Weaverham CW8 77 B1
Church College Cl CH1 118 A2
Church Coppenhall Jun Sch
CW1 190 A3
Church Cotts
Rainow SK10 88 C3
Waverton CH3 143 B2
Church Croft CH4 162 A3
Church Ct
Altrincham WA15 238 E1
Ashton CH3 121 C4
Farndon CH3 180 C1
Church Dr
Newton-le-W WA12 2 B1
Warrington WA2 9 A1
Church End L24 21 B1
Church Farm CW5 216 C2
Church Farm Ct
Heswall CH60 40 C4
Willaston CH64 67 C4
Church Fields TF9 236 B1
Church Gn WA13 19 A4
Church Hall Cl CH1 117 C2
Church Hill WA16 57 A1
Church La
Alderley Edge SK9 60 A1
Aldford CH3 163 C2
Backford CH1 95 A2
Bebington CH62 44 A2
Chester CH2 118 B4
Congleton CW12 134 C1
Culcheth WA3 4 C2
Ellesmere Port CH66 69 B2
Elton WA6 72 B1
Farndon CH3 180 C1
Golborne WA3 3 B4
Guilden Sutton CH3 119 C3
Henbury SK11 111 B4
Lawton-gate ST7 194 B2
Mobberley WA16 58 B3
Mow Cop ST7 195 C4
Nantwich CW5 204 C3
Neston CH64 66 C4
New Mills SK22 39 B4
Rainow SK10 88 C3
Church La *continued*
Romiley SK6 241 C2
Sandbach CW11 175 C4
Scholar Green ST7 194 B4
Smallwood CW11 176 C2
Stoak CH2 96 A4
Sutton Lane Ends SK11 112 C2
Warren SK11 134 B4
Warrington WA4 17 A1
Weaverham CW8 77 B1
Wistaston CW2 205 C4
Woodford SK7 35 B1
Church Lawton Prim Sch
ST7 194 A3
Church Manor SK4 240 B8
Church Mdw
Dukinfield SK14 241 C7
Norton in Hales TF9 236 B1
Church Mdws
Little Leigh CW8 77 B3
Whitchurch SY13 226 A1
Church Mead CH3 181 A3
Church Meadow Gdns
SK14 241 C7
Church Meadow La CH60 40 C4
Church Meadow Wlk
WA8 22 A3
Church Mews
Bollington SK10 88 A4
Knutsford WA16 57 A1
Church Par 2 CH65 70 B3
Church Rd Alsager ST7 193 B2
Ashton CH3 121 C4
Barnton CW8 78 A1
Broughton CH4 139 B2
Burwardsley CH3 184 A3
Cheadle SK8 35 A4
Eccleston CH4 141 C1
Frodsham WA6 74 B4
Gatley SK8 239 A5
Hale L24 47 C4
Handforth SK9 34 B2
Haydock WA11 1 C4
Little Leigh CW8 77 B2
Lymm WA13 18 C1
New Mills SK22 39 B4
Northwich CW9 104 A4
Sale M33 242 D6
Saughall CH1 94 A1
Shocklach CH3 197 B1
Stockport SK4 240 E6
Thornton Hough CH63 42 A3
Tilston SY14 198 A2
Wilmslow SK9 59 C2
Worleston CW5 188 B3
Church Rd E M33 242 D6
Church Rd W M33 242 D6
Church Rise CW8 102 A1
Church Row CW6 168 C1
Church St
Altrincham WA14 238 D5
Audley ST7 209 B1
Audley ST7 210 A1
Bollington SK10 88 A4
Cheadle SK8 239 D6
Chester CH2 237 B4
Connah's Quay CH5 91 B1
Davenham CW9 104 A2
Ellesmere Port CH65 70 B3
Farndon CH3 180 C1
Frodsham WA6 74 A4
Great Budworth CW9 79 A4
Higher Wincham CW9 79 C3
Holt LL13 180 C1
Hyde SK14 241 D5
Kelsall CW6 122 B2
Kidsgrove, Butt Lane ST7 194 B1
Kidsgrove, The Rookery
ST7 195 A2
Macclesfield SK11 112 B4
Malpas SY14 213 A2
Moulton CW9 126 C4
Mount Pleasant ST7 195 B3
Newton-le-W WA12 2 C2
Runcorn WA7 23 A2
Sandbach CW11 175 B3
Stalybridge SK15 242 D2
Stockport SK4 240 E7
Tarvin CH3 121 B1
Warrington WA1 16 B3
Weaverham CW8 77 B1
Widnes WA8 23 A3
Wilmslow SK9 60 A4
Winsford CW7 126 C1
Church St N CW6 122 B3
Church St W SK11 112 B4
Church Steadings CH3 143 B2
Church Terr
Handforth SK9 34 B2
Sale M33 242 A8
Church View
Audlem CW3 230 A2
Handforth SK9 34 A1
Haslington CW1 191 B3
Hyde SK14 241 D5
Kingsley WA6 75 A1
13 Knutsford WA16 57 A1
Lymm WA13 19 A2
Church View Terr SK11 112 C2
Church View Wlk CW2 205 C4
Church Way Blacon CH1 117 C3
Wybunbury CW5 220 A4
Church Wlk Crowton CW8 76 B1
1 Ellesmere Port CH65 70 B3
Holmes Chapel CW4 130 B2
Knutsford WA16 57 A1
Lower Peover WA16 81 C1
Northwich CW9 104 A4
Church Wlk *continued*
Stalybridge SK15 242 D3
Wilmslow SK9 59 C3
Winwick WA2 8 A3
Church Wlks
Christleton CH3 142 C4
Norton in Hales TF9 236 B1
Church Wood View
WA13 18 C2
Churche's Ct 9 CW5 204 C3
Churche's Mansion*
CW5 204 C3
Churchfield Rd WA6 74 B4
Churchfields
Altrincham WA14 238 B1
Audlem CW3 230 A2
Barnton CW8 78 A2
Croft WA3 9 A4
Cuddington CW8 102 A1
Helsby WA6 73 B2
Knutsford WA16 57 B1
Widnes WA8 13 A3
Wybunbury CW5 220 A4
Churchgate SK1 240 F5
Churchill Ave WA3 5 A2
Churchill Cl CW12 156 A2
Churchill Dr CW6 146 B1
Churchill Parkway CW7 149 B4
Churchill Rd WA14 238 D7
Churchill St SK4 240 D7
Churchill Way
Macclesfield SK11 112 B4
Neston CH64 66 C4
Churchley Cl SK3 240 A2
Churchley Rd SK3 240 A3
Churchmere Cl CW1 190 B4
Churchside SK11 112 B4
Churchside Wlk CH4 140 C4
Churchward Cl CH2 118 B2
Churchway Alvanley WA6 73 B1
Macclesfield SK10 86 C1
Churchway Rd L24 21 A1
Churchyard Side CW5 204 C3
Churton Cl
3 Davenham CW9 103 C2
Hough Common CW2 206 C2
Churton Rd Chester CH3 119 A1
Farndon CH3 180 C1
Churton St CH3 119 A1
Cicely Mill La WA16 30 B2
Cinder Cl CH3 119 C3
Cinder Hill CW7 125 C3
Cinder Hill La ST7 194 C4
Cinder La Chelford SK11 83 C1
Guilden Sutton CH3 119 C3
Lostock Green CW9 105 A4
Peover WA16 108 B4
Warrington WA4 17 C1
Worleston CW5 188 B1
Cinnamon Brow CE Prim Sch
WA2 8 C2
Cinnamon La WA2 8 C1
Cinnamon La N WA2 8 C2
Cinnamon Pk WA2 9 A2
Circle Ave CW5 205 C3
Circle The Crewe CW2 190 B1
Mere WA16 30 B1
Circuit The
Alderley Edge SK9 60 A2
Bramhall SK8 35 A4
Stockport SK3 240 C2
Wilmslow SK9 59 B3
Circular Dr CH4 140 C2
City Bank ST8 179 B1
City Rd CH2 237 C3
City Walls Rd CH1 237 A2
Civic Way
Ellesmere Port CH65 70 A2
Middlewich CW10 128 B1
Clair Ave CH5 116 A2
Claire Pl CW7 149 B4
Clamhunger La WA16 56 B4
Clamley Ct L24 21 A2
Clamley Gdns L24 21 C1
Clanfield Ave WA8 12 B2
Clap Gate Cres WA8 22 A3
Clap Gates Cres WA5 15 C4
Clap Gates Rd WA5 15 C4
Clare Ave Chester CH2 119 A2
Wilmslow SK9 34 B2
Clare Dr
Ellesmere Port CH65 70 A1
Macclesfield SK10 87 B2
Wistaston CW2 189 C1
Clare Rd SK5 240 F8
Clare St Kidsgrove ST7 195 C2
Mount Pleasant ST7 195 B3
Claremont Ave
Altrincham WA14 238 E8
Widnes WA8 13 B2
Claremont Cl 15 CW9 103 C2
Claremont Dr
Altrincham WA14 238 E8
Widnes WA8 13 A2
Claremont Gdns OL6 242 B4
Claremont Gr WA15 238 E3
Claremont Rd
Cheadle SK8 35 A4
Crewe CW2 190 A1
Culcheth WA3 4 B2
Runcorn WA7 23 A1
Sale M33 242 B7
Claremont St OL6 242 B4
Clarence Ave
Chester CH3 119 A1
Warrington WA5 14 B3
Widnes WA8 13 A2
Clarence Ct
Newton-le-W WA12 2 A2
Wilmslow SK9 60 A3
Clarence Gr CW1 190 A3
Clarence Rd
Altrincham WA15 238 F3
Bollington SK10 63 A1
Warrington WA4 17 A1
Clarence St Hyde SK14 241 E8
Newton-le-W WA12 1 C2
Runcorn WA7 22 C2
Stalybridge OL6,SK15,
SK16 242 B1
Warrington WA1 16 C4
Clarence Terr
Bollington SK10 63 A1
Runcorn WA7 23 A2
Clarendon Ave
Altrincham WA15 238 E5
Stockport SK4 240 B7
Clarendon Cl
Chester CH4 141 C3
Runcorn WA7 50 B4
Clarendon Cres M33 242 D7
Clarendon Ct WA2 7 C2
Clarendon Dr SK10 88 A1
Clarendon Ind Est SK14 241 E7
Clarendon Pl SK14 241 E6
Clarendon Rd
Denton M34 241 B6
Hyde SK14 241 E7
Irlam M44 11 C4
Sale M33 242 D6
Clarendon St Hyde SK14 241 D7
Stockport SK5 240 F7
Clares Farm Cl WA1 17 C4
Clark Way SK14 241 D7
Clarke Ave Culcheth WA3 5 A2
Warrington WA4 16 B1
Clarke Gdns 17 WA8 23 A4
Clarke La Bollington SK10 87 C3
Langley SK11 113 B2
Clarke St WA14 238 D7
Clarke Terr SK11 112 B3
Clarks Terr WA7 48 B4
Clary Mdw CW8 78 C1
Clatterbridge Hospl
CH63 42 B4
Clatterbridge Rd CH63 42 B4
Claude St WA1 16 B3
Claughton Ave CW2 190 B1
Claverton Cl WA7 49 A3
Clay Heyes SK11 84 A2
Clay La Burtonwood WA5 6 C3
Handforth SK9 34 B3
Peover WA16 108 A4
Sandbach CW11 174 A1
Wilmslow SK9 59 B2
Winsford CW7 125 A2
Claydon Gdns WA3 10 C1
Clayhill CH64 41 C1
Clayhill Gn CH66 69 B4
Clayhill Gr WA3 4 A4
Clayhill Light Ind Pk
CH64 41 C1
Claypit Rd CH4 141 A3
Claypitts La CH3 142 C3
Clayton Ave
Congleton CW12 157 A3
Golborne WA3 3 C4
Clayton Cl CW1 190 A4
Clayton Cres
Runcorn WA7 22 C1
Widnes WA8 12 C1
Clayton Dr SY13 226 A1
Clayton Rd WA3 9 C3
Clayton's Row CW5 204 C4
Clayton-by-pass CW12 156 B2
Cleaver Mews SK11 112 B3
Cleaver Rd CH1 117 C2
Cledford Cres CW10 151 C3
Cledford Inf Sch CW10 151 B4
Cledford Jun Sch CW10 151 B4
Cledford La CW10 151 C4
Cledwen Rd CH4 139 B3
Cleethorpes Rd WA7 50 B4
Cleeve Way SK8 35 A3
Cleeves Cl WA1 16 B3
Clegg Pl OL6 242 A4
Clegg St SK11 112 C4
Clegge St WA2 16 A4
Cleggs Cl CH3 142 A4
Clelland St WA4 16 B2
Clement St SK4 240 E7
Clemley Cl CW6 122 B3
Clerewood Ave SK8 34 A4
Clevedon Cl SK11 112 A4
Cleveland Ave SK14 241 C6
Cleveland Dr CH66 69 A3
Cleveland Rd
Altrincham WA15 238 F3
Stockport SK4 240 A8
Warrington WA2 8 A2
Cleveland Way CW7 149 A4
Cleveleys Ave Gatley SK8 239 B1
Widnes WA8 13 B1
Cleveleys Rd WA5 15 A2
Cleves Cl CH1 117 B3
Cliff Gr SK4 240 B8
Cliff La Acton Bridge CW8 76 B2
Lymm WA13 28 A3
Macclesfield SK10 88 A1
Rainow SK10 88 A1
Warrington WA4 17 B1
Cliff Rd Acton Bridge CW8 76 C2

Cliff Rd *continued*
Wilmslow SK9 .60 A4
Cliff Side SK9 .60 A4
Cliff View WA6 .74 A4
Cliffbrook Gr 2 SK9 .34 B1
Cliffe Rd Crewe CW1 .190 A4
Neston CH64 .66 C3
Warrington WA4 .26 B4
Cliffe St 3 WA8 .13 B1
Cliffmere Cl SK8 .239 F3
Clifford Dr CH4 .140 C3
Clifford Gr CW1 .191 B2
Clifford Pl 6 CW7 .149 B4
Clifford Rd
Macclesfield SK11 .112 A4
Poynton SK12 .36 B2
Warrington WA5 .15 A2
Wilmslow SK9 .59 C3
Clifton Ave
Altrincham WA15 .238 E5
Bebington CH62 .43 C2
Crewe CW2 .190 A2
Culcheth WA3 .4 B2
Gatley SK8 .239 A2
Clifton Cl WA1 .17 B4
Clifton Cres WA6 .49 B1
Clifton Ct WA7 .49 A3
Clifton Dr Blacon CH1 .117 C2
Cheadle, Heald Green SK8 239 A2
Cheadle,Gatley SK8 .239 A6
Northwich CW9 .104 A3
Wilmslow SK9 .59 C2
Clifton Gdns CH65 .70 B2
Clifton La WA7 .49 C2
Clifton Park Ave CH5 .91 B1
Clifton Rd Runcorn WA7 .49 C2
Runcorn, Heath WA7 .49 A3
Sale M33 .242 B5
Sandbach CW11 .174 B4
Stockport SK4 .240 A8
Clifton St
Alderley Edge SK9 .60 A1
Crewe CW2 .190 A2
Warrington WA4 .16 B2
Cliftonmill Mdws WA3 .2 C4
Cliftonville Rd WA1 .17 B3
Clincton Cl WA8 .22 A4
Clincton View WA8 .22 A4
Clinton St OL6 .242 A4
Clipsley Cres WA11 .1 A4
Clipsley La WA11 .1 B3
Clitheroe Rd CW8 .77 C1
Clive Ave WA2 .8 B1
Clive La CW7 .150 B4
Cliveden Rd CH4 .140 C3
Clivegreen La CW10 .150 C4
Clock Face Rd WA8 .13 C4
Clock Tower Cl SK14 .241 E5
Cloister Way CH65 .70 C3
Cloisters The Sale M33 .242 D6
Stockport SK8 .240 A1
Clonners Field CW5 .205 A2
Close La Alsager ST7 .192 C2
Mow Cop ST7 .195 B4
Close The Alsager ST7 .193 A2
Altrincham WA14 .238 C5
Blacon CH1 .117 B2
Newton-le-W WA12 .2 C1
Northwich CW8 .103 B3
Saughall CH1 .94 A1
Stalybridge SK15 .242 C4
Tarporley CW6 .146 B1
Closeburn Ave CH60 .40 C3
Cloud The* CW12 .158 A2
Cloud View CW12 .157 A1
Cloudberry Wlk M31 .11 C2
Clough Ave Handforth SK9 34 A1
Warrington WA2 .8 A1
Clough Bank SK10 .87 C4
Clough Fold Rd SK14 .241 D5
Clough Hall Dr ST7 .210 C3
Clough Hall Rd ST7 .210 C4
Clough Hall Tech Sch
ST7 .194 C1
Clough La CW8 .103 B3
Clough Rd CW7 .126 C1
Clough The WA7 .23 C1
Clough Wlk CW2 .206 B4
Cloughside SK12 .38 C3
Cloughwood Sch CW8 .103 B3
Clovelly Ave WA5 .14 C4
Clovelly Gr WA7 .50 B3
Clover Ave Frodsham WA6 .74 B4
Stockport SK3 .240 D1
Clover Ct WA7 .50 A3
Clover Dr Pickmere WA16 .79 C4
Winsford CW7 .126 B2
Clover La CH4 .140 C3
Clover Pl CH4 .140 C3
Clover Rd SK6 .241 E3
Cloverdale CW8 .103 B4
Cloverdale Rd SK11 .112 A3
Cloverfield WA7 .50 B4
Cloverfield Gdns CH66 .69 B4
Cloverfields CW1 .191 A2
Clowes Ave ST7 .193 C1
Clowes St SK11 .112 A4
Clumber Cl SK12 .36 C2
Clumber Rd SK12 .36 C2
Clutton CE Prim Sch
CH3 .182 B1
Clwyd Ave SK3 .240 D3
Clwyd Cl CH4 .139 A3
Clwyd Way CH66 .69 A3
Clyde Ave ST8 .179 C1
Clyde Cres CW7 .127 A1
Clyde Gr CW2 .190 A2
Clyde Rd SK3 .240 C3
Clydesdale CH65 .70 A2
Clydesdale Ave CW2 .190 A2
Clydesdale Rd WA4 .26 B4
Coach Rd Broxton CH3 .183 A2
Edge Green SY14 .199 B1
Little Budworth CW6 .147 B4
Coachway SK10 .86 C4
Coalbrookdale Rd CH64 .41 C1
Coalpit Hill ST7 .210 B4
Coalpit La Langley SK11 .113 B3
Mollington CH1 .94 B2
Winsford CW10 .127 C1
Coalport Dr CW7 .126 C2
Coare St SK10 .87 B1
Coastguard La CH64 .41 A1
Cob Hall La WA6 .98 B3
Cob Moor Rd ST7 .195 A2
Cobal Ct WA6 .74 A4
Cobbett's Way SK9 .59 C2
Cobblers Cross La CW6 146 C1
Cobblers La LL12 .161 A1
Cobbles The
Chester CH4 .141 B4
Cuddington CW8 .101 B2
Lower Peover WA16 .81 C1
Cobblestone Ct CH2 .119 C4
Cobbs Inf Sch The WA4 .26 C4
Cobbs La
Hough Common CW2 .206 C1
Warrington WA4 .26 C4
Cobden St
Ashton-u-Lyne OL6 .242 A2
Newton-le-W WA12 .2 B2
Warrington WA2 .16 A3
Cock Hall La SK11 .113 B2
Cock La CW9 .78 C4
Cock Lane Ends WA8 .22 A2
Cocker Hill SK15 .242 E2
Cockhedge Ctr WA1 .16 A3
Cockhedge La WA1 .16 A3
Cockhedge Way WA1 .16 A3
Cockington Cl CW9 .104 A2
Cocklade La L24 .21 B1
Cockpit La CW8 .102 A1
Cocksheadhey Rd SK10 .63 B1
Cocksmoss La SK11 .133 B2
Coe La WA14 .30 B4
Coerdon Dr WA4 .17 B1
Cogshall La
Comberbach CW9 .78 A4
Little Leigh CW8,CW9 .77 C4
Northwich CW9 .78 B3
Colborne Ave SK6 .241 C2
Colchester Pl SK4 .240 C7
Colchester Sq CH4 .140 C3
Coldmoss Dr CW11 .175 B2
Coldstream Cl WA2 .8 C2
Coldstream Dr CH66 .68 C3
Cole Ave WA12 .2 B2
Colebrook Cl WA3 .10 A2
Coleclough Pl WA3 .4 C2
Colehill Bank CW12 .156 C1
Colehill Pl CH5 .91 B1
Colemere Cl WA1 .17 A4
Colenso Gr SK4 .240 B7
Coleridge Cl Blacon CH1 118 A3
Sandbach CW11 .174 B3
Coleridge Gr WA8 .12 C1
Coleridge Way CW1 .190 C3
Colin Rd SK4 .240 E8
Colinwood Ave CH4 .139 A2
Coliseum Way CH65 .70 B1
Collar House Dr SK10 .86 C3
College Cl
Warrington WA1 .16 B3
Warrington, Fearnhead WA2 .9 A1
Wilmslow SK9 .59 C4
College Fields CW2 .190 A1
College Gn CH4 .141 B4
College Ho
Altrincham WA14 .238 C1
Stockport SK4 .240 B8
College La CW6 .168 C1
College of Law (Christleton
Hall) CH3 .142 B4
College Rd ST7 .193 A3
College View CH5 .91 B1
Colley La CW11 .175 B3
Colleys La Nantwich CW2 205 B4
Willaston (nr Nantwich)
CW2 .205 B4
Collier St WA7 .22 C2
Collier's Row WA7 .48 C4
Colliers La CW9 .54 C1
Colliery Green Cl CH64 .66 C3
Colliery Green Ct CH64 .66 C3
Colliery Green Dr CH64 .66 C3
Collin St WA5 .15 C3
Collinbrook Ave CW2 .190 A1
Collingham Gn CH66 .69 A3
Collingham Way CW7 .126 B1
Collingtree Ave CW7 .127 A2
Collingwood Cl
Macclesfield SK10 .87 A1
Poynton SK12 .37 A2
Collingwood Rd WA12 .2 A2
Collins Green La WA5 .1 C1
Collins St CW2 .190 A2
Collinson Ct 3 WA6 .74 A4
Colmere Cl WA2 .9 A1
Colmere Ct CH65 .70 B4
Colne Rd WA5 .6 C3
Colorado Cl WA5 .15 B4
Colshaw Dr SK9 .34 B1
Colshaw La SK11 .109 C1
Colson Ct CH1 .237 A4
Coltsfoot Dr WA14 .238 B8
Columbine Cl
Huntington CH3 .142 A3
Widnes WA8 .12 A2
Columbine Way WA9 .6 A4
Columbine Wlk 15 M31 .11 C2
Colville Ct WA2 .8 A2
Colville Rd SK11 .111 C4
Colwick Ave WA14 .238 E6
Colwyn Cl WA5 .7 C1
Colwyn Rd Bramhall SK7 .35 C4
Cheadle SK8 .239 E1
Comber Way WA16 .82 A4
Comberbach Dr CW5 .205 A2
Comberbach Prim Sch
CW9 .78 B4
Combermere Cl SK8 .239 F4
Combermere Pl CW1 .190 A3
Comboy Dr CW9 .104 B3
Combs Cl SK22 .39 A4
Comer Terr M33 .242 A6
Commercial Ave SK8 .34 C3
Commercial Brow SK14 241 E8
Commercial Rd SK10 .112 C4
Commercial St SK14 .241 E7
Common Farm La SK11 .83 C1
Common La Betley CW3 .221 C3
Chelford SK11 .83 C1
Culcheth WA3 .4 C2
Duddon CW6 .145 A4
Kelsall CW6 .122 B2
Lach Dennis CW9 .105 C3
Stretton WA4 .52 C4
Warrington WA4 .16 C1
Waverton CH3 .143 A2
Winsford CW7 .125 A3
Common Rd WA12,WA5 .1 C2
Common St WA12 .1 C2
Common The WA7 .49 C4
Commonhall St CH1 .237 A2
Commons Mill CW11 .175 A4
Commons The CW11 .175 A3
Commonside WA6 .73 C1
Commonwealth Cl CW7 149 B3
Company's Cl WA7 .48 C3
Compass Cl WA7 .50 B3
Compstall Rd SK6 .241 E2
Compton Cl WA11 .1 B4
Compton Pl Chester CH4 141 A3
Ellesmere Port CH65 .70 A3
Compton St SK15 .242 E1
Concorde Pl WA2 .8 B1
Concourse Way WA9 .1 A1
Condliffe Cl CW11 .175 B3
Conery Cl WA6 .73 B2
Coney Gr WA7 .50 A3
Coneymead SK15 .242 D4
Congleton Bsns Ctr
CW12 .156 C2
Congleton Bsns Pk
CW12 .156 B2
Congleton Cl SK9 .85 A4
Congleton Edge Rd
CW12 .179 A3
Congleton High Sch
CW12 .155 C2
Congleton La SK11 .109 B3
Congleton Rd
Alderley Edge SK9 .60 A1
Biddulph ST7 .178 C1
Biddulph ST8 .179 B1
Broughton CH4 .139 B2
Kidsgrove ST7 .194 B1
Macclesfield SK11 .112 A3
Marton SK11 .133 A3
Nether Alderley SK10 .85 A3
Sandbach CW11 .175 A4
Sandbach CW11 .175 C4
Scholar Green CW12,ST7 .177 C2
Siddington SK11 .110 A3
Smallwood CW11 .177 A3
Swettenham CW4,CW12 .131 C2
Talke ST7 .210 B4
Warren SK11 .111 C1
Congleton Rd N ST7 .194 C3
Congleton Rd S ST7 .194 B2
Congleton Sta CW12 .157 A1
Congleton War Meml Hospl
CW12 .156 C1
Conifer Cl CH1 .95 A4
Conifer Gr WA5 .14 C4
Conifer Wlk M31 .11 C2
Conifers The ST7 .193 A2
Coningsby Dr CW7 .126 C1
Coniston Ave
Bebington CH63 .43 B2
Congleton CW12 .155 C1
Dukinfield SK14 .241 C8
Warrington WA5 .14 B2
Winsford CW7 .126 B1
Coniston Cl
Alderley Edge SK9 .84 A4
Hooton CH66 .44 A1
Nantwich CW5 .205 A3
Runcorn WA7 .49 B3
Coniston Dr
Frodsham WA6 .74 B4
Handforth SK9 .34 B2
Holmes Chapel CW4 .130 A2
Stalybridge SK15 .242 D3
Coniston Rd
Chester CH2 .118 C3
Gatley SK8 .239 B5
High Lane SK6 .37 B4
Neston CH64 .66 C3
Partington M31 .11 C2
Coniston Way SK11 .111 C3
Connah's Quay High Sch
CH5 .91 B1
Connaught Ave WA1 .16 C4
Connaught Cl SK9 .60 B4
Connaught Dr WA12 .2 B1
Conrad Cl CW1 .190 C2
Conroy Way WA12 .7 B4
Consort Cl SK10 .87 C4
Consort Pl WA14 .238 B3
Constable Dr SK9 .60 C4
Constables Cl WA7 .24 A1
Constance Rd M31 .11 C2
Constance Way WA8 .23 A3
Convamore Rd SK7 .35 B4
Conway Ave Irlam M44 .11 C4
Warrington WA5 .7 C1
Winsford CW7 .149 B4
Conway Cl
Broughton CH4 .140 B3
Crewe CW1 .190 B4
Knutsford WA16 .82 A4
Warrington WA5 .14 C3
Conway Cres SK10 .87 C1
Conway Ct CH65 .70 B2
Conway Dr
Newton-le-W WA12 .2 C2
Stalybridge SK15 .242 D3
Conway Rd Cheadle SK8 .239 E2
Sale M33 .242 D5
Conway St SK5 .240 E8
Coogee Ave WA5 .14 C4
Cook Ave WA11 .1 C4
Cook St
Ellesmere Port CH65 .70 B3
Stockport SK3 .240 E5
Cooke's La CW9 .104 C3
Cookes Ct CH3 .166 A1
Cooks La SY13 .225 B4
Cooksmere La CW11 .175 A4
Coole La Nantwich CW5 .218 C2
Newhall CW3 .229 B3
Coombe Dr WA7 .49 A4
Coombe Park Ct 1 CH66 69 B3
Coombe Pk CH66 .69 B3
Coombes Ave SK14 .241 F5
Coope Rd SK10 .87 C3
Cooper Ave
Newton-le-W WA12 .1 C2
Warrington WA2 .8 A1
Cooper La WA11 .1 B3
Cooper St
Congleton CW12 .156 C2
Runcorn WA7 .23 A2
Stockport SK1 .240 F3
Widnes WA8 .13 A1
Cooper Terr CW6 .146 B1
Cooper's Croft CH3 .142 A4
Cooper's Fold SK8 .34 C3
Cooper's La CH5 .91 B1
Coopers Opening CW11 175 A4
Cop Mdw SK11 .112 C1
Copage Dr SK6 .241 A4
Cope Ave CW5 .204 B2
Copeland Gr WA7 .49 C3
Copeland Rd WA4 .16 A1
Copes La CW5 .204 B2
Copeswood Cl CH4 .139 B2
Copgrove Wlk M22 .33 C4
Copley Ave SK15 .242 F2
Copley High Sch SK15 .242 F2
Copley Park Mews SK15 242 F2
Coppenhall Gr CW2 .190 A2
Coppenhall Heyes CW2 190 A2
Coppenhall High Sch
CW1 .190 C3
Coppenhall La CW2 .189 B2
Copper Beach Cl CH4 .139 B2
Copper St SK11 .112 C3
Copper Wood CW8 .101 C3
Copperfield Cl WA3 .9 B3
Copperfield Rd
Bramhall SK8 .35 A3
Poynton SK12 .36 B1
Copperfields
Poynton SK12 .36 B1
Tarporley CW6 .146 B1
Wilmslow SK9 .60 B4
Copperhill Rd CW12 .179 A4
Coppermine La SY14 .184 A1
Copperwood WA7 .24 B1
Coppice Ave SK12 .38 A3
Coppice Cl High Lane SK12 38 A3
Romiley SK6 .241 B4
Runcorn WA7 .24 A1
Willaston (nr Nantwich)
CW5 .205 B3
Coppice Dr CW10 .151 C3
Coppice Gn WA5 .7 A1
Coppice Gr WA16 .57 A2
Coppice Ho ST7 .210 B4
Coppice La SK12 .38 A3
Coppice Rd
Haslington CW11 .192 A4
Poynton SK12 .37 A2
Talke ST7 .210 B4
Willaston (nr Nantwich)
CW5 .205 B3
Coppice Rise SK11 .112 B3
Coppice The
Altrincham WA15 .32 A4
Cuddington CW8 .101 B3
Higher Wincham CW9 .79 B2
Sandbach CW11 .174 C4
Whaley Bridge SK23 .65 C3
Coppice Way SK9 .34 C2
Coppins Cl Chester CH3 .119 A1
Helsby WA6 .73 A2
Coppins The
Warrington WA2 .8 B1
Wilmslow SK9 .59 C2
Copse The
Altrincham WA15 .32 B4
Newton-le-W WA12 .2 A2
Runcorn WA7 .50 A3
Copthorne Cl CW12 .156 C1
Copthorne Dr CW3 .229 C2
Copyhold CW8 .102 B4
Corbet Ave WA2 .16 A4
Corbet Dr TF9 .235 A2
Corbet St WA2 .16 A4
Corcoran Dr SK6 .241 F2
Corfe Way CW7 .149 B4
Coriander Cl CW10 .128 B2
Corkland Cl OL6 .242 B2
Corkland St OL6 .242 B2
Corks La SK12 .38 C3
Corley Ave SK3 .239 F7
Cormorant Cl CW1 .190 C2
Cormorant Dr WA7 .22 C1
Cornbrook Rd SK11 .112 B2
Corner Croft SK9 .60 A2
Corner Ct SK8 .239 F6
Cornerhouse La WA8 .12 B2
Corners The CW8 .102 C4
Cornfield Cl
Ellesmere Port CH66 .69 C1
Macclesfield SK10 .87 B2
2 Sale M33 .242 F5
Cornfield Rd SK6 .241 E3
Cornforth Way WA8 .12 C2
Cornhill Cl ST5 .210 B1
Cornish Cl M22 .33 B4
Cornishway M22 .33 B4
Cornishway Ind Est 4
M22 .33 B4
Cornubia Rd WA8 .23 B4
Cornwall Ave WA7 .23 A1
Cornwall Cl
3 Congleton CW12 .157 A1
High Lane SK6 .37 C4
Macclesfield SK10 .86 C1
Runcorn WA7 .23 C1
Cornwall Gr CW1 .190 A3
Cornwall Rd
Chester CH2 .118 C4
Gatley SK8 .34 A4
Irlam M44 .11 B3
Widnes WA8 .13 A2
Cornwall St Chester CH2 237 B4
Warrington WA1 .16 C4
Cornwell Cl SK9 .60 B4
Corona Ave SK14 .241 E7
Coronation Ave
Alsager ST7 .193 A2
Glazebury WA3 .5 B4
Hyde SK14 .241 E5
Warrington WA4 .17 B1
Winsford CW7 .126 C1
Coronation Bldgs SK10 .88 A4
Coronation Cres
Crewe CW1 .190 C3
Kidsgrove ST7 .194 C1
Sandbach CW11 .175 A3
Coronation Dr
Frodsham WA6 .49 B1
Haydock WA11 .2 A4
Newton-le-W WA12 .2 C1
Warrington WA5 .14 C2
Widnes WA8 .22 B4
Coronation Gr CW8 .78 A2
Coronation Ho WA7 .49 B4
Coronation Rd
Broughton CH4 .139 A2
Congleton CW12 .156 C2
Ellesmere Port CH65 .70 B2
Middlewich CW10 .151 B3
Runcorn, Higher Runcorn
WA7 .23 A1
Runcorn, Preston Brook
WA7 .50 C3
Coronation Sq 16 WA16 .57 A1
Coronation St
Chester CH4 .140 C4
Crewe CW1 .190 B3
Macclesfield SK11 .112 B3
Stockport SK5 .240 E8
Coronation Terr CW6 .146 B1
Coroner's La WA8 .13 A2
Coronet Ave CW9 .103 C2
Coronet Way WA8 .22 A4
Corporation St
Hyde SK14 .241 D6
Stalybridge SK15 .242 D1
Stockport SK1 .240 F6
Correction Brow SK12 .37 B3
Corridor Rd CH65 .71 A3
Corstons La CH64 .67 A3
Corwen Cl WA5 .7 C1
Cossack Ave WA2 .8 B1
Cote Lea Ct WA7 .49 C3
Cotebrook Dr CH2 .118 C4
Cotebrook Rd CW9 .104 B4
Cotes Pl CH1 .117 C2
Cotgreaves Cl CH4 .141 A3
Cotswold Ave WA3 .3 B3
Cotswold Cl Chester CH2 118 C3
Cuddington CW8 .102 A1
Macclesfield SK10 .86 C1
Cotswold Gr WA9 .1 A2
Cotswold Pl WA2 .8 A2
Cotswold Rd
Stockport SK4 .240 D7
Warrington WA2 .8 A2
Cotswold Way CW7 .149 A4
Cottage Cl Bebington CH63 43 B3

Cottage Cl *continued*
Neston CH64 66 C4
Cottage Dr E CH60 40 C3
Cottage Dr W CH60 40 C3
Cottage Gr SK9 59 C3
Cottage La Heswall CH60 40 C3
Macclesfield SK10 112 C4
Cottage Lawns SK9 60 A1
Cottage Rd CH4 141 A3
Cottage St SK11 112 A4
Cottages The CW4 129 B1
Cottam Dr WA2 9 A2
Cotterdale Cl WA5 14 C4
Cotterill WA7 49 B4
Cotterill Dr WA1 17 B4
Cotterill St CW2 190 B1
Cottesmore Dr CH60 41 B4
Cottesmore Gdns WA15 32 B4
Cotton Cl SK14 241 E5
Cotton La Duddon CW6 145 B4
Runcorn WA7 49 B4
Sandbach CW11 175 A2
Cotton Mews CW3 230 A2
Cotton Tree St SK4 240 E5
Cottons Bridge WA7 50 C3
Cottonwood Dr ST7 195 C2
Cottrell Rd WA15 32 B4
Coulton Rd WA8 13 C2
Council Hos
Audlem CW3 229 C1
Newhall CW5 228 A4
Countess Ave SK8 34 C3
Countess Cl SK11 111 C4
Countess Ct CH1 118 A3
Countess of Chester Hospl CH2 118 A3
Countess Rd SK11 112 A4
Countess St OL6 242 A2
Countess Way CH2 118 B2
Counting House Rd SK12 38 C3
Country Ctr The★ CH3 165 C3
County Ave OL6 242 B4
County Terr WA16 56 C1
Courier Row SK10 87 C4
Court Ho The 6 CH65 70 B3
Court La CW8 77 A1
Court The CH64 66 C3
Courtney Gn SK9 34 B1
Courtney Pl WA14 238 A1
Courtney Rd CH4 140 C2
Courts View M33 242 C7
Courtyard The
Congleton CW12 156 A2
Cuddington CW8 101 C1
Haughton CW6 186 C2
Middlewich CW10 127 B3
Newton-le-W WA12 2 C2
Stalybridge SK15 242 D2
Weaverham CW8 102 A4
Cousens Way CH1 118 A2
Cove The WA15 238 F3
Covell Rd SK12 36 B3
Covent Gdn 18 SK1 240 F5
Coventry Ave
Ellesmere Port CH66 94 C4
Gatley SK3 239 F7
Coverdale Cl WA5 14 C4
Coverdale Fold CW11 174 B3
Covert Cl CW7 149 A4
Covert Gdns ST7 210 B4
Covert Rise CH3 166 A1
Covington Pl SK9 60 A3
Cow Hey La WA7 49 A3
Cow La Ashley WA15 31 C3
Bollington SK10 88 A4
Hargrave CH3 144 A1
Macclesfield SK11 112 B3
Norley WA6 101 A3
Rainow SK10 88 B2
Sale M33 242 E7
Winsford CW7 149 C4
Cowanway WA8 12 C3
Cowbrook La SK11 135 A3
Cowdell St WA2 16 A4
Cowfields CW5 204 C3
Cowhey Cl CH4 141 A3
Cowley Way CW1 190 C1
Cowlishaw Rd SK14,SK6 241 F4
Cowper Cl CW2 206 A4
Cowthorne Dr CH3 143 A2
Coyt Rd SK23 65 C3
Crab La WA2 9 A2
Crab Tree Cl L24 21 C1
Crabmill Dr CW11 174 C4
Crabmill La Norley WA6 100 C3
Sandbach CW11 174 A3
Warmingham CW11 173 C4
Crabtree Ave
Altrincham WA15 32 B4
Disley SK12 38 C3
Crabtree Cl WA12 2 C2
Crabtree Ct SK12 38 B3
Crabtree Fold WA7 50 B4
Crabtree Gr CW1 190 C3
Crabtree Green Ct CW8 101 B1
Crabtree La WA16 29 A3
Crabwall Pl CH1 117 C3
Crackley Bank ST5 210 C1
Crackley Bank CE Prim Sch ST5 210 C1
Cradley WA8 12 B1
Cragside Way SK9 60 B3
Craig Cl
Macclesfield SK11 112 A3
Stockport SK4 240 B5
Craig Dr SK23 65 C3
Craig Gdns CH66 69 C4
Craig Rd Congleton CW12 156 C2
Craig Rd *continued*
Macclesfield SK11 112 A3
Stockport SK4 240 B5
Craig Wlk ST7 193 C1
Craigleigh Gr CH62 43 C2
Craigside ST8 179 B1
Craithe Rd CH3 119 A1
Crampton Dr WA15 32 B4
Cranage Cl WA7 49 B4
Cranage Ct 3 CW12 156 C2
Cranage Rd CW2 190 A2
Cranage Way 16 SK9 34 B3
Cranberry Cl WA14 238 B8
Cranberry Dr ST5 210 B1
Cranberry Inf Sch ST7 193 A2
Cranberry Jun Sch ST7 193 A2
Cranberry La ST7 193 A2
Cranberry Moss La ST7 193 A2
Cranberry Rd M31 11 C2
Cranborne Rd
Crewe CW1 190 B3
Warrington WA4 16 A1
Cranbourne Ct SK4 240 B8
Cranbourne Rd SK4 240 B8
Crandon Dr M20 239 C8
Cranebrook Cl CW1 190 A4
Cranfield Dr ST7 193 A2
Cranford Ave
Knutsford WA16 56 C1
Macclesfield SK11 112 C4
Sale M33 242 C8
Cranford Cl CH62 43 C2
Cranford Ct Chester CH4 141 A3
Warrington WA1 17 C4
Cranford Mews ST7 193 A2
Cranford Rd SK9 34 A1
Cranham Ave WA3 3 C4
Cranleigh Cl WA4 26 A4
Cranleigh Cres CH1 118 A2
Cranleigh Dr
Cheadle SK8 239 F6
Hazel Grove SK7 37 A4
Sale M33 242 A7
Cranmere Cl CW9 104 A2
Cranshaw La WA8 13 A3
Cransley Sch CW9 53 C1
Cranston Dr
Manchester M20 239 B8
Sale M33 242 E5
Cranswick Gn CH66 69 B3
Crantock Dr SK8 34 B4
Cranwell Ave WA3 4 C2
Cranworth St SK15 242 E1
Crauford Rd CW12 157 A4
Craven Ave WA3 3 C4
Craven Ct WA2 7 C2
Craven Dr WA14 238 C8
Craven Rd WA14 238 C7
Craven Terr M33 242 C6
Crawford Ave WA8 12 A1
Crawford Pl WA7 49 A3
Crawford St OL6 242 A2
Crawford's Wlk CH2 118 C2
Crawley Ave WA2 8 A2
Crayford Ave CW12 157 A3
Crediton Cl WA14 238 B6
Cresanne Cl 6 CW10 151 B4
Crescent Ct M33 242 B5
Crescent Dr Helsby WA6 73 A2
Whaley Bridge SK23 39 B1
Crescent Gr SK8 239 C6
Crescent Pk SK4 240 C6
Crescent Rd
Alderley Edge SK9 60 A1
Altrincham WA14 238 A6
Altrincham, Hale WA15 238 E1
Cheadle SK8 239 C6
Congleton CW12 156 B1
Crange CW4 129 C3
Ellesmere Port CH65 70 B3
Rostherne WA16 30 A2
Crescent The
Altrincham WA14 238 A5
Altrincham, Timperley WA15 238 F7
Cheadle SK8 239 D6
Chester CH2 118 B2
Congleton CW12 156 B1
Ellesmere Port CH65 69 C3
Hartford CW8 103 A3
Heswall, Gayton CH60 41 A3
Lymm WA13 18 C1
Macclesfield SK10 87 C1
Middlewich CW10 128 A1
Mottram St Andrew SK10 61 A1
Nantwich CW5 204 C3
New Mills SK22 39 A4
Northwich CW9 103 C3
Rostherne WA16 30 A2
Utkinton CW6 146 A4
Weaverham CW8 77 C1
Cressbrook Rd WA4 16 B1
Cressington Gdns 4 CH65 70 B3
Cresswell Ave
New Mills SK22 39 B4
Newcastle-u-L ST5 210 B1
Cresswell Cl WA5 7 B1
Cresswell St SK22 39 B4
Cresswellshawe Rd ST7 193 B2
Cresta Dr WA7 48 C3
Crestwood Cl CW2 206 A4
Crew Ave SK10 87 C1
Crew Rd ST7 193 C2
Crewe Bsns Pk CW1 190 C1
Crewe Gates Farm Ind Est CW1 190 C1
Crewe Gates Ind Est CW1 207 A4
Crewe Green Ave CW1 191 A2
Crewe Green Rd CW1 191 A2
Crewe Hall Ent Pk CW1 207 B4
Crewe Hill La CH3 197 A3
Crewe La CH3 180 C1
Crewe La S CH3 197 A4
Crewe Rd Alsager ST7 193 A2
Crewe CW1 190 C1
Haslington CW1,CW11 191 B3
Hatherton CW5 219 C2
Nantwich CW2,CW5 205 B3
Sandbach CW11 175 A2
Shavington CW2 206 B3
Crewe St Chester CH2 237 C3
Crewe CW1 190 B2
Crewe Sta CW1 190 C1
Crewood Common Rd CW8 76 A2
Crib La CW6 168 A4
Criccieth Ct CH65 70 B1
Criccieth Rd SK3 240 A3
Cricket St M34 241 A8
Cricket's La OL6 242 A3
Criftin Cl CH66 69 B1
Crimes La CH3,CW6 167 B2
Cringle Dr SK8 239 C3
Crisham Ave CW5 218 C4
Crispin Rd M22 33 C4
Critchley Cl SK14 241 F5
Critchley Rd L24 21 A2
Croasdale Dr WA7 49 C3
Crocus St CW8 78 A2
Croesmere Dr CH66 69 B1
Croft Cl Altrincham WA15 32 B3
Congleton CW12 156 C1
Utkinton CW6 146 A4
Waverton CH3 143 A3
Croft Ct CH65 70 C2
Croft Gdns WA4 27 A4
Croft Heath Gdns WA3 9 A4
Croft La Dodleston CH4 162 A4
Knutsford WA16 82 A4
Croft Prim Sch WA3 9 A4
Croft Rd SK9 59 C2
Croft St Golborne WA3 3 A4
Hyde SK14 241 D6
Stalybridge SK15 242 E2
Widnes WA8 23 A3
Croft The Chester CH2 118 B3
Norton in Hales TF9 236 A2
Runcorn WA7 23 C1
Croften Dr CH64 66 C3
Crofters Cl
8 Ellesmere Port CH66 69 C1
Pickmere WA16 80 A4
Wistaston CW2 206 A4
Crofters Ct
Holmes Chapel CW4 130 B2
Newcastle-u-L ST5 210 B2
Crofters Gn SK9 59 C3
Crofters Heath CH66 69 C1
Crofters Lea CW8 103 B4
Crofters Pk CH5 116 A2
Crofters The M33 242 F5
Crofters Way CH1 116 C4
Crofton Cl WA4 27 B3
Crofton Gdns WA3 4 C2
Crofton Rd WA7 22 C1
Crofts The CH3 180 C1
Croftside WA1 17 C4
Croftside Way SK9 60 B3
Croftsway CH60 40 B4
Croftwood Cl 11 CW7 149 A4
Cromdale Way WA5 14 C3
Cromer Dr CW1 190 A4
Cromer Rd Cheadle SK8 239 E6
Sale M33 242 C5
Cromford Ct SK23 65 C3
Cromford Mews SK23 65 C3
Cromley Rd SK6 37 C3
Crompton Dr WA2 8 A3
Crompton Rd SK11 112 B4
Crompton St OL6 242 B4
Cromwell Ave
Gatley SK8 239 A6
Warrington WA5 15 B4
Cromwell Ave S WA5 15 B2
Cromwell Cl WA12 2 A2
Cromwell Ct Irlam M44 11 C4
10 Nantwich CW5 204 C3
4 Warrington WA1 16 A3
Cromwell Dr CW2 206 B2
Cromwell Rd
Bramhall SK7 35 B3
Ellesmere Port CH65 70 B3
Irlam M44 11 C4
Northwich CW8 103 C4
Cromwell St
Stockport SK4 240 D7
Widnes WA8 23 A3
Cronkinson Ave CW5 204 C2
Cronkinson Oak CW5 204 C2
Cronton CE Prim Sch WA8 12 B3
Cronton La
Cronton WA8,L35 12 A4
Widnes WA8 12 C3
Cronton Park Ave WA8 12 B3
Cronton Park Cl WA8 12 B3
Cronton Rd WA8 12 B3
Cronulla Dr WA5 14 C4
Crook La CW7 127 A1
Crook St Chester CH1 237 A2
Hyde SK14 241 E6
Crooked La CH3,CW6 145 B2
Crookedyard Rd SK11 113 C4
Crookenden Cl CH2 95 B1
Crookenden Rd CH2 95 B1
Croppers Rd WA2 8 C2
Crosby Ave WA5 16 A4
Crosby Gr CH64 68 A4
Crosby St SK2 240 F3
Crosfield St WA1 16 A3
Cross Farm WA2 9 A1
Cross Gn CH2 118 C3
Cross Gr WA15 238 F8
Cross Hey CH4 237 C1
Cross La Audley ST7 209 C3
Church Minshull CW1,CW5 172 B3
Congleton CW12 157 A1
Croft WA3 9 B4
Frodsham WA6 73 A4
Haslington CW11 191 C4
Middlewich CW10 151 B3
Neston CH64 66 C3
Newton-le-W WA12 2 A2
Sandbach CW11 175 B3
Smallwood CW11 176 C3
Swettenham CW12 131 C2
Warrington WA4 17 A2
Wilmslow SK9 60 C4
Cross La E M31 11 C2
Cross La W M31 11 C1
Cross Lane S WA3 9 B3
Cross Lanes Tarvin CH3 121 B1
Tarvin, Old Moss CH3 144 B4
Cross O' Th' Hill Rd SY14 214 A2
Cross Rd Gatley SK8 34 A4
Haslington CW1 191 B2
Cross St Alsager ST7 193 B2
3 Altrincham WA14 238 D4
Barnton CW8 78 A2
Chester CH2 118 C1
Congleton CW12 156 B2
Crewe CW1 190 B2
Golborne WA3 3 A4
Haslington CW1 191 B2
Holt LL13 196 C4
Hyde SK14 241 D6
Macclesfield SK11 112 C3
Marston CW9 79 B2
Neston CH64 66 C4
New Mills SK22 39 B4
Runcorn WA7 23 A2
Sale M32,M33 242 B8
Warrington WA2 16 A4
Widnes WA8 13 B1
Cross The Holt LL13 196 C4
Kingsley WA6 75 B1
Lymm WA13 18 C2
Cross Wood St CW5 204 B3
Crossall St SK11 112 B4
Crossdale Rd CH62 43 B3
Crossfield Ave
Culcheth WA3 4 C1
Winsford CW7 149 B4
Crossfield Cl
Denton M34 241 A6
Stalybridge SK15 242 D1
Crossfield Rd
Bollington SK10 87 C3
Handforth SK9 34 B2
Crossfields CH3 121 A1
Crossgates WA8 13 C2
Crossings The WA12 2 B2
Crosskeys Cl CW6 145 A3
Crossland Terr WA6 73 A1
Crosslands
Congleton CW12 157 A1
Haslington CW1 191 B2
Crossledge CW12 156 A2
Crossley Ave CH66 69 C3
Crossley Cres CH2 119 A3
Crossley Dr CH60 40 B4
Crossley Pk WA6 99 B4
Crossley Rd M33 242 A8
Crossley St
Stalybridge SK15 242 C2
Warrington WA1 16 B3
Crossmoor Cres SK6 241 C1
Crossmoor Gr SK6 241 C2
Crossway Bramhall SK7 35 C3
Crewe CW1 190 B3
Widnes WA8 22 B4
Crossway The CH63 42 B2
Crossways ST8 179 C1
Crossways Rd ST7 194 A2
Crosthwaite Ave CH62 43 C2
Croston Cl
Alderley Edge SK9 60 B1
Widnes WA8 12 B2
Crotia Ave CW2 207 A3
Crouch La CW12 157 B2
Crouchley Hall Mews WA13 18 C1
Crouchley La WA13 18 C1
Croughton Ct CH66 69 C4
Croughton Rd
Ellesmere Port CH66 69 C4
Stoak CH2 96 A4
Stoak, Croughton CH2 95 C3
Crow La E WA12 2 B2
Crow La W WA12 2 A2
Crow Wood La WA8 13 B1
Crow Wood Pl WA8 13 B2
Crow's Nest Cotts CH3 166 B3
Crowbrook Gr 20 SK9 34 B1
Crowder's La CW9 105 A2
Crowe Ave WA2 8 A1
Crowland Gdns SK8 35 A3
Crowley La CW9,WA16 28 A2
Crown Ave WA8 22 A4
Crown Bank
3 Sandbach CW11 175 A3
Talke ST7 210 B3
Crown Bank Cres ST7 210 B3
Crown Cotts CW8 124 A4
Crown Ctyd CW3 229 C2
Crown Fields Cl WA12 2 A3
Crown Gate WA7 49 C4
Crown Gdns
Newton-le-W WA12 2 A2
Talke ST7 210 B3
Crown Gn WA13 19 A2
Crown Ind Est WA14 238 E7
Crown La WA16 106 B4
Crown Mews CW3 229 C2
Crown Park Dr WA12 2 A3
Crown Pasages WA15 238 E2
Crown Royal Ind Pk 11 SK1 240 F4
Crown St
Newton-le-W WA12 2 A2
8 Northwich CW8 103 C4
7 Warrington WA1 16 A3
Crown St W SK11 112 B4
Crownest La CW9 78 C4
Crowther Ct 6 SK4 240 A7
Croxton Gn SY14 201 B3
Croxton La CW10 128 A2
Croxton Way CW8 103 A2
Croyde Cl M22 33 C4
Croyde Rd L24 21 A2
Crum Hill 2 CW9 104 A4
Crummock Rd SK8 239 B3
Cryers La Elton CH2 72 A1
Thornton-le-M CH2 96 C4
Cty High Sch Leftwich The CW9 104 A2
Cuckoo Clock Mus★ WA16 80 C4
Cuckoo La Acton CW5 203 C4
Neston CH64 67 B4
Cuckstoolpit Hill 3 SK11 112 C4
Cuddington Cres SK3 240 D2
Cuddington La CW8 101 B2
Cuddington Prim Sch CW8 101 C1
Cuddington Sta CW8 102 A2
Cuddington Way 7 SK9 34 B3
Cuerdley Gn WA5 14 A1
Cuerdley Rd WA5 14 B2
Culbin Cl WA3 10 A3
Culcheth Com Prim Sch WA3 5 A2
Culcheth Hall Dr WA3 4 C2
Culcheth Hall Prep Sch WA14 238 D3
Culcheth High Sch WA3 5 A2
Culcheth Rd WA14 238 D3
Culford Cl WA7 24 B1
Culland St CW2 190 B1
Cullen Cl CH63 43 B2
Cullen Rd WA7 48 B4
Culver Rd SK3 240 D1
Cumber Cl SK9 59 B2
Cumber Dr SK9 59 B2
Cumber La SK9 59 B2
Cumberland Ave
Irlam M44 11 B3
Nantwich CW5 204 C3
Cumberland Cl
Crewe CW1 190 B3
Talke ST7 210 C4
Cumberland Cres WA11 1 A3
Cumberland Dr
Altrincham WA14 31 A4
Bollington SK10 88 A4
Cumberland Gr CH66 69 B2
Cumberland Rd
Congleton CW12 156 A2
Partington M31 11 C1
Sale M33 242 C5
Cumberland Sports Ctr CW1 190 B3
Cumberland St
37 Macclesfield SK11 112 B4
Stalybridge SK15 242 C2
Warrington WA4 16 B2
Cumbermere Dr CW11 174 C4
Cumbers Dr CH64 67 A3
Cumbers La CH64 67 A3
Cumbrae Dr 8 CH65 70 B1
Cumbria Cl 4 CH66 69 C1
Cuncliffe Cl WA7 50 A4
Cundiff Cl SK11 112 C3
Cundy St SK14 241 E8
Cunliffe Ave WA12 2 A3
Cunliffe Dr M33 242 C5
Cunliffe St
Dukinfield SK14 241 C8
Stockport SK3 240 C4
Cunningham Cl WA5 14 C3
Cunningham Dr
Bebington CH63 43 B4
Gatley M22 34 A4
Runcorn WA7 22 C1
Cunningham Rd WA8 22 B4
Cuppin St CH1 237 A2
Curlender Way L24 21 C1
Curlew Cl Golborne WA3 3 B4
Winsford CW7 149 B3
Curlew Gr WA3 9 C2
Currans Rd WA2 8 A1
Currier La OL6 242 A2
Curtis Rd SK4 240 A6

Curzon Ave ST7 193 B3
Curzon Cl CH4 141 A4
Curzon Dr WA4 27 A4
Curzon Gr CW7 126 C1
Curzon Mews SK9 60 A3
Curzon Pk N CH4 141 A4
Curzon Pk S CH4 141 A4
Curzon Rd
Ashton-u-Lyne OL6 242 A4
Gatley SK8 34 A4
Poynton SK12 36 C1
6 Sale M33 242 B7
Curzon St Chester CH4 140 C4
3 Runcorn WA7 22 C1
Cuthbert Rd SK8 239 E6
Cybnet Ct WA1 16 A2
Cygnet Cl CH66 69 B2
Cyman Cl CH1 117 B2
Cymbal Ct SK5 240 F7
Cynthia Ave WA1 17 A4
Cynthia Rd WA7 22 C1
Cypress Ave
Ellesmere Port CH66 69 C1
Widnes WA8 13 A1
Cypress Cl Stockport SK3 240 C4
Warrington WA1 17 C4
Cypress Gr Denton M34 241 A7
Runcorn WA7 49 B4
Cypress Mews CW8 102 C4
Cypress Way SK6 38 A4
Cyril Bell Cl WA13 18 C2
Cyril St WA2 16 A4

D

D'Arcy Cotts CH63 42 A3
Daffodil Cl WA8 13 C2
Dagfields Craft & Antiques Ctr* CW5 220 A2
Dagnall Ave WA5 7 C1
Daintry St SK11 112 C4
Daintry Terr 4 SK11 112 C4
Dairy Farm Cl 8 WA13 18 C2
Dairy House La SK7 35 A2
Dairy House Rd SK7,SK8 35 A3
Dairy House Small Holdings SK7 35 A2
Dairy House Way CW2 189 C1
Dairy La CW5 188 B3
Dairyground Rd SK7 35 C4
Dairyhouse La WA14 238 B7
Dairylands Rd ST7 193 C2
Daisy Ave WA12 2 B1
Daisy Bank Culcheth WA3 4 C2
Nantwich CW5 204 B3
Daisy Bank Cres CW3 229 C3
Daisy Bank La
Anderton CW9 78 B2
Cheadle SK8 239 A1
Daisy Bank Rd
Lymm WA13 18 B2
Warrington WA5 14 C2
Daisy St SK1,SK2 240 F3
Daisy Way SK6 37 C4
Daisybank Dr
Congleton CW12 156 B2
Sandbach CW11 175 B3
Daisyhill Cl M33 242 E6
Dalby Cl WA3 10 A3
Dalby Ct CW9 104 C3
Dale Ave Bebington CH62 43 B4
Bramhall SK7 35 C4
Ellesmere Port CH66 69 B3
Dale Cl Warrington WA5 15 B2
Widnes WA8 22 A4
Dale Cres CW12 156 C1
Dale Ct Heswall CH60 40 C4
Middlewich CW10 151 B4
Dale Dr Chester CH2 118 B4
Ellesmere Port CH65 69 C3
Dale Gdns CH65 70 A2
Dale Gr Altrincham WA15 238 F7
Congleton CW12 157 A1
Irlam M44 11 C3
Dale Head Rd SK10 86 C2
Dale Hey CH66 43 C1
Dale House Fold SK12 37 A2
Dale La WA4 26 C4
Dale Rd Bebington CH62 43 B3
Golborne WA3 3 A4
New Mills SK22 39 B4
Dale St Chester CH3 119 A1
Macclesfield SK11 112 C4
Runcorn WA7 23 A1
Stalybridge SK15 242 C1
Stockport SK3 240 D3
Dale The Neston CH64 66 C3
Tiverton CW6 168 B3
Warrington WA5 14 C3
Dale View Kidsgrove ST7 195 B3
Newton-le-W WA12 2 C2
Dale's Sq CW9 103 C3
Dalebrook Ct SK4 240 C6
Dalecroft WA6 72 C1
Dalefords La
Cuddington CW8 102 A1
Whitegate CW8 125 B4
Dales Green Rd ST7 195 B3
Dalesford Cl WN7 4 B4
Dalesford Cres SK11 111 C4
Daleside CH2 118 B4
Dalesway CH60 40 C4
Dalewood Cl WA2 16 A3
Dalewood Cres CH2 72 A2
Dalham La WA2 16 A4
Dallam Com Prim Sch WA5 7 C1
Dalmahoy Cl CW7 126 B1
Dalrybrook Gr 7 SK9 34 C1
Dalston Dr SK7 35 B3
Dalton Ave WA5 15 C4
Dalton Bank WA1 16 B3
Dalton Cl CH1 117 C2
Dalton Ct Runcorn WA7 23 C2
Sandbach CW11 174 C4
Dalton Gr SK4 240 C8
Dalton St Runcorn WA7 23 B1
Sale M33 242 C8
Warrington WA3 9 C3
Dalton Way CW10 128 B1
Dalveen Dr WA15 238 F7
Dalwood Cl WA7 50 C4
Dam Head La WA3 11 A3
Dam La Hollinfare WA3 11 A2
Mobberley WA16 58 B2
Warrington WA1 17 B4
Winwick WA3 8 C4
Dame Hollow SK8 34 B4
Dameny Ct SK7 35 C4
Damery Rd SK7 35 C4
Damhead La CH64 67 C4
Damian Dr WA12 2 A3
Dams La WA16 106 B3
Damson La WA16 58 A2
Damson Wlk M31 11 B2
Dan's Rd WA8 13 C1
Danby Cl Hyde SK14 241 F8
Runcorn WA7 49 B3
Warrington WA5 15 C4
Danby Pl SK14 241 F8
Danby Rd SK14 241 F8
Dane Ave Partington M31 11 C2
Stockport SK3 240 A4
Dane Bank Ave
Congleton CW12 156 C2
Crewe CW2 190 A1
Dane Bank Dr SK12 38 B3
Dane Bank Rd CW9 104 A4
Dane Cl Alsager ST7 193 A2
Sandbach CW11 174 C4
Dane Dr Biddulph ST8 179 C1
Wilmslow SK9 60 B3
Dane Gdns ST7 195 B1
Dane Gr CH2 119 C4
Dane Hill Cl SK12 38 B3
Dane Mews M33 242 B6
Dane Mill Bsns Ctr CW12 156 B2
Dane Pl CW7 127 A1
Dane Rd M33 242 D7
Dane Road Sta M33 242 C8
Dane St Congleton CW12 156 B2
Middlewich CW10 128 B1
Northwich CW9 103 C4
Danebank Rd WA13 18 C2
Danebank Rd E WA13 18 C2
Danefield Ct SK8 34 B4
Danefield Rd
Holmes Chapel CW4 130 B2
Northwich CW9 104 A4
Sale M33 242 C8
Danes Sq SK11 112 B3
Danesbury Rise SK8 239 D5
Danescroft WA8 12 A2
Daneside Bsns Pk CW12 156 C2
Daneswell Rd L24 21 A1
Daniel Adamson Ave M31 11 B2
Daniel Cl WA3 10 A2
Daniel Ct M31 11 C2
Daniel's La SK1 240 E6
Daniell Way CH3 142 A4
Danwood Cl M34 241 B5
Dappleheath Rd CW2 190 A1
Darby Cl CH64 66 C2
Darent Rd WA11 1 A4
Daresbury Ave WA15 238 E5
Daresbury Cl
Holmes Chapel CW4 130 A2
Sale M33 242 F5
Stockport SK3 240 D1
Wilmslow SK9 60 B4
Daresbury Ct WA8 13 C2
Daresbury Expressway
Daresbury WA4 25 A2
Runcorn WA7 24 B2
Daresbury La WA4 25 B1
Daresbury Prim Sch WA4 25 A1
Dargle Rd M33 242 B8
Darian Ave M22 33 B4
Dark Ark La CH3,WA6 99 A2
Dark La Henbury SK11 111 A4
Kingsley WA6 75 A1
Marston CW9 79 B3
Tattenhall CH3 183 C4
Warren SK11 111 B2
Whitchurch SY13 227 A1
Whitley WA4 52 B3
Darkie Mdw CW6 185 C4
Darland La LL12 162 B1
Darley Ave Crewe CW2 190 A2
Gatley SK8 239 B5
Warrington WA2 8 C2
Darley Cl WA8 12 A2
Darley Rd SK7 36 C4
Darley St M33 242 B6
Darleydale Dr CH62 43 C3
Darlington Ave CW1 189 C3
Darlington Cres CH1 94 A1
Darlington Ct 19 WA8 23 A4
Darlington St CW10 128 B1
Darnaway Cl WA3 10 A3
Darnhall Prim Sch CW7 149 B3
Darnhall School La CW7 149 B3
Darnton Gdns OL6 242 B3
Darnton Rd OL6,SK15 242 B3
Dart Cl Alsager ST7 193 A2
Biddulph ST8 179 B1
Dart Wlk CW7 127 A1
Dartnall Cl SK12 38 A3
Darwen Gdns WA2 8 C1
Darwin Gr SK7 35 C3
Darwin Rd CH1 117 B2
Darwin St CW8 103 C4
Daryl Rd CH60 41 A4
Dashwood Cl WA4 27 A4
Daten Ave WA3 9 C3
Daten Pk WA3 9 C3
Dauncey Cl CH2 95 B1
Davehall Ave SK9 60 A4
Daven Prim Sch CW12 156 C1
Daven Rd CW12 156 C1
Davenham Ave WA1 16 C4
Davenham CE Prim Sch CW9 103 C1
Davenham Cres CW2 190 A2
Davenham Ct CW9 104 A2
Davenham Rd
Davenham CW9 104 C2
Handforth SK9 34 B2
Davenham Way CW10 151 B3
Davenport Ave
Crewe CW2 206 B4
Nantwich CW5 204 C4
Warrington WA4 16 C3
Wilmslow SK9 59 C2
Davenport Cl CW11 175 B4
Davenport La
Altrincham WA14 238 C7
Brereton Green CW11 154 B1
Marton SK11 132 C3
Mobberley WA16 58 B3
Davenport Lodge SK3 240 F1
Davenport Park La
Brereton Green CW12 154 B4
Swettenham CW12 131 B1
Davenport Rd CH60 40 C4
Davenport Row WA7 49 B4
Davenport St
Congleton CW12 156 B1
Crewe CW1 190 B3
Macclesfield SK11 112 C4
Davenport Sta SK3 240 F1
Davey La SK9 60 A1
Daveylands SK9 60 B4
David Cl M34 241 A5
David Lewis Sch SK9 83 C3
David Rd WA13 18 B2
David St Denton M34 241 A6
Northwich CW8 103 C4
David's Ave WA5 15 A3
Davidson Ave CW12 157 A3
Davies Ave Gatley SK8 34 A3
Newton-le-W WA12 2 B2
Warrington WA4 16 C2
Davies Cl WA8 23 A2
Davies Way WA13 18 C2
Davis Cl ST7 193 C2
Davy Ave WA3 9 C3
Davy Rd WA7 23 C2
Daw Bank SK3 240 E5
Dawlish Ave SK8 34 C4
Dawlish Cl Bramhall SK7 35 C4
Hollinfare WA3 11 A2
Dawn Cl CH64 67 A3
Dawn Gdns CH65 70 A2
Dawpool Cl CH2 118 B3
Dawpool Dr CH62 43 B4
Dawson Dr CH2 237 A4
Dawson Rd
Altrincham WA14 238 D8
Bollington SK10 88 A4
Gatley SK8 34 B4
Macclesfield SK11 111 C4
Dawson St SK14 241 E5
Dawstone Rd CH60 41 A4
Dawstone Rise CH60 40 C4
Daylesford Cl SK8 239 D4
Daylesford Cres SK8 239 D4
Daylesford Rd SK8 239 D4
De Lacy Row WA7 24 A1
De Trafford Mews 6 SK9 34 B1
Deacon Cl WA14 238 B1
Deacon Rd WA8 13 A1
Deacon Trad Est WA12 2 A1
Deacons Cl WA3 9 A4
Deadman's La CW5 205 A1
Deakin's Rd CW7 127 A2
Deal Sq SK14 241 E6
Deal St SK14 241 E6
Dean Bank CW6 168 B2
Dean Cl Bollington SK10 88 A4
Handforth SK9 34 B1
Partington M31 11 C2
Sandbach CW11 174 C4
7 Widnes WA8 23 A4
Dean Cres WA2 8 A1
Dean Ct Bollington SK10 88 A4
Golborne WA3 3 A4
Dean Dr Altrincham WA14 238 B1
Handforth SK9 34 B1
Dean Hollow ST7 209 B1
Dean La SK7 36 C4
Dean Meadow WA12 2 B2
Dean Pk SY14 214 A3
Dean Rd Golborne WA3 3 A4
Dean Rd continued
Handforth SK9 34 C2
Irlam M44 11 C3
Dean Row Ct 14 SK9 34 B1
Dean Row Jun Sch SK9 34 C1
Dean Row Rd SK9 61 A4
Dean St Middlewich CW10 128 B1
Northwich CW9 104 B4
Stalybridge SK15 242 D1
Widnes WA8 23 A4
Winsford CW7 126 B1
Dean Valley Com Sch SK10 87 C4
Dean's La ST5 210 B1
Deane Ave SK8 239 F5
Deane Ct CW5 205 A2
Deanery Cl CH2 118 B2
Deanery Way SK1 240 F6
Deans Cl Chester CH2 118 B3
Tarvin CH3 121 A1
Deans La
Barthomley CW2 208 B2
Sandbach CW11 174 C3
Warrington WA4 17 C2
Deans Rd CH65 70 C2
Deans Way
Higher Kinnerton CH4 161 A4
Tarvin CH3 121 A1
Deansgate CH65 70 A3
Deansgate La WA14, WA15 238 E7
Deansway WA8 22 B4
Deanwater Cl WA3 9 B2
Deanwater Ct SK8 34 B4
Deanway SK9 34 B1
Deanway Trad Est SK9 34 B2
Dearden St SK15 242 D2
Dearnford Ave CH62 43 B3
Dearnford Cl CH62 43 B3
Debra Cl CH66 69 B2
Debra Rd CH66 69 B2
Decade Cl ST5 210 C1
Dee Banks CH4 141 C4
Dee Banks Sch CH3 142 A4
Dee Cl Biddulph ST8 179 C1
Sandbach CW11 174 C4
Talke ST7 210 C4
Dee Cres CH3 180 C1
Dee Fords Ave CH3 119 A1
Dee Hills Pk CH2 237 C2
Dee La Chester CH2 237 C2
Holt LL13 196 B4
Dee Mdws LL13 196 B4
Dee Park Cl CH60 41 A3
Dee Park Rd CH60 41 A3
Dee Pk LL13 196 B4
Dee Point Prim Sch CH1 117 B2
Dee Side CH60 40 B4
Dee View CH3 180 C1
Dee View Rd
Connah's Quay CH5 91 B1
Heswall CH60 40 C4
Dee Way CW7 127 A1
Deep Dale WA5 14 C3
Deepdale WA8 12 B2
Deer Park Ct WA7 49 C3
Deerwood Cl
Ellesmere Port CH66 69 B4
Macclesfield SK10 86 C1
Deerwood Cres CH66 69 B4
Deeside
Ellesmere Port CH65 70 A2
Holt LL13 196 C4
Deeside Cl CH65 70 A1
Deeside Coll of F Ed (Coleg Glannau Dyfrdwy) CH5 91 B1
Deeside Cres CH1 116 C3
Deeside Ct CH64 41 A1
Deeside Ind Est (Parc Ddiwydiannol Glannau Dyfrdwy) CH5 93 A1
Deeside La CH1 116 B2
Deirdre Ave WA8 13 A1
Delafield Cl WA2 8 C2
Delamer Rd WA14 238 C3
Delamere Ave
Bebington CH62 43 C2
Ellesmere Port CH66 69 C3
Golborne WA3 3 C3
Sale M33 242 E5
Widnes WA8 12 B1
Delamere CE Prim Sch CW6 123 B3
Delamere Cl Barnton CW8 78 A2
Bebington CH62 43 C2
Sandbach CW11 174 C4
Delamere Ct Alsager ST7 192 C2
Bebington CH62 43 C2
Delamere Dr
Ellesmere Port CH66 69 C3
Macclesfield SK10 87 C1
Delamere Forest Sch WA6 100 B2
Delamere Forest Visitor Ctr* CW8 100 A1
Delamere Gn CH66 69 C3
Delamere La CH3 99 A1
Delamere Park Way E CW8 101 B3
Delamere Park Way W CW8 101 B3
Delamere Rd
Congleton CW12 155 C2
Gatley SK8 239 B5
Handforth SK9 34 C2
Nantwich CW5 204 C2
Norley WA6 100 A3
Delamere Rise CW7 126 A1
Delamere St
Chester CH1 237 A3
Crewe CW1 190 B2
Warrington WA5 15 C3
Winsford CW7 126 A1
Delamere Sta CW8 100 B1
Delamore's Acre CH64 68 A4
Delavor Cl CH60 40 C4
Delavor Rd CH60 40 C4
Delenty Dr WA3 9 C2
Delery Dr WA1 16 C4
Delfur Rd SK7 35 C4
Delhi Rd M44 11 C4
Dell Cl CH63 43 A3
Dell Dr WA2 9 A1
Dell La CH60 41 A4
Dell The Cuddington CW8 101 B3
Guilden Sutton CH3 119 C3
Kelsall CW6 122 B2
Delmar Rd WA16 57 B1
Delph La Daresbury WA4 25 A1
Winwick WA2 8 C3
Delphfield WA7 50 B4
Delphfields Rd WA4 26 B4
Delphside ST7 209 C1
Delta Cres WA5 7 B1
Delta Ct CH4 140 A3
Delves Ave WA5 15 C4
Delves Broughton Ct CW1 191 B3
Delves Cl CW2 206 A2
Delves Wlk CH3 142 A4
Delvine Dr CH2 118 B3
Demage Dr CH66 69 B2
Demage La Backford CH1 94 C2
Chester CH2 118 B4
Demage La S CH2 118 B4
Demesne Cl SK15 242 F1
Demesne Cres SK15 242 F1
Demesne Dr SK15 242 F1
Demmings Inf Sch SK8 239 F5
Demmings Rd SK8 239 F5
Den La CW3,CW5 221 B2
Denbigh Cl
Hazel Grove SK7 36 B4
Helsby WA6 73 A1
Denbigh Cres CW10 151 B4
Denbigh Ct CH65 70 B2
Denbigh Dr CW7 149 A4
Denbigh Gdns CH65 70 B2
Denbigh St Chester CH1 118 A2
Stockport SK4 240 D7
Denbury Ave WA4 16 C1
Denbury Dr WA14 238 B5
Denby La SK4 240 D8
Dene Ave WA12 1 C2
Dene Ct SK4 240 C6
Dene Dr CW7 149 B4
Denehurst Cl WA5 14 C2
Denehurst Park Way CW8 101 B3
Denesgate 11 CW7 149 B4
Deneside Ave CW1 190 B3
Deneway Bramhall SK7 35 B4
High Lane SK6 37 C4
Stockport SK4 240 C6
Deneway Cl SK4 240 C6
Deneway Mews SK4 240 C6
Denewood Ct 3 SK9 60 A3
Denford Cl CH4 139 B2
Denford Pl ST7 193 B3
Denhall Cl CH2 118 C3
Denhall La CH64 67 A2
Denham Ave WA5 15 A3
Denham Dr SK7 35 B4
Denholm Rd M20 239 C8
Denise Ave WA5 14 C3
Denison Rd SK7 36 C4
Denmark Rd M33 242 B8
Denmark St WA14 238 D4
Dennett Cl WA1 17 C3
Dennis Dr CH4 141 A3
Dennis Rd WA8 23 B4
Dennison Rd SK8 35 A4
Densham Ave WA2 8 A1
Denston Cl CW2 190 A1
Denstone Dr CH4 141 A2
Dentdale Wlk M22 33 B4
Dentith Dr CH1 117 C3
Denton Cl CW7 126 B1
Denton Dr CW9 79 B1
Denton Drive Ind Est CW9 79 B1
Denton St WA8 13 B1
Denver Ave CW2 190 A2
Denver Rd WA4 17 A2
Denwall Ho 5 CH64 66 C2
Depenbech Cl SY14 213 A2
Depleach Rd SK8 239 D5
Depmore La WA6 75 A1
Deramore Cl OL6 242 B3
Derby Cl Irlam M44 11 B3
Newton-le-W WA12 2 A2
Derby Ct M33 242 C5
Derby Dr WA1 16 C4
Derby Knoll SK23 39 C1
Derby Pl CH2 118 C2
Derby Range SK4 240 B8
Derby Rd
Ashton-u-Lyne OL6 242 A3
Golborne WA3 3 B4
Hyde SK14 241 E8
Stockport SK4 240 C8
Talke ST7 210 B4
Warrington WA4 16 B1
Widnes, Barrow's Green WA8 13 B2

Derby Rd *continued*
Widnes, Lunts Heath WA8 . . 13 A2
Derby Row WA12 . . . 7 B4
Derby St
Altrincham WA14 . . . 238 E5
Congleton CW12 . . . 156 B2
Crewe CW1 . . . 190 A3
Newton-le-W WA12 . . . 2 A2
Stockport SK3 . . . 240 D4
Derbyshire Hill Rd WA9 . . 1 A1
Derbyshire Rd
High Lane SK12 . . . 37 B3
Partington M31 . . . 11 C1
Sale M33 . . . 242 C6
Dereham Way WA7 . . . 24 B2
Derek Ave WA2 . . . 8 C1
Derfel Terr 5 WA6 . . . 74 A4
Derrington Ave CW2 . . . 190 B2
Derwen Prim Sch CH4 . 161 A4
Derwen Rd SK3 . . . 240 E3
Derwent Ave CW7 . . . 127 A1
Derwent Cl Alsager ST7 . 193 A2
Culcheth WA3 . . . 5 A1
Holmes Chapel CW4 . . . 130 A2
Macclesfield SK11 . . . 112 A3
Partington M31 . . . 11 C2
Willaston (nr Nantwich) CW5 . . . 205 B3
Derwent Cres ST7 . . . 195 B1
Derwent Dr Biddulph ST8 179 C1
Bramhall SK7 . . . 35 B3
Congleton CW12 . . . 156 C1
Handforth SK9 . . . 34 B3
Hooton CH66 . . . 44 A1
Derwent Rd Chester CH2 118 C3
High Lane SK6 . . . 37 C4
Warrington WA4 . . . 16 A1
Widnes WA8 . . . 12 B1
Derwent Terr SK15 . . . 242 D4
Derwent Way
Neston CH64 . . . 66 C4
Alderley Edge SK9 . . . 83 C4
Desoto Rd WA8 . . . 22 C3
Desoto Rd E WA8 . . . 22 C3
Desoto Rd W WA8 . . . 22 C3
Deva Ave CH4 . . . 140 B3
Deva Bsns Pk CH5 . . . 116 A4
Deva Cl SK12 . . . 36 A2
Deva Ct CH2 . . . 118 C1
Deva La CH2 . . . 118 B3
Deva Link CH1 . . . 118 A2
Deva Rd CW2 . . . 189 B2
Deva Stad (Chester City FC) CH1 . . . 117 C1
Deva Terr CH2 . . . 237 C2
Devisdale Grange WA14 238 B3
Devisdale Rd WA14 . . . 238 B4
Devon Cl
Macclesfield SK10 . . . 86 C1
Middlewich CW10 . . . 128 B1
Devon Gr ST8 . . . 179 B1
Devon Pl
Congleton CW12 . . . 156 C2
Widnes WA8 . . . 13 A2
Devon Rd Chester CH2 . . 118 C3
Irlam M44 . . . 11 B3
Partington M31 . . . 11 C1
Devonshire Dr SK9 . . . 60 A1
Devonshire Gdns WA12 . . 2 B1
Devonshire Pl
Chester CH4 . . . 141 C4
Runcorn WA7 . . . 23 A1
Devonshire Rd
Altrincham WA14 . . . 238 D6
Broughton CH4 . . . 139 B2
Hazel Grove SK7 . . . 36 C4
Stockport SK4 . . . 240 B7
Warrington WA1 . . . 16 C4
Dewar Ct WA7 . . . 23 C2
Dewar St WA3 . . . 9 C3
Dewes St CW1 . . . 190 A3
Dewhurst Rd WA3 . . . 9 B1
Dexter Way CW10 . . . 128 B1
Dial Cotts CH64 . . . 67 A3
Dial La CW12 . . . 158 A1
Dial Rd WA15 . . . 32 B4
Dial St WA1 . . . 16 B3
Diamond Ave 12 ST7 . . . 195 A1
Diamond Cl OL6 . . . 242 A4
Diamond St OL6 . . . 242 A4
Dibbins Gn CH63 . . . 43 A4
Dibbinsdale Rd CH63 . . . 43 A4
Dickens Cl Cheadle SK8 . . 35 A3
Sandbach CW11 . . . 174 B3
Dickens La SK12 . . . 36 C1
Dickenson St WA2 . . . 16 B4
Dickinson Cl WA11 . . . 1 A3
Dickinson Way ST7 . . . 193 A2
Dickson Cl WA8 . . . 23 A4
Dickson St 2 WA8 . . . 23 A4
Dicksons Dr CH2 . . . 118 B2
Didsbury Rd SK4 . . . 240 B6
Dierden St CW7 . . . 127 A1
Dierdens Terr CW10 . . . 128 B1
Dig La Acton CW5 . . . 203 C2
Frodsham WA6 . . . 74 A4
Shavington CW2 . . . 206 A2
Diglake Cl ST7 . . . 210 B3
Diglake St ST7 . . . 209 C2
Diglee Rd SK23 . . . 39 B2
Dillors Croft CW1 . . . 173 A1
Dinas Cl CH1 . . . 117 B2
Dingle Ave
Alderley Edge SK9 . . . 59 B2
Denton M34 . . . 241 B6
Newton-le-W WA12 . . . 1 C1
Dingle Bank CH4 . . . 141 B4
Dingle Bank Cl WA13 . . . 18 C2
Dingle Cl
Macclesfield SK10 . . . 87 A2
Romiley SK6 . . . 241 D2
Dingle La
Bridgemere CW5 . . . 231 C3
Kelsall CW6 . . . 122 C3
Sandbach CW11 . . . 175 B3
Warrington WA4 . . . 26 C3
Winsford CW7 . . . 126 B1
Dingle Prim Sch The CW1 . . . 191 B3
Dingle The Barnton CW8 . . 78 A2
Haslington CW1 . . . 191 B3
Lymm WA13 . . . 18 C2
Dingle Way CW8 . . . 101 C3
Dingle Wlk CW7 . . . 126 B1
Dinglebrook Gr 22 SK9 . . 34 B1
Dingleway WA4 . . . 26 B4
Dinnington Ct WA8 . . . 12 C2
Diploma Dr CW10 . . . 128 B1
Dipping Brook Ave WA4 . 26 C2
Dirty La WA14 . . . 31 A3
Disley Prim Sch SK12 . . . 38 B3
Disley Sta SK12 . . . 38 B3
Disley Wlk M34 . . . 241 A5
Distaff Rd SK12 . . . 36 A2
District CE Prim Sch The WA12 . . . 2 A2
Ditchfield La WA16 . . . 29 B2
Ditchfield Pl WA8 . . . 22 A4
Ditchfield Rd
Warrington WA5 . . . 14 C2
Widnes WA8 . . . 22 A4
Ditton CE Prim Sch WA8 12 A1
Ditton Prim Sch WA8 . . 12 C1
Ditton Rd WA8 . . . 22 B3
Dixon Ave WA12 . . . 2 B3
Dixon Cl WA11 . . . 2 A4
Dixon Ct SK8 . . . 239 D5
Dixon Dr SK11 . . . 84 A2
Dixon Rd
Congleton CW12 . . . 157 A3
Hyde M34 . . . 241 B5
Dixon St
Ashton-u-Lyne OL6 . . . 242 A4
Irlam M44 . . . 11 C4
Warrington WA1 . . . 16 A3
Dixon's Ho CH3 . . . 142 C4
Dobb Hedge Cl WA15 . . . 32 B3
Dobell's Rd CW9 . . . 103 C3
Dobers La WA6 . . . 74 B2
Dobson Sq SY14 . . . 213 A2
Dock Rd Northwich CW9 . 103 C4
Widnes WA8 . . . 22 C3
Dock Road Edwardian Pumping Station The★ CW9 . . . 103 C4
Dock St
Ellesmere Port CH65 . . . 70 B4
Widnes WA8 . . . 23 A3
Dock Yard Rd CH65 . . . 70 C3
Dodd's Green La SY13 . . 228 B2
Dodd's La
Appleton Thorn WA4 . . . 27 A3
Bell o 'th' Hill SY13,SY14 . 224 C4
Doddington Cl CW11 . . . 175 B4
Doddington Rd CW2 . . . 190 A2
Doddlespool Barns CW3 . . . 221 C4
Dodds La CW12 . . . 178 B3
Doddswood Dr CW12 . . 156 C2
Dodge Hill SK4 . . . 240 E6
Dodgsley Dr WA6 . . . 75 B1
Dodleston CE Prim Sch CH4 . . . 162 A4
Dodleston La CH4 . . . 162 B2
Doe's Meadow Rd CH63 . 43 A4
Doeford Cl WA3 . . . 4 C3
Dog La
Brereton Green CW4, CW11 . . . 153 C4
Nantwich CW5 . . . 204 C3
Tattenhall CH3 . . . 182 B2
Threapwood SY14 . . . 223 B4
Dogmore La CW6 . . . 147 B2
Dolly La SK23 . . . 39 C2
Dolmas La 11 WA1 . . . 16 A3
Dolphin Cres CH66 . . . 69 C1
Dolphin Ct CH4 . . . 141 A4
Dombey Rd SK12 . . . 36 B1
Domestic App M90 . . . 33 B3
Domville Cl WA13 . . . 18 C2
Don Wlk CH65 . . . 70 A4
Donagh Cl SK10 . . . 86 C1
Donald Ave SK14 . . . 241 F5
Donkey La SK9 . . . 60 A3
Donne Pl CH1 . . . 117 C3
Donnington Ave SK8 . . 239 F6
Donnington Way CH4 . . 140 C4
Dooley's Grig SK11 . . . 108 C1
Dooley's La SK9 . . . 33 B1
Dorac Ave SK8 . . . 34 B4
Dorchester Cl
Kidsgrove ST7 . . . 195 A2
Wilmslow SK9 . . . 60 B4
Dorchester Pk WA7 . . . 24 C2
Dorchester Rd
Chester CH4 . . . 140 C3
Warrington WA5 . . . 15 B3
Dorchester Way
Burtonwood WA5 . . . 6 C3
Macclesfield SK10 . . . 87 B2
Doreen Ave CW12 . . . 179 A4
Doreold Dr CW5 . . . 204 B3
Dorfold Cl CW11 . . . 175 B4
Dorfold Hall★ CW5 . . . 204 A3
Dorfold St CW1 . . . 190 B2
Dorfold Way CH2 . . . 118 C3
Doric Ave WA6 . . . 74 B4
Dorin Park Sch CH2 . . . 118 B3
Doris Rd SK3 . . . 240 C4
Dormer Cl CH3 . . . 143 A3
Dorney Cl WA4 . . . 26 C3
Dornoch Ct CW4 . . . 130 A1
Dorothea St WA2 . . . 16 B4
Dorric Way CW1 . . . 190 B4
Dorrington Cl WA7 . . . 50 B4
Dorrington Rd SK3 . . . 240 A3
Dorrit Cl SK12 . . . 36 C1
Dorset Ave SK8 . . . 240 C1
Dorset Cl CW12 . . . 156 C2
Dorset Ct WA7 . . . 50 A3
Dorset Dr ST8 . . . 179 B1
Dorset Pl Chester CH2 . . 119 A3
Kidsgrove ST7 . . . 195 A1
Dorset Rd
Altrincham WA14 . . . 238 B5
Chester CH2 . . . 118 C4
Irlam M44 . . . 11 B3
Dorset St OL6 . . . 242 A2
Dorset Way WA1 . . . 17 A4
Dorset Wlk SK10 . . . 86 C1
Douglas Ave WA9 . . . 6 A3
Douglas Cl Hartford CW8 103 B3
Widnes WA8 . . . 13 C2
Douglas La CW7 . . . 171 A3
Douglas Pl CH4 . . . 140 C3
Douglas St
Ashton-u-Lyne OL6 . . . 242 A3
Hyde SK14 . . . 241 E6
Doulton Cl CW7 . . . 126 C2
Doune Ct CH65 . . . 70 B2
Dounrey Cl WA2 . . . 9 A1
Douthwaite Dr SK6 . . . 241 E1
Dove Bank Prim Sch ST7 . . . 195 A1
Dove Cl
Ellesmere Port CH66 . . . 70 A4
Elton CH2 . . . 72 B2
Helsby WA6 . . . 73 B3
Sandbach CW11 . . . 175 A4
Warrington WA3 . . . 9 C2
Dove Gr ST8 . . . 179 B1
Dove Pl CW7 . . . 127 A1
Dovecot Dr WA11 . . . 1 B4
Dovecote Bsns & Tech Pk M33 . . . 242 F6
Dovecote Cl CW2 . . . 206 A4
Dovecote Gn WA5 . . . 7 A1
Dovedale Ave CH62 . . . 43 C3
Dovedale Cl
Congleton CW12 . . . 157 A2
High Lane SK6 . . . 37 C4
Warrington WA2 . . . 8 C2
Dovedale Ct WA8 . . . 12 A2
Dover Cl WA7 . . . 50 C3
Dover Ct CH65 . . . 70 B1
Dover Dr
Ellesmere Port CH65 . . . 70 B1
Winsford CW7 . . . 149 A4
Dover Rd Chester CH4 . . 141 A3
Macclesfield SK10 . . . 87 C1
Warrington WA4 . . . 17 A2
Dover St WA7 . . . 23 A2
Dovesmead Rd CH60 . . . 41 B4
Doveston Gr M33 . . . 242 B8
Doveston Rd M33 . . . 242 B8
Doward St WA8 . . . 13 B1
Downes Cl SK10 . . . 87 A1
Downesway SK9 . . . 59 C1
Downham Ave WA3 . . . 4 C1
Downham Ct CH60 . . . 41 A4
Downham Dr CH60 . . . 41 A4
Downham Pl CH1 . . . 117 C2
Downham Rd S CH60 . . . 41 A4
Downing Cl SK11 . . . 112 C2
Downs Dr WA14 . . . 238 E8
Downs End WA16 . . . 57 B1
Downs Rd WA7 . . . 23 A1
Downs The
Altrincham WA14 . . . 238 D3
Cheadle SK8 . . . 239 D3
Cuddington CW8 . . . 101 B3
Downsfield Rd CH4 . . . 141 A3
Downside WA8 . . . 12 A2
Downswood Ct CH2 . . . 118 B2
Downswood Dr CH2 . . . 118 B2
Downway La WA9 . . . 1 A1
Dragon Yd WA8 . . . 13 A2
Dragon's La CW11 . . . 152 A1
Dragons Wharf CW11 . . 152 B1
Drake Ave M44 . . . 11 C3
Drake Cl WA5 . . . 7 B1
Drake Ct SK5 . . . 240 E8
Drake La CW5 . . . 203 C2
Drake Rd
Altrincham WA14 . . . 238 B8
Neston CH64 . . . 41 C1
Drakelow La CW10 . . . 128 C4
Drakes Way SY14 . . . 213 A3
Draycott Dr ST5 . . . 210 B1
Drayton Ave SK8 . . . 34 A4
Drayton Cl Runcorn WA7 . . 22 C1
16 Handforth SK9 . . . 34 B1
Drayton Cres CW1 . . . 190 C3
Drayton Manor M20 . . . 239 B8
Drenfell Rd ST7 . . . 194 C4
Drift Cotts LL12 . . . 162 B1
Drill Field Rd CW9 . . . 103 C4
Drive A CH5 . . . 93 A1
Drive B CH5 . . . 93 A1
Drive C CH5 . . . 93 A1
Drive The
Altrincham WA15 . . . 32 B4
Broomedge WA13 . . . 19 B1
Holmes Chapel CW4 . . . 130 B1
Drome Rd CH5 . . . 93 A1
Drovers Way CW11 . . . 175 A3
Droxford Ct SK9 . . . 60 A3
Drs Green & Slater Rest Hos 4 SK4 . . . 240 A7
Drumber La ST7 . . . 195 A4
Drumber The CW7 . . . 126 B1
Drumble Field SK11 . . . 84 A2
Drummond Ave CH66 . . . 69 B2
Drummond Ct WA8 . . . 13 B1
Drummond Way SK10 . . . 86 C1
Druridge Dr WA5 . . . 14 C2
Drury Cl CW1 . . . 190 C3
Drury La Knutsford WA16 . 57 A1
Warmingham CW1 . . . 173 B2
Dryden Ave SK8 . . . 239 F6
Dryden Cl CW2 . . . 190 A1
Dryden Pl WA2 . . . 8 B1
Dryhurst Dr SK12 . . . 38 B3
Dryhurst La SK12 . . . 38 B3
Dublin Croft CH66 . . . 69 C1
Duchess Pl CH2 . . . 237 A4
Duchy Rd CW1 . . . 207 A4
Duchy St SK3 . . . 240 D3
Duck La CH3 . . . 121 C4
Duckworth Gr WA2 . . . 9 A1
Duddon Cl
8 Davenham CW9 . . . 103 C2
Duddon CW6 . . . 145 A3
Duddon Hook La CW6 . . 144 C3
Duddon Rd CW6 . . . 145 A3
Dudleston Rd CH66 . . . 69 A3
Dudley Ave WA7 . . . 23 B1
Dudley Cres CH65 . . . 44 A2
Dudley Rd
Ellesmere Port CH65 . . . 70 A3
Irlam M44 . . . 11 B2
Sale M33 . . . 242 C8
Dudley St WA2 . . . 16 A4
Dudley Wlk SK11 . . . 111 C4
Dudlow Green Rd WA4 . . 26 C3
Dufton Wlk M22 . . . 33 C4
Duke Ave Cheadle SK8 . . . 34 C3
Glazebury WA3 . . . 5 B4
Duke Cl WA7 . . . 22 C1
Duke St Alderley Edge SK9 . 60 A1
Chester CH4 . . . 237 B1
Congleton CW12 . . . 156 B1
Crewe CW2 . . . 190 B2
Macclesfield SK11 . . . 112 B4
Newton-le-W WA12 . . . 2 A2
Stalybridge SK15 . . . 242 C1
9 Stockport SK1 . . . 240 F5
Duke's Cres CW11 . . . 175 A4
Duke's Ct CH4 . . . 237 B1
Dukes Way CW9 . . . 103 C3
Dukes Wharf WA7 . . . 50 C4
Dukesway CH2 . . . 118 C4
Dukinfield Rd SK14 . . . 241 C8
Dulas Ct CH2 . . . 118 C4
Dulverton Ave CH3 . . . 119 B1
Dumbah La SK10 . . . 87 B3
Dumbers SK11 . . . 136 A1
Dumbill Ho ST7 . . . 210 B4
Dunbar Cl
Connah's Quay CH5 . . . 91 B1
Ellesmere Port CH66 . . . 69 B3
Holmes Chapel CW4 . . . 130 B1
Dunbar Ct CH66 . . . 69 B3
Dunblane Ave SK4 . . . 240 D6
Duncan Ave
Newton-le-W WA12 . . . 2 B3
Runcorn WA7 . . . 23 B1
Duncan St WA2 . . . 16 B4
Duncansby Cres WA5 . . . 14 C3
Duncansby Dr CH63 . . . 43 B2
Dundalk La WA8 . . . 22 B4
Dundalk Rd WA8 . . . 22 C4
Dundee Cl WA2 . . . 8 C2
Dundee Ct CH65 . . . 70 C2
Dundonald Ave WA4 . . . 16 B1
Dundonald Rd SK8 . . . 35 A4
Dundonald St SK2 . . . 240 F2
Dundrennan Cl SK12 . . . 36 B3
Dunecroft M34 . . . 241 A8
Dunge Valley Gdns★ SK23 . . . 89 C4
Dunham Cl
Bebington CH62 . . . 43 C2
Sandbach CW11 . . . 175 B3
Dunham Cres CW2 . . . 206 A4
Dunham Ct WA6 . . . 97 C3
Dunham Hill Prim Sch WA6 . . . 97 C3
Dunham Lawn WA14 . . 238 B4
Dunham Massey Hall★ WA14 . . . 20 B2
Dunham Pk★ WA14 . . . 20 B2
Dunham Rd
Altrincham WA14 . . . 238 B4
Northwich CW9 . . . 104 A2
Partington WA13 . . . 19 C4
Dunham Rise WA14 . . . 238 C4
Dunham Way CH2 . . . 118 C3
Dunkirk Ave CW7 . . . 149 B4
Dunkirk Dr CH65 . . . 70 A1
Dunkirk La
Capenhurst CH1 . . . 94 B4
Ellesmere Port CH65 . . . 70 A1
Hyde SK14 . . . 241 B8
Dunley Cl WA3 . . . 10 A3
Dunlin Ave WA12 . . . 2 B2
Dunlin Cl Poynton SK12 . . 36 A2
Runcorn WA7 . . . 49 C3
Warrington WA2 . . . 8 C2
Dunlin Wlk WA14 . . . 238 B8
Dunlop St WA4 . . . 16 A2
Dunmore Cl CW10 . . . 151 B4
Dunmore Cres CH66 . . . 69 A3
Dunmore Rd
Ellesmere Port CH66 . . . 69 A3
Gatley SK8 . . . 239 B6
Dunmow Rd WA4 . . . 17 B2
Dunn's La CH3 . . . 121 C4
Dunnillow Field CW5 . . 205 A2
Dunnock Cl WA2 . . . 8 C2
Dunnock Gr WA3 . . . 9 C2
Dunnocksfold Rd ST7 . . 193 A2
Dunnockswood ST7 . . . 193 A2
Dunollie Rd M33 . . . 242 E5
Dunoon Cl CW4 . . . 130 A1
Dunraven Rd CH64 . . . 67 A4
Dunscar Cl WA3 . . . 9 B3
Dunsford WA8 . . . 12 A2
Dunsmore Cl WA11 . . . 1 B4
Dunstan La CH64 . . . 67 C2
Dunster Cl CW9 . . . 104 A2
Dunster Gr CH60 . . . 41 A4
Dunster Rd SK10 . . . 87 C1
Dunstone Cl CW2 . . . 190 A1
Dunwood Dr ST7 . . . 193 B3
Dunwoody Way CW1, CW2 . . . 190 A2
Durban Ave CH3 . . . 142 B4
Durber Cl ST7 . . . 209 B1
Durham Cl
Macclesfield SK10 . . . 86 C1
Romiley SK6 . . . 241 A1
Warrington WA1 . . . 17 C4
Durham Ct CH65 . . . 70 C2
Durham Dr CW7 . . . 149 B3
Durham Gr M44 . . . 11 B3
Durham Rd Blacon CH1 . 117 C3
Handforth SK9 . . . 34 B3
Widnes WA8 . . . 13 A2
Durlston Cl WA8 . . . 12 B1
Durrell Way WA3 . . . 3 C4
Dutton Gn CH2 . . . 70 C2
Dutton La CW8,WA6 . . . 101 B3
Dutton Way CW5 . . . 204 C2
Dutton's La CW6 . . . 122 B3
Duttons Bsns Ctr CW9 . 103 C4
Duxford Ct WA2 . . . 8 C1
Dyar Terr CW8 . . . 78 B1
Dye House La SK22 . . . 39 B4
Dye La SK6 . . . 241 B2
Dyers Cl WA13 . . . 19 A2
Dyers La WA13 . . . 19 A2
Dykin Cl WA8 . . . 13 C2
Dykin Rd WA8 . . . 13 C2
Dysart St OL6 . . . 242 A2
Dyserth Gr 2 SK5 . . . 240 F8
Dyserth Rd CH1 . . . 117 B2
Dystelegh Rd SK12 . . . 38 B3

E

Eadie Gr CW1 . . . 190 A4
Eaglais Way SK10 . . . 86 C1
Eagland Pl CW12 . . . 156 C2
Eagle Brow WA13 . . . 18 B2
Eagle La CH66 . . . 69 B4
Eagle Lodge WA15 . . . 238 F2
Eagle Mount WA4 . . . 16 B1
Eagle Park Dr WA2 . . . 8 A1
Eagles Way WA7 . . . 49 C3
Eaglesfield CW8 . . . 103 B2
Ealing Cl WA7 . . . 24 B1
Ealing Rd WA5 . . . 15 A3
Eanlewood La WA7 . . . 50 B4
Eardley Cres CW12 . . . 156 C2
Eardley Pl CW1 . . . 190 A3
Eardleyend Rd ST7 . . . 209 C4
Eardswick Cl CH2 . . . 237 B4
Eardswick La CW1 . . . 172 B3
Eardswick Rd CW10 . . . 151 B3
Earl Rd Handforth SK8,SK9 . 34 C3
Stockport SK4 . . . 240 C8
Earl St Sale M33 . . . 242 C7
Stockport SK3 . . . 240 D4
Warrington WA2 . . . 16 A4
Earl's Port CH1 . . . 118 A1
Earle Cl WA12 . . . 1 C2
Earle Cres CH64 . . . 41 B1
Earle Dr CH64 . . . 41 B1
Earle Rd WA8 . . . 23 B4
Earle St Crewe CW1 . . . 190 B2
Newton-le-W WA12 . . . 2 A2
Earle's La CW6 . . . 122 B3
Earles La CW9 . . . 79 C3
Earlestown Sta WA12 . . . 2 A2
Earls Gdns CH65 . . . 70 A3
Earls Oak CH2 . . . 118 B4
Earls Rd CW2 . . . 206 A2
Earls Way
Davenham CW9 . . . 103 C2
Runcorn WA7 . . . 49 C3
Earlscliffe Ct WA14 . . . 238 B4
Earlston Ct CH2 . . . 237 C2
Earlsway Chester CH4 . . 141 A4
Macclesfield SK11 . . . 111 C4
Earlswood Mews CW9 . . 103 C2
Easby Cl Bramhall SK8 . . . 35 A3
Poynton SK12 . . . 36 B2
Runcorn WA7 . . . 23 B1
Easenhall Cl WA8 . . . 13 B3
Easingwold 2 WA14 . . . 238 C4
East Ave Bollington SK10 . . 87 C4
Gatley SK8 . . . 34 B4
Northwich CW9 . . . 104 B3
Stalybridge SK15 . . . 242 D3
Warrington WA2 . . . 16 B4

East Ave *continued*
Warrington, Great Sankey WA5 ....15 A2
Warrington, Stockton Heath WA4 ....16 B1
Weston CW2 ....207 B3
East Ct ST7 ....193 C2
East Dam Wood Rd L24 ....21 A1
East Downs Rd
Altrincham WA14 ....238 C2
Cheadle SK8 ....239 F2
East Dudley St CW7 ....126 C1
East Gn CH5 ....116 A3
East La Cuddington CW8 ....102 A2
Runcorn WA7 ....49 C4
East Lancashire Rd
Ashton-u-Lyne WA11,WA12, WA3 ....2 B4
Haydock WA11 ....1 B4
East Lea M34 ....241 A6
East Mains L24 ....21 A2
East Millwood Rd L24 ....21 A2
East Park Rd SK11 ....112 A3
East Rd Halewood L24,L26 ....21 A3
Middlewich CW10 ....128 A1
Wythenshawe M90 ....33 B4
East St Ashton-u-Lyne OL6 ....242 A4
Widnes WA8 ....13 B1
East View WA4 ....17 A1
Eastbury Cl WA8 ....13 B3
Eastcott Cl CW12 ....155 C2
Eastdale Pl WA14 ....238 D7
Eastdale Rd WA1 ....17 A4
Easter Ct WA5 ....7 A1
Eastern Pathway CH4 ....237 C1
Eastern Rd
Shavington CW5 ....205 C3
Willaston (nr Nantwich) CW5 ....205 C3
Eastfields Gr CH1 ....117 A4
Eastford Rd WA4 ....16 A1
Eastgate Rd
Holmes Chapel CW4 ....130 B2
Runcorn WA7 ....24 C3
Eastgate Row N CH1 ....237 B2
Eastgate Row S CH1 ....237 B2
Eastgate St CH1 ....237 B2
Eastham Ctry Pk★ CH62 ....44 A4
Eastham Mews CH62 ....44 A2
Eastham Rake CH62,CH64 ....43 B2
Eastham Rake Sta CH63 ....43 B2
Eastham Village Rd CH62 ....44 A3
Eastham Way 11 SK9 ....34 B2
Eastleigh Rd SK8 ....239 B1
Easton Dr SK8 ....240 A1
Eastview M33 ....242 B5
Eastward Ave SK9 ....59 C3
Eastway
Ellesmere Port CH66 ....69 B4
Widnes WA8 ....12 B1
Eastwood WA7 ....24 B1
Eastwood Ave WA12 ....2 C2
Eastwood Ct CH4 ....139 A3
Eastwood Rd WA5 ....6 C4
Eaton Ave CH4 ....141 B4
Eaton Bank CW12 ....156 C2
Eaton Bank Ind Est CW12 ....156 C2
Eaton Bank Sch CW12 ....156 C3
Eaton Cl Broughton CH4 ....139 B2
Cheadle SK8 ....239 F3
Poynton SK12 ....37 A2
Sandbach CW11 ....175 B4
Eaton Cres CW9 ....103 C1
Eaton Ct
Altrincham WA14 ....238 C1
Wilmslow SK9 ....60 A3
Eaton Dr
Alderley Edge SK9 ....59 C1
Middlewich CW10 ....151 A4
Eaton Gr CH4 ....140 C3
Eaton La Davenham CW9 ....103 C1
Eaton CW6 ....147 A3
Goostrey CW4 ....107 B1
Macclesfield SK11 ....112 B3
Tarporley CW6 ....168 C4
Eaton Mews CH4 ....141 B4
Eaton Pl CW8 ....102 C2
Eaton Prim Sch CW6 ....147 A2
Eaton Rd Alsager ST7 ....193 B2
Altrincham WA14 ....238 C1
Chester CH4 ....141 C2
Sale M33 ....242 A6
Tarporley CW6 ....146 B1
Wettenhall CW7 ....170 B4
Eaton St Crewe CW2 ....190 B2
Runcorn WA7 ....23 A1
Eaton View CW9 ....126 C4
Eaton Way CW3 ....230 A2
Eaves Brow Rd WA3 ....9 A4
Eaves Knoll Rd SK22 ....39 A4
Ebnal La SY14 ....213 C2
Ebury Pl CH4 ....141 B4
Eccles Cl SK23 ....65 B4
Eccles Rd SK23 ....65 C3
Eccleston Ave
Bebington CH62 ....43 B4
Chester CH4 ....141 B3
Ellesmere Port CH66 ....69 C3
Eccleston CE Prim Sch CH4 ....141 C1
Eccleston Cl WA3 ....9 B3
Eccleston Dr WA7 ....23 B1
Eccleston Rd CH4 ....161 A4
Eccleston Way 3 SK9 ....34 B2
Eccups La SK9 ....59 B4
Echo Cl CH4 ....140 C3
Ecton Ave SK10 ....113 A4
Ecton Cl CW7 ....127 A2
Edale Cl
Altrincham WA14 ....238 C1
Bebington CH62 ....43 C3
Gatley SK8 ....34 B4
Edale Dr CW6 ....122 B3
Edburton Ct WA3 ....3 A4
Eddisbury Cl SK11 ....112 C4
Eddisbury Dr ST5 ....210 B1
Eddisbury Hill CW6,CW8 ....123 B4
Eddisbury Rd CH66 ....69 C1
Eddisbury Sq WA6 ....74 A4
Eddisbury Terr SK11 ....112 C4
Eddisbury Way CW9 ....103 C2
Eddisford Dr WA3 ....4 B3
Edelsten St WA5 ....15 C3
Edelston Hall La CW5 ....203 C1
Eden Ave
Fowley Common WA3 ....5 B2
High Lane SK6 ....37 C4
Winsford CW7 ....126 C1
Eden Cl Biddulph ST8 ....179 C1
10 Ellesmere Port CH66 ....69 B3
Kidsgrove ST7 ....195 A1
Wilmslow SK9 ....59 C3
Eden Dr SK10 ....87 C1
Eden Pl SK8 ....239 D6
Edenbridge Gdns WA4 ....26 C2
Edendale WA8 ....12 A1
Edenfield Cl WA16 ....58 A2
Edenfield Rd WA16 ....58 A2
Edenhall Cl CW4 ....130 A2
Edgar Ct CH4 ....237 B1
Edgar Pl CH4 ....237 B1
Edgars Dr WA2 ....9 A1
Edge Gr CH2 ....118 C1
Edge La SY14 ....199 B1
Edge View La SK9 ....59 A1
Edgecroft CH3 ....166 A1
Edgehill Chase SK9 ....60 C4
Edgeley Fold SK3 ....240 C3
Edgeley Rd SK3 ....240 B3
Edgemoor WA14 ....238 A2
Edgerley La CH3 ....181 A3
Edgerton Rd WA3 ....3 C4
Edgeview Rd CW12 ....179 A4
Edgeway Henbury SK11 ....111 B4
Wilmslow SK9 ....60 A3
Edgewell La CW6 ....147 A2
Edgewood CH3 ....142 A4
Edgewood Dr
Bebington CH62 ....43 B3
Wistaston CW2 ....206 A4
Edgworth St WA2 ....16 A3
Edinbridge Cl CW2 ....207 A1
Edinburgh Cl SK8 ....239 F6
Edinburgh Ct CH65 ....70 B2
Edinburgh Dr
Macclesfield SK10 ....87 A1
Romiley SK6 ....241 C4
Edinburgh Pl CW12 ....156 C1
Edinburgh Rd
Congleton CW12 ....156 C1
Widnes WA8 ....22 A4
Wistaston CW2 ....205 C4
Edinburgh Way CH4 ....237 C1
Edison Rd WA7 ....23 B2
Edith St WA7 ....22 C2
Edleston Prim Sch CW2 ....190 B2
Edleston Rd CW2 ....190 B2
Edlestone Gr 2 SK9 ....34 C1
Edmund Cl SK4 ....240 E8
Edna St Chester CH2 ....118 C2
Hyde SK14 ....241 D6
Edward Bright Way CW5 ....204 B3
Edward Ct WA14 ....238 B7
Edward Gdns WA1 ....17 C3
Edward Rd WA5 ....14 B3
Edward St
Ashton-u-Lyne OL6 ....242 B2
Audley ST7 ....209 C2
Crewe CW2 ....190 B1
Dukinfield SK14 ....241 C7
Ellesmere Port CH65 ....70 B4
Haydock WA11 ....1 A3
Macclesfield SK11 ....112 A4
Northwich CW9 ....104 B4
Sale M33 ....242 E6
Stockport SK1 ....240 F4
Widnes WA8 ....13 B1
Edwards Ave CW2 ....206 B3
Edwards Cl CW2 ....206 B3
Edwards Rd CH4 ....141 A3
Edwards Way
Alsager ST7 ....193 C2
Widnes WA8 ....22 B4
Edwin St WA8 ....13 B1
Egdon Cl WA8 ....13 C1
Egerton WA16 ....29 B3
Egerton Ave
Hartford CW8 ....103 A2
Partington WA13 ....19 B4
Warrington WA1 ....16 C4
Egerton Ct
Dukinfield M34 ....241 A8
Kelsall CW6 ....122 A3
Egerton Dr Chester CH2 ....118 B3
Sale M33 ....242 B7
Egerton Lodge M34 ....241 A8
Egerton Moss WA15 ....31 C3
Egerton Prim Sch WA16 ....56 C1
Egerton Rd Blacon CH1 ....117 B3
Handforth SK9 ....34 A1
Egerton Rd *continued*
Lymm WA13 ....18 B1
Egerton Rd S SK4 ....240 C8
Egerton Sq 6 WA16 ....57 A1
Egerton St Chester CH2 ....237 C3
Congleton CW12 ....156 B1
Ellesmere Port CH65 ....70 B3
Runcorn WA7 ....22 C2
Warrington, Howley WA1 ....16 B3
Warrington, Stockton Heath WA4 ....16 B1
Egerton Street Sch CH2 ....237 C3
Egerton Wlk CH4 ....162 A4
Eggbridge La CH3 ....143 A3
Egremont Gr 2 SK3 ....240 B4
Egypt St
5 Warrington WA1 ....16 A3
Widnes WA8 ....22 C4
Eilison Ct CH2 ....237 B3
Eisenhower Cl WA5 ....15 A3
Elaine Cl
Ellesmere Port CH66 ....69 B2
Widnes WA8 ....13 B1
Elaine St WA1 ....16 B4
Elanor Rd CW11 ....174 B4
Elcho Rd WA14 ....238 B3
Elcombe Ave WA3 ....3 C4
Elder Dr CH4 ....140 C3
Elderberry Way SK9 ....60 C4
Elderberry Wlk M31 ....11 C2
Eldon Rd
Macclesfield SK11 ....111 C4
Stockport SK3 ....240 C3
Eldon St WA1 ....16 B3
Eldon Terr CH64 ....66 C4
Eleanor Cl CW1 ....189 C3
Eleanor St
Ellesmere Port CH65 ....70 B3
18 Widnes WA8 ....23 A4
Electra Way CW1 ....191 A1
Electricity St CW2 ....190 B2
Elf Mill Cl SK3 ....240 E2
Elgar Ave CH62 ....43 C3
Elgar Cl CH65 ....69 C2
Elgin Ave
Holmes Chapel CW4 ....130 A1
Macclesfield SK10 ....87 A1
Warrington WA4 ....16 A1
Elgin Cl CH3 ....119 A2
Elgin Dr M33 ....242 E5
Elgin St SK15 ....242 E1
Elgol Cl SK3 ....240 F1
Eliot Cl CW1 ....191 A2
Elizabeth Ave Disley SK12 ....38 B3
Stalybridge SK15 ....242 D2
Stockport SK1 ....240 F4
Elizabeth Cl Kelsall CW6 ....122 B3
Sandbach CW11 ....174 B4
Elizabeth Cres CH4 ....237 C1
Elizabeth Ct
Stockport SK4 ....240 C6
Talke ST7 ....210 B3
Widnes WA8 ....23 A4
Elizabeth Dr WA1 ....17 A4
Elizabeth Gaskell Ct WA16 ....56 C1
Elizabeth Rd Haydock WA11 ....1 C4
Partington M31 ....11 C2
Elizabeth St
Congleton CW12 ....156 B1
Crewe CW1 ....190 A3
Hyde SK14 ....241 D7
Macclesfield SK11 ....112 B4
Elizabeth Terr WA8 ....12 B1
Elizabethan Way CW9 ....104 C3
Elk View SY14 ....222 C3
Elkan Cl WA8 ....13 C1
Elkan Rd WA8 ....13 C1
Ella Gr WA16 ....57 A1
Elland Dr CH66 ....69 B3
Ellen Brook Rd M22 ....33 B4
Ellen St Stockport SK4 ....240 D7
Warrington WA5 ....15 C4
Ellerby Cl WA7 ....50 C4
Ellerton Ave CH66 ....69 B3
Ellerton Cl WA8 ....12 B2
Ellesmere Ave
Broughton CH4 ....139 B2
Chester CH2 ....118 B3
Ellesmere Cl CW11 ....174 C4
Ellesmere Dr SK8 ....240 A1
Ellesmere Pl CW1 ....190 A3
Ellesmere Port Hospl CH65 ....70 A1
Ellesmere Port RC High Sch CH65 ....70 A2
Ellesmere Port Sta CH65 ....70 B3
Ellesmere Port Stadium The CH65 ....70 C2
Ellesmere Rd
Altrincham WA14 ....238 E6
Culcheth WA3 ....4 C2
Northwich CW9 ....104 A2
Stockport SK3 ....240 A3
Warrington WA4 ....16 A1
Ellesmere St
Runcorn WA7 ....23 A1
Warrington WA1 ....16 B3
Ellesworth Cl WA5 ....15 B4
Ellingham Way CW9 ....103 C2
Elliot Ave WA1 ....16 C4
Elliot Ho CH1 ....118 A3
Elliot St 9 WA8 ....23 A4
Ellis La WA6 ....49 B1
Ellis St Crewe CW1 ....190 A3
Hyde SK14 ....241 F6
Widnes WA8 ....22 C4
Ellison St
Warrington, Howley WA1 ....16 B3
Warrington, Stockton Heath WA4 ....16 B1
Elloway Rd L24 ....21 A2
Ellwood Cl L24 ....21 C1
Ellwood Gn CW2 ....206 C2
Elm Ave Newton-le-W WA12 ....2 B1
Widnes WA8 ....13 A1
Elm Beds Rd SK12 ....37 B1
Elm Cl 9 Partington M31 ....11 C2
Poynton SK12 ....36 C2
Tarporley CW6 ....146 B1
Wistaston CW2 ....189 C1
Elm Cres SK9 ....60 A2
Elm Ct CW1 ....190 B3
Elm Dr Crewe CW1 ....190 C3
Holmes Chapel CW4 ....130 B2
Macclesfield SK10 ....87 C1
Elm Gn CH64 ....67 C4
Elm Gr Alderley Edge SK9 ....60 A1
Alsager ST7 ....193 C2
Broughton CH4 ....140 C3
Ellesmere Port CH66 ....70 A1
Handforth SK9 ....34 B2
Hyde SK14 ....241 F6
Sale M33 ....242 B8
Warrington WA1 ....16 C4
Widnes WA8 ....13 A1
Winsford CW7 ....127 A1
Elm Ho 9 CW11 ....175 A3
Elm Rd Altrincham WA15 ....238 E3
Congleton CW12 ....156 A2
Gatley SK8 ....239 A5
Haydock WA11 ....1 C4
High Lane SK6 ....37 C4
Hollinfare WA3 ....11 A1
Middlewich CW10 ....151 B4
Runcorn WA7 ....49 B4
Warrington, Cinnamon Brow WA5 ....14 C2
Warrington, Winwick Quay WA2 ....8 A2
Weaverham CW8 ....102 B4
Willaston CH64 ....67 C4
Elm Rd S SK3 ....240 A3
Elm Rise Frodsham WA6 ....74 B4
Prestbury SK10 ....86 C3
Elm Sq CH4 ....140 C3
Elm St Ellesmere Port CH65 ....70 B4
Northwich CW9 ....79 A1
Elm Terr CW1 ....190 C3
Elm Tree Ave Lymm WA13 ....18 B1
Warrington WA1 ....16 C4
Elm Tree Cotts CH3 ....167 A4
Elm Tree Ct CW6 ....147 A2
Elm Tree Dr ST7 ....209 C1
Elm Tree La CW11 ....174 B4
Elm Tree Rd Golborne WA3 ....3 C4
Lymm WA13 ....18 B1
Elmdale Ave SK8 ....239 B2
Elmfield Cl SK9 ....60 A1
Elmfield Rd
Alderley Edge SK9 ....60 A1
Stockport SK3 ....240 F1
Elmir CH1 ....117 C2
Elmore Cl
Holmes Chapel CW4 ....130 A2
Runcorn WA7 ....24 B1
Elmridge Ct WA3 ....3 C4
Elmridge Dr WA15 ....32 B4
Elmridge Prim Sch WA15 ....32 B4
Elms The Golborne WA3 ....3 C4
Mobberley WA16 ....58 C1
Runcorn WA7 ....22 C1
Threapwood SY14 ....222 C2
Elmsett Cl WA5 ....14 C3
Elmsleigh Rd SK8 ....239 A2
Elmstead Cres CW1 ....189 C4
Elmstead Rd SK11 ....84 A2
Elmsway Altrincham WA15 ....32 A4
Bollington SK10 ....88 A4
Bramhall SK7 ....35 B4
High Lane SK6 ....37 C3
Elmtree Dr SK4 ....240 C6
Elmwood WA7 ....24 B1
Elmwood Ave
Chester CH2 ....118 C2
Warrington WA1 ....16 C4
Elmwood Cl ST7 ....194 A2
Elmwood Gr CW7 ....149 C4
Elmwood Rd CW8 ....78 A2
Elnor Ave SK23 ....65 C3
Elnor La SK23 ....65 C2
Elsby Rd ST7 ....193 C1
Elsinore Hts L26 ....21 A4
Elston Ave WA12 ....2 B3
Elstree Ave CH3 ....119 A2
Elstree Gr SK3 ....240 D4
Elswick Ave SK7 ....35 C4
Eltham Cl WA8 ....13 C2
Eltham Wlk WA8 ....13 C2
Elton Cl Bebington CH62 ....43 C2
Golborne WA3 ....3 C4
Handforth SK9 ....34 C1
Warrington WA3 ....9 B2
Elton Crossings Rd CW11 ....174 B3
Elton Dr SK7 ....36 B4
Elton La Elton CH2 ....72 C2
Haslington CW11 ....174 B1
Elton Lordship La WA6 ....73 A4
Elton Prim Sch CH2 ....72 A2
Elton Rd CW11 ....174 B3
Elvington Cl
Congleton CW12 ....156 C1
Runcorn WA7 ....49 C2
Elwood Way CW5 ....205 A2
Elworth Ave WA8 ....13 A3
Elworth CE Prim Sch CW11 ....174 C4
Elworth Ct
12 Congleton CW12 ....156 C2
Sandbach CW11 ....174 B4
Elworth Hall Prim Sch CW11 ....174 C4
Elworth Rd CW11 ....174 C3
Elworth St CW11 ....175 A4
Elworth Way 6 SK9 ....34 B2
Elwyn Dr L26 ....21 A4
Ely Cl CH66 ....94 C4
Ely Pk WA7 ....24 C1
Embassy Cl CH1 ....117 B2
Emberton Pl CW3 ....230 A3
Embleton Ct WA7 ....49 B3
Embridge Cswy SK10, SK17 ....90 A3
Emerald Rd M22 ....33 C4
Emery Cl
Altrincham WA14 ....238 C1
Stockport SK4 ....240 A8
Emily St 14 WA8 ....23 A4
Emlyn Gr SK8 ....240 A2
Emmett St CW8 ....78 A2
Empire Ct WA1 ....16 A2
Empress Dr Crewe CW2 ....190 A2
Stockport SK4 ....240 D8
Emral Ct SY14 ....211 A1
Emslie Ct CH64 ....66 B4
Enderby Rd CH1 ....237 A3
Endon Av SK10 ....88 A4
Endsleigh Cl CH2 ....118 C4
Endsleigh Gdns CH2 ....118 C4
Enfield Cl CW2 ....206 A2
Enfield Park Rd WA2 ....8 C2
Enfield Rd CH65 ....70 A3
Engelsea Brook La CW2 ....208 A2
Engineer Pk CH5 ....116 A2
Englefield Ave CH4 ....140 B3
Englefield Cl CW1 ....190 A4
Englesea Brook Mus of Primitive Methodism★ CW2 ....208 A2
Englesea Gr CW2 ....190 A1
English Martyrs RC Sch WA11 ....1 C4
Ennerdale Chester CH2 ....118 C3
Macclesfield SK11 ....111 C3
Ennerdale Ave
Bebington CH62 ....43 C2
Warrington WA2 ....8 A2
Ennerdale Cl
Alderley Edge SK9 ....83 C4
Winsford CW7 ....126 B2
Ennerdale Dr
Congleton CW12 ....156 A1
Frodsham WA6 ....74 B4
Gatley SK8 ....239 B3
Ennerdale Rd
Crewe CW2 ....189 B2
Partington M31 ....11 C2
Romiley SK6 ....241 B4
Ennerdale Terr SK15 ....242 D3
Ennis Cl L24 ....21 B1
Ensor Way SK22 ....39 B4
Enterprise Ctr The CW12 ....156 C2
Enterprise Way WA3 ....4 A4
Enticott Rd M44 ....11 B3
Enville Rd WA14 ....238 C3
Enville St WA4 ....16 B2
Epping Dr WA1 ....17 B4
Epsom Ave SK8,SK9 ....34 C2
Epsom Gdns WA4 ....26 C4
Epworth Cl WA5 ....6 C4
Epworth Ct SK4 ....240 B7
Era St M33 ....242 B6
ERF Way CW10 ....151 C4
Eric Ave WA1 ....16 C4
Eric St WA8 ....13 B1
Erindale Cres WA6 ....74 A3
Erlesmere Ave M34 ....241 A8
Ermine Rd CH2 ....237 C4
Ernest St Cheadle SK8 ....239 C6
Crewe CW2 ....190 B1
Errington Ave CH65 ....70 B3
Errwood Forest Walks★ SK17 ....90 C1
Erskine Rd M31 ....11 C2
Erwood St WA2 ....16 A3
Esk Dale Cl CW7 ....126 B1
Esk Rd CW7 ....127 A1
Eskdale Cheadle SK8 ....239 C4
Ellesmere Port CH65 ....70 A2
Eskdale Ave
Bebington CH62 ....43 C3
Bramhall SK7 ....35 B3
Warrington WA2 ....8 B2
Eskdale Cl WA7 ....49 B3
Eskdale Terr SK15 ....242 D4
Essex Ave SK3 ....240 B4
Essex Cl CW12 ....156 C3
Essex Dr Biddulph ST8 ....179 B1
Kidsgrove ST7 ....194 C1
Essex Gdns M44 ....11 B2
Essex Rd CH2 ....119 A3
Essex Wlk SK10 ....86 C1
Esther St WA8 ....13 B1
Esthers La CW8 ....102 B4
Etchells Prim Sch SK8 ....239 C1
Etchells Rd SK8 ....239 D1
Etchells St 6 SK1 ....240 F5
Etharow Ct 6 SK14 ....241 E6
Ethelda Dr CH2 ....119 A3
Etherow Ave SK6 ....241 E2
Etherow Cl CW11 ....174 C4

Eton Dr CH63 .... 41 C3
Eton Rd CH65 .... 70 B2
Etterick Pk CH3 .... 119 A1
Ettiley Ave CW11 .... 174 B3
Euclid Ave WA4 .... 17 A1
Europa Bsns Pk SK3 ... 240 B2
Europa Bvd WA5 .... 7 B2
Europa Way
Ellesmere Port CH65 ...... 70 B3
Stockport SK3 .... 240 B2
Eustace St WA2 .... 16 A3
Eva Rd SK3 .... 240 A3
Eva St CW11 .... 174 B4
Evans Cl WA11 .... 1 C4
Evans Pl WA4 .... 16 B2
Evans St
Ashton-u-Lyne OL6 ...... 242 A4
Crewe CW1 .... 190 B3
Evansleigh Dr CH5 ..... 116 A2
Evelyn St WA5 .... 15 B2
Evelyn Street Prim Sch
WA5 .... 15 C2
Evenholme WA14 ...... 238 B2
Evenwood Cl WA7 ...... 24 C2
Everdon Cl CW7 ...... 126 C2
Everest Cl CH66 ...... 69 C2
Everest Rd ST7 ...... 195 B2
Everglade Cl SK11 ..... 112 A3
Evergreen Way WA9 ...... 6 A4
Everite Rd WA8 .... 22 A4
Eversley WA8 .... 12 A1
Eversley Cl Frodsham WA6 74 B3
Warrington WA4 .... 26 C3
Eversley Ct CH2 ...... 118 B2
Eversley Pk CH2 ...... 118 B2
Evesham Ave SK4 ...... 240 B7
Evesham Cl
Macclesfield SK10 .... 87 C2
Warrington WA4 .... 26 B4
Evesham Dr SK9 .... 34 B1
Evesham Gr M33 ...... 242 E6
Ewart St CH4 .... 140 A4
Ewloe Ct CH65 .... 70 B1
Ewrin La SK10 .... 89 B3
Excalibur Ind Est ST7 .. 193 C2
Excalibur Prim Sch ST7 193 C1
Excalibur Way M44 ..... 11 C4
Exchange Cl 25 SK11 ... 112 B4
Exchange St
Macclesfield SK11 .... 112 B4
Stockport SK3 .... 240 E5
Exeter Cl SK8 .... 34 C4
Exeter Pl CH1 .... 117 C3
Exeter Rd CH65 .... 70 B3
Exeter Wlk SK7 .... 35 C4
Exit Rd W M90 .... 33 A4
Exmouth Cres WA7 ...... 50 C3
Exmouth Way WA5 .... 6 C3
Express Ind Est WA8 .... 22 A4
Exton Pk CH2 .... 237 A4
Eyam Rd SK7 .... 36 C4
Eyebrook Rd WA14 .... 238 A2
Eyre Pl CH65 .... 70 A3
Eyston Cl CW9 .... 103 C3

F

Factory La Disley SK12 ... 38 C4
Warrington WA1,WA5 ..... 15 C2
Widnes WA8 .... 13 A2
Factory Rd CH5 .... 116 A2
Fair Haven's Ct WA8 .... 23 A4
Fair Isle Cl CH65 .... 70 B1
Fair Mead WA16 .... 82 A4
Fair Oak Rd ST5 .... 210 B1
Fair View Cl CW8 .... 77 C2
Fairacre Dr CW10 ...... 151 C3
Fairacres Rd SK6 .... 37 C4
Fairbourne Ave
Alderley Edge SK9 .... 60 A2
Wilmslow SK9 .... 59 C2
Fairbourne Cl
Warrington WA5 .... 7 C2
Wilmslow SK9 .... 59 C2
Fairbourne Dr SK9 ...... 59 C2
Fairbrook CW2 .... 189 C1
Fairbrother Cres WA2 .... 8 B1
Fairburn Ave CW2 ...... 189 C2
Fairburn Cl WA8 .... 13 C2
Fairclough Ave WA1 ..... 16 B2
Fairclough Cres WA11 .... 1 A3
Fairclough St
Burtonwood WA5 .... 6 C3
Newton-le-W WA12 .... 2 A2
Fairfax Dr Runcorn WA7 .. 23 B1
Wilmslow SK9 .... 59 C2
Fairfield Ave
Cheadle SK8 .... 239 F2
Ellesmere Port CH65 ...... 70 A1
Romiley SK6 .... 241 A4
Sandbach CW11 .... 175 A3
Fairfield Gdns WA4 ..... 16 C1
Fairfield High Sch WA8 .13 A2
Fairfield Jun & Inf Sch
WA8 .... 13 A1
Fairfield Rd
Broughton CH4 .... 139 A2
Chester CH2 .... 119 A2
Irlam M44 .... 11 B3
Lymm WA13 .... 18 C2
Northwich CW9 .... 104 A2
Warrington WA4 .... 16 C1
Widnes WA8 .... 13 A1
Fairfield St WA1 .... 16 B3
Fairfields ST7 .... 209 C1
Fairford Rd CH4 .... 140 C3
Fairford Way SK9 .... 60 B4
Fairhaven CW2 .... 207 A1
Fairhaven Cl Bramhall SK7 35 C4
Macclesfield SK10 .... 87 A2
Warrington WA5 .... 15 A2
Fairhaven Dr CH63 .... 43 B3
Fairhaven Rd WA8 .... 13 B1
Fairhills Ind Est M44 .... 11 C4
Fairhills Rd M44 .... 11 C4
Fairholm Rd CW9 ...... 127 A4
Fairholme Ave CH64 ...... 41 B1
Fairholme Cl CH1 .... 94 A1
Fairholme Rd SK4 ...... 240 C7
Fairlawn SK4 .... 240 D7
Fairlawn Cl CH63 .... 43 A3
Fairlea M34 .... 241 A6
Fairmeadow CH4 .... 162 B1
Fairmile Dr M20 .... 239 C8
Fairoak Cl 13 CW7 ...... 149 A4
Fairoak Ct WA7 .... 50 C2
Fairoak La WA7 .... 50 C2
Fairview LL13 .... 196 C4
Fairview Ave
Alsager ST7 .... 193 B2
Weston CW2 .... 207 A3
Fairview Rd
Ellesmere Port CH65 ...... 70 A1
Macclesfield SK11 .... 112 A3
Fairway Bramhall SK7 ..... 35 B3
Gatley SK8 .... 239 B4
Hawarden CH5 .... 116 A1
Fairway The ST7 .... 193 B2
Fairways Frodsham WA6 .. 74 B4
Warrington WA4 .... 26 B3
Fairways Dr
Ellesmere Port CH66 ...... 69 B4
Whitchurch SY13 .... 226 A1
Fairways The
Macclesfield SK10 .... 87 A2
Winsford CW7 .... 126 A1
Fairywell Cl SK9 .... 34 B1
Falcon Cl
Middlewich CW10 .... 151 B3
New Mills SK22 .... 39 B4
Winsford CW7 .... 149 B3
Falcon Dr CW1 .... 190 A4
Falcon Rd CH66 .... 69 C2
Falcondale Rd WA2 .... 8 A3
Falconers Gn WA5 .... 7 A1
Falcons Way WA7 .... 49 C3
Fallibroome Cl SK11 ... 111 C4
Fallibroome High Sch
SK10 .... 86 C1
Fallibroome Rd SK11 ... 111 C4
Fallow Ct CW10 .... 151 B4
Fallowfield WA7 .... 23 B1
Fallowfield Cl CW7 ...... 125 C1
Fallowfield Ct CW1 ...... 190 A3
Fallowfield Gr WA2 .... 9 A1
Falls Gr SK8 .... 239 A3
Falmouth Cl SK10 ...... 111 C4
Falmouth Dr WA5 .... 14 C2
Falmouth Pl WA7 .... 50 C3
Falmouth Rd
Congleton CW12 .... 178 C4
Crewe CW1 .... 190 A3
Falstaff Mews SK6 ...... 241 A3
Falstone Cl WA3 .... 10 A3
Falstone Dr WA7 .... 50 C4
Fanner's La WA16 .... 28 B3
Fanny's Croft ST7 .... 193 B1
Fanshawe La SK11 ...... 110 C3
Fanshawe Wlk CW2 ...... 206 B4
Far Ridings SK6 .... 241 D3
Faraday Rd
Ellesmere Port CH65 ...... 70 A2
Runcorn WA7 .... 23 B2
Faraday St WA3 .... 9 C2
Farams Rd ST7 .... 193 C4
Farbailey Cl CH4 .... 141 A3
Farfields Cl SK11 .... 111 C1
Faringdon Rd WA2 .... 8 A3
Farlands Dr M20 .... 239 B7
Farley Cl CW10 .... 151 A4
Farley Ct SK8 .... 239 F3
Farm Cl CW8 .... 77 B1
Farm Dr CH5 .... 91 B1
Farm La High Lane SK12 .. 38 A3
Warrington WA4 .... 26 C4
Withington Green SK11 .. 108 C1
Farm Rd Northwich CW9 .104 C4
Oakmere CW8 .... 124 A4
Weaverham CW8 .... 77 B1
Farm Way WA12 .... 2 C1
Farm Wlk WA14 .... 20 C1
Farmdale Dr CH2 .... 72 A2
Farmer Cl CW2 .... 190 A2
Farmer St SK4 .... 240 E7
Farmer's La WA5 .... 7 A3
Farmers Heath CH66 ..... 69 B1
Farmfield Dr SK10 .... 87 B2
Farmfields Rise CW3 .... 232 B1
Farmfold SK9 .... 33 C2
Farmleigh Dr CW1 ...... 189 C4
Farmleigh Gdns WA5 ..... 15 B3
Farmside Cl WA5 .... 15 C4
Farmstead Way CH66 .... 69 C1
Farndale WA8 .... 13 A3
Farndale Cl
Warrington WA5 .... 14 C4
Wistaston CW2 .... 206 A3
Farndon Cl
Broughton CH4 .... 139 B2
Cuddington CW8 .... 102 A2
Sale M33 .... 242 E5
Farndon Prim Sch CH3 .180 C1
Farndon Rd CH66 .... 69 C3
Farne Cl CH2 .... 95 B4
Farnham Ave SK11 ...... 112 A3
Farnham Cl Cheadle SK8 .. 35 A4
Warrington WA4 .... 26 C4
Farnhill Cl WA7 .... 50 B4
Farnley Cl WA7 .... 24 B1
Farnworth CE Prim Sch
WA8 .... 13 A2
Farnworth Cl WA8 .... 13 A2
Farnworth Rd WA5 .... 14 B2
Farnworth St WA8 .... 13 A2
Farr Hall Dr CH60 .... 40 C4
Farr Hall Rd CH60 .... 40 C4
Farr St SK3 .... 240 D4
Farrant St WA8 .... 23 A4
Farrell Rd WA4 .... 26 B4
Farrell St WA1 .... 16 B3
Farriers Way CW7 ...... 126 A1
Farthing La CW9 .... 79 A4
Farwood Cl SK10 .... 86 C1
Faulkner Dr CW10 ...... 151 C3
Faulkner St CH2 .... 118 C2
Faulkner's La WA16 .... 58 C1
Faulkners Cl CH4 .... 161 A4
Faulkners La CH3 .... 142 B4
Fawley Ave SK14 .... 241 D5
Fawns Keep SK9 .... 60 B4
Fawns Leap CW8 .... 101 C3
Fearndown Way SK10 .... 87 B2
Fearnhead Cross WA2 .... 8 C1
Fearnhead La WA2 .... 9 A1
Fearnley Way WA12 .... 2 B1
Feather La CH60 .... 40 C4
Feilden Ct CH1 .... 94 C1
Felix Rd CW8 .... 103 C4
Fellside Gn SK15 .... 242 D3
Felskirk Rd M22 .... 33 B4
Fence Ave SK10 .... 112 C4
Fence Ave Ind Est SK10 112 C4
Fence La CW12 .... 178 B2
Fenham Dr WA5 .... 14 C2
Fennel St WA1 .... 16 B3
Fenton Cl
Congleton CW12 .... 157 A1
Widnes WA8 .... 12 B2
Fenwick La WA7 .... 49 B3
Fenwick Rd CH66 .... 69 C1
Ferguson Ave CH66 ...... 69 C3
Ferguson Dr WA2 .... 8 B1
Ferma La CH3 .... 120 B3
Fern Ave WA12 .... 2 B1
Fern Bank SK15 .... 242 F1
Fern Cl WA3 .... 9 B2
Fern Cres
Congleton CW12 .... 157 A2
Stalybridge SK15 .... 242 F1
Fern Ct CW1 .... 190 C2
Fern Lea SK8 .... 239 B1
Fern Lea Dr SK11 .... 112 A4
Fern Rd CH65 .... 70 A1
Fern Way CW8 .... 77 B1
Fernacre M33 .... 242 C7
Fernally St SK14 .... 241 E6
Fernbank Cl Crewe CW1 190 C2
Warrington WA3 .... 9 C2
Winsford CW7 .... 127 A1
Fernbank Rise SK10 ...... 88 A4
Ferndale Ave CH2 .... 72 A2
Ferndale Cl
Bold Heath WA8 .... 13 C4
Sandbach CW11 .... 175 B3
Warrington WA1 .... 17 B4
Weston CW2 .... 207 A3
Ferndale Cres SK11 ...... 111 C4
Fernhill Rd CH1 .... 117 C3
Fernhurst WA7 .... 49 B4
Fernilee Cotts SK23 ...... 65 C1
Fernlea WA15 .... 238 F1
Fernlea Rd Heswall CH60 .41 A4
Marston CW9 .... 79 A3
Fernleaf Cl ST7 .... 193 C4
Fernleigh CW8 .... 103 B4
Fernleigh Cl
Middlewich CW10 .... 151 C3
Winsford CW7 .... 126 A1
Fernley Ave M34 .... 241 A6
Fernway CW7 .... 127 A1
Fernwood WA7 .... 24 A1
Fernwood Gr SK9 .... 60 B4
Fernyess La CH64 .... 67 C4
Ferrous Way M44 .... 11 C3
Ferry Cl CH5 .... 116 A3
Ferry La Sealand CH1 ... 117 B1
Warrington WA4 .... 17 C2
Ferry Rd CH62 .... 44 A3
Ferryview Wlk WA7 ...... 23 C1
Festival Ave
Buerton CW3 .... 230 C2
Warrington WA2 .... 8 B1
Festival Cres WA2 .... 8 B1
Festival Dr SK10 .... 85 C3
Festival Hill CW12 ...... 156 C1
Festival Rd CH65 .... 69 C3
Festival Way WA7 .... 49 B4
Fiddler's Ferry Rd WA8 .. 13 B1
Fiddlers La CH1 .... 94 B1
Field Ave CW2 .... 189 C1
Field Cl Bollington SK10 .. 87 C4
Bramhall SK7 .... 35 B2
Northwich CW8 .... 103 B4
Tarvin CH3 .... 121 A1
Field Hey La CH64 .... 43 A1
Field La Tarvin CH3 ...... 121 A1
Tattenhall CH3 .... 166 A1
Warrington WA4 .... 26 B3
Wistaston CW2 .... 189 C1
Field Side Cl WA16 .... 58 A2
Field St SK6 .... 241 A3
Field View ST8 .... 179 B1
Field View Dr SK11 ...... 112 C3
Field Way ST7 .... 193 C2
Field Wlk 2 M31 .... 11 C2
Fieldbank Rd SK11 ...... 112 A4
Fieldfare CW7 .... 150 A4
Fieldfare Cl Golborne WA3 .3 B4
Warrington WA3 .... 9 C2
Fieldgate WA8 .... 22 A3
Fieldhead Mews SK9 ...... 60 C4
Fieldhead Rd SK9 .... 60 C4
Fieldhouse Row WA7 .... 49 B4
Fielding Ave SK12 .... 36 C1
Fields Cl ST7 .... 193 C2
Fields Cres CW12 .... 156 B1
Fields Dr CW11 .... 175 A3
Fields Rd Alsager ST7 ... 193 C2
Congleton CW12 .... 178 C4
Haslington CW1 .... 191 B2
Fields The CW5 .... 205 B3
Fields View SY13 .... 228 B1
Fields View Cl CW5 ...... 220 A4
Fieldsend Dr WN7 .... 4 B4
Fieldside CW6 .... 145 A3
Fieldsway WA7 .... 49 A3
Fieldview Dr WA2 .... 8 B1
Fieldway Chester CH2 ... 118 C2
Ellesmere Port CH66 ...... 69 A4
Frodsham WA6 .... 74 B4
Saughall CH1 .... 94 A1
Weaverham CW8 .... 77 B1
Widnes WA8 .... 13 C1
Fieldways 2 WA13 .... 18 B2
Fife Rd WA1 .... 16 C4
Fifth Ave Kidsgrove ST7 .. 194 C1
Runcorn WA7 .... 49 C4
Fildes Cl WA5 .... 15 B3
Filkin's La CH3 .... 119 A1
Finch La L26 .... 21 A4
Finchdale Gdns WA3 ..... 4 A4
Finchett Ct CH1 .... 118 A2
Finchett Dr CH1 .... 118 A2
Finchley Rd WA15 ...... 238 E3
Findlay Cl WA12 .... 2 B1
Finlan Rd WA8 .... 22 C4
Finland Rd SK3 .... 240 D3
Finlay Ave WA5 .... 14 C2
Finlow Hill La SK10 ...... 85 C3
Finney Cl SK9 .... 34 B1
Finney Dr SK9 .... 34 B1
Finney Gr WA11 .... 1 C3
Finney La SK8 .... 239 C1
Finney's La CW10 .... 128 A1
Finningley Ct WA2 .... 8 C1
Finny Bank Rd M33 ...... 242 A8
Finsbury Cl WA5 .... 15 B2
Finsbury Pk WA8 .... 13 B3
Finsbury Way SK9 .... 34 C1
Finsbury Wlk CW7 ...... 149 A4
Fir Ave Bramhall SK7 ...... 35 C4
Halewood L26 .... 21 A4
Fir Cl Halewood L26 .... 21 A4
Poynton SK12 .... 36 C2
Tarporley CW6 .... 146 B1
Fir Ct SK10 .... 86 C1
Fir Gr Macclesfield SK11 .112 B3
Warrington WA1 .... 16 C4
Weaverham CW8 .... 102 C4
Fir La CW8 .... 102 A1
Fir Rd Bramhall SK7 ...... 35 C4
Denton M34 .... 241 A7
Fir St Irlam M44 .... 11 B3
Stockport SK4 .... 240 E6
Widnes WA8 .... 13 B1
Fir Tree Ave
Chester CH4 .... 141 A3
Golborne WA3 .... 3 C4
Knutsford WA16 .... 82 B4
Fir Tree Cl WA4 .... 26 B1
Fir Tree La
Burtonwood WA5 .... 7 A4
Chester CH3 .... 119 C1
Faddiley CW5 .... 202 A2
Fir Tree Wlk WA3 .... 3 C4
Fir Way CH60 .... 41 A3
Firbank CH2 .... 72 B2
Firbank Cl WA7 .... 24 B1
Firbeck Cl
Broughton CH4 .... 139 A2
Congleton CW12 .... 155 C2
Firbeck Gdns CW2 ...... 189 B2
Firdale Rd CW8 .... 103 B4
Firecrest Ct WA1 .... 16 A2
Firemans Sq CH1 .... 237 A3
Firman Cl WA5 .... 15 A4
Firs Cl SK8 .... 239 A3
Firs Gr SK8 .... 239 A4
Firs La WA4 .... 26 A3
Firs Pottery The* CW5 .217 B1
Firs Rd SK8 .... 239 A4
Firs Sch The CH2 .... 118 C3
Firs The Altrincham WA14 238 B3
Wilmslow SK9 .... 60 A3
Firs View WA6 .... 73 B2
First Ave
Congleton CW12 .... 156 A2
Connah's Quay CH5 ...... 93 A1
Crewe CW1 .... 190 C1
Kidsgrove ST7 .... 194 C1
Poynton SK12 .... 36 B1
Sandbach CW11 .... 175 A3
First Dig La CW5 .... 219 B4
First Wood St CW5 ...... 204 B3
Firswood Mount SK8 ..... 239 A4
Firthfields Cl CW9 ...... 103 C1
Firths Fields CW9 .... 103 C1
Firtree Ave WA1 .... 17 A4
Firtree Cl Barnton CW8 .... 78 A2
Winsford CW7 .... 127 A1
Firtree Gr CH1 .... 95 A4
Firvale Ave SK8 .... 239 B1
Firwood Rd ST8 .... 179 C1
Firwood Wlk CW2 .... 190 B1
Fisher Ave WA2 .... 8 A1
Fisher Rd CH1 .... 117 C2
Fisher St WA7 .... 23 A2
Fisherfield Dr WA3 .... 10 A3
Fishermans Cl CW11 .... 191 C4
Fishers Gn CW6 .... 146 A3
Fishers La CW5 .... 203 B4
Fishpool Rd CW8 .... 123 C2
Fishwicks Ind Est WA11 .. 1 C4
Fistral Ave SK8 .... 34 B4
Fitton St CW9 .... 80 A1
Fitton's Cl CW5 .... 217 C3
Fitz Cl SK10 .... 87 B2
Fitz Cres SK10 .... 87 B2
Fitz Walter Rd WA1 ...... 17 B4
Fitzherbert St WA2 .... 16 B4
Fitzwilliam Ave SK11 ... 112 C2
Fitzwilliam Wlk WA7 ..... 24 A1
Five Ashes Rd CH4 ...... 141 A3
Five Ways CH64 .... 41 C2
Fivelanes End WA6 .... 74 B3
Fiveways Par SK7 .... 36 C4
Flacca Ct CH3 .... 166 A1
Flag La Crewe CW1,CW2 .190 B2
Neston CH64 .... 66 C4
Flag La N CH2 .... 118 C4
Flag La S CH2 .... 118 C4
Flamingo Cl CW1 .... 189 C4
Flander Cl WA8 .... 12 B1
Flash La Antrobus CW9 ... 53 C3
Bollington SK10 .... 87 B4
Flashes La CH64 .... 67 A3
Flat La Kelsall CW6 ...... 122 B2
Sandbach CW11 .... 175 A3
Flatt La CH65 .... 70 A3
Flatts La SK23 .... 64 C2
Flaxley Cl WA3 .... 10 A3
Flaxmere Dr CH3 .... 142 A4
Flaxyards CW6 .... 146 C1
Fleet La WA9 .... 1 A1
Fleet St
Ellesmere Port CH65 ...... 70 A3
Hyde SK14 .... 241 E7
Fleetwood Cl WA5 .... 15 A2
Fleetwood Dr WA12 .... 2 A2
Fleetwood Wlk WA7 .... 50 B3
Fleming Dr WA2 .... 8 A3
Fleming St CH65 .... 70 B3
Flemish Rd M34 .... 241 B6
Flers Ave WA4 .... 16 B2
Fletcher Dr
Altrincham WA14 .... 238 C1
High Lane SK12 .... 37 C3
Fletcher Gr CW9 .... 104 B3
Fletcher St Crewe CW1 .190 A3
Stockport SK1 .... 240 F5
Warrington WA4 .... 16 A2
Fletchers La WA13 .... 18 C2
Fletsand Rd SK9 .... 60 B3
Flint Cl CH64 .... 66 C3
Flint Ct CH65 .... 70 B1
Flint Dr CH64 .... 66 C3
Flint Gr M44 .... 11 B3
Flint Mdw CH64 .... 66 C4
Flint St Macclesfield SK11 112 C4
Stockport SK3 .... 240 E3
Flittogate La WA16 .... 80 C4
Flixton Dr CW2 .... 190 A1
Florence Ct SK3 .... 240 B2
Florence St Sale M33 .... 242 B8
6 Stockport SK4 .... 240 E6
Warrington WA4 .... 16 B2
Florida Cl WA5 .... 15 B4
Florist St SK3 .... 240 E3
Flower St CW8 .... 103 C4
Flowers La CW1 .... 172 C1
Flowerscroft CW5 .... 205 A2
Flowery Field Gn SK14 . 241 C8
Flowery Field Prim Sch
SK14 .... 241 D8
Fluin La WA6 .... 74 B4
Foden Ave ST7 .... 194 A2
Foden La
Alderley Edge SK9 .... 59 B1
Woodford SK7 .... 35 B2
Foden St SK10 .... 87 B1
Foden Wlk 8 SK9 .... 34 B1
Fogg's La CW9,WA4 ...... 53 A3
Fol Hollow CW12 .... 156 A1
Fold La Biddulph ST8 .... 179 C2
Bosley SK11 .... 135 B1
Fold The SK10 .... 87 A4
Folden Cl CH66 .... 69 A3
Folds La SK23 .... 65 C2
Folds The CH63 .... 42 A3
Foley Wlk M22 .... 33 C4
Folkestone Cl SK10 ...... 87 A1
Folkstone Way WA7 ...... 50 B4
Folly La WA5 .... 15 C4
Forbes Cl WA3 .... 9 C2
Forbes Pk SK7 .... 35 B4
Ford Cl CW1 .... 190 A3
Ford Ct CW7 .... 149 B3
Ford La Crewe CW1 ...... 190 A3
Tattenhall CH3 .... 166 C2
Ford St Stockport SK3 .... 240 D5
Warrington WA1 .... 16 B3
Ford's La SK7 .... 35 B3
Fordington Rd WA5 ...... 15 A3
Fords La ST7 .... 195 B3
Fordton Leisure Ctr WA2 .8 A2
Foregate St CH1 .... 237 B2

Foreland Cl WA5 . . . . .14 B4
Forest Ave CW4 . . . . . . .107 B1
Forest Cl
 Cuddington CW8 . . . . . . .101 C2
 Rainow SK10 . . . . .88 C3
Forest Dr
 Altrincham WA15 . . . . .238 F6
 Broughton CH4 . . . . . . .139 A2
Forest Gate La CW6 . . . .122 C4
Forest Ho SK10 . . . . .87 C1
Forest La WA6 . . . . .100 B3
Forest Pl 3 CW9 . . . . . . .79 A1
Forest Rd
 Cuddington CW8 . . . . . . .101 C2
 Ellesmere Port CH66 . . . . .69 C4
 Heswall CH60 . . . . .41 A4
 Macclesfield SK11 . . . . . .113 C3
 Tarporley CW6 . . . . .146 B2
 Winsford CW7 . . . . .149 A4
Forest Sch WA15 . . . . . .238 F6
Forest St Chester CH1 . . .237 C2
 Weaverham CW8 . . . . . . .102 B4
Forester Ave WA16 . . . . . .57 B1
Forester Dr SK15 . . . . . .242 D1
Foresters Cl WA6 . . . . . .101 A4
Forge Cl Cronton WA8 . . . .12 B3
 Warren SK11 . . . . .111 B1
Forge Fields CW11 . . . . .174 C2
Forge La
 Congleton CW12 . . . . . . .156 A2
 Norton in Hales TF9 . . . . .236 B1
Forge Mill La CW10 . . . . .151 B1
Forge Rd
 Ellesmere Port CH66 . . . . .69 B3
 Warrington WA5 . . . . .14 C3
 Whaley Bridge SK23 . . . . . .65 C4
Forge Sh Ctr The WA4 . . .16 B1
Forge St CW1 . . . . .190 B2
Forge Way CH4 . . . . .140 C2
Formby Cl WA5 . . . . .14 C2
Formby Dr SK8 . . . . .34 A4
Forrest Dr SK11 . . . . .113 B2
Forrest Rd M34 . . . . .241 B5
Forshaw St WA2 . . . . .16 B4
Forshaw's La WA5 . . . . . . .6 C4
Forster Ave CW8 . . . . . . .102 C4
Forster St WA2 . . . . .16 A4
Forsythia Wlk 2 M31 . . . .11 C1
Forty Acre La CW4,
 CW12 . . . . .131 B3
Forum The Chester CH1 . .237 A2
 Romiley SK6 . . . . .241 C2
Forwood Rd CH62 . . . . . . .43 B4
Fossa CW10 . . . . .128 B1
Foster Rd CW12 . . . . .157 A3
Foster St WA3 . . . . .13 A1
Fothergill St WA1 . . . . . . .16 B4
Fotheringay Ct 3 CH65 . . .70 B1
Foulkes Ave CW1 . . . . . . .189 C3
Foundry Bank CW12 . . . .156 C2
Foundry Ct
 13 Macclesfield SK11 . . . .112 B4
 New Mills SK22 . . . . .39 B4
Foundry La
 Sandbach CW11 . . . . .174 B4
 Scholar Green ST7 . . . . . .194 C4
 Widnes WA8 . . . . .22 B3
Foundry St
 Bollington SK10 . . . . .88 A4
 Newton-le-W WA12 . . . . . . .2 A2
 Warrington WA2 . . . . .16 A3
Fountain Ct Biddulph ST8 .179 B1
 Winsford CW7 . . . . .126 B1
Fountain Ho SK11 . . . . . .112 C4
Fountain La
 Davenham CW9 . . . . .103 C1
 Frodsham WA6 . . . . .74 A4
Fountain Pl SK12 . . . . .36 B2
Fountain St
 Ashton-u-Lyne OL6 . . . . .242 B4
 Congleton CW12 . . . . . . .156 B1
 Hyde SK14 . . . . .241 F7
 Macclesfield SK11 . . . . . .112 C4
Fountains Ave WA11 . . . . . .1 C4
Fountains Cl
 Middlewich CW10 . . . . . .128 A1
 Poynton SK12 . . . . .36 B2
 Runcorn WA7 . . . . .50 B3
Fountains Rd SK7,SK8 . . . .35 B3
Fountains Wlk WA3 . . . . . . .4 A4
Four Lane Ends WA6 . . . . .74 A4
Four Lanes End
 Betley CW2 . . . . .207 C1
 Thornton Hough CH63 . . . .42 B3
Fourseasons Cl CW2 . . . .206 A4
Fourth Ave
 Connah's Quay CH5 . . . . . .92 C1
 Crewe CW1 . . . . .190 C1
 Kidsgrove ST7 . . . . .194 C4
 Runcorn WA7 . . . . .49 C4
Fourway Tech Pk CW11 . .176 C2
Fourways CW2 . . . . .207 A3
Fowey Cl SK10 . . . . .86 B1
Fowler Rd CH1 . . . . .117 B2
Fowler St SK10 . . . . .87 B1
Fowlers Bench La CH3 . . .184 B3
Fowley Common La WA3 . . .5 B3
Fox Bank Ct SK3 . . . . . . .240 D4
Fox Bench Cl SK7,SK8 . . . .35 B3
Fox Cl WA15 . . . . .238 F6
Fox Cover CH3 . . . . .119 C3
Fox Cover Rd CH60 . . . . . .41 A4
Fox Covert WA7 . . . . .50 B4
Fox Covert La CH2 . . . . . .96 A1

Fox Covert Way CW1 . . . .173 A1
Fox Gdns Lymm WA13 . . . .18 B2
 Talke ST7 . . . . .210 B4
Fox Gr WA16 . . . . .57 B1
Fox Hill CW6 . . . . .122 B2
Fox La Clutton CH3 . . . . . .182 B1
 Waverton CH3 . . . . .143 A3
Fox Lea CH1 . . . . .117 A4
Fox St Congleton CW12 . . .156 C2
 Runcorn WA7 . . . . .23 A1
 Stockport SK3 . . . . .240 D4
 Warrington WA5 . . . . .15 C3
Fox Wood Sch WA3 . . . . . .9 C2
Fox's Dr CH5 . . . . .116 A3
Foxall Way CH66 . . . . .69 B1
Foxcote WA8 . . . . .12 A1
Foxcote Cl CH1 . . . . .117 B3
Foxcovert La WA16 . . . . .106 C4
Foxdale Ct WA4 . . . . .26 B4
Foxendale Cl CW8 . . . . . .103 B4
Foxes Fold CW8 . . . . .78 C1
Foxes Hey CW8 . . . . .101 B3
Foxes Hollow CW1 . . . . . .190 C4
Foxes Wlk CH3 . . . . .142 A4
Foxfield La CW7 . . . . .126 A1
Foxglove Cl
 Bollington SK10 . . . . .88 B4
 2 Golborne WA3 . . . . .3 B4
 Huntington CH3 . . . . .142 A3
 Wistaston CW2 . . . . .206 A4
Foxglove Ct WA6 . . . . .74 B4
Foxglove Dr WA14 . . . . . .238 C8
Foxglove La SK15 . . . . . .242 D3
Foxglove Way CH64 . . . . . .66 C3
Foxglove Wlk M31 . . . . . . .11 C1
Foxhall Rd WA15 . . . . . . .238 F6
Foxhill WA14 . . . . .238 A5
Foxhill Ct CW6 . . . . .146 C1
Foxhill Gr WA5 . . . . .73 B2
Foxhills Cl WA4 . . . . .26 B2
Foxhunter Cl CH3 . . . . . .121 C4
Foxland Rd SK8 . . . . .239 B4
Foxlea CW9 . . . . .78 B4
Foxley Cl WA13 . . . . .19 A1
Foxley Hall Mews WA13 . . .19 A1
Foxley Heath WA8 . . . . . . .22 C4
Foxwist Cl CH2 . . . . .237 B4
Foxwist Gr CW7 . . . . .125 C3
Foxwood Dr WA16 . . . . . .108 A4
Foxwood Way 1 SK9 . . . . .60 A3
Frances Ave SK8 . . . . . . .239 A6
Frances Dr Cheadle SK8 . .239 E6
 Crewe CW2 . . . . .190 B1
 Dukinfield SK14 . . . . .241 C7
 Irlam M44 . . . . .11 C3
 Macclesfield SK11 . . . . . .112 A4
 Stockport SK1,SK3 . . . . . .240 E4
Frances St W SK14 . . . . . .241 C7
Francis Cl WA8 . . . . .22 B4
Francis Ct CH2 . . . . .237 C3
Francis La LL13 . . . . .196 A3
Francis Rd Frodsham WA6 . .49 B1
 Irlam M44 . . . . .11 C4
 Warrington WA4 . . . . .16 B1
Francis St CH2 . . . . .237 C3
Frank Bott Ave CW1 . . . . .190 A4
Frank Perkins Way M44 . .11 C4
Frank St Hyde SK14 . . . . .241 E6
 Widnes WA8 . . . . .13 B1
Frank Webb Ave CW1 . . . .190 A3
Franklin Cl
 Macclesfield SK11 . . . . . .112 A3
 Warrington WA5 . . . . .15 B4
Fraser Ave M33 . . . . .242 E5
Fraser Ct CH4 . . . . .141 B4
Fraser Rd WA5 . . . . .14 B3
Frawley Ave WA12 . . . . . . .2 B3
Freckleton Ct WA5 . . . . . .15 A2
Frederick St
 Ashton-u-Lyne OL6,SK15 . .242 B2
 Warrington WA4 . . . . .16 C3
 Widnes WA8 . . . . .23 A4
Frederick Terr WA8 . . . . . .22 A1
Fredric Pl WA7 . . . . .23 A2
Free Green La WA16 . . . . .107 A4
Freedom Dr ST7 . . . . .195 C2
Freeman Ave OL6 . . . . . . .242 A3
Freemantle St SK3 . . . . . .240 D4
French Ave SK15 . . . . . . .242 F1
French La CW5 . . . . .218 B3
French St
 Ashton-u-Lyne OL6 . . . . .242 A4
 Stalybridge SK15 . . . . . . .242 F1
 Widnes WA8 . . . . .13 B1
Freshfield SK8 . . . . .34 A4
Freshfield Ave SK14 . . . . .241 D5
Freshfield Dr SK10 . . . . . .87 B2
Freshfields
 Comberbach CW9 . . . . . . .78 B4
 Wistaston CW2 . . . . .206 A4
Freshfields Dr WA2 . . . . . . .9 B1
Freshmeadow La WA6 . . . .73 A1
Freshwater Cl WA5 . . . . . .14 B4
Friar's Cl SK9 . . . . .59 C4
Friar's Rd M33 . . . . .242 B6
Friars Ave WA5 . . . . .14 C3
Friars Cl
 Altrincham WA14 . . . . . . .238 B1
 Rainow SK10 . . . . .88 B3
Friars Gate Chester CH1 . .237 B2
 Warrington WA1 . . . . .16 A2
Friars La WA1 . . . . .16 A2
Friars Way SK10 . . . . .86 C1
Frida Cres CW8 . . . . .103 C3
Friends La WA5 . . . . .14 B3
Friesian Gdns ST5 . . . . . .210 B1
Frieston Rd WA14 . . . . . . .238 E8
Frith Ave CW8 . . . . .123 B4
Frith La CW5 . . . . .216 B2

Frith Terr SK11 . . . . .112 B2
Frobisher Cl WA5 . . . . .15 B4
Frobisher Pl SK5 . . . . . . .240 E8
Frobisher Rd CH64 . . . . . .66 C4
Froda Ave WA6 . . . . .74 A4
Frodsham Ave SK4 . . . . . .240 C7
Frodsham CE Prim Sch
 WA6 . . . . .74 A4
Frodsham Rd WA6 . . . . . . .73 B1
Frodsham Sch WA6 . . . . . .74 A4
Frodsham St
 Chester CH1 . . . . .237 B3
 Kelsall CW6 . . . . .122 A3
Frodsham Sta WA6 . . . . . .74 A4
Frodsham Way SK9 . . . . . .34 C2
Frog La Holt LL13 . . . . . . .196 B4
 Milton Green CH3 . . . . . .165 C1
 Pickmere WA16 . . . . .55 A1
 Tattenhall CH3 . . . . .166 A1
 Worthenbury SY14 . . . . . .211 A1
Froghall La
 High Legh WA16 . . . . .29 B4
 Warrington WA2,WA5 . . . . .15 C3
Frome Ct CH65 . . . . .70 A4
Front St CW11 . . . . .175 A4
Frosts Mews CH65 . . . . . .70 A3
Fryer Rd CW9 . . . . .80 A2
Fuchsia Cl CH66 . . . . .69 C1
Fulbeck WA8 . . . . .12 B1
Fulbeck Cl CW2 . . . . .206 A4
Fulbrook Dr SK8 . . . . .35 A4
Fuller Dr CW2 . . . . .206 A4
Fullerton Rd
 Hartford CW8 . . . . .103 A2
 Stockport SK4 . . . . .240 B6
Fulmar Cl SK12 . . . . .36 A2
Fulmar Ct CW7 . . . . .189 C4
Fulmards Cl SK9 . . . . .60 B4
Fulshaw Ave SK9 . . . . .60 A3
Fulshaw CE Prim Sch
 SK9 . . . . .59 C3
Fulshaw Cross SK9 . . . . . .60 A3
Fulshaw Ct SK9 . . . . .60 A3
Fulshaw Pk SK9 . . . . .60 A3
Fulshaw Pk S SK9 . . . . . . .60 A3
Fulton Gr CW9 . . . . .103 C1
Fulwood Gdns CH66 . . . . .69 B3
Fulwood Mews CH66 . . . . .69 B3
Fulwood Rd
 Ellesmere Port CH66 . . . . .69 B3
 Golborne WA3 . . . . .3 C4
Furber St CW1 . . . . .190 B2
Furnace St SK14 . . . . . . .241 C8
Furne Rd CH1 . . . . .117 C2
Furness Cl
 Holmes Chapel CW4 . . . .130 A2
 Poynton SK12 . . . . .36 B2
 Winsford CW7 . . . . .149 A4
Furness Ct WA7 . . . . .24 C2
Furness Gr SK4 . . . . .240 A5
Furness Lodge Cl SK23 . . .39 B2
Furness Rd SK8 . . . . .35 B3
Furness Vale Bsns Ctr
 SK23 . . . . .39 B2
Furness Vale Prim Sch
 SK23 . . . . .39 B2
Furness Vale Sta SK23 . . . .39 B2
Furnival St Crewe CW2 . . .190 B1
 Sandbach CW11 . . . . .175 A4
Furrocks Cl CH64 . . . . .66 C3
Furrocks La CH64 . . . . . . .66 C3
Furrocks Way CH64 . . . . . .66 C3
Furrows The CH66 . . . . . . .94 C4
Fylde Ave SK8 . . . . .34 B4
Fylde Rd SK4 . . . . .240 A6
Fytton Cl SK11 . . . . .111 A6

G

Gable Ave SK9 . . . . .60 A4
Gable St WA12 . . . . .2 A4
Gables Cl WA2 . . . . .8 C2
Gables The ST7 . . . . .193 B2
Gabriel Bank CW8 . . . . . . .76 A1
Gadbrook Bsns Ctr
 CW9 . . . . .104 B3
Gadbrook Pk CW9 . . . . . .104 B3
Gadbrook Rd CW9 . . . . . .104 B3
Gaddum Rd WA14 . . . . . .238 B1
Gail Ave SK4 . . . . .240 D6
Gail Cl SK9 . . . . .60 A1
Gainford Ave SK8 . . . . . . .239 B4
Gainford Cl WA8 . . . . .12 B2
Gainsborough Cl SK9 . . . .60 B4
Gainsborough Ct WA8 . . . .12 A1
Gainsborough Dr SK8 . . . .239 F6
Gainsborough Inf Sch
 CW2 . . . . .190 A2
Gainsborough Jun Sch
 CW2 . . . . .190 A1
Gainsborough Rd
 Crewe CW2 . . . . .190 A2
 Warrington WA4 . . . . .16 A1
Gair Rd SK5 . . . . .240 F8
Gair St SK14 . . . . .241 D8
Gairloch Cl WA2 . . . . .8 C2
Gaisgill Ct WA8 . . . . .12 B1
Gala Cl CH4 . . . . .139 B2
Galbraith Cl CW12 . . . . . .156 B1
Gale Ave WA5 . . . . .7 C1
Gale Rd SK22 . . . . .39 B4
Galion Way WA8 . . . . .12 C2
Galleys Bank ST7 . . . . . . .195 A2
Gallimore Ho ST7 . . . . . . .210 B4
Galloway Cl CW4 . . . . . . .130 B1
Gallowsclough La WA6 . . .100 C4
Galway Gr CW2 . . . . .206 A2

Game St CW11 . . . . .175 A2
Gamul Pl CH4 . . . . .237 B1
Ganton Cl WA8 . . . . .13 A2
Garden Ave CW7 . . . . .126 A1
Garden Cl SK10 . . . . .87 C1
Garden Ct CH1 . . . . .237 A3
Garden La
 Altrincham WA14 . . . . . . .238 D5
 Chester CH1 . . . . .237 A3
 Harthill CH3 . . . . .183 C2
Garden Rd WA16 . . . . .56 C2
Garden St Bollington SK10 .87 C4
 Congleton CW12 . . . . . . .156 B2
 Hyde SK14 . . . . .241 E8
 Macclesfield SK10 . . . . . . .87 C1
Garden Terr
 Chester CH1 . . . . .237 A3
 Chester, Hoole Park CH2 . .118 C1
 Stalybridge SK15 . . . . . . .242 D2
Garden Wlk 1 M31 . . . . . .11 B3
Gardens The Holt LL13 . . .196 B4
 Sandbach CW11 . . . . .175 A3
Gardiner Ave WA11 . . . . . . .1 B3
Garfit St CW10 . . . . .128 B1
Garlick St SK14 . . . . .241 F7
Garner Cl WA14 . . . . .238 D2
Garner St WA2 . . . . .16 B4
Garner's La SK3 . . . . .240 E1
Garnett Ave WA4 . . . . .17 A4
Garnett St SK1 . . . . .240 F5
Garnetts La WA8 . . . . .22 A2
Garrett Field WA3 . . . . .9 B3
Garrett Wlk SK3 . . . . .240 C4
Garrigill Cl WA8 . . . . .13 B3
Garsdale Cl WA5 . . . . .15 A4
Garside Ave WA3 . . . . .3 B4
Garside St SK14 . . . . .241 E5
Garston Cl SK4 . . . . .240 C7
Garth Ave WA15 . . . . .238 E6
Garth Dr CH2 . . . . .118 B3
Garth Hts SK9 . . . . .60 B4
Garth Rd CH65 . . . . .71 A3
Garven Pl WA1 . . . . .16 A3
Garwood Cl WA5 . . . . .15 B4
Gas Rd SK11 . . . . .112 B4
Gas St SK4 . . . . .240 E5
Gaskell Ave
 Knutsford WA16 . . . . .56 C1
 Warrington WA4 . . . . .17 A2
Gaskell Rd WA14 . . . . . . .238 D6
Gaskell St WA4 . . . . .17 A2
Gatcombe Mews 1 SK9 . . .60 A3
Gate Warth St WA5 . . . . . .15 B2
Gateacre Ct CH66 . . . . . . .69 C4
Gatefield St CW1 . . . . . . .190 B2
Gatesheath Dr CH2 . . . . . .118 C4
Gatesheath La CH3 . . . . . .165 C3
Gatewarth Ind Est WA5 . . .15 B2
Gateway Crewe CW1 . . . . .190 C1
 Newcastle-u-L ST5 . . . . . .210 B1
Gathill Cl SK8 . . . . .239 F1
Gathurst Ct WA8 . . . . .22 B4
Gatley Gn SK8 . . . . .239 A5
Gatley Prim Sch SK8 . . . . .239 A5
Gatley Rd Cheadle SK8 . . .239 C5
 Sale M33 . . . . .242 E5
Gatley Sta SK8 . . . . .239 B5
Gauntley Bird of Prey Ctr★
 SK10 . . . . .85 A1
Gaunts Way WA7 . . . . .49 C3
Gavin Rd WA8 . . . . .22 A3
Gawend La SK11 . . . . .112 B1
Gawer Pk CH2 . . . . .118 B2
Gawsworth Ave CW2 . . . .189 C2
Gawsworth Cl
 Alsager ST7 . . . . .193 B2
 Bramhall SK7 . . . . .35 C3
 Holmes Chapel CW4 . . . .130 A2
 Northwich CW9 . . . . .104 A2
 Poynton SK12 . . . . .36 C1
 Stockport SK3 . . . . .240 D1
Gawsworth Ct WA3 . . . . . . .9 C3
Gawsworth Dr CW11 . . . . .175 B4
Gawsworth Hall★ SK11 . .134 C4
Gawsworth Mews SK8 . . .239 B5
Gawsworth Prim Sch
 SK11 . . . . .111 B1
Gawsworth Rd
 Ellesmere Port CH66 . . . . .69 C3
 Macclesfield SK11 . . . . . .111 B3
Gawsworth Way
 4 Denton M34 . . . . .241 A5
 Handforth SK9 . . . . .34 C2
Gayhurst Ave WA2 . . . . . . .8 C1
Gaymoore Cl CH2 . . . . . . .237 A4
Gaynor Ave WA11 . . . . .1 C4
Gayton Cl CH2 . . . . .118 C3
Gayton Farm Rd CH60 . . . .41 A3
Gayton La CH60 . . . . .41 A3
Gayton Mill Cl CH60 . . . . . .41 A4
Gayton Parkway CH60 . . . .41 B3
Gayton Prim Sch CH60 . . . .41 A3
Gayton Rd CH60 . . . . .41 A3
Gee St SK3 . . . . .240 D3
Gemini Bsns Pk WA5 . . . . . .7 B2
Gemmull Cl CW3 . . . . .229 C2
General St WA1 . . . . .16 B3
Genesis Ctr The WA3 . . . . .9 C3
Geneva Rd CW7 . . . . .126 C1
Geo Hampson's Bldgs
 WA3 . . . . .5 B4
George Bates St ST7 . . . . .193 B2
George Kenyon Mews
 CH4 . . . . .140 C3
George La SK6 . . . . .241 A4
George Richards Way
 WA14 . . . . .238 C7

George St
 Alderley Edge SK9 . . . . . . .60 A1
 Altrincham WA14 . . . . . . .238 D4
 Audley ST7 . . . . .209 B1
 Barnton CW8 . . . . .78 A2
 Chester CH1 . . . . .237 A3
 Denton M34 . . . . .241 A4
 Ellesmere Port CH65 . . . . .70 A4
 Knutsford WA16 . . . . .57 A1
 Macclesfield SK11 . . . . . .112 B4
 Newton-le-W WA12 . . . . . . .2 A2
 Sandbach CW11 . . . . .174 C4
 Stalybridge SK15 . . . . . . .242 D2
 Whaley Bridge SK23 . . . . . .65 C4
 Winsford CW7 . . . . .126 C1
George St W SK11 . . . . . .112 B4
George VI Ave CW10 . . . . .151 B3
George VI Cl CW10 . . . . . .151 B3
George's Cl SK12 . . . . .36 C2
George's La CW9 . . . . .54 B1
George's Prec WA5 . . . . . .14 B3
George's Rd Sale M33 . . . .242 B5
 Stockport SK4 . . . . .240 D6
George's Rd E SK12 . . . . . .36 C2
George's Rd W SK12 . . . . .36 C2
George's Wlk CW11 . . . . . .175 A3
Georges Cres WA4 . . . . . . .17 A1
Georges Way ST7 . . . . . . .209 C1
Gerard Dr CW5 . . . . .204 B2
Gerosa Ave WA2 . . . . .8 A4
Gerrard Ave
 Ellesmere Port CH66 . . . . .69 B2
 Warrington WA5 . . . . .15 C4
Gerrard Dr CW8 . . . . .77 B1
Gerrard Rd WA3 . . . . .9 A4
Gerrard St
 Stalybridge SK15 . . . . . . .242 E1
 Widnes WA8 . . . . .23 A4
Gerrards Ave CH3 . . . . . . .119 A1
Giantswood La CW12 . . . . .156 B3
Gibb Hill CW9 . . . . .53 B1
Gibbon Dr CW9 . . . . .80 A2
Gibson Cres CW11 . . . . . .174 B3
Gibson St
 Warrington, Howley WA1 . . .16 B3
 Warrington, Stockton Heath
 WA4 . . . . .16 B1
Gibson Way WA14 . . . . . .238 C8
Gibsons Rd SK4 . . . . .240 B8
Gig La WA1 . . . . .17 C4
Gigg La Moore WA4 . . . . . .25 A3
 Warrington WA4 . . . . .17 C2
Gilbert Cl 2 ST7 . . . . . . .195 A1
Gilbert Rd WA15 . . . . .238 E1
Gilbertbank SK6 . . . . .241 B4
Gilchrist Ave SK11 . . . . . .111 C4
Gilchrist Rd M44 . . . . .11 C3
Gilderdale Cl WA3 . . . . . . .10 A3
Gillan Cl WA7 . . . . .50 B3
Gillbent Rd SK8 . . . . .35 A4
Gillow Cl CW1 . . . . .190 A4
Gilmore St SK3 . . . . .240 E3
Giltbrook Cl WA8 . . . . .12 C2
Gilwell Cl WA4 . . . . .17 B1
Gingerbread La CW5 . . . . .205 A3
Girton Cl CH65 . . . . .70 B2
Girton Rd CH65 . . . . .70 B2
Girvin Dr CH64 . . . . .66 C3
Glade The SK4 . . . . .240 A5
Gladewood Cl SK9 . . . . . . .60 B4
Gladstone Ave CH1 . . . . . .118 A1
Gladstone Ct 1 SK4 . . . . .240 B7
Gladstone Gr SK4 . . . . . . .240 A7
Gladstone Rd
 Altrincham WA14 . . . . . . .238 D8
 Broughton CH4 . . . . .139 A4
 Chester CH1 . . . . .118 A2
 Neston CH64 . . . . .66 C4
Gladstone St Crewe CW1 .190 B2
 Northwich CW9 . . . . .103 C4
 Warrington WA2 . . . . .16 A3
 8 Widnes WA8 . . . . .23 A4
Gladstone Way WA12 . . . . .2 A2
 Winsford CW7 . . . . .149 B4
Gladville Dr SK8 . . . . .240 A2
Glaisdale Cl CW2 . . . . . . .206 A3
Glamis Cl Chester CH3 . . .119 A1
 Wistaston CW2 . . . . .205 C4
Glan Aber Pk CH4 . . . . . . .141 A4
Glanaber Ct CH4 . . . . .141 A4
Glandon Dr SK8 . . . . .35 B4
Glanvor Rd SK3 . . . . .240 C4
Glastonbury Ave
 Bramhall SK8 . . . . .35 B3
 Chester CH2 . . . . .118 C4
 Golborne WA3 . . . . .4 B4
Glastonbury Cl WA7 . . . . . .24 C2
Glastonbury Dr
 Middlewich CW10 . . . . . .128 B3
 Poynton SK12 . . . . .36 B3
Glaswen Gr SK5 . . . . .240 F8
Glazebrook La WA3 . . . . . .11 A3
Glazebrook St WA1 . . . . . .16 B3
Glazebrook Sta WA3 . . . . .11 A3
Glazebury CE Prim Sch
 WA3 . . . . .5 B4
Glaziers La WA3 . . . . .4 B1
Gleadmere WA8 . . . . .12 B1
Gleave Av SK10 . . . . .88 A4
Gleave Rd Burtonwood WA5 .6 C3
 Weaverham CW8 . . . . .77 B1
Gleave St M33 . . . . .242 B8
Glebe Ave WA4 . . . . .17 A1
Glebe Cl CW5 . . . . .220 A4
Glebe Farm Mews CH2 . . .71 C1
Glebe Green Dr CW7 . . . . .149 B3

Glebe La WA8 13 A3
Glebe Mdws CH2 96 C1
Glebe Rd CW8 102 A2
Glebe St ST7 194 B1
Glebe The WA7 23 C1
Glebecroft Ave CH2 72 A2
Glebeland WA3 4 C1
Glebelands Rd
Knutsford WA16 57 A1
Sale M33 242 A8
Glebeway Rd CH65 70 C3
Gledhall St SK15 242 D2
Glen Aber Dr CH4 140 C4
Glen Ave M33 242 A8
Glen Cl WA3 11 A1
Glen Maye M33 242 C6
Glen Rd CH66 69 B2
Glen The Blacon CH1 117 C3
Runcorn WA7 49 C3
Glenathol Rd CH66 69 B2
Glenbourne Pk SK7 35 B3
Glenburn Ave CH62 43 C2
Glencoe Cl CW4 130 B1
Glencoe Rd CH66 69 B2
Glencourse Rd WA8 13 A3
Glendale Ave Elton CH2 72 A2
Hawarden CH5 116 A2
Glendale Bsns Pk CH5 116 A2
Glendale Cl
Buerton CW3 230 C2
Wistaston CW2 189 B2
Glendale Pk CH5 116 A2
Glendene Ave SK7 35 B3
Glendyke Rd CH66 69 B2
Gleneagles Cl
Bramhall SK7 36 A4
Chester CH3 119 A2
Wilmslow SK9 60 B4
Gleneagles Dr
Haydock WA11 1 A3
Holmes Chapel CW4 130 A1
Macclesfield SK10 87 B2
Widnes WA8 13 A3
Winsford CW7 126 B1
Gleneagles Rd
Ellesmere Port CH66 69 B2
Gatley SK8 239 C1
Glenesk Rd CH66 69 B2
Glenfield WA14 238 B4
Glenfield Dr SK12 36 B2
Glenfield Rd SK4 240 D8
Glenholme Rd SK7 35 B4
Glenlea Dr M20 239 B8
Glenmaye Rd CH66 69 B2
Glenmere Rd M20 239 C8
Glenn Pl WA8 12 C1
Glenorchy Cl CW4 130 B1
Glenside Cl CH1 117 B3
Glenside Dr SK9 60 B3
Glent View SK15 242 D4
Glenthorn Gr M33 242 B5
Glenton Pk CH64 66 C3
Glenville Cl WA7 49 A3
Glenville Way M34 241 A6
Glenville Wlk SK15 242 D1
Glenwood WA7 24 B1
Glenwood Cl 3 CH66 69 B3
Glenwood Gdns CH66 69 B3
Glenwood Rd CH66 69 B3
Gleyve WA16 29 B3
Gloucester Ave 2 WA3 3 A4
Gloucester Cl
Ellesmere Port CH66 94 C4
Macclesfield SK10 87 C2
Warrington WA1 17 B4
Gloucester Rd Gatley SK8 34 B4
Kidsgrove ST7 194 C1
Knutsford WA16 81 C4
Poynton SK12 36 B2
Widnes WA8 13 A2
Gloucester St
Chester CH2 237 B4
Stockport SK3 240 D3
Glover Dr SK14 241 E6
Glover Rd WA3 9 B2
Glover St Crewe CW1 190 A3
Newton-le-W WA12 2 B2
Glovers Loom CH3 142 A4
Gloverstone Ct CH4 237 B1
Glyn Ave CH62 43 C4
Goathland Way SK11 112 B3
Goddard Rd WA7 23 C2
Goddard St CW1 190 A3
Godfrey St WA2 16 B4
Godley Ct SK14 241 F6
Godley Prim Sch SK14 241 F7
Godley St SK14 241 F8
Godscroft La WA6 73 C3
Godshill Cl WA5 14 B4
Godstall La CH1 237 B2
Godstow WA7 24 C2
Godward Rd SK22 39 A4
Golborne Cty Prim Sch
WA3 3 A4
Golborne Dale Rd WA12 3 A3
Golborne Rd Golborne WA3 3 B4
Winwick WA12,WA2 8 A4
Golborne St
Newton-le-W WA12 2 C2
Warrington WA1 16 A3
Gold Triangle Complex
WA8 22 B3
Goldborne La WA16 28 C1
Goldcliffe Cl WA5 7 B2
Goldcrest Cl Crewe CW1 189 C4
Runcorn WA7 49 C3
Winsford CW7 149 B3
Golden Sq WA1 16 A3
Goldfinch Cl CW12 156 C1
Goldfinch Dr ST7 193 A2
Goldfinch La WA3 9 C2
Goldford La SY14 199 C3
Goldsmith Dr CW11 174 B3
Golf Rd Altrincham WA15 238 F3
Sale M33 242 F6
Golftyn Dr CH5 91 B1
Golftyn La CH5 91 B1
Gongar La CH3 98 C1
Gonsley Cl CH2 237 B4
Gonville Ave SK11 112 C2
Gooch Dr WA12 2 B1
Goodall St SK11 112 C4
Goodall's Cnr CW2 206 B2
Goodier St M33 242 A6
Goodrington Rd SK9 34 C2
Goodwood Cl
Barnton CW8 78 A2
Chester CH1 118 A1
Goodwood Gr CH66 69 B2
Goodwood Rise CW10 128 A1
Goose Gn WA14 238 D4
Goose La WA4 26 A1
Gooseberry La
Kelsall CW6 122 C2
Runcorn WA7 24 B1
Goosebrook Cl CW9 78 B4
Goosebrook La WA4,CW9 52 C1
Goosetrey Cl SK9 34 C1
Goostrey Com Prim Sch
CW4 130 C4
Goostrey Com Prim Sch (The Annexe) CW4 107 C1
Goostrey Ct 4 CW12 156 C2
Goostrey La CW4 130 A4
Goostrey Sta CW4 131 A4
Gordale Cl
Congleton CW12 157 A3
Warrington WA5 14 C4
Gordon Ave
Bebington CH62 43 C4
Haydock WA11 1 C4
Sale M33 242 B8
Warrington WA1 17 A4
Gordon La CH1 95 A3
Gordon St
Ashton-u-Lyne OL6 242 A4
Hyde SK14 241 E6
Stalybridge SK15 242 E1
Stockport SK4 240 E7
Gordon Terr SK15 242 D2
Gore La SK9 59 B2
Gorse Bank Rd WA15 32 B4
Gorse Cl WA6 101 A3
Gorse Covert CW9 79 B2
Gorse Covert Prim Sch
WA3 10 A3
Gorse Covert Rd WA3 10 A3
Gorse Hall Dr SK15 242 C1
Gorse Hall Prim Sch
SK15 242 D1
Gorse La CW12 178 B3
Gorse Sq M31 11 B2
Gorse Stacks CH1 237 B3
Gorse The WA14 31 A4
Gorse Way CH3 142 A3
Gorsefield CH3 166 A1
Gorsefield Ave CH62 43 B3
Gorsefield Cl CH62 43 B3
Gorsefield Hey SK9 60 C4
Gorselands SK8 35 A3
Gorsewood Prim Sch
WA7 50 B4
Gorsewood Rd WA7 50 B3
Gorsey Bank Cres CW5 220 A4
Gorsey Bank Prim Sch
SK9 59 C4
Gorsey Bank Rd SK3 240 B4
Gorsey Brow SK6 241 A2
Gorsey La
Altrincham WA14 238 B5
Partington WA13 20 A4
St Helens WA5,WA9 6 B3
Warrington WA1,WA2 16 B4
Widnes WA8 13 C1
Gorsey Rd SK9 59 C4
Gorseywell La WA7 50 C3
Gorsley Cl CW10 151 B3
Gorstage La CW8 102 B4
Gorsthills Com Prim Sch
CH66 69 B2
Gorston Wlk M22 33 B4
Gorsty Hill Cl CW2 207 C1
Gosberryhole La CW12 158 A1
Gosforth Ct WA7 49 C4
Gosforth Pl CH2 118 C2
Gosling Cl WA4 26 A1
Gosling Rd WA3 9 A4
Gosling Way CW12 156 A2
Gosport Cl WA2 8 C1
Goss St CH1 237 A2
Gotherage Cl SK6 241 E2
Gotherage La SK6 241 E2
Gothic Cl SK6 241 F2
Gough Ave WA2 8 A1
Gough St SK3 240 D5
Gough's La WA16 82 B4
Goulden St Crewe CW1 190 A3
Warrington WA5 15 C3
Goulders Ct WA7 50 A3
Gourham Dr SK8 239 F2
Gower Rd Hyde SK14 241 D5
Stockport SK4 240 D8
Gowy Cl Alsager ST7 192 C2
Sandbach CW11 174 C4
Wilmslow SK9 34 C1
Gowy Cres CH3 121 A1
Gowy Ct Alpraham CW6 169 C1
Ellesmere Port CH66 69 C4
Gowy Rd CH2 96 C1
Gowy Wlk CW7 127 A2
Goyt Pl SK23 65 C4
Goyt Rd Disley SK12 38 B3
New Mills SK22 39 B3
Goyt Valley Ind Est SK23 39 B2
Goyt View SK22 39 A3
Grace Ave WA2 16 A4
Grace Cl CW1 191 B2
Gradbach Mill* SK17 138 A1
Gradwell St SK3 240 D4
Grafton Mall 5 WA14 238 D4
Grafton Mews CH2 237 B4
Grafton Rd CH65 70 B4
Grafton St
Altrincham WA14 238 D4
Ashton-u-Lyne OL6 242 A2
Hyde SK14 241 D7
Newton-le-W WA12 2 A2
Stockport SK4 240 E7
Warrington WA5 15 C3
Graham Ave CH66 69 B3
Graham Cl WA8 12 B1
Graham Cres M44 11 B2
Graham Dr Disley SK12 38 B3
Halewood L26 21 A4
Graham Rd Blacon CH1 117 C2
Widnes WA8 22 B4
Grainger's Rd CW9 103 C3
Grammar School Ct WA4 16 C2
Grammar School Rd
Lymm WA13 18 C1
Warrington WA4 16 C2
Grampian Way
Bebington CH62 43 C2
Neston CH64 66 C3
Winsford CW7 149 A4
Granby Cl WA7 50 B3
Granby Rd Cheadle SK8 35 A4
Warrington WA4 26 A4
Grand Junction Ret Pk
CW1 190 B2
Grandford La CW5 217 B1
Granford Cl WA14 238 D7
Grange Ave Barnton CW8 78 A2
Cheadle SK8 239 F3
Denton M34 241 B6
Warrington WA4 16 C2
Grange Cl Crewe CW1 190 C2
Golborne WA3 3 B3
Hyde SK14 241 F5
Sandbach CW11 174 C4
Grange Comp Sch The
WA7 23 B1
Grange Cres CH66 44 A1
Grange Ct
Altrincham WA14 238 C1
Biddulph ST8 179 B1
11 Knutsford WA16 57 A1
Winsford CW7 126 A1
Grange Dr Hartford CW8 103 A3
Thornton Hough CH63 42 A4
Warrington WA5 15 A2
Widnes WA8 12 B1
Grange Farm Cl WA5 15 B3
Grange Green Manor
WA4 25 C4
Grange Inf Sch The WA7 23 B1
Grange Jun Sch The
Hartford CW8 103 A3
Runcorn WA7 23 B1
Grange La Tilston SY14 198 C2
Weaverham CW8 102 A4
Whitegate CW8 125 C4
Winsford CW7 126 A2
Grange Lea CW10 128 A1
Grange Park Ave
Cheadle SK8 239 D5
Runcorn WA7 23 B1
Wilmslow SK9 60 A4
Grange Park Rd SK8 239 D5
Grange Pk Dr ST8 179 C2
Grange Pl M44 11 B3
Grange Prim Sch CW7 126 A1
Grange Rd
Altrincham WA14 238 C1
Ashton CH3 99 A1
Barnton CW8 78 A2
Biddulph ST8 179 C2
Chester CH3 119 B1
Chester, Bache CH2 118 B2
Cuddington CW8 101 C1
Ellesmere Port CH65 70 B2
Haydock WA11 1 B3
Macclesfield SK11 112 B3
Northwich, Rudheath CW9 104 B3
Runcorn WA7 23 B1
Sale M33 242 A6
Grange Rd N Hyde SK14 241 F6
Runcorn WA7 23 B1
Grange Rd W CH3 119 B1
Grange Sch The CW8 103 A3
Grange The
Hartford CW8 103 A3
Hyde SK14 241 F5
Macclesfield SK11 112 A3
Grange Valley WA11 1 B3
Grange Valley Prim Sch
WA11 1 B3
Grange Villas CH3 142 C3
Grange Way CW11 174 C4
Grangebrook Dr CW7 126 B2
Grangefields ST8 179 C2
Grangelands SK10 86 C1
Grangemoor WA7 49 B4
Grangeside CH2 118 B4
Grangeway Runcorn WA7 49 B4
Wilmslow SK9 34 B2
Grangeway Ct WA7 49 B4
Grangewood Dr SK11 83 C2
Granston Cl WA5 7 C1
Grant Cl WA5 7 B1
Grant Rd WA5 15 A3
Grantham Ave
Warrington WA1 16 C4
Warrington, Walton WA4 26 A4
Grantham Cl CW9 104 B4
Grantham Rd SK4 240 C6
Granville Dr CH66 69 A4
Granville Rd
Chester CH1 118 A2
Northwich CW9 104 A3
Stockport SK8 240 C1
Wilmslow SK9 59 C3
Granville Sq CW7 149 C4
Granville St
Ashton-u-Lyne OL6 242 A2
Runcorn WA7 23 A2
Warrington WA1 16 B3
Winsford CW7 149 C4
Grapes St SK11 112 B4
Grappenhall Hall Sch
WA4 17 A1
Grappenhall Heys Com Prim Sch WA4 27 A4
Grappenhall La WA4 27 C3
Grappenhall Rd
Ellesmere Port CH65 69 C2
Warrington WA4 16 B1
Grappenhall St Wilfred's CE Prim Sch WA4 17 A1
Grasmere SK11 111 C3
Grasmere Ave
Congleton CW12 155 C1
Crewe CW2 189 C3
Warrington WA2 8 C2
Grasmere Cl
Stalybridge SK15 242 D4
Winsford CW7 126 B1
Grasmere Cres SK7 35 C4
Grasmere Dr
Holmes Chapel CW4 130 A2
Runcorn WA7 49 B3
Grasmere Rd
Alderley Edge SK9 60 A1
Chester CH2 118 C3
Ellesmere Port CH65 70 B1
Frodsham WA6 74 B4
Gatley SK8 239 B3
9 Lymm WA13 18 C2
Neston CH64 66 C3
Partington M31 11 C2
Grason Ave SK9 34 B1
Grasscroft Rd SK15 242 D1
Grassfield Way WA16 82 A4
Grassmoor Cl CH62 43 C4
Grassygreen La ST7 209 C1
Gratrix La M33 242 F5
Gratrix Rd CH62 43 B4
Gravel La SK9 59 C3
Graveyard La WA16 58 C3
Gray Ave WA11 1 B3
Gray's Cl ST7 195 A4
Graylag Cl WA7 49 C3
Graymarsh Dr SK12 36 C1
Graysands Rd WA15 238 F3
Greasby Dr CH66 69 C2
Great Ashfield WA8 12 B2
Great Budworth CE Prim Sch
CW9 79 A4
Great Delph WA11 1 B4
Great Egerton St SK1 240 E6
Great King St SK11 112 B4
Great Norbury St SK14 241 D6
Great Portwood St SK1 240 F6
Great Queen St SK11 112 B4
Great Riding WA7 50 B4
Great Sankey High Sch
WA5 14 C4
Great Sankey L Ctr WA5 14 C4
Great Sankey Prim Sch
WA5 15 A3
Great Underbank SK1 240 F5
Greatoak Rd ST7 209 C2
Greave SK6 241 D4
Greave Fold SK6 241 D4
Greave Prim Sch SK6 241 D4
Greaves La SY14 222 C3
Greaves Lane E SY14 222 C4
Greaves Rd SK9 59 C4
Grebe Cl Knutsford WA16 57 A2
Poynton SK12 36 A2
Greeba Ave WA4 16 A2
Greek St Runcorn WA7 22 C2
Stockport SK3 240 E4
Green Acre Cl WA16 82 A4
Green Ave
Alpraham CW6 169 B2
Barnton CW8 78 A2
Davenham CW9 103 C2
Green Bank
Adderley TF9 235 A3
Chester CH4 141 C3
Green Bridge Cl WA7 24 A1
Green Cl SK8 239 A6
Green Coppice WA7 50 B4
Green Courts WA14 238 B3
Green Croft SK6 241 E3
Green Dr Alsager ST7 193 B2
Handforth SK9 34 B1
Green End Farm CH4 139 B1
Green Farm CH4 163 A1
Green Gables Cl SK8 239 B1
Green Hall Mews SK9 60 A3
Green Hill St SK3 240 D3
Green Hill Terr SK3 240 D3
Green Jones Brow WA5 6 C3
Green La Acton CW5 204 A2
Appleton Thorn WA4 27 A3
Audlem CW3 229 C1
Barbridge CW5 187 A4
Bollington SK10 63 A1
Burtonwood WA5 6 C4
Chester CH3 119 A2
Chester, Lache CH4 140 C2
Davenham CW9 103 C2
Disley SK12 38 B2
Ellesmere Port CH65 70 B2
Ellesmere Port, Great Sutton CH66 69 B2
High Lane SK12 37 B2
Higher Kinnerton CH4 161 A3
Higher Wincham CW9 79 C2
Irlam M44 11 C3
Kelsall CW6 122 B2
Knutsford WA16 56 B2
Lindow End SK9 84 C4
Peover WA16 83 B1
Picton CH2 96 B2
Plumley WA16 80 C3
Romiley SK6 241 B2
Sandbach CW11 173 C4
Saughall CH1 117 B4
Shocklach SY14 211 B4
Stockport SK4 240 B7
Stockport SK4 240 C6
Stockport SK4 240 D5
Tattenhall CH3 182 C3
Tilston SY14 212 A4
Warrington WA1 17 A4
Widnes WA8 12 C1
Willaston (nr Nantwich) CW5 205 C3
Wilmslow SK9 60 A4
Winwick WA2 8 A4
Green La E CH5 116 B4
Green La W CH5 93 A2
Green Lake La CH3 163 C2
Green Lane Cl WA2 8 A4
Green Lane Com Specl Sch
WA1 17 A4
Green Lane Est CH5 116 B4
Green Lane Ind Est SK4 240 C5
Green Lawns Dr CH66 94 C4
Green Mdws Golborne WA3 3 C3
Macclesfield SK11 111 C3
Green Oaks Path WA8 23 B4
Green Oaks Way WA8 23 B4
Green Pk CW8 102 C4
Green Rd M31 11 C2
Green St
3 Alderley Edge SK9 60 A1
Holt LL13 180 C1
Hyde SK14 241 E5
Knutsford WA16 57 A1
Macclesfield SK11 112 C4
Sandbach CW11 175 A4
Stockport SK3 240 F2
Warrington WA5 15 C3
Green The Cheadle SK8 34 C4
Congleton CW12 156 B1
Ellesmere Port CH65 70 A1
Hale L24 21 B1
Handforth SK9 34 C2
Hartford CW8 103 A3
Harthill CH3 183 C2
Higher Kinnerton CH4 161 A4
Lawton-gate ST7 194 A2
Middlewich CW10 151 B3
Neston CH64 66 B4
Neston, Little Neston CH64 66 C3
Partington M31 11 C2
Stockport SK4 240 C6
Tarvin CH3 121 C1
Thornton Hough CH63 42 B2
Green Tree Gdns SK6 241 B2
Green View WA13 19 A3
Green Villa Pk SK9 59 C2
Green Way CH1 94 A1
Green Wlk
Altrincham WA14 238 B3
Cuddington CW8 102 A2
Gatley SK8 239 A6
Partington M31 11 C2
Greenacre SK8 34 B4
Greenacre Dr CH63 43 B4
Greenacre Rd CH4 140 C2
Greenacres Crewe CW1 190 B3
Duddon CW6 145 A3
Frodsham WA6 74 B3
Sandbach CW11 175 A4
Chester CH2 95 C1
Greenacres Cl WA3,WN7 4 A4
Greenacres Rd CW12 155 C1
Greenacres The WA13 19 A2
Greenall Ave WA5 14 B2
Greenall Rd CW9 104 A4
Greenall's Ave WA4 16 B1
Greenbank Ave
Ellesmere Port CH66 69 B4
Gatley SK8 239 A5
Greenbank Cl CW5 205 B3
Greenbank Dr SK10 88 A4
Greenbank Gdns WA4 16 C1
Greenbank La CW8 103 B3
Greenbank Pk CW11 175 A1
Greenbank Rd
Chester CH2 119 A2
Gatley SK8 239 A6

Greenbank Rd continued
Warrington WA4 16 C1
Greenbank Residential Sch
CW8 103 B3
Greenbank St WA4 16 B1
Greenbank Sta CW8 103 B3
Greenbridge Rd WA7 24 A1
Greencourts Bsns Pk
M22 34 A4
Greendale Dr
Middlewich CW10 151 A4
Newcastle-u-L ST5 210 B1
Greendale Gdns CW1 190 C3
Greendale La SK10 86 B4
Greenfield Ave CH4 161 A4
Greenfield Cl
New Mills SK22 39 A4
Newton-le-W WA12 2 B2
Stockport SK3 240 E2
Greenfield Cres
Chester CH2 119 A3
Waverton CH3 143 A3
Greenfield Gdns CH2 72 A2
Greenfield Ind Est
CW12 156 A2
Greenfield La
Chester CH2 119 A3
Frodsham WA6 49 A1
Greenfield Prim Sch
SK14 241 E6
Greenfield Rd
Bollington SK10 88 A4
Broughton CH4 139 B2
Congleton CW12 156 A2
Ellesmere Port CH66 69 A4
Waverton CH3 143 A3
Greenfield St SK14 241 D6
Greenfield Way CW8 102 A2
Greenfields Chester CH2 95 C1
Winsford CW7 127 A1
Greenfields Ave
Bebington CH62 43 B4
Shavington CW2 206 A2
Warrington WA4 26 B4
Greenfields Cl
Neston CH64 66 C3
Warrington WA1 17 B4
Greenfields Cres CH62 43 B4
Greenfields Croft CH64 66 C3
Greenfields Dr CH64 66 C3
Greenfields La SY14 213 A2
Greenfields Lodge CH3 120 B3
Greenfields Prim Sch
CW7 126 A1
Greenfields Rd ST7 193 C2
Greengate WA15 32 B4
Greengate Rd Hyde M34 241 A8
Lawton-gate ST7 193 C3
Greengates Cres CH64 66 B4
Greenhalgh St SK4 240 E6
Greenhaven Ct CW5 219 C3
Greenhead Fold SK6 241 A1
Greenhill Ave M33 242 A8
Greenhill La WA4 52 A3
Greenhill Wlk SK12 38 B3
Greenhills Cl SK11 112 C4
Greenhouse Farm Rd
WA7 50 A4
Greenhythe Rd SK8 34 B3
Greenland Cl CW6 146 B1
Greenlands CH3 166 A2
Greenlands Cl 3 SK8 34 C4
Greenlaw Cl CW9 104 A3
Greenlea Cl CH65 70 A1
Greenoaks Farm Ind Est
WA8 23 B4
Greenore Dr L24 21 B1
Greenshall La SK12 38 C3
Greenshank Cl WA12 2 B2
Greenside SK4 240 A5
Greenside Ave WA6 74 B4
Greenside Ct CW9 105 B3
Greenside Dr
Altrincham WA14 238 E1
Lostock Green CW9 105 A4
Greensway CH4 141 A4
Greenvale Dr SK8 239 C6
Greenview Dr M20 239 C8
Greenway Alsager ST7 193 A3
Altrincham WA14 238 A5
Bramhall SK7 35 B3
Congleton CW12 156 A2
Crewe CW1 190 B4
Farndon CH3 180 C1
Hyde SK14 241 D5
Romiley SK6 241 E1
Tilston SY14 198 B2
Warrington WA4 26 B4
Warrington, Great Sankey
WA5 14 C4
Warrington, Paddington
WA1 16 C4
Wilmslow SK9 60 A3
Greenway Cl Helsby WA6 73 A2
Rode Heath ST7 193 C4
Greenway Dr CW9 104 B4
Greenway Rd
Biddulph ST8 179 C1
Gatley SK8 34 B3
Runcorn WA7 23 A1
Sale WA15 238 F8
Speke L24 21 A2
Widnes WA8 13 A1
Greenway St CH4 237 B1
Greenway Wlk CW9 104 B4
Greenways ST7 209 C1
Greenwell Rd WA11 1 B3
Greenwich Ave WA8 13 B2
Greenwood Ave
Chester CH4 141 B4
Congleton CW12 156 C2
Greenwood Cl
Culcheth WA3 4 C1
Weaverham CW8 77 B1
Greenwood Cres WA2 8 C1
Greenwood Dr
Newton-le-W WA12 2 B1
Runcorn WA7 24 C2
Wilmslow SK9 60 B4
Greenwood Rd WA13 18 C1
Greenwood St 1 WA14 238 D4
Greenwood Terr WA16 58 A2
Greg Ave SK10 87 C4
Greg Mews SK9 34 A1
Gregory Ave SK6 241 C1
Gregory Cl WA5 15 B4
Gregson Rd WA8 13 B1
Grenfell Cl CH64 41 B1
Grenfell Pk CH64 41 B1
Grenfell St 11 WA8 23 A4
Grenville Cl CW1 191 B3
Grenville Cres CH63 43 B4
Grenville Rd CH64 41 C1
Grenville St SK3 240 D4
Grenville Terr OL6 242 A2
Gresford Ave CH2 237 C4
Gresford Cl WA5 7 C1
Gresley Way ST7 209 C1
Gresty Green Rd CW2 206 B4
Gresty La CW2 206 A4
Gresty Rd CW2 190 B1
Gresty Road Football Gd (
Crewe Alexandra FC)
CW2 190 B1
Gresty Terr CW1 190 C2
Greta Ave SK8 34 B3
Greville Dr CW7 127 A1
Grey Cl SK6 241 A4
Grey Friars CH1 237 A2
Grey Rd WA14 238 C5
Grey St Stalybridge SK15 242 F1
Warrington WA1 16 B3
Greyhound Park Rd
CH1 117 C2
Greyhound Pk CH1 118 A1
Greyhound Rd SK10 86 A3
Greylands Rd M20 239 C8
Greymist Ave WA1 17 B4
Greys Ct WA1 9 B1
Greystoke Ave M33 242 B5
Greystoke Dr SK9 60 A1
Greystoke Rd SK10 87 A3
Greystone Pk CW1 190 B2
Greystone Rd WA5 14 C2
Greystones CH66 69 B2
Greystones Rd CH3 119 B1
Grice St WA4 16 B1
Griffin Cl Blacon CH1 117 C3
New Mills SK22 39 B3
Norton in Hales TF9 236 B1
Griffin Mews WA8 13 A2
Griffith Ave WA3 9 C3
Griffiths Dr CW9 104 B3
Griffiths Rd
Lostock Gralam CW9 79 C1
Northwich CW9 104 C4
Griffiths St WA4 16 C2
Grig Pl ST7 193 B3
Grimsditch La WA4 52 A3
Grimshaw Ave SK10 88 A4
Grimshaw Cl SK6 241 A4
Grimshaw La SK10 88 A4
Grindley Bank CH2 119 C4
Grindley Gdns CH65 70 B1
Grisedale Ave WA2 8 A2
Grisedale Cl WA7 49 C3
Grisedale Rd CH62 43 C4
Grisedale Way SK11 112 A3
Gritstone Dr SK11 112 A4
Grizedale WA8 12 A1
Grizedale Cl CW2 189 B1
Grizedale Rd SK6 241 B4
Groarke Dr WA5 14 B3
Groby Ct WA14 238 C4
Groby Pl WA14 238 D5
Groby Rd
Altrincham WA14 238 C4
Crewe CW1 190 C4
Groby St SK15 242 F1
Grosvenor Ave
Alsager ST7 193 B3
3 Golborne WA3 3 B4
Hartford CW8 103 A2
Warrington WA1 16 C4
Grosvenor Cl
Warrington WA5 15 B3
Wilmslow SK9 60 A2
Grosvenor Cres SK14 241 C5
Grosvenor Ct
Cheadle SK8 239 D6
Chester CH1 237 C2
Winsford CW7 149 B4
Grosvenor Dr SK12 36 B2
Grosvenor Gdns
Newton-le-W WA12 2 B1
Stalybridge SK15 242 D1
Grosvenor Grange WA1 9 A1
Grosvenor Ho SK15 242 D1
Grosvenor Mus★ CH4 237 A1
Grosvenor Nuffield Hospl
CH4 141 B3
Grosvenor Pk Rd CH2 237 C2
Grosvenor Pk Terr CH2 237 C2
Grosvenor Pl CH4 237 B1
Grosvenor Rd
Altrincham WA14 238 E5
Chester CH4 141 B4
Congleton CW12 156 A2
Haydock WA11 1 A4
Hyde SK14 241 D5
Stockport SK4 240 B7
Tarvin CH3 121 A1
Widnes WA8 13 A3
Grosvenor Sh Ctr The
CH1 237 B2
Grosvenor Sq M33 242 A6
Grosvenor St
Chester CH1 237 A2
Crewe CW1 190 A3
6 Macclesfield SK11 112 B4
Runcorn WA7 23 A2
Stalybridge SK15 242 D1
9 Stockport SK1 240 F4
Winsford CW7 149 C4
Grotsworth La SY14 214 C4
Grotto La WA16 108 A4
Grounds St WA2 16 A4
Grove Arc SK9 60 A1
Grove Ave Chester CH3 119 A2
Kidsgrove ST7 194 C1
Lawton-gate ST7 194 A2
Lostock Gralam CW9 80 A2
Lymm WA13 18 B2
Wilmslow SK9 60 A4
Grove Cl CW7 149 A4
Grove Cres CW3 232 B1
Grove Ct Alsager ST7 193 C2
Lymm WA13 18 B2
Sale M33 242 D6
Grove Gdns CH3 119 C1
Grove Ho SK8 35 A3
Grove La SK7,SK8 35 A3
Grove Park Ave ST7 194 A2
Grove Pk WA16 57 A1
Grove Rd
Altrincham WA15 238 E3
Backford CH1 94 C2
Grove Rise WA13 18 C2
Grove St New Mills SK22 39 A4
Runcorn WA7 22 C2
Stalybridge SK16 242 A1
Warrington WA4 16 B2
Wilmslow SK9 60 A4
Grove Terr WA6 73 B2
Grove The Bramhall SK8 35 A3
Knutsford WA16 57 B2
Lawton-gate ST7 194 A2
Lymm WA13 18 C2
Sale M33 242 B5
Stockport SK3 240 E3
Warrington WA5 14 C2
Grove Way SK9 60 A4
Grovemount CW9 103 C1
Groves The Chester CH1 237 B2
Ellesmere Port CH1 95 A4
Tarporley CW6 146 B1
GroveThe SY13 225 C1
Grovewood Mews SK11 112 B3
Grub La CW6 122 B3
Grundy Cl WA8 12 C2
Grundy St WA3 3 A4
Guardian Ct M33 242 A7
Guardian St WA5 15 C3
Guernsey Cl
Congleton CW12 157 A1
Middlewich CW10 128 B1
Warrington WA4 26 B4
Guernsey Dr CH65 70 B1
Guernsey Ho CH2 119 A3
Guernsey Rd WA8 13 C2
Guest St WA8 23 A4
Guests Slack WA6 100 A4
Guilden Gn CH3 119 C2
Guilden Sutton CE Prim Sch
CH3 119 C3
Guilden Sutton La CH3 119 B3
Guildford Ave SK8 35 A3
Guildford Cl WA2 9 A1
Guildford Rd CH4 140 C3
Guillemot Cl CW1 190 C3
Gull Cl SK12 36 A2
Gullane Cl SK10 87 A2
Gullet The CW5 204 C3
Gullivers World Theme Pk★
WA5 7 C1
Gulls Way CH60 40 C4
Gunco La
Macclesfield SK11 112 C3
Prestbury SK10 87 B4
Gunn Gr CH64 66 C4
Gutterscroft CW1 191 B3
Gutticar Rd WA8 12 A1
Guy La CH3 143 B3
Guywood Cotts SK6 241 C3
Guywood La SK6 241 C3
Gypsey Cnr SY13 224 C1

H

Hack Green Secret Nuclear
Bunker★ CW5 218 B2
Hackberry Cl WA14 238 B8
Hacked Way La SK11 113 C3
Haddon Cl
Alderley Edge SK9 59 C1
High Lane SK6 37 C3
Holmes Chapel CW4 130 A2
Macclesfield SK11 112 A3
Wistaston CW2 206 A4
Haddon Dr WA8 12 B2
Haddon Gr
Altrincham WA15 238 F7
Sale M33 242 A6
Haddon Ho 4 CH64 66 C4
Haddon La CH64 67 B2
Haddon Rd Burton CH64 67 B1
Gatley SK8 34 B4
Hadfield Cl WA8 13 C1
Hadfield St CW9 79 A1
Hadleigh Cl WA5 14 C3
Hadley Ave CH62 43 B4
Hadley Cl SK8 239 F1
Hadlow La CH64 67 C4
Hadlow Rd CH64 67 C3
Hadrian Dr CH1 117 C3
Hadrian Way
Cuddington CW8 102 A1
Middlewich CW10 128 B1
Hafod Cl Blacon CH1 117 B2
Connah's Quay CH5 91 B1
Hag Bank La SK12 38 B4
Hague Bar Prim Sch
SK22 38 C4
Hague Bar Rd SK22 39 A4
Hague Fold Rd SK22 38 C4
Hague Pl SK15 242 D2
Hague St OL6 242 A4
Haig Ave Irlam M44 11 B2
Warrington WA5 15 A3
Haig Ct WA16 57 B2
Haig Rd Knutsford WA16 57 B2
Widnes WA8 13 A1
Haigh Lawn WA14 238 B3
Hale Ave SK12 36 B1
Hale Bank Rd WA8 21 C3
Hale Bank Terr WA8 22 A2
Hale CE Prim Sch L24 21 C1
Hale Ct WA14 238 D2
Hale Gate Rd Hale WA8 21 C2
Widnes WA8 22 A2
Hale Gr WA5 15 A3
Hale Low Rd WA15 238 F3
Hale Prep Sch WA15 238 E3
Hale Rd Altrincham WA15 32 B4
Hale L24 21 A1
Stockport SK4 240 C7
Widnes WA8 22 B4
Widnes, Ditton WA8 22 B4
Hale Road Ind Est WA8 22 A2
Hale St WA2 16 A4
Hale Sta WA14 238 D2
Hale View WA7 48 C4
Hale View Rd WA6 73 B2
Halebank CE Prim Sch
WA8 22 A3
Halewood Lane Ends
L26 21 A4
Haley Rd N WA5 6 C3
Haley Rd S WA5 6 C3
Half St SK11 112 B3
Halfacre La WA4 17 C1
Halghton La LL13 222 A1
Halifax Cl WA2 8 B1
Halkett Cl CH4 140 C3
Halkyn Rd CH2 237 C4
Hall Ave Altrincham WA15 238 F7
Widnes WA8 12 A1
Hall Bank WA16 58 B2
Hall Bank N WA16 58 B2
Hall Bank S WA16 58 B2
Hall Cl SK10 87 B2
Hall Dr Alsager ST7 193 B2
Marston CW9 79 A3
Warrington WA4 26 B3
Willaston (nr Nantwich)
CW5 205 B3
Hall Gr Cheadle SK8 239 C6
Macclesfield SK10 87 B2
Hall Hill SK10 87 C4
Hall La Antrobus CW9 53 A1
Appleton Thorn WA4 27 A4
Audlem CW3 230 B4
Brown Knowl CH3 199 B4
Cronton WA8,L35 12 B4
Daresbury WA4 25 B1
Haughton CW6 186 B3
Higher Wincham CW9 79 C2
Kelsall CW6 122 B3
Little Leigh CW9 77 C4
Mobberley WA16 58 B2
Newton-le-W WA5 7 A4
Partington M31 11 C2
Pickmere WA16 55 A1
Sandbach CW11 174 A3
St Helens WA9 6 A2
Stretton WA4 52 C4
Sutton Lane Ends SK11 112 C2
Utkinton CW6 146 B3
Warmingham CW11 173 C2
Winsford CW7 149 A2
Hall La The CW6 147 B1
Hall Mdw SK8 239 E1
Hall Moss La SK7 35 B2
Hall Nook WA5 14 C2
Hall O'shaw St CW1 190 C2
Hall Rd Altrincham WA14 238 C1
Handforth SK9 34 C2
Haydock WA11 1 C4
Warrington WA1 17 B4
Wilmslow SK9 60 A4
Hall St Ashton-u-Lyne OL6 242 B2
Audley ST7 209 B1
Cheadle SK8 239 D6
Denton SK14 241 B7
Macclesfield SK11 112 B4
New Mills SK22 39 A4
Warrington WA1 16 B3
Hall Terr WA5 14 C4
Hall View CH3 166 A1
Hall View Cl CW8 102 A4
Hall Wood Ave WA11 1 C4
Halla Way WA4 16 C2
Hallastone Rd WA6 73 A2
Hallcroft M31 11 C2
Hallcroft Pl WA4 17 A1
Hallefield Cres SK11 112 C4
Hallefield Dr 6 SK11 112 C4
Hallefield Rd 7 SK11 112 C4
Hallfield Dr CH2 72 A2
Hallfield Pk CH66 69 B2
Hallfields Rd Tarvin CH3 121 B1
Warrington WA2 8 B1
Hallgate Dr SK8 239 A2
Hallgreen La CW12 155 B4
Halliday Cl WA3 9 C2
Halliwell's Brow WA16 29 A2
Hallows Ave WA2 16 B4
Hallows Cl CW6 122 B2
Hallows Dr CW6 122 B2
Hallowsgate Ct CW6 122 B2
Halls Rd Biddulph ST8 179 B1
Mow Cop ST7 195 B4
Hallsgreen La CH2 96 C4
Hallshaw Ave CW1 190 C3
Hallside Pk WA16 57 B1
Hallwood Cl WA7 49 A3
Hallwood Dr CH66 68 B2
Hallwood Link Rd WA7 49 C3
Hallwood Park Ave WA7 49 C3
Hallwood Park Prim Sch
WA7 49 C3
Hallwood Rd SK9 34 B1
Halsall Ave WA2 16 B4
Halsall Cl WA7 50 B3
Halsall's Cotts WA8 21 C3
Halston Cl SK5 240 F8
Halstone Ave SK9 59 C2
Halton Brook Ave WA7 23 B1
Halton Castle★ WA7 23 C1
Halton Coll of F Ed WA8 23 A4
Halton Coll of F Ed (Annexe)
Runcorn WA7 23 C2
Widnes WA8 23 A4
Halton Cres CH66 69 C1
Halton Ct WA7 23 B1
Halton Dr CW2 189 B3
Halton General Hospl
WA7 49 C3
Halton Link Rd WA7 49 C4
Halton Lodge Ave WA7 49 B4
Halton Lodge Prim Sch
WA7 49 B4
Halton Rd Chester CH2 118 C3
Ellesmere Port CH66 69 C1
Runcorn WA7 23 B1
Warrington WA5 14 C3
Halton St Haydock WA11 1 C3
Hyde SK14 241 F7
Halton Station Rd WA7 49 C2
Halton View Rd WA8 13 B1
Halton Way CH66 69 C1
Hamble Dr WA5 14 C2
Hamble Way SK10 86 C1
Hambledon Cl CH66 69 A3
Hambleton Cl WA8 12 B2
Hambleton Rd SK8 34 B4
Hambleton Way CW7 149 A4
Hambletts Hollow WA6 100 C3
Hamilton Ave
Hawarden CH5 116 A2
Irlam M44 11 B2
Hamilton Cl
Haslington CW1 191 B2
Macclesfield SK10 113 A4
Neston CH64 41 A1
Hamilton Cres SK4 240 B5
Hamilton Ct M33 242 B6
Hamilton Pl CH1 237 A2
Hamilton Rd
Connah's Quay CH5 91 B1
Lymm WA13 18 B2
Hamilton Sq SK4 240 E7
Hamilton St Chester CH2 118 C2
Stalybridge SK15 242 C2
Hammond Sch
Chester CH2 119 A4
Chester CH2 237 A4
Hammond St CW2 190 B2
Hamnett Ct WA3 9 C2
Hamnett St SK14 241 D7
Hamon Rd WA15 238 E4
Hampden Rd M33 242 A5
Hampshire Cl CW12 156 B2
Hampshire Rd M31 11 B1
Hampshire Wlk SK10 86 C1
Hampson Ave WA3 4 C2
Hampson Cres SK9 34 B2
Hampson St M33 242 D6
Hampstead Ct 8 CW7 149 A4
Hampton Cl Neston CH64 66 C3
Widnes WA8 13 C2
Hampton Cres
Neston CH64 66 C3
No Man's Heath SY14 214 A2
Hampton Ct WA7 24 B2
Hampton Dr Cronton WA8 12 B3
Warrington WA5 15 B2
Hampton Gdns CH65 70 A3
Hampton Gr SK8 239 E2
Hampton Rd
Chester CH4 140 C3
Irlam M44 11 B2
Hamson Dr SK10 63 A1
Hamsterley Cl WA3 10 A3
Hanbury Cl CW2 206 A4
Hancock Ct WA4 16 B2

Hancock Rd CW12 ... 156 C2
Hand St SK11 ... 112 A4
Handa Dr CH65 ... 95 A4
Handbridge CH4 ... 237 B1
Handel Mews M33 ... 242 C6
Handford Ave CH62 ... 43 C3
Handford Rd CH2 ... 118 C3
Handforth Cl WA4 ... 17 B2
Handforth La WA7 ... 49 B3
Handforth Rd
Crewe CW2 ... 189 C2
Handforth SK9 ... 34 C1
Handforth Sta SK9 ... 34 B2
Handley Cl SK3 ... 240 C1
Handley Hill CW7 ... 149 B4
Handley Hill Prim Sch
CW7 ... 149 A4
Handley St WA7 ... 22 C2
Hangman's La CW9 ... 105 B4
Hankelow Cl
Chester CH2 ... 237 B4
Middlewich CW10 ... 151 B3
Hankey St WA7 ... 22 C1
Hankins Heys La CW3 ... 231 A1
Hankinson Cl M31 ... 11 C1
Hanley Cl Disley SK12 ... 38 B3
Widnes WA8 ... 12 B1
Hanley Rd WA8 ... 12 B1
Hannah's Wlk 2 CW10 ... 151 B4
Hanns Hall Farm CH64 ... 67 B4
Hanns Hall Rd CH64 ... 67 B4
Hanover Bsns Pk WA14 ... 238 B7
Hanover Ct WA7 ... 50 A3
Hanover Dr 2 CW7 ... 149 B3
Hanover Rd WA14 ... 238 B7
Hanover St
Stalybridge SK15 ... 242 C2
Warrington WA1 ... 16 A2
Hapsdale View WA6 ... 72 C1
Hapsford Cl WA3 ... 9 B2
Hapsford La
Dunham-on-t-H WA6 ... 97 C4
Elton CH2 ... 72 B2
Elton, Hapsford WA6 ... 72 C1
Hapton Pl SK4 ... 240 E7
Harbord St WA1 ... 16 B2
Harbour Cl Chester CH2 ... 118 C4
Runcorn WA7 ... 50 B3
Harbour La SK11 ... 111 B1
Harburn Wlk M22 ... 33 C4
Harcourt Cl WA3 ... 9 C2
Harcourt Rd
Altrincham WA14 ... 238 D6
Sale M33 ... 242 A8
Hardcastle Rd SK3 ... 240 D3
Harden Pk SK9 ... 60 A2
Harding Ave
Tattenhall CH3 ... 166 B1
Warrington WA2 ... 8 C1
Harding Rd Chester CH2 ... 118 A4
Nantwich CW5 ... 204 B2
Hardings Mdw ST7 ... 194 C1
Hardingswood Rd ST7 ... 194 C1
Hardknott Rd CH62 ... 43 C4
Hardman Ave SK6 ... 241 A3
Hardman St SK3 ... 240 D4
Hardwick Cl SK6 ... 37 C3
Hardwick Dr SK11 ... 112 A3
Hardwick Grange WA1 ... 17 C4
Hardwick Rd WA7 ... 23 B2
Hardwicke Rd SK12 ... 36 C2
Hardy Cl
Ellesmere Port CH66 ... 69 C2
Wistaston CW2 ... 205 C4
Hardy Dr
Altrincham WA15 ... 238 F7
Bramhall SK7 ... 35 B4
Hardy Rd WA13 ... 18 B1
Hardy St WA2 ... 16 A3
Hare La CH3 ... 119 B2
Hare's La WA6 ... 73 C4
Harebell Cl CH3 ... 142 A3
Harebell Gr ST7 ... 195 C1
Harecastle Ave ST7 ... 194 C1
Harefield Dr SK9 ... 60 A3
Harefield Rd SK9 ... 34 C2
Harehill Gdn* SK10 ... 86 A3
Harewood Ave CH66 ... 69 B2
Harewood Cl
Northwich CW9 ... 103 C2
Winsford CW7 ... 126 A1
Harewood Ct M33 ... 242 C5
Harewood Way SK11 ... 112 A3
Harewood Wlk 6 M34 ... 241 A5
Harfield Gdns CH66 ... 69 B3
Harford Cl WA5 ... 14 C2
Hargrave Ave CW2 ... 189 C2
Hargrave Dr CH66 ... 69 C3
Hargrave La
Bebington CH64 ... 43 A2
Thornton Hough CH63,CH64 42 C3
Hargreaves Ct WA8 ... 13 B1
Hargreaves Rd CW9 ... 104 B4
Harington Cl CH2 ... 95 B1
Harington Rd CH2 ... 118 B4
Harlech Cl WA5 ... 7 C1
Harlech Ct CH65 ... 70 B2
Harlech Way CH65 ... 70 B2
Harley Rd M33 ... 242 C7
Harlow Cl WA4 ... 17 B2
Harlyn Ave SK7 ... 35 C4
Harlyn Gdns WA5 ... 14 B2
Harn The CH66 ... 69 B2
Harold Rd WA11 ... 1 C4
Haroldgate SY13 ... 225 C1
Harper Cl
Ellesmere Port CH66 ... 69 B2
Macclesfield SK11 ... 112 B3
Harper Gr CW12 ... 156 C2
Harpers Rd WA2 ... 9 A1
Harpur Cres ST7 ... 193 A3
Harraps Pl 2 SK11 ... 112 A3
Harrier Cl CW1 ... 189 C4
Harrier Rd WA2 ... 8 C1
Harriet St M44 ... 11 C3
Harrington Dr SK11 ... 111 B1
Harrington Rd WA14 ... 238 B5
Harris Cl CW1 ... 173 A1
Harris Rd CW9 ... 80 A1
Harris St WA8 ... 13 B1
Harriseahead La ST7 ... 195 B2
Harrison Dr
Allostock CW4 ... 107 A1
Haydock WA11 ... 1 A3
Harrison Gr CH5 ... 116 A2
Harrison Sq WA5 ... 7 C1
Harrison St
Stalybridge SK15 ... 242 D2
Stockport SK1,SK2 ... 240 F3
Widnes WA8 ... 22 A3
Harrison Way WA12 ... 2 B2
Harrisons Pl 17 CW8 ... 103 C4
Harrogate Cl
Bebington CH62 ... 43 B2
Warrington WA5 ... 7 A1
Harrogate Rd CH62 ... 43 B2
Harrop La SK10 ... 62 C3
Harrop Rd
Altrincham WA15 ... 238 F2
Bollington SK10 ... 88 B4
Runcorn WA7 ... 23 A1
Harrop St SK15 ... 242 D2
Harrow Cl Crewe CW2 ... 190 A1
Warrington WA4 ... 26 C3
Harrow Dr WA7 ... 23 C1
Harrow Gr CH62 ... 43 C4
Harrow Rd CH65 ... 70 B2
Harrow Way CW9 ... 103 C2
Harrytown SK6 ... 241 A3
Harrytown RC High Sch
SK6 ... 241 A2
Hart Ave M33 ... 242 F5
Hart St WA14 ... 238 E5
Hartford Ave SK9 ... 59 C3
Hartford Bsns Ctr CW8 ... 102 C2
Hartford Cl CW11 ... 175 B4
Hartford Dr CH65 ... 69 C2
Hartford High Sch CW8 103 B3
Hartford Manor Com Prim
Sch CW8 ... 103 B3
Hartford Prim Sch CW8 103 A2
Hartford Rd CW9 ... 103 C1
Hartford Sta CW8 ... 103 A2
Hartford Way CH1 ... 118 A1
Harthill Cl CW9 ... 103 C3
Harthill La CH3 ... 183 C2
Harthill Prim Sch CH3 ... 183 C2
Harthill Rd Blacon CH1 ... 117 C3
Burwardsley CH3 ... 184 A3
Hartington Dr SK7 ... 36 C4
Hartington Rd
Altrincham WA14 ... 238 D8
Bramhall SK7 ... 35 C3
Gatley SK8 ... 34 B4
High Lane SK12,SK6 ... 37 C4
Hartington St CH4 ... 141 C4
Hartland Cl Poynton SK12 ... 36 B3
Widnes WA8 ... 13 A3
Hartley Cl WA13 ... 18 C2
Hartley Gdns CW12 ... 179 A4
Hartley Gn SK10 ... 87 C4
Hartley Rd WA14 ... 238 C5
Hartley St SK3 ... 240 D4
Hartshead Ave SK15 ... 242 D3
Hartshead View SK14 ... 241 F5
Hartswood Cl Hyde M34 ... 241 A8
Warrington WA4 ... 26 C2
Hartwell Gr CW7 ... 126 C2
Harty Rd WA11 ... 1 A3
Harvard Cl WA7 ... 24 B1
Harvard Ct WA2 ... 8 A2
Harvest Cl CW9 ... 126 C4
Harvest Rd SK10 ... 87 B2
Harvey Ave
Nantwich CW5 ... 205 A3
Newton-le-W WA12 ... 1 C2
Harvey Ct WA2 ... 8 A2
Harvey Rd CW12 ... 157 A3
Harvey St SK1 ... 240 F5
Harvin Gr M34 ... 241 A6
Harwood Gdns WA4 ... 17 A1
Harwood St SK4 ... 240 E7
Haryngton Ave WA5 ... 15 C4
Haseley Cl SK12 ... 36 C3
Haslam Rd SK3 ... 240 E2
Haslemere Ave WA15 ... 32 B3
Haslemere Dr WA5 ... 14 B2
Haslemere Way CW1 ... 190 B3
Haslin Cres CH3 ... 142 B4
Haslington Cl ST5 ... 210 B1
Haslington Gr L26 ... 21 A3
Haslington Prim Sch
CW1 ... 191 B2
Hassall Rd Alsager ST7 ... 193 A3
Haslington CW11 ... 192 A4
Sandbach CW11 ... 175 B2
Hassall St SK15 ... 242 E1
Hassall Way 7 SK9 ... 34 C3
Hastings Ave WA2 ... 8 A2
Hasty La Altrincham WA15 ... 32 C4
Wythenshawe M90 ... 33 A4
Hatch Mere* WA6 ... 100 B3
Hatchery Cl WA4 ... 27 A2
Hatchings The WA13 ... 18 C1
Hatchmere Cl
Sandbach CW11 ... 174 C4
Hatchmere Cl *continued*
Warrington WA5 ... 15 C3
Hatchmere Dr CH3 ... 142 A4
Hatchmere Rd SK8 ... 239 F4
Hatfield Ct CW4 ... 130 A2
Hatfield Gdns WA4 ... 26 C2
Hathaway Cl SK8 ... 34 A4
Hathaway Dr SK11 ... 112 B3
Hatherlow SK6 ... 241 A1
Hatherlow Hts SK6 ... 241 A1
Hatherton Cl
10 Davenham CW9 ... 103 C2
Newcastle-u-L ST5 ... 210 B1
Hatherton Gr L26 ... 21 A3
Hatherton Way CH2 ... 237 B4
Hatley La WA6 ... 73 C4
Hatter St CW12 ... 156 C2
Hatton Ave CH62 ... 43 C2
Hatton La Northwich CW8 103 B3
Stretton WA4 ... 26 A1
Hatton Rd CH1 ... 117 C3
Hatton St
Macclesfield SK11 ... 112 B4
3 Stockport SK1 ... 240 E6
Haughton Cl SK10 ... 86 C1
Haughton Hall Rd M34 ... 241 A7
Haughton St SK14 ... 241 E5
Havannah La
Congleton CW12 ... 156 C3
St Helens WA9 ... 1 A2
Havannah Prim Sch
CW12 ... 157 A3
Havannah St CW12 ... 156 C2
Haven The
Altrincham WA15 ... 238 F3
Crewe CW1 ... 190 B4
Havergal St 2 WA7 ... 22 C1
Haverhill Cl CW2 ... 207 A2
Havisham Cl WA3 ... 9 B3
Hawarde Cl WA12 ... 2 A2
Hawarden Airport CH4,
CH5 ... 139 B4
Hawarden Gdns CH65 ... 70 B1
Hawarden Ind Pk CH4 ... 139 A3
Hawarden Rd WA14 ... 238 D6
Haweswater Ave
Crewe CW1 ... 173 A1
Haydock WA11 ... 1 A3
Haweswater Cl WA7 ... 50 A3
Haweswater Dr CW7 ... 126 B1
Hawick Cl CH66 ... 69 A3
Hawk Rd SK22 ... 39 C4
Hawk St CW11 ... 175 A3
Hawke St SK15 ... 242 F1
Hawker Cl CH4 ... 139 B2
Hawkins La SK10 ... 88 B2
Hawkins Rd CH64 ... 41 C1
Hawkins St SK5 ... 240 E8
Hawkins View CH3 ... 120 C3
Hawks Ct WA7 ... 49 C3
Hawks Way CH60 ... 40 C4
Hawksey Dr CW5 ... 204 C2
Hawkshaw Cl WA3 ... 9 B2
Hawkshead Rd WA5 ... 6 C3
Hawkshead Way CW7 ... 126 B1
Hawkstone Gr WA6 ... 73 B2
Hawley Dr WA15 ... 32 A4
Hawley La WA15 ... 32 A4
Hawley's Cl WA5 ... 7 C1
Hawley's La WA2,WA5 ... 8 A1
Haworth Ave CW12 ... 157 A3
Haworth Cl SK11 ... 112 A3
Hawthorn Ave
Altrincham WA15 ... 238 F8
16 Nantwich CW5 ... 204 C3
Newton-le-W WA12 ... 2 B2
Runcorn WA7 ... 23 A1
Widnes WA8 ... 13 A1
Wilmslow SK9 ... 60 A4
Hawthorn Bank SK22 ... 39 A3
Hawthorn Bsns Pk WA5 ... 16 A4
Hawthorn Cl
Altrincham WA15 ... 238 F7
Holmes Chapel CW4 ... 130 B2
Winsford CW7 ... 126 B2
Hawthorn Cotts CH60 ... 40 C4
Hawthorn Dr M44 ... 11 B3
Hawthorn Gdns ST7 ... 210 B4
Hawthorn Gn SK9 ... 60 A4
Hawthorn Gr
Bramhall SK7 ... 35 B3
Crewe CW1 ... 190 B4
Hyde SK14 ... 241 D5
Stockport SK4 ... 240 B7
Warrington WA4 ... 16 B2
Wilmslow SK9 ... 60 A4
Hawthorn La
Bebington CH62 ... 43 B4
Wilmslow SK9 ... 60 A4
Wistaston CW2 ... 189 C1
Hawthorn Pk SK9 ... 60 A4
Hawthorn Rd
Altrincham WA15 ... 238 E3
Bollington SK10 ... 87 C4
Chester CH4 ... 140 C3
Christleton CH3 ... 142 C4
Ellesmere Port CH66 ... 69 B3
Gatley SK8 ... 239 A5
Neston CH64 ... 41 B1
Newcastle-u-L ST5 ... 210 C1
Plumley WA16 ... 80 C2
Weaverham CW8 ... 102 B4
Hawthorn Rise SK10 ... 86 C3
Hawthorn St SK9 ... 60 A3
Hawthorn Terr
Stockport SK4 ... 240 B7
Wilmslow SK9 ... 60 A3
Hawthorn View
Connah's Quay CH5 ... 116 A4
Wilmslow SK9 ... 60 A4
Hawthorn Villas CW4 ... 130 B2
Hawthorn Way SK10 ... 87 C1
Hawthorn Wlk
Higher Wincham CW9 ... 79 B2
4 Partington M31 ... 11 C2
Wilmslow SK9 ... 60 A4
Hawthorne Ave
Audley ST7 ... 209 C1
Fowley Common WA3 ... 5 B3
Warrington, Great Sankey
WA5 ... 15 A3
Warrington, Woolston WA1 ... 17 A4
Hawthorne Cl
Congleton CW12 ... 156 A2
Haydock WA11 ... 1 A3
Hawthorne Ct ST7 ... 193 C2
Hawthorne Dr
Sandbach CW11 ... 175 B3
Willaston CH64 ... 43 A1
Hawthorne Gr
Barnton CW8 ... 77 C2
High Lane SK12 ... 37 B2
Warrington WA1 ... 16 C4
Winsford CW7 ... 127 A1
Hawthorne Rd WA4 ... 26 B4
Hawthorne St WA5 ... 16 A4
Hawthorne View WA16 ... 59 A1
Hawthorns The
Bunbury CW6 ... 185 C4
Ellesmere Port CH66 ... 69 C4
Northwich CW8 ... 103 B4
Tarporley CW6 ... 146 B1
Hay Croft SK8 ... 34 C4
Haycroft Cl CH66 ... 69 B1
Haydan Mews WA6 ... 73 C3
Haydn Jones Dr CW5 ... 204 C2
Haydock Cl Chester CH1 ... 118 A1
5 Macclesfield SK10 ... 87 B2
Haydock High Sch WA11 ... 1 A3
Haydock La WA11 ... 1 B4
Haydock La Ind Est WA11 ... 1 C4
Haydock St
Newton-le-W WA12 ... 2 A2
Warrington WA2 ... 16 A3
Haye's Rd M44 ... 11 C3
Hayes Cl CW5 ... 204 C4
Hayes Cres WA6 ... 49 B1
Hayes Dr CW8 ... 78 B2
Hayes Pk CH2 ... 237 A4
Hayfield Ave SK6 ... 241 A4
Hayfield Cl SK10 ... 87 A2
Hayfield Rd Romiley SK6 ... 241 A4
Warrington WA1 ... 17 B4
Hayfield St M33 ... 242 B7
Hayfields WA16 ... 57 B2
Hayfields Gr CW3 ... 229 C2
Hayhead Cl ST7 ... 195 A1
Hayhurst Ave CW10 ... 151 B4
Hayhurst Cl CW9 ... 103 C4
Hayle Cl SK10 ... 86 B1
Hayling Cl CW1 ... 190 A4
Haymakers Cl CH4 ... 140 C2
Haymakers Way CH1 ... 117 A4
Haymoor Green Rd
CW5 ... 205 C2
Hayscastle Cl WA5 ... 7 C1
Hayside Wlk SY14 ... 213 A2
Hayton St WA16 ... 56 C1
Haywood Cres WA7 ... 24 B1
Hazel Ave Cheadle SK8 ... 239 E5
Macclesfield SK11 ... 112 A3
Romiley SK6 ... 241 D2
Runcorn WA7 ... 48 C4
Sale M33 ... 242 B5
Hazel Cl
9 Ellesmere Port CH66 ... 69 C1
Kidsgrove ST7 ... 195 A2
Hazel Dr Gatley M22 ... 34 A4
Lymm WA13 ... 18 C1
Poynton SK12 ... 36 C2
Weaverham CW8 ... 102 B4
Winsford CW7 ... 149 B4
Hazel Gr Alsager ST7 ... 194 A2
Crewe CW1 ... 190 B4
Golborne WA3 ... 3 A4
Warrington WA1 ... 17 A4
Hazel Grove High Sch
SK7 ... 36 B4
Hazel Rd
Altrincham WA14 ... 238 D6
Chester CH4 ... 140 C3
Stalybridge SK15 ... 242 F3
Hazel St WA1 ... 16 B4
Hazel Wlk M31 ... 11 C2
Hazelbadge Cl SK12 ... 36 B2
Hazelbadge Rd SK12 ... 36 B2
Hazelbank CH65 ... 69 C2
Hazelborough Cl WA3 ... 10 A3
Hazelcroft SK9 ... 85 A4
Hazelcroft Gdns SK9 ... 85 A4
Hazeldean Ct 17 SK9 ... 34 C1
Hazelehurst Rd WA6 ... 74 B3
Hazelhurst Dr SK10 ... 88 A4
Hazelhurst Rd SK15 ... 242 D4
Hazelmere Cl CW8 ... 103 B3
Hazelwood Mews WA4 ... 17 B1
Hazelwood Rd
Altrincham WA15 ... 238 E2
Barnton CW8 ... 78 A2
Wilmslow SK9 ... 60 B4
Hazlemere Ave SK11 ... 112 A3
Headland Cl WA3 ... 3 C3
Headlands The CH2 ... 237 C2
Headworth Cl CW9 ... 103 C2
Heald Cl WA14 ... 238 C2
Heald Dr WA14 ... 238 C2
Heald Gr SK8 ... 239 A1
Heald Green Sta M22 ... 34 A4
Heald Rd WA14 ... 238 C2
Heald St WA12 ... 1 C2
Healdwood Rd SK6 ... 241 C4
Healey Cl CW1 ... 190 A4
Hearn's La CW5 ... 202 C3
Heary St SK11 ... 112 C3
Heath Ave
Ellesmere Port CH65 ... 70 A1
Rode Heath ST7 ... 193 C4
Sandbach CW11 ... 175 C3
Heath Bank CH3 ... 119 B3
Heath Cl Chester CH3 ... 142 A4
Sandbach CW11 ... 175 B3
Tarvin CH3 ... 121 A1
Heath Cres SK2 ... 240 F1
Heath Ct Alsager ST7 ... 193 C3
Ellesmere Port CH66 ... 69 A3
Heath Dr Runcorn WA7 ... 49 A4
Tarvin CH3 ... 121 A1
Heath End Rd ST7 ... 193 A3
Heath Gn CW6 ... 146 B2
Heath Gr CH66 ... 69 A4
Heath La Chester CH3 ... 142 A4
Culcheth WA3 ... 4 A1
Golborne WA3 ... 3 B3
Great Barrow CH3 ... 120 C3
Great Budworth CW9 ... 54 A1
High Legh WA16 ... 28 B3
Little Leigh WA4,CW8 ... 77 A4
Lower Peover WA16 ... 106 C3
Marbury SY13 ... 226 C3
Stoak CH2 ... 95 C4
Willaston CH66 ... 68 B4
Heath Park Gr WA7 ... 48 C4
Heath Rd
Altrincham WA14 ... 238 D2
Bollington SK10 ... 87 C3
Chester CH2 ... 118 C4
Congleton CW12 ... 156 A1
Runcorn WA7 ... 23 A1
Sale WA15 ... 238 F8
Sandbach CW11 ... 175 B3
Stockport SK2 ... 240 F2
Warrington WA5 ... 14 C3
Weaverham CW8 ... 77 C1
Widnes WA8 ... 12 B1
Heath Rd S WA7 ... 48 C3
Heath Sch The WA7 ... 49 A4
Heath St Crewe CW1 ... 190 B2
Golborne WA3 ... 3 A4
Warrington WA4 ... 26 B4
Heath Terr Chester CH2 ... 118 C4
Smallwood CW11 ... 154 A1
Heath View Alsager ST7 ... 193 C3
Weston CW2 ... 207 A3
Heath Way CW6 ... 168 B4
Heathbank Rd
Cheadle SK8 ... 34 C4
Stockport SK3 ... 240 B3
Heathbrook CW9 ... 104 C4
Heathcote Ave SK4 ... 240 C7
Heathcote Cl CH2 ... 118 B2
Heathcote Gdns
Northwich CW9 ... 104 B4
Romiley SK6 ... 241 E1
Heathcote St ST7 ... 195 A1
Heather Ave M44 ... 11 B3
Heather Brae WA12 ... 2 A2
Heather Cl
Ellesmere Port CH66 ... 69 C2
Macclesfield SK11 ... 112 B2
Runcorn WA7 ... 49 C2
Warrington WA3 ... 9 B3
Heather Ct CH3 ... 142 A4
Heather Lea M34 ... 241 A6
Heather Rd WA14,WA15 ... 238 E1
Heather Wlk M31 ... 11 C2
Heatherfield Ct SK9 ... 60 C4
Heathergate Pl CW2 ... 206 A4
Heatherside ST7 ... 195 B3
Heatherways CW6 ... 146 B2
Heathfield SK9 ... 60 A3
Heathfield Ave
Crewe CW1 ... 190 B2
Gatley SK8 ... 239 B5
Heathfield Cl
Congleton CW12 ... 155 C2
Nantwich CW5 ... 204 C3
Sale M33 ... 242 F6
Heathfield Ct CH65 ... 70 A3
Heathfield Dr ST5 ... 210 B1
Heathfield Pk
Warrington WA4 ... 17 A1
Widnes WA8 ... 12 B2
Heathfield Rd
Audlem CW3 ... 230 A3
Ellesmere Port CH65 ... 70 A3
Stockport SK2 ... 240 F2
Heathfield Sq WA16 ... 56 C1
Heathfields WA14 ... 238 C3
Heathfields Cl CH2 ... 237 B4
Heathgate Ave L24 ... 21 A1
Heathland Terr SK3 ... 240 E3
Heathlands Ho WA16 ... 56 C1
Heathlands Rd CH66 ... 69 A4
Heathmoor Ave WA3 ... 3 B3
Heaths La CW6 ... 123 B1
Heathside CW5 ... 204 C3
Heathside Park Rd SK3 ... 239 F7
Heathside Rd SK3 ... 240 A3
Heathview CW1 ... 191 B2
Heathview Cl WA8 ... 22 A3

Heathview Rd WA8 ......22 A3
Heathway CH60 ....41 A4
Heathwood Dr ST7 .....193 A3
Heathwood Gr WA1 ....17 A4
Heatley Cl WA13 ....19 A2
Heatley La CW5 ....217 C2
Heatley Way 5 SK9 .....34 B2
Heaton Cl
Middlewich CW10 ....151 B3
Stockport SK4 ....240 A7
Heaton Ct Stockport SK4 .240 B8
Warrington WA3 ....9 C3
Heaton La SK4 ....240 E5
Heaton Moor Rd SK4 ...240 B8
Heaton Rd SK4 ....240 C7
Heaton Sq CW7 ....149 B4
Heaward Cl CW2 ....206 A2
Hebden Ave
Fowley Common WA3 ......5 A3
Romiley SK6 ....241 A4
Hebden Green Com Specl Sch CW7 ....149 A4
Heber Wlk CW9 ....104 A4
Heber's Cl SY14 ....213 B3
Hedge Hey WA7 ....24 A1
Hedge Row SK10 ....63 C1
Hedgerow Dr CW9 ....79 B2
Hedgerows The WA11 ......1 C4
Hedingham Cl 6 SK10 .111 C4
Hefferston Grange Dr CW8 ....102 A4
Hefferston Rise CW8 ...102 A4
Heights The WA6 ....73 B2
Helena Cl WA16 ....57 B1
Helford St CW12 ....156 B2
Hellath View CW5 ....204 C1
Hellyar-Brook Rd ST7 ..193 A2
Helmsdale Cl CW1 ......190 A3
Helmsdale La WA5 ....15 B3
Helmsley Cl WA5 ....15 C4
Helsby Ave CH62 ....43 C2
Helsby High Sch WA6 ...73 B3
Helsby Rd WA6 ....73 B1
Helsby St WA1 ....16 B3
Helsby Sta WA6 ....73 A2
Helsby Way 4 SK9 ....34 B2
Helston Cl Bramhall SK7 ..35 C4
Runcorn WA7 ....50 A3
Warrington WA5 ....14 C3
Helston Gr SK8 ....34 B4
Helton Cl CW4 ....130 A2
Hemingford Cl CH66 ....69 B1
Hemlegh Vale WA6 ....73 A1
Hemming St CW8 ....78 B1
Hemmingshaw La CW11 ....176 A4
Hemswell Cl CW7 ....149 C4
Hemsworth Ave CH66 ...69 B3
Henbury Cl CW10 ....151 B4
Henbury High Sch SK10 111 C4
Henbury La SK8 ....34 C3
Henbury Pl WA7 ....49 A3
Henbury Rd SK9 ....34 B2
Henbury Rise SK11 .....111 B4
Henderson Cl WA5 ....14 B3
Henderson Rd
2 Widnes WA8 ....13 A1
Widnes, Lower House WA8 .22 C4
Henderson St SK11 ....112 B4
Hendham Dr WA14 .....238 B5
Hendon Cl CW1 ....190 C3
Hendon Dr SK3 ....240 A3
Henley Ave Cheadle SK8 .239 F2
Irlam M44 ....11 C3
Henley Cl
Macclesfield SK10 ....87 A2
Neston CH64 ....66 C3
Warrington WA4 ....26 C3
Henley Ct WA7 ....23 B1
Henley Dr
Altrincham WA15 ....238 F7
Winsford CW7 ....126 C1
Henley Rd Chester CH4 ..140 C3
Hough Common CW2 ....207 A1
Neston CH64 ....66 C3
Henrietta St CW12 .....156 B2
Henry Pl CH2 ....237 B3
Henry St Crewe CW1 ...190 B3
Haslington CW1 ....191 B2
Hyde SK14 ....241 D6
2 Lymm WA13 ....18 C2
Tarporley CW6 ....146 B1
Warrington WA1 ....16 A3
4 Widnes WA8 ....13 B1
Henry Wood Ct CH4 ....140 C3
Henshall Ave WA4 ....16 C2
Henshall Dr CW11 ......175 B4
Henshall Hall Dr CW12 .157 A1
Henshall La WA14 ....20 B3
Henshall Rd SK10 ....87 C4
Henshall St CH2 ....237 A4
Henshaw La SK11 ......110 C1
Hepherd St WA5 ....15 B2
Hepley Rd SK12 ....37 A2
Herald Dr CW1 ....190 C2
Herald Pk CW1 ....190 C2
Heralds Cl WA8 ....22 B4
Heralds Gn WA5 ....7 A1
Herbert St Burtonwood WA5 6 C3
Congleton CW12 ....156 C2
Crewe CW1 ....191 A3
Dukinfield M34 ....241 A8
Lostock Gralam CW9 .....80 A1
Stockport SK3 ....240 D3
Herdman St CW2 ....190 B1
Hereford Ave
Ellesmere Port CH66 ......94 C4
1 Golborne WA3 ....3 A4
Hereford Cl
Macclesfield SK10 ....86 C1
Warrington WA1 ....17 B4
Hereford Dr SK9 ....34 C2
Hereford Pl CH1 ....118 A3
Hereford St M33 ....242 B6
Hereford Way CW10 ....128 B1
Hereford Wlk SK6 ......241 A1
Hereward Rd CH3 ......119 A1
Hermitage Ave SK6 ....241 F2
Hermitage Ct
Holmes Chapel CW4 .....130 B2
Saughall CH1 ....117 A4
Hermitage Dr CW4 .....130 B2
Hermitage Gdns SK6 ...241 F2
Hermitage Green La WA2, WA12 ....8 A4
Hermitage La CW4 .....130 B4
Hermitage Prim Sch CW4 ....130 B2
Hermitage Rd CH1 .....117 A4
Heron Cl Broughton CH4 .139 A2
Farndon CH3 ....180 C1
Knutsford WA16 ....57 A2
Runcorn WA7 ....50 B4
Winsford CW7 ....149 B3
Heron Cres CW1 ....190 C3
Heron Ct Neston CH64 ....66 B4
Northwich CW9 ....79 B1
Stockport SK3 ....240 E3
Heron Dr SK12 ....36 A2
Heron Pl CH2 ....237 B4
Heron St SK3 ....240 D3
Herons Way Chester CH4 141 A2
Runcorn WA7 ....24 C2
Herrick Cl CW2 ....206 A4
Herries St OL6 ....242 A4
Hertford Cl
Congleton CW12 ....156 C2
Warrington WA1 ....17 C4
Hertford Gr M44 ....11 B3
Hesketh Cl WA5 ....14 C2
Hesketh Croft CW1 ....190 A4
Hesketh Dr CW9 ....80 A2
Hesketh Grange Cotts CH63 ....42 A4
Hesketh Meadow La WA3 .4 A4
Hesketh Rd L24 ....21 C1
Hesketh St Stockport SK4 240 E7
Warrington WA5 ....15 B2
Hesketh St N WA5 ....15 B2
Hesnall Cl WA3 ....5 B4
Hessle Dr CH60 ....40 C4
Heswall Ave WA3 ....4 C2
Heswall Rd CH66 ....69 B2
Heswall Sta CH60 ....41 B4
Hewitt Dr CW7 ....150 B4
Hewitt Gr CW9 ....79 C3
Hewitt St Chester CH2 ..118 C2
Crewe CW2 ....190 B1
Northwich CW9 ....79 B1
Warrington WA4 ....16 B2
Hexham Way 4 SK10 ....87 B2
Hey Lock Cl WA12 ....7 B4
Hey Shoot La WA3 ....5 B3
Hey Wood Cl WA12 ....7 B4
Heybridge La SK10 ......87 A3
Heyes Ave WA11 ....1 B3
Heyes Dr WA13 ....18 B1
Heyes Farm Rd SK11 ...111 C4
Heyes La
Alderley Edge SK9 ....60 A2
Warrington WA4 ....26 C4
Heyes Pk CW8 ....102 C2
Heyes Rd WA8 ....22 B4
Heyeswood La CW8 ....103 A2
Heyfield Park Rd CH66 ..69 A4
Heygarth Prim Sch CH62 43 C3
Heygarth Rd CH62 ....43 C3
Heys Ave Bebington CH62 .43 B4
Romiley SK6 ....241 E3
Heys Farm Cotts SK6 ..241 E3
Heys La SK6 ....241 E3
Heys Prim Sch The OL6 242 A3
Heys Rd OL6 ....242 A3
Heys The Bebington CH62 .43 C3
Runcorn WA7 ....23 C1
Heysbank Rd SK12 ....38 B3
Heyscroft Rd SK4 .....240 A6
Heysham Cl WA7 ....50 B3
Heysoms Ave CW8 ......103 B4
Heysoms Cl CW8 ....103 B4
Heythrop Dr CH60 ....41 B4
Heywood Cl SK9 ....60 A1
Heywood Gn CW2 ....206 B4
Heywood Gr M33 ....242 B8
Heywood La CW3,SY13 ..234 B4
Heywood Rd
Alderley Edge SK9 ....60 A1
Ellesmere Port CH66 .....69 B3
Sale M33 ....242 B5
Heywood St CW12 ......156 B1
Heywoods Ridge CW3 ..229 C2
Heywoods The CH2 .....118 B2
Heyworth Ave SK6 .....241 D3
Hibbert Ave 5 SK14 ...241 E5
Hibbert St New Mills SK22 39 A3
6 Widnes WA8 ....23 A4
Hibel Rd SK10 ....87 B1
Hickhurst La CW6 ......147 B2
Hickmore Heys CH3 ....119 C3
Hickory Cl WA1 ....17 C4
Hickson St CW8 ....78 A2
Hickton Dr WA14 ....238 B6
Hidcote Cl CW2 ....206 A4
Hield Gr CW9 ....79 B4
Hield La CW9 ....79 B4
Higginbotham Gn SK11 .112 C3
Higginson Cl CW12 ....179 B4
High Bank WA14 ....238 D5
High Bank Cl M44 ....11 B3
High Bank Rd SK14 ....241 F7
High Bank Side SK1 ...240 F5
High Bent Ave SK8 ......35 A3
High Carr Bsns Pk ST5 .210 C1
High Cross La CH3 .....182 B1
High Ct SK10 ....88 A4
High Elm Dr WA15 ....32 B4
High Elm Rd WA15 ....32 B4
High Elms SK8 ....35 A3
High Field WA14 ....20 A1
High Gates M33 ....242 E7
High Gates Cl WA5 ......15 C4
High Gates Lodge WA5 ..15 C4
High Grove Rd SK8 ....239 C5
High La SK6 ....241 B4
High Lane Prim Sch SK6 37 C4
High Lea SK8 ....239 C5
High Lea Rd SK22 ....39 A4
High Lee Ho M33 ......242 D6
High Legh Prim Sch WA16 ....29 B3
High Legh Rd WA13 ......29 B4
High Lowe Ave CW12 ..157 A2
High Mdw 2 SK8 ....34 C4
High Mdws SK6 ....241 C3
High Mount CH60 ....40 C4
High St Altrincham WA14 .238 D4
Audley ST7 ....210 A1
Bollington SK10 ....88 A4
Broughton CH4 ....140 C4
Cheadle SK8 ....239 D6
Congleton CW12 ....156 B1
Crewe CW2 ....190 B2
Duddon CW6 ....145 B2
Farndon CH3 ....180 C1
Frodsham WA6 ....49 A1
Golborne WA3 ....3 A4
Great Budworth CW9 .....79 A4
Hale L24 ....21 B1
Hyde SK14 ....241 F7
Kidsgrove, Harriseahead ST7 ....195 C3
Kidsgrove, Newchapel ST7 195 C1
Kidsgrove, The Rookery ST7 ....195 B2
Macclesfield SK11 ......112 B3
Malpas SY14 ....213 A2
Mow Cop ST7 ....195 B4
Nantwich CW5 ....204 C3
Neston CH64 ....66 C4
New Mills SK22 ....39 B4
Newton-le-W WA12 ....2 B2
Norley WA6 ....100 C3
Northwich CW9 ....103 C4
Runcorn WA7 ....23 A1
Sandbach CW11 ....175 A3
Stalybridge SK15 ....242 D1
Stockport SK1 ....240 F5
Talke ST7 ....210 B3
Tarporley CW6 ....146 B1
Tarvin CH3 ....121 A1
Tattenhall CH3 ....166 A1
Warrington WA1 ....16 B3
Weaverham CW8 ....77 B1
Winsford CW7 ....126 B1
High View Helsby WA6 ...73 B2
Mount Pleasant ST7 ....195 A3
High Warren Cl WA4 .....26 B3
Higham Ave WA5 ....7 C1
Highbank Cl CW8 ....78 A2
Highbank Dr M20 ......239 B8
Highbank Rd
Kingsley WA6 ....75 B1
Northwich CW8 ....103 B4
Highcliffe Ave CH1 ....118 A2
Highcroft Ave CW12 ...156 C1
Highcroft Rd SK6 ......241 C3
Higher Ash Rd ST7 ....210 B4
Higher Ashton WA8 ......12 C2
Higher Barlow Row SK1 240 F4
Higher Bents La SK6 ..241 A3
Higher Bury St SK4 ...240 D6
Higher Carden La SY14 .198 B3
Higher Downs
Altrincham WA14 ....238 C3
Knutsford WA16 ....57 B1
Higher Fence Rd SK10 ...87 C1
Higher Ferry CH1 ......140 A4
Higher Gn OL6 ....242 A4
Higher Henry St SK14 ..241 E5
Higher Heyes Dr WA6 ...75 B1
Higher Hillgate SK1 ...240 F4
Higher Knutsford Rd WA4 ....16 C1
Higher La Bollington SK10 .88 A3
Dutton WA4 ....51 B2
Kettleshulme SK23 ....64 C3
Lymm WA13 ....19 A1
Higher Rd Hale L26,WA8 ..21 B3
Halewood L26 ....21 A3
Higher Tame St SK15 ..242 E2
Higherland Ct 6 ST7 ..195 A1
Highfield Elton CH2 .....72 A2
Prestbury SK10 ....87 A3
Sale M33 ....242 C5
Highfield Ave
Audlem CW3 ....230 A2
Golborne WA3 ....2 C4
Kidsgrove ST7 ....195 A1
Lostock Gralam CW9 .....80 A2
Warrington, Appleton WA4 .26 B2
Highfield Ave continued
Warrington, Great Sankey WA5 ....15 A3
Highfield Cl CH64 ....66 C4
Highfield Com Prim Sch CH1 ....117 C2
Highfield Cres
Widnes WA8 ....13 A1
Wilmslow SK9 ....34 B1
Highfield Dr Lymm WA13 .18 B1
Macclesfield SK10 ....87 A1
Nantwich CW5 ....205 A3
Highfield Est SK9 ....34 B1
Highfield Gdns SK14 ..241 F7
Highfield La
Coddington CH3 ....181 C2
Golborne WA3 ....3 B3
Winwick WA2 ....8 B4
Highfield Parkway SK7 ..35 B2
Highfield Pl 14 CW8 ...103 C4
Highfield Rd Blacon CH1 117 B3
Bollington SK10 ....88 A4
Cheadle SK8 ....239 F1
Congleton CW12 ....156 C1
Ellesmere Port CH65 .....70 B3
Ellesmere Port, Little Sutton CH66 ....69 A3
Lymm WA13 ....18 B1
Macclesfield SK11 ......112 B4
Neston CH64 ....66 C4
Northwich CW8 ....103 C4
Poynton SK12 ....36 A2
Widnes WA8 ....13 A1
Highfield Rd N 7 CH65 ..70 B3
Highfield Sch L26 ....21 A4
Highfield St 2 SK3 ....240 C4
Highfield Terr SK22 .....39 B4
Highfields SY13 ....224 A1
Highfields Com Prim Sch CW5 ....204 C3
Highgate Cl Crewe CW1 .190 A4
Runcorn WA7 ....24 B1
Highgate Rd WA14 .....238 B4
Highgrove Mews 2 SK9 .60 A3
Highland Ave SK6 ......241 A2
Highland Way WA16 .....82 A4
Highlands Rd WA7 ....48 C4
Highlands The CW6 ....185 C4
Highmarsh Cres WA12 ....2 A2
Hightown Crewe CW1 ...190 B2
Middlewich CW10 ....128 B1
Sandbach CW11 ....175 A3
Hightree Dr SK11 ......111 B4
Highwood Rd WA4 ....26 B4
Higifield Ave M33 .....242 C5
Hignett Ave WA9 ....1 A1
Hilary Ave SK8 ....34 B4
Hilary Cl Chester CH3 ..119 A1
Stockport SK4 ....240 D6
Warrington WA5 ....14 B3
Widnes WA8 ....13 C2
Hilbre Ave CH60 ....40 C3
Hilbre Bank CW6 ......169 B2
Hilbre Dr CH65 ....70 B1
Hilda Ave SK8 ....239 E5
Hilda Gr SK5 ....240 F8
Hilda St 5 SK5 ....240 F8
Hilden Pl WA2 ....8 C1
Hilden Rd WA2 ....8 C1
Hill Cl CH64 ....67 A3
Hill Cliffe Rd WA4 ......26 A4
Hill Cotts CH3 ....164 A2
Hill Court Mews SK6 ..241 B2
Hill Crest Ave SK4 ....240 A6
Hill Croft CW11 ....191 C4
Hill Ct CH64 ....67 A3
Hill Dr SK9 ....34 C2
Hill Fields Cl CW12 ...156 B2
Hill La Brown Knowl CH3 .199 B4
Burwardsley CW6 ....184 C3
Hill Rd CH4 ....141 C1
Hill Rd N WA6 ....73 B2
Hill Rd S WA6 ....73 B2
Hill Rise
Altrincham WA14 ....238 A5
Romiley SK6 ....241 B2
Hill St Altrincham WA14 ..238 C8
Crewe CW1 ....190 B2
Macclesfield SK11 ......112 B3
Romiley SK6 ....241 B2
Runcorn WA7 ....23 A1
Sandbach CW11 ....174 B4
Winsford CW7 ....126 C1
Hill Terr ST7 ....209 B1
Hill The Knutsford WA16 ..82 A4
Sandbach CW11 ....175 B3
Hill Top Altrincham WA15 ..32 A4
Barnton CW8 ....78 A1
Romiley SK6 ....241 B3
Hill Top Ave Cheadle SK8 .35 A4
Wilmslow SK9 ....60 A4
Winsford CW7 ....126 B1
Hill Top La Heswall CH60 .41 A4
Neston CH64 ....67 A3
Hill Top Rd
Acton Bridge CW8 ....76 C1
Dutton WA4 ....51 B1
Warrington, Stockton Heath WA4 ....16 C1
Warrington, Woolston WA1 .17 B4
Hill Top Rise SK23 ......65 B4
Hill View Bollington SK10 .87 C4
Whaley Bridge SK23 .....65 B4
Widnes WA8 ....12 C3
Hill View Ave WA6 ....73 A1
Hill View Prim Sch WA7 .49 C2
Hillary Ave CW12 ......157 A1
Hillary Dr CW3 ....230 A2
Hillary Rd Bebington CH62 43 C3
Kidsgrove ST7 ....195 A2
Hillberry Cres WA4 ......16 A2
Hillbre Way Handforth SK9 34 C2
1 Wilmslow SK9 ....34 B2
Hillbrook Rd SK7 ....35 B3
Hillcourt Rd
High Lane SK6 ....37 C4
Romiley SK6 ....241 C4
Hillcrest Ave CW4 .....130 A2
Hillcrest Dr Denton M34 .241 B5
Ellesmere Port CH66 .....69 A3
Hillcrest Gram Sch SK3 240 F2
Hillcrest Rd
Bollington SK10 ....87 C4
Ellesmere Port CH66 .....69 A3
Kelsall CW6 ....122 C3
Warren SK11 ....112 A2
Hillcroft Rd WA14 .....238 A5
Hillesden Rise CW12 ..156 C1
Hillfield Frodsham WA6 ..74 A4
Runcorn WA7 ....50 B4
Hillfield Gdns CW5 ....204 C2
Hillfield Pl CW5 ......204 C2
Hillfield Rd CH66 ....69 B4
Hillfield View CW5 ....204 C2
Hillfields CW12 ....156 B2
Hillfoot Cres WA4 ....26 A4
Hillfoot La WA6 ....74 C2
Hillgate Bsns Ctr 10 SK1 ....240 F4
Hillington Rd SK3 .....240 C4
Hillock La WA1 ....17 B4
Hillsboro Ave WA6 ......74 B4
Hillsdown Way CH66 ....69 B1
Hillside Broomedge WA13 .19 C1
Northwich CW8 ....103 B4
Hillside Ave
Newton-le-W WA12 ....1 C1
Runcorn WA7 ....48 C4
Hillside Bird Oasis* WA16 ....58 A2
Hillside Cl Bramhall SK7 ..36 A4
Disley SK12 ....38 C3
Kidsgrove ST7 ....195 B4
Hillside Ct SK10 ....88 A1
Hillside Dr Crewe CW1 ..190 C3
Ellesmere Port CH66 .....69 C4
Macclesfield SK10 ....88 A1
Hillside Gr WA5 ....14 C2
Hillside La CW9 ....126 C4
Hillside Prim Sch WA6 ..73 B2
Hillside Rd Blacon CH1 ..117 C2
Frodsham WA6 ....74 B4
Heswall CH60 ....41 A4
Kelsall CW6 ....122 B2
Knutsford WA16 ....57 A1
Warrington WA4 ....26 B2
Hillside View SK22 ......39 A4
Hilltop WA7 ....50 B4
Hilltop Pk WA16 ....79 C4
Hilltop Prim Sch ST7 ..210 B4
Hilltop Rd
Guilden Sutton CH3 ....119 C3
Lymm WA13 ....18 B1
Hillview Cl WA6 ....74 B4
Hillview Rise CW8 ......78 C1
Hilton Ave WA5 ....15 A3
Hilton Cl
Macclesfield SK11 ......111 C4
Middlewich CW10 ....151 A4
Hilton Dr M44 ....11 B3
Hilton Gr SK12 ....36 B2
Hilton Rd Disley SK12 ...38 A4
High Lane SK12 ....37 B3
Hilton St SK3 ....240 D4
Hinchley Cl CW8 ....103 A2
Hinckley Ct CW12 .....156 A2
Hind Heath La CW11 ...174 C2
Hind Heath Rd CW11 ...174 C2
Hinde St CW5 ....204 B2
Hinderton Dr CH60 ......40 C3
Hinderton Gn CH64 .....66 C4
Hinderton La CH64 .....67 A4
Hinderton Rd CH64 .....66 C4
Hinderton Sch CH65 ....69 C2
Hindle Ave WA5 ....7 C1
Hindley Cres CW8 ....78 A2
Hindley St SK1 ....240 F4
Hinton Cres WA4 ....26 C4
Hinton Rd Crewe CW2 ..206 B4
Runcorn WA7 ....23 A1
Hitch Lowes SK11 ....84 A2
Hitchen's Cl WA7 ....50 B4
Hitchens La SY14 ......184 B1
Hob Hey La WA3 ....4 B2
Hob Hill SK15 ....242 C1
Hob La Churton CH3 ....180 C3
Dunham-on-t-H WA6 ......97 B3
Hobart Cl SK7 ....35 C2
Hobart Way CH1 ....117 B2
Hobb La WA4 ....25 B3
Hobbs Cl CW1 ....191 B2
Hobbs Hill La WA16 .....28 C1
Hobby Ct WA7 ....49 C3
Hobcroft La WA16 ....58 A4
Hobson St SK11 ....112 B3
Hockenhull Ave CH3 ...121 A1
Hockenhull Cres CH3 ..121 B1
Hockenhull La CH3 ....121 A1
Hocker La SK10 ....85 B2
Hockerley Ave SK23 ....65 B4
Hockerley Cl SK23 ......65 B4
Hockerley La SK23 ......65 B4
Hockley Cl SK12 ....37 A2
Hockley Rd SK12 ....37 A2
Hodge La Hartford CW8 .103 A3
Weaverham CW8 ....102 B3

Hodgehill La SK11 .....132 C3
Hodgkin Cl CW5 ....204 C2
Hodgkinson Ave WA5 .....7 C1
Hoghton Rd L24 ....21 C1
Hogshead La CW8 .....124 B4
Holbeck WA7 ....50 B4
Holbein Cl CH4 ....141 C3
Holborn Ct WA8 ....12 C2
Holborn St 11 SK1 .....240 F5
Holbrook Cl WA5 ....14 C3
Holbury Cl CW1 ....190 A4
Holcombe Ave WA3 ......3 B4
Holcombe Cl WA14 .....238 B6
Holcombe Dr SK10 ......87 A2
Holcroft La WA3 ....5 B1
Holden Pl WA2 ....16 B4
Hole House Fold SK6 ..241 B2
Hole House La CW8 .....77 C2
Holehouse La
Adlington SK10 ....62 B1
Langley SK11 ....113 B2
Scholar Green ST7 ......194 B4
Holes La WA1 ....17 A4
Holford Ave
Lostock Gralam CW9 ......80 A2
Warrington WA5 ....15 C4
Holford Cres WA16 ......57 A1
Holford Way WA12 ....2 C2
Holgrave Cl WA16 ....29 B2
Holker Cl SK12 ....36 C2
Holkham Cl WA8 ....12 C1
Holkham The CH3 ....119 A1
Holland Ave SK15 ......242 D2
Holland Cl CW11 ....175 B3
Holland Rd SK7 ....35 C4
Holland St Crewe CW1 ..190 A3
18 Macclesfield SK11 ....112 B4
Hollands La CW6 ......122 B3
Hollands Pl SK11 ......112 C4
Hollands Rd CW9 ......103 C4
Hollies Ct M33 ....242 B6
Hollies La SK9 ....60 C4
Hollies The Gatley SK8 ..239 B5
Moulton CW9 ....126 C4
Runcorn WA7 ....49 B4
Shavington CW2 ....206 A2
3 Stockport SK4 ....240 B7
Hollin Green La CW5 ...202 C3
Hollin La Newhall CW5 ..228 B4
Styal SK9 ....33 C3
Sutton Lane Ends SK11 ...136 B3
Hollin Rd SK10 ....88 A4
Hollingford Pl WA16 ....82 A4
Hollingreen La CW5 ...229 A4
Hollinhey Prim Sch
SK11 ....112 C2
Hollins Cres ST7 ....194 C1
Hollins Dr WA2 ....8 A3
Hollins Gr M33 ....242 A6
Hollins Grange ST7 ....210 B4
Hollins Hill CW6 ....146 C4
Hollins La Antrobus CW9 ..53 C2
Winwick WA2 ....7 C3
Hollins Park Hospl WA2 ..7 C3
Hollins Rd SK11 ....112 C3
Hollins Terr SK11 ......112 C3
Hollins Way WA8 ....22 A3
Hollinshead Cl ST7 ....194 C4
Hollinwood Cl ST7 .....210 C4
Hollinwood Rd
Disley SK12 ....38 B3
Talke ST7 ....210 C4
Hollow Dr WA4 ....16 C1
Hollow La Kingsley WA6 ..75 A2
Knutsford WA16 ....57 A1
Hollow Oak La CW8 ....101 B2
Hollow The Cheadle SK8 .239 C1
Mount Pleasant ST7 .....195 A3
Holloway WA7 ....22 C1
Hollowood Rd SY14 ....213 A3
Hollows The SK8 ......239 C1
Holly Ave Cheadle SK8 ..239 D5
Newton-le-W WA12 ....2 B2
Holly Bank Frodsham WA6 74 B4
Helsby WA6 ....73 B1
Lymm WA13 ....18 B1
Sale M33 ....242 C5
Stalybridge OL6 ....242 A2
Holly Bank Rd SK9 .....34 A1
Holly Bank Sch CH2 ...237 A4
Holly Bush La WA3 ......10 B1
Holly Cl Connah's Quay CH5 91 B1
Hale L24 ....21 B1
Mickle Trafford CH2 .....119 C4
Holly Ct Helsby WA6 .....73 B3
Middlewich CW10 ....128 A1
Stockport SK3 ....240 E1
Holly Dr Sale M33 .....242 A6
Winsford CW7 ....149 B4
Holly Gr Denton M34 ...241 A7
Sale M33 ....242 D6
Tabley WA16 ....56 A2
Warrington WA1 ....17 A4
Holly Grange WA14 ....238 D2
Holly Hedge La WA4 ....25 B3
Holly Heys 5 M33 .....242 D6
Holly House Est CW10 ..129 B3
Holly La Alsager ST7 ...193 C2
Kidsgrove ST7 ....195 C3
Styal SK9 ....33 C3
Holly Mount CW2 ......206 C3
Holly Rd Bramhall SK7 ...35 C3
Chester CH4 ....140 C3
Ellesmere Port CH65 ......70 B3
Golborne WA3 ....3 B4
Haydock WA11 ....1 A3
High Lane SK6 ....37 C4
Lymm WA13 ....19 A3
Holly Rd *continued*
Macclesfield SK11 ......112 A4
Newcastle-u-L ST5 ......210 C1
Poynton SK12 ....36 C2
Warrington WA5 ....14 C3
Weaverham CW8 ....102 B4
Holly Rd N SK9 ....60 A3
Holly Rd S SK9 ....60 A3
Holly Terr Tilston SY14 ..198 B2
Warrington WA5 ....14 C3
Holly Tree Dr
Biddulph ST8 ....179 B1
Lower Peover WA16 .....106 B4
Holly Wlk Northwich CW8 103 B4
Partington M31 ....11 B2
Hollybank Audlem CW3 ..229 C2
Moore WA4 ....25 A3
Hollybank Rd WA7 ......49 C4
Hollybush Cres CW5 ...205 B3
Hollyfield Rd CH65 ......70 A3
Hollyfields CW11 ......191 C4
Hollyheath Cl CW11 ....175 B3
Hollythorn Ave SK8 .....35 B4
Hollythorn Mews SK8 ...35 B4
Hollytree Rd WA16 ......80 C2
Hollywood WA14 ....238 D2
Hollywood Twrs SK3 ...240 D4
Hollywood Way SK3 ...240 D5
Holm Cl CH3 ....142 C4
Holm Dr CH2 ....72 B2
Holm Oak Way CH66 ....94 C4
Holme St Hyde SK14 ....241 D6
Tarvin CH3 ....120 C1
Holmedale Ct M33 .....242 C6
Holmefield M33 ....242 B6
Holmes Chapel Comp Sch
CW4 ....130 A1
Holmes Chapel Prim Sch
CW4 ....130 A2
Holmes Chapel Rd
Allostock WA16 ....106 A2
Brereton Green CW4,
CW12 ....154 B4
Congleton CW12 ....155 B2
Knutsford WA16 ....82 B2
Lach Dennis CW9 ....105 C2
Middlewich CW10 ....128 C1
Ollerton WA16 ....82 B2
Sandbach CW11 ....153 C1
Sproston Green CW4 ....129 B1
Withington Green SK11 ..109 A4
Holmes Chapel Sta
CW4 ....130 B2
Holmes Ct WA3 ....9 B2
Holmes St Cheadle SK8 ..239 E6
Stockport SK2 ....240 E3
Holmesville Ave CW12 .156 A2
Holmeswood Cl SK9 .....60 B4
Holmfield Ave WA7 .....23 B1
Holmfield Cl SK4 ......240 D7
Holmfield Dr Cheadle SK8 35 A4
Ellesmere Port CH66 ......69 B2
Holmlea Dr CW1 ....190 C2
Holmlee Way SK10 ......86 B3
Holmrook WA14 ....238 B5
Holmsfield Rd WA1 .....16 B3
Holmshaw La CW1 .....192 A2
Holmwood WA14 ....238 A3
Holmwood Dr CH65 .....70 A1
Holset Dr WA14 ....238 B5
Holt Hey CH64 ....67 A3
Holt La WA7 ....49 C4
Holt St Altrincham WA14 .238 C8
Crewe CW1 ....190 A2
Stockport SK1 ....240 F4
Holt's La SK9 ....33 C2
Holy Family RC Prim Sch
Cronton WA8 ....12 B3
Sale M33 ....242 E6
Holy Spirit RC Prim Sch The
WA7 ....49 B4
Holyhead Cl WA5 ....7 B2
Holyrood Ave WA8 ......13 A2
Holyrood Dr CW2 ......205 C4
Holyrood Way CH3 .....119 A1
Holywell Cl CH64 ....41 A1
Holywell La CH3 ......182 B1
Home Farm Ave SK10 ...86 C1
Home Pk CH1 ....94 C1
Homebeck Ho SK8 .....239 A5
Homecrofts CH64 ....66 C3
Homedee Ho CH1 ......237 A3
Homeshire Ho ST7 .....193 B2
Homestead Ave WA11 ....1 C3
Homestead Ct CW9 ....104 B4
Homestead Rd SK12 ....38 B3
Homesteads The CW5 ..172 A3
Homeway WA6 ....73 A1
Homewood Cres CW8 ..103 A3
Honey Fields CW6 .....146 B1
Honey Suckle Cl CH66 ...94 C4
Honeysuckle Cl
Broughton CH4 ....139 B2
Widnes WA8 ....13 A2
Honeysuckle Dr SK15 ..242 F2
Hong Kong Ave M90 ....33 A4
Honister Ave WA2 ....8 B1
Honiton Way
Altrincham WA14 ....238 B6
Warrington WA5 ....14 C2
Hood La WA5 ....15 B2
Hood La N WA5 ....15 B3
Hood Manor Prim Sch
WA5 ....15 B3
Hood Rd WA8 ....12 C1
Hoofield La Duddon CH3 .145 A1
Huxley CH3 ....167 A4
Hoogreen La WA16 ......29 C1
Hooker St CW8 ....103 C4
Hookstone Dr CH66 .....69 B3
Hoole Cl SK8 ....240 A1
Hoole Gdns CH2 ....119 A2
Hoole Ho CH2 ....119 A2
Hoole La CH2 ....119 A2
Hoole Rd CH2 ....119 A2
Hoole Way CH2 ....237 B3
Hooley Range SK4 .....240 B7
Hooleyhey La SK10,SK11 .89 B2
Hoolpool La WA6 ....72 C3
Hooper St SK1 ....240 E5
Hooton Gn CH66 ....44 A1
Hooton La CH66 ....44 A1
Hooton Rd CH64,CH66 ...43 B1
Hooton Sta CH66 ....43 B1
Hooton Way Hooton CH66 .44 A1
14 Warrington SK9 ....34 B3
Hope Ave SK9 ....34 B2
Hope Croft CH66 ....69 C1
Hope Farm Prec CH66 ...69 C1
Hope Farm Rd CH66 ....69 C1
Hope Green Way SK10 ...36 B1
Hope La SK10 ....36 C1
Hope Rd Broughton CH4 .139 A2
Sale M33 ....242 B6
Hope St
Ashton-u-Lyne OL6 ......242 A4
Audley ST7 ....209 C2
Chester CH4 ....140 C4
Crewe CW2 ....190 B1
Macclesfield SK11 ......112 C4
Newton-le-W WA12 ....2 A2
Northwich CW8 ....103 C4
Sandbach CW11 ....175 A3
Stockport SK4 ....240 D5
Hope St W SK11 ....112 B4
Hope Terr SK3 ....240 E4
Hopefield Rd WA13 .....19 A2
Hopes Carr SK1 ....240 F5
Hopkins Cl CW12 ......156 A2
Hopkins Field WA14 ...238 B1
Hopkins St SK14 ......241 E8
Hopley Ct CW2 ....190 A2
Hopwood Cl 16 WA3 ......3 C4
Hopwood St WA1 ....16 B3
Horace Black Gdns CH65 70 B3
Horace Gr SK4 ....240 E8
Horace Lawton Ct
CW12 ....156 B2
Horbury Gdns CH66 .....69 B3
Hornbeam Ave CH66 ....69 C1
Hornbeam Cl WA7 ....24 B1
Hornbeam Rd L26 ....21 A4
Hornby Dr
Congleton CW12 ....156 A2
Nantwich CW5 ....205 A3
Hornby La WA2 ....8 A3
Horncastle Cl 15 WA3 ....3 C4
Horns Mill Prim Sch
WA6 ....73 A1
Horridge Ave WA12 ......2 B3
Horrocks La WA1 ....16 A3
Horrocks Rd CH2 ......118 C3
Horsemarket St WA1 ....16 A3
Horseshoe Cl WA6 ......75 A1
Horseshoe Cres WA2 .....8 C2
Horseshoe Dr SK11 ....112 A4
Horseshoe La SK9 ......60 A1
Horsley La CW6 ....167 C1
Horstone Cres CH66 ....69 C1
Horstone Gdns CH66 ....70 A1
Horstone Rd CH66 ......69 C1
Hospital La CW5 ......203 C1
Hospital Of St John
Almhouses CH1 ....237 A3
Hospital St Crewe CW1 ..190 B3
Nantwich CW5 ....204 C3
Hospital Way WA7 ......49 C4
Hotel Rd M90 ....33 B4
Hotel St WA12 ....2 A2
Hothersall Cl CW1 .....173 A1
Hough Cl SK10 ....88 B3
Hough Gn Ashley WA15 ...31 C3
Chester CH4 ....141 A4
Hough Green Rd WA8 ....12 A2
Hough Green Sta WA8 ...12 A1
Hough La
Barnton CW8,CW9 ....78 A2
Norley WA6 ....100 C3
Wilmslow SK9 ....60 B2
Hough's La WA4 ....26 A3
Hougher Wall Rd ST7 ..209 B1
Houghley Cl SK10 ....87 B1
Houghton Cl
Chester CH2 ....118 C2
Newton-le-W WA12 ....2 A2
14 Northwich CW9 ....103 C2
Widnes WA8 ....13 B1
Houghton Croft WA8 ....12 B3
Houghton St
Newton-le-W WA12 ....2 A2
Warrington WA2 ....16 A3
Widnes WA8 ....13 B1
Houldsworth Ave WA14 .238 E7
Houndings La CW11 ...175 A3
Hourd Way CH66 ....94 C4
Housesteads Dr CH2 ...118 C2
Housman Cl CH1 ......118 A3
Hove Cl CW1 ....190 A4
Hove The WA7 ....50 B3
Hoverty Prec WA12 ......2 A1
Hovis Mill SK11 ....112 C4
Howard Ave
Bebington CH62 ....43 B4
Lymm WA13 ....19 A2
Howard Cl SK6 ....241 A2
Howard Ct Neston CH64 ..41 C1
Howard Ct *continued*
Runcorn WA7 ....24 B2
Howard Pl 5 SK14 .....241 D6
Howard Rd
Broughton CH4 ....140 B3
Culcheth WA3 ....5 A1
Howard St Crewe CW1 ..191 A3
Stockport SK1 ....240 F6
Howards Way CH64 .....67 A3
Howarth Ct WA7 ....23 A1
Howbeck Cres CW5 ....220 A4
Howbeck Wlk CW2 .....206 B4
Howe Rd CH4 ....141 A4
Howe St SK10 ....87 C1
Howells Ave
Ellesmere Port CH66 ......69 B2
Sale M33 ....242 B7
Howey Hill CW12 ......156 B1
Howey La
Congleton CW12 ....156 B1
Frodsham WA6 ....74 A4
Howey Rise WA6 ....74 A4
Howgill Cl CH66 ....68 C3
Howley La WA1 ....16 C3
Howley Quay Ind Est
WA1 ....16 B3
Howson Rd WA2 ....8 B2
Howty Cl SK9 ....34 B1
Hoxton Cl SK6 ....241 A4
Hoylake Cl WA7 ....50 B3
Hoylake Rd Sale M33 ...242 F5
Stockport SK3 ....240 B4
Hoyle St WA5 ....15 C4
Hubert Dr CW10 ....151 B4
Hubert Worthington Ho 8
SK9 ....60 A1
Hudson Cl WA5 ....15 B4
Hudson Gr 9 WA3 ....3 C4
Hugh St CH4 ....141 B4
Hughes Ave WA2 ....8 B1
Hughes Dr CW2 ....189 C2
Hughes Pl WA2 ....8 B1
Hughes St WA4 ....16 B2
Hulley Pl SK10 ....87 C1
Hulley Rd SK10 ....87 C1
Hullock's Pool Rd ST7 .209 C3
Hully St SK15 ....242 C2
Hulme Hall Ave SK8 ....35 A4
Hulme Hall Cres SK8 ...35 A4
Hulme Hall La WA16 ...106 A2
Hulme Hall Rd SK8 .....35 A4
Hulme Hall Schs SK8 ...35 A4
Hulme La WA16 ....106 B4
Hulme Rd M33 ....242 D5
Hulme Sq SK11 ....112 B3
Hulme St
Ashton-u-Lyne OL6 ......242 A4
Crewe CW1 ....189 C3
Hulse La CW9 ....105 B3
Hulseheath La WA16 ....30 A2
Humber Cl WA8 ....13 C2
Humber Dr ST8 ....179 C1
Humber Rd
Ellesmere Port CH66 ......69 C1
Warrington WA2 ....8 C1
Humble Bee Bank Cotts
CW5 ....187 B4
Hume St WA1 ....16 B3
Humphrey's Cl WA7 .....50 B4
Hungerford Ave CW1 ...190 C2
Hungerford Pl
Barthomley CW2 ....208 B3
Sandbach CW11 ....175 A3
Hungerford Prim Sch
CW1 ....190 C2
Hungerford Rd CW1 ...190 C2
Hungerford Terr CW1 ..190 C2
Hunsterson Rd
Bridgemere CW5 ....231 B4
Hatherton CW5 ....220 A2
Hunt Cl WA5 ....15 A4
Hunt Rd WA11 ....1 C3
Hunter Ave
Shavington CW2 ....206 B4
Warrington WA2 ....8 A2
Hunter St CH1 ....237 A3
Hunter's Cres CH3 ....121 B1
Hunter's Dr CH3 ......121 B1
Hunter's View SK9 .....34 B2
Hunters Cl SK9 ....34 C1
Hunters Ct Helsby WA6 ...73 B2
Runcorn WA7 ....49 C3
Hunters Field CW8 ....103 B4
Hunters Hill Kingsley WA6 75 B1
Weaverham CW8 ....77 B1
Hunters Lo SK9 ....34 C1
Hunters Mews Sale M33 242 A7
Wilmslow SK9 ....60 B4
Hunters Pool La SK10 ...86 B4
Hunters Rise CW7 .....126 B1
Hunters Way CH64 ......66 B4
Hunters Wlk CH1 ......237 A3
Huntersfield CW2 .....206 A2
Huntington Com Prim Sch
CH3 ....142 A3
Huntley Rd SK3 ....240 B3
Huntley St WA5 ....15 B2
Huntly Chase SK9 ......60 B4
Hunts Cl CH3 ....119 A1
Hunts Field Cl WA13 ....18 B1
Hunts La WA4 ....16 C1
Huntsbank Bsns Pk
CW2 ....205 C4
Huntsbank Dr ST5 .....210 B1
Huntsham Cl WA14 ....238 B6
Huntsman Dr M44 ....11 C4
Hurdsfield Cl CW10 ...151 B4
Hurdsfield Com Prim Sch
SK10 ....87 C1
Hurdsfield Gn SK10 .....87 C1
Hurdsfield Ho SK10 .....87 C1
Hurdsfield Ind Est SK10 .87 C2
Hurdsfield Rd SK10 .....87 C1
Hurford Ave CH65 ......69 C2
Hurlbote Cl SK9 ....34 B3
Hurlestone Cl CH2 .....96 C1
Hurley Cl WA5 ....15 B3
Hurley Dr SK8 ....239 E2
Hurn Cl CW1 ....190 A4
Hurst Ave SK8 ....35 B3
Hurst Bank Rd OL6 ....242 B4
Hurst Cl ST7 ....210 B3
Hurst Ct CW6 ....185 C4
Hurst Hill Cres OL6 ...242 A4
Hurst La Bollington SK10 ..88 A4
Glazebury WA3 ....5 B4
Hurst Lea Ct SK9 ....60 A1
Hurst Lea Rd SK22 .....39 B4
Hurst Mews WA6 ....75 B1
Hurst Mill La WA3 ....5 B4
Hurst Rd ST8 ....179 C2
Hurst St WA8 ....23 A2
Hurst The WA6 ....75 B1
Hursthead Inf Sch SK8 ..35 B3
Hursthead Jun Sch SK8 ..35 B4
Hursthead Rd SK8 ......35 A4
Hurstvale Ave SK8 ....239 B1
Hurstwood CH3 ....143 A2
Huskisson Way WA12 .....2 A2
Hutchins' Cl CW10 ....151 C3
Hutchinson St WA8 .....22 C3
Huttfield Rd L24 ....21 A2
Hutton Ave OL6 ....242 B3
Hutton Cl
Congleton CW12 ....157 A1
Culcheth WA3 ....4 C3
Hutton Dr CW12 ......157 A1
Huxley CE Prim Sch
CH3 ....167 A4
Huxley Cl Bramhall SK7 ..35 C4
Macclesfield SK10 ....87 A1
Huxley Ct CH66 ....69 C4
Huxley Dr SK7 ....35 C4
Huxley La CH3,CW6 ....167 B3
Huxley St
Altrincham WA14 ....238 D7
Northwich CW8 ....103 C4
Huxley Terr WA14 .....238 C1
Hyacinth Cl Haydock WA11 .1 C3
Stockport SK3 ....240 D1
Hyde Bank Ct SK22 .....39 B4
Hyde Bank Rd SK22 .....39 B4
Hyde Central Sta SK14 .241 C6
Hyde Cl
Ellesmere Port CH65 ......69 C2
Runcorn WA7 ....49 B3
Hyde Gr M33 ....242 B6
Hyde Hospl SK14 .....241 F5
Hyde Rd M34,SK14 ....241 A7
Hyde Sixth Form Coll
SK14 ....241 E8
Hyde Tech Sch SK14 ...241 D8
Hydes Terr SK15 ......242 E2
Hyldavale Ave SK8 ....239 B6
Hylton Ct CH65 ....70 C1
Hylton Dr SK8 ....35 B4
Hythe Ave CW1 ....190 A4
Hythe Rd SK3 ....240 B4

I

Ian Rd ST7 ....195 B1
Ibis Ct WA1 ....16 A2
Ikey La CW5 ....202 C3
Ikins Dr ST7 ....209 C1
Ilex Ave WA2 ....8 A4
Ilford Gdns WA4 ....26 B2
Illingworth Ave SK15 ...242 F2
Imperial Ave CH1 .....117 B2
Imperial Mews
Crewe CW2 ....190 B2
Ellesmere Port CH65 ......70 A3
Imperial Terr M33 .....242 A6
Ince & Elton Sta CH2 ....72 A2
Ince Ave CH62 ....43 C2
Ince Cl SK4 ....240 E7
Ince Dr CH3 ....180 C1
Ince La Elton CH2 ....72 A2
Wimbolds Trafford CH2 ....96 C3
Ince Orch CH2 ....72 A2
Ince St SK4 ....240 E7
Indigo Rd CH65 ....70 C3
Ingersley Rd SK10 ......88 B4
Ingham Ave WA12 ....2 B1
Ingham Cl CH3 ....119 A1
Ingham Rd WA8 ....12 C2
Ingle Rd SK8 ....240 A2
Inglegreen CH60 ....41 A4
Inglehead Cl M34 .....241 A6
Inglenook Rd WA5 ......14 C2
Ingleton Cl Cheadle SK8 .239 C6
Holmes Chapel CW4 .....130 A2
Newton-le-W WA12 ....2 A2
Ingleton Gr WA7 ....49 B3
Ingleton Rd SK3 ......240 C3
Inglewood WA14 ......238 B3
Inglewood Ave CW10 ..151 B3
Inglewood Cl
Partington M31 ....11 C2
Warrington WA3 ....10 A3
Inkerman St SK14 .....241 D8

Inman Ave WA9 . . . . .1 A1
Inner Gosling Cl WA4 . . . .25 C1
Innisfree Cl 9 CH66 . . . . . .69 B3
Innovation Ho 15 CW7 . .149 A4
Insall Rd WA2 . . . . .8 C1
Inscape House Specl Sch
　SK8 . . . . .239 D3
Int Peace Ctr WA5 . . . . . .15 B3
Intack La WA16 . . . . .28 A2
Intake Cl CH64 . . . . .68 A4
International App M90 . . .33 B4
Inveresk Rd SY14 . . . . . .198 B2
Inward Way CH65 . . . . . . .70 A4
Ion Path CW7 . . . . .127 B1
Ipswich Way 1 M34 . . . .241 A5
Irby Cl CH66 . . . . .69 C2
Ireland Cl Hale L24 . . . . . .21 C1
　Haydock WA11 . . . . .1 B3
Ireland St Warrington WA2 16 A4
　Widnes WA8 . . . . .13 B1
Iris Cl WA8 . . . . .12 B1
Iris Wlk 7 M31 . . . . .11 C1
Irlam & Cadishead Com High
　Sch M44 . . . . .11 C4
Irlam Rd M33 . . . . .242 C6
Irlam Sta M44 . . . . .11 C4
Ironbridge Dr CW4 . . . . .130 B1
Irons La CH3 . . . . .120 C4
Irvin Dr M22,SK8 . . . . . . .34 A4
Irving's Cres CH4 . . . . . .140 C3
Irwell Ave WA4 . . . . .16 A1
Irwell La WA7 . . . . .23 A2
Irwell Rise SK10 . . . . .87 C4
Irwell St WA8 . . . . .23 A2
Irwin Ct SK8 . . . . .239 F3
Irwin Dr SK9 . . . . .34 B3
Irwin Rd WA14 . . . . .238 D8
Isabella Ct CH4 . . . . .140 C3
Isherwood Cl WA2 . . . . . . .8 C1
Isis Cl CW12 . . . . .156 C1
Islay Cl CH65 . . . . .70 B1
Iveagh Cl WA7 . . . . .50 A4
Iver Cl Chester CH2 . . . . .118 C4
　Cronton WA8 . . . . .12 B3
Iver Rd CW3 . . . . .118 C4
Ivy Ave WA12 . . . . .2 B1
Ivy Bank Prim Sch SK11 112 A3
Ivy Bank Trad Est WA16 . .58 A2
Ivy Ct CH4 . . . . .162 B1
Ivy Dr CW8 . . . . .102 A1
Ivy Farm Ct L24 . . . . .21 B1
Ivy Farm Dr CH64 . . . . . . .66 C3
Ivy Farm Gdns WA3 . . . . . .4 B2
Ivy Farm Rd CH3 . . . . . .183 B1
Ivy Gdns CW12 . . . . .156 B1
Ivy Ho SK11 . . . . .112 A4
Ivy House Rd ST8 . . . . . .179 B1
Ivy La Alsager ST7 . . . . .193 C1
　Macclesfield SK11 . . . . .112 A3
Ivy Meade Cl SK11 . . . . .111 C4
Ivy Meade Rd SK11 . . . . .111 C3
Ivy Mews CW2 . . . . .119 A3
Ivy Rd Golborne WA3 . . . . .3 A4
　Macclesfield SK11 . . . . .112 A4
　Poynton SK12 . . . . .36 C2
　Warrington WA1 . . . . . . .17 C4
Ivy St WA7 . . . . .23 A1
Ivy Wlk M31 . . . . .11 B2
Ivychurch Mews WA7 . . . .23 B1

J

Jack La
　Moulton CW9,CW10 . . . .127 A3
　Weston CW2 . . . . .207 B3
Jackie Stewart Bsns Ctr
　CW6 . . . . .147 B3
Jackson Ave Culcheth WA3 .4 C2
　Nantwich CW5 . . . . .204 C3
　Warrington WA1 . . . . . . .16 C3
Jackson Ct CH4 . . . . .139 A3
Jackson La SK10 . . . . .88 A4
Jackson Rd CW12 . . . . . .156 C2
Jackson St
　Burtonwood WA5 . . . . . . .6 C3
　Cheadle SK8 . . . . .239 E6
　Haydock WA11 . . . . .1 A4
　Hyde SK14 . . . . .241 D6
　Macclesfield SK11 . . . . .112 B3
　Sale M33 . . . . .242 D7
Jackson's La SK7 . . . . . . .36 B4
Jacksons Cl SK10 . . . . . . .88 A4
Jacksons Edge Rd SK12 .38 A3
Jacob Way WA16 . . . . .79 C4
Jacobsen Ave SK14 . . . . .241 F8
Jamage Rd ST7 . . . . .210 B3
James Atkinson Way
　CW1 . . . . .189 C4
James Ave CH66 . . . . .69 B2
James Cl WA8 . . . . .23 A2
James Dr SK14 . . . . .241 E6
James Hall St CW5 . . . . .204 C3
James Leech St SK1 . . . .240 E4
James Pl CH2 . . . . .118 C1
James Rd WA11 . . . . .1 C4
James St Chester CH2 . . .237 B3
　Dukinfield M34 . . . . . . .241 A8
　Macclesfield SK11 . . . . .112 A4
　Northwich CW9 . . . . . . .104 B4
　Sale M33 . . . . .242 D6
　Stockport SK3 . . . . .240 E3
　6 Warrington WA1 . . . . .16 A3
Jamieson Cl Alsager ST7 193 C2
　Chester CH3 . . . . .119 A1

Jan Palach Ave CW5 . . .204 C2
Jarman SK11 . . . . .112 C2
Jasmin Way ST7 . . . . . . .195 C1
Jasmine Gdns WA9 . . . . . .6 A4
Jasmine Gr WA8 . . . . .22 B4
Jasmine Wlk M31 . . . . . . .11 C1
Jay Cl WA3 . . . . .10 A2
Jayton Ave M20 . . . . . . .239 B8
Jedburgh Ave CH66 . . . . .69 A3
Jellicoe Ave M44 . . . . . . .11 C3
Jennet's La WA3 . . . . .5 B4
Jennings St SK3 . . . . . . .240 D3
Jenny La SK7 . . . . .35 C2
Jensen Ct WA7 . . . . .23 B2
Jersey Ave CH65 . . . . .70 B1
Jersey Cl CW12 . . . . .157 A1
Jersey Rd SK5 . . . . .240 F8
Jersey Way CW10 . . . . . .128 B1
Jervis Cl WA2 . . . . .9 A4
Jesmond Cres CW2 . . . . .190 A1
Jesmond Gr SK8 . . . . .35 A4
Jesmond Rd CH1 . . . . . . .118 A1
Jessop Way CW1 . . . . . . .191 B2
JH Godwin Prim Sch
　CH1 . . . . .117 B2
Jockey St WA2 . . . . .16 A4
Jodrell Bank Science Ctr★
　SK11 . . . . .108 B2
Jodrell Cl
　Holmes Chapel CW4 . . . .130 A2
　Macclesfield SK11 . . . . .112 C4
Jodrell Mdw SK23 . . . . . .65 C4
Jodrell Rd SK23 . . . . .65 B4
Jodrell St
　Macclesfield SK11 . . . . .112 C4
　New Mills SK22 . . . . . . .39 A4
John Ave SK8 . . . . .239 E5
John Brunner Cres
　CW8 . . . . .103 A3
John Fryer Ave CW9 . . . . .80 A3
John Gresty Dr CW5 . . . .205 B3
John Lloyd Ct M44 . . . . . .11 C4
John May Ct SK10 . . . . . .87 B1
John Middleton Cl L24 . . .21 C1
John Morris Ho 1 WA1 . .16 B2
John Nicholas Cres CH65 70 B3
John Rd WA13 . . . . .18 B2
John Shepley St SK14 . . .241 E6
John St Altrincham WA14 238 D4
　Bollington SK10 . . . . .88 A4
　Congleton CW12 . . . . . .156 B1
　Crewe CW1 . . . . .190 B2
　Ellesmere Port CH65 . . . . .70 A3
　Golborne WA3 . . . . .3 A4
　Hyde SK14 . . . . .241 D7
　Irlam M44 . . . . .11 C3
　Macclesfield SK11 . . . . .112 B3
　1 Northwich CW9 . . . . .104 A4
　Romiley SK6 . . . . .241 C2
　Sale M33 . . . . .242 B7
　Stockport SK1 . . . . .240 F5
　Utkinton CW6 . . . . .146 A4
　Warrington WA2 . . . . . . .16 A3
　Winsford CW7 . . . . .126 B1
John Street Prim Sch
　CH65 . . . . .70 A3
John's Pl SK6 . . . . .241 C2
Johns Ave Haydock WA11 . .1 C4
　Runcorn WA7 . . . . .48 C4
Johns Cl SK10 . . . . .88 B3
Johnson Ave WA12 . . . . . .2 A3
Johnson Cl CW12 . . . . . .157 A1
Johnson St SK23 . . . . . . .65 C4
Johnson's La WA8 . . . . . .23 C4
Johnsons Cl CH4 . . . . . . .141 A3
Join Rd M33 . . . . .242 D6
Jonathan's Way CH1 . . . .117 C3
Jones Sq SK1 . . . . .240 F3
Jones's La CW10 . . . . . . .152 B3
Jonson Rd CH64 . . . . .66 C4
Jordangate 36 SK11 . . . .112 B4
Joseph Cres ST7 . . . . . . .193 C1
Joseph St WA8 . . . . .13 B1
Joules Ct SK1 . . . . .240 F4
Jowett St SK5 . . . . .240 F8
Joy La WA5 . . . . .6 C2
Joyce Ave CW7 . . . . .126 B1
Joynson St M33 . . . . .242 B7
Jubilee Ave Crewe CW2 . .190 A2
　Stalybridge SK16 . . . . . .242 B1
　Warrington, Padgate WA1 . .16 C4
　Warrington, Penketh WA5 . .14 C2
Jubilee Cres 1 C4
Jubilee Ct CW4 . . . . .130 A2
Jubilee Gdns
　Nantwich CW5 . . . . .204 C2
　New Mills SK22 . . . . . . .39 B4
Jubilee Gr WA13 . . . . .18 B2
Jubilee Ho WA7 . . . . .49 B4
Jubilee Rd CW12 . . . . . . .156 C1
Jubilee St SK22 . . . . .39 B4
Jubilee Terr CW5 . . . . . . .204 C2
Jubilee Villas CW7 . . . . . .175 B1
Jubilee Way Widnes WA8 .12 C1
　Winsford CW7 . . . . .126 B1
Jubit's La WA8 . . . . .13 A4
Juddfield St WA11 . . . . . . .1 A4
Judy La SK11 . . . . .113 A2
Julian Way WA8 . . . . .12 C2
July Cotts CH4 . . . . .141 C1
Jumper La SK10 . . . . .88 C4
Junction Eight Bsns Ctr
　CH65 . . . . .70 A4
Junction La WA12 . . . . .2 A2
Junction Rd SK1,SK2 . . . .240 F3
June Ave Bebington CH62 .43 C4
　Stockport SK4 . . . . .240 B6

Juniper Cl
　Newcastle-u-L ST5 . . . . .210 C1
　Sale M33 . . . . .242 A6
Juniper Dr CH66 . . . . .69 C1
Juniper Gr CH66 . . . . .69 C1
Juniper La WA3 . . . . .18 A4
Juniper Rise SK10 . . . . . . .86 C1
Jupiter Dr CH1 . . . . .117 C1
Jurby Cl WA2 . . . . .8 C1
Justice St SK10 . . . . .87 B1

K

Karen Cl WA5 . . . . .7 A3
Karen Way CH66 . . . . .69 B2
Kay La WA13 . . . . .29 A4
Kay St SK15 . . . . .242 D1
Kaye Ave WA3 . . . . .4 C2
Keats Cl
　Ellesmere Port CH66 . . . . .94 C4
　Widnes WA8 . . . . .22 C4
Keats Dr Macclesfield SK10 86 C1
　Rode Heath ST7 . . . . . . .193 C4
　Wistaston CW2 . . . . . . .206 A4
Keats Gr WA2 . . . . .8 B1
Keats La CW9 . . . . .80 A3
Keats Terr CH1 . . . . .118 A3
Keble St WA8 . . . . .23 A4
Keckwick La
　Daresbury WA4 . . . . .25 A2
　Runcorn WA4 . . . . .24 C2
Keele Cres SK11 . . . . . . .112 A3
Keeper's La CW8 . . . . . . .102 C4
Keeper's Rd WA4 . . . . .27 A4
Keepers Cl WA16 . . . . . . .57 B2
Keepers La CW9 . . . . .53 B2
Keepers Wlk WA7 . . . . . . .23 C1
Keith Ave WA5 . . . . .14 C3
Keith Dr Bebington CH63 . .43 B3
　Stockport SK3 . . . . .240 B3
Kelburn Ct WA3 . . . . .9 C3
Kelmscott Cl CH66 . . . . . .69 B1
Kelsall Ave CH62 . . . . .43 C2
Kelsall Cl Bebington CH62 .43 C2
　Warrington WA3 . . . . .9 B2
　Widnes WA8 . . . . .12 B1
Kelsall Com Prim Sch
　CW6 . . . . .122 B2
Kelsall Cres SK3 . . . . . . .240 D2
Kelsall Rd Ashton CH3 . . .121 C4
　Stockport SK8 . . . . .240 A1
　Tarvin CH3 . . . . .121 B2
Kelsall St
　Congleton CW12 . . . . . .156 C2
　Sale M33 . . . . .242 B6
Kelsall Way Audley ST7 . .209 B1
　6 Wilmslow SK9 . . . . . .34 B3
Kelsborrow Cl CW9 . . . . .103 C2
Kelsborrow Way CW6 . . .122 B2
Kelso Way SK10 . . . . .87 B2
Kelstern Cl 7 CW9 . . . . .104 A4
Kelsterton Ct CH5 . . . . . . .91 B1
Kelsterton La CH6 . . . . . . .91 A1
Kelsterton Rd CH6,CH5 . . .91 A1
Kelvin Ave M33 . . . . .242 B6
Kelvin Cl WA3 . . . . .9 B3
Kelvin Gr CH2 . . . . .118 C2
Kelvin St WA3 . . . . .9 C3
Kemberton Dr WA8 . . . . . .13 A3
Kemble Cl CW2 . . . . .206 A4
Kemmel Ave WA4 . . . . . . .16 B2
Kemp St SK14 . . . . .241 E8
Kempsell Way L26 . . . . . . .21 A4
Kempsell Wlk L26 . . . . . . .21 A4
Kempton Ave CW1 . . . . . .190 B4
Kempton Cl Chester CH1 118 A1
　Newton-le-W WA12 . . . . . .2 B3
　Runcorn WA7 . . . . .49 B3
Kempton Way SK10 . . . . . .87 B2
Kendal Ave Denton M34 . .241 A5
　Sale M33 . . . . .242 C5
　Warrington WA2 . . . . .8 B1
Kendal Cl Chester CH2 . . .119 A3
　Ellesmere Port CH66 . . . . .69 B1
　Macclesfield SK11 . . . . .111 C3
Kendal Ct CW12 . . . . . . .156 A1
Kendal Dr Bramhall SK7 . . .35 B3
　Ellesmere Port CH66 . . . . .69 C1
　Gatley SK8 . . . . .239 C4
Kendal Gdns SK6 . . . . . .241 B4
Kendal Ho SK15 . . . . . . .242 D3
Kendal Rd
　Macclesfield SK11 . . . . .111 C3
　Widnes WA8 . . . . .12 B1
Kendal Rise WA7 . . . . .49 B3
Kendrick Cl CW8 . . . . .77 B1
Kendrick St WA1 . . . . .16 A3
Kenilworth Ave
　Handforth SK9 . . . . .34 B2
　Knutsford WA16 . . . . . . .57 B1
　Runcorn WA7 . . . . .49 A4
Kenilworth Cl
　Macclesfield SK11 . . . . .111 C3
　Wistaston CW2 . . . . . . .206 A4
Kenilworth Ct CH65 . . . . . .70 C1
Kenilworth Dr
　Hazel Grove SK7 . . . . . . .36 B4
　Warrington WA1 . . . . . . .16 C4
Kenilworth Gdns WA12 . . .2 B1
Kenilworth Gn SK3 . . . . . .240 B3
Kenilworth Ho CH2 . . . . .237 C3
Kenilworth Rd
　Cheadle SK3 . . . . .239 F7
　Golborne WA3 . . . . .3 C4
　Macclesfield SK11 . . . . .111 C3
　Neston CH64 . . . . .66 C3
Kenley Ave WA8 . . . . .12 B3

Kenmare Bank CW9 . . . .104 A3
Kenmore Cl M44 . . . . .11 B3
Kennard Pl WA14 . . . . . .238 E6
Kennedy Ave SK10 . . . . . .86 C1
Kennedy Cl CH2 . . . . . . .119 A3
Kennedy Way SK4 . . . . . .240 C6
Kennel La CW8 . . . . .102 A1
Kennelwood Rd CW9 . . . . .78 B4
Kennerley St SK9 . . . . .60 A4
Kennerley's La SK9 . . . . . .60 A4
Kennet Cl SK9 . . . . .34 B1
Kennet Dr CW12 . . . . . . .156 C1
Kennet Rd WA11 . . . . .1 B3
Kenneth Rd WA8 . . . . .22 B4
Kennington Pk WA8 . . . . .12 C2
Kenrick Cl CW3 . . . . .232 B1
Kensington Ave
　Ashton-u-Lyne OL6 . . . . .242 B4
　Warrington WA4 . . . . . . .17 B1
Kensington Cl
　Chester CH4 . . . . .141 A3
　Widnes WA8 . . . . .13 B2
Kensington Ct
　Alsager ST7 . . . . .192 C2
　Wilmslow SK9 . . . . .60 A3
　Winsford CW7 . . . . .149 B4
Kensington Dr CW5 . . . . .205 B2
Kensington Gdns
　Altrincham WA15 . . . . . .238 F1
　Hyde SK14 . . . . .241 F5
Kensington Gn CH4 . . . . .140 C3
Kensington Gr
　Sale WA14 . . . . .238 E8
　Stalybridge SK15 . . . . . .242 D1
Kensington Rd
　Chester CH4 . . . . .141 A3
　Ellesmere Port CH65 . . . . .70 A3
　Stockport SK3 . . . . .240 B3
Kensington Way CW9 . . .103 C2
Kent Ave Bollington SK10 .87 C3
　Stockport SK3 . . . . .240 C1
Kent Cl CH63 . . . . .43 A4
Kent Dr CW12 . . . . .156 B2
Kent Gdns CH2 . . . . .118 C3
Kent Gr WA7 . . . . .23 A1
Kent Ho ST7 . . . . .210 B3
Kent Rd Chester CH2 . . . .118 C3
　Irlam M44 . . . . .11 B3
　Partington M31 . . . . .11 C1
　Stockport SK3 . . . . .240 B4
　Warrington WA5 . . . . . . .15 B2
Kent St Warrington WA4 . . .16 B2
　Widnes WA8 . . . . .13 A1
Kent Way WA12 . . . . .2 B1
Kent Wlk SK10 . . . . .86 C1
Kent's Green La CW1,
　CW11 . . . . .191 C4
Kent's La CW1 . . . . .173 B1
Kentmere Ave CW7 . . . . .126 B1
Kentmere Cl SK8 . . . . . . .239 B3
Kentmere Pl WA2 . . . . .8 A2
Kenton Rd L26 . . . . .21 A4
Kentridge Dr CH66 . . . . . .69 B2
Kentwell Dr SK10 . . . . .87 B2
Kenview Cl WA8 . . . . .22 A4
Kenwick Cl CH66 . . . . .69 B2
Kenwood Ave
　Altrincham WA15 . . . . . .238 F2
　Bramhall SK7 . . . . .35 B3
　Gatley SK8 . . . . .239 A6
Kenworthy St SK15 . . . . .242 D1
Kenyon Ave WA5 . . . . . . .14 C3
Kenyon La WA3 . . . . .4 A2
Kenyon's La N WA11 . . . . .1 C4
Kenyon's La S WA11 . . . . .1 C4
Kerfoot Bsns Pk WA2 . . . .16 A4
Kerfoot St WA2 . . . . .16 A4
Keristal Ave CH3 . . . . . . .142 A4
Kerridge Cl CW10 . . . . . .151 A4
Kerridge Rd SK10 . . . . . . .88 A2
Kerry Cft CH66 . . . . .69 C1
Kershaw Gr SK11 . . . . . . .112 A4
Kershaw St WA8 . . . . .12 B1
Kershaw Way WA12 . . . . . .2 B3
Kestrel Ave WA16 . . . . . . .57 C4
Kestrel Cl
　Congleton CW12 . . . . . .156 C1
　Middlewich CW10 . . . . .151 B3
　Winsford CW7 . . . . .149 B3
Kestrel Dr CW1 . . . . .190 A4
Kestrel La WA3 . . . . .9 C2
Kestrel Rd Heswall CH60 . .41 B4
　Northwich CW8 . . . . . . .103 B4
Kestrels Way WA7 . . . . . . .49 C3
Keswick Ave
　Bebington CH63 . . . . . . .43 B2
　Dukinfield SK14 . . . . . . .241 C8
　Gatley SK8 . . . . .239 B4
　Macclesfield SK11 . . . . .111 C3
　Warrington WA2 . . . . .8 B1
Keswick Cl Chester CH2 . .119 A3
　Crewe CW2 . . . . .189 C3
　Irlam M44 . . . . .11 B2
　Macclesfield SK11 . . . . .111 C3
　Stalybridge SK15 . . . . . .242 D4
　Widnes WA8 . . . . .12 B1
　Winsford CW7 . . . . .126 B1
Keswick Cres CW2 . . . . . . .8 B1
Keswick Ct CW12 . . . . . .156 A1
Keswick Dr Bramhall SK7 . .35 B3
　Frodsham WA6 . . . . .74 B4
Keswick Gdns CH63 . . . . .43 B2
Keswick Rd SK6 . . . . .37 C4
Ketlan Ct CH4 . . . . .140 C4
Kettell Ave CW1 . . . . .190 A3
Kettle La CW3 . . . . .230 B1
Kettleshulme Way SK12 . .37 A2

Kettleshulme Wlk 4 SK9 34 C1
Kew Dr WA3 . . . . .239 E2
Keyes Cl WA3 . . . . .9 C1
Keyes Gdn WA3 . . . . .9 C2
Keysbrook CH3 . . . . .166 B1
Keysbrook Ave CH3 . . . . .166 B1
Kidderton Cl CW5 . . . . . .202 C4
Kidderton La CW5 . . . . . .202 C4
Kidsgrove Sta ST7 . . . . . .194 C1
Kilbuck La WA11 . . . . .2 A4
Kilburn Ave CH62 . . . . . . .43 C3
Kilburn Cl SK8 . . . . .34 A4
Kilburn Rd SK3 . . . . .240 C3
Kildare Cl L24 . . . . .21 B1
Kildonnan Rd WA4 . . . . . .17 A1
Kilford Cl WA5 . . . . .7 C1
Killingworth La WA3 . . . . .10 A3
Kilmorey Park Rd CH2 . . .118 C2
Kilmorey Pk CH2 . . . . . . .118 C2
Kilmorey Pk Ave CH2 . . . .237 C4
Kiln Croft La SK9 . . . . .34 C2
Kiln La CW5 . . . . .220 A4
Kilncroft WA7 . . . . .50 A3
Kilsby Dr WA8 . . . . .13 C1
Kilshaw Rd WA5 . . . . .6 C3
Kilsyth Cl WA2 . . . . .8 C2
Kimberley Ave SK6 . . . . .241 C2
Kimberley Dr WA4 . . . . . . .16 B1
Kimberley St
　Stockport SK3 . . . . .240 E3
　Warrington WA5 . . . . . . .15 C3
Kimberley Terr CH2 . . . . .118 C1
Kinder Dr CW2 . . . . .189 B2
Kinder Gr SK6 . . . . .241 E2
Kinder St
　Stalybridge SK15 . . . . . .242 D2
　Stockport SK3 . . . . .240 E3
Kinder View SK22 . . . . . . .39 B4
Kinderton Cl WA16 . . . . . .29 B2
Kinderton St CW10 . . . . .128 B1
King Arthur's Wlk WA7 . . .24 A1
King Edward Bldgs 6
　CH3 . . . . .119 A1
King Edward Cl CW9 . . . .103 C2
King Edward Rd
　Knutsford WA16 . . . . . . .57 A1
　2 Macclesfield SK11 . . .112 B4
King Edward St
　Macclesfield SK11 . . . . .112 B4
　Middlewich CW10 . . . . .128 B2
　Warrington WA1 . . . . . . .16 C4
King George Ave CW9 . . .104 A4
King George Cres WA1 . . .16 C4
King George Rd WA11 . . . .2 A4
King James Ct WA7 . . . . . .49 C3
King Pl CW5 . . . . .204 C3
King St Audley ST7 . . . . .209 B1
　Chester CH1 . . . . .237 A3
　Congleton CW12 . . . . . .156 C2
　Crewe CW1 . . . . .190 B2
　Ellesmere Port CH65 . . . . .70 B1
　Hartford CW8 . . . . .103 A3
　Hyde SK14 . . . . .241 D7
　Kidsgrove ST7 . . . . .195 A1
　Knutsford WA16 . . . . . . .57 A1
　Macclesfield SK10 . . . . .112 C4
　Middlewich CW10 . . . . .128 A3
　Newton-le-W WA12 . . . . . .2 A2
　Northwich CW9 . . . . . . .104 C3
　Runcorn WA7 . . . . .23 A2
　Sandbach CW11 . . . . . .174 C4
　Stalybridge SK15 . . . . . .242 D2
　Talke ST7 . . . . .210 B2
King St E SK1 . . . . .240 F6
King Street Trad Est
　CW10 . . . . .128 B1
King's Ave WA3 . . . . .3 C4
King's Bldgs CH1 . . . . . . .237 B3
King's Cres CW10 . . . . . .128 B1
King's Cres E CH3 . . . . . .119 A1
King's Cres W CH3 . . . . . .119 A1
King's Dr SK4 . . . . .240 C3
King's La Allostock CW10 106 B3
　Nantwich CW5 . . . . .204 B3
King's Rd Romiley SK6 . . .241 A3
　Wilmslow SK9 . . . . .59 C4
King's Sch Chester CH4 . .141 A2
　Macclesfield SK10 . . . . .112 C4
　Macclesfield SK10 . . . . . .87 C1
Kingfisher Cl
　Congleton CW12 . . . . . .156 C1
　Crewe CW1 . . . . .189 C4
　Farndon CH3 . . . . .180 C1
　Nantwich CW5 . . . . .204 C4
　Runcorn WA7 . . . . .49 C3
　Warrington WA3 . . . . .9 C2
Kingfisher Ct CW9 . . . . . . .79 B1
Kingfisher Dr 5 CW7 . . . .149 B3
Kingfisher Gr WA3 . . . . . . .79 C3
Kingham Cl WA8 . . . . .13 B1
Kinglsey Ct CW11 . . . . . .174 B4
Kings Acre WA14 . . . . . . .238 A1
Kings Ave SK8 . . . . .239 A4
Kings Cl Chester CH4 . . . .140 C3
　Wilmslow SK9 . . . . .60 A3
Kings Croft CH5 . . . . .91 B1
Kings Ct Nantwich CW5 . .204 B3
　Runcorn WA7 . . . . .24 B2
　Stockport SK5 . . . . .240 F7
Kings Dr Helsby WA6 . . . . .73 A2
　Wistaston CW2 . . . . . . .205 C4
Kings Gate CW8 . . . . .102 A1
Kings Grove Sch CW2 . . .190 A2
Kings La CW5 . . . . .147 B2
Kings Lea Ho CH3 . . . . . .142 A4
Kings Mdw Runcorn WA7 . .50 B4
　Shavington CW2 . . . . . .206 C1
Kings Mews CH66 . . . . . . .69 B4

Kings Rd
Connah's Quay CH5 .... 91 B1
Ellesmere Port CH66 ...... 69 B4
Golborne WA3 .... 3 A4
Irlam M44 .... 11 C3
Warrington WA1 .... 9 A1
Kingsbury Cl WA4 ...... 26 B2
Kingsbury Dr 18 SK9 .... 34 B1
Kingsdale Rd WA5 ...... 14 C4
Kingsfield Ct CH4 ...... 141 B2
Kingshead Cl WA7 ...... 24 A1
Kingsland Grange WA1 ... 9 B1
Kingsland Rd SK3 ...... 240 A3
Kingsley Ave
Bebington CH62 .... 43 C2
Handforth SK9 .... 34 B1
Stockport SK4 .... 240 E8
Kingsley Cl Hartford CW8 103 B3
Talke ST7 .... 210 B3
Kingsley Com Prim Sch
WA6 .... 74 C1
Kingsley Cres WA7 ...... 23 A1
Kingsley Dr
Northwich CW9 .... 104 A3
Warrington WA4 .... 26 B4
Kingsley Gdns CH3 .... 142 A4
Kingsley Gn WA6 .... 74 C3
Kingsley Rd Chester CH3 142 A4
Congleton CW12 .... 157 A2
Crowton CW8 .... 76 A1
Ellesmere Port CH65 ...... 70 B3
Frodsham WA6 .... 74 C2
Haslington CW1 .... 191 B2
Runcorn WA7 .... 23 A1
Talke ST7 .... 210 B3
Kingsley Wlk CW7 ..... 126 A1
Kingsmead Chester CH2 . 118 B4
Davenham CW9 .... 103 C2
Northwich CW9 .... 103 C3
Kingsmead Ct WA3 ...... 9 A4
Kingsmead Sq CW9 .... 103 C2
Kingston Ave
Macclesfield SK11 ...... 112 C4
Warrington WA5 .... 14 C3
Kingston Cl WA7 .... 23 C1
Kingston Ct
14 Handforth SK9 .... 34 C1
Saughall CH1 .... 94 A1
Kingston Dr M33 ...... 242 D7
Kingston Gdns SK14 ... 241 B7
Kingston Hill SK8 ...... 239 D4
Kingston Pl Biddulph ST8 179 C1
Cheadle SK8 .... 239 E2
Kingston Rd SK9 .... 34 B3
Kingston St SK3 .... 240 D5
Kingsway
Altrincham WA14 .... 238 D5
Bollington SK10 .... 87 C4
Cheadle M20,SK8 .... 239 C6
Chester CH2 .... 118 C3
Crewe CW2 .... 190 A1
Frodsham WA6 .... 74 A4
Heswall CH60 .... 41 B3
Newton-le-W WA12 .... 2 B1
Northwich CW9 .... 104 A4
Widnes WA8 .... 13 A1
Winsford CW7 .... 126 C1
Kingsway High Sch
CH2 .... 118 C3
Kingsway Ho WA4 ...... 16 C2
Kingsway N WA1 .... 16 C3
Kingsway S WA1,WA4 .... 16 C2
Kingsway Sec Sch The
SK8 .... 239 C4
Kingsway W CH2 ...... 118 C2
Kingswood ST7 .... 195 A1
Kingswood Ave
Chorlton CW2 .... 207 A2
Saughall CH1 .... 94 B1
Kingswood Cres CW10 . 151 C3
Kingswood La CH1 ...... 94 B1
Kingswood Rd WA5 ...... 7 A1
Kingswood Wlk CW6 ... 122 B3
Kinloch Cl Crewe CW1 .. 190 A3
Halewood L26 .... 21 A4
Kinnerley Rd CH65 ...... 70 A2
Kinnersley Ave ST7 .... 210 C4
Kinnersley St 1 ST7 ... 195 A1
Kinnerton Cl CH4 ...... 140 C3
Kinnerton Hts CH4 ..... 161 A4
Kinnerton La CH4 ...... 161 A4
Kinnington Way CH1 .... 94 C4
Kinnock Pk WA5 .... 6 C3
Kinross Cl WA2 .... 8 C2
Kinsale Dr WA3 .... 9 B2
Kinsey Rd CH65 .... 70 B1
Kinsey St CW12 .... 156 C1
Kinsey's La CH2 .... 71 C3
Kintore Cl Bebington CH63 43 B2
Winsford CW7 .... 127 A2
Kintore Dr WA5 .... 14 B3
Kintyre Cl CH65 .... 70 B1
Kipling Ave WA2 .... 8 B1
Kipling Cres WA8 ...... 22 C4
Kipling Rd CH1 .... 117 C3
Kipling Way CW1 ...... 190 C2
Kirby Cl CH2 .... 118 B3
Kirkacre Ave WA12 ...... 7 B4
Kirkby Rd WA3 .... 4 C2
Kirkcaldy Ave WA5 ...... 14 B3
Kirkfell Dr SK6 .... 37 C4
Kirkham Ave WA3 .... 3 C3
Kirkham Cl WA5 .... 15 A2
Kirkham Rd Gatley SK8 ... 34 B4
Widnes WA8 .... 13 B1
Kirkley St SK14 .... 241 E5
Kirkstall Cl
Macclesfield SK10 .... 87 A1
Kirkstall Cl *continued*
Poynton SK12 .... 36 B2
Kirkstead Rd SK8 ...... 35 B3
Kirkstead Way WA3 ...... 3 A4
Kirkstone Ave WA2 ...... 8 B1
Kirkstone Cres WA7 ..... 50 A2
Kirkstone Ct CW12 ..... 156 A1
Kirkwall Dr WA5 .... 15 A2
Kirkwood Cl CH3 ...... 119 A1
Kishfield La SK23 ...... 65 A3
Kitchen St CH1 .... 118 A1
Kitchener Ave M44 ...... 11 B2
Kite Gr ST7 .... 195 B2
Kitfield Ave CW10 ...... 151 B4
Kitt's Moss La SK7 ...... 35 B3
Kitty Wheeldon Gdns
M33 .... 242 A7
Knap The CH60 .... 41 A3
Knebworth Ct CW12 ... 179 A4
Knight Rd WA5 .... 6 C3
Knight St Hyde SK14 ... 241 E5
Macclesfield SK11 ...... 112 C4
Knight's Cl SK11 ...... 112 C4
Knight's Grange (Sports
Complex) CW7 ...... 126 B2
Knights La CW6 ...... 123 C1
Knights Mdw CW7 ...... 126 B2
Knights Way CW2 ...... 206 A2
Knightsbridge SK1 ..... 240 F6
Knightsbridge Ave
4 Davenham CW9 ...... 103 C2
Warrington WA4 .... 17 B1
Knightsbridge Cl
17 Handforth SK9 .... 34 B1
Widnes WA8 .... 13 B2
Knightwake Rd SK22 .... 39 A4
Knivton St SK14 ...... 241 F7
Knole Ave SK12 .... 36 C2
Knoll St SK22 .... 39 A4
Knoll The WA7 .... 49 C4
Knott Fold SK14 ...... 241 D5
Knott's Hos WN7 .... 4 A4
Knottingley Dr CH66 .... 69 B3
Knotty La CW12 ...... 179 C4
Knowe The CH64 ...... 68 A4
Knowl Hey Rd L26 ...... 21 A3
Knowl La CH3 .... 180 C3
Knowl St SK15 .... 242 E2
Knowl The CH3 .... 180 C3
Knowle Cl CH66 .... 69 C2
Knowle Gn SK9 .... 34 B2
Knowle Pk SK9 .... 34 B2
Knowles Ind Est SK23 .... 39 B2
Knowles St 6 WA8 ...... 13 B1
Knowsley Ave WA3 ...... 3 A4
Knowsley La ST7 ...... 194 C2
Knowsley Rd
Chester CH2 .... 118 C2
Hazel Grove SK7 .... 36 C4
Macclesfield SK11 ...... 112 B3
Knutsford & Dist Hospl
WA16 .... 56 C1
Knutsford Ave M33 ..... 242 E6
Knutsford High Sch (Lower
Sch) WA16 .... 56 C1
Knutsford High Sch (Upper
Sch) WA16 .... 56 C1
Knutsford Rd
Antrobus CW9 .... 53 B2
Appleton Thorn WA4 ...... 27 C4
Chelford SK11 .... 84 A1
Great Budworth CW9 ...... 54 A1
Holmes Chapel CW4 ...... 130 A3
Lawton-gate ST7 ...... 193 C3
Mobberley WA16 .... 57 C2
Warrington WA4 .... 16 B2
Wilmslow SK9,WA16 ...... 59 B2
Knutsford Road Wlk 12
SK11 .... 112 C4
Knutsford Sta WA16 ...... 57 A1
Knutsford View WA15 .... 32 B4
Knutsford Way CH1 .... 117 C1
Kohima Cres CH3 ...... 142 A3
Kronsbec Ave CH66 ...... 69 B3
KUS Ind Est CH5 ...... 139 A3
Kynaston Dr CH4 ...... 140 B4

L

Laburnam Cl
Congleton CW12 ...... 156 A2
Talke ST7 .... 210 C4
Laburnham Farm Cl
CH64 .... 67 A3
Laburnum Ave
15 Nantwich CW5 ...... 204 C3
Warrington WA1 .... 17 B4
Wistaston CW2 .... 189 C1
Laburnum Cres CW8 .... 78 A2
Laburnum Gr
Broughton CH4 .... 140 C3
Crewe CW1 .... 190 B3
Ellesmere Port CH1 ...... 95 A4
Runcorn WA7 .... 49 B4
Weaverham CW8 ...... 102 B4
Laburnum La
Altrincham WA15 .... 31 C4
Warrington WA5,WA8 ...... 14 B3
Laburnum Pl ST5 ...... 210 B1
Laburnum Rd
Davenham CW9 .... 103 C2
Golborne WA3 .... 3 C4
Irlam M44 .... 11 B3
Macclesfield SK11 ...... 112 C3
Northwich CW9 .... 104 B3
Laburnum Way
Holt LL13 .... 180 B1
Laburnum Way *continued*
Stockport SK3 .... 240 B4
Lacey Ave SK9 .... 34 A1
Lacey Ct Widnes WA8 .... 23 A4
Wilmslow SK9 .... 34 A1
Lacey Gn SK9 .... 34 A1
Lacey Gr SK9 .... 34 B1
Lacey Green Prim Sch
SK9 .... 34 A1
Lacey St WA8 .... 23 A4
Lache Hall Cres CH4 ... 140 C2
Lache La Chester CH4 ... 141 A3
Dodleston CH4 .... 140 C2
Lache Park Ave CH4 ... 141 A3
Lache Prim Sch CH4 ... 141 A3
Lacy Ct CW12 .... 156 C1
Lacy St SK1 .... 240 F4
Ladies Mile WA16 ...... 56 C1
Ladies Wlk CH64 ...... 66 C4
Lady Acre Cl WA13 ...... 18 B1
Lady Barn House Sch
SK8 .... 239 D3
Lady Helen Wlk CW5 ... 204 C3
Lady Kelvin Rd WA14 ... 238 C6
Lady La Croft WA3 .... 9 B4
Mobberley WA16 .... 58 B4
Lady Richeld Cl WA7 .... 24 B2
Ladybarn Ave WA3 .... 2 C4
Ladybarn Cres SK7 ...... 35 C3
Ladybarn Manor SK7 .... 35 C4
Ladybridge Prim Sch
SK8 .... 240 B1
Ladybrook Gr 7 SK9 .... 34 B1
Ladybrook Prim Sch SK7 35 C4
Ladycroft Cl WA1 ...... 17 C4
Ladyfield St SK9 .... 60 A4
Ladyfield Terr SK9 ...... 60 B4
Ladypit Rd SK23 .... 39 C2
Ladypool L24 .... 21 B1
Ladys Cl SK12 .... 36 C2
Ladysmith Rd SK15 .... 242 D4
Ladysmith St SK3 ...... 240 E3
Ladythorn Cres SK7 .... 35 C3
Ladythorn Gr SK7 ...... 35 C3
Ladythorn Rd SK7 ...... 35 C3
Ladywood Rd WA5 .... 7 B1
Lagos Gr CW7 .... 126 C1
Laira Ct WA2 .... 16 B4
Laira St WA2 .... 16 B4
Lake House Cl CW8 ...... 77 B1
Lake La WA4 .... 52 C3
Lake Rd SK15 .... 242 C4
Lake View Alsager ST7 ... 193 B1
Congleton CW12 .... 156 A1
Whaley Bridge SK23 ...... 39 B2
Lakelands Cl SK10 ..... 112 C4
Lakeside Bosley SK11 .... 158 B4
Chester CH4 .... 141 A1
Gatley SK8 .... 239 C3
Lakeside Cl Chester CH2 118 C4
Widnes WA8 .... 22 A4
Lakeside Ctry Pk★ CW1 174 B1
Lakeside Dr Poynton SK12 36 C3
Warrington WA1 .... 16 A2
Lakeside Rd WA13 ...... 18 B1
Lakeside View
Moulton CW7 .... 126 C4
Nantwich CW5 .... 204 C2
Lakewood CH4 .... 141 A1
Laleston Cl WA8 .... 22 C4
Lamb La WA14 .... 31 B2
Lamb St ST7 .... 195 A1
Lambert Ct WA8 .... 23 A4
Lambert Way CW8 ...... 103 A2
Lambert's La CW12 .... 156 C1
Lamborne Gr CW10 .... 128 B1
Lambourn Ave WA8 ...... 12 B3
Lambourn Cl SK12 ...... 36 B2
Lambourn Dr CW1 ...... 173 A1
Lambourne Cl
Ellesmere Port CH66 ...... 94 C4
Wythenshawe M22 .... 33 B4
Lambourne Gr WA9 ...... 1 A2
Lambs La WA1 .... 17 A4
Lambsickle Cl WA7 ...... 48 C3
Lambsickle La WA7 ...... 49 A3
Lamerton Cl WA5 ...... 14 B2
Lamerton Way SK9 ...... 34 C1
Lampeter Cl WA5 .... 7 C1
Lampits La CH3 .... 120 C3
Lamport Cl WA8 .... 13 C2
Lampton Cl WA14 ...... 238 D7
Lanark Wlk SK10 .... 86 C1
Lancashire Hill SK4,SK5 . 240 E7
Lancashire Rd M31 ...... 11 C1
Lancaster Ave
Golborne WA3 .... 3 B4
Runcorn WA7 .... 48 C4
Stalybridge SK15 .... 242 D3
Widnes WA8 .... 12 A1
Lancaster Cl
Hazel Grove SK7 .... 36 B4
Newton-le-W WA12 .... 1 C2
Romiley SK6 .... 241 A1
Warrington WA2 .... 8 C1
Winsford CW7 .... 149 B3
Lancaster Ct 3 WA4 .... 16 C1
Lancaster Dr CH3 ...... 119 A1
Lancaster Fields CW1 .. 191 A1
Lancaster Gdns CH65 .... 70 B2
Lancaster Pk CH4 ...... 139 A2
Lancaster Rd
Handforth SK9 .... 34 C1
Irlam M44 .... 11 B3
Widnes WA8 .... 13 A2
Lancaster St WA5 ...... 15 C3
Lanceley Ct SY14 ...... 213 A2
Lancelyn Dr SK9 .... 60 B4
Lancer Ct WA7 .... 23 C2
Lancers Cft CH66 ...... 69 C1
Lancing Ave WA2 .... 8 A2
Lancing Rd CH65 .... 70 B2
Land Cut La WA3 .... 9 B2
Land La SK9 .... 60 B3
Lander Cl WA5 .... 15 B4
Landor Cl WA3 .... 3 C4
Landscape Dean WA6 ... 73 B2
Landsdowne St SK10 .... 87 C1
Landseer Ave
Neston CH64 .... 66 C4
Warrington WA4 .... 16 A1
Landseer Dr SK11 ...... 111 C4
Landswood Pk CW8 .... 103 A2
Lane Ends Hale WA8 ...... 21 B3
Romiley SK6 .... 241 D3
Lane Head Ave WA3 ...... 3 C4
Lane Head Rd SK23 ...... 65 B3
Lane The SY13,SY14 .... 223 B2
Laneside Rd
Manchester M20 .... 239 C8
New Mills SK22 .... 39 C4
Langcliffe Cl WA3 .... 4 C2
Langdale Ave 10 WA13 .. 18 C2
Langdale Cl
Altrincham WA15 ...... 238 E5
Gatley SK8 .... 239 C3
High Lane SK6 .... 37 C4
Macclesfield SK11 ...... 111 C3
Warrington WA2 .... 8 C1
Widnes WA8 .... 22 B4
Winsford CW7 .... 126 B1
Langdale Ct CW12 ..... 156 A1
Langdale Rd Bramhall SK7 35 B3
Partington M31 .... 11 C2
Romiley SK6 .... 241 B4
Runcorn WA7 .... 23 A1
Wistaston CW2 .... 189 B1
Langdale Terr SK15 .... 242 D4
Langdale Way WA6 ...... 49 B1
Langden Cl WA3 .... 4 B2
Langdon Ho CH4 ...... 141 A4
Langfield WA3 .... 3 C4
Langfield Gr CH62 ...... 43 B3
Langford L24 .... 21 B1
Langford Ct CH3 ...... 121 B1
Langford Rd
Lostock Gralam CW9 ...... 80 A2
Stockport SK4 .... 240 C8
Langford St 11 SK11 .... 112 B4
Langford Way WA4 ...... 27 B2
Langham Rd
Altrincham WA14 ...... 238 C2
Stockport SK4 .... 240 B5
Langland Cl WA5 .... 7 C1
Langley Ave WA12 .... 2 B1
Langley Cl
Newcastle-u-L ST5 ...... 210 B1
Sandbach CW11 .... 175 B4
Langley Ct CH65 .... 70 C2
Langley Dr Chester CW2 . 190 A1
Handforth SK9 .... 34 C2
Langley Hall Cl SK11 ... 113 A2
Langley Rd
Northwich CW9 .... 104 A3
Sutton Lane Ends SK11 ... 113 A2
Langport Dr CH3 ...... 119 B1
Langton Cl
Newton-le-W WA12 .... 2 A2
Widnes WA8 .... 12 A2
Langton Gn WA1 .... 17 B4
Langwell Cl WA3 .... 10 A3
Lanreath Cl SK10 .... 86 B1
Lansdown Cl SK7,SK8 .... 35 B4
Lansdown Rd CH4 ...... 139 A2
Lansdowne Culcheth WA3 .. 4 C1
Frodsham WA6 .... 74 B3
Lansdowne Ave SK6 ... 241 D2
Lansdowne Gr CH4 .... 141 A4
Lansdowne Rd
Altrincham WA14 ...... 238 D6
Connah's Quay CH5 ...... 91 B1
Crewe CW1 .... 190 C3
Great Barrow CH3 ...... 120 B2
Sale M33 .... 242 A8
Lapwing Cl Golborne WA3 .. 3 B4
Newton-le-W WA12 .... 2 B2
Stalybridge SK15 .... 242 D4
Winsford CW7 .... 149 B3
Lapwing Gr WA7 .... 50 A3
Lapwing La Moore WA4 ... 25 A4
Withington Green SK11 ... 109 B2
Withington Green SK11 ... 109 B3
Lapwing Rd ST7 ...... 195 B2
Larch Ave
Macclesfield SK11 ...... 112 A3
Newton-le-W WA12 .... 2 B1
Shavington CW2 ...... 206 C3
Warrington WA5 .... 14 C3
Widnes WA8 .... 13 A1
Larch Cl Golborne WA3 .... 3 C3
Poynton SK12 .... 36 C2
Runcorn WA7 .... 49 B4
Weaverham CW8 ...... 102 B4
Larch Rd Denton M34 ... 241 A7
Haydock WA11 .... 1 C4
Partington M31 .... 11 C2
Runcorn WA7 .... 49 B4
Wistaston CW2 .... 189 C1
Larch Rise SK10 .... 86 B3
Larch Way CH4 .... 140 C3
Larchdale Cl CH66 ...... 94 C4
Larches The WA16 ...... 58 C1
Larchfields CH1 .... 117 A4
Larchtree Cl CW8 ...... 78 A2
Larchway Bramhall SK7 ... 35 B4
High Lane SK6 .... 37 C4
Larchways WA4 .... 26 B3
Larchwood SK8 .... 239 D6
Larchwood Dr SK9 ...... 60 C4
Lark Ave ST7 .... 195 B2
Lark Hall Cl SK10 ...... 113 A4
Lark Hall Cres SK10 .... 113 A4
Lark Hall Rd SK10 ...... 113 A4
Lark Hill SK15 .... 242 D4
Lark Hill Cotts SK22 .... 39 A4
Lark Hill Prim Sch SK3 . 240 C4
Lark Hill Rd SK3 ...... 240 D4
Larkfield ST7 .... 195 A1
Larkfield Ave WA1 ...... 17 A3
Larkhill Rd SK8 ...... 240 C1
Larkhill View SK8 ...... 240 C1
Larkspur Cl Chester CH4 140 C2
Nantwich CW5 .... 204 C4
Runcorn WA7 .... 49 C2
Larkstoke Cl WA4 ...... 26 C3
Larksway CH60 .... 41 A4
Larkwood Way SK10 .... 87 C3
Larne Ave SK3 .... 240 B3
Larwood Ave SK4 ...... 240 B5
Lasky La WA4 .... 17 C2
Latchford CE Prim Sch
WA4 .... 16 A2
Latchford Rd CH60 ...... 41 A3
Latchford St WA4 ...... 17 A2
Latham Ave Helsby WA6 .. 73 A1
Newton-le-W WA12 .... 2 B2
Runcorn WA7 .... 23 B1
Warrington WA2 .... 16 A4
Latham Ho WA12 .... 2 A2
Latham Rd CW11 ...... 175 A3
Latham St CW7 .... 126 B1
Lathom Gr M33 .... 242 E5
Lathom Rd M44 .... 11 C4
Lathom Way SK10 ...... 87 C1
Launceston Cl
Runcorn WA7 .... 50 B3
Winsford CW7 .... 149 A4
Launceston Dr
Bramhall SK7 .... 35 C4
Warrington WA5 .... 14 C2
Laura St CW2 .... 190 B1
Laurel Ave Cheadle SK8 . 239 D5
Newton-le-W WA12 .... 2 B2
Warrington WA1 .... 17 B4
Laurel Bank
Warrington WA4 .... 17 B1
Widnes WA8 .... 13 A2
Winsford CW7 .... 149 B4
Laurel Cl Barnton CW8 ... 78 A2
Middlewich CW10 ...... 128 A1
Sandbach CW11 .... 175 B3
Laurel Dr
Ellesmere Port CH65 ...... 70 A1
Kidsgrove ST7 .... 195 C2
Willaston CH64 .... 43 A1
Wistaston CW2 .... 189 C1
Laurel End La SK4 ..... 240 A7
Laurel Gn M34 .... 241 A6
Laurel Gr Chester CH2 .. 119 A2
Golborne WA3 .... 3 B4
Laurel Pk CW6 .... 145 A3
Laurel Rd 1 SK4 ...... 240 B8
Laurel St SK4 .... 240 E6
Laurel Way SK8 .... 35 B4
Laurel Wlk M31 .... 11 C1
Laurels Farm Ct CH2 .... 72 A2
Laurelwood Dr 6 CH66 .. 69 C1
Laureston Ave CW1 .... 190 C2
Laurieston Ct SK8 .... 239 C5
Lavender Cl WA7 ...... 23 B1
Lavender Dr CW9 ...... 104 C4
Lavender Wlk M31 ...... 11 C1
Lavenders Brow 22 SK1 . 240 F5
Lavenham Cl
Hazel Grove SK7 .... 36 C4
Macclesfield SK10 .... 87 B1
Lavington Ave SK8 ..... 240 A2
Lavister Cl 11 CW9 ..... 103 C2
Lavister Wlks LL12 .... 162 B1
Law St CH2 .... 118 C2
Lawford Cl CW1 .... 189 C4
Lawford Dr CH60 .... 41 B4
Lawn Ave WA1 .... 16 C4
Lawn Dr
Altrincham WA15 ...... 238 E6
Chester CH2 .... 118 B4
Lawnhurst Trad Est SK8 240 B1
Lawns Ave CH63 .... 43 A3
Lawns The
Altrincham WA14 ...... 238 C3
Wilmslow SK9 .... 59 C2
Lawnsdale CW8 .... 101 B3
Lawnswood Gr CH2 ..... 72 A2
Lawrence Ave CW9 .... 126 C4
Lawrence Ave E CW10 .. 128 B1
Lawrence Cl
Cranage CW4 .... 130 A3
3 Sandbach CW11 ...... 174 B3
Lawrence Pl SK12 ...... 36 B1
Lawrence Rd WA14 .... 238 C6
Lawrence St Crewe CW1 190 B2
Hawarden CH5 .... 116 A2
Stockport SK1 .... 240 E5
Laws Gdns CH3 .... 142 A4
Lawson Ave SK8 ...... 239 B5
Lawson Cl WA1 .... 17 C4
Lawson Gr M33 ...... 242 A8
Lawton Ave Bramhall SK7 . 35 C4
Lawton-gate ST7 ...... 194 B2
Lawton Cl WA3 .... 4 C2
Lawton Coppice ST7 ... 194 C2

Lawton Heath Rd ST7 . .193 C3
Lawton Rd Alsager ST7 . .193 C2
Stockport SK4 . . . . .240 C8
Lawton St
Congleton CW12 . . . . .156 C1
Crewe CW2 . . . . .190 B2
Hyde SK14 . . . . .241 E7
Kidsgrove ST7 . . . . .195 B2
Stalybridge SK15 . . . . . . .242 E1
Lawton Way CW11 . . . . .174 C4
Lawtongate Est ST7 . . . .194 A2
Laxey Ave WA1 . . . . .17 B3
Laxton Cl CH66 . . . . .94 C4
Laxton Way CW10 . . . . . .128 B1
Layland Ave WA3 . . . . .4 C2
Layton Ave SK14 . . . . . . .241 C6
Layton Cl WA3 . . . . .9 C2
Layton Dr SK6 . . . . .241 C3
Lea Ave Crewe CW1 . . . . .190 C2
Goostrey CW4 . . . . .107 B1
Lea Bank Cl SK11 . . . . . .112 A4
Lea Cl CW11 . . . . .175 B3
Lea Cross Gr WA8 . . . . . . .12 B2
Lea Ct SK4 . . . . .240 B8
Lea Dr Nantwich CW5 . . .204 B2
Wimboldsley CW10 . . . . . .151 A2
Lea Hall Pk CH1 . . . . .95 A2
Lea La CH3 . . . . .164 B2
Lea Rd Gatley SK8 . . . . . .239 B1
Stockport SK4 . . . . .240 C8
Lea St SK22 . . . . .39 A4
Lea Way ST7 . . . . .193 B2
Lea's Pas CW10 . . . . . . .128 A1
Leacroft Rd WA3 . . . . .10 A4
Leadbeaters Cl SK11 . . .112 C4
Leadbeaters Rd SK11 . . .112 C4
Leadgate La CH3 . . . . . . .144 C1
Leadsmithy St CW10 . . .128 B1
Leadworks La CH2 . . . . .237 C3
Leaf La CW7 . . . . .127 A1
Leaf Lane Inf Sch CW7 .127 A1
Leafield Dr SK8 . . . . .34 C3
Leafield Rd SK12 . . . . .38 B3
Leafy Way CW8 . . . . .102 B4
Leahurst Cl CH2 . . . . . . .118 C2
Leam St OL6 . . . . .242 A4
Leamington Ave WA12 . . . .2 B1
Leamington Cl
Neston CH64 . . . . .66 C3
Warrington WA5 . . . . .15 A4
Leamington Rd
Congleton CW12 . . . . .155 C2
Macclesfield SK10 . . . . . . .86 C1
Lear Dr CW2 . . . . .205 C4
Leas Cl 8 CH66 . . . . .69 B3
Leaside WA7 . . . . .23 B1
Leaside Rd CH1 . . . . . . .117 C3
Leaside Way SK9 . . . . .60 B3
Leatham Cl WA3 . . . . .9 C2
Leather's La L26 . . . . .21 A4
Leawood Cl CW8 . . . . . . .103 A3
Ledbury Dr CW2 . . . . . . .206 A4
Ledge Ley SK8 . . . . .34 C4
Ledger Rd WA11 . . . . .1 A3
Ledley St SK10 . . . . .87 C4
Ledsham Cl WA3 . . . . .9 B2
Ledsham Hall La CH66 . . .68 C2
Ledsham La CH66 . . . . . . .68 C2
Ledsham Park Dr CH66 . .69 A3
Ledsham Rd CH66 . . . . . . .69 A3
Ledsham Village CH66 . . .68 C1
Ledston Cl WA7 . . . . .24 B1
Ledward La WA14 . . . . . .238 B2
Ledward St CW7 . . . . . . .127 A1
Ledyard Cl WA5 . . . . .15 B4
Lee Ave WA14 . . . . .238 C7
Lee Cl WA16 . . . . .56 C1
Lee Dale Cl M34 . . . . . . .241 A6
Lee Dr CW8 . . . . .103 C4
Lee Rd WA5 . . . . .15 A3
Lee St Chester CH2 . . . . .237 C3
16 Stockport SK1 . . . . . . .240 F5
Leech Rd SY14 . . . . .213 A2
Leech St Hyde SK14 . . . .241 F6
Stalybridge SK15 . . . . . . .242 D1
Leegate Gdns SK4 . . . . .240 A8
Leegate Rd SK4 . . . . . . .240 A8
Leek Old Rd SK11 . . . . . .112 C1
Leek Rd CW12 . . . . .179 A4
Leen La CH1 . . . . .237 B2
Lees La
Ellesmere Port CH65 . . . . . .70 C2
Mottram St Andrew SK10 . .61 A4
Neston CH64 . . . . .67 A4
Lees Rd SK7 . . . . .35 B3
Lees St SK15 . . . . .242 D2
Leeside SK4 . . . . .240 A5
Leesway Dr M34 . . . . . .241 A6
Leewood Ct 7 SK4 . . . . .240 B7
Leftwich Com Prim Sch
CW9 . . . . .104 A2
Legh Cl SK12 . . . . .36 C2
Legh Ct M33 . . . . .242 E5
Legh Gdns WA16 . . . . .57 A1
Legh Rd Adlington SK10 . . .62 B3
Haydock WA11 . . . . .1 A3
High Lane SK12 . . . . .38 A3
Knutsford WA16 . . . . .82 A4
Prestbury SK10 . . . . .87 A4
Sale M33 . . . . .242 E5
Legh St Golborne WA3 . . . .3 A4
Newton-le-W WA12 . . . . . . .2 A2
Warrington WA1 . . . . .16 A3
Legh Vale Prim Sch WA11 .1 A3
Leicester Ave ST7 . . . . . .193 B3
Leicester Rd
Altrincham WA15 . . . . . . .238 F2
Sale M33 . . . . .242 B7
Leicester St
Northwich CW9 . . . . .79 A1
Warrington WA5 . . . . .15 C3
Leigh Ave Knutsford WA16 .57 B2
Widnes WA8 . . . . .13 A1
Leigh Green Cl 4 WA8 . . .22 B4
Leigh La CW8 . . . . .77 B3
Leigh Prim Sch
Hyde SK14 . . . . .241 E6
Hyde SK14 . . . . .241 F6
Leigh Rd
Altrincham WA15 . . . . . . .238 E2
Congleton CW12 . . . . .157 A3
Wilmslow SK9 . . . . .59 B3
Leigh St Hyde SK14 . . . .241 E6
3 Lymm WA13 . . . . .18 C2
Macclesfield SK11 . . . . . .112 C4
Leigh Way CW8 . . . . .77 B1
Leigh's Brow CW8 . . . . . . .77 C2
Leighstone Ct CH2 . . . . .237 A4
Leighton Chase CH64 . . . .41 B1
Leighton Ct CH64 . . . . . . .66 B4
Leighton Hospl CW1 . . .172 C1
Leighton Pk CH64 . . . . . . .66 B4
Leighton Prim Sch CW1 189 C4
Leighton Rd CH64 . . . . . . .41 B1
Leighton St CW1 . . . . . . .190 A3
Leighton View CW1 . . . .190 A4
Leightons The CH64 . . . . .66 B4
Leinster Gdns WA7 . . . . . .22 C2
Leinster St WA7 . . . . .22 C2
Leiria Way WA7 . . . . .23 A1
Leith Ave M33 . . . . .242 E6
Leith Rd M33 . . . . .242 E6
Lenham Wlk M22 . . . . . . .33 B4
Lenthall Ave CW12 . . . . .178 C4
Leon Cl WA5 . . . . .14 B4
Leonard St Blacon CH1 . .118 A2
Runcorn WA7 . . . . .48 B4
Warrington WA2 . . . . .16 B4
Warrington, Stockton Heath
WA4 . . . . .16 B1
Leslie Rd CW7 . . . . .149 A4
Lessingham Rd WA8 . . . .12 C2
Lester Cl ST7 . . . . .193 B2
Leven Ave CW7 . . . . .126 C1
Leven Wlk CH66 . . . . .70 A4
Levens Cl SK8 . . . . .239 B4
Levens Way 1 WA8 . . . . .22 B4
Leveret Rd L24 . . . . .21 A2
Leverett Cl WA14 . . . . . .238 A5
Levisham Gdns WA5 . . . .15 C4
Lewin St CW10 . . . . .128 B1
Lewis Ave WA5 . . . . .7 C1
Lewis Cl
Ellesmere Port CH65 . . . . .95 B4
Nantwich CW5 . . . . .205 A3
Lewis Cres WA8 . . . . .23 A4
Lewis Gr WA8 . . . . .12 B1
Lewis St CW1 . . . . .190 B2
Lexden St WA5 . . . . .15 C3
Leyburn Gr SK6 . . . . . . .241 C2
Leycester Cl WA16 . . . . . .82 B4
Leycester Rd
Knutsford WA16 . . . . .82 A4
Mobberley WA16 . . . . .57 C4
Leyfield Ave SK6 . . . . . .241 C2
Leyfield Ct Chester CH4 .140 C3
Romiley SK6 . . . . .241 C2
Leygate View SK22 . . . . . .39 A4
Leyland Ave SK8 . . . . . .239 B6
Leyland Dr CH4 . . . . . . .140 B3
Leyland Gr
Haslington CW1 . . . . .191 B2
Haydock WA11 . . . . .1 A3
Leyland St SK1 . . . . .240 E5
Leyland Wlk CW7 . . . . . .149 B3
Leys Rd WA14 . . . . .238 E8
Leyton Cl WA7 . . . . .49 A3
Libson Cl WA2 . . . . .9 A2
Lichfield Ave WA3 . . . . . . .3 B4
Lichfield Cl WA16 . . . . . . .57 B1
Lichfield Ct CW7 . . . . . . .149 B4
Lichfield Dr CH66 . . . . . . .94 C4
Lichfield Rd Blacon CH1 .117 C3
Talke ST7 . . . . .210 B4
Lichfield St CW10 . . . . . .128 B1
Lichfield Wlk SK6 . . . . . .241 A1
Lidgetts La SK10 . . . . . . .88 B2
Liebig St WA8 . . . . .23 A4
Light Alders La SK12 . . . .38 A3
Light Oaks Rd WA3 . . . . . .5 B3
Lightburn St 4 WA7 . . . . .22 C1
Lightfoot Cl CH60 . . . . . . .41 A4
Lightfoot La Eaton CW6 .147 A2
Heswall CH60 . . . . .41 A4
Lightfoot St CH2 . . . . . . .118 C1
Lighthorne Ave SK3 . . . .239 F7
Lighthorne Gr SK3 . . . . .239 F7
Lighthorne Rd SK3 . . . . .239 F7
Lighthouse Rd L24 . . . . . .47 C4
Lightley Cl CW11 . . . . . .175 A2
Lightwood Green Ave
CW3 . . . . .229 A1
Lightwood Rd ST5 . . . . .210 B1
Lilac Ave Knutsford WA16 .56 C1
Warrington WA5 . . . . .15 A3
Widnes WA8 . . . . .13 A1
Lilac Cl Kelsall CW6 . . . .122 C1
Newcastle-u-L ST5 . . . . . .210 B1
Lilac Cres WA7 . . . . .49 B4
Lilac Ct CW12 . . . . .156 C1
Lilac Dr CW8 . . . . .103 B3
Lilac Gr
Ellesmere Port CH1 . . . . . .95 A4
Lilac Gr *continued*
Warrington WA4 . . . . .16 C1
Lilac St SK2 . . . . .240 F2
Lilac Wlk M31 . . . . .11 C2
Lilford Ave WA5 . . . . .15 C4
Lilford Dr WA5 . . . . .14 C3
Lilford Sq SK11 . . . . . . .112 B3
Lilford St WA5 . . . . .15 C4
Lillyfield CH60 . . . . .40 C3
Lily Ave WA12 . . . . .2 B1
Lily Cl SK3 . . . . .240 D1
Lily La CW10 . . . . .129 A3
Lime Ave Frodsham WA6 . .74 B4
Northwich CW9 . . . . .103 C3
Weaverham CW8 . . . . . . .102 B4
Widnes WA8 . . . . .13 A1
Lime Cl Hollinfare WA3 . . .11 A1
Middlewich CW10 . . . . . .128 A1
Sandbach CW11 . . . . .175 A4
Tarporley CW6 . . . . .146 B1
Lime Ct CW9 . . . . .103 C3
Lime Gr Alsager ST7 . . . .193 C1
Broughton CH4 . . . . .140 B3
Cheadle SK8 . . . . .239 D6
Chester CH2 . . . . .119 A2
Elton CH2 . . . . .72 A2
Golborne WA3 . . . . .3 C3
Macclesfield SK10 . . . . . .112 C4
Runcorn WA7 . . . . .49 B4
Shavington CW2 . . . . . . .206 B2
Winsford CW7 . . . . .127 A1
Lime Kiln La ST7 . . . . . .194 C1
Lime St Congleton CW12 .156 B1
Crewe CW1 . . . . .190 B3
Ellesmere Port CH65 . . . . .70 B4
Lime Tree Ave
Congleton CW12 . . . . .156 A2
Crewe CW1 . . . . .190 C3
Lime Tree Cl CH1 . . . . . . .95 A4
Lime Tree Dr CH3 . . . . . .180 C1
Lime Tree Gr CH60 . . . . . .41 B4
Lime Tree La WA16 . . . . . .29 B3
Lime Tree Prim Sch
M33 . . . . .242 E5
Lime View SK11 . . . . . . .112 B1
Lime Wlk
21 Handforth SK9 . . . . .34 B1
Partington M31 . . . . .11 B2
Limefield Ave WA13 . . . . .18 C1
Limehurst Gr CH62 . . . . . .43 B3
Limekiln La WA5 . . . . .6 C2
Limekiln Row WA7 . . . . . .50 A4
Limes La WA4 . . . . .52 B3
Limes The Culcheth WA3 . . .4 B2
Golborne WA3 . . . . .3 B3
Middlewich CW10 . . . . . .128 A1
Limetree Ave
Warrington WA1 . . . . .17 A4
Warrington, Stockton Heath
WA4 . . . . .16 C1
Limeways WA4 . . . . .26 C3
Limewood Cres CW8 . . . . .78 A2
Limewood Gr CW8 . . . . . .78 A2
Lincoln Ave Gatley SK8 . . .34 A4
Irlam M44 . . . . .11 B2
Lincoln Cl Golborne WN7 . . .4 B4
Macclesfield SK10 . . . . . . .86 C1
Rainow SK10 . . . . .88 C3
Runcorn WA7 . . . . .49 B3
Warrington WA1 . . . . .17 C3
Lincoln Ct WA6 . . . . .73 A2
Lincoln Dr CH2 . . . . .119 A3
Lincoln Gr M33 . . . . .242 F6
Lincoln Pl SK10 . . . . .86 C1
Lincoln Rd Blacon CH1 . .117 C3
Ellesmere Port CH66 . . . . . .69 B2
Handforth SK9 . . . . .34 C1
Kidsgrove ST7 . . . . .194 C1
Lincoln Rise SK6 . . . . . .241 A1
Lincoln Sq WA8 . . . . .13 A1
Lincoln St CW1 . . . . .190 A3
Lincoln Wlk SK10 . . . . . . .86 C1
Lincombe Hey SK10 . . . . .87 B4
Lincombe Rd M22 . . . . . . .33 B4
Lindale Cl CW12 . . . . . . .157 A3
Linden Ave WA15 . . . . . .238 E5
Linden Cl
Congleton CW12 . . . . .179 A4
Denton M34 . . . . .241 A7
Ellesmere Port CH66 . . . . . .94 C4
Lymm WA13 . . . . .19 A2
Warrington WA1 . . . . .17 B4
Linden Ct
Sandbach CW11 . . . . .174 C2
Widnes WA8 . . . . .12 C2
Linden Dr Biddulph ST8 . .179 B1
Crewe CW1 . . . . .190 C2
Helsby WA6 . . . . .73 A1
Mickle Trafford CH2 . . . . . .96 C1
Linden Gr Bramhall SK7 . . .35 B2
Broughton CH4 . . . . .140 B3
Chester CH2 . . . . .119 A2
Linden Rd M34 . . . . .241 A7
Linden Road Prim Sch
M34 . . . . .241 A7
Linden Way High Lane SK6 38 A4
Widnes WA8 . . . . .12 C2
Lindens The CW10 . . . . .128 A1
Lindfield Cl WA4 . . . . .25 A3
Lindfield Est N SK9 . . . . .60 A3
Lindfield Est S SK9 . . . . .59 C3
Lindi Ave WA4 . . . . .17 B1
Lindisfarne Ave
Ellesmere Port CH65 . . . . . .70 B1
Golborne WA3 . . . . .4 B4
Lindisfarne Cl CW10 . . . .128 A1
Lindisfarne Dr SK12 . . . . .36 B2
Lindley Ave WA4 . . . . .16 C2
Lindley Dro SK3 . . . . . . .240 D1
Lindop Cl WA16 . . . . .57 B1
Lindop Rd WA15 . . . . . . .238 F1
Lindow Com Prim Sch
SK9 . . . . .59 B2
Lindow Ct M33 . . . . .242 F5
Lindow Fold Dr SK9 . . . . .59 B3
Lindow La SK9 . . . . .59 C3
Lindow Par SK9 . . . . .59 C3
Lindow St M33 . . . . .242 F5
Lindrick Cl SK10 . . . . .87 B2
Lindrum Ave SK11 . . . . .112 B1
Linds Worth Cl WA5 . . . . .15 B3
Lindsay St SK15 . . . . . . .242 E1
Lindsay Way ST7 . . . . . .193 A2
Lindsay Wlk CW8 . . . . . .102 A2
Lindsell Rd WA14 . . . . . .238 C8
Linear View WA12 . . . . . . .2 B1
Lines Rd M44 . . . . .11 C4
Linfields CH4 . . . . .140 C3
Lingdale Rd SK8 . . . . . . .239 F2
Lingdale Wlk SK11 . . . . .112 B3
Lingfield Cl SK10 . . . . . . .87 B2
Lingfield Dr CW1 . . . . . .190 B4
Lingfield Rd WA7 . . . . . . .22 C1
Lingley Green Ave WA5 . .14 B4
Lingley Rd WA5 . . . . .14 B3
Linglongs Ave SK23 . . . . .65 B3
Linglongs Rd SK23 . . . . . .65 B3
Lingmell Gdns CW4 . . . .129 C2
Lingwell Ave WA8 . . . . . . .12 B1
Lingwood Rd WA5 . . . . . .14 C3
Link The SK9 . . . . .34 B2
Link Wlk M31 . . . . .11 B1
Links Ave CH66 . . . . .69 B4
Links Cl CH63 . . . . .43 A3
Links Rd Romiley SK6 . . .241 D2
Wilmslow SK9 . . . . .59 C2
Linkside Ave WA2 . . . . .8 A3
Linkside Way CH66 . . . . . .94 C4
Linksway Chester CH2 . . .118 B4
Congleton CW12 . . . . .178 C4
Gatley SK8 . . . . .239 A4
Linksway Cl CW12 . . . . .178 C4
Linkway WA7 . . . . .49 B4
Linley Gr Alsager ST7 . . .193 C2
Stockport SK3 . . . . .240 D1
Linley La ST7 . . . . .194 A1
Linley Rd Alsager ST7 . . .193 C1
Cheadle SK8 . . . . .35 A4
Sale M33 . . . . .242 B7
Talke ST7 . . . . .210 B4
Linley Trad Est ST7 . . . .194 B1
Linnards La CW9,WA16 . . .80 A3
Linnet Cl
Newton-le-W WA12 . . . . . . .2 B2
Warrington WA2 . . . . .8 B2
Winsford CW7 . . . . .150 A4
Linnet Gr
Macclesfield SK10 . . . . . . .87 A1
Warrington WA3 . . . . .9 C2
Linnets Way CH60 . . . . . .40 C4
Linnett Cl CW1 . . . . .190 A4
Linton Rd M33 . . . . .242 C8
Linum Gdns WA9 . . . . .6 A4
Linwood Cl WA7 . . . . .50 B3
Lion Salt Works Mus*
CW9 . . . . .79 B2
Lion St CW12 . . . . .156 B1
Lisburn Ave M33 . . . . . .242 A5
Liskeard Cl WA7 . . . . .50 A3
Liskeard Dr SK7 . . . . .35 C4
Lismore WA15 . . . . .238 F2
Lismore Ave SK3 . . . . . .240 B4
Lismore Wlk M22 . . . . . . .33 C4
Lisson Gr WA15 . . . . . . .238 E2
Lister Cl CW10 . . . . .151 B3
Lister Rd WA7 . . . . .23 B2
Litherland Rd M33 . . . . .242 E5
Little Abbey Gateway
CH1 . . . . .237 A3
Little Aston Cl SK10 . . . . .87 B2
Little Bollington CE Prim Sch
WA14 . . . . .20 A1
Little Budworth Ctry Pk
CW6 . . . . .147 B4
Little Delph WA11 . . . . . . .1 B4
Little Egerton St 5 SK1 240 E6
Little Gn CH66 . . . . .69 B2
Little Heath Cl CW3 . . . .230 A3
Little Heath La WA14 . . . .20 B3
Little Heath Rd
Chester CH3 . . . . .119 C1
Christleton CH3 . . . . .142 C4
Little La CH64 . . . . .41 B1
Little Leigh Prim Sch
CW8 . . . . .77 B3
Little Meadow Cl SK10 . .87 A4
Little Meadow Rd WA14 238 B1
Little Moreton Hall*
CW12 . . . . .177 C1
Little Moss Cl ST7 . . . . .194 C3
Little Moss La ST7 . . . . .194 C3
Little Roodee CH5 . . . . .139 A4
Little Row 14 ST7 . . . . . .195 A1
Little St Congleton CW12 .156 B1
3 Macclesfield SK11 . . . .112 B4
Little St John St CH1 . . .237 B2
Little Stanney La CH2 . . .95 C4
Little Sutton CE Prim Sch
CH66 . . . . .69 A3
Little Sutton Sta CH66 . . .69 B3
Little Underbank 1
SK1 . . . . .240 F5
Little Wissage CH66 . . . . .69 C1
Littlebourne WA7 . . . . . . .50 C4
Littlecote Ave WA4 . . . . . .26 B2
Littledale Rd WA5 . . . . . .14 C4
Littledales La CW8 . . . . .102 C2
Littlegate WA7 . . . . .49 C4
Littler Grange Ct CW7 . .126 A1
Littler La CW7 . . . . .125 C1
Littler Rd WA11 . . . . .1 A3
Littlestone Cl WA8 . . . . . .13 A2
Littleton Cl
6 Davenham CW9 . . . . . . .103 C2
Warrington WA5 . . . . .15 B2
Littleton La CH3 . . . . . . .119 C1
Littondale Cl CW12 . . . .157 A3
Liverpool Pl WA8 . . . . . . .12 B1
Liverpool Rd
Backford CH1,CH2 . . . . . . .95 A2
Chester CH2 . . . . .118 B3
Haydock WA11 . . . . .1 A4
Irlam M44,WA3 . . . . .11 B2
Kidsgrove ST7 . . . . .195 A1
Neston CH64 . . . . .41 C1
Newcastle-u-L ST5 . . . . . .210 B1
Warrington WA5,WA1 . . . . .15 C3
Warrington, Great Sankey
WA5,WA8 . . . . .14 C3
Widnes WA8 . . . . .12 B1
Liverpool Rd E ST7 . . . .194 C1
Liverpool Rd W ST7 . . . .194 A2
Liverpool Row WA12 . . . . .7 B4
Liverpool St CW9 . . . . . .104 B4
Livingstone Cl
Macclesfield SK11 . . . . . .111 C4
Warrington WA5 . . . . .15 B4
Livingstone Rd CH65 . . . .70 B4
Livingstone Way CW10 .151 B3
Liz Kaye Ho SK11 . . . . . .112 C4
Llanberis Rd SK8 . . . . . .239 E1
Llandaff Cl CH66 . . . . . . .69 C1
Llandovery Cl CW7 . . . . .149 A4
Llanfair Rd 7 SK3 . . . . .240 C4
Lloyd Ave SK8 . . . . .239 A6
Lloyd Cl CH3 . . . . .180 C1
Lloyd Cres WA12 . . . . .1 C2
Lloyd Dr CH65 . . . . .70 B1
Lloyd Gdns WA14 . . . . . .238 D3
Lloyd Pl CH1 . . . . .117 C2
Lloyd Sq 6 WA14 . . . . . .238 D4
Lloyd St
Altrincham WA14,WA15 . .238 D4
Stockport SK4 . . . . .240 D7
Lloyd's Ct WA14 . . . . . .238 D4
Llyndir La LL12 . . . . . . .162 A1
Llys Caer CH4 . . . . .139 A2
Llys Derwen CH4 . . . . . .161 A4
Loachbrook Ave CW12 . .156 A1
Lobelia Gr WA7 . . . . .49 C3
Lobelia Wlk 6 M31 . . . . .11 C1
Loch St WA7 . . . . .23 A2
Lochinvar Ave CH66 . . . . .68 C3
Lochleven Rd CW2 . . . . .206 A4
Lochmaben Cl CW4 . . . . .130 A1
Lock La M31 . . . . .11 C2
Lock Rd Altrincham WA14 238 C6
Bebington CH62 . . . . .44 A4
Warrington WA1 . . . . .16 C3
Locker Ave WA2 . . . . .8 A1
Lockerbie Cl
Holmes Chapel CW4 . . . . .130 B1
Warrington WA2 . . . . .8 C2
Lockett Rd WA8 . . . . .13 A2
Lockett St WA4 . . . . .16 C2
Lockgate E WA7 . . . . .24 B1
Lockgate W WA7 . . . . .24 A1
Locking Stumps Com Prim
Sch WA3 . . . . .9 B2
Locking Stumps La WA3 . .9 A2
Lockitt St CW2 . . . . .190 B2
Locksley Cl SK4 . . . . . . .240 C6
Lockton La WA5 . . . . .15 C4
Lockwood View WA7 . . . .50 C3
Lodge Brow SK10 . . . . . . .63 A1
Lodge Cl WA13 . . . . .19 A2
Lodge Dr Culcheth WA3 . . . .4 C2
Moulton CW9 . . . . .126 C4
Winsford CW7 . . . . .127 A1
Lodge Gdns CH2 . . . . . . .118 B3
Lodge Hollow WA6 . . . . . .73 A2
Lodge La Antrobus CW9 . .54 A3
Dutton WA4 . . . . .76 B4
Hartford CW8 . . . . .103 A2
Hatherton CW5 . . . . .220 A2
Hyde SK14 . . . . .241 D8
Lostock Gralam CW9 . . . . .80 A1
Newton-le-W WA12 . . . . . . .2 A4
Runcorn WA7 . . . . .49 C4
Saughall CH1 . . . . .94 A1
Warrington WA5 . . . . .15 C4
Widnes WA8 . . . . .12 A2
Lodge Rd Alsager ST7 . . .193 B2
Knutsford WA16 . . . . .57 B2
Sandbach CW11 . . . . .174 C3
Talke ST7 . . . . .210 B3
Widnes WA8 . . . . .22 A4
Lodge The CH2 . . . . .237 C3
Lodgefields Dr CW2 . . . .189 C2
Lodgefields Prim Sch
CW2 . . . . .189 C2
Lodmore La SY13 . . . . . .233 B3
Lofthouse Gate WA8 . . . .12 C2
Lomas Sq SK11 . . . . . . .112 B3
Lomas St SK3 . . . . .240 D3
Lomax Rd CW5 . . . . .205 B3
Lomond Gr CH66 . . . . . . .69 C2
London Pl 13 SK1 . . . . . .240 F5
London Rd Adlington SK10 62 B3
Alderley Edge SK9 . . . . . . .60 A1
Allostock WA16 . . . . .107 A3
Bridgemere CW5 . . . . . . .232 A3
Davenham CW9 . . . . .104 A1
Frodsham WA6 . . . . .74 A4

London Rd *continued*
Hatherton CW5 . . . . .220 B2
Holmes Chapel CW4 . . . . .130 B1
Macclesfield SK11 . . . . . . .112 B2
Nantwich CW5 . . . . .204 C3
Northwich CW9 . . . . .103 C4
Sandbach CW11 . . . . .174 B4
Stapeley CW5 . . . . .205 A2
Warrington WA4 . . . . .26 B3
London Rd N SK12 . . . . . .36 C3
London Rd S SK12 . . . . . .36 B2
London Rd Terr SK11 . . . .112 B3
London Row WA12 . . . . . . .7 B4
London Sq 10 SK1 . . . . .240 F5
Loney St SK11 . . . . .112 B4
Long Acre CW8 . . . . .77 B1
Long Acres Rd CH64 . . . . .41 C1
Long Barn La WA1 . . . . . .17 B4
Long Croft La SK8 . . . . . .239 F1
Long Hill SK23 . . . . .65 C1
Long La Alpraham CW6 . . .169 C2
Bickerton SY14 . . . . .199 C2
Bollington SK10 . . . . .63 A1
Burland CW5 . . . . .203 A4
Chester CH2 . . . . .119 A3
Hargrave CH3 . . . . .143 B1
Haughton CW6 . . . . .186 B2
Huxley CH3 . . . . .166 B4
Kidsgrove ST7 . . . . .195 C2
Lower Peover WA16 . . . . .107 B4
Middlewich CW10 . . . . . . .151 B4
Saughall CH1 . . . . .94 A1
Swettenham CW12 . . . . . .131 C3
Tilston SY14 . . . . .198 A2
Warrington WA2 . . . . .8 A1
Wettenhall CW6,CW7 . . . .170 B3
Whaley Bridge SK23 . . . . .65 C2
Long La S CW10 . . . . . . .151 B4
Long Lane Com Prim Sch
WA2 . . . . .8 A1
Long Looms CH3 . . . . . .120 C3
Long Marl Dr SK9 . . . . . .34 C2
Long Mdw CH60 . . . . . . .40 C3
Long Meadow Pas
SK14 . . . . .241 D7
Long Row ST7 . . . . .195 A1
Long Shoot WA4 . . . . . . .130 B4
Long Shoot Rd SK11 . . . .108 C1
Long Spinney WA7 . . . . . .50 B4
Long Valley Rd ST8 . . . . .179 B1
Long Wlk M31 . . . . .11 B2
Longacre St SK11 . . . . . .112 B4
Longacres Rd WA15 . . . . .32 B4
Longbarn Bvd WA2 . . . . . .9 B1
Longbarn Com Prim Sch
WA3 . . . . .9 A1
Longbenton Way WA7 . . .24 A2
Longburgh Cl CH2 . . . . . .118 C2
Longbutt La WA13 . . . . . .19 A1
Longbutts La SK11 . . . . .111 C1
Longclough Rd ST5 . . . . .210 B1
Longcroft Dr WA14 . . . . .238 B4
Longcross CW10 . . . . . . .128 B1
Longdale Dr CH1 . . . . . . .117 B3
Longden Ct SK7 . . . . .35 C3
Longden La SK11 . . . . . . .113 A3
Longden St SK11 . . . . . . .112 C4
Longdin St WA4 . . . . .16 C2
Longdown Rd CW12 . . . . .155 C2
Longfield Ave
Chester CH2 . . . . .118 C4
Gatley SK8 . . . . .34 B4
Longfield Rd WA2 . . . . . . .8 B1
Longford St Crewe CW2 . .190 B1
Warrington WA2 . . . . .16 A4
Longhill La CW3 . . . . . . .230 C3
Longhorn Cl CW2 . . . . . .128 B1
Longlands Dr SK22 . . . . . .39 A4
Longlands Rd SK22 . . . . . .39 A4
Longley Ave CW6 . . . . . .122 B3
Longlooms Rd CH65 . . . . .70 B1
Longmeade Gdns SK9 . . . .60 B1
Longmeadow Cheadle SK8 .35 B4
Weaverham CW8 . . . . . . .102 B4
Longmoss Cl CW10 . . . . .151 B4
Longmynd Rise CW7 . . . .149 A4
Longnor Rd Gatley SK8 . . .34 B4
Hazel Grove SK7 . . . . .36 C4
Longridge WA16 . . . . .57 B2
Longridge Ave SK15 . . . .242 D4
Longridge Trad Est
WA16 . . . . .57 B2
Longsdon St ST5 . . . . . . .210 B1
Longshaw St WA5 . . . . . . .15 C4
Longshut La SK1,SK2 . . . .240 F3
Longshut La W SK2 . . . . .240 F3
Longsides Rd WA15 . . . . . .32 B4
Longsight La SK8 . . . . . . .34 C3
Longsons The SK5 . . . . . .240 F7
Longster Cl WA6 . . . . .73 A1
Longstone La CW6 . . . . . .124 C2
Longton Ave WA3 . . . . .3 B4
Longview Ave ST7 . . . . . .193 C2
Longwood Cl
Middlewich CW10 . . . . . . .151 B4
Romiley SK6 . . . . .241 E3
Longwood Rd
Stretton WA4 . . . . .26 C3
Warrington WA4 . . . . .26 C3
Lonsdale Cl
Warrington WA5 . . . . .14 C4
3 Widnes WA8 . . . . .22 B4
Lonsdale Ct CH4 . . . . . . .140 C2
Looe Cl WA5 . . . . .14 C1
Looms The CH64 . . . . .41 A4
Loonies Ct 1 SK1 . . . . . .240 F4
Loont The CW7 . . . . .149 B4
Lord Kitchener Ct M33 . .242 B7

Lord Nelson St WA1 . . . . .16 B3
Lord St Bollington SK10 . . .88 A4
Chester CH1 . . . . .118 C1
Crewe CW2 . . . . .190 B2
Croft WA3 . . . . .9 A4
Macclesfield SK11 . . . . . . .112 B4
Newton-le-W WA12 . . . . . . .2 A2
Runcorn WA7 . . . . .22 C2
Stockport SK1 . . . . .240 F5
Warrington WA4 . . . . .16 A4
Lord's St M44 . . . . .11 B3
Lords La WA3 . . . . .9 B2
Lords Mill Rd CW2 . . . . . .206 A2
Lordship La WA4 . . . . . . .73 A4
Lordshire Pl ST7 . . . . . . .195 C1
Loreto Convent Gram Sch
WA14 . . . . .238 C5
Loreto Convent Prep Sch
WA14 . . . . .238 C5
Lorland Rd SK3 . . . . .240 B3
Lorne Gr SK3 . . . . .240 E2
Lorne St CH1 . . . . .237 A3
Lorraine St ST7 . . . . .195 C1
Lostock Ave Poynton SK12 . .36 A4
Sale M33 . . . . .242 E6
Warrington WA5 . . . . .15 C4
Lostock Ct SK9 . . . . .34 B2
Lostock Gralam CE Prim Sch
CW9 . . . . .80 A1
Lostock Gralam Sta CW9 . .80 A1
Lostock Hall Prim Sch
SK12 . . . . .36 A2
Lostock Hall Rd SK12 . . . . .36 A2
Lostock Hollow CW9 . . . . .80 A1
Lostock Rd SK12 . . . . .36 B1
Lostock Way SK9 . . . . . . .34 B2
Lottery St SK3 . . . . .240 D5
Louise St CH1 . . . . .237 A3
Loushers La WA4 . . . . . . .16 B1
Loushers Lane Sch WA4 . .16 B1
Lovage Cl WA2 . . . . .9 B1
Lovat Dr WA16 . . . . .82 A4
Lovatt Ct WA13 . . . . .19 A2
Love La
Hassall Green CW11 . . . . .176 B2
Nantwich CW5 . . . . .204 C3
Stockport SK4 . . . . .240 E6
Love St CH1 . . . . .237 B2
Lovel Terr WA8 . . . . .22 A3
Lovell Dr SK14 . . . . .241 F8
Lovely La WA5 . . . . .15 C3
Low Hill WA6 . . . . .97 B3
Low Leighton Rd SK22 . . .39 B4
Low Mdw SK23 . . . . .65 B4
Low St ST7 . . . . .193 C4
Lowcross La SY14 . . . . . .198 B2
Lowe Ave
Congleton CW12 . . . . .156 C1
Warrington WA4 . . . . .16 C2
Lowe Cres CW9 . . . . .53 B2
Lowe Dr WA16 . . . . .57 A1
Lowe St Denton M34 . . . . .241 B7
Golborne WA3 . . . . .3 A4
Macclesfield SK11 . . . . . . .112 B4
15 Stockport SK1 . . . . . .240 F5
Lower Appleton Rd WA8 . .13 A1
Lower Ash Rd ST7 . . . . . .194 C1
Lower Bank St 10 SK11 . .112 C4
Lower Beech Cotts SK10 . .87 B1
Lower Bridge St CH4 . . . .237 B1
Lower Brook St CH5 . . . . .91 B1
Lower Bury St SK4 . . . . . .240 D6
Lower Carrs 21 SK1 . . . .240 F5
Lower Church St WA8 . . . .23 A3
Lower Cl L26 . . . . .21 A4
Lower Darwin St CW8 . . .103 C3
Lower Exchange St
SK11 . . . . .112 B4
Lower Field Rd CH4 . . . . .141 A3
Lower Fold M34 . . . . .241 A6
Lower Greenshall La
SK12 . . . . .38 C3
Lower Hague SK22 . . . . . . .38 C4
Lower Haigh St 12 CW7 . .149 B4
Lower Hall La CH3 . . . . . .182 B1
Lower Hall Mews CH3 . . . .182 B1
Lower Heath CW12 . . . . . .156 C2
Lower Heath Ave CW12 . .156 C2
Lower High St ST7 . . . . . .195 B4
Lower Hillgate SK1 . . . . .240 F5
Lower House La WA8 . . . . .22 A3
Lower La CW6 . . . . .147 A2
Lower Macclesfield Rd
SK23 . . . . .65 C3
Lower Meadow Rd SK9 . . . .34 C2
Lower Mersey St CH65 . . . .70 B4
Lower Moat Cl SK4 . . . . .240 E7
Lower Park Cres SK12 . . . .36 B3
Lower Park Rd
Chester CH4 . . . . .237 C2
Poynton SK12 . . . . .36 A3
Lower Park St SK12 . . . . . .36 B2
Lower Park St CW12 . . . . .156 C2
Lower Peover CE Prim Sch
WA16 . . . . .81 C1
Lower Rake La WA6 . . . . . .73 A2
Lower Rd L26,WA8 . . . . . . .21 B4
Lower Robin Hood La
WA6 . . . . .73 A2
Lower Sandy La CH3 . . . .199 B4
Lower Wash La WA4 . . . . .16 C2
Lowerfield Rd SK10 . . . . . .87 C1
Lowerhouse SK10 . . . . . . .87 C4
Lowerlea SK10 . . . . .87 C4
Lowerlea CW12 . . . . .38 B3
Lowes La SK11 . . . . .111 C1
Loweswater Cl WA2 . . . . . .8 A2
Loweswater Cres WA11 . . .1 A3

Loweswater Rd SK8 . . . .239 B3
Loweswater Terr SK15 . . .242 B4
Lowfield Gdns WA3 . . . . . . .5 B4
Lowfield Gr SK2 . . . . .240 F3
Lowfield Rd SK2,SK3 . . . .240 E3
Lowfields Ave CH62 . . . . . .43 C2
Lowfields Cl CH62 . . . . . . .43 C2
Lowland Way WA16 . . . . . .82 A4
Lowlands Rd WA7 . . . . . . .22 C1
Lownorth Rd M22 . . . . . . .33 C4
Lowry Cl WA5 . . . . .15 B3
Lowther Ave WA3 . . . . .4 C2
Lowther St SK10 . . . . .88 B4
Lowton Bsns Pk WA3 . . . . .4 A4
Lowton Com High Sch
WA3 . . . . .4 A4
Lowton Gdns WA3 . . . . .3 B4
Lowton Jun & Inf Sch
WA3 . . . . .4 A4
Lowton Rd WA3 . . . . .3 B4
Lowton St Mary's CE Prim
Sch WA3 . . . . .4 A4
Lowton West Prim Sch
WA3 . . . . .3 B4
Loxdale Dr CH65 . . . . .69 C2
Loxley Cl
Macclesfield SK11 . . . . . . .112 A4
Warrington WA5 . . . . .15 A4
Loyola Hey L35 . . . . .12 C4
Lucerne Cl CH3 . . . . .142 A3
Lucy St SK3 . . . . .240 E4
Ludford Cl ST5 . . . . .210 B1
Ludford Rd CW1 . . . . . . .190 B3
Ludlow Ave CW1 . . . . . . .190 C2
Ludlow Cl
Macclesfield SK10 . . . . . . .87 C1
Winsford CW7 . . . . .149 A4
Ludlow Cres WA7 . . . . . . .49 A4
Ludlow Dr CH65 . . . . .70 C2
Ludlow Rd CH1 . . . . .118 A3
Ludwell Cl CH4 . . . . .141 A3
Lugsdale Rd WA8 . . . . . . .23 A4
Lulworth Cl CW7 . . . . . . .149 A4
Lum Head Prim Sch
SK8 . . . . .239 B3
Lumb Brook La WA4 . . . . .27 A3
Lumb Brook Rd WA4 . . . . .26 C4
Lumb Cl SK7 . . . . .35 C3
Lumb La SK7 . . . . .35 C3
Lumber La WA5 . . . . .6 C4
Lumbrook Mews 5 WA4 . .26 C4
Lumley Pl CH1 . . . . .237 B2
Lumley Rd Chester CH2 . . .118 B2
Macclesfield SK11 . . . . . . .111 C4
Lumley Wlk L24 . . . . .21 C1
Lumn Hollow 4 SK14 . . . .241 E6
Lumn Rd SK14 . . . . .241 E6
Lumpy St CW12 . . . . .156 B2
Lundy Dr CH2 . . . . .95 B4
Lune Cl 1 CW12 . . . . . . .157 A1
Lune Way WA8 . . . . .12 B1
Lunehurst 18 WA3 . . . . .3 A4
Lunt Ave CW2 . . . . .190 B1
Lunt's Heath Rd WA8 . . . . .13 A3
Lunts Heath Prim Sch
WA8 . . . . .13 A3
Lupin Dr Haydock WA11 . . . .1 C3
Huntington CH3 . . . . .142 A3
Lupus Way CH66 . . . . .69 C2
Lurgan Ave M33 . . . . .242 C5
Luscombe Cl L26 . . . . .21 A4
Lutener Ave WA14 . . . . . .238 C8
Luther Gr WA9 . . . . .1 A1
Luton Cl CH65 . . . . .70 A3
Luton St WA8 . . . . .23 A4
Lutyens Cl SK11 . . . . . . .111 C4
Lyceum Cl CW1 . . . . .190 A4
Lyceum Way CW1 . . . . . .190 A4
Lychgate WA4 . . . . .25 C4
Lycroft Cl WA7 . . . . .49 A3
Lydbury Cl WA5 . . . . .7 B1
Lydden Rd CH65 . . . . .70 A4
Lydgate Cl Denton M34 . . .241 B5
Wistaston CW2 . . . . .205 A4
Lydiate La SK9 . . . . .60 A1
Lydiate La Runcorn WA7 . . .48 B4
Willaston CH64 . . . . .42 C1
Lydiate The CH60 . . . . . . .40 C4
Lydney Ave SK8 . . . . .34 B4
Lydstep Cl WA5 . . . . .7 C1
Lydyett La SK8 . . . . .78 A2
Lymcote Dr CW8 . . . . . . .103 A2
Lyme Ave
Macclesfield SK11 . . . . . . .112 B3
Wilmslow SK9 . . . . .34 A1
Lyme Com Prim Sch
WA12 . . . . .1 C2
Lyme Gr
Altrincham WA14 . . . . . . .238 C4
Lymm WA13 . . . . .18 A1
Romiley SK6 . . . . .241 D2
Stockport SK4 . . . . .240 F3
Lyme Green Bsns Pk
SK11 . . . . .112 B2
Lyme Green Settlement
SK11 . . . . .112 B1
Lyme Park* SK12 . . . . . . .38 A1
Lyme Park Ctry Pk SK12 . .38 A1
Lyme Rd Disley SK12 . . . . .37 B2
High Lane SK12 . . . . .38 A3
Lyme St Haydock WA11 . . . .1 C3
Newton-le-W WA12 . . . . . . .1 C1
Lyme View Ct SK6 . . . . . .241 D2
Lymewood Dr Disley SK12 . .38 B3
Wilmslow SK9 . . . . .60 C1
Lymm Brook 1 WA13 . . . .18 C2
Lymm Cl SK3 . . . . .240 D2
Lymm High Sch WA13 . . . .19 A2

Lymm Rd
Little Bollington WA14 . . . .20 A1
Warrington WA4 . . . . .17 C2
Lymmhay La WA13 . . . . . .18 C2
Lymmington Ave WA13 . . .18 B2
Lynalls Cl CW12 . . . . .155 C2
Lynbrook Rd CW1 . . . . . .190 C2
Lyncastle Rd WA4 . . . . . . .27 B2
Lyncastle Way WA4 . . . . . .27 B2
Lyncombe Cl SK8 . . . . .35 A3
Lyncroft Cl CW1 . . . . .190 C2
Lyndale Ave
Bebington CH62 . . . . .43 C2
Warrington WA2 . . . . .16 B4
Warrington, Fearnhead WA2 .8 C1
Lyndale Ct CW7 . . . . .127 A2
Lyndene Gdns SK8 . . . . . .239 B6
Lyndhurst Cl SK9 . . . . .59 B3
Lyndon Gr WA7 . . . . .49 A4
Lyngard Cl SK9 . . . . .34 C1
Lyngarth Ho 1 WA14 . . . .238 F6
Lynham Ave WA3 . . . . .4 C3
Lynn Ave Sale M33 . . . . . .242 D8
Talke ST7 . . . . .210 B4
Lynn Cl WA7 . . . . .49 B4
Lynn Gr SK11 . . . . .112 B3
Lynndene CH66 . . . . .69 B4
Lynneal Ave CH66 . . . . . . .69 B2
Lynside WA8 . . . . .33 C4
Lynthorpe Ave M44 . . . . . .11 B3
Lynton Ave M44 . . . . .11 C3
Lynton Cl Heswall CH60 . . .41 A3
Knutsford WA16 . . . . .57 B1
Warrington WA5 . . . . .14 C2
Lynton Cres WA8 . . . . .12 C1
Lynton Dr SK6 . . . . .37 C4
Lynton Gdns WA4 . . . . . . .26 B2
Lynton Gr
Altrincham WA15 . . . . . . .238 F5
Haslington CW1 . . . . .191 B3
Lynton La SK9 . . . . .60 A1
Lynton Mews SK9 . . . . . . .60 A1
Lynton Park Rd SK8 . . . . . .34 C4
Lynton Pl Alsager ST7 . . . .193 B2
Broughton CH4 . . . . .139 A2
Lynton Rd SK8 . . . . .239 C5
Lynton Way CW2 . . . . . . .206 A4
Lyntonvale Ave SK8 . . . . .239 B6
Lynwood Altrincham WA15 . .32 A4
Wilmslow SK9 . . . . .60 A3
Lynwood Ave
Golborne WA3 . . . . .3 C3
Warrington WA4 . . . . .26 B4
Lynwood Gr M33 . . . . . . .242 C7
Lynwood Rd CH1 . . . . . . .117 C3
Lyon Ct WA4 . . . . .16 C2
Lyon Ind Est WA4 . . . . . . .238 B7
Lyon Rd WA14 . . . . .238 C7
Lyon St Chester CH2 . . . . .237 B3
Crewe CW1 . . . . .190 B2
Macclesfield SK11 . . . . . . .112 B4
Warrington WA4 . . . . .16 C2
Lyon's La WA4 . . . . .26 C3
Lyons Fold M33 . . . . .242 B8
Lyons Rd WA5 . . . . .15 A2
Lyster Cl WA3 . . . . .9 C2
Lytham Dr SK7 . . . . .36 A4
Lytham Rd Gatley SK8 . . . .239 B1
Widnes WA8 . . . . .13 B1
Lytham St SK3 . . . . .240 F2
Lytherton Ave M44 . . . . . .11 B2
Lythgoes La WA2 . . . . .16 A3

M

Mableden Cl SK8 . . . . .34 B4
Mablins La CW1 . . . . .190 A4
Mablins Lane Com Prim Sch
CW1 . . . . .190 A4
Mabs Ct OL6 . . . . .242 B4
Macarthur Dr WA5 . . . . . . .15 A3
Macbeth Ho ST7 . . . . .210 B4
Macclesfield Coll
Macclesfield SK11 . . . . . . .112 A3
Macclesfield SK11 . . . . . . .112 B4
Macclesfield District General
Hospl SK11 . . . . .112 A4
Macclesfield Rd
Alderley Edge SK9 . . . . . . .85 B4
Chelford SK11 . . . . .84 A1
Congleton CW12 . . . . .156 C3
Hazel Grove SK7 . . . . .36 C4
Holmes Chapel CW4 . . . . .130 C2
Kettleshulme SK23,SK10 . . .64 B2
Prestbury SK10 . . . . .86 C2
Rainow SK10 . . . . .89 A4
Whaley Bridge SK23 . . . . .65 B3
Wilmslow SK9 . . . . .60 B3
Macclesfield Sta SK11 . . . .112 B4
Macdermott Rd WA8 . . . . . .22 C3
Macdonald Rd M44 . . . . . . .11 C4
Mackenzie Ind Pk SK3,
SK8 . . . . .240 B2
Mackeson Dr OL6 . . . . . . .242 B4
Mackeson Rd OL6 . . . . . . .242 B4
Macon Ct CW1 . . . . .190 C2
Macon Ind Pk CW1 . . . . . .190 C2
Macon Way CW1 . . . . .190 C2
Maddock St ST7 . . . . .209 B1
Maddocks Hill WA6 . . . . . .100 C3
Madeley Cl
Altrincham WA14 . . . . .31 C4
Broughton CH4 . . . . .139 A2
Madeley St CW2 . . . . .190 B1
Madeline McKenna Ct
WA8 . . . . .12 B2

Madras Rd SK3 . . . . .240 C3
Madron Ave SK10 . . . . .86 B1
Maelor Cl CH63 . . . . .43 B3
Maes-y-coed CH4 . . . . . . .140 C3
Mag La WA13,WA16 . . . . . .28 C3
Magdala Pl CW9 . . . . .104 B4
Magdalen Ct CW2 . . . . . . .190 A1
Magecroft CW1 . . . . .173 A1
Magenta Ave M44 . . . . . . .11 C3
Maggoty La SK11 . . . . . . .111 B1
Magnolia Cl
11 Ellesmere Port CH66 . .69 C1
5 Partington M31 . . . . . .11 C1
Warrington WA1 . . . . .17 C4
Magnolia Dr WA7 . . . . .49 C2
Magnolia Rise SK10 . . . . . .86 C3
Magpie Cres 18 ST7 . . . .195 A1
Mahood St SK3 . . . . .240 D3
Maiden Est CW5 . . . . .228 B4
Maiden Gdns CH65 . . . . . . .70 B2
Maidenhills CW10 . . . . . . .128 B3
Maidstone Cl SK10 . . . . . . .87 A1
Maidstone Wlk M34 . . . . .241 A5
Maidwell Cl CW7 . . . . . . .127 A2
Main Cl WA11 . . . . .1 B3
Main La WA3 . . . . .3 C2
Main Rd Betley CW2,CW3 . .221 C4
Broughton CH4 . . . . .139 A2
Goostrey CW4 . . . . .107 C1
Higher Kinnerton CH4 . . . .161 A4
Langley SK11 . . . . .113 B2
Moulton CW9 . . . . .126 C4
Norton in Hales TF9 . . . . .236 B1
Shavington CW2 . . . . .206 A2
Weston CW2 . . . . .207 B3
Worleston CW5 . . . . .188 C3
Wybunbury CW5 . . . . .220 A4
Main St Frodsham WA6 . . . .74 A4
Great Barrow CH3 . . . . . .120 C3
Hyde SK14 . . . . .241 D8
Runcorn WA7 . . . . .49 C4
Maintree Cres L24 . . . . . . .21 A4
Mainwaring Cl CW5 . . . . . .205 A2
Mainwaring Dr
Broughton CH4 . . . . .140 B4
Wilmslow SK9 . . . . .60 B4
Mainwaring Rd
Bebington CH62 . . . . .43 B4
Peover WA16 . . . . .108 A4
Mairesfield Ave WA4 . . . . .17 A1
Maisterson Ct 11 CW5 . . .204 C3
Maitland Way CH1 . . . . . . .117 B2
Maitland Wood Cl CW9 . . .104 B4
Maizefield Cl M33 . . . . . . .242 F6
Major Cross St 15 WA8 . . .23 A4
Makepeace Cl CH3 . . . . . .119 B2
Malaga Ave M90 . . . . .33 A4
Malakoff St SK15 . . . . . . .242 B4
Malam Dr CW9 . . . . .104 B3
Malbank CW5 . . . . .204 C3
Malbank Rd CW2 . . . . .189 C2
Malbank Sch CW5 . . . . . . .204 B3
Malcolm Ave WA2 . . . . .8 B1
Malcolm Cres CH63 . . . . . .43 B3
Malcolm St WA7 . . . . .23 A1
Malgam Dr M20 . . . . .239 B8
Malhamdale Rd CW12 . . . .157 A2
Malin Cl L24 . . . . .21 B1
Maliston Rd WA5 . . . . .15 A3
Mall The Hyde SK14 . . . . .241 D6
Sale M33 . . . . .242 B7
Mallaig Cl CW4 . . . . .130 B1
Mallard Cl
Knutsford WA16 . . . . .57 A1
Runcorn WA7 . . . . .49 C3
Warrington WA2 . . . . .8 B2
Mallard Cres SK12 . . . . . . .36 A2
Mallard Ct Cheadle SK8 . . .34 B4
Chester CH2 . . . . .118 C4
Mallard Gn WA14 . . . . . . .238 B4
Mallard La WA3 . . . . .9 C2
Mallard Way Crewe CW1 . .191 A1
Winsford CW7 . . . . .149 B3
Mallards Reach SK6 . . . . .241 D2
Mallards The SK11 . . . . . .112 A4
Mallory Ct
Altrincham WA14 . . . . . . .238 C2
Congleton CW12 . . . . .155 C2
Mallory Rd CH65 . . . . .70 A2
Mallory Wlk CH4 . . . . . . .162 A4
Mallow Cl CH3 . . . . .142 A3
Mallow Wlk M31 . . . . .11 C1
Mallowdale Cl CH62 . . . . . .43 C3
Malmesbury Cl
Middlewich CW10 . . . . . . .128 A1
Poynton SK12 . . . . .36 B2
Malmesbury Pk WA7 . . . . .24 C1
Malmesbury Rd SK8 . . . . . .35 A3
Malory Cl CW1 . . . . .190 C2
Malpas Alport Prim Sch
SY14 . . . . .213 A2
Malpas Cl Handforth SK9 . . .34 C1
Northwich CW9 . . . . .104 B4
Malpas Dr WA5 . . . . .15 B2
Malpas Rd
Ellesmere Port CH65 . . . . .69 C2
Northwich CW9 . . . . .104 B4
Runcorn WA7 . . . . .49 B4
Malpas Way WA5 . . . . .15 B2
Malrae WA15 . . . . .238 E1
Malt Kiln Rd WA16 . . . . . . .80 C2
Malt Rd CH4 . . . . .95 A1
Malta Rd CH2 . . . . .237 A3
Maltmans Rd WA13 . . . . . .18 B2
Malton Ave WA3 . . . . .3 C4

Malton Cl WA8 ....12 B3
Malton Dr
  Altrincham WA14 ......238 A6
  Hazel Grove SK7 ....36 B4
Malton Rd SK4 ....240 A8
Malvern Ave CH65 .....70 B2
Malvern Cl
  Congleton CW12 ......155 C2
  Shavington CW2 .....206 A2
  Stockport SK4 ....240 D7
  Warrington WA5 ....15 A4
Malvern Dr
  Altrincham WA14 ......238 B5
  Macclesfield SK10 .....87 C2
Malvern Rd Blacon CH1 .118 A3
  Haydock WA9 ....1 A2
  Knutsford WA16 ....81 C4
Malvern Way CW7 ....149 A4
Manchester Airport Sta
  M90 ....33 A4
Manchester Bridge
  CW1 ....190 C4
Manchester International
  Airport M90 ....33 A4
Manchester Met Univ, Crewe
  & Alsager Faculty, (Alsager
  Campus) ST7 ....193 A3
Manchester Met Univ, Crewe
  & Alsager Faculty, (Crewe
  Campus) CW1 ....190 C2
Manchester New Rd M31 11 C2
Manchester Rd
  Altrincham WA14 ......238 D7
  Cheadle M20,SK8 ....239 D7
  Congleton CW12 ......156 C3
  Dukinfield SK14 ......241 C7
  Handforth SK9 ....34 B1
  Hollinfare WA3 ....11 A1
  Knutsford WA16 ....56 C2
  Macclesfield SK10 .....87 B2
  Northwich CW9 ....79 B1
  Partington M31 ....11 C2
  Stockport SK4 ....240 E8
  Warrington WA3 ....18 A4
  Warrington, Bruche WA1 .16 C4
Manchester Row WA12 ...7 B4
Mancroft Cl WA1 ......17 C4
Mandarin Dr WA14 ....238 B8
Manifold Cl CW11 ....174 C4
Manifold Dr SK6 ......37 C3
Manley Cl Antrobus CW9 .53 B2
  Holmes Chapel CW4 ..130 A2
  Northwich CW9 ....104 A3
Manley Gdns WA5 ......15 C3
Manley Gr SK7 ....35 C3
Manley La
  Dunham-on-t-H WA6 ...97 C3
  Manley WA6 ....98 B2
Manley Rd Frodsham WA6 .74 A2
  Manley WA6 ....98 C4
  Warren SK11 ....112 A3
Manley View CH2 ......72 B2
Manley Village Sch WA6 .99 A3
Manna Dr CH2 ....72 B2
Manners La CH60 ......40 C3
Manning La S CH2 ....119 A3
Manning St CW2 ......190 B1
Mannings La CH2 .....119 A3
Manor Ave Crewe CW2 .190 A1
  Golborne WA3 ....3 B4
  Goostrey CW4 ....107 C1
  Marston CW9 ....79 A3
  Newton-le-W WA12 .....1 C2
Manor CE Jun Sch The
  WA12 ....1 C2
Manor Cl Broughton CH5 .139 B4
  Cheadle SK8 ....35 B4
  Congleton CW12 ......157 A1
  Denton M34 ....241 B6
  Great Barrow CH3 ....120 C3
  Lymm WA13 ....18 C1
  Neston CH64 ....66 B4
  Warrington WA1 ....17 B4
  Wilmslow SK9 ....59 C4
Manor Cres
  Broughton CH4 ....139 B4
  Knutsford WA16 ....57 A1
  Macclesfield SK10 .....87 B2
  Middlewich CW10 ....151 B4
Manor Ct Crewe CW2 .190 A1
  Golborne WA3 ....3 B4
  Knutsford WA16 ....57 A1
Manor Dr Barnton CW8 ..78 A1
  Chester CH3 ....119 B1
  Northwich, Rudheath CW9 104 B4
Manor Farm Cl CH2 ..119 C4
Manor Farm Cres CH1 ..94 B4
Manor Farm Ct
  Broughton CH5 ....139 A4
  Frodsham WA6 ....49 B1
Manor Farm Rd WA7 ...24 B2
Manor Fell WA7 ....50 A4
Manor Fields CW10 ...151 B4
Manor Gdns SK9 ....60 B4
Manor Gr CW8 ....103 B3
Manor Ho Bebington CH62 43 B4
  Ellesmere Port CH66 ..69 B2
Manor House Prim Sch
  WA6 ....49 B1
Manor Ind Est WA4 ....16 C2
Manor La Broughton CH5 139 A4
  Davenham CW9 ....104 B1
  Ellesmere Port CH66 ..69 B2
  Holmes Chapel CW4 ..130 B2
  3 Middlewich CW10 ...151 B4

Manor La *continued*
  Ollerton WA16 ....82 C3
Manor Park Ave WA7 ...24 B2
Manor Park Dr CH66 ...69 B1
Manor Park N WA16 ....57 B1
Manor Park Rd CW12 .134 B1
Manor Park S WA16 ....57 B1
Manor Park Sch WA16 .57 B1
Manor Pk
  Great Barrow CH3 ....120 C3
  Hawarden CH4 ....139 A4
Manor Pl WA8 ....12 A1
Manor Rd
  Altrincham WA15 .....238 E4
  Bebington CH62 ....43 C3
  Chester CH4 ....141 A3
  Cuddington CW8 .....101 C1
  Denton M34 ....241 B6
  Frodsham WA6 ....49 B1
  Haydock WA11 ....1 C4
  Lymm WA13 ....18 C1
  Mow Cop ST7 ....195 B4
  Nantwich CW5 ....204 C3
  Runcorn WA7 ....23 B1
  Sale M33 ....242 B7
  Sandbach CW11 ......175 B3
  Sealand CH5 ....116 A3
  Thornton Hough CH63 .42 A4
  Whaley Bridge SK23 ...65 C3
  Widnes WA8 ....12 A1
  Wilmslow SK9 ....59 C4
Manor Rd N CW5 ......204 C4
Manor Sq CW7 ....149 A4
Manor St CW8 ....103 B3
Manor Way Crewe CW2 .190 B1
  Sandbach CW11 ......175 C3
Manora Rd WA9 ....104 A4
Manorfield Cl CH1 .....69 A1
Manorial Rd S CH64 ...66 B4
Manse Field Rd WA6 ...75 A1
Manse Gdns WA12 ......2 B1
Mansell Cl WA8 ....13 B3
Mansfield Cl WA3 .....10 A2
Mansfield Prim Sch
  CH65 ....69 C2
Mansfield Rd
  Ellesmere Port CH65 ..70 B1
  Hyde SK14 ....241 F5
Mansion Ct **18** CW5 .204 C3
Mansion Dr WA16 ......57 A1
Manston Rd WA5 ......14 C2
Manuel Perez Rd WA5 .15 A3
Manvers St SK5 ......240 E7
Manx St WA4 ....16 A2
Maori Dr WA6 ....74 A4
Maple Ave Alsager ST7 .193 C1
  Cheadle SK8 ....239 B4
  Disley SK12 ....39 A3
  Ellesmere Port CH66 ..69 B3
  Golborne WA3 ....3 C4
  Haydock WA11 ....1 A4
  Macclesfield SK11 ...112 B3
  Newcastle-u-L ST5 ...210 C1
  Newton-le-W WA12 .....2 B1
  Poynton SK12 ....36 C2
  Runcorn WA7 ....49 B4
  Sutton WA7 ....50 A2
  Talke ST7 ....210 B4
  Widnes WA8 ....13 A1
Maple Cl
  Brereton Green CW11 .153 C2
  Congleton CW12 ......155 C2
  Holmes Chapel CW4 ..130 B2
  Sandbach CW11 ......175 B3
Maple Cres WA5 ....14 C2
Maple Ct SK4 ....240 C8
Maple Gr Barnton CW8 ..78 A2
  Bebington CH62 ....43 B4
  Broughton CH4 ......140 B3
  Chester CH2 ....119 A2
  Crewe CW1 ....190 C4
  Ellesmere Port CH1 ...95 A4
  Northwich, Greenbank
    CW8 ....103 B3
  Warrington WA4 ....16 B2
  Winsford CW7 ....127 A1
Maple La CW8 ....101 C1
Maple Pl ST7 ....193 C4
Maple Rd
  Alderley Edge SK9 ....60 A2
  Bramhall SK7 ....35 C3
  Partington M31 ....11 C2
  Warrington WA1 ......17 C4
  Winwick WA2 ....8 A3
Maples SK9 ....59 C3
Maples The
  Mobberley WA16 ......58 C1
  Winsford CW7 ....127 A2
Mapleton Dr WA7 ......49 C2
Maplewood Gr CH1 ...117 A4
Maplewood Rd SK9 ....60 C4
Mapplewell Cres WA5 .15 A3
Marble Arch **4** WA16 ..57 A1
Marbury Gdns CH65 ...69 C3
Marbury La CW9 ....78 C3
Marbury Pk Ctry Pk★
  CW9 ....78 C3
Marbury Rd Chester CH3 119 B1
  Comberbach CW9 ......78 B3
  Handforth SK9 ....34 A1
Marbury St WA4 ....16 B2
March Ave SK4 ....240 B6
March St CW1 ....190 C2
Marchbank Dr SK8 ...239 C6
Marchwiel Rd CH65 ...70 B2
Marcien Way WA8 .....12 C2
Marcliff Gr
  Knutsford WA16 ......57 A1

Marcliff Gr *continued*
  Stockport SK4 ....240 B6
Marcross WA5 ....7 C1
Mardale Ave WA2 ......8 B2
Mardale Cl
  Congleton CW12 ......157 A3
  Stalybridge SK15 ....242 D3
Mardale Cres WA13 ...18 C2
Mardale Ct WA4 ......130 A1
Mardon Cl WA16 ......57 B2
Marfields Prim Sch
  CW12 ....156 B1
Marford CW10 ....103 C3
Marfords Ave CH63 ...43 B4
Margaret Ave WA1 ....17 A4
Margaret Ct WA8 ......23 A4
Margaret Rd M34 ....241 A8
Margaret's La CH66 ...69 A4
Margery Ave ST7 ....194 C4
Marian Ave WA12 ......1 C2
Marian Dr CH3 ....142 A4
Marian Rd WA11 ....1 C4
Marie Cl CW5 ....216 C2
Marie Dr WA1 ....17 B1
Marigold Cl SK11 ....111 C4
Marigold Way WA9 .....6 A4
Marina Ave Hyde M34 .241 A5
  Warrington WA5 ....15 A2
Marina Cl SK9 ....34 B3
Marina Dr Chester CH2 .118 C3
  Ellesmere Port CH65 ..70 A3
  Warrington WA2 ....8 B1
Marina Gr WA7 ....23 A1
Marina La WA7 ....50 C4
Marina Village WA7 ...50 C4
Marina Wlk CH5 ......70 A3
Marine Ave M31 ......11 B2
Marine Dr CH60 ....40 B3
Marine Flats CH3 ....142 C4
Mariner Cl WA7 ....50 B3
Marion Dr WA7 ....48 C3
Mark Ave CH66 ....69 B2
Mark Cl CH2 ....118 C1
Market Cl CW1 ....190 B3
Market Ct CW6 ....146 B1
Market Ctr The CW1 .190 B2
Market Gate WA1 .....16 A3
Market Pl Bollington SK10 .88 A4
  Hampton SY14 ....213 B4
  1 Hyde SK14 ....241 D6
  Macclesfield SK11 ...112 B4
  Stockport SK1 ......240 F6
  Winsford CW7 ....126 C1
Market Sq Chester CH1 .237 A2
  Congleton CW12 ......156 C3
  Crewe CW1 ....190 B2
  4 Sandbach CW11 ....175 A3
Market St
  Altrincham WA14 .....238 D4
  Congleton CW12 ......156 B1
  Crewe CW1 ....190 B2
  Crewe CW1 ....190 B3
  Disley SK12 ....38 B3
  Hyde SK14 ....241 D6
  Kidsgrove ST7 ....195 A1
  Nantwich CW5 ....204 C3
  New Mills SK22 ....39 A4
  Newton-le-W WA12 .....2 A2
  9 Northwich CW9 ....103 C4
  Stalybridge SK15 ....242 D2
  Whaley Bridge SK23 ...65 C3
  Widnes WA8 ....23 A4
Market Way **7** CW9 .103 C4
Market Wlk M33 .....242 B6
Markland St SK14 ....241 E5
Marl Croft CH3 ......142 A4
Marl Edge SK10 ....87 A3
Marl Heys CH2 ....118 C4
Marland Ave SK8 ....239 F2
Marlborough Ave
  Alderley Edge SK9 ....60 A1
  Winsford CW7 ....126 B2
Marlborough Cl
  Knutsford WA16 ......57 B2
  Macclesfield SK10 ....87 B2
  Wistaston CW2 ......205 C2
Marlborough Cres
  Warrington WA4 ......16 C1
  Widnes WA8 ....13 A3
Marlborough Ct
  1 Chester CH3 ......119 A1
  24 Macclesfield SK11 ..112 B4
Marlborough Dr
  Helsby WA6 ....73 A1
  Macclesfield SK10 ....87 B2
  Stockport SK4 ......240 D8
Marlborough Ho **7**
  SK11 ....111 C4
Marlborough Prim Sch The
  SK10 ....87 B2
Marlborough Rd
  Altrincham WA14 .....238 D2
  Ellesmere Port CH66 ..70 B2
  Sale M33 ....242 B6
Marlborough Wlk CH65 .70 B2
Marlcroft Ave SK4 ...240 B6
Marler Rd SK14 .....241 E8
Marleston Ct CH4 ....140 C1
Marley Ave CW1 .....190 A4
Marley Cl WA15 .....238 F7
Marley Dr M33 ......242 A8
Marley Rd SK12 ......36 C1
Marley Way CH4 .....140 C4
Marlfield Rd
  Altrincham WA15 .....32 B4
  Warrington WA4 ......17 A1

Marline Ave CH63 .....43 B3
Marling Cl WA6 ....74 B3
Marling Pk WA8 ....12 A1
Marloes WA14 ....238 B2
Marlow Ave CW12 ....118 C4
Marlow Cl Cheadle SK8 .239 F2
  9 Sandbach CW11 ....174 B3
  Warrington WA3 ....9 A3
Marlow Dr
  Altrincham WA14 .....20 C1
  Handforth SK9 ....34 B3
Marlowe Cl Blacon CH1 .118 A3
  Widnes WA8 ....12 C1
Marlowe Cl SK11 ....112 B3
Marlowe Dr CW5 .....204 C2
Marlowe Rd
  1 Neston CH64 ......66 C4
  Northwich CW9 ......104 B3
Marlston Ave CH4 ...141 A3
Marlston Pl WA7 ......49 A3
Maroon Rd M22 ....33 C4
Marple Cres CW2 ....189 C2
Marple Rd CW9 ......104 B4
Marquis Dr SK8 ......34 B4
Marrick Ave SK8 ....239 C5
Marriott Rd CW11 ...174 C2
Marriott St SK1 .....240 F4
Marron Ave WA2 ....8 A1
Marsden Ave WA4 ....17 A2
Marsden Ct WA8 ......12 C2
Marsden Rd SK6 ....241 C3
Marsden Terr **16** SK11 .112 B4
Marsh Cl Alsager ST7 .193 A2
  Stockport SK3 ......240 D2
Marsh Gr ST8 ....179 B3
Marsh Green Cl ST8 .179 B3
Marsh Green Rd
  Biddulph ST8 ....179 B1
  Sandbach CW11 .....174 C4
Marsh Hall Pad WA8 .13 A2
Marsh Hall Rd WA8 ..13 A2
Marsh House La WA1,
  WA2 ....16 B4
Marsh La Acton CW5 .204 A4
  Alsager ST7 ....193 A2
  Barton CH3,SY14 ....181 C2
  Churton CH3 ....181 A3
  Crowton SW4,WA6 ...101 A4
  Dutton WA4 ....51 C2
  Elton CH2 ....72 A2
  Elton CH2 ....72 B1
  Frodsham WA6 ....74 A4
  Holmes Chapel CW4 ..130 C1
  Mere WA14 ....30 C2
  Nantwich CW5 ....204 B3
  New Mills SK22,SK23 ..39 B3
  Ravensmoor CW5 ....203 C1
  Runcorn WA7 ....23 C2
  Warrington WA5 ......14 B1
Marsh Lane Trad Est
  SK22 ....39 B4
Marsh Rd WA4 ....27 A2
Marsh St Warrington WA1 .16 A2
  Widnes WA8 ....23 A3
Marshall Ave WA5 .....7 C1
Marshall Ct OL6 ....242 A2
Marshall Gr WA2 ....179 A4
Marshall La CW8 ....103 B3
Marshall Rd WA1 .....17 B4
Marshalls Ct CW8 ...103 B3
Marshfield Bank CW2 .189 B2
Marshfield La ST8 ..179 B1
Marshfield Rd CW2 .189 B2
Marshgate WA8 ....22 A3
Marshgate Pl WA6 ...49 B1
Marshlands Rd CH64 ..66 C3
Marshway Dr WA12 ....2 A3
Marsland Rd M33 ...242 B5
Marsland St SK1 ....240 F6
Marson St WA2 ....16 A3
Marston Cl CH62 .....43 C2
Marston Gdns CH65 ..69 C3
Marston La CW9 ......79 B3
Marten Ave CH63 .....43 B4
Martens Rd M44 ......11 C3
Marthall La
  Chelford SK10 ....83 A4
  Ollerton WA16 ....82 C3
Marthall Way **8** SK9 .34 C3
Martham Cl WA4 .....17 A2
Martin Ave
  Newton-le-W WA12 .....2 B3
  Warrington WA2 ....8 C1
Martin Cl Chester CH2 .118 B4
  Runcorn WA7 ....50 A4
Martin Rd Chester CH2 .118 B4
  Frodsham WA6 ....74 A4
Martin St SK14 .....241 E6
Martin's La CH3 ....143 C2
Martindale Gr WA7 ...49 B3
Martins Fields CW8 ..77 A3
Martins Hill CW12 ...157 B1
Martland Ave WA3 ....3 C4
Martlet Ave SK12 ....38 C2
Marton & District CE Prim
  Sch SK11 ....133 C2
Marton Cl
  Congleton CW12 ......156 C3
  Culcheth WA3 ....4 C2
  Hough Common CW2 .206 C2
  Macclesfield SK10 ....86 C1
Marton Gn SK3 ......240 D1
Marton Hall La SK11 .133 C2
Marton La
  Congleton SK11 .....134 A2
  Marton SK11 ....133 B4
  Warren SK11 ....111 A1

Marton Pl M33 ......242 A6
Marton Rd CH4 ......139 B2
Marton Way **5** SK9 ..34 C3
Marwood Cl WA14 ...238 B6
Mary Dendy Unit (Soss Moss)
  SK10 ....84 B3
Mary St Cheadle SK8 ..239 D6
  Crewe CW1 ....190 C3
  Dukinfield M34 .....241 A8
  Hyde SK14 ....241 D7
  Widnes WA8 ....23 B4
Maryfield Cl WA3 ......3 A4
Maryhill Cl ST7 .....195 A2
Maryhill High Sch ST7 195 A2
Maryhill Prim Sch ST7 195 A2
Maryhill Rd WA7 .....49 A4
Marys Gate CW2 ....205 B2
Masefield Ave WA8 ...22 C4
Masefield Dr Blacon CH1 117 C3
  Crewe CW1 ....190 C4
  Stockport SK4 ......240 A6
Maskery Pl CW12 ....156 B2
Mason Ave
  Warrington WA1 ......16 C4
  Widnes WA8 ....13 A2
Mason Cl CH66 ....69 B1
Mason St Chester CH2 .237 A3
  Runcorn WA7 ....23 B2
  Warrington WA1 ......16 B3
Mason's Row CW6 ...169 C1
Masons La SK10 ......87 C1
Massals Cl CH2 ......96 C1
Massey Ave
  Hartford CW8 ....103 A3
  Lymm WA13 ....18 A1
  Warrington WA5 ....7 C1
  Winsford CW7 ......126 C1
Massey Brook La WA13 .18 A1
Massey Hall Specl Sch
  WA4 ....17 C1
Massey Rd
  Altrincham WA15 .....238 E8
  Sale M33 ....242 E6
Massey St
  4 Alderley Edge SK9 ..60 A1
  17 Stockport SK4 ....240 F5
Masseyfield Rd WA7 ..50 A3
Massie St SK8 ......239 B4
Masters Ct WA16 .....56 C1
Mates La SY14 ......213 A3
Mather Ave Golborne WA3 ..3 C3
  Runcorn WA7 ....48 B4
Mather Cl CW10 .....151 B4
Mather Dr
  Comberbach CW9 ......78 B4
  Northwich CW9 ......104 B4
Mathers Cl WA2 ....9 A2
Mathieson Rd WA8 ...22 C3
Matlock Cl Sale M33 .242 C6
  Warrington WA5 ....15 A4
Matlock Dr SK7 ......36 C4
Matlock Mews WA14 .238 E5
Matlock Rd SK8 ......34 B4
Matterdale Cl WA6 ...74 B4
Matterdale Terr SK15 .242 D4
Matthew Cl CH2 .....118 C1
Matthews Pl CW12 ..157 A1
Matthews St WA1 .....16 B4
Matty's La WA6 ......74 A4
Mauldeth Cl SK4 ....240 A7
Mauldeth Rd SK4 ...240 A7
Mavor Ct CW1 ....190 A2
Maw Green Cl CW1 ..190 C4
Maw Green Rd CW1 .190 C4
Maw La CW1 ....191 B4
Mawdsley Ave WA1 ...17 C4
Mawdsley Cl ST7 ....193 A2
Mawson Cl WA5 ....15 A4
Maxfield Cl SK11 ....111 C4
Maxwell Cl CH65 .....70 A1
Maxwell Rd CW12 ...179 A4
Maxwell St Crewe CW2 .190 B2
  Warrington WA3 ....9 C3
May Ave Bramhall SK8 ..35 A3
  Stockport SK4 ......240 C6
May Rd Bramhall SK8 .35 A3
  Heswall CH60 ....41 A4
May Wlk **3** M31 ......11 C2
Mayberry Gr WA2 .....9 A1
Maybrook Pl WA4 ....16 C2
Maydews Pas **22** SK11 .112 B4
Maydor Ave CH4 ....140 B4
Mayfair Cl Poynton SK12 ..36 C2
  Warrington WA5 ......14 B4
Mayfair Dr CW9 .....103 C2
Mayfair Gr WA8 ......12 B1
Mayfield Ave
  Macclesfield SK11 ...112 B3
  Sale M33 ....242 E6
  Widnes WA8 ....12 A1
Mayfield Cl CW4 ....130 B2
Mayfield Ct WA8 .....13 A1
Mayfield Dr
  Bebington CH62 ......44 A3
  Cuddington CW8 .....102 A2
  Golborne WA3,WN7 ....4 B3
Mayfield Gdns CH64 ..41 C1
Mayfield Gr
  Cuddington CW8 .....102 A2
  Wilmslow SK9 ....59 C3
Mayfield Mews CW1 .189 C4
Mayfield Rd Blacon CH1 117 B3
  Bramhall SK7 ....35 C2
  Mobberley WA16 .....57 C2
  Northwich CW9 ......104 B4
  Warrington WA1 ......17 A1
Mayfield Terr SK11 .112 B4
Mayfield View WA13 .18 C1

Mayflower Rd CW5 204 C2
Mayor's Rd WA15 238 E4
Maythorn Ave WA3 9 A4
Maytree Ave CH3 119 A1
Maywood Ave M20 239 B8
Mc Clellan Pl WA8 13 A1
McCarthy Cl WA3 10 A2
McGarva Way CH65 70 B2
Mcgowan Ho ST7 210 B4
McKee Ave WA2 8 A1
Mckellin Cl ST7 209 C1
McLaren St CW1 190 B4
McMinnis Ave WA9 1 A1
McNeill Ave CW1 190 A3
Mead Ave ST7 194 C4
Mead Cl WA16 56 C1
Mead Rd WA1 17 A4
Meade The SK9 60 B4
Meadow Ave
Congleton CW12 156 B1
Goostrey CW4 107 B1
Warrington WA4 16 A1
Weston CW2 207 A3
Meadow Bank
Adderley TF9 235 A2
Kelsall CW6 122 B2
Stockport SK4 240 B6
Meadow Brow SK9 60 A1
Meadow Cl
Cuddington CW8 102 A2
Goostrey CW4 107 C1
Helsby WA6 73 A2
High Lane SK6 37 C4
Neston CH64 66 C3
Newton-le-W WA12 1 C2
Shavington CW2 206 B3
Tarvin CH3 121 A1
Whaley Bridge SK23 65 B4
Widnes WA8 12 B2
Willaston CH64 67 C4
Wilmslow SK9 59 C2
Winsford CW7 126 B2
Meadow Croft
Alsager ST7 193 C1
Willaston CH64 67 C4
Meadow Ct
Mollington CH1 94 C1
No Man's Heath SY14 214 A2
Packmoor ST7 195 C1
Meadow Dr Barnton CW8 78 A2
Knutsford WA16 81 C4
Prestbury SK10 87 A4
Wistaston CW2 205 C4
Meadow Field Rd CH4 141 A3
Meadow Gate CW9 79 C3
Meadow Gr
Northwich CW9 104 A3
Winsford CW7 126 C3
Meadow Home Pk CW7 126 B3
Meadow Ind Est SK5 240 F7
Meadow La
Comberbach CW9 78 B4
Disley SK12 38 B3
Ellesmere Port CH65 70 B3
Huntington CH3 142 A3
Moulton CW9 126 C4
Warrington WA2 9 A1
Willaston CH64 67 C4
Meadow Lane Ind Est
CH65 70 B3
Meadow Prim Sch CH66 69 C1
Meadow Rd
Broughton CH4 139 B2
Weaverham CW8 102 C4
Meadow Rise
Clutton CH3 182 B1
Winsford CW7 126 A1
Meadow Row WA7 24 A1
Meadow St Hyde SK14 241 E5
New Mills SK22 39 B4
3 Northwich CW9 104 A4
Meadow The CW4 130 B4
Meadow View Elton CH2 72 A2
Lymm WA13 18 B2
Middlewich CW10 128 A1
Sealand CH5 116 A3
Meadow View Dr WA6 74 A4
Meadow Way
Lawton-gate ST7 194 A3
Macclesfield SK10 87 C1
Wilmslow SK9 59 C2
Meadow Wlk 3 M31 11 C2
Meadowbank Gdns WA3 5 B4
Meadowcroft
Higher Kinnerton CH4 161 A4
Saughall CH1 94 A1
Meadowfield
Tarporley CW6 146 B1
Whaley Bridge SK23 65 B4
Meadowfield Ct SK14 241 D8
Meadowgate Cl CW11 174 B3
Meadowgate Farm WA6 49 C1
Meadows La
Chester CH4 237 C1
Saughall CH1 117 A4
Meadows Pl CH4 141 C4
Meadows Rd Cheadle SK8 34 C4
Gatley SK8 239 B1
Kidsgrove ST7 194 C1
Sale M33 242 C8
Meadows The
Ashton CH3 121 C4
Congleton CW12 156 C2
Irlam M44 11 C3
Neston CH64 66 C3
Romiley SK6 241 B4
Meadowside
Adlington SK10 63 A4
Meadowside *continued*
Disley SK12 39 A3
Northwich CW8 103 B4
Whaley Bridge SK23 65 B4
Meadowside Ave ST7 209 B1
Meadowside La ST7 195 A4
Meadowside Mews CH1 118 A2
Meadowside Rd CH62 43 B4
Meadowsway CH2 118 B4
Meadowsweet Rd WA16 57 C2
Meadowvale Cl CW5 204 C4
Meads Rd ST7 193 B2
Meadscroft Dr SK9 59 C1
Meadway Bramhall SK7 35 C3
Ellesmere Port CH66 69 A4
Golborne WA3 3 B4
Heswall CH60 40 C3
High Lane SK6 37 C4
Poynton SK12 36 A2
Prestbury SK10 87 A3
Runcorn WA7 49 C4
Widnes WA8 12 A1
Meakin Cl CW12 157 A1
Meal St New Mills SK22 39 B4
Stockport SK4 240 E7
Mealhouse Brow 2
SK1 240 F5
Meddings Cl SK9 85 A4
Medina Ave CW7 126 C1
Medina Way ST7 195 A1
Medlar Cl CH4 140 C3
Medway Cl Golborne WN7 4 B4
Handforth SK9 34 B1
Warrington WA2 8 C1
Medway Cres WA14 238 C6
Medway Dr ST8 179 B1
Medway Rd WA3 5 A1
Mee St SK11 112 C3
Meeanee Dr CW5 204 B2
Meerbrook Rd SK3 240 A4
Meeting House La WA6 74 C1
Meeting La WA5 14 C3
Meg La Antrobus CW9 53 A2
Macclesfield SK11 111 C4
Sutton Lane Ends SK11 113 B1
Megacre ST7 210 A1
Melbourne Ave M90 33 A4
Melbourne Gr CW1 191 B3
Melbourne Rd
Blacon CH1 117 B2
Bramhall SK7 35 C3
Melbourne St SK15 242 D1
Melbury Ct WA3 9 C3
Melbury Rd SK8 35 A3
Melchett Cres CW9 104 B4
Melford Cl CW2 206 B4
Melford Ct WA1 17 B4
Melford Dr
Macclesfield SK10 87 B1
Runcorn WA7 23 A1
Meliden Gr WA6 73 A1
Melkridge Cl CH2 119 A2
Melksham Cl SK11 112 A4
Mellard St ST7 209 B1
Mellington Ave M20 239 C8
Mellock Cl CH64 66 C3
Mellock La CH64 66 C3
Mellor Cl Runcorn WA7 24 B1
Stalybridge OL6 242 B2
Mellor Cres WA16 56 C1
Mellor Rd OL6 242 B3
Mellor St Crewe CW1 190 B3
Packmoor ST7 195 C1
Mellors Bank ST7 195 B3
Melrose Ave
Burtonwood WA5 6 C4
Cheadle SK3 239 F7
Chester CH3 119 A1
Sale M33 242 B6
Warrington WA4 26 B4
Melrose Cres SK12 37 B3
Melrose Ct 15 SK9 34 C1
Melrose Dr Crewe CW1 190 A4
Ellesmere Port CH66 94 C4
Melton Ave WA4 26 A4
Melton Cl CW12 155 C2
Melton Dr CW12 155 C2
Melton Rd WA7 49 B4
Melton St SK5 240 F8
Melverly Dr CH1 117 B2
Melville Cl
Warrington WA2 16 A4
Widnes WA8 13 B1
Melville Rd M44 11 B3
Menai Gr SK8 240 A2
Menai Rd SK3 240 E2
Mendell Cl CH62 43 C4
Mendell Prim Sch CH62 43 C4
Mendip Ave WA2 8 A2
Mendip Cl
Ellesmere Port CH66 69 C2
Gatley SK8 34 A4
Stockport SK4 240 E7
Mendip Ct SK4 240 E7
Menin Ave WA4 16 B2
Menlow Cl WA4 17 B1
Mentmore Gdns WA4 26 C3
Mentone Rd SK4 240 C7
Meols Cl
Ellesmere Port CH66 69 C2
Hale L24 21 C1
Mercer Cl SY14 213 A2
Mercer Rd WA11 1 B3
Mercer St Burtonwood WA5 6 C3
Newton-le-W WA12 2 B2
Mercer Way Chester CH4 140 C3
Nantwich CW5 204 C4
Mercer Wlk CH65 70 B2
Mercian Cl CW2 206 A2
Mercian Way SK3 240 E3
Mercury Ct CH1 117 C1
Mere Ave CH63 43 A3
Mere Bank CW9 127 A4
Mere Brook Wlk CW2 190 B1
Mere Cl
Ellesmere Port CH66 69 B1
Haslington CW1 191 B2
Pickmere WA16 80 A4
Sale M33 242 F5
Mere Cres CW8 123 C3
Mere Ct Alsager ST7 193 B2
Chelford SK11 83 C2
5 Knutsford WA16 57 A1
Mere Home Farm WA16 56 A4
Mere La Cuddington CW8 102 A1
Pickmere WA16 79 C4
Mere Rd Marston CW9 79 A3
Newton-le-W WA12 2 C2
Warrington WA2 9 A1
Weston CW2 207 A3
Mere Side SK15 242 C4
Mere St CW1 191 B2
Mere View Gdns WA4 26 C3
Merebank Rd CW2 190 A1
Merebrook Rd SK11 111 C4
Merecroft 3 CH3 119 A1
Meredith Ave WA4 17 A1
Meredith St CW1 190 B3
Merehaven Cl WA16 80 A4
Mereheath La WA16 56 C3
Mereheath Pk WA16 56 C2
Merelake Rd ST7 210 A4
Meremore Dr ST5 210 B1
Mereside Ave CW12 156 A2
Mereside Cl Cheadle SK8 239 F4
Macclesfield SK10 87 A1
Mereside Rd WA16 30 B1
Merevale Cl WA7 49 C3
Merewood Cl WA2 8 B2
Mereworth Dr CW9 103 C3
Merganser Cl CW1 189 C4
Meriton Rd SK9 34 B2
Merlin Ave WA16 57 A2
Merlin Cl Runcorn WA7 24 A1
Winsford CW7 150 A4
Merlin Way Crewe CW1 190 A4
Kidsgrove ST7 195 B2
Merlyn Ave M33 242 C8
Merrick Cl WA2 8 C2
Merridale The WA15 32 A4
Merriden Rd SK10 87 A1
Merrill's Ave CW2 189 C3
Merriman Ave WA16 57 B2
Merrivale Rd CW2 206 A4
Merrydale Cl SK10 86 C1
Merryman's La SK9 84 A4
Mersey Pl CW7 127 A1
Mersey Rd Runcorn WA7 23 A2
Sale M33 242 B8
Mersey Sq SK1 240 E5
Mersey St Runcorn WA7 23 A2
St Helens WA9 1 A2
Warrington WA1 16 A3
Mersey Vale Prim Sch
SK4 240 A5
Mersey Valley Visitor Ctr★
M33 242 F7
Mersey View WA7 48 B4
Mersey View Rd WA8 22 A2
Mersey Wlk WA4 16 C3
Merseyton Rd CH65 70 B4
Merseyton Road Workshops
CH65 70 B4
Merseyway SK1 240 F6
Mersham Ct WA8 12 C2
Merston Dr M20 239 C8
Merton Ave
Hazel Grove SK7 36 C4
Romiley SK6 241 A4
Merton Cl CH64 66 C3
Merton Dr CH4 141 A2
Merton House Sch CH2 118 B2
Merton House Sch
(Downswood) CH2 237 A4
Merton Rd
Bebington CH65 44 A2
Ellesmere Port CH66 69 C2
Sale M33 242 A8
5 Stockport SK3 240 B4
Mertoun Rd WA4 16 A1
Mervyn Rd CW8 77 C1
Merwood Ave SK8 34 B4
Messuage La CW12 132 C2
Meteor Cres WA2 8 B1
Metron Rd SK12 36 A2
Mevagissey Rd WA7 50 B3
Mevril Rd SK23 65 C3
Mews The Barnton CW8 78 A1
Gatley SK8 239 B5
Sale M33 242 C5
Tarporley CW6 168 B4
Wilmslow SK9 33 B2
Meyer St SK3 240 F2
Meynell Cl CW2 190 A1
Meynell Pl CH1 118 A3
Meyrick Ct WA12 2 A2
Micawber Rd SK12 36 C1
Mickle Trafford Village Sch
CH2 119 C4
Micklegate WA7 50 B4
Micklewright Ave CW1 190 B3
Mickley Hall La CW5 218 A2
Mid Cheshire Coll (London
Road Studios) CW9 103 C3
Mid Cheshire Coll (Verdin
Ctr) CW7 126 B1
Mid-Cheshire Coll (Hartford
Campus) CW8 103 B3
Middle Hillgate SK1 240 F4
Middle La Aldford CH3 163 C2
Congleton CW12 157 B2
Kingsley WA6 74 C1
Middle Wlk
Frodsham WA6 74 A4
Knutsford WA16 57 A1
Middlecroft CH3 119 C3
Middlehills SK11 113 A3
Middlehurst Ave CW8 102 C4
Middlehurst Rd WA4 17 A1
Middlewich High Sch
CW10 151 B4
Middlewich Prim Sch
CW10 151 A4
Middlewich Rd
Allostock WA16 106 B3
Church Minshull CW1,
CW10 172 C3
Cranage CW10 129 C3
Crewe CW1,CW2 189 B2
Holmes Chapel CW4 130 A2
Lower Peover WA16 81 C1
Nantwich CW5 204 C4
Northwich CW9 104 B4
Ollerton WA16 82 A2
Sandbach CW11 174 C4
Winsford CW7,CW10 127 C1
Middlewich Road Ind Est
CW10 129 A3
Middlewich St CW1 190 B3
Middlewood WA3 3 C4
Middlewood Dr SK4 240 A5
Middlewood Rd
High Lane SK6 37 B4
Poynton SK12 37 A2
Middlewood Sta SK6 37 B3
Middlewood View SK6 37 B4
Midfield Cl ST8 179 B1
Midgley Cres OL6 242 B4
Midhurst Cl SK8 34 C4
Midland St WA8 13 A1
Midland Terr SK22 39 B4
Midland Way WA1,WA5 16 A3
Midlothian Ho CH2 237 C3
Midpoint 18 Motorway Ind
Est CW10 128 C1
Midway SK8 35 A3
Milborne Cl CH2 118 C3
Mile Bank Rd SY13 226 B2
Miles Cl WA3 9 C2
Miles St SK14 241 F6
Milk St Congleton CW12 156 B2
Hyde SK14 241 D6
Mill Ave WA5 14 C4
Mill Bank CH64 67 A3
Mill Bridge Cl CW1 190 C2
Mill Brow WA8 13 B1
Mill Cl Chester CH2 118 B3
Culcheth WA3 4 C2
Knutsford WA16 57 B2
Warrington WA2 8 C2
Mill Cotts SK10 88 A4
Mill Ct CH65 69 C3
Mill Farm Cl WA2 8 C2
Mill Farm Est CW5 217 A2
Mill Field Cl CH3 180 C1
Mill Gn Congleton CW12 156 B2
Willaston CH64 67 C4
Mill Gr Bulkeley SY14 184 C1
Kidsgrove ST7 194 B1
Mill Green La WA8 13 C3
Mill Green Specl Sch
WA12 2 C2
Mill Hill Ave SK12 36 B4
Mill Hill Dr CW11 175 A2
Mill Hill Hollow SK12 36 B4
Mill Hill La CW11 175 A2
Mill La Adlington SK10 62 A3
Altrincham WA15 32 C2
Audlem, Little Heath CW3 230 A2
Audlem, Swanbach CW3 229 C1
Barthomley CW2 208 B4
Blakenhall CW5 221 A2
Bold Heath WA8 13 B3
Brereton Green CW4 153 C4
Burton CH64 67 B1
Cheadle SK8 239 D6
Chester CH2 118 B3
Congleton CW12 179 B4
Cronton WA8 12 B3
Cuddington CW8 101 C3
Denton M34,SK14 241 B6
Duddon CW6 145 A4
Eaton CW6 147 A1
Ellesmere Port CH66 69 C3
Frodsham WA6 49 C1
Goostrey CW4 107 C1
Great Barrow CH3 120 C3
Hazel Grove SK7 36 C4
Heswall CH60 41 A4
Higher Walton WA4 25 C4
Huxley CH3 144 B1
Kelsall CW6 122 B1
Kingsley WA6 75 C2
Lindow End SK9 84 A4
Little Budworth CW6 125 A1
Lymm WA13 19 B2
Macclesfield SK11 112 B4
Marton CW12 132 C1
Middlewich CW10 128 A1
Middlewich CW10 128 B1
Mobberley WA16 58 A2
Mottram St Andrew SK10 61 B3
Neston CH64 67 B3
Newton-le-W WA12 2 C2
Mill La *continued*
Peover WA16,SK11 108 B4
Prestbury SK10 61 C3
Sandbach CW11 174 B4
Siddington SK11 109 C3
Smallwood CW11 175 A1
Tarvin CH3 121 B2
The Bank ST7 195 A4
Warrington WA2 7 C2
Warrington, Stockton Heath
WA4 16 C1
Weston CW2 207 A3
Whitegate CW7 126 A3
Willaston CH64 42 C1
Mill Lane Cotts CH3 120 C3
Mill Mdw WA12 2 C2
Mill Park Dr CH62 43 C2
Mill Pool La CW5 187 B3
Mill Rd Macclesfield SK11 112 B3
Wilmslow SK9 60 A4
Mill Rise ST7 195 A1
Mill Row CW11 175 B3
Mill St Altrincham WA14 238 E5
Chester CH4 237 B1
Congleton CW12 156 B2
Congleton, Buglawton
CW12 156 C2
Crewe CW2 190 B2
Golborne WA3 3 A4
Macclesfield SK11 112 B4
Neston CH64 66 B4
Stalybridge SK15 242 F1
Warrington WA1 16 A3
Wilmslow SK9 60 A4
Mill St Mall 31 SK11 112 B4
Mill Stream Cl CW4 107 C1
Mill View Cl SY14 184 C1
Mill View Prim Sch
CH2 118 C3
Mill Way CW5 204 C1
Mill Wharf CH3 143 A3
Millar Cres WA8 23 A4
Millbank WA13 18 C2
Millbank Cl SK11 84 A2
Millbank Ct WA6 74 A4
Millbank Dr SK10 86 C1
Millbeck Cl CW2 207 A3
Millbridge Gdns WA12 2 C2
Millbrook Cl Glazebury WA3 5 B3
Winsford CW7 148 C4
Millbrook End CH3 166 A1
Millbrook Fold SK7 36 C4
Millbrook Gr 10 SK9 34 B1
Millbrook St SK1 240 F4
Millbuck Way CW11 174 B3
Milldale Rd WN7 4 A4
Millend La ST7 209 B3
Millenium Ct CH64 41 C1
Millenium Way ST5 210 C1
Miller St WA4 16 B2
Millers Croft SK11 112 B4
Millers La Lymm WA13 19 A3
Waverton CH3 143 A2
Millers Mdw SK10 88 C3
Millers View ST7 195 A1
Millers Wharf ST7 193 C4
Millersdale Cl CH62 43 C3
Millersdale Gr WA7 49 B3
Milley La WA16 80 B4
Millfield Bsns Ctr WA11 1 C4
Millfield Ct WA15 238 F2
Millfield La Haydock WA11 1 C4
Saighton CH3 142 C1
Tarporley CW6 146 B1
Millfield Rd WA8 13 B1
Millfield Terr CH66 69 B4
Millfields CW5 204 B2
Millfields Prim Sch
Bebington CH62 43 C2
Nantwich CW5 204 B3
Millgate Cuddington CW8 101 C2
Stockport SK1 240 F6
Millgate La M20 239 A8
Millhouse Ave WA4 16 B1
Millhouse La Croft WA3 9 A3
Warrington WA3 9 A3
Milling Field The CW4 130 B1
Millingford Ind Est WA3 3 A4
Millington Cl
Runcorn WA7 49 C2
Widnes WA8 22 C4
Millington Hall La WA14 30 A3
Millington La
Rostherne WA14 30 A3
Weaverham CW8 102 A3
Millmead ST7 193 C4
Millom Pl SK8 239 B3
Millrace Dr CW2 206 A4
Mills Way CW1 173 A1
Millstone Ave ST7 194 C1
Millstone Cl SK12 36 C3
Millstone La CW5 204 C3
Millstone Pas SK11 112 C3
Millway Altrincham WA15 32 B4
Waverton CH3 143 A3
Millway Rd L24 21 A2
Millwood WA7 24 B1
Millwood Cl 4 SK8 34 C4
Millwood Ct L24 21 A2
Millwood Cty Prim Sch
L24 21 A2
Millwood Terr 2 SK14 241 D6
Milne Cl CW2 189 C1
Milner Ave WA14 238 B7
Milner Cop CH60 41 A4

Milner Rd Heswall CH60 . . . . .41 A4
Northwich CW8 . . . . .103 B3
Milner St WA5 . . . . .15 C3
Milnthorpe Rd WA5 . . . . .6 C3
Milton Ave Irlam M44 . . . . . . .11 C3
Newton-le-W WA12 . . . . .2 A2
Widnes WA8 . . . . .22 C4
Milton Cl
Higher Wincham CW9 . . . . . .80 A3
Middlewich CW10 . . . . .151 B3
Milton Cres Cheadle SK8 239 C5
Talke ST7 . . . . .210 B4
Milton Ct SK7 . . . . .35 C3
Milton Dr Poynton SK12 . . . .36 B2
Sale M33 . . . . .242 B8
Wistaston CW2 . . . . .206 A4
Milton Gr Helsby WA6 . . . . . .73 A1
Sale M33 . . . . .242 A8
Warrington WA4 . . . . .16 B2
Milton Rd Blacon CH1 . . . . .117 C3
Bramhall SK7 . . . . .35 C4
Ellesmere Port CH65 . . . . . .70 B2
Golborne WA3 . . . . .3 B4
Widnes WA8 . . . . .23 A4
Milton Rough CW8 . . . . .76 C1
Milton St Chester CH2 . . . . .237 B1
Hyde SK14 . . . . .241 D8
Widnes WA8 . . . . .23 A4
Milton Way CW11 . . . . .174 B3
Milvain Dr WA2 . . . . .8 B1
Milverton Dr SK7,SK8 . . . . . .35 A3
Mine Way WA11 . . . . .1 C4
Miners Way Speke L24 . . . . .21 A4
Widnes WA8 . . . . .23 A4
Minerva Ave CH1 . . . . .117 C1
Minerva Ct WA4 . . . . .16 B1
Minerva Ct CH1 . . . . .117 C1
Minister Cl CW7 . . . . .149 B3
Minn-End-La SK11 . . . . .159 A3
Minor Ave SK11 . . . . .112 B2
Minshull La CW5,CW7 . . . . .171 B2
Minshull New Rd CW1 . . . . .189 C4
Minshull St WA16 . . . . .57 A1
Minster Ct Runcorn WA7 . . . .48 C4
Wistaston CW2 . . . . .205 C4
Minster Dr
Altrincham WA14 . . . . .31 A4
Stockport SK8 . . . . .240 A1
Minton Cl CW12 . . . . .157 A1
Minton Way WA8 . . . . .13 A3
Mirfield Ave SK4 . . . . .240 B6
Mirfield Cl WA3 . . . . .3 B4
Mirion St CW1 . . . . .190 B2
Misty Cl WA8 . . . . .12 B1
Mitchell Ave
Burtonwood WA5 . . . . .6 C3
Kidsgrove ST7 . . . . .194 B1
Mitchell Dr ST7 . . . . .194 B1
Warrington WA4 . . . . .26 B4
Mitchell St Golborne WA3 . . .3 A4
Warrington WA4 . . . . .26 B4
Mithril Cl WA8 . . . . .13 C2
Mitton Cl WA3 . . . . .4 C3
Moadlock SK6 . . . . .241 C4
Moat La Audley ST7 . . . . . . .209 A2
Hollins Green WA3 . . . . . . .10 C1
Mobberley CE Prim Sch
WA16 . . . . .58 B3
Mobberley Cl WA4 . . . . .17 B2
Mobberley Rd
Ashley WA14,WA15,WA16 . .31 C2
Knutsford WA16 . . . . .57 B2
Wilmslow SK9 . . . . .33 B1
Mobberley Sta WA16 . . . . . .57 C4
Moelfre Dr SK8 . . . . .35 B4
Moggie La SK10 . . . . .36 C3
Mold Rd CH4 . . . . .139 A2
Mollington Ct CH1 . . . . .94 C1
Mollington Rd M22 . . . . .33 A3
Molly Pitcher Way WA5 . . . .15 A3
Molly Potts Cl WA16 . . . . . . .82 A4
Molyneux Ave WA5 . . . . .15 C4
Mona Ave SK8 . . . . .239 D1
Mona St SK14 . . . . .241 E6
Monarch Cl Crewe CW2 . . . .189 C2
Irlam M44 . . . . .11 C3
Monarch Dr CW9 . . . . .103 C3
Mond Rd WA8 . . . . .23 A4
Mond St CW8 . . . . .78 A2
Money Ash Rd WA15 . . . . . .238 E3
Monica Dr WA8 . . . . .13 A3
Monk St CW1 . . . . .190 A3
Monk's La CW3 . . . . .230 B3
Monks Coppenhall Prim Sch
CW1 . . . . .190 C4
Monks Gr CH65 . . . . .70 A3
Monks La Acton CW5 . . . . . .203 C4
Crewe CW1 . . . . .189 C3
Nantwich CW5 . . . . .204 C3
Monks St WA5 . . . . .15 C3
Monks Way CW8 . . . . .103 C3
Monksheath Hall Wrkshps
SK10 . . . . .85 A1
Monkswood Cl WA5 . . . . .7 C1
Monmouth Cl WA1 . . . . .17 A4
Monroe Cl WA1 . . . . .17 A4
Monsall Cl SK11 . . . . .112 C4
Monsall Dr SK11 . . . . .112 C4
Montague Ho SK3 . . . . .240 D4
Montague Rd
Ashton-u-Lyne OL6 . . . . . . .242 A3
Sale M33 . . . . .242 B6
Montague Way WA15 . . . . . .242 D2
Montclare Cres WA4 . . . . . . .16 C1
Montcliffe Cl WA3 . . . . .9 B3

Montgomery Cl WA16 . . .57 B2
Montgomery Rd WA8 . . . .22 B4
Montgomery Way CW7 .149 A4
Montmorency Rd WA16 . .57 B2
Montpelier Ave WA7 . . . .48 C3
Montrose Cl
Macclesfield SK10 . . . . .87 A1
Shavington CW2 . . . . .206 A3
Warrington WA2 . . . . .8 C2
Montrose Ct
Chester CH4 . . . . .140 C4
Holmes Chapel CW4 . . . . . .130 A1
Monument Rd ST7 . . . . .210 B3
Monument View ST7 . . . . . .209 C1
Moody St CW12 . . . . .156 B1
Moon St WA8 . . . . .23 A4
Moor Cl ST8 . . . . .179 C1
Moor Cres CH4 . . . . .139 B1
Moor La Elton WA6 . . . . .72 C1
Frodsham WA6 . . . . .74 A4
Hawarden CH5 . . . . .116 A1
Heswall CH60 . . . . .40 C4
Higher Kinnerton CH4 . . . . .161 B4
Higher Kinnerton, Kinnerton Green
CH4 . . . . .161 B3
Waverton CH3 . . . . .143 A3
Widnes WA8 . . . . .22 A4
Widnes WA8 . . . . .23 A4
Wilmslow SK9 . . . . .59 C3
Woodford SK7 . . . . .35 C2
Moor La S SK4 . . . . .22 C4
Moor Lodge SK4 . . . . .240 B8
Moor Nook M33 . . . . .242 D5
Moor Park Rd M20 . . . . .239 C8
Moor Park Way CW9 . . . . . .103 C2
Moor Platt M33 . . . . .242 D5
Moor St CW12 . . . . .156 C1
Moor Top Pl SK4 . . . . .240 B7
Moorcroft WA16 . . . . .80 C2
Moorcroft Ave CH3 . . . . .119 A1
Moorcroft Cres CH3 . . . . . . .119 B2
Moorcroft Mews CH4 . . . . . .140 B3
Moordale Rd WA16 . . . . .57 A1
Moorditch La WA6 . . . . .48 B1
Moore Ave St Helens WA9 . . .1 C4
Warrington WA4 . . . . .17 B2
Moore Cl WA8 . . . . .13 B1
Moore Dr WA11 . . . . .1 C3
Moore Gr WA13 . . . . .19 A3
Moore La WA4 . . . . .25 B3
Moore Prim Sch WA4 . . . . . .25 A3
Moorfield Ave M34 . . . . .241 A6
Moorfield Cres WA3 . . . . .4 A4
Moorfield Dr Neston CH64 41 B1
Wilmslow SK9 . . . . .59 C3
Moorfield Gr Sale M33 . . . . .242 D5
Stockport SK4 . . . . .240 B8
Moorfield Prim Sch WA8 13 B2
Moorfield Rd WA8 . . . . .13 B2
Moorfields
Willaston (nr Nantwich)
CW5 . . . . .205 C3
Wistaston CW5 . . . . .205 C3
Moorhead La CW11 . . . . . . .154 B2
Moorhill Rd SK11 . . . . .112 B2
Moorhouse Ave ST7 . . . . . .193 C2
Moorhouse Cl CH2 . . . . .118 B3
Mooring Cl WA7 . . . . .50 B3
Moorings CW12 . . . . .156 C1
Moorings Cl CH64 . . . . .41 A1
Moorings The
Christleton CH3 . . . . .142 C4
Disley SK12 . . . . .38 C3
Heswall CH60 . . . . .40 B4
Middlewich CW10 . . . . .128 B1
Moorland Ave M33 . . . . .242 C5
Moorland Cl CH60 . . . . .41 A4
Moorland Dr Cheadle SK8 .34 C4
Runcorn WA7 . . . . .50 C4
Moorland Pk CH60 . . . . .41 A4
Moorland Rd
Biddulph ST8 . . . . .179 B1
Ellesmere Port CH66 . . . . . .69 C4
Kidsgrove ST7 . . . . .195 B4
Moorlands Ave CW8 . . . . . . .102 A2
Moorlands Cl SK10 . . . . .87 B2
Moorlands Dr CW5 . . . . .206 A1
Moorlands Jun Sch
M33 . . . . .242 E7
Moorlands Pk CW8 . . . . .102 A2
Moors La CW7 . . . . .149 B3
Moorsbrook Gr [9] SK9 . . . . .34 C1
Moorsfield Ave CW3 . . . . . . .229 C2
Moorside WA16 . . . . .57 A1
Moorside Ave CH64 . . . . .66 B4
Moorside Ct
Dukinfield M34 . . . . .241 A8
Sale M33 . . . . .242 B6
Widnes WA8 . . . . .22 C4
Moorside La Hyde M34 . . . . .241 A8
Neston CH64 . . . . .66 B4
Pott Shrigley SK10 . . . . .63 C2
Moorside Rd SK4 . . . . .240 A6
Moorson Ave ST7 . . . . .194 C4
Moorview Gdns ST7 . . . . . . .195 C3
Moorway CH60 . . . . .41 A4
Moran Cl SK9 . . . . .34 C1
Moran Cres SK11 . . . . .112 A4
Moran Rd SK11 . . . . .112 A4
Morcott La L24 . . . . .21 B1
Moresby Cl WA7 . . . . .50 C4
Moresby Dr M20 . . . . .239 B8
Moreton Ave SK7 . . . . .35 C3
Moreton Dr Alsager ST7 . . . .193 B2
Handforth SK9 . . . . .34 C2
Holmes Chapel CW4 . . . . . .130 A2
Poynton SK12 . . . . .36 C2
Sandbach CW11 . . . . .175 B4

Moreton Ho WA14 . . . . .238 B4
Moreton Rd CW2 . . . . . .189 C2
Moreton St 78 B1
Moreton Terr [1] WA6 . . . .74 A4
Moreville Cl CW9 . . . . . . .103 C2
Morgan Ave WA2 . . . . .8 B1
Morgan Cl Blacon CH1 . . . .117 C3
Crewe CW2 . . . . .190 A2
Morgan Pl SK5 . . . . .240 F8
Morland Ave
Bebington CH62 . . . . .43 B3
Neston CH64 . . . . .66 C4
Morley Cl CH2 . . . . .119 C4
Morley Dr CW12 . . . . .157 A1
Morley Gn SK9 . . . . .33 B1
Morley Rd Runcorn WA7 . . . .23 A1
Warrington WA4 . . . . .16 A1
Morley St WA1 . . . . .16 B3
Mornant Ave CW8 . . . . .103 A2
Morningside WA14 . . . . .238 B5
Morningside Dr M20 . . . . . .239 C8
Mornington Ave
Cheadle SK8 . . . . .239 D4
Ellesmere Port CH65 . . . . . .70 B2
Mornington Cl CW11 . . . . . .174 B4
Mornington Rd
Cheadle SK8 . . . . .239 D4
Sale M33 . . . . .242 D7
Morphany La WA4 . . . . .51 C3
Morreys La CW6 . . . . .122 C4
Morris Ave WA4 . . . . .16 C2
Morris Cl WA11 . . . . .1 A3
Morris Dr CW8 . . . . .77 B1
Morris Pk CW8 . . . . .103 A4
Morrison Cl WA5 . . . . .15 A3
Mort Ave WA4 . . . . .17 A3
Mortimer Ave WA2 . . . . .16 A4
Mortimer Dr CW11 . . . . .175 B2
Mortlake Cl WA8 . . . . .12 B2
Mortlake Cres CH3 . . . . .119 A1
Morton Ave WA6 . . . . .73 A1
Morton Cl WA5 . . . . .15 B4
Morton Dr SK11 . . . . .112 C2
Morton Rd Blacon CH1 . . . . .117 C2
Runcorn WA7 . . . . .50 B4
Morton St SK4 . . . . .240 E8
Morven Cl WA2 . . . . .8 C2
Moscow Rd SK3 . . . . .240 D3
Moscow Rd E SK3 . . . . .240 D3
Mosedale Gr WA7 . . . . .49 C3
Moseley Ave WA4 . . . . .17 A2
Moseley Grange SK8 . . . . . .239 F3
Moseley Rd SK8 . . . . .239 F3
Moseley St [2] SK3 . . . . .240 E4
Moses Ct CH2 . . . . .237 A4
Mosley Cl WA15 . . . . .238 F7
Moss Bank
Bramhall SK7,SK8 . . . . .35 B3
Chester CH2 . . . . .118 B2
Winsford CW7 . . . . .126 B1
Moss Bank Rd WA8 . . . . .23 B4
Moss Bower Rd SK11 . . . . . .112 B2
Moss Brow SK10 . . . . .87 C4
Moss Brow La WA16 . . . . . . .28 B3
Moss Cl Warrington WA4 . . . .16 C1
Willaston CH64 . . . . .68 A4
Moss Croft CW1 . . . . .190 A4
Moss Dr Manley WA6 . . . . . . .98 C2
Middlewich CW10 . . . . .151 B3
Moss Farm Recn Ctr
CW8 . . . . .103 B4
Moss Fields Alsager ST7 .193 A2
Crewe CW1 . . . . .173 A1
Moss Gate WA3 . . . . .10 A3
Moss Gr Broughton CH4 . . . .140 B3
Lymm WA13 . . . . .19 A2
Newcastle-u-L ST5 . . . . . . .210 B2
Moss Green Way WA9 . . . . . .1 A1
Moss Hey Prim Sch SK7 .35 B3
Moss La Alderley Edge SK9 60 A1
Altrincham WA14,WA15 . . . .238 E4
Altrincham, Timperley
WA15 . . . . .238 F7
Bollington SK10 . . . . .87 C4
Bramhall SK7 . . . . .35 A3
Brereton Green CW12 . . . . .154 C3
Congleton CW12 . . . . .156 C3
Crewe CW1 . . . . .173 A1
Cuddington CW8 . . . . .102 A2
Fowley Common WA3 . . . . . .5 B3
Golborne WA3 . . . . .3 A3
High Legh WA16 . . . . .29 C3
High Legh, Sink Moss WA16 28 B2
Hollins Green WA3 . . . . .10 C3
Irlam M44 . . . . .11 B3
Knutsford WA16 . . . . .56 B3
Lawton-gate ST7 . . . . .194 C2
Lostock Green CW9 . . . . . . .105 B4
Macclesfield SK11 . . . . .112 B2
Manley WA6 . . . . .99 A2
Middlewich CW10 . . . . .129 A4
Mobberley WA16 . . . . .58 C2
Moore WA4 . . . . .25 A3
Mottram St Andrew SK10 . . .61 A1
Norley WA6 . . . . .101 A3
Northwich CW8 . . . . .103 B4
Ollerton SK10 . . . . .83 B2
Partington M31 . . . . .11 C1
Sandbach CW11 . . . . .174 B4
Siddington SK11 . . . . .109 C1
St Helens, Moss Nook WA9 . .1 A1
Styal SK9 . . . . .33 C3
Warmingham CW1 . . . . .173 B2
Moss Lane Bsns Ctr
CW11 . . . . .174 B3
Moss Pl CW7 . . . . .126 B1
Moss Rd Alderley Edge SK9 60 B1
Congleton CW12 . . . . .178 C4

Moss Rd continued
Irlam M44 . . . . .11 B4
Northwich CW8 . . . . .103 B4
Warrington WA4 . . . . .17 A2
Moss Rose SK9 . . . . .60 A1
Moss Rose Football Gnd
SK11 . . . . .112 B2
Moss Side La
Antrobus CW9 . . . . .53 B4
Hollins Green WA3 . . . . . . .10 C2
Moore WA4 . . . . .24 C4
Moss Side Rd M44 . . . . .11 C3
Moss Sq Crewe CW1 . . . . . .190 B2
Moss St Weaverham CW8 . . .77 B1
Widnes WA8 . . . . .23 A4
Moss Terr Northwich CW8 . . .78 B1
Warren SK11 . . . . .112 A3
Wilmslow SK9 . . . . .60 C4
Moss The CW9 . . . . .78 B4
Moss View Rd SK11 . . . . . . .112 A2
Moss Way ST7 . . . . .193 A2
Mossdale Cl Crewe CW2 189 C2
Warrington WA5 . . . . .15 A4
Mossfield Cl SK4 . . . . .240 B6
Mossfield Cres [13] ST7 . . . .195 A1
Mossford Ave WA1 . . . . .190 A4
Mossgrove Rd WA15 . . . . . .238 F6
Mosshall La WA4 . . . . .26 C1
Mosslands Cl CH66 . . . . .69 C1
Mossley Ave CH62 . . . . .43 B4
Mossley CE Prim Sch
CW12 . . . . .179 A4
Mossley Ct CW12 . . . . .178 C4
Mossley Rd OL6 . . . . .242 B4
Mossvale CH66 . . . . .69 B4
Mosswood Pk M20 . . . . .239 B8
Mosswood Rd SK9 . . . . .34 C1
Moston Ct [5] CW12 . . . . . . .156 C2
Moston Gr WA13 . . . . .18 B2
Moston Rd Chester CH2 . . . .118 B4
Sandbach CW11 . . . . .174 B3
Moston Way CH66 . . . . .69 C2
Mostyn Ave Cheadle SK8 .239 E1
Heswall CH60 . . . . .40 B4
Mostyn Gdns CH64 . . . . .41 A1
Mostyn House Sch CH64 .66 B4
Mostyn Pl CH1 . . . . .117 C3
Mostyn Sq CH64 . . . . .41 A1
Motcombe Farm Rd
SK8 . . . . .239 B1
Motcombe Gr SK8 . . . . .239 A3
Motcombe Rd SK8 . . . . .239 A2
Motram Cl WA4 . . . . .17 A2
Mottershead Rd WA8 . . . . . .23 A4
Mottram Cl
Middlewich CW10 . . . . .151 A4
Stockport SK8 . . . . .240 A1
Mottram Fold SK1 . . . . .240 F4
Mottram Rd
Alderley Edge SK9 . . . . .60 B1
Sale M33 . . . . .242 F6
Mottram St [5] SK1 . . . . .240 F4
Mottram St Andrew Prim Sch
SK10 . . . . .61 A1
Mottram Way SK10 . . . . .87 C1
Moughland La WA7 . . . . .49 A4
Moulders La WA1 . . . . .16 A2
Mouldsworth Cl [2]
CW9 . . . . .103 C2
Mouldsworth Motor Mus★
CH3 . . . . .98 C1
Mouldsworth Sta CH3 . . .99 A1
Moulton Cl
Davenham CW9 . . . . .103 C2
Knutsford WA16 . . . . .57 C2
Runcorn WA7 . . . . .49 C2
Moulton Sch CW9 . . . . . . .126 C4
Mount Ave CH60 . . . . .40 C4
Mount Cl CW5 . . . . .204 C3
Mount Ct CH60 . . . . .40 C4
Mount Farm Way CH66 . . . .69 B1
Mount Mews CH60 . . . . .40 C4
Mount Pl CH2 . . . . .118 C1
Mount Pleasant
Audlem CW3 . . . . .230 A2
Bollington SK10 . . . . .88 A4
Chester CH4 . . . . .140 C4
Congleton CW12 . . . . .156 C1
Crewe CW1 . . . . .190 A3
Elton CH2 . . . . .72 A2
Haslington CW1 . . . . .191 B2
Kidsgrove ST7 . . . . .195 A1
Macclesfield SK10 . . . . .87 A1
Rainow SK10 . . . . .88 B2
Widnes WA8 . . . . .13 A1
Wilmslow SK9 . . . . .60 C4
Mount Pleasant Ave WA9 . .1 A2
Mount Pleasant Dr
CW7 . . . . .149 A4
Mount Pleasant Rd
Davenham CW9 . . . . .103 C2
The Bank ST7 . . . . .195 A4
Mount Pleasant Residential
Pk CW7 . . . . .130 B4
Mount Rd Kidsgrove ST7 . . .195 A1
Runcorn WA7 . . . . .49 C4
Stockport SK4 . . . . .240 C6
Mount St Hyde SK14 . . . . . .241 E6
Widnes WA8 . . . . .13 A1
Mount Terr SK11 . . . . .112 C4
Mount The
Altrincham WA14 . . . . .238 D5
Altrincham, Halebarns
WA15 . . . . .32 B4
Ashton-u-Lyne OL6 . . . . . . .242 A3
Chester CH2 . . . . .118 C1
Congleton CW12 . . . . .156 C2

Mount The continued
Great Budworth CW9 . . . . . .79 A4
Heswall CH60 . . . . .40 C4
Kidsgrove ST7 . . . . .195 A1
Scholar Green ST7 . . . . . . .194 C4
Mount Way CH3 . . . . .143 A2
Mountain View
Broughton CH4 . . . . .140 A3
Helsby WA6 . . . . .73 A2
Mountbatten Ct CW2 . . . . . .190 A2
Mountbatten Way
CW12 . . . . .156 B2
Mountfield Rd
Bramhall SK7 . . . . .35 C3
Stockport SK3 . . . . .240 C3
Mourne Cl CH66 . . . . .69 A3
Mow Cop Rd ST7 . . . . .195 B3
Mow La Biddulph ST7,ST8 179 A1
Mount Pleasant ST7 . . . . . .195 A3
Mowbray Ave M33 . . . . .242 C5
Mowbray Rd [4] SK1 . . . . . .240 F4
Mowcroft La WA5 . . . . .14 A3
Mowpen Brow WA16 . . . . . . .29 A3
Moxon Ave WA4 . . . . .16 C3
Moyles Cl WA8 . . . . .12 B1
Mudhouse La CH64 . . . . .67 C1
Mudhurst La SK12 . . . . .38 C2
Muir Rd CH1 . . . . .117 C2
Muirfield Ave SK6 . . . . .241 C4
Muirfield Cl
Northwich CW9 . . . . .104 A3
Warrington WA2 . . . . .9 A4
Wilmslow SK9 . . . . .60 B4
Muirfield Dr
Macclesfield SK10 . . . . .87 B2
Winsford CW7 . . . . .126 B3
Muirfield Mews CW7 . . . . . .126 B1
Mulberry Ave WA3 . . . . .3 C4
Mulberry Cl Elton CH2 . . .72 C4
Gatley SK8 . . . . .34 B4
Warrington WA1 . . . . .17 C3
Mulberry Ct
Altrincham WA14 . . . . .238 D6
Macclesfield SK11 . . . . .112 B2
Warrington WA4 . . . . .16 B1
Mulberry Gdns CW11 . . . . . .174 B2
Mulberry Mews SK4 . . . . . . .240 C6
Mulberry Mount St SK3 . . . .240 E4
Mulberry Rd CW2 . . . . .189 C1
Mulberry Rise CW8 . . . . . . .103 B4
Mulcaster Ct CW1 . . . . .191 B3
Mull Cl CH65 . . . . .70 B1
Mullein Cl WA3 . . . . .3 B4
Mullen Cl WA5 . . . . .7 C1
Mullins Ave WA12 . . . . .2 B4
Mullion Cl WA7 . . . . .50 A3
Mullion Dr WA15 . . . . .238 C5
Mullion Gr WA2 . . . . .9 A1
Mulsford Ct LL13 . . . . .222 A4
Mulsford La LL13,SY14 . . . .222 A4
Murdishaw Ave WA7 . . . . . . .50 B3
Murdishaw West Prim Sch
WA7 . . . . .50 B3
Muriel Cl WA5 . . . . .14 A4
Murieston Rd WA15 . . . . . . .238 E2
Murray Cl SK10 . . . . .87 A1
Murrayfield SK10 . . . . .87 A3
Murrayfield Dr CW5 . . . . . . .205 B3
Museum of Hatting Stockport
The★ SK1 . . . . .240 E5
Museum St WA1 . . . . .16 A2
Music Hall Pass CH1 . . . . . .237 B2
Mustard La WA3 . . . . .4 A1
Myddleton La WA2 . . . . .8 B3
Myrica Gr CH2 . . . . .119 A2
Myrtle Ave Haydock WA11 . . .1 A4
Higher Kinnerton CH4 . . . . .161 A4
Newton-le-W WA12 . . . . .2 B1
Myrtle Gr Chester CH2 . . . . .119 A2
Warrington WA4 . . . . .16 B2
Widnes WA8 . . . . .22 B4
Myrtle Rd M31 . . . . .11 B2
Myrtle St
Ellesmere Port CH65 . . . . . .70 B4
Stockport SK3 . . . . .240 E4
Mythorne Ave M44 . . . . .11 B2

N

Nab Cl SK10 . . . . .63 B1
Nab La SK10 . . . . .63 B1
Nabbs Cl ST7 . . . . .195 A1
Nabbswood Rd ST7 . . . . . . .195 A1
Nairn Ave CW4 . . . . .130 A1
Nairn Cl Bebington CH63 . . .43 B2
Warrington WA2 . . . . .9 A2
Nancy View SK10 . . . . .88 A4
Nansen Cl WA5 . . . . .15 B4
Nansen Rd SK8 . . . . .239 A4
Nansmoss La SK9 . . . . .33 B1
Nantwich Mus★ CW5 . . .204 C3
Nantwich Rd
Barbridge CW5 . . . . .187 A4
Betley ST7 . . . . .208 C1
Broxton CH3 . . . . .183 B1
Crewe CW2 . . . . .190 B1
Ellesmere Port CH66 . . . . . .69 C2
Middlewich CW10 . . . . .151 A4
Sound CW5 . . . . .217 A3
Tarporley CW6 . . . . .168 B4
Wimboldsley CW10 . . . . . . .150 C3
Woore CW3 . . . . .232 A1
Worleston CW2,CW5 . . . . . .189 B1
Wrenbury CW5 . . . . .201 C1
Nantwich Sta CW5 . . . . .204 C2
Nantwich Way [6] SK9 . . . .34 C3
Naomi Cl CH1 . . . . .117 B3

Napier Ct 5 SK4 .240 B7
Napier Gdns 3 ST7 .195 A1
Napier Rd Chester CH2 .118 B4
Stockport SK4 .240 B7
Napier St Hyde SK14 .241 E5
Warrington WA1 .16 B3
Naples Rd SK3 .240 B3
Napley Dr TF9 .236 B1
Napley Rd TF9 .236 B1
Nares Cl WA5 .7 B1
Narrow La SK10 .37 A1
Narrows The WA14 .238 C4
Naseby Rd CW12 .156 A2
Nasmyth Ave M34 .241 A8
Nat La CW7 .126 C1
Nat Lane Ret Pk CW7 .126 C1
Nathan Dr WA11 .1 C3
Naughton Lea WA8 .12 B2
Naughton Rd WA8 .23 A4
Navan Ct CW1 .190 A3
Navigation Cl WA7 .50 B3
Navigation Prim Sch WA14 .238 D6
Navigation Rd
Altrincham WA14,WA15 .238 D6
Northwich CW8 .103 C4
Navigation Road Sta WA14 .238 E6
Navigation St WA1 .16 B3
Naylor Ave WA3 .3 A4
Naylor Cres CH66 .69 C4
Naylor Ct 12 CW9 .103 C4
Naylor Rd WA8 .13 B1
Naylor St WA1 .16 A3
Neal Ave
Ashton-u-Lyne OL6 .242 A3
Gatley SK8 .239 A1
Neath Cl SK12 .36 B3
Needham Cl WA7 .23 B1
Needham Dr
Cranage CW4 .130 A3
Hartford CW8 .103 A2
Needhams Wharf Cl SK10 .88 A1
Neil St WA8 .13 B1
Neills Rd WA5 .6 A3
Nelson Ave SK12 .37 A2
Nelson Bldgs ST7 .195 A1
Nelson Cl SK12 .37 A2
Nelson Dr M44 .11 C3
Nelson Gr ST7 .193 C1
Nelson Ind Est ST7 .194 B1
Nelson Rd CH65 .70 B4
Nelson St Chester CH2 .237 C3
Congleton CW12 .156 B1
Crewe CW2 .190 B1
Hyde SK14 .241 E6
Macclesfield SK11 .112 B4
Newton-le-W WA12 .2 A2
Runcorn WA7 .23 A2
Widnes WA7 .23 A1
Nemos Cl WA6 .73 B1
Neptune Cl WA7 .50 B4
Nesfield Cl CW11 .191 C4
Nesfield Dr CW11 .191 C4
Ness Botanic Gdns* CH64 .67 A2
Nessina Gr CW2 .205 C4
Neston Dr CH2 .118 C3
Neston Gn CH66 .69 B2
Neston Gr SK3 .240 D1
Neston Prim Sch CH64 .66 C4
Neston Rd
Heswall CH63,CH64 .41 C3
Neston CH64 .67 A2
Willaston CH64 .67 C4
Neston St Mary's CE Prim Sch CH64 .41 C1
Neston Sta CH64 .66 C4
Neston Way SK9 .34 B2
Neston,High Sch CH64 .41 C1
Nether Alderley Mill* SK10 .85 A3
Nether Alderley Prim Sch SK10 .85 A3
Nether Fold SK10 .87 A4
Nether Lea CW4 .130 B4
Nethercroft Ct WA14 .238 C5
Netherfield WA8 .22 C4
Netherfields SK9 .85 A4
Netherley Rd WA8 .12 A1
Netherlow Ct SK14 .241 E6
Netherpool Rd CH66 .69 C4
Netherton Dr WA6 .74 A4
Neumann St CW9 .104 A4
Nevada Cl WA5 .15 B4
Neville Ave St Helens WA9 .1 A1
Warrington WA2 .8 B1
Neville Cres WA5 .15 A2
Neville Dr 9 CH3 .119 A1
Neville Rd Bebington CH62 43 C4
Chester CH3 .119 A1
Neville St Crewe CW2 .190 B1
Newton-le-W WA12 .2 A2
Nevin Ave SK8 .239 E1
Nevin Cl SK7 .36 A4
Nevin Rd CH1 .117 B2
Nevis Dr CW2 .189 B2
New Bank Pl WA8 .12 A1
New Bank Rd WA8 .12 A1
New Barnet WA8 .12 C2
New Chester Rd
Bebington CH62 .43 C3
Hooton CH62,CH66 .44 A1
New Cotts Hampton SY14 213 C4
Manley WA6 .99 B4
New Crane Bank CH1 .118 A1
New Crane St CH1 .118 A1
New Cut Ind Est WA1 .17 B4
New Cut La WA1 .17 A4
New Farm Cotts WA3 .11 A4
New Farm Ct CH3 .120 C3
New Grosvenor Rd CH65 70 A4
New Hall Ave SK8 .34 A4
New Hall Cl M33 .242 F6
New Hall La Culcheth WA3 .4 C1
Culcheth WA3 .5 A1
New Hall St SK10 .87 B1
New Hey La CH64 .68 A3
New Hey Rd SK8 .239 E6
New Horwich Rd SK23 .65 C4
New Hos CW5 .187 B3
New Houses CH3 .143 A4
New Inn Cotts WA16 .108 B4
New Inn La CW11 .176 A1
New King St Audley ST7 .209 B1
Middlewich CW10 .128 B1
New La
Appleton Thorn WA4 .27 A3
Churton CH3 .180 C3
Croft WA3 .9 A4
Harthill CH3 .183 C2
Winsford CW7 .149 C2
New Manchester Rd WA1 .17 A4
New Manor Rd WA4 .51 A3
New Mills Central Sta SK22 .39 A4
New Mills Newtown Sta SK22 .39 A3
New Mills Prim Sch SK22 .39 A4
New Mills Sch SK22 .39 B4
New Moss Rd M44 .11 B3
New Pale Rd WA6 .99 B3
New Platt La CW4 .107 A1
New Rd Anderton CW9 .78 B2
Antrobus CW9 .27 B1
Astbury CW12 .178 A2
Audley ST7 .209 C2
Duddon CW6 .145 A3
Ellesmere Port CH66 .69 A4
Lymm WA13 .18 C2
Marton CW12 .132 B1
Mere WA16 .30 C2
Prestbury SK10 .87 A4
Warrington WA4 .16 A2
Whaley Bridge SK23 .65 C3
Whaley Bridge, Bridgemont SK23 .39 C1
Winsford CW7 .126 C1
Wrenbury CW5 .216 B2
New School La CH66 .44 A1
New St Altrincham WA14 .238 D4
Congleton CW12 .156 C1
Haslington CW1 .191 B3
Neston CH64 .66 C3
New Mills SK22 .39 B4
Runcorn WA7 .23 A1
Sandbach CW11 .174 B4
Widnes WA8 .23 A4
Wilmslow SK9 .59 C3
New St Cotts CW12 .157 A3
New Warrington Rd CW9 79 A1
New Wellington Sch WA15 .238 F6
Newall Cl CH3 .166 A1
Newall Cres CW7 .127 A1
Newberry Gr SK3 .240 D1
Newbold Ct 9 CW12 .156 C2
Newbold Way CW5 .204 C2
Newborough Cl WA5 .7 C1
Newboult Rd SK8 .239 E6
Newbridge Cl
Runcorn WA7 .50 B3
Warrington WA5 .7 B1
Newbridge Rd CH65,CH2 .70 C2
Newburgh Cl WA7 .24 B1
Newbury Ave
Crewe CW1 .190 B4
6 Winsford CW7 .149 A4
Newbury Cl Cheadle SK8 .35 A3
Widnes WA8 .13 A2
Newbury Ct SK9 .60 A3
Newbury Rd
Chester CH4 .140 C3
Gatley SK8 .34 B4
Newby Ct CW12 .156 A1
Newby Dr
Altrincham WA14 .238 D6
Gatley SK8 .239 A6
Sale M33 .242 E5
Newby Rd SK4 .240 C6
Newcastle Rd
Astbury CW12 .178 A4
Brereton Green CW11 .153 C2
Congleton CW12 .156 A1
Hassall Green CW11 .176 A2
Haymoor Green CW5 .205 B2
Shavington CW2,CW5 .206 B2
Smallwood CW11 .176 B3
Talke ST7 .210 C4
Woore CW3 .232 C1
Newcastle Rd N CW11 .153 C3
Newcastle Rd S CW11 .153 C3
Newcastle St CW1 .190 A3
Newchapel Obsy* ST7 .195 C1
Newchapel Rd ST7 .195 B2
Newchurch Com Prim Sch WA3 .4 C1
Newchurch La WA3 .4 C1
Newcombe Ave WA2 .16 C4
Newcroft CH1 .94 A1
Newcroft Dr SK3 .240 D2
Newdigate St
Crewe CW1 .190 B2
Newdigate St *continued*
Crewe CW1 .190 B3
Newfield Ct WA13 .19 A3
Newfield Dr CW1 .190 C3
Newfield Rd WA13 .18 B2
Newfield St CW11 .175 A4
Newfield Terr WA6 .73 A1
Newgate
Macclesfield SK11 .112 B4
Wilmslow SK9 .59 B4
Newgate St CH1 .237 B2
Newhall Ave CW11 .175 A3
Newhall Ct CH2 .118 C3
Newhall Rd CH2 .118 C3
Newham Cl SK11 .112 C2
Newhaven Rd WA2 .8 A2
Newington Ct WA14 .238 B3
Newland Cl WA8 .12 B2
Newland Mews WA3 .4 C3
Newland Way CW5 .205 A2
Newlands Ave
Bramhall SK7 .35 C4
Cheadle SK8 .35 A4
Newlands Cl Cheadle SK8 .35 A4
Frodsham WA6 .74 B3
Newlands Dr Golborne WA3 3 B4
Manchester M20 .239 C8
Wilmslow SK9 .59 C3
Newlands Rd
Cheadle SK8 .239 D6
Macclesfield SK10 .111 C4
Warrington WA4 .16 C1
Newlyn Ave
Congleton CW12 .178 C4
Macclesfield SK10 .86 B1
Newlyn Cl WA7 .50 A3
Newlyn Dr SK6 .241 A3
Newlyn Gdns WA5 .14 B2
Newman Cl CW12 .156 A2
Newman RC High Sch WA4 .16 C3
Newman St Hyde SK14 .241 E7
Warrington WA4 .16 C2
Newman's La CW5 .219 B4
Newmarket Cl 1 SK10 .87 B2
Newmarket Wlk 12 WA1 .16 A3
Newmoore La WA7 .24 C2
Newnham Dr CH65 .70 B2
Newport Gr ST5 .210 C1
Newquay Cl WA7 .50 A3
Newquay Ct CW12 .178 C4
Newquay Dr Bramhall SK7 35 C4
Macclesfield SK10 .111 B4
Newry Ct CH2 .118 B2
Newry Pk CH2 .118 B2
Newry Pk E CH2 .118 B2
Newsham Cl WA8 .12 A2
Newsholme Cl WA3 .4 C2
Newstead Cl SK12 .36 B3
Newstead Terr WA15 .238 F7
Newton Ave WA3 .9 C3
Newton Bank CW10 .128 A1
Newton Bank Prep Sch WA12 .2 C2
Newton Comm Hospl WA12 .2 A1
Newton Cotts CH3 .166 B2
Newton for Hyde Sta SK14 .241 F8
Newton Gr WA2 .8 C2
Newton Hall Ct CH2 .118 C3
Newton Hall Dr CH2 .118 C3
Newton Hall La WA16 .58 C3
Newton Hall Mews 1 CW10 .151 B4
Newton Heath CW10 .128 A1
Newton Hollow WA6 .74 B1
Newton La Chester CH2 .118 C2
Daresbury WA4 .51 C4
Golborne WA12 .2 C3
Tattenhall CH3 .166 B2
Newton Park Dr WA12 .2 C2
Newton Park View CH2 .118 B2
Newton Pl CW12 .156 C1
Newton Prim Sch CH2 .118 C2
Newton Rd
Altrincham WA14 .238 E7
Ellesmere Port CH65 .70 B3
Golborne WA3 .3 B3
Handforth SK9 .34 A1
St Helens WA9 .1 A2
Winwick WA2 .8 A3
Newton St Crewe CW1 .190 B3
Hyde SK14 .241 D8
Macclesfield SK11 .112 B4
Stalybridge SK15 .242 C2
1 Stockport SK3 .240 E4
Newton-le-Willows Com High Sch WA12 .2 B3
Newton-le-Willows Prim Sch WA12 .2 B2
Newton-le-Willows Sta WA12 .2 C2
Newtons Cres CW11 .191 C4
Newtons Gr CW11 .191 C4
Newtons La CW11 .191 C4
Newtown Kidsgrove ST7 .195 C1
Neston CH64 .66 C4
Newtown Cl CH2 .237 B3
Newtown Prim Sch SK22 39 A3
Nicholas Ave CW9 .104 B3
Nicholas Ct CH1 .237 A2
Nicholas Rd
Weaverham CW8 .77 B1
Widnes WA8 .22 B4
Nicholas St CH1 .237 A2
Nicholas St Mews CH1 .237 A2
Nicholls St WA4 .17 A1
Nicholson Ave SK10 .87 C1
Nicholson Cl SK10 .87 C1
Nicholson St
Stockport SK4 .240 E6
Warrington WA1 .15 C3
Nickleby Rd SK12 .36 C2
Nickolson Cl CH2 .119 C4
Nicol Ave WA1 .17 C4
Nidderdale Cl CW12 .157 A3
Niddries Ct CW9 .126 C4
Niddries La CW9 .126 C4
Nield Ct CH2 .118 B4
Nield's Brow WA14 .238 C2
Nigel Gresley Cl CW1 .191 A2
Nigel Rd CH60 .41 B4
Nigel Wlk WA7 .24 A1
Nightgale Cl CW1 .189 C4
Nightingale Cl
Farndon CH3 .180 C1
Middlewich CW10 .151 B3
Runcorn WA7 .49 C3
Warrington WA3 .9 C2
Wilmslow SK9 .34 A1
Nightingale Ct 4 CW7 .149 B3
Nightingale Way ST7 .193 A2
Nile St CW2 .190 B1
Nine Hos The CH3 .166 A1
Nixon Dr CW7 .126 A1
Nixon Rd CW8 .101 C2
Nixon St Crewe CW1 .189 C3
Macclesfield SK11 .112 A4
3 Stockport SK3 .240 E4
Nixon's Row CW5 .204 B3
No 1 Road N CW2 .192 C1
No 1 Road S CW2 .192 C1
No 2 Pas SK3 .240 D5
No 2 Road N CW2 .192 C1
No 2 Road S CW2 .192 C1
Noahs Ark La WA16 .58 C1
Noble Cl WA3 .9 C2
Noel Dr M33 .242 D6
Nook La Antrobus CW9 .53 C3
Golborne WA3 .3 A4
Warrington WA4 .17 A2
Warrington, Fearnhead WA2 .9 A1
Nook The Bramhall SK7 .35 B3
Broughton CH4 .140 C3
Chester CH2 .118 C2
Guilden Sutton CH3 .119 B2
Noon Ct WA12 .2 A1
Nora St WA1 .16 B3
Norbreck Ave
Crewe CW2 .190 A1
Stockport SK8 .240 A2
Norbreck Dr WA5 .15 A2
Norbury Ave
4 Hyde SK14 .241 D6
Warrington WA2 .16 B4
Norbury Cl
Hough Common CW2 .206 C2
Knutsford WA16 .57 B2
Norbury Dr
Congleton CW12 .156 C2
Middlewich CW10 .151 A4
Norbury Hollow Rd SK7 .37 A4
Norbury St
Macclesfield SK11 .112 B4
Northwich CW9 .104 A4
12 Stockport SK1 .240 F5
Norbury Way 9 SK9 .34 B3
Norcott Ave WA4 .16 C1
Norcott Dr WA5 .6 C3
Norden Cl WA3 .9 B3
Norfolk Cl M44 .11 B3
Norfolk Dr WA5 .14 C3
Norfolk Gr ST8 .179 B1
Norfolk Ho 1 Sale M33 .242 D6
Talke ST7 .210 B3
Norfolk Pl WA8 .22 B4
Norfolk Rd Chester CH2 .118 C2
Congleton CW12 .156 C2
Ellesmere Port CH65 .70 B3
Kidsgrove ST7 .194 C1
Norfolk St Hyde SK14 .241 D6
Runcorn WA7 .23 A2
Norfolk Wlk SK10 .86 C1
Norgrove Cl WA7 .50 B4
Norland St WA8 .13 B1
Norland's La L35 .12 C4
Norleane Cres WA7 .49 A4
Norley Ave
Bebington CH62 .43 C2
Ellesmere Port CH65 .69 C3
Norley CE Prim Sch WA6 .100 C3
Norley Dr Chester CH3 .119 B1
Sale M33 .242 E6
Norley La Crowton CW8 .76 A1
Norley CW8 .101 A4
Norley Rd
Cuddington CW8 .101 C2
Kingsley WA6 .75 A1
Norley WA6 .100 B4
Norman Ave Haydock WA11 2 A4
Newton-le-W WA12 .2 C2
Norman Cl CH66 .94 C4
Norman Dr CW7 .149 B3
Norman Rd
Altrincham WA14 .238 C6
Runcorn WA7 .23 A1
Sale M33 .242 B5
Stalybridge SK15 .242 C2
Stockport SK4 .240 B7
Norman St Hyde SK14 .241 E6
Warrington WA2 .16 A3
Norman Way CH1 .117 C3
Norman's La WA4 .52 C2
Norman's Pl WA14 .238 D4
Normanby Chase WA14 .238 B4
Normanby Cl WA5 .15 C4
Normandy Ave 10 CW7 .149 B4
Normandy Rd CH2 .95 B1
Normans Cotts 9 CH64 .66 C4
Normanton Rd SK3 .240 A2
Norreys Ave WA5 .15 C4
Norris Ave SK4 .240 C6
Norris Bank Prim Sch SK4 .240 B7
Norris Bank Terr SK4 .240 C5
Norris Hill Dr SK4 .240 C6
Norris Rd Blacon CH1 .117 C3
Sale M33 .242 F5
Norris St WA2 .16 B4
North Ave
Stalybridge SK15 .242 D3
Warrington WA2 .16 A4
North Brook Rd CW6 .146 A4
North Cestrian Gram Sch WA14 .238 C5
North Cheshire Hospl WA4 .26 B1
North Cheshire Jewish Prim Sch SK8 .239 C2
North Crofts CW5 .204 C3
North Downs WA16 .57 B1
North Downs Rd SK8 .239 F3
North Dr Heswall CH60 .41 A4
High Legh WA16 .29 B2
Northwich CW9 .104 C4
North Fields WA16 .57 B2
North Florida Rd WA11 .1 B4
North Gn CH5 .116 A3
North Harvey St 8 SK1 .240 F5
North Mead SK10 .87 A3
North Par CH64 .41 A1
North Park Brook Rd WA5 7 C1
North Pl 5 SK1 .240 F5
North Rd Altrincham WA15 32 A4
Bebington CH65 .44 C2
Ellesmere Port CH65 .70 A4
Halewood L26 .21 A3
North St Broughton CH4 .140 A4
Chester CH3 .119 A1
Congleton CW12 .156 B2
Crewe CW1 .190 B4
Hawarden CH5 .116 A2
Haydock WA11 .1 C3
Mount Pleasant ST7 .195 A3
Newton-le-W WA12 .1 C2
North Stafford St CW1 .190 B2
North Vale Rd WA15 .238 F6
North View Crewe CW1 .190 A3
Warrington WA5 .14 C4
North Way
Holmes Chapel CW4 .130 B2
Hyde SK14 .241 E6
Shavington CW2 .206 B3
Northbank Ind Pk M44 .11 C4
Northbank Wlk CW2 .206 B4
Northbury Rd CH66 .69 C1
Northcombe Rd SK3 .240 E1
Northcote Rd SK7 .35 C4
Northdale Rd WA1 .17 A4
Northend Rd SK15 .242 E2
Northenden Rd
Gatley SK8 .239 A6
Sale M33 .242 C6
Northern La WA8 .12 A2
Northern Pathway CH4 .237 C1
Northern Rise CH66 .69 C2
Northfield Dr
Biddulph ST8 .179 C1
Wilmslow SK9 .60 B4
Northfield Pl CW2 .206 B3
Northgate CW6 .146 A4
Northgate Ave
Chester CH2 .237 B4
Macclesfield SK10 .87 B1
Northgate Rd SK3 .240 C4
Northgate Row CH1 .237 B2
Northgate St CH1 .237 A3
Northlands CW3 .232 B1
Northolt Ct WA2 .8 C1
Northstead Ave M34 .241 B6
Northumberland Rd M31 11 C1
Northward Rd SK9 .59 C3
Northway
Altrincham WA14 .238 E6
Chester CH4 .141 A4
Lymm WA13 .18 B2
Northwich CW8 .78 B1
Runcorn WA7 .49 C4
Warrington WA2 .8 A1
Widnes WA8 .12 B1
Northwich Rd
Antrobus CW9,WA4 .53 A2
Cranage CW4,WA16 .106 C1
Dutton WA4 .51 A1
Great Budworth CW9 .78 C4
Knutsford WA16 .56 B1
Runcorn WA7 .50 C2
Runcorn, Brookvale WA7 .50 B3
Stretton WA4 .52 C4
Weaverham CW8 .102 C4
Northwich Sta CW9 .104 A4
Northwick Ret Pk CW9 .79 B1
Northwood Ave
Middlewich CW10 .151 C3
Newton-le-W WA12 .2 C2
Northwood Gr M33 .242 B6
Northwood La WA16 .28 C1
Northwood Rd WA7 .23 C1

Norton Ave
Broughton CH4 140 B3
Warrington WA5 14 C2
Norton Cotts WA7 50 C4
Norton Gate WA7 50 B4
Norton Gr SK4 240 B5
Norton Hill WA7 24 B1
Norton La
Runcorn, Norton WA7 24 B1
Runcorn, Town Park WA7 50 A4
Norton Priory High Sch WA7 24 A1
Norton Priory Mus★ WA7 24 A2
Norton Priory Walled Gdns★ WA7 24 A2
Norton Rd CH3 119 B1
Norton Station Rd WA7 50 B4
Norton View WA7 50 A4
Norton Village WA7 24 B1
Norton Way CW11 174 B4
Norton's La CH3 98 A1
Norton-in-Hales CE Prim Sch TF9 236 B1
Nortons La CW6 122 C4
Nortonwood La WA7 24 B1
Norview Dr M20 239 B8
Norville CH66 69 B4
Norway Gr 6 SK5 240 F8
Norwich Ave WA3 3 B4
Norwich Dr CH66 94 C4
Norwood Ave
Bramhall SK7 35 B3
Golborne WA3 3 C4
High Lane SK6 37 B4
Norwood Dr CH4 141 A3
Norwood Rd SK8 239 B6
Nottingham Cl WA1 17 C3
Nun House Cl CW7 127 A1
Nun House Dr CW7 127 A1
Nuns Rd CH1 237 A1
Nunsmere Cl CW7 127 A1
Nursery Ave WA15 31 C4
Nursery Cl Kidsgrove ST7 194 B1
Sale M33 242 D6
Shavington CW2 206 B2
Widnes WA8 13 B2
Nursery Dr Biddulph ST8 179 B1
Poynton SK12 36 B2
Nursery Gr M31 11 C2
Nursery La
Congleton CW12 156 C1
Nether Alderley SK10 84 B3
Siddington SK11 110 A2
Stockport SK3 240 A3
Wilmslow SK9 59 C3
Nursery Rd Barnton CW8 78 A2
Bollington SK10 87 C4
Haslington CW1,ST7 192 C2
Scholar Green ST7 194 C3
Stockport SK4 240 C6
Nursery The Norley WA6 100 A4
Northwich CW8 103 B3
Nutfield Ave CW1 190 A4
Nuthurst Gdns 17 CW5 204 C3
Nuttall Ct WA3 9 B2
Nuttall St M44 11 C3

O

O'Connell Cl WA11 1 B3
O'Leary St WA2 16 B4
Oak Ave Alsager ST7 193 C1
Disley SK12 39 A3
Golborne WA3 3 A4
Haydock WA11 1 C4
Irlam M44 11 B3
Macclesfield SK11 112 A3
Newton-le-W WA12 2 B2
Romiley SK6 241 C2
Stockport SK4 240 B6
Wilmslow SK9 59 C3
Winsford CW7 149 B4
Oak Bank SK12 39 A3
Oak Bank Cl CW5 205 C2
Oak Bank Dr SK10 63 A1
Oak Bank La CH2 119 B3
Oak Brow Cotts SK9 33 C2
Oak Cl SK9 59 C3
Oak Cotts Styal SK9 33 C2
Wrenbury CW5 216 C2
Oak Dr Bramhall SK7 35 B4
Higher Kinnerton CH4 161 A4
Middlewich CW10 151 B4
Runcorn WA7 49 B4
Oak Gr Cheadle SK8 239 E5
Ellesmere Port CH65 70 A2
Nantwich CW5 204 C2
Poynton SK12 36 B2
Oak Ho 7 CW11 175 A3
Oak House La CW7 149 A4
Oak La Bollington SK10 88 A3
Cuddington CW8 101 C1
Marton SK11 133 B3
Wilmslow SK9 59 C3
Oak Lea Ave SK9 60 A3
Oak Lodge SK7 35 C4
Oak Mdw CW8 102 C4
Oak Mews SK9 34 B1
Oak Rd Altrincham WA15 238 E3
Cheadle SK8 239 E5
Chelford SK11 84 A2
Chester CH4 140 C3
Hooton CH66 43 C1
Oak Rd *continued*
Lymm WA13 18 B2
Mottram St Andrew SK10 86 A4
Partington M31 11 B1
Sale M33 242 D6
Warrington WA5 14 C2
Oak St Crewe CW2 190 B2
Croft WA3 9 A4
Ellesmere Port CH65 70 B4
Hyde SK14 241 E8
Northwich CW9 79 A1
Rode Heath ST7 193 C4
Sandbach CW11 174 B4
Stockport SK3 240 B4
Oak Tree Cl CW1 190 C3
Oak Tree Dr CW1 190 C3
Oak Tree Gate CW3 229 C2
Oak Tree La
Cranage CW10 129 C4
Newcastle-u-L ST7 210 B3
Oak View Knutsford WA16 57 B1
Marton SK11 133 B3
Speke L24 21 A2
Oak Villas CW5 216 C2
Oak Wood Rd WA16 29 C1
Oakdale Ave
Frodsham WA6 74 B3
Warrington WA4 16 B1
Oakdale Cl
Broughton CH4 139 A2
Chorlton CW2 207 A2
Oakdale Ct
Altrincham WA14 238 C5
Stalybridge SK15 242 E2
Oakdale Dr SK8 239 B2
Oakdene Ave
Ellesmere Port CH66 69 B3
Gatley SK8 34 B4
Warrington WA1 17 B4
Oakdene Cl CH62 43 B3
Oakdene Way CW6 168 B4
Oakenclough Cl SK9 34 B1
Oakenclough Prim Sch SK9 34 B1
Oakes Cnr CW5 219 C2
Oakfield M33 242 A7
Oakfield Ave
Cheadle SK8 239 E6
Chester CH2 118 C4
Knutsford WA16 57 B2
Wrenbury CW5 216 C2
Oakfield Cl
Alderley Edge SK9 60 A2
Bramhall SK7 35 C2
Wrenbury CW5 216 C2
Oakfield Ct WA15 238 F6
Oakfield Cty Inf Sch WA8 22 A4
Oakfield Cty Jun Sch WA8 22 A4
Oakfield Dr Chester CH2 118 C4
Widnes WA8 22 A4
Oakfield Mews M33 242 A6
Oakfield Rd
Alderley Edge SK9 60 A1
Altrincham WA15 238 E4
Bebington CH62 43 B4
Blacon CH1 117 B2
Ellesmere Port CH66 68 C4
Plumley WA16 80 C2
Poynton SK12 36 C2
Stockport SK3 240 F1
Oakfield Rise CW4 130 A2
Oakfield St WA15 238 E5
Oakfield Trad Est WA15 238 E5
Oakgrove Prim Sch SK8 34 B4
Oakham Rd M34 241 A5
Oakhill Cl SK10 87 A2
Oakhurst Chase SK9 60 A1
Oakhurst Dr
Stockport SK3 240 B1
Wistaston CW2 206 A4
Oakland Ave CW1 191 B2
Oakland Ct SK12 36 B2
Oakland St
Warrington WA1 16 C4
Widnes WA8 23 A2
Oaklands CH3 119 C2
Oaklands Ave CH3 166 A1
Oaklands Cl SK9 34 C1
Oaklands Com Inf Sch SK9 34 C1
Oaklands Cres CH3 166 A1
Oaklands Dr Lymm WA13 18 B1
Sale M33 242 A7
Oaklands Rd Golborne WA3 3 C4
Ollerton WA16 82 C3
Oaklands Sch CW7 149 A4
Oaklea Ave CH2 118 C2
Oakleaf Lodge SK11 112 B3
Oakleigh Knutsford WA16 82 B4
2 Stockport SK4 240 B7
Oakleigh Ct CW12 155 C2
Oakleigh Rd SK8 34 C4
Oakleigh Rise CW8 78 C1
Oakley Cl CW11 175 A4
Oakley St CW1 190 B3
Oakley Villas SK4 240 B7
Oakmere Cl CW11 174 C4
Oakmere Dr Chester CH3 142 A4
Ellesmere Port CH66 69 C1
Warrington WA5 14 C2
Oakmere Hall CW8 101 C1
Oakmere Rd Cheadle SK8 239 F4
Handforth SK9 34 B3
Winsford CW7 125 C1
Oakmere St WA7 23 A1
Oakmoore WA7 24 C2
Oaks Dr The CH2 118 B4
Oaks Pl WA8 23 A4
Oaks The
Alderley Edge SK9 60 A1
Bebington CH62 43 B4
Gatley SK8 239 A2
Goostrey CW4 130 B4
Mobberley WA16 58 C1
Oakside Cl SK8 239 E6
Oaksway CH60 41 B3
Oakthorn Gr WA11 1 B3
Oaktree Cl Barnton CW8 78 A2
Tarporley CW6 146 B1
Oaktree Cotts SK8 239 F3
Oaktree Ct Cheadle SK8 239 D5
Chester CH2 119 A2
Oakway M20 239 C8
Oakways WA4 26 B3
Oakwood Ave Gatley SK8 239 B5
Warrington WA1 16 C4
Wilmslow SK9 59 C3
Oakwood Avenue Com Prim Sch WA1 16 B4
Oakwood Cl CH66 69 B1
Oakwood Com Prim Sch M31 11 B2
Oakwood Cres
Crewe CW2 189 C2
Sandbach CW11 175 C3
Oakwood Ct WA14 31 A4
Oakwood Dr SK10 87 B3
Oakwood Gate WA3 9 B2
Oakwood La
Altrincham WA14 238 B1
Barnton CW8 78 A1
Sandbach CW11 174 A4
Oakwood Pk CH62 43 B3
Oakwood Rd Disley SK12 38 B3
Rode Heath ST7 193 C4
Romiley SK6 241 C2
Oat Market 8 CW5 204 C3
Oathills SY14 213 A3
Oathills Cl CW6 146 B1
Oathills Dr CW6 146 B1
Oatlands SK9 85 A4
Oban Dr Heswall CH60 41 A4
Sale M33 242 E5
Oban Gr WA2 9 A2
Obelisk Way CW12 156 B2
Ocean St WA14 238 B6
Ocean Street Trad Est WA14 238 B7
Odeon Bldg CH1 237 A3
Off Ridge Hill La SK15 242 C2
Offley Ave CW11 175 A4
Offley Inf Sch CW11 175 A4
Offley Jun Sch CW11 175 A4
Offley Rd CW11 175 A4
Ogden Ct SK14 241 E6
Ogden Rd SK7 35 B3
Oglet La L24 46 C4
Oil Sites Rd CH65 71 B3
Okell St WA7 23 A1
Old Applecroft CW11 174 B3
Old Bank Cl SK6 241 A3
Old Bedions Sports Ctr M20 239 A8
Old Boston WA11 2 A4
Old Boston Trad Est WA11 2 A4
Old Brickworks Ind Est SK10 63 C2
Old Butt La ST7 194 B1
Old Chapel St SK3 240 D3
Old Cherry La WA13 28 A4
Old Chester Ct CW5 187 B3
Old Chester Rd
Barbridge CW5 187 B3
Ellesmere Port CH66 69 B2
Helsby WA6 73 B2
Higher Walton WA4 25 C4
Old Church Cl CH65 70 B4
Old Coach Rd
Broxton SY14,CH3 199 A3
Kelsall CW6 122 B3
Old Constabulary The CW5 204 B3
Old Court Ho The 8 WA16 57 A1
Old Farm Cl
Macclesfield SK10 87 A1
Willaston CH64 68 A4
Old Gardens St 3 SK1 240 F4
Old Gate Cl CW10 151 A4
Old George The CH2 237 B3
Old Gorse Cl CW2 189 C2
Old Hall Ave SK23 65 C2
Old Hall Cl WA4 26 A4
Old Hall Cres SK9 34 C2
Old Hall Ct Ashton CH3 121 C4
Malpas SY14 213 A2
Sale M33 242 E6
Old Hall Dr CH65 70 A2
Old Hall Gdns CH2 237 C4
Old Hall La Elton CH2 72 A2
Knutsford WA16 56 A2
Tabley WA16 55 C2
Woodford SK7 35 B1
Old Hall Pk CH3 119 C3
Old Hall Pl CH1 237 A2
Old Hall Rd Gatley SK8 239 A6
Northwich CW9 104 A3
Sale M33 242 E6
Warrington WA5 15 B4
Old Hall St SK10 87 B1
Old Hey Wlk WA12 2 B1
Old Higher Rd WA8 21 B3
Old Hutte La L26 21 A3
Old La Acton Bridge CW8 76 C2
Old La *continued*
Antrobus CW9 53 B2
Davenham CW9 104 B1
Pulford CH4 162 C1
Heswall CH60 41 B4
Old Liverpool Rd WA5 15 C2
Old Man of Mow★ ST7 195 B4
Old Market Pl
4 Altrincham WA14 238 D5
7 Knutsford WA16 57 A1
Old Mill Cl Heswall CH60 41 A4
Lymm WA13 19 B3
Old Mill Ct CH2 118 B3
Old Mill La
Hazel Grove SK7 37 A4
Macclesfield SK11 112 C3
Whitley WA4 52 C2
Old Mill Pl CH3 166 A1
Old Mill Rd CW11 175 B3
Old Moss La
Fowley Common WA3 5 C3
Tarvin CH3 144 B4
Old Oak Dr M34 241 A7
Old Orchard SK9 60 A4
Old Orchard The
Antrobus CW9 53 B2
Cuddington CW8 101 C2
Old Paddock The CW4 130 C4
Old Park Rd CW1 207 B4
Old Pearl La CH3 119 A1
Old Pewterspear La WA4 26 C2
Old Pump Ho The CH66 68 C4
Old Quay Cl CH64 66 B4
Old Quay La CH64 66 B4
Old Quay St WA7 23 A2
Old Rd Anderton CW9 78 B2
Audley ST7 209 C2
Cheadle SK8 239 F6
Handforth SK9 34 B2
Hyde SK14 241 D8
Stockport SK4 240 E7
Warrington WA4 16 A2
Whaley Bridge SK23 65 C2
Whaley Bridge, Furness Vale SK23 39 B2
Whaley Bridge, New Horwich SK23 65 C3
Wilmslow SK9 60 A4
Old Rectory Gdns SK8 239 D5
Old School Cl
Farndon CH3 180 C1
Neston CH64 66 C3
Old School House La WA2 8 A4
Old Smithy La WA13 18 B1
Old St SK15 242 D2
Old Stack Yd CH3 120 C3
Old Upton La WA8 12 C2
Old Vicarage Gdns CW3 229 C2
Old Vicarage Rd CH64 68 A4
Old Wargrave Rd WA12 2 B2
Old Warrington Rd CW9 79 A1
Old Whint Rd WA11 1 A3
Old Woman's La CH3 142 B4
Old Wool La SK8 239 F4
Old Wrexham Rd CH4 141 B4
Oldcastle La SY14 222 C4
Oldfield Brow Prim Sch WA14 238 A5
Oldfield Cres CH4 140 C3
Oldfield Dr
Altrincham WA15 238 F6
Chester CH3 119 B1
Mobberley WA16 58 A2
Oldfield Gr M33 242 C7
Oldfield La WA14 20 C2
Oldfield Mews WA14 238 C5
Oldfield Prim Sch CH3 119 B2
Oldfield Rd
Altrincham WA14 238 B5
Ellesmere Port CH65 70 A3
Lymm WA13 18 B2
Sale M33 242 C7
Sandbach CW11 174 C2
Oldgate WA8 22 B4
Oldhall St SY14 213 A2
Oldham Dr SK6 241 A4
Oldham St Bollington SK10 88 A4
Hyde SK14 241 D6
Warrington WA4 16 B2
Oldham's Rise SK10 87 B2
Oldhams Hill CW8 78 C1
Oldhill Cl ST7 210 C3
Olive Dr CH64 66 C4
Olive Gr ST5 210 B1
Olive Rd CH64 66 C4
Oliver Cl SK10 87 C4
Oliver La CH66 69 B2
Oliver St
Stockport SK1,SK3 240 F4
Warrington WA2 16 A3
Ollerbarrow Rd WA15 238 E2
Ollersett Ave SK22 39 B4
Ollershaw La CW9 79 B2
Ollerton Cl WA4 17 A2
Ollerton Rd SK9 34 C3
Ollier St 21 WA8 23 A4
Omega Blvd WA5 6 B1
On The Air', Broadcasting & Sound Shop★ CH1 237 B2
One Oak La SK9 60 C4
Onneley La CW3 232 C2
Onslow Rd Blacon CH1 117 B2
Stockport SK3 240 C4
Onston La CW8 101 C4
Onward St SK14 241 D6
Openshaw La M44 11 C3
Orange Gr WA2 8 C1
Orange La CW9 79 B1
Orchard Ave
Acton Bridge CW8 76 C2
Lymm WA13 18 C2
Partington M31 11 C2
Whaley Bridge SK23 65 B4
Orchard Brow WA3 11 A1
Orchard Cl Barnton CW8 78 A2
Bramhall SK8 35 B4
Bunbury CW6 185 C4
Chester CH2 118 B3
Ellesmere Port CH66 69 C1
Frodsham WA6 74 A3
Goostrey CW4 107 C1
Higher Wincham CW9 80 A3
Macclesfield SK11 112 A3
Middlewich CW10 151 B4
Poynton SK12 36 C2
Weaverham CW8 77 B1
Wilmslow SK9 59 C3
Winsford CW7 149 B4
Orchard Cotts CW6 146 B1
Orchard Cres
Kidsgrove ST7 194 B1
Nantwich CW5 204 C2
Nether Alderley SK10 84 C4
Orchard Croft CH3 119 C3
Orchard Ct Alsager ST7 193 C2
5 Chester CH3 119 A1
Haslington CW1 191 B3
Orchard Dene CW8 101 B3
Orchard Dr Handforth SK9 34 C1
Little Leigh CW8 77 B3
Neston CH64 66 C3
Orchard Gdns
Congleton CW12 156 A2
Weaverham CW8 77 A1
Orchard Gn SK9 60 A1
Orchard Gr CH3 180 C1
Orchard Haven CH66 69 C1
Orchard La CH66 69 A4
Orchard Park La CH2 72 B2
Orchard Pl Helsby WA6 73 B2
Poynton SK12 36 B2
5 Sale M33 242 B7
Orchard Rd
Altrincham WA15 238 E5
Ellesmere Port CH65 70 A1
Lymm WA13 19 A3
Whaley Bridge SK23 65 B4
Orchard Rise CW9 126 C4
Orchard St Chester CH1 237 A3
Crewe CW1 190 B3
Hyde SK14 241 E6
Northwich CW9 104 A4
Stockport SK1 240 F5
Warrington WA1 16 B3
Warrington, Fearnhead WA2 9 A1
Warrington, Hillcliffe WA4 26 B4
Willaston (nr Nantwich) CW5 205 B3
Orchard The
Alderley Edge SK9 85 A4
Chester CH3 142 A4
Disley SK12 38 B3
Helsby WA6 73 A1
Orchard Vale SK3 240 C2
Orchard Way
Congleton CW12 156 A2
Kelsall CW6 122 B3
Widnes WA8 12 A2
Orchards The
Broughton CH4 140 B3
Pickmere WA16 79 C4
Shavington CW2 206 B2
Orchid Cl Huntington CH3 142 A3
Irlam M44 11 C4
Orchid Way WA9 6 A4
Orchil Cl CH66 69 A3
Ordnance Ave WA3 9 C2
Ordsall Cl CW11 174 C2
Orford Ave
Warrington WA1,WA2 16 B4
SK12 38 B3
Orford Cl Hale L24 21 C1
High Lane SK6 37 C4
Orford Gn WA2 8 B1
Orford La WA2 16 A4
Orford Rd WA1,WA2 16 C4
Orford St WA1 16 A3
Organsdale Cotts CW6 123 A3
Orhcards The LL13 196 B4
Oriel Bank Sch SK3 240 F1
Oriel Ho CH2 118 B2
Orion Blvd WA5 6 C1
Orion Bsns Pk SK8 240 B1
Orkney Cl
7 Ellesmere Port CH65 70 B1
Widnes WA8 13 C2
Orme Cl Macclesfield SK10 87 B2
Prestbury SK10 87 A4
Orme Cres SK10 87 B2
Orme St SK9 60 A1
Ormerod Cl Romiley SK6 241 A1
Sandbach CW11 175 B3
Ormesby Gr CH63 43 A3
Ormond Cl WA8 12 B1
Ormonde Rd CH2 118 B2
Ormonde St CH2 237 C3
Orphanage St SK4 240 E7
Orrell Cl WA5 15 A3
Orrishmere Rd SK8 239 F3
Orton Cl CW7 127 A2
Ortonbrook Prim Sch M31 11 C1
Orwell Cl SK9 34 B1
Osborne Ave WA2 8 B1
Osborne Gr Gatley SK8 239 A3
Shavington CW2 206 B3

Osborne Rd
Altrincham WA15 . . . . . . .238 E5
Golborne WA3 . . . . .3 C4
Hyde SK14 . . . . .241 E5
Stockport SK2 . . . . .240 F3
Warrington WA4 . . . . .16 A1
Osborne Terr M33 . . . . . .242 B6
Osbourne Cl
Bebington CH62 . . . . .43 C4
Sandbach CW11 . . . . . . .174 B3
Wilmslow SK9 . . . . .60 B3
Osbourne Pl 7 WA14 . .238 D4
Osier Cl CH2 . . . . .72 B2
Osmere Cl SY13 . . . . . . .226 A1
Osprey Ave CW7 . . . . . .149 B3
Osprey Cl
Middlewich CW10 . . . . . .151 B3
Runcorn WA7 . . . . .49 C3
Warrington WA2 . . . . .8 C2
Osprey Ct CH2 . . . . .237 A4
Osprey Dr SK9 . . . . .60 B4
Osprey View ST7 . . . . . .195 B2
Ossett Cl WA7 . . . . .50 B4
Ossmere Cl CW11 . . . . .174 C4
Ostler's La WA16 . . . . . .58 C4
Oteley Ave CH62 . . . . . .43 B4
Otters Bank CW7 . . . . .126 A1
Oughtrington Cres WA13 19 A2
Oughtrington La WA13 . .19 A1
Oughtrington Prim Sch
WA13 . . . . .19 A2
Oughtrington View
WA13 . . . . .19 A2
Oulton Ave Chester CH2 .118 C4
Sale M33 . . . . .242 E7
Oulton Dr CW12 . . . . . . .155 C2
Oulton Mill La CW6 . . . .147 A4
Oulton Pl CH1 . . . . .237 B3
**Our Lady Mother of the
Saviour RC Prim Sch**
WA7 . . . . .50 A3
**Our Lady of Lourdes RC Prim
Sch** M31 . . . . .11 C2
**Our Lady of Perpetual
Succour RC Inf Sch**
WA8 . . . . .12 A1
**Our Lady of Perpetual
Succour RC Jun Sch**
WA8 . . . . .22 A1
Our Lady's RC Inf & Jun Sch
CH65 . . . . .70 A2
Our Lady's RC Prim Sch
Stockport SK3 . . . . .240 E4
Warrington WA4 . . . . . . .16 C2
Out La CH3 . . . . .184 B3
Outwood Dr SK8 . . . . . .34 A4
Outwood La M90 . . . . . .33 B4
Outwood La W M90 . . . .33 A4
Outwood Prim Sch SK8 .34 B4
Outwood Rd SK8 . . . . . .34 A4
Oval The
Ellesmere Port CH65 . . . .70 B2
Gatley SK8 . . . . .34 A4
Ovenhouse La SK10 . . . .87 A3
Over Hall Com Sch
CW7 . . . . .149 A4
Over Hill Dr CW7 . . . . . .149 B4
Over Pl WA16 . . . . .82 B4
Over Rd CW5 . . . . .172 A4
Over St John's CE Prim Sch
CW7 . . . . .126 A1
Overdale WA16 . . . . . . .238 B5
Overdale La CW8 . . . . .101 B4
Overdale Rd
New Mills SK12 . . . . .38 C3
Willaston CH64 . . . . .43 A1
Overdene Rd CW7 . . . . .149 B4
Overfields WA16 . . . . . .57 B2
Overhill Dr SK9 . . . . . . .60 C4
Overhill La SK9 . . . . . . .60 C4
Overhill Rd SK9 . . . . . . .60 B4
Overleigh Ct CH4 . . . . .141 B4
Overleigh Rd CH4 . . . . .141 B4
**Overleigh St Mary's CE Prim
Sch** CH4 . . . . .141 B4
Overleigh Terr CH4 . . . .141 B4
Overpool Gdns CH66 . . .69 C2
Overpool Rd CH66 . . . . .69 C3
Overpool Sta CH66 . . . . .69 C3
Overton Cl
Congleton CW12 . . . . . .156 B2
Middlewich CW10 . . . . . .151 A4
Overton Dr WA6 . . . . . . .74 B3
Overton Rd ST8 . . . . . . .179 C3
Overton Way 2 SK9 . . .34 B3
Overway CW7 . . . . .126 C1
Overwood Ave CH1 . . . . .94 C1
Overwood La Blacon CH1 117 B2
Mollington CH1 . . . . .94 B1
Ovington Cl WA7 . . . . . .49 C2
Owen Cl CH1 . . . . .117 C4
Owen St Crewe CW2 . . .190 B1
Northwich CW9 . . . . . . .104 A4
Stockport SK3 . . . . .240 D5
Warrington WA2 . . . . . . .16 A4
Owl Ind Est The CH5 . . .116 A3
Owley Wood Rd CW8 . . .77 C1
Owlsfield WA12 . . . . . . .2 C2
Ox-Hey Cres ST8 . . . . . .179 B1
Ox-Hey Dr ST8 . . . . . . .179 B1
Oxborough Cl WA8 . . . . .12 C2
Oxenham Rd WA2 . . . . . .8 A2
Oxford Cl CH66 . . . . . . .94 C4
Oxford Dr Halewood L26 .21 A4
Heswall CH63 . . . . .41 C3
Romiley SK6 . . . . .241 C4
Oxford Gr M44 . . . . .11 B3

Oxford Rd
Altrincham WA14 . . . . . .238 D3
Chester CH4 . . . . .140 D3
Macclesfield SK11 . . . . .112 A4
Runcorn WA7 . . . . .49 A4
Oxford St Crewe CW1 . .190 A3
Newton-le-W WA12 . . . . .2 A2
Stalybridge SK15 . . . . . .242 F1
Warrington WA4 . . . . . . .16 B2
Widnes WA8 . . . . .23 A4
Oxford Way WA4 . . . . . .240 D7
Oxhey Fst Sch ST8 . . . .179 C1
Oxheys WA7 . . . . .50 B4
Oxmead Cl WA2 . . . . . . .9 A1
Oxmoor Cl WA7 . . . . . . .50 A4
Oxney Cl SK11 . . . . . . .111 C4
Oxton Cl WA8 . . . . .12 C1
Oxton Gn CH66 . . . . . . .69 B2

P

Pacific Rd WA14 . . . . . .238 A6
Packmoor Prim Sch
ST7 . . . . .195 C1
Packsaddle Pk SK10 . . .86 C3
Padarn Cl CH4 . . . . .140 B3
Padden Brook SK6 . . . . .241 B2
Padden Brook Mews
SK6 . . . . .241 B2
Paddington Bank WA1 . .16 C3
Paddock Brow SK10 . . . .87 A3
Paddock Chase SK12 . . .36 C3
Paddock Cl SK23 . . . . . .64 C2
Paddock Dr CH64 . . . . . .41 B1
Paddock Hill La WA14 . .59 A2
Paddock La Audlem CW3 230 A1
Kettleshulme SK23 . . . . . .64 C2
Lymm WA13 . . . . .19 B4
Partington WA13,WA14 . .20 A3
Whaley Bridge SK23 . . . .65 C3
Paddock Rd CH4 . . . . . .141 C1
Paddock Rise WA7 . . . . .49 C2
Paddock The
Cheadle SK8 . . . . .239 E5
Chester CH4 . . . . .141 A4
Ellesmere Port CH66 . . . .69 B2
Elton CH2 . . . . .72 A2
Handforth SK9 . . . . .34 B2
Hartford CW8 . . . . .103 B2
Hassall Green CW11 . . . .175 C1
Helsby WA6 . . . . .73 B1
Heswall CH60 . . . . .41 B4
Lymm WA13 . . . . .19 B4
Tarporley CW6 . . . . .146 B1
Whaley Bridge SK23 . . . .65 C3
Willaston (nr Nantwich)
CW5 . . . . .205 B2
Paddock View CW10 . . .128 B1
Paddock Way CW4 . . . .161 A4
Paddock Wlk CW8 . . . . .101 B3
Paddocks Gn CW12 . . . .178 C4
Paddocks The
Prestbury SK10 . . . . .87 A3
Whitegate CW8 . . . . . . .125 A3
Padgate Bsns Ctr WA1 . .17 A4
Padgate CE Prim Sch
WA2 . . . . .9 A1
Padgate Com High Sch
WA2 . . . . .8 C1
Padgate La WA1 . . . . . . .16 C4
Padgate Sta WA1 . . . . . .9 A1
Padgbury Cl CW12 . . . . .156 A1
Padgbury La CW12 . . . . .156 A1
Padmore Cl CW1 . . . . . .190 A4
Padston Dr ST7 . . . . . . .193 A2
Padstow Cl Crewe CW1 .190 B4
Macclesfield SK10 . . . . . .111 C4
Warrington WA5 . . . . . . .14 C2
Padstow Dr SK7 . . . . . . .35 C4
Padstow Sq WA7 . . . . . .50 A3
Padworth Pl CW1 . . . . . .173 A1
Page Gr CW2 . . . . .206 A2
Page La WA8 . . . . .13 B1
Paignton Cl WA5 . . . . . .14 C2
Painswick Rd CH66 . . . . .69 C1
Paisley Ave CH62 . . . . . .43 C4
Palace Fields Ave WA7 . .50 A4
Palace Fields Local Ctr
WA7 . . . . .50 A3
Palace Hey CH64 . . . . . .67 A3
Palace Rd M33 . . . . . . .242 A7
Palacefields Prim Sch
WA7 . . . . .50 A3
Palatine Cl CH1 . . . . . . .117 B3
Palatine Ind Est WA4 . . .16 B2
Palgrave Cl CW1 . . . . . .118 A3
Palin Dr WA5 . . . . .14 C3
Pall Mall CW5 . . . . .204 C3
Pallard Ave WA6 . . . . . . .74 B4
Palliser Cl WA3 . . . . .10 A2
Palm Gr CH66 . . . . .70 A1
Palma Ave M90 . . . . . . .33 A4
Palmer Ave SK8 . . . . . . .239 F6
Palmer Cres WA5 . . . . . .15 B4
Palmer Cl CW9 . . . . . . .103 C3
Palmer St M33 . . . . . . .242 A6
Palmer Rd CW11 . . . . . .175 B3
Palmerston Cl CW1 . . . .191 B3
Palmerston Rd SK11 . . .112 A4
Palmerston St SK10 . . . .88 A4
Palmerston Way ST8 . . .179 B1
Palmerstone Cl CH1 . . . .118 A2
Palmyra Sq N WA1 . . . .16 A3
Palmyra Sq S WA1 . . . .16 A3
Panda Way CW1 . . . . . .175 A4
Pangbourne Cl
Stockport SK3 . . . . .240 C2

Pangbourne Cl *continued*
Warrington WA4 . . . . .26 C3
Panton Pl CH2 . . . . .118 C2
Panton Rd CH2 . . . . . . .118 C2
Parade Rd M90 . . . . .33 B4
Parade The
1 Alderley Edge SK9 . . . .60 A1
Blacon CH1 . . . . .117 C3
Neston CH64 . . . . .41 A1
Romiley SK6 . . . . .241 B1
Paradise CH4 . . . . .237 B1
Paradise La CW5 . . . . . .171 C4
Paradise Mill (Mus)★
SK11 . . . . .112 B4
Paradise St SK11 . . . . . .112 B4
Paragon Cl WA8 . . . . . . .13 A3
Parbold Ct WA8 . . . . . . .22 B4
Parchments The WA12 . . .2 A2
Parish Cl ST7 . . . . .193 A2
Park Ave
Altrincham, Hale WA15 . .238 F1
Altrincham, Timperley
WA14 . . . . .238 E8
Bramhall SK7 . . . . .35 B3
Broughton CH4 . . . . .140 C3
Cheadle SK3 . . . . .239 F7
Cheadle SK8 . . . . .239 F1
Haydock WA11 . . . . .1 A3
Hyde SK14 . . . . .241 D8
Poynton SK12 . . . . .36 C2
Romiley SK6 . . . . .241 C2
Sale M33 . . . . .242 A8
Saughall CH1 . . . . .94 A1
Talke ST7 . . . . .210 C4
Tattenhall CH3 . . . . .166 A1
Warrington WA4 . . . . . . .16 B2
Weaverham CW8 . . . . . . .77 B1
Whaley Bridge SK23 . . . .39 B2
Widnes WA8 . . . . .13 A1
Wilmslow SK9 . . . . .60 B4
Winsford CW7 . . . . .127 A2
Park Ave N WA12 . . . . . .2 B1
Park Ave S WA12 . . . . . .2 B1
Park Bank CW12 . . . . . .156 C1
Park Brook Rd SK11 . . . .112 A4
Park Bvd WA4 . . . . .16 A2
Park Cl Sale WA14 . . . . .238 F8
Stalybridge SK15 . . . . . .242 C3
Tarvin CH3 . . . . .121 A1
Park Court Mews SK8 . .239 E4
Park Cres
Ashton-u-Lyne OL6 . . . . .242 B2
Cuddington SK8 . . . . . . .101 C2
Handforth SK9 . . . . .34 A1
Warrington WA4 . . . . . . .26 B3
Whaley Bridge SK23 . . . .39 B2
Park Ct Chester CH2 . . . .237 C2
Frodsham WA6 . . . . .74 A4
Runcorn WA7 . . . . .49 A4
Sale M33 . . . . .242 A7
2 Warrington WA1 . . . . .16 A3
Park Dr Altrincham WA15 .238 F1
Chester CH2 . . . . .119 A2
Ellesmere Port CH65 . . . .70 A4
Hyde SK14 . . . . .241 D8
Stockport SK4 . . . . .240 B6
Wistaston CW2 . . . . . . .205 C4
Park Dr S CH2 . . . . .119 A2
Park Est CW2 . . . . .206 B3
Park Gn SK11 . . . . .112 B4
Park Gr SK4 . . . . .240 B8
Park House Dr
Prestbury SK10 . . . . .87 A4
Sandbach CW11 . . . . . . .175 B4
Park House La SK10 . . . .87 A4
Park House Mews
CW11 . . . . .175 B4
Park La Audley ST7 . . . .209 A2
Congleton CW12 . . . . . .156 C1
Frodsham WA6 . . . . .74 C1
Hargrave CH3 . . . . .144 C2
Hartford CW8 . . . . .103 A2
Hatherton CW5 . . . . . . .219 C2
Higher Walton WA4 . . . . .25 C3
Little Bollington WA14 . . .20 A1
Macclesfield SK11 . . . . .112 B3
Moulton CW9 . . . . .126 C4
Pickmere CW9,WA16 . . . .79 C4
Poynton SK12 . . . . .36 C2
Sandbach CW11 . . . . . .174 C3
Park Lane Sch SK11 . . . .112 A3
Park Lodge Cl SK8 . . . . .239 E4
Park Mills Cl CW5 . . . . .205 B3
Park Mount SK8 . . . . . . .239 A5
Park Mount Cl SK11 . . . .112 A3
Park Mount Dr SK11 . . . .112 A3
Park Prim Sch The WA7 .24 A1
Park Rd
Altrincham, Bowdon WA14 238 A2
Altrincham, Hale WA15 . .238 F1
Altrincham, Timperley
WA14,WA15 . . . . .238 F8
Bebington, Eastham CH62 .43 C3
Cheadle SK8 . . . . .239 E6
Congleton CW12 . . . . . .156 C2
Congleton, North Rode
CW12 . . . . .134 C1
Ellesmere Port CH65 . . . .70 B2
Golborne WA3 . . . . .3 A4
Haslington CW1 . . . . . . .191 B3
Heswall CH60 . . . . .41 A4
High Lane SK12 . . . . .37 C3
Hyde SK14 . . . . .241 D8
Little Budworth CW6 . . . .124 C1
Lymm WA13 . . . . .29 B4
Macclesfield SK11 . . . . .112 B3
Middlewich CW10 . . . . . .128 B1

Park Rd *continued*
Nantwich CW5 . . . . .204 C2
New Mills SK22 . . . . .39 B4
Northwich CW8 . . . . .78 B1
Partington WA13 . . . . . . .19 B4
Romiley SK6 . . . . .241 C3
Runcorn WA7 . . . . .49 A4
Sale M33 . . . . .242 A8
Sandbach CW11 . . . . . .175 B4
Stalybridge SK15,SK16 . .242 A1
Tarporley CW6 . . . . .146 B1
Thornton-le-M CH2 . . . . .71 C1
Warrington WA5 . . . . . . .14 C3
Warrington, Orford WA2 . .8 B1
Whaley Bridge SK23 . . . .65 B3
Widnes WA8 . . . . .13 A1
Willaston CH64 . . . . .68 A4
Willaston (nr Nantwich)
CW5 . . . . .205 B3
Wilmslow SK9 . . . . .59 C4
Park Rd N WA12 . . . . . . .2 C2
Park Rd S WA12 . . . . . . .2 B1
Park Rd W CH4 . . . . . . .141 A4
Park Rise SK6 . . . . .241 C3
Park Road Com Prim Sch
WA5 . . . . .14 C3
Park Road Prim Sch
Altrincham WA14 . . . . . .238 E8
Sale M33 . . . . .242 A8
Park St Bollington SK10 . .88 A4
Chester CH1 . . . . .237 B2
Congleton CW12 . . . . . .156 C1
Haydock WA11 . . . . .1 A3
Macclesfield SK11 . . . . .112 B4
Neston CH64 . . . . .66 C4
Northwich CW8 . . . . .103 C4
Stalybridge SK15 . . . . . .242 E1
6 Stockport SK1 . . . . . .240 F6
Park The Christleton CH3 .142 C4
Warrington WA5 . . . . . . .14 B2
Park Vale Rd SK11 . . . . .112 B3
Park View Audlem CW3 . .230 B4
Bebington CH62 . . . . . . .43 B4
Cheadle SK3 . . . . .239 F7
Congleton CW12 . . . . . .156 C2
Gatley SK8 . . . . .239 A6
High Lane SK7 . . . . .37 A4
Little Bollington WA14 . . .20 A1
Nantwich CW5 . . . . .204 C3
Newton-le-W WA12 . . . . .2 C2
Park View Ct
Poynton SK12 . . . . .36 C2
Romiley SK6 . . . . .241 C2
Park View Rd ST7 . . . . . .195 A2
Park W Blacon CH1 . . . .117 C1
Heswall CH60 . . . . .40 C4
Park Way CH1 . . . . .94 A1
Park Wlk CH2 . . . . .118 C2
Parkdale Ind Est WA1 . . .16 B2
Parkdale Rd WA1 . . . . . .17 A4
Parker Ave CW8 . . . . . .103 A3
Parker Dr CH3 . . . . .180 C1
Parker Dr S CH3 . . . . . .180 C1
Parker St
Macclesfield SK11 . . . . .112 C1
Runcorn WA7 . . . . .23 A2
Warrington WA1 . . . . . . .16 A3
Parker's Rd CW1 . . . . . .190 A4
Parker's Row CH3 . . . . .180 C3
Parkett Heyes Rd SK11 . .111 C4
Parkfield Crewe CW1 . . .173 A1
Ellesmere Port CH65 . . . .70 A1
Parkfield Ave WA4 . . . . .17 A2
Parkfield Cl WA14 . . . . .238 C4
Parkfield Dr
Ellesmere Port CH65 . . . .70 A2
Helsby WA6 . . . . .73 A2
Nantwich CW5 . . . . .204 C2
Parkfield Rd
Altrincham WA14 . . . . . .238 C4
Broughton CH4 . . . . .139 B2
Cheadle SK8 . . . . .239 F1
Knutsford WA16 . . . . . . .82 A4
Northwich CW9 . . . . .104 B4
Parkfields La WA2 . . . . . .8 C1
Parkgate
Altrincham WA14 . . . . . .238 A4
Knutsford WA16 . . . . . . .57 B2
Parkgate Ave WA16 . . . .108 A4
Parkgate Ct CH1 . . . . . .118 A2
Parkgate La Heswall CH64 41 C3
Knutsford WA16 . . . . . . .57 B2
Parkgate Prim Sch CH64 .41 B1
Parkgate Rd
Chester CH1 . . . . .118 A2
Macclesfield SK11 . . . . .112 B2
Mollington CH1 . . . . .117 C4
Neston CH64 . . . . .66 B4
Puddington CH66 . . . . . .68 B1
Saughall CH1 . . . . .94 B2
Shotwick CH1 . . . . .93 C4
Warrington WA4 . . . . . . .16 B1
Parkgate Trad Est WA16 .57 B2
Parkgate Way
7 Handforth SK9 . . . . . .34 B2
Runcorn WA7 . . . . .50 B4
Parkhill Ct WA16 . . . . . .57 A1
Parkhouse Ind Est ST5 . .210 C1
Parkhouse Rd E ST5 . . . .210 C1
Parkhouse Rd W ST5 . . .210 C1
Parkland Cl WA4 . . . . . . .27 A4
Parkland Dr CH2 . . . . . . .72 A2
Parklands
Ellesmere Port CH66 . . . .69 B3
Kidsgrove ST7 . . . . .195 A1
Sale M33 . . . . .242 C4
Widnes WA8 . . . . .12 B2

Osb – Pea 275

Parklands Com Prim Sch
CH66 . . . . .69 B3
Parklands Dr Elton CH2 . .72 B2
Heswall CH60 . . . . .41 B3
Parklands Gdns CH66 . . .69 B3
Parklands The
Congleton CW12 . . . . . .157 A1
Stockport SK4 . . . . .240 E8
Parklands View CH66 . . .69 B3
Parklands Way SK12 . . . .36 C2
Parklea CH66 . . . . .69 B3
Parkleigh CW12 . . . . . . .156 C1
Parkroyal Com Sch
SK11 . . . . .112 B4
Parkside SK6 . . . . .37 A4
Parkside Cl SK6 . . . . . . .37 B4
Parkside Ct WA8 . . . . . . .13 A1
Parkside Rd
Culcheth WA12,WA2 . . . . .3 A1
Sale M33 . . . . .242 D5
Parkstone Dr CW1 . . . . .190 A4
Parksway WA1 . . . . .17 B4
Parkview Ct CH60 . . . . . .40 C4
Parkway Cheadle SK8 . . .239 F7
Connah's Quay CH5 . . . . .92 C1
Holmes Chapel CW4 . . . .130 B2
Wilmslow SK9 . . . . .60 A3
Parkway Bsns Ctr CH5 . .92 C1
Parkwood Cl
Bebington CH62 . . . . . . .43 C4
Lymm WA13 . . . . .18 B1
Parliament St 22 CW8 . .103 C4
Parliament Way CH66 . . .94 C4
Parlington Cl WA8 . . . . . .22 B4
Parnell Sq CW12 . . . . . .157 A1
Parochial CE Prim Sch
OL6 . . . . .242 A4
Parr Gr WA11 . . . . .1 A3
Parr St Macclesfield SK11 112 B4
Warrington WA1 . . . . . . .16 B2
1 Widnes WA8 . . . . .13 B1
Parrs Wood Rd M20 . . . .239 B8
Parrs Wood View WA4 . .17 A1
Parry Dr WA4 . . . . .17 C2
Parry Mead SK6 . . . . . . .241 A4
Parry Wlk OL6 . . . . .242 A4
Parson St CW12 . . . . . . .156 B1
Parsonage Ct SK8 . . . . .239 C8
Parsonage Gn Hale L24 . .21 C1
Wilmslow SK9 . . . . .60 A4
Parsonage Rd
Stockport SK4 . . . . .240 C8
Widnes WA8 . . . . .23 A4
Parsonage St Hyde SK14 241 D5
Macclesfield SK11 . . . . .112 B4
Stockport SK4 . . . . .240 E6
Parsonage Way
Stockport SK8 . . . . .240 B1
Warrington WA5 . . . . . . .15 A3
Parsons La CH2 . . . . . . .118 A4
Partington Pl 4 M33 . . .242 B7
Partington Prim Sch
M31 . . . . .11 C2
Partridge Cl
Congleton CW12 . . . . . .156 C1
Warrington WA3 . . . . .9 C2
Winsford CW7 . . . . .149 B3
Partridge Way CW7 . . . . .79 C3
Parvey La SK11 . . . . . . .112 C1
Pasture Cl Kelsall CW6 . .122 B2
Macclesfield SK10 . . . . . .87 B2
Pasture Dr WA3 . . . . .9 A4
Pasture La WA2 . . . . .9 A4
Pasturefield Cl 1 M33 . .242 F5
Pastures The WA9 . . . . . .6 A4
Patch La SK7 . . . . .35 B3
Patmos La WA16 . . . . . .105 C4
Patrivale Cl WA1 . . . . . . .16 C3
Patten La WA1 . . . . .16 A3
Patterdale Ave WA2 . . . . .8 B1
Patterdale Cl
Crewe CW2 . . . . .189 B2
Stalybridge SK15 . . . . . .242 D3
Patterdale Rd
Partington M31 . . . . .11 C2
Romiley SK6 . . . . .241 B4
Patterson Cl WA3 . . . . . . .9 C2
Patterson St WA12 . . . . .2 A2
Paul Cl WA5 . . . . .14 B3
Paul St WA2 . . . . .16 A3
Paulden Rd CW9 . . . . . . .80 A1
Pavement La WA16 . . . . .57 C2
Pavilion Way
Congleton CW12 . . . . . .156 B2
Macclesfield SK10 . . . . . .86 C1
Pavilions The
Cheadle SK8 . . . . .239 D4
Davenham CW9 . . . . . . .103 C1
Eccleston CH4 . . . . .141 A2
Paxford Pl SK9 . . . . .60 A3
Paxhill Ct SK4 . . . . .240 A6
Payne Cl WA5 . . . . .15 B3
Paythorne Cl WA3 . . . . . .4 C1
Peace Dr WA5 . . . . .15 B3
Peach Field CH3 . . . . . . .142 A4
Peach Gr WA11 . . . . .1 C4
Peach La CW5 . . . . .189 A1
Peach Tree Cl L24 . . . . . .21 C1
Peacock Ave Gatley SK8 . .34 A4
Warrington WA1 . . . . . . .16 C2
Winsford CW7 . . . . .149 B3
Peacock Hay Rd ST7 . . . .210 C2
Peacock La WA16 . . . . . .29 C3

Peacock Way 5 SK9 ....34 B3
Peak Bank SK6 ....241 B3
Peak Rd SK22 ....39 B4
Peakdale Ave SK8 ....239 B4
Pear Tree Ave
  Crewe CW1 ....190 A4
  Runcorn WA7 ....49 B4
Pear Tree Cl
  Frodsham WA6 ....49 B1
  Hale L24 ....21 C1
  Winsford CW7 ....149 B4
Pear Tree Dr
  Higher Wincham CW9 ...80 A3
  Stalybridge SK15 ....242 E2
Pear Tree Farm Cotts
  CW9 ....104 C2
Pear Tree Field CW5 ..205 A2
Pear Tree La
  Acton Bridge CW8 ....76 C2
  Whitchurch SY13 ....225 B1
Pear Tree Rd ST7 ....209 C1
Pear Tree Way
  Chester CH2 ....118 C3
  7 Ellesmere Port CH66 ..69 C1
Pearl La CH3 ....119 B1
Pearl St SK10 ....87 A4
Pearle St SK10 ....87 B1
Pearlings The CH3 ....119 A1
Pearson Ave WA4 ......16 B1
Pearson St
  15 Macclesfield SK11 ..112 C4
  Stockport SK5 ......240 F7
Peartree Cl CW11 ....175 C3
Peartree La SY14 ....222 B1
Peartree Pl WA4 ......16 B2
Pearwood Cl CW6 ....146 B1
Peaslake Cl SK6 ......241 D2
Peasley Cl WA2 ....9 A1
Pebble Brook Prim Sch
  CW2 ....190 B1
Pebble Cl SK15 ......242 D4
Peck Mill La WA6 ......98 A4
Peckfield Cl WA7 ......50 A3
Peckforton Castle ★
  CW6 ....167 C1
Peckforton Cl
  Gatley SK8 ....239 A5
  Sandbach CW11 ......174 C4
Peckforton Dr
  Ellesmere Port CH66 ..69 C2
  Runcorn WA7 ....49 C2
Peckforton Hall La
  CW6 ....185 A3
Peckforton Rd CW6 ..168 A1
Peckforton Way
  Chester CH2 ....118 C3
  20 Northwich CW8 ....103 C4
Peckmill Cl SK9 ......34 C1
Peckforton Wlk 11 SK9 ..34 C1
Pedley Hill Adlington SK10 62 C4
  Rainow SK10 ....88 C2
Pedley House La WA16 ..58 C1
Pedley La Chelford WA16 ..83 B4
  Congleton CW12 ....157 C2
Pedley St CW2 ....190 B1
Peebles Cl
  Ellesmere Port CH66 ..68 C3
  Holmes Chapel CW4 ..130 A1
Peel Ave WA14 ......238 D2
Peel Cl WA1 ....17 B3
Peel Cres CH3 ....121 C4
Peel Ct 4 ST7 ......195 C4
Peel Dr Astbury CW12 ..178 A4
  Sale M33 ....242 E6
Peel Hall La CH3 ....121 C4
Peel Hollow ST7 ....209 A1
Peel House La WA8 ..13 A1
Peel La CW12 ....178 B4
Peel Rd WA15 ....238 E3
Peel Sq WA1 ....190 A3
Peel St Crewe CW1 ..190 A4
  Hyde SK14 ....241 F5
  Macclesfield SK11 ..112 B3
  Newton-le-W WA12 ....2 A1
  Runcorn WA7 ....22 C2
  Stalybridge SK15 ..242 C1
  Stockport SK2 ......240 F2
Peel Terr CH2 ......237 C3
Peelgate Dr SK8 ......239 A2
Peerglow Park Est
  WA14 ....238 E8
Peerswood Ct CH64 ..66 C3
Peewit Cl CW7 ......149 B3
Pegasus Ct M33 ....242 D7
Peggie's La SK10 ....62 B1
Pelham Cl CW1 ......191 B3
Pelham Rd WA4 ......17 B2
Pelican Cl CW1 ......191 A4
Pemberton Cl CH64 ..68 A4
Pemberton Rd CH1 ..237 C2
Pembridge Ct CH65 ..70 C2
Pembridge Gdns CH65 ..70 C2
Pembroke Ct CH4 ....141 C3
Pembroke Dr CH65 ..70 A2
Pembroke Gdns WA4 ..26 B2
Pembroke Gr M44 ....11 B3
Pembroke Rd SK11 ..111 C4
Pembroke Way CW7 ..149 A4
Penare WA7 ....50 B3
Penbrook Cl CW2 ....189 B2
Pendennis Rd SK4 ..240 C7
Pendine Cl WA5 ....7 B1
Pendle Cl Crewe CW1 ..191 A3
  Ellesmere Port CH66 ..68 C3

Pendle Gdns WA3 ......4 C1
Pendlebury Rd SK8 ..239 B6
Pendlebury St WA4 ....17 A2
Penfold Cl CH1 ....94 A4
Penfold Hey CH2 ....118 B4
Penfold Way CH4 ....162 A4
Penfolds WA7 ....23 B1
Penhale Mews SK7 ....35 C4
Penistone Dr CH66 ....69 A3
Penkeith's La WA7 ....23 A2
Penketh Ave WA5 ....15 C4
Penketh Bsns Pk WA5 ..15 A2
Penketh Ct WA5 ......23 A1
Penketh High Sch WA5 ..15 A3
Penketh Prim Sch WA5 ..14 B2
Penketh South Com Prim Sch
  WA5 ....14 C2
Penkford La WA5 ....1 B1
Penkford Sch WA12 ....1 C1
Penkford St WA12 ......1 C1
Penlington Ct CW5 ..204 C3
Penmann Cres L26 ....21 A4
Penmark Cl WA5 ....7 B1
Penmon Cl CH1 ......117 B2
Penn Gdns CH65 ......70 A3
Penn House St SK7 ....35 C4
Penn La WA7 ....22 C1
Pennant Cl WA3 ......10 A2
Pennine Ct SK10 ......87 C1
Pennine Dr
  Altrincham WA14 ....238 B5
  Ashton-u-Lyne OL6 ..242 B4
Pennine Rd WA2 ....8 C1
Pennine View SK15 ..242 F4
Pennine Way
  Biddulph ST8 ......179 C1
  Winsford CW7 ......149 A4
Pennine Wlk CH66 ....69 A3
Pennington Cl WA6 ....49 B1
Pennington Dr WA12 ..2 C2
Pennington Gn CH66 ..69 B2
Pennington La WA5,WA9 ..1 B1
Penningtons La SK11 ..111 C3
Penny Bank Cl CH4 ..139 A2
Penny La Collins Green WA5 1 B1
  Cronton WA8,L35 ....12 A3
  Haydock WA11 ....2 A1
  Rainow SK10 ....88 B2
  Stockport SK5 ......240 F7
Penny's La
  Lach Dennis CW9 ....105 A3
  Northwich CW9 ......104 C3
Pennyfields Rd ST7 ..195 B1
Pennymoor Dr WA14 ..238 B6
Pennypleck La CW9 ....28 A1
Penrhyn Ave SK8 ....239 E1
Penrhyn Cres
  Hazel Grove SK7 ....36 B4
  Runcorn WA7 ....49 A4
Penrhyn Rd
  Northwich CW8 ......103 C4
  Stockport SK3 ......240 C4
Penrith Ave
  Macclesfield SK11 ..111 C3
  Warrington WA2 ......8 B1
Penrith Cl Frodsham WA6 ..49 B1
  Partington M31 ......11 C2
Penrose Gdns WA5 ....14 B2
Penry Ave M44 ....11 C3
Penryn Cl WA5 ......14 C2
Pensarn Gdns WA5 ....7 B1
Pensarn Gr SK5 ....240 F8
Pensby Ave CH2 ......118 B3
Pensby Dr CH66 ......69 B2
Pensby Rd CH60 ......40 C4
Penshaw Ct WA7 ......49 A4
Penshurst Wlk 7 M34 ..241 A5
Pentland Ave WA2 ....8 A2
Pentland Cl Chester CH3 ..119 A1
  Winsford CW7 ......149 A4
Pentland Pl WA2 ......8 A2
Pentre Cl CH3 ......121 C4
Pentre La CH3 ......121 C4
Penzance Cl SK10 ....111 C4
Peony Gdns WA9 ......6 A4
Peover Ave M33 ....242 E6
Peover Hall ★ WA16 ..107 C4
Peover La Chelford SK11 ..108 C4
  Congleton CW12 ....157 C2
Peover Prim Sch WA16 ..108 A4
Peover Rd SK9 ....34 C3
Pepper Ct SK9 ....60 A3
Pepper St
  Appleton Thorn WA4 ..27 A2
  Ashley WA16 ....31 C1
  Chelford SK11 ......83 C1
  Chester CH1 ......237 B2
  Christleton CH3 ....142 B4
  Hale L24 ....21 B1
  Henbury SK11 ......111 A4
  Lymm WA13 ....18 C2
  Middlewich CW10 ....128 B1
  Nantwich CW5 ......204 C3
Peppers The WA13 ....18 C2
Percival Cl CH2 ....118 B4
Percival La Ollerton WA16 ..83 A2
  Runcorn WA7 ....23 A1
Percival Rd Chester CH2 ..118 B4
  Ellesmere Port CH65 ..70 A3
Percival St WA1 ......16 B3
Percy James Cl ST7 ..193 C2
Percy St Northwich CW9 ..104 A4
  Stalybridge SK15 ..242 E2
  Stockport SK1 ......240 F6
  Warrington WA5 ......15 C3

Peregrine Cl CW7 ....149 B3
Perimeter Rd CH2 ....72 B3
Perrey St WA7 ....23 A1
Perrin Ave WA7 ......48 C4
Perrin St SK14 ......241 D6
Perrins Rd WA5 ....6 C3
Perry Fields CW1 ....173 A1
Perth Cl Bramhall SK7 ..35 C3
  Holmes Chapel CW4 ..130 A1
  Warrington WA2 ......8 C2
Peter House Rd SK11 ..112 C2
Peter Pl CW1 ....190 A4
Peter Salem Dr WA5 ..15 A3
Peter St
  Altrincham WA14 ..238 D3
  Denton M34 ....241 A4
  Golborne WA3 ....3 A4
  Macclesfield SK11 ..112 B4
  Northwich CW9 ......79 A1
  Peter St W WA7 ......112 B4
Peter St W SK11 ....112 B4
Peterborough Cl
  Ellesmere Port CH66 ..94 C4
  Macclesfield SK10 ..87 A1
Peterhouse Gdns SK6 ..241 C4
Peters Cl SK10 ....87 A4
Petersburg Rd SK3 ..240 D2
Petersfield Gdns WA3 ..4 C2
Petersgate WA7 ......50 B4
Petersham Dr WA4 ....26 C3
Peterstone Cl WA5 ....7 B1
Petham Ct WA8 ......12 C2
Petrel Ave SK12 ......36 A2
Petrel Cl Stockport SK3 ..240 B2
  Winsford CW7 ......149 B3
Petunia Cl
  Macclesfield SK11 ..112 A3
  St Helens WA9 ....6 A4
Petworth Ave WA2 ....8 A2
Petworth Cl CW2 ....206 A4
Pevensey Dr WA16 ....82 A4
Peveril Cl WA4 ......26 B4
Peveril Dr SK7 ......36 C4
Peveril Gdns SK12 ....39 A3
Peveril Mews SK12 ....39 A3
Peveril Rd WA14 ....238 C7
Peveril Wlk SK11 ....111 C4
Pewit La CW5 ....231 A4
Pewithall Prim Sch WA7 ..49 A4
Pewterspear Green Rd
  WA4 ....26 C2
Pewterspear La WA4 ..26 B2
Pexhall Rd CW12,SK11 ..134 B2
Pexhill Ct SK4 ......240 A6
Pexhill Dr SK10 ......111 C4
Pexhill Rd
  Macclesfield SK11 ..111 B3
  Siddington SK11 ....110 B2
Pheasant Cl WA3 ......9 C2
Pheasant Dr CW9 ......79 C3
Pheasant Field L24 ....21 B1
Pheasant Rise WA14 ..238 D1
Pheasant Way CW7 ..149 B3
Pheasant Wlk WA16 ..29 B2
Philip Rd WA8 ....22 A4
Philip St CH5 ....116 A1
Philips Dr WA5 ......14 C4
Philips La CH66 ......69 B2
Phillip St CH2 ......118 C2
Phillips Rd CH1 ......117 B2
Phillips Way CH60 ....40 C4
Phipps' La WA5 ......6 C4
Phoenix Ave WA5 ......7 C1
Phoenix Cl ST7 ......195 B1
Phoenix St CH5 ......116 A2
Phythian Cres WA5 ..14 C2
Piccadilly SK1 ......240 F5
Pichael Nook WA4 ....17 A2
Pickenham Cl SK11 ..111 C3
Pickering Cres WA4 ..17 B2
Pickering Rd WA8 ....22 A3
Pickering St CH2 ....118 C2
Pickering's Pasture (Nature Reserve) ★ WA8 ......22 A2
Pickerings Cl WA7 ....49 B3
Pickford St SK11 ....112 B4
Pickford's Brow 3 SK1 ..240 F5
Pickmere Cl
  Sandbach CW11 ....174 C4
  Stockport SK3 ......240 C2
Pickmere Ct 10 SK9 ..34 B3
Pickmere Dr
  Bebington CH62 ......43 C2
  Chester CH3 ......142 A4
  Runcorn WA7 ....50 B3
Pickmere Gdns SK8 ..239 F4
Pickmere La
  Higher Wincham CW9 ..79 C3
  Pickmere WA16 ......55 B1
  Tabley WA16 ....55 B1
Pickmere Rd SK9 ......34 B3
Pickmere St WA5 ......15 C3
Pickwick Cl CW11 ..175 B4
Pickwick Pl ST7 ....194 B1
Pickwick Rd SK12 ....36 B2
Picow Farm Rd WA7 ..22 C1
Picow St 1 WA7 ......22 C1
Picton Ave
  Ellesmere Port CH65 ..70 B3
  Runcorn WA7 ....23 A1
Picton Cl Bebington CH62 ..43 C2
  7 Davenham CW9 ....103 C2
  Warrington WA3 ......9 A2
Picton Dr Wilmslow SK9 ..34 C1
  Winsford CW7 ......126 A1
Picton Gorse La CH2 ..119 A4
Picton La CH2 ....96 B2
Picton Sq CW4 ......130 A2
Piele Rd WA11 ....1 C4

Pierce St SK11 ......112 B4
Pierpoint La CW11 ..237 B2
Pierpoint St Golborne WA3 ..3 A4
  Warrington WA5 ......15 C4
Pigot Pl WA4 ....16 C3
Pike La WA6 ....75 A2
Pike Rd SK10 ....89 A3
Pike St WA4 ....16 B1
Pike The CW5 ....204 C2
Pikemere Rd ST7 ....193 A3
Pikemere Sch ST7 ..193 A3
Pikenall La CW8 ......76 B2
Pilgrim Cl WA2 ....8 A3
Pilgrims Way WA7 ....24 B1
Pillar Box La CW11 ..153 C2
Pillmoss La WA4 ......52 A4
Pillory St CW5 ......204 C3
Pimblett Rd WA11 ....1 C4
Pimblett St WA3 ......3 A4
Pimlico Rd WA7 ......22 C1
Pincot Rd SK22 ......39 B4
Pine Ave Newton-le-W WA12 2 B1
  Widnes WA8 ....13 A1
Pine Cl Haydock WA11 ....1 B3
  Macclesfield SK10 ..87 C1
  Talke ST7 ....210 B4
Pine Ct ST7 ....193 C2
Pine Gdns CH2 ......118 B3
Pine Gr Chester CH2 ..119 A2
  Denton M34 ....241 A4
  Ellesmere Port CH66 ..70 A1
  Golborne WA3 ....3 B4
  Sandbach CW11 ....175 B3
  Warrington WA1 ......17 A4
  Winsford CW7 ......127 A1
Pine Lodge SK7 ......35 C4
Pine Rd Bramhall SK7 ..35 C4
  Heswall CH60 ......41 B4
  Macclesfield SK10 ..87 C1
  Poynton SK12 ......36 C2
  Runcorn WA7 ....49 B4
Pine St SK3 ....240 D4
Pine Tree Cl CH4 ....139 B2
Pine Trees WA16 ......57 C4
Pine Wlk Nantwich CW5 ..204 C2
  6 Partington M31 ..11 C2
Pineapple Pk CW7 ..127 A1
Pinedale Cl CH1 ......95 A4
Pinehey CH64 ....41 B1
Pinehurst SK10 ......86 C3
Pinellas WA7 ....23 A2
Pines The WA16 ......58 C1
Pinetree Cl Barnton CW8 ..78 A2
  Winsford CW7 ......127 A1
Pineways WA4 ....26 B3
Pinewood WA14 ......238 A2
Pinewood Ave WA1 ....16 A4
Pinewood Cl Elton CH2 ..72 B2
  Stockport SK4 ......240 A7
Pinewood Ct
  Altrincham WA14 ..238 E1
  Sale M33 ....242 D7
  Wistaston CW2 ......206 A4
Pinewood Dr CH60 ....41 A4
Pinewood Gr ST5 ....210 C1
Pinewood Rd
  Burtonwood WA5 ......6 C4
  Wilmslow SK9 ....60 C4
Pinfold Cl WA15 ......32 B4
Pinfold Craft Ctr ★ CW5 188 A2
Pinfold Ct CH4 ......141 C2
Pinfold La Chelford WA16 ..83 B3
  Chester CH4 ....141 C4
  Little Budworth CW6 ..147 C4
  Middlewich CW10 ....128 A3
  Plumley WA16 ......81 A2
  Romiley SK6 ....241 E4
  Wythenshaw M90,WA15 ..32 C4
Pinfold St 12 SK11 ..112 B4
Pinfold The LL13 ....196 B4
Pinfold Way CW8 ......77 B1
Pingard's La CW8 ....101 B3
Pingate Dr SK8 ......35 A3
Pingate La SK8 ......35 A3
Pingate La S SK8 ....35 A3
Pingot Croft CH3 ....142 A4
Pingot La WA6 ....99 A3
Pinmill Brow WA6 ....74 A4
Pinmill Cl WA6 ......74 B4
Pinners Brow WA2 ....16 A3
Pinners Brow Ret Pk
  WA2 ....16 A3
Pinners Fold WA7 ....24 A1
Pinsley Green Rd CW5 ..216 C3
Pinsley View CW5 ....216 C2
Pintail Ave SK3 ......240 B2
Pintail Pl CW7 ......149 B3
Pinwood Cl 13 SK9 ..34 C1
Piper's Cl CH60 ......40 B4
Piper's End CH60 ....40 B4
Piper's La CH60 ......40 B4
Pipers Ash CW7 ......126 A1
Pipers Ct CH2 ......119 A2
Pipers La Chester CH2 ..119 A2
  Puddington CH64 ....93 A4
Pipers The WA3 ......3 C4
Pipit Ave WA12 ....2 B2
Pipit La WA3 ....9 C2
Pippin Cl CW10 ......151 B4
Pippits Row WA7 ......49 C2
Pirie Cl CW12 ......157 A2
Pirie Rd CW12 ......157 A2
Pit La
  Hough Common CW2 ..206 C1
  Talke ST7 ....210 B3
  Widnes WA8 ....23 A4
Pitt St Hyde SK14 ..241 D7
  Macclesfield SK11 ..112 B3

Pitt St continued
  Stockport SK3 ......240 D4
  Warrington WA5 ......15 C4
  Widnes WA8 ....23 A3
Pitts Cl CH3 ....121 B1
Pitts Heath La WA7 ..24 C2
Pitville Terr WA8 ....22 B4
Pius XII RC Prim Sch
  CH66 ....69 B3
Place Rd WA14 ......238 C6
Plaistow Ct WA7 ......49 C4
Plane Gr ST5 ....210 C1
Plane Tree Dr CW1 ..190 C3
Plane Tree Gr WA11 ..2 A4
Plane Tree Rd M31 ..11 B3
Plant Cl M33 ....242 A7
Plant La CW11 ......174 A4
Plant St CW11 ......175 A4
Plantagenet Cl 3 CW7 ..149 B3
Plantation Cl WA7 ....24 C2
Plantation Dr CH66 ..69 C4
Plantation Ind Est OL6 ..242 A4
Plantation St OL6 ....242 A2
Plas Newton La CH2 ..118 C3
Platt Ave CW11 ......175 A4
Platt St SK8 ....239 E6
Platt's La CH3 ......164 C3
Platts La Christleton CH3 ..143 B4
  Duddon CH3,CW6 ....144 C4
  Tarvin CH3 ....121 A1
  Tarvin, Broom Bank CH3 ..144 A4
  Tattenhall CH3 ....183 C4
Platts St WA11 ....1 A3
Play St SK1 ....240 F4
Pleasance Way WA12 ..2 B2
Pleasant St
  Macclesfield SK10 ..87 C1
  Northwich CW8 ....103 C4
Pleasant Way SK7,SK8 ..35 B3
Pleck Rd CH65 ......70 A4
Plemstall Cl CH2 ....119 C4
Plemstall La CH2 ....97 A1
Plemstall Way CH2 ..96 C1
Plemston Ct CH66 ....69 C4
Plex The ST7 ....193 B2
Plinston Ave WA4 ....16 C2
Plough Croft ST7 ....193 A2
Plough La CH3 ......143 A4
Ploughmans Cl CH66 ..94 C4
Ploughmans Way
  Ellesmere Port CH66 ..94 C4
  Macclesfield SK10 ..87 A2
Plover Ave CW7 ......149 B3
Plover Cl Farndon CH3 ..180 C1
  Newton-le-W WA12 ....2 B2
Plover Dr
  Altrincham WA14 ..238 B8
  Runcorn WA7 ....50 B4
Plover Way WA3 ......3 C4
Plovers La WA6 ......73 B3
Plum Terr CH1 ......237 A3
Plumbs Fold CW8 ....78 A1
Plumley Cl Chester CH3 ..119 B1
  Stockport SK3 ......240 F1
Plumley Gdns WA8 ..12 A1
Plumley Moor Rd WA16 ..81 B3
Plumley Rd SK9 ......34 B3
Plumley Sta WA16 ....81 A2
Plumpstons La WA6 ..49 A1
Plumtre Ave WA5 ....15 C4
Plymouth Cl WA7 ....50 C3
Plymouth Dr SK7 ....35 C4
Plymouth Gr SK3 ....240 B3
Plymyard Ave CH62 ..43 B3
Plymyard Cl CH62 ....43 B3
Plymyard Copse CH62 ..43 B3
Poachers La WA4 ....16 C2
Pochard Ave CW7 ..149 B3
Pochard Dr
  Altrincham WA14 ..238 B7
  Poynton SK12 ......36 A2
Pochard Rise WA7 ....50 B4
Pochin Way CW10 ..128 C1
Pocket Nook La WA3 ..4 A4
Pocklington Ct WA2 ..8 C1
Pole La CW9 ....53 C1
Pole Lane Ends CW9 ..53 B2
Poleacre Dr WA8 ....12 B1
Police St 1 WA14 ..238 D5
Pollard Dr CW5 ......205 A2
Polldean Ho SK8 ....239 D3
Pollen Rd WA14 ......238 C6
Polperro Cl
  Macclesfield SK10 ..86 B1
  Warrington WA5 ......14 C2
Pond Cotts CH2 ......72 A2
Pond St WA3 ....4 A4
Pond View Cl CH60 ..41 B4
Pond Wlk WA9 ....1 A1
Pool Bank Bsns Pk CH3 121 B2
Pool End Cl SK10 ....87 B2
Pool End Rd SK10 ....87 B2
Pool Hall Ind Est CH5,
  CH66 ....70 A4
Pool House Rd SK12 ..37 B3
Pool La Elton CH2 ....71 C2
  Haslington CW11 ....192 A4
  Lymm WA13 ....18 A2
  Runcorn WA7 ....23 A2
  Tarvin CH3 ....121 B2
  Warrington WA3 ......16 A1
Pool Meadows Rd CW1 191 A2
Pool Rd WA3 ....11 A2
Pool Side ST7 ......194 A4
Pool St Macclesfield SK11 112 C3
  Widnes WA8 ....23 A4
Pool View CW11 ....191 C4
Poolcroft M33 ......242 F5

Poole Ave WA2 8 A1
Poole Cres WA2 8 A1
Poole Hall La CH66 69 C4
Poole Hall Rd CH66 69 C4
Poole La CH2 71 C1
Poole Old Hall La CW5 188 B2
Poolford La CW4 129 C1
Pools La CW11 177 A3
Pools Platt La CW9 53 C3
Poolside Ct ST7 193 C2
Poolside Rd WA7 23 A1
Pooltown Com Jun Sch CH65 69 C3
Pooltown Rd CH65 69 C3
Poplar Ave
Altrincham WA14 238 E6
Culcheth WA3 4 C2
Moulton CW9 126 C4
Newton-le-W WA12 2 B2
Runcorn WA7 49 B4
Warrington WA5 14 C2
Wilmslow SK9 59 C3
Poplar Cl
Congleton CW12 156 A2
Cuddington CW8 102 A2
Ellesmere Port CH65 70 A2
Gatley SK8 239 B5
Runcorn WA7 49 B4
Winsford CW7 149 A4
Poplar Dr Alsager ST7 193 C1
Kidsgrove ST7 195 A1
Middlewich CW10 151 B4
Poplar Gr Bollington SK10 88 A4
Crewe CW1 190 C3
Elton CH2 72 A2
Haydock WA11 1 B3
Irlam M44 11 B3
Sale M33 242 B5
Poplar La TF9 236 C3
Poplar Rd Chester CH4 140 C3
Haydock WA11 1 B3
Macclesfield SK11 112 B3
Weaverham CW8 102 B4
Poplar Way SK6 38 A4
Poplar Weint 2 CH64 66 C4
Poplar Wlk M31 11 B2
Poplars Ave WA2 8 B2
Poplars Pl WA2 8 B1
Poplars The Golborne WN7 4 B4
Lymm WA13 18 B2
Wistaston CW2 205 C4
Poppyfields ST7 193 A2
Porlock Cl Heswall CH60 41 A3
Warrington WA5 14 C2
Port Arcs The CH65 70 B3
Port St SK1 240 E6
Portal Gr M34 241 B5
Porter Ave WA12 2 B3
Porter Dr CW9 104 B3
Porter St WA7 23 B1
Porter Way CW9 104 B3
Porters Croft CH3 119 C3
Portford Cl SK10 86 C1
Porthcawl Cl WA8 12 B2
Portland Dr Biddulph ST8 179 B1
Scholar Green ST7 194 C3
Portland Gr
Haslington CW1 191 B3
5 Stockport SK4 240 B8
Portland Pl WA6 73 B2
Portland Rd WA14 238 D3
Portland St
Newton-le-W WA12 1 C2
Runcorn WA7 22 C2
Portland Wlk SK11 111 C4
Portleven Rd WA7 50 A3
Portloe Rd SK8 34 A4
Portman Pl 4 CW7 149 A4
Portmarnock Cl SK10 87 A2
Portola Cl WA4 17 B1
Portrea Cl SK3 240 F1
Portree Ave CH63 43 B3
Portree Dr CW4 130 A1
Portrush Dr SK10 87 B2
Portside WA7 50 C4
Portside Bsns Pk CH65 70 A4
Portsmouth Pl WA7 50 C3
Portway M22 33 B4
Portwood Pl SK1 240 F6
Posnett St SK3 240 C4
Post Office La
Betley CW2 207 C1
Hampton SY14 213 B4
Norley WA6 100 C3
Runcorn WA7 48 B4
Post Office Pl 1 CW9 79 A1
Post Office St WA14 238 D5
Postles Pl CW9 103 C3
Pott Shrigley Church Sch SK10 63 B2
Potter Cl CW5 205 B2
Potters Barn The★ CW11 176 A1
Potters End ST8 179 B1
Potters La WA8 21 C3
Poulton Cres WA1 17 B4
Poulton Dr WA8 22 B4
Poulton Hall Rd CH63 43 A4
Poulton Rd CH63 43 A4
Pound Rd CH66 69 B4
Povey Rd WA2 8 B1
Powell Ave Hyde SK14 241 E7
Warrington WA3 9 C2
Powell St WA4 16 C2
Powell's Orch CH4 141 B4
Powey La Mollington CH1 94 A3
Saughall CH1 94 A3
Powicke Wlk SK6 241 A1
Pownall Ave SK7 35 C4
Pownall Ct SK9 59 C4
Pownall Green Prim Sch SK7 35 C4
Pownall Hall Sch SK9 59 C4
Pownall Rd
Altrincham WA14 238 D3
Wilmslow SK9 59 C4
Pownall Sq SK11 112 B4
Pownall St SK10 87 B1
Powy Dr ST7 195 A1
Powys St WA5 15 C3
Poynton Cl WA4 17 A2
Poynton High Sch SK12 36 C1
Poynton Ind Est SK10 36 B1
Poynton St 9 SK11 112 B4
Poynton Sta SK12 36 B2
Pratchitts Row CW5 204 C3
Precinct The CW2 189 C1
Preece Cl WA8 12 B2
Preece Ct CW1 190 A3
Preesall Ave SK8 34 A4
Prenton Pl CH4 141 C4
Prescot Rd
Altrincham WA15 238 F2
Widnes WA8 12 B1
Prescot St CH2 118 C2
Prescott Rd SK9 34 A1
Prescott St WA4 16 C2
Prescott Wlk M34 241 B5
Prestbury Ave WA15 238 E6
Prestbury CE Prim Sch SK10 86 C4
Prestbury Cl
13 Northwich CW9 103 C2
Widnes WA8 22 C4
Prestbury Ct SK10 86 C3
Prestbury Dr WA4 17 B2
Prestbury La SK10 87 A4
Prestbury Pk SK10 86 C3
Prestbury Rd
Macclesfield SK10 87 A1
Nether Alderley SK10 86 A3
Nether Alderley, Adder's Moss SK10 85 C3
Wilmslow SK10,SK9 60 C3
Prestbury Sta SK10 87 A4
Preston Ave M44 11 C4
Preston On The Hill WA4 50 C3
Preston St W SK11 112 A3
Prestwich Ave WA3 4 C2
Prestwick Cl
Macclesfield SK10 87 B3
Winsford CW7 126 B1
Prestwood Ct WA3 10 A4
Pretoria St CH4 141 B4
Price Ave CW11 175 A3
Price Gr WA9 1 A1
Pride Cl WA12 2 C1
Priest Ave SK8 239 A4
Priest La SK10 61 A1
Priest St SK1 240 F3
Priestfield Rd CH65 70 B3
Priestley Coll WA1 16 B2
Priestley St WA5 15 C3
Priestner Dr WA6 73 A2
Priestway La CH64 67 C1
Priesty Ct CW12 156 B1
Priesty Fields CW12 156 B1
Primary Cl M44 11 B3
Primitive St ST7 195 B4
Primrose Ave
Haslington CW1 191 B3
Macclesfield SK11 112 A3
Primrose Bank WA14 238 C1
Primrose Chase CW4 130 B4
Primrose Cl
Huntington CH3 142 A3
Runcorn WA7 50 A4
Warrington WA2 8 B1
Widnes WA8 12 C1
Primrose Cotts WA14 238 C1
Primrose Gr WA11 1 C4
Primrose Hill
Crewe CW2 189 C3
Cuddington CW8 101 C2
Kelsall CW6 122 C3
Primrose La WA6 73 A1
Primula Dr WA3 3 B4
Prince Albert St CW1 190 B2
Prince Edward St CW5 204 C3
Prince Henry Sq 10 WA1 16 A3
Prince Rd SK12 37 B3
Prince William Ave CH5 116 A2
Prince's Ave SK6 241 A3
Prince's Rd SK6 241 A3
Prince's St
4 Stockport SK1 240 E6
Widnes WA8 23 A4
Princes Ave
Bebington CH62 43 C3
Chester CH2 237 C3
Northwich CW9 104 A4
Princes Cl WA7 23 C1
Princes Ct CW5 204 C4
Princes Dr M33 242 D5
Princes Pk CW8 78 A1
Princes Pl WA8 12 C1
Princes Rd
Altrincham WA14 238 D6
Ellesmere Port CH65 70 A3
Sale M33 242 D5
Stockport SK4 240 A8
Princes St WA12 2 A2
Princes Way SK11 111 C4
Princess Ave Audley ST7 209 B1
Haydock WA11 2 A4
Warrington WA1 16 C3
Princess Ave *continued*
Warrington, Great Sankey WA5 14 C4
Warrington, Padgate WA1 17 A4
Princess Cl CW2 205 C4
Princess Cres
Middlewich CW10 151 B3
Warrington WA1 16 C3
Princess Ct ST7 210 B3
Princess Dr
Bollington SK10 87 C4
Nantwich CW5 205 A3
Sandbach CW11 175 A4
Wistaston CW2 205 C4
Princess Gr CW2 205 C4
Princess Rd Lymm WA13 18 B2
Wilmslow SK9 59 C3
Princess St
Altrincham WA14 238 C8
Ashton-u-Lyne OL6 242 A4
Bollington SK10 87 C4
Chester CH1 237 A2
Congleton CW12 156 B2
Crewe CW1 190 B3
Hyde SK14 241 E6
Knutsford WA16 57 A1
Northwich CW9 79 C1
Runcorn WA7 23 A2
Talke ST7 210 B3
Warrington WA5 15 B2
Winsford CW7 127 A1
Princess Wlk SK7 36 A4
Princeway WA6 74 A4
Printworks Rd SK15 242 F3
Prior Cl CW2 189 C1
Priory Ave CW9 103 C2
Priory Cl Chester CH2 118 B2
Congleton CW12 179 A4
Crewe CW1 190 A4
Runcorn WA7 24 A1
Sale M33 242 D8
Winsford CW7 126 B2
Priory Ct SK10 86 C1
Priory Dr SK10 86 C1
Priory La SK10 86 C1
Priory Pl Chester CH1 237 B2
Kidsgrove ST7 195 A2
Priory Rd
Altrincham WA14 31 A4
Runcorn WA7 24 B1
Sale M33 242 D7
Stockport SK8 240 A1
Wilmslow SK9 59 C4
Priory Specl Sch M33 242 A6
Priory St
Altrincham WA14 238 C1
Northwich CW9 104 A4
Warrington WA4 16 A2
Priory The Neston CH64 41 C1
Winwick WA2 8 A4
Priory Way CW8 103 A2
Priscilla St CW1 190 C2
Pritchard Dr CW9 103 C1
Probert Cl CW2 190 A2
Proctors Cl WA8 13 B1
Proctors La CW11 174 C3
Proffits La WA6 73 C2
Promised Land La CH3 142 C3
Prospect Ave M44 11 C3
Prospect Dr
Altrincham WA15 32 B4
Davenham CW9 103 C1
Prospect La WA3 10 B2
Prospect Rd M44 11 C3
Prospect Row WA7 48 C4
Prospect St CW12 156 B1
Prospect Vale SK8 239 B1
Prospect Vale Prim Sch SK8 239 B1
Prosperity Way CW10 128 B1
Prosser Rd CH2 95 B1
Protector Way M44 11 C4
Provan Way CH1 117 B3
Providence St OL6 242 A4
Provident St WA9 1 A2
Prunus Rd CW1 190 C3
Pryors The CH3 121 B2
Ptarmigan Pl 7 CW7 149 B3
Public Hall St WA7 23 A2
Pudding La CW6 168 A4
Puddington La
Neston CH64 92 C4
Puddington CH64 93 A4
Puffin Ave SK12 36 A2
Puffin Cl CH65 95 B4
Pulford Cl
Davenham CW9 103 C2
Runcorn WA7 49 C3
Pulford Ct CH4 162 B1
Pulford La CH4 162 A3
Pulford Rd Blacon CH1 117 C3
Ellesmere Port CH65 69 C2
Winsford CW7 126 B1
Pullman Cl CH60 41 B4
Pullman Dr CW9 104 B4
Pump La Churton CH3 181 A3
Runcorn WA7 49 C4
Pumptree Mews SK11 111 C4
Purdy Cl WA5 7 B1
Puritan Bldgs WA7 23 B1
Purley Dr M44 11 B3
Purser La SY14 211 C2
Puss Bank Prim Sch SK10 112 C4
Putney Ct WA7 49 C4
Pye Cl WA11 2 A4
Pye Rd CH60 41 A4
Pyecroft Cl WA5 14 B3
Pyecroft Rd WA5 14 B3
Pyecroft St CH4 141 B4
Pym's La CW1 189 C3
Pymgate Dr SK8 239 A2
Pyrus Ave CW1 190 C3
Pyrus Gr WA6 73 B2
Pytcheley Hollow WA6 100 C3

Q

Quad The CH1 117 C1
Quadrant Cl WA7 50 B3
Quadrant The
Blacon CH1 117 C1
Romiley SK6 241 A2
Warrington WA3 9 C3
Quail Cl WA2 8 B2
Quakers Coppice CW1 191 A1
Quakers Way LL13 180 C1
Quantock Cl
Ellesmere Port CH66 69 A3
Stockport SK4 240 E6
Winsford CW7 149 A4
Quarry Ave CH3 180 C1
Quarry Bank CW6 146 B4
Quarry Bank Mill★ SK9 33 C1
Quarry Bank Rd SK9 33 C2
Quarry Cl Chester CH4 141 B4
Runcorn WA7 23 B1
Quarry Ct WA8 12 B1
Quarry Hill CH3 180 C1
Quarry Hts SK15 242 C1
Quarry La
Christleton CH3 142 C4
Kelsall CW6 122 B3
Neston CH64 42 A1
Warrington WA4 26 B3
Quarry Rd Neston CH64 42 B1
New Mills SK22 39 B4
Romiley SK6 241 B2
Quarry Rise SK6 241 B3
Quarry St SK15 242 C1
Quarry Terr ST7 195 A1
Quarrybank CW6 184 C3
Quarrybank Cotts CW6 184 C3
Quay Fold WA5 15 C3
Quay Pl WA7 50 C4
Quay Side WA6 49 B1
Quay The WA6 49 B1
Quayle Cl WA11 1 B3
Quayside
Congleton CW12 156 C1
Neston CH64 66 C3
Quayside Mews WA13 18 C2
Quayside Way SK11 112 C4
Queastybirch La WA4 26 A1
Quebec Rd WA2 16 B4
Queen Anne Ct
1 Macclesfield SK11 112 A3
Wilmslow SK9 60 B3
Queen Sq OL6 242 A4
Queen St Audley ST7 209 B1
Bollington SK10 88 A4
Bunbury CW6 185 C4
Cheadle SK8 239 F6
Chester CH1 237 B2
Congleton CW12 156 B1
Congleton, Buglawton CW12 156 C2
Crewe CW1 190 C3
Ellesmere Port CH65 70 B4
Golborne WA3 3 A4
Hyde SK14 241 E6
Kidsgrove ST7 195 A1
Knutsford WA16 56 C1
Macclesfield SK11 112 B4
Middlewich CW10 128 B1
Nantwich CW5 204 C3
Newton-le-W WA12 2 A2
Northwich CW9 103 C4
Runcorn WA7 23 A2
Shavington CW2 206 B2
Stalybridge SK15 242 D2
Queen Victoria St 26 SK11 112 B4
Queen's Ave Chester CH2 237 C3
Connah's Quay CH5 91 B1
Glazebury WA3 5 B4
Hawarden CH5 116 A2
Macclesfield SK10 87 C1
Romiley SK6 241 A3
Widnes WA8 22 A4
Queen's Cl
Macclesfield SK10 87 C1
Runcorn WA7 22 C1
Queen's Cres CW1 172 C1
Queen's Dr Chester CH4 237 C1
Middlewich CW10 151 B4
Nantwich CW5 204 B2
Sandbach CW11 175 A4
Stockport SK4 240 A6
Queen's Gdns SK8 239 E6
Queen's Par CW7 126 B1
Queen's Park Gdns CW2 189 C2
Queen's Park Ho CH4 237 B1
Queen's Park Rd CH4 237 B1
Queen's Rd
Altrincham WA15 238 F3
Cheadle SK8 239 F4
Chester CH2 237 C3
Romiley SK6 241 A3
Runcorn WA7 22 C1
Wilmslow SK9 60 A3
Queen's Sch CH1 237 A2
Queen's Sch (Jun Dept) CH2 118 B2
Queen's Way CH4 139 A2
Queens Ave
Ellesmere Port CH65 70 A2
Warrington WA1 16 C4
Queens Cl Bollington SK10 87 C3
Stockport SK4 240 A6
Queens Cres
Chester CH2 118 C4
Warrington WA1 17 A4
Queens Ct
1 Stockport SK4 240 A7
Winsford CW7 126 B1
Queens Dr Golborne WA3 3 B4
Helsby WA6 73 A2
Heswall CH60 40 C4
Newton-le-W WA12 2 B3
Warrington WA4 17 A1
Queens Gdns
Ellesmere Port CH65 70 A3
Talke ST7 210 B3
Queens Park Golf Course CW2 189 C2
Queens Park High Sch CH4 237 B1
Queens Pl CH1 237 B3
Queens Rd Chester CH3 119 A2
Ellesmere Port CH66 69 B4
Haydock WA11 2 A4
Queens Terr SK9 34 B2
Queensbury Cl 19 SK9 34 B1
Queensbury Way WA8 12 C2
Queensgate Bramhall SK7 35 C3
Northwich CW8 103 C4
Queensgate Prim Sch SK7 35 C2
Queensway Alsager ST7 193 A3
Chester CH2 118 C3
Crewe CW1 190 B2
Frodsham WA6 74 A4
Gatley SK8 34 B4
Heswall CH60 41 B3
Knutsford WA16 56 C2
Partington M31 11 C2
Poynton SK12 36 B2
Runcorn WA7 22 C2
Widnes WA8 22 C3
Winsford CW7 149 B4
Queensway Trad Est WA8 23 A3
Quill Ct M44 11 C3
Quillet The CH64 66 C4
Quinn St WA8 23 A4
Quinta Prim Sch The CW12 156 A1
Quinta Rd CW12 156 A2

R

Raby Ave CH63 43 A3
Raby Cl Bebington CH63 43 A4
Heswall CH60 40 C4
Widnes WA8 13 C1
Raby Ct CH65 70 B2
Raby Dr CH63 43 A3
Raby Gdns CH64 66 C4
Raby Hall Rd CH63 43 A3
Raby Mere Rd CH63 42 B3
Raby Park Cl CH64 66 C4
Raby Park Rd CH64 41 C1
Raby Rd Neston CH64 66 C4
Thornton Hough CH63 42 A3
Race The SK9 34 B1
Racecourse La CW6 124 A1
Racecourse Pk SK9 59 C3
Racecourse Rd SK9 59 C3
Racefield Cl WA13 18 C2
Racefield Rd
Altrincham WA14 238 C4
Knutsford WA16 56 C1
Radbroke Cl CW11 175 B4
Radcliffe Ave WA3 4 C2
Radcliffe Cl CH3 121 B2
Radcliffe Rd
Sandbach CW11 174 C2
Sutton Lane Ends SK11 135 B4
Raddel La WA4 52 B3
Raddle Wharf CH65 70 B4
Raddon Pl WA4 16 C2
Radford Cl WA8 22 B4
Radlett Cl WA5 14 C2
Radley Dr CH63 41 C3
Radley La WA2 8 C2
Radnor Cl
Congleton CW12 156 A2
Sandbach CW11 174 C4
Radnor Dr Chester CH4 141 A2
Widnes WA8 12 B1
Radnor Park Ind Ctr CW12 156 A2
Radnor Park Trad Est CW12 156 A2
Radnor St WA5 15 C3
Radway Gn CH66 69 C3
Radway Green Rd CW2 208 C4
Rae St SK3 240 C4
Raeburn Ave
Bebington CH62 43 C3
Neston CH64 66 C4
Raeburn Prim Sch CH62 43 B3
Raglan Ct WA3 9 C3
Raglan Dr WA14 238 E8
Raglan Rd
Macclesfield SK10 87 C1
Sale M33 242 A5

Raglan St SK14 ......241 C6
Ragley Cl SK12 ......36 C2
Railbrook Ct CW2 ......190 B1
Railton Ave CW1 ......190 A4
Railway Age Mus The★
CW1 ......190 B2
Railway Bank SK14 ......241 C6
Railway Cotts
Congleton CW12 ......157 A1
Hollinfare WA3 ......11 A3
Hooton CH66 ......43 B1
Railway Rd SK1 ......240 E4
Railway St
Altrincham WA14 ......238 D4
Crewe CW2 ......190 B1
Hyde SK14 ......241 D6
Newton-le-W WA12 ......2 A2
Stockport SK1 ......240 E6
Railway Terr Disley SK12 ..38 B3
Hawarden CH5 ......116 A2
Railway View WA5 ......1 B1
Rainbow Cl WA8 ......12 B2
Rainbow Dr SK12 ......37 A1
Rainbow St CW1 ......190 B2
Rainford Cl ST7 ......195 C1
Rainmoor Cl CW10 ......151 A4
Rainow Prim Sch SK10 ..88 B2
Rainow Rd
Macclesfield SK10 ......88 A1
Rainow SK10 ......88 A1
Stockport SK3 ......240 C2
Rainow View SK10 ......63 B1
Rainow Way 10 SK9 ......34 C1
Rajar Cotts WA16 ......57 C2
Rake House Mews WA6 ..73 C4
Rake La Backford CH2 ....95 B3
Christleton CH3 ......143 A4
Dunham-on-t-H WA6 ....97 C4
Eccleston CH4 ......141 B4
Hawarden CH5 ......139 A4
Helsby WA6 ......73 A4
Helsby, Helsby Marsh WA6 ..73 A3
Stoak CH2 ......95 B3
Rake The Bebington CH62 ..43 B4
Burton CH64 ......67 B1
Rake Way CH1 ......94 A1
Raleigh Cl WA5 ......7 B1
Raleigh Rd CH64 ......41 C1
Raleigh St SK5 ......240 E8
Ramp Rd E M90 ......33 B4
Ramp Rd S M90 ......33 B4
Ramp Rd W M90 ......33 A4
Rampit Cl WA11 ......1 C4
Ramsbottom St CW1 ....190 A3
Ramsbrook La L24,WA8 ...21 B2
Ramsdale Rd SK7 ......35 C4
Ramsden Ct CH4 ......140 C2
Ramsey Cl Warrington WA3 ..9 C4
Widnes WA8 ......13 C2
Ramsey Rd CH65 ......70 B1
Ramsfield Rd L24 ......21 A2
Randall Cl WA12 ......2 A2
Randle Bennett Cl
CW11 ......174 C4
Randle Mdw CH66 ......69 C1
Randle Meadow Ct 2
CH66 ......69 C1
Randolph Pl SK3 ......240 E3
Range Ct SK10 ......87 C1
Range Rd SK3 ......240 E3
Rangemoor Cl WA3 ......10 A3
Rannoch Cl CH66 ......69 C2
Ranulph Cl WA6 ......74 B4
Ranwonath Ct CH2 ......237 B4
Ranworth Dr WA3 ......3 C4
Ranworth Rd WA5 ......14 C3
Rappax Rd WA15 ......32 A4
Raquets Ct The CW10 ..127 B3
Rassbottom Brow SK15 242 C2
Rassbottom Ind Est
SK15 ......242 C2
Rassbottom St SK15 ....242 C2
Ratcliffe St 6 SK1 ....240 F4
Rathbone Pk CW6 ......146 B1
Rathlin Cl WA8 ......13 C2
Rathmell Cl WA3 ......4 C2
Rathvale Dr M22 ......33 B4
Raven Cl CW11 ......175 A4
Raven Cotts TF9 ......235 A3
Raven's La CW5 ......203 C3
Ravenbank Com Prim Sch
WA13 ......18 C2
Ravendale Cl CW7 ......149 C4
Ravenfield Dr WA8 ......12 B2
Ravenho La SK10 ......88 B2
Ravenhurst Ct WA3 ......9 C3
Ravenoak Park Rd SK8 ..35 A4
Ravenoak Rd SK8 ......35 A4
Ravens Cl ST7 ......209 C2
Ravens La CW5 ......203 C3
Ravenscar Cres M22 ....33 B4
Ravenscliffe Rd ST7 ....195 A1
Ravenscroft CW4 ......130 A2
Ravenscroft Cl CW11 ..175 B4
Ravenscroft Rd CW2 ....189 C2
Ravensdale Cl WA2 ......8 B2
Ravensfield CW8 ......101 B2
Ravensholme Cl CH3 ...166 A1
Ravensholme La CH3 ...166 A1
Ravensmead Prim Sch
ST7 ......209 C2
Ravenstone Dr M33 ....242 E7
Ravenswood CW8 ......103 A2
Ravenswood Ave SK4 ...240 A5
Ravenswood Dr SK8 ....35 A4

Ravenswood Rd SK9 ....59 C2
Ravenswood Dr WA15 ...32 B4
Rawcliffe Cl WA8 ......12 C2
Rawdon Cl WA7 ......50 A4
Rawlings Cl WA3 ......9 C2
Rawlinson Cres L26 ....21 A4
Rawson Rd CH1 ......117 C2
Ray Ave CW5 ......204 C4
Rayleigh Ave CW9 ......127 A4
Rayleigh Way SK10 ......86 C1
Raymond Ave WA1 ......16 B1
Raymond St CH1 ......237 B1
Raymond Way CH64 ......67 A4
Rayners Cl SK15 ......242 C1
Rays Brow CW8 ......78 A1
Read St SK14 ......241 C7
Read St W SK14 ......241 C7
Reades La CW12 ......179 B4
Readesdale Ave CW2 ...189 C1
Reading Room La SY14,
CH3 ......199 B4
Rean Mdw CH3 ......166 A1
Reaper Cl WA5 ......15 B3
Reaseheath Coll CW5 ..188 B1
Reay St WA8 ......13 B1
Record Bsns Pk WA2 ....16 A4
Rectory Ave WA3 ......3 B4
Rectory Cl Denton M34 ..241 A6
Farndon CH3 ......180 C1
Heswall CH60 ......40 C4
12 Nantwich CW5 ......204 C3
Winwick WA2 ......8 A3
Wistaston CW2 ......205 C4
Rectory Gdns Lymm WA13 18 C2
Talke ST7 ......210 B3
Rectory La Adderley TF9 ..235 A3
Capenhurst CH1 ......94 A4
Heswall CH60 ......40 C4
Ledsham CH66 ......68 C1
Lymm WA13 ......18 C2
Winwick WA2 ......8 A3
Rectory View ST7 ......210 B3
Red Brow La WA4 ......50 C4
Red Cow Yd 10 WA16 ....57 A1
Red Ct CH66 ......69 B4
Red Gables WA4 ......27 A2
Red Ho SK10 ......87 C1
Red House La WA14 ....20 B4
Red La Disley SK12 ......38 B3
Frodsham WA6 ......74 B4
Huxley CH3 ......166 B3
Sandbach CW11 ......174 B3
Warrington WA4 ......26 B4
Whitley WA4 ......52 B1
Red Lion Cl ST7 ......210 B4
Red Lion La
Ellesmere Port CH66 ....69 B4
Nantwich CW5 ......204 B3
Red Pike CH66 ......69 B4
Red Rose Ct M33 ......242 B8
Red Row SK7 ......37 A4
Red Stone Hill WA6 ....73 B2
Redacre SK12 ......36 C3
Redacre Cl WA4 ......51 A2
Redbourne Dr
Chorlton CW2 ......207 B1
Widnes WA8 ......12 A4
Redbrook Cl CH62 ......43 B3
Redbrook Gr 11 SK9 ....34 B1
Redbrook Rd M31 ......11 C1
Redbrook Way SK10 ....62 B3
Redcar Dr CH62 ......43 B3
Reddish Ave SK23 ......65 B3
Reddish Cres WA13 ......18 C2
Reddish La Lymm WA13 ..19 A3
Whaley Bridge SK23 ....65 B3
Reddish Rd SK23 ......65 B3
Reddy La WA14 ......30 A4
Redesdale Cl
Sandbach CW11 ......174 C4
Warrington WA2 ......8 C1
Redesmere Cl
Macclesfield SK10 ......87 A1
Northwich CW9 ......104 A3
Redesmere Dr
Alderley Edge SK9 ......60 A1
Cheadle SK8 ......239 F4
Redesmere La SK11 ....110 A2
Redesmere Rd SK9 ......34 B3
Redfern Ave
Congleton CW12 ......156 C2
Sale M33 ......242 E5
Redfern Ho SK6 ......241 A4
Redgate CW8 ......103 B4
Redhill Rd Chester CH4 ..140 C3
Kelsall CW6 ......122 B3
Redhills Mews CH65 ....70 A3
Redhouse La Disley SK12 .38 C4
Romiley SK6 ......241 A4
Redhouses SK11 ......113 B2
Redland Cl CH4 ......141 A4
Redland Ho CH4 ......141 A4
Redmain Gr WA3 ......3 C4
Redmayne Cl WA12 ......2 A2
Redmere Dr CH60 ......41 B4
Redmoor La Disley SK12 ..39 A2
New Mills SK22 ......39 A3
Redpoll La WA3 ......9 C2
Redruth Ave SK10 ......86 C1
Redruth Cl WA7 ......50 B3
Redshank Ave CW7 ....149 B3
Redshank Cl WA12 ......2 B1
Redshank La WA3 ......9 C2
Redshaw Cl CW10 ......151 B3
Redstart Cl 4 WA3 ......9 B2
Redstone Dr CW7 ......126 A1
Redvales Ct WA3 ......9 B2

Redvers Ave CH66 ......44 A1
Redway La SK10 ......88 A4
Redwood Cl Barnton CW8 .78 A4
Broughton CH4 ......140 C3
Holt LL13 ......196 B4
Warrington WA1 ......17 C4
Redwood Ct SK10 ......87 C3
Redwood Dr
Ellesmere Port CH66 ....69 C1
Elton CH2 ......72 B2
Reece Cl CH2 ......119 C4
Reed La CW9 ......53 B3
Reedgate La CW9 ......27 C1
Reedsmere Cl WA4 ......16 C1
Reedsmere Wlk CW9 ....78 B4
Reeman Cl SK6 ......241 A4
Reeman Ct SK9 ......34 A1
Rees Cres CW4 ......130 B2
Reeve St WA3 ......4 A4
Reeves Rd CH3 ......142 A4
Regal Cl
Ellesmere Port CH66 ....69 C2
Northwich CW9 ......103 C2
Regal Cres WA8 ......22 A4
Regency Cl ST7 ......210 B3
Regency Ct Chester CH2 .119 C4
Winsford CW7 ......149 B3
Neston CH64 ......41 A1
Regency Gdns SK8 ......34 C4
Regency Hospl SK10 ....112 A4
Regency Prep Sch SK11 112 A4
Regency Way CW9 ......103 C2
Regent Ave Haydock WA11 .1 A4
Macclesfield SK11 ......112 A3
Warrington WA1 ......17 A4
Regent Cl Bramhall SK7 ..35 B4
Shavington CW2 ......206 A4
Wilmslow SK9 ......59 C3
Regent Ct
Altrincham WA14 ......238 D4
Altrincham, Halebarns
WA15 ......32 B4
Regent Rd
Altrincham WA14 ......238 D4
Widnes WA8 ......13 A1
Regent St
Ellesmere Port CH65 ....70 A3
Moulton CW9 ......126 C4
Newton-le-W WA12 ......2 A2
Runcorn WA7 ......23 A2
Warrington WA1 ......16 A3
Regents Cl CH3 ......119 A1
Regents Gate CW5 ......205 A3
Regents Theological Coll
CW5 ......205 A3
Regents Way 5 CW7 ....149 A4
Regina St SK15 ......242 D2
Reginald Mitchell Prim Sch
ST7 ......194 B1
Registry Cl CW9 ......103 C2
Reid Ave WA5 ......15 C4
Reid St CW1 ......190 B3
Remer St CW1 ......190 C4
Rena Cl SK4 ......240 D7
Renaissance Ct CW1 ...191 A2
Renaissance Way CW1 ..191 A2
Renbury Pl WA4 ......51 A2
Rendel Cl WA12 ......2 B1
Rendlesham Cl WA3 ....10 A3
Renfrew Ave CH62 ......43 C3
Renfrew Cl SK10 ......86 C1
Renown Cl WA3 ......9 B2
Renshaw Rd CW9 ......79 B1
Renshaw St WA14 ......238 E5
Rensherds Pl WA16 ....29 B3
Renton Ave WA7 ......23 B1
Repton Ave SK14 ......241 E7
Repton Cl WA16 ......29 B3
Repton Dr CW1 ......191 B3
Repton Rd CH65 ......70 B2
Reservoir Rd
Stockport SK3 ......240 D3
Whaley Bridge SK23 ....65 B4
Reservoir Terr CH2 ....118 C1
Retreat The Crewe CW1 .190 B1
Romiley SK6 ......241 C1
Reuben St SK4 ......240 E8
Revesby Cl WA8 ......12 B1
Rex Bldgs SK9 ......60 A3
Reynard St SK14 ......241 D7
Reyner St OL6 ......242 B2
Reynold St SK14 ......241 D6
Reynold's La CW11 ....175 C3
Reynolds Ave
St Helens WA9 ......1 A1
Warrington WA5 ......15 C2
Reynolds Mews SK9 ....60 C4
Reynolds St WA4 ......16 C2
Rhoden St CW1 ......191 A3
Rhodes Cl CW1 ......191 B2
Rhodes St
Dukinfield SK14 ......241 C7
Warrington WA2 ......16 B4
Rhodes St N SK14 ......241 C7
Rhodesway CH60 ......41 A4
Rhona Cl CH63 ......43 B2
Rhona Dr WA5 ......14 C3
Rhone Ct CH3 ......142 A4
Rhos Ave SK8 ......239 E1
Rhuddlan Ct CH65 ......70 B1
Rhuddlan Rd CH1 ......117 B2
Rhum Cl CH65 ......70 B1
Rhyl St WA8 ......22 C4
Ribble Ave CW7 ......127 A1
Ribble Cl Culcheth WA3 ..4 C1
Widnes WA8 ......13 C2

Ribble Dr ST8 ......179 C1
Ribble Pl CW7 ......127 A1
Ribblesdale CH65 ......70 A2
Ribblesdale Ave CW12 .157 A3
Ribblesdale Cl CH62 ....43 C3
Ribchester Gdns WA3 ....5 A2
Richard Cl WA7 ......24 A1
Richard Evans Com Prim Sch
WA11 ......1 A3
Richard Moon St CW1 ..190 A2
Richard Reynolds Ct
M44 ......11 C3
Richard St Crewe CW1 ..190 A3
Northwich CW9 ......104 B4
1 Stockport SK1 ......240 F6
Richards Croft CH3 ....142 A4
Richardson Cl
4 Sandbach CW11 ....174 B3
Shavington CW2 ......206 B3
Richardson St WA2 ....16 B4
Richbell Cl M44 ......11 C4
Richmond Ave
Handforth SK9 ......34 B2
Haydock WA11 ......1 A4
Runcorn WA7 ......23 C1
Warrington WA4 ......17 A2
Warrington, Grappenhall
WA4 ......17 B2
Richmond Care Village
CW5 ......205 A3
Richmond Cl Culcheth WA3 .4 B2
Lymm WA13 ......19 A2
Sale M33 ......242 F5
Sandbach CW11 ......174 C4
Stalybridge SK15 ......242 D1
Richmond Cres CH3 ....119 B1
Richmond Ct
Altrincham WA14 ......238 B2
Cheadle SK8 ......239 C5
Ellesmere Port CH65 ....70 B2
Richmond Dr Lymm WA13 19 A2
Northwich CW9 ......104 A2
Richmond Gdns WA12 ...2 B1
Richmond Gn WA14 ....238 B2
Richmond Gr SK8 ......239 F1
Richmond Hill
17 Knutsford WA16 ......57 A1
Macclesfield SK11 ......112 C3
Richmond Hill Rd SK8 ..239 C6
Richmond Ho SK15 ....242 C1
Richmond Mews CH1 ...118 C1
Richmond Pl SK11 ......112 C3
Richmond Rd
Altrincham WA14 ......238 D5
Altrincham, Bowdon WA14 238 C2
Crewe CW1 ......190 C3
Romiley SK6 ......241 C3
Richmond St
2 Hyde SK14 ......241 E6
Stalybridge SK15 ......242 F2
Warrington WA4 ......17 A2
Widnes WA8 ......13 B1
Rickaby Cl CH63 ......43 B4
Ridding La WA7 ......50 A4
Riddings Ct
Altrincham WA15 ......238 F8
Northwich CW8 ......103 A2
Riddings La
Hartford CW8 ......103 A2
Wybunbury CW5 ......220 A4
Riddings Rd WA15 ......238 F2
Riddings The CH65 ......70 A2
Ridge Ave WA15 ......32 B3
Ridge Cl SK6 ......241 F2
Ridge Danyers Coll SK8 239 F3
Ridge Hill
Sutton Lane Ends SK11 .113 A1
Utkinton CW6 ......146 A3
Ridge Hill La SK15 ....242 D3
Ridge Hill Prim Sch
SK15 ......242 C3
Ridge Pk SK7 ......35 B3
Ridge The CW8 ......123 B4
Ridge View SK11 ......112 B3
Ridgeborne Cl WA5 ......7 B1
Ridgemont Ave SK4 ....240 B6
Ridgeway Golborne WA3 ..3 C4
Wilmslow SK9 ......60 C4
Ridgeway Cl CH66 ......69 B1
Ridgeway Gdns WA13 ...18 B2
Ridgeway Ho CH3 ......121 B2
Ridgeway The
Alvanley WA6 ......74 A1
Cronton WA8 ......12 B3
Disley SK12 ......38 B3
Heswall CH60 ......41 A4
Runcorn WA7 ......50 B3
Tarvin CH3 ......121 B2
Ridgewell Ave 4 WA3 ...3 B4
Ridgmont Rd SK7 ......35 C3
Ridgway St Crewe CW1 .190 B3
Warrington WA2 ......16 B4
Ridgway The SK6 ......241 A1
Ridings Com Inf Sch The
CH1 ......94 A1
Ridings The
Saughall CH1 ......117 A4
Wilmslow SK9 ......59 B2
Ridley Cl CW2 ......206 C1
Ridley Dr WA5 ......15 B2
Ridley Rd SK10 ......87 C4
Ridley Wood Rd LL13 ..196 A4
Ridling La SK14 ......241 E6
Ridsdale 2 WA8 ......22 B4
Rifle Rd M21,M33 ......242 F7
Rigby Ave CW1 ......190 A4
Rigby Rd ST7 ......195 A3

Rigby St
Altrincham WA14 ......238 D3
Golborne WA3 ......3 A4
Rigby's Row CW5 ......204 C3
Rigg St CW1 ......190 A3
Riley Bank Mews WA6 ...74 A1
Riley Cl CW11 ......174 C3
Riley Dr WA7 ......49 A4
Rileys Way ST7 ......209 C1
Rilshaw La CW7 ......150 A4
Rilston Ave WA3 ......4 B2
Rimington Cl WA3 ......4 C1
Rimsdale Cl Gatley SK8 ..239 A3
Wistaston CW2 ......206 A4
Ring Rd CH3 ......119 B2
Ring-o-Bells La SK12 ....38 B3
Ringsfield Rd L24 ......21 A1
Ringstead Cl SK9 ......34 B1
Ringstead Dr 18 SK9 ....34 B1
Ringstone Way SK23 ....65 B4
Ringway
Ellesmere Port CH66 ....69 C2
Neston CH64 ......41 C1
Waverton CH3 ......143 A3
Ringway Cl SK10 ......87 A2
Ringway Rd Runcorn WA7 23 B1
Wythenshawe M22,M90 ..33 B4
Ringway Rd W M22,M90 .33 B4
Ringway Trad Est M22 ...33 C4
Ringwood Cl WA3 ......10 A3
Ripley Ave SK8 ......35 A3
Ripley Cl SK7 ......36 C4
Ripley St WA5 ......15 C3
Ripon Ave
Ellesmere Port CH66 ....69 B3
Golborne WA3 ......3 B4
Ripon Cl Macclesfield SK10 87 B2
Newton-le-W WA12 ......2 B3
Ripon Dr CW2 ......206 A4
Ripon Row WA7 ......49 B3
Ripon Wlk SK6 ......241 A1
Rise The SK23 ......65 B3
Riseley St SK11 ......112 A4
Riseley's Pas 33 SK11 ..112 B4
Rising Sun Cl SK11 ....112 A3
Rising Sun Rd SK11 ....112 A2
Risley Moss Local Nature
Reserve Visitor Ctr★
WA3 ......10 A2
Risley Rd WA3 ......9 C3
Rivacre Brow CH66 ......69 C4
Rivacre Bsns Ctr CH66 ..69 B4
Rivacre Rd CH62,CH65,
CH66 ......44 B1
Rivacre Valley Ctry Pk★
CH66 ......69 B4
Rivacre Valley Prim Sch
CH66 ......69 C4
River La Broughton CH4 ..140 C4
Chester CH4 ......141 B4
Farndon CH3 ......180 C1
Partington M31 ......11 C2
River Rd WA4 ......16 A2
River St Congleton CW12 .156 B2
Macclesfield SK11 ......112 C3
Wilmslow SK9 ......60 A4
River View CW7 ......126 C3
Riverbank Cl
Bollington SK10 ......87 C4
Heswall CH60 ......40 C3
Nantwich CW5 ......204 C4
Riverbank Rd CH60 ......40 C3
Riverdane Rd CW12 ....156 C2
Rivermead Ave WA15 ...32 B4
Riversdale Frodsham WA6 .49 B1
Warrington WA1 ......17 C4
Riversdale Rd
Cheadle SK8 ......239 C5
Runcorn WA7 ......49 C4
Rivershill M33 ......242 B4
Rivershill Gdns WA15 ...32 B4
Riverside Nantwich CW5 .204 B3
Northwich CW9 ......104 A3
Riverside Bsns Pk SK9 ..60 A4
Riverside Cres WA4 ....130 B2
Riverside Ct Chester CH4 141 C4
Langley SK11 ......113 A2
Riverside Dr
Northwich CW8 ......103 C3
Prestbury SK10 ......87 A3
Riverside Gr CW2 ......189 B2
Riverside Pk CH5 ......116 A4
Riverside Ret Pk WA1 ...16 B2
Riverside Trad Est CW8 .103 C4
Riverside Wlk CH64 ......66 B3
Riversmead CH3 ......142 A3
Riverton Rd M20 ......239 B8
Riverview Rd CH64 ......66 C3
Rivington Ct WA1 ......17 C4
Rivington Gr M44 ......11 B3
Rivington Rd
Altrincham WA15 ......238 F2
Ellesmere Port CH65 ....70 B3
Runcorn WA7 ......50 C2
Rixton Ave WA5 ......15 C4
Rixton Clay Pits Nature
Reserve★ WA3 ......10 C1
Roaches The SK11 ......112 A3
Roachill Cl WA14 ......238 B5
Road Beta CW10 ......151 B4
Road Five CW7 ......127 B1
Road Four CW7 ......127 A1
Road One Crewe CW1 ...207 B4
Winsford CW7 ......127 A2
Road St CW6 ......146 A2
Road Three CW7 ......127 B1
Road Two Crewe CW1 ...207 B4

Road Two *continued*
Winsford CW7 127 A1
Roadside Ct WA3 3 B4
Roan Ct SK11 112 C4
Roan House Way SK11 112 C4
Roan Mews SK11 112 C4
Roan Way SK9 85 A4
Rob La WA12 2 C3
Robert Moffat WA16 29 B3
Robert Salt Ct WA14 238 E6
Robert St Dukinfield SK14 241 C7
Northwich CW8 103 C3
Runcorn WA7 23 B1
Sale M33 242 E6
Warrington WA5 15 C3
Widnes WA8 13 A1
Robert's Terr CH1 118 A1
Roberts Ave WA11 1 A3
Roberts Ct WA7 49 C3
Roberts Dr CW9 104 B3
Roberts Rd CW9 80 A1
Robin Cl Rainow SK10 88 C3
Runcorn WA7 50 B4
Sandbach CW11 175 A4
Robin Cres SK11 112 B1
Robin Hood Ave SK11 112 B3
Robin Hood La WA6 73 A1
Robin La Chelford SK11 84 A2
Sutton Lane Ends SK11 112 B1
Robin's La SK7 35 B4
Robins Cft CH66 69 C1
Robins Cl SK7 35 C4
Robins La WA3 4 B1
Robins Way SK10 88 A4
Robinsbay Rd M22 33 C4
Robinson St Hyde SK14 241 F7
Stockport SK3 240 D3
Robinsons Croft CH3 142 A4
Robinsway WA14 238 C1
Robson St WA1 16 B3
Robson Way 14 WA3 3 C4
Roby Gr WA5 15 A3
Roche Gdns SK8 35 A3
Rochester Cl Golborne WA3 3 A4
Warrington WA5 15 B3
Rochester Cres CW1 190 C3
Rochester Dr CH65 70 B2
Rochester Ho SK10 86 C1
Rochford Ave M22 33 B4
Rock Bank SK23 65 C3
Rock Cotts CH5 91 B1
Rock Dr WA6 49 B1
Rock Farm Cl CH64 67 A3
Rock Farm Dr CH64 67 A3
Rock Farm Gr CH64 67 A3
Rock La
Burwardsley CW6 184 B3
Chester CH2 237 A4
Widnes WA8 12 C2
Rock Rd CH5 91 C1
Rock St SK22 39 B4
Rock The WA6 73 B1
Rockfield Cl WA8 12 B1
Rockfield Dr WA6 73 B1
Rockford Lodge WA16 57 B1
Rockhouse La ST7 210 B4
Rockingham Cl WA3 10 B3
Rocklands La CH63 42 B4
Rocklee Gdns CH64 67 A3
Rocklife La CH6 91 A2
Rocklynes SK6 241 B2
Rocksavage Expressway
WA7 49 B3
Rockside ST7 195 B3
Rockwood Ave CW2 190 A2
Rockwood Cl CW2 190 A2
Rocky La Heswall CH60 40 C4
Tattenhall CH3 182 C4
Rocky La S CH60 41 A4
Roddy La WA6 75 C1
Rode Ct 7 CW12 156 C2
Rode Hall* ST7 194 A4
Rode Heath Prim Sch
ST7 193 C4
Rode House Cl ST7 193 C4
Rode The ST7 193 B2
Rodeheath Cl SK9 60 B4
Rodepool Cl SK9 34 B1
Rodgers Cl WA6 49 A1
Rodmill Dr SK8 239 A4
Rodney St
Ashton-u-Lyne OL6 242 A4
Macclesfield SK11 112 B4
Roe Pk CW12 178 C1
Roe St Congleton CW12 156 C1
Macclesfield SK11 112 B4
Roebourne Rise CH1 117 B2
Roebuck La M33 242 A6
Roebuck St CW1 190 B3
Roeburn Way WA5 14 B2
Roedean Wlk CW1 190 B3
Roehampton Dr WA7 49 C4
Roehurst La CW7 126 B1
Roemarsh Ct WA7 49 C3
Roewood La
Macclesfield SK10 88 A1
Macclesfield, Higherfence
SK10 113 A4
Roften Ind Est CH66 43 B1
Rokeby Ct WA7 24 B3
Rokeden WA12 2 B2
Roland Ave WA7 22 C1
Rolands Wlk WA7 23 C1
Rolleston St WA2 16 A3
Rolls Ave CW1 190 A4
Rolt Cres CW10 151 B4
Roman Cl
Newton-le-W WA12 2 B1

Roman Cl *continued*
Runcorn WA7 23 C1
Roman Ct CH64 66 C4
Roman Dr CH1 117 B3
Roman Rd Stockport SK4 240 E6
Warrington WA4 16 B1
Roman Rise CW8 78 A2
Roman Way CW11 174 C4
Romanes St CW8 103 C4
Romford Ave M34 241 A8
Romiley Prec SK6 241 C2
Romiley Prim Sch SK6 241 C2
Romiley Rd CH66 69 C3
Romiley Sta SK6 241 C2
Romney Cl Neston CH64 66 C4
Widnes WA8 13 C1
Romney Croft CH64 66 C4
Romney Way CH64 66 C4
Romsey Dr SK8 35 B3
Rona Ave CH65 70 B1
Ronald Dr WA2 9 A1
Ronaldshay WA8 13 C1
Ronaldsway Halewood L26 21 A4
Heswall CH60 40 C3
Ronan Rd WA8 22 C3
Rood Hill CW12 156 B2
Rook Rd WA4 16 C2
Rook St CW2 190 B1
Rookery Cl
14 Nantwich CW5 204 C3
Sandbach CW11 174 B3
Rookery Ct 14 CW11 174 B3
Rookery Dr
Nantwich CW5 204 C2
Tattenhall CH3 166 A1
Rookery Gdns CW9 103 C2
Rookery Rd
Kidsgrove ST7 195 B2
Tilston SY14 198 A2
Rookery Rise CW7 127 A1
Rookery The
Broughton CH4 139 A2
Newton-le-W WA12 2 B2
Rookerypool Cl SK9 34 B1
Rookfield M33 242 C7
Rookfield Ave M33 242 C7
Rooks Way CH60 40 C4
Roome St WA2 16 B4
Rooth St SK4 240 D6
Rope Bank Ave CW2 206 A4
Rope La CW2 206 A3
Rope Wlk CW12 156 B2
Ropewalk The CH64 41 B1
Rosam Ct WA7 49 C3
Roscoe Ave
Newton-le-W WA12 2 C2
Warrington WA2 16 B4
Roscoe Cres WA7 48 C4
Roscoe Park Est WA14 238 E8
Roscoe Rd M44 11 C4
Roscoe St SK3 240 D4
Roscoes Yd 3 WA16 57 A1
Roscote Cl CH60 40 C4
Roscote The CH60 40 C4
Rose Ave WA11 1 C3
Rose Bank WA13 18 C2
Rose Cl WA7 50 B3
Rose Cnr CH3 166 A1
Rose Cotts CW12 154 C3
Rose Cres WA8 22 C4
Rose Gdns CH64 66 C3
Rose Lea Cl WA8 13 A2
Rose St Stockport SK5 240 F7
Widnes WA8 22 C4
Rose Terr Crewe CW1 190 B3
Stalybridge SK15 242 D1
Rose Vale SK8 239 B1
Rose View Ave WA8 13 A1
Rose Wlk 7 M31 11 C2
Roseacre Dr SK8 239 C1
Rosebank Cl CW7 149 C4
Rosebank Rd M44 11 B2
Rosebank Sch CW8 78 A2
Rosebank Wlk CW8 78 A2
Roseberry Way CW1 191 B2
Rosecroft CH62 43 B3
Rosedale Ave
Golborne WA3 3 B4
Warrington WA1 17 B4
Rosedale Rd SK4 240 D8
Rosedene Cl CH2 118 C4
Rosefield Ave WA13 18 C2
Rosefield Cl SK3 240 E1
Roseheath Com Prim Sch
L26 21 A4
Roseheath Dr L26 21 A3
Rosehill Ave WA9 6 A3
Rosehill Rd CW2 190 A1
Rosemary Ave
Runcorn WA7 49 C2
Warrington WA4 16 C1
Rosemary Cl
Broughton CH4 139 B2
Warrington WA5 15 B3
Rosemary Dr WA12 2 C2
Rosemary La LL12 161 B1
Rosemary Row CH3 166 A1
Rosemary Wlk M31 11 C1
Rosemere Dr CH66 94 C4
Rosemoor Gdns WA4 26 C3
Rosendale Dr WA3 10 A3
Rosetree Mdw CW9 80 A1
Rosevale Rd ST5 210 C1
Roseville Dr CW12 179 A4
Roseway SK11 112 B3
Rosewood Ave
Chester CH2 118 B3
Frodsham WA6 74 B4

Rosewood Ave *continued*
Stockport SK4 240 A5
Warrington WA1 16 C4
Rosewood Cl CW1 190 C3
Rosewood Dr CW7 126 A1
Rosewood Gdns 4 M33 242 F5
Rosewood Gr CH1 117 A4
Roslyn Rd SK3 240 E1
Ross Ave SK3 240 E1
Ross Cl WA5 15 B4
Ross Dr CH66 69 B3
Ross Rd CH65 70 A3
Ross St WA8 13 A1
Rossall Cl L24 21 C1
Rossall Dr SK7 35 C3
Rossall Gr CH66 69 B3
Rossall Rd
Warrington WA5 15 A2
Widnes WA8 13 B1
Rossbank Rd CH65 70 A4
Rosscliffe Rd CH65 70 A3
Rossenclough Rd SK9 34 B1
Rossendale Rd SK8 34 B4
Rossett Ave 1 M22 33 B4
Rossett Bsns Village
LL12 162 B1
Rossett Cl
Northwich CW9 103 C2
Warrington WA5 7 C1
Rossett Pk LL12 162 B1
Rossfield Rd CH65 70 A3
Rossfield Rd N CH65 70 A4
Rosslyn Cl CH5 116 A1
Rosslyn La CW8 102 A2
Rosslyn Rd Cheadle SK8 239 D1
Chester CH3 119 A2
Rossmill La WA15 32 A4
Rossmore Bsns Pk CH65 70 A4
Rossmore Gdns CH66 69 B3
Rossmore Ind Est CH65 70 A3
Rossmore Rd E CH65 69 C4
Rossmore Rd W CH66 69 B4
Rossmore Sch CH66 69 B4
Rossmount Rd CH65 70 A3
Rosswood Rd CH65 70 A3
Rostherne Ave
Ellesmere Port CH66 69 C2
Golborne WA3 3 B4
High Lane SK6 37 C4
Rostherne Cl WA5 15 B2
Rostherne Cres WA8 12 B1
Rostherne Ct WA14 238 D3
Rostherne Rd Sale M33 242 F5
Stockport SK3 240 E1
Wilmslow SK9 59 C2
Rostherne St 1 WA14 238 D3
Rostherne Way CW11 174 C4
Rosthernmere Rd SK8 239 F4
Rostrevor Rd SK3 240 E1
Rothay Dr WA5 14 B2
Rothbury Cl WA7 49 B3
Rother Dr CH65 70 A4
Rother Dr Bsns Ctr CH65 70 A4
Rotherhead Dr SK11 112 A3
Rotherwood Rd SK9 59 B3
Rothesay Cl WA7 23 C1
Rothesay Dr CH62 43 C2
Rothesay Rd CH4 141 A4
Rough Bank CW12 179 C4
Rough Heys La SK11 111 A4
Roughlea Ave WA3 4 B2
Roughley Ave WA5 15 B2
Roughlyn Cres CH4 140 C1
Roughwood La CW11 176 A1
Round Gdns SK10 88 A4
Round Hill Mdw CH3 142 A4
Round Mdw SK10 88 C3
Round Thorn WA3 9 A4
Round Way SK22 39 B4
Roundabout The WA8 12 B3
Roundcroft SK6 241 E3
Roundhey SK8 34 B4
Roundway SK7 35 B3
Roundy La SK10 62 C3
Routledge St WA8 13 A1
Row The CW7 126 B1
Rowan Ave WA3 3 C4
Rowan Cl Alsager ST7 193 B2
Middlewich CW10 151 C3
Runcorn WA7 49 B4
Sandbach CW11 174 C4
Warrington WA5 14 C3
Winsford CW7 126 B2
Rowan Ct 4 Hyde SK14 241 E5
Wilmslow SK9 60 A4
Rowan Dr SK8 35 B4
Rowan Gr CH5 91 B1
Rowan Lodge SK7 35 C4
Rowan Pk CH3 142 C4
Rowan Pl CH2 119 A2
Rowan Rd CW8 102 B4
Rowan St SK14 241 F5
Rowan Way SK10 87 C1
Rowan Wlk M31 11 C1
Rowans The CH4 139 A2
Rowanside SK10 86 C3
Rowanside Dr SK9 60 C4
Rowcliffe Ave CH4 141 A2
Rowena Ct CH2 118 C2
Rowland Cl WA2 9 A2
Rowlands View CW6 146 A4
Rowley Bank La WA16 29 A1
Rowley Rd SK7 36 C4
Rowley Way WA16 82 A4
Rowson Ct 2 M33 242 D6
Rowson Dr M44 11 B3
Rowswood Farm WA4 25 C3
Rowthorn Cl WA8 22 C4

Rowton Brideg Rd CH3 142 C4
Rowton Cl 12 CW9 103 C2
Rowton La CH3 142 C3
Rowton Rd CW2 189 B2
Roxborough Cl WA5 7 A3
Roxburgh Cl SK10 87 A1
Roxburgh Rd CH66 68 C3
Roxby Way WA16 82 A4
Roxholme Wlk M22 33 B4
Royal Ave WA8 12 A1
Royal Gdns
Altrincham WA14 20 C1
Northwich CW9 103 C2
Royal George St SK1,
SK3 240 F4
Royal La CW6 147 A2
Royal Mdws SK10 87 A1
Royal Mews CW9 104 B3
Royal Oak Yd 4 SK1 240 F5
Royal Pl WA8 22 A4
Royal Rd SK12 38 B3
Royal Schools for the Deaf
The SK8 34 B3
Royal Sh Arc The 7
CH64 66 C4
Royce Ave WA15 238 E5
Royce Cl CW1 190 A4
Royce Ct WA16 56 C1
Royden Ave Irlam M44 11 C4
Runcorn WA7 49 A4
Royds Cl CW8 103 A2
Royds Ct CW11 174 B3
Roylands Dr CW10 151 B4
Royle St Congleton CW12 156 B2
Northwich CW9 104 A4
Stockport SK1 240 F3
Winsford CW7 126 C1
Royle's Pl CW8 103 B3
Royleen Dr WA6 74 B3
Royley Carr Flats SK6 241 A3
Royon Dr SK3 240 B3
Royston Ave WA1 17 A4
Royston Cl
Ellesmere Port CH66 69 C2
2 Golborne WA3 3 C4
Rozel Cres WA5 15 A3
Rudd Ave WA9 1 A1
Rudheath Cl CW2 189 B3
Rudheath Com Prim Sch
CW9 104 B3
Rudheath High Sch
CW9 104 B4
Rudheath Way CW9 104 C3
Rudloe Ct WA2 8 C1
Rudstone Cl CH66 69 A3
Rudyard Cl SK11 112 A3
Rue De Bohars CW6 168 B4
Rufford Ave SK14 241 F6
Rufford Cl Widnes WA8 12 B1
Wistaston CW2 206 A4
Rufford Ct WA1 17 C4
Rufus Ct CH1 237 A3
Rugby Cl SK10 87 C2
Rugby Dr SK10 87 C2
Rugby Ho SK10 87 B2
Rugby Rd CH65 70 B2
Ruislip Ct WA2 8 C1
Runcorn Docks Rd WA7 22 C1
Runcorn East Sta WA7 50 B4
Runcorn Rd Barnton CW8 78 A1
Little Leigh CW8 77 B3
Moore WA4 25 B3
Runcorn Spur Rd WA7 49 B4
Runcorn Sta WA7 22 C1
Runger La M90,WA15 32 C4
Runnell The CH64 41 B2
Runnymede WA1 17 B4
Runnymede Cl SK3 240 C2
Runnymede Ct
Stockport SK3 240 C2
2 Widnes WA8 13 B1
Runnymede Dr WA11 1 A3
Runnymede Gdns 5
WA8 13 B1
Runnymede Wlk 7 WA8 13 B1
Rupert Row WA7 50 A4
Ruscoe Ave CW11 174 C3
Ruscolm Cl WA5 14 B4
Rush Gdns WA13 19 A2
Rushes Mdw WA13 19 A3
Rushey Cl WA15 32 B4
Rushfield Cres WA7 50 A3
Rushfield Rd Cheadle SK8 35 A3
Chester CH4 141 A3
Rushgreen Rd WA13 19 A2
Rushmere Cl SK10 62 C1
Rushmere La CH3 163 C2
Rushmore Gr WA1 17 A4
Rusholme Cl L26 21 A3
Rushside Rd SK8 35 A3
Rushton Ave WA12 2 A2
Rushton CE Prim Sch
SK11 159 A1
Rushton Cl
Northwich CW9 104 B4
Widnes WA8 12 C2
Rushton Dr Chester CH2 118 C4
Hough Common CW2 206 C1
Middlewich CW10 151 B4
Romiley SK6 241 C3
Rushton Fold SK10 61 A1
Rushton La CW6 147 B3
Rushton Rd Cheadle SK8 35 A3
Stockport SK3 240 B3
Rushy View WA12 2 A2
Rushyfield Cres SK6 241 D3
Ruskin Ave
Newton-le-W WA12 2 B2

Ruskin Ave *continued*
Warrington WA2 8 B1
Ruskin Ct WA16 57 A1
Ruskin Dr CH65 70 B2
Ruskin Gdns SK6 241 A3
Ruskin Gr SK6 241 A3
Ruskin Rd
Congleton CW12 156 B1
Crewe CW2 190 B1
Ruskin Sch The CW2 190 B1
Ruskin Way WA16 57 A2
Rusland Ct M33 242 A7
Russel Ct WA8 13 A2
Russell Ave Alsager ST7 193 B3
High Lane SK6 37 C4
Sale M33 242 D7
Russell Cl CW12 179 A4
Russell Dr CW1 191 B2
Russell Rd Runcorn WA7 48 C4
Winsford CW7 149 B4
Russell St
Ashton-u-Lyne OL6 242 A4
Chester CH2 237 C3
Hyde SK14 241 D7
Russet Cl CW10 128 A1
Russet Rd CW8 102 B4
Russett Sch The CW8 102 C4
Rutherford Cl SK14 241 D6
Rutherford Dr WA16 82 B4
Rutherford Way 6
SK14 241 D6
Ruthin Ave SK8 239 E2
Ruthin Cl WA5 7 C2
Ruthin Ct CH65 70 B2
Ruthin Wlk WA6 73 A1
Rutland Ave Denton M34 241 B6
Golborne WA3 3 B4
Halewood L26 21 A4
Warrington WA4 26 A4
Rutland Cl
Ashton-u-Lyne OL6 242 A2
Congleton CW12 156 C2
Gatley SK8 239 B6
Sandbach CW11 174 B3
Rutland Dr
Middlewich CW10 151 B4
Weaverham CW8 77 B1
Rutland La M33 242 F6
Rutland Pl CH2 119 A3
Rutland Rd
Altrincham WA14 238 D6
Hazel Grove SK7 36 C4
Irlam M44 11 B3
Kidsgrove ST7 195 A1
Macclesfield SK11 112 B2
Partington M31 11 C1
Rutland St
Ashton-u-Lyne OL6 242 A2
Runcorn WA7 22 C1
Rutter Ave WA5 7 C1
Ryburn Cl CW2 207 A2
Ryburn Rd SK11 112 A3
Rydal Ave High Lane SK6 37 C4
Warrington WA4 16 A1
Rydal Cl
Ellesmere Port CH65 70 B1
Gatley SK8 239 B4
Holmes Chapel CW4 130 A1
Neston CH64 66 C3
Winsford CW7 126 B2
Rydal Ct CW12 156 A1
Rydal Dr WA15 32 B4
Rydal Gr Chester CH4 141 A3
Helsby WA6 73 A1
Runcorn WA7 49 A4
Rydal Mount CW1 173 A1
Rydal Pl SK11 112 A3
Rydal St WA12 2 B2
Rydal Way Alsager ST7 193 B3
Widnes WA8 12 B1
Rydal Wlk SK15 242 D3
Ryde Ave SK4 240 B6
Ryde Cl CW1 190 A4
Ryder Ave WA14 238 E7
Ryder Rd Warrington WA1 17 B4
Widnes WA8 13 A2
Ryders St CW8 103 C4
Rye Cl ST7 193 A2
Ryebank Ave CW1 190 A4
Ryebank Way SK10 87 B2
Ryecroft CH2 72 A2
Ryecroft Cl CW10 151 A4
Ryecroft La
Duddon CH3,CW6 144 B3
Mobberley WA16 57 C2
Ryecroft Rd CH60 41 B4
Ryedale Cl SK4 240 B7
Ryedale Way CW12 179 B4
Ryehills ST7 209 C1
Rylands Cl SY14 213 A2
Rylands St
Warrington WA1 16 A3
5 Widnes WA8 23 A4
Ryle St SK11 112 B3
Ryle's Park Rd SK11 112 B3
Ryles Cl SK11 112 B3
Ryles Cres SK11 112 B3
Ryles Ho SK11 112 B3
Ryles Park High Sch
SK11 112 B3
Ryleys La SK9 59 C1
Ryleys Sch The SK9 59 C1

S

Sabre Cl WA7 . . . . .50 B4
Sack La CW9 . . . . .54 C3
Sacred Heart RC Prim Sch
WA5 . . . . .15 C3
Saddleback Dr SK10 . . . . .86 C4
Saddlers Rise WA7 . . . . . .50 B4
Sade Ct CW1 . . . . .190 A3
Sadler Cl CW4 . . . . .126 B1
Sadler Rd CW7 . . . . .126 B1
Sadler St WA8 . . . . .13 B1
Sadler's Cl CW4 . . . . .130 A2
Sadlers La CW6 . . . . .124 A1
Sadlers Wells CW6 . . . . . .185 C4
Safferon Cl WA2 . . . . .9 A1
Saffron Cl WA3 . . . . .9 B1
Saffron Wlk M31 . . . . .11 C1
Sagars Rd SK9 . . . . .34 B2
Sage Cl WA2 . . . . .9 B1
Saighton CE Prim Sch
CH3 . . . . .142 C1
Saighton La CH3 . . . . .142 C1
SS Peter & Paul RC High Sch
WA8 . . . . .12 C1
St Aelred's RC Tech Coll
WA12 . . . . .2 B2
St Alban Rd WA5 . . . . .14 C3
St Alban's RC Prim Sch
SK10 . . . . .86 C1
St Alban's RC Sch WA5 . . .15 C3
St Albans Cl WA11 . . . . .2 A4
St Albans Cres WA14 . . . .238 C8
St Albans Dr CW5 . . . . . . .204 C2
St Albans Pl SK22 . . . . . . .39 B4
St Albans St SK22 . . . . . . .39 B4
St Ambrose Coll WA15 . . . .32 A4
St Ambrose Prim Sch
L24 . . . . .21 A1
St Ambrose RC Prim Sch
SK3 . . . . .240 E1
St Ambrose Rd WA8 . . . . . .13 B1
St Andrew's Ave WA15 . . .238 F7
St Andrew's CE Prim Sch
WA2 . . . . .8 B2
St Andrew's Cl SK6 . . . . . .241 B1
St Andrew's Gdns ST7 . . . .193 C1
St Andrew's Rd
Ellesmere Port CH65 . . . . . .70 C2
Macclesfield SK11 . . . . .112 A4
St Andrews Cl
Northwich CW9 . . . . .104 C4
Stockport SK4 . . . . .240 B8
Warrington WA2 . . . . .9 A2
St Andrews Ct
Altrincham WA15 . . . . . . .238 F3
Crewe CW2 . . . . .190 B1
Ellesmere Port CH65 . . . . . .70 C1
St Andrews Dr
Holmes Chapel CW4 . . . . .130 A1
Kidsgrove ST7 . . . . .195 B2
St Andrews Rd
Gatley SK8 . . . . .239 C1
Stockport SK4 . . . . .240 B8
St Andrews Sch (Special
Needs) CH4 . . . . .141 B4
St Andrews Wlk
Mickle Trafford CH2 . . . . . .96 C1
New Mills SK22 . . . . .39 B4
St Ann's Ave CW10 . . . . . .151 B4
St Ann's CE Prim Sch
WA2 . . . . .16 B4
St Ann's Rd CW10 . . . . . . .151 B4
St Ann's Rd N SK8 . . . . . .239 B2
St Ann's Rd S SK8 . . . . . . .34 B4
St Ann's Sq SK8 . . . . .34 B4
St Anne St CH2 . . . . .237 B3
St Anne's Cl M33 . . . . . . .242 C6
St Anne's Dr M34 . . . . . . .241 A8
St Anne's Hospl WA14 . . . .238 C3
St Anne's La CW5 . . . . . . .204 B3
St Anne's Prim Sch
M34 . . . . .241 A8
St Anne's RC Prim Sch
CW5 . . . . .204 C2
St Anne's Rd Hyde M34 . . .241 A8
Widnes WA8 . . . . .13 A1
St Annes Ave WA4 . . . . . . .17 A1
St Annes Ave E WA4 . . . . .17 A1
St Annes CE Prim Sch
M33 . . . . .242 D6
St Annes RC High Sch
SK4 . . . . .240 D8
St Anns St M33 . . . . .242 F5
St Anthony Pl WA2 . . . . . . .8 A3
St Anthony's RC Prim Sch
CH4 . . . . .140 C3
St Asaph Dr WA5 . . . . .7 C2
St Asaph Rd CH66 . . . . . . .69 C2
St Augustine's Ave WA4 . . .16 C2
St Augustine's RC Prim Sch
Runcorn WA7 . . . . .24 A1
Warrington WA4 . . . . .16 C2
St Augustine's Rd SK3 . . .240 B4
St Austel Cl WA5 . . . . .14 C2
St Austell Ave SK10 . . . . . .86 C1
St Austell Cl
Macclesfield SK10 . . . . . . .86 C1
Runcorn WA7 . . . . .50 A3
St Austell Dr SK8 . . . . .34 A4
St Austins La WA1 . . . . . . .16 A2
St Barnabas CE Prim Sch
Macclesfield SK11 . . . . . .112 B3

St Barnabas CE Prim Sch
continued
Warrington WA5 . . . . .15 C3
St Barnabas St SK11 . . . . .112 B3
St Barnabas Pl WA5 . . . . . .15 B3
St Basil's RC Prim Sch
WA8 . . . . .12 A1
St Bede's Ave CW8 . . . . . .77 B1
St Bede's RC Inf Sch
WA8 . . . . .13 A1
St Bede's RC Jun Sch
WA8 . . . . .13 A1
St Bede's RC Prim Sch
CW8 . . . . .102 C4
St Bees Cl SK8 . . . . .239 B3
St Benedict's RC Prim Sch
Warrington WA2 . . . . .16 B4
Wilmslow SK9 . . . . .34 C2
St Benedicts Cl WA2 . . . . . .16 A4
St Bernard's RC Prim Sch
CH65 . . . . .70 B2
St Berteline's CE Prim Sch
WA7 . . . . .50 B4
St Brannocks Rd SK8 . . . . .35 A4
St Brides Cl WA5 . . . . .14 C2
St Bridget's RC Prim Sch
WA2 . . . . .8 C2
St Bridgets Cl WA2 . . . . . . .8 C2
St Bridgets Ct CH4 . . . . . .141 A3
St Catherine's RC Prim Sch
WA3 . . . . .3 C4
St Catherines Dr CW8 . . . .103 A2
St Chad's Ave SK6 . . . . . .241 C2
St Chad's CE Prim Sch
ST5 . . . . .210 B1
St Chad's Fields CW7 . . . . .149 B3
St Chad's Gr SK6 . . . . . . .241 C2
St Chad's RC High Sch
WA7 . . . . .49 B4
St Chad's Rd CH1 . . . . . . .117 C3
St Chads Cl CW5 . . . . . . .220 A4
St Chads Way TF9 . . . . . .236 B1
St Christopher's Dr SK6 . . .241 A2
St Christopher's RC Prim Sch
SK6 . . . . .241 A2
St Christophers Cl CH2 . . .118 B4
St Clairs St CW2 . . . . .190 B1
St Clare's RC Prim Sch
CH4 . . . . .141 A4
St Clement's RC Prim Sch
WA7 . . . . .49 A4
St David Rd CH62 . . . . .44 A3
St David's Ave SK6 . . . . . .241 B2
St David's High Sch
CH4 . . . . .140 B3
St David's Terr CH4 . . . . . .140 B3
St Davids Cl M33 . . . . . . .242 A5
St Davids Dr
Ellesmere Port CH66 . . . . . .94 C4
Warrington WA5 . . . . .7 C1
St Davids' Ret Pk CH4 . . . .140 B4
St Edward's RC Prim Sch
Macclesfield SK11 . . . . . .112 B3
Runcorn WA7 . . . . .23 A2
St Edwards Cl SK11 . . . . . .112 B3
St Elmo Pk SK12 . . . . .37 B2
St Elphin's (Fairfield) CE
Prim Sch WA1 . . . . .16 B3
St Elphins Cl WA1 . . . . . . .16 B3
St Gabriel's RC Prim Sch
ST7 . . . . .193 B2
St Gabriels Ct ST7 . . . . . .193 B2
St George's CE Prim Sch
Hyde SK14 . . . . .241 D5
Stockport SK2 . . . . .240 F2
St George's Cl WA16 . . . . . .82 B4
St George's Cres
Chester CH4 . . . . .237 C1
Waverton CH3 . . . . .143 A3
St George's Ct
Altrincham WA14 . . . . . . .238 B7
Widnes WA8 . . . . .22 B4
St George's Gdns SK8 . . . .241 A5
St George's Pl SK11 . . . . .112 B4
St George's Rd CW7 . . . . .149 B4
St George's St
Macclesfield SK11 . . . . . .112 B3
Stalybridge SK15 . . . . . . .242 D3
St George's Way
Northwich CW9 . . . . .103 C3
Thornton Hough CH63 . . . . .42 A4
St Georges Ave CH66 . . . . .94 C4
St Georges Cl WA4 . . . . . . .26 C2
St Georges Ct 5 SK14 . . . .241 E6
St Georges Dr SK14 . . . . .241 D5
St Georges Rd SK22 . . . . . .39 B4
St Gerards RC Prim Sch
WA8 . . . . .23 A4
St Giles Dr SK14 . . . . .241 F6
St Gregory's RC High Sch
WA5 . . . . .15 B3
St Gregory's RC Prim Sch
SK10 . . . . .87 C4
St Helen's Coll (Newton
Campus) WA12 . . . . .2 A1
St Helens CE Prim Sch
WA3 . . . . .11 A1
St Helens Rd WA3 . . . . . . .11 A2
St Helens Rd Golborne WN7 4 A4
5 Northwich CW9 . . . . . .104 A4
St Hilary's Sch
Alderley Edge SK9 . . . . . . .60 A1
Alderley Edge SK9 . . . . . . .85 A4
St Hilda's Dr WA6 . . . . .49 B1
St Hugh's Cl WA14 . . . . . .238 E8
St Hugh's RC Prim Sch
WA15 . . . . .238 F8
St Ives Ave SK8 . . . . .240 A2

St Ives Cl SK10 . . . . .86 C1
St Ives Pk CH5 . . . . .116 A2
St Ives Way CH5 . . . . .116 A2
St James Ave
Chester CH2 . . . . .118 C4
Congleton CW12 . . . . . . .156 B1
Warren SK11 . . . . .111 C1
St James CE Prim Sch
Haydock WA11 . . . . .1 C3
Kettleshulme SK23 . . . . . . .64 C2
St James Cl Audlem CW3 230 A2
Frodsham WA6 . . . . .49 B1
St James Ct
Altrincham WA15 . . . . . . .238 E4
Audley ST7 . . . . .209 B1
Connah's Quay CH5 . . . . . .91 B1
Manchester M20 . . . . . . .239 B8
St James Dr M33 . . . . . . .242 A5
St James St
Ashton-u-Lyne OL6 . . . . . .242 A2
Chester CH2 . . . . .237 B3
St James Terr 10 CW7 . . . .149 A4
St James Wlk 19 CW8 . . . .103 C4
St James' CE Prim Sch
CW3 . . . . .230 A3
St James' Ct ST8 . . . . .179 C2
St James' Dr SK9 . . . . .60 A3
St James' RC High Sch
SK8 . . . . .34 C4
St James' Sq SK22 . . . . . . .39 B4
St James' Way SK8 . . . . . . .34 C4
St James's CE Jun Sch
CH2 . . . . .119 A2
St John Ave WA4 . . . . .16 A1
St John Fisher RC Prim Sch
Denton M34 . . . . .241 B5
Widnes WA8 . . . . .13 B1
St John St Chester CH1 . . . .237 B2
Newton-le-W WA12 . . . . . . .2 A2
St John The Evangelist CE
Prim Sch SK11 . . . . . . .112 A4
St John The Evangelist RC
Prim Sch (Annexe)
ST7 . . . . .194 C1
St John Vianney Sch
SK4 . . . . .240 B6
St John's Ave
Knutsford WA16 . . . . .56 C1
Lostock Gralam CW9 . . . . . .79 C2
St John's CE Prim Sch
Bollington SK10 . . . . .88 A4
Kingsley WA6 . . . . .75 B1
Sandbach CW11 . . . . . . .175 C3
St John's Cl
Northwich CW9 . . . . .104 C3
Romiley SK6 . . . . .241 B2
St John's Ct
Altrincham WA14 . . . . . . .238 D3
Hyde SK14 . . . . .241 F7
Knutsford WA16 . . . . .57 B1
St John's Dr SK14 . . . . . . .241 F7
St John's Rd
Altrincham WA14 . . . . . . .238 D3
Bebington CH62 . . . . .44 A3
Chester CH4 . . . . .237 C1
Congleton CW12 . . . . . . .156 C3
Knutsford WA16 . . . . .57 A1
19 Macclesfield SK11 . . . .112 B4
Wilmslow SK9 . . . . .59 C2
St John's Rear Rd CH4 . . .237 C1
St John's St WA7 . . . . .23 A2
St John's Way
Cuddington CW8 . . . . . . .102 A1
Sandbach CW11 . . . . . . .175 C3
St John's Wood ST7 . . . . .194 C1
St John's Wood Com Sch
WA16 . . . . .57 B1
St Johns Dr CW7 . . . . .149 A4
St Joseph's Cl WA5 . . . . . .14 C3
St Joseph's RC Prim Sch
Sale M33 . . . . .242 B6
Stockport SK1 . . . . .240 F5
Warrington WA5 . . . . .14 C1
Winsford CW7 . . . . .149 A4
St Josephs Way CW5 . . . . .205 A3
St Katherines Way WA1 . . .16 B3
St Kilda Cl CH65 . . . . .70 B1
St Lawrence Ct CW5 . . . . .204 C3
St Lawrence Rd
Frodsham WA6 . . . . .74 A4
Hyde M34 . . . . .241 A7
St Leonard's Way CW3 . . .232 B1
St Leonards Dr WA15 . . . . .238 F6
St Lesmo Ct SK3 . . . . .240 C3
St Lesmo Rd SK3 . . . . . . .240 C3
St Lewis RC Prim Sch
WA3 . . . . .4 A1
St Luke's Ave WA3 . . . . .3 B4
St Luke's CE Prim Sch
WA3 . . . . .3 C4
St Luke's Cres WA8 . . . . . .13 A2
St Luke's RC Prim Sch
WA6 . . . . .74 B4
St Luke's Way WA6 . . . . . . .49 A1
St Lukes Cl CW4 . . . . .130 B2
St Margaret's Ave WA2 . . . .8 B1
St Margaret's CE Prim Sch
WA2 . . . . .8 B1
St Margaret's Cl WA14 . . . .238 C4
St Margaret's Rd
Altrincham WA14 . . . . . . .238 C4
Stockport SK8 . . . . .240 A2
St Mark's Ave WA14 . . . . .238 A5
St Mark's CE Prim Sch
WA6 . . . . .53 B2
St Mark's Prim Sch SK6 241 A4
St Mark's St Haydock WA11 1 A3

St Mark's St continued
Romiley SK6 . . . . .241 A4
St Marks Cres CH66 . . . . . .94 C4
St Marks Rd CH4 . . . . . . .140 C2
St Martin's Ave SK4 . . . . . .240 C6
St Martin's Cl SK14 . . . . . .241 F6
St Martin's Rd ST7 . . . . . .210 C3
St Martins Dr CH66 . . . . . .69 B1
St Martins La WA7 . . . . . . .50 B4
St Martins RC Prim Sch
WA7 . . . . .50 B4
St Mary's Ave CW8 . . . . . . .77 B1
St Mary's CE Prim Sch
CW12 . . . . .178 A4
St Mary's CE Prim Sch
Bebington CH62 . . . . .44 A3
Bosley SK11 . . . . .158 B4
Irlam M44 . . . . .11 B3
Sale M33 . . . . .242 A6
St Mary's Cl Alsager ST7 193 B3
Hale L24 . . . . .21 C1
Warrington WA4 . . . . .26 B3
St Mary's Ct CW12 . . . . . .156 A1
St Mary's Dr Cheadle SK8 239 F6
Whitegate CW7 . . . . .126 A4
St Mary's Halton CE Prim Sch
WA7 . . . . .50 A4
St Mary's Hill CH4 . . . . . . .237 B1
St Mary's Inf Sch CH1 . . . .237 B1
St Mary's RC Inf Sch WA12 2 B2
St Mary's RC Jun Sch
WA12 . . . . .2 A2
St Mary's RC Prim Sch
Ashton-u-Lyne OL6 . . . . . .242 A4
Congleton CW12 . . . . . . .156 B2
Crewe CW2 . . . . .190 A1
Middlewich CW10 . . . . . . .151 B4
New Mills SK22 . . . . .39 A4
Stockport SK4 . . . . .240 E6
St Mary's Rd
Altrincham WA14 . . . . . . .238 C3
Disley SK12 . . . . .38 B3
Dodleston CH4 . . . . .162 A4
Nantwich CW5 . . . . .204 C4
New Mills SK22 . . . . .39 A4
Runcorn WA8 . . . . .23 C1
Warrington WA5 . . . . .14 C3
Widnes WA7 . . . . .23 A2
St Mary's St Crewe CW1 . .190 B2
Warrington WA4 . . . . .16 B2
St Marys Ct CW5 . . . . . . .204 A4
St Matthew's CE Prim Sch
SK3 . . . . .240 E4
St Matthew's Rd SK3 . . . . .240 D4
St Matthew's Terr SK3 . . . .240 D4
St Matthews CE Prim Sch
WA4 . . . . .26 C1
St Matthews Cl
Haslington CW1 . . . . .191 B2
Warrington WA4 . . . . .26 B4
St Mawes Cl WA8 . . . . .12 C1
St Mawes Ct SK10 . . . . . . .86 C1
St Mawgan Ct WA2 . . . . . . .8 C1
St Michael's Ave SK7 . . . . .35 C4
St Michael's Cl
Little Leigh CW8 . . . . .77 B3
Widnes WA8 . . . . .22 B4
St Michael's RC Prim Sch
WA8 . . . . .22 B4
St Michael's Rd WA8 . . . . . .22 B4
St Michael's Road Ind Est
WA8 . . . . .22 B3
St Michael's View CW1 . . . .190 A3
St Michael's Way CW10 . . .128 B1
St Monica's RC Prim Sch
WA4 . . . . .26 B4
St Monicas Cl WA4 . . . . . . .26 B4
St Nicholas Ct CW5 . . . . . .204 C3
St Nicholas RC High Sch
CW8 . . . . .103 B3
St Olave St CH4 . . . . .237 B1
St Oliver Plunkett RC Prim
Sch WA3 . . . . .9 C2
St Oswald's CE Prim Sch
CH1 . . . . .94 C1
St Oswald's Cres CW11 . . .153 C3
St Oswald's Way
WA1 . . . . .16 C4
St Oswalds Cl
Malpas SY14 . . . . .213 A2
Winwick WA2 . . . . .8 A3
St Oswalds Way CH1 . . . . .237 B3
St Paul of the Cross RC Prim
Sch WA5 . . . . .6 C3
St Paul's CE Prim Sch
SK15 . . . . .242 F2
St Paul's CE Prim Sch
CW6 . . . . .146 A4
St Paul's Cl CW1 . . . . .190 B2
St Paul's Ct Hyde SK14 . . .241 E7
Warrington WA2 . . . . .16 A3
St Paul's Hill Rd SK14 . . . .241 F6
St Paul's Inf Sch CH2 . . . .237 C3
St Paul's Pl 2 CW9 . . . . . . .79 A1
St Paul's RC Prim Sch
SK14 . . . . .241 F8
St Paul's Rd
5 Macclesfield SK11 . . . .112 C4
Stockport SK4 . . . . .240 B8
Widnes WA8 . . . . .23 A4
St Paul's St Crewe CW1 . . .190 B2
Hyde SK14 . . . . .241 F7
Stalybridge SK15 . . . . . . .242 F2
St Pauls Cl SK15 . . . . . . .242 F2
St Pauls Gdns CH66 . . . . . .69 A4
St Pauls Rd WA7
SK12 . . . . .36 C1

St Pauls Trad Est SK15 . . .242 F2
St Peter's Ave WA16 . . . . . .56 C1
St Peter's CE Prim Sch
Duddon CW6 . . . . .145 A3
Heswall CH60 . . . . .40 C4
Newton-le-W WA12 . . . . . . .2 C2
St Peter's Cl Heswall CH60 40 C4
Lymm WA13 . . . . .19 A2
St Peter's Ct WA2 . . . . .16 B4
St Peter's Dr Hyde SK14 . .241 F6
Little Budworth CW6 . . . . .147 C4
St Peter's RC Prim Sch
Stalybridge SK15 . . . . . .242 D1
Warrington WA1 . . . . .17 B4
St Peter's Rise CW11 . . . . .174 C4
St Peter's Sq SK1 . . . . . . .240 F5
St Peter's Way WA2 . . . . . .16 B4
St Peters Rd CW12 . . . . . .156 C1
St Peters Way CH2 . . . . . .119 C4
St Petersgate SK1 . . . . . . .240 F5
St Philip (Westbrook) CE
Prim Sch WA5 . . . . .7 A1
St Saviour's CE Prim Sch
ST7 . . . . .194 B1
St Saviour's RC Inf Sch
CH66 . . . . .69 C2
St Saviour's RC Jun Sch
CH66 . . . . .69 C2
St Saviour's St ST7 . . . . . .194 B1
St Stephen Rd WA5 . . . . . .14 C3
St Stephen's Ave WA2 . . . . .8 A2
St Stephen's RC Prim Sch
WA2 . . . . .8 A1
St Stephens Cl CH60 . . . . .41 B4
St Stephens Ct
11 Congleton CW12 . . . . .156 C2
Sandbach CW11 . . . . . . .174 B4
St Teresa's RC Prim Sch
M44 . . . . .11 C1
St Theresa's Prim Sch
CH1 . . . . .117 C3
St Thomas CE Prim Sch
ST7 . . . . .195 A1
St Thomas Ct WA8 . . . . . . .12 C1
St Thomas Hospl SK3 . . . .240 E4
St Thomas More RC High Sch
CW2 . . . . .190 A1
St Thomas of Canterbury CE
Jun Sch CH2 . . . . .237 A4
St Thomas St ST7 . . . . . . .195 A1
St Thomas' View CH65 . . . .70 A2
St Thomas's CE Prim Sch
SK1 . . . . .240 F5
St Thomas's CE Prim Sch
WA4 . . . . .16 B1
St Thomas's Pathway
CH1 . . . . .237 B2
St Thomas's Pl SK1 . . . . . .240 F4
St Vincent Dr CW8 . . . . . .102 C4
St Vincent Rd WA5 . . . . . . .14 C3
St Vincent St WA14,
WA15 . . . . .238 E4
St Vincent's RC Inf Sch
WA15 . . . . .238 E5
St Vincent's RC Jun Sch
WA15 . . . . .238 E5
St Vincent's RC Prim Sch
Knutsford WA16 . . . . .57 C1
St Helens WA9 . . . . .1 A2
Warrington WA5 . . . . .14 C2
St Wenefredes Gn SY13 . . .214 C3
St Werburgh St CH1 . . . . .237 B2
St Werburgh's & St
Columba's RC Prim Sch
CH2 . . . . .118 C4
St Werburgh's CE Prim Sch
WA4 . . . . .16 A1
St Wilfred's Dr WA4 . . . . . .17 B1
St Wilfrid's Cl CW9 . . . . . .104 A2
CW8 . . . . .103 B3
St Wilfrids Cl CW9 . . . . . . .104 A2
St Winefride's RC Prim Sch
Neston CH64 . . . . .66 C3
Neston CH64 . . . . .66 C4
St Winifred's Pl SK15 . . . .242 C4
St Winifred's RC Prim Sch
SK4 . . . . .240 A4
Salander Cres CW2 . . . . . .206 A4
Sale Gram Sch M33 . . . . .242 C5
Sale Sta M33 . . . . .242 B6
Sale Water Pk* M21 . . . . .242 E8
Salerno Rd CH2 . . . . .95 A1
Salesbrook La CW5 . . . . . .228 B3
Salford CW3 . . . . .230 A2
Salford Pl CW12 . . . . .156 C2
Salisbury Ave
Broughton CH4 . . . . .140 C3
Crewe CW2 . . . . .190 B1
Salisbury Cl Crewe CW2 . .190 B1
Ellesmere Port CH66 . . . . . .94 C4
Salisbury Pl SK10 . . . . .87 C2
Salisbury Rd
Altrincham WA14 . . . . . . .238 D7
Haydock WA11 . . . . .1 C4
Salisbury St Blacon CH1 . .118 A2
Golborne WA3 . . . . .3 A4
Runcorn WA7 . . . . .23 A1
Warrington WA1 . . . . .16 B3
Widnes WA8 . . . . .23 A4
Salkeld St 12 CW9 . . . . . .104 A4
Salop Pl ST7 . . . . .195 A2
Salop Wlk SK10 . . . . .86 C1
Salt Line Way CW11 . . . . . .174 B3
Salt Mdws CW5 . . . . .204 B3
Salt Mus The* CW9 . . . . . .103 C4
Saltash Cl WA7 . . . . .50 A3
Salter's La
Bickerton SY14 . . . . .199 C4

Salter's La continued
Broxton CH3 . . . . .183 C1
Picton CH2 . . . . .119 B4
Salters La
Siddington SK11 . . . . . . .109 C1
Withington SK11 . . . . . .132 A4
Saltersbrook Gr 12 SK9 .34 C1
Saltersford Cnr CW4 . . . .130 C2
Saltersgate CH66 . . . . . . .69 C3
Saltney Bsns Ctr CH4 .140 C4
Saltney Ferry Prim Sch
CH4 . . . . .140 A3
Saltney Ferry Rd CH4 . . .140 A4
Saltney Terr CH4 . . . . . . .140 A4
Salton Gdns WA5 . . . . .15 C4
Saltwood Dr WA7 . . . . .50 B3
Saltworks Cl WA6 . . . . .49 B1
Samuel Laycock Specl Sch
SK15 . . . . .242 C4
Samuel St Chester CH2 .237 C3
Crewe CW1 . . . . .190 A4
Macclesfield SK11 . . . . .112 B4
Packmoor ST7 . . . . .195 C1
Stockport SK4 . . . . .240 D7
Warrington WA5 . . . . .15 C2
Sanbec Gdns WA8 . . . . . . .12 B3
Sand La SK10 . . . . .84 C3
Sandalwood WA7 . . . . .24 B1
Sandalwood Cl WA2 . . . . . .8 B1
Sandbach Com Prim Sch
CW11 . . . . .175 A3
Sandbach Crosses★
CW11 . . . . .175 A3
Sandbach High Sch & Sixth
Form Coll CW11 . . . . . .175 A4
Sandbach Rd
Congleton CW12 . . . . . .156 A2
Hassall Green CW11,ST7 .176 B1
Lawton Heath ST7 . . . . .193 C3
Rode Heath ST7 . . . . . .193 C4
Sale M33 . . . . .242 F5
Sandbach Rd N ST7 . . . . .193 B2
Sandbach Rd S ST7 . . . . .193 B2
Sandbach Sch CW11 . . . .175 A3
Sandbach Sta CW11 . . . . .174 B4
Sanderling Rd WA12 . . . . . .2 B2
Sanders Hey Cl WA7 . . . . .50 C4
Sanders Sq SK11 . . . . . . .112 B3
Sanderson Cl
Crewe CW2 . . . . .206 B4
Warrington WA3 . . . . .14 B3
Sandfield Ave CW5 . . . . .216 C2
Sandfield Cl 3 WA3 . . . . . .3 C4
Sandfield Cres WA3 . . . . . .5 B4
Sandfield Ct
4 Frodsham WA6 . . . . . .74 A4
Wrenbury CW5 . . . . . . .216 C2
Sandfield La
Acton Bridge CW8 . . . . . .76 C1
Hartford CW8 . . . . .103 B2
Sandfield Pk CH60 . . . . . . .40 B4
Sandfields WA6 . . . . .74 A4
Sandford Cres CW2 . . . . .207 B1
Sandford Rd
Nantwich CW5 . . . . . . .204 C4
Sale M33 . . . . .242 F5
Sandgate Rd SK10 . . . . . . .87 C1
Sandham Gr CH60 . . . . . . .41 B4
Sandham Rd L24 . . . . .21 A2
Sandheys CH64 . . . . .41 B1
Sandhill St SK14 . . . . . . .241 F8
Sandhole Cotts 1 CW7 .149 A4
Sandhole La
Chelford WA16 . . . . .83 B2
Crowton CW8 . . . . .101 A4
Sandhurst Ave CW2 . . . . .190 A1
Sandhurst Dr SK9 . . . . . . .60 B4
Sandhurst Rd L26 . . . . . . .21 A3
Sandhurst St WA4 . . . . . . .16 C2
Sandicroft Cl WA3 . . . . .9 B3
Sandiford Rd CW4 . . . . . .130 B2
Sandileigh CH2 . . . . .118 C2
Sandileigh Ave
Altrincham WA15 . . . . . .238 F3
Knutsford WA16 . . . . . . .56 C1
Stockport SK8 . . . . .240 A2
Sandileigh Dr WA15 . . . . .238 F3
Sandington Dr CW8 . . . . .101 C1
Sandiway Bebington CH63 .43 B3
Knutsford WA16 . . . . . . .57 A1
Sandiway Ave WA8 . . . . . .12 A1
Sandiway Cl CW8 . . . . . . .102 A1
Sandiway La CW9 . . . . . . .53 A1
Sandiway Pk CW8 . . . . . . .102 C2
Sandiway Pl WA14 . . . . . .238 D5
Sandiway Prim Sch
CW8 . . . . .102 A2
Sandiway Rd
Altrincham WA14 . . . . . .238 D6
Crewe CW2 . . . . .190 A4
Handforth SK9 . . . . .34 B3
Sandle Bridge La WA16,
SK9 . . . . .83 C3
Sandle Bridge Rise
WA16 . . . . .83 C3
Sandon Cres CH64 . . . . . .66 C3
Sandon Park Gdns CW2 189 B2
Sandon Pl WA8 . . . . .13 C2
Sandon Rd CH2 . . . . .118 C2
Sandon St CW1 . . . . .190 B2
Sandown Cl Culcheth WA3 . .4 C2
Middlewich CW10 . . . . . .151 B4
Runcorn WA7 . . . . .49 B3
Wilmslow SK9 . . . . .60 B4
Sandown Cres CW8 . . . . .102 A4
Sandown Dr WA15 . . . . . . .32 B3
Sandown Pl SK11 . . . . . . .111 C4
Sandown Rd Crewe CW1 190 B4

Sandown Rd continued
Stockport SK8 . . . . .240 B4
Sandown Terr CH3 . . . . . .118 C1
Sandpiper Cl
Crewe CW1 . . . . .189 C2
Newton-le-W WA12 . . . . . .2 B2
Sandpiper Ct
Chester CH4 . . . . .141 A1
Kidsgrove ST7 . . . . .195 B1
Sandpiper Dr SK3 . . . . . . .240 D2
Sandpiper Way CH4 . . . . .141 A2
Sandra Dr WA12 . . . . .2 C2
Sandringham Ave
Chester CH3 . . . . .119 A1
Helsby WA6 . . . . .73 A2
Stalybridge SK15 . . . . . .242 D3
Sandringham Cl
Altrincham WA14 . . . . . . .20 C1
Davenham CW9 . . . . . . .103 C2
Winsford CW7 . . . . .126 B2
Sandringham Ct 5 SK9 . .60 A3
Sandringham Dr
Poynton SK12 . . . . .36 B2
Stockport SK4 . . . . .240 A5
Warrington WA5 . . . . . . .15 B2
Wistaston CW2 . . . . . . .205 C4
Sandringham Gdns 2
CH65 . . . . .70 B1
Sandringham Rd
Macclesfield SK10 . . . . . .87 C1
Widnes WA8 . . . . .13 C3
Sandringham Way 4
SK9 . . . . .60 A3
Sandrock Rd CH3 . . . . . . .142 C4
Sands Rd ST7 . . . . .195 C3
Sandsdown Cl ST8 . . . . . .179 B1
Sandside Rd ST7 . . . . .193 A2
Sandstone Wlk CH60 . . . . .41 A4
Sandwell Dr M33 . . . . . . .242 B8
Sandwich Dr SK10 . . . . . . .87 B2
Sandwood Ave CH4 . . . . .139 A2
Sandy Brow La WA3 . . . . . .3 C1
Sandy Cl SK10 . . . . .87 C4
Sandy La Allostock WA16 .106 C3
Astbury CW12 . . . . .177 C3
Aston CW5 . . . . .217 B1
Bold Heath WA8 . . . . . . .14 A3
Broughton CH4 . . . . . . .140 B3
Brown Knowl CH3 . . . . .199 B4
Bulkeley SY14 . . . . .184 B1
Chester CH3 . . . . .119 A1
Congleton CW12 . . . . . .155 B2
Congleton, Astbury Marsh
CW12 . . . . .156 A1
Croft WA3 . . . . .9 A4
Cronton WA8 . . . . .12 B3
Golborne WA3 . . . . .2 C4
Golborne, Lowton WA3 . . .4 A4
Goostrey WA16 . . . . . . .107 B1
Haslington CW11 . . . . . .192 A4
Hatherton CW5 . . . . . . .219 C3
Helsby WA6 . . . . .73 A1
Higher Kinnerton CH4 . . .161 A3
Lymm WA13 . . . . .19 A2
Macclesfield SK10 . . . . . .86 B1
Neston CH64 . . . . .67 A4
Romiley SK6 . . . . .241 D3
Runcorn, Preston Brook
WA7 . . . . .50 C3
Runcorn, Weston Point
WA7 . . . . .48 C4
Saighton CH3 . . . . .142 B2
Sandbach CW11 . . . . . .174 B3
Stockport SK4,SK5 . . . . .240 E7
Swettenham CW12 . . . . .131 B2
Tarvin CH3 . . . . .121 B2
Threapwood SY14 . . . . .222 C4
Warrington, Cobbs WA4 . . .26 B4
Warrington, Longford WA2 . .8 B1
Warrington, Penketh WA5 . .15 A2
Weaverham CW8 . . . . . .77 B1
Whitegate CW8 . . . . . . .125 B3
Wilmslow SK9 . . . . .59 C4
Sandy La W WA2 . . . . .8 A2
Sandy Moor La WA7 . . . . . .24 B2
Sandy Rd ST8 . . . . .179 B1
Sandyhill Pl 1 CW7 . . . . .149 B3
Sandyhill Rd CW7 . . . . . . .149 B3
Sandylands Cres ST7 . . . .193 C3
Sandylands Pk CW2 . . . . .205 B4
Sandylane Mews CW12 .156 B3
Sandymoor La WA7 . . . . . .24 B2
Sankey Bridges Ind Est
WA5 . . . . .15 B2
Sankey St Golborne WA3 . . .3 A4
Newton-le-W WA12 . . . . .16 A3
Warrington WA1 . . . . . . .16 A3
Widnes WA8 . . . . .23 A3
Sankey Sta WA5 . . . . .14 C3
Sankey Valley Ind Est
WA12 . . . . .2 A1
Sankey Valley Pk★ Haydock
WA11,WA12 . . . . .1 B2
★ Warrington WA5 . . . . .15 B3
Sankey Way WA5 . . . . . . .15 B3
Sanky La WA4 . . . . .25 C1
Santon Dr WA3 . . . . .3 C4
Sapling La CW6 . . . . .146 C2
Sark Ave CH65 . . . . .95 A4
Sark Ho CH2 . . . . .119 A2
Sarl Williams Ct CW1 . . .237 A3
Sarn Bank Rd SY14 . . . . .222 B3
Sarn Rd SY14 . . . . .222 B4
Sarra La CH3 . . . . .184 A3
Sarsfield Ave 1 WA3 . . . . .3 B4
Saughall Cl CW9 . . . . .103 C2
Saughall Hey CH1 . . . . . . .94 A1
Saughall Rd CH1 . . . . . . .117 C3

Saunders St CW1 . . . . . .190 A2
Saundersfoot Cl WA5 . . . . .7 C1
Saunderton Cl WA11 . . . . . .1 B4
Saville Ave WA5 . . . . .15 C4
Saville Rd SK8 . . . . .239 B6
Saville St SK11 . . . . .112 C3
Savoy Rd CW1 . . . . .207 A2
Sawley Cl Culcheth WA3 . . .5 A1
Warrington WA7 . . . . .50 C4
Sawley Dr SK8 . . . . .35 B3
Sawpit St WA13,WA14 . . . .20 A3
Sawyer Brow SK14 . . . . . .241 F8
Sawyer Dr ST8 . . . . .179 B1
Saxon Cl WA4 . . . . .26 B3
Saxon Crossway CW7 . . . .126 A1
2 Sandbach CW11 . . . . .174 B3
Saxon Terr WA8 . . . . .13 A1
Saxon Way Blacon CH1 . . .117 C3
Ellesmere Port CH66 . . . .94 C4
Sandbach CW11 . . . . . .175 B3
Saxons La
Northwich CW8 . . . . . . .103 C3
Northwich, Greenbank
CW8 . . . . .103 B4
Sayce St WA3 . . . . .13 A1
Scafell Ave WA2 . . . . .8 A3
Scafell Cl Bebington CH62 .43 B2
High Lane SK6 . . . . .37 C3
Scaife Rd CW5 . . . . .204 C3
Scaliot Cl SK22 . . . . .39 A4
Scar La SY14 . . . . .198 C1
Sceptre Cl 1 WA12 . . . . . .2 A2
Scholar Green Prim Sch
ST7 . . . . .194 C3
Scholar's Ct 3 CH64 . . . .66 C4
Scholars Cl Chester CH4 140 C3
Macclesfield SK10 . . . . .111 B4
Scholars Green La WA13 18 C1
School Ave CH64 . . . . .66 C3
School Bank WA6 . . . . . . .101 A4
School Brow
Romiley SK6 . . . . .241 A2
Warrington WA1 . . . . . . .16 B3
School La Audley ST7 . . . .210 A1
Knutsford WA16 . . . . . . .56 C1
Marbury SY13 . . . . .226 C4
Poynton SK12 . . . . .36 C2
School Cres Crewe CW1 .190 C2
Stalybridge SK15 . . . . . .242 D4
School Ct SK3 . . . . .240 F2
School Dr ST8 . . . . .78 A2
School Field Cl CW3 . . . .230 C4
School Gn CH3 . . . . .182 B1
School Hill CH60 . . . . .40 C4
School La Aldford CH3 . . .163 C1
Antrobus CW9 . . . . .53 B2
Astbury CW12 . . . . .178 A4
Audlem CW3 . . . . .230 A2
Bold Heath WA8 . . . . . . .13 C4
Brereton Green CW11 . . .153 C3
Bunbury CW6 . . . . .168 C1
Burwardsley CH3 . . . . . .184 A3
Cheadle SK8 . . . . .35 A4
Cuddington CW8 . . . . . .102 A1
Eaton (nr Congleton)
CW12 . . . . .156 C4
Ellesmere Port CH66 . . . .69 A4
Elton CH2 . . . . .72 A2
Frodsham WA6 . . . . .74 B4
Great Budworth CW9 . . . .79 A4
Guilden Sutton CH3 . . . .119 C3
Hartford CW8 . . . . .103 B2
Henbury SK11 . . . . .111 A3
Hollinfare WA3 . . . . .11 A1
Hooton CH66 . . . . .43 C1
Irlam M44 . . . . .11 B3
Lostock Gralam CW9 . . . .80 A1
Manley WA6 . . . . .99 A3
Marbury SY13 . . . . .215 C1
Marton SK11 . . . . .133 B3
Mickle Trafford CH2 . . . . .119 C4
Moulton CW9 . . . . .126 C4
5 Nantwich CW5 . . . . .204 C3
Neston CH64 . . . . .42 A1
Neston, Little Neston CH64 .66 C3
Neston, Parkgate CH64 . . .41 A1
Nether Alderley SK10 . . . .86 A3
Norley WA6 . . . . .100 B3
Ollerton WA16 . . . . .83 A2
Partington WA14 . . . . . . .20 B3
Poynton SK12 . . . . .36 C2
Runcorn WA7 . . . . .49 C4
Sandbach, Betchton CW11 175 C2
Sandbach, Ettiley Heath
CW11 . . . . .174 B4
Smallwood CW11 . . . . . .176 C3
Warmingham CW11 . . . . .173 C4
Warrington WA3 . . . . . . .10 B3
Whitley WA4 . . . . .52 C3
School Mews SK7 . . . . . . .35 C4
School Rd
Altrincham WA15 . . . . . .238 F3
Ellesmere Port CH65 . . . .70 A3
Handforth SK9 . . . . .34 B2
Lach Dennis CW9 . . . . . .104 B3
Sale M33 . . . . .242 B7
Warrington WA2 . . . . .8 B1
Winsford CW7 . . . . .127 A1
Winsford, Meadow Bank
CW7 . . . . .126 C3
School Rd N CW9 . . . . . . .104 C3
School Rd S CW9 . . . . . . .104 C3
School Terr Chester CH2 . .118 C2
Golborne WA3 . . . . .3 A4
Haslington CW1 . . . . . . .191 B4
Newton-le-W WA12 . . . . . .2 A3
Warrington WA4 . . . . .16 A2
School Terr WA3 . . . . .3 A4

School Way
Northwich CW9 . . . . . . .104 A4
Widnes WA8 . . . . .13 B2
Schoolfold La SK10 . . . . . .63 A4
Schools Hill SK8 . . . . .239 D3
Schooner Cl WA7 . . . . .50 B3
Scilly Cl CH65 . . . . .70 B1
Scotch Hall La CW9 . . . . . .53 A2
Scotia Wlk 12 WA3 . . . . . . .3 C4
Scotland Rd WA1 . . . . .16 A3
Scott Ave Crewe CW1 . . . .190 C2
Widnes WA8 . . . . .22 C4
Scott Cl
Macclesfield SK10 . . . . .113 A4
Rode Heath ST7 . . . . . . .193 C4
Scott Rd SK10 . . . . .87 A4
Scott St WA2 . . . . .16 B3
Scott Wlk WA12 . . . . .2 A3
Scotthorpe Cl SK11 . . . . . .111 C3
Scotton Ave CH66 . . . . . . .69 A3
Scroggins La M31 . . . . . . .11 C2
Sea Bank CW10 . . . . .128 B1
Sea La WA7 . . . . .23 B1
Sea View CH64 . . . . .66 C2
Seabank Rd CH60 . . . . . . .40 C3
Seabury St WA4 . . . . .17 A2
Seacombe Dr CH66 . . . . . .69 C2
Seacombe Gr SK3 . . . . . . .240 B4
Seafield Ave CH60 . . . . . . .40 C3
Seaford Cl WA2 . . . . .24 B1
Seaford Pl WA2 . . . . .8 A2
Seagrave Cl CW9 . . . . . . .103 C3
Seagull Cl CW1 . . . . .190 C1
Seahill Rd CH1 . . . . .116 C4
Seal Rd SK7 . . . . .36 A4
Sealand Cl WA5 . . . . .8 C1
Sealand Ind Est CH1 . . . .117 C1
Sealand Rd Blacon CH1 . . .117 C3
Chester CH1 . . . . .118 A1
Sealand CH5 . . . . .116 B3
Sealand Trad Pk CH1 . . . .117 C1
Sealand Way 2 SK9 . . . . .34 C2
Seamon's Dr WA14 . . . . . .238 A6
Seamon's Rd WA14 . . . . . .238 A6
Seamons Wlk WA14 . . . . . .238 B5
Seathwaite Cl WA7 . . . . . .49 C3
Seaton Cl CW1 . . . . .190 A4
Seaton Pk WA7 . . . . .24 C2
Seaton St CW7 . . . . .127 B1
Seaview Ave CH62 . . . . . . .44 A3
Seaville St CH2 . . . . .237 C3
Secker Ave WA9 . . . . .16 B1
Secker Cl WA4 . . . . .16 B1
Second Ave
Congleton CW12 . . . . . .156 A2
Connah's Quay CH5 . . . . .92 C2
Crewe CW1 . . . . .190 C1
Kidsgrove ST7 . . . . .194 C1
Poynton SK12 . . . . .36 B1
Runcorn WA7 . . . . .49 C4
Sandbach CW11 . . . . . .175 A3
Second Dig La CW5 . . . . .219 B4
Second Wood St CW5 . . . .204 B3
Sedbergh Gr WA7 . . . . . . .49 C3
Sedburgh Cl WA4 . . . . . . .130 A2
Seddon Rd WA14 . . . . . . .238 D2
Seddon St CW10 . . . . . . .128 B1
Sedgefield Cl 3 SK10 . . . .87 B2
Sedgefield Rd CH1 . . . . . .118 A1
Sedgeford Cl SK9 . . . . . . .34 B1
Sedgewick Cres WA5 . . . . .6 C3
Sedgmere Ave CW1 . . . . .190 A4
Sedum Cl CH3 . . . . .142 A3
Sefton Ave
Congleton CW12 . . . . . .157 A1
Widnes WA8 . . . . .13 A2
Sefton Cres M33 . . . . . . .242 B8
Sefton Dr SK9 . . . . .34 B1
Sefton Rd Chester CH2 . . .119 A2
Sale M33 . . . . .242 B7
Sefton St WA2 . . . . .1 C2
Selby Cl Poynton SK12 . . . .36 B3
Runcorn WA7 . . . . .24 C2
Selby Gdns SK8 . . . . .35 B3
Selby Gn CH66 . . . . .69 A3
Selby St Stockport SK4 . . .240 D8
Warrington WA5 . . . . . . .15 C2
Selkirk Ave
Bebington CH62 . . . . . . .43 C2
Warrington WA4 . . . . . . .17 A2
Selkirk Cl
Ellesmere Port CH66 . . . .68 C3
Macclesfield SK10 . . . . . .86 C1
Selkirk Dr Chester CH4 . . .141 A4
Holmes Chapel CW4 . . . .130 A1
Selkirk Rd CH4 . . . . .141 A4
Seller St CH2 . . . . .237 C3
Selsdon Ct CH4 . . . . .141 B4
Selsey Ave SK3 . . . . .239 F7
Selsey Dr M20 . . . . .239 C8
Selworth Ave M33 . . . . . . .242 E6
Selworth Cl 5 WA15 . . . . .238 E6
Selworthy Dr
Crewe CW1 . . . . .190 A4
Warrington WA4 . . . . . . .17 B2
Selwyn Cl
Newton-le-W WA12 . . . . . .2 A3
Widnes WA8 . . . . .13 C2
Selwyn Dr Cheadle SK8 . . .35 B4
Sutton Lane Ends SK11 . . .112 C2
Semper Cl CW12 . . . . . . .157 A2
Seneschal Ct WA7 . . . . . . .49 C3
Senna La Antrobus CW9 . . .53 A1
Comberbach CW9 . . . . . .78 B4
Sennen Cl WA7 . . . . .50 B3

Sens Cl CH1 . . . . .237 A2
Sephton Ave WA3 . . . . .4 C2
Sergeant York Loop
WA5 . . . . .15 A3
Serin Cl WA2 . . . . .2 B2
Serpentine The CH4 . . . . .141 C4
Service St SK3 . . . . .240 B4
Servite Cl CH65 . . . . .69 C3
Servite Pl 8 CH64 . . . . . . .66 C4
Set St SK15 . . . . .242 C1
Sett Cl SK22 . . . . .39 A4
Seven Sisters La WA16 . . .82 C3
Sevenoaks Cl SK10 . . . . . .87 A1
Sevenoaks Rd SK8 . . . . . .239 B6
Severn Cl
Altrincham WA14 . . . . . .238 C6
Biddulph ST8 . . . . .179 C1
Congleton CW12 . . . . . .156 C1
Macclesfield SK10 . . . . . .86 C1
Warrington WA2 . . . . .8 C1
Widnes WA8 . . . . .13 C2
Severn Dr SK7 . . . . .35 B3
Severn Rd WA3 . . . . .4 C1
Severn Wlk CW7 . . . . .127 A1
Severnvale CH65 . . . . .70 A2
Sewell St WA7 . . . . .23 A1
Sextant Cl WA7 . . . . .50 B3
Sexton Ave WA9 . . . . .1 A1
Seymour Chase WA16 . . . .82 A4
Seymour Ct WA7 . . . . .24 B2
Seymour Dr
Ellesmere Port CH66 . . . .69 C3
Warrington WA1 . . . . . . .17 A4
Seymour Gr M33 . . . . .242 B6
Seymour Ho 16 SK9 . . . . .34 C1
Seymour Rd SK8 . . . . .35 A4
Shackleton Cl WA5 . . . . . .15 A3
Shade Terr SK6 . . . . .37 C4
Shadewood Cres WA4 . . . .17 A1
Shadewood Rd SK11 . . . . .112 A3
Shadowmoss Rd M22 . . . . .33 C4
Shady Brook La CW8 . . . . .77 B1
Shady Gr ST7 . . . . .193 B2
Shaftesbury Ave
Chester CH3 . . . . .119 C1
Warrington WA5 . . . . . . .14 C1
Shaftesbury Rd SK3 . . . . .240 B2
Shaftesbury Way WA5 . . . . .6 C4
Shaftway Cl WA11 . . . . .1 C4
Shakerley Ave CW12 . . . . .156 C2
Shakespeare Cl CW9 . . . . .104 B4
Shakespeare Dr
Cheadle SK8 . . . . .239 F6
Crewe CW1 . . . . .191 A2
Shakespeare Gr WA2 . . . . . .8 B1
Shakespeare Rd
Neston CH64 . . . . .41 C1
Widnes WA8 . . . . .13 A1
Shalcombe Cl L26 . . . . . . .21 A4
Shalford Dr M22 . . . . .33 C4
Shallacres CH65 . . . . .69 C4
Shallcross Ave SK23 . . . . .65 C2
Shallcross Cres SK23 . . . .65 C2
Shallcross Rd SK23 . . . . . .65 C2
Shambles The WA16 . . . . . .57 A1
Shanklin Cl WA5 . . . . .14 B3
Shannon Cl Chester CH4 . .140 C3
Willaston (nr Nantwich)
CW5 . . . . .205 B3
Shargar Cl WA5 . . . . .34 B1
Sharnbrook Dr CW2 . . . . .189 B2
Sharon Park Cl WA4 . . . . . .17 A1
Sharp St Warrington WA2 . .16 B3
Widnes WA8 . . . . .23 A4
Sharples St SK4 . . . . .240 E7
Sharpley St SK11 . . . . . . .112 B4
Sharston Cres WA16 . . . . . .57 A1
Shavington Ave CH2 . . . . .118 C1
Shavington High Sch
CW2 . . . . .206 A3
Shavington Prim Sch
CW2 . . . . .206 B4
Shavington Sports Ctr
CW2 . . . . .206 A3
Shavington Way CW9 . . . .103 C2
Shaw Dr WA16 . . . . .57 B2
Shaw Entry WA8,L35 . . . . .12 A4
Shaw Heath SK2 . . . . .240 E3
Shaw Heath View WA16 . . .57 B2
Shaw Moor Ave SK15 . . . .242 F1
Shaw Rd SK4 . . . . .240 B8
Shaw Rd S SK3 . . . . .240 B8
Shaw St
Ashton-u-Lyne OL6 . . . . .242 A3
Culcheth WA3 . . . . .5 A2
Haydock WA11 . . . . .1 C3
Macclesfield SK11 . . . . .112 B4
Runcorn WA7 . . . . .22 C1
Shaw's Rd WA14 . . . . .238 D4
Shawbury Gr WA1 . . . . . . .17 A4
Shawcross Fold 5 SK1 .240 F6
Shawell Ct WA8 . . . . .13 C1
Shaws Ave WA2 . . . . .16 B4
Shaws Fold SK9 . . . . .33 C2
Shaws La
Mottram St Andrew SK10 . .86 B4
Winsford CW7 . . . . .126 C2
Winsford CW7 . . . . .127 A2
Shay La Ashton CH3 . . . . .122 A4
Hampton SY14 . . . . .200 A1
Tarvin CH3 . . . . .121 C2
Shay's La CW6 . . . . .124 C2
Sheaf Cl CH3 . . . . .121 B1
Shearbrook La CW4 . . . . .107 C3
Sheardhall Ave SK12 . . . . .38 C3

Sheath St CW9 104 A4
Shed La CH3 119 A1
Sheepfield Cl CH66 69 B4
Sheerwater Cl WA1 16 C4
Sheffield Cl WA5 15 B3
Sheffield Rd SK14 241 F8
Sheffield Row WA12 7 B4
Sheffield St SK4 240 E7
Sheiling Ct WA14 238 C4
Sheilings The WA3 3 C4
Shelagh Ave WA8 13 A1
Shelbourne Mews 2 SK11 111 C4
Shelburne Dr CW1 191 B3
Sheldon Ave
Chester CH3 119 A1
Congleton CW12 157 A1
Sheldon Cl M31 11 C2
Sheldon Rd
Hazel Grove SK7 36 C4
Poynton SK12 37 B1
Sheldrake Dr CH64 66 C3
Sheldrake Rd WA14 238 B8
Shellbrook Gr 12 SK9 34 B1
Shelley Ave CW9 80 A3
Shelley Cl Crewe CW1 190 C2
Rode Heath ST7 193 C4
Shelley Ct 5 CW11 174 B3
Shelley Dr CW2 189 C1
Shelley Gr WA4 16 C2
Shelley Rd Blacon CH1 117 C3
Widnes WA8 13 A1
Shellow La CW12,SK11 134 B3
Shellway Rd CH2 71 A2
Shelly Cl CW10 151 C3
Shelton Cl WA8 13 C2
Shenhurst Cl SK9 59 C2
Shenton St SK14 241 C8
Shepcroft La WA4 26 B1
Shepherd's Brow WA14 238 A3
Shepherd's La CH2 118 B3
Shepherds Fold Dr CW7 126 B2
Shepherds Row WA7 23 C1
Shepley Cl SK7 36 B4
Shepley St 1 Hyde SK14 241 E6
Stalybridge SK15 242 D2
Sheppard Cl CW1 190 B3
Sheppenhall Gr CW5 217 B1
Sheppenhall La CW5 228 B3
Shepperton Cl WA4 26 C3
Shepsides Cl CH66 69 B2
Shepton Rd CH66 69 C1
Sheraton Rd CH3 143 A3
Sherborne Cl WA7 24 C2
Sherborne Rd
Crewe CW1 190 B3
Stockport SK3 240 A3
Sherbourne Ave CH4 141 A3
Sherbourne Cl SK8 35 A3
Sherbourne Rd
Ellesmere Port CH65 70 B2
Macclesfield SK11 111 C4
Sherbourne Way WA5 6 C3
Sherbrook Rise SK9 60 B3
Sherbrooke Rd SK12 38 B3
Sheri Dr WA12 2 C1
Sheridan Ave WA3 3 B4
Sheridan Cl CW1 173 A1
Sheridan Pl WA2 8 A3
Sheridan Way WA7 24 B1
Sheringham Cl CH4 140 C3
Sheringham Dr CW1 190 A4
Sheringham Rd WA5 14 C3
Sherlock Ave WA11 1 C4
Sherratt Cl CW12 156 C1
Sherrington's La CH3 199 B4
Sherwin St CW2 190 B1
Sherwood Ave
Cheadle SK8 239 F2
Sale M33 242 D7
Stockport SK4 240 A5
Sherwood Cl WA8 12 B1
Sherwood Cres WA5 6 C3
Sherwood Gr WA6 73 A2
Sherwood Rd SK11 112 B3
Shetland Cl
Warrington WA2 8 C2
Widnes WA8 13 C2
Shetland Dr
Bebington CH62 43 C4
Ellesmere Port CH65 70 B1
Shevington Cl WA8 13 C2
Shevington Wlk WA8 13 C2
Shield St SK3 240 E4
Shiers Dr SK8 239 E4
Shiggins Cl WA5 15 B3
Shillingford Cl WA4 26 C3
Shilton Cl CW10 151 C3
Ship St WA6 49 B1
Shipbrook Rd
Chester CH2 118 C3
Lach Dennis CW9 104 B2
Northwich CW9 104 B3
Shipgate St CH4 237 B1
Shipton Cl
Warrington WA5 15 A4
Widnes WA8 12 B2
Shirley Ave SK8 34 B3
Shirley Ct M33 242 C6
Shirley Dr WA4 17 A1
Shirley Gr SK3 240 E2
Shirleys Cl SK10 87 A3
Shirleys Dr SK10 87 A3
Shocklach Oviatt CE Prim Sch SY14 211 B4
Shocklach Rd CH2 118 C3
Shones Croft CH64 67 A3
Shop La Congleton CW12 156 C1
Little Budworth CW6 124 C1
Shopping Precinct The CH2 72 A2
Shoreham Dr WA5 15 A2
Shores Green Dr CW9 79 C3
Shores La CW5 203 B4
Short Cl WA12 1 C2
Short St Haydock WA11 1 C3
28 Macclesfield SK11 112 B4
Newton-le-W WA12 1 C2
Stockport SK4 240 E7
Widnes WA8 23 A3
Short St E SK4 240 E7
Shorthorn Cl CW10 128 B1
Shorwell Cl WA5 14 B4
Shotwick La CH1 93 B3
Shotwick Rd CH5 93 A2
Shrewbridge Cres CW5 204 C2
Shrewbridge Rd CW5 204 B2
Shrewsbury Dr ST5 210 C1
Shrewsbury Gdns SK8 35 B3
Shrewsbury Rd 11 CH65 70 B3
Shrewsbury St WA4 16 B2
Shrewsbury Way CH4 140 C3
Shrigley Cl SK9 34 B1
Shrigley Rd SK10 63 A3
Shrigley Rd N SK12 37 B2
Shrigley Rise SK10 63 B1
Shropshire Cl
Middlewich CW10 151 A4
Warrington WA1 17 C3
Shropshire La SY13 227 C1
Shropshire Rd CH2 70 C2
Shropshire St CW3 229 C2
Shuldham Cl WA16 29 B2
Shurlach Rd CW9 104 B3
Shutley La CW8 77 B3
Shutlingsloe Way SK11 112 A4
Sibbersfield La CH3 180 C2
Sibell St CH2 237 C3
Sibley Rd SK4 240 B7
Sibson Rd M33 242 B6
Siddall St 11 CW9 104 A4
Siddeley Cl CH4 139 B2
Siddeley Dr WA12 1 C2
Siddington Ave
Northwich CW9 104 A2
Stockport SK3 240 D2
Siddington Bank SK11 109 C2
Siddington Rd
Handforth SK9 34 B3
Poynton SK12 36 C1
Siddorn St CW7 126 C1
Side Ave WA14 238 C1
Side End La SK23 64 C2
Side La CW6 144 C3
Sidebottom St SK15 242 D2
Sidlaw Cl CH66 69 A3
Sidley Pl SK14 241 F7
Sidley St SK14 241 F7
Sidmouth Cl WA5 14 C2
Sidmouth Gr SK8 34 C4
Sidney Rd CH64 41 C1
Siemens Rd M44 11 C3
Sienna Cl M44 11 C3
Signal Ct CH2 118 C1
Silk Hill SK23 65 C4
Silk Mill
Macclesfield SK11 112 B4
Poynton SK12 36 B2
Silk Mill St WA16 57 A1
Silk Mus & Heritage Ctr* SK11 112 B4
Silk Rd The
Bollington SK10 87 C2
Macclesfield SK10 87 C2
Silk St CW12 156 B1
Silkstone Cres WA7 50 A4
Silsden Ave WA3 4 A4
Silvan Ct SK10 87 A1
Silver Ave WA11 1 A3
Silver Birches M34 241 B5
Silver Hill Rd SK14 241 E5
Silver La Croft WA3 9 C4
Warrington WA3 10 B3
Silver St Bollington SK10 88 A4
Congleton CW12 156 C1
Warrington WA2 16 A3
Silver Terr CW11 175 B3
Silverbirch Croft CH4 139 A2
Silverbirch Way CH66 94 C4
Silverdale
Altrincham WA14 238 C4
Northwich CW8 103 B4
Silverdale Ave M34 241 A6
Silverdale Cl
Frodsham WA6 74 B4
High Lane SK6 37 C4
Silverdale Dr SK9 60 A2
Silverdale Rd Gatley SK8 239 B4
Newton-le-W WA12 2 A2
Stockport SK4 240 D8
Warrington WA4 16 A1
Silvergate Ct CW12 178 C4
Silvermine Cl 17 ST7 195 A1
Silvermuir CH1 117 C2
Silverne Dr CH65 70 A1
Silverthorne Cl SK15 242 D1
Silverwood ST7 195 A1
Simmonds Cl CW9 103 C2
Simms Cross Prim Sch WA8 23 A4
Simon Cl M33 242 A5
Simons La WA6 74 A3
Simonside WA8 12 B1
Simonstone Rd CH4 139 B2
Simonswood Cl CW10 151 A4
Simpkin Ave WA4 16 C2
Simpson Cl CH2 95 B1
Simpson Ct CW1 173 A1
Simpson La SK10 63 B4
Simpson Rd CH2 95 B1
Simpson St Hyde SK14 241 D6
Wilmslow SK9 59 C3
Simpsons Way CH4 139 A2
Sinclair Ave Alsager ST7 193 A2
Warrington WA2 8 A1
Widnes WA8 23 A4
Sinderland La WA13 20 A4
Sinderland Rd WA14 238 C8
Singapore Ave M90 33 A4
Singleton Ave CW1 190 B3
Singleton Rd
Ellesmere Port CH65 69 C2
2 Stockport SK4 240 B8
Sir John Deane's Coll CW9 103 C3
Sir Thomas Boteler High Sch WA4 16 C2
Siskin Cl WA12 2 B2
Six Acre Gdns WA4 25 A3
Six Acre La WA4 25 A3
Sixpenny Wlk WA1 16 B3
Sixth Ave CH5 92 C1
Skaife Rd M33 242 E6
Skeath Cl CW11 175 C3
Skellern St ST7 194 B1
Skellorn Green La SK10 62 C4
Skelton Rd WA14 238 E7
Skiddaw Cl WA7 50 A2
Skip's La CH3 142 C4
Skipton Cl SK7 36 B4
Skipton Dr CH66 69 B3
Skye Cl
Ellesmere Port CH65 70 B1
Widnes WA8 13 C2
Skye Croft SK6 241 D3
Skylark Cl CW1 189 C4
Slack St Hyde SK14 241 F8
Macclesfield SK11 112 C3
Slacken La ST7 194 B1
Slade La Mobberley WA16 58 A4
Nether Alderley SK10 85 C3
Slade St 9 CW9 104 A4
Slag La Golborne WA3 3 B4
Haydock WA11 1 A4
Slater St
Macclesfield SK11 112 B3
Warrington WA4 16 B2
Slicks Bsns Ctr CW8 78 B1
Slindon Cl ST5 210 B1
Slutchers La WA1 16 A2
Small Ave WA2 8 B1
Small Cres WA2 8 B1
Small La WA16 58 A4
Smallbrook Wlk CW2 206 B4
Smallman Rd CW2 190 B1
Smallwood CE Prim Sch CW11 176 C3
Smallwood Cl
5 Middlewich CW10 151 B4
Newcastle-u-L ST5 210 B1
Smallwood Ct 1 CW12 156 C2
Smallwood Forge CW11 176 B3
Smethwick La CW11, CW12 154 C2
Smith Cl ST7 193 A2
Smith Cres WA2 16 B4
Smith Dr WA2 16 B4
Smith Gr CW1 190 A3
Smith La Mobberley WA16 57 C3
Rainow SK10 89 A3
Smith Rd WA8 22 C4
Smith St Cheadle SK8 239 F6
Macclesfield SK11 112 B3
Warrington WA1 16 A3
Smith's La CW8 77 B1
Smithfield Dr LL13 196 B4
Smithfield La CW11 175 B3
Smithfield St LL13 196 B4
Smithfields CH3 166 B1
Smithills Cl WA3 9 B3
Smiths Lawn SK9 60 A3
Smithy Bank CW7 149 A2
Smithy Brow
Bollington SK10 88 B4
Winwick WA3 8 C4
Smithy Cl Cronton WA8 12 B3
Saughall CH1 94 A1
Willaston CH64 67 A2
Smithy Ct
Christleton CH3 142 C4
5 Ellesmere Port CH66 69 B3
Smithy Gn Cheadle SK8 35 A4
Milton Green CH3 165 C3
Smithy Gr CW11 176 A1
Smithy Hill CH63 42 A3
Smithy La
Altrincham WA14 20 B2
Barthomley CW2 208 B3
Barthomley CW2 208 B4
Biddulph ST8 179 B1
Bosley SK11 158 C3
Broxton CH3 183 B1
Congleton CW12 156 B4
Crewe CW1 189 C4
Croft WA3 9 A4
Cronton WA8 12 B3
Cuddington CW8 102 A3
Ellesmere Port CH66 69 B3
Great Budworth CW9 79 A4
Smithy La *continued*
Helsby WA6 73 B3
Hyde SK14 241 E5
Kingsley WA6 75 A1
Little Leigh CW8 77 A3
Lostock Gralam CW9 80 A1
Malpas SY14 213 A1
Mottram St Andrew SK10 61 B1
Mouldsworth CH3 98 C1
Partington M31 11 C2
Utkinton CW6 146 B3
Weston CW2 207 B3
Willaston CH64 68 A4
Smithy Pathway CH4 140 C2
Smithy The CH2 118 C4
Smithy Wlk CW11 174 C2
Smokehall La CW7,CW9 126 C3
Smokehall Lane Ind Est CW7 127 A3
Smokey La SY13 224 A1
Smokies Way ST8 179 B1
Smyth Rd WA8 13 B1
Snab La CH64 66 C2
Snabwood Cl CH64 66 C3
Snaefell Rise WA4 26 B4
Snape Hollow CW2 207 C2
Snape La CW2 207 C2
Snape Rd Crewe CW2 206 B4
Macclesfield SK10 87 C1
Snapebrook Wlk 6 SK9 34 C1
Snelson La
Chelford SK11 108 C4
Chelford, Marthall WA16, SK9 83 B2
Snipe Cl SK12 36 A2
Snow Hill SK11 112 C3
Snowberry Cl WA8 13 C2
Snowberry Wlk M31 11 C2
Snowdon Cl
Ellesmere Port CH66 69 A3
Warrington WA5 14 C3
Snowdon Cres CH4 141 A3
Snowdon Dr CW2 189 B2
Snowdon St CW8 77 C2
Snowdonia Way CW7 149 A4
Snowdrop Cl WA7 49 C2
Solly Cres CW12 156 A1
Solway Cl WA2 8 C2
Solway Gr WA7 49 B3
Solway Rd CW8 78 B1
Somerford Ave CW2 190 A2
Somerford Cl CW11 175 B4
Somerford Ct 2 CW12 156 C2
Somerford Rd CH4 139 B2
Somerford Way 3 SK9 34 C3
Somerford Wlk WA8 13 C2
Somerley Cl CW1 190 A4
Somerset Ave ST7 194 C1
Somerset Cl
Congleton CW12 156 B2
Irlam M44 11 B3
Somerset Pl M33 242 B8
Somerset Rd
Altrincham WA14 238 D6
Chester CH2 118 C3
Somerset St CH2 237 B4
Somerset Way WA1 17 A4
Somerton Ave M33 242 C5
Somerton Cl SK11 111 C4
Somerton Rd SK11 111 C4
Somerville Cl
Bebington CH63 43 A3
High Legh WA16 29 B2
Neston CH64 66 C3
Somerville Cres CH65 70 B2
Somerville Gdns WA15 238 F7
Somerville Rd WA8 22 B4
Somerville St CW2 190 A1
Soot Hill CW8,CW9 78 B2
Sorbus Cl CH2 72 B2
Sorbus Dr CW1 190 C3
Sorrel Cl Huntington CH3 142 A3
Warrington WA2 9 B1
Sossmoss La SK10 84 B3
Sound & District Prim Sch CW5 217 C3
Sound La
Ravensmoor CW5 203 C1
Sound CW5 217 B4
Souracre Fold SK15 242 E3
Souter's La CH1 237 B2
South Acre Dr
Macclesfield SK11 113 A4
Wilmslow SK9 34 B2
South Ave Chester CH2 237 C4
Haslington CW1 191 B2
Warrington WA2 16 A4
Warrington, Stockton Heath WA4 16 B1
South Bank CH2 118 B2
South Bank Cl SK9 60 A1
South Bank Gr CW12 156 C1
South Bank Terr WA7 22 C2
South Cft CW6 185 B4
South Cheshire Coll CW2 190 A1
South Cheshire Coll (Annexe) CW1 190 B2
South Cl Tarporley CW6 146 B1
Wilmslow SK9 59 C3
South Crescent Rd CH4 237 C1
South Crofts CW5 204 C3
South Dale WA5 14 C3
South Downs WA16 57 B1
South Downs Dr WA14 238 D1
South Downs Rd WA14 238 D1
South Dr Gatley SK8 239 A4
Heswall CH60 41 A4
South Dr *continued*
Northwich CW9 104 B3
Plumley WA16 80 C2
South Gn CH5 116 A3
South Gr
7 Alderley Edge SK9 60 A1
Sale M33 242 B5
South La
Warrington WA5,WA8 14 C3
Widnes WA8 13 C2
South Lane Entry WA8 13 C3
South Mead SK12 36 A3
South Meadway SK6 37 C4
South Oak La SK9 59 C3
South Par WA7 48 B4
South Park Dr SK12 36 C3
South Park Rd
Gatley SK8 239 B6
Macclesfield SK11 112 B4
South Pier Rd CH65 70 B4
South Rd
Altrincham, Bowdon WA14 238 C2
Altrincham, Hale WA14 31 C4
Ellesmere Port CH65 70 B2
Halewood L24 21 A2
Runcorn WA7 48 B4
Stanlow CH65 70 C2
South St Alderley Edge SK9 60 A1
Chester CH3 119 A1
Congleton CW12 156 B2
Crewe CW2 190 B1
Mount Pleasant ST7 195 A3
3 Widnes WA8 23 A4
South Trafford Coll WA14 238 D8
South Vale Cres WA15 238 F5
South View Chester CH4 141 B4
Christleton CH3 142 C4
New Mills SK22 39 A4
Withington SK11 132 A4
South View Ave SK11 111 B1
South View Cotts ST7 193 C2
South View Gdns SK8 239 C3
South View La CW7 170 C1
South View Rd CH1 118 A1
South Way CH1 117 C2
South West Ave SK10 87 C3
South Wirral High Sch CH62 43 B2
Southampton Way WA7 50 C3
Southbank CW9 79 A4
Southbank Ave CW2 206 B3
Southdale Rd WA1 17 A4
Southdown Cl
Macclesfield SK10 87 B2
Stockport SK4 240 E6
Southdown Cres SK8 34 C4
Southern Rd M33 242 A8
Southern St WA4 16 B1
Southey Cl
8 Sandbach CW11 174 B3
Widnes WA8 22 C4
Southfield SK10 87 A2
Southfield Cl SK9 34 B2
Southfield Rd CH66 69 B4
Southfields WA16 57 B2
Southfields Ave WA5 14 C3
Southfields Cl CW5 220 A4
Southgate Ct M33 242 C7
Southlands CW4 130 B1
Southlands Ave WA5 14 C2
Southlands Ct WA7 48 C4
Southlands Mews 6 WA7 22 C1
Southlands Rd CW12 179 A4
Southlands View CW4 107 C1
Southlawn SK9 60 A3
Southport St WA9 1 A2
Southward Rd WA11 2 A4
Southwark Pl CW7 149 A4
Southway
Altrincham WA14 238 E6
Runcorn WA7 49 C4
Widnes WA8 22 B4
Southway Ave WA4 26 B4
Southwell Cl Golborne WA3 3 B4
Romiley SK6 241 A1
Southwood Ave WA7 24 B1
Southworth Ave WA5 15 C4
Southworth La WA2,WA3 8 C4
Southworth Rd WA12 2 C2
Sovereign Cl Golborne WA3 3 C4
Northwich CW9 104 C3
Runcorn WA7 50 B4
Sovereign Ct WA3 9 B2
Sovereign Way CH1 117 C1
Spark Hall Cl WA4 26 C1
Spark La Runcorn WA7 23 C1
Smallwood CW11 154 B1
Sparks Cl CH3 142 A4
Sparrow La WA16 57 A1
Sparrowbutts Gr ST7 195 B1
Sparrowhawk Cl WA7 50 A4
Sparth La SK4 240 D7
Sparthfield Rd SK4 240 D7
Spath La SK8 34 C3
Spath La E SK8 35 A3
Spath Wlk SK8 35 A3
Spawell Cl WA3 3 C4
Speakman Ave WA12 2 B3
Speakman St WA7 22 C2
Speed's Way CH3 180 C1
Speedwell Cl
7 Golborne WA3 3 C4
Heswall CH60 41 B4
Huntington CH3 142 A3
Speedwell Dr CH60 41 B4
Speedwell Rd ST5 210 C1

Speke Bvd L24,WA8 . . . . . . .21 A3
Speke Rd WA8 . . . . .22 B3
Spencer Brook SK10 . . . . . . .86 C3
Spencer Cl Alsager ST7 . . .192 C2
Widnes WA8 . . . . .12 C1
Wistaston CW2 . . . . .206 A4
Spencer Mews WA8
Northwich CW8 . . . . .103 C4
Spencer St Barnton CW8 . .78 A2
Northwich CW8 . . . . .103 C4
Spenlow Cl SK12 . . . . .36 C1
Spennymoor Ct WA7 . . . . . .49 C4
Spenser Rd CW64 . . . . .41 C1
Spey Cl Altrincham WA14 .238 C6
Winsford CW7 . . . . .126 C1
Spey Dr ST7 . . . . .195 B1
Spike Island (Nature
Reserve)★ WA8 . . . . .23 A3
Spindle Ave SK15 . . . . . .242 F3
Spindle St CW12 . . . . .156 C1
Spink La WA16 . . . . .80 A3
Spinnaker Cl WA7 . . . . .50 B3
Spinner Cres CW9 . . . . .78 B4
Spinners La SK10 . . . . .36 B2
Spinners Way SK10 . . . . . . .87 C4
Spinney CW8 . . . . .101 B3
Spinney Ave
Goostrey CW4 . . . . .107 C1
Widnes WA8 . . . . .12 A1
Spinney Cl Handforth SK9 . .34 B2
Winsford CW7 . . . . .150 A1
Spinney Dr
Ellesmere Port CH66 . . . . . .69 B1
Weston CW2 . . . . .207 A3
Spinney End CH3 . . . . .166 A1
Spinney Gdns WA4 . . . . . . .27 A2
Spinney La WA16 . . . . .56 C2
Spinney Mead SK10 . . . . . . .87 C1
Spinney The
Cheadle SK8 . . . . .239 E3
Heswall CH60 . . . . .41 B3
Lawton-gate ST7 . . . . .194 C2
Neston CH64 . . . . .41 B1
Norley WA6 . . . . .100 C3
Sandbach CW11 . . . . .175 B3
Willaston (nr Nantwich)
CW5 . . . . .205 B3
Spinney Wlk WA7 . . . . .24 A1
Spires Gdns WA2 . . . . .8 A4
Spirewood Gdns SK6 . . . .241 A2
Spital Wlk CH2 . . . . .118 C1
Spodegreen La WA14 . . . .30 B4
Spout La WA16 . . . . .58 A2
Spragg St CW12 . . . . .156 C2
Spring Ave 2 CH66 . . . . . .69 B3
Spring Bank
Altrincham WA14 . . . . . . .238 D3
Stalybridge SK15 . . . . . . .242 E1
The Bank ST7 . . . . .195 A4
Spring Bank La SK10 . . . . . .63 A3
Spring Bank Pl SK1 . . . . . .240 E4
Spring Bank Rd SK22 . . . . .39 B4
Spring Cl ST7 . . . . .193 C4
Spring Ct WA7 . . . . .23 A1
Spring Gdns Crewe CW1 .190 C3
Ellesmere Port CH66 . . . . . .69 B3
Hyde SK14 . . . . .241 D8
Macclesfield SK10 . . . . .87 B1
Nantwich CW5 . . . . .204 C3
Spring Hill CW6 . . . . .168 B4
Spring La
Coddington CH3 . . . . .181 C3
Croft WA3 . . . . .9 A3
Lymm WA13 . . . . .19 C2
Spring Mdw CW8 . . . . .78 C1
Spring Mount SK22 . . . . . . .39 B4
Spring Rd
Altrincham WA14 . . . . . . .238 D2
Poynton SK12 . . . . .36 C1
Spring St
Stalybridge SK15 . . . . . . .242 D2
Widnes WA8 . . . . .23 A3
Wilmslow SK9 . . . . .60 A4
Springbank SK10 . . . . .87 C4
Springbank Cl WA7 . . . . . . .49 A3
Springbank Cres CW7 . . .149 B4
Springbourne WA3 . . . . . . .74 B3
Springburn Gdns WA1 . . .17 C4
Springcroft CH64 . . . . .41 B1
Springe La CW5 . . . . .203 A3
Springfield Ave
Golborne WA3 . . . . .2 C4
Helsby WA6 . . . . .73 C4
Lymm WA13 . . . . .19 A3
Malpas SY14 . . . . .213 B2
Warrington, Grappenhall
WA4 . . . . .17 A2
Warrington, Padgate WA1 .17 A4
Springfield Cl CH4 . . . . . .161 A4
Springfield Cres CW8 . . . .77 C2
Springfield Ct CH4 . . . . . .161 A4
Springfield Dr
Chester CH2 . . . . .118 C2
Wilmslow SK9 . . . . .59 B3
Wistaston CW2 . . . . .205 C4
Springfield Pk WA11 . . . . . .1 B4
Springfield Prim Sch
M33 . . . . .242 B6
Springfield Rd
Altrincham WA14 . . . . . . .238 D1
Gatley SK8 . . . . .239 B5
Macclesfield SK11 . . . . . . .111 C4
Malpas SY14 . . . . .213 A2
Mobberley WA16 . . . . .57 C2
Sale M33 . . . . .242 B6
Widnes WA8 . . . . .22 A4
Springfield Sch CW1 . . . .190 C2
Springfield Specl Sch
CW1 . . . . .191 A2

Springfield St WA1 . . . . . .16 A3
Springfields
Cuddington CW8 . . . . .101 B2
Knutsford WA16 . . . . .57 B2
Mickle Trafford CH2 . . . . . .119 C4
Prestbury SK10 . . . . .87 A4
Springfields Dr CW12 . . .156 B2
Springhead Cl ST7 . . . . . .210 B3
Springhead Prim Sch
ST7 . . . . .210 B3
Springhill SK10 . . . . .88 A1
Springhill Cl CH62 . . . . . . .43 B3
Springholm Dr WA4 . . . . . .26 B2
Springmount WA3 . . . . .3 C4
Springs La SK15 . . . . .242 C3
Springs The WA14 . . . . . .238 B2
Springvale Ind Est
CW11 . . . . .174 B3
Springwell Cl CW2 . . . . . .206 B4
Springwood Ave WA1 . . . .57 B2
Springwood Cl
Blacon CH1 . . . . .117 B2
Macclesfield SK10 . . . . .87 B3
Springwood Cres SK6 . . .241 E2
Springwood La SK6 . . . . .241 F3
Springwood Prim Sch
SK6 . . . . .241 E2
Springwood Way SK10 . . .87 B3
Sprink La CW12 . . . . .157 B3
Sproston Way CW9 . . . . . .103 C2
Spruce Ave CW8 . . . . .102 A2
Spruce Cl Golborne WA3 . .3 C4
Warrington WA1 . . . . .17 C4
Spruce Gr ST7 . . . . .193 C4
Spruce Lodge SK8 . . . . . .239 D6
Spuley La SK10 . . . . .63 B1
Spunhill Ave CH66 . . . . . . .69 B1
Spurling Rd WA5 . . . . .6 C3
Spurston Cl WA16 . . . . .29 B2
Square St SK11 . . . . .112 C3
Square The
Altrincham WA15 . . . . .32 B4
Audlem CW3 . . . . .229 C2
Christleton CH3 . . . . .142 C4
Elton CH2 . . . . .71 C3
Holmes Chapel CW4 . . . . .130 B2
Hyde SK14 . . . . .241 D6
Lymm WA13 . . . . .18 C2
Stockport SK4 . . . . .240 C7
Woore CW3 . . . . .232 B1
Squires Ave WA8 . . . . .23 A4
Squires Cl WA11 . . . . .1 A3
Squirrel Ct WA8 . . . . .103 B4
Squirrel Dr WA14 . . . . . . .238 C8
Squirrel's Jump SK9 . . . . .60 B1
Squirrels Chase SK10 . . . .86 C3
Stable La
Mouldsworth CH3 . . . . .99 A2
Utkinton CW6 . . . . .123 C1
Stables The
Guilden Sutton CH3 . . . . . .119 C3
Winsford CW10 . . . . .127 B3
Stablings The SK9 . . . . .60 A3
Stadium Ind Est CH1 . . . .118 A2
Stadium Way CH1 . . . . . . .118 A2
Stadmorslow La ST7 . . . .195 C2
Staffin Ave CH65 . . . . .95 A4
Stafford Cl SK10 . . . . .86 C1
Stafford Gdns CH65 . . . . . .70 A3
Stafford Rd WA4 . . . . .16 B1
Stafford St Audlem CW3 . .230 A2
Crewe CW1 . . . . .190 B3
Stafford Way 2 M34 . . . .241 A5
Stafford Wlk SK10 . . . . . . .86 C1
Stag Ind Est WA14 . . . . . .238 B6
Stage La WA13 . . . . .19 B2
Stainer Cl WA12 . . . . .2 A3
Staines Cl WA4 . . . . .26 C3
Stainforth Cl WA3 . . . . .4 B2
Stainmore Cl WA3 . . . . . . .10 A3
Staithes Rd M22 . . . . .33 B4
Stalbridge Rd CW2 . . . . . .190 B1
Staley Cl SK15 . . . . .242 F2
Staley Hall Cres SK15 . . .242 F3
Stallard Way CW10 . . . . . .151 B4
Stalmine Ave SK8 . . . . .34 A4
Staly Hall Rd SK15 . . . . . .242 F2
Staly Ind Est SK15 . . . . . .242 E2
Stalybridge Sta SK15 . . . .242 C2
Stamford Ave
Altrincham WA14 . . . . . . .238 A5
Crewe CW2 . . . . .190 B2
Stalybridge SK15 . . . . . . .242 B2
Stamford Cl
Macclesfield SK11 . . . . . . .112 B2
Stalybridge SK15 . . . . . . .242 B2
Stamford Com High Sch
OL6 . . . . .242 B4
Stamford Ct Chester CH3 119 B1
7 Lymm WA13 . . . . .18 C2
Macclesfield SK11 . . . . . . .112 B3
Stalybridge OL6 . . . . .242 A2
Stamford Dr SK15 . . . . . . .242 C2
Stamford Gr SK15 . . . . . . .242 C2
Stamford Grange 1
WA14 . . . . .238 C4
Stamford La CH3 . . . . .120 A1
Stamford New Rd
WA14 . . . . .238 D4
Stamford Park Inf Sch
WA15 . . . . .238 E3
Stamford Park Jun Sch
WA15 . . . . .238 E3
Stamford Park Rd
WA15 . . . . .238 E3
Stamford Pl M33 . . . . .242 C6
Stamford Rd
Alderley Edge SK9 . . . . . . .60 A1

Stamford Rd continued
Altrincham WA14 . . . . . . .238 C2
Blacon CH1 . . . . .117 C3
Handforth SK9 . . . . .34 A1
Little Bollington WA14 . . . . .20 A1
Macclesfield SK11 . . . . . . .112 B2
Stamford Sq
3 Altrincham WA14 . . . . .238 D5
Ashton-u-Lyne OL6 . . . . . .242 A2
Stamford St
Altrincham WA14 . . . . . . .238 D5
Ellesmere Port CH65 . . . . . .70 A3
Sale M33 . . . . .242 A8
Stalybridge SK15 . . . . . . .242 C2
Stamford St E OL6 . . . . . .242 A2
Stamford Way 2 WA14 .238 D5
Stamore Rd WA7 . . . . .23 B1
Stamp Ave CW1 . . . . .190 B3
Stanbank St SK4 . . . . .240 E8
Stanbridge Ct SK4 . . . . . .240 E6
Standford Dr CW9 . . . . . . .104 A3
Standish Ct WA8 . . . . .22 B4
Stanford Cl CW9 . . . . .103 C3
Stanhope Ave CW1 . . . . . .190 C2
Stanhope Cl SK9 . . . . .60 B4
Stanhope Rd WA14 . . . . . .238 A4
Stanhope St OL6 . . . . .242 A4
Stanier Cl WA7 . . . . .191 A2
Stanlaw Abbey Prim Sch
CH65 . . . . .70 C1
Stanlaw Rd CH65 . . . . .70 B2
Stanley & Brocklehurst Ct
SK11 . . . . .112 B4
Stanley Ave Hyde SK14 . .241 E8
Warrington, Great Sankey
WA5 . . . . .14 B4
Warrington, Stockton Heath
WA4 . . . . .16 C1
Stanley Bank Rd WA11 . . . .1 A4
Stanley Cl Hartford CW8 .103 A3
Widnes WA8 . . . . .13 B1
Stanley Ct ST7 . . . . .193 B2
Stanley Dr Gatley SK8,SK9 .34 B3
Newcastle-u-Lyt ST5 . . . . .210 B1
Stanley Gr Northwich CW9 79 C1
Stockport SK4 . . . . .240 B8
Stanley Green Ind Est
SK8 . . . . .34 C3
Stanley Green Ret Pk
SK8 . . . . .34 C3
Stanley Hall La SK12 . . . . .38 B3
Stanley La CH62 . . . . .43 C2
Stanley Mount M33 . . . . . .242 A5
Stanley Park Ct CH4 . . . . .140 C3
Stanley Park Dr CH4 . . . . .140 C3
Stanley Pl Chester CH1 . .237 A2
Warrington WA4 . . . . .16 C1
Stanley Rd Biddulph ST8 .179 B1
Ellesmere Port CH65 . . . . . .70 B4
Handforth SK8,SK9 . . . . . . .34 C3
Irlam M44 . . . . .11 C4
Knutsford WA16 . . . . .56 C1
Stockport SK4 . . . . .240 B7
Stanley Rd Ind Est WA16 57 A1
Stanley Sq SK15 . . . . .242 C1
Stanley St Chester CH1 . .237 A2
Crewe CW1 . . . . .190 B2
Macclesfield SK11 . . . . . . .112 B4
Newton-le-W WA12 . . . . . . .2 A1
Northwich CW9 . . . . .104 B4
Runcorn WA7 . . . . .23 A2
Stalybridge SK15 . . . . . . .242 C1
Warrington WA1 . . . . .16 A2
Stanley Villas 5 WA7 . . . .22 C1
Stanley Woods Ave CH2 . .95 B4
Stanlow & Thornton Sta
CH2 . . . . .71 B3
Stanlow Abbey Bsns Ctr
CH65 . . . . .70 B1
Stannage La CH3 . . . . .180 C3
Stanner Cl WA5 . . . . .7 B1
Stannerhouse La CW11 .175 C2
Stanney Cl
Bebington CH62 . . . . .43 C2
Neston CH64 . . . . .66 C4
Stanney Grange Com Prim
Sch CH65 . . . . .70 B2
Stanney Grange Sports
Complex The CH65 . . . . . . .70 C1
Stanney High Sch CH65 . .70 B1
Stanney La
Ellesmere Port CH65 . . . . . .70 A3
Stoak CH2 . . . . .70 C1
Stanney Mill Ind Est CH2 .70 C2
Stanney Mill La CH2 . . . . .70 C1
Stanney Mill Rd CH2 . . . . .70 C1
Stanney Ten Ind Est CH2 .70 C1
Stanney Woods Ave
CH65 . . . . .70 B1
Stanney Woods Ctry Pk★
CH65 . . . . .70 A1
Stanneybrook Cl WA6 . . .101 A3
Stanneylands Cl SK9 . . . . .34 B1
Stanneylands Dr SK9 . . . . .34 A1
Stanneylands Rd SK9 . . . . .34 A1
Stansfield Ave WA1 . . . . . .16 C3
Stansfield Dr WA4 . . . . .27 A4
Stansfield Rd SK14 . . . . . .241 E8
Stanstead Ave WA5 . . . . . .14 C2
Stanthorne Ave CW2 . . . .190 A2
Stanton Cl WA11 . . . . .1 B3
Stanton Ct CH64 . . . . .66 C4
Stanton Dr CH2 . . . . .118 B3
Stanton Rd WA4 . . . . .17 B2
Stanway Dr WA15 . . . . .31 B4
Stapeley Broad Lane CE Prim
Sch CW5 . . . . .205 A1
Stapeley Ct CW1 . . . . .190 A3
Stapeley Gdns L26 . . . . . . .21 A3

Stapeley Terr CW5 . . . . . .205 A2
Stapeley Water Gdns★
CW5 . . . . .205 A2
Stapleford Cl M33 . . . . . . .242 E7
Stapleford Ct CH66 . . . . . . .69 C4
Stapleton Ave WA2 . . . . . .16 B4
Stapleton Cl WA6 . . . . .74 B4
Stapleton Rd SK10 . . . . . . .87 A1
Stapleton Way WA8 . . . . . .22 C3
Stapley Cl
Northwich CW9 . . . . .103 C2
Runcorn WA7 . . . . .22 C1
Star La Lymm WA13 . . . . . .18 B2
Macclesfield SK11 . . . . . . .112 B2
Starbeck Dr CH66 . . . . .69 A3
Starkey Gr 2 WA7 . . . . . . .16 C2
Starling Cl Farndon CH3 . .180 C1
Kidsgrove ST7 . . . . .195 B2
Runcorn WA7 . . . . .50 A3
Start La SK23 . . . . .65 A4
Statham Ave Lymm WA13 .18 B2
Warrington WA2 . . . . .8 B1
Statham Cl Hyde M34 . . . .241 A7
Lymm WA13 . . . . .18 B2
Statham Com Prim Sch
WA13 . . . . .18 B2
Statham Dr WA13 . . . . .18 B2
Statham La WA13 . . . . .18 A3
Statham St SK11 . . . . .112 B4
Station Ave
Ellesmere Port CH66 . . . . . .69 B4
Helsby WA6 . . . . .73 A2
Station Cl Hyde SK14 . . . .241 D6
Neston CH64 . . . . .66 C4
Station Gn CH66 . . . . .69 B4
Station Hill CW8 . . . . .76 C1
Station La
Guilden Sutton CH2 . . . . . .119 C4
Rushton Spencer SK11 . . .159 A1
Station Rd Adderley TF9 . .235 A3
Alpraham CW6 . . . . .169 C1
Alsager ST7 . . . . .193 B2
Astbury ST7,CW12 . . . . . .178 A1
Backford CH1 . . . . .95 A2
Biddulph ST8 . . . . .179 B1
Bosley SK11 . . . . .135 A1
Chelford SK11 . . . . .84 A1
Chester CH2 . . . . .237 C4
Crowton CW8 . . . . .76 B1
Delamere CW8 . . . . .123 B4
Ellesmere Port, Little Sutton
CH66 . . . . .69 B3
Elton CH2 . . . . .72 A4
Goostrey CW4 . . . . .131 A4
Hawarden CH5 . . . . .116 A1
Haydock WA11 . . . . .1 B3
Heswall CH60 . . . . .40 C3
Holmes Chapel CW4 . . . . .130 B3
Kidsgrove ST7 . . . . .194 C1
Kidsgrove, Newchapel ST7 195 C1
Lostock Gralam CW9 . . . . .80 A1
Mobberley WA16 . . . . .57 C4
Mouldsworth CH3 . . . . .99 A1
Mow Cop ST7 . . . . .195 B4
Nantwich CW5 . . . . .204 C3
Neston CH64 . . . . .66 C4
Neston, Burton CH64 . . . . .67 A1
Neston, Parkgate CH64 . . .66 B4
New Mills SK22 . . . . .39 A4
4 Northwich CW9 . . . . . . .79 A1
Partington WA14 . . . . .20 A3
Runcorn WA7 . . . . .22 C1
Sandbach CW11 . . . . .174 C1
Scholar Green ST7 . . . . . . .195 A4
Stockport SK3 . . . . .240 E4
Sutton WA7 . . . . .50 A2
Warrington WA4 . . . . .16 C1
Warrington, Fearnhead WA2 .9 A1
Warrington, Great Sankey
WA5 . . . . .14 C3
Warrington, Penketh WA5 .14 C2
Weaverham WA8 . . . . .77 A1
Whaley Bridge SK23 . . . . .39 B2
Wilmslow SK9 . . . . .60 A4
Wilmslow, Handforth SK9 . .34 B2
Wilmslow, Styal SK9 . . . . . .34 A2
Winsford CW7 . . . . .127 A1
Worleston CW5 . . . . .188 C3
Station Rd N WA2 . . . . .9 A1
Station Rd S WA2 . . . . .9 A1
Station St SK10 . . . . .87 B1
Station View
Chester CH2 . . . . .118 C1
Nantwich CW5 . . . . .204 C2
Sandbach CW11 . . . . .174 B4
Staveley Ave SK15 . . . . . .242 D3
Staveley Dr CW7 . . . . .126 B1
Stayley Dr SK15 . . . . .242 F2
Steadings The CH3 . . . . . .120 A3
Steam Mill St CH2 . . . . . .237 C3
Stearns Cl CH1 . . . . .118 A3
Stearns Ho CH1 . . . . .118 A3
Steel St WA1 . . . . .16 C4
Steele Rd CW10 . . . . .151 B3
Steele St CH1 . . . . .237 B2
Steeles Ave SK14 . . . . . . .241 E7
Steeple Cl CW4 . . . . .66 C4
Steeple St SK10 . . . . .87 C1
Stein Ave WA3 . . . . .3 C4
Stenhills Cres WA7 . . . . . . .23 B1
Step Hill 30 SK11 . . . . . . .112 B4
Stephen St WA1 . . . . .16 B3
Stephen's Gr WA6 . . . . . . .73 A1
Stephens Gdns CH66 . . . . .69 A3
Stephens Rd SK15 . . . . . .242 C4
Stephens Terr CH66 . . . . . .69 A3

Stephens Way ST7 . . . . . .209 C1
Stephenson Dr CW1 . . . . .191 A2
Stephenson Rd WA12 . . . . .2 B1
Stephenson Wlk CW7 . . . .149 A4
Sterling Cl CW9 . . . . .103 C3
Sterndale Rd
Romiley SK6 . . . . .241 B1
Stockport SK3 . . . . .240 F1
Sterne Cl CW11 . . . . .174 B3
Stetchworth Rd WA4 . . . . .16 A1
Steven Ct CH2 . . . . .237 C3
Stevenage Cl SK11 . . . . . .112 A4
Stevenage Dr SK11 . . . . . .112 A4
Stevens Rd CH60 . . . . .41 B4
Stevens St WA1 . . . . .60 A1
Steventon WA7 . . . . .24 C2
Steward's Ave WA8 . . . . . .22 C4
Stewart St CW2 . . . . .190 A2
Stile End CH2 . . . . .119 C4
Stiles The 101 B3
Stiperstones Cl CH66 . . . . .69 A3
Stirling Cl Chester CH3 . . .119 A1
Macclesfield SK10 . . . . .86 C1
Stockport SK3 . . . . .240 C2
Warrington WA1 . . . . .17 C4
Winsford CW7 . . . . .127 C1
Stirling Ct
Ellesmere Port CH65 . . . . . .70 B2
Holmes Chapel CW4 . . . . .130 A1
Stirling Dr SK15 . . . . .242 D3
Stirrup Cl WA2 . . . . .9 A2
Stitch La SK4 . . . . .240 D7
Stoak Lodge CH65 . . . . . . .70 B2
Stock La CW2,CW5 . . . . . .206 A1
Stockdale Ave SK3 . . . . . .240 F1
Stockham Cl WA7 . . . . .50 A4
Stockham La WA7 . . . . .50 A4
Stockholm Rd SK3 . . . . . .240 E2
Stockley Farm★ CW9 . . . .54 C4
Stockley La WA4 . . . . .52 C4
Stockport Air Raid Shelters★
SK1 . . . . .240 E5
Stockport Coll of F & H Ed
SK1 . . . . .240 F4
Stockport Rd
Altrincham WA15 . . . . . . .238 F5
Cheadle SK8 . . . . .239 E6
Romiley SK6 . . . . .241 B2
Stockport SK3 . . . . .240 A3
Warrington WA4 . . . . .17 C2
Stockport Rd E SK6 . . . . .241 A4
Stockport St SK3 . . . . .240 C4
Stockport Trad Est SK4 . .240 B4
Stocks Ave 7 CH3 . . . . . .119 A1
Stocks Gdns SK15 . . . . . .242 F1
Stocks Hill CW7 . . . . .149 C4
Stocks La Chester CH3 . . .119 A1
Knutsford WA16 . . . . .82 C1
Rainow SK10 . . . . .88 C3
Stalybridge SK15 . . . . . . .242 F1
Warrington WA5 . . . . .14 B3
Stockswell Rd WA8 . . . . . .12 A2
Stockton Ave 4 SK3 . . . . .240 F4
Stockton Heath Prim Sch
WA4 . . . . .16 B1
Stockton La WA4 . . . . .16 C1
Stockton Rd SK9 . . . . .59 C2
Stoke Abbott Cl SK7 . . . . .35 C4
Stoke Cl CH62 . . . . .43 C2
Stoke Gdns CH65 . . . . .70 B2
Stoke Wlk CH65 . . . . .70 B2
Stokehall La CW5 . . . . . . .187 C3
Stokes St WA3 . . . . .9 C3
Stokesay Ct CH65 . . . . . . .70 C2
Stokoe Ave WA14 . . . . . . .238 A6
Stone Barn La WA7 . . . . . . .50 A3
Stone Chair La ST7 . . . . . .194 C4
Stone Cotts CW12 . . . . . . .157 C1
Stone Croft CH3 . . . . .142 A4
Stone Cross La N WA3 . . . .3 B4
Stone Cross La S WA3 . . . .3 B3
Stone Heyes La CW8,CW9 77 C3
Stone House La CW6 . . . .184 C3
Stone Mead SK6 . . . . .241 E3
Stone Mead Ave WA15 . . .32 B4
Stone Pit La WA3 . . . . .3 C1
Stone Pl CH2 . . . . .118 C2
Stoneacre Gdns WA4 . . . .26 C2
Stonebank Dr CH64 . . . . . .67 A3
Stonebridge Rd CW5 . . . .204 C2
Stonechat Cl
Crewe CW1 . . . . .189 C4
8 Golborne WA3 . . . . .3 C4
Runcorn WA7 . . . . .49 C3
Stonecliffe Ave SK15 . . . .242 D2
Stonecliffe Terr SK15 . . .242 D3
Stonecrop Cl
Runcorn WA7 . . . . .49 C2
Warrington WA3 . . . . .9 B2
Stonehaven Dr WA2 . . . . . .9 A2
Stoneheads SK23 . . . . .65 B4
Stoneheads Rise SK23 . . . .65 B4
Stonehill Cl WA4 . . . . .26 B2
Stonehills Ct WA7 . . . . .23 B1
Stonehills La WA7 . . . . .23 B1
Stonehouse Gn CW12 . . .156 B2
Stonelea 24 A1
Stoneleigh Cl SK10 . . . . . . .87 B1
Stoneleigh Gdns WA4 . . . .17 B1
Stoneley Ave CW1 . . . . . .190 B4
Stoneley Rd CW1 . . . . . . .190 B4
Stonemill Terr SK5 . . . . . .240 F7
Stones Manor La CW8 . . .103 B3
Stoney Holt WA7 . . . . .50 B4

Stoney La Delamere CW6 123 B3
Wilmslow SK9 .59 C3
Stoneyfield SK15 .242 D4
Stoneyfold La SK11 .113 A3
Stoneyford La CW8 .101 B1
Stoneyhurst Cres WA3 .4 B3
Stoneyland Dr SK22 .39 A4
Stony La CW12 .156 B1
Stonyford Rd M33 .242 D6
Stopford St SK3 .240 D4
Stopsley Cl CW12 .155 C2
Stour Cl WA14 .238 C6
Stour Ct CH65 .70 A4
Stourport Cl SK6 .241 A1
Stradbroke Cl WA3 .4 A4
Straight Length WA6 .73 C4
Straight Mile CH4 .162 C3
Straker Ave CH65 .69 C3
Stratford Rd Blacon CH1 117 C2
Neston CH64 .66 B3
Stratford Sq SK8 .34 B4
Stratford Way SK11 .112 B3
Strathaven Ave CW2 .205 C4
Strathearn Rd CH60 .40 C4
Strathmore Ave M34 .241 B6
Strathmore Cl CW4 .130 A1
Stratton Cl WA7 .50 A3
Stratton Pk WA8 .12 C3
Stratton Rd WA5 .15 A3
Strawberry Cl
Altrincham WA14 .238 B7
Warrington WA3 .9 B2
Strawberry Dr CH1 .95 A4
Strawberry Fields CH3 .142 A4
Strawberry Gn CH1 .95 A4
Strawberry La
Acton Bridge CW8 .76 C2
Mollington CH1 .94 B2
Wilmslow SK9 .59 C3
Street Forest Walks The★
SK17 .90 C2
Street Hey La CH64 .43 A1
Street La Adlington SK10 .62 B4
Rode Heath ST7 .176 C1
Whitley WA4 .52 B2
Street The
Mickle Trafford CH2 .119 B4
Whaley Bridge SK10,SK17 .90 B3
Stretton Ave WA3 .3 C4
Stretton Cl CH62 .43 C2
Stretton Hall Mews WA4 52 C4
Stretton Mill★ SY14 .198 A3
Stretton Rd WA4 .26 C1
Stretton Way 3 SK9 .34 B3
Stretton Wlk CW9 .103 C2
Strickland Cl WA4 .27 A4
Strines Ct SK14 .241 E8
Strines Rd SK6 .38 B4
Stringer Ave CW11 .175 B3
Stringer Cres WA4 .16 C2
Stringer's La LL12,CH4 .161 A2
Strumness Cl WA2 .8 C2
Stuart Cl Chester CH3 .119 B2
Winsford CW7 .149 B3
Stuart Ct SK10 .87 A1
Stuart Dr WA4 .16 C1
Stuart Hampson Ct 8
M31 .11 C2
Stuart Pl CH2 .237 B3
Stuart Rd
Altrincham WA14 .238 B7
Runcorn WA7 .24 B2
Stubbs La
Lostock Gralam CW9 .80 A1
Mobberley WA16 .58 C2
Stubbs Pl CH1 .117 C2
Stubbs Terr SK11 .112 C4
Stubby La SK10 .84 C1
Sturgess St WA12 .1 C2
Styal Cl 9 CW9 .103 C2
Styal Ctry Pk★ SK9 .33 C2
Styal Gn SK9 .33 C2
Styal Gr SK8 .239 A3
Styal Prim Sch SK9 .33 C2
Styal Rd
Gatley M22,SK8,SK9 .239 A3
Wilmslow SK9 .60 A4
Wythenshawe M22 .33 C4
Styal Sta SK9 .34 A2
Styal View SK9 .34 A1
Styperson Way SK12 .36 C2
Sudbrook Cl WA3 .3 C4
Sudbury Dr SK8 .34 B4
Sudbury Rd SK7 .36 C4
Sudlow La Knutsford WA16 56 B1
Plumley WA16 .81 B4
Suez St Newton-le-W WA12 .2 A2
Warrington WA1 .16 A3
Suffolk Ave CH65 .69 C3
Suffolk Cl
Congleton CW12 .156 B2
Macclesfield SK10 .86 C1
Warrington WA1 .17 C3
Suffolk Dr SK9 .34 B1
Suffolk Pl WA8 .22 B4
Suffolk Rd WA14 .238 B5
Suffolk St WA7 .22 C2
Sugar La Adlington SK10 .63 A2
Manley WA6 .98 C3
Rainow SK10 .88 B3
Sugar Pit La WA16 .56 C2
Sugden St OL6 .242 A3
Sulby Ave WA4 .16 A2
Sulgrave Ave SK12 .36 C2
Summer Cl WA7 .23 C1
Summer La
Daresbury WA4 .51 B4
Runcorn WA7 .23 C1
Summerfield ST7 .195 A1
Summerfield Ave WA5 .7 C1
Summerfield Cl CH4 .139 A2
Summerfield Dr CW9 .126 C4
Summerfield Pl SK9 .60 A3
Summerfield Rd
Guilden Sutton CH3 .119 C3
Mobberley WA16 .57 C2
Summerfields WA16 .57 B2
Summerfields Ctr SK9 .34 B1
Summerhill Dr ST5 .210 B1
Summerhill Rd SK10 .86 C2
Summerlea SK8 .35 A4
Summerlea Cl SK10 .87 B1
Summers Ave SK15 .242 F2
Summers Cl WA16 .82 A4
Summers Way WA16 .82 A4
Summertrees Rd CH66 .69 C2
Summerville Gdns WA4 .16 C1
Summit Cl WA4 .26 C1
Sumner Rd CH1 .117 C2
Sumner St WA11 .1 A3
Sumpter Pathway CH2 .118 C2
Sunart Cl CW2 .206 A3
Sunbank La WA15 .32 C3
Sunbeam St WA12 .2 B2
Sunbury Cl SK9 .34 C1
Sunbury Cres CH4 .140 C3
Sunbury Gdns WA4 .26 C4
Suncroft Cl WA1 .17 C4
Suncroft Rd CH60 .41 B4
Sundale Dr CW2 .189 B2
Sunderland St SK11 .112 B4
Sundown Cl SK22 .39 A4
Sunfield SK6 .241 C3
Sunfield Cl CH66 .69 B2
Sunningdale Ave
Sale M33 .242 E5
Widnes WA8 .12 A1
Sunningdale Cl
Burtonwood WA5 .6 C3
Northwich CW9 .104 C4
Winsford CW7 .126 A1
Sunningdale Ct M33 .242 E5
Sunningdale Dr
Bebington CH63 .43 A3
Bramhall SK7 .36 A4
Sunningdale Rd
Denton M34 .241 B5
Macclesfield SK11 .112 A3
Sunningdale Way CH64 .66 C2
Sunninghey Ct SK9 .59 C1
Sunny Bank Wilmslow SK9 59 B2
Wilmslow SK9 .60 A3
Sunny Bank Cl SK11 .112 B3
Sunny Bank Cotts WA8 .14 A2
Sunny Bank Rd WA14 .31 B4
Sunny Lea Mews SK9 .60 A3
Sunnybank Cl WA12 .2 B2
Sunnybank Rd CW1,
CW2 .189 C3
Sunnyside Alsager ST7 .193 A2
Malpas SY14 .212 C1
Warrington WA5 .14 C3
Sunnyside Cres OL6 .242 A2
Sunnyside Gr OL6 .242 A2
Sunnyside La WA7 .24 C2
Sunset Cotts CH64 .67 A2
Surrey Dr CW12 .156 C3
Surrey Rd Chester CH2 .119 A3
Kidsgrove ST7 .195 A1
Warren SK11 .112 A2
Surrey St Crewe CW1 .190 C2
Runcorn WA7 .23 A1
Warrington WA4 .16 B2
Surridge WA16 .29 B3
Susan Dr WA5 .14 B3
Susan St WA8 .13 B1
Sussex Ave SK11 .112 A3
Sussex Dr ST7 .194 C1
Sussex Pl CW12 .156 C3
Sussex Rd Chester CH2 .118 C2
Irlam M44 .11 B3
Partington M31 .11 C1
Stockport SK3 .240 B4
Sussex St WA8 .13 B1
Sussex Way CH2 .118 C2
Sutch La WA13 .19 A2
Sutherland Ct WA7 .23 A1
Sutherland Dr
Bebington CH62 .43 B2
Macclesfield SK10 .87 A1
Sutherland St OL6 .242 B3
Sutherland Way CH3 .119 A2
Sutton Ave Culcheth WA3 .4 C2
Neston CH64 .66 C3
Sutton Causeway WA6,
WA7 .49 C1
Sutton Cl Bebington CH62 .43 C2
Higher Wincham CW9 .79 C3
Macclesfield SK11 .112 B3
Mickle Trafford CH2 .119 C4
Sutton Dr CH2 .118 C3
Sutton Green Prim Sch
CH66 .69 B3
Sutton Hall Dr CH66 .69 A3
Sutton Hall Gdns CH66 .69 A3
Sutton High Sch CH66 .69 C3
Sutton La CW10 .151 B4
Sutton Quays Bsns Pk
WA7 .49 C2
Sutton Rd
Alderley Edge SK9 .59 C1
Poynton SK12 .37 A1
Stockport SK4 .240 C7
Sutton St Runcorn WA7 .23 A1
Warrington WA1 .16 B2
Sutton Way
Ellesmere Port CH66 .69 C2
1 Handforth SK9 .34 C3
Sutton's La WA8 .23 A4
Swaine St SK3 .240 E5
Swale Cl SK9 .34 C1
Swale Dr WA14 .238 C6
Swale Rd CH65 .70 A4
Swaledale Ave CW12 .157 A3
Swaledale Cl
Bebington CH62 .43 C3
Warrington WA5 .14 C4
Swallow Cl
9 Kidsgrove ST7 .195 A1
Macclesfield SK10 .113 A4
Warrington WA3 .9 C2
Swallow Ct CW7 .149 B3
Swallow Dr Alsager ST7 .193 A2
Sandbach CW11 .175 A4
Swallow St SK1 .240 F3
Swallowfield Cl CW2 .206 A4
Swallowfield Gdns WA4 .26 C3
Swallowfields CH3 .180 C1
Swallowmore View ST7 .210 B4
Swan Ave WA9 .1 A1
Swan Bank
Congleton CW12 .156 B1
Talke ST7 .210 B4
Swan Cl
Ellesmere Port CH66 .69 C2
Poynton SK12 .36 A2
Talke ST7 .210 B4
Swan Ct CW8 .101 C4
Swan Farm La CW3 .232 A1
Swan Gr WA16 .106 B4
Swan La CW6 .185 C4
Swan Rd WA12 .1 C2
Swan St Congleton CW12 .156 B1
Wilmslow SK9 .60 A4
Swanage Cl WA4 .16 C1
Swanage Ct 6 CW7 .149 B3
Swanbourne Gdns SK3 .240 C2
Swanley La CW5 .203 B2
Swanlow Ave CW7 .149 B3
Swanlow Dr CW7 .149 B3
Swanlow La CW7 .149 C3
Swann La SK8 .35 A4
Swanscoe Av SK10 .88 A4
Swanscoe Cl CW10 .151 A4
Swanscoe La SK10 .88 A2
Swanwick Cl CW4 .107 B1
Sweet Briar Cres CW2 .189 C2
Sweet Brier Cl CW8 .78 A2
Sweetenham Cl ST7 .193 B2
Sweetfield Gdns CH66 .69 B4
Sweetfield Rd CH66 .69 B4
Sweettooth La CW11 .175 A4
Swettenham Cl CW11 .175 B4
Swettenham La CW12 .131 C2
Swettenham Rd
Swettenham CW12 .132 A1
Wilmslow SK9 .34 B3
Swettenham St SK11 .112 C4
Swift Cl Kidsgrove ST7 .195 A1
Warrington WA2 .8 C2
Wistaston CW2 .205 C4
Swinburne Dr CW1 .190 C2
Swindale Ave WA2 .8 A2
Swinden Cl WA7 .24 B1
Swine Market 7 CW5 .204 C3
Swineyard La WA16 .28 B2
Swinford Ave WA8 .13 C1
Swinley Chase SK9 .34 C1
Swinleys Hey CH3 .142 A4
Swinnerton St CW2 .190 B1
Swinton Sq 15 WA16 .57 A1
Swireford Rd WA6 .73 A1
Swiss Cott SK10 .87 A1
Swiss Hill SK9 .60 A1
Swithin Rd M22 .33 C4
Swynnerton Way WA8 .13 A3
Swythamley Cl SK3 .240 A4
Swythamley Rd SK3 .240 A4
Sycamore Ave
Alsager ST7 .193 C1
Altrincham WA14 .238 A5
Congleton CW12 .155 C2
Crewe CW1 .190 B3
Haydock WA11 .1 A3
Newton-le-W WA12 .2 B2
Rode Heath ST7 .193 C4
Widnes WA8 .13 A1
Winsford CW7 .149 B4
Sycamore Cl
Ashton-u-Lyne OL6 .242 B2
Audlem CW3 .230 A2
Biddulph ST8 .179 C1
Handforth SK9 .34 A1
Holmes Chapel CW4 .130 B2
Talke ST7 .210 C4
Sycamore Cres
Barnton CW8 .78 A2
Hollinfare WA3 .11 A1
Macclesfield SK11 .112 A4
Sycamore Ct CW5 .204 C4
Sycamore Dr
Chester CH4 .140 C3
Ellesmere Port CH66 .70 A1
Lymm WA13 .18 B2
Middlewich CW10 .151 C3
Sutton WA7 .50 A2
Sycamore Gr
Broughton CH4 .139 A2
Sandbach CW11 .175 A4
Sycamore La WA5 .15 A3
Sycamore Lane Prim Sch
WA5 .15 A3
Sycamore Lodge SK7 .35 C4
Sycamore Rd
Partington M31 .11 C2
Romiley SK6 .241 A4
Runcorn WA7 .49 B4
Sycamore Rise SK11 .112 A3
Sycamore St Sale M33 .242 E6
Stockport SK3 .240 B4
Sycamore Wlk SK8 .239 D6
Sycamores The WA16 .58 C1
Syddal Cl SK7 .35 B3
Syddal Cres SK7 .35 B2
Syddal Gn SK7 .35 B3
Syddal Park Prep Sch
SK7 .35 B3
Syddal Park Sch SK7 .35 B3
Syddal Rd SK7 .35 B3
Syddall Ave SK8 .34 B4
Syddall St SK14 .241 D6
Sydney Ave M90 .33 A4
Sydney Rd Blacon CH1 .118 A2
Cheadle SK7 .35 C3
Crewe CW1 .190 C3
Sydney St
Northwich CW8 .103 B4
Runcorn WA7 .48 B4
Syers Ct WA1 .16 C4
Sykes Mdw SK3 .240 D2
Sykes St SK14 .241 F5
Sylvan Ave
Altrincham WA15 .238 F8
Sale M33 .242 C5
Wilmslow SK9 .59 C3
Sylvan Cl CW8 .103 B4
Sylvan Gr WA14 .238 D5
Sylvan Mews CH1 .117 C3
Sylvia Cres WA2 .8 B1
Symondley Rd SK11 .112 C1
Symons Rd M33 .242 B7
Synge St WA2 .16 B4
Sytch Croft CH64 .66 C4

T

Tabley Ave WA8 .12 B1
Tabley Cl Knutsford WA16 .56 C2
Macclesfield SK11 .112 A4
Sandbach CW11 .174 C4
Tabley Gr WA16 .56 C1
Tabley Hill La WA16 .56 A1
Tabley Ho★ WA16 .81 A4
Tabley Mere Gdns SK8 .239 F3
Tabley Rd Crewe CW2 .189 C2
Handforth SK9 .34 B3
Knutsford WA16 .56 C2
Tabley St CW9 .79 A1
Tabor St SK11 .112 C3
Tadgers La WA6 .73 B4
Tadman Gr WA14 .238 A6
Tailors View CW5 .204 C3
Talbot Ave CH64 .66 C3
Talbot Cl Neston CH64 .66 C3
Shavington CW2 .206 A2
Warrington WA3 .9 C2
Talbot Gdns CH64 .66 C3
Talbot Rd
Alderley Edge SK9 .60 A1
Altrincham WA14 .238 B2
Dunham-on-t-H WA6 .97 C4
Ellesmere Port CH66 .69 C2
Sale M33 .242 E6
Talbot St Chester CH2 .237 B4
Golborne WA3 .3 A4
Stockport SK1 .240 E5
Talfryn Cl CH5 .91 B1
Talisman Cl WA7 .50 B4
Talke Rd Alsager ST7 .193 C2
Audley ST5 .210 C1
Newcastle-u-L ST7,ST5 .210 B2
Tall Ash Ave CW12 .157 A2
Tall Trees Cl CW8 .103 B3
Tally Ho La CW5 .203 C2
Tamar Cl
Congleton CW12 .156 C1
Macclesfield SK10 .86 C1
Tamar Rd Haydock WA11 .1 B3
Kidsgrove ST7 .195 A1
Tamar Wlk CW7 .127 A1
Tame Cl Biddulph ST8 .179 B1
Sandbach CW11 .174 C4
Stalybridge SK15 .242 F3
Tame St SK15 .242 B1
Tame Wlk 9 SK9 .34 B1
Tameside Coll
Ashton-u-Lyne OL6 .242 A3
Hyde SK14 .241 E6
Tameside General Hospl
OL6 .242 B4
Tameside Leisure Pk
SK14 .241 F6
Tamworth Cl SK7 .36 B4
Tamworth St WA12 .2 A2
Tan House La
Burtonwood WA5 .7 A3
Widnes WA8 .23 B4
Tanfield Rd M20 .239 B8
Tang The SK6 .241 B1
Tanhouse Ind Est WA8 .23 B4
Tankersley Gr WA5 .15 A3
Tanner St
Congleton CW12 .156 C1
Hyde SK14 .241 D7
Tanner's La WA3 .3 A4
Tanners La WA2 .16 A3
Tanners Way CW5 .204 C2
Tannery La Neston CH64 .66 C4
Warrington WA5 .14 B2
Tannery Way WA14 .238 E7
Tanning Ct 3 WA1 .16 B3
Tanyard Dr WA15 .32 B3
Tanyard La WA15 .32 A3
Tapley Ave SK12 .36 C1
Taplow Cl WA4 .26 C3
Taplow Gr SK8 .239 F2
Taporley War Meml Hospl
CW6 .146 B1
Target Cl ST7 .210 C3
Target Rd CH60 .40 B4
Tarn Cl CW7 .126 B1
Tarn Ct WA1 .17 C4
Tarn Mount SK11 .112 A3
Tarnbeck WA7 .50 B4
Tarns The SK8 .239 B3
Tarnway WA3 .3 C4
Tarporley Bsns Ctr CW6 168 B4
Tarporley CE Prim Sch
CW6 .146 B1
Tarporley Cl SK3 .240 D1
Tarporley Com High Sch
CW6 .146 B1
Tarporley Rd
Duddon CW6 .145 A3
Ellesmere Port CH66 .69 C2
Little Budworth CW6,CW8 .124 B3
Tarvin CH3 .121 B1
Utkinton CW6 .146 C3
Whitchurch SY13 .225 C2
Whitley WA4 .52 B2
Tarporley Wlk SK9 .34 C1
Tarran Gr M34 .241 B5
Tarran Pl WA14 .238 E6
Tarrant Ct CH1 .94 C1
Tarvin Ave CW2 .189 B2
Tarvin Cl
Ellesmere Port CH65 .70 B2
Golborne WA3 .3 C4
Macclesfield SK11 .112 C3
Middlewich CW10 .151 B3
Runcorn WA7 .49 B3
Tarvin Prim Sch CH3 .121 A1
Tarvin Rd Alvanley WA6 .73 C2
Bebington CH62 .43 C2
Chester, Boughton CH3 .119 A1
Chester, Vicarscross CH3 .119 C1
Christleton CH3 .120 B2
Frodsham WA6 .73 C2
Manley WA6 .99 A2
Tarvin Sands Industries
CH3 .121 A2
Tarvin Way 1 SK9 .34 B3
Tasman Cl WA5 .15 B4
Tate Cl WA8 .12 B1
Tate Dr CW1 .191 B2
Tattenhall La
Beeston CW6 .167 C1
Tattenhall CH3 .167 A1
Tattenhall Rd CH3 .166 B2
Tatton Cl Alsager ST7 .193 B2
Chester CH4 .140 C3
Davenham CW9 .103 C2
Winsford CW7 .126 A1
Tatton Ct
4 Handforth SK9 .34 C3
2 Knutsford WA16 .57 A1
Stockport SK4 .240 C8
Tatton Dr CW11 .175 B4
Tatton Hall★ WA16 .56 C4
Tatton Lodge 14 WA16 .57 A1
Tatton Pk★ WA16 .57 A4
Tatton Pl M33 .242 B7
Tatton Rd Crewe CW2 .189 C1
Denton M34 .241 A5
Handforth SK9 .34 C3
Sale M33 .242 B7
Tatton Rd S SK4 .240 C8
Tatton St Knutsford WA16 .57 A1
Stalybridge SK15 .242 E1
7 Stockport SK1 .240 F5
Tatton Stile WA16 .58 A2
Taunton Wlk 3 M34 .241 A5
Taurus Pk WA5 .7 B2
Tavener Cl CH63 .43 B3
Tavistock Rd WA5 .14 C2
Tavlin Ave WA5 .7 C1
Tawney Cl ST7 .195 A1
Tawny Ct WA7 .49 C4
Taxal & Fernilee CE Prim Sch
SK23 .65 B3
Taxal Ctr The SK23 .65 B3
Taxal Moor Rd SK23 .65 B2
Taxi Rd M90 .33 A4
Taxmere Cl CW11 .174 C4
Tay Cl ST8 .179 C1
Taylor Ind Est WA3 .4 C1
Taylor Rd
Altrincham WA14 .238 A5
Haydock WA11 .1 C4
Taylor St Hyde SK14 .241 F7
Stalybridge SK15 .242 E1
Warrington WA4 .16 A1
Widnes WA8 .13 B1
Taylor's La WA5 .14 A1
Taylors La CW1 .192 B1
Taylors Row WA7 .23 B1
Teal Ave Knutsford WA16 .57 A1
Poynton SK12 .36 A2
Teal Cl Altrincham WA14 .238 B8
Warrington WA2 .8 C2
Warrington, Oakwood WA3 .9 C2
Winsford CW7 .149 B3
Tealby Cl CW9 .104 A4
Teals Way CH60 .40 C4
Tebay Rd CH62 .43 C4

Tedder Dr M22 33 C4
Tedder Sq WA8 22 B4
Teddington Cl WA4 26 C3
Tees Ct CH65 70 A4
Teesdale Cl WA5 14 C4
Teesdale Rd WA11 1 B4
Tefler Ct CW10 151 C3
Tegg's Nose Ctry Pk★ SK11 113 B3
Teggsnose La SK11 113 B3
Tegid Way CH4 140 B3
Tegsnose Mt SK11 113 B2
Telegraph Rd CH60 41 A4
Telford Cl
Congleton CW12 157 A1
Macclesfield SK10 88 A1
Talke ST7 210 C4
Widnes WA8 12 B2
Telford Gdns CW11 174 C2
Telford Pl CW5 204 B3
Telford Rd CH65 70 C2
Telford Way
Audlem CW3 229 C2
Chester CH4 140 C3
Middlewich CW10 128 C1
Telford's Quay CH65 70 B4
Tempest Rd SK9 60 B1
Templar Ct SK10 87 A1
Temple Ct WA3 9 C3
Temple Rd M33 242 D6
Templemoor Inf Sch M33 242 E6
Templeton Cl WA14 238 B6
Tenbury Cl WA5 15 A4
Tenby Cl WA5 7 C1
Tenby Dr WA7 23 B1
Tenby Rd
Macclesfield SK11 111 C3
Stockport SK3 240 B3
Tenchersfield CW5 205 A2
Tennyson Ave CW1 190 C2
Tennyson Cl
Macclesfield SK11 111 C3
Northwich CW9 104 B3
Rode Heath ST7 193 C4
Stockport SK4 240 B6
Wistaston CW2 190 A1
Tennyson Dr WA2 8 B1
Tennyson Rd
Cheadle SK8 239 F6
Ellesmere Port CH65 70 A2
Widnes WA8 13 A1
Tennyson Wlk CH1 118 A3
Tensing Cl WA5 15 A4
Terence Ave WA1 16 C3
Terminal Rd E M90 33 B4
Terminal Rd N M90 33 A4
Terminal Rd S M90 33 A4
Tern Ave ST7 195 B1
Tern Cl Altrincham WA14 238 B8
Widnes WA8 13 A2
Tern Dr SK12 36 A2
Terra Nova Sch CW4 108 B1
Terrace Rd WA8 23 A3
Terrick Rd SY13 226 A1
Tetchill Cl
Ellesmere Port CH66 69 B1
Runcorn WA7 50 B4
Tetton Ct 8 CW12 156 C2
Tetton La CW10 151 C2
Tewkesbury Cl
Bramhall SK8 35 A3
Chester CH2 118 C4
Ellesmere Port CH66 94 C4
Middlewich CW10 128 A1
Poynton SK12 36 B2
Tewkesbury Dr SK10 87 C2
Tewkesbury Rd
Golborne WA3 3 A4
Stockport SK3 240 B2
Thackeray Dr CH3 119 B2
Thackery Ct 6 CW11 174 B3
Thames Cl
Congleton CW12 156 C1
Warrington WA2 8 B1
Thames Dr ST8 179 B1
Thames Gdns CH65 70 A2
Thames Rd WA3 5 A1
Thames Side CH65 70 A2
Thames Trad Ctr M44 11 C4
Thamesdale CH65 70 A2
Thatcher Cl WA14 238 C1
Thaxted Wlk M22 33 B4
The Catholic High Sch CH4 141 B3
The Verdin High Sch CW7 126 B1
Theatre Ct CW9 103 C4
Thelwall Cl 3 WA15 238 E6
Thelwall Com Inf Sch WA4 17 B2
Thelwall Com Jun Sch WA4 17 B2
Thelwall Ind Est WA4 17 B2
Thelwall La WA4 16 C2
Thelwall New Rd WA4 17 B2
Thelwall Rd
Ellesmere Port CH66 69 C2
Sale M33 242 E5
Theobald Rd WA14 238 D1
Thetford Cl SK10 87 B2
Thetford Rd WA5 14 C3
Thewlis St WA5 15 C3
Third Ave
Congleton CW12 156 A2
Connah's Quay CH5 92 C1
Crewe CW1 190 C1
Kidsgrove ST7 194 C1
Third Ave *continued*
Poynton SK12 36 B1
Runcorn WA7 49 C4
Sandbach CW11 175 A3
Thirlmere SK11 111 C3
Thirlmere Ave WA2 8 B2
Thirlmere Cl
Alderley Edge SK9 59 C1
Frodsham WA6 49 B1
Holmes Chapel CW4 130 A2
Stalybridge SK15 242 D4
Winsford CW7 126 C2
Thirlmere Ct CW12 156 A1
Thirlmere Dr WA13 18 C2
Thirlmere Lodge 5 WA13 18 C2
Thirlmere Rd
Chester CH2 119 A3
Ellesmere Port CH65 70 B1
Neston CH64 66 C3
Partington M31 11 C2
Wistaston CW2 190 A1
Thirlmere Way WA8 22 B4
Thirsk Cl WA7 49 B3
Thirsk Way 6 SK10 87 B2
Thistle Cl WA16 79 C4
Thistle Sq M31 11 C1
Thistle Wlk 4 M31 11 C1
Thistleton Cl SK11 112 B3
Thistlewood Dr SK9 60 B4
Thomas Brassey Cl CH2 237 C4
Thomas Cl Alsager ST7 193 C2
Blacon CH1 117 C3
Ellesmere Port CH65 70 A1
Hyde M34 241 A8
Mickle Trafford CH2 119 C4
Thomas Ct WA7 49 C4
Thomas Ho CH1 118 A3
Thomas Hodges Ct CW4 130 B2
Thomas Pl CW7 127 A1
Thomas St
Altrincham WA15 238 E4
Biddulph ST8 179 B1
Congleton CW12 156 C2
Crewe CW1 190 B2
Golborne WA3 3 A4
Packmoor ST7 195 C1
Romiley SK6 241 A3
Runcorn WA7 23 A2
Stockport SK1 240 F3
Talke ST7 210 B4
20 Widnes WA8 23 A4
Thomas St W SK1 240 F3
Thomas Wedge CE Jun Sch The CH1 94 A1
Thomasons Bridge La WA4 25 C3
Thompson Ave WA3 4 C2
Thompson Cl WA12 2 B1
Thompson Ct SK15 242 C2
Thompson Fold SK15 242 C2
Thompson St WA3 9 C2
Thomson St SK3 240 E4
Thoresway Rd SK9 59 C3
Thoriby Rd WA3 4 C2
Thorley Gr CW2 190 A1
Thorley La M90 33 A4
Thorley Mews SK7 35 C4
Thorn Cl Runcorn WA7 49 B4
Warrington WA5 14 C2
Thorn Ct SK15 242 D2
Thorn Dr M22 34 A4
Thorn Gr
Altrincham WA15 238 E3
Bramhall SK8 35 A4
Sale M33 242 B6
Thorn Grove Prim Sch SK8 35 A4
Thorn Ho Chester CH4 141 A3
Stalybridge SK15 242 D2
Thorn La CW8 103 B3
Thorn Rd Bramhall SK7 35 C3
Runcorn WA7 49 B4
Warrington WA1 17 A4
Thorn Tree Cl L24 21 C1
Thorn Tree Dr CW1 173 A1
Thorn Wlk M31 11 C1
Thornberry Cl CH1 117 A4
Thornbury Ave WA3 3 C4
Thorne Cl SK10 87 A3
Thorne Dr CH66 69 A2
Thorney Dr SK7,SK8 35 B3
Thorneyholme Dr WA16 57 A1
Thornfield SK9 60 A2
Thornfield Cl WA3 3 B4
Thornfield Ct 2 SK4 240 A7
Thornfield Hey SK9 60 C4
Thornfield Rd SK4 240 A7
Thornfield Sch SK4 240 A7
Thornfields CW1 173 A1
Thorngrove Dr SK9 60 B3
Thorngrove Hill SK9 60 B3
Thorngrove Rd SK9 60 B3
Thornleigh Ave CH62 43 C2
Thornleigh Dr CH66 69 C3
Thornley Cl 3 WA13 18 B2
Thornley Cres SK6 241 A4
Thornley Rd
Dukinfield M34 241 A8
Lymm WA13 18 B2
Thornley St SK14 241 E5
Thornsgreen Rd M22 33 B4
Thornton WA8 22 C4
Thornton Ave SK11 112 A3
Thornton Bank CW6 169 B2
Thornton Common Rd CH63 42 B4
Thornton Cres CH60 41 A3
Thornton Dr
Chester CH2 118 B3
Wilmslow SK9 34 B2
Wistaston CW2 206 A4
Thornton Gate SK8 239 A6
Thornton Green La CH2 71 C1
Thornton Ho CH63 42 A3
Thornton Hough Prim Sch CH63 42 A4
Thornton Mews CH66 69 A4
Thornton Pl 4 SK4 240 B8
Thornton Rd
Ellesmere Port CH65 70 C2
Gatley SK8 34 B4
Warrington WA5 15 A2
Thornton Sq SK11 112 A3
Thorntondale Dr WA5 14 C4
Thorntree Bglws SK11 132 A4
Thorntree Gn WA4 27 A3
Thornway Bollington SK10 88 A4
Bramhall SK7,SK8 35 B4
High Lane SK6 37 C4
Thornwythe Gr CH66 69 C2
Thornycroft CW7 126 A1
Thornycroft Cl SK11 111 C1
Thornycroft St 8 SK11 112 C4
Thorold Gr M33 242 E6
Thorp St SK10 112 B4
Thorpe Cl CW1 189 C4
Thorsby Ave SK14 241 F6
Thorsby Rd WA15 238 E5
Thorsby Way 5 M34 241 A5
Thowler La WA14 30 A3
Threaphurst La SK7 37 B4
Three Fields Cl CW12 156 A2
Threeways CW8 101 B2
Thresher Cl 3 M33 242 F5
Throstle Bank St SK14 241 C8
Thurlestone Rd WA14 238 B6
Thurlow WA3 3 C4
Thursfield Ave ST7 195 B2
Thursfield Prim Sch ST7 195 C2
Thurstaston Rd CH60 40 C4
Thurston Cl WA5 15 B3
Thurston Gn SK9 60 A1
Thurston Rd CH4 140 C3
Thynne St WA1 16 A2
Tib St M34 241 A6
Tibb St ST7 209 C1
Tibbs Cross La WA8 13 B4
Tidal La WA1 16 C4
Tideswell Cl SK8 34 B4
Tideswell Rd SK7 36 C4
Tidnock Ave CW12 156 C3
Tiffild Ct CW7 127 A2
Tilbury Pl WA7 50 C3
Tildsley Cres WA7 48 C3
Tilestone Paddocks CW6 168 C3
Tilewright Cl ST7 195 A1
Tillard Ave SK3 240 B4
Tilley St WA1 16 B3
Tilman Cl WA5 15 A4
Tilston Ave WA4 17 A2
Tilston CE Prim Sch SY14 198 A2
Tilston Rd SY14 213 A3
Tilston Wlk 5 SK9 34 C1
Tilstone Cl
Hough Common CW2 206 C1
Northwich CW9 104 A3
Timber La 2 CW9 103 C4
Timber St SK10 87 C1
Timberfields Rd CH1 117 A4
Timberley Ave WA4 17 A2
Timbersbrook Gr 5 SK9 34 B1
Timberscombe Gdns WA1 17 C3
Timbrell Ave CW1 190 A3
Timmis Cl WA2 9 A2
Timmis Cres WA8 13 A1
Timperley St WA8 23 A4
Timperley Sta WA15 238 F8
Tinkersfield CW5 205 A2
Tinkwood La SY14 211 C1
Tinsley St WA4 16 C2
Tintagel Cl
Macclesfield SK10 111 C4
Runcorn WA7 50 A3
Tintagel Ct SK15 242 C2
Tintern Ave CH2 118 C3
Tintern Cl Poynton SK12 36 B3
Warrington WA5 7 C1
Tintern Rd SK8 35 A3
Tipping Brow WA16 58 B2
Tipping St WA14 238 D3
Tirley La CW6 123 A1
Tithe Barn Prim Sch SK4 240 A7
Tithebarn Cl CH60 40 C4
Tithebarn Dr CH64 41 A1
Tithebarn Rd WA15 32 B4
Tithings The WA7 23 C1
Tiverton Cl Chester CH2 118 C3
Sandbach CW11 175 B4
Widnes WA8 12 B2
Tiverton Dr 13 SK9 34 B1
Tiverton Sq WA5 14 C2
Tiveton Ct CW9 103 C3
Tiviot Dale SK1 240 F6
Tiviot Way SK1,SK5 240 F7
Tobermory Cl WA11 1 A3
Tobermory Rd SK8 239 C1
Todbrook Cl SK23 65 B3
Toft Cl Chester CH4 140 C3
Widnes WA8 12 C1
Toft Rd WA16 82 A4
Toft Way SK9 34 C2
Toll Bar Ave SK11 112 C4
Toll Bar Pl WA2 8 A2
Toll Bar Rd
Christleton CH3 142 B4
Macclesfield SK11 111 C4
Warrington WA2 8 A2
Tolland La WA15 31 C4
Tollard Cl SK8 35 A3
Tollbar St SK1 240 F4
Tollemache Dr CW1 190 A4
Tollemache Terr CH2 118 C1
Tollgate Cl ST7 210 B4
Tollgate Dr CW3 229 C2
Tollitt St CW1 190 B2
Tom Brads Croft SK23 65 C4
Tom Fields ST7 209 C1
Tom La WA14 30 C3
Tom Shepley St SK14 241 E6
Tomkinson Cl CW1 189 C4
Tomkinson St CH2 237 C4
Tomlins Terr CH1 117 C3
Tomlinson Ave WA2 16 B4
Tommy's La
Congleton CW12 156 C2
Crewe CW1 190 C1
Tonbridge Cl SK10 87 A1
Toogood Cl CH2 119 C4
Top Farm La CW7 170 C1
Top Rd Frodsham WA6 74 B3
Kingsley WA6 75 A1
Top Station Rd ST7 195 B4
Topgate Cl CH60 41 A4
Topping Ct WA3 9 A2
Toppings The SK6 241 A3
Torbrook Gr 1 SK9 34 B1
Torkington Rd
Gatley SK8 239 B5
Wilmslow SK9 60 B3
Torkington St SK3 240 D4
Toronto Ave M90 33 A4
Torr Rd SK11 112 B2
Torr Rise CW6 146 B1
Torr Top St SK22 39 B4
Torridon Gr CH66 69 C2
Torrin Cl SK3 240 F1
Torrs Valley SK22 39 B4
Torrvale Rd SK22 39 A4
Totland Cl WA5 14 B4
Totland Gr CH2 118 C2
Totton Ct WA1 9 B1
Tourney Gn WA5 7 A1
Tower Hill SK10 88 B2
Tower Hill Rd ST7 195 C4
Tower La Lymm WA13 18 C1
Runcorn WA7 50 B4
Weaverham CW8 77 A1
Tower Rd CH1 118 A1
Tower St SK14 241 D5
Tower Way CW1 190 B2
Towers Cl Poynton SK12 36 C3
Wistaston CW2 206 A4
Towers Ct WA5 15 C4
Towers La WA6 98 B4
Towers Rd SK12 36 C3
Towers The SK10 86 C1
Town Farm La WA6 100 C4
Town Gn The WA4 52 B3
Town Hill WA1 16 A3
Town La Hale L24 21 C1
Mobberley WA16 58 A2
Neston CH64 66 C3
Town Sq
4 Northwich CW9 103 C4
Runcorn WA7 49 C4
Sale M33 242 B6
Town Well WA6 75 B1
Town's View SK15 242 E1
Towncroft M34 241 A8
Towneley Ct WA8 13 A1
Townend St SK14 241 E6
Townfield Ave CH3 180 C1
Townfield Cl ST7 194 B1
Townfield Ct CW8 78 A2
Townfield Gdns WA14 238 D5
Townfield La
Allostock WA16 106 C3
Barnton CW8 78 A2
Farndon CH3 180 B1
Frodsham WA6 74 B4
Lymm WA13 19 A4
Mollington CH1 94 B1
Tarvin CH3 121 A1
Tiverton CW6 168 B3
Townfield Rd
Altrincham WA14 238 D5
Mobberley WA16 58 A2
Townfield View WA7 24 B1
Townfields
Knutsford WA16 57 B1
Sandbach CW11 175 A3
Townfields Cotts 8 CW7 149 B4
Townfields Cres CW7 149 B4
Townfields Dr CW7 149 B4
Townfields Gdns 9 CW7 149 B4
Townfields Rd CW7 149 B4
Townley Pl 23 SK11 112 B4
Townley St SK11 112 B4
Townsend La ST7 194 A4
Townsend Rd CW12 156 C1
Townsfield Dr CW6 147 C4
Townshend Rd CW9 80 A2
Township Cl CH3 182 B1
Townwell Ct CW5 204 B3
Tracy Dr WA12 2 C2
Trafalgar Ave SK12 37 A2
Trafalgar Cl
Northwich CW9 103 C2
Poynton SK12 37 A2
Trafalgar Ct WA8 23 A3
Trafalgar Rd M33 242 C8
Trafford Ave WA5 15 C4
Trafford Cres WA7 49 B3
Trafford Rd
Alderley Edge SK9 60 A1
Handforth SK9 34 A1
Trafford St CH2 237 B3
Tragan Dr WA5 14 B2
Tramway Rd M44 11 C4
Tramway St CH2 237 C3
Tranmere Dr SK9 34 C1
Tranmere Rd 1 SK3 240 B4
Trap Rd CW12 132 B2
Trap St SK11 132 A3
Travers' Entry WA9 6 A4
Travis Brow SK4 240 D5
Travis St Hyde SK14 241 E6
10 Widnes WA8 23 A4
Treborth Rd CH1 117 B2
Tree Bank Cl WA7 49 A4
Tree Tops CH64 66 C2
Tree Way WA16 82 A4
Treen Cl SK10 86 B1
Treetops Cl WA1 16 C4
Trefoil Cl Huntington CH3 142 A3
Warrington WA3 9 B3
Tregele Cl CH1 117 B2
Trenance Cl WA7 50 B3
Trenchard Dr M22 33 C4
Trent Ave CW7 127 A1
Trent Cl Bramhall SK7 35 B3
Widnes WA8 13 A2
Winsford CW7 127 A1
Trent Way CH60 41 B3
Trentdale CH65 70 A2
Trentham Cl WA8 13 A2
Trentham St WA7 22 C2
Tresham Dr WA4 27 A4
Trevithick Cl CW1 191 A2
Trevone Cl WA16 57 A1
Tribune Ave WA14 238 B7
Tricketts La CW5 205 C3
Tricketts Mews CW5 205 C3
Trident Ind Est WA3 9 C3
Trident Pk WA7 49 C4
Trinity Ave M33 242 D6
Trinity Cl CW2 190 A1
Trinity Ct
4 Congleton CW12 157 A1
1 Knutsford WA16 57 A1
Warrington WA3 9 C3
Trinity La SK11 112 C2
Trinity Pl
Congleton CW12 179 A4
13 Widnes WA8 23 A4
Trinity Rd M33 242 D6
Trinity Sch SK15 242 C1
Trinity Sq SK10 87 C1
Trinity St Chester CH1 237 A2
Runcorn WA7 23 A2
Stalybridge SK15 242 D1
Trinity Terr 15 CW8 103 C4
Troon Cl Bebington CH63 43 B3
Bramhall SK7 36 A4
Haydock WA11 1 A3
Holmes Chapel CW4 130 B1
Troon Dr SK8 239 C1
Trossach Cl WA2 8 C1
Troutbeck Ave
Congleton CW12 156 A1
Newton-le-W WA12 1 C2
Warrington WA5 15 C4
Troutbeck Gr CW7 126 B1
Troutbeck Rd SK8 239 B3
Trouthall La WA16 81 A1
Trowbridge Rd M34 241 A5
Trubshaw Ct ST7 195 B2
Trubshaw Pl ST7 195 A2
Trumans La CH66 69 B4
Truro Cl Bramhall SK7 35 C4
Congleton CW12 178 C4
Ellesmere Port CH66 94 C4
Macclesfield SK10 86 C1
Runcorn WA7 50 B3
Warrington WA1 17 A4
Tudor Cl
Ellesmere Port CH66 94 C4
Northwich CW9 104 C3
Warrington WA4 17 A1
Winsford CW7 149 B3
Tudor Ct 4 WA4 16 C1
Tudor Dr SK10 86 B4
Tudor Gn Blacon CH1 117 C3
Wilmslow SK9 34 C1
Tudor Rd
Altrincham WA14 238 B7
Handforth SK9 34 C1
Runcorn WA7 24 B2
Tudor Way Chester CH3 142 A4
Congleton CW12 156 B1
Nantwich CW5 204 C2
Tudors The SK7 35 B3
Tudorway CH60 41 A4
Tue La WA8 12 A3
Tulip Cl SK3 240 D1
Tulip Dr WA15 238 F6
Tulip Rd Haydock WA11 1 C3
Partington M31 11 C1
Tully Ave WA12 1 C2
Tulworth Rd SK12 36 B2

Tumblewood Dr SK8 ....239 E4
Tunbridge Cl
 Warrington WA5 ....15 A4
 Wistaston CW2 ....206 A4
Tunnel Rd CW8 ....78 A1
Tunnicliffe Rd SK11 .....112 C2
Tunnicliffe St ◨ SK11 ...112 B4
Tunstall Rd Bosley SK11 .158 B4
 Congleton CW12 ....157 C1
Tunstall St SK4 ....240 E6
Turf La SK11 ....112 B2
Turn St OL6 ....242 A4
Turnall Rd WA8 ....22 A4
Turnberry Cl Lymm WA13 ..18 B2
 Macclesfield SK10 ......87 B2
 Northwich CW9 ....104 C4
 Winsford CW7 ....126 B1
Turnberry Dr SK9 ....60 B4
Turnberry Rd SK8 ......239 C1
Turnbury Cl M33 ....242 B8
Turner Ave ST7 ....210 A1
Turner Cl Crewe CW1 ...190 A4
 Widnes WA8 ....12 B2
Turner Gdns SK14 ......241 E8
Turner La SK14 ....241 F8
Turner St Bollington SK10 ..88 A4
 Nantwich CW5 ....204 C3
Turnfield Ho SK8 ......239 D3
Turnfield Rd SK8 ......239 D3
Turnhurst Rd ST7 ......195 C1
Turnock St SK11 ....112 C4
Turnstone Ave WA12 ....2 B1
Turret Hall Dr ◨ WA3 ...3 C4
Turriff Dr CH63 ....43 B2
Turrocks Cl CH64 ......66 C3
Turrocks Croft CH64 ...66 C3
Turton Hale L24 ....21 C1
 Warrington WA3 ....9 B3
Turton St WA3 ....3 A4
Turves Rd SK8 ....239 F1
Turville Ho SK9 ....34 B1
Tuscan Cl WA8 ....13 A3
Tuscan Rd M20 ....239 B8
Tushingham Cl WA3 ....142 A4
**Tushingham-with-Grindley
 CE Prim Sch** SY13 ...214 B1
Tuson Dr WA8 ....12 C1
Tutor Bank Dr WA12 ....2 B2
Tweed Cl WA14 ....238 C6
Tweedsmuir Cl WA3 .....9 A2
Twemlow Ave CW11 ....175 A4
Twemlow La CW4 ......130 B3
Twenty Acre Rd WA5 ...15 B4
Twinnies Ct SK9 ....34 A1
Twinnies Rd SK9 ....34 A1
Twiss Green Com Prim Sch
 WA3 ....4 C2
Twiss Green Dr WA3 .....4 C2
Twiss Green La WA3 .....4 C2
Twist Ave WA3 ....3 B4
Two Acre Gr CH66 ....69 C1
Two Trees Com High Sch
 M34 ....241 A5
Two Trees La M34 .....241 A5
Twyford Cl WA8 ....13 A3
Twyford La WA8 ....13 B3
Tyler St SK9 ....60 A1
Tyler Wlk ◨ WA3 ....3 C4
Tyne Cl WA2 ....8 C1
Tynedale Ave CW2 .....190 B1
Tynedale Cl SK11 ......112 B4
Tynemouth Rd WA7 .....50 B3
Tynesdale CH65 ....70 A2
Tynwald Cres WA8 ......12 C3
Tynwald Dr WA4 ....26 B4
Tyrer Rd WA12 ....2 B1
Tytherington Bsns Pk
 SK10 ....87 B3
Tytherington Ct SK10 ...87 B1
Tytherington Dr SK10 ...87 C2
Tytherington Gn SK10 ...87 B2
Tytherington High Sch
 SK10 ....87 B1
Tytherington La SK10 ...87 B3
Tytherington Park Rd
 SK10 ....87 B2
Tytherington Sh Ctr ◨
 SK10 ....87 B2

U

Ullapool Cl CH66 ....68 C3
Ullswater SK11 ....111 C3
Ullswater Ave
 Crewe CW2 ....189 C2
 Warrington WA2 ....8 B2
 Winsford CW7 ....126 B1
Ullswater Cres CH2 ....119 A3
Ullswater Dr SK9 ....83 C4
Ullswater Gr WA7 ....49 B3
Ullswater Mans SK11 ...111 C3
Ullswater Rd
 Congleton CW12 ....156 A1
 Ellesmere Port CH65 ...70 B1
 Handforth SK9 ....34 B2
Ullswater Terr SK15 ....242 D4
Ulverston Ave WA2 ......8 A2
Ulverston Cl WA11 ......1 A3
Ulviet Gate WA5 ....29 B2
Under Rainow Rd CW12 157 C1
Underbridge La WA4 ....25 C3
Undercliffe Ho WA4 ....241 C2
Underway The WA7 .....49 C4

Underwood Cl SK10 .....86 C1
Underwood Dr CH65 ....70 B1
Underwood Ind Pk CW1 190 A3
Underwood La CW1 .....190 A3
Underwood Rd SK9 ......60 B1
Underwood West Inf Sch
 CW1 ....190 A3
Underwood West Jun Sch
 CW1 ....190 A3
Unicorn Gateway SK11 .112 B4
Union Cl CW12 ....156 B2
Union Ind Est SK11 ....112 C4
Union Rd
 Macclesfield SK11 .....112 C4
 New Mills SK22 ....39 B4
Union St Chester CH1 ..237 C2
 Congleton CW12 ....156 B2
 Crewe CW2 ....190 B2
 Hyde SK14 ....241 E6
 Macclesfield SK11 .....112 B4
 Runcorn WA7 ....23 A1
 Sandbach CW11 ....175 A3
 Stockport SK1 ....240 F4
 Warrington WA1 ....16 A3
Union Terr CH1 ....237 B3
Union Wlk CH1 ....237 B3
Unity Way ST7 ....210 A4
**Univ of Liverpool (Chester
 Coll)** CH2 ....237 A4
**Univ of Liverpool, Faculty of
 Veterinary Science
 (Leahurst)** CH64 .....67 B4
Unsworth Ct WA2 ....8 C1
Upcast La SK9 ....59 C2
Uplands CW8 ....101 B2
Uplands Rd CW9 ....78 C2
Uplands The
 Biddulph ST8 ....179 C1
 Runcorn WA7 ....50 A4
Upper Cambrian Rd
 CH1 ....118 A1
Upper Downs WA14 ....238 C3
Upper Haigh St CW7 ...149 B4
Upper Mersey Rd WA8 ..22 A3
Upper Mersey St CH65 ..70 B4
Upper Northgate St
 CH1 ....237 A3
Upper Raby Rd CH64 ....42 A1
Upton SK8 ....35 A4
Upton Bridle Path WA8 ..12 C2
Upton Cl Golborne WA3 ..3 B4
 Winsford CW7 ....126 C2
Upton Dr
 Altrincham WA14 ......238 E8
 Chester CH2 ....118 B3
 Warrington WA5 ....14 C3
Upton Grange WA8 .....12 B2
Upton Heath CE Prim Sch
 CH2 ....118 C4
Upton La Chester CH2 ..118 B4
 Widnes WA8 ....12 C2
Upton Pk CH2 ....118 B3
Upton Priory Inf Sch
 SK10 ....86 C1
Upton Priory Jun Sch
 SK10 ....86 C1
Upton Rd CH66 ....69 B2
Upton Way ◨ SK9 ......34 B3
Upton Westlea Prim Sch
 CH2 ....118 C4
Upton-by-Chester High Sch
 CH2 ....118 C4
Upwood Rd WA3 ....3 B4
Urban Ave WA15 ......238 E4
Urban Dr WA15 ....238 E4
Urban Rd
 Altrincham WA15 ......238 E4
 Sale M33 ....242 A6
Ure Ct CH65 ....70 A4
Urmston Ave WA12 ......2 A3
Urwick Rd SK6 ....241 B2
Utkinton La CW6 ....146 C4
Utkinton Rd CW6 ......146 B3

V

Vahler Terr WA7 ....23 B1
Vale Ave Sale M33 .....242 E7
 Warrington WA2 ....16 A4
Vale Cl Broughton CH4 .139 B2
 Romiley SK6 ....241 F2
Vale Cotts SK14 ....241 C8
Vale Cres SK8 ....239 F2
Vale Ct WA4 ....51 A2
Vale Gdns Alsager ST7 .193 C2
 Ellesmere Port CH65 ...70 A2
 Helsby WA6 ....73 A2
Vale Head SK9 ....34 B1
Vale Owen Rd WA2 ......8 B1
Vale Rd Alpraham CW6 .169 A2
 Altrincham WA14 ......238 B1
 Ellesmere Port CH65 ...70 A2
 Hartford WA8 ....103 B2
 Marston CW9 ....79 A3
 Tiverton CW6 ....168 C3
 Wilmslow SK9 ....59 C4
Vale Royal Ctyd CW8 ..126 C4
Vale Royal Dr CW8 ....126 A4
Vale View CW9 ....79 C4
Valebrook Dr CW5 .....220 A4
Valentine Rd
 Kidsgrove ST7 ....195 A1
 Newton-le-W WA12 .....1 C4
Valewood Ave SK4 .....240 A5
Valiant Cl WA2 ....8 C1
Valley Brook Bsns Ctr
 CW2 ....190 B2

Valley Cl Alsager ST7 ..192 C2
 Cheadle SK8 ....239 E3
 Knutsford WA16 ....82 A4
Valley Ct WA2 ....8 C1
Valley Dr Chester CH2 ..118 B3
 Ellesmere Port CH66 ...69 B3
 Wilmslow SK9 ....34 B2
Valley Gr M34 ....241 B6
Valley La SK8 ....101 C2
Valley Rd Bebington CH62 .43 B4
 Bramhall SK7 ....35 C4
 Cheadle SK8 ....239 E3
 Crewe CW2 ....190 A1
 Macclesfield SK11 .....112 A3
 Stockport SK4 ....240 A5
 Weaverham CW8 ....77 B1
 Wistaston CW2 ....189 C1
Valley Sch SK7 ....35 B3
Valley View
 Congleton CW12 ....156 B2
 Ellesmere Port CH66 ...69 B3
 Newton-le-W WA12 .....2 A1
 Northwich CW9 ....104 B4
Valley Way
 Knutsford WA16 ....82 A4
 Stalybridge SK15 .....242 F1
Vanguard Ct WA3 ....9 B2
Varden Gr SK3 ....240 D1
Varden Rd SK12 ....36 C2
Vardon Dr SK9 ....60 B3
Varey Rd CW12 ....156 C2
Vaudrey Cres CW12 ....156 C2
Vaudrey Dr WA1 ....17 B4
Vaudrey La M34 ....241 A6
Vaudrey St SK15 ......242 D1
Vaughan Rd
 Stockport SK4 ....240 D7
 Whaley Bridge SK23 ...65 C3
Vaughans La CH3 ......142 A4
Vauxhall Rd CW5 ......204 C4
Vauxhall Cl WA5 ....14 C2
Vauxhall Way CW7 .....149 B3
Vearows Pl ◨ CW8 ....103 C4
Venable's Rd CH1 .....117 C2
Venables Rd CW9 ....79 A1
Venables Way
 High Legh WA16 ....29 B2
 Middlewich CW10 .....151 C3
Venns Rd WA2 ....16 B4
Ventnor Ave M33 ......242 B8
Ventnor Cl
 Middlewich CW10 .....151 B4
 Warrington WA5 ....14 B4
Ventnor Rd SK4 ....240 A6
Venture Way SK12 ......36 C2
Verbena M31 ....11 C2
Verbina Cl WA7 ....49 C2
Verdin Ave CW8 ....78 C1
Verdin Cl Moulton CW9 .126 C4
 Winsford CW7 ....126 B1
Verdin Ct CW1 ....190 A4
Verdin St CW9 ....104 B4
Vere St CW1 ....190 B3
Verity Cl CW1 ....191 B2
Vermont Cl WA5 ....15 B4
Vernay Gn CH4 ....141 A3
Vernon Ave Audley ST7 .209 B1
 Congleton CW12 ....178 C2
 Hooton CH66 ....44 A1
Vernon Cl Audley ST7 ..209 B1
 Cheadle SK8 ....239 E1
 Poynton SK12 ....36 B1
 Saughall CH1 ....117 A3
Vernon Dr CW3 ....230 C2
Vernon Gr M33 ....242 E5
Vernon Jun & Inf Schs
 SK12 ....36 C2
Vernon Rd Chester CH1 .118 A1
 Poynton SK12 ....36 C1
Vernon St Crewe CW1 ..190 A4
 Hyde SK14 ....241 E6
 Macclesfield SK10 .....112 C4
 ◨ Stockport SK1 .....240 F6
 Warrington WA1 ....16 A2
Vernon Way CW1 ......190 B2
Veronica Way CH66 .....69 B4
Vetch Cl WA3 ....11 A3
Vetches The CH3 ......119 C3
Viaduct Rd WA14 ......238 D7
Viaduct St
 Newton-le-W WA12 .....2 A2
 Stockport SK3 ....240 E5
Vicar's La CH1 ....237 B2
Vicarage Ave SK8 ....35 A4
Vicarage Cl
 Guilden Sutton CH3 ...119 C3
 Hale L24 ....21 C1
Vicarage Ct LL13 ......196 C4
Vicarage Dr WA11 ....1 A4
Vicarage Gdns
 Hyde SK14 ....241 F6
 Sandbach CW11 ....174 C4
Vicarage Gr CW7 ......149 B2
Vicarage Hill WA6 ......73 B2
Vicarage La
 Altrincham WA14 ......238 C1
 Audlem CW3 ....230 A2
 Bunbury CW6 ....168 C1
 Burton CH64 ....67 B1
 Frodsham WA6 ....74 B4
 Hassall Green CW11 ..175 C3
 Helsby WA6 ....73 B2
 Little Budworth CW6 ..147 C4
 Poynton SK12 ....36 C3
 Sandbach CW11 ....174 C4
Vicarage Rd
 Chester CH2 ....118 C2
 Haslington CW1 ....191 B3

Vicarage Rd continued
 Haydock WA11 ....1 A4
 Northwich CW9 ....104 A4
 Stockport SK3 ....240 E2
 Widnes WA8 ....23 A4
Vicarage Row CH62 ....44 A3
Vicarage Way SK11 ....111 C4
Vicarage Wlk CW9 .....104 A4
Vicars Cross Ct ◨ CH3 .119 A1
Vicars Cross Rd CH3 ...119 B1
Vicker's Cl CH3 ....121 C4
Vickers Rd WA4 ....22 C2
Vickers Way CW9 ......104 A4
Victoria Ave
 Altrincham WA15 ......238 F7
 Crewe CW2 ....190 A2
 Haslington CW1 ....191 B2
 Heswall CH60 ....41 A3
 Holmes Chapel CW4 ...130 B1
 Kidsgrove ST7 ....194 C1
 Warrington, Grappenhall
  WA4 ....17 A1
 Warrington, Great Sankey
  WA5 ....14 B3
 Widnes WA8 ....13 A2
Victoria Chase SK8 .....34 C4
Victoria Cl Bramhall SK7 .35 B3
 Stockport SK3 ....240 E3
Victoria Com High Sch
 CW1 ....190 B3
Victoria Cres
 Chester CH2 ....237 A4
 Chester, Handbridge CH4 .237 C1
Victoria Ct Chester CH2 .237 A4
 Crewe CW1 ....190 B2
 Haslington CW1 ....191 B2
 ◨ Kidsgrove ST7 .....195 A1
Victoria Dr M33 ....242 D5
Victoria Gdns SK14 ....241 F8
Victoria Gr WA8 ....13 A2
Victoria Inf Sch CH2 ...237 A4
Victoria Infmy CH4 ....103 C1
Victoria Mews CH65 .....70 A3
Victoria Mill Dr CW5 ...205 B3
Victoria Mkt SK15 .....242 D1
Victoria Pathway CH4 ..237 C1
Victoria Pk CW8 ....78 C1
Victoria Pl Chester CH1 .237 B3
 Warrington WA4 ....16 B1
Victoria Rd
 Altrincham WA15 ......238 D3
 Broughton CH4 ....140 D3
 Chester CH1 ....237 A4
 Chester CH2 ....237 A4
 Ellesmere Port CH65 ..70 B3
 Macclesfield SK10 .....87 A1
 Neston CH64 ....67 A3
 Northwich CW9 ....104 A4
 Runcorn WA7 ....23 A1
 Sale M33 ....242 D5
 Warrington, Great Sankey
  WA5 ....15 A2
 Warrington, Penketh WA5 .14 B2
 Warrington, Stockton Heath
  WA4 ....16 B1
 Widnes WA8 ....23 A3
 Wilmslow SK9 ....60 A3
Victoria Road Prim Sch
 Northwich CW9 ....104 A4
 Runcorn WA7 ....23 A1
Victoria Sq
 Warrington WA1 ....16 B1
 Winsford CW7 ....149 A4
Victoria St
 Altrincham WA14 ......238 D5
 Congleton CW12 ....156 B1
 Crewe CW1 ....190 B2
 Knutsford WA16 ....56 C1
 New Mills SK22 ....39 A3
 Northwich CW9 ....79 C1
 Sandbach CW11 ....175 A4
 Stalybridge SK15 .....242 C2
 Warrington WA1 ....16 B3
 Widnes WA8 ....23 A4
Victoria Trad Ctr WA8 ..23 A3
Victoria Way SK7 ....35 B3
Victoria Wlk SK10 .....112 C4
Victory Rd M44 ....11 B2
Vienna Rd SK3 ....240 D2
Vienna Rd E SK3 ......240 E2
Viewlands Dr SK9 ......34 B1
Villa Farm CW11 ....176 A4
Villa Rd CH5 ....116 A4
Village Cl
 Lostock Green CW9 ...105 A4
 Runcorn WA7 ....50 A4
 Warrington WA4 ....17 C2
Village Ct SK9 ....34 B1
Village Farm CW5 .....172 A3
Village La WA4 ....52 B2
Village Mews SK10 .....87 A3
Village Rd
 Christleton CH3 ....142 C4
 Great Barrow CH3 ....120 C3
 Heswall CH60 ....40 C4
 Waverton CH3 ....143 B2
Village St WA7 ....24 C1
Village The
 Astbury CW12 ....178 A4
 Burton CH64 ....67 B1
 Prestbury SK10 ....86 C3
Village Way SK9 ....34 B1
Villars St WA1 ....16 B3
Villas The CW4 ....131 A4
Villiers Russell Cl CW1 .190 B3
Villiers St
 Ashton-u-Lyne OL6 ...242 A2

Villiers St continued
 Hyde SK14 ....241 F6
Vincent Cl WA5 ....15 C4
Vincent Dr CH4 ....141 B3
Vincent St Crewe CW1 .190 C2
 Macclesfield SK11 .....112 B4
Vine Bank Rd ST7 .....195 A1
Vine Cl SK11 ....112 A3
Vine Cres WA5 ....14 C3
Vine Rd CH66 ....69 C1
Vine St Bollington SK10 ..88 A4
 Runcorn WA7 ....23 A1
 Widnes WA8 ....23 A4
Vine Terr WA8 ....12 A1
Vine Tree Ave
 Crewe CW2 ....190 A1
 Shavington CW2 ......206 A3
Vine Tree Prim Sch
 CW2 ....190 A1
Violet Cl WA3 ....9 B3
Violet St Stockport SK2 .240 F2
 Widnes WA8 ....23 A4
Virginia Chase SK8 .....34 C4
Virginia Dr CH1 ....117 B2
Virginia Gdns WA5 .....15 A4
Virginia Terr CH66 ......69 A4
Virtual Bsns Ctr CH1 ..117 C1
Viscount Dr Gatley SK8 .34 B4
 Wythenshaw M90 ....32 C4
Viscount Rd WA2 ....2 A2
Vista Ave
 Newton-le-W WA11,WA12 .2 A3
 Runcorn WA7 ....49 A4
Vista The M44 ....11 B2
Vista Way WA2 ....2 A2
Volunteer Ave ◨ CW5 .204 C3
Volunteer Fields CW5 ..204 C3
Volunteer St
 Chester CH1 ....237 B2
 Frodsham WA6 ....49 B1
Vose Cl WA5 ....15 B3
Vulcan Cl
 Newton-le-W WA12 .....2 B1
 Warrington WA2 ....8 C1
Vulcan Ind Est WA12 ....2 B1
Vyrnwy Rd CH4 ....140 B1

W

Waddington Cl
 Golborne WA3 ....3 C1
 Warrington WA2 ....8 C1
Wade Cres CW8 ....78 A2
Wade Deacon High Sch
 WA8 ....13 A1
Wade St CW9 ....79 C1
Wadebrook Gr ◨ SK9 ..34 B1
Wades La CW7 ....126 B2
Wadeson Way WA3 ......9 A4
Wadham Gdns SK6 ....241 C4
Wadham Way WA15 ....238 F1
Wadsworth Cl SK9 ......34 C2
Wagg St CW12 ....156 B1
Waggs Rd CW12 ....156 B1
Wagon La WA11 ....1 A3
Waine St CW1 ....190 B3
Wainwright Rd WA14 ..238 C5
Wainwright St SK16 ...242 A1
Waitney Croft SK10 ....113 A4
Wakefield Cl CW1 ......189 C4
Wakefield Cres SK6 ....241 A4
Wakefield Ho WA5 ......15 C3
Wakefield Rd
 Ellesmere Port CH66 ..69 C1
 Stalybridge SK15 .....242 E3
Wakefield St WA3 ....3 A4
Wakefield Wlk M34 ....241 A5
Wakeham Cl SK11 .....111 C4
Wakes Mdw CW6 ......185 C4
Walden Cl WA4 ....17 B2
Walden Dr CH1 ....93 B4
Waldon Ave SK8 ....239 D5
Waldon Rd SK11 ......112 A3
Waldron Gdns CW2 ....189 C1
Waldron Rd CW1 ......191 B2
Waldron's La CW1 .....173 B1
Walfield Ave CW12 ....156 B3
Walford Ave CW2 .....190 A4
Walgrove Cl CW12 ....156 A2
Walker Ave SK15 ......242 F2
Walker Cl
 Haslington CW1 ....191 B2
 Hyde SK14 ....241 F6
Walker Dr CW10 ......151 B4
Walker Fold SK14 .....241 F6
Walker La Hyde SK14 ..241 F6
 Sutton Lane Ends SK11 .112 C1
Walker St Chester CH2 .237 C4
 ◨ Crewe CW1 ....190 A3
 Stockport SK1 ....240 E6
 Warrington WA2 ....16 A3
Walkers La
 Ellesmere Port CH66 ..69 C3
 Scholar Green ST7 ...177 A1
 Tarporley CW6 ....146 B1
 Warrington WA5 ....14 C2
Walkersgreen Rd ST5 ..210 B3
Wall Fields Rd CW5 ....204 C4
Wall Hill Way CW8 .....76 C2
Wall La CW5 ....204 C3
Wallace Ct CW7 ....127 B1
Wallace St
 Northwich CW8 ....103 C4
 Widnes WA8 ....23 A4
Wallcroft CH64 ....68 A4

Walled Gdn The CW10 . .127 B3
Waller St SK11 . . . . . . .112 C3
Wallerscote Cl CW8 . . . .102 C4
Wallerscote Com Sch
  CW8 . . . . .102 C4
Wallerscote Rd CW8 . . .102 C4
Walleys Cl CW5 . . . . . . .204 B4
Wallfields Cl CW5 . . . . .204 C4
Wallhill La CW11 . . . . . .177 B4
Wallingford Rd SK9 . . . . .34 B3
Wallis St Crewe CW1 . . .190 B2
  Warrington WA4 . . . . . .16 A2
Wallrake CH60 . . . . .40 C4
Walls Ave CH1 . . . . .118 A1
Wallsend Ct WA8 . . . . . .12 C2
Wallworth Terr SK9 . . . . .59 C4
Wallworth's Bank CW12 156 C1
Walmer Pl CW7 . . . . . . .149 B3
Walmoor Pk CH3 . . . . . .119 A1
Walmsley St
  Newton-le-W WA12 . . . . .2 B2
  Stockport SK5 . . . . . . .240 F7
  Widnes WA8 . . . . .23 B4
Walnut Ave CW8 . . . . . .102 B4
Walnut Cl Chester CH2 . .118 B4
  Warrington WA4 . . . . . .17 C4
  Wilmslow SK9 . . . . .60 C4
Walnut Cotts LL13 . . . . .196 B4
Walnut Croft CH3 . . . . .180 C3
Walnut Dr CW7 . . . . . . .127 A1
Walnut Gr
  Ellesmere Port CH66 . . . .70 A1
  Sale M33 . . . . .242 A6
Walnut La CW8 . . . . . . .103 A3
Walnut Rd M31 . . . . .11 B2
Walnut Rise CW12 . . . . .156 C1
Walnut Tree La
  Bradwall Green CW11 . . .153 A2
  Warrington WA4 . . . . . .26 C2
Walnut Tree Rd SK3 . . . .240 A4
Walpole Cl CW1 . . . . . . .191 B3
Walpole Gr WA2 . . . . .8 B1
Walpole Rd WA7 . . . . . . .49 B3
Walpole St CH2 . . . . . . .237 A4
Walsh Cl WA12 . . . . .2 B3
Walsingham Dr WA7 . . . . .24 B1
Walsingham Rd WA5 . . . .14 C3
Walter St Chester CH2 . .237 B4
  Warrington WA1 . . . . . .16 C4
  Widnes WA8 . . . . .13 B1
Walthall St CW2 . . . . . .190 B1
Waltham Ave WA3 . . . . . .5 B4
Waltham Ct WA7 . . . . . . .24 C2
Waltham Dr SK8 . . . . . . .35 A3
Waltham Pl CH4 . . . . . . .141 A3
Walton Ave WA5 . . . . . . .14 C3
Walton Gr ST7 . . . . .210 B4
Walton Hall★ WA4 . . . . .25 C3
Walton Hall Gdns★ WA4 25 C3
Walton Heath Dr SK10 . . .87 A2
Walton Heath Rd WA4 . . .16 A1
Walton La WA3 . . . . .9 C3
Walton Lea Rd WA4 . . . . .26 A4
Walton New Rd WA4 . . . .26 A4
Walton Pl CH1 . . . . .117 C1
Walton Rd
  Altrincham WA14 . . . . . .238 B5
  Culcheth WA3 . . . . .4 C1
  Warrington WA4 . . . . . .26 B4
Walton St Runcorn WA7 . .23 A1
  ☑ Stockport SK1 . . . . .240 F3
Walton Way Hyde M34 . . .241 B5
  Talke ST7 . . . . .210 B4
Waltons The CH4 . . . . . .141 C3
Wandsworth Way WA8 . . .22 C3
Wansfell Pl WA2 . . . . . . .8 A2
Warbreck Gr WA4 . . . . .242 D5
Warburton Bridge Rd
  WA3 . . . . .11 A1
Warburton Cl
  Altrincham WA15 . . . . . .32 B3
  Lymm WA13 . . . . .19 A2
  Romiley SK6 . . . . .241 A4
Warburton Dr WA15 . . . . .32 B3
Warburton La M31,WA13 . .11 C1
Warburton Rd SK9 . . . . . .34 B2
Warburton St WA4 . . . . . .16 B1
Warburton View WA3 . . . .11 A1
Ward Ave SK10 . . . . .88 A4
Ward Cl WA5 . . . . .7 A1
Ward La SK12 . . . . .38 C2
Ward St SK14 . . . . .241 E6
Ward's La CW11 . . . . . . .153 B3
Ward's Terr CH2 . . . . . .118 C2
Wardle Ave CW5 . . . . . .187 B4
Wardle Cres SK9 . . . . . . .84 A4
Wardle Ct M33 . . . . .242 C6
Wardle Cotts CW5 . . . . .187 B4
Wardle Cres SK11 . . . . .111 C1
Wardle Ind Est CW5 . . . .187 A4
Wardle Mews CW10 . . . .151 B4
Wardle Rd M33 . . . . . . .242 C6
Wardley Rd WA4 . . . . . . .16 A1
Wardour Cl SK11 . . . . . .111 C4
Wardour St WA5 . . . . . . .15 C3
Wards La CW12 . . . . . . .179 B4
Wareham Cl WA1 . . . . . . .17 B4
Wareham Dr CW1 . . . . . .190 A4
Warford Ave SK12 . . . . . .37 A1
Warford Cres SK9 . . . . . .84 A4
Warford Hall Dr SK9 . . . . .84 A3
Warford La WA16 . . . . . . .59 A1
Warford Pk SK9 . . . . .58 C1
Warford Terr WA16 . . . . . .59 A1
Wargrave CE Prim Sch
  WA12 . . . . .2 B1
Wargrave House Sch
  WA12 . . . . .2 B1
Wargrave Mews WA12 . . .2 B1

Wargrave Rd WA12 . . . . . .2 B1
Warham St WA12 . . . . . . .60 A4
Waring Ave St Helens WA9 . .1 A1
  Warrington WA4 . . . . . .16 C3
Warkworth Cl WA8 . . . . . .12 B2
Warkworth Ct CH65 . . . . .70 C2
Warley Cl SK8 . . . . .239 E6
Warmingham CE Prim Sch
  CW11 . . . . .173 C4
Warmingham Ct ☑
  CW10 . . . . .151 B4
Warmingham La
  Middlewich CW10 . . . . . .151 B3
  Sandbach CW11 . . . . . .174 A4
Warmingham Rd CW1 . . .173 B2
Warnley Cl WA8 . . . . .12 B1
Warren Ave Cheadle SK8 239 D5
  Knutsford WA16 . . . . . . .56 C1
  Lostock Gralam CW9 . . . .80 A2
Warren Cl Knutsford WA16 56 C1
  Middlewich CW10 . . . . . .151 A4
  Poynton SK12 . . . . .36 A3
Warren Croft WA7 . . . . . .50 B4
Warren Ct
  Ellesmere Port CH66 . . . .69 B2
  Frodsham CW8 . . . . .74 B3
Warren Dr
  Altrincham WA15 . . . . . .32 B4
  Broughton CH4 . . . . . . .139 A2
  Ellesmere Port CH66 . . . .69 C4
  Newton-le-W WA12 . . . . .2 C1
  Warren SK11 . . . . .111 B1
  Warrington WA4 . . . . . .26 B4
Warren Gr SK11 . . . . . . .111 B1
Warren Hey SK9 . . . . . . .60 C4
Warren La Hartford CW8 . .103 A2
  Warrington WA1 . . . . . .17 B4
Warren Lea SK12 . . . . . .36 C3
Warren Rd Stockport SK3 240 E2
  Warrington WA2 . . . . . . .8 B1
Warren St SK1 . . . . .240 F6
Warren The CW8 . . . . . .101 B4
Warren Way WA6 . . . . . .168 B4
Warrener St M33 . . . . . .242 D6
Warrilow Heath Rd ST5 210 B1
Warrington Ave
  Crewe CW1 . . . . .190 B3
  Ellesmere Port CH65 . . . .70 A1
Warrington Bank Quay Sta
  WA1 . . . . .16 B3
Warrington Bsns Pk WA2 .8 B1
Warrington Central Sta
  WA2 . . . . .16 A3
Warrington Collegiate Inst
  WA2 . . . . .8 A1
Warrington District General
  Hospl WA5 . . . . .15 C3
Warrington La WA13 . . . . .19 C1
Warrington Mus & Art
  Gallery★ WA1 . . . . . . .16 A3
Warrington Rd
  Bold Heath L35,WA8 . . . . .13 B4
  Comberbach CW9 . . . . . .78 B4
  Cronton L35 . . . . .12 C4
  Cuddington CW8 . . . . . .102 A4
  Dunham-on-t-H WA6 . . . .97 B3
  Fowley Common WA3,WN7 . .3 A3
  Golborne WA12,WA3 . . . . .3 A3
  Hatton WA4 . . . . .25 C2
  Little Leigh CW8 . . . . . . .77 A3
  Lymm WA13 . . . . .18 A2
  Mere WA16 . . . . .56 B4
  Mickle Trafford CH2 . . . .119 C4
  Runcorn, Castlefields WA7 . .23 C1
  Runcorn, Manor Park WA7 . .24 A2
  Warrington, Birchwood WA3 . .9 C4
  Warrington, Locking Stumps
    WA3 . . . . .9 B2
  Widnes WA8 . . . . .13 B1
Warrington St SK15 . . . . .242 E1
Warrington Trad Est
  WA2 . . . . .16 A3
Warrington Univ Coll
  (Padgate Campus) WA2 . .9 A2
Warton Cl Bramhall SK7 . .36 A4
  Warrington WA5 . . . . . .15 A2
Warwick Ave
  Newton-le-W WA12 . . . . .2 C1
  Warrington, Bewsey WA5 . .15 C4
  Warrington, Great Sankey
    WA5 . . . . .14 B4
Warwick Cl
  Kidsgrove ST7 . . . . .195 A2
  Knutsford WA16 . . . . . . .57 B1
  Macclesfield SK11 . . . . .111 C3
  Neston CH64 . . . . .66 C3
  Stockport SK4 . . . . .240 D8
Warwick Com Prim Sch
  SK11 . . . . .111 C3
Warwick Ct
  Ellesmere Port CH65 . . . .70 C1
  Stockport SK4 . . . . .240 D8
Warwick Dr
  Altrincham WA15 . . . . . .238 F1
  Sale M33 . . . . .242 D6
Warwick Ho ☑ M33 . . . .242 D6
Warwick Mall SK8 . . . . .239 D6
Warwick Pl CW7 . . . . . .149 B3
Warwick Rd
  Altrincham WA15 . . . . . .238 E1
  Blacon CH1 . . . . .117 C3
  Irlam M44 . . . . .11 B3
  Macclesfield SK11 . . . . .111 C3
  Romiley SK6 . . . . .241 A2
  Stockport SK4 . . . . .240 C7
Warwick Wlk SK11 . . . . .111 C3
Wasdale Dr SK8 . . . . . . .239 B3

Wasdale Gr CW1 . . . . . . .173 A1
Wasdale Terr SK15 . . . . .242 D4
Wash La Allostock WA16 . .106 C2
  Warrington WA4 . . . . . .16 C2
Washington Cl
  Biddulph ST8 . . . . .179 B1
  Cheadle SK8 . . . . .34 C4
Washington Dr WA5 . . . . .15 B4
Washway Rd M33 . . . . . .242 A6
Wasley Cl WA2 . . . . .8 C2
Waste La
  Cuddington CW8 . . . . . .101 C2
  Delamere CW8 . . . . . . .123 C3
  Kelsall CW6 . . . . .122 C2
Watch La CW11 . . . . . . .174 A3
Water La CW5 . . . . .60 A4
Water Lode CW5 . . . . . . .204 A3
Water Rd SK15 . . . . .242 C2
Water St Bollington SK10 . .88 A4
  Hyde SK14 . . . . .241 D6
  Macclesfield SK11 . . . . .112 B4
  Newcastle-u-L ST5 . . . . .210 B1
  Northwich CW9 . . . . . . .104 A4
  Runcorn WA7 . . . . .23 A2
  Stalybridge SK15 . . . . . .242 D2
  Stockport SK1 . . . . .240 F7
  Widnes WA8 . . . . .23 A3
Water's Reach SK6 . . . . . .37 C4
Waterbank Row CW9 . . . .103 C4
Waterbridge Ct
  ☐ Lymm WA13 . . . . .18 B2
  Warrington WA4 . . . . . .26 B4
Waterfoot La SK23 . . . . . .65 B3
Waterford Ave WA8 . . . . .241 F2
Waterford Dr CH64 . . . . . .67 A4
Waterford Pl WA8 . . . . . . .34 A4
Waterford Way WA7 . . . . .50 B3
Waterfront WA7 . . . . .50 C3
Watergate Row CH1 . . . .237 A2
Watergate Sq CH1 . . . . .237 A2
Watergate St CH1 . . . . . .237 A2
Waterhouse Ave SK10 . . . .87 C4
Waterloo ☑ CH65 . . . . . . .70 B3
Waterloo Gdns OL6 . . . . .242 B4
Waterloo Gr ST7 . . . . . . .195 A1
Waterloo La WA6 . . . . . . .74 C1
Waterloo Rd Bramhall SK7 35 C4
  Chester CH2 . . . . .118 B2
  Haslington CW1 . . . . . . .191 B2
  Northwich CW8 . . . . . . .103 C4
  Poynton SK12 . . . . .37 A1
  Romiley SK6 . . . . .241 E2
  Runcorn WA7 . . . . .22 C2
  Stalybridge SK15 . . . . . .242 D2
  Stockport SK1 . . . . .240 F5
  Widnes WA8 . . . . .23 A4
Waterloo St
  Ashton-u-Lyne OL6 . . . . .242 A4
  Macclesfield SK11 . . . . .112 C4
Waterloo St W SK11 . . . .112 B4
Waterly La WA6 . . . . .74 C3
Watermead Dr WA7 . . . . .50 C3
Watermeetings La SK6 . .241 F1
Watermill Dr SK11 . . . . .112 C4
Waters Edge
  Anderton CW9 . . . . .78 B2
  Chester CH1 . . . . .118 A1
Waters Gn SK11 . . . . . . .112 B4
Waters Reach SK12 . . . . .36 C3
Waters Reams CH3 . . . . .142 A4
Watersedge M33 . . . . . . .49 B1
Watersfield Cl SK8 . . . . . .34 C4
Waterside
  Macclesfield SK11 . . . . .112 C4
  Warrington WA4 . . . . . .26 B4
Waterside Cotts CW5 . . .216 C3
Waterside Dr WA6 . . . . . .49 B1
Waterside La WA8 . . . . . .22 B3
Waterside Mews CW11 . .174 C2
Waterside Rd SK12,SK22 . .38 C4
Waterside View CW9 . . . .104 C3
Waterside Way CW10 . . .128 A1
Watertower View CH2 . . .118 C1
Waterway CH3 . . . . .143 A3
Waterways WA5 . . . . .15 B3
Waterworks Dr WA12 . . . .2 C2
Watery La
  Ellesmere Port CH66 . . . .68 C4
  Winwick WA2 . . . . .8 A4
Watery La Astbury CW12 . .178 B3
  Winwick WA2 . . . . .7 C3
Watkin St Hawarden CH5 116 A1
  Warrington WA1 . . . . . .16 A4
Watkins Ave WA12 . . . . . .1 C2
Watkinson Way WA8 . . . . .13 B3
Watlands Rd ST7 . . . . . .209 C1
Watling Cres CH4 . . . . . .141 C4
Watling Ct CH3 . . . . .119 B1
Watling Dr CW6 . . . . . . .123 B3
Watling St CW9 . . . . . . .103 C4
Watson Sq ☑ SK1 . . . . .240 F5
Watson St M34 . . . . .241 B7
Watson's Cl CH4 . . . . . . .139 B2
Watton Cl WA4 . . . . .17 B2
Wavell Ave WA8 . . . . .22 B4
Wavells Way CH3 . . . . . .142 A3
Waveney Dr
  Altrincham WA14 . . . . . .238 C6
  Handforth SK9 . . . . .34 B1
Waverley Ave WA4 . . . . . .26 B4
Waverley Cl SK10 . . . . . .113 A4
Waverley Dr SK8 . . . . . . .35 A4
Waverley Rd Sale M33 . . .242 C8
  Stockport SK3 . . . . .240 C3
Waverley Terr CH2 . . . . .118 C2
Waverton Cl
  Davenham CW9 . . . . . . .103 C2

Waverton Cl continued
  Hough Common CW2 . . . .206 C1
Waverton Com Prim Sch
  CH3 . . . . .143 A3
Waverton Mill Quays
  CH3 . . . . .143 A3
Waverton Pk CH3 . . . . . .143 A3
Waverton Rd CH66 . . . . . .69 C3
Wavertree Ave
  Scholar Green ST7 . . . . .194 C4
  Widnes WA8 . . . . .23 A4
Wavertree Ct CH66 . . . . . .69 C4
Wavertree Dr CW10 . . . . .151 A4
Wavertree Rd CH1 . . . . . .117 B3
Way's Gn CW7 . . . . .149 C4
Waybutt La CW2 . . . . . . .221 B4
Wayfarers Dr WA12 . . . . . .2 C1
Wayford Cl WA6 . . . . .49 A1
Wayside ST7 . . . . .193 C1
Wayside Cl WA13 . . . . . . .18 B1
Wayside Ct CW2 . . . . . . .119 C4
Wayside Dr SK12 . . . . . . .36 B3
Wayside Rd SK10 . . . . . .112 C4
Waystead Cl CW9 . . . . . .103 C2
Waywell Cl WA2 . . . . .8 C2
Weal Stone La CH2 . . . . .118 C3
Weald Dr CH66 . . . . .69 A3
Wealstone Ct CH2 . . . . . .118 C3
Wealstone La CH2 . . . . . .118 C3
Wearhead Cl WA3 . . . . . . .2 C1
Weaste La WA4 . . . . .17 C1
Weates Cl WA8 . . . . .13 C1
Weathercock La CW12 . . .157 C2
Weatherstone Cotts
  CH64 . . . . .67 B4
Weaver Bank CW5 . . . . .204 B3
Weaver Cl Alsager ST7 . . .193 A2
  Altrincham WA14 . . . . . .238 C1
  Biddulph ST8 . . . . .179 B1
  Sandbach CW11 . . . . . .174 C4
Weaver Cres WA6 . . . . . .49 B1
Weaver Ct
  Macclesfield SK11 . . . . .112 B4
  Northwich CW9 . . . . . . .103 C4
Weaver Gr
  Mickle Trafford CH2 . . . .119 C4
  St Helens WA9 . . . . .1 A2
Weaver Grange CW9 . . . .126 C4
Weaver La WA6 . . . . .49 A1
Weaver Park Ind Est
  WA6 . . . . .49 B1
Weaver Prim Sch CW5 . .204 C2
Weaver Rd Culcheth WA3 . .5 A1
  Ellesmere Port CH65 . . . .70 B1
  Frodsham WA6 . . . . .49 B1
  Moulton CW9 . . . . .126 C4
  Nantwich CW5 . . . . . . .204 C3
  Northwich CW8 . . . . . . .103 C4
  Runcorn WA7 . . . . .49 A3
Weaver St Chester CH1 . .237 A2
  Winsford CW7 . . . . .126 C1
Weaver Vale Prim Sch
  WA6 . . . . .49 B1
Weaver Valley Rd CW7 . .126 C2
Weaver View
  Audlem CW3 . . . . .229 C2
  Church Minshull CW5 . . . .172 A3
  Northwich CW8 . . . . . . .103 C4
  Weaverham CW8 . . . . . .77 B1
Weaver Way CW9 . . . . . . .78 C1
Weaverhall La CW7 . . . . .150 A3
Weaverham Forest Prim Sch
  CW8 . . . . .77 B1
Weaverham High Sch
  CW8 . . . . .102 B4
Weaverham Rd CW8 . . . .102 A4
Weaverham Way SK9 . . . .34 C2
Weaverham Wlk M33 . . . .242 E5
Weavers La SK7 . . . . .35 B3
Weaverside CW5 . . . . . . .204 C1
Weaverside Ave WA7 . . . .49 C2
Webb Dr WA5 . . . . .6 C3
Webb's La CW10 . . . . . . .128 B1
Webbs Orch SK23 . . . . . .65 B4
Webster Cl CH4 . . . . . . .139 B2
Websters La CH66 . . . . . .69 C1
Weddell Cl WA5 . . . . .15 B4
Wedge Ave WA11 . . . . . . .1 A3
Wedgwood Ave ST7 . . . .210 A1
Wedgwood Dr WA8 . . . . .13 B2
Wedgwood La CW10 . . . .128 A1
Wedgwood Rd ST7 . . . . .210 B4
Wednesbury Dr WA5 . . . .14 C3
Weedon Ave WA12 . . . . . .1 C1
Weighbridge Rd CH5 . . . .92 B3
Weint The WA3 . . . . .11 A2
Weir Gr ST7 . . . . .195 A1
Weir La WA1 . . . . .17 C3
Weir St Northwich CW9 . .103 C4
  Warrington WA4 . . . . . .16 A1
Welbeck Ave WA12 . . . . . .2 B2
Welbeck Cl CW10 . . . . . .128 A1
Welbeck Rd SK14 . . . . . .241 F6
Welch Rd SK14 . . . . .241 F8
Welcroft St ☑ SK1 . . . . .240 F4
Weldon Rd WA14 . . . . . .238 D6
Welford Ave WA3 . . . . . . .3 B4
Welford Cl SK9 . . . . .60 C4
Well Ave SY14 . . . . .213 A2
Well Bank WA11 . . . . .1 A3
Well Bank Cotts WA16 . . .108 B4
Well Bank La WA16,
  SK11 . . . . .108 B3
Well Cl CH64 . . . . .67 A2
Well Farm Cl
  Malpas SY14 . . . . .213 A2
  Warrington WA1 . . . . . .17 B4
Well Field Cl WA16 . . . . . .80 A4
Well La Alsager ST7 . . . . .193 B2

Well La continued
  Antrobus CW9 . . . . .53 A2
  Biddulph ST8 . . . . .179 B1
  Chester CH2 . . . . .118 C3
  Heswall CH60 . . . . .41 A3
  Kingsley WA6 . . . . .75 B1
  Little Budworth CW6 . . . .147 C4
  Macclesfield SK10 . . . . . .88 A1
  Manley WA6 . . . . .98 C2
  Mollington CH1 . . . . . . .94 C1
  Neston CH64 . . . . .66 C3
  Prestbury SK10 . . . . .87 B4
  Stretton WA4 . . . . .52 C4
  Warrington WA5 . . . . . . .14 C2
  Weaverham CW8 . . . . . .77 B1
Well Meadow SK14 . . . . .241 D8
Well Meadow Dr SK14 . . .241 D8
Well St Malpas SY14 . . . .213 A1
  Mow Cop ST7 . . . . .195 B4
  New Mills SK22 . . . . .39 A4
  Winsford CW7 . . . . .126 B1
Welland Cl ☑ CW11 . . . .174 B3
Welland Rd SK9 . . . . .34 C1
Wellbank Ct CW12 . . . . .156 C1
Wellbrook Cl WA7 . . . . . .50 B3
Wellcroft Cl CW2 . . . . . .206 A4
Weller Ave SK12 . . . . .36 B1
Weller Cl SK12 . . . . .36 B1
Welles St SK11 . . . . .175 A3
Wellesbourne Cl
  Macclesfield SK10 . . . . . .86 C1
  Neston CH64 . . . . .66 B3
Wellesley Ave
  Ellesmere Port CH65 . . . .70 B3
  Haslington CW1 . . . . . . .191 B2
Wellesley Cl WA12 . . . . . .2 A3
Wellesley Wlk ☑ CH65 . . .70 B3
Wellfield
  Preston on the Hill WA7 . .50 C3
  Romiley SK6 . . . . .241 C4
  Widnes WA8 . . . . .13 A2
  Winsford CW7 . . . . .127 A1
Wellfield Rd WA3 . . . . . . .4 C2
Wellfield St WA5 . . . . .15 C3
Wellfield Way SY13 . . . . .225 C1
Wellington Circ SK11 . . .112 C4
Wellington Cl
  Congleton CW12 . . . . . .156 B2
  ☑ Ellesmere Port CH65 . .70 B3
  Knutsford WA16 . . . . . . .57 B2
  Newton-le-W WA12 . . . . .2 A2
  Sale M33 . . . . .242 C8
  Warrington WA2 . . . . . . .8 C1
Wellington Gate L24 . . . . .21 C1
Wellington Gdns WA12 . . .2 A2
Wellington Gr SK2 . . . . .240 F3
Wellington Pl
  Altrincham WA14 . . . . . .238 D4
  Chester CH2 . . . . .237 B3
Wellington Rd
  Altrincham WA15 . . . . . .238 F6
  Bollington SK10 . . . . . . .87 C4
  Broughton CH4 . . . . . . .139 A2
  Ellesmere Port CH65 . . . .70 B2
  Ellesmere Port CH65 . . . .70 B3
  High Lane SK7 . . . . .37 A4
  Kidsgrove ST7 . . . . .195 A1
  Nantwich CW5 . . . . . . .204 C2
Wellington Rd N
  Ellesmere Port CH65 . . . .70 B3
  Stockport SK4 . . . . .240 D7
Wellington Rd S SK1,
  SK2 . . . . .240 F4
Wellington St
  Dukinfield SK14 . . . . . . .241 C7
  Macclesfield SK11 . . . . .112 B4
  Newton-le-W WA12 . . . . .2 A2
  Northwich CW8 . . . . . . .103 C4
  Runcorn WA7 . . . . .23 A2
  Stockport SK1 . . . . .240 F5
  Warrington WA1 . . . . . .16 B3
  Widnes WA8 . . . . .23 A3
Wellington St Wrkshps ☑
  WA1 . . . . .16 B3
Wells Ave CW1 . . . . .191 B3
Wells Cl
  Ellesmere Port CH66 . . . .94 C4
  Gatley SK8 . . . . .34 B4
  Mickle Trafford CH2 . . . .119 C4
  Warrington WA1 . . . . . .17 A4
Wellswood Dr CW2 . . . . .205 C4
Wellswood Rd CH66 . . . . .69 C4
Welsby Cl WA2 . . . . .8 C2
Welsh La CW7 . . . . .149 B3
Welsh Rd
  Ellesmere Port CH66 . . . .68 C2
  Shotwick CH1 . . . . .93 B3
Welsh Road Cotts CH1 . . .93 B3
Welsh Row
  Nantwich CW5 . . . . . . .204 A3
  Nether Alderley SK10 . . . .84 C3
Welshampton Cl CH66 . . .69 B1
Welshmen's La CW5 . . . .204 B4
Welshpool Cl WA5 . . . . . . .7 B1
Welton Cl SK9 . . . . .59 C2
Welton Dr SK9 . . . . .59 C2
Welton Gr SK9 . . . . .59 C2
Welwyn Cl WA4 . . . . .17 B2
Wem Gr ST5 . . . . .210 C1
Wemyss Rd CH1 . . . . . . .117 B2
Wendover Cl WA11 . . . . . .1 B4
Wenger Rd WA8 . . . . .13 A3
Wenlock
  Macclesfield SK10 . . . . . .87 A1
  Newcastle-u-L ST5 . . . . .210 C1

Wenlock Cl continued
Warrington WA1 . . . .**17** A4
Wenlock Gdns CH66 . . . . .**69** C1
Wenlock La CH66 . . . .**69** C1
Wenlock Rd WA7 . . . .**50** A2
Wenlock Way CH4 . . . . . .**140** C3
Wensley Dr SK7 . . . .**36** B4
Wensley Rd Cheadle SK8 **239** C6
Golborne WA3 . . . .**3** C4
1 Stockport SK5 . . . .**240** F8
Wensleydale Ave
Bebington CH62 . . . .**43** C3
Cheadle SK8 . . . .**239** C6
Congleton CW12 . . . .**157** A2
Wensleydale Cl WA5 . . . . .**14** C4
Wentworth Ave
Macclesfield SK11 . . . .**111** C3
Warrington WA1 . . . .**17** A4
Wentworth Cl
Northwich CW9 . . . .**104** C4
Widnes WA8 . . . .**13** A3
Wentworth Dr
Bebington CH63 . . . .**43** B3
Bramhall SK7 . . . .**36** A4
Kidsgrove ST7 . . . .**195** B2
Wentworth Gr CW7 . . . . .**126** A1
Wereton Rd ST7 . . . .**209** B1
Werneth Low Rd SK6 . . . .**241** D4
Werneth Rd Hyde SK14 . . .**241** F6
Romiley SK6 . . . .**241** D4
Werneth Sch SK6 . . . .**241** A2
Wervin Rd CH2 . . . .**96** A2
Wesley Ave Alsager ST7 . .**193** B2
Haydock WA11 . . . .**1** C4
2 Sandbach CW11 . . . . . .**175** A3
Wesley Cl CW7 . . . .**156** B1
Wesley Cl Nantwich CW5 .**204** C3
Neston CH64 . . . .**66** B4
Wesley Ct CW7 . . . .**126** C1
Wesley Gdns 7 ST7 . . . . .**195** A1
Wesley Pl Crewe CW2 . . . .**190** B1
4 Northwich CW9 . . . .**104** A4
Wesley St Audley ST7 . . . .**210** A1
19 Stockport SK1 . . . .**240** F5
Weson Sq SK11 . . . .**111** C4
Wessex Cl
Shavington CW2 . . . .**206** B2
Warrington WA1 . . . .**17** C4
Wessex Dr CW9 . . . .**104** B3
West Ave
Altrincham WA14 . . . .**238** A5
Crewe CW1 . . . .**190** A2
Gatley SK8 . . . .**239** C1
Kidsgrove ST7 . . . .**194** B1
Middlewich CW10 . . . .**128** B1
Northwich CW9 . . . .**104** B4
Stalybridge SK15 . . . .**242** D3
Warrington WA2 . . . .**16** A4
Warrington, Stockton Heath
  WA4 . . . .**16** B1
Weston CW2 . . . .**207** A3
West Bank
Alderley Edge SK9 . . . .**85** A4
Chester CH2 . . . .**118** B2
West Bank Dock Est
  WA8 . . . .**22** C3
West Bank Prim Sch
  WA8 . . . .**23** A2
West Bank Rd SK10 . . . . . .**87** A1
West Bank St WA8 . . . .**23** A3
West Bond St SK11 . . . . . .**112** B4
*West Cheshire Coll (Grange
  Ctr)* CH66 . . . .**70** A3
*West Cheshire Coll
  (Handbridge Ctr)* CH4 . .**141** B4
West Cl SK10 . . . .**87** C4
West Downs Rd SK8 . . . .**239** F3
West Dr Gatley SK8 . . . . .**239** A4
Heswall CH60 . . . .**41** A4
Neston CH64 . . . .**66** C3
Warrington WA5 . . . .**15** A2
Winsford CW7 . . . .**127** A1
West Dudley St CW7 . . . .**126** C1
West End CH3 . . . .**121** C4
West End Ave SK8 . . . . . .**239** A6
West End Cotts CW12 . . .**156** B1
West End Gr WA11 . . . .**1** A3
West End Rd WA11 . . . .**1** A3
West Gr Alsager ST7 . . . . .**193** C2
Heswall CH60 . . . .**40** C4
Sale M33 . . . .**242** B5
West Hall Ct WA16 . . . .**29** B3
West Heath Gr WA13 . . . . .**18** B2
West Heath Sh Ctr
  CW12 . . . .**156** A2
West Hill SK15 . . . .**242** C2
West Hill Sch SK15 . . . . . .**242** C2
West House Ct SK10 . . . . . .**86** C1
West Hyde WA13 . . . .**18** B2
West La Cuddington CW8 .**101** C2
High Legh WA16 . . . .**29** B3
Runcorn WA7 . . . .**49** C4
West Lea M34 . . . .**241** A6
West Lorne St CH1 . . . . . .**237** A3
West Mains L24 . . . .**21** A2
West Oak Pl SK8 . . . .**239** F1
West Over SK6 . . . .**241** A1
West Park Ave
Denton M34 . . . .**241** B6
Poynton SK12 . . . .**36** A2
West Park Dr CH66 . . . .**94** C4
West Park Mus★ SK10 . . . .**87** B1
West Quay Rd WA2 . . . .**7** C2
West Rd
Altrincham WA14 . . . .**238** C2

West Rd continued
Congleton CW12 . . . .**156** B2
Ellesmere Port CH65 . . . . . .**70** B2
Runcorn WA7 . . . .**48** B4
Weaverham CW8 . . . .**77** A1
West Side Ave WA11 . . . . . .**1** A3
West St Alderley Edge SK9 .**60** A1
Chester CH2 . . . .**237** C4
Congleton CW12 . . . .**156** B2
Crewe CW1 . . . .**190** A3
Haslington CW1 . . . .**191** B3
Macclesfield SK11 . . . .**112** A4
Middlewich CW10 . . . .**128** B1
Mount Pleasant ST7 . . . . . .**195** A3
Stalybridge SK15 . . . .**242** C2
Stockport SK3 . . . .**240** D5
Warrington WA2 . . . .**16** A4
West Thorpe WA14 . . . . .**238** B2
West Vale CH64 . . . .**66** C3
West Vale Rd WA15 . . . . .**238** F6
West View
Ellesmere Port CH66 . . . . . .**69** A4
Lach Dennis CW9 . . . .**104** A4
Warrington WA2 . . . .**9** A1
West View Rd WA6 . . . . . .**101** A3
West Way
Holmes Chapel CW4 . . . . .**130** A2
Sandbach CW11 . . . .**174** C2
Shavington CW2 . . . .**206** B3
West Wing The CW10 . . . .**127** B3
Westage La CW9 . . . .**79** A4
Westbourne Ave CW1 . . . .**190** A3
Westbourne Gr M33 . . . . .**242** A6
Westbourne Mews
CW12 . . . .**156** A1
Westbourne Rd
Blacon CH1 . . . .**118** A2
Warrington WA4 . . . .**26** A4
Westbrook Ave WA4 . . . . . .**16** B1
Westbrook Cres WA5 . . . . . .**7** A1
Westbrook Ctr WA5 . . . .**7** B1
Westbrook Dr SK10 . . . .**87** B1
Westbrook Old Hall Prim Sch
  WA5 . . . .**15** B4
Westbrook Rd WA6 . . . .**75** A1
Westbrook Way WA5 . . . . . .**7** A1
Westbury Cl
Middlewich CW10 . . . .**151** A4
Warrington WA1 . . . .**17** A4
Wistaston CW2 . . . .**206** A3
Westbury Ct SK11 . . . .**112** A4
Westbury Dr SK11 . . . .**112** A4
Westbury Way CH4 . . . . . .**140** C3
Westby Cl SK7 . . . .**36** A4
Westcliff Gdns WA4 . . . . . .**26** C2
Westcourt Rd M33 . . . . . .**242** A8
Westdale Rd WA1 . . . .**17** A4
Westend Ct LL13 . . . .**196** B4
Westenra Ave CH65 . . . . . .**69** C3
Westerham Ct SK10 . . . . . .**87** A1
Western App CH2 . . . .**118** C2
Western Ave Blacon CH1 .**117** B2
Ellesmere Port CH65 . . . . . .**69** C4
Macclesfield SK11 . . . .**112** B3
Milton Green CH3 . . . .**165** B1
Nantwich CW5 . . . .**204** C2
Western Ct CH2 . . . .**118** C2
Western Dr SK11 . . . .**112** B3
Western Pk CW11 . . . .**191** C4
Westfield WA14 . . . .**238** C3
Westfield Ave
Audley ST7 . . . .**209** B1
Macclesfield SK10 . . . .**87** A1
Westfield Cl
Chester CH4 . . . .**141** A4
Winsford CW7 . . . .**149** B3
Westfield Cres WA7 . . . . . .**22** C1
Westfield Dr
Knutsford WA16 . . . .**56** C1
Willaston (nr Nantwich)
  CW2 . . . .**205** C4
Westfield Gr CW8 . . . .**77** C2
Westfield Inf Sch CW2 . . .**205** C4
Westfield Mews WA7 . . . . .**22** C1
Westfield Prim Sch WA7 . .**22** C1
Westfield Rd Cheadle SK8 .**34** C4
Mow Cop ST7 . . . .**195** B4
Northwich CW9 . . . .**104** A4
Runcorn WA7 . . . .**22** C1
Westfields WA15 . . . .**31** C4
Westfields Rise CW3 . . . . .**232** B1
Westford Rd WA4 . . . .**16** A1
Westgate
Altrincham WA15 . . . .**238** E2
Sale M33 . . . .**242** A6
Widnes WA8 . . . .**22** A4
Wilmslow SK9 . . . .**60** A3
Westgate Ave CW7 . . . . . .**126** A1
Westgate Pk CW2 . . . .**206** C1
Westholme Cl
Congleton CW12 . . . .**156** B2
Wistaston CW2 . . . .**206** B4
Westholme Ct SK9 . . . .**60** A1
Westhouse Cl CH63 . . . . . .**43** B3
Westlands ST7 . . . .**209** C1
Westlands Cl CH64 . . . .**41** C1
Westlands Rd CW10 . . . . .**128** A4
Westlands The CW12 . . . .**156** B1
Westmere Cl CW2 . . . .**207** A3
Westmere Dr CW1 . . . .**190** C1
Westminster Ave CH4 . . . .**141** A3
Westminster Cl
Middlewich CW10 . . . .**128** A1
Warrington WA4 . . . .**17** B1
Widnes WA8 . . . .**22** A4
Westminster Dr
Bebington CH62 . . . .**43** B4
Bramhall SK8 . . . .**35** A3

Westminster Dr continued
Haydock WA11 . . . .**1** C4
Wilmslow SK9 . . . .**60** A2
Westminster Gn CH4 . . . .**141** B4
Westminster Gr
Ellesmere Port CH65 . . . . . .**70** B3
9 Winsford CW7 . . . .**149** A4
Westminster Ind Pk
  CH65 . . . .**69** C3
Westminster Pl 9 WA1 . . .**16** A3
Westminster Rd
Broughton CH4 . . . .**139** A4
Chester CH2 . . . .**118** C2
Ellesmere Port CH65 . . . . . .**70** B3
Macclesfield SK10 . . . .**87** B1
Westminster St
Crewe CW2 . . . .**190** B1
5 Macclesfield SK11 . . . .**112** B4
Westminster Terr CH4 . . .**141** B4
Westmoor Gables SK4 . . .**240** A8
Westmoreland Cl WA14 . . .**31** A4
Westmorland Ave
Talke ST7 . . . .**210** C4
Widnes WA8 . . . .**13** A1
Westmorland Cl SK10 . . . . .**86** C1
Westmorland Rd M31 . . . . .**11** C1
Westmorland Terr CW4 . . .**130** A2
Weston Cl CW10 . . . .**151** B4
Weston Cres WA7 . . . .**49** A3
Weston Ct WA7 . . . .**48** C4
Weston Dr M34 . . . .**241** A4
Weston Gr Chester CH2 . . .**118** C4
Halewood L26 . . . .**21** A3
Weston La CW2 . . . .**206** C3
Weston Point Expressway
  WA7 . . . .**49** A3
Weston Point Prim Sch
  WA7 . . . .**48** C4
Weston Prim Sch WA7 . . . .**49** A3
Weston Rd Crewe CW1 . . .**207** A4
Runcorn WA7 . . . .**48** C4
Wilmslow SK9 . . . .**60** C3
Weston St SK5 . . . .**240** E8
Weston View WA7 . . . .**49** B2
Weston Village Prim Sch
  CW2 . . . .**207** B3
Westover Rd WA1 . . . .**16** C4
Westrees WA8 . . . .**101** B3
Westville Dr CW12 . . . . . .**156** A1
Westward Rd
Chester CH3 . . . .**142** A4
Wilmslow SK9 . . . .**59** C3
Westway CH60 . . . .**40** C3
Westway Cres WA3 . . . .**10** A3
Westwood
Altrincham WA14 . . . .**238** B4
Runcorn WA7 . . . .**24** B1
Westwood Ave WA15 . . . .**238** F7
Westwood Cl CW2 . . . .**207** A1
Westwood Ct CH64 . . . .**41** C1
Westwood Lodge WA15 . .**238** F2
Westwood Rd SK8 . . . .**34** A4
Westy La WA4 . . . .**16** C2
Wet Gate La WA13 . . . .**19** C2
Wetheral Rd SK10 . . . .**87** A1
Wetherby Cl
Chester CH1 . . . .**118** A1
Newton-le-W WA12 . . . .**2** B3
Wetherby Way CH66 . . . . . .**69** B3
Wetreins La SY14,CH3 . . .**197** B3
Wettenhall Rd CW5 . . . . .**188** A2
Wetton La CW8 . . . .**76** C2
Wexford Ave L24 . . . .**21** B1
Weybourne Cl CH4 . . . . . .**140** C3
Weybridge Cl WA4 . . . .**26** C4
Weybridge Dr SK10 . . . . . .**87** A2
Weygates Dr WA15 . . . .**32** B4
Weymouth Cl WA7 . . . .**50** C3
Weymouth Rd WA5 . . . .**6** C3
Whaddon Dr CH4 . . . .**140** C2
Whaley Bridge Prim Sch
  SK23 . . . .**65** C4
Whaley Bridge Sta SK23 .**65** C4
Whaley La SK23 . . . .**65** B4
Whalley Ave Glazebury WA3 .**5** B4
Sale M33 . . . .**242** C7
Whalley Cl WA15 . . . .**238** F8
Whalley Dr CW6 . . . .**147** A2
Whalley Gr WA8 . . . .**13** B2
Whalley Hayes SK11 . . . . .**112** B4
Whalley Rd CW9 . . . .**104** A4
Whalley St WA1 . . . .**16** B3
Wharams Bank CW11 . . . .**176** C3
Wharburton Cl CW8 . . . . .**101** C1
Wharf Cl SK23 . . . .**65** C4
Wharf La CW12 . . . .**178** A2
Wharf Rd
Altrincham WA14 . . . .**238** D7
Collins Green WA12 . . . .**1** C1
Sale M33 . . . .**242** C7
Whaley Bridge SK23 . . . . . .**65** C4
Wharf St Stockport SK4 . .**240** E7
Warrington WA1 . . . .**16** B2
Wharf The WA7 . . . .**50** C3
Wharfdale Cl WA5 . . . .**15** A4
Wharfdale Rd
Congleton CW12 . . . .**157** A3
Crewe CW1 . . . .**173** A1
Wharfe Cl CW12 . . . .**156** C1
Wharfe La CH65 . . . .**70** A4
Wharfedale WA7 . . . .**50** A3
Wharfedale Dr CH62 . . . . . .**43** C3
Wharford La WA7 . . . .**24** C2
Wharfside Ct 6 WA4 . . . . .**16** C1
Wharmby Rd WA11 . . . .**1** C3
Wharton (Donefields) Ind Est
  CW7 . . . .**126** C1

Wharton CE Jun Sch
  CW7 . . . .**127** A1
Wharton Gdns CW7 . . . . .**127** A1
Wharton Park CW7 . . . . . .**126** C1
Wharton Rd CW7 . . . .**127** A1
Wharton Ret Pk CW7 . . . .**126** C2
Whatcroft Cl WA7 . . . .**49** B3
Wheat Croft SK3 . . . .**240** F1
Wheat Moss SK11 . . . .**84** A2
Wheatcroft Cl WA5 . . . .**15** B3
Wheatfield Cl
Barnton CW8 . . . .**78** A2
Ellesmere Port CH66 . . . . . .**69** B2
Macclesfield SK10 . . . .**87** B2
Romiley SK6 . . . .**241** A4
Wheatfield Rd WA8 . . . .**12** B3
Wheatland Rd CH60 . . . . . .**41** B4
Wheatlands WA7 . . . .**23** C1
Wheatley Ave WA12 . . . .**2** B3
Wheatley Rd CW1 . . . .**190** C3
Wheatsheaf La CW9 . . . . . .**53** A2
Wheatsheaf Rd SK23 . . . . .**65** C3
Wheelman Rd CW1 . . . . . .**190** A4
Wheelock Cl Alsager ST7 .**193** A2
Wilmslow SK9 . . . .**34** B1
Wheelock Ct CW11 . . . . . .**175** A1
Wheelock Dr CW7 . . . .**127** A1
Wheelock Prim Sch
  CW11 . . . .**175** A2
Wheelock St CW10 . . . . . .**128** B1
Wheelock Way 10 ST7 . . . .**195** A1
Wheldon Cl CH2 . . . .**118** C4
Wheldrake Cl CH66 . . . .**69** A3
Whernside WA8 . . . .**12** B2
Whernside Cl SK4 . . . .**240** E7
Whetstone Hey CH66 . . . . .**69** B3
Whetstone Rd ST8 . . . . . .**179** B1
Whickham Cl WA8 . . . .**12** C2
Whimbrel Ave WA12 . . . .**2** B2
Whimbrel Cl WA7 . . . .**49** C3
Whinberry Rd WA14 . . . . .**238** B7
Whinchat Ave WA12 . . . .**2** B2
Whinchat Cl WA3 . . . .**9** C2
Whinchat Dr WA3 . . . .**9** C2
Whinfell Gr WA7 . . . .**49** C3
Whipcord La CH1 . . . .**118** A1
Whirley Cl CW10 . . . .**151** B4
Whirley La SK10 . . . .**85** C1
Whirley Prim Sch SK10 . . .**86** B1
Whirley Rd SK10 . . . .**86** B1
Whirlow Rd CW2 . . . .**206** A4
Whisterfield La SK11 . . . . .**109** C2
Whiston Cl
High Legh WA16 . . . .**29** B2
Winsford CW7 . . . .**127** A2
Whiston Mews SK11 . . . . .**113** A2
Whiston St SK11 . . . .**112** B4
Whitbarrow Rd WA8 . . . . . .**18** B2
Whitby Ave Chester CH2 . .**118** B3
Warrington WA2 . . . .**8** B1
Whitby Cl Cheadle SK8 . . .**239** C6
Crewe CW1 . . . .**190** A4
Poynton SK12 . . . .**36** B2
Whitby Heath Prim Sch
  CH65 . . . .**70** A2
Whitby High Sch The
  CH66 . . . .**70** A1
Whitby La CH1 . . . .**95** A3
Whitby Rd
Ellesmere Port CH65 . . . . . .**70** B3
Runcorn WA7 . . . .**23** A1
Whitby's La CW7 . . . .**126** A1
Whitchurch Cl WA1 . . . .**17** A4
Whitchurch Gr ST5 . . . . . .**210** C1
Whitchurch Rd
Audlem CW3 . . . .**229** B2
Broxton CH3 . . . .**183** A2
Chester CH3 . . . .**119** A1
Christleton CH3 . . . .**142** C4
Edge Green SY14,CH3 . . . .**199** A2
Milton Green CH3 . . . .**165** B2
Newhall CW3 . . . .**229** B1
Royal's Green CW3,SY13 . .**228** B1
Sound CW5 . . . .**217** C2
Waverton CH3 . . . .**143** A2
Whitchurch Way WA7 . . . . .**49** B4
White Ave CW2 . . . .**189** C2
White Bear Yd 12 WA16 . . .**57** A1
White Broom WA13 . . . .**19** A2
White Friars CH1 . . . .**237** A2
White Hall La CW11 . . . . . .**173** C4
White Hart Gdns CW8 . . . .**102** C2
White Hart La CW2 . . . . . .**205** C4
White Hart St SK11 . . . . . .**241** D8
White House Cl WA11 . . . . . .**1** A3
White House Dr WA1 . . . . . .**17** C4
White La CH3 . . . .**142** B4
White Lodge Cl CH62 . . . . .**43** B3
White Lodge Mews
  CW8 . . . .**102** A2
White Park Cl CW10 . . . . .**128** C4
White St
Macclesfield SK11 . . . .**112** B3
Warrington WA1 . . . .**16** A3
Warrington, Stockton Heath
  WA4 . . . .**16** B1
Widnes WA8 . . . .**23** A3
Whiteacre Rd OL6 . . . .**242** A4
Whitebarn Rd SK9 . . . .**85** A4
Whitebeam Cl 13 CH66 . . .**69** C1
Whitebeam Cl
Newcastle-u-L ST5 . . . .**210** B1
Runcorn WA7 . . . .**24** B1
Whitebeam Row CW8 . . . .**102** C4
Whitecroft Rd CH66 . . . . . .**69** C1
Whitecross Rd WA5 . . . . . .**15** C3
Whitefield Lymm WA13 . . . .**19** A2

Whitefield continued
Stockport SK4 . . . .**240** D7
Whitefield Ave
Newton-le-W WA12 . . . .**2** C1
Warrington WA1 . . . .**16** C4
Whitefield Cl
Golborne WA3 . . . .**3** A4
Lymm WA13 . . . .**19** A3
Whitefield Ct WA3 . . . .**4** C1
Whitefield Gr WA13 . . . . . .**19** A3
Whitefield Rd Sale M33 . .**242** A7
Warrington WA4 . . . .**26** A4
Whitefields CH2 . . . .**72** A2
Whitefriars Wlk 2 M22 . . .**33** B2
Whitegate CH3 . . . .**121** C4
Whitegate Ave WA3 . . . .**4** C1
Whitegate CE Prim Sch
  CW8 . . . .**125** C4
Whitegate Cl CW10 . . . . . .**151** B3
Whitegate Fields LL13 . . .**180** B1
Whitegate Rd CW7 . . . . . .**125** C2
Whitegates SK8 . . . .**239** D5
Whitegates Cl CH64 . . . . . .**42** C1
Whitegates Cres CH64 . . . .**42** C1
Whitegates Rd SK8 . . . . . .**239** D5
Whitehall Ave ST7 . . . .**194** C1
Whitehall Cl Barnton CW8 .**78** A2
Wilmslow SK9 . . . .**60** A3
Whitehall Ct CW5 . . . .**204** B3
Whitehall Dr
Hartford CW8 . . . .**103** B3
Shavington CW2 . . . .**206** A2
Whitehall La CW6 . . . .**124** C1
Whitehall Pl 6 WA6 . . . .**74** A4
Whitehall Rd M33 . . . .**242** B5
Whitehaven La CW5 . . . . .**203** A4
Whitehaven Rd SK7 . . . .**35** B3
Whitehill Prim Sch SK4 . .**240** E8
Whitehill Rd ST7 . . . .**195** A1
Whitehill St W SK4 . . . . . .**240** E8
Whitehouse Dr WA15 . . . .**32** A4
Whitehouse Expressway
  WA7 . . . .**50** A3
Whitehouse Ind Est WA7 . .**50** C1
Whitehouse La
Nantwich CW5 . . . .**204** C4
Partington WA14 . . . .**20** B4
Plumley WA16 . . . .**80** C2
Whitehouse Rd WA16 . . . . .**30** A2
Whitelands Rd OL6,SK15 .**242** C4
Whitelea Dr SK3 . . . .**240** D1
Whiteleas Rd SK23 . . . .**65** B2
Whiteley Pl WA14 . . . .**238** D6
Whitelow Rd SK4 . . . .**240** A4
Whitemere Ct CH65 . . . . . .**70** B4
Whitemore Rd CW10 . . . . .**151** B3
Whiteridge Rd ST7 . . . . . .**195** A1
Whites La CW2 . . . .**207** A3
Whites Mdw CH3 . . . .**142** A4
Whitesands Rd WA13 . . . . .**18** B2
Whiteside Rd WA11 . . . .**1** C1
Whitesmead Cl SK12 . . . .**38** B3
Whitethorn Ave WA5 . . . . .**14** C3
Whitethorn Way ST5 . . . . .**210** C1
Whitewell Cl CW5 . . . .**204** C3
Whitewood La SY14 . . . . . .**212** B4
Whitfield Gr WA11 . . . .**1** A3
Whitfield Rd ST7 . . . .**195** A1
Whitfields The SK10 . . . . . .**87** A1
Whitley Ave Barnton CW8 .**78** A2
Warrington WA4 . . . .**17** A2
Whitley Cl
Middlewich CW10 . . . .**151** A4
Runcorn WA7 . . . .**48** C4
Whitley Dr CW8 . . . .**103** A2
Whitley La WA16 . . . .**55** A4
Whitley Rd SK4 . . . .**240** B7
Whitley Village Sch WA4 . .**52** B2
Whitlow Ave
Altrincham WA14 . . . .**238** B8
Nantwich CW5 . . . .**204** C2
Whitlow La CW9 . . . .**126** C4
Whitstable Pk WA8 . . . .**12** C2
Whittaker Ave WA2 . . . .**8** B1
Whittaker Cl CW1 . . . .**190** A4
Whittington Gdns CW9 . .**104** A1
Whittle Ave Haydock WA11 . .**1** A4
Warrington WA5 . . . .**15** A4
Whittle Cl CH5 . . . .**116** A2
Whittle Hall La WA5 . . . . . .**14** C3
Whittles Ave M34 . . . .**241** A6
Whittles Wlk M34 . . . .**241** A6
Whittlewood Cl WA3 . . . . . .**10** A3
Whitton Dr CH2 . . . .**118** C3
Whitwell Cl WA5 . . . .**14** B4
Whitworth Cl WA3 . . . .**9** C2
Wickenby Dr M33 . . . .**242** A6
Wicker La
Altrincham WA15 . . . .**32** B4
Guilden Sutton CH3 . . . . . .**120** A2
Wicklow Ave SK3 . . . .**240** B3
Wicklow Cl CH66 . . . .**69** A3
Wickson La CH3,CW6 . . . .**167** B2
Wicksten Dr WA7 . . . .**23** B1
Widdale Cl WA5 . . . .**14** C4
Widgeon Cl SK12 . . . .**36** A2
Widgeon Rd WA14 . . . . . .**238** B8
Widgeons Covert CH63 . . .**41** C3
Widnes Rd
Warrington WA5 . . . .**14** B2
Widnes WA8 . . . .**23** A4
Widnes Sixth Form Coll
  WA8 . . . .**12** C3
Widnes Sta WA8 . . . .**13** A2
Wiend The CH2 . . . .**118** B2
Wight Cl CH65 . . . .**70** B1
Wightman Ave WA12 . . . . . .**2** B3
Wigmore Cl WA3 . . . .**10** A3

Wigmore St OL6 ....242 A4
Wigsey La WA13 ....19 A4
Wigshaw La WA3 ....4 B1
Wigwam Cl SK12 ....36 B2
Wilbraham Cl CW5 ....204 A4
Wilbraham Rd
  Acton CW5 ....204 A4
  Congleton CW12 ....156 C2
  Weaverham CW8 ....77 C1
Wilbraham's Wlk ST7 ..209 B1
Wilbrahams Way ST7 ..193 B2
Wilcock Rd WA11 ....2 A4
Wilcott Dr SK9 ....59 C2
Wilcott Rd SK8 ....239 A5
Wild Arum Cl 6 WA3 ......3 C4
Wild Clough SK14 ......241 F5
Wild Goose Ave ST7 ..195 B4
Wildcote Cl WA8 ....13 B2
Wilderhope Cl WA2 ....206 B4
Wilderspool Cres WA4 ..16 A1
Wilderspool Cswy WA4 ..16 B2
Wilding Ave WA7 ....23 A1
Wilding Bsns Pk CH3 ..119 B2
Wilding St CW1 ....190 C2
Wildings Old La WA3 ......9 A4
Wildwood Gr WA1 ....17 A4
Wilkin Croft SK8 ......239 E1
Wilkins La SK9 ....33 C3
Wilkinson Ave WA1 ......16 C3
Wilkinson Cl WA8 ....23 A3
Wilkinson Rd SK4 ......240 E6
Wilkinson St
  Ellesmere Port CH65 ....70 B3
  4 Sale M33 ....242 D6
  Warrington WA2 ....16 B4
Wilkinson St N CH65 ....70 B3
Willan Rd CH1 ....117 B2
Willaston CE Prim Sch
  CH64 ....67 C4
Willaston Dr L26 ....21 A3
Willaston Farm CH64 ....67 C4
Willaston Green Mews
  CH64 ....67 C4
Willaston Hall Gdns
  CW5 ....205 B3
Willaston Prim Sch
  CW5 ....205 B3
Willaston Rd CH63,CH64 ..42 B2
Willaston Way 8 SK9 ....34 B3
Willbank La WA5 ....202 B3
Willdor Gr SK3 ....240 B2
Willerby Cl SK11 ......112 B4
Willeymoor La SY13 ....225 B4
William Beamont Com High
  Sch WA2 ....8 B1
William Johnson Gdns
  CH65 ....70 B3
William Penn Cl WA5 ....14 C3
William Rd ST7 ....195 A1
William St Chester CH1 ..237 B3
  Chester, Hoole Park CH2 ..118 C2
  Congleton CW12 ....157 A2
  Macclesfield SK10 ....112 C4
  10 Northwich CW9 ....104 A4
  Widnes WA8 ....13 B1
  Winsford CW7 ....126 C1
William Stockton Com Sch
  CH65 ....70 A3
William Wlk 2 WA14 ..238 D3
Williams Ave WA12 ....2 B3
Williams Cl CH2 ....118 B2
Williams Way WA11 ....111 B4
Williamson Ave SK6 ..241 A4
Williamson Cres SK23 ..65 B4
Williamson Rd SK23 ....65 B4
Willington Ave CH62 ....43 C2
Willington La
  Duddon CW6 ....145 C4
  Kelsall CW6 ....122 B2
Willington Rd
  Duddon CW6 ....145 A4
  Kelsall CW6 ....122 B2
  Tarvin CW6 ....122 B1
Willis Rd SK3 ....240 E2
Willis St WA1 ....16 B3
Willmer Cres ST7 ......195 A3
Willotts Hill Rd ST5 ..210 B1
Willoughby Cl Sale M33 ..242 A4
  Warrington WA5 ....7 B1
Willow Ave Cheadle SK8 ..239 F2
  Newton-le-W WA12 ....2 C2
  Stockport SK5 ....240 F8
  Widnes WA8 ....13 A1
Willow Bank Bramhall SK8 ..35 A3
  Helsby WA6 ....73 B1
Willow Bank Ct M20 ..239 B8
Willow Bank Est WA12 ....2 C2
Willow Cl Chester CH2 ..118 B4
  Lymm WA13 ....18 C2
  Newcastle-u-L ST5 ....210 B1
  Poynton SK12 ....36 C2
  Runcorn WA7 ....49 B4
  Winsford CW7 ....126 B2
Willow Cres Chester CH2 119 A2
  Warrington WA1 ....17 A4
  Wistaston CW2 ....189 C1
Willow Ct Alsager ST7 ..193 C2
  Connah's Quay CH5 ......91 B1
  Gatley SK8 ....239 A6
  Higher Kinnerton CH4 ..161 A4
  Macclesfield SK10 ......87 A1
  Middlewich CW10 ......128 B1
  Nantwich CW5 ....204 C4
  Sale M33 ....242 E7
Willow Dr Blacon CH1 ..117 B3
  Bunbury CW6 ....185 C4
  Handforth SK9 ....34 B2
  Sandbach CW11 ....175 C4

Willow Dr continued
  Warrington WA4 ....16 C1
Willow Gn
  Knutsford WA16 ....56 C2
  Weaverham CW8 ....102 B4
Willow Gr Barnton CW8 ..78 A2
  Chester CH2 ....119 A2
  Ellesmere Port CH1 ......95 A4
  Elton CH2 ....72 A2
Willow Hayes CH3 ......121 C4
Willow La Goostrey CW4 .107 C1
  Thornton Hough CH63,CH64 42 B2
  Warrington WA4 ....26 B2
Willow Lea CH1 ....94 C1
Willow Rd Chester CH4 ..140 C3
  Haydock WA11 ....1 C4
  High Lane SK6 ....37 C4
  Newton-le-W WA12 ....2 C2
  Partington M31 ....11 C1
Willow Sq CW7 ....127 A1
Willow St CW12 ....156 C2
Willow Tree Gr ST7 ....193 B4
Willow Tree Mews SK8 ..239 B1
Willow Tree Rd WA14 ..238 D3
Willow Way Bramhall SK7 ..35 B4
  Broughton CH4 ....139 A2
  Prestbury SK10 ....87 A3
Willow Wood Cl 6 WA3 ..3 C4
Willow Wood Com Jun Sch
  CW7 ....127 A1
Willow Wood Inf Sch
  CW7 ....127 A1
Willoway Rd CH3 ......119 A1
Willowbank Dr SK10 ....88 B4
Willowbrow Rd CH63,
  CH64 ....42 B2
Willowcroft Way ST7 ..195 C2
Willowdale WA12 ....2 C1
Willowdale Ave SK8 ..239 B2
Willowdale Way CH66 ..94 C4
Willowgreen La CW8 ....77 A3
Willowherb Cl CH3 ....142 A3
Willowmead Dr SK10 ....87 A3
Willows SK9 ....59 C3
Willows Cl CW2 ....206 A4
Willows The
  Frodsham WA6 ....74 B4
  Higher Wincham CW9 ..79 C3
  Partington M31 ....11 C2
  Sandbach CW11 ....175 A4
  5 Stockport SK4 ......240 A7
  Warrington WA5 ....14 C3
Wilmere La WA8 ....13 A3
Wilmot Ave WA5 ....14 C3
Wilmot Dr WA3 ....2 C4
Wilmslow Ave CH66 ....69 C3
Wilmslow Cres WA4 ....17 B2
Wilmslow Dr CH66 ....69 C3
Wilmslow Grange Sch
  SK9 ....34 B2
Wilmslow High Sch SK9 ..60 A3
Wilmslow Old Rd
  Mottram St Andrew SK10 ..61 A1
  Wythenshawe M90,WA15 ..33 A3
Wilmslow Park Rd SK9 ..60 B4
Wilmslow Prep Sch
  Alderley Edge SK9 ......60 A1
  Cheadle SK8 ....239 D5
  Gatley SK8,SK9 ....34 B3
  Handforth SK9 ....34 B2
  Mottram St Andrew SK10 ..61 A2
  Mottram St Andrew SK10 ..61 B3
  Mottram St Andrew, Greendale
    SK10 ....86 B4
  Woodford SK7 ....35 B1
  Wythenshaw M90,WA15,
    SK9 ....32 C3
Wilmslow Sta 5 SK9 ....32 C3
Wilmslow Wlk 13 SK11 ..112 C4
Wilsbury Grange CW8 ..103 A3
Wilsden Rd WA8 ....12 A1
Wilson Cl Warrington WA4 ..17 B2
  Widnes WA8 ....13 B1
Wilson Cres
  Lostock Gralam CW9 ....80 A2
  Stalybridge OL6 ......242 B4
Wilson Dr CW9 ....126 C4
Wilson La WA3 ....9 C3
Wilson Patten St WA1 ..16 A2
Wilson Rd SK4 ....240 B8
Wilson St Hyde SK14 ..241 E6
  3 Sale M33 ....242 B7
  Warrington WA5 ....16 A4
Wilsons La CH65 ....70 A2
Wilton Ave SK8 ....34 B4
Wilton Cl CW9 ....103 C1
Wilton Cres
  Alderley Edge SK9 ......59 C1
  Macclesfield SK11 ....111 C3
Wilton Dr WA15 ....32 B4
Wilton La WA3 ....4 A3
Wiltshire Cl
  Macclesfield SK10 ......86 C1
  Warrington WA1 ....17 B3
Wiltshire Dr CW12 ....156 C2
Wiltshire Rd M31 ....11 C1
Wiltshire Wlk SK10 ....86 C1
Wilwick La SK11 ......111 C4
Wimberry Dr ST5 ......210 B1
Wimbledon Dr SK3 ....240 C1
Wimboldsley Com Prim Sch
  CW10 ....150 C2
Wincham Ave CW9 ......79 B2
Wincham Bsns Pk CW9 ..79 B2
Wincham Com Prim Sch
  CW9 ....79 C3
Wincham La CW9 ....79 B2

Winchester Ave
  Ellesmere Port CH65 ....70 B2
  Warrington WA5 ....15 B3
Winchester Cl
  Shavington CW2 ....206 A2
  Wilmslow SK9 ....59 C3
Winchester Dr SK4 ....240 B6
Winchester Pl WA8 ......22 B4
Winchester Sq CW12 ..140 C3
Wincle Ave SK12 ....37 A1
Wincle CE Prim Sch
  SK11 ....136 C1
Windemere Ave CH2 ..119 A3
Windermere Ave
  Warrington WA2 ....8 B2
  Widnes WA8 ....13 A2
Windermere Cl CH64 ..66 C4
Windermere Dr
  Alderley Edge SK9 ......59 C1
  Congleton CW12 ....156 A1
Windermere Rd
  Ellesmere Port CH65 ....70 B1
  Haydock WA11 ....1 A3
  High Lane SK6 ....37 C4
  Stalybridge SK15 ......242 D4
  Winsford CW7 ....126 B1
  Wistaston CW2 ....189 C1
Windermere St WA8 ....13 A2
Windfield Gdns CH66 ..69 B4
Windings The CW10 ....128 A1
Windle Ct Neston CH64 ..41 C1
  Warrington WA3 ....9 B2
Windlehurst Ct SK6 ....37 B4
Windlehurst Rd SK6 ....37 B4
Windmill Cl
  Buerton CW3 ....230 C2
  Warrington WA4 ....26 B3
Windmill Ctr The WA8 ..23 A4
Windmill Dr CW3 ......229 C2
Windmill Hill Ave WA7 ..24 B1
Windmill Hill Ave E WA7 ..24 B1
Windmill Hill Ave N WA7 24 B2
Windmill Hill Ave S WA7 24 B1
Windmill Hill Ave W
  WA7 ....24 B1
Windmill Hill Prim Sch
  WA7 ....24 B1
Windmill La
  Bollington SK10 ....88 A3
  Buerton CW3 ....230 C2
  Christleton CH3 ......142 B4
  Preston on the Hill WA4 ..51 A3
  Warrington, Appleton WA4 ..26 B3
  Warrington, Penketh WA5 ..14 C3
Windmill Rd M33 ......242 F5
Windmill Rise CH2 ....118 B4
Windmill St
  Macclesfield SK11 ....112 C3
  Runcorn WA7 ....23 A1
Windscale Rd WA2 ......9 A1
Windsor Ave Crewe CW1 190 A3
  Gatley SK8 ....239 A5
  Nantwich CW5 ....204 C2
  Newton-le-W WA12 ....2 B1
  Sale M33 ....242 B8
  Stockport SK4 ....240 A7
  Tarporley CW6 ....146 B1
  Wilmslow SK9 ....59 C4
Windsor Cl
  Bollington SK10 ....87 C3
  Cuddington CW8 ......101 C2
  Poynton SK12 ....36 B2
Windsor Ct Chester CH4 ..237 B1
  1 Warrington WA4 ....16 C1
Windsor Dr Alsager ST7 ..192 C2
  Altrincham WA14 ......20 C1
  Broughton CH4 ....139 A2
  Ellesmere Port CH65 ....70 A2
  Faddiley CW5 ....202 C4
  Haydock WA11 ....2 A4
  Helsby WA6 ....73 A1
  Sale WA14 ....238 F8
  Stalybridge SK15 ......242 D3
  Warrington WA4 ....17 A1
  Winsford CW7 ....149 B3
Windsor Gr Cheadle SK8 ..34 C4
  Romiley SK6 ....241 E2
  Runcorn WA7 ....49 A4
Windsor Ho ST7 ....210 B3
Windsor Pl CW12 ......156 C1
Windsor Rd Chester CH4 140 C1
  Golborne WA3 ....3 B4
  Widnes WA8 ....13 A2
  Wistaston CW2 ....205 C4
Windsor Sq SK11 ......112 B2
Windsor St WA5 ....15 C3
Windsor Way WA16 ....56 C1
Windsor Wlk SK2 ......240 F2
Windways CH66 ....69 B4
Windy Bank Ave WA3 ..3 C4
Winfield St SK14 ......241 F6
Winfield Way WA8 ......23 A4
Winfrith Rd WA2 ....9 A1
Wingate Rd
  Bebington CH62 ....43 C3
  Stockport SK4 ....240 C8
Wingfield Ave SK9 ......59 C3
Wingfield Dr SK9 ....59 C3
Wingfield Pl CW7 ......149 A3
Winghay Rd ST7 ......195 B1
Wingrove Rd WA2 ....16 B4
Winifred St WA2 ....16 A4
Winkwell Dr CH4 ......141 A4
Winmarith Dr WA15 ....31 A4
Winmarleigh St WA1 ....16 A2
Winnington Ave CW8 ..103 B4
Winnington La CW8 ....78 B1

Winnington Park Com Prim
  Sch CW8 ....103 B4
Winnington St CW7 ..126 C1
Winnows The WA7 ......23 B1
Winscombe Dr CH3 ....119 B1
Winsfield Rd SK7 ....36 C4
Winsford Cl WA11 ....1 C4
Winsford Dr WA5 ....6 C1
Winsford Gr CH66 ......69 B2
Winsford High Street Com
  Sch CW7 ....126 B1
Winsford Ind Est CW7 ..127 B2
Winsford Rd
  Cholmondeston CW7 ..171 A1
  Wettenhall CW7 ......170 C3
Winsford St Chad's CE Prim
  Sch CW7 ....149 C1
Winsford Sta CW7 ....127 B1
Winsford Way CH1 ....117 C1
Winsford Wlk M33 ....242 E5
Winslow Cl WA7 ....50 B4
Winstanley Cl WA5 ....15 B3
Winstanley Ind Est WA2 ..8 A1
Winstanley Rd
  Neston CH64 ....66 C3
  Sale M33 ....242 C7
Winston Ave Alsager ST7 193 B3
  Newton-le-W WA12 ....1 A1
  St Helens WA9 ....1 A1
Winston Ct CH2 ....119 A3
Winter Gr WA9 ....1 A2
Winter La SY14 ....147 A1
Winterbottom La WA16 ..55 C4
Winterford La CW6 ....147 A1
Wintergreen Wlk 10 M31 11 C2
Winterlea Dr L26 ....21 A3
Winterside Cl ST5 ....210 B1
Winterton Way SK11 ..112 B2
Winton Ct WA14 ......238 C2
Winton Gr WA7 ....24 B1
Winton Rd
  Altrincham WA14 ......238 C2
  Golborne WA3 ....3 C3
Winton St SK15 ......242 E1
Winwick CE Prim Sch
  WA2 ....8 A3
Winwick La WA3 ....3 C2
Winwick Link Rd WA2,WA3 8 B3
Winwick Park Ave WA2 ..8 A3
Winwick Rd
  Newton-le-W WA12 ......2 C1
  Warrington WA2 ....8 A1
Winwick St WA2 ....16 A3
Winwick View WA5 ......1 B1
Winwood Rd M20 ......239 C8
Wirksmoor Rd SK22 ....39 A4
Wirral Cl WA3 ....4 C2
Wirral Cres Neston CH64 ..66 C3
  Stockport SK3 ....240 A4
Wirral Ctry Pk ★ CH64 ..67 B4
Wirral Ed Ctr CH62 ....43 B4
Wirral Met Coll (Carlett Park
  Campus) CH62 ....44 A4
Wirswall Rd SY13 ....226 B4
Wisenholme Cl WA7 ....49 C3
Wistaston Ave CW2 ..189 C1
Wistaston Green Cl
  CW2 ....189 C1
Wistaston Green Inf Sch
  CW2 ....189 C1
Wistaston Green Jun Sch
  CW2 ....189 C1
Wistaston Green Rd
  CW2 ....189 C1
Wistaston Jun Sch CW2 205 C4
Wistaston Pk CW2 ....189 C1
Wistaston Rd
  Crewe CW2 ....190 B2
  Willaston (nr Nantwich)
    CW5 ....205 C3
  Wistaston CW5 ....205 C3
Wistaston Road Bsns Ctr
  CW2 ....190 A2
Wisterdale Cl CW2 ....206 A4
Witchcroft Heath Rd
  SK11 ....109 A2
Witham Cl CW2 ....206 A4
Witham Rd CH66 ......242 B4
Witham Way ST8 ......179 C1
Withens Cl CW8 ......102 B4
Withens La CW8 ......102 B4
Withenshaw La SK11 ..136 C3
Wither's La WA16 ......28 B3
Withers Ave WA2 ....16 B4
Witherwin Ave WA4 ....26 C4
Within Way L24 ....47 C4
Withington Ave WA3 ....5 A2
Withington Cl
  Northwich CW9 ....104 A3
  Sandbach CW11 ......175 B4
Withinlee Rd SK10 ......86 B3
Withins Rd Culcheth WA3 ..4 C2
  Haydock WA11 ....1 C4
Withy Cl WA6 ....74 B4
Withy Croft CH3 ......142 A4
Withy Tree Gr 1 M34 ..241 A6
Withycombe Rd WA5 ..14 C2
Withyfold Dr SK10 ......87 C1
Witney Gdns WA4 ......26 C3
Witney La SY14 ......213 B4
Witt Rd WA2 ....23 A4
Wittenbury Rd SK4 ..240 B6
Wittenham Ho SK9 ....34 B1
Witter Pl CH2 ....237 C3
Wittering La CH60 ....40 B4
Witterings The CH64 ..41 C1
Witton Church Walk CE Prim
  Sch CW9 ....104 A4

Witton St CW9 ....79 A1
Witton Wlk 5 CW9 ....103 C4
Wivern Pl WA7 ....23 A2
Woburn Ave WA3 ....1 C4
Woburn Cl Haydock WA11 ..1 C4
  Macclesfield SK10 ......87 B1
  Northwich CW9 ....103 C3
Woburn Ct SK12 ....36 C2
Woburn Dr Chester CH2 ..118 C3
  Congleton CW12 ....179 A4
  Cronton WA8 ....12 B3
Woburn Rd WA2 ....8 A2
Woking Rd SK8 ....35 A4
Wolfe Cl
  Grappenhall Heys WA4 ..27 A4
  Knutsford WA16 ....57 B2
Wolseley Ho M33 ......242 C8
Wolseley Rd M33 ......242 C8
Wolsey Dr WA14 ......238 A1
Wolstanholme Cl CW12 156 C1
Wolverham Prim Sch
  CH65 ....70 B2
Wolverham Rd CH65 ..70 B2
Wolverton Dr
  Runcorn WA7 ....24 B1
  Wilmslow SK9 ....34 B1
Wolvesey Pl CW7 ......149 A3
Wood Croft CH3 ......119 C2
Wood Dr ST7 ....193 A2
Wood End Ct WA8 ......13 B1
Wood End La CH64 ....67 C2
Wood Gdns SK9 ....60 A1
Wood Hey Gr 2 M34 ..241 A6
Wood La Altrincham WA16 ..32 B1
  Bradwall Green CW10,
    CW11 ....152 C2
  Broughton CH4 ....139 A2
  Burton CH64 ....67 B1
  Duddon CW6 ....145 C4
  Goostrey CW4 ....107 B1
  Mobberley WA16 ....58 A4
  Neston CH64 ....41 B1
  Partington M31 ....11 B2
  Runcorn WA7 ....49 C2
  Runcorn, Brookvale WA7 ..50 B3
  Tattenhall CH3 ....167 A1
  Utkinton CW6 ....146 A3
  Warrington WA4 ....26 C4
  Weaverham CW8 ......102 C3
Wood La E SK10 ....63 A4
Wood La N SK10 ....63 A4
Wood La S SK10 ....63 A4
Wood La W SK10 ....63 A4
Wood Lane Prim Sch
  ST7 ....210 A1
Wood Meml Sch CH4 ..140 C3
Wood Orchard La CW3 ..230 A1
Wood Sorrel Way WA3 ..3 C4
Wood St
  Altrincham WA14 ......238 D4
  Audley ST7 ....209 C2
  Cheadle SK8 ....239 D6
  Congleton CW12 ....156 C2
  Crewe CW2 ....190 B1
  Golborne WA3 ....3 A4
  Hawarden CH5 ....116 A1
  Hyde SK14 ....241 E6
  Macclesfield SK11 ....112 B4
  Mow Cop ST7 ....195 B4
  New Mills SK22 ....39 B4
  Stalybridge SK15 ......242 D2
  Stockport SK3 ....240 E5
  Warrington WA1 ....16 B3
  Widnes WA8 ....13 B1
Wood View ST7 ....210 A1
Wood's La CW8 ....101 B3
Woodacre Gr CH66 ....69 C4
Woodacre Rd CH66 ....69 C4
Woodacres Ct SK9 ....59 C4
Woodale Rd WA5 ....14 C4
Woodall Cl M33 ......242 D6
Woodall Dr WA7 ....23 A1
Woodavens Gr CW3 ..229 A1
Woodbank Cl CW2 ....206 A4
Woodbank La CH1 ......93 B3
Woodbank Rd
  Ellesmere Port CH65 ....70 A1
  Warrington WA5 ....15 A2
Woodbine Ave M44 ....11 B2
Woodbine Cres SK2 ..240 F3
Woodbine Rd WA13 ....19 A2
Woodbourne Rd SK22 ..39 A3
Woodbridge Cl WA4 ....26 C2
Woodbrook SK23 ....65 C4
Woodbrook Ave SK14 ..241 F6
Woodbrook Ct SK23 ....65 C4
Woodbrook Rd SK9 ....60 B1
Woodburn Dr CH60 ....40 C3
Woodbury Rd SK3 ....240 B3
Woodchurch La CH66 ..69 C2
Woodchurch Wlk 5
  M33 ....242 F5
Woodclose CH66 ....44 A1
Woodcock La ST7 ....195 B3
Woodcocks' Well CE Prim
  Sch ST7 ....195 B3
Woodcote Ave CH65 ..70 A1
Woodcote Cl WA2 ....8 B1
Woodcote Pl CW11 ..191 C4
Woodcote View SK9 ..34 C1
Woodcotes The CH62 ..43 B3
Woodcott Ave CW2 ..126 A1
Woodcott Cl CW2 ....206 C1
Woodcott Gr 3 SK9 ....34 C1
Woodcotthill La CW5 ..217 A2

Woodcroft ST7 210 A1
Woodend WA7 50 C4
Woodend Cl CW10 151 B3
Woodend La
Altrincham WA16 32 C1
Hollins Green WA3 10 B1
Hyde SK14 241 D5
Mobberley WA16 58 C4
Woodend Rd CH65 69 C3
Woodfall Cl CH64 67 A3
Woodfall Gr CH64 67 A3
Woodfall Inf Sch CH64 67 A3
Woodfall Jun Sch CH64 67 A3
Woodfall La CH64 67 A3
Woodfield Ave SK6 241 A4
Woodfield Cl CH4 139 A2
Woodfield Gr
Chester CH2 119 A3
Sale M33 242 A8
Woodfield Ho CH2 119 A3
Woodfield Prim Sch
CH2 119 A3
Woodfield Rd
Altrincham WA14 238 C6
Bramhall SK8 35 A4
Ellesmere Port CH65 70 B3
Woodfield Rd N 9 CH65 70 B3
Woodfields CH3 142 C4
Woodfin Croft SK11 84 A2
Woodford Ave
Dukinfield M34 241 A8
Golborne WA3 3 B4
Woodford Cl Crewe CW2 189 C1
Helsby WA6 73 A1
Runcorn WA7 49 A3
Warrington WA4 17 B2
Woodford Court Ind Est
CW7 149 A4
Woodford La
Prestbury SK10 61 B4
Winsford CW7 149 A4
Woodford La W CW7 149 A4
Woodford Lodge High Sch
CW7 149 A4
Woodford Park Ind Est
CW7 148 C4
Woodford Prep Sch SK7 35 B1
Woodford Rd
Bramhall SK7 35 C2
Poynton SK12 36 A3
Wilmslow SK9 61 A4
Woodgate Ave ST7 194 A3
Woodgreen La CW5 171 B3
Woodhall Cl
Warrington WA5 15 A4
Woodford SK7 35 C2
Woodhall Rd
Kidsgrove ST7 195 B2
Stockport SK5 240 F8
Woodham Cl CW8 103 B3
Woodham Gr CH64 66 C3
Woodhatch Rd WA7 50 A3
Woodhead Dr WA15 238 F1
Woodhead Rd WA15 238 F1
Woodhey Hall La CW5 202 A3
Woodhey La CW5 202 B3
Woodhill Ave CH4 140 C3
Woodhouse Cl WA3 9 C2
Woodhouse End Rd
SK11 135 A4
Woodhouse La
Biddulph ST8 179 C1
Buerton CW3 235 B4
Partington WA14 20 B2
Warren SK11 111 C1
Wythenshawe M22 33 B4
Woodhouse Mid Sch
ST8 179 C1
Woodhouse Park Prim Sch
M22 33 B4
Woodhouse Rd M22 33 B4
Woodland Ave
Crewe CW1 190 C2
Lymm WA13 19 A1
Nantwich CW5 205 A3
Newton-le-W WA12 2 C2
Widnes WA8 12 C1
Woodland Bank CH2 96 C1
Woodland Cl SK11 84 A2
Woodland Ct ST7 193 B2
Woodland Dr WA13 19 A1
Woodland End SK11 84 A2
Woodland Gdns CW1 190 B3
Woodland Rd
Ellesmere Port CH65 70 A1
Rode Heath ST7 193 C4
Woodland View
Ellesmere Port CH66 69 A4
Whaley Bridge SK23 65 C1
Woodland Wlk
Bebington CH62 43 B4
Runcorn WA7 24 A1
Woodlands Ave
Chester CH1 118 A2
Congleton CW12 156 B2
Kidsgrove ST7 194 B1
Woodlands Cl
Cheadle SK8 35 A4
Eaton CW6 147 A4
Neston CH64 66 B4
Woodlands Cres WA16 29 B2
Woodlands Ct
Altrincham WA15 238 E5
18 Knutsford WA16 57 A1
Woodlands Dr
Chester CH2 118 C2
Goostrey CW4 107 C1
Knutsford WA16 57 A1
Warrington WA4 17 B2
Woodlands Gr CW8 77 C2
Woodlands Ind Est WA12 2 B3
Woodlands Inf Sch CH66 69 C1
Woodlands Jun Sch
CH66 69 C1
Woodlands La
Altrincham WA15 238 E5
Chester CH3 119 A1
Woodlands Parkway
WA15 238 E6
Woodlands Pk CW12 156 B2
Woodlands Rd
Altrincham WA14,WA15 238 E5
Handforth SK9 34 C2
Hartford CW8 103 B3
High Lane SK12 38 A3
Huntington CH3 142 A3
Macclesfield SK11 112 B3
Neston CH64 66 B4
New Mills SK22 39 A4
Sale M33 242 C6
Wilmslow SK9 33 C1
Woodlands Rd E CW8 103 B3
Woodlands The
Higher Wincham CW9 80 A3
Northwich CW8 78 C1
Woodlands Way CW6 146 B1
Woodlark Cl CW7 150 A4
Woodlea Ave CH2 118 C4
Woodlea Cl CH62 43 B3
Woodlea Ct CW8 103 B4
Woodlea Dr SK10 87 C4
Woodleigh WA14 238 A5
Woodleigh Ct SK9 60 A1
Woodley Fold WA5 14 C2
Woodman St 2 SK1 240 E6
Woodmount Cl SK6 241 F2
Woodnoth Dr CW2 206 B3
Woodpecker Cl WA3 9 C2
Woodpecker Dr CW9 103 C2
Woodridge WA7 24 B1
Woodridings WA14 238 B3
Woodrow Way M44 11 C4
Woodruff Cl ST7 195 C1
Woodruff Wlk 14 M31 11 C2
Woods Ct WA12 2 A2
Woods Gr SK8 35 A4
Woods La SK8 35 A4
Woods Rd M44 11 C4
Woods The 4 WA14 238 E6
Woodsfin La CH3 183 C4
Woodshutt's St ST7 194 C1
Woodside
Ellesmere Port CH65 70 B1
Knutsford WA16 57 A1
Lawton-gate ST7 194 C2
Siddington SK11 110 A2
Woodside Ave
Alsager ST7 193 C2
Frodsham WA6 74 B4
Kidsgrove ST7 195 A1
Wistaston CW2 189 C1
Woodside Ct CH2 118 B2
Woodside Dr
High Lane SK6 37 C4
Sandbach CW11 175 B3
Woodside La Lymm WA13 19 A1
Poynton SK12 36 C2
Wistaston CW2 189 C1
Woodside Prim Sch WA7 49 B4
Woodside Rd
Blacon CH1 117 B3
Haydock WA11 1 C4
Warrington WA5 14 C3
Woodside St SK22 39 A3
Woodside Terr CW9 104 A2
Woodslands Rd CH4 141 A4
Woodsome Cl CH65 70 A1
Woodsome Dr CH65 70 A1
Woodstock Ave
Bramhall SK8 35 A4
Newton-le-W WA12 2 B1
Woodstock Cl SK10 87 A1
Woodstock Dr CW10 151 C3
Woodstock Gdns WA4 26 C3
Woodstock Gr WA8 12 B1
Woodstock Rd WA14 238 C8
Woodthorn Cl WA4 24 C2
Woodvale WA14 238 C2
Woodvale Cl WA2 8 C1
Woodvale Rd
Ellesmere Port CH66 69 B3
Knutsford WA16 82 A4
Woodview Cres WA8 22 A4
Woodview Rd WA8 22 A4
Woodville Dr M33 242 A7
Woodville Pl WA8 12 B1
Woodville Rd
Altrincham WA14 238 C3
Sale M33 242 A7
Woodward St CW8 77 B1
Woodward Wlk CH3 121 B2
Woodyear Rd CH62 43 C4
Woolacombe Cl WA4 16 B1
Woolaston Dr ST7 193 B2
Woolden Rd M44 11 A4
Woollam Dr CH66 69 B4
Woolley Ave SK12 36 B1
Woolley Cl WA6 49 B1
Woolmer Cl WA3 10 A3
Woolston Ave CW12 157 A1
Woolston CE Prim Sch
WA1 17 B4
Woolston Com High Sch
WA1 17 A4
Woolston Com Prim Sch
WA1 17 B4
Woolston Dr CW2 206 C1
Woolston Grange Ave
WA1 9 B1
Woolston Rd WA11 1 B4
Woolton Ct CH66 69 C4
Woore Prim Sch CW3 232 A1
Woore Rd Audlem CW3 230 B2
Buerton CW3 230 B2
Wootton St SK14 241 D8
Worcester Ave
Denton M34 241 A5
3 Golborne WA3 3 A4
Worcester Cl
Romiley SK6 241 A1
Talke ST7 210 B4
Warrington WA5 15 B3
Worcester Pl CH1 118 A2
Worcester St CH65 70 B3
Worcester Wlk 3 CH65 70 B3
Wordsworth Ave
Warrington WA4 16 A1
Widnes WA8 22 C4
Wordsworth Cl
7 Sandbach CW11 174 B3
Wistaston CW2 189 C1
Wordsworth Cres CH1 118 A3
Wordsworth Dr CW1 190 C2
Wordsworth Ho SK10 86 C1
Wordsworth Mews CH1 118 A3
Wordsworth Sq CH1 118 A3
Wordsworth Way
Alsager ST7 193 B2
Ellesmere Port CH66 69 C1
Works La CW9 79 C1
World Way M90 33 A4
Worleston CE Prim Sch
CW5 188 C3
Worleston Cl CW10 151 B3
Wornish Nook CW11 154 C1
Worrall St
Congleton CW12 156 C2
Stockport SK3 240 E3
Worsborough Ave WA5 15 A3
Worsley Ave
Saughall CH1 117 A4
Warrington WA4 16 C2
Worsley Dr CW12 157 A1
Worsley Rd WA4 16 A1
Worsley St Golborne WA3 3 A4
Warrington WA5 15 C4
Worth Prim Sch SK12 36 C1
Worthing St CW9 104 B4
Worthington Ave 16 M31 11 C2
Worthington Cl
Henbury SK11 111 B4
Nantwich CW5 205 A3
Runcorn WA7 50 A4
Worthington Ct
Chester CH2 118 B2
Sale M33 242 E6
Worthington Prim Sch
M33 242 F6
Worthington Rd
Denton M34 241 B5
Sale M33 242 F6
Worthington St SK15 242 C1
Wr Twr (Mus)★ CH1 118 A1
Wr Twr Rd CH64 41 C1
Wr Twr St CH1 237 A3
Wrayton Lodge M33 242 B5
Wrekin Way CH4 140 C3
Wren Ave CW4 129 B1
Wren Cl Crewe CW1 189 C4
Macclesfield SK10 87 A1
Runcorn WA7 50 A3
Warrington WA3 9 C2
Wrenburry Cl ST5 210 B1
Wrenbury Cres SK3 240 C2
Wrenbury Dr SK8 239 E6
Wrenbury Hall Dr CW5 217 A3
Wrenbury Heath Rd
CW5 217 B3
Wrenbury Ind Est CW5 217 A2
Wrenbury Prim Sch
CW5 216 C2
Wrenbury Rd Aston CW5 217 A2
Marbury SY14 201 B1
Wrenbury Sta CW5 217 A2
Wrenbury Wlk M33 242 E5
Wrenmere Cl CW11 174 C4
Wrenshot La WA16 29 B3
Wrexham Cl
Biddulph ST8 179 B1
Warrington WA5 7 C1
Wrexham Ind Est (Ystad Ddiwdiannol Wrecsam)
LL13 196 A1
Wrexham Rd
Bickerton SY14 200 A4
Bulkeley SY14,CW6 184 C1
Burland CW5 203 B4
Chester CH4 141 A2
Faddiley CW5,CW6 202 B3
Holt LL13 196 A4
Malpas SY14 212 C1
Pulford CH4 162 C3
Wright Ave CW9 104 B3
Wright Cres WA8 23 A3
Wright St
Ashton-u-Lyne OL6 242 A4
Kidsgrove ST7 194 B1
Wright Tree Villas M44 11 B3
Wright's La
Burtonwood WA5 6 C2
Sandbach CW11 175 B3
Wrights La WA5 13 C1
Wrigley La SK10 86 A2
Wrigley Rd WA11 1 C3
Wrinehill Rd CW5 220 C4
Wroxham Cl Chester CH2 237 B4
Helsby WA6 73 A2
Wroxham Rd WA5 14 C3
Wrynose Rd CH62 43 C4
Wyatt St SK4 240 E6
Wybersley Rd SK6 38 A4
Wybunbury Delves CE Prim
Sch CW5 220 A4
Wybunbury La CW5 205 C2
Wybunbury Rd
Willaston (nr Nantwich)
CW5 205 B3
Wybunbury CW5 220 A4
Wych House Bank CW5 204 B3
Wych House La CW10 128 B1
Wych La SK10 62 B3
Wyche Ave CW5 204 B3
Wyche Cl CW9 104 C3
Wyche La CW6 185 C4
Wyche Prim Sch CW5 204 C3
Wyche Rd CW6 185 C4
Wychelm Rd M31 11 C2
Wychwood WA14 238 B1
Wychwood Ave WA13 18 B2
Wychwood Pk CW2 207 A1
Wycliffe Ave SK9 60 A4
Wycliffe Ct CH2 119 A1
Wycliffe Rd
Ellesmere Port CH65 69 C2
Haydock WA11 1 C4
Wycliffe St SK4 240 D6
Wyedale CH65 70 A2
Wyedale Rd WA11 1 B3
Wyncroft Cl
Ellesmere Port CH65 70 A2
Widnes WA8 22 B4
Wyncroft Ct CW8 77 B1
Wyncroft Rd WA8 22 B4
Wynd The CW6 122 B2
Wyndham Cl Bramhall SK7 35 C4
Northwich CW9 103 C3
Wyndham Cres CH66 69 C1
Wyndham Rd CH1 117 B2
Wynfield Ave M22 33 C4
Wyngate Rd
Altrincham WA15 31 C4
Cheadle SK8 239 F1
Wynnstay Rd
Broughton CH4 139 B2
Sale M33 242 B7
Wynter Cl SY14 198 A2
Wythburn Gr WA7 49 C3
Wythens Rd SK8 34 A4
Wythenshawe Rd M33 242 F6

Y

Yagol Gynradd Holt Com
Prim Sch LL13 196 B4
Yardley Ave WA5 15 C4
Yarmouth Rd WA5 14 C3
Yarrow Cl CH4 139 B2
Yarwood Cl CW8 103 C4
Yarwood St WA14 238 D3
Yarwoodheath La WA14 30 C4
Yatehouse La CW10 128 B4
Yates Cl WA5 15 B3
Yates Rd New Mills SK22 39 B4
Thornton-le-M CH2 71 C1
Yates St CW2 190 B1
Yealand Ave SK4 240 D7
Yeald Brow WA13 18 A2
Yeardsley Ave SK23 39 B2
Yeardsley Gn SK23 65 B4
Yeardsley La SK23 39 B2
Yearsleys La WA6 101 A3
Yeld La CW6 122 C4
Yeoford Dr WA14 238 B6
Yeoman Way CH66 69 C1
Yeovil Cl WA1 17 B4
Yerburgh St CH2 118 B2
Yew St SK4 240 C5
Yew Tree Ave WA12 2 A2
Yew Tree Bank CW6 145 A3
Yew Tree Cl
Broughton CH4 139 B2
Bulkeley SY14 184 B1
Little Budworth CW6 147 C4
Lymm WA13 18 C2
Macclesfield SK11 112 A3
Middlewich CW10 128 A1
Prestbury SK10 87 A4
Thornton-le-M CH2 71 C1
Wilmslow SK9 60 B4
Yew Tree Ct Alsager ST7 193 C1
Wimboldsley CW10 150 C2
Yew Tree Dr Barnton CW8 78 A2
Nantwich CW5 204 B3
Sale M33 242 E6
Yew Tree Farm Trad Est
WA11 2 A4
Yew Tree Gr SK8 239 A3
Yew Tree La
Appleton Thorn WA4 27 B3
Astbury CW12 178 B2
Bridgemere CW5 232 A3
Yew Tree Park Rd SK8 35 A3
Yew Tree Rd
Poynton SK10 37 A1
Wistaston CW2 206 A4
Yew Tree Way
Golborne WA3 3 A4
Prestbury SK10 87 B3
Yew Wlk 1 M31 11 C1
Yewdale Dr CH66 69 C1
Yewlands CW8 101 B3
Yewlands Dr WA16 57 B1
Yewtree Cl CH64 66 C4
Yewtree La SK12 36 C2
Yewtree Rd WA16 80 C2
Yonne The CH1 237 A2
York Ave Culcheth WA3 4 C1
Sale M33 242 B7
Warrington WA5 14 C4
York Cl Biddulph ST8 179 B1
Stockport SK8 240 A1
Talke ST7 210 B4
York Cres SK9 60 B4
York Ct 2 WA4 16 C1
York Dr Altrincham WA14 238 D1
Mickle Trafford CH2 96 C1
Warrington WA4 17 A1
Winsford CW7 149 B3
Wythenshaw M90 32 C4
York Ho 1 M33 242 B7
York Pl WA7 23 A1
York Rd Altrincham WA14 238 C1
Connah's Quay CH5 91 B1
Ellesmere Port CH65 70 B3
Irlam M44 11 B3
Sale M33 242 A7
Warrington WA4 17 A1
Widnes WA8 22 B4
York St Altrincham WA15 238 E3
Chester CH1 237 B3
Macclesfield SK10 112 C4
Stockport SK3 240 E4
Warrington WA4 16 B2
York Terr M33 242 A6
Yorkshire Rd M31 11 C1
Yorston Lodge Sch
WA16 56 C1
Yule St SK3 240 D4

Z

Zan Dr CW11 175 A2
Zan Ind Pk CW11 175 A2
Zara Ct WA11 1 B4
Zinnia Dr M44 11 C4
Zion St 21 CW8 103 C4

NG	NH	NJ	NK	
NM	NN	NO	NP	
NR	NS	NT	NU	
NX	NY	NZ		
	SC	SD	SE	TA
	SH	SJ	SK	TF	TG
SM	SN	SO	SP	TL	TM
SR	SS	ST	SU	TQ	TR
SW	SX	SY	SZ	TV

Any feature in this atlas can be given a unique reference to help you find the same feature on other Ordnance Survey maps of the area, or to help someone else locate you if they do not have a Street Atlas.

The grid squares in this atlas match the Ordnance Survey National Grid and are at 1 kilometre intervals. The small figures at the bottom and sides of every other grid line are the National Grid kilometre values (**00** to **99** km) and are repeated across the country every 100 km (see left).

To give a unique National Grid reference you need to locate where in the country you are. The country is divided into 100 km squares with each square given a unique two-letter reference. Use the administrative map to determine in which 100 km square a particular page of this atlas falls.

The bold letters and numbers between each grid line (**A** to **C, 1** to **4**) are for use within a specific Street Atlas only, and when used with the page number, are a convenient way of referencing these grid squares.

Example *The railway bridge over DARLEY GREEN RD in grid square A1*

Step 1: Identify the two-letter reference, in this example the page is in **SP**

Step 2: Identify the 1 km square in which the railway bridge falls. Use the figures in the southwest corner of this square: Eastings **17**, Northings **74**. This gives a unique reference: **SP 17 74**, accurate to 1 km.

Step 3: To give a more precise reference accurate to 100 m you need to estimate how many tenths along and how many tenths up this 1 km square the feature is. This makes the bridge about **8** tenths along and about **1** tenth up from the southwest corner.

This gives a unique reference: **SP 178 741**, accurate to 100 m.

Eastings (read from left to right along the bottom) come before Northings (read from bottom to top). If you have trouble remembering say to yourself "Along the hall, THEN up the stairs"!

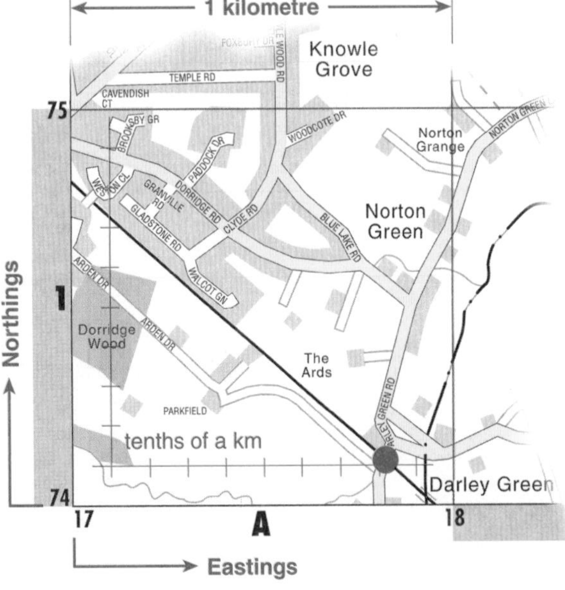

Addresses

Name and Address	Telephone	Page	Grid reference

Name and Address	Telephone	Page	Grid reference

Street Atlases from Philip's

Philip's publish an extensive range of regional and local street atlases which are ideal for motoring, business and leisure use. They are widely used by the emergency services and local authorities throughout Britain.

Key features include:

◆ Superb county-wide mapping at an extra-large scale of 3½ inches to 1 mile, or 2½ inches to 1 mile in pocket editions

◆ Complete urban and rural coverage, detailing every named street in town and country

◆ Each atlas available in two handy sizes – standard spiral and pocket paperback

'The mapping is very clear... great in scope and value'
★★★★ BEST BUY   AUTO EXPRESS

1 Anglesey, Conwy and Gwynedd
2 Bedfordshire
3 Berkshire
4 Birmingham and West Midlands
5 Bristol and Bath
6 Buckinghamshire
7 Cambridgeshire
8 Cardiff, Swansea and The Valleys
9 Cheshire
10 Cornwall
11 Cumbria
12 Denbighshire, Flintshire and Wrexham
13 Derbyshire
14 Devon
15 Dorset
16 County Durham and Teesside
17 Edinburgh and East Central Scotland
18 Essex
19 North Essex
20 South Essex
21 Fife and Tayside
22 Glasgow and West Central Scotland
23 Gloucestershire
24 North Hampshire
25 South Hampshire
26 Herefordshire and Monmouthshire
27 Hertfordshire
28 East Kent
29 West Kent
30 Lancashire
31 Leicestershire and Rutland
32 Lincolnshire
33 London
34 Greater Manchester
35 Merseyside
36 Norfolk
37 Northamptonshire
38 Nottinghamshire
39 Oxfordshire
40 Shropshire
41 Somerset
42 Staffordshire
43 Suffolk
44 Surrey
45 East Sussex
46 West Sussex
47 Tyne and Wear and Northumberland
48 Warwickshire
49 Wiltshire and Swindon
50 Worcestershire
51 East Yorkshire and Northern Lincolnshire
52 North Yorkshire
53 South Yorkshire
54 West Yorkshire

How to order

The Philip's range of street atlases is available from good retailers or directly from the publisher by phoning 01903 828503